Fodor's Affordable Caribbean

"The Fodor's series puts a premium on showing its readers a good time."
—*Philadelphia Inquirer*

"Concentrates on life's basics...without skimping on literary luxuries."
—*New York Daily News*

"Good helpmates for the cost-conscious traveler."
—*Detroit Free Press*

"These books succeed admirably; easy to follow and use, full of cost related information, practical advice and recommendations...maps are clear and easy to use."
—*Travel Books Worldwide*

"The books can help you fill the gap between deprivation and ostentation when you travel."
—*Dawson Sentinel*

Parts of this book appear in *Fodor's Caribbean*

Fodor's Travel Publications, Inc.
New York•Toronto•London•Sydney•Auckland

Fodor's Affordable Caribbean

Editor: Suzanne De Galan
Editorial Contributors: Pamela Acheson, Harriet Edleson, Nigel Fisher, Jane Hershey, Amy Hunter, Joan Iaconetti, Karl Luntta, Denise Nolty, Carolyn Price, Marcy Pritchard, Laurie Senz, Jordan Simon, Heidi Waldrop, Simon Worrall
Creative Director: Fabrizio La Rocca
Cartographer: David Lindroth
Illustrator: Karl Tanner
Cover Photograph: S. Achernar/Image Bank

Design: Vignelli Associates

Special Sales

Contents

Maps and Plans

How This Guide Will Save You Money

The Affordables are aimed at people like you and me—people with discriminating tastes and limited budgets.

This is a new series that combines essential budget travel information with quality writing, authoritative hotel and restaurant reviews, detailed exploring tours, and wonderful maps.

The idea behind these guides is that you, the budget traveler, have the same curiosity and high expectations as those who travel first class, and you need information with the same depth and detail as readers of Fodor's gold guides. But as a budget traveler you also need to know about low-cost activities, meals, and lodging.

These are guides not for the hotdog-on-the-run-it's-okay-to-sleep-on-a-beach crowd but for those of you who insist on at least two good meals a day and a safe, comfortable place to put your head at night. The hotels we recommend offer good value, and there are no dives, thank you—only clean, friendly places with an acceptable level of comfort, convenience, and charm. There's also a wide range of inexpensive and moderately priced dining options, mostly small, family-run restaurants offering healthy, home-cooked, regional cuisine.

Fodor's has made every effort to provide you with accurate, up-to-date information, but time always brings change, and consequently the publisher cannot accept responsibility for errors that may occur. Hotel rates in particular may change, so we encourage you to call ahead.

We also encourage you to write and share your travel experiences with us—pleasant and unpleasant. When a hotel or restaurant fails to live up to its billing, please let us know, and we'll investigate the complaint and revise our entries when the facts warrant it. Send your letters to The Editor, Fodor's Affordables, 201 East 50th Street, New York, NY 10022.

Have a great trip!

Michael Spring
Editorial Director

Fodor's Choice for Budget Travelers

No two people will agree on what makes a perfect vacation, but it's fun and helpful to know what others think. We hope you'll have the chance to experience some of Fodor's Choices yourself while visiting the Caribbean. For detailed information about each entry, refer to the appropriate chapter in this guidebook.

Beaches

Shoal Bay, Anguilla

Palm Beach, Aruba

Seven Mile Beach, Grand Cayman

Negril, Jamaica

Anse du Gouverneur, St. Barts

Magens Bay, St. Thomas, U.S. Virgin Islands

Trunk Bay, St. John, U.S. Virgin Islands

Diving/Snorkeling

Reefs around Bonaire

Virgin Gorda, British Virgin Islands

Cayman Islands (especially Sting Ray City)

Southern Coast of Curaçao

Scott's Head, Dominica

Saba's pinnacles

St. Vincent

Reefs around Speyside, Tobago

Turks and Caicos Islands' reefs

Buck Island Reef, St. Croix, U.S. Virgin Islands

Hiking

Washington/Slagbaai National Park, Bonaire

Morne Diablotin, Dominica

Parc Naturel, Basse-Terre, Guadeloupe

Bamboo Forest, Montserrat

Dunn's River Falls, Jamaica

El Yunque Rain Forest, Puerto Rico

The Quill, St. Eustatius

National Park, St. John

Hotels

Fort Recovery, Tortola, British Virgin Islands (*Moderate*)

Boscobel Beach (for families), Jamaica (*Moderate*)

Relais Caraibes, Martinique (*Moderate*)

Golden Rock, Nevis (*Moderate*)

Passangrahan Royal Guest House, St. Martin (*Inexpensive–Moderate*)

Admiral's Inn, Antigua (*Inexpensive*)

Maho Bay Camp, St. John (*Inexpensive*)

Hibiscus Lodge, Jamaica (*Budget–Inexpensive*)

Bruce Bowker's Carib Inn, Bonaire (*Budget*)

Restaurants

Bon Appetit, Aruba (*Moderate*)

Ile de France, Barbados (*Moderate*)

Canboulay, Grenada (*Moderate*)

Le Balata, Guadeloupe (*Moderate*)

Le Coq Hardi, Martinique (*Moderate*)

Cooperage, Nevis (*Moderate*)

Roy's, Anguilla (*Inexpensive*)

Niggy's, Montserrat (*Inexpensive*)

Turtle Pier Bar & Restaurant, St Maarten (*Inexpensive*)

Veni Mange, Trinidad (*Inexpensive*)

Skyworld, Tortola, British Virgin Islands (*Budget–Inexpensive for lunch*)

Jerk Centres on Boston Beach, Jamaica (*Budget*)

Lolo snack stands, St. Martin (*Budget*)

Value Vacations

Villa rental, Montserrat

Campground, St. John

Parador, Puerto Rico

Dive package, Bonaire

Bare-boat charter, British Virgin Islands (for experienced sailors)

Plantation-house hotel, Nevis (off-season)

The Caribbean

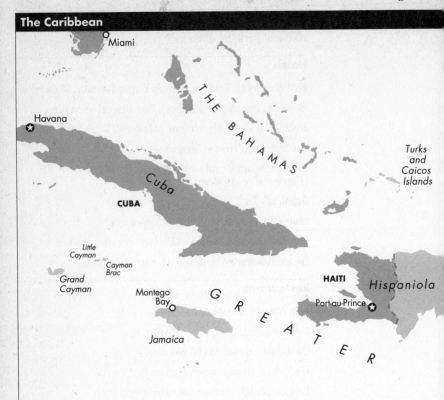

Miami

THE BAHAMAS

Turks and Caicos Islands

Havana

Cuba

CUBA

Little Cayman

Cayman Brac

Grand Cayman

Montego Bay

Jamaica

G R E A T E R

HAITI

Hispaniola

Port-au-Prince

Caribbean

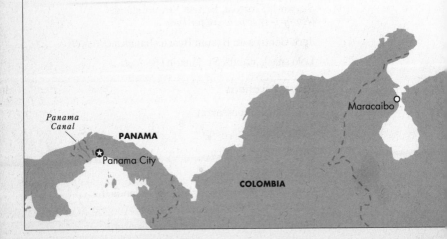

Panama Canal

PANAMA

Panama City

Maracaibo

COLOMBIA

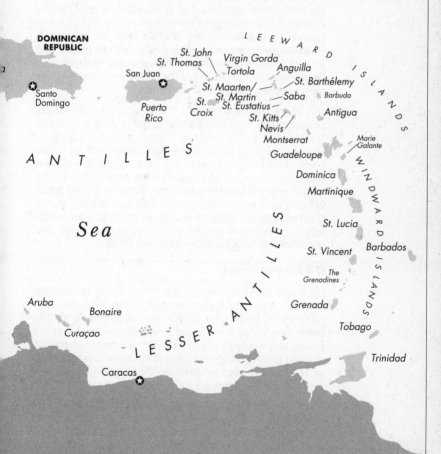

0   200 miles

0   300 km

N

ATLANTIC OCEAN

LEEWARD ISLANDS

DOMINICAN REPUBLIC

St. John
St. Thomas
Virgin Gorda
Tortola
Anguilla

San Juan

St. Barthélemy

St. Maarten/
St. Martin
Saba
Barbuda

Santo
Domingo

St.
Croix

St. Eustatius
Antigua

*Puerto
Rico*

St. Kitts
Nevis

Montserrat

*Marie
Galante*

Guadeloupe

A N T I L L E S

WINDWARD ISLANDS

Dominica

Martinique

Sea

St. Lucia

St. Vincent

Barbados

*The
Grenadines*

Aruba

Grenada

Bonaire

L E S S E R   A N T I L L E S

Tobago

Curaçao

Trinidad

Caracas

VENEZUELA

Making Your Vacation Affordable

By Jane Hershey

Jane Hershey's work has appeared in Good Housekeeping, US, *and* Elle. *She is a frequent traveler to the Caribbean.*

What traveler hasn't dreamed of a vacation in the Caribbean, with its near-perfect weather, stunning beaches, exotic cultures, and multitude of outdoor activities? Sadly, the cost of paradise can be a rude awakening. Many of these islands are expensive—some shockingly so. It's telling that some of our island chapters list hotels costing under $125 a night in a budget category—not out of line when you consider that hotel rates of $600 a night are common on these islands. There are reasons for the hefty price tags you find in the Caribbean. A lack of airlines flying directly to the region means higher costs. Islands must import much of their food and beverages, which keeps dining prices high. And it can't be denied that jet-setters have made the Caribbean one of their stops on the glamour circuit—many of the region's resorts and villas have been designed with them in mind.

But there are ways to save. Traveling in the off-season, choosing less expensive islands, going with a group of friends and renting a villa, taking advantage of a package deal—all of these can bring a Caribbean vacation within reach of the budget traveler. And once you are on your fantasy island, there are more ways to save: eating West Indian food in local cafés and beach shacks, listening to steel bands in funky bars, snorkeling on public beaches, and hiking pristine forest trails. With a few rules to guide you and a willingness to research and ask questions, you'll discover that your faraway island is closer than you think.

Off-Season Travel

Choosing an off-season date for your Caribbean vacation may be your single biggest money-maker. High season is fairly short, from about mid-December to mid-April, (the exact date varies from island to island and from hotel to hotel), and when it's over prices for accommodations and just about everything can plummet by as much as 50%, even at the most deluxe properties. While not quite as discounted, airline prices are sometimes lower, too.

There is much to be said for off-season travel to the Caribbean. Without the prime-time crowds, it's easier to rent a car, enjoy a local historic site, or find a deserted beach without the prime-time crowds. While temperatures are fairly constant year-round, brief storms are almost as likely to occur in January as they are in August. (The one time of year many travelers avoid is September and October—hurricane season.) In the drier summer months you'll find fewer mosquitoes and other flying nuisances. The water tends to be calmer and clearer, which means better snorkeling and sailing. Spring and summer are also when many Caribbean countries hold local festivals, such as St. Thomas's Frenchtown Carnival in June and Antigua's Windsurfing Week and calypso competition in July.

Besides the region's traditional low season, the Caribbean has other small "windows" during high season, when hotels that face sharp drops in occupancy quietly lower their rates for a week or so. A common window occurs in early January, right after New Year's; another is at the end of January, right before the February surge in visitors. Dates and price decreases vary among hotels and islands; a good travel agent can be useful in helping you find deals. (*see* Travel Agents, *below*). Note that rates are fairly stable year-round at city hotels that cater to business travelers and small inns and B&Bs with already-rock-bottom prices. But be sure to ask: Many are willing to negotiate during slack periods.

Choice of Destination

Your choice of island is vital in determining affordability. The Caribbean consists of many nations, and in some ways they differ from one another as much as, say, France differs from Holland, or the United Kingdom from the United States. Prices can differ as dramatically. Some islands, such as St. Barts and Antigua, tend to attract a jet-set clientele, so their hotel and restaurant prices are higher than those on popular family and couple-oriented destinations such as the U. S. Virgin Islands, Jamaica, and Puerto Rico. Not that these and other islands don't have world-class facilities, or that there are no budget lodgings on expensive islands; it's just that larger islands tend to pay more attention to the needs of a wider spectrum of the vacation market. You'll notice that the price charts for Dining and Lodging in each of our island chapters differ greatly from one another: What's moderately priced in Puerto Rico, for instance, may be considered inexpensive on Antigua. Aim for a specific atmosphere rather than a specific island. Laid-back, casual elegance isn't only found on pricey islands like Anguilla; look for it in the many charming, small hotels tucked into intimate bays and hillsides on unknown "treasure islands" like Saba or Dominica. Our Finding Your Place in the Sun chart (*see below*) categorizes each island in terms of cost.

Setting Priorities

Deciding what's most important to you can save a surprising amount of money. If activity-filled informality is what you're seeking, steer clear of destinations and resorts that emphasize fine dining and elegant atmosphere, or you'll likely end up paying for someone else's bone china and imported caviar. If golf and tennis aren't your games, put your dollars where the best diving, snorkeling, or beach-combing are found. All that turf—whether astro or natural—

costs a fortune in upkeep and staffing, and you end up paying for facilities you may not even use.

If you prefer an active vacation, it's wise to research which properties and destinations offer the best values. Various hotels and airlines offer many sports-specific packages. Many hotels in some countries, like Jamaica, feature rafting and horseback riding. Other hotel and all-inclusive companies have properties catering to dive enthusiasts. (If you prefer not to use a package, think about taking the least expensive room available and cutting back on extra luxuries so you'll have more money for your sport.)

Lodging

Unless you go camping, your accommodations will almost certainly be the most expensive portion of your trip. Here are savvy ways to save.

Hotels Sometimes it makes sense to deal with a larger hotel or resort, even though the initial price tag looks higher. Even in season, these facilities usually have rooms to fill, and they can be more flexible about upgrades and discounts on food, drink, and activities. Smaller, independent properties can't afford to be as generous.

Is a popular resort going through a change of management or redecoration? If you're willing to put up with minor nuisances like staff training and repainting, you might take advantage of special rates. Just make certain that the rock drill won't be outside your door at 6 AM and that the swimming pool will be filled.

How important is an oceanfront room to you? Many properties have a category for rooms that are off the beach. Amenities in these rooms, often referred to as "mountain" or "garden" view, are similar to those on the ocean, but rates can be 50% less, even in high season.

There are also ways to save if you take your family. A number of hotel chains have children's day camps and teen programs. Most of these programs are free to guests; some charge a small amount for meals and excursions. Many chains (and individual properties) allow children under 18 to stay free in their parents' room. Some have low-price children's menus and other discounts. Do not hesitate to ask about such offers when you book—you may be pleasantly surprised, even in high season.

All-Inclusives All-inclusives—where guests pay one preset price that covers room, meals, and all activities—have a reputation for being expensive, and many are. But some can actually help you save money, particularly if you plan on an active vacation with plenty of sports, recreation, eating, and drinking. If nothing else, you'll know up front exactly how much your vacation will cost. The popularity of these resorts has mushroomed over the past decade, and now all-inclusives for every taste and budget have emerged. Some cater to sports enthusiasts, others are designed especially for families. Still others emphasize romantic tranquillity and comparative luxury at an affordable price. Evaluate carefully the personality of the all-inclusive you are considering, and find out exactly what's included before you book. Some resorts throw in everything down to the last rum punch and paddleboat; others require separate payment for drinks, as at Club Meds, or certain menu items. Better rooms or rooms with better views will cost you more at some all-inclusives. Remember that affordably priced all-inclusives will not offer the same levels of comfort and service as all-inclusives charging three times as much.

Apartment and Villa Rentals Many couples and families are discovering the pleasures of renting a private or semiprivate villa. In fact, many resorts are developing such options as part of their facilities. Most villas are upscale properties, often with several bedrooms, a pool, a gourmet kitchen, elaborate home entertainment system, a cook, maid—even a car. Although weekly high-season rates at such posh digs can seem like a king's ransom, prices drop dramatically in the off-season. If you share the cost among more than one couple or family, some of the rentals are quite affordable. On St. Barts and Montserrat, villas are cheaper and more attractive than many hotels.

Even if you don't plan to travel with a group, rental cottages and houses can still be affordable. Just keep in mind that you will probably need your own car (many villas are in remote settings far from beaches and grocery stores), and will have to do your own cooking (or at least, make your own coffee if you choose to eat out), and wash your own beach towels. In general, renting lower-priced properties requires a slightly adventurous and independent spirit. If you're the type that won't let less-than-perfect plumbing or faded furnishings interfere with your enjoyment of glorious sunsets and a secluded pool, this route may be your ticket to paradise. For a list of companies offering villa rentals throughout the Caribbean, *see* Apartment and Villa Rentals in Chapter 1, Essential Information. *See also* Lodging in island chapters for additional companies on specific islands.

Camping Ecological awareness has sparked a renewed interest in camping vacations, and even if you're not on a budget, it can be one of the most delightful ways to vacation in the Caribbean. However, camping is not an option on all islands. Many have no campgrounds or camp sites, and some forbid or discourage independent campers on beaches and protected forest areas. What camping exists comes in all stripes. At **Cinnamon Bay,** on St. John, U.S. Virgin Islands, you can get cabins, linens, and personal barbecue grills, or opt for simpler accommodations at lower rates. **Mojacasabe,** on Puerto Rico, has a pool and beach. Other islands have nothing more than sites where you can pitch a tent. For those who enjoy camping with a group, the **Sierra**

Club (Outing Dept., 730 Polk St., San Francisco, CA 94109, tel. 415/776–2211) and **American Youth Hostels** (Box 37613, Washington, DC 20013–7613, tel. 202/783–6161) offer hiking, biking, and other tours that involve camping. A growing number of specialty tour operators combine camping with archaeological or ecological tourism. A good source of information on such companies is the advertising sections of Caribbean specialty magazines, such as *Caribbean Travel & Life*, or publications like *Outdoors. See also* Lodging in island chapters for campgrounds on specific islands.

Guest Houses and B&Bs Although this form of lodging is not as developed as in Europe or the United States, it does exist in the Caribbean—with wildly differing degrees of quality. Some properties may not meet your standards of comfort and hygiene, while others can be sparkling, well-run establishments— with the bonus of warmth and charm you find only in privately owned establishments. It's best to approach B&Bs and guest houses here with a flexible attitude about things like private baths and modern furnishings. Those who do are rewarded with accommodations that almost always cost less than all but the most bare-bones hotel rooms.

To investigate this option, start by looking at advertising sections in reputable travel monthlies or major newspapers (the Sunday *New York Times* travel section, for instance, features weekly listings). Another good source of information is the **Bed & Breakfast Reservation Services Worldwide** (Box 39000, Washington, D.C. 20016, tel. 800/842–1486), a trade association that offers a comprehensive list of B&Bs for a nominal fee. Note that most B&Bs do not accept credit cards; ask when you book and make your initial deposit. For more information about guest houses and B&Bs on a particular island, *see* Lodging in each island chapter.

Special Deals

Smart travelers never pay the full rate for anything. They know that a little research will yield packages, limited offers, and all kinds of ways to save.

Doing Your Homework **Magazines** such as *Caribbean Travel & Life* and *Islands* not only run in-depth articles on Caribbean destinations, but also have large advertising sections full of hotels, property rentals, and group and special-interest travel opportunities. In addition, general-interest travel magazines usually do at least one annual issue on Caribbean travel. There are also a number of Caribbean travel newsletters. Look for some of their advertisements in magazines, or check your local library.

Most national and regional **newspapers** carry regular travel sections, usually on Sunday. Check the ads for packages offered by chain agencies such as **Empress** and **Liberty** and airlines such as **American, United,** and **BWIA.** Larger newspapers have large sections of small ads; these include dozens of villa and condominium companies and smaller hotels, along with a few fairly sizable properties, such as Puerto Rico's **Palmas Del Mar.** Many of the rates are highly competitive, even during high season.

Travel Agents These can be the budget traveler's best friend when it comes to finding quality bargains. Agents have access to one or more airline computer booking systems that allow them to see a broad spectrum of flights and fares. Experienced agents also know which properties are offering special packages; which have changed management, policy, or price structures to your advantage or disadvantage; and who's actively looking for business during high and low seasons. They can also be more aggressive than most individual travelers when it comes to striking a hard bargain. A good agent is personally familiar with the destinations and type of travel you have in mind. However, the more specific information you can be about your budget, priorities, and preferences for lodging, meals, sports, and atmosphere, the more helpful an agent can be.

Packages Both airline and hotel packages include accommodations. Airline packages also include airfare and may include car rental and other options. Hotel packages seldom include airfare but usually pile on extras like champagne breakfasts and free use of sports facilities. Either can mean significant savings over the same components purchased separately, but you must be prepared to use a calculator and compare costs: Sometimes making your own arrangements can be cheaper.

Airline packages frequently work with hotels at all price levels. You can usually have your pick of properties and room types, especially during low season. Airline packages also take care of airport transfers—which can be costly on some islands. For a list of airlines offering packages to the Caribbean, *see* Independent Packages in Chapter 1, Essential Information.

Hotel packages include the popular honeymoon variety, with extra pampering like breakfast in bed and complimentary cocktails on arrival. Some of the best include massages, sunset sailing trips, and even a free round of golf. These packages frequently incorporate a better class of rooms (and baths). Often the best time to book this type of deluxe package is during low season. Caribbean hotels also offer tennis, golf, diving, sailing, and other sports packages. For a list of hotel chains with properties in the Caribbean that offer packages, *see* Independent Packages in Chapter 1, Essential Information. In addition, individual properties throughout the book may be featuring package deals when you call to book; be sure to inquire.

Discount Flights Most major U.S. carriers have only limited flights to the region; thus cheap airfares are few and far between. Nev-

Caribbean Island-Finder

	Cost of Island	Number of rooms	Nonstop flights	Cruise ship port	U.S. dollars accepted	Historic sites	Natural beauty	Lush	Arid	Mountainous	Rain forest	Beautiful beaches	Good roads	
Anguilla	$$$	863			•				•			•		
Antigua	$$$$	2752	•	•	•	•	•		•			•		
Aruba	$$	5459	•	•	•				•			•	•	
Barbados	$$	6650	•	•	•	•							•	
Bonaire	$$	714	•		•								•	
British Virgin Islands	$$$	1163		•	•	•	•	•		•	•	•		
Cayman Islands	$$$$	2573	•	•	•				•			•	•	
Curaçao	$$	2159	•	•	•	•							•	
Dominica	$	547					•	•		•	•			
Dominican Republic	$	22555	•			•		•				•		
The Grenadines	$$	400					•	•		•	•	•		
Grenada	$$$	1118		•	•		•	•		•		•		
Guadeloupe	$$	7016		•			•	•		•	•		•	
Jamaica	$	17337		•			•	•				•	•	
Martinique	$$$	5802		•			•	•		•	•		•	
Montserrat	$$	233		•			•	•		•	•			
Nevis	$$$	363		•		•				•			•	
Puerto Rico	$	8500	•	•	•	•	•	•		•	•	•	•	
Saba	$	100		•						•	•			
St. Barthélemy	$$$$	1130					•			•		•	•	
St. Eustatius	$	102		•	•						•			
St. Kitts	$$$	705		•			•	•		•	•	•	•	
St. Lucia	$$	2464	•				•	•		•	•			
St. Martin/St. Maarten	$$$	3400		•								•	•	
St. Vincent	$$	700		•		•	•	•		•	•	•		
Trinidad	$	1300	•								•			
Tobago	$$	1000							•			•		
Turks and Caicos	$$$	1004	•		•				•			•		
U.S. Virgin Islands:														
St. Croix	$$	1000		•	•	•				•	•			
St. John	$$	500			•		•	•		•		•		
St. Thomas	$$	2419	•	•	•					•		•	•	

	Public transportation	Fine dining	Local cuisine	Shopping	Music	Casinos	Nightlife	Diving and Snorkeling	Sailing	Golfing	Hiking	Ecotourism	Villa rentals	All-inclusives	Campgrounds	Luxury resorts	Secluded getaway	Good for families	Romantic hideaway	
		•	•	•	•			•								•	•		•	
		•	•	•		•	•	•	•	•				•		•		•		
	•	•	•	•	•	•	•		•					•		•		•		
	•	•			•		•		•					•		•		•		
								•	•		•	•								
	•	•	•	•	•		•	•	•	•	•	•	•	•	•	•	•	•	•	
		•		•			•	•		•	•		•	•		•		•		
	•	•	•	•		•	•	•	•		•							•		
	•							•			•	•					•			
			•			•	•		•					•				•		
	•		•				•	•	•	•	•					•		•	•	
		•	•				•	•	•		•	•			•					
	•		•		•		•	•		•			•	•	•			•	•	
			•				•	•	•						•					
	•	•	•				•	•	•	•	•	•				•	•			
		•	•		•			•		•					•			•		
	•	•	•	•	•	•	•	•	•	•	•			•	•		•	•	•	
								•						•		•		•		
		•	•	•				•		•					•		•			
								•				•				•		•		
		•	•	•	•	•	•	•	•	•	•	•	•		•	•	•	•	•	
	•						•		•			•		•		•		•	•	
	•	•	•	•		•	•	•		•			•	•		•		•		
	•		•					•	•		•	•						•		
	•				•			•										•		
								•	•	•	•	•	•	•		•	•		•	
			•					•		•	•					•				
	•							•		•		•	•		•	•		•	•	
	•	•	•	•			•	•		•			•	•		•				

ertheless, options such as airline packages, charter flights, and discount travel clubs do offer some hope. For information on researching **discount flights,** *see* Cutting Flight Costs in Chapter 1, Essential Information.

Money-Saving Tips

- Choose a less-expensive island. (*See* our Finding Your Place in the Sun chart.)

- Choose islands that offer activities such as hiking and snorkeling, rather than those catering primarily to golfers or tennis buffs.

- Take advantage of hotels that offer cheaper rates for garden-view, rather than ocean-view, rooms. Ask about other discounts at hotels when you call. Find out if a hotel is undergoing renovations, and ask for a rate reduction. At expensive properties, ask whether smaller rooms are available at a lower price, even if not advertised.

- If you are traveling with more than one couple or with a large family, consider renting a condominium or villa.

- Go camping.

- Research airline packages and hotel packages.

- If you are traveling with children, find out which hotels offer special programs and rates. In low season, try to negotiate a standard suite with sofabed or larger accommodation for the price of a regular room. Many such units come with their own wet bars, microwaves, and other cooking equipment.

- Check your frequent flier miles and combine this low airfare with a land-only package. Some flier programs have hotel and car rental discounts, too. Read all fine print to check restrictions.

- Use a travel agent to help you find the best deals, including lesser-known or new properties with introductory rates.

- It's not uncommon for associations, such as university alumnae groups, to offer discounted airline tickets to members; check with yours.

- If you're not participating in a meal plan at your hotel, eat your main meal at lunch and go light on dinner. Check out local cafés; on larger islands, save at chain restaurants such as Pizza Hut. Or, at midday, consider a picnic or lunch at a roti stand or other casual spot.

- If your room has a kitchen, buy local produce and cook at least one dinner.

- In bars, stick with the local rum punch and avoid imported wines, liquors, soft drinks, or juices. Better yet, buy your rum and mixers at a convenience store and make your own.

- Rent a moped instead of a car on islands that have suitable roads. (Be sure to rent helmets, too.)

- Take minivans instead of private cabs on the islands that have them.

- Compare the cost of guided island tours with that of a rental car for a day. Prices are comparable on some islands. On many, car rental is less. Surprisingly, on some islands a guided tour—especially on a smaller island that takes only half a day to see—is less.

- Bring your own snorkeling gear, tennis racket and balls, and other portable sports equipment.

- Shop wisely. Look only for legitimate bargains or unique finds like spices at local markets. Bargains on luxury items like cameras and jewelry *can* be found at duty-free ports, but you'll need to do your homework before your trip: Check stateside prices on items you intend to buy before you leave home. Put all purchases on a credit card—if there's a dispute later, the card company can help.

- Make local phone calls from a pay phone. For long-distance calls, make sure your hotel allows you to use your discount calling card.

- Choose local nightlife, such as a steel band at a small bar, over a hotel casino or cabaret show.

- Think off-season.

- Remember that you're on vacation. This is a time to cut your costs, but not your losses. It's no bargain if you can't relax and have fun, too.

1 Essential Information

Before You Go

Government Tourist Offices

Each island has a U.S.–based tourist board, listed with its name and address under Important Addresses in the individual island chapters that follow; they're good sources of general information, up-to-date calendars of events, and listings of hotels, restaurants, sights, and shops. The **Caribbean Tourism Organization** (20 E. 46th St., New York, NY 10017–2452, tel. 212/682–0435) is another resource.

The Department of State's Citizens Emergency Center issues Consular Information Sheets, which cover crime, security, and health risks as well as embassy locations, entry requirements, currency regulations, and other routine matters. (Travel Warnings, which counsel travelers to avoid a country entirely, are issued in extreme cases.) For the latest travel advisories, stop in at any passport office, consulate, or embassy; call the interactive hotline (tel. 202/647–5225); or, with your PC's modem, tap into the Bureau of Consular Affairs' computer bulletin board (tel. 202/647–9225).

Tours and Packages

Should you buy your travel arrangements to the Caribbean packaged or do it yourself? There are advantages either way. Buying packaged arrangements saves you money, particularly if you can find a program that includes exactly the features you want. You also get a pretty good idea of what your trip will cost from the outset. For most destinations, you have two options: fully escorted tours and independent packages. Since most travelers to the Caribbean visit one island and stay at one resort, there is little need for escorted tours. Independent packages to the Caribbean, on the other hand, are wildly popular and exist for every budget and taste. In addition to general hotel-and-airfare packages, there are specialized programs of diving, golf, tennis, activities for kids, and more. Travel agents are your best source of recommendations. They will have the largest selection, and the cost to you is the same as buying direct. Whatever program you ultimately choose, be sure to find out exactly what is included: taxes, tips, transfers, meals, baggage handling, ground transportation, entertainment, excursions, sports or recreation (and rental equipment for any sport you plan to pursue). Ask about the level of hotel used, its location, the size of its rooms, the kind of beds, and its amenities, such as pool, room service, or programs for children, if they're important to you. One other important point: If the beach is the centerpiece of your vacation, ask exactly where your hotel is located with respect to the nearest one—the words "beach nearby" can have a disturbing number of meanings.

Find out the operator's cancellation penalties. Nearly everyone charges them, and the only way to avoid them is to buy trip-cancellation insurance (*see* Insurance, *below*). Also ask about the single supplement, a surcharge assessed to solo travelers. Some operators do not make you pay it if you agree to be matched up with a roommate of the same sex, even if one is not found by departure time. Remember that a program that has features you won't use, whether for rental sporting equipment or discounted museum admissions, may not be the most cost-wise choice for you. Note that when pricing different packages, it sometimes pays to purchase the same arrangements separately, as when a rock-bottom promotional airfare is being offered. Base your choice on what's available at your budget for the destinations you want to visit.

Independent Packages
Independent packages are offered by airlines, tour operators who may also do escorted programs, hotels, and any number of other companies from large, established firms to small, new entrepreneurs. Such programs come in a wide range of prices based on levels of luxury and options—in addition to hotel and airfare, sightseeing, car rental, transfers, admission to local attractions, and other extras.

General
One excellent source is **Tour-Scan, Inc.** (Box 2367, Darien, CT 06820, tel. 203/655–8019 or 800/962–2080), a one-stop travel shop that sells, direct to the public, more than 15,000 Caribbean packages, from the least to the most expensive, for all kinds of interests, most containing hotel and airfare along with transfers and various activities. Attesting that his staff checks out each resort personally, President Arthur Mehmel promises savings of "up to several hundred dollars" and says it makes the Caribbean affordable, even on islands with a reputation for being pricey. The $4 you pay for the catalogue listing all the offerings is refundable if you book, which entails no fee. Independent packages are also available from **American Express Vacations** (300 Pinnacle Way, Norcross, GA 30093, tel. 800/241–1700); **Horizon Tours** (1010 Vermont Ave. NW, Suite 202, Washington, DC 20005, tel. 202/393–8390 or 800/395–0025) with over 50 different programs; **GWV International** (300 First Ave., Needham, MA 02194, tel. 617/449–5460 or 800/225–5498); and **Cavalcade Tours** (465 Smith St., Farmingdale, NY 11735, tel. 800/284–0044 in the eastern U.S. or 800/284–0077 in the West).

Airline
Airline packages almost always include round-trip airfare, accommodations, and transfers. Contact **American Airlines Fly AAway Vacations** (tel. 800/321–2121), **Cayman Airtours** (tel. 800/247–2966), **Continental Airlines' Grand Destinations** (tel. 800/634–5555), **Delta Dream Vacations** (tel. 800/872–7786), and **TWA Getaway Vacations** (tel. 800/438–2929; Puerto Rico only).

Hotels
Packages offered directly through hotel chains or individual resorts do not commonly include airfare, but they often feature luxury add-ons, such as champagne breakfasts or room upgrades, that would be more expensive if purchased separately. In addition, many offer special-interest packages such as unlimited golf or diving. As with most deals, you'll find the best bargains in the off-season. The following hotel chains have several properties in the Caribbean, and offer frequent packages: **Club Med** (tel. 800/258–2633), **Divi Divi** (tel. 800/367–3484), **Hilton** (tel. 800/445–8667), **Holiday Inn** (tel. 800/465–4329), **Hyatt** (tel. 800/233–1234), **Marriott** (tel. 800/331–3131), **Radisson** (tel. 800/333–3333), **Ramada** (tel. 800/228–9898; 800/272–6232 in Canada), **Sandals** (tel. 800/726–3257), **Super Clubs** (tel. 800/858–8009), and **Wyndham** (tel. 800/822–4200). Also, individual properties listed in each island chapter may be offering one or more packages when you call; be sure to inquire.

Tips for British Travelers

Tourist Information   Contact the **Caribbean Tourism Organization** (Vigilant House, 120 Wilton Rd., London SW1V 1JZ, tel. 071/233–8382).

Passports and Visas   See the Before You Go section in each island chapter for specific passport and visa requirements. Some islands require passports; others do not, but may require a British visitor's passport.

How to Apply   Applications for new and renewal passports are available from main post offices as well as at the six passport offices, located in Belfast, Glasgow, Liverpool, London, Newport, and Peterborough. You may apply in person at all passport offices, or by mail to all except the London office. Children under 16 may travel on a parent's passport when accompanying them. All passports are valid for 10 years. Allow a month for processing.

A British visitor's passport can include both partners of a married couple. A British visitor's passport is valid for one year and will be issued on the same day that you apply. You must apply in person at a main post office.

Customs   Exact customs regulations vary slightly from island to island, but in general, from countries outside the EC, you may bring home duty-free 200 cigarettes, 100 cigarillos, 50 cigars or 250 grams of tobacco; 1 liter of spirits or 2 liters of fortified or sparkling wine; 2 liters of still table wine; 60 milliliters of perfume; 250 milliliters of toilet water; plus £36 worth of other goods, including gifts and souvenirs.

For further information or a copy of "A Guide for Travellers," which details standard customs procedures as well as what you may bring into the United Kingdom from abroad, contact HM Customs and Excise (New King's Beam House, 22 Upper Ground, London SE1 9PJ, tel. 071/620–1313).

Insurance   Most tour operators, travel agents, and insurance agents sell specialized policies covering accident, medical expenses, personal liability, trip cancellation, and loss or theft of personal property. Some policies include coverage for delayed departure and legal expenses, winter sports, accidents, or motoring abroad. You can also purchase an annual travel-insurance policy valid for every trip you make during the year in which it's purchased (usually only trips of less than 90 days). Before you leave, make sure you will be covered if you have a preexisting medical condition or are pregnant; your insurers may not pay for routine or continuing treatment, or may require a note from your doctor certifying your fitness to travel.

For advice by phone or a free booklet, "Holiday Insurance," that sets out what to expect from a holiday-insurance policy and gives price guidelines, contact the Association of British Insurers (51 Gresham St., London EC2V 7HQ, tel. 071/600–3333; 30 Gordon St., Glasgow G1 3PU, tel. 041/226–3905; Scottish Provincial Bldg., Donegall Sq. W, Belfast BT1 6JE, tel. 0232/249176; call for other locations).

Tour Operators   Packages to the Caribbean are available from **Caribbean Connection** (Concorde House, Forest St., Chester CH1 1QR, tel. 0244/341131), with a 100-page catalogue devoted to Caribbean holidays; **Caribtours** (161 Fulham Rd., London SW3 6SN, tel. 071/581–3517), another Caribbean specialist; **Kuoni Travel**

(Kuoni House, Dorking, Surrey RH5 4AZ, tel. 0306/742222); and **Tradewinds Faraway Holidays** (Station House, 81/83 Fulham High St., London SW6 3JP, tel. 071/731–8000).

Travelers with Disabilities Main information sources include the **Royal Association for Disability and Rehabilitation** (RADAR, 25 Mortimer St., London W1N 8AB, tel. 071/637–5400), which publishes travel information for the disabled in Britain, and **Mobility International** (228 Borough High St., London SE1 1JX, tel. 071/403–5688), the headquarters of an international membership organization that serves as a clearinghouse of travel information for people with disabilities.

Festivals and Seasonal Events

Regardless of when Carnival season starts on each island, it always means days and nights of continuous partying. There's a celebration going on from January through August, it's just a matter of being on the right island!

Curaçao's Carnival season, which lasts from late January to early February, is the first to hit the Caribbean; it features music, dance, and a costumed parade. **Guadaloupe's** Carnival, also in January, begins on a Sunday late in the month and continues until Lent, finishing with a parade of floats and costumes on "Mardi Gras" and a huge bash on Ash Wednesday.

February brings a flood of Carnival events including those on **Bonaire, Martinique, Puerto Rico, St. Lucia, St. Maarten,** and **Trinidad and Tobago,** all of which combine feasting, dancing, music, and parades. **Martinique,** one of the biggest and best celebrations, offers six weeks of *zouks* (all-night revelries). During Carnival on **Trinidad and Tobago,** adults and children alike are swept up in the excitement of Playing Mas'—the state of surrendering completely to the rapture of fantastic spectacle, parades, music, and dancing. For those who feel the urge, places in a genuine "mas' band" can be purchased (long in advance) for fees that vary according to the prestige of the group and the intricacy of the costumes.

Spring brings the **Cayman Islands'** Carnival, which begins on Grand Cayman in May. In July, the season reaches **Saba** and the **Dominican Republic,** whose popular 10-day Merengue Festival features entertainment from outdoor bands and orchestras and the best cuisine from local hotel chefs. **Anguilla's** Carnival begins in early August with street dancing, calypso competitions, the Carnival Queen Coronation, and sumptuous beach barbecues. The **Turks and Caicos** finish the string of festivals during the last days of the month.

There are many other festivals each year around the islands that celebrate their rich local cultures. Barbados' **Holetown Festival** commemorates the first settlement of Barbados on February 17, 1627, with a week of fairs, street markets, and revelry. The Historical and Cultural Foundations organize the **St. Martin Food Festival** in May. During the **Tobago Heritage Festival** in July, each village on Trinidad and Tobago mounts a different show or festivity. Beginning in July and continuing through August, Barbados celebrates the **Crop-Over Festival,** a month-long cheer for the end of the sugarcane harvest. Calypsonians battle for the coveted Calypso Monarch award, and Bajan cooking abounds at the massive Bridgetown Market street fair. The **Hatillo Festival of the Masks,** held in December in Puerto Rico, is a carnival featuring folk music and dancing, as well as parades in which islanders don brightly colored masks and costumes.

Swimming, splashing, and snorkeling aren't the only things going on in these gorgeous green and blue waters. Sportsmen, tourists and islanders travel throughout the Caribbean to watch the many regattas. Grenada's **New Year Fiesta Yacht Race** in late January is highlighted by the "Around Grenada" sailing contest. Antigua's **Sailing Week** in April brings together more than 300 yachts from around the world. The British Virgin Islands' **Spring Regatta, The Curacao Regatta, The Grenada Easter Regatta,** and the U.S. Virgin Islands' **International Rolex Cup Regatta** take place in April. Boat racing is the national sport in Anguilla, and the most important competitions take place on **Anguilla Day,** May 30. Just about every type of competition that can be held on or in water constitutes the week-long "Aqua Action" Festival held in St. Lucia at the end of June. Canoe racing, Sunfish sailing, windsurfing, sportfishing, waterskiing, and a nonmariners' race are some of the main attractions. The U.S. and British Virgin Islands share the **Hook In & Hold On Boardsailing Regatta** in June and July. Grenada's annual **Carriacou Regatta,** which takes place on this island some 16 miles to the north, brings a week of racing and partying at the end of July. Martinique hosts the **Tour des Yoles Rondes** point-to-point yawl race in early August, and the annual **Sailing Regatta** in Bonaire takes place in October. The **Route du Rose,** a transatlantic regatta of tall ships that set sail from St-Tropez in early November, is welcomed to St. Barts in December with a round of festivities.

Music lovers should also take note of several annual events. In January, St. Barts is host to an international collection of soloists and musicians as part of the **Annual St. Barts Music Festival. The Barbados Caribbean Jazz Festival** in Bridgetown features performances of original compositions and traditional jazz for three days at the end of May. At the end of June, the **Aruba Jazz and Latin Music Festival** is held in Oranjestad, offering well-known entertainers performing Latin, pop, jazz, and salsa music at Mansur Stadium. And the **August Reggae Sunsplash International Music Festival** is getting hotter every year, as the best, brightest, and newest of the reggae stars perform in open-air concerts in MoBay on Jamaica.

When to Go

The Caribbean "season" has traditionally been a winter one, usually extending from December 15 to April 14. The winter months are the most fashionable, the most expensive, and the most popular, and most hotels are heavily booked. You have to make your reservations at least two or three months in advance for the very best places. Hotel prices are at their highest in winter; the 20%–50% drop in rates for "summer" (after April 15) is one of the chief advantages of off-season travel. Saving money isn't the only reason to visit the Caribbean during the off-season. Temperatures in summer are virtually the same as in winter. Some restaurants close, and many hotels offer limited facilities, but reservations are easy to get, even at top establishments, and you'll have the beaches virtually to yourself. The flamboyant flowering trees are at their height in summer, and so are most of the flowers and shrubs of the West Indies. In May, June, and July the water is clearer for snorkeling and smoother for sailing in the Virgin Islands and the Grenadines.

Climate The Caribbean climate approaches the ideal of perpetual June. Average year-round temperature for the region is 78°F–85°F. The extremes of temperature are 65°F low, 95°F high, but as everyone knows, it's the humidity, not the heat, that makes you suffer, especially when the two go hand in hand. You can count on downtown shopping areas being hot at midday any time of the year, but air-conditioning provides some respite. Stay near the beaches, where water and trade winds can keep you cool, and shop early or late in the day.

High places can be cool, particularly when the Christmas winds hit Caribbean peaks (they come in late November and last through January). Since most Caribbean islands are mountainous (notable exceptions being the Caymans, Aruba, Bonaire, and Curaçao), the altitude always offers an escape from the latitude. Kingston (Jamaica), Port-of-Spain (Trinidad), and Fort-de-France (Martinique) swelter in summer; climb 1,000 feet or so, though, and everything is fine.

Hurricanes occasionally sweep through the Caribbean, and officials on many islands are not well equipped to warn locals, much less tourists. Check the news daily and keep abreast of brewing tropical storms by reading stateside papers if you can get them. The rainy season, usually in fall, consists mostly of brief showers interspersed with sunshine. You can watch the clouds come over, feel the rain, and remain in your lounge chair for the sun to dry you off. A spell of overcast days is "unusual," as everyone will tell you.

Generally speaking, there's more planned entertainment in winter. The peak of local excitement on many islands, most notably Trinidad, St. Vincent, and the French West Indies, is Carnival (*see* Festivals and Seasonal Events, *above*).

For More Information For current weather conditions for cities in the United States and abroad, plus the local time and helpful travel tips, call the **Weather Channel Connection** (tel. 900/WEATHER; 95¢ per minute) from a touch-tone phone.

What to Pack

Pack light, because baggage carts are nonexistent at most Caribbean airports and luggage restrictions are tight, particularly on small island-hopper planes.

Clothing Dress on the islands is light and casual. Bring loose-fitting clothes made of natural fabrics to see you through days of heat and high humidity. Take a coverup for the beaches, not only to protect you from the sun but also to wear to and from your hotel room. Bathing suits and immodest attire are frowned upon off the beach on many islands. A sun hat is advisable, but you don't have to pack one, since inexpensive straw hats are available everywhere. For shopping and sightseeing, bring walking shorts, jeans, T-shirts, long-sleeve cotton shirts, slacks, and sundresses. You'll need a sweater in the many glacially air-conditioned hotels and restaurants, for protection from the trade winds, and at higher altitudes. Evenings are casual; jacket and tie are rarely required except in the fancier casinos.

Adapters, The general rule in the Caribbean is 110 and 120 volts AC, and
Converters, the outlets take the same two-prong plugs found in the United
Transformers States, but there are a number of exceptions. To be sure, check
with your hotel when making reservations.

You may need an adapter plug, plus a converter, which reduces
the voltage entering the appliance from 220 to 110 volts. There
are converters for high-wattage appliances (such as hair dryers), low-wattage items (such as electric toothbrushes and ra-
zors), and combination models. Hotels sometimes have outlets
marked "For Shavers Only" near the sink; these are 110-volt
outlets for low-wattage appliances; don't use them for a high-
wattage appliance. For more information get a copy of the free
brochure "Foreign Electricity is No Deep Dark Secret," published by adapter-converter manufacturer Franzus (Murtha
Industrial Park, Box 142, Beacon Falls, CT 06403, tel. 203/723–
6664; send a stamped, self-addressed envelope when ordering).

Miscellaneous Bring a spare pair of eyeglasses and sunglasses, and if you have
a health problem that may require you to purchase a prescrip-
tion drug, have your doctor write a prescription using its generic name, since nomenclature varies from island to island.
Better still, take enough to last the duration of the trip: Although you can probably find what you need in the pharmacies,
you may need a local doctor's prescription. You'll want an umbrella during the rainy season; leave the plastic or nylon raincoats at home, since they're extremely uncomfortable in hot,
humid weather. Bring suntan lotion and film from home;
they're much more expensive on the islands. You'll need insect
repellent, too, especially if you plan to walk through rain forests or visit during the rainy season. Don't forget to pack a list
of the addresses of offices that supply refunds for lost or stolen
traveler's checks.

Luggage Free baggage allowances on an airline depend on the airline,
Regulations the route, and the class of ticket. In general, on domestic flights
and on international flights between the United States and foreign destinations, you are entitled to check two bags—neither
exceeding 62 inches, or 158 centimeters (length + width +
height), or weighing more than 70 pounds (32 kilograms). A
third piece may be brought aboard as a carryon; its total di-
mensions are generally limited to less than 45 inches (114 centimeters), so it will fit easily under the seat in front of you or
in the overhead compartment. There are variations, so ask in
advance; small island-hopper planes, especially, have little
room for luggage. The only rule, a Federal Aviation Administration safety regulation that pertains to carry-on baggage on
U.S. airlines, requires only that carryons be properly stowed
and allows the airline to limit allowances and tailor them to
different aircraft and operational conditions. Charges for excess, oversize, or overweight pieces vary, so inquire before you
pack.

If you are flying between two foreign destinations, note that
baggage allowances may be determined not by the piece
method but by the weight method, which generally allows 88
pounds (40 kilograms) of luggage in first class, 66 pounds (30
kilograms) in business class, and 44 pounds (20 kilograms) in
economy. If your flight between two cities abroad *connects* with
your transatlantic or transpacific flight, the piece method still
applies.

Safeguarding Your Before leaving home, itemize your bags' contents and their
Luggage worth; this list will help you estimate the extent of your loss if
your bags go astray. To minimize that risk, tag them inside and
out with your name, address, and phone number. (If you use
your home address, cover it so that potential thieves can't see
it.) At check-in, make sure that the tag attached by baggage
handlers bears the correct three-letter code for your destination. If your bags do not arrive with you, or if you detect damage, do not leave the airport until you've filed a written report
with the airline.

Taking Money Abroad

Traveler's checks and all major U.S. credit cards are accepted
in the Caribbean. Although large hotels, restaurants, and department stores accept credit cards readily, some budget hotels and smaller restaurants and shops operate on a cash-only
basis. U.S. dollars are also accepted on most islands; paying in
dollars may even allow you to bargain for a lower price.

Traveler's Checks Although you will want plenty of cash when visiting small cities
or rural areas, traveler's checks are usually preferable. The
most widely recognized are **American Express, Barclay's, Thomas Cook,** and those issued by major commercial banks such
as **Citibank** and **Bank of America.** American Express also issues **Traveler's Cheques for Two,** which can be signed and used
by you or your traveling companion. Some checks are free; usually the issuing company or the bank at which you make your
purchase charges 1% of the checks' face value as a fee. Be sure
to buy a few checks in small denominations to cash toward the
end of your trip, when you don't want to be left with more foreign currency than you can spend. Always record the numbers
of checks as you spend them, and keep this list separate from
the checks.

You can also buy traveler's checks in the currency of some of
the islands, a good idea if the dollar is dropping in relation to
the local currency. The value of some currencies changes with
great frequency and very radically; some are subject to infla-
tion, others to devaluation, while still others float with the U.S.
dollar. Banks and government-approved exchange houses give
the best rates; hotels will also change currency, but generally
at lower rates. Remember to take the addresses of offices in
the islands where you can get refunds for lost or stolen traveler's checks.

Currency Banks and bank-operated exchange booths at airports are usu-
Exchange ally the best places to change money. Hotels, stores, and privately run exchange firms typically offer less favorable rates.

Before your trip, pay attention to how the dollar is doing vis-
à-vis your destination's currency. If the dollar is losing
strength, try to pay as many travel bills as possible in advance,
especially the big ones. If it is getting stronger, pay for costly
items overseas, and use your credit card whenever possible—
you'll come out ahead, whether the exchange rate at which your
purchase is calculated is the one in effect the day the vendor's
bank abroad processes the charge, or the one prevailing on the
day the charge company's service center processes it at home.

To avoid lines at airport currency-exchange booths, arrive in a
foreign country with a small amount of the local currency al-

ready in your pocket—a so-called tip pack. **Thomas Cook Currency Services** (630 5th Ave., New York, NY 10111, tel. 212/757–6915) supplies foreign currency by mail.

Getting Money from Home

Cash Machines Automated-teller machines (ATMs) are proliferating; many are tied to international networks such as **Cirrus** and **Plus,** both of which have expanded their service in the Caribbean. You can use your bank card at ATMs away from home to withdraw money from your checking account and get cash advances on a credit-card account (providing your card has been programmed with a personal identification number, or PIN). Check in advance on limits on withdrawals and cash advances within specified periods. Ask whether your bank-card or credit-card PIN number will need to be reprogrammed for use in the area you'll be visiting—a possibility if the number has more than four digits. Remember that finance charges apply on credit-card cash advances from ATMs as well as on those from tellers. And note that, although transaction fees for ATM withdrawals abroad will probably be higher than fees for withdrawals at home, Cirrus and Plus exchange rates tend to be good. Be sure to plan ahead: Obtain ATM locations and the names of affiliated cash-machine networks before departure. For specific foreign Cirrus locations, call 800/4–CIRRUS; for foreign Plus locations, consult the Plus directory at your local bank.

American Express Cardholder Services The company's **Express Cash** system lets you withdraw cash and/or traveler's checks from a worldwide network of 57,000 American Express dispensers and participating bank ATMs. You must *enroll first* (call 800/CASH–NOW for a form and allow two weeks for processing). Withdrawals are charged not to your card but to a designated bank account. You can withdraw up to $1,000 per seven-day period on the basic card, more if your card is gold or platinum. There is a 2% fee (minimum $2.50, maximum $10) for each cash transaction, and a 1% fee for traveler's checks (except for the platinum card), which are available only from American Express dispensers.

At AmEx offices, cardholders can also cash personal checks for up to $1,000 in any seven-day period in U.S. territory (21 days abroad); of this, $200 can be in cash, more if available, with the balance paid in traveler's checks, for which all but platinum cardholders pay a 1% fee. Higher limits apply to the gold and platinum cards.

Wiring Money You don't have to be a cardholder to send or receive an **American Express MoneyGram** for up to $10,000. To send one, go to an American Express MoneyGram agent, pay up to $1,000 with a credit card and anything over that in cash, and phone a transaction reference number to your intended recipient, who needs only to present identification and the reference number to the nearest MoneyGram agent to pick up the cash. There are MoneyGram agents in more than 60 countries (call 800/543–4080 for locations). Fees range from 5% to 10%, depending on the amount and how you pay. You can't use American Express,— only Discover, MasterCard, and Visa credit cards.

You can also use **Western Union.** To wire money, take either cash or a check to the nearest office. (Or you can order money sent by phone, using a credit card.) Money sent from the

United States or Canada will be available for pickup at agent locations in the Caribbean within minutes, and fees are roughly 5%–10%. (Note that once the money is in the system it can be picked up at *any* location.) There are approximately 20,000 agents worldwide (call 800/325–6000 for locations).

Passports and Visas

If your passport is lost or stolen abroad, report it immediately to the nearest embassy or consulate and to the local police. If you can provide the consular officer with the information contained in the passport, they will usually be able to issue you a new passport. For this reason, it is a good idea to keep a copy of the data page of your passport in a separate place, or to leave the passport number, date, and place of issuance with a relative or friend at home.

U.S. Citizens You can pick up new and renewal application forms at any of the 13 U.S. Passport Agency offices and at some post offices and courthouses. Although passports are usually mailed within two weeks of your application's receipt, it's best to allow three weeks for delivery in low season, five weeks or more from April through summer. Call the Department of State Office of Passport Services' information line (1425 K St. NW, Washington, DC 20522, tel. 202/647–0518) for fees, documentation requirements, and other details.

Canadian Citizens Application forms are available at 23 regional passport offices as well as post offices and travel agencies. Whether applying for a first or subsequent passport, you must apply in person. Children under 16 may be included on a parent's passport, but must have their own passport to travel alone. Passports are valid for five years and are usually mailed within two weeks of an application's receipt. For fees, documentation requirements, and other information in English or French, call the passport office (tel. 514/283–2152).

Customs and Duties

U.S. Customs Provided you've been out of the country for at least 48 hours and haven't already used the exemption, or any part of it, in the past 30 days, you may bring $600 worth of goods home duty-free from *most* Caribbean countries. This amount—more generous than the $400 duty-free exemption allowed on return from almost everywhere else—applies to two dozen Caribbean Basin Initiative beneficiary countries. If you're returning from the U.S. Virgin Islands, the duty-free allowance is even higher—$1,200. A flat 10% duty applies to the next $1,000 of goods; above that, the rate varies with the merchandise. These exemptions may be pooled among family members, regardless of age, so that one may bring in more if another brings in less. If the 48-hour or 30-day limits apply, your duty-free allowance drops to $25, which may *not* be pooled.

Some wrinkles to the above: If you are visiting more than one island, say the U.S. Virgins and the Dominican Republic (a beneficiary country), you may bring in a total of $1,200 duty-free, of which no more than $600 may be from the Dominican Republic. If you visit a beneficiary country and an excluded one, such as Martinique, you may bring in a total of $600 goods duty-free, of which no more than $400 may be from Martinique.

In addition, the Generalized System of Preferences, aimed at helping developing countries improve their economies through trade, exempts certain items from the same beneficiary countries entirely, meaning that they do not count toward the duty-free total at all. (At press time, the future of GSP beyond its July 4, 1994, expiration date was unknown.)

Travelers 21 or older may bring back two liters of alcohol duty-free from most Caribbean countries, provided the beverage laws of the state through which they reenter the U.S. allow it. (This is again more generous than the usual limit, which is one liter.) In the case of the U.S. Virgin Islands, five liters are allowed. If you are visiting a beneficiary country and an excluded one, no more than one of the two liters allowed may be from the excluded country; if you are visiting the U.S. Virgin Islands and a beneficiary country, no more than two liters of the five allowed may be from the beneficiary country.

Regardless of age, you may bring 100 non-Cuban cigars and 200 cigarettes back to the U.S. From the U.S. Virgin Islands, 1,000 cigarettes are allowed, but only 200 of them may have been acquired elsewhere.

Gifts under $50 may be mailed duty-free to stateside friends and relatives, with a limit of one package per day per addressee (do not send alcohol or tobacco products, nor perfume valued at more than $5). These gifts do not count as part of your exemption, although if you bring them home with you, they do. Mark the package "Unsolicited Gift" and include the nature of the gift and its retail value.

The free brochure "Know Before You Go" lists all Caribbean Basin Initiative beneficiary countries and details what you may and may not bring back to this country, rates of duty, and other pointers; to obtain it, contact the U.S. Customs Service (Box 7407, Washington, DC 20044, tel. 202/927–6724). A copy of "GSP and the Traveler" is available from the same source.

Canadian Customs Once per calendar year, when you've been out of Canada for at least seven days, you may bring in $300 worth of goods duty-free. If you've been away less than seven days but more than 48 hours, the duty-free exemption drops to $100 but can be claimed any number of times (as can a $20 duty-free exemption for absences of 24 hours or more). You cannot combine the yearly and 48-hour exemptions, use the $300 exemption only partially (to save the balance for a later trip), or pool exemptions with family members. Goods claimed under the $300 exemption may follow you by mail; those claimed under the lesser exemptions must accompany you on your return.

Alcohol and tobacco products may be included in the yearly and 48-hour exemptions, but not in the 24-hour exemption. If you meet the age requirements of the province through which you reenter Canada, you may bring in, duty-free, 1.14 liters (40 imperial ounces) of wine or liquor *or* two dozen 12-ounce cans or bottles of beer or ale. If you are 16 or older, you may bring in, duty-free, 200 cigarettes, 50 cigars or cigarillos, and 400 tobacco sticks or 400 grams of manufactured tobacco. Alcohol and tobacco must accompany you on your return.

Gifts may be mailed to friends in Canada duty-free. These do not count as part of your exemption. Each gift may be worth up to $60—label the package "Unsolicited Gift—Value under

$60." There are no limits on the number of gifts that may be sent per day or per addressee, but you can't mail alcohol or tobacco.

For more information, including details of duties on items that exceed your duty-free limit, ask the Revenue Canada Customs and Excise Department (Connaught Bldg., MacKenzie Ave., Ottawa, Ont., K1A OL5, tel. 613/957–0275) for a copy of the free brochure "I Declare/Je Déclare."

Traveling with Cameras and Camcorders

About Film and Cameras If your camera is new or if you haven't used it for a while, shoot and develop a few rolls of film before leaving home. Pack some lens tissue and an extra battery for your built-in light meter, and invest in an inexpensive skylight filter, to both protect your lens and provide some definition in hazy shots. Store film in a cool, dry place—never in the car's glove compartment or on the shelf under the rear window.

Films above ISO 400 are more sensitive to damage from airport security X-rays than others; very high speed films, ISO 1,000 and above, are exceedingly vulnerable. To protect your film, don't put it in checked luggage; carry it with you in a plastic bag and ask for a hand inspection. Such requests are honored at U.S. airports, but may not be by the inspector abroad. Don't depend on a lead-lined bag to protect film in checked luggage—the airline may very well turn up the dosage of radiation to see what you've got in there. Airport metal detectors do not harm film, although you'll set off the alarm if you walk through one with a roll in your pocket. Call the Kodak Information Center (tel. 800/242–2424) for details.

About Camcorders Before your trip, put new or long-unused camcorders through their paces and practice panning and zooming. Invest in a skylight filter to protect the lens and check the lithium battery that lights up the LCD (liquid crystal display) modes. As for the rechargeable nickel-cadmium batteries that are the camera's power source, take along an extra pair, so while you're using your camcorder you'll have one battery ready and another recharging. Most newer camcorders are equipped with the battery (which generally slides or clicks onto the camera body) and, to recharge it, with what's known as a universal or worldwide AC adapter charger (or multivoltage converter) that can be used whether the voltage is 110 or 220. All that's needed is the appropriate plug. Airport security personnel may want you to turn the camcorder on to prove that that's what it is, so make sure the battery is charged when you get to the airport.

About Videotape Unlike still-camera film, videotape is not damaged by X-rays. However, it may well be harmed by the magnetic field of a walk-through metal detector. Note that while most Caribbean islands operate on the National Television System Committee video standard (NTSC), like the United States and Canada, Guadeloupe and Martinique use a different technology known as Secam. For that reason, you will not be able to view your tapes through the local TV set or view movies bought there in your home VCR. (Blank tapes bought in the Caribbean can be used for NTSC camcorder taping, however—although you'll probably find they cost more in the islands and wish you'd brought an adequate supply along.)

Staying Healthy

Few real hazards threaten the health of a visitor to the Caribbean. The small lizards that seem to have overrun the islands are harmless, and poisonous snakes are hard to find, although you should exercise caution while bird-watching in Trinidad. Beware of a tiny sand fly known as the "no see'um," which tends to appear after a rain, near wet or swampy ground, and around sunset. If you feel particularly vulnerable to insect bites, bring along a good repellent.

The worst problem tends to be sunburn or sunstroke. Even people who are not normally bothered by strong sun should head into this area with a long-sleeve shirt, a hat, and long pants or a beach wrap. These are essential for a day on a boat, but are also advisable for midday at the beach and whenever you go out sightseeing. Also carry some sun-block lotion for nose, ears, and other sensitive areas such as eyelids, ankles, etc. Limit your sun time for the first few days until you become used to the heat. And be sure to drink enough liquids.

Since health standards vary from island to island, inquire about local conditions before you go. No special shots are required for most destinations; where they are, we have made note of it.

Scuba divers take note: PADI recommends that you not scuba dive and fly within a 24-hour period.

Finding a Doctor The International Association for Medical Assistance to Travelers (IAMAT, 417 Center St., Lewiston, NY 14092, tel. 716/754–4883; 40 Regal Rd., Guelph, Ont. N1K 1B5; 57 Voirets, 1212 Grand-Lancy, Geneva, Switzerland) publishes a worldwide directory of English-speaking physicians whose qualifications meet IAMAT standards and who have agreed to treat members for a set fee. Membership is free.

Assistance Companies Pretrip medical referrals, emergency evacuation or repatriation, 24-hour telephone hot lines for medical consultation, dispatch of medical personnel, relay of medical records, up-front cash for emergencies, and other personal and legal assistance are among the services provided by several membership organizations specializing in medical assistance to travelers. Among them are **International SOS Assistance** (Box 11568, Philadelphia, PA 19116, tel. 215/244–1500 or 800/523–8930; Box 466, Pl. Bonaventure, Montréal, Qué., H5A 1C1, tel. 514/874–7674 or 800/363–0263), **Near Services** (450 Prairie Ave., Suite 101, Calumet City, IL 60409, tel. 708/868–6700 or 800/654–6700), and **Travel Assistance International** (1133 15th St. NW, Suite 400, Washington, DC 20005, tel. 202/331–1609 or 800/821–2828), part of Europ Assistance Worldwide Services, Inc. Because these companies will also sell you death-and-dismemberment, trip-cancellation, and other insurance coverage, there is some overlap with the travel-insurance policies discussed below, which may include the services of an assistance company among the insurance options or reimburse travelers for such services without providing them.

Insurance

Most tour operators, travel agents, and insurance agents sell specialized health-and-accident, flight, trip-cancellation, and luggage insurance as well as comprehensive policies with some or all of these features. But before you make any purchase, review your existing health and homeowner policies to find out whether they cover expenses incurred while travelling.

Health-and-Accident Insurance Supplemental health-and-accident insurance for travelers is usually a part of comprehensive policies. Specific policy provisions vary, but they tend to address three general areas, beginning with reimbursement for medical expenses caused by illness or an accident during a trip. Such policies may reimburse anywhere from $1,000 to $150,000 worth of medical expenses; dental benefits may also be included. A second common feature is the personal-accident, or death-and-dismemberment, provision, which pays a lump sum to your beneficiaries if you die or to you if you lose one or both limbs or your eyesight. This is similar to the flight insurance described below, although it is not necessarily limited to accidents involving airplanes or even other "common carriers" (buses, trains, and ships) and can be in effect 24 hours a day. The lump sum awarded can range from $15,000 to $500,000. A third area generally addressed by these policies is medical assistance (referrals, evacuation, or repatriation and other services). Some policies reimburse travelers for the cost of such services; others may automatically enroll you as a member of a particular medical-assistance company.

Flight Insurance This insurance, often bought as a last-minute impulse at the airport, pays a lump sum to a beneficiary when a plane crashes and the insured dies (and sometimes to a surviving passenger who loses eyesight or a limb); thus it supplements the airlines' own coverage as described in the limits-of-liability paragraphs on your ticket (up to $75,000 on international flights, $20,000 on domestic ones—and that is generally subject to litigation). Charging an airline ticket to a major credit card often automatically signs you up for flight insurance; in this case, the coverage may also embrace travel by bus, train, and ship.

Baggage Insurance In the event of loss, damage, or theft on international flights, airlines limit their liability to $20 per kilogram for checked baggage (roughly about $640 per 70-pound bag) and $400 per passenger for unchecked baggage. On domestic flights, the ceiling is $1,250 per passenger. Excess-valuation insurance can be bought directly from the airline at check-in, but leaves your bags vulnerable on the ground.

Trip Insurance There are two sides to this coin. Trip-cancellation-and-interruption insurance protects you in the event you are unable to undertake or finish your trip. Default or bankruptcy insurance protects you against a supplier's failure to deliver. Consider the former if your airline ticket, cruise, or package tour does not allow changes or cancellations. The amount of coverage to buy should equal the cost of your trip should you, a traveling companion, or a family member get sick, forcing you to stay home, plus the nondiscounted one-way airline ticket you would need to buy if you had to return home early. Read the fine print carefully; pay attention to sections defining "family member" and "preexisting medical conditions." A characteristic quirk of default policies is that they often do not cover default by travel agencies or default by a tour operator, airline, or cruise line if you bought your tour and the coverage directly from the firm in question. To reduce your need for default insurance, give preference to tours packaged by members of the United States Tour Operators Association (USTOA), which maintains a fund to reimburse clients in the event of member defaults. Even better, pay for travel arrangements with a major credit card, so you can refuse to pay the bill if services have not been rendered—and let the card company fight your battles.

Comprehensive Policies Companies supplying comprehensive policies with some or all of the above features include **Access America, Inc.,** underwritten by BCS Insurance Company (Box 11188, Richmond, VA 23230, tel. 800/284–8300); **Carefree Travel Insurance,** underwritten by The Hartford (Box 310, 120 Mineola Blvd., Mineola, NY 11501, tel. 516/294–0220 or 800/323–3149); **Tele-Trip** (Mutual of Omaha Plaza, Box 31762, Omaha, NE 68131, tel. 800/228–9792), a subsidiary of Mutual of Omaha; **The Travelers Companies** (1 Tower Sq., Hartford, CT 06183, tel. 203/277–0111 or 800/243–3174); **Travel Guard International,** underwritten by Transamerica Occidental Life Companies (1145 Clark St., Stevens Point, WI 54481, tel. 715/345–0505 or 800/782–5151); and Wallach and Company, Inc. (107 W. Federal St., Box 480, Middleburg, VA 22117, tel. 703/687–3166 or 800/237–6615), underwritten by Lloyds, London. These companies may also offer the above types of insurance separately.

Student and Youth Travel

The Caribbean is not as far out of a student's budget as you might expect. Many islands have fine camping facilities, inexpensive guest houses, and small no-frills hotels. You're most likely to meet students from other countries in the French and Dutch West Indies, where many go on holiday or sabbatical. Puerto Rico, Jamaica, Grenada, and Dominica, among others, have large resident international student populations at their universities.

Travel Agencies The foremost U.S. student travel agency is **Council Travel,** a subsidiary of the nonprofit Council on International Educational Exchange. It specializes in low-cost travel arrangements, is the exclusive U.S. agent for several discount cards, and, with its sister CIEE subsidiary, **Council Charter,** is a source of airfare bargains. The Council Charter brochure and CIEE's twice-yearly *Student Travels* magazine, which details its programs, are available at the Council Travel office at CIEE headquarters (205 E. 42nd Street, New York, NY 10017, tel. 212/661–1450) and at 37 branches in college towns nationwide (free in person, $1 by mail). The **Educational Travel Center** (ETC, 438 N. Francis St., Madison, WI 53703, tel. 608/256–5551) also offers low-cost rail passes, domestic and international airline tickets (mostly for flights departing from Chicago), and other budgetwise travel arrangements. Other travel agencies catering to students include **Travel Management International** (TMI, 18 Prescott St., Suite 4, Cambridge, MA 02138, tel. 617/661–8187) and **Travel Cuts** (187 College St., Toronto, Ont. M5T 1P7, tel. 416/979–2406).

Discount Cards For discounts on transportation and on museum and attractions admissions, buy the **International Student Identity Card** (ISIC) if you're a bona fide student, or the **International Youth Card** (IYC) if you're under 26. In the United States, the ISIC and IYC cards cost $15 each and include basic travel accident and sickness coverage. Apply to CIEE (*see* address *above,* tel. 212/661–1414; the application is in *Student Travels*). In Canada, the cards are available for $15 each from Travel Cuts (*see* *above*). In the United Kingdom, they cost £5 and £4, respectively, at student unions and student travel companies, including Council Travel's London office (28A Poland St., London W1V 3DB, tel. 071/437–7767).

Traveling with Children

The Caribbean islands and their resorts are increasingly sensitive to the needs of families. Children's programs are part of all major new hotel developments. Baby food is easy to find, but except at major hotels you may not find such items as high chairs and cribs. Another thing to consider is whether or not English is spoken widely; the language barrier can be frustrating for children.

Getting There All children, including infants, must have a passport for foreign travel.

Airfares What you will pay for your children's tickets depends on your starting and ending points. In some cases, the fare for infants under 2 not occupying a seat is 10% of the accompanying adult's fare, and children ages 2–11 pay half to two-thirds of the adult fare. In other instances, children under 2 not occupying a seat travel free, and older children currently travel on the "lowest applicable" adult fare, as on flights within the United States. Other routes have still other rules, so check ahead.

Safety Seats The FAA recommends the use of safety seats aloft and details approved models in the free leaflet **"Child/Infant Safety Seats Recommended for Use in Aircraft"** (available from the Federal Aviation Administration, APA–200, 800 Independence Ave. SW, Washington, DC 20591, tel. 202/267–3479). Airline policy varies. U.S. carriers must allow FAA-approved models, but because these seats are strapped into a regular passenger seat, they may require that parents buy a ticket even for an infant under 2 who would otherwise ride free. Foreign carriers may not allow infant seats, may charge the child's rather than the infant's fare for their use, or may require you to hold your baby during takeoff and landing, thus defeating the seat's purpose.

Facilities Aloft Airlines do provide other facilities and services for children, such as children's meals and freestanding bassinets (to those sitting in seats on the bulkhead, where there's enough legroom to accommodate them). Make your request when reserving. The annual February/March issue of *Family Travel Times* gives details of the children's services of dozens of airlines (*see below*). "Kids and Teens in Flight" (free from the U.S. Department of Transportation, tel. 202/366–2220) offers tips for children flying alone.

Tour Operators **GrandTravel** (6900 Wisconsin Ave., Suite 706, Chevy Chase, MD 20815, tel. 301/986–0790 or 800/247–7651) offers international and domestic tours for grandparents traveling with their grandchildren. The catalogue, as charmingly written and illustrated as a children's book, positively invites armchair traveling with lap-sitters aboard. **Rascals in Paradise** (650 5th St., Suite 505, San Francisco, CA 94107, tel. 415/978–9800 or 800/872–7225) specializes in programs for families.

Accommodations Children are welcome except in the most exclusive resorts;
Hotels many hotels allow children under 12 or 16 to stay free in their parents' room (be sure to find out the cut-off age when booking). In addition, several hotel chains have developed children's

programs that free parents to explore or relax, and many hotels and resorts arrange for baby-sitting. The following brief list is representative of the kinds of services and activities offered by some of the major chains and resorts. Although some of these hotels are expensive during high season, many offer dramatically lower rates and packages during the summer, when most families with children travel to the Caribbean.

In **Aruba, Aruba Sonesta Hotel, Beach Club & Casino** (tel. 800/766–3782) operates a complimentary "Just Us Kids" program for children ages 5–12. The daily, year-round program features field trips to local Aruban attractions, sports and games, arts-and-crafts classes, and special bonfire nights. Baby-sitting services are also offered.

In **Puerto Rico,** the **Hyatt Regency Cerromar Beach** and the **Hyatt Dorado Beach** operate a camp (tel. 800/233–1234) for children ages 5–12 all summer, at Christmastime, and at Easter. One of the camp's main attractions is a meandering, free-form freshwater pool with waterfalls, bridges, and a 187-foot water slide. The camp's staff includes bilingual college-age counselors. The cost at both hotels is $25 per child per day. The **El San Juan** (tel. 800/468–2818) in Puerto Rico has a program for children in the same age group that features swimnastics, treasure hunts, beach walks, exercise classes, tennis, and an always-open games room.

SuperClubs Boscobel Beach (tel. 800/858–8009) in **Jamaica** is an all-inclusive resort that specializes in families. Seven-night packages are in the $1,000-per-person range, and two children under 14 are allowed to stay free if they occupy the same room as their parents. A small army of SuperNannies is on hand to take charge. The activities are scheduled in half-hour periods so children can drop in and out. For younger children there are morning "Mousercises," a petting zoo, shell hunts, and crafts classes; for teens, "Coke-tail" parties at a disco and "No-Talent" shows.

On **St. Thomas** in the U.S. Virgin Islands the **Stouffer Grand Beach Resort** (tel. 800/233–4935) has half-day and full-day programs for children ages 3–12. In addition to supervising volleyball matches, arts-and-crafts classes, water games, and iguana hunts, the staff arranges outings to the Coral World Marine Life Park and Observatory.

Club Med (tel. 800/CLUB–MED) has Mini Club programs for children as well as a regular roster of activities at resorts in the **Dominican Republic** and **St. Lucia.** Designed for children ages 2–11 and scheduled from 9 AM to 9 PM, the fully supervised Mini Club activities include tennis, waterskiing, sailing, scuba experience in a pool, costume parties, painting and pottery classes, and circus workshops.

Villa Rentals Villa rentals are abundant, often economical, and great for families; island tourist boards can usually refer you to the appropriate realtors. When you book these, be sure to ask about the availability of baby-sitters, housekeepers, and medical facilities (*see* Staying in the Caribbean, *below.*)

Publications **Family Travel Times,** published 10 times a year by Travel With
Newsletter Your Children (TWYCH, 45 W. 18th St., 7th Floor Tower, New York, NY 10011, tel. 212/206–0688; annual subscription $55), covers destinations, types of vacations, and modes of travel; an

airline issue comes out every other year (the last one, February/March 1993, is sold to nonsubscribers for $10). On Wednesday, the staff answers subscribers' questions on specific destinations.

Books   *Great Vacations with Your Kids,* by Dorothy Jordon and Marjorie Cohen ($13; Penguin USA, 120 Woodbine St., Bergenfield, NJ 07621, tel. 800/253–6476), and *Traveling with Children—And Enjoying It,* by Arlene K. Butler ($11.95 plus $3 shipping per book; Globe Pequot Press, Box 833, Old Saybrook, CT 06475, tel. 800/243–0495 or 800/962–0973 in CT), both help you plan your trip with children from toddlers to teens. Also from Globe Pequot is *Recommended Family Resorts in the United States, Canada, and the Caribbean,* by Jane Wilford with Janet Tice ($12.95), which describes 100 resorts at length and includes a "Children's World" section describing activities and facilities as part of each entry.

Hints for Travelers with Disabilities

The Caribbean has not progressed as far as other areas of the world in terms of accommodating travelers with disabilities, and very few attractions and sights are equipped with ramps, elevators, or wheelchair-accessible rest rooms. However, major new properties are beginning to do their planning with the needs of travelers with mobility problems and hearing and visual impairments in mind.

Accommodations   To make sure that a given establishment provides adequate access, ask about specific facilities when making a reservation or consider booking through a travel agent who specializes in travel for the disabled (*see below*). A number of **cruise ships,** such as the *QE II* and the Norwegian Cruise Line's *Seaward,* also recently adapted some of their cabins to meet the needs of passengers with disabilities.

Divi Hotels (tel. 800/367–3484), which has six properties in the Caribbean, runs one of the best dive programs for the disabled at its resort in **Bonaire.** The facility is equipped with ramps; guest rooms and bathrooms can accommodate wheelchairs; and the staff is specially trained to assist divers with disabilities.

Travel Agencies and Tour Operators   **Tomorrow's Level of Care** (TLC, Box 470299, Brooklyn, NY 11247, tel. 718/756–0794 or 800/932–2012) was started by two Barbadian nurses who develop unique vacation programs tailored to travelers with mobility problems and their families. They can arrange everything from accommodations to entire packages. **Directions Unlimited** (720 N. Bedford Rd., Bedford Hills, NY 10507, tel. 914/241–1700), a travel agency, has expertise in tours and cruises for the disabled. **Evergreen Travel Service** (4114 198th St. SW, Suite 13, Lynnwood, WA 98036, tel. 206/776–1184 or 800/435–2288) operates Wings on Wheels Tours for those in wheelchairs, White Cane Tours for the blind, and tours for the deaf; it makes group and independent arrangements for travelers with any disability. **Flying Wheels Travel** (143 W. Bridge St., Box 382, Owatonna, MN 55060, tel. 800/535–6790 or 800/722–9351 in MN), a tour operator and travel agency, arranges international tours, cruises, and independent travel itineraries for people with mobility disabilities. **Nautilus,** at the same address as TIDE (*see below*), packages tours for the disabled internationally.

Information Sources Several organizations provide travel information for people with disabilities, usually for a membership fee, and some publish newsletters and bulletins. Among them are the **Information Center for Individuals with Disabilities** (Fort Point Pl., 27–43 Wormwood St., Boston, MA 02210, tel. 617/727–5540 or 800/462–5015 in MA between 11 and 4, or leave message; TDD/TTY tel. 617/345–9743); **Mobility International USA** (Box 3551, Eugene, OR 97403, voice and TDD tel. 503/343–1284), the U.S. branch of an international organization based in Britain and present in 30 countries; **MossRehab Hospital Travel Information Service** (1200 W. Tabor Rd., Philadelphia, PA 19141, tel. 215/456–9603, TDD tel. 215/456–9602); **The Society for the Advancement of Travel for the Handicapped** (SATH, 347 5th Ave., Suite 610, New York, NY 10016, tel. 212/447–7284, fax 212/725–8253); the **Travel Industry and Disabled Exchange** (TIDE, 5435 Donna Ave., Tarzana, CA 91356, tel. 818/368–5648); and **Travelin' Talk** (Box 3534, Clarksville, TN 37043, tel. 615/552–6670).

Publications In addition to the fact sheets, newsletters, and books mentioned above, several free publications are available from the Consumer Information Center (Pueblo, CO 81009): "New Horizons for the Air Traveler with a Disability," a U.S. Department of Transportation booklet describing changes resulting from the 1986 Air Carrier Access Act and those still to come from the 1990 Americans with Disabilities Act (include Department 608Y in the address), and the Airport Operators Council's *Access Travel: Airports* (Dept. 5804), which describes facilities and services for the disabled at more than 500 airports worldwide.

Twin Peaks Press (Box 129, Vancouver, WA 98666, tel. 206/694–2462 or 800/637–2256) publishes the *Directory of Travel Agencies for the Disabled* ($19.95), listing more than 370 agencies worldwide; *Travel for the Disabled* ($19.95), listing some 500 access guides and accessible places worldwide; the *Directory of Accessible Van Rentals* ($9.95) for campers and RV travelers worldwide; and *Wheelchair Vagabond* ($14.95), a collection of personal travel tips. Add $2 per book for shipping.

Hints for Older Travelers

Special facilities, rates, and package deals for older travelers are not common in the Caribbean. When planning your trip, be sure to inquire about everything from senior-citizen discounts to available medical facilities. Focus on your vacation needs: Are you interested in sightseeing, activities, golf, ecotourism, the beach? Accessibility may be an important consideration for you. When booking, inquire whether you can easily get to the things that you enjoy. The more remote islands have fewer options and amenities.

Organizations The **American Association of Retired Persons** (AARP, 601 E St. NW, Washington, DC 20049, tel. 202/434–2277) provides independent travelers the Purchase Privilege Program, which offers discounts on hotels, car rentals, and sightseeing. AARP also arranges group tours, cruises, and apartment living through AARP Travel Experience from American Express (400 Pinnacle Way, Suite 450, Norcross, GA 30071, tel. 800/927–0111); these can be booked through travel agents, except for the cruises, which must be booked directly (tel. 800/745–4567).

AARP membership is open to those 50 and over; annual dues are $8 per person or couple.

Two other membership organizations offer discounts on lodgings, car rentals, and other travel products, along with such nontravel perks as magazines and newsletters. The **National Council of Senior Citizens** (1331 F St. NW, Washington, DC 20004, tel. 202/347–8800) is a nonprofit advocacy group with some 5,000 local clubs across the United States; membership costs $12 per person or couple annually. **Mature Outlook** (6001 N. Clark St., Chicago, IL 60660, tel. 800/336–6330), a Sears Roebuck & Co. subsidiary with 800,000 members, charges $9.95 for an annual membership.

Note: When using any senior-citizen identification card for reduced hotel rates, mention it when booking, not when checking out. At restaurants, show your card before you're seated; discounts may be limited to certain menus, days, or hours. If you are renting a car, ask about promotional rates that might improve on your senior-citizen discount.

Educational Travel **Elderhostel** (75 Federal St., 3rd floor, Boston, MA 02110, tel. 617/426–7788) is a nonprofit organization that has offered inexpensive study programs for people 60 and older. Programs take place at more than 1,800 educational institutions in the United States, Canada, and 45 countries overseas, and courses cover everything from marine science to Greek myths and cowboy poetry. Participants generally attend lectures in the morning and spend the afternoon sightseeing or on field trips; they live in dorms on the host campuses. Unique home-stay programs are offered in a few countries. Fees for the two- to three-week international trips—including room, board, tuition, and transportation from the United States—range from $1,800 to $4,500.

Tour Operators **Saga International Holidays** (222 Berkeley St., Boston, MA 02116, tel. 800/343–0273), which specializes in group travel for people over 60, offers a selection of variously priced tours and cruises covering five continents. If you want to take your grandchildren, look into GrandTravel (*see* Traveling with Children, *above*).

Arriving and Departing

By Plane

Flights are either nonstop, direct, or connecting. A **nonstop** flight requires no change of plane and makes no stops. A **direct** flight stops at least once and can involve a change of plane, although the flight number remains the same; if the first leg is late, the second waits. This is not the case with a **connecting** flight, which involves a different plane and a different flight number.

Generally, nonstop flights are available from major East Coast cities—usually New York, Boston, Atlanta, and Miami—to Puerto Rico, St. Maarten, Antigua, Jamaica, Aruba, the Dominican Republic, St. Thomas, St. Lucia, and Barbados. Direct flights are usually available from other major cities, such as Toronto, Chicago, Los Angeles, Dallas, Houston, Minneapolis, San Francisco, and Seattle. If you're flying to islands other than the above, you'll probably be changing planes, most likely in Puerto Rico, Antigua, or Aruba.

Airports Most Caribbean airports are one-strip affairs, with a waiting room, bar, and little else. The largest is San Juan's **Luis Muños Marín,** a major hub for American and Continental. Other large airports where you're likely to catch inter-island flights: Antigua's **V.C. Bird,** Barbados's **Grantley Adams,** The Dominican Republic's **Las Américas** and **La Unión,** Jamaica's **Donald Sangster** and **Norman Manley,** St. Maarten's **Juliana,** and St. Thomas's **Cyril E. King.**

Airlines North American carriers serving the Caribbean from various U.S. and Canadian gateways include the largest, **American** (tel. 800/433–7300), as well as **Air Canada** (tel. 800/776–3000), **Continental** (tel. 800/231–0856), **Delta** (tel. 800/221–1212), **Northwest** (tel. 800/447–4747), **TWA** (tel. 800/892–4141), **United** (tel. 800/241–6522), and **USAir** (tel. 800/428–4322). Major European carriers serving the Caribbean (mostly out of New York and Miami) include **Air France** (tel. 800/237–2747), **British Airways** (tel. 800/247–9297), **Iberia** (tel. 800/772–4642), and **Lufthansa** (tel. 800/645–3880). The primary international regional carriers are **Air Aruba** (tel. 800/827–8221), **Air Jamaica** (tel. 800/523–5585), **BWIA** (tel. 800/327–7401), **Cayman Airways** (tel. 800/422–9626), **Dominican** (tel. 212/765–7310), **LACSA** (tel. 800/225–2272), and **VIASA** (tel. 800/327–5454). By far the largest inter-island carriers are **LIAT** (tel. 800/791–3838) and Windward Islands Airways, or **Winair** (tel. 599/5–42255).

Cutting Flight Costs The Sunday travel section of most newspapers is a good source of deals. When booking, particularly through an unfamiliar company, call the Better Business Bureau to find out whether any complaints have been registered against the company, pay with a credit card if you can, and consider trip-cancellation and default insurance.

Promotional Airfares All the less expensive fares, called promotional or discount fares, are round-trip and involve restrictions. The exact nature of the restrictions depends on the airline, the route, and the season and on whether travel is domestic or international, but you must usually buy the ticket—commonly called an APEX (advance purchase excursion) when it's for international travel—in advance (seven, 14, or 21 days is usual). You must also respect certain minimum- and maximum-stay requirements (for instance, over a Saturday night or at least seven and no more than 30, 45, or 90 days), and you must be willing to pay penalties for changes. Airlines generally allow some changes for a fee. But the cheaper the fare, the more likely the ticket is nonrefundable; it would take a death in the family for the airline to give you any of your money back, if you had to cancel. The cheapest fares are also subject to availability; because only a certain percentage of the plane's total seats will be sold at that price, they may go quickly.

Consolidators Consolidators or bulk-fare operators—also known as bucket shops—buy blocks of seats on scheduled flights that airlines anticipate they won't be able to sell. They pay wholesale prices, add a markup, and resell the seats to travel agents or directly to the public at prices that still undercut the airline's promotional or discount fares. You pay more than on a charter, but ordinarily less than for an APEX ticket, and, even when there is not much of a price difference, the ticket usually comes without the advance-purchase restriction. Moreover, although tickets are marked nonrefundable so you can't turn them in to the airline for a full-fare refund, some consolidators sometimes give you your money back. Carefully read the fine print detailing penalties for changes and cancellations. If you doubt the reliability of a company, call the airline once you've made your booking and confirm that you do, indeed, have a reservation on the flight.

The biggest U.S. consolidator, C.L. Thomson Express, sells only to travel agents. Well-established consolidators selling to the public include **UniTravel** (Box 12485, St. Louis, MO 63132, tel. 314/569–0900 or 800/325–2222); **Council Charter** (205 E. 42nd St., New York, NY 10017, tel. 212/661–0311 or 800/800–8222), a division of the Council on International Educational Exchange and a longtime charter operator now functioning more as a consolidator; and **Travac** (989 6th Ave., New York, NY 10018, tel. 212/563–3303 or 800/872–8800), also a former charterer.

Charter Flights Charters usually have the lowest fares and the most restrictions. Departures are limited and seldom on time, and you can lose all or most of your money if you cancel. (Generally, the closer to departure you cancel, the more you lose, although sometimes you will be charged only a small fee if you supply a substitute passenger.) The charterer, on the other hand, may legally cancel the flight for any reason up to 10 days before departure; within 10 days of departure, the flight may be canceled only if it becomes physically impossible to operate it. The charterer may also revise the itinerary or increase the price after you have bought the ticket, but if the new arrangement constitutes a "major change," you have the right to a refund. Before buying a charter ticket, read the fine print for the company's refund policy and details on major changes. Money for charter flights is usually paid into a bank escrow account, the name of which should be on the contract. If you don't pay by credit card, make your check payable to the escrow account (unless you're dealing with a travel agent, in which case, his or her check should be payable to the escrow account). The Department of Transportation's Consumer Affairs Office (I–25, Washington, DC 20590, tel. 202/366–2220) can answer questions on charters and send you its "Plane Talk: Public Charter Flights" information sheet.

Charter operators may offer flights alone or with ground arrangements that constitute a charter package. Well-established charter operators include **Council Charter** (205 E. 42nd St., New York, NY 10017, tel. 212/661–0311 or 800/800–8222), now largely a consolidator, despite its name, and **Travel Charter** (1120 E. Long Lake Rd., Troy, MI 48098, tel. 313/528–3500 or 800/521–5267), with Midwestern departures. **DER Tours** (Box 1606, Des Plains, IL 60017, tel. 800/782–2424), a charterer and consolidator, sells through travel agents. Charter flights to the Caribbean are also offered by **Carnival Airlines** (tel. 800/824–7386).

Discount Travel Travel clubs offer their members unsold space on airplanes,
Clubs cruise ships, and package tours at nearly the last minute and at well below the original cost. Suppliers thus receive some revenue for their "leftovers," and members get a bargain. Membership generally includes a regular bulletin or access to a toll-free telephone hot line giving details of available trips

departing anywhere from three or four days to several months in the future. Packages tend to be more common than flights alone, so if airfares are your only interest, read the literature before joining. Reductions on hotels are also available. Clubs include **Discount Travel International** (114 Forrest Ave., Suite 203, Narberth, PA 19072, tel. 215/668–7184; $45 annually, single or family), **Moment's Notice** (425 Madison Ave., New York, NY 10017, tel. 212/486–0503; $45 annually, single or family), **Travelers Advantage** (CUC Travel Service, 49 Music Sq. W, Nashville, TN 37203, tel. 800/548–1116; $49 annually, single or family), and **Worldwide Discount Travel Club** (1674 Meridian Ave., Miami Beach, FL 33139, tel. 305/534–2082; $50 annually for family, $40 single).

Smoking   Since February 1990, smoking has been banned on all domestic flights of less than six hours' duration; the ban also applies to domestic segments of international flights aboard U.S. and foreign carriers.

Staying in the Caribbean

Getting Around

Many islands are so small that a day or two of exploring in a rental car or with an organized tour are all the transportation you'll need; the rest of your vacation may be spent strolling between the beach and your hotel's dining room. If you're staying in a villa or budget hotel far from the beach and your hotel does not provide a shuttle, on the other hand, you'll probably need a car for the duration of your stay. But whether you need wheels for a day or for two weeks, it pays to look into the options available and compare costs. In general, a full day's guided tour on a Caribbean island is more expensive than a single day of car rental, but not always: Car rental costs can vary widely from island to island (from $30 a day up to $80), and there are also gas and local driving license purchases to be considered. On a smaller island, where a drive of a few hours is sufficient to see the sights, you may find half-day tours are comparable or even cheaper than renting your own car. And although guided tours usually charge per person, many private taxi drivers charge the same price for up to four people in a single cab. If you're with a group, you may find that hiring a cab and driver is actually the cheapest way to see the island.

Other transportation options that can save you money include minivans, scooters, bicycles, and buses. Although public transportation is practically nil in much of the Caribbean, you can find reliable bus systems on some of the larger islands, such as Barbados. In some cases such buses are good choices for short trips; most are not recommended for touring an island. In general, traveling by public transportation requires a more flexible attitude and a willingness to endure erratic schedules and crowded, sometimes dilapidated vehicles. For local color, however, it can't be beat. Look into bicycling if your island is small enough and flat enough to make this a practical means of getting around. There are even some islands where hitchhiking is the preferred method of getting places. Be sure to study the Getting Around section in each island's chapter; it explains the transportation options and costs on that island.

Shopping

Many Caribbean ports of call are duty-free. Don't assume that this automatically means prices are cheap. It pays to know the standard prices stateside and to comparison shop. You may do better at your local store's clearance sale (especially if you live in the New York area). In general, you'll realize the most substantial savings (often 25%–50% off) on items manufactured outside the United States. Local crafts usually make the best buys and gifts. Seek out crafts markets, and remember that bargaining is expected. Some of the indigenous items to look for are spices in Grenada; rums in Jamaica, Barbados, and Martinique; *santos* in Puerto Rico, straw work in Dominica, and Saba lace on Saba. Shells, batiks, and locally made bay rum fragrances are other possibilities. Even if some of these items *seem* pricey, they're usually a fraction of the cost stateside (assuming you can find them).

Dining

For the longest time, cuisine in the Caribbean was thought to be the weakest part of many an island vacation. Many hotels and restaurants assumed that visitors weren't interested in local foods, and instead served poorly prepared Continental fare garnished with a dismal papaya slice or banana leaf. Happily, this is now changing.

The cuisine of the islands is difficult to pin down because of the region's history as a colonial battleground and ethnic melting pot. The gracefully sauced French presentations of Martinique, for example, are far removed from the hearty Spanish casseroles of Puerto Rico, and even further removed from the pungent curries of Trinidad.

The one quality that best defines Caribbean-style cooking has to be its essential spiciness. While reminiscent of Tex-Mex and Cajun, Caribbean cuisine is more varied and more subtle than its love of peppers implies. The region's abundant seafood has also helped define Caribbean cooking. Caribbean lobster, closer to crawfish than to Maine lobster, has no claws and tends to be much tougher than the New England variety. Another local favorite is conch, biologically quite close to land-loving escargots. Conch chowder, conch fritters, conch salad, conch cocktail—no island menu would be complete without at least a half-dozen conch dishes.

For many vacationers, much of the Caribbean experience has to do with the consumption of frothy blended fruit drinks whose main and potent ingredient is Caribbean rum. Whether you are staying in a superdeluxe resort or a small, locally operated guest house, you will find that rum flows as freely as water. Hard liquors other than rum, as well as wine, are usually fairly expensive in the Caribbean. The local beers (Carib and Jamaica's Red Stripe) are light, flavorful, and inexpensive.

Unless you've chosen a money-saving meal plan at your hotel, seek out informal restaurants and casual cafés and sample the island's local Creole and West Indian specialties. Don't be afraid of the barbecue stands found on most islands; the food is usually fresh, cheap, and tasty. If all you need is something quick and cheap, you can always resort to American fast-food stops on larger islands such as St. Thomas and Jamaica. The restaurant reviews in the chapters that follow indicate only when reservations are necessary or advised. Since dining is usually informal throughout the region, we have mentioned attire only when something more elegant or formal than casual dress is called for.

Lodging

Although the Caribbean is best known for its exclusive hideaways and deluxe resorts, affordable accommodations abound, from large, mid-priced hotels and all-inclusives to charming small inns and cost-effective apartment and home rentals. In addition to the information provided here, each chapter includes a detailed look at that island's over-all lodging situation: what's available, in what areas, and at what prices (*see* Lodging introductions in chapters that follow). *See also* Lodging in the Introduction, *above,* for general tips on how to save.

Plan ahead and reserve a room well before you travel to the Caribbean. If you have reservations but expect to arrive later than 5 or 6 PM, advise the hotel, inn, or guest house in advance. Also be sure to find out what the rate quoted includes—use of sports facilities and equipment, airport transfers, and the like—and whether it operates on the **European Plan** (EP, with no meals), **Continental Plan** (CP, with Continental breakfast), **Breakfast Plan** (BP, with full breakfast), **Modified American Plan** (MAP, with two meals), or **Full American Plan** (FAP, with three meals), or is **All-inclusive** (with three meals, all facilities, and drinks unless otherwise noted). Be sure to bring your deposit receipt with you in case any questions arise when you arrive at your hotel. Above all, find out what's included in the price! Some hotels neglect to mention you'll be paying a tax and service charge on top of the quoted rate. Some may charge extra for the use of sports equipment or even beach chairs. A Full American Plan may be ideal for travelers on a budget who don't want to worry about additional expenses, but those who enjoy a different dining experience each night will prefer to book rooms on a European Plan. Since many hotels insist on a Modified American Plan, particularly during high season, find out whether you can exchange dinners for lunch. In lodging reviews throughout the book, we have indicated what meal plans are available in each review's service information.

Decide whether you want a hotel on the leeward side of the island (with calm water, good for snorkeling) or on the windward (with waves, for good surfing). Inquire about the view; in most cases you pay more to look at the ocean than at the garden or another part of the property. Also find out how close the property is to a beach; at some hotels you can walk barefoot from your room onto the sand; others are across a road or are a 10-minute drive away. This information is essential to help you determine whether you must rent a vehicle to get to the beach (unless your hotel provides a shuttle).

Air-conditioning is not a necessity on all islands, most of which are cooled by trade winds, but an air conditioner can be a plus if you enjoy an afternoon snooze. Breezes are stronger in second-floor rooms, particularly corner rooms, which enjoy cross ventilation. If you like to sleep without air-conditioning, make sure that windows can open and come with screens. Many budget properties do not have air-conditioning. Don't automatically be put off by this: Even many super-luxe hideaways known for their "barefoot elegance" have rooms cooled exclusively by trade winds and ceiling fans. Many sophisticated Caribbean visitors wouldn't have it any other way.

Given the vast differences in standards and accommodations in the various islands covered in this book, it would be impossible (and misleading) to establish uniform categories such as first class, second class, and so on. Instead, we have used categories to indicate price rather than quality. Price estimates throughout are for high season: Although we strongly recommend that travelers on a budget visit the Caribbean during the off-season (*see* Introduction, *above*), not everyone will be able to or will want to do so. You'll be better prepared if you know the worst. Prices are given in ranges rather than exact amounts, and are intended as a guideline only.

Apartment and Villa Rentals Apartment rentals are plentiful on some islands and are usually reasonably priced. Villas, on the other hand, tend to be expensive, but often only because they have several bedrooms; if you are traveling with another family or a group and split the cost, even large properties become affordable. Smaller, one- and two-bedroom house rentals are also available on some islands. A good villa rental company will be able to match your tastes and budget to a suitable property. Some send an illustrated catalogue, and others send photographs of specific properties, sometimes at a charge; up-front registration fees may apply.

Among the companies with properties in the Caribbean are **At Home Abroad** (405 E. 56th St., Suite 6H, New York, NY 10022, tel. 212/421–9165); **Overseas Connection** (31 N. Harbor Dr., Sag Harbor, NY 11963, tel. 516/725–9308); **Rent a Home International** (7200 34th Ave. NW, Seattle, WA 98117, tel. 206/789–9377 or 800/488–7368); **Vacation Home Rentals Worldwide** (235 Kensington Ave., Norwood, NJ 07648, tel. 201/767–9393 or 800/633–3284); **Villa Leisure** (Box 209, Westport, CT 06881, tel. 407/624–9000 or 800/526–4244); **Villas and Apartments Abroad** (420 Madison Ave., Suite 1105, New York, NY 10017, tel. 212/759–1025 or 800/433–3020); **Villas International** (605 Market St., Suite 510, San Francisco, CA 94105, tel. 415/281–0910 or 800/221–2260); **Caribbean Escapes, Inc.** (Box 550, New York, NY 11018, tel. 718/855–8737 or 800/231–5303); **Prestige Villas** (Box 1046, Southport, CT 06490, tel. 203/254–1302 or 800/336–0080); **Villas Caribe** (9403 E. Chenango, Englewood, CO. 80111, tel. 303/741–2219 or 800/645–7498, fax 303/741–2520); and **Villas of Distinction** (Box 55, Armonk, N.Y. 10504, tel. 914/273–3331 or 800/289–0900). **Hideaways International** (15 Goldsmith St., Box 1270, Littleton, MA 01460, tel. 508/486–8955 or 800/843–4433), with properties in the Caribbean, functions as a travel club. Membership ($79 yearly per person or family at the same address) includes two annual guides plus quarterly newsletters; rentals are arranged directly between members, not by the club staff.

For a more detailed description of the Caribbean villa rental experience, *see* Introduction, *above. See also* Lodging in island chapters for additional rental companies on specific islands.

Credit Cards

The following credit card abbreviations have been used: AE, American Express; D, Discover Card; DC, Diners Club; MC, MasterCard; V, Visa. It's a good idea to call ahead to check current credit card policies.

Boating

Cruises Although standard brochure rates for cruise lines that ply these lovely waters are on the pricey side, there are definitely deals to be had. The key to cruising the Caribbean on a budget is to connect with the special packages and rates offered by cruise lines through your local travel agent. Currently popular are early booking programs, which slash prices by as much as half the standard rate when you book early. Lines that offer such programs include **Carnival Cruise Lines** (3655 N.W. 87th Ave., Miami, FL 33178, tel. 800/327–9501); **Holland America Line** (300 Elliott Ave. W, Seattle, WA 98119, tel. 800/426–0327); **Norwegian Crusie Line** (95 Merrick Way, Coral Gables, FL 33134, tel. 305/447–9660 or 800/327–7030); and **Royal Caribbean Cruise Line** (1050 Caribbean Way, Miami, FL 33132, tel. 800/327–6700).

Charters If you are an experienced sailor, bare-boat chartering can be an affordable way to visit the Caribbean, particularly during the off season. Indeed, off-season prices for even crewed charters can fit your budget when the cost is divided among several couples. As always, be sure to find out exactly what is included in the price. A good broker can help you select a charter that matches your needs and budget. These include **Blue Water Cruises** (Box 292, Islesboro, ME 04848, tel. 800/524–2020); **Ed Hamilton & Co.** (Box 430, N. Whitefield, ME 04353, tel. 800/621–7855); **Lynhollen Yacht Charters** (601 University Ave. #150, Sacramento, CA 95825, tel. 916/920–0820); **Lynn Jachney** (Box 302, Marblehead, MA 01945, tel. 800/223–2050); **Regency Yacht Vacations** (Long Bay Rd., St. Thomas, USVI 00802, tel. 800/524–7676); **Russell Yacht Charters** (2750 Black Rock Turnpike, Suite 27, Fairfield, CT 06430, tel. 800/635–8895); **Shannon Webster Charters** (1126 S. Federal Hwy., Suite 254, Fort Lauderdale, FL 33316, tel. 800/525–8860); **Ann-Wallis White** (Box 4100, Horn Point Harbor, Annapolis, MD 21403, tel. 800/732–3861); and **Yacht Charters International** (10 Vineyard Hill Rd., Woodside, CA 94062, tel. 800/835–7090).

2 Anguilla

*Updated by
Jordan Simon*

At first glance, the charms of Anguilla (which rhymes with vanilla) may be difficult to detect. It is not a particularly pretty
island. There are no lush rain forests or majestic mountains.
It's a dry limestone isle with a thin covering of soil over the
rock and has neither streams nor rivers, only saline ponds used
for salt production. Nevertheless, this long, skinny, eel-shaped
island just 20 minutes from the bustle of St. Martin-St.
Maarten's resorts and casinos has debuted and become a very
popular, and so far unspoiled, princess at the Caribbean ball.

Anguilla is noted for expensive, luxurious enclaves that exist
to pamper. But the island also offers a wide range of affordable
guest houses, apartments, and small hotels, many right on the
water. That's where you're likely to find yourself, for Anguilla
has no glittering casinos, fascinating historic sites, or duty-free
shops to distract you. The most rewarding activities here are
getting to know the warm inhabitants and the sparkling
beaches surrounded by clear waters and brilliant coral reefs.

Anguilla is the most northerly of the Leeward Islands, lying
between the Caribbean Sea and the Atlantic Ocean. Stretching
from northeast to southwest, it's about 16 miles long and only
3 miles across at its widest point. The keen eye of Christopher
Columbus seems not to have spotted this island. *Anguilla*
means "eel" in Italian, but the Spanish *anguila* or French *anguille* (both of which also mean "eel") may have been the original name. New archaeological evidence shows that the island
was inhabited as long as 2,000 years ago by Indians who named

Anguilla

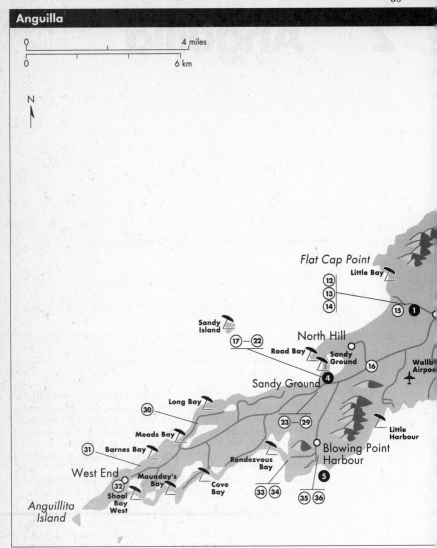

0 — 4 miles
0 — 6 km

N

Flat Cap Point
Little Bay
⑫
⑬
⑭
⑮ ❶

Sandy Island
⑰ — ㉒
North Hill
Road Bay
Sandy Ground
⑯
Wallb
Airpo

Sandy Ground ❹

Long Bay
㉚
㉓ — ㉙
Little Harbour

Meads Bay
㉛ Barnes Bay
West End
㉜
Maunday's Bay
Shoal Bay West
Cove Bay
Rendezvous Bay
Blowing Point Harbour
❺
㉝ ㉞
㉟ ㊱

Anguillita Island

Exploring
Blowing Point
Harbour, **5**
The Fountain, **2**
Sandy Ground, **4**
Sandy Hill Bay, **3**
Wallblake House, **1**

Lodging
Blue Waters Inn, **32**
Easy Corner Villas, **27**
Ferryboat Inn, **35**
Harbour Lights, **7**
Harbour Villas, **8**
Inter-Island Hotel, **28**
La Palma, **20**
La Sirena, **30**

The Mariners, **21**
The Pavillion, **36**
Rainbow Reef, **38**
Rendezvous Bay
Hotel, **33**
The Seahorse, **34**
Skiffles Villas, **29**
Sydan's, **22**
Yellow Banana, **11**

Dining
Aquarium, **23**
Arlo's, **24**
Brothers Cafeteria, **12**
Chillie's, **17**
Cross Roads, **13**
Johnno's, **18**
La Fontana, **9**

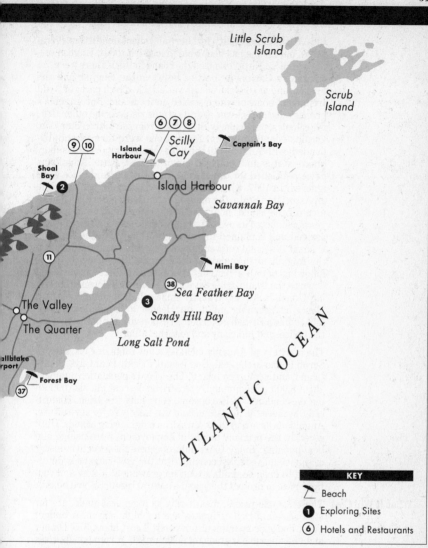

Little Scrub
Island

Scrub
Island

⑥⑦⑧
Scilly
Cay

Captain's Bay

⑨⑩
Island
Harbour

Shoal
Bay

❷

Island Harbour

Savannah Bay

⑪

Mimi Bay

㊳ Sea Feather Bay

❸

Sandy Hill Bay

The Valley

The Quarter

Long Salt Pond

allblake
rport

Forest Bay

㊲

ATLANTIC OCEAN

KEY

Beach

❶ Exploring Sites

⑥ Hotels and Restaurants

the island Malliouhana, a more mellifluous title that's been adopted by some of the island's shops and resorts.

In 1631, the Dutch built a fort here and maintained it for several years, but no one has been able to locate it today. English settlers from St. Kitts colonized the island in 1650. There were the obligatory Caribbean battles between the English and the French, and in 1688 the island was attacked by a party of "wild Irishmen," some of whom settled on the island. But Anguilla's primary discontent was over its status vis-à-vis the other British colonies, particularly St. Kitts. From the 19th century on, various island units and federations were formed and disbanded, with Anguilla all the while simmering over its subordinate status and enforced union with St. Kitts. Anguillans twice petitioned for direct rule from Britain, and twice were ignored. In 1967, when St. Kitts, Nevis, and Anguilla became an Associated State, the mouse roared, kicked St. Kitts policemen off the island, held a self-rule referendum, and for two years conducted its own affairs. In 1968, a senior British official arrived and remained for a year working with the Anguilla Council. A second referendum in 1969 confirmed the desire of the Anguillans to remain apart from St. Kitts-Nevis, and the following month a British "peacekeeping force" parachuted down to the island, where it was greeted with flowers, fluttering Union Jacks, and friendly smiles. Today Anguilla elects a House of Assembly and its own leader to handle internal affairs, while a British governor is responsible for public service, the police, and judiciary and external affairs.

The territory of Anguilla includes a few islets or cays, such as Scrub Island to the east, Dog Island, Prickly Pear Cays, Sandy Island, and Sombrero Island. The island's population numbers about 8,000, predominantly of African descent but also including descendants of Europeans, especially the Irish. Historically, because the limestone land was hardly fit for agriculture, Anguillans have had to seek work on neighboring islands. Until recently, the primary means of employment were fishing and boat building. Today, tourism has become the growth industry of the island's stable economy. But the government is determined to keep Anguilla's tourism growing at a slow and cautious pace to protect the island's natural resources and beauty.

What It Will Cost These sample prices, meant only as a general guide, are for high season. Price estimates are for high season. A budget guest house or apartment for two will cost about $75. Dinner at an inexpensive restaurant is about $20. A rum punch, glass of wine, or other cocktail is about $3; a beer at a local bar costs $2.50. Car-rental rates are reasonable here, about $35–$45. Taxis are expensive; the trip from Sandy Ground or Road Bay to the Valley is around $15. A sailing excursion, with snorkeling and lunch provided, is around $40. Snorkel equipment rents for about $6.

Before You Go

Tourist Information Contact the very helpful **Anguilla Tourist Information and Reservation Office** (c/o Medhurst & Associates, 271 Main St., Northport, NY 11768, tel. 212/869–0402, 516/261–1234, or 800/553–4939). In the United Kingdom, contact the **Anguilla Tourist Office** (3 Epirus Rd., London SW6 7UJ, tel. 071/937–7725).

Arriving and Departing **American Airlines** (tel. 800/433–7300) is the major airline with
By Plane nonstop flights from the United States to its hub in San Juan,
from which the airline's **American Eagle** flies twice daily to Anguilla, the first flight connecting with East Coast and Canadian
flights, the second with those from the Midwest and West.
Windward Islands Airways (Winair) (tel. 809/775–0183) wings
in daily from St. Thomas and four times a day from St.
Maarten's Juliana Airport. **Air BVI** (tel. 809/774–6500) flies in
five times daily from St. Thomas and from San Juan three
times a week, and **LIAT** (tel. 809/465–2286) comes in from St.
Kitts and Antigua. **Air Anguilla** (tel. 809/497–2643) has regularly scheduled daily flights from St. Thomas, St. Maarten, San
Juan, and Tortola. It also provides air-taxi service on request
from neighboring islands, as does **Tyden Air** (tel. 809/497–
2719).

From the Airport At **Wallblake Airport** you'll find taxis lined up to meet the
planes. A trip from the airport to Sandy Ground will cost about
$7. Fares, which are government regulated, should be listed in
brochures the drivers carry. If you are traveling in a group, the
fares apply to the first two people; each additional passenger
adds $2 to the total. There are no buses or shuttles.

By Boat There are ferry-boat journeys across the water from Marigot
on St. Martin several times a day between 8 AM and 5:30 PM to
Blowing Point on Anguilla. You pay the $9 one-way fare on
board, plus a 15F ($3) departure tax before boarding. Don't
buy a round-trip ticket because it restricts you to the boat on
which you bought the ticket. The trip can be bouncy, but it takes
only 15–20 minutes, so even if you suffer from motion sickness,
you may not need medication. Check the schedules for the return ferries. The last hourly ferry departs Anguilla at 5 PM. The
next ferry is at 6:15, and a late ferry departs at 10:15 PM. There
is a $2 departure tax. An information booth outside the customs
shed in Blowing Point, Anguilla, is usually open daily from 8:30
AM to 5 PM, but sometimes the attendant wanders off.

From the Docks Taxis are always waiting to pick passengers up at the Blowing
Point landing. It costs $12 to get to the Malliouhana Hotel and
$15 to the most distant point, the Cap Juluca Hotel. Rates are
fixed by the government and quoted in the local paper *What
We Do in Anguilla.* The taxi driver should have a list of these
fares. There are no buses or shuttles.

Passports and Visas U.S. and Canadian citizens need proof of identity. A passport
is preferred (even one that's expired, but not more than five
years ago). A photo ID, along with a birth certificate (original
with raised seal), a voter registration card, or a driver's license
is also acceptable. Visitor's passes are valid for stays of up to
three months. British citizens must have a passport. All visitors
must also have a return or ongoing ticket.

Language English, with a West Indian lilt, is spoken on Anguilla.

Precautions The manchineel tree, which resembles an apple tree, shades
many beaches. The tree bears poisonous fruit, and the sap from
the tree causes painful blisters, so avoid sitting beneath the
tree because even dew or raindrops falling from the leaves can
blister your skin. Be *sure* to take along a can of insect repellent—mosquitoes are all over the place. Anguilla is a quiet, relatively safe island, but there's no point in tempting fate by
leaving your valuables unattended in your hotel room or on the
beach.

Staying in Anguilla

Important Addresses

Tourist Information: The **Anguilla Tourist Office** (The Social Security Building, The Valley, tel. 809/497–2759) is open weekdays 8–noon and 1–4.

Emergencies **Police** and **Fire:** tel. 809/497–2333; **Hospital:** There is a 24-hour emergency room at the **Cottage Hospital** (The Valley, tel. 809/497–2551). By 1994, the new Princess Alexandra Hospital in Stoney Ground, under construction at press time, may have supplanted it. **Ambulance:** tel. 809/497–2551; **Pharmacies:** The **Government Pharmacy** (The Valley, tel. 809/497–2551) is located in the Cottage Hospital. The **Paramount Pharmacy** (Waterswamp, tel. 809/497–2366) is open Monday–Saturday 8:30 AM–8:30 PM and has a 24-hour emergency service.

Currency Legal tender here is the Eastern Caribbean dollar (E.C.), but U.S. dollars are widely accepted. (You'll usually get change in E.C. dollars.) The E.C. is fairly stable relative to the U.S. dollar, hovering between E.C. $2.60 and $2.70 to U.S. $1. Credit cards are not widely accepted, but some places accept personal and traveler's checks. Be sure to carry lots of small bills; change for a $20 bill is often difficult to obtain.

Taxes and Service Charges The government imposes an 8% tax on accommodations. A 10% service charge is added to all hotel bills and most restaurant bills. If you're not certain about the restaurant service charge, ask. If you are particularly pleased with the service, you can certainly leave a little extra. Tip taxi drivers 10% of the fare. The departure tax is $7 at the airport, $2 by boat.

Getting Around There are rumors on Anguilla about public transportation, but bus routes and schedules are extremely erratic; if you don't rent a car, you'll probably have to rely on taxis to take you significant distances. Hitchhiking is common and considered safe here.

Taxis The somewhat stiff taxi rates are regulated by the government and there are fixed fares from point to point. Posted rates are for one to two people; each additional person pays $2. The fare from the airport and from Blowing Point Landing to most hotels ranges from $10 to $15.

Rental Cars This is your best bet for maximum mobility, if you're comfortable driving on the left. For the most part, Anguilla's roads are narrow, paved two-laners, and many of the beaches are reachable only via ghastly dirt roads. Watch out for the four-legged critters that amble across the road, and observe the 30 mph speed limit. To rent a car you'll need a valid driver's license and a local license, which can be obtained for $6 at any of the car-rental agencies. Among the agencies are **Avis** (tel. 809/497–6221 or 800/331–2112), **Budget** (tel. 809/497–2217 or 800/527–0700), **Connors (National)** (tel. 809/497–6433 or 800/328–4567), and **Island Car Rental** (tel. 809/497–2723). Count on $35–$45 per day's rental, plus insurance. Motorcycles and scooters are available for about $30 per day from **R & M Cycle** (tel. 809/497–2430).

Telephones and Mail To call Anguilla from the United States, dial area code 809 + 497 + the local four-digit number. International direct-dial is available on the island. **Cable & Wireless** (Wallblake Rd., tel. 809/497–3100) is open weekdays 8–6, Saturday 9–1, Sunday and holidays 10–2. A pay phone is accessible 24 hours a day for credit card and collect calls. To make a local call (E.C. 25¢) on the island, dial the four-digit number. Inside the departure lounge at the Blowing Point Ferry and at the airport, there is an AT&T USADIRECT access telephone for collect or credit card calls to the United States.

Airmail letters to the United States cost E.C. 60¢; postcards, E.C. 25¢.

Opening and Closing Times Banks are open Monday–Thursday 8–1, Friday 8–1 and 3–5. Shopping hours are variable. No two shops seem to have the same hours. Your best bet is to call the shop you're interested in, or ask at the Tourist Office for opening and closing times.

Guided Tours A round-the-island tour by taxi will take about 2½ hours and will cost $40 for one or two people, $5 for each additional passenger. The cost is about the same as a full-day's car rental.

Bennie's Tours (Blowing Point, tel. 809/497–2788), and **Malliouhana Travel and Tours** (The Valley, tel. 809/497–2431) put together personalized package tours on and around the island.

Exploring Anguilla

Numbers in the margin correspond to points of interest on the Anguilla map.

Exploring on Anguilla means deciding which beach is best, with perhaps a time-out for lunch at one of the resorts along the way. For this, a rental car or scooter is necessary. Since Anguilla is relatively flat, bikes are an excellent way to tour, although the cost for two people nearly equals that of a rental car. Guided tours are another possibility (*see above*), but these cost the same for a couple of hours as does a rental car for the day.

If you have not collected maps and brochures from the tourist booths either at the airport or on the boat ferry, then make the Tourist Office in The Valley your first stop on the island. Here you can pick up a large, colorful map of the island with splashy pictures of Anguilla's beaches. The island is sprinkled with salt ponds and small villages, the most important of which is The Valley, where administrative offices, banks, a few boutiques, guest houses, eateries, and markets are located. Take a look at the island's historic house, then go beachcombing.

① **Wallblake House** is a plantation house that was built around 1787 by Will Blake (Wallblake is probably a corruption of his name). Legends of murders, invasions by the French in 1796, and high living surround the house. Now owned and used by the Catholic Church, the plantation has spacious rooms, some with tray ceilings edged with handsome carving. The long, narrow pantry with red and black baked brick tiles is now being converted to a kitchen. On the grounds there is an ancient vaulted stone cistern and an outbuilding called the Bakery (which used not for bread-making but for baking turkeys and hams). The oven measures 12 feet across and rises 3 feet up through a stepped chimney. *Cross Roads, The Valley. Call Father John, tel. 809/497–2405, to make an appointment to tour the plantation.*

If you follow the road west toward the Cottage Hospital, you'll come to a dirt road that leads to **Crocus Bay** and several strips of white-sand beaches.

② Four miles northeast of The Valley on the main road, as you approach the coast at **Shoal Bay,** you'll pass near **The Fountain,** where Arawak petroglyphs have been discovered. Presently closed to the public, the area is being researched by the Anguilla Archaeological and Historical Society. The AAHS (tel. 809/497–2767) plans to open a museum in the former Customs House in The Valley.

Two miles farther east, the fishing village of **Island Harbour** nestles in its sheltered cove.

Follow rutted dirt roads from Island Harbour to the eastern-most tip of the island. On the way to the aptly named **Scrub Island** and **Little Scrub Island** off the eastern tip of Anguilla, you'll pass Captain's Bay, with its isolated beach, on the north coast.

You can also choose to bypass the east end of the island, because there isn't much to see there. From Island Harbour, a paved road leads south, skirts Savannah Bay on the southeast coast, **③** and continues to **Sandy Hill Bay.** If you're an aficionado of ruined forts, there's one here you may want to explore.

Four miles down the coast, beyond the Long Salt Pond, is **Forest Bay,** a fit place for scuba diving. South of Forest Bay lies **Little Harbour,** with a lovely horseshoe-shape bay and the splendid **Cinnamon Reef Beach Club.**

From Little Harbour, follow the paved road past Wallblake Airport, just outside The Valley, and turn left on the main road. In **④** 4 miles you'll come to **Sandy Ground,** one of the most active and most developed of the island's beaches. It is home to the **Mariners Hotel, Tamariain Watersports,** a dive shop, a commercial pier, and several small guest houses and restaurants. The *Shauna* departs from here for Sandy Island 2 miles offshore.

⑤ On the south coast is **Blowing Point Harbour,** where you'll have docked if you arrived by ferry from Marigot in St. Martin.

The main paved road travels more or less down the center of the island, which at this west end is quite narrow. Teeth-jarring dirt roads lead to the coasts, the beaches, and some of the best resorts on the island.

On the south coast, west of Blowing Point, is the crescent-shape home of **Rendezvous Bay,** the island's first hotel, built in 1959. The white sand drifts down the coastline to **Cove Bay,** a pretty coconut palm–fringed beach. **Maunday's Bay,** on the extreme southwest coast, is the home of **Cap Juluca,** a stunning resort that looks as if it were plucked out of Marrakech.

On the opposite side of the island is **Coccoloba Plantation,** one of the largest resorts on the island, overlooking the white sands of **Barnes Bay.** A five-minute walk from Barnes Bay is **Meads Bay,** and **Long Bay** is farther to the north.

Beaches

The island's big attractions are its beaches. All are free to the public and all are white sand. Nude bathing is a no-no, but is nevertheless not uncommon. Most of the island's beaches are on coral reefs that are great for snorkeling. Most apartment complexes and guest houses are within a 15-minute walk of the nearest beach, if not actually on it. You *will* need a car to go beach-hopping.

One of the prettiest beaches in the Caribbean, **Shoal Bay** is a 2-mile L-shape beach of talcum-powder-soft white sand. There are beach chairs, umbrellas, a backdrop of sea-grape and coconut trees, and for seafood and tropical drinks there's Trader Vic's, Uncle Ernie, and the Round Rock. Souvenir shops for T-shirts, suntan lotion, and the like abound. Head to Shoal Bay for good snorkeling in the offshore coral reefs, and visit the water-sports center to arrange diving, sailing, and fishing trips.

Island Harbor, another busy beach, is shaded by coconut trees and lined with colorful fishing boats. Depart from here for **Scilly Cay,** a three-minute motorboat ride away. You can get snorkeling equipment on the ferrying motorboat, but at times the waters are too rough to see much. On Scilly Cay there is a beach bar that serves drinks and grilled lobster and seafood.

The reward for traveling along an inhospitable dirt road via four-wheel drive is complete isolation at **Captain's Bay** on the northeastern end of the island. The surf slaps the sands with a vengeance, and the undertow is quite strong here. Wading is the safest water sport.

Mimi Bay is a difficult-to-reach, isolated, half-mile beach east of Sea Feathers Bay. But the trip is worth it. When the surf is not too rough, the barrier reef makes for great snorkeling.

Also not far from Sea Feathers is **Sandy Hill,** a base for fishermen. Here you can buy fresh fish and lobster right off the boats and snorkel in the warm waters. Don't plan to sunbathe—the beach is quite narrow here.

Rendezvous Bay is 1½ miles of pearl-white sand. Here the water is calm, and there's a great view of St. Martin. The Anguilla Great House's open-air beach bar is handy for snacks and Happy Jacks (rum punches).

The good news and the bad news about **Cove Bay** are the same—it's virtually deserted. There are no restaurants or bars, just calm waters, coconut trees, and soft sand that stretches down to Maunday's Bay.

One of the most popular beaches, wide, mile-long **Maunday's Bay** is known for good swimming and snorkeling. Rent watersport gear at Tropical Watersports.

Adjacent to Maunday's Bay, **Shoal Bay West** is a pleasant beach with a backdrop of the white stucco buildings of Cove Castles, a set of futuristic villas where Chuck Norris has a home, set apart by its pink-colored stone. The snorkeling is best in the area of the Oasis restaurant. Comb this beach for lovely conch shells as well.

Barnes Bay is a superb spot for windsurfing and snorkeling. The elegant Coccoloba Plantation perches above and offers a poolside bar. In high season this beach can get a bit crowded with day-trippers from St. Martin.

The clear blue waters of **Road Bay** beach are usually dotted with yachts. The Mariners Hotel (*see* Lodging, *below*), several restaurants, a water-sports center, and lots of windsurfing and waterskiing activity make this an active commercial area. It's a typical Caribbean scene, as fishermen set out in their boats and goats ramble the littoral at will. The snorkeling is not very good here, but do visit this bay for its glorious sunsets.

Sandy Island, nestled in coral reefs about 2 miles offshore from Road Bay, is a tiny speck of sand and sea, equipped with a beach boutique, beach bar and restaurant, and free use of snorkeling gear and underwater cameras. The *Shauna* (tel. 809/497–6395 or 809/497–6845) will ferry you there from Sandy Ground.

At **Little Bay** sheer cliffs embroidered with agave and creeping vines plummet to a small gray sand beach, usually accessible only by water (it's a favored spot for snorkeling and night dives). But, virtually assured of total privacy, the hale and hearty can clamber down a rope to explore the caves and surrounding reef.

Sports and the Outdoors

Bicycling There are plenty of flat stretches, making wheeling pretty easy. Bikes can be rented at **Boothes** (tel. 809/497–2075) for about $15–$20 a day.

Fitness Lest you go flabby lolling around on the beach, you'll find exercise equipment, aerobics, and martial arts instruction at **Highway Gym** (George Hill Rd., tel. 809/497–2363). A day pass costs $8.

Tennis Hotel guests have priority; occasionally resorts will rent out an empty court, usually at $30–$40 an hour. If you're determined to play, there are two courts at the **Carimar Beach Club** (tel. 809/497–6881), three championship courts at **Malliouhana** (tel. 809/497–6111), two Deco Turf tournament courts at **Cinnamon Reef** (tel. 809/497–2727), and two courts at **Fountain Beach and Tennis Club** (tel. 809/497–6395). Tennis is also available at **Cap Juluca** (tel. 809/497–6666), **Cove Castles** (tel. 809/497–6801), **Mariners** (tel. 809/497–2671), **Masara** (tel. 809/497–3200), **Rendezvous Bay** (tel. 809/497–6549), **Pelicans** (tel. 809/497–6593), **Sea Grapes** (tel. 809/497–6433), and **Spindrift Apts.** (tel. 809/497–4164).

Sea Excursions Picnic, swimming, and diving excursions to Prickly Pear, Sandy Island, and Scilly Cay are available through **Sandy Island Enterprises** (tel. 809/497–6395), **Enchanted Island Cruises** (tel. 809/497–3111), **Suntastic Cruises** (tel. 809/497–3400), and **Tropical Watersports** (tel. 809/497–6666 or 809/497–6779). Prices average $20–$40 per person, depending on the activity and whether meals or drinks are included. Use of snorkeling equipment is usually free. Local fisherman Rollin Ruan (tel. 809/497–3394) is a font of knowledge and will take you out on one of his boats for a half- or full-day excursion, including snorkeling and refreshments; cost ranges from $20 to $40 per person.

Water Sports The major resorts offer complimentary Windsurfers, paddleboats, and water skis to their guests. If your hotel has no watersports facilities, you can get in gear at **Tropical Watersports** (tel. 809/497–6666 or 809/497–6779) or **Tamariain Watersports** (tel. 809/497–2020). Tamariain Watersports also has PADI instructors, short resort courses, and more than a dozen dive sites, including several spectacular wrecks and reefs. Single-tank dives are $40; snorkel-gear rental, $6.

Shopping

Shopping tips are readily available in the informative free publications *Anguilla Life* and *What We Do in Anguilla,* but you have to be a really dedicated shopper to peel yourself off the beach and poke around in Anguilla's few shops.

Beach Stuff (Back St., South Hill, tel. 809/497–6814) has a fun collection of sportswear. **The Valley Gap** (Shoal Bay Beach, tel. 809/497–2754) has local crafts, T-shirts, and swimwear. **Vanhelle Boutique** (Sandy Ground, tel. 809/497–2965) carries gift items, as well as Brazilian swimsuits for men and women. **Java Wraps** (George Hill Rd., tel. 809/497–5497) carries superb batik-wear.

The **Anguilla Arts and Crafts Center** (The Valley, tel. 809/497–2200) has a wide selection of island crafts. **Alicea's Place** (The Quarter, tel. 809/497–3540) has some locally made ceramics and pottery. The **Scruples Gift Shop** (Social Security Bldg., tel. 809/497–2800) has shells, handmade baskets, wood dolls, hand-crocheted mats, lace tablecloths, and bedspreads. **Devonish Art Gallery** (The Valley, tel. 809/497–2949) displays the ceramics and sculpture of Courtney Devonish, as well as works by other prominent local artists. **Cheddie's Carving Shop** (The Cove, tel. 809/497–6027), just down the road from Coccoloba Plantation, showcases Cheddie's wonderfully textured, fanciful creatures fashioned from driftwood. Even the whimsically carved desk and balustrade in his studio testify to his vivid imagination. Many other local artists hold open studios where you can find true bargains; the tourism board can provide brochures.

Dining

Anguilla is one of those islands where the restaurants tend to fall into two categories: those serving expensive Continental cuisine and those dishing up budget Creole. With careful ordering you can keep the former within your budget; at the latter you'll enjoy delicious food and good company at affordable prices. Call ahead—in the winter to make a reservation, and in the summer to see if the place you've chosen is open. Most restaurants not affiliated with a hotel tack an additional 5% on to the service charge if you pay by credit card.

If you're cooking in, **Vista Food Market** (South Hill, tel. 809/497–2804) is usually well stocked. If you plan to picnic (on the beach or in your room), try the **Fat Cat** (George Hill, tel. 809/497–2307) for escargots to go, as well as takeout quiche, soups, chili, chicken, and conch dishes. **Amy's Bakery** (Blowing Point, tel. 809/497–6775) turns out homemade pies, cakes, tarts, cookies, and breads.

Highly recommended restaurants are indicated by a star ★.

Category	Cost*
Moderate	$25–$35
Inexpensive	$15–$25
Budget	under $15

per person, excluding drinks, service, and sales tax (8%)

Arlo's. Pasta, pizza, and other simple fare are served in this Italian- American restaurant beside the sea. The large bar is a popular gathering place, with animated conversation lasting long into the evening. *South Hill, tel. 809/497–6810. Reservations advised. No credit cards. Moderate.*

La Fontana. Set back from the beach, this small restaurant has an ambitious northern Italian menu, deftly seasoned with island touches by the Rastafarian chef. You can select from a range of pastas for your *primi piatti,* including fettuccine al limone and rasta pasta (usually tossed with crayfish and radicchio). For the main course, there is a wide selection, from chicken to T-bone steak and duck to fish. *Fountain Beach Hotel, Shoal Bay, tel. 809/497–3491. No credit cards. Moderate.*

★ **Lucy's Harbour View Restaurant.** Passing through a swinging wood gate, you'll step up to a terrace restaurant with a splendid sea view. The specialty is "Lucy's delicious whole red snapper," but there is a wide selection here, including several curried and Creole dishes such as conch and goat. Be sure to try Lucy's sautéed potatoes. Live music Wednesday and Friday. *South Hill, tel. 809/497–6253. No credit cards. Closed Sun. Moderate.*

Mango's. Husband-and-wife team Bob and Melinda Blanchard sold their hugely successful operation last year, but the new owners have retained much of the staff and Melinda's most popular inventions, including pumpkin shrimp bisque and sesame swordfish with ginger-mango sauce. Try one of the unusual pizza combinations for lunch. *Barnes Bay, tel. 809/497–6479. Reservations advised in high season. MC, V. Usually closed on Tues. Moderate.*

Riviera Bar & Restaurant. This is a beachside bistro serving French and Creole specialties with an Oriental accent. A fourcourse lobster meal is featured, and the fish soup à la Provençale is highly recommended. Sushi, sashimi, and oysters sautéed in soy sauce and sake are also among the eclectic offerings. There's a very happy Happy Hour from 6 to 7 daily. Live entertainment is featured frequently in season. *Sandy Ground, tel. 809/497–2833. AE, V. Moderate.*

Smuggler's Grill. Somewhat out of the way on Forest Bay, this romantic, nautically themed restaurant offers 10 different preparations of lobster at very reasonable prices, in addition to the usual bistro fare. Animated, energetic owner/hostess Marysa is a fresh wind blown in from Paris. *Forest Bay, tel. 809/497–3728. AE, MC, V. Closed Sun. Moderate.*

The Old House. Hanging vines and local artwork adorn the walls of this converted turn-of-the-century dining room where mainly seafood is served. Try the Potfish Anguilla: catch of the day simmered with herbs, tomatoes, onion, lemon, and butter. Entrées are less expensive at lunch. *George Hill, tel. 809/497–2228. AE, D, MC, V. Inexpensive–Moderate.*

★ **Aquarium.** An upstairs terrace, the Aquarium is all gussied up with gingerbread trim, bright blue walls, and red cloths. The lunch menu lists sandwiches and burgers. Stewed lobster, curried chicken, barbecued chicken, and mutton stew are offered at night. This is a popular spot with locals. *South Hill, tel. 809/497–2720. No credit cards. Closed Sun. Inexpensive.*

★ **Roy's.** The dainty pink-and-white–covered deck belies the rowdy reputation of Roy and Mandy Bosson's pub, an Anguillan mainstay. One of the island's best buys, it features Roy's fish-and-chips, cold English beer, pork fricassee, and a wonderful chocolate rum cake. Sunday lunch special is roast beef and

Yorkshire pudding. A faithful clientele gathers in the lively bar. *Crocus Bay, tel. 809/497–2470. No credit cards. Closed Mon. and Sat. lunch. Inexpensive.*

Chillie's. For a change of pace, stop in this beach bar for killer margaritas and surprisingly decent Tex-Mex fare, including chili potato soup and seafood quesadillas. Dishes tend to be bland unless you request otherwise. *Sandy Ground, tel. 809/497–3171. AE, MC, V. Budget–Inexpensive.*

Cross Roads. Millie Philip's roadside bar features hearty breakfasts and, at lunch, seafood salads, fish, and chicken. Satisfying fare at low prices. *Wallblake, The Valley, tel. 809/497–2581. No credit cards. Budget–Inexpensive.*

Johnno's. This is *the* place to be on Sunday afternoons for barbecue and music by the island band Dumpa and the AnVibes, but grilled or barbecued lobster, chicken, and fish are good any time. This is a classic Caribbean beach bar, attracting a funky, eclectic crowd, from locals to movie stars. *Sandy Ground, tel. 809/497–2728. No credit cards. Budget–Inexpensive.*

Short Curve. You'll get tasty homemade sea moss, maubey and ginger beer, steamy fish soup, delectable stewed chicken, and other island specialties at this quiet spot off the main road. Already huge portions are dressed with mounds of rice and peas, fresh potato salad, and greens. *South Hill, tel. 809/497–6600. No credit cards. Budget–Inexpensive.*

Smitty's. The tempting aroma of barbecue wafts through this small, trellised shack on the sand overlooking colorful Island Harbour. Try the succulent crayfish or juicy ribs. Smitty's rocks with live music Thursdays and Sundays. *Island Harbour, tel. 809/497–4300. No credit cards. Budget–Inexpensive.*

Brothers Cafeteria. This Caribbean coffee shop has the same Naugahyde and Formica you'll find the world over. But the West Indian food—goat stew, panfried fish—is sensational, and the portions gargantuan. Even locals wonder how the owners do it. *The Valley, tel. 809/497–3550. No credit cards. Budget.*

Pepper Pot. Cora Richardson's small eatery in the center of town offers *roti* aficionados their favorite dish, made of boneless chicken, *tanias* (poi), celery, pepper, onion, garlic, and local peas, all wrapped in a crepe and panfried. A full meal in itself, it sells for E.C. $5. Dumpling dinners, lobster, whelk, and conch are also good choices. *The Valley, tel. 809/497–2328. No credit cards. Budget.*

Uncle Ernie's. No one is saying whether this beach shack is named after the "wicked" character in the rock opera *Tommy,* but it does serve a mean ribs and coleslaw for $6 and ice cold beer for a buck. Lots of regulars call it home. *Shoal Bay, no telephone. No credit cards. Budget.*

Lodging

Even in the island's lowest season (mid-June–mid-September), standard room rates at luxury resorts are expensive. Note that the high ranges in our price chart reflect the realities of this tony island. Yet unlike some expensive islands that have few or no options for the budget traveler, Anguilla does offer some affordable smaller properties. Guest houses here are usually simple, locally owned properties, with few if any of a larger hotel's amenities and facilities, but they often represent substantial savings. As a rule, lodgings clustered around Sandy Ground, Shoal Bay, and Island Harbour represent the best value, if only for the shops and restaurants within walking distance. Hotels usually include air-conditioning; cheaper apartments and guest houses often substitute ceiling fans. Ask the **Tourist Office** (tel. 809/497–2759) for its Inns of Anguilla list. When you call to reserve a room in a resort, be sure to inquire about special packages.

Highly recommended lodgings are indicated by a star ★.

Category	Cost*
Moderate	$150–$225
Inexpensive	$80–$150
Budget	under $80

All prices are for a standard double room for two, excluding 8% tax and a 10% service charge. To estimate rates for hotels offering MAP, add about $35–$40 per person per day to the above price ranges. For all-inclusives, add about $75–$100 per person per day.

Hotels   **The Mariners.** This is Anguilla's first all-inclusive resort, though EP is just as popular with the honeymooners and businesspeople on retreat who make up much of the clientele. Accommodations vary considerably, from deluxe cottages to simple rooms; the studios and one-bedroom suites are at the top end of our Moderate range. The Thursday-night barbecue and Saturday West Indian night in the beachfront restaurant are popular island events. Unlike other top Anguillan resorts, the Mariners is very West Indian in attitude and ambience; that means 19th-century gingerbread cottages, muted pastel decor, and friendly, laid-back service that verges on the lackadaisical. *Box 139, Sandy Ground, tel. 809/497–2671, 809/497–2815 or 800/223–0079; in NY, 212/545–7688. 25 suites, 25 studios. Facilities: 2 restaurants, 2 bars, jacuzzi, laundry service, boutique, pool, lighted tennis court, water-sports center. AE, MC, V. EP, MAP, FAP, All-inclusive (drinks not included). Moderate.*

★   **La Sirena.** Overlooking Meads Bay—and a 2-minute walk by a path—La Sirena offers the best value on Anguilla. After taking over in 1988, Rolf and Viviane Masshardt, who are from Switzerland, have made this into an extremely comfortable, personable, and well-run hotel. Each of the 20 attractive doubles has a small patio overlooking lovely Mead's Bay. Upstairs are two small restaurants open to the sea breezes, one serving Swiss cuisine, the other, of all things, Southwestern fare. The key to the hotel's success is the personal service offered by the owner-managers. Not surprisingly, it's wildly popular with Europeans. *Box 200, The Valley, tel. 809/497–6827 or 800/331–9358. 20 rooms, 7 suites. Facilities: 2 pools, 2 restaurants, bar, car rental, picnic and snorkeling equipment. No credit cards. EP. Moderate.*

Blue Waters Inn. These gleaming, whitewashed units are set on shimmering, isolated Shoal Bay West. The one- and two-bedroom apartments (the latter are just within our price range) all feature full kitchens, cable TV, ceiling fans, and patios overlooking the water. The effect is very simple, very breezy, very peaceful—even for Anguilla it's quiet. *Box 69, Shoal Bay West, tel. 809/497–6292, fax 809/497–3309. 9 apartments. AE, MC, V. EP. Moderate.*

Ferryboat Inn. This airy, light-filled complex opens onto a rather poky beach. But the units are fully equipped with kitchen, cable TV, shower bath, and ceiling fans. A constant breeze wafts through the rooms, stirring the potted plants. The beautifully situated restaurant is a pleasant place for a drink or snack. Children under 12 stay free. *Blowing Point, tel. 809/497–6613. 6 apartments, 1 two-bedroom beach house. Facilities: restaurant, bar. AE, MC, V. EP; dive packages available. Inexpensive–Moderate.*

★ **Rendezvous Bay Hotel.** Anguilla's first hotel sits amid 60 acres of coconut groves and fine white sand. The water here is as clear as Perrier. The main building is low and rose-colored, with a broad front patio, tile floors, and wicker chairs. The rooms are clean, simple, and very quaint, with one double and one single bed; a private shower bath; and Haitian art, bamboo, and wicker everywhere. Suites in two-story buildings along the broad beach are spacious, decorated in muted earth tones, with modern furnishings and some with kitchenettes. On the other side of the main house are more new units, which are stepped back from a secluded beach area. Rooms in the new units can be joined together to form suites for families or two or more couples. *Box 31, Rendezvous Bay, tel. 809/497–6549; in the United States, 201/738–0246 or 800/274–4893; in Canada, 800/468–0023. 20 rooms, 26 suites. Facilities: restaurant, lounge, game and TV room, 2 tennis courts, water-sports center. No credit cards. EP. Inexpensive–Moderate.*

Inter-Island Hotel. The West Indian cottage is modestly furnished (no air-conditioning) with wicker and rattan, and the hotel has some rooms with balconies. Most rooms have refrigerators and cramped shower baths that give new meaning to the term "water closet." There are also two small one-bedroom apartments, each with a separate entrance on the ground floor. A homey dining room serves hearty breakfasts and fine West Indian dinners. *Box 194, The Valley, tel. 809/497–6259 or 800/223–9815; in Canada, 800/468–0023. 10 rooms, 2 one-bedroom apartments. Facilities: restaurant, bar, TV lounge, transportation to beach ¹/2 mi away. AE, D, MC, V. EP. Inexpensive.*

The Pavillion. This modern, boxy three-story building already needs a new coat of paint, and the apartments are rather starkly appointed. Still, with kitchenette, cable TV, and shower bath, these neat units are a fairly good buy. The nearest beach is a five-minute walk away. *Blowing Point, tel. 809/497–6395. 10 one-bedroom apartments. No credit cards. EP. Budget–Inexpensive.*

Guest Houses   **La Palma.** This pink-and-white private home may be plain, but it's right on Road Bay. The immaculate white terrace gleams, the doors are a lovely carved mahogany, and owner Marie Richardson's welcome couldn't be warmer. She's a superb cook, too: Reserve at least one night in her sweet dollhouse of a restaurant to feast on the likes of pumpkin soup and baked chicken smothered in onions. The one-bedroom apartment and one of the three tidy rooms include a kitchenette. *Sandy Ground, tel. 809/497–3260. 3 studios, 1 one-bedroom apartment. Facilities: restaurant, bar. AE. EP. Budget.*

Yellow Banana. This defines basic: Only two of the rooms have their own shower bath, and there aren't even ceiling fans. Yet the ultra-simple decor is homey, and at $30–$40 a night, it's nicer than many properties costing twice as much. Larger units have kitchenettes. Shoal Bay is a 15-minute walk away.

Stoney Ground, tel. 809/497–2626. 12 rooms. Facilities: breakfast room, grocery. No credit cards. EP. Budget.

Villa and Apartment Rentals Private villas are generally not affordable on Anguilla. Apartment complexes, while modest, are clean, well-run, and often tastefully furnished. The Tourist Office has a complete listing of vacation rentals. You can also contact **Sunshine Villas** (Box 142, Blowing Point, tel. 809/497–6149) or **Property Real Estate Management Services** (Box 256, George Hill, tel. 809/497–2596), which represents more moderate choices. Housekeeping accommodations are plentiful and well organized. The following are a selection:

Easy Corner Villas. These one-, two-, and three-bedroom apartments with kitchens are furnished right down to microwaves. Only three of the units are air-conditioned; all have only shower baths. No. 10 is a deluxe two-bedroom villa. Not located on the beach but on a bluff overlooking Road Bay, this is a good buy for families. *Box 65, South Hill, tel. 809/497–6433, 809/497–6541, or 800/223–8815. 17 units. AE, MC, V. Moderate.*

Rainbow Reef. David and Charlotte Berglund's secluded units are set on three dramatic seaside acres. A gazebo, with beach furniture and barbecue facilities, perches right over the beach. Each self-contained villa has two bedrooms, fully equipped kitchen, spacious dining and living area, and a large gallery overlooking the sea. *Box 130, Sea Feather Bay, tel. 809/497–2817 or 708/325–2299. 14 units. No credit cards. Moderate.*

★ **Skiffles Villas.** These self-catering villas, perched on a hill overlooking Road Bay, are usually booked a year in advance. The one-, two-, and three-bedroom apartments have fully equipped kitchens, floor-to-ceiling windows, and pleasant porches. *Box 82, Lower South Hill, tel. 809/497–6619, 219/642–4855, or 219/642–4445. 5 units. Facilities: pool. No credit cards. Moderate.*

Harbour Villas. Located across from all the activity of Island Harbour and its small beach, these charming Mediterranean-style villas all feature a full kitchen, shower bath, and appealing, homey decor. The area surrounding this property—less developed than other hotel locations on Anguilla—is bursting with local flavor. *Island Harbour, tel. 809/497–4433. 16 villas. No credit cards. Inexpensive.*

The Seahorse. These cozy, secluded cottages overlook Rendezvous Bay, arguably Anguilla's most exquisite beach. Each recently renovated apartment is equipped with kitchenette, shower bath, and private ocean-view terrace. *Cul de Sac, tel. 809/497–6751. 5 one-bedroom apartments. No credit cards. Inexpensive.*

Harbour Lights. The pretty, slightly weathered blue-and-white buildings front their own tiny private beach. The units are nothing special, but are breezy and pleasant, with kitchenettes and shower baths. *Island Harbour, tel. 809/497–4435. 4 one-bedroom apartments. No credit cards. Budget–Inexpensive.*

★ **Sydan's.** Just across the street from all the activity on Road Bay, these very pleasant, clean efficiencies contain comfortable furnishings, kitchenettes, and shower baths. A tremendous bargain. *Sandy Ground, tel. 809/497–3180. 6 studios. Facilities: gift shop. AE, MC, V. Inexpensive.*

Off-Season Bets If you're in luck, the deluxe, sumptuous **Cap Juluca** (Maunday's Bay, tel. 809/497–6666) or **Malliouhana** (Mead's Bay, tel. 809/497–6111) may offer a special package during the off-season (April 15–December 15). You'll have a chance to experience pampering and elegance usually reserved for royalty, rock stars, and Rothschilds. The tranquil, lovely villas at **Cinnamon Reef Beach Club** (Little Harbour, tel. 809/497–2727) can also sneak into our Moderate category during low season.

Nightlife

The **Mayoumba Folkloric Group** performs song-and-dance skits depicting Antillean and Caribbean culture, replete with African drums and a string band. They entertain every Thursday night at **La Sirena** (The Valley, tel. 809/497–6827). Be on the lookout for Bankie Banx, Anguilla's own reggae superstar. He has his own group called New Generations. Other local groups include Keith Gumbs and The Mellow Tones; Spracka; Megaforce; Sleepy and the All-Stars, a string-and-scratch band; Joe and the Invaders; and Dumpa and the AnVibes. Steel Vibrations, a pan band, often entertains at barbecues and West Indian evenings. The **Mariners** (Sandy Ground, tel. 809/497–2671) has regularly scheduled Thursday night barbecues and Saturday night West Indian parties, both with live entertainment by local groups. Things are pretty loose and lively at **Johnno's** beach bar (tel. 809/497–2728) in Sandy Ground, which has alfresco dancing on weekends. The **Red Dragon Disco** (South Hill, tel. 809/497–2687) is a hot spot on weekends after midnight. The **Coconut Paradise** restaurant (Island Harbour, tel. 809/497–4150) has nightly entertainment ranging from disco to limbo. For soft dance music after a meal, go to **Lucy's Palm Palm** (tel. 809/497–2253) at Sandy Ground. There is usually a live band on Tuesday and Friday evenings. Sunday is the big night in restaurants. In addition to the above, **Uncle Ernie's** (Shoal Bay, no tel.), **Round Rock** (Shoal Bay, tel. 809/497–2076), and **Smitty's** (Island Harbour, tel. 809/497–4300) swing all day and well into the night.

3 Antigua

Updated by
Simon Worrall

One could spend an entire year—and a leap year, at that—exploring the beaches of Antigua (*An-TEE-ga*); the island has 366 of them, many with snow-white sand. All the beaches are public, and many are backed by lavish resorts offering sailing, diving, windsurfing, and snorkeling. These resorts have given Antigua a reputation as one of the most expensive islands in the Caribbean.

The largest of the British Leewards, Antigua is where Lord Horatio Nelson headquartered during his forays into the Caribbean to do battle with the French and pirates in the late 18th century, and there is still a decidedly British atmosphere here, with Olde-English public houses that will raise the spirits of Anglophiles. Since becoming independent from Great Britain in 1981, however, Antigua has gone Floridian in a big way. Large resorts catering to an international (mostly North American and European) package-tour clientele have proliferated. Club Antigua, for instance, is the largest resort in the eastern Caribbean: 481 rooms the size of a monk's cell and still growing. Not all of these large, mainly all-inclusive resorts are affordable in high season, though, despite their democratic feel. If you're traveling to Antigua in the winter, you'll find better value in the smaller, self-catering hotels, particularly around St. John's and English Harbour. Good guest house and B&B accommodations here are rare. On the other hand, budget dining is plentiful at small restaurants and cafés, especially in St. John's.

Antigua is still a place with a rich history and a strong sense of national identity. Its cricketers, like the legendary Viv Richards, arguably the greatest batsman the game has ever seen, are famous throughout the Caribbean. English Harbour, on the southeast end of the island, is still steeped in the history of the colonial era and Lord Horatio Nelson. Nelson's Dockyard is Antigua's answer to Williamsburg, Virginia: a carefully restored gem of British Georgian architecture that still evokes a vanished era and the world-famous admiral who gave it its name. For history buffs, English Harbour and the surrounding villages and historic sites offer much of interest.

Those who want beaches, nightlife, and resorts should head for Dickenson Bay, at the northwest end of the island. It's here that a lively, Florida-style tourist trade has grown up, centered on the bustling capital of St. John's. You can parasail and waterski, bounce across the azure water on an inflatable rubber banana, lie in a Jacuzzi, or sip piña coladas at a swim-up bar as you listen to Bob Marley and the Wailers. Swingers and singles abound, as do restaurants, discos, and casinos. The least developed part of the island is in the southwest, in the shadow of Antigua's highest mountain, Boggy Peak. At Fry's Bay and Darkwood Beach, visitors will find long, unspoiled beaches and, on weekends, Antiguan families who come to swim and picnic under the tamarind trees. Antigua's sister island of Barbuda, about 30 miles to the north, offers shelling, diving, and snorkeling for day-trippers from Antigua.

What It Will Cost These sample prices, meant only as a general guide, are for high season. Price estimates are for high season. A budget hotel is about $55 a night; a bed-and-breakfast for two, about $45; and a modest two-bedroom villa, about $900 a week. Expect to pay around $200 a night for a moderately priced hotel. A budget restaurant meal will be $6–$10; a sandwich lunch is about $5. A rum punch here costs around $3.50, a glass of house wine anywhere from $3 to $5, and a beer is about $1.50. Car rental here is expensive—about $50 a day, plus $12 for a temporary license. It's $6 for a taxi from St. John's to Dickenson Bay; from St. John's to English Harbour is $17. A single-tank dive averages $40, while snorkel equipment rents for about $5 a day.

Before You Go

Tourist Information Contact the **Antigua and Barbuda Tourist Offices** (610 5th Ave., Suite 311, New York, NY 10020, tel. 212/541–4117; 121 S.E. 1st St., Suite 1001, Miami, FL 33131, tel. 305/381–6762; 60 St. Clair Ave. E, Suite 205, Toronto, Ont. M4T 1N5, Canada, tel. 416/961–3085; Antigua House, 15 Thayer St., London W1M 5LD, England, tel. 071/486–7073).

Arriving and Departing
By Plane **American Airlines** (tel. 800/433–7300) has daily direct service from New York, as well as several flights from San Juan that connect with flights from more than 100 U.S. cities. **BWIA** (tel. 800/JET–BWIA) has direct service from New York, Miami, and Toronto; **Air Canada** (tel. 800/422–6232) from Toronto; **British Airways** (tel. 800/247–9297) from London; and **Lufthansa** (tel. 800/645–3880) from Frankfurt. **LIAT** (tel. 809/462–0701) has daily flights from Antigua to Barbuda, 15 minutes away, as well as to down-island destinations.

48

Exploring

Curtain Bluff, **11**

Devil's Bridge, **15**

Dows Hill Interpretation Center, **9**

English Harbour, **6**

Falmouth, **5**

Fig Tree Drive, **10**

Fort George, **4**

Fort James, **2**

Harmony Hall, **16**

Indian Town, **14**

Liberta, **3**

Megaliths of Greencastle Hill, **12**

Nelson's Dockyard, **7**

Parham, **13**

St. John's, **1**

Shirley Heights, **8**

Dining

Admiral's Inn, **36**

Brother B's , **19**

Calypso, **21**

Coconut Grove, **26**

The Dolphin, **24**

Home, **25**

Ital, **22**

Lemon Tree, **18**

Lobster Pot, **27**

Mandalay, **35**

Redcliffe Tavern, **23**

Shirley Heights Lookout, **37**

Lodging

Admiral's Inn, **36**

Barrymore Beach Club, **28**

The Catamaran Hotel, **33**

Club Antigua, **32**

Falmouth Beach Apartments, **34**

Lord Nelson Beach Hotel, **17**

Murphy's Place, **20**

Pillar Rock Hotel and Condominiuns, **30**

Sunset Cove, **29**

Yepton Beach Resort, **31**

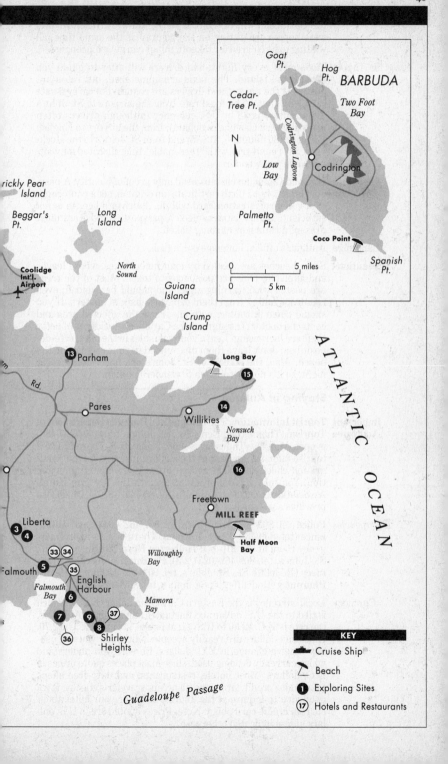

BARBUDA

Goat Pt.

Hog Pt.

Cedar-Tree Pt.

Two Foot Bay

Codrington Lagoon

Low Bay

Codrington

Palmetto Pt.

Coco Point

Spanish Pt.

N

0   5 miles

0   5 km

rickly Pear Island

Beggar's Pt.

Long Island

Coolidge Int'l. Airport

North Sound

Guiana Island

Crump Island

Parham **13**

Rd.

Pares

Long Bay

15

Willikies

14

Nonsuch Bay

16

Freetown

MILL REEF

Half Moon Bay

Liberta

3

4

Willoughby Bay

33 **34**

Falmouth

5

35

Falmouth Bay

English Harbour

Mamora Bay

6

7

9

37

8

36

Shirley Heights

ATLANTIC OCEAN

Guadeloupe Passage

KEY

Cruise Ship

Beach

1 Exploring Sites

17 Hotels and Restaurants

V. C. Bird International Airport is, on a much smaller scale, to the Caribbean what O'Hare is to the Midwest. When several wide-bodies are sitting on the runway at the same time, all waiting to be cleared for takeoff, things can get a bit congested.

From the Airport Taxis meet every flight, and drivers will offer to guide you around the island. The taxis are unmetered, but rates are posted at the airport and drivers are required to carry a rate card with them. The fixed rate from the airport to St. John's (20 minutes) is $8 in U.S. currency (although drivers often *quote* Eastern Caribbean dollars); from the airport to English Harbour (30 minutes), $18.75; and from St. John's to the Dockyard, $33 round-trip, with "reasonable" time allocated for waiting while you wander.

Passports and Visas U.S. and Canadian citizens need only proof of identity. A passport is best, but a birth certificate (an original, not a photocopy) or a voter registration card will do. A driver's license is *not* sufficient. British citizens need a passport. All visitors must present a return or ongoing ticket.

Language Antigua's official language is English.

Precautions Some beaches are shaded by manchineel trees, whose leaves and applelike fruit are poisonous to touch. Most of the trees are posted with warning signs and should be avoided; even raindrops falling from them can cause painful blisters. If you should come in contact with one, rinse the affected area and contact a doctor. Throughout the Caribbean, incidents of petty theft are increasing. Leave your valuables in the hotel safe-deposit box; don't leave them unattended in your room or on the beach. Also, the streets of St. John's are fairly deserted at night, so it's not a good idea to wander out alone.

Staying in Antigua

Important Addresses Tourist Information: The **Antigua and Barbuda Department of Tourism** (Thames and Long Sts., St. John's, tel. 809/462–0480) is open Monday–Thursday 8–4:30, Friday 8–3. There is also a tourist-information desk at the airport, just beyond the immigration checkpoint. The tourist office gives limited information. You may have more success with the **Antigua Hotels Association** (Long St., St. John's, tel. 809/462–3702), which also provides assistance.

Emergencies **Police** (tel. 809/462–0125), **Fire** (tel. 809/462–0044), and **Ambulance** (tel. 809/462–0251). **Hospital:** There is a 24-hour emergency room at the 210-bed **Holberton Hospital** (Hospital Rd., St. John's, tel. 809/462–0251/2/3). **Pharmacies: Joseph's Pharmacy** (Redcliffe St., St. John's, tel. 809/462–1025) and **Health Pharmacy** (Redcliffe St., St. John's, tel. 809/462–1255).

Currency Local currency is the Eastern Caribbean dollar (E.C.$), which is tied to the U.S. dollar and fluctuates only slightly. At hotels, the rate is E.C. $2.60 to U.S. $1; at banks, it's about E.C. $2.70. American dollars are readily accepted, although you will usually receive change in E.C. dollars. Be sure you understand which currency is being used, since most places quote prices in E.C. dollars. Most hotels, restaurants, and duty-free shops take major credit cards, and all accept traveler's checks. It's a good idea to inquire at the Tourist Office or your hotel about current credit-card policy. Note: Prices quoted are in U.S. dollars unless indicated otherwise.

Taxes and Service Charges Hotels collect a 7% government room tax and add a 10% service charge to your bill. In restaurants, a 10% service charge is usually added to your bill. Taxi drivers expect a 10% tip. The departure tax is $10.

Getting Around Antigua is a fairly large island, as Caribbean islands go (it's a 40-minute drive from Dickenson Bay to English Harbour, for instance). You will need at least one very full day, and preferably two, to really explore. Roads are extensive but not particularly good. Driving is on the left-hand side. The standard forms of transportation are cab or private car. There is no public bus service as such. If you are staying at an all-inclusive resort, you will probably only leave your accommodation once or twice for shopping or a sightseeing excursion. Almost all resorts and hotels either have their own stretch of beach or are within walking distance of one. Hitchhiking is not encouraged on Antigua.

Taxis Taxis are abundant on Antigua, and you won't have to look far to find one. Most hotels and resorts have their own cab drivers. In St. John's, there is a busy taxi stand, appropriately near the King's Casino, in the Heritage Quay complex. Taxis are unmetered, but rates are fixed by the government and drivers are required to carry a rate sheet. A cab from resorts in Dickenson Bay to St. John's costs $6; from St. John's to English Harbour, $17.

Public Transportation There is no scheduled bus service on Antigua. However, an extensive network of privately owned minibuses (mostly 16-seater Nissans) connects the main centers of St. John's and English Harbour with the rest of the island. These are mostly used by local people traveling to work or to shop, but they do offer a cheap, if unreliable, alternative to cabs.

Cross-island buses leave from St. John's at the West Bus Station at the end of Market Street and travel by three different routes. One route travels via the village of All Saints to English Harbour. Another services the southwest coast, via Ebenezer and Johnson's Point. A third goes to the southeast coast via the village of Philip's. Buses from the East Bus Station in St. John's, on Independence Avenue, service points east, passing via Potter's and Seeton's to Pineapple Beach. Fares are computed by distance, but are low (St. John's to English Harbour costs E.C. $2). There are no set timetables and no fixed bus stops (just flag down the bus). Most depart St. John's and the villages early, about 6:30 AM, and return as needed, usually about two hours later.

Rental Cars To rent a car, you'll need a valid driver's license and a temporary permit ($12), which is available through the rental agent. Rentals average about $50, in season, per day, with unlimited mileage. Most agencies provide both automatic and stick shift and both right- and left-hand-drive vehicles. If you plan on driving, be careful! Not only is driving on the left, but Antiguan roads are generally unmarked and full of potholes. Jeeps are also available from most of the rental agencies. Among the agencies are **Budget** (St. John's, tel. 809/462–3009 or 800/527–0700), **National** (St. John's, tel. 809/462–2113 or 800/468–0008), **Carib Car Rentals** (St. John's, tel. 809/462–2062), and **Avis** (at the airport or the St. James's Club, tel. 809/462–2840).

Telephones and Mail To call Antigua from the United States, dial 1, then area code 809, then the local seven-digit number (and cross your fingers for luck). Many numbers are restricted from receiving incoming international calls. In addition, the telephone system is primitive, and even local connections crackle. Few hotels have direct-dial telephones, but connections are easily made through the switchboard. A local call costs E.C. 25¢. Recently introduced is the phone card, to be used in new public telephones, that permits the placing of local and overseas telephone calls. You may purchase the phone card from most hotels or from a post office.

To place a call to the United States, dial 1, the appropriate area code, and the seven-digit number. AT&T's USADIRECT is available only from a few designated telephones, such as those at the airport departure lounge, the cruise terminal at St. John's, the English Harbour Marina, the Pineapple Beach Club, and the Sugar Mill Hotel. To place an interisland call, dial the local seven-digit number.

In an emergency, you can make calls from **Cable & Wireless (WI) Ltd.** (42–44 St. Mary's St., St. John's, tel. 809/462–9840, and Nelson's Dockyard, English Harbour, tel. 809/463–1517).

Airmail letters to North America cost E.C. 60¢; postcards, E.C. 40¢. The post office is at the foot of High Street in St. John's.

Opening and Closing Times In general, shops are open Monday–Saturday 8:30–noon and 1–4. Some close at noon on Thursday and Saturday. Duty-free shops that cater to tourists often have flexible hours. Banks are open Monday–Wednesday 8–2, Thursday 8–1, Friday 8–1 and 3–5.

Guided Tours The cheapest way to see the island is to rent a car for the day (*see above*). But if you don't want to brave left-hand driving and potholed roads, elect for a guided tour. Nearly all **taxi drivers** on Antigua double as guides; a four-hour island tour costs about $70, though prices are usually negotiable. The most reliable and informed driver/guides are at **Capital Car Rental** (High St., St. John's, tel. 809/462–0863). Other operators include **Bryson's Travel** (St. John's, tel. 809/462–0223); **Alexander, Parrish Ltd.** (St. John's, tel. 809/462–0387); and **Antours** (St. John's, tel. 809/462–4788).

If you want to venture off the beaten track, **Tropikelly** (tel. 809/461–0383) is the best operation on the island. Run by Kelly Scales, a native Antiguan, and her husband, Patrick, it offers four-wheel-drive tours for $55 a person, which includes drinks and a picnic lunch. The tours give an insider's look at Antigua: deserted plantation houses, rain-forest trails, and ruined sugar mills and forts. The highlight is the luxuriant tropical forest around the island's highest point, Boggy Peak. The going is sometimes rough, and stout walking shoes are recommended.

Exploring Antigua

Numbers in the margin correspond to points of interest on the Antigua (and Barbuda) map.

St. John's
❶ The capital city of **St. John's,** home to some 40,000 people (nearly half the island's population), lies at sea level on the northwest coast of the island. Stop in at the Tourist Bureau, at the corner of Long and Thames streets, to pick up free map and island brochures.

Cross Long Street and walk one block to Church Street. The **Museum of Antigua and Barbuda** is a "hands-on history" opportunity. Signs say Please Touch, with the hope of welcoming both citizens and visitors into Antigua's past. Exhibits interpret the history of the nation from its geological birth to political independence in 1981. There are fossil and coral remains from some 34 million years ago, a life-size Arawak house, models of a sugar plantation, a wattle-and-daub house, and a minishop with handicrafts, books, historical prints, and paintings. The colonial building that houses the museum is the former courthouse, which dates from 1750. *Church and Market Sts., tel. 809/463–1060 or 809/462–3946. Admission free. Open weekdays 8:30–4, Sat. 10–1.*

Walk two blocks east on Church Street to **St. John's Cathedral.** The Anglican church sits on a hilltop, surrounded by its churchyard. At the south gate, there are figures of St. John the Baptist and St. John the Divine, said to have been taken from one of Napoleon's ships and brought to Antigua. The original church on this site was built in 1681 and replaced by a stone building in 1745. An earthquake destroyed that church in 1843, and the present building dates from 1845. With an eye to future earthquakes, the parishioners had the interior completely encased in pitch pine, hoping to forestall heavy damage. The church was elevated to the status of cathedral in 1848. *Between Long and Newcastle Sts., tel. 809/461–0082. Admission free.*

Recross Long Street, walk one block, and turn left on High Street. At the end of High Street, you'll see the **Cenotaph,** which honors Antiguans who lost their lives in World Wars I and II.

Trek seven blocks to the **Westerby Memorial,** which was erected in 1888 in memory of the Moravian bishop George Westerby. One block south of the memorial is **Heritage Quay,** a multimillion-dollar complex, which opened some of its 40 shops in summer 1988. Now that the 500-foot pier and 200-foot causeway are completed, cruise-ship passengers can disembark in the middle of Heritage Quay.

Redcliffe Quay, just south of Heritage Quay, is an attractive waterfront marketplace with more of an upscale feel to its shops, restaurants, and boutiques. This is the shopping area favored by both residents and return guests. Goods here are not duty-free as they are at Heritage Quay, but prices are comparable, and the charm of the restored buildings around small courtyards is far greater.

At the far south end of town, where Market Street forks into Valley Road and All Saints Road, a whole lot of haggling goes on every Friday and Saturday during the day, when locals jam the public **marketplace** to buy and sell fruits, vegetables, fish, and spices. Be sure to ask before you aim a camera, and expect the subject of your shot to ask for a tip.

Elsewhere on the Island To tour the rest of the island you'll need to rent a car or take a guided tour. You could do it by minibus, but it would be a long, arduous day. After seeing Fort James, we will divide the island into two more tours. First, we'll take in English Harbour and Nelson's Dockyard on the south coast, returning to St. John's along the Caribbean (western) coast. Then we'll travel to the eastern side of the island for sights ranging from historical churches to Devil's Bridge.

It's a good idea to wear a swimsuit under your clothes while you're sightseeing—one of the sights to strike your fancy may be an enticing, secluded beach. Be sure to bring your camera along. There are some picture-perfect spots around the island.

Fort James   Follow Fort Road northwest out of town. In 2 miles, you'll come
②   to **Fort James,** named after King James II. The fort was constructed between 1704 and 1739 as a lookout point for the city and St. John's Harbour. The ramparts overlooking the small islands in the bay are in ruins, but 10 cannons still point out to sea. If you continue on this road, you'll come to Dickenson Bay, with its string of smart, expensive resorts.

English Harbour   Take All Saints Road south out of St. John's. Eight miles out
③   of town—almost to the south coast—is **Liberta,** one of the first settlements founded by freed slaves. East of the village, on
④   Monk's Hill, is the site of **Fort George,** built from 1689 to 1720. The fort wouldn't be of much help to anybody these days, but among the ruins, you can make out the sites for its 32 cannons, its water cisterns, the base of the old flagstaff, and some of the original buildings.

⑤   **Falmouth,** 1½ miles farther south, sits on a lovely bay, backed by former sugar plantations and sugar mills. **St. Paul's Church** was rebuilt on the site of a church once used by troops during the Nelson period.

⑥   **English Harbour** lies on the coast, just south of Falmouth. This is the most famous of Antigua's attractions. In 1671, the governor of the Leeward Islands wrote to the Council for Foreign Plantations in London pointing out the advantages of this landlocked harbor, and by 1704, English Harbour was in regular use as a garrisoned station.

In 1784, 26-year-old Horatio Nelson sailed in on HMS *Boreas* to serve as captain and second in command of the Leeward Island Station; he made frequent stops there for a period of three years.

The Royal Navy abandoned the station in 1889, and it fell into a state of decay. The Society of the Friends of English Harbour began restoring it in 1951, and on Dockyard Day, November
⑦   14, 1961, **Nelson's Dockyard** was opened with much fanfare.

Within this compound are crafts shops, hotels, and restaurants. It is a hub for oceangoing yachts and serves as headquarters for the annual Sailing Week Regatta. A lively community of mariners keeps the area active in season. Visitors who do not want to spend their entire vacation on the beach should make this their base. One of the Dockyard's former storehouses is now the beautifully restored and very British **Copper and Lumber Store Hotel.** Another fine hostelry, the **Admiral's Inn,** started out as a pitch-and-tar store built of bricks that had been used as ballast in British ships.

The **Admiral's House Museum** has several rooms displaying ship models, a model of English Harbour, silver trophies, maps, prints, and Nelson's very own telescope and tea caddy. *English Harbour, tel. 809/463–1053 or 809/463–1379. Admission: $1.60. Open daily 8–6.*

On a ridge overlooking the dockyard is **Clarence House** (tel. 809/463–1026), built in 1787 and once the home of the duke of Clarence. Princess Margaret and Lord Snowdon spent part of their honeymoon here in 1960, and Queen Elizabeth and Prince Philip have dined here. It is now used by the governor-general; visits are possible when he is not in residence. Slip a tip to the caretaker, who will give you a fascinating tour; the place is worth a visit. As you leave the dockyard, turn right at the cross-

8 roads in English Harbour and drive to **Shirley Heights** for a spectacular view of English Harbour. The heights are named for Sir Thomas Shirley, the governor who fortified the harbor in 1787.

9 Not far from Shirley Heights is the new **Dows Hill Interpretation Center,** with viewing platforms for sweeping views of the English Harbour area. Inside you can view a cheery but rather bland multimedia presentation on Antigua. Visitors watch as different displays, incorporating lifelike figures and colorful tableaux, are illuminated. A commentary, synchronized TV displays, and music combine to portray the island's history and culture from Amerindian times to the present. *For more information, contact the Parks Department, tel. 809/460–1053. Admission: E.C. $15. Open daily 9–5.*

Drive back up to Liberta. Four and a half miles north of town, opposite the Catholic church, turn left and head southwest on

10 **Fig Tree Drive.** (Forget about plucking figs; *fig* is the Antiguan word for banana.) This drive takes you through the rain forest, which is rich in mangoes, pineapples, and banana trees. This is also the hilliest part of the island—**Boggy Peak,** to the west, is the highest point, rising to 1,319 feet. Fig Tree Drive runs into

11 Old Road, which leads down to **Curtain Bluff,** an unforgettable sight. On this peninsula, between Carlisle Bay and Morris Bay, the Atlantic Ocean meets the Caribbean Sea, resulting in wonderful color contrasts in the water. From here, the main road sweeps along the southwest coast, where there are lovely beaches and spectacular views. The road then veers off to the northeast and goes through the villages of Bolans and Jennings.

12 From Jennings, a road turns right to the **Megaliths of Greencastle Hill,** an arduous climb away (you'll have to walk the last 500 yards). Some say the megaliths were set up by humans for the worship of the sun and moon; others believe they are nothing more than unusual geological formations.

The East End St. John's is 6 miles northeast of Jennings. To explore the other half of the island, take Parham Road east out of St. John's. Three and a half miles to the east, you'll see on your left the now-defunct sugar refinery. Drive 2 miles farther and turn left on the side road that leads 1¼ miles to the settlement of

13 **Parham.** Built in 1840 by Thomas Weekes, an English architect, **St. Peter's Church** is an octagonal Italianate building whose facade was once richly decorated with stucco, though it suffered considerable damage during the earthquake of 1843.

Backtrack and continue east on Parham Road for about three-quarters of a mile, to a fork in the road. One branch veers to the right in a southeasterly direction toward Half Moon Bay, and the other continues toward the northeast coast. The latter

14 route runs through the villages of Pares and Willikies to **Indian Town,** a national park, where archaeological digs have revealed evidence of Carib occupation.

15 Less than a mile further along the coast is **Devil's Bridge,** a natural formation sculpted by the crashing breakers of the Atlantic at Indian Creek. The bluffs took their name from the slaves who committed suicide there in the 18th century because they believed they had the devil in them. Surf gushes out through blowholes that were carved by the breakers.

Backtrack again to Parham Road and take the fork that runs southeast. You'll travel 9 miles to Half Moon Bay. Just before the coast are the village of **Freetown** and the **Mill Reef area,** where many pre-Columbian discoveries have been made.

16 **Harmony Hall,** northeast of Freetown, is an interesting art gallery. A sister to the Jamaican gallery near Ocho Rios, Harmony Hall is built on the foundation of a 17th-century sugar-plantation great house. Artist Graham Davis and Peter and Annabella Proudlock, who founded the Jamaican gallery, teamed up with local entrepreneur Geoffrey Pidduck to create an Antiguan art gallery specializing in high-quality West Indian art. A large gallery is used for one-man shows, and another exhibition hall displays watercolors. A small bar and an outside restaurant under the trees are open in season. *Brown's Mill Bay, tel. 809/463–2057. Open daily 10–6.*

Beaches

Antigua's beaches are public, and many are dotted with resorts that provide water-sports equipment rentals and a place to grab a cool drink. Sunbathing topless or in the buff is strictly illegal.

Antigua **Dickenson Bay** has a lengthy stretch of powder-soft white sand and a host of hotels (the Siboney, Sandals, Antigua Beach Village, and Halcyon Cove) that cater to water-sports enthusiasts. Don't come here seeking solitude.

The white sand of **Runaway Beach,** just south of Dickenson Bay, is home to the Barrymore Beach Club and the Runaway Beach Club, so things can get crowded. Refresh yourself with hot dogs and beer at the Barrymore's Satay Hut.

Five Islands, in the northwest, has four secluded beaches of fine tan sand and coral reefs for snorkeling.

Lignumvitae Bay, on the west coast, is a beautiful beach at the edge of a saltwater swamp that is currently being dredged for a condominium-and-marina complex.

Johnson's Point is a deliciously deserted beach of bleached white sand on the southwest coast.

A large coconut grove adds to the tropical beauty of **Carlisle Bay,** a long snow-white beach over which the estimable Curtain Bluff resort sits. Standing on the bluff of this peninsula, you can see the almost blinding blue waters of the Atlantic Ocean drifting into the Caribbean Sea.

Half Moon Bay is a three-quarter-mile crescent of sand on the eastern end of the island; it's a prime area for snorkeling and windsurfing. Half Moon Bay Hotel will let you borrow gear with a refundable deposit.

Long Bay, on the far eastern coast, has coral reefs in water so shallow that you can actually walk out to them. Here is a lovely beach, as well as the Long Bay Hotel and the rambling Pineapple Beach Club.

Barbuda **Coco Point,** on Barbuda, is an uncrowded 8-mile stretch of white sand. Barbuda is great for scuba diving, with dozens of shipwrecks off reefs that encircle the island.

Sports and the Outdoors

Almost all the resort hotels can come up with fins and masks, Windsurfers, Sunfish, glass-bottom boats, catamarans, and other water-related gear (*see* Lodging, *below*).

Bicycling Biking hasn't caught on here. Distances are comparatively large, and the terrain away from the coast is arid and sparsely vegetated. **Sun Cycles** (tel. 809/461–0324), in St. John's, rents bikes for about $20 a day.

Golf There is an 18-hole course at **Cedar Valley Golf Club** (tel. 809/462–0161), and a nine-hole course at **Half Moon Bay Hotel** (tel. 809/460–4300). An 18-hole round will cost $40.

Scuba Diving Antigua doesn't have the most spectacular diving in the Caribbean, though there are a number of exciting sites, including the Sunken Rock and the wreck of the Mimosa. Captain A.G. Fincham, a British ex-merchant seaman, runs a shipshape shop at **Dockyard Divers** (tel. 809/464–8591). As well as offering resort courses and PADI/NAUI certification, he leads day trips for certified divers and has dive packages. Other specialists include **Dive Antigua** (tel. 809/462–0256) and **Aquanaut Dive Centre** at the Halcyon Cove Hotel (tel. 809/462–3483). **Pirate Divers** at the Lord Nelson Beach Hotel (tel. 809/462–3094) and **Dive Runaway** (tel. 809/462–2626) also offer dive packages. Average price for a single-tank dive is $40. Snorkel equipment rents for about $10 a day.

Sea Excursions The 50-foot catamaran *Cariba* offers full-day sails (10–4) with lunch or half-day sails (9:30–12:30 or 1:30–4:30) that include an on-board picnic. There are swim and snorkel stops on all trips, but the *Cariba* also has underwater viewing windows for those who prefer to stay dry. **Wadadli Watersports** (tel. 809/462–2890) makes trips to Bird Island and Barbuda that include soft drinks and barbecue on the beach. The *Jolly Roger* (tel. 809/462–2064) has a "fun cruise," complete with "pirate" crew, limbo dancing, plank walking, and other pranks. *Paradise 1* (tel. 809/462–4158) is a 45-foot Beneteau yacht that offers lunch or sunset cruises. The *Falcon* (tel. 809/462–4792) is a catamaran schooner that cruises to Bird Island and Barbuda for snorkeling and barbecue; it also makes sunset cruises.

Tennis Many of the larger resorts have their own tennis courts. The **St. James's Club** (tel. 809/460–5000) has seven (five lighted for night play); **Sandals** (tel. 809/462–0267) has two; **Halcyon Cove** (tel. 809/462–0256) four (lighted); and **Curtain Bluff** (tel. 809/462–8400), four Har-Tru and a grass court. For nonguests, court fees are about $30 an hour. The **Temo Sports Complex** (Falmouth Bay, tel. 809/463–1781) has floodlit courts, glass-backed squash courts, showers, a sports shop, and a small restaurant. Squash-court rental is E.C. $30 for 40 minutes; tennis is E.C. $30 an hour.

Waterskiing Many all-inclusive resorts provide this free to guests; others will make arrangements through local outfitters. Dickenson Bay is the center for waterskiing (watch out you don't collide with an inflatable banana). **Wadadli Watersports** (tel. 809/462–2890) will whiz you around for $20 for a half-hour.

Windsurfing The **High Wind Centre** at the Lord Nelson Hotel is *the* spot for serious board sailors, run by expert Patrick Scales (tel. 809/462–3094). Rentals are also available at **Wadadli Watersports** (tel. 809/462–2890) and **Hodges Bay Club** (tel. 809/462–2300); most major hotels offer boardsailing equipment. Equipment rental averages $20 an hour.

Shopping

If you haven't already seen enough designer clothes, Gucci bags, and Luis Vuitton suitcases back home, you can get your fill at **Heritage Quay.** Cruise-ship passengers must pass through this complex when they arrive on the island. The small shops around the historic **Redcliffe Quay** section of St. John's are better, but prices are comparable to those in the United States. Other tourist shops in St. John's are on **St. Mary's, High,** and **Long streets**. At the other end of the scale, endless street stalls sell garish T-shirts and cheap jewelry. Quality crafts are few and far between, but try some of the following:

Janie Easton designs many of the original finds in her **Galley Boutique** (the main shop in a historic building in English Harbour, tel. 809/462–1525) with pizzazz and reasonable prices. Trinidadian Natalie White sells her sculptured cushions and wall hangings, all hand-painted on silk and signed, from her home-studio (tel. 809/463–2519). Artist-filmmaker Nick Maley, with his wife, Gloria, have turned the **Island Arts Galleries** (Alton Place, on Sandy Lane, behind the Hodges Bay Club, tel. 809/461–3332) into a melting pot for Caribbean artists. **Harmony Hall** (at Brown's Bay Mill, near Freetown, tel. 809/460–4120) is the Antiguan sister to the original Jamaica location. In addition to "Annabella Boxes," books, and cards, there are pottery and ceramic pieces, carved wooden fantasy birds, and an ever-changing roster of exhibits. John and Katie Shears have opened **Seahorse Studios** (at Cobbs Cross, en route to English Harbour, tel. 809/463–1417), presenting the works of good artists in a good setting. **Bona** (Redcliffe Quay, tel. 809/462–2036) presents antiques, select crystal and porcelain, leaf-of-lettice pottery from Italy, and "wedding frogs" from Thailand, collected during the world travels of owners Bona and Martin Macy. The **CoCo Shop** (St. Mary's St., tel. 809/462–1128) is a favorite haunt for Sea Island cotton designs, Daks clothing, and Liberty of London fabrics. **Karibbean Kids** (Redcliffe Quay, tel. 809/462–4566) has great gifts for youngsters. A "must" buy at the **Map Shop** (St. Mary's St., tel. 809/462–3993) for those interested in Antiguan life, is the paperback *To Shoot Hard Labour (The Life and Times of Samuel Smith, an Antiguan Workingman);* it costs $12, but you won't regret spending it. Also check out any of the books of Jamaica Kincaid, whose works on her native Antigua have won international, albeit controversial, acclaim.

Dining

Travelers on a budget can save on the many West Indian fast-food and street-food options on Antigua, especially in St. John's. Inexpensive restaurants, most serving local cuisine or an international (mainly Italian) mix, are also easy to find. Local specialties include *funghi* (pronounced foon-ji), cornmeal paste usually served with swordfish and pumpkin; *ducana,* a boiled dumpling filled with grated sweet potato and coconut; goatwater, or kiddi, stew, a rich, soupy mix seasoned with cloves; *souse*, pig's trotters cooked with hot peppers, onions, and lime juice; and *pepper pot*, or spinach, *eddo* (a local vegetable), and okra cooked with salted meat. A typical breakfast snack, costing about E.C. $3, is freshly baked bread covered in melted cheese and butter.

In St. John's, **Speedy Joe's**, on Nevis Street, and **Big Bite**, on Long Street, have a good selection of sandwiches, *rotis* (West Indian sandwiches of curried meat or chicken wrapped in pastry), and fresh juices. **Billigan's**, on Camacho Avenue, has a menu of local dishes. At **Jap's Snack Shop**, a tiny bakery-cum-café on Vivien Richards Street, the legendary Viv Richards still comes for his funghi and swordfish whenever he returns to the island. In **Redcliffe Quay**, several attractive cafés serve sandwiches, quiches, and the like, good with passion fruit juice or homemade ginger beer. At Fort James, just outside St. John's, a group of cheerfully painted **fish-and-chip stalls** near the water serve lunch to locals and anyone else on weekends. Also at Fort James is **Russell's**, a small bar and restaurant built into the ruins of a former fort; it serves simple fish dishes.

For those who'll be cooking, the biggest supermarkets are in St. John's, including **Dew's**, on Long Street, and **Food City**. At the **public market** on Independence Avenue (open Fri.–Sat. 6 AM–2 PM), you'll find a large selection of local fruits and vegetables, as well as fresh fish (snapper, swordfish, grunt, mullet), meat, and poultry. Other stalls sell local products, radios, and cassettes (good calypso music).

At the other end of the scale from budget cafés and restaurants are the island's sophisticated, expensive dining rooms serving fine Continental and American cuisine. If you decide to give any of these a try, you'll need to make reservations (in high season). Restaurants listed below do not need reservations unless stated otherwise. Also inquire about dress, as some places require a jacket and tie in winter; in listings below, dress is casual unless stated otherwise.

Most menu prices are listed in E.C. dollars; some are listed in both E.C. and U.S. dollars. Be sure to ask if credit cards are accepted and in which currency the prices are quoted. Prices below are in U.S. dollars. Highly recommended restaurants are indicated by a star ★.

Category	Cost*
Moderate	$15–$25
Inexpensive	$8–$15
Budget	under $8

per person, excluding drinks, service, and sales tax (7%)

★ **Admiral's Inn.** Known as the Ad to yachtsmen around the world, this historic inn, in the heart of English Harbour, is a must for Anglophiles and mariners. At the bar inside, you can sit and soak up the centuries under dark, timbered wood (the bar top even has the names of sailors from Nelson's fleet carved into it), but most guests sit on the terrace under shady Australian pines to enjoy the splendid views of the harbor complex and Clarence House opposite. Specialties include curried conch, fresh snapper with equally fresh limes, and lobster thermidor. The pumpkin soup is the best on the island. *Nelson's Dockyard, tel. 809/460–1027. Reservations required. AE, MC, V. Moderate.*

★ **Coconut Grove.** There are few more pleasant places to eat in Antigua than this waterfront restaurant at the Siboney Beach Club, where coconut palms grow through the roof and waves lap white coral sand a few feet away. Service is friendly and attentive, and the English owner is a charming hostess. The Trinidad-born chef makes good use of local produce, though the menu is mainstream European. Start with a chilled gazpacho or the superb terrine of broccoli with lobster. Follow this with lamb, steak, or fish. The fish is especially good, with the sauces that complement the flavor of the marlin, kingfish, or snapper. Lobsters are available for the asking. Vegetarian dishes and low-cholesterol recipes are also offered. *Box 1760, Dickenson Bay, tel. 809/462–1538, fax 809/461–4555. Reservations advised in high season. MC, V. Moderate.*

Lemon Tree. On the second floor of a historic building in the old part of St. John's, this upbeat eatery is popular with cruiseship passengers. Owner Janet Ferraro animates the restaurant with her winning smile and *bon vivant* presence. The menu is eclectic, with minipizzas, ribs, beef Wellington, Cornish hen, lobster, vegetarian crepes, a very spicy Cajun garlic shrimp, and pasta dishes. For those who like Mexican food, the Lemon Tree makes unbeatable burritos, as well as chili, nachos, and fajitas. Live music nightly varies from soft, classical piano to funky reggae. *Long and Church Sts., St. John's, tel. 809/462–1689. AE, DC, MC, V. Moderate.*

Lobster Pot. This bistro-style restaurant has improved considerably since being taken over by current owner Tony Sayers. The large stone-flagged dining room, with its timbered roof supported on stone columns and its fishing boat smack in the center, is airy and open to the sea breeze. Best seats are in the gallery right on the water. Specialties on the varied menu include coconut-milk curry; baked breast of chicken stuffed with goat's cheese, broccoli, and sun-dried tomatoes; and flavorful local seafood (lobster, mahi-mahi, and red snapper). For Anglophiles, there is bread-and-butter pudding and, for children, hamburgers and 4-oz. steaks. *Runaway Bay, tel. 809/462–2855. Reservations advised in high season. D, MC, V. Moderate.*

Shirley Heights Lookout. This restaurant is in part of an 18th-century fortification, and the view of English Harbour below is breathtaking. There's a breezy pub downstairs that opens onto the lookout point and, upstairs, a cozy, windowed room with hardwood floors and beamed ceilings. Pub offerings include burgers, sandwiches, and barbecue, while the upstairs room serves the likes of pumpkin soup and lobster in lime sauce. The best time to come is on Sunday after 3 PM, when crowds troop up the hill for the barbecue livened by island music from a steel band from 3 to 6 and reggae from 6 to 9. *Shirley Heights, tel. 809/463–1785. Reservations required in season. AE, MC, V. Moderate.*

Calypso. This snappy outdoor bistro has become a favorite with the St. John's professional set since its opening in 1992. At lunchtime it's packed with dapper lawyers and upwardly mobile Antiguan ladies. Tables are ranged under green umbrellas on a sunny patio dominated by the remains of a brick kiln. Specials change every day, but generally include stewed lamb; grilled lobster; and baked chicken served with funghi, rice, and dumplings. The pumpkin soup and garlic bread are excellent. You may find the owner is somewhat haughty. *Redcliffe St., St. John's, tel. 809/462–1965. No credit cards. No dinner except Fri. Closed Sun. Inexpensive–Moderate.*

The Dolphin. The honey-colored hurricane shutters; rattan chairs from Dominica; and Madras cotton tablecloths, hand-sewn by the redoubtable Mrs. Murphy (the owner's mother, who runs the guest house opposite) make this small restaurant in a suburb of St. John's worth the $4 cab fare from the center of town to get there. The menu is traditional Caribbean, with dishes like salt fish and ducana; shrimp in a freshly grated ginger and garlic sauce; and *orpionos,* delicious batter-dipped, deep-fried vegetables served with a Creole sauce. Mrs. Murphy's coconut meringue pie is to die for. The young Antiguan owner and his Toronto-born wife make pleasant hosts, and on Saturday evenings there is live jazz. *All Saint's Rd., St. John's, tel. 809/462–1183. MC, V. Inexpensive–Moderate.*

Home. When Carl Thomas came back to his native Antigua after years in New York, he decided to open a restaurant in his boyhood home, a '50s bungalow in a quiet suburb of St. John's. So he completely refurbished the original house, knocked down walls to create one large space, planted an herb and vegetable garden, and hired a Dutch cook. Furnishing is Ikea-style stripped pine, with polished wood floors and walls hung with African and Caribbean art (Carl's own watercolors are in the rest room). At press time, the restaurant had only been open two weeks, and the quality of the food—dubbed "Caribbean haute cuisine" was very uneven. (Smoked fish, a house specialty, and bread pudding with whisky sauce were delicious.) In addition, the brand-new, squeaky-clean interior still lacks atmosphere. *Gambles Terr., St. John's, tel. 809/461–7651. Reservations advised in high season. AE, MC, V. Inexpensive–Moderate.*

Redcliffe Tavern. Here's a good stop when you're shopping at Redcliffe Quay in St. John's. The beautiful, antique water-pumping equipment here, still bearing the original maker's crests from England, was salvaged from all over the island and imaginatively integrated into the restaurant's structure (one supports the buffet bar, for instance). The warm brick and black-and-white painted woodwork of this former colonial warehouse also charm. The menu has an especially good selection of local fishes, including wahoo, marlin, shark, and mahi-mahi. Other specialties include mango-stuffed chicken breast with curry sauce and beer-battered flying fish from Trinidad. *Redcliffe Quay, St. John's, tel. 809/461–4557. AE, MC, V. Inexpensive–Moderate.*

Mandalay. Located at Falmouth Harbour, it's the only Indian restaurant on the island. Mary, the owner's wife and the chef, is from Sri Lanka and knows her *somosas* and *chappatis* like the back of her own cooking pot. Though the menu is limited, the green-and-white checked tablecloths, handmade wall hangings, and well-stocked bar make this a pleasant spot for a reasonably priced meal. The specialty is Lobster Malay, cooked in ginger and garlic. Only the bar is open during off-season. *Falmouth Harbour, tel. 809/460–1198. AE, MC, V. Dinner only. Inexpensive.*

Brother B's. It's impossible to miss this funky restaurant in the appropriately named Soul Alley, with its yellow-painted wooden fence and hand-painted boards advertising its fare. And if you want to try such local specialties as pepper pot, funghi, pilau (seasoned rice with chicken, meat, and peas), or salt fish and ducana, this is the place to do it. They even have bull's foot soup, a Caribbean variant of a 19th-century dish from England. The mostly local clientele, the Guinness ads, the framed picture of Viv Richards, Antigua's cricketing folk hero; and the rather surly waitresses make Brother B's as authentically Antiguan as you will find. You can also get breakfast here. *Soul Alley, St. John's, tel. 809/462–0616. No credit cards. Budget.*

Ital. Kimba, the owner of this tiny back-street café (also known as the Best Health Vegetarian Restaurant), is a man with a mission. An earnest, imposing-looking Rastafarian with a mass of dreadlocks piled under his cap and a beard down to his navel, he presides over his four tables in the shade of a lemon tree with almost biblical authority, preparing food in keeping with his philosophy. No animal products or cooking oil (only coconut butter) are used. Tofu, rice, barley, and local cassava bread figure prominently. Everything is cooked in clay pots, and the "Ital-juices" (carrot, papaya, mango) are all fresh-squeezed. For E.C. $16 he will cook you all you can eat under faded pictures of Haile Selassie, Marcus Garvey, and a print bearing the inscription "Behold the conquering lion of Judah." Seriously alternative. *Lower Newgate St., St. John's, no tel. No credit cards. Lunch only. Closed Sun. Budget.*

Lodging

The dominant form of accommodation on Antigua is the large resort catering to an international clientele. Despite the package-tour feel of a lot of these places, they are not cheap, at least not during high season. Those that are moderately priced are included below; more expensive ones drop their rates dramatically during the summer (*see* Off-Season Bets, *below*). Most of these larger hotels and resorts are located on or within walking distance of a beach; you won't need a car if you'll be eating at your hotel. Those seeking cheaper alternatives should know that guest houses and B&Bs, with a few notable exceptions (*see below*) are rare on Antigua, as are villa and apartment rentals. Don't count on these budget properties being on a beach. If you're looking for active nightlife and opportunities for meeting other island guests, you'll want to stay in one of the hotels in Dickenson Bay, where properties are close together and St. John's is just a five-minute cab ride away.

Highly recommended lodgings are indicated by a star ★.

Category	Cost*
Moderate	$150–$225
Inexpensive	$80–$150
Budget	under $80

All prices are for a standard double room for two, excluding 7% tax and a 10% service charge. To estimate rates for hotels offering MAP, add about $45 per person per day to the above price ranges. For all-inclusives, add about $100 per person per day.

Barrymore Beach Club. Situated on Runaway Bay, this mid-priced resort offers standard rooms or one-bedroom apartments, both with kitchens, in two-story, condominium-style buildings. The gardens, with hibiscus and bougainvillea plants much in evidence, are well maintained. Although individual units are generously spaced from one another, the standard rooms are small for two people and tend to be rather airless. Another drawback is the cramped beach here. But the resort is quiet and attractive, and there's a small restaurant nearby where guests can eat reasonably priced meals. *Box 1774, Runaway Bay, tel. and fax 809/462–4101. 36 rooms. AE, MC, V. EP. Moderate.*

Club Antigua. Formerly known as the Jolly Beach Resort, this sprawling, all-inclusive resort is in one of the least attractive parts of the island. The nearby saltwater lagoon, a mosquito breeding ground, has been dredged to create a vast marina and condominium complex. With 570 rooms, it is the largest resort in the Caribbean and about to get even larger. Club Antigua caters to a fun-loving, budget clientele (the cruise on the resort's repro pirate ship is a notorious drinking binge), many of whom come from Europe. The rooms are the size of a monk's cell, and you'll have to face long queues in the dining hall for meals, but the sports facilities are extensive and the nearby beaches, as everywhere on the island, are attractive. If you want a cheap, all-inclusive vacation and don't expect too much *savoir vivre,* this will be your best bet on Antigua. *Box 744, St. John's, tel. 809/462–0061; in FL, 800/432–6083; in Canada, 800/368–6669, fax 809/462–4900. 570 rooms. Facilities: 3 restaurants, 4 bars, disco, pool, 8 tennis courts, movie room, shops, car-rental desk, water-sports center, excursion boat. AE, MC, V. All-inclusive. Moderate.*

Yepton Beach Resort. Set on Hog John Bay on the Five Islands peninsula, this Swiss-designed, all-suites resort still feels, five years after opening, somewhat isolated and unlived-in. But it's a splendid location on a beautiful beach. Accommodations are in a row of four Mediterranean-style, white-stucco blocks that look onto the resort's own beach in one direction and a lagoon dotted with pelicans and egrets on the other. Some of the rooms are two-room suites, with a bedroom and large living-room-cum-kitchenette. Others are studios, with a Murphy bed and kitchenette in one room. It's possible to combine a double bedroom and a studio to make an apartment sleeping four. Lou Belizaire, an operatic Antiguan, works wonders in the kitchen of the on-property restaurant. *Box 1427, St. John's, tel. 809/462–2520 or 800/361–4621. Facilities: restaurant, tennis courts, pool, water sports. AE, MC, V. EP, MAP. Moderate.*

★ **Admiral's Inn.** Lovingly restored 30 years ago to its former glory, this 18th-century Georgian inn is the centerpiece of the magnificent Nelson's Dockyard complex. Once an engineers' office and warehouse (the bricks were originally used as ballast for British ships), the Admiral's Inn reverberates with history; whether you're a sailing buff or not, you can't help being drawn into the historic, maritime ambience of the place. The best rooms are upstairs in the main building. They have the original timbered ceilings complete with iron braces, and massive, whitewashed brick walls. Straw mats from Dominica on the floors and views through wispy Australian pines to the sunny harbor beyond complete the effect. The rooms in the garden annex are smaller and tend to be a little airless. The best-kept secret here is The Loft, a simple, timbered space upstairs in a separate building that used to be the dockyard's joinery. It has two big bedrooms, an enormous kitchen, and a magnificent view from the timbered living room onto the busy harbor. The inn's boat ferries guests to a nearby beach. *Box 713, St. John's, tel. 809/460–1027 or 800/223–5695, 914/833–3303 in NY, 416/447–2335 in Canada, fax 809/460–1534. 14 rooms. Facilities: restaurant, pub. AE, MC, V. EP, MAP. Inexpensive.*

★ **The Catamaran Hotel.** Renovation in 1989 was careful to retain the historical ambience of this plantation-style house, with its attractive apricot, white, and black trim and wraparound veranda supported on white, classical-style pediments. The property sits on the water at Falmouth Harbour, on a beach lined with palm and almond trees. The best rooms are the eight first-floor suites, with four-poster beds, full baths, kitchenettes, and private balconies. None of the rooms has air-conditioning, TV, or telephone. English Harbour is only 2 miles and a $6 cab ride away, and a nearby supermarket stocks provisions for cooking. There's also a restaurant here serving à la carte meals. For those who want a low-key, low-priced, tranquil resort, this offers excellent value. *Box 958, Falmouth, tel. 809/460–1036, fax 809/460–1506. 16 rooms. Facilities: restaurant, bar, sailing. AE, MC, V. EP. Inexpensive.*

★ **Lord Nelson Beach Hotel.** This small, weathered mom-and-pop resort is run by the Fullers, expatriate Americans who have been here since 1949. As they have a vast, extended family of their own, it's a perfect place for children to scamper about and explore. If you don't mind a bit of chipped paint and organized chaos, you'll love it, too. In recent years it's become a mecca for windsurfers, who like its windsurfing boards, easy access to the water, and dedicated professional staff. The best rooms here are in a two-story, apricot-colored building that looks directly onto the property's own horseshoe-shaped beach. Each room is slightly different (one has beautiful tiled floors and an ornately carved bed from Dominica that is so high you almost need to be a pole-vaulter to get into it). Guests eat in the timbered dining room, dominated by a replica of the boat in which Captain Bligh was cast off from the *Bounty*; expect hearty dishes such as stuffed pork chops, wahoo, and snapper. As the resort is fairly isolated (5 miles from St. John's), figure into your budget about E.C. $20 for cab fare to any meal you have elsewhere. *Box 155, St. John's, tel. 809/462–3094, fax 809/462–0751. Facilities: restaurant, bar, dive shop, windsurfing. AE, MC, V. EP, MAP, FAP. Inexpensive.*

Guest Houses and B&Bs
★

Murphy's Place. Mrs. Murphy, a hard-working, talkative woman, started taking guests into her home, a modern bungalow on the outskirts of St. John's, to pay for her children's education. Now she gets calls from places like Miami from people begging for a room. The units, in a plain wooden annex hung with yellow bella flowers, are of two kinds: Singles each have a double bed, shower, and fan; two-bedroom units have a large living-room area and a well- equipped kitchen. The furnishing is simple enough, but Mrs. Murphy sews many of the curtains and bedspreads herself and takes a lot of trouble seeing that everything is shipshape and clean. On a patio festooned with plants she serves afternoon tea for those who want it and a pancake breakfast on Saturday. As a result, the guest book is full of the signatures of (mostly young) people from all over the world. At The Dolphin Restaurant (*see* Dining, *above*), a few yards away, her son serves good Caribbean food at reasonable prices. The beach is about 3 miles away. *Box 491, St. John's, tel. 809/461–1183. 4 rooms. Facilities: patio. No credit cards. EP. Inexpensive.*

Villa and Apartment Rentals

Few villas designed for vacationers have been built on Antigua. Instead, the island has a number of condominium- and apartment-style resorts. Units in many of these have limited cooking facilities or Pullman kitchens.

Sunset Cove. Accommodations in this new complex on Dickenson Bay are in white, two-story blocks, festooned with bougainvillea. Units range from standard rooms (barely enough space to squeeze past the end of the bed) to studios to villas, which are basically a room and studio combined and can sleep four. The best suites are ocean-view (forget what the brochure says about the views of the others; they look across at the suites opposite). All units come with air-conditioning, ceiling fans, TVs, VCRs, and microwave ovens. Many units are very close together, and you may end up hearing a good bit of your neighbor's holiday, too. But the property is attractive, well maintained, and uncrowded, and a little beach of white coral sand is only a stone's throw away. *Runaway Bay, Box 1262, St. John's, tel. 809/462–3762. 32 units. Facilities: pool, maid service, bar. AE, DC, MC, V. EP. Inexpensive–Moderate.*

Falmouth Beach Apartments. This is the quiet sister hotel of the famous Admiral's Inn at English Harbour. The best accommodations are in an attractive colonial-style house on its own small palm-lined beach. Apartments here are basically one large room comprising a bed room-cum-living-room, a shower bath, and a kitchenette screened off from the main living area. A door opens directly onto a timbered, wraparound veranda with a view of the water and the mountainous peninsula opposite. Other rooms, in four modern buildings perched on the hillside, have a separate kitchen, a bedroom with twin beds, and a shower bath. There is no air-conditioning, telephones, or TVs. All apartments have daily maid service, which includes washing up. The sheltered beach is ideal for toddlers and small children learning to swim. *Box 713, Falmouth Harbour, tel. 809/460–1094 or 800/223–5695, fax 809/460–1534. 28 rooms. Facilities: sailing. AE, MC, V. EP. Inexpensive.*

Pillar Rock Hotel and Condominiums. At press time, this hilltop complex of efficiency apartments and one-bedroom villas overlooking Hog John Bay on the Five Islands peninsula was offering a recession-driven rate of 50% off the regular price in high season. (Regular high-season rates are high-end Moder-

ate.) The good news is that for $125 you will probably be able
to rent a small villa for two. The bad news is that services are
probably also running at half-steam. The property is attractive, with a swimming pool at its center and spectacular views
to the west. Studios have kitchenettes, a single bed, and a fold-
out bed. The best rooms are immediately above the sea, on the
Hog John Bay side (overwise you overlook the Ramada Renaissance). There's a surcharge for air-conditioning. *Box 1226,
St. John's, tel. 809/462–2623. 60 units. Facilities: pool, snack bar,
bar. AE, MC, V. EP. Inexpensive.*

Off-Season Bets The following properties offer substantial reductions in the off-
season, making them particularly good choices: **The Copper
and Lumber Store Hotel** (Box 184, St. John's, tel. 809/463–
1058); **Halcyon Cove Beach Resort and Casino** (Box 251, St.
John's, tel. 809/462–0256 or 800/223–1588); the **Inn at English
Harbour** (Box 187, St. John's, tel. 809/463–1014); the **Ramada
Renaissance Royal Antiguan Resort** (Deep Bay, St. John's, tel.
809/462–3733); **Sandals** (Box 147, St. John's, tel. 809/462–0267
or 800/SANDALS); and **Siboney Beach Club** (Box 222, St.
John's, tel. 809/462–0806 or 800/533–0234).

Nightlife

Most of Antigua's evening entertainment centers on the resort
hotels, which feature calypso singers, steel bands, limbo dancers, and folkloric groups on a regular basis. Check with the
Tourist Board for up-to-date information.

Shirley Heights Lookout (Shirley Heights, tel. 809/463–1785)
does Sunday-afternoon barbecues that continue into the night
with music and dancing. It's a favorite local spot on Sunday
night for residents, visitors, and the ever-changing yachting
crowd. (Best gossip on the island!) **Hemingway's** (St. Mary's
St., St. John's, tel. 809/462–2783), a restaurant serving West
Indian fare, is a popular gathering spot for Yuppie locals.

Casinos Most casinos on Antigua are fairly declassé. There is usually
no cover charge, and casual dress is fine. There are five hotel
casinos open from early evening until 4 AM. The "world's largest slot machine" as well as gaming tables are at the **King's
Casino** (tel. 809/462–1727), at Heritage Quay. Slot machines
and gaming tables attract gamblers to the **Flamingo** (Michaels
Mount, tel. 809/462–1266). The **St. James's Club** (Mamora Bay,
tel. 809/463–1113) has a private casino with a European ambience. Ramada has turned the casino at the **Ramada Renaissance Royal Antiguan Resort** (tel. 809/462–3733) into an
Atlantic City–style casino.

Discos **Tropix** (Redcliffe Quay, St. John's, tel. 809/462–2317) is very
popular. Open Wednesday through Saturday, from 9 PM till
whenever, it draws locals, residents, and energetic visitors; an
insider's favorite remains **Peter Scott's Cafe** (St. John's, no
phone). Owner Scott is his own best entertainment, playing the
guitar and mixing songs from reggae to ballads. On Wednesday
nights, **Columbo's** (Galleon Beach Club, English Harbour, tel.
809/463–1081) is the place to be for live reggae, and the **Lemon
Tree Restaurant** (Long and Church Sts., St. John's, tel.
809/461–2507) swings every night in season until at least 11 PM.

4 Aruba

Updated by
Laurie Senz

The *A* in the ABC Islands, Aruba is small—only 19.6 miles long and 6 miles across at its widest point, approximately 70 square miles. Most of its 25 hotels sit side by side down one major strip along the southwestern shore, with restaurants, exotic boutiques, fiery floor shows, and glitzy casinos right on their premises. Nearly every night there are organized theme parties, treasure hunts, beachside barbecues, and fish fries with steel bands and limbo dancers.

Budget-minded travelers have much to celebrate. Aruba has a cheap, safe, and reliable bus system; abundant fast-food franchises; and a glut of overbuilding that's kept room rates stable for the past few years. Although standard high-season rates for large resort hotels and time-share units here are pricey (you generally need to spend at least $150 a night to get good value), these complexes offer numerous package deals in the high season, as well as much discounted rates in low season. In addition, the island has several small apartment hotels and guest houses with rock-bottom rates.

The island's national anthem proclaims, "The greatness of our people is their great cordiality," and this is no exaggeration. Once a member of the Netherlands Antilles, Aruba became an independent entity within the Netherlands in 1986, with its own royally appointed governor, a democratic government, and a 21-member elected Parliament. With education, housing, and health care financed by an economy based on tourism, the island's population of 70,000 recognizes visitors as valued guests. Waiters serve you with smiles and solid eye contact,

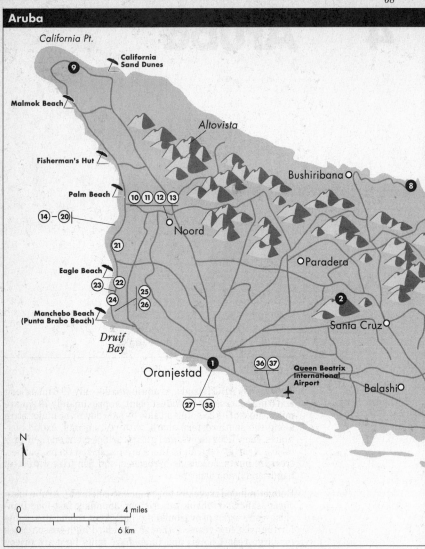

Aruba

California Pt.

California
Sand Dunes

Malmok Beach

Altovista

Fisherman's Hut

Bushiribana

Palm Beach

⑩ ⑪ ⑫ ⑬

⑭ — ⑳

Noord

㉑

Paradera

Eagle Beach

㉓ ㉒

㉔ ㉕

㉖

❷

Manchebo Beach
(Punta Brabo Beach)

Santa Cruz

Druif
Bay

❶

㊱ ㊲

Oranjestad

Queen Beatrix
International
Airport

Balashi

㉗ — ㉟

N

0   4 miles

0   6 km

Exploring
Balashi Gold
Mine, **4**
California
Lighthouse, **9**
Frenchman's Pass, **3**
Guadirikiri/Fontein
caves, **7**

Hooiberg (Haystack
Hill), **2**
Natural Bridge, **8**
Oranjestad, **1**
San Nicolas, **6**
Spanish Lagoon, **5**

Dining
Bali Floating
Restaurant, **28**
Bon Appetit, **15**
Boonoonoonoos, **29**
Brisas del Mar, **38**
Buccaneer
Restaurant, **30**
Captain's Table, **22**
Coco Plum, **34**
La Paloma, **11**
Mi Cushina, **39**

New Old Cunucu
House, **16**
Olé, **14**
Papamiento, **21**
Reubens, **32**
Roseland, **25**
The Steamboat, **17**
Talk of the Town
Restaurant, **37**
Twinklebone's House
of Roastbeef, **12**
The Waterfront, **33**

KEY

⌐ Beach

① Exploring Sites

⑩ Hotels and Restaurants

Caribbean Sea

○ Andicouri

Arikok

Boca Prins
(sand dunes)

○ Miralamar

⑦

③
④

Yamanota

Boca
Grandi

*Spanish
Lagoon*

⑤

Savaneta ○

③⑨
⑥
San
Nicolas

Grapefield
Beach

*Colorado
Pt.*

○ Seroe
Colorado

③⑧

Rodger's
Beach

Baby Beach

Lodging

Amsterdam Manor
Beach Resort, **23**

Aruba Beach Club, **26**

Aruba Hilton Hotel
& Casino, **18**

Aruba Palm Beach
Hotel & Casino, **19**

Best Western Talk of
the Town Resort, **37**

Bushiri Beach
Resort, **27**

Cactus
Apartments, **10**

Coconut Inn, **13**

Harbourtown Beach
Resort & Casino, **35**

La Cabana All Suite
Beach Resort &
Casino, **22**

La Quinta Beach
Resort, **24**

The Mill Resort, **20**

Sonesta Hotel, Beach
Club & Casino, **31**

Vistalmar, **35**

English is spoken everywhere, and hotel-hospitality directors appear delighted to serve your special needs. Good, direct air service from the United States makes Aruba an excellent choice for even a short vacation.

The island's distinctive beauty lies in its countryside—an almost extraterrestrial landscape full of rocky deserts, cactus jungles, secluded coves, and aquamarine vistas with crashing waves. With its low humidity and average temperatures of 82°F, Aruba has the climate of a paradise; rain comes mostly during November.

What It Will Cost These sample prices meant only as a general guide, are for high season. Price estimates are for high season. Moderately priced hotels and time-share units cost $150–$185 a night. Small budget apartment hotels offer basic, air-conditioned lodging for under $85 a night. Dinner at an inexpensive restaurant costs $15–$20 or less; at a budget restaurant, about $12; and cheaper still at the many fast-food spots around the island. All-you-can-eat buffets have also become popular, charging around $10 per person. A rum punch costs about $2.50; a glass of wine or other cocktail, $3.50; and a glass of beer, $2. Car rental averages $30–$35 a day. Taxi rates are fixed; from the airport to your hotel, figure about $12–$16, depending upon your hotel's location. Round-trip bus fare from hotels along Eagle and Palm beaches to Oranjestad is $1.50. A single-tank dive is about $30. Snorkel equipment rents for around $9 a day.

Before You Go

Tourist Information Contact the **Aruba Tourism Authority** (1000 Harbor Blvd., Weehawken, NJ 07087, tel. 201/330–0800 or 800/TO–ARUBA, fax 201/330–8757; 2344 Salezdo St., Miami, FL 33134, tel. 305/567–2720, fax 305/567–2721; 86 Bloor St. W, Suite 204, Toronto, Ont., Canada M5S 1M5, tel. 416/975–1950).

Arriving and Departing *By Plane* Flights leave daily to Aruba from New York area airports and Miami International airport, with easy connections from most American cities. **Air Aruba** (tel. 800/882–7822), the island's official airline, flies nonstop to Aruba daily from Miami and five days a week from Newark. **American Airlines** (tel. 800/433–7300) offers daily nonstop service from both Miami International and New York's JFK International airports. **ALM** (tel. 800/327–7230), the major airline of the Dutch Caribbean islands, flies five days a week nonstop from Miami to Aruba; two nonstop and two direct flights a week leave out of Atlanta with connecting services (throughfares) to most major U.S. gateways tied in with Delta. Air Aruba and ALM also have connecting flights to Caracas, Bonaire, Curaçao, and St. Maarten as well as other Caribbean islands. ALM also offers a "Visit Caribbean Pass" for interisland travel. From Toronto and Montreal, you can fly to Aruba on American Airlines via San Juan. American also has connecting flights from several U.S. cities via San Juan. **VIASA** (tel. 800/327–5454) has Monday and Thursday nonstop flights out of Houston. **AeroPostal** (tel. 800/468–9419) offers nonstop flights from Atlanta four times a week and from Orlando three times a week.

From the Airport Aruba has one airport, Queen Beatrix International, about 3½ miles from downtown Oranjestad. There is no public transportation to the hotels. A taxi to properties at Eagle Beach will run about $12 for up to four people; to Palm Beach, $16. Some hotels include transfers in their package rates. If you're staying at a small guest house, it's advisable to rent a car at the airport.

Passports and Visas U.S. and Canadian residents need only show proof of identity—a valid passport, birth certificate, naturalization certificate, green card, valid nonquota immigration visa, or a valid voter registration card. All other nationalities must submit a valid passport.

Precautions For this hot, dry island, bring moisturizer, sunscreen, sunglasses, and a hat. You'll also need repellent for the mosquitoes that plague the island, especially when the trade winds die down. Aruba has a very low crime rate, so you should have no problems if you use basic caution; lock your valuables in your hotel's vault, and lock your car if you are leaving anything in it. Exercise care if you rent a scooter, and do wear the helmet provided. If you plan to do a full island tour, stick to a car or other four-wheel-drive vehicle. Help Arubans conserve water and energy: Turn off air-conditioning when you leave your room and keep your faucets turned off. Aruba is a party island, but only up to a point. A police dog sniffs for drugs at the airport.

Staying in Aruba

Important Addresses **Tourist Information:** The **Aruba Tourism Authority** (L.G. Smith Blvd. 172, Box 1019, tel. 297/8–23777) has free brochures and guides who are ready to answer any questions.

Emergencies **Police:** (tel. 100). **Hospital:** Horaceo Oduber (tel. 24300). **Pharmacy:** Botica del Pueblo (tel. 21254), **Ambulance and Fire** (tel. 115). All hotels have house doctors on call 24 hours a day. Call the front desk.

Currency Arubans happily accept U.S. dollars virtually everywhere, so there's no real need to exchange money, except for necessary pocket change (cigarettes, soda machines, or pay phones). The currency used, however, is the Aruban florin (AFl), which at press time exchanged to the U.S. dollar at AFl 1.77 for cash, AFl 1.79 for traveler's checks, and to the Canadian dollar at AFl 1.30. The Netherlands Antilles florin (used in Bonaire and Curaçao) is not accepted in Aruba. Major credit cards and traveler's checks are widely accepted, but you will probably be asked to show identification when cashing a traveler's check. Prices quoted here are in U.S. dollars unless otherwise noted.

Taxes and Service Charges Hotels charge a 5% government room tax and usually add 11% onto the bill for gratuity charges. Some restaurants also add a 10%–15% service charge onto the bill. There is no sales tax in Aruba. The departure tax is $10.

Getting Around Aruba is small and easy to explore. Car rentals are reasonably priced, and navigation is simple: It's hard to get lost when all you have to do is follow the pointing divi-divi trees back to hotel row along Palm Beach. If you're staying at one of the larger hotels or time-shares, you'll already be on the beach, and Aruba's safe, cheap, and reliable bus system will shuttle you into town and back. We recommend renting a car for a day to explore the island, longer if you are staying somewhere away from the beach. A few rental car agencies offer one day free with a three-day or longer rental.

Taxis A dispatch office is located at **Alhambra Bazaar and Casino** (tel. 297/8–21604 or 297/8–22116); you can also flag down taxis on the street. Since taxis do not have meters, rates are fixed and should be confirmed before your ride begins. All Aruba's taxi drivers have participated in the government's Tourism Awareness Programs and have received their Tourism Guide Certificate. An hour's tour of the island by taxi will run you about $30 with a maximum of four people per car.

Rental Cars You'll need a valid U.S. or Canadian driver's license to rent a car, and you must be able to meet the minimum age requirements of each rental service, implemented for insurance reasons. Jeeps are wonderful for exploring off the beaten path, but they're twice as expensive as a basic rental car. Local rental car agencies are cheaper than well-known major companies. Their rates average $30–$35 a day (less if you rent for three or more days) for a Nissan Sunny Centra or a Toyota Tercel; air-conditioning is an unnecessary option. Three reputable local agencies, with several locations including one at the airport, are: **Hedwina Car Rental** (tel. 297/8–26442 or 297/8–37393, fax 297/8–48744), **Optima** (tel. 297/8–36263 or 297/8–35622), and **Marcos** (tel. 297/8–65889). Gas runs about $2.75 for an imperial gallon (5 liters). For a small car, plan on $25 a week for gas.

If you prefer to rent from a major company, the addresses and phone numbers for the rental agencies are **Avis** (Kolibristraat 14, tel. 297/8–28787; airport tel. 297/8–25496), **Budget Rent-A-Car** (Kolibristraat 1, tel. 297/8–28600; airport tel. 297/8–25423; at Divi resorts tel. 297/8–35000), **Hertz, De Palm Car Rental** (L.G. Smith Blvd. 142, Box 656, tel. 297/8–24545; airport tel. 297/8–24886), **Dollar Rent-a-Car** (Grendeaweg 15, tel. 297/8–22783; airport tel. 297/8–25651; Manchebo tel. 297/8–26696), **National** (Tank Leendert 170, tel. 297/8–21967; airport tel. 297/8–25451; Holiday Inn tel. 297/8–23600), and **Thrifty** (airport tel. 297/8–35335).

Scooter Rentals More economical than car rental, scooters cost about $15–$20 a day for a 50cc single-seater, $18–$25 for an 80cc double-seater. Rates are lower with two-day or longer rentals, and it's worth calling several services to get the best rate. The following offer free pickup and drop-off service at your hotel: **Semver Cycle Rentals** (tel. 297/8–66851), **Ron's** (tel. 297/8–62090), **George's** (tel. 297/8–25975), and **Pardo's** (tel. 297/8–24573 or 297/8–23524).

Buses For inexpensive trips between the beach hotels and Oranjestad, buses run hourly. One-way fare is 90¢; round-trip fare is $1.50, and exact change is preferred. In Oranjestad, the main terminal is located on South Zoutmanstraat, next to Fort Zoutman and just behind the yellow government building on L.G. Smith Boulevard (the one across from the Harbourtown shopping mall). Public buses run approximately every 20 minutes from 7:30 AM to 11 PM Monday–Saturday, less frequently on Sunday. Contact the Aruba Tourism Authority (tel. 297/8–27089) for a bus schedule or inquire at the front desk of your hotel. A free Shopping Tour Bus (you'll know it by its wild colors) departs every hour beginning at 9:15 AM and ending at 3:15 PM from the Holiday Inn, making stops at all the major hotels on its way toward Oranjestad. Be aware that you'll have to find your own way back to your hotel.

Telephones and Mail To dial direct to Aruba from the United States, dial 011–297–8, followed by the number in Aruba. Local and international calls in Aruba can be made via hotel operators or from the Government Long Distance Telephone Office, SETAR, which is in the Post Office in Oranjestad. When dialing locally in Aruba, simply dial the five-digit number. A local telephone call costs AFl 25¢. To reach the United States, dial 001, then the area code and number.

Telegrams and telexes can be sent through SETAR, the Government Telegraph and Radio Office at the Post Office Building in Oranjestad or via your hotel. There is also a SETAR office in front of the Hyatt Regency Hotel, adjacent to the hotel's parking lot (tel. 297/8–37138).

You can send an airmail letter from Aruba to anywhere in the world for AFl 1, a postcard for AFl 70¢.

Opening and Closing Times Shops are generally open Monday–Saturday 8 AM–6 PM. Most stores stay open through the lunch hour, noon–2 PM. Many stores open when cruise ships are in port on Sunday and holidays. Nighttime shopping at the Alhambra Bazaar runs 5 PM–midnight. Bank hours are weekdays 8–noon and 1:30–4. The Aruba Bank at the airport is open Saturday 9–4 and Sunday 9–1.

Guided Tours
Orientation Most of Aruba's highways are in excellent condition, but guided tours save time and energy. **De Palm Tours** (L.G. Smith Blvd. 142, tel. 297/8–24400 or 297/8–24545) offers a basic 3½-hour tour that hits the island's high spots. Wear tennis or hiking shoes (there'll be optional climbing) and note that the air-conditioned bus can get cold. The tour, which begins at 9:30 AM, picks you up in your lobby and costs $17.50 per person. **Friendly Tours** (tel. 297/8–23230) offers guided 3½-hour sightseeing tours to the island's main sights twice a day ($20).

Special-Interest While not inexpensive, these take visitors off the beaten track, offer good photo opportunities, and lend insight into the island's architectural, botanical, and environmental history. **Corvalou Tours** (tel. 297/8–21149) offers unusual excursions for specialized interests. The Archaeological/Geological Tour involves a four- to six-hour field trip through Aruba's past, including the huge monoliths and rugged, desolate north coast. Also available are architectural, bird-watching, and botanical tours. The fee for all tours is $40 per person, $70 per couple, with special prices for parties of five or more.

For a three-in-one tour of prehistoric Indian cultures, volcanic formations, and natural wildlife, contact archaeologist Eppie Boerstra of **Marlin Booster Tracking, Inc.,** at Charlie's Bar (tel. 297/8–45086 or 297/8–41513). The fee for a six-hour tour is $35 per person, including a cold picnic lunch and beverages. Tours can be given in English, Dutch, German, French, and Spanish.

Hikers will enjoy a guided three-hour trip to remote sites of unusual natural beauty, accessible only on foot. The fee is $25 per person, including refreshments and transportation; a minimum of four people is required. Contact **De Palm Tours** (tel. 297/8–24545).

Private Safaris Educational Tours (tel. 297/8–34869) offers adventure safaris by land cruiser into Aruba's interior. The half-day ($30) and full-day ($40) tours explore the island's history, geology, and wildlife.

Boat Cruises These are popular diversions. **Pelican Watersports** (tel. 297/8–24739) offers daily glass-bottom boat tours for $17 a person. It also offers two-hour morning or afternoon sailing, swimming, and snorkeling cruises aboard a 50-foot catamaran for $25 a person, and "happy hour" sunset cruises for $20 a person (prices include an open bar). **De Palm Tours** (tel. 297/8–24400 or 297/8–24545) offers 1½-hour glass-bottom boat tours for $15 a person, moonlight or sunset party cruises for $25 a person, and three-hour sailing and snorkeling cruises with sandwiches and an open bar for $22.50 a person. **Red Sail Sports** (tel. 297/8–31603) offers four-hour snorkel, sail, and lunch cruises, with an open bar, aboard a 53-foot catamaran; sunset sails; party sails; and even a romantic dinner cruise, at prices that range from $27.50 to $49.50 a person.

If you've ever wanted to walk the plank, take a swing from the yardarm, or be a swashbuckler defending his lady, then take a Pirate Cruise aboard the *Topaz*, the original tall ship used in Walt Disney's production *Return to Treasure Island.* The $39.50 cost includes unlimited drinks, a barbecue dinner, and a sunset swim. Runs daily. Call De Palm Tours (*see above*).

Exploring Aruba

Numbers in the margin correspond to points of interest on the Aruba map.

Oranjestad Aruba's charming Dutch capital, **Oranjestad,** is best explored
❶ on foot. Take a bus from your hotel to the **Port of Call Marketplace,** a new shopping mall. After exploring the boutiques and shops, head up L.G. Smith Boulevard to the colorful **Fruit Market,** located along the docks on your right.

Stop in for lunch at the **Bali Floating Restaurant,** where you can enjoy *rijsttafel* (a buffet of Indonesian foods served over rice) or sip a cool drink and watch the fishermen bringing in their catch (*see* Dining, *below*).

Continue walking along the harbor until you come to **Harbourtown Market,** a festive shopping, dining, and entertainment mall. Next door (one block southwest) is **Wilhelmina Park,** a small grove of palm trees and flowers overlooking the sea.

Cross L.G. Smith Boulevard to Oranjestraat and walk one block to **Fort Zoutman,** one of the island's oldest buildings. It was built in 1796 and used as a major fortress in the skirmishes between British and Curaçao troops. The Willem III Tower, named for the Dutch monarch of that time, was added in 1868. The fort's Historical Museum displays centuries' worth of Aruban relics and artifacts in an 18th-century Aruban house. *Oranjestraat, tel. 297/8–26099. Admission: $1. Open weekdays 9–noon and 1–4.*

Turn left onto Zoutmanstraat and walk two blocks to the **Archeology Museum,** where there are two rooms of Indian artifacts, farm and domestic utensils, and skeletons. *Zoutmanstr. 1, tel. 297/8–28979. Admission free. Open weekdays 8–noon and 1:30–4:30.*

From here, cross the street to the Protestant Church. You're now on Wilhelminastraat. Walk one block and turn right on Kazernestraat. On your right side is the **Strada Complex I** and on your left, **Strada Complex II.** Both are shopping malls, and both are excellent examples of Dutch Colonial architecture. Behind Strada Complex II is the **Holland Aruba Mall,** a new shopping complex built to resemble a Dutch Colonial village. Upstairs is an international food court.

At the intersection of Kazernestraat and Caya G.F. Betico Croes, turn right. This is Oranjestad's main street. When you come to Hendrikstraat, turn left and continue walking until you come to the **Saint Francis Roman Catholic Church.** Next to the church is the **Numismatic Museum,** displaying coins and paper money from more than 400 countries. *Iraussquilnplein 2-A, tel. 297/8–28831. Admission free. Open weekdays 8:30–noon and 1–4:30.*

Diagonally across from the church is the **Post Office,** where you can buy colorful Aruban stamps. Next door is the SETAR, where you can place overseas phone calls.

The Countryside   The "real Aruba"—what's left of a wild, untamed beauty—can be found only in the countryside. Either rent a car, take a sightseeing tour, or hire a cab for $30 an hour (for up to four people). The main highways are well paved, but on the north side of the island some roads are still a mixture of compacted dirt and stones. A four-wheel-drive vehicle will allow you to explore the unpaved interior. Traffic is sparse, and you can't get lost. If you do lose your way, just follow the divi-divi trees (because of the direction of the trade winds, the trees are bent toward the leeward side of the island, where all the hotels are).

Few beaches outside the hotel strip have refreshment stands, so take your own food and drink. And one more caution: Note that there are *no* public bathrooms—anywhere—once you leave Oranjestad, except in the infrequent restaurant.

East to San Nicolas   For a shimmering vista of blue-green sea, drive east on L.G. Smith Boulevard toward San Nicolas, on what is known as the Sunrise side of the island. Past the airport, you'll soon see the towering 541-foot peak of **Hooiberg** (Haystack Hill). If you have the energy, climb the 562 steps up to the top for an impressive view of the city.

Turn left where you see the drive-in theater (a popular hangout for Arubans). Drive to the first intersection, turn right, and follow the curve to the right to **Frenchman's Pass,** a dark, luscious stretch of highway arbored by overhanging trees. Local legend claims the French and native Indians warred here during the 17th century for control of the island. Nearby are the cement ruins of the **Balashi Gold Mine** (take the dirt road veering to the right)—a lovely place to picnic, listen to the parakeets, and contemplate the towering cacti. A magnificent gnarled divi-divi tree guards the entrance.

Backtrack all the way to the main road, past the drive-in, and drive through the area called **Spanish Lagoon,** where pirates once hid to repair their ships.

Back on the main highway, pay a visit to **San Nicolas,** Aruba's oldest village. During the heyday of the Exxon refineries, the town was a bustling port; now it's dedicated to tourism, with the main-street promenade full of interesting kiosks. The **China Clipper Bar** on Main Street used to be a famous "whore" bar frequented by sailors docked in port.

Anyone looking for geological exotica should head for the northern coast, driving northwest from San Nicolas. Stop at

7 the two old Indian caves **Guadirikiri** and **Fontein.** Both were used by the native Indians centuries ago, but you'll have to decide for yourself whether the "ancient Indian inscriptions" are genuine—rumor has it they were added by a European film company that made a movie here years ago. You may enter the caves, but there are no guides available, and bats are known to make appearances. Wear sneakers and take a flashlight or rent one from the soda vendor who has set up shop here.

8 A few miles up the coast is the **Natural Bridge,** sculpted out of coral rock by centuries of raging wind and sea. To get to it, you'll have to follow the main road inland and then the signs that lead the way. Nearby is a café overlooking the water and a souvenir shop stuffed with trinkets, T-shirts, and postcards for reasonable prices.

West of Palm Beach Drive west from the hotel strip to Malmok, where Aruba's wealthiest families reside. Open to the public, **Malmok Beach** is considered one of the finest spots for shelling, snorkeling, and windsurfing (*see* Beaches, *below*). Right off the coast here is the wreck of the German ship *Antilla*, which was scuttled in 1940—a favorite haunt for divers. At the very end of the island

9 stands the **California Lighthouse,** now closed, which is surrounded by huge boulders that look like extraterrestrial monsters; in this stark landscape, you'll feel as though you've just landed on the moon.

Beaches

Beaches in Aruba are legendary in the Caribbean: white sand, turquoise waters, and virtually no garbage, for everyone takes the "no littering" sign—"No Tira Sushi"—very seriously, especially with an AFl 500 fine. The influx of tourists in the past decade, however, has crowded the major beaches, which back up to the hotels along the southwestern strip. These beaches are public, and you can make the two-hour hike from the Holiday Inn on Fisherman's Hut Beach south to the Bushiri Beach Hotel free of charge and without ever leaving sand. If you go strolling during the day, make sure you are well protected from the sun—it scorches fast. Luckily, there's at least one covered bar (and often an ice-cream stand) at virtually every hotel you pass. If you take the stroll at night, you can hotel-hop for dinner, dancing, gambling, and late-night entertainment. On the northern side of the island, heavy trade winds make the waters too choppy for swimming, but the vistas are great and the terrain is wonderfully suited to sunbathing and geological explorations. Most of the major hotels are located on the beach, or within a few minutes' walk. The only exception is the **Sonesta Hotel,** which provides free transportation to its private beach. The public bus runs from town to Eagle, Palm, and Manchebo beaches; fare is 90¢ one way; $1.50 round-trip. You can also take the bus to the Holiday Inn and walk to Fisherman's Hut Beach. A car is necessary to get to the other beaches listed below. Among the finer beaches are:

Baby Beach. On the island's eastern tip, this semicircular beach bordering a bay is as placid as a wading pool and only four to five feet deep—perfect for tots and terrible swimmers. Thatched shaded areas are good for cooling off.

Grapefield Beach. On the north of San Nicolas, this gorgeous beach is perfect for professional windsurfing.

Boca Prins. Near the Fontein Cave and Blue Lagoon, this beach is about as large as a Brazilian bikini, but with two rocky cliffs and tumultuously crashing waves, it's as romantic as you get in Aruba. This is not a swimming beach, however. Boca Prins is famous for its backdrop of enormous vanilla sand dunes. Most folks bring a picnic lunch, a beach blanket, and sturdy sneakers.

Malmok Beach. On the southwestern shore, this lackluster beach borders shallow waters that stretch out 300 yards from shore, making it perfect for beginners learning to windsurf.

Fisherman's Hut. Next to the Holiday Inn, this beach is a windsurfer's haven. Take a picnic lunch (tables are available) and watch the elegant purple, aqua, and orange Windsurfer sails struggle in the wind.

Palm Beach. Once called one of the 10 best beaches in the world by the *Miami Herald*, this is the center of Aruban tourism, offering the best in swimming, sailing, and fishing. During high season, however, it's a sardine can.

Eagle Beach. Across the highway from what is quickly becoming known as Time-Share Lane is Eagle Beach on the southern coast. Not long ago, it was a nearly deserted stretch of pristine sands dotted with the occasional thatched picnic hut. Now that the new time-share resorts are completed, this beach is one of the more hopping on the island.

Manchebo Beach (formerly Punta Brabo Beach). In front of the Manchebo Beach Resort, this impressively wide stretch of white powder is where officials turn a blind eye to those who wish to sunbathe topless. Elsewhere on the island, topless sunbathing is not permitted.

Sports and the Outdoors

Bowling Opened in 1991, the **Eagle Bowling Palace** (Pos Abou, tel. 297/8–35038) has 12 lanes, a cocktail lounge, and snack bar. The cost is $8.25 a game from 10 AM to 3 PM, $10.25 a game from 3 PM to 2 AM, and $1.20 for shoe rentals. Open 10 AM–2 AM.

Golf The **Aruba Golf Club** (Golfweg 82, near San Nicolas, tel. 297/8–42006) features a nine-hole course with 25 sand traps, roaming goats, and lots of cacti. There are 11 Astroturf greens, permitting 18-hole tournaments. The clubhouse contains a bar, storage rooms, workshop, and separate men's and women's locker rooms. The course's official U.S. Golf Association rating is 67; greens fees are $7.50 for 9 holes, $10 for 18 holes. There are no caddies, but golf carts are available. Golfers should also check with the Tourism Authority on the status of the par-72 Robert Trent Jones, Jr., 18-hole golf course, which, at press time, was planned for the area known as Arashi.

Land Sailing Carts with a Windsurfer-type sail are rented at **Aruba Sail Cart** (Bushire 23, tel. 297/8–35133) at $15 (single seater) and $20 (double seater) for 30 minutes of speeding back and forth across a dirt field. The sport is new to Aruba and thrilling for land-bound sailors. Anyone can learn the rudiments of driving the cart in just a few minutes. Open 10 AM–7 PM. Food and drinks are served until 10 PM. Unique, if expensive.

Miniature Golf Two elevated 18-hole minigolf courses surrounded by a moat are available at **Joe Mendez Adventure Golf** (Eagle Beach, tel. 297/8–36625). There are also paddleboats and bumper boats, a bar, and a snack stand. Fees are $6 for a round of minigolf, $5 for 30 minutes of paddleboating, and $5 for 10 minutes of bumper boating.

Snorkeling and With visibility up to 90 feet, Aruban waters are excellent for
Scuba Diving snorkeling in shallow waters, and scuba divers will discover exotic marine life and coral. Certified divers can go wall diving, reef diving, or explore wrecks sunk during World War II. The *Antilla* shipwreck—a German freighter sunk off the northwest coast of Aruba near Palm Beach—is a favorite spot with divers and snorkelers.

Pelican Watersports (J.G. Emanstraat 1, Oranjestad, tel. 297/8–31228 or 297/8–23600, ext. 329), **Red Sail Sports** (L.G. Smith Blvd. 83, tel. 297/8–31603, 297/8–24500, ext. 109, or 800/255–6425) and **De Palm Tours** (L.G. Smith Blvd. 142, tel. 297/8–24545 or 297/8–24400) are the island's three largest water-sports operators. All offer snorkeling trips that cost $15–$19 a person, including equipment. They also offer beginner dive courses and day and night dives. Prices vary among operators, so call around. Beginner courses ("resort" courses) range from $60 to $80 a person. Single-tank dives average $30; two-tank dives, $50, and night dives are about $35. Prices include tanks and weight belts; if you need to rent additional equipment, figure on an extra $15–$25.

Many operators also offer package dives and PADI-certification courses. They include Red Sail Sports, **Aruba Pro Dive** (Ponton 88, tel. 297/8–25520), **Charlie's Buddies S.E.A. Scuba** (San Nicholas, tel. 297/8–41640 or 800/252–0557), **Mermaid Sports Divers** (Manchebo Beach Resort, tel. 297/8–35546 or 800/223–1108), and **Hallo Aruba Dive Shop** (Talk of the Town Hotel, L.G. Smith Blvd. 2, tel. 297/8–38270).

Windsurfing **Pelican Watersports** (J.G. Emanstraat 1, tel. 297/8–23600) rents equipment and offers instruction with a certified Mistral instructor. Stock boards and custom boards rent for $30 per 2 hours, $55 per day. **Red Sail Sports** (L.G. Smith Blvd. 83, tel. 297/8–31603 or 800/255–6425) offers two-hour beginner lessons for $44 and advanced lessons for $33 per hour. It also offers Fanatic board and regular windsurfing board rentals by the hour, day, and week.

Windsurfing instruction and board rental are also available through **Carib Asurf** (Manchebo Beach Resort, tel. 297/8–23444), **Sailboard Vacation** (L.G. Smith Blvd. 462, tel. 297/8–21072), **Roger's Windsurf Place** (L.G. Smith Blvd. 472, tel. 297/8–21918), **Windsurfing Aruba** (Boliviastraat 14, Box 256, tel. 297/8–33472), and **De Palm Tours** (L.G. Smith Blvd. 142, Box 656, tel. 297/8–24545).

Shopping

Caya G.F. Betico Croes—Aruba's chief shopping street—makes for a pleasant diversion from the beach and casino life. Major credit cards are welcome virtually everywhere, U.S. dollars are accepted almost as often as local currency, and traveler's checks can be cashed with proof of identity. Shopping malls have arrived in Aruba, so when you finish walking the main street, stop in at a mall to browse through the chic new boutiques.

Many shops sell duty-free merchandise such as jewelry, perfume, hand-embroidered linens, watches, china, and crystal. Others sell name-brand designer clothing. The best bargains are island crafts, both those made on Aruba and those imported from Latin America and other Caribbean islands. Several souvenir and crafts stores are full of Dutch porcelains and figurines, as befits the island's Netherlands heritage. Dutch cheese is a good buy (you are allowed to bring up to one pound of hard cheese through U.S. customs), as are hand-embroidered linens and any products made from the native plant aloe vera—sunburn cream, face masks, and skin refresheners. Since there is no sales tax, the price you see on the tag is the price you pay. But one word of warning: Don't pull any bargaining tricks. Arubans consider it rude to haggle.

One good craft store is **Artesania Arubiano** (L.G. Smith Blvd. 142, next to the Aruba Tourism Authority, tel. 297/8–37494), where you'll find charming Aruban home-crafted pottery, silkscreened T-shirts and wall hangings, and folklore objects. Inexpensive souvenirs can also be found at the **Bon Bini Festival** (*see* Nightlife, *below*) craft stalls.

Shopping Malls   **Seaport Village Mall** (located on L.G. Smith Blvd., tel. 297/8–23754) is landmarked by the Crystal Casino Tower. This covered mall is located only five minutes away from the cruise terminal. It has more than 85 stores, boutiques, and perfumeries, featuring merchandise to meet every taste and budget. The arcade is lined with tropical plants and caged parrots, and the casino is located just at the top of the escalator.

There are several other shopping malls in Oranjestad, all of which are worth visiting. The **Holland Aruba Mall** (Havenstr. 6, right downtown) houses a collection of smart shops and eateries. Nearby are the **Strada I** and **Strada II,** two small complexes of shops in tall Dutch buildings painted in pastels.

In **Harbourtown** (Swain Wharf), a blue-and-white postmodern version of a seaside village, look for handmade china by Venezuelan artists, discounted perfumes, and embroidered linens from China.

Port of Call Marketplace (L.G. Smith Blvd. 17) features fine jewelry, perfumes, duty-free liquors, batiks, crystal, leather goods, and fashionable clothing.

Dining

Aruba's restaurants serve a cosmopolitan variety of cuisines, although most menus are specifically designed to please American palates—you can get fresh surf and New York turf almost anywhere. Make the effort to try Aruban specialties—*pan bati* is a delicious beaten bread that resembles a pancake, and plantains are similar to cooked bananas. Dress ranges from casual to elegant, but even the finest restaurants require at the most only a jacket for men and a sundress for women. The air-conditioning does get cold, so don't go bare-armed. And anytime you plan to eat in the open air, remember to douse yourself first with insect repellent—the mosquitoes can get unruly, especially in July and August, when the winds drop.

For good or for bad, fast food has arrived in Aruba. For those who are homesick, there's McDonald's, Kentucky Fried Chicken, Burger King, and Wendy's. For breakfast and lunch, the restaurances in the hotels tend to be more expensive than the ones in town, although on Sundays, it may be difficult to find any other kind of restaurant that's open before dinner. Some hotels offer several food plans, which you can purchase either in advance or upon arrival. But before you purchase a Full American Plan (FAP), which includes breakfast, lunch, and dinner, remember that Aruba has numerous excellent and reasonably priced restaurants from which to choose and that eating at different places can be part of the fun of a vacation.

If your hotel room or apartment has a kitchen, save money by making breakfast and lunch and eating it, island-style, on your terrace. For American brands and good quality meats, shop at **Pueblo** (L.G. Smith Blvd. 156). Other grocery stores include **Ling & Sons** (Weststraat 29); **Favorito Supermercado** (Hendrikstraat 28); and **Kong Hing** (Havenstraat 16).

Highly recommended restaurants are indicated by a star ★.

Category	Cost*
Moderate	$15–$25
Inexpensive	$10–$15
Budget	under $10

Prices are for a main course only and are per person, excluding drinks and service (15%).

Bali Floating Restaurant. Floating in its own Oriental houseboat and anchored in Oranjestad's harbor, the Bali has one of the island's best *rijsttafel* dinners (an Indonesian buffet table with 21 different meat, chicken, shrimp, vegetable, fruit, and relish dishes, served over rice). It runs $39 for two people. Bamboo rooftops and Indonesian antiques add to the charm of this popular restaurant. Recently, the owners of the Japanese & Thai Dynasty Restaurant took over the management of the restaurant and have added less-spicy fare. The service is slow, but well meaning. Happy hour 6–8 PM. *L.G. Smith Blvd., Oranjestad, tel. 297/8–22131. AE, MC, V. Moderate.*

★ **Bon Appetit.** A savory aroma and a glowing interior of white tablecloths, clay-potted plants, low lighting, and warm wood beams greet you as you enter. The international cuisine wins acclaim, and the kitchen won a Dutch award for being the cleanest in Aruba. Look forward to generous portions of seafood and beef (with Dutch specialties). The winning prime rib will satisfy even the largest appetites. Leave room for the flaming Max dessert, named after owner and charming host Max Croes. *Palm Beach 29, tel. 297/8–25241. Reservations advised. AE, D, DC, MC, V. Moderate.*

Buccaneer Restaurant. Imagine you're in a sunken ship—fish nets and turtle shells hang from the ceiling, and through the portholes you see live sharks, barracudas, and groupers swimming by. That's the Buccaneer, snug in an old stone building flanked by heavy black chains and boasting a fantastic 5,000-gallon saltwater aquarium, plus 12 more porthole-size tanks. The surf-and-turf cuisine is prepared by the chef-owners with

European élan, and the tables are always full. Order the fresh catch of the day or more exotic fare, such as shrimps with Pernod; smoked pork cutlets with sausage, sauerkraut, and potatoes; or the turtle steak with a light cream sauce. Go early (around 5:45 PM) to get a booth next to the aquariums. *Gasparito 11-C., Oranjestad, tel. 297/8–26172. AE, MC, V. Closed Sun. Moderate.*

Olé. Spain comes alive within the coral stone walls of this romantic restaurant. Waiters and waitresses croon Spanish love songs tableside to the melodic music of a classical guitarist, while an illuminated waterfall tumbles into a moat just outside. The ambience makes up for the limited menu. Order some sangria, share a few *tapas*, and then split a *paella* for two. Honeymooners will want to request, in advance, the sole table on the private terrace overlooking the waterfall. *Hyatt Regency Aruba Resort, L.G. Smith Blvd. 85, tel. 297/8–31234. Reservations required. AE, DC, MC, V. Moderate.*

Papiamento. Veteran restaurateurs Lenie and Eduardo Ellis have converted their 130-year-old home into this intimate, romantic dining spot with impeccable service. Guests can dine indoors surrounded by antiques or outdoors on the patio garden, beneath ficus and palm trees adorned with lights. The chef utilizes flavors from both Continental and Caribbean cuisines in such dishes as Dover sole, Caribbean lobster, shrimp and red snapper cooked tableside on a hot marble stone, and "claypot" for two—seafood medley cooked in a sealed clay pot. *Washington 61, Noord, tel. 297/8–64544. Reservations advised. AE, MC, V. Dinner only. Moderate.*

Talk of the Town Restaurant. Here you'll find candlelight dining and some of the best steaks in town—the owner comes from a family of Dutch butchers. Located in the Best Western Talk of the Town Resort, between the airport and Oranjestad, this fine restaurant is now a member of the elite honorary restaurant society, Chaine de Rotisseurs. Saturday night is prime-rib-as-much-as-you-can-eat night ($18.95), but seafood specialties—such as the crabmeat crepes and the *escargots à la bourguignonne* —are popular too. For late-night suppers, the poolside grill stays open until 2 AM. *L.G. Smith Blvd. 2, Oranjestad, tel. 297/8–23380. AE, DC, MC, V. Moderate.*

Twinklebone's House of Roastbeef. Prime rib with Yorkshire pudding is the kitchen's pride, but there's a full international menu with dishes named after local friends and residents. The chef is known to leave the stove and sing Aruban tunes with the maître d'. In fact, the owner, hostess, and waiters are all known to break into song and encourage the patrons to sing along. There are two seatings, so be sure to call ahead. *Turibana Plaza, Noord 124, tel. 297/8–69800 or 297/8–26780. Reservations advised. AE, MC, V. Closed Sun. Moderate.*

The Waterfront. At this happening harborside eatery you can sit on the wide patio and people-watch, or choose the air-conditioned indoors beneath huge murals of mermaids, dolphin, manatees, and tropical fish. Choose a lobster from the live tank at the entrance and have it steamed, broiled, stuffed with crabmeat, or served *fra diablo*. There's also Alaskan king crab, garlic crab, snow crab, and fresh fish grilled over an open fire. It's open for breakfast too. *Harbourtown Mall, tel. 297/8–35858. Reservations advised. AE, MC, V. Moderate.*

Captain's Table. Within La Cabana All Suite Beach Resort is this gem offering everything from health salads and herbal teas to barbecued Sunset burgers and grilled T-bone steaks. A special treat is the weekend prime rib special, served with a baked potato and salad for $14. Breakfast is an all-you-can-eat for $8. *L.G. Smith Blvd. 250, tel. 297/8–39000. AE, DC, MC, V. Closed Mon. Inexpensive–Moderate.*

Boonoonoonoos. The name—say it just as it looks!—means "extraordinary," which is a bit of hyperbole for this Austrian-owned Caribbean bistroquet in the heart of town. The decor is simple in bright and pastel colors, but the tasty food, served with hearty portions of peas-and-rice and plantains, makes up for the lack of tablecloths, china, and crystal. It should be avoided when crowded, since the service and the quality of the food deteriorate. The roast chicken Barbados is sweet and tangy, marinated in pineapple and cinnamon and simmered in fruit juices. The Jamaican jerk ribs (a 300-year-old recipe) are tiny and spicy, and the satin-smooth hot pumpkin soup drizzled with cheese and served in a pumpkin shell may as well be dessert. The place is small, and the tables are close together. *Wilhelminastr. 18A, Oranjestad, tel. 297/8–31888. Reservations advised. AE, V. Dinner only. Closed Sun. Inexpensive.*

Brisas del Mar. This friendly 10-table place is popular with tourists who like to feel as if they're dining in an Aruban home overlooking the sea. The menu features mostly fried fish with Creole sauces of tomatoes and onions. Try the baby-shark steak and the turtle soup. The pan bati is some of the best on the island. It's a good choice for lunch if you'll be exploring the area, but the food does not justify a taxi ride to reach it—10 miles east of Oranjestad in the town of Saveneta. *Savaneta 22A, tel. 297/8–47718. Reservations advised. No credit cards. Closed Mon. Inexpensive.*

Coco Plum. Fresh fruit drinks, seafood, and hearty Aruban dishes are the specialties at this pleasant and casual alfresco eatery owned by three sisters. The average price for a filling breakfast or lunch is $5. (Saturday mornings, the breakfast special is $2.25.) For dinner, try the fish soup followed by red snapper *crioyo* (a sauce of sweet peppers, onions, and tomatoes) or *keshi yena* (Edam cheese stuffed with meat and baked). *Caya G.F. Betico Croes 100, tel. 297/8–31176. AE, MC, V. Closed Sun. Inexpensive.*

★ **La Paloma.** "The Dove" is not the place for a romantic interlude; come for the family atmosphere (it's usually packed), American-style Italian food, and reasonable prices. The restaurant has its own fishing boat, so the fish is always fresh. There's conch stew with pan bati and fried plantains for exotic tastes. The Caesar salad and minestrone soup are house specialties. *Noord 39, tel. 297/8–62770. AE, MC, V. Closed Tues. Inexpensive.*

Mi Cushina. The name means "My Kitchen," and the menu lists such Aruban specialties as *sopi di mariscos* (seafood soup) and *kreeft stoba* (lobster stew). The walls are hung with antique farm tools, and there's a small museum devoted to the aloe vera plant. You'll need a car to get here, about a mile from San Nicolas. *Cura Cabai 24, San Nicolas, tel. 297/8–48335. Reservations advised. AE, MC, V. Closed Thurs. Inexpensive.*

New Old Cunucu House. Situated on a small estate in a residential neighborhood three minutes from the high-rise hotels, this 72-year-old Aruban home has been renovated into a seafood and international restaurant of casual élan. Dine on local recipes for red snapper, coconut-fried shrimp, Cornish hen, and New York sirloin, or beef fondue à deux. Private dining rooms hold groups up to 20. An Aruban trio sings and plays background music every Friday, and on Saturday evenings a mariachi band serenades the patrons. Happy hour 5–6 PM. *Palm Beach 150, tel. 297/8–61666. Reservations advised. AE, DC, MC. Closed Mon. Inexpensive.*

The Steamboat. The motto of this large, well-lit restaurant with nautical decor is "eat as much as you wish and never come out hungry." Breakfast ($6.95; served until noon) and dinner ($12.95) are all-you-can-eat buffets (children under nine eat for half price). Dinner includes a huge salad and dessert bar. Sunday and Thursday are barbecue nights, with chicken, spare ribs, corn on the cob, and rice. Deli sandwiches are served until 4 AM. A 15% gratuity is added to all bills. *L.G. Smith Blvd. 370 (across from the Americana Aruba hotel), tel. 297/8–36700. AE, MC, V. Inexpensive.*

Reubens. Stop by this clean coffee shop for deli sandwiches, hamburgers, and Aruban snacks. It's open for breakfast and lunch only. *Harbourtown Mall, tel. 297/8–36565. No credit cards. No dinner. Budget.*

Roseland. This former nightclub in the Alhambra Casino complex now dedicates itself to serving copious buffets to hungry tourists. There are different specials for every night of the week. A mere $10.95 buys you all you can eat, including 20 salads and four desserts; children under 10 eat free. *L.G. Smith Blvd. 93, tel. 297/8–35000, ext. 469. AE, DC, MC, V. No lunch. Budget.*

Lodging

Most of the hotels in Aruba are located west of Oranjestad along L.G. Smith Boulevard. Most include a host of facilities—drugstores, boutiques, health spas, beauty parlors, casinos, restaurants, pool bars, and gourmet delis.

Unfortunately, $100-a-night hotel rooms on Aruba are not standouts; you're better off paying more for a good hotel with full facilities (around $150–$185 a night) or putting up with less and saving money at one of the island's $50-a-night guest houses or small budget apartment hotels. Aruba has an abundance of time-share resorts, which are booked more or less the same as a hotel room but often with a one-week minimum. Accommodations are generally in apartment/condominium-type complexes, but often with the addition of restaurants, shops, and sports facilities. The island also has a number of small guest houses and budget apartment hotels with older but adequate kitchen facilities. Several are listed below; contact the Tourism Authority (tel. 800/TO-ARUBA or 201/330–0800) for a complete list. If you choose this route, be sure to ask the property for a written confirmation of your reservation.

Do not arrive in Aruba without a reservation; many hotels are booked months in advance, especially in the winter season. All hotels offer packages, and these are considerably less expensive than the one-night rate. Hotel restaurants and clubs are open to all guests on the island, so you can visit other properties no matter where you're staying. Most hotels, unless specified, do not include meals in their room rates. Off-season, roughly mid-April to mid-December, rates drop from 30% to 45%. There are no bed-and-breakfasts or campgrounds on Aruba.

Highly recommended lodgings are indicated by a star ★.

Category	Cost*
Moderate	$150–$185
Inexpensive	$85–$150
Budget	under $85

All prices are for a standard double room for two, excluding 5% tax and a 10% service charge. To estimate rates for hotels offering MAP/FAP, add about $30–$40 per person per day to the above price ranges. For all-inclusives, add about $65 per person per day.

Resort Hotels **Aruba Hilton Hotel and Casino.** Hilton Hotels recently took over this run-down, 18-story high rise and gutted it completely. At press time, the renovations were impressive but still ongoing: Thus far, $20 million dollars had been poured into the rooms, the pool, the lobby, and the casino—all new and all of which should be open and serving guests by the 1993–94 season. Because the resort was still being renovated at press time, be sure to call to verify rates, meal plans, and facilities. *L.G. Smith Blvd. 77, Palm Beach, tel. 800/445-8667. 500 rooms. Facilities: 5 restaurants, nightclub, casino, 3 cocktail lounges, pool, children's wading pool, 2 lighted tennis courts, massage room, games room, car rental, tour desk, water-sports desk, beach, beach bar, ballroom with meeting and banquet rooms, shops, beauty parlor, deli, children's corner. AE, DC, MC, V. EP, CP, BP, MAP, FAP. Moderate.*

Aruba Palm Beach Hotel & Casino. Formerly a Sheraton, this pink, eight-story Moorish palazzo even has pink-swaddled palm trees dotting its drive. The lobby, with its impressive grand piano, is a haze of pink and purple, underlaid with cool marble. The large backyard sunning grounds are a well-manicured tropical garden, with a fleet of pesky parrots guarding the entrance. The guest rooms are roomy and cheerful, decorated in either burgundy and mauve or emerald and pink. Each has a walk-in closet, color cable TV, and a tiny balcony. All overlook either the ocean, the pool, or the gardens. For a peaceful meal, eat alfresco in the rock-garden setting of the Seawatch Restaurant. For live music, try the Players Club lounge, open nightly until 3 AM. Every Wednesday there's a popular limbo and barbecue party around the pool for $23 per person. *L.G. Smith Blvd. 79, Palm Beach, tel. 297/8-23900 or 800/428-9933, 305/539-9933 in FL, fax 297/8-21941. 202 rooms. Facilities: 2 restaurants, pool, coffee shop, disco, TV, shops, casino, 2 lighted tennis courts, water sports, tour desk, beauty salon. AE, DC, MC, V. EP, MAP. Moderate.*

Bushiri Beach Resort. Two long, low buildings—built around a lush Jacuzzi garden and situated on a wide expanse of beach—make up this all-inclusive resort, Aruba's first. These buildings are old and nondescript, and although the rooms were recently renovated, they remain ordinary. But the Bushiri is a hotel-training school, a factor that shows in the enthusiastic staff. The best rooms are in the West Wing; "deluxe" rooms, the largest, have balconies that face the ocean, minifridges, and safe-deposit boxes. Where this resort shines is in its full daily activities program for adults. Snorkeling (with instruction and equipment), tennis, sailing, windsurfing, pool volleyball, and casino gambling classes are among the offerings. Kids are kept busy with their own day-long supervised program. Three sightseeing tours around the island, three meals daily, a poolside barbecue, and a midnight buffet, as well as all soft-drinks and alcoholic beverages, are included in the single tab of about $140 per person per day, an excellent value for those who'd like to take advantage of the many facilities here. *L.G. Smith Blvd. 35, Oranjestad, tel. 297/8–25216, 800/GO–BOUNTY, or 800/462–6868, fax 297/8–26789. 150 rooms. Facilities: 2 restaurants, pool bar, cocktail lounge, piano bar, pool, satellite TV, 2 tennis courts, nightly entertainment, beach, water-sports center, drugstore, health club, 3 Jacuzzis, free nightly shuttle to the Holiday Inn casino. AE, DC, MC, V. All-inclusive. Moderate.*

Sonesta Hotel, Beach Club & Casino. For the most part, this luxury hotel in Oranjestad is out of our price range, but the lowest room rates just sneak into the top end of our Moderate category. If your budget allows it, consider the Sonesta if you like to shop, eat, and gamble rather than fall out of bed and onto a beach. It stands out amid the Dutch architecture of Oranjestad: In the lobby, sleek low couches wrap around pink stucco pillars while glass elevators rise above the circular deepwater grotto, and motor skiffs board guests headed for the hotel's 40-acre private island. The 300 tropical green-and-pink guest rooms and suites are spacious and modern, with tiny balconies, cable TV, hair dryers, safe-deposit boxes, and stocked minibars. The free daily "Just Us Kids" program offers children ages 5 to 12 supervised activities, including kite flying, bowling, movies, storytelling, and field trips. Children under 12 (maximum two per family) stay free in their parents' room. For adults there are free casino classes, volleyball, and beach bingo. The neighboring Crystal Casino houses the Caribbean's largest $1 slot machine. Dancers should head for the Desires Lounge, which features live entertainment every night except Sunday. The hotel is popular with businessmen and those who do not wish to depend on taxis or a rental car every time they leave their hotel. *L.G. Smith Blvd. 82, tel. 297/8–36000, 800/SONESTA, or 800/343–7170, fax 297/8–34389. 274 rooms, 25 suites. Facilities: minispa and fitness center, pool, 40-acre private island with water-sports center, 3 restaurants, bar, casino, nightclub, 85 shops, children's program, tour desk, beauty salon. AE, DC, MC, V. EP. Moderate.*

★ **Best Western Talk of the Town Resort.** Originally a run-down chemical plant, Talk of the Town was transformed by Ike and Grete Cohen into a top-notch budget resort. It gets its name from the excellent on-premises restaurant (*see* Dining, *above*). There are two other restaurants here, and various meal plans let you try all three. A huge pool is at the center of this two-story motellike structure, with most of the rooms in the new wing overlooking the charming Spanish-style courtyard. Some accommodations have kitchens and all offer TVs, air-conditioning, and minifridges. There's also a Jacuzzi. Though the resort is on the outskirts of Oranjestad, there is a beach just across the street, where guests have the run of the Surfside Beach Club, complete with pool, two Jacuzzis, snack bar, and a water-sports and dive center. *L.G. Smith Blvd. 2, Oranjestad, tel. 297/8–23380 or 800/233–1108, fax 297/8–32446. 63 rooms. Facilities: 3 restaurants, nightclub, cable TV, facilities exchange with Manchebo Beach Hotel, gift shop, beach club with pool, 2*

Jacuzzis, snack bar, water-sports and dive center. AE, MC, V. EP, BP, MAP. Inexpensive.

Time-Share Resorts

Aruba Beach Club. This attractive low-rise property is almost exclusively a time-share resort, although a handful of rooms remain regular hotel rooms. The open-air lobby leads to a patio, gardens, and pool, with the beach only a few steps beyond. Action settles around the pool bar, with a clientele that's mostly American, mostly young-to-middle-aged couples with children. The pastel rooms are more basic than luxurious, even though they're refurbished every two years. Each features a kitchenette and a balcony. Guests may use all the facilities at the Casa Del Mar resort next door. *L.G. Smith Blvd. 53, Punta Brabo Beach, tel. 297/8–23000 or 800/346–7084, fax 297/8–26557. 131 studio and 1-bedroom suites. Facilities: 2 restaurants, cocktail lounge, pool bar, ice-cream parlor, satellite TV, adults' and children's pools, 2 lighted tennis courts, children's playground, baby-sitting. AE, MC, V. EP. Moderate.*

Harbourtown Beach Resort & Casino. This new time-share resort is in the center of town overlooking the marina. The five-story property is sleekly tropical, with a two-story alfresco lobby, glass elevators, and neon lights around a huge free-form pool with swim-up bar. Units are lovely one-bedroom suites with emerald carpets, beige Formica furnishings, track lighting, and full baths. Room amenities include a kitchenette, two remote control TVs, two phones, a king-size bed, a sofa bed, and a terrace. The resort is adjacent to a large shopping plaza containing many moderately priced restaurants and a few coffee shops. *9 Swain Wharf, Oranjestad, tel. 297/8–35600 or 800/824–0953. 236 suites. Facilities: 2 pools, man-made beach, semicircular swimming lagoon, deli, baby-sitting, tour desk, library, 2 bars, casino, 30-slip marina. AE, MC, V. EP. Moderate.*

La Cabana All Suite Beach Resort & Casino. At the top end of Eagle Beach and across the road from the sand is Aruba's largest time-sharing condominium/hotel complex. The large four-story building forms a horseshoe around a huge free-form pool complex with a water slide, poolside bar, outdoor café, and water-sports center. The entire complex faces the pristine white sands of Eagle Beach just across the street. One-third of the rooms have a full sea view; two-thirds have a partial view. All rooms—studios or one-bedroom suites—come with a fully equipped kitchenette, a small balcony, and a Jacuzzi, and have both air-conditioning and ceiling fans. The tropically decorated suites have interconnecting doors so that three of them may be linked together to form two- and three-bedroom units. Ground-floor living rooms, overlooking the pool area, do not offer as much privacy as higher floors. Claustrophobic elevators (or stairs) lead to upper floors with plain open-air corridors. This complete resort has much to offer: a modern fitness and health center, an ice-cream and espresso shop, a budget restaurant, a small grocery store, several shops, and an activities center in the main complex. Shuttle buses run guests to the upscale casino, the island's largest, where the hotel has another three restaurants and the *rouge et noir* Tropicana nightclub, which features top shows and comedy acts. In addition to EP and MAP plans, the hotel offers numerous meal plan combinations, such as 10 breakfasts and seven dinners, for adults and children. *L.G. Smith Blvd. 250, tel. 297/8–39000 or 800/835–7193, 212/251–1710 in NY, fax 297/8–37208. 440 rooms. Facilities: 5 restaurants, including poolside bar; shops; casino; racquetball,* *squash, and tennis courts; health and fitness center. AE, DC, MC, V. EP, MAP. Moderate.*

The Mill Resort. Two-story, red-roof buildings flank the open-air common areas of this small condominium hotel, which opened in September 1990. Unlike time-share resorts, this hotel sells each unit to an individual, who then leases the unit back to the resort for use as a hotel room. The decor is soft, country French, with a delicate rose-and-white color scheme, white wicker furniture, and wall-to-wall silver carpeting. The junior suites feature a king-size bed, sitting area, and kitchenette. The studios have a full kitchen, but only a queen-size convertible sofa bed and a tiny bathroom. There's no kitchen in the hedonistic Royal Den, but there's a marble Jacuzzi tub big enough for two. This resort is popular with couples seeking a quiet getaway and with families vacationing with small children. There's a coffee shop on the premises, and the Mill Restaurant is next door. There are also no bars, no tour desk, and no organized evening activities. The theme here is one of peaceful bliss. Action can be found at the nearby large resorts, and the beach is only a five-minute walk away. *L.G. Smith Blvd. 330, Palm Beach, tel. 297/8–37700, fax 297/8–37271. 99 studio, junior, and Royal Den suites. One- and 2-bedroom suites are available by combining two of the above units. Facilities: coffee shop, pool, kiddie pool, mini food market, baby-sitting, car rental, 2 lighted tennis courts, fitness center, pool snack bar. AE, DC, MC, V. EP, BP. Moderate.*

Amsterdam Manor Beach Resort. Built to resemble a small Spanish hacienda, this new, mustard-colored time-share complex is popular with Europeans and offers good value. There's a pool on the property, Eagle Beach is just across the street, and water sports can be arranged through next-door neighbor La Cabana All Suite Beach Resort. Accommodations range from studio rooms (some with a kitchenette) to two-bedroom suites. The small, modern units are air-conditioned and feature white tile floors, ceiling fans, and terraces. If a bathtub is important, ask for one, as some rooms have only a shower. *L.G. Smith Blvd. 252, tel. 297/8–31492, fax 297/8–31463. 60 units. Facilities: minimarket, pool, VCRs available for rental, poolside restaurant and bar. MC, V. EP. Inexpensive.*

La Quinta Beach Resort. Twenty-four new units are slated for construction in 1993 at this time-share complex across the road from Eagle Beach. Existing efficiency and one-bedroom units are small but well designed and stylish, with full cooking facilities, TVs, and hair dryers in the tiled bathrooms. One-, two-, and three-bedroom units also have sleep sofas and VCRs. (The two- and three-bedroom units are not affordable for one couple.) There's a restaurant, but it's scheduled to be torn down to make room for the new units; be sure to ask about its status when you call, as meal plans won't be available once the restaurant closes. Staff here is friendly. *Eagle Beach, tel. 297/8–35010 or 800/223–9815, fax 297/8–26263. Facilities: bar, 2 pools, cable TV, tennis courts. AE, DC, MC, V. EP, MAP, FAP. Inexpensive.*

Small Apartment Hotels

Vistalmar. There's no beach, but the sea is just across the street, along with a swimming pier; guests can also use the beach from the Best Western Talk of the Town hotel. Air-conditioned units are one-bedroom apartments with a full kitchen, living room/dining room, and decent-sized sun porch. There are TVs but no phones in the rooms. The only drawback to this small hotel is its distance from town, making a rental car a necessity. *A.O. Yarzagaray, Bucutiweg 28, tel. 297/8–28579. 8 rooms. Facilities: laundry room. EP. Inexpensive.*

Cactus Apartments. A fence of tall cacti surrounds this mustard-colored apartment hotel. Public buses stop nearby, but a car is highly recommended, especially because the property is not on the beach. All units are air-conditioned, with beige tile floors, a kitchenette, tiny bathroom (shower only), color TV, and double bed. There's no pool and only one public telephone, but there's daily maid service and washer and dryer facilities. It's no more than a clean, cheap place to sleep, but for $40 a night in high season, it's hard to do better. *Jacinto Tromp, Matadera 5, Noord, tel. 297/8–22903, fax 297/8–20433. 13 units. EP. Budget.*

Coconut Inn. It's best to have a car if you're staying at this budget hotel, a five-minute drive inland from hotel row on Palm Beach. Request one of the 11 "superior studio" rooms in the two-story white building and accept no substitute, as the rest of the rooms are old, musty, dark, and lacking in cheer. Also ask about the four new studio rooms planned for early 1993. All superior studios are air-conditioned, with one double bed, a second bed meant for a small child, a bathroom with tiled shower, color TV, kitchenette, and small balcony or patio. Plans call for a pool by the end of 1993, and the public bus stops a short walk away. *Angelo Rojer, Noord 31, tel. 297/8–66288, fax 297/8–65433. 24 rooms. EP. Budget.*

Off-Season Bets From mid-April to mid-December, many luxury resorts on Aruba slash their rates by as much as 45%, placing them in our Moderate and even Inexpensive price categories. Some of the best off-season rates can be found at the following: **Sonesta Hotel, Beach Club & Casino** (*see above*); **Divi Divi Doral Beach Resort** (Divi Beach, tel. 297/8–23300 or 800/22-DORAL); **Playa Linda Beach Resort** (L.G. Smith Blvd. 87, Palm Beach, tel. 297/8–31000 or 800/346–7084); **Radisson Aruba Caribbean Resort & Casino** (L.G. Smith Blvd. 81, Palm Beach, tel. 297/8–33555 or 800/777–1700); and the **Divi Doral Tamarjin Beach Resort** (Divi Beach, tel. 297/8–24150 or 800/22-DORAL).

Nightlife

Casinos Casinos are all the rage in Aruba. At last count there were 10. The crowds seem to flock to the newest of the new: The Crystal Casino enjoyed the business until the Hyatt Regency's ultramodern gaming room stole the show (the marquee above the bar at this casino opens to reveal a live band). Now both are getting stiff competition from the popular (and new) **Royal Cabana Casino** (L.G. Smith Blvd. 250, tel. 297/8–39000) with its sleek interior, multitheme three-in-one restaurant, and showcase Tropicana nightclub.

Most major hotels have a casino either on or adjacent to their premises. There's no entry fee to the casinos, and many have free shuttles from major hotels. But keep in mind that gambling can blow any budget fast; if you must try your luck, stick to the slot machines. Hours of operation vary, but many are open during the day for slots and from mid-afternoon or early evening until 4 AM for all games. Dress is casual (meaning pants, not shorts or swimsuits) except on Saturday nights at the fancier spots, where men may wear jackets.

Theater One of the island's better entertainment deals is the Tropicana's **Comedy Hour** (in the Royal Cabana Casino, L.G. Smith Blvd. 250, tel. 297/8–39000), featuring comedians from New York, Miami, Atlantic City, Chicago, and Las Vegas. It's a regular feature every Friday and Saturday at midnight and Sunday at 9:30 PM. Cost: $5 a person.

Specialty Theme Nights One of the unique things about Aruba's nightlife is the number of specialty theme nights offered by the hotels: At last count there were more than 30. Each "party" features dinner and entertainment, followed by dancing, and some of them offer excellent value. The Hyatt Regency Aruba's **Fajitas & 'ritas** (tel. 297/8–31234, ext. 37) Mexican fiesta is held Friday nights from 7 PM to 1 AM at their Palms restaurant by the beach. The $13.95 price includes all of the beef and chicken fajitas you can eat plus one 16-ounce margarita. La Cabana All Suite Beach Resort hosts **The Captain's Barbecue** (tel. 297/8–39000) every Monday 7 PM–10 PM, with live entertainment and a fashion show. The $22.40 cost includes one free cocktail plus all the barbecued chicken, ribs, fish, vegetables, salads, and pastry desserts you can eat. For a complete list, contact the Aruba Tourism Authority (tel. 297/8–23777).

An Aruban must is the **Bon Bini Festival**, held every Tuesday evening from 6:30 to 8:30 PM in the outdoor courtyard of the Fort Zoutman Museum. *Bon Bini* is Papiamento for "welcome," and this tourist event is the Aruba Institute of Culture and Education's way of introducing visitors to all things Aruban. Stroll by the stands of Aruban foods, drinks, and crafts, or watch Aruban entertainers perform Antillean music and folkloric dancing. A master of ceremonies explains the history of the dances, instruments, and music. It's a fun event, and a good way to meet other tourists. Look for the clock tower. *Oranjestr., tel. 297/8–22185. Admission: Afl 2. adults, Afl 1. children.*

5   Barbados

Updated by
Nigel Fisher

Genuinely proud of their country, the quarter million Bajans on Barbados welcome visitors as privileged guests. Barbados is fine for people who want nothing more than to offer their bodies to the sun; yet, unlike many islands in the Caribbean, it is also ideal for travelers who want to discover another life and culture.

You can pay a lot for a vacation on Barbados, but you don't have to. This large island has everything from superluxury resorts to tiny B&Bs for $30 a night. Restaurants serving Continental cuisine are expensive, but travelers on a budget can opt for West Indian fare from local cafés, or try the pricier places at lunch. This is also one of the few Caribbean islands where you can really get around by bus. For a small fare, hop aboard, rub shoulders with other straphangers, and get acquainted with diverse sights and attractions.

Beaches here are lovely, though you won't have them to yourself. Many along the tranquil west coast—in the lee of the northwest trade winds—are backed by first-class resorts. Most of the hotels are situated along the beaches on the southern and southwestern coasts. The British and Canadians often favor the hotels of St. James Parish; Americans tend to prefer the large south-coast resorts. The south is also where you'll find smaller, less expensive hotels and guest houses. Since this area is compact, especially around St. Lawrence, you can walk to neighboring restaurants and local night spots without relying on taxis.

To the northeast are rolling hills and valleys covered by acres of impenetrable sugarcane. The Atlantic surf pounds the gigantic boulders along the rugged east coast, where the Bajans themselves have their vacation homes. Elsewhere on the island, linked by almost 900 miles of good roads, are historic plantation houses, stalactite-studded caves, a wildlife preserve, and the Andromeda Gardens, one of the most attractive small tropical gardens in the world.

No one is sure whether the name *los Barbados* ("the bearded ones") refers to the beardlike root that hangs from the island's fig trees or to the bearded natives who greeted the Portuguese "discoverer" of the island in 1536. The name Los Barbados was still current almost a century later when the British landed— by accident—in what is now Holetown in St. James Parish. They colonized the island in 1627 and remained until it achieved independence in 1966.

Barbadians retain a British accent. Afternoon tea is habitual at numerous hotels. Cricket is still the national sport, producing some of the world's top cricket players. Polo is played in winter. The British tradition of dressing for dinner is firmly entrenched; although jackets are not necessary at moderately priced restaurants, they are not out of place. Sundresses are suitable for women. A daytime stroll in a swimsuit is as inappropriate in Bridgetown as it would be on New York's 5th Avenue. Yet the island's atmosphere is hardly stuffy. When the boat you ordered for noon doesn't arrive until 12:30, you can expect a cheerful response, "He okay, mon, he just on Caribbean time." Translation: No one, including you, needs to be in a hurry here.

What It Will Cost These sample prices, meant only as a general guide, are for high season. Price estimates are for high season. Expect to pay around $80 and up at a small hotel close to the sea. A B&B costs anywhere from $25–$50 a night, while a room at a guest house can be as low as $30 a night. A moderately priced dinner can cost as much as $30 a person, but more careful selection from a menu can keep the price to around $12. A generous plateful of curry with rice from a local café will be $5 or less. Avoid wine here, since it's imported and therefore expensive. Local beer is good and reasonably priced at $1.50. Local rum, notable Mount Gay, is excellent and, at $4.50 a bottle, a steal. Cars rent for about $45–$55 a day. Taxis are expensive—an average trip within Bridgetown will cost about $5. Public transportation is efficient and a bargain—BDS $1.50 (about U.S. 75¢) for any distance. A single-tank dive is about $35; multiple dives will save you money. Snorkel-equipment rental is about $5 a day.

Before You Go

Tourist Information Contact the **Barbados Board of Tourism** (800 2nd Ave., New York, NY 10017, tel. 212/986–6516; or 3440 Wilshire Blvd., Suite 1215, Los Angeles, CA 90010, tel. 213/380–2199. In Canada: 5160 Yonge St., Suite 1800, N. York, Ont. M2N–6L9, tel. 416/512–6569; 615 Dorchester, Montreal, Suite 960, Montreal, P.Q. H3B 1P5, tel. 514/861–0085. In the United Kingdom: 263 Tottenham Court Rd., London W1P 9AA, tel. 441/636–9448).

Arriving and Departing
By Plane Grantley Adams International Airport in Barbados is a Caribbean hub. **American Airlines** (tel. 800/433–7300), and **BWIA** (tel. 800/JET–BWIA) both have nonstop flights from New

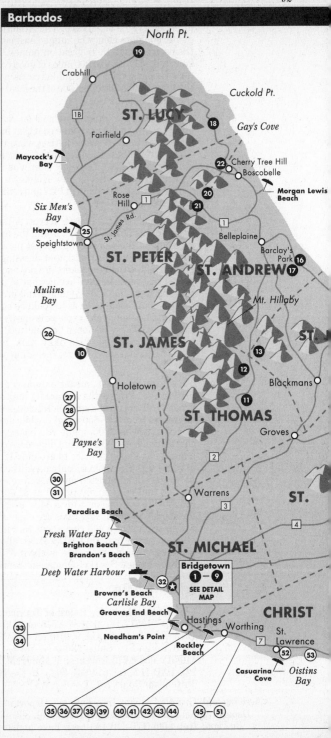

Barbados

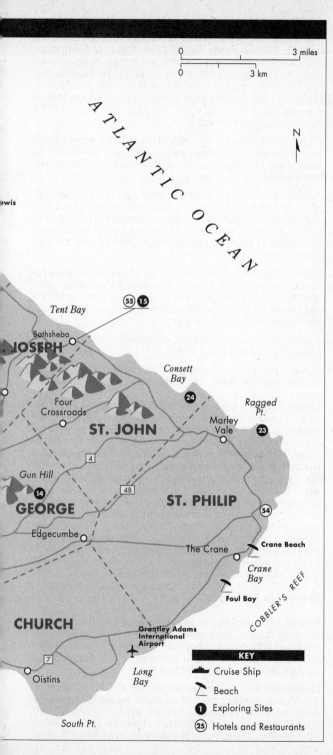

ATLANTIC OCEAN

N

0 ——————— 3 miles
0 ——————— 3 km

Tent Bay

55 **15**

Bathsheba

JOSEPH

Consett Bay

Four Crossroads

24

ST. JOHN

Marley Vale

Ragged Pt.

23

4

Gun Hill

4B

ST. PHILIP

14

54

GEORGE

Edgecumbe

The Crane

Crane Beach

Crane Bay

Foul Bay

COBBLER'S REEF

CHURCH

Grantley Adams International Airport

7

Oistins

Long Bay

South Pt.

KEY

⛴ Cruise Ship

⚓ Beach

1 Exploring Sites

25 Hotels and Restaurants

York. There are direct flights from Miami on BWIA. A new charter airline, **North American Airlines** (tel. 800/221–9831) began in 1993 operating weekly direct flights to Bridgetown from New York between January and March. At press time, fares were around $300. From Canada, **Air Canada** (tel. 800/776–3000) connects from Montreal through New York or Miami and flies nonstop from Toronto. From London, **British Airways** (tel. 800/247–9297) has nonstop service and BWIA connects through Trinidad.

Flights to St. Vincent, St. Lucia, Trinidad, and other islands are scheduled on LIAT (tel. 809/462–0801) and BWIA; Air St. Vincent/Air Mustique links Barbados with St. Vincent and the Grenadines.

From the Airport   Airport taxis are not metered. A large sign at the airport announces the fixed rate to each hotel or area, stated in both Barbados and U.S. dollars (about $20 to the west coast hotels, $13 to the south coast ones). You can also catch a bus into Bridgetown (BDS $1.50), then transfer to another for west and east coast hotels.

Passports and Visas   U.S. and Canadian citizens need proof of citizenship plus a return or ongoing ticket to enter the country. Acceptable proof of citizenship is a valid passport or an original birth certificate and a photo ID; a voter registration card is not acceptable. British citizens need a valid passport.

Language   English is spoken everywhere, sometimes accented with the phrases and lilt of a Bajan dialect.

Precautions   Beach vendors of coral jewelry and beachwear will not hesitate to offer you their wares. The degree of persistence varies, and some of their jewelry offerings are good; sharp bargaining is expected on both sides. One hotel's brochure gives sound advice: "Please realize that encouraging the beach musicians means you may find yourself listening to the same three tunes over and over for the duration of your stay." The water on the island, both in hotels and in restaurants, has been treated and is safe to drink. Insects aren't much of a problem on Barbados, but if you plan to hike or spend time on secluded beaches, it's wise to use insect repellent. Little green apples that fall from the large branches of the manchineel tree may look tempting, but they are poisonous to eat and toxic to the touch. Even taking shelter under the tree when it rains can give you blisters. If you do come in contact with one, go to the nearest hotel and have someone there phone for a physician. Don't invite trouble by leaving valuables unattended on the beach or in plain sight in your room, and don't pick up hitchhikers.

Staying in Barbados

Important Addresses   **Tourist Information: The Barbados Board of Tourism** is on Harbour Road in Bridgetown (tel. 809/427–2623). Hours are weekdays 8:30–4:30. There are also information booths, staffed by Board representatives at Grantley Adams International Airport and at Bridgetown's Deep Water Harbour.

Emergencies   **Emergency:** tel. 119. **Ambulance:** tel. 809/426–1113. **Police:** tel. 112. **Fire department:** tel. 113. **Scuba diving accidents:** Divers' Alert Network (DAN) (tel. 919/684–8762 or 919/684–2948). Barbados decompression chamber, Barbados Defense Force, St. Ann's Fort, Garrison, St. Michael Parish (tel. 809/427–8819).

Currency One Barbados dollar (BDS $1) equals about U.S. 50¢. Because the value of the Barbados dollar is pegged to that of the U.S. dollar, the ratio remains constant. Both currencies and the Canadian dollar are accepted everywhere on the island, but changing your money to Barbados dollars will get you slightly better value. Prices quoted throughout this chapter are in U.S. dollars unless noted otherwise.

Taxes and Service Charges At the airport you must pay a departure tax of BDS $25 (about U.S. $12) in either currency before leaving Barbados.

A 10% service charge is added to your hotel bill and to most restaurant checks; any additional tip recognizes extraordinary service. When no service charge is added, tip maids $1 per room per day, waiters 10% to 15%, taxi drivers 10%. Airport porters and bellboys expect BDS $2 (U.S. $1) per bag. There is no sales tax.

Getting Around Barbados is relatively flat, with almost 900 miles of good roads. It's easy to get around by taxi and public buses. This is one island where a rental car is not critical to your mobility. One inexpensive option is to rent a bicycle and explore on your own, at least in the vicinity of your hotel.

Taxis Taxis operate at a fixed rate (BDS $30 for the first hour, less after that). From Bridgetown to Crane Beach the fare is BDS $35; from Bridgetown to Harrison's Cave, it's BDS $30. The most expensive fare, from the southern part of the island to the north, is BDS $55. Always settle on a price before you enter the taxi, and agree on whether it's in U.S. or Barbados dollars. Taxis outside the major hotels are less open to negotiation. One to five persons may travel at the same rate.

Buses Public buses are an excellent means of inexpensive transportation. The fare is a fixed BDS $1.50 for whatever distance. The government-owned buses, painted blue with yellow trim, leave from Bridgetown for destinations throughout the island approximately every 30 minutes. North- and westbound buses use the terminals at Lower Green Street and Princess Alice Highway; southbound buses leave from the Fairchild Street Bus Terminal. Destinations are marked over the front windshield. Bus stops are marked "To City" and "Out of City." You need to flag buses down; they do not stop automatically for those standing at the stop.

Privately owned minibuses also operate for the same fixed fare. Most of these ply shorter routes and usually keep to the coastal roads. Board these at the terminals at Temple Yard, Probyn Street, and River Road in Bridgetown. Routes are usually painted on the side of the vehicles and their destination displayed on a card in the bottom left-hand corner of the windshield.

Rental Cars It's a pleasure to explore Barbados by car, provided you take the time to study a good map and don't mind asking directions frequently. The more remote roads are in good repair, yet few are well lighted at night, and night falls quickly—at about 6 PM. Even in full daylight, the tall sugarcane fields lining a road can create near-zero visibility. Yet local residents are used to pointing travelers in the right direction, and some confused but intelligent drivers have been known to flag a passing taxi and pay to follow it back to a city area. Use caution: Pedestrians are everywhere. And remember, traffic keeps to the left throughout the island.

To rent a car you must have an international driver's license, obtainable at the airport and major car-rental firms for BDS $10 (U.S. $5) if you have a valid driver's license. More than 40 offices rent minimokes for upwards of $45 a day plus insurance (about $215 a week), usually with a three-day or four-day minimum; cars with automatic shift are $45–$55 a day, or approximately $285 a week. Gas costs just over BDS $1 a liter (about $2 a gallon) and is extra. The speed limit, in keeping with the pace of life, is 37 miles per hour (60 kilometers per hour) in the country, 21 miles per hour in town. Operating a motorbike also requires an international driver's license—and some skill and daring. Cost is about $16 a day for a single-seater and $31 for a two-seater.

The principal car-rental firms are **National** (tel. 809/426–0603), **Dear's Garage** on the south coast (tel. 809/429–9277 or 809/427–7853), **Sunny Isle** in Worthing (tel. 809/428–8009 or 809/428–2965), and **Sunset Crest Rentals** in St. James (tel. 809/432–1482). **P&S Car Rentals** (Spring Garden Hwy., tel. 809/424–2052) offers air-conditioned cars and Jeeps with free customer delivery.

Bicycles You can rent bikes for about $10 a day from numerous outlets. In Hastings, try **M.A. Williams Bicycle Rentals** (tel. 809/427–3955).

Telephones and Mail The area code for Barbados is 809. Except for emergency numbers, all phone numbers have seven digits and begin with 42 or 43. A local call costs BDS 10¢.

An airmail letter from Barbados to the United States or Canada costs BDS 95¢ per half-ounce; an airmail postcard costs BDS 65¢. Letters to the United Kingdom are BDS $1.10; postcards are BDS 70¢.

Opening and Closing Times Stores are open weekdays 8–4, Saturday 8–1. Some supermarkets remain open daily 8–6. Banks are open Monday–Thursday 9–3, Friday 9–1 and 3–5.

Guided Tours For an island of its size (14 miles by 21 miles), Barbados has a lot to see. A bus or taxi tour, which can be arranged by your hotel, is a good way to get your bearings. **L. E. Williams Tour Co.** (tel. 809/427–1043) offers an 80-mile island tour for about $50 a person; a bus picks you up between 8:30 and 9:30 AM and takes you through Bridgetown, the St. James beach area, past the Animal Flower Cave, Farley Hill, Cherry Tree Hill, Morgan Lewis Mill, the east coast, St. John's Church, Sam Lord's Castle, Oistin's fishing village, and to St. Michael Parish, with drinks along the way and a West Indian lunch at the Atlantis Hotel in Bathsheba.

Custom Tours (tel. 809/425–0099) arranges personalized tours for one to four persons at a cost of U.S. $25 per hour (minimum four hours). Staff members determine your particular interests (such as gardens, plantation houses, swimming at secluded beaches), pack a picnic lunch, and drive you in their own cars. They offer a familiarization tour for first-time visitors and often can take you to places that aren't normally open to the public. Ask for Margaret Leacock, the owner.

Alternatively, customize your own tour by hiring a taxi. Most drivers narrate with enthusiasm their island's history and can give you off-the-cuff insights to local attractions. You will need to agree upon where you want to go and for how long in order to settle on a price somewhere in the region of $60 for a half-day tour (this is per car, not per person, so four people traveling together will save money).

Exploring Barbados

Numbers in the margin correspond to points of interest on the Bridgetown map.

The island's most popular sights and attractions can be seen comfortably in four or five excursions, each lasting less than a day, but you may want to combine some of them into one very full day of sightseeing. Bridgetown is best explored on foot. After Bridgetown, tours take in central Barbados, the eastern shore, north-central Barbados, and the south shore. Before you set out in a car, bus, or taxi, ask at your hotel or the Board of Tourism for a free copy of the detailed Barbados Holiday Map.

Bridgetown **Bridgetown** is a bustling city, complete with rush hours and traffic congestion; avoid hassle by taking a bus to town and touring on foot. Sightseeing will take only an hour or so, and the shopping areas are within walking distance.

❶ In the center of town, overlooking the picturesque harbor known as the Careenage, is **Trafalgar Square,** with its impressive monument to Horatio, Lord Nelson. It predates the Nelson's Column in London's Trafalgar Square by about two decades (and for more than a century Bajans have petitioned to replace it with a statue of a Bajan). Here are also a war memorial and a three-dolphin fountain commemorating the advent of running water in Barbados in 1865.

❷ Bridgetown is a major Caribbean free port. The principal shopping area is **Broad Street,** which leads west from Trafalgar Square past the House of Assembly and Parliament buildings. These Victorian Gothic structures, like so many smaller buildings in Bridgetown, stand beside a growing number of modern office buildings and shops. Small colonial buildings, their balconies trimmed with wrought iron, reward the visitor who has patience and an appreciative eye.

❸ The water that bounds Trafalgar Square is called the **Careenage,** a finger of sea that made early Bridgetown a natural harbor and a gathering place. Here working schooners were careened (turned on their sides) to be scraped of barnacles and repainted. Today the Careenage serves mainly as a berth for fiberglass pleasure yachts.

❹ Although no one has proved it conclusively, George Washington, on his only visit outside the United States, is said to have worshiped at **St. Michael's Cathedral** east of Trafalgar Square. The structure was nearly a century old when he visited in 1751, and it has since been destroyed by hurricanes and rebuilt twice, in 1780 and 1831.

❺ The two bridges over the Careenage are the Chamberlain Bridge and the Charles O'Neal Bridge, both of which lead to Highway 7 and south to the **Fairchild Market.** On Saturdays
❻ the activity there and at the **Cheapside Market** (on the north

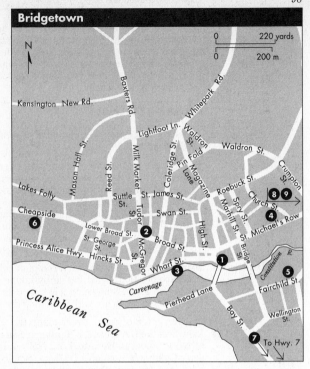

Bridgetown

end of Lower Broad Street, across from St. Mary's Church Square) recall the lively days before the coming of the supermarket and the mall, when the outdoor markets of Barbados were the daily heart and soul of shopping and socializing.

7 About a mile south of Bridgetown on Highway 7, the **Barbados Museum** has artifacts and mementos of military history and everyday life in the 19th century. Here you'll see cane-harvesting implements, lace wedding dresses, ancient (and frightening) dentistry instruments, and slave sale accounts kept in a spidery copperplate handwriting. Wildlife and natural-history exhibits, a well-stocked gift shop, and a good café are also here, in what used to be the military prison. *Hwy. 7, Garrison Savannah, tel. 809/427–0201. Admission: BDS $7. Open Mon.–Sat. 10–6.*

8 East of St. Michael's Cathedral, **Queen's Park,** now being restored to its original splendor, is home to one of the largest trees in Barbados: an immense baobab more than 10 centuries **9** old. The historic **Queen's Park House,** former home of the commander of the British troops, has been converted into a theater—with an exhibition room on the lower floor—and a restaurant. Queen's Park is a long walk from Trafalgar Square or the museum; you may want to share a taxi. *Open daily 9–5.*

Central Barbados *Numbers in the margin correspond to points of interest on the Barbados map.*

For nervous swimmers, the most interesting place for getting **10** into the water is the **Folkstone Underwater Park,** north of Holetown. While Folkstone has a land museum of marine life, the real draw is the underwater snorkeling trail around Dottin's Reef, with glass-bottom boats available for use by nonswimmers. A dredge barge sunk in shallow water is home to myriad fish, and it and the reef are popular with scuba divers. Huge sea fans, soft coral, and the occasional giant turtle are sights to see.

⓫ Highway 2 will take you to **Harrison's Cave.** These pale-gold limestone caverns, complete with subterranean streams and waterfalls, are entirely organic and said to be unique in the Caribbean. Open since 1981, the caves are so extensive that tours are made by electric tram (hard hats are provided, but all that may fall on you is a little dripping water). *Tel. 809/438–6640. Admission: BDS $15 adults, BDS $7.50 children. Reservations advised. Open daily 9–4.*

⓬ The nearby **Welchman Hall Gully,** a part of the National Trust in St. Thomas, affords another ideal opportunity to commune with nature. Here are acres of labeled flowers and trees, the occasional green monkey, and great peace and quiet. *Tel. 809/438–6671. Admission: BDS $5 adults, BDS $2.50 children. Open daily 9–5.*

⓭ Continue along Highway 2 to reach the **Flower Forest,** 8 acres of fragrant flowering bushes, canna and ginger lilies, and puffball trees. Another hundred species of flora combine with the tranquil views of Mt. Hillaby to induce in visitors what may be a relaxing and very pleasant light-headedness. *Tel. 809/433–8152. Admission: BDS $10. Open daily 9–5.*

⓮ Go back toward Bridgetown and take Highway 4 and smaller roads to **Gun Hill** for a view so pretty it seems almost unreal: Shades of green and gold cover the fields all the way to the horizon, the picturesque gun tower is surrounded by brilliant flowers, and the white limestone lion behind the garrison is a famous landmark. Military invalids were once sent here to convalesce. *No phone. Admission: BDS $5 adults, BDS $2.50 children.*

The Eastern Shore Take Highway 3 across the island to Bathsheba and the phenomenal view from the **Atlantis,** one of the oldest hotels in Barbados, where you may need help getting up from the table after sampling the lunch buffet.

⓯ In the nearby **Andromeda Gardens,** a fascinating small garden set into the cliffs overlooking the sea, are unusual and beautiful plant specimens from around the world, collected by the late horticulturist Iris Bannochie and now administered by the Barbados National Trust. *Tel. 809/433–1524. Admission: BDS $10. Open daily 9–5.*

⓰ North of Bathsheba, **Barclay's Park** offers a similar view and picnic facilities in a wooded seafront area. At the nearby **⓱** **Chalky Mount Potteries,** you'll find craftspersons making and selling their wares.

⓲ A drive north to the isolated Morgan Lewis Beach (*see* Beaches, *below*) or to Gay's Cove, which every Bajan calls Cove Bay, will put you in reach of the town of **Pie Corner.** Pie Corner is known not for baked goods but for artifacts left by the Carib and Arawak tribes who once lived here.

⓳ The **Animal Flower Cave** at North Point, reached by Highway 1B, displays small sea anemones, or sea worms, that resemble jewellike flowers as they open their tiny tentacles. For a small fee you can explore inside the cavern and see the waves breaking just outside it. *Tel. 809/439–8797. Admission: BDS $3 adults, BDS $1.50 children under 12. Open daily 9–5.*

North-Central Barbados The attractions of north-central Barbados may well be combined with the tour of the eastern shore.

20 The **Barbados Wildlife Reserve** can be reached on Highway 1 from Speightstown on the west coast. Here are herons, land turtles, a kangaroo, screeching peacocks, innumerable green monkeys and their babies doing all manner of things, geese, brilliantly colored parrots, and a friendly otter. The fauna are not in cages, so step carefully and keep your hands to yourself. The preserve has been much improved in recent years with the addition of a giant walk-in aviary and natural-history exhibits. Terrific photo opportunities are everywhere. *Tel. 809/422–8826. Admission: BDS $10 adults, BDS $5 children under 12 with adult. Open daily 10–5.*

21 Just to the south is **Farley Hill,** a national park in northern St. Peter Parish; the rugged landscape explains why they call this the Scotland area. Gardens; lawns; gigantic mahogany, white-wood, and casuarina trees; and an avenue of towering royal palms surround the imposing ruins of a once magnificent plantation great house. Partially rebuilt for the filming of *Island in the Sun,* the structure was later destroyed by fire. *Admission: BDS $2 per car; walkers free. Open daily 8:30–6.*

22 **St. Nicholas Abbey** near Cherry Tree Hill, named for a former owner and the oldest (c. 1650) great house in Barbados, is well worth visiting for its stone and wood architecture in the Jacobean style. Fascinating home movies, made by the present owner's father, record scenes of Bajan town and plantation life in the 1920s and 1930s. There are no set showing times; you need only ask to see them. *Tel. 809/422–8725. Admission: BDS $2.50. Open weekdays 10–3:30.*

The South Shore Driving east from Bridgetown on Highways 4 and 4B, you'll note the many **chattel houses** along the route; the property of tenant farmers, these ever-expandable houses were built to be dismantled and moved when necessary. On the coast, the ap-
23 propriately named **Ragged Point Lighthouse** is where the sun first shines on Barbados and its dramatic Atlantic seascape. About 4 miles to the northwest, in the eastern corner of St. John Parish, the coralstone buildings and serenely beautiful
24 grounds of **Codrington Theological College,** founded in 1748, stand on a cliff overlooking Consett Bay.

Beaches

Barbados is blessed with some of the Caribbean's most beautiful beaches, all of them open to the public. (Access to hotel beaches may not always be public, but you can walk onto almost any beach from another one.)

West Coast Beaches The west coast has the stunning coves and white-sand beaches that are dear to postcard publishers—plus calm, clear water for snorkeling, scuba diving, and swimming. The afternoon clouds and sunsets may seem to be right out of a Turner painting; because there is nothing but ocean between Barbados and Africa, the sunsets are rendered even more spectacular by the fine red sand that sometimes blows in from the Sahara.

While beaches here are seldom crowded, the west coast is not the place to find isolation. Owners of private boats stroll by, offering waterskiing, parasailing, and snorkel cruises. There are no concession stands per se, but hotels welcome nonguests for terrace lunches (wear a cover-up). Picnic items and necessities can be bought at the Sunset Crest shopping center in Holetown.

Beaches begin in the north at **Heywoods** (about a mile of sand) and continue almost unbroken to Bridgetown at **Brighton Beach,** a popular spot with locals. There is public access through the Barbados Beach Club and the Barbados Pizza House (both good for casual lunches), south of the Discovery Bay Hotel.

Good spots for swimming include **Paradise Beach,** just off the Cunard Paradise Village & Beach Club; **Brandon's Beach,** a 10-minute walk south; **Browne's Beach,** in Bridgetown; and **Greaves End Beach,** south of Bridgetown at Aquatic Gap, between the Grand Barbados Beach Resort and the Hilton in St. Michael Parish.

South Coast Beaches The heavily traveled south coast of Christ Church Parish is much more built up than the St. James Parish coast in the west; here you'll find condos, high-rise hotels, many places to eat and shop, and the traffic (including public transportation) that serves them. These busier beaches generally draw a younger, more active crowd. The quality of the beach itself is consistently good, the reef-protected waters safe for swimming and snorkeling.

Needham's Point, with its lighthouse, is one of Barbados's best beaches, crowded with locals on weekends and holidays. Two others are in the St. Lawrence Gap area, near **Casuarina Cove.** The **Benston Windsurfing Club Hotel** in Maxwell caters specifically to windsurfing aficionados, and most hotels and resorts provide boards or rent them for a nominal fee.

The sands of **Rockley Beach** are usually crowded with guests from the hotels along this part of the shore.

Crane Beach has for years been a popular swimming beach. As you move toward the Atlantic side of the island, the waves roll in bigger and faster; the waves at the nearby Crane Hotel are a favorite with bodysurfers. (But remember that this is the ocean, not the Caribbean, and exercise caution.)

Nearby **Foul Bay** lives up to its name only for sailboats; for swimmers and alfresco lunches, it's lovely.

North Coast Beaches Those who love wild natural beauty will want to head north up the east-coast highway. With secluded beaches and crashing ocean waves on one side, rocky cliffs and verdant landscape on the other, the windward side of Barbados won't disappoint anyone who seeks dramatic views. But be cautioned: Swimming here is treacherous and *not* recommended. The waves are high, the bottom tends to be rocky, and the currents are unpredictable. Limit yourself to enjoying the view and watching the surfers—who have been at it since they were kids.

A worthwhile little-visited beach for the adventurous who don't mind trekking about a mile off the beaten track is **Morgan Lewis Beach,** on the coast east of Morgan Lewis Mill, the oldest intact windmill on the island. Turn east on the small road that goes to the town of Boscobelle (between Cherry Tree Hill and Morgan Lewis Mill), but instead of going to the town, take the even less traveled road (unmarked on most maps; you will have to ask for directions) that goes down the cliff to the beach. What awaits is more than 2 miles of unspoiled, uninhabited white sand and sweeping views of the Atlantic coastline. You may see a few Bajans swimming, sunning, or fishing, but for the most part you'll have privacy.

Return to your car, cross the island's north point on the secondary roads until you reach the west coast. About a mile west from the end of Highway 1B is **Maycock's Bay,** an isolated area in St. Lucy Parish about 2 miles north of Heywoods, the west coast's northernmost resort complex.

Sports and the Outdoors

Golfing The Royal Westmoreland Golf and Country Club is still in its planning stages and until it is completed, golfers favor the 18 holes at the **Sandy Lane Club** (tel. 809/432–1145), whose dramatic 7th hole is famous both for its elevated tee and its view. There is also a 9-hole course at the **Rockley Resort** (tel. 809/435–7873), and another 9 holes at **Heywoods** (tel. 809/422–4900). All are open to nonguests, with fees ranging from BDS $32 at Heywoods to BDS $120 ($80 in summer) at Sandy Lane.

Hiking Hilly but not mountainous, the interior of Barbados is ideal for hiking. The **Barbados National Trust** (Belleville, St. Michael, tel. 809/436–9033) sponsors free walks year-round on Sunday, from 6:30 AM to about 9:30 AM and from 3:30 PM to 5:30 PM, as well as special moonlight hikes when the heavens permit. Newspapers announce the time and meeting place (or you can call the Trust).

Jogging The **Hash House Harriers** is an international running group with relaxed jogging at different points each week. Contact John Carpenter (tel. 809/429–5151 days or 809/429–3818 evenings).

Sea Excursions The west coast is the area for scuba diving, sailing, and lunch-and-rum cruises on the red-sailed *Jolly Roger* "pirate" party ship (Fun Cruises, tel. 809/436–6424 or 809/429–4545). Somewhat more sedate sea experiences can be had on the *Wind Warrior* (tel. 809/425–5800) and the *Secret Love* (tel. 809/425–5800). Cruises cost about $40 per person.

Scuba Diving Barbados, with a rich and varied underwater world, offers activity for both divers and nondivers. Many dive shops provide instruction (the three-hour beginner's "resort courses" and the week-long certification courses) followed by a shallow dive, usually on Dottin's Reef. Trained divers can explore reefs, wrecks, and the walls of "blue holes," the huge circular depressions in the ocean floor. Not to be missed by certified, guided divers is the *Stavronikita*, a 368-foot Greek freighter that was deliberately sunk at about 125 feet; hundreds of butterfly fish hang out around its mast, and the thin rays of sunlight that filter down through the water make exploring the huge ship a wonderfully eerie experience. The cost for a single-tank dive on Barbados is approximately $35. Discounts come with multiple dives; two, for example, are $50, three are $70. Equipment, other than tank and weights, is extra.

Dive Barbados (Watersports, Sunset Crest Beach, near Hole-town, St. James Parish, tel. 809/432–7090) provides beginner's instruction (resort course) and reef and wreck dives with a friendly, knowledgeable staff. At **The Dive Shop, Ltd.** (Grand Barbados Beach Resort, tel. 809/426–9947), experienced divers can participate in deep dives to old wrecks to look for bottles and other artifacts (and you can usually keep what you find). **Willie's Watersports** (Heywoods Hotel, tel. 809/422–4900, ext. 2831) offers instruction and a range of diving excursions. **Exploresub Barbados** (Divi Southwinds Beach Resort, tel. 809/428–7181) operates a full range of daily dives. **Dive Boat Safari** (Barbados Hilton, tel. 809/427–4350) offers full diving and instruction services.

Snorkeling Snorkeling gear can be rented for about BDS $10 (U.S. $5) from nearly every hotel.

Squash and Tennis Squash courts can be reserved at the **Rockley Resort** (tel. 809/435–7880) and **Barbados Squash Club** (Marine House, Christ Church, tel. 809/427–7913). Most hotels have tennis courts that can be reserved day and night. Be sure to bring your whites; appropriate dress is expected on the court. Fees average BDS $30 (U.S. $15).

Surfing The best surfing is available on the east coast, and most wave riders congregate at the Soup Bowl, near Bathsheba. An annual international surfing competition is held on Barbados every November.

Waterskiing Waterskiing is widely available, often provided along St. James and Christ Church by the private speedboat owners. Cost is about BDS $35 (U.S. $18) for 15 minutes. Inquire at your hotel, which can direct you to the nearest Sunfish sailing and Hobie Cat rentals as well.

Windsurfing Windsurfing boards and equipment are often guest amenities at the larger hotels and can be rented by nonguests. The best place to learn and to practice is on the south coast at the **Barbados Windsurfing Club Hotel** (Maxwell, Christ Church Parish, tel. 809/428–9095).

Shopping

Traditionally, Broad Street and its side streets in Bridgetown have been the center for shopping action. Hours are generally weekdays 8–4, Saturday 8–1. Many stores have an in-bound (duty-free) department where you must show your travel tickets or a passport in order to buy duty-free goods. Bridgetown stores have values on fine bone china, crystal, cameras, stereo and video equipment, jewelry, perfumes, and clothing. But remember that these are luxury items—expensive even without taxes. You are advised to check stateside prices before deciding upon a purchase here: The item may be cheaper at home.

Island handicrafts are everywhere: woven mats and place mats, dresses, dolls, handbags, shell jewelry. The **Best of Barbados** shops, at the Sandpiper Inn, Mall 34 in Bridgetown (tel. 809/436–1416), and three other locations, offer the highest-quality artwork and crafts, both "native style" and modern designs. A resident artist, Jill Walker, sells her watercolors and prints here and at **Walker's World** shops near the south shore hotels in St. Lawrence Gap. **Artwox** in Shop 5 of the Quayside

Shopping Center (at Rockley in Christ Church) has handmade articles from Barbados, Trinidad, St. Lucia, and Guyana.

At the **Pelican Village Handicrafts Center** on the Princess Alice Highway near the Cheapside Market in Bridgetown, in a cluster of conical shops, you can watch goods and crafts being made before you purchase them. Rugs and mats made from pandanus fiber and khuskhus grass are good buys.

For native Caribbean arts and crafts, including items from Barbados and Haiti, try the Guardhouse Gallery near the Grand Barbados Hotel in St. Michael. A selection of wooden, straw, and ceramic items is available.

Best 'N The Bunch is both a wildly colored chattel house at The Chattel House Village (at St. Lawrence Gap) and its own best advertisement. Here the expertly crafted jewelry of Bajan David Trottman sells for that rarity—reasonable prices. **Perfections** also has good finds—all from Bajan artists—for men, women, and children, and **Beach Bum** offers teens "barely" bikinis.

Dining

Restaurant prices are high on Barbados. Continental fare is standard at restaurants here, and for this you'll pay $25 and up per person for dinner. The better hotels and restaurants of Barbados have employed chefs trained in New York and Europe to attract and keep their sophisticated clientele. Gourmet dining here usually means fresh seafood, beef, or veal with finely blended sauces. Fortunately, many of these restaurants offer the same cuisine at lunch for about half the cost.

Budget diners will fare much better with the native West Indian cuisine. You can enjoy delicious fried flying fish, for example, for less than $10 at local restaurants. Small cafés typically offer zesty goat curry with rice for under $5. The island's West African heritage brought rice, peas, beans, and okra to its table, the staples that make a perfect base for slowly cooked meat and fish dishes. Many side dishes are cooked in oil (the pumpkin fritters can be addictive). And be cautious at first with the West Indian seasonings; like the sun, they are hotter than you think.

Every menu features dolphin (the fish, not the mammal), kingfish, snapper, and flying fish prepared every way imaginable. Shellfish abound; so does steak. Everywhere for breakfast and dessert you'll find mangoes, soursop, papaya (called pawpaw), and, in season, mammyapples, a basketball-size, thick-skinned fruit with giant seeds.

Cou-cou is a mix of cornmeal and okra with a spicy Creole sauce made from tomatoes, onions, and sweet peppers; steamed flying fish is often served over it. A version served by the Brown Sugar restaurant, called red herring, is smoked herring and breadfruit in Creole sauce. Pepper pot stew, a hearty mix of oxtail, beef chunks, and "any other meat you may have," simmered overnight, is flavored with cassareep, an ancient preservative and seasoning that gives the stew its dark, rich color. *Christophines* and *eddoes* are tasty, potatolike vegetables that are often served with curried shrimp, chicken, or goat. *Buljol* is a cold salad of codfish, tomatoes, onions, sweet peppers, and celery, marinated and served raw. Callaloo is a soup made from okra, crabmeat, a spinachlike vegetable that gives the dish its name, and seasonings.

Among the liquid refreshments of Barbados, in addition to the omnipresent Banks Beer and Mount Gay rum, there are Falernum, a liqueur concocted of rum, sugar, lime juice, and almond essence, and *maubey,* a refreshing nonalcoholic beerlike drink made by boiling bitter bark and spices, straining the mixture, and sweetening it.

Increasingly, hotels here are offering MAP plans or are becoming all-inclusive, but if no meals are included in your hotel rate, take advantage of the island's grocery stores, found in every neighborhood. These are better stocked with local and imported foods than those on many other islands. Convenience stores in shopping plazas located along the coast road are another option.

Highly recommended restaurants are indicated by a star ★.

Category	Cost*
Moderate	$25–$40
Inexpensive	$15–$25
Budget	under $15

*per person, excluding drinks and 5% service charge

Moderate **Brown Sugar.** A special-occasion atmosphere prevails at Brown Sugar, located just behind the Island Inn outside Bridgetown. Dozens of ferns and hanging plants decorate the breezy multi-level restaurant. The extensive and authentic West Indian lunch buffets, served between 11:30 and 2:30 and popular with local businessmen, include cou-cou, pepperpot stew, Creole orange chicken, and such homemade desserts as angel-food chocolate mousse cake, passion fruit, and nutmeg ice cream. *Aquatic Gap, St. Michael Parish, tel. 809/426–7684. Reservations advised. AE, MC.*

★ **Fathoms.** Veteran restaurateurs Stephen and Sandra Toppin have opened their newest property seven days a week, for lunch and dinner, with 22 well-dressed tables scattered from the inside dining rooms to the patio's ocean edge. Dinner may bring grilled lobster, island rabbit, jumbo baked shrimp, or cashew-crusted kingfish. This place is casual by day, candlelit by night. *Payne's Bay, St. James Parish, tel. 809/432–2568. Reservations advised for dinner. AE, MC, V.*

★ **Ile de France.** French owners Martine (from Lyon) and Michel (from Toulouse) Gramaglia have adapted the pool and garden areas of the Windsor Arms Hotel and turned them into an island "in" spot. White latticework opens to the night sounds; soft taped French music plays; and a single, perfect hibiscus dresses each table. Just a few of their specialties: foie gras; tournedos Rossini; lobster-and-crepe flambé; and filet mignon with a choice of pepper, béarnaise, or champignon sauces. This is the one place on the island where you can eat decent French food. Even if the prices here strain your budget, your taste buds will reassure you that all is not lost. *Windsor Arms Hotel, Hastings, Christ Church Parish, tel. 809/435–6869. Reservations required. No credit cards. Dinner only. Closed Mon.*

Josef's. Nils Ryman, a former chef for the Swedish embassy, offers a menu combining Caribbean and Scandinavian fare. His blackened fish is rolled in Cajun spices, seared in oil, then baked. *Toast Skagen* blends diced shrimp with mayonnaise and fresh dill. Start with a drink in the garden before moving to the upstairs dining room for a table that looks seaward. *Waverly House, St. Lawrence Gap, tel. 809/435–6541. Reservations advised. AE, DC, MC, V.*

La Maison. The elegant, colonial-style Balmore House reopened in October 1990 under the ownership of Geoffrey Farmer. The atmosphere is created by English country furnishings and a paneled bar opening onto a seaside terrace for dining. A French chef from the Loire Valley creates seafood specials, including a flying-fish parfait appetizer. Passion-fruit ice cream highlights the dessert menu. *Holetown, St. James Parish, tel. 809/432–1156. Reservations advised. D, MC, V.*

★ **Ocean View.** This elegant pink grande dame of a hotel is dressed in fresh fabrics, with great bunches of equally fresh flowers and sparkling crystal chandeliers. Bajan dishes are featured for lunch and dinner, and the Sunday-only Planter's Luncheon Buffet in the downstairs Club Xanadu (which fronts the beach) offers course after course of traditional dishes. Pianist Jean Emerson plays Hoagy Carmichael tunes and sings in dusky tones. *Hastings, Christ Church Parish, tel. 809/427–7821. Reservations advised. AE, MC, V.*

Plantation. Wednesday's Bajan buffet and Tuesday's entertainment are big attractions here. The Plantation is set in a renovated Barbadian residence surrounded by spacious grounds above the Southwinds Resort; its cuisine combines French and Barbadian influences, and you can eat indoors or on the terrace. *St. Lawrence, Christ Church Parish, tel. 809/428–5048. Reservations advised. AE, MC, V. Dinner only.*

Rose and Crown. The casual Rose and Crown serves a variety of fresh seafood, but it's the local lobster that's high on diners' lists. Indoors is a paneled bar, outdoors are tables on a wraparound porch. *Prospect, St. James Parish, tel. 809/425–1074. Reservations advised. AE, MC, V. Dinner served 6–10.*

Inexpensive **Atlantis Hotel.** While the surroundings may be simple and the rest room could use a coat of paint, the nonstop food and the magnificent ocean view at the Atlantis Hotel in Bathsheba make it a real find. Owner-chef Enid Maxwell serves up an enormous Bajan buffet daily, where you're likely to find pickled souse (marinated pig parts and vegetables), pumpkin fritters, spinach balls, pickled breadfruit, fried "fline" (flying) fish, roast chicken, pepper pot stew, and West Indian–style okra and eggplant. Among the homemade pies are an apple and a dense coconut. *Bathsheba, St. Joseph Parish, tel. 809/433–9445. Reservations advised. No credit cards.*

Nico's. This small second-floor bistro is a cheery, intimate gathering spot for expatriates and visitors alike. Tables in the main room surround an oval bar; a terrace above the street has a few more tables. The blackboard menu offers snacks, such as deep-fried Camembert, and more substantial dishes, such as seafood thermidor. *2nd St., Holetown, tel. 809/432–6386. MC, V. Inexpensive.*

Pisces. For Caribbean seafood at the water's edge, this restaurant in lively St. Lawrence Gap specializes in seasonal dishes. Fish is the way to go here—flying fish, dolphin, crab, kingfish, shrimp, prawns, and lobster—prepared any way from charbroiled to sautéed. There are also some chicken and beef dishes. Other items include conch fritters, tropical gazpacho, and seafood terrine with a mango sauce. Enjoy a meal in a contemporary setting filled with hanging tropical plants. *St. Lawrence Gap, Christ Church Parish, tel. 809/435–6564. Reservations advised. Dinner only during low season. AE, MC, V.*

The Virginian. The locally popular Virginian offers intimate surroundings and some of the island's best dining values. The specialties are seafood, shrimp, and steaks. *Sea View Hotel, Hastings, Christ Church Parish, tel. 809/427–7963, ext. 121. Reservations advised. AE, MC, V. Dinner only.*

Witch Doctor. The walls are decorated with pseudo-African art; the menu features traditional Barbadian dishes, European fare, and local seafood. *St. Lawrence Gap, Christ Church Parish, tel. 809/435–6581. Reservations advised. MC, V. Dinner only.*

Budget
★

David's Place. Here you'll be served first-rate dishes in a first-rate location—a black-and-white Bajan cottage overlooking St. Lawrence Bay. Specialties include Baxters Road chicken, local flying fish, pepper pot (salt pork, beef, and chicken boiled and bubbling in a spicy cassareep stock), and curried shrimp. Homemade cheese bread is served with all dishes. Desserts might be banana pudding, coconut-cream pie, or carrot cake with rum sauce. *St. Lawrence Main Rd., Worthing, Christ Church Parish, tel. 809/435–6550. Reservations advised. AE, MC, V.*

The Waterfront Café. Located on the Careenage, a sliver of sea in Bridgetown, this is the perfect place to enjoy a drink, snack, or meal. Locals and tourists gather here for sandwiches, salads, fish, steak-and-kidney pie, and casseroles. The panfried flying-fish sandwich is especially tasty. From the brick and mirrored interior you can gaze through the arched windows, enjoy the cool trade winds and let time pass. *Bridgetown, St. Michael Parish, tel. 809/427–0093. MC, V. Live jazz Mon.–Sat. Food served 10–10, open until midnight.*

Lodging

The southern and western shores of Barbados are lined with accommodations of every size and price, from superluxury resorts to B&Bs and rental apartments. Besides looking at rates, budget travelers should consider location when choosing their hotel. Those north of Bridgetown, in the parishes of St. Peter, St. James, and St. Michael, tend to be self-contained resorts that carry a high price tag. Furthermore, the stretches of empty road between them do not encourage strolling to a neighborhood bar or restaurant. In contrast, the area southwest of Bridgetown, in Christ Church Parish, contains both expensive and inexpensive hotels that cluster near or along the busy strip known as St. Lawrence Gap, where small restaurants, bars, and nightclubs abound.

In addition to hotels, Barbados has a range of alternative accommodations. Guest houses, best described as small hotels with meals provided on request, provide simple lodgings at around $30 a double per night. B&Bs are another option. About 20 are listed with the **Board of Tourism** (tel. 809/427–2623); roughly half are in Christ Church parish. B&Bs here tend to be humble rooms in family homes; prices range from $25–$50 a night. Finally, apartment and home Øentals are becoming increasingly popular among visitors to the island (*see* Villa and Apartment Rentals, *below*).

Hotels listed are grouped here by parish, beginning with St. James in the west and St. Peter to the north, then St. Michael, Christ Church, St. Philip, and St. Joseph. You'll notice that most of the affordable hotels are located in Christ Church.

Highly recommended lodgings are indicated by a star ★.

Category	Cost*
Moderate	$130–$225
Inexpensive	$80–$130
Budget	under $80

All prices are for a standard double room, excluding 5% government tax and 10% service charge. To estimate rates for hotels offering MAP/FAP, add about $35–$45 per person per day to the above price ranges. For all-inclusives, add about $75 per person per day.

Hotels and Resorts
St. James Parish
★

Almond Beach Club. Formerly the Pineapple Beach Club, this hotel includes everything in the price of the room—all you want to eat and drink (that includes wine and liquor); water sports; boat trips; tennis; tours of the island; shopping excursions to Bridgetown; departure transportation to the airport; and service and taxes. Accommodations are mostly in double rooms and one-bedroom suites with balconies. The food is consistently good, from the breakfast buffet and a four-course lunch to the afternoon tea and pastries and the extensive dinner menu. Menus offer plenty of choice, but if your stay is seven days or more and you want something different, the resort offers a dine-around program: dinner or lunch at a number of area restaurants, with round-trip transportation included. The Almond Beach Club has none of the enforced-activity or "whistle-blowing" atmosphere of some all-inclusives. Be sure to inquire closely about the various room options when you call: Pool views are cheaper than beachfront units, and a two-bedroom, pool-view unit that can accommodate two couples is only $200 more—food and all—than a standard double room. *Vauxhall, St. James, tel. 809/432–7840 or 800/966–4737, fax 407/994–6344. 147 units. Facilities: restaurant, 3 pools, snorkeling, fishing, windsurfing, waterskiing, tennis, squash, sauna, fitness center. AE, MC, V. All-inclusive. Moderate.*

Barbados Beach Village. Vacationers choose from twin-bed rooms, studios, apartments, and duplexes here. The beach has a terrace bar; and the restaurant is seaside. The hotel is a lively spot and one of the least expensive on this strip of glittering resorts. *Hwy. 1, St. James Parish, tel. 809/425–1440, fax 809/424–0996. 60 rooms, 28 suites. Facilities: pool, restaurant, disco nightclub. AE, DC, MC, V. EP. Moderate.*

St. Peter Parish **Heywoods Barbados.** This huge resort attracts large groups who have plenty of room on the mile-long beach and in the hundreds of rooms located in seven buildings. Now a Wyndham property, the resort has recently become all-inclusive, an advantage considering its northern location, away from the tourist pleasures of St. Lawrence. *Hwy. 1, St. Peter Parish, tel. 809/422–4900, fax 809/422–1581. 306 rooms. Facilities: 3 pools, 5* *lighted tennis courts, squash courts, 9-hole golf course, restaurants, bars, boutiques, entertainment. AE, DC, MC, V. All-inclusive. Moderate.*

St. Michael Parish **Barbados Hilton International.** This large resort, just five minutes from Bridgetown, is for those who like activity and plenty of people around. Expect to rub shoulders with delegates attending seminars and with conventioneers, and don't be surprised by the occasional odor from the nearby oil refinery. Its attractions include an atrium lobby, a 1,000-foot-wide, man-made beach with full water sports, and lots of shops. All rooms have balconies; unfortunately, those within our price category face the gardens, not the sea. *Needham's Point, St. Michael Parish, tel. 809/426–0200, fax 809/436–8646. 183 rooms, 2 suites. Facilities: pool, tennis courts, restaurant, lounge, health club. AE, DC, MC, V. EP. Moderate.*

Christ Church **Casuarina Beach Club.** This luxury apartment hotel on 900 feet
Parish of pink sand takes its name from the casuarina pines that surround it. Its quiet setting provides a dramatic contrast to that of the platinum-coast resorts. The bar and restaurant are on the beach, and the surrounding gardens enhance the feeling of seclusion. A new reception area includes small lounges where guests can get a dose of TV—there aren't any in the bedrooms. Scuba diving, golf, and other activities can be arranged. The Casuarina Beach is popular with those who prefer self-catering holidays in a setting that feels remote, yet is convenient to nightlife and shopping. *St. Lawrence Gap, Christ Church Parish, tel. 809/428–3600, fax 809/428–1970. 134 units. Facilities: pool, tennis courts, squash courts, restaurant, bar, minimarket, duty-free shop. AE, MC, V. EP. Moderate.*

Divi Southwinds Beach Resort. This hotel, situated on 20 lush acres, has a tour-package feel, with its barracklike buildings, self-service dining facilities, and rollicking good-time atmosphere. Rooms are pleasant enough: Newer one-bedroom suites include balconies and kitchenettes; older standard rooms and one-bedroom suites are located right on the fine, white-sand beach, but are smaller and in need of repair. Complete scuba and water-sports facilities are available. *St. Lawrence, Christ Church Parish, tel. 800/367–3484, fax 809/428–4674. 140 rooms, 26 suites. Facilities: 2 restaurants, 3 pools, 2 lighted tennis courts, putting green, shopping arcade. AE, DC, MC, V. EP, MAP. Moderate.*

Sandy Beach Hotel. On a wide, sparkling white beach, this comfortable hotel has a popular poolside bar and the Green House Restaurant, which serves a weekly West Indian buffet. Although the hotel is in the top end of our Moderate price category, you can offset costs by preparing your own meals (all rooms have kitchenettes) and by skipping a car rental (St. Lawrence Gap, with restaurants and entertainment, is within walking distance). Water sports, which cost extra, include scuba-diving certification, deep-sea fishing, harbor cruises, catamaran sailing, and windsurfing. *Worthing, Christ Church Parish, tel. 809/435–8000, fax 809/435–8053. 89 units. Facilities: pool, restaurant, bar, entertainment. AE, D, DC, MC, V. EP. Moderate.*

Southern Palms. A plantation-style hotel on a 1,000-foot stretch of pink sand near the Dover Convention Center, Southern Palms is popular with businesspeople as well as beach lovers. Standard rooms are at the top of our price range. Each wing of the hotel has its own small pool. *St. Lawrence, Christ*

Church Parish, tel. 809/428–7171, fax 809/428–7175. 93 rooms. Facilities: 2 pools, duty-free shop, small conference center; miniature-golf course, tennis court, dining room, water sports. AE, D, DC, MC, V. EP. Moderate.

Sichris Hotel. The Sichris is a "discovery," more attractive inside than from the road, and a comfortable, convenient resort. It's minutes from Bridgetown and a five-minute walk to the beach. Units are smallish one-bedroom suites with kitchenettes and private balconies where you can enjoy your culinary creations. The pool is quite small and literally a hot spot—it's encircled by low white buildings that reflect the sun's rays. *Worthing, Christ Church Parish, tel. 809/ 435–7930, fax 809/435–8232. 24 rooms. Facilities: pool, restaurant, bar. AE, MC, V. EP. Inexpensive–Moderate.*

Accra Beach Hotel. At press time, the Accra was undergoing a room renovation that should inject new life into this utilitarian hotel, located on the beach in Christ Church Parish. The rooms, in two-story buildings, face a small lawn and permit an angled view of the sea. Guests gather for al fresco dining by the pool in the evenings. Nightlife is a walk away. *Rockley Beach, Christ Church Parish, tel. 809/427–7866 or 800/223–9815, fax 809/435–6794. 52 rooms. Facilities: dining room, lounge, beach bar; water-sports center. AE, MC, V. EP. Inexpensive.*

Benston Windsurfing Club Hotel. A small hotel that began as a gathering place for windsurfing enthusiasts, the Benston is now a complete school and center for the sport. The rooms are spacious and sparsely furnished to accommodate the active young crowd that chooses this bare-bones hotel right on the beach. The bar and restaurant overlook the water, and other restaurants are within walking distance. All sports can be arranged, but windsurfing (learning, practicing, and perfecting it) is king. *Maxwell Main Rd., Christ Church Parish, tel. 809/428–9095, fax 809/435–6621. 15 rooms. Facilities: restaurant, bar; entertainment. AE, MC, V. EP. Inexpensive.*

Club Rockley Barbados. At press time, some of these timeshare condominiums 5 miles south of Bridgetown were being transformed into an all-inclusive resort. This new section of the property features air-conditioned studios and one- and two-bedroom accommodations; most have either a balcony or a patio. A free shuttle bus transports guests to the beach, about five minutes away. Two dining rooms, one buffet and the other à la carte, varies the dining experience here; you can also dine one evening at a participating hotel. A children's program makes this resort a good family choice. *Christ Church Parish, tel. 809/435–7880, fax 809/435–8015. 150 units. Facilities: 2 restaurants, bar; disco, tennis courts, squash courts, golf, gym, children's game room, disco, water sports, entertainment, disco. AE, DC, MC, V. All-inclusive. Inexpensive.*

Little Bay Hotel. This small hotel just a five-minute walk from great beaches is a find. Each unit has a private balcony, bedroom, small lounge, and kitchenette. Plans are afoot to replace the drab carpets with clay tiled floors. Room 100—a corner unit with small sitting room and a balcony overlooking the bay—is a favorite. The popular restaurant is open to the bay and features delicious seafood; guests can watch TV in the small lounge. Nightlife is a stroll away. *St. Lawrence Gap, Christ Church Parish, tel. 809/435–8574, fax 809/435–8586. 10 rooms. Facilities: lounge, bar; restaurant. AE, MC, V. EP. Budget–Inexpensive.*

★ **Ocean View.** One of the best-kept secrets on the island, this unique hideaway with its 40 rooms and suites is a stopping place for celebrities on their commute to private villas in Mustique. Owner John Chandler places his antiques throughout his three-story grande dame nestled against the sea (the beach is not good for swimming), adds great bouquets of tropical flowers everywhere, and calls it home. Rooms vary considerably, and their charm depends on whether you appreciate the eclectic furnishings. Smaller, sparsely furnished rooms fall into our Budget category, while larger rooms stretch into the upper reaches of our Inexpensive range. A car is not essential here, since the property is on the main coastal road: Restaurants are within walking distance, and popular beaches are a short bus ride away. Those who enjoy this old colonial-style building for what it is and don't mind the lack of modern amenities will be happiest here. Cat lovers will be wooed by the owner's pets, which drape themselves over lounge chairs. *Hastings, Christ Church Parish, tel. 809/427-7821, fax 809/427-7826. 40 rooms. Facilities: restaurant and bar, supper club with Off-Broadway shows during high season. AE, MC, V. CP. Budget–Inexpensive.*

Pegwell Inn. Across the road from the beach, this small, friendly guest house run by Mrs. Phillip has four double rooms with twin beds and private baths. Coffee- and tea-making facilities are available, and you can pick up snacks from the nearby food plaza for picnics. Prices are low. *Welches, Christ Church Parish, tel. 809/428-6150. 4 rooms. No credit cards. EP. Budget.*

Rio. Mr. Harding runs this small family-owned inn 3 miles outside Bridgetown and within walking distance of the beach. Inexpensive restaurants, food shops, pubs, and nightclubs are all within walking distance. Rooms are not large, but rates are rock bottom. *St. Lawrence Gap, Christ Church Parish, tel. 809/428-1546. 5 doubles with bath, 2 singles with shared bath. No credit cards. EP. Budget.*

St. Philip Parish **Marriott's Sam Lord's Castle.** Set on the Atlantic coast about 14 miles east of Bridgetown, Sam Lord's Castle is a sprawling great house surrounded by 72 acres of grounds, gardens, and beach. The rooms, most in buildings angling off the main house toward the beach, are conventionally furnished in international Marriott style. Only the standard doubles facing the gardens are within our Moderate price category. The beach, fronting ocean waters with large breakers, is a mile long; there are also three freshwater pools. The hotel is miles from any other resort or activity, but the two restaurants, evening entertainment, and even a few slot machines are designed to keep everyone busy. *Long Bay, St. Philip Parish, tel. 809/423-7350, fax 809/423-5918. 256 rooms. Facilities: 3 pools, lighted tennis courts, 3 restaurants, entertainment. AE, DC, MC, V. EP, MAP. Moderate.*

St. Joseph Parish **Atlantis Hotel.** If you'd rather experience the Bajan side of Barbados than the international tourist scene, come to this modest hotel in a pastoral location, overlooking a majestically rocky Atlantic coast. You'll need your own wheels here (a bike will do for the energetic), as the nearest swimming beach with sand is a good 15-minute drive away. Spartan rooms feature little more than a bed, writing table, and a couple of chairs. The restaurant (*see* Dining, *above*) serves bountiful Bajan buffets, and the congenial atmosphere is welcome indeed. *Bathsheba,*

St. Joseph Parish, tel. 809/433–9445. 16 rooms. Facilities: restaurant. AE. EP. Budget–Inexpensive.

Rental Homes and Apartments These are a popular option on Barbados. Apartments range from studios to two-bedroom units. **Husband Heights Apartments** (Hotel Management Services, Hastings, Christ Church Parish, tel. 809/429–9039) manages units with rates of $20–$100 per person per day in Christ Church Parish.

Villas and private homes are available for rent south of Bridgetown in the Hastings–Worthing area, along the St. James Parish coast, and in St. Peter Parish. Rentals are available through Barbados realtors, including **Alleyne, Aguilar & Altman,** Rosebank, St. James (tel. 809/432–0840); **Bajan Services,** St. Peter (tel. 809/422–2618); and **Ronald Stoute & Sons Ltd.,** St. Philip (tel. 809/423–6800). In the United States, contact **At Home Abroad** (tel. 212/421–9165) or **Villa Vacations** (tel. 617/593–8885 or 800/800–5576). The **Barbados Board of Tourism** has a listing of rental properties and prices.

Off-Season Bets During the off-season (mid-April–mid-December), hotel prices tumble as much as 50%. Because Barbados is in the southern Caribbean and is a flat island, it receives less rain than some other islands, making it a good choice for an autumn vacation. (Be aware, however, that some properties discount less dramatically during the shoulder season, from November to mid-December.) Although some properties, such as Sandy Lane and Glitter Bay, still charge more than $300 a night in the off-season, other glamorous resorts do become affordable. **Treasure Beach** (Payne's Bay, St. James Parish, tel. 809/432–1346, fax 809/432–1094) has 24 one-bedroom suites, a delightful beach, and a cozy, intimate atmosphere. The seven-acre **Colony Club** (Box 429, Bridgetown, Hwy. 1, St. James Parish, tel. 809/422–2335, fax 809/422–1726), a cottage colony on the beach, has rooms with private patios and a dining room and cocktail terrace that curve along the beach. One of our most highly recommended hotels is the **Crane Beach Hotel** (Crane Bay, St. Philip Parish, tel. 809/423–6220, fax 809/423–5343), on a remote hilltop overlooking the dramatic Atlantic coast. A Roman-style pool with columns separates the main house from the dining room. To reach the beach, guests descend about 200 steps to a beautiful stretch of sand thumped by waves.

The Arts and Nightlife

The Arts **Barbados Art Council.** The gallery shows drawings, paintings, and other art, with a new show about every two weeks. *2 Pelican Village, Bridgetown, tel. 809/426–4385. Admission free. Open weekdays 10–5, Sat. 9–1.*

Nightlife When the sun goes down, the musicians come out, and folks go "limin' " (which means anything from hanging out to a chat-up or jump-up—Caribbean for an informal street party). Competitions among reggae groups, steel bands, and calypso singers are major events, and tickets can be hard to come by, but give it a try.

Island residents have their own favorite night spots that change with the seasons. The most popular one is still **After Dark** (St. Lawrence Gap, Christ Church, tel. 809/435–6547), with the longest bar on the island and a jazz-club annex.

Harbour Lights claims to be the "home of the party animal," and most any night features live music with dancing under the stars. *On the Bay, Marine Villa, Bay St., St. Michael, tel. 809/436–7225.*

Another "in" spot, **Front Line** (Wharf St., tel. 809/429–6160) at the Wharf in Bridgetown, attracts a young crowd for its reggae music.

Disco moves are made on the floor at the **Hippo Disco** in the Barbados Beach Village Hotel (St. James, tel. 809/425–1440), and above it, where dancers gyrate until the early hours of the morning.

Another dusky disco, **Club Miliki** (tel. 809/422–4900), takes center stage at the Heywoods Resort in St. Peter. Live music begins at 9 PM Friday and Saturday.

A late-night (after 11) excursion to **Baxter Road** is de rigueur for midnight Bajan street snacks, local rum, great gossip, and good lie-telling. **Enid & Livy's** and **Collins** are just two of the many long-standing favorites. The later, the better.

Bars and Inns   Barbados supports the rum industry in more than 1,600 "rum shops," simple bars where men congregate to discuss the world's ills; and in more sophisticated inns where you'll find world-class rum drinks and the island's renowned Mount Gay and Cockspur rums. The following offer welcoming spirits: **The Ship Inn** (St. Lawrence Gap, Christ Church Parish, tel. 809/435–6961), **The Coach House** (Paynes Bay, St. James Parish, tel. 809/432–1163), and **Harry's Oasis** (St. Lawrence, Christ Church Parish, no phone); **Bert's Bar** at the Abbeville Hotel; (Rockley, Christ Church Parish, tel. 809/435–7924), serves the best daiquiris in town—any town. Also try **The Boat Yard** (Bay Street, Bridgetown, tel. 809/436–2622), **The Waterfront Cafe** (Bridgetown, tel. 809/427–0093), **The Warehouse** (Bridgetown, tel. 809/436–2897), and **TGI Boomers** (St. Lawrence Gap, Christ Church Parish, tel. 809/428–8439).

6　**Bonaire**

*Updated by
Laurie Senz*

Bonaire is a stark desert island, perfect for the rugged individualist who is turned off by the overcommercialized high life of the other Antillean islands. The island boasts a spectacular array of exotic wildlife—from fish to fowl to flowers—that will keep nature-watchers awestruck for days. It's the kind of place where you'll want to rent a Jeep and go dashing off in search of the wild flamingo, the wild iguana, or even the wild yellow-winged parrot named the Bonairian lora.

A mecca for divers, Bonaire offers one of the most unspoiled reef systems in the world. The water is so clear that you can lean over the dock and look the fish straight in the eye.

Kudos for the preservation of the 112-square-mile isle go to the people and government of Bonaire, who in 1970, with the help of the World Wildlife Fund, developed the Bonaire Marine Park—a model of ecological conservation. The underwater park includes, roughly, the entire coastline, from the high-water tidemark to a depth of 200 feet, all of which is protected by strict laws. Because the Bonairians are determined to keep their paradise intact, any diver with a reckless streak is firmly requested to go elsewhere.

This is not the island for connoisseurs of fine cuisine, shopping maniacs, beachcombers, or those who prefer hobnobbing with society. Instead, it's an island for divers, ecotourists, bird-watchers, hikers, and seekers of serene getaways. While several upscale and expensive hotels have been built here, Bonaire remains rich in reasonably priced inns, guest houses, small hotels, and inexpensive apartments. Fast food has not arrived on this sleepy island, but you can control food costs here by choosing lodgings with a kitchen and cooking your meals. Scuba diving is an expensive sport, but with so many excellent dive sites just offshore, visitors can stick to beach diving and forego the more expensive boat dives. All of the island's dive operators offer boat-dive packages, which offer substantial savings over the price of individual boat dives. At night, find out which hotel has a band playing and drop in to listen for free. On Bonaire, you're always welcome. With only 11,000 inhabitants, the island has a feeling of a small community with a gentle pace.

What It Will Cost These sample prices, meant only as a general guide, are for high season. Price estimates are for high season. A decent room on Bonaire can cost as little as $50 a night in high season. Apartments with kitchens run a bit more, but can be found for $60–$90 a night. Two couples traveling together can rent a two-bedroom, two-bath villa with a fully equipped kitchen for about $150 a night. Because most of the food on Bonaire is imported, prices tend to be high; try to stick to local places and order dishes such as the fish of the day with rice, fried bananas, and vegetables, which can run as low as $5. Expect to pay about $2.50 for a rum punch, $3 for a cocktail, and $2 for a beer. Car rental begins at about $28 a day and includes unlimited mileage. A taxi from the airport to your hotel costs $6–$10 for up to four passengers; fare from most hotels into town is about $4–$6. Snorkel-gear rental costs from $5 to $11 a day. Six full days of unlimited shore diving, which includes tanks, air, and weight belts, ranges from $80–$110. Individual boat dives cost from $12 to $40, depending on the dive operator. A week of unlimited shore dives plus six boat dives costs about $170. Your best bet is to check around and choose a package and price that fit your needs.

Before You Go

Tourist Information Contact the **Tourism Corporation of Bonaire** (444 Madison Ave., Suite 2403, New York, N.Y. 10022, tel. 212/832–0779, fax 212/838–3407; in Canada: 512 Duplex Ave., Toronto, Ont. M4R 2E3, tel. 416/484–4864) for advice and information on planning your trip.

Arriving and Departing
By Plane **ALM** (tel. 800/327–7230) and **Air Aruba** (tel. 800/882–7822) will get you to Bonaire. ALM has eight direct flights (through Curaçao) a week, two nonstop flights a week from Miami, and five flights a week from Atlanta through Curaçao, with connecting service (throughfares) to most U.S. gateways tied in with Delta and other airlines, making ALM Bonaire's major airline. ALM also flies to Caracas, Aruba, Curaçao, and St. Martin, as well as other Caribbean islands, using Curaçao as its Caribbean hub. Air Aruba flies four days a week from Newark and daily from Miami to Aruba with connecting service to Bonaire. **American Airlines** (tel. 800/433–7300) offers daily flights from New York to Aruba, but you must connect to Bonaire through ALM or Air Aruba. ALM also offers a Visit Caribbean Pass, which allows easy interisland travel.

From the Airport Bonaire's Flamingo Airport is tiny, but you'll appreciate its welcoming ambience. The customs check is perfunctory if you are arriving from another Dutch isle; otherwise you will have to show proof of citizenship, plus a return or ongoing ticket. There is no public transportation to the hotels, but rental cars

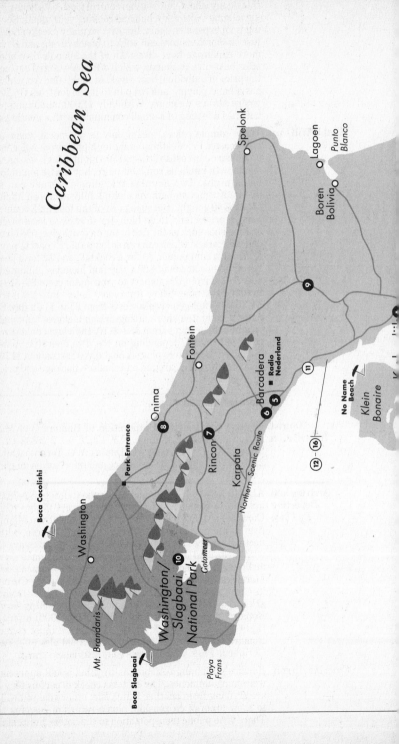

Bonaire

Caribbean Sea

Boca Cocolishi

Washington

Mt. Brandaris

Boca Slagbaai

Playa Frans

Cotomeer

Washington/ Slagbaai National Park

⑩

Park Entrance

Onima

Fontein

Spelonk

⑧

Rincon

⑦

Karpata

Northern Scenic Route

Barcadera

■ Radio Nederland

⑥ ⑤

⑨

Boren Bolivia

Lagoen

Punto Blanco

⑪

No Name Beach

Klein Bonaire

⑫ – ⑯

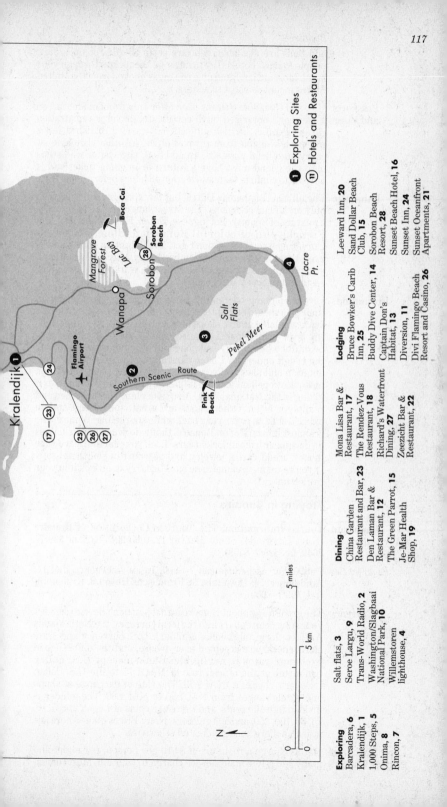

Boca Cai

Mangrove Forest

Lac Bay

Sorobon Beach

Soraбon

Wanapa

Salt Flats

Pekel Meer

Lacre Pt.

Flamingo Airport

Southern Scenic Route

Pink Beach

Kralendijk

24

17 — 23

25 26 27

N

5 miles

5 km

Exploring
Barcadera, **6**
Kralendijk, **1**
1,000 Steps, **5**
Onima, **8**
Rincon, **7**

Salt flats, **3**
Seroe Largu, **9**
Trans-World Radio, **2**
Washington/Slagbaai
National Park, **10**
Willemstoren
lighthouse, **4**

Dining
China Garden
Restaurant and Bar, **23**
Den Laman Bar &
Restaurant, **12**
The Green Parrot, **15**
Je-Mar Health
Shop, **19**

Mona Lisa Bar &
Restaurant, **17**
The Rendez-Vous
Restaurant, **18**
Richard's Waterfront
Dining, **27**
Zeezicht Bar &
Restaurant, **22**

Lodging
Bruce Bowker's Carib
Inn, **25**
Buddy Dive Center, **14**
Captain Don's
Habitat, **13**
Diversion, **11**
Divi Flamingo Beach
Resort and Casino, **26**

Leeward Inn, **20**
Sand Dollar Beach
Club, **15**
Sorobon Beach
Resort, **28**
Sunset Beach Hotel, **16**
Sunset Inn, **24**
Sunset Oceanfront
Apartments, **21**

1 Exploring Sites

11 Hotels and Restaurants

and taxis are available; cab fare costs $6–$10 for up to four people to most hotels. Try to arrange the pickup through your hotel. Most air, land, and dive packages booked from the United States include airport transfers.

Passports and Visas U.S. and Canadian citizens need offer only proof of identity, so a passport, notarized birth certificate, or voter registration card will suffice. British subjects may carry a British visitor's passport, available from any post office. All other visitors must carry an official passport. In addition, any visitor who steps onto the island must have a return or ongoing ticket and is advised to confirm that reservation 48 hours before departure.

Language The official language is Dutch, but few speak it, and even then only on official occasions. The street language is Papiamento, a mixture of Spanish, Portuguese, Dutch, English, African, and French—full of colorful Bonairian idioms that even Curaçaoans sometimes don't get. You'll light up your waiter's eyes, though, if you can remember to say *Masha danki* (thank you). English is spoken by most people working at the hotels, restaurants, and tourist shops.

Precautions Divers planning on renting a car and going shore diving on their own should buy the excellent *Guide to the Bonaire Marine Park*, available at dive shops around the island, which specifies the level of diving skill required for 44 sites. No matter how beautiful a beach may look, heed all warning signs regarding the rough undertow. Listen carefully to the Marine Park orientation and always dive with a buddy. Take plenty of roll-on mosquito repellent and use it liberally, especially at night, or if hiking in the National Park. Also take plenty of sunscreen and reapply it often. Other musts are a hat, sunglasses, and an extra T-shirt to cover your back while snorkeling. While crime is almost unheard of on Bonaire, thefts do occur, and valuables do disappear from unlocked cars. Lock your car and leave your money, credit cards, jewelry, and passport in your hotel safe. If you're taking a camera, be sure to carry it, or lock it in your car's trunk.

Staying in Bonaire

Important Addresses **Tourist Information:** The **Tourism Corporation of Bonaire** (Kaya Libertador Simon Bolivar 12, tel. 599/7–8322 or 599/7–8649, fax 599/7–8408).

Emergencies **Police:** For assistance call 7–8000. In an emergency, dial 11. **Ambulance: 14. Hospitals: St. Franciscus Hospital,** Kralendijk (tel. 599/7–8900).

Currency The great thing about Bonaire is that you don't need to convert your American dollars into the local currency, the Netherlands Antilles florin (also called guilder). U.S. currency and traveler's checks are accepted everywhere, and the difference in exchange rates is negligible. Banks accept U.S. dollar banknotes at the official rate of NAf 1.77 to the U.S. dollar, traveler's checks at NAf 1.79. The rate of exchange at shops and hotels ranges from NAf 1.75 to NAf 1.80. The guilder is divided into 100 cents, and there are coins of 1 cent, 2½, 5, 10, 25, 50, 100, 250, and 500 guilders. Note: Prices quoted here are in U.S. dollars unless indicated otherwise.

Taxes and Service Charges Hotels charge a room tax of $4.10 per person, per night, and many add a 10% maid service charge to your bill. Most restaurants add a 10% service charge to your bill. There's no sales tax on purchases in Bonaire. Departure tax when going to Curaçao is $5.65. For all other destinations it's $10.

Getting Around There's no public transportation on Bonaire, but hitchhiking is considered a respectable way to get around. You can ask someone for a lift or stick out your thumb at a passing vehicle. You can also zip about the island in a car or a Suzuki Jeep. Scooters and bicycles, which are also available, are less practical but can be fun, too. Just remember that there are at least 20 miles of unpaved road; the roller-coaster hills at the national park require strong stomachs; and during the rainy season, mud—called Bonairian snow—is unpleasant. All traffic stays to the right and, delightfully, there is yet to be a single traffic light.

Rental Cars **Budget** has cars and Jeeps available from its six locations, but reservations can be made only at the Head Office (tel. 599/7–8300, ext. 225). Pickups are at the airport (tel. 599/7–8315) and at several hotels. It's always a good idea to make advance reservations (fax 599/7–8865 or 599/7–8118; cable BUDGET BONAIRE; in the U.S., tel. 800/472–3325). Prices range from $28 a day for a Volkswagen to $60 a day for an automatic, air-conditioned four-door sedan. Other agencies are **Avis** (tel. 599/7–5795, fax 599/7–5791; telex 1900 ROCAR), **Dollar Rent-A-Car** (tel. 599/7–5588, at the airport; tel. 599/7–8888; fax 599/7–7788), **Sunray** (tel. 599/7–5230, fax 599/7–4888), and **AB Car Rental** (tel. 599/7–8980 or 599/7–5410, fax 599/7–5034). There is also a new government tax of $2 per day per car rental.

Scooters Two-seater scooters are available from **Bonaire Bicycle & Motorbike Rental** (tel. 599/7–8226) and **S. F. Wave Touch** (tel. 599/7–4246) for about $26 a day and $165 a week.

Bicycles Bicycling is a safe way to get around Kralendijk. Bring a water bottle to safeguard against dehydration, and wear plenty of sunscreen. For exploring the National Park, however, a car or Jeep is recommended. **Bonaire Bicycle & Motorbike Rental** (tel. 599/7–8226) rents bicycles for $15 a day. **Captain Don's Habitat** (tel. 599/7–8290 or 599/7–8913) rents mountain bicycles for $6 per day plus a $250 deposit. **Harbour Village Beach Resort** (tel. 599/7–7500) occasionally rents bikes to nonguests for $11 a day.

Taxis Taxis are unmetered; they have fixed rates controlled by the government. A trip from the airport to your hotel will cost $6 to $10 for up to four passengers. A taxi from most hotels into town costs between $4 and $6. Fares increase from 7 PM to midnight by 25% and from midnight to 6 AM by 50%. Call **Taxi Central Dispatch** (tel. 599/7–8100 or dial 10), or inquire at your hotel.

Telephones and Mail It's difficult for visitors to Bonaire to get involved in dramatic, heart-wrenching phone conversations or in *any* phone discussions requiring a degree of privacy: Only about one-third of the major hotels have phones in their rooms, so calls must be made from hotel front desks or from the central telephone company office in Kralendijk. Telephone connections have improved, but static is still common. To call Bonaire from the United States, dial 011–599–7 + the local four-digit number. When making inter-island calls, dial the local four-digit number. Local phone calls cost NAf 25¢. Airmail postage rates to the United States are NAf 1.15 for letters and NAf 70¢ for postcards; to Canada,

NAf 1.45 for letters and NAf 70¢ for postcards; to Britain, NAf 1.90 for letters and NAf 75¢ for postcards.

Opening and Closing Times Stores in the Kralendijk area are generally open Monday through Saturday 8–noon and 2–6 PM. On Sundays and holidays, when cruise ships arrive, most shops open for a few extra hours. Most restaurants are open for lunch and dinner, but few not affiliated with hotels are open for breakfast.

Guided Tours If you don't like to drive, **Bonaire Sightseeing Tours** (tel. 599/7–8778 or 599/7–8300, ext. 212) will chauffeur you around the island on four different tours. A two-hour Northern Island Tour ($12) visits the 1,000 steps, Goto Lake, and Rincon, the oldest settlement on the island. A two-hour Southern Island Tour ($12) covers Akzo Salt Antilles N.V., a modern salt-manufacturing facility where flamingos gather; Lac Bay; and the oldest lighthouse on the island. A half-day tour ($17) visits sites in both the north and south. For $25, you can take a half-day tour of Bonaire's Washington/Slagbaai National Park (entrance fee included), 13,500 acres of majestic scenery, wildlife, unspoiled beaches, and tropical flora. A full-day tour of the park costs $45. **Ayubi's Tours** (tel. 599/7–5338) also offers several half- and full-day island tours. Taxi drivers are usually knowledgeable enough about the island to conduct half-day tours; they charge about $60 for a northern-route tour and $40 for a southern-route tour.

Exploring Bonaire

Numbers in the margin correspond to points of interest on the Bonaire map.

Kralendijk Bonaire's capital city of **Kralendijk** (population: 2,500) is five
❶ minutes from the airport and a short walk from the Carib Inn and the Flamingo Beach Resort. There's really not much to explore here, but there are a few sights worth noting in this small, very tidy city.

Kralendijk has one main drag, J. A. Abraham Boulevard, which turns into **Kaya Grandi** in the center of town. Along it are most of the island's major stores, boutiques, restaurants, duty-free shops, and jewelry stores (*see* Shopping, *below*).

Walk down the narrow waterfront avenue called Kaya C.E.B. Hellmund, which leads straight to the **North** and **South piers**. In the center of town, stop in at the new Harborside Mall, which has 13 chic boutiques. Along this route you will see **Fort Oranje**, with cannons pointing to the sea.

The elegant white structure that looks like a tiny Greek temple is the **Fish Market,** where local fishermen sell their early-morning haul, along with vegetables and fruits.

Elsewhere on the Island Two tours, north and south, are possible of the 24-mile-long island; both will take from a few hours to a full day, depending upon whether you stop to snorkel, swim, dive, or lounge. If you like to explore at your own pace, you'll need to rent a car. While it's possible to see the whole island in one whirlwind day, it's more enjoyable to pack a swimsuit and snorkel gear and take your time over two or more days. In dry weather, a scooter is fine for exploring the southern end of Bonaire. If you prefer to leave the driving to others and like to hear anecdotal information about what you're seeing, a guided tour will be more to your liking (*see* Guided Tours, *above*).

South Bonaire The trail south from Kralendijk is chock-full of icons—both natural and man-made—that tell the minisaga of Bonaire. Heading south along the Southern Scenic Route, the first icon you'll come to is the unexpected symbol of modernism—the **②** towering 500-foot antennae of **Trans-World Radio,** one of the most powerful stations in Christian broadcasting. From here, evangelical programs and gospel music are transmitted daily in five languages to all of North, South, and Central America, as well as the entire Caribbean.

③ Keep on cruising past the salt pans until you come to the **salt flats,** voluptuous white drifts that look something like huge mounds of vanilla ice cream. Harvested twice a year, the "ponds" are owned by the Akzo Salt Antilles N.V. company, which has reactivated the 19th-century salt industry with great success. Keep a lookout for the three 30-foot obelisks—white, blue, and red—that were used to guide the trade boats coming to pick up the salt. On this stark landscape, these obelisks look decidedly phallic; today, they are photographed as historical curiosities.

Along the sea just a bit farther south is **Pink Beach,** a half-mile-long stretch of incredibly soft sand that derives its name from the delicate pink hue of the sand at the shoreline (*see* Beaches, *below*).

The gritty history of the salt industry is revealed down the road in **Rode Pan,** the site of two groups of tiny slave huts. During the 19th century, the salt workers, imported slaves from Africa, worked the fields by day, then crawled into these huts at night to sleep. Each Friday afternoon, they walked seven hours to Rincon to spend the weekend with their families, returning each Sunday to the salt pans. In recent years, the government has restored the huts to their original simplicity. Only very small people will be able to go inside, but take a walk around and put your head in for a look.

④ Continue heading south to **Willemstoren,** Bonaire's first lighthouse, built in 1837 and still in use (although closed to visitors).

Rounding the tip of the island, head north to two more picturesque beaches—**Sorobon Beach** and **Boca Cai** at Lac Bay. The road here winds through otherworldly desert terrain, full of organ-pipe cacti and spiny-trunk mangroves—huge stumps of saltwater trees that rise out of the marshes like witches. At Boca Cai, you'll be impressed by the huge piles of conch shells discarded by local fishermen. (Sift through them; they make great gifts—but pack them carefully.) On Sundays at Cai, live bands play from noon to 4, and there's beer and food available at the local restaurant. When the mosquitoes arrive at dusk, it's time to hightail it home.

North Bonaire The northern tour takes you right into the heart of Bonaire's natural wonders—desert gardens of towering cacti, tiny coastal coves, dramatically shaped coral grottoes, and plenty of fantastic panoramas. A snappy excursion with the requisite photo stops will take about 2½ hours, but if you pack your swimsuit and a hefty picnic basket (forget finding a Burger King), you could spend the entire day exploring this northern sector, including a few hours snorkeling in Washington Park.

Head out from Kralendijk on the Kaya Gobernador N. Debrot until it turns into the Northern Scenic Route, a one-lane, one-way street on the outskirts of town. Fifteen minutes north of **⑤** the Sunset Beach Hotel is a site called **1,000 Steps,** a limestone staircase carved right out of the cliff on the left side of the road. If you take the trek down them, you'll discover a great place to snorkel and scuba dive. (It's 67 steps going down, but more like 1,000 going up with scuba gear.)

Following the route northward, look closely for a turnoff marked Vista Al Mar Restaurant. A few yards ahead, you'll discover some stone steps that lead down into a cave full of stalactites and vegetation. Once used to trap goats, this cave, **⑥** called **Barcadera,** is one of the oldest in Bonaire; there's even a tunnel that looks intriguingly spooky.

Note that once you pass the antennae of the Radio Nederland, you cannot turn back to Kralendijk. The road becomes one-way, and you will have to follow the cross-island road to Rincon and return via the main road through the center of the island.

If you continue toward the northern curve of the island, the green storage tanks of the Bonaire Petroleum Corporation become visible. Follow the sign to **Goto Meer,** a popular flamingo **⑦** hangout. The road will loop around and pass through **Rincon,** a well-kept cluster of pastel cottages and century-old buildings that constitute Bonaire's oldest village. Watch your driving— both goats and dogs often sit right in the middle of the main drag.

Rincon was the original Spanish settlement on the island: It became home to the slaves brought from Africa to work on the plantations and salt fields. Superstition and voodoo lore still have a powerful impact here, more so than in Kralendijk, where they work hard at suppressing the old ways. Rincon has a couple of local eateries. **Verona's Bar & Restaurant** (no phone) on Kaya Para Mira, on the road south, has tasty local dishes, but the real temptation is **Prisca's Ice Cream** (tel. 599/7–6334), to be found at her house on Kaya Komkomber.

Pass through Rincon on the road that heads toward Fontein, **⑧** but take the left-hand turn before Fontein to **Onima.** Small signposts direct the way to the **Indian inscriptions** found on a three-foot limestone ledge that juts out like a partially formed cave entrance. Look up to see the red-stained designs and symbols inscribed on the limestone, said to have been the handiwork of the Arawak Indians when they inhabited the island centuries ago.

Backtrack to the main road and continue on to Fontein and then **⑨** to **Seroe Largu,** the highest point on the southern part of the island. During the day, a winding path leads to a magnificent view of Kralendijk's rooftops and the island of Klein Bonaire; at night, the twinkling city lights below make this a romantic stop. If you've got some time, sit on one of the stone benches and watch the friendly turquoise-footed lizards slithering about. Tourists are their main source of crumbs, but if they should happen to ignore you, throw a pebble near them and they'll trot right over.

Washington/
Slagbaai National
Park
10 Once a plantation producing divi-divi trees (whose pods were used for tanning animal skins), aloe (used for medicinal lotions), charcoal, and goats, **Washington/Slagbaai National Park** is now a model of conservation, designed to maintain fauna, flora, and geological treasures in their natural state. Visitors may easily tour the 13,500-acre tropical desert terrain along the dirt roads. As befits a wilderness sanctuary, the well-marked, rugged roads force you to drive slowly enough to appreciate the animal life and the terrain. Four-wheel drive is a must. (Think twice about coming here if it rained the day before—the mud you may encounter will be more than inconvenient.) If you are planning to hike, bring a picnic lunch, camera, sunscreen, and plenty of water. There are two different routes: The long one, 22 miles (about 2½ hours), is marked by yellow arrows; the short one, 15 miles (about 1½ hours), is marked by green arrows. Goats and donkeys may dart across the road, and if you keep your eyes peeled, you may catch sight of large, camouflaged iguanas in the shrubbery.

Bird-watchers are really in their element here. Right inside the park's gate, flamingos roost on the salt pad known as **Salina Mathijs,** and exotic parakeets dot the foot of **Mt. Brandaris,** Bonaire's highest peak at 784 feet. Some 130 species of colorful birds fly in and out of the shrubbery in the park. Keep your eyes open and your binoculars at hand. (For choice beach sites in the park, *see* Beaches, *below.*) Swimming, snorkeling, and scuba diving are permitted, but visitors are requested not to frighten the animals or remove anything from the grounds. There is absolutely no hunting, fishing, or camping allowed. A useful guidebook to the park is available at the entrance for about $6. *Admission: $3 adults, 50¢ children under 15. The park is open daily 8–5, but you must enter before 3:30.*

Beaches

Beaches in Bonaire are not the island's strong point. Don't come expecting Aruba-length stretches of glorious white sand. Bonaire's beaches are smaller, and though the water is indeed blue (several shades of it, in fact), the sand is not always white. You can have your pick of beach in Bonaire according to color: pink, black, or white.

All Bonaire's beaches are open to the public, and good places to swim can be found all along the island's west coast. If you're staying in the vicinity of Kralendijk, you can walk or hitch a ride to beaches at the **Harbour Village Beach Resort** or the **Sunset Beach Hotel.** Another option is to take a water taxi (available from several hotels and dive shops for $12 round-trip) over to **No Name Beach** on Klein Bonaire. Here, with a picnic basket and snorkeling gear, you can play king of the dune in style. Except for a few forgotten sneakers, there is absolutely *nothing* on Klein Bonaire, so remember to take whatever you'll need along. And don't miss the boat back home.

Hermit crabs can be found along the shore at **Boca Cocolishi,** a black-sand beach in Washington/Slagbaai Park on the northeast coast. The dark hues of tiny bits of dried coral and shells that form the basin and beach give the sand an unusual look. Located on the windward side of the island, the water is too rough for anything more than wading; however, the spot is perfect for an intimate picnic à deux. To get there, take the Northern Scenic Route to the park, then ask for directions at the gate.

Also inside Washington Park is **Boca Slagbaai,** a beach of coral fossils and rocks, with interesting coral gardens just offshore that make for fine snorkeling. Bring scuba boots or canvas sandals to walk into the water because the "beach" is rough on bare feet. The gentle surf makes it an ideal place for picnicking or swimming, especially for children.

You'll need a car or strong legs to bicycle south to **Pink Beach,** where the sand boasts a pinkish tint that takes on a magical shimmer in the late-afternoon sun. The water is suitable for swimming, snorkeling, and scuba diving. Take the Southern Scenic Route on the western side of the island, past the Trans-World Radio station, close to the slave huts. A favorite hangout for Bonairians on the weekend, it is virtually deserted during the week.

For uninhibited sun worshipers who'd rather enjoy the rays in the altogether, the private "clothes-optional" **Sorobon Beach Resort** offers calm water, soft clean sand, and refreshing tropical breezes. Nonguests are welcome, but must purchase a $15 day resort pass at the entrance gate.

Boca Cai is across Lac Bay, which is an ideal spot for windsurfing.

Sports and the Outdoors

Scuba Diving   Bonaire has some of the best reef diving this side of Australia's Great Barrier Reef. The island is unique primarily for its incredible dive sites; it takes only 5–25 minutes to reach your site, the current is usually mild, and while some reefs have very sudden, steep drops, most begin just offshore and slope gently downward at a 45° angle. General visibility runs 60 to 100 feet, except during surges in October and November. An enormous range of coral can be seen, from knobby brain and giant brain coral to elkhorn, staghorn, mountainous star, gorgonian, and black coral. You're also likely to encounter schools of parrotfish, surgeonfish, angelfish, eels, snappers, and groupers. Beach diving is excellent just about everywhere on the leeward side of the island.

The well-policed Bonaire Marine Park, which encompasses the entire coastline around Bonaire and Klein Bonaire, remains an underwater wonder because visitors take the rules here seriously. Do not even think about (1) spearfishing, (2) dropping anchor, or (3) touching, stepping on, or collecting coral. Divers must pay an admission charge of $10, for which they receive a colored plastic tag (to be attached to an item of scuba gear) entitling them to one calendar year of unlimited diving in the Marine Park. The fees are used to maintain the underwater park. Tags are available at all scuba facilities and from the Marine Park headquarters in the Old Fort in Kralendijk (tel. 599/7–8444). To help preserve the reef, all dive operations on Bonaire now offer free buoyancy-control, advanced-buoyancy control, and photographic buoyancy-control classes. Check with any dive shop for the schedule.

There is a hyperbaric decompression chamber located next to the hospital in Kralendijk (tel. 599/7–8187 or 599/7–8900 for emergencies).

Dive Operations Most of the hotels listed in this guide have dive centers. The competition for quality and variety is fierce. Before making a room reservation, inquire about specific dive/room packages that are available. The prices for unlimited shore diving (you pay for tanks and weights), boat dives, and rental equipment vary with each dive facility, so it pays to comparison shop. For instance, snorkel-equipment rental costs $5 a day at the Carib Inn Dive Shop, but $11 a day at Great Adventure's Bonaire (at the Harbour Village Beach Resort). Scuba-gear rental ranges from $20 to $40 a day, again depending on the dive shop. **Peter Hughes Dive Bonaire** (Divi Flamingo Beach Resort, tel. 599/7–8285 or 800/367–3484), **Sand Dollar Dive and Photo** (Sand Dollar Beach Club, Caya Gob. de Brot 79, tel. 599/7–5252), and **Habitat Dive Center** (Captain Don's Habitat, Kaya Gob. Debrot 103, tel. 599/7–8290 or 800/327–6709) are all PADI five-star dive facilities qualified to offer both PADI and NAUI certification courses. Sand Dollar Dive and Photo is also qualified to certify dive instructors. Other centers include **Bonaire Scuba Center** (Black Durgon Inn; in the U.S., write Box 775, Morgan, NJ 08879, or call 908/566–8866 or 800/526–2370), **Buddy Dive Resort** (Kaya Gob. N., Debrot 85, tel. 599/7–8647), **Dive Inn** (Kaya C.E.B. Hellmund 27, tel. 599/7–8761 and at the Sunset Beach Hotel, tel. 599/7–8448), **Neal Watson's Bonaire Undersea Adventures** (Coral Regency Resort, Kaya Gob. Debrot 90, tel. 599/7–5580 or 800/327–8150), **Great Adventures Bonaire** (Harbour Village Beach Resort, tel. 599/7–7500 or 800/424–0004), and **Bruce Bowker's Carib Inn Dive Center** (Bruce Bowker's Carib Inn, tel. 599/7–8819, fax 599/7–5295).

Americans Jerry Schnabel and Suzi Swygert of **Photo Tours N.V.** (Kaya Grandi 68, tel. 599/7–8060) specialize in teaching and guiding novice-through-professional underwater photographers. They also offer land-excursion tours of Bonaire's birds, wildlife, and vegetation. **Dee Scarr's Touch the Sea** (Box 369, tel. 599/7–8529) is a personalized (two people at a time) diving program that provides interaction with marine life; it is available to certified divers.

Dive Sites The *Guide to the Bonaire Marine Park* lists 44 sites that have been identified and marked by moorings. In the past few years, however, an additional 42 designated mooring and shore diving sites have been added through a conservation program called Sea Tether. Guides associated with the various dive centers can give you more complete directions. The following are a few popular sites to whet your appetite; these and selected other sites are pinpointed on our Bonaire Diving map.

Take the track down to the shore just behind Trans-World Radio station; dive in and swim south to **Angel City,** one of the shallowest and most popular sites in a two-reef complex that includes **Alice in Wonderland.** The boulder-size green and tan coral heads are home to black margates, Spanish hogfish, gray snappers, and the large, purple tube sponges.

Calabas Reef is located off the Flamingo Beach Hotel. All divers using the hotel's facilities take their warm-up dive here where they can inspect the wreck sunk by Don Stewart for just this purpose. The site is replete with Christmas-tree sponges and fire coral adhering to the ship's hull. Fish life is frenzied, with the occasional octopus putting in an appearance.

Bonaire Diving

Washington/
Slagbaai
National Park

Playa
Funchi

Nukove

Gotomeer

Onima

Rincon

Karpata

Karpata

Rappel

Barcadera

Cliff

Small Wall

Sampler

La Machaca

Ebo's Special

Carl's Hill

Klein
Bonaire

Something
Special

Southwest Corner

Calabas
Reef

Forest

Kralendijk

Caribbean
Sea

Windsock Steep

Flamingo
Airport

Angel City

Southern Scenic Route

Trans-World
Radio

Wanapa

Alice in Wonderland

Salt Pier/Salt City

N

Pink Beach

Pekel Meer

Salt
Flats

0   5 miles
0   5 km

Lighthouse

Lacre Pt.

You'll need to catch a boat to reach **Forest,** a dive site off the coast of Klein Bonaire, so named for the abundant black-coral forest found there. Responsible for occasional currents, this site gets a lot of fish action, including what's been described as a "friendly" spotted eel that lives in a cave.

Small Wall is one of Bonaire's only complete vertical wall dives. Located off the Black Durgon Inn, it is one of the island's most popular night diving spots. Access is made by boat (Black Durgon guests can access it from shore). The 60-foot wall is frequented by sea horses, squid, turtles, tarpon, and barracudas and has dense hard and soft coral formations; it also allows for excellent snorkeling.

Rappel, near the Karpata Ecological Center, is one of the most spectacular dives. The shore is a sheer cliff, and the lush coral growth is home to an unusual variety of marine life, including orange sea horses, squid, spiny lobsters, and a spotted trunk-fish named Sir Timothy that will befriend you for a banana or a piece of cheese.

Something Special, just south of the entrance of the marina, is famous for its garden eels, which slither around the relatively shallow sand terrace.

Windsock Steep, situated in front of the small beach opposite the airport runway, is an excellent first-dive spot and a popular place for snorkeling close to town.

Snorkeling Don't consider snorkeling the cowardly diver's sport; in Bonaire the experience is anything but elementary. For only $8–$11 per day, you can rent a mask, fins, and snorkel at any hotel with a water-sports center (*see* Lodging, *below*). The better spots for snorkeling are on the leeward side of the island, where you have access to the reefs.

Tennis Tennis is available free to guests at the **Sunset Beach Hotel, Divi Flamingo Beach Resort & Casino,** and the **Sand Dollar Beach Club.** Nonguests can play for free during the day at the **Divi Flamingo Beach Resort & Casino** and even take the free tennis clinics on Tuesday and Wednesday mornings (8:30–10). At night, there's a $10 an hour charge. At press time, the Sunset Beach Hotel was considering charging nonguests $10 an hour to use its two courts (currently, only guests can play here).

Windsurfing Lac Bay, a protected cove on the east coast, is ideal for wind-surfing. Novices will find it especially comforting, since there's no way to be blown out to sea. **Windsurfing Bonaire,** known locally as "Jibe City," (fax 599/7–5363; U.S. representative, 800/748–8733) offers courses for beginning to advanced board sailors. Lessons cost $20; board rentals start at $20 an hour; $40 for a half day. There are free regular pickups at all the hotels at 9 AM and 1 PM.

Sea Excursions You can also see the island by boat. The 56-foot Samur (tel. 599/7–5433), an authentic Siamese junk built in Bangkok, offers a four-hour sail, snorkel, and swim cruise to Klein Bonaire for $35 a person, including lunch; a five-hour trip that includes a barbecue on Klein Bonaire's beach is $45. Prices also include as much rum, vodka, and soft drinks as you can handle, snorkel gear, and plenty of food. A two-hour sunset cruise for $25 (half price for children 5–12) is also available. The 37-food trimaran *Windwood* (tel. 599/7–8285) also offers half-day sail, swim, and snorkel cruises to Klein Bonaire four mornings a week. The $29 cost includes snacks, an open bar, and snorkel gear. The two-hour happy hour sunset cruise costs $19 a person; the late afternoon sunset snorkel tour is $22.50 per person. Glass-bottom boat tours are offered aboard the *Bonaire Dream* (no phone). The 1½-hour trip ($15 adults, $7.50 children) leaves Monday–Saturday from the Harbour Village Marina.

Shopping

You can get to know all the shops in Bonaire in a matter of a few hours, but sometimes there's no better way to enjoy some time out of the sun and sea than to go shopping, particularly if your companion is a dive fanatic and you're not. Almost all the shops are situated on the Kaya Grandi or in adjacent streets and tiny malls. There are several snazzy boutiques worth a browse. One word of caution: Buy as many flamingo T-shirts as you want, but don't take home anything made of goatskin or tortoiseshell; they are not allowed into the United States. There are no outdoor craft markets on Bonaire, but some of the better stores carrying unusual handicrafts or reasonably priced Dutch items are listed below.

Kibrahacha Souvenir and Gifts (Bonaire Shopping Gallery, 33 Kaya Grandi, tel. 599/7–8434) features wall hangings, exotic shells and driftwood, embroidered dresses, and Dutch curios. **Littman Gifts** (35 Kaya Grandi, tel. 599/7–8091) is the place for gourmet foods—mouth-watering Dutch cheeses, rye breads, Dutch and American chocolates, and fine wines. Batik cloth by the yard, European costume jewelry, T-shirts, framed underwater pictures, wooden divers, and glass flamingos are also sold. **Caribbean Arts and Crafts** (38-A Kaya Grandi, tel. 599/7–5051) is a welcome newcomer to Bonaire's shopping scene. Here you'll find Mexican onyx, papier-mâché clowns, woven wall tapestries, painted wooden fish and parrots, straw bags, and hand-blown glass vases. **Things Bonaire** (Sunset Beach Hotel, Kaya Grandi 38C, tel. 599/7–8423) offers T-shirts, shorts, colorful earrings, batik dresses, souvenirs, and guidebooks. A government-funded crafts center, **Fundashon Arte Industri Bonairiano** (J. A. Abraham Blvd., Kralendijk, next to the post office, no phone), offers locally made necklaces of coral in a variety of colors, hand-painted shirts and dresses, and the "fresh craft of the day."

Dining

Gourmets aren't sneaking off to Bonaire for five-star cuisine, but restaurants offer a mix of tasty and hearty meals. Happily, fresh local dishes are generally the most reasonably priced menu items. Sample a restaurant's fresh catch of the day, which could be snapper, wahoo, grouper, tuna, or swordfish, all prepared over the grill or panfried in a Creole sauce (usually, a spicy sauce of sweet peppers, tomatoes, and onions). Other favorites are goat stew, stewed conch, fried conch, and *nasi goreng,* an Indonesian meat and rice dish. Most local meals include *funghi* (a medium-firm cornmeal dish), sweet potatoes, and fried plantains. Local appetizers include Kadushi soup, made from the flesh of the Kadushi cactus; iguana soup (available only when someone has caught one of the fleet-footed lizards); and fish soup. Besides the restaurants listed below, budget local food can be found in town at **Julius Place** (Kaya L.D. Gerharts, tel. 599/7–5544) and **La Sonrisa** (Kaya Grande 13, tel. 599/7–5017). The three Chinese restaurants in town also offer budget fare. **Cozzoli's Pizza** (Harbourside Mall, Kralenkijk, tel. 599/7–5195) serves New York–style pizza and is as close as Bonaire comes to a fast-food eatery.

Many accommodations on Bonaire have kitchens. Several larger apartment resorts, such as Sand Dollar Condominiums, will, upon advance request, stock an arriving guest's refrigerator with breakfast basics. Supermarkets on Bonaire tend to be small and carry a limited number of items. Fresh fish, fruit, and vegetables can be found at the harborside **Fish Market** on Caya C.E.B. Hellmund in Kralendijk. **Sand Dollar Grocery** (Sand Dollar Shopping Center; open daily 8–6) has everything from diapers to Dewars on the shelves, plus frozen precooked meals in the freezer. Guests of the Carib Inn usually shop at **Joke's Minimarket** (Kaya Suecia 23), located just across the street. Other popular markets include **Korona Supermarket** (Kaya Korona 89) and **Supermarket Montecatini** (Kaya Grandi 51).

Most restaurants add a 10% service charge to the bill. If not, you should tip your waiter 10%–15%. Hotel restaurants tend to be more pricey than the restaurants in town.

Highly recommended restaurants are indicated by a star ★.

Category	Cost*
Moderate	$15–$20
Inexpensive	$10–$15
Budget	under $10

*Per person, excluding drinks and service. There is no sales tax.

Den Laman Bar & Restaurant. A 6,000-foot aquarium provides the backdrop to this nautically decorated, sea-breezy restaurant. Eat indoors next to the glass-enclosed "ocean show" (request a table in advance) or outdoors on the noisier patio overlooking the sea. Pick a fresh Caribbean lobster from the tank, or choose red snapper Creole, which is a hands-down winner. *77 Gob. Debrot, next to the Sunset Beach Hotel, tel. 599/7–8599. Reservations advised. AE, MC, V. Closed Tues. Dinner only. Moderate.*

★ **The Rendez-Vous Restaurant.** From the terrace of this bistro-like café in Kralendijk, watch the world of Bonaire go by as you fill up on warm bread, hearty soups, seafood, steaks, and vegetarian specialties. Or munch on light pastries accompanied by steamy espresso. *3 Kaya L. D. Gerharts, tel. 599/7–8454. AE. Dinner only. Closed Tues. Moderate.*

★ **Richard's Waterfront Dining.** This casually romantic alfresco eatery on the water may be the best restaurant on the island. Located on the airport side of Kralendijk and next door to a seafood stand, Richard's specializes in grilled seafood dishes. Chef Bonito caters to an American palate, serving up flavorful, not spicy, dishes. Although the menu is limited, the food is consistently excellent. Among the best dishes are conch *alajillo* (fillet of conch with garlic and butter), shrimp primavera, and grilled wahoo. Start with the fish soup, a tasty broth with chunks of the catch of the day. A new pier lets you arrive by boat. The sunset happy hour is popular with locals. *60 J. A. Abraham Blvd., a few houses away from the Carib Inn, tel. 599/7–5263. Reservations advised. AE, MC, V. Dinner only. Closed Mon. Inexpensive–Moderate.*

The Green Parrot. This family-run restaurant, on the dock of the Sand Dollar Beach Club, features the biggest hamburgers and the best strawberry margaritas on the island. Try the onion-string appetizer, which consists of onion rings shaped into a small bread loaf. Bagels with cream cheese, chargrilled steaks, Creole fish, and barbecue chicken and ribs are also served. American expatriates like to hang out here and watch the setting sun. *Sand Dollar Beach Club, tel. 599/7–5454. Reservations advised in high season. AE, MC, V. Inexpensive.*

Zeezicht Bar & Restaurant. Zeezicht (pronounced *zay-zeekt* and meaning sea view) is one of the better restaurants open for both breakfast and lunch in town. At lunch you'll get basic American fare with an Antillean touch, such as fish omelet. Dinner is either on the terrace overlooking the harbor or upstairs inside a romantic, air-conditioned enclave that's popular with couples and honeymooners. Locals are dedicated to this hangout, especially for the ceviche, conch sandwiches, local snails in hot sauce, and the Zeezicht special soup with conch, fish, shrimps, and oysters. After dessert, stop in the garden to see the monkey and parrots. *10 Kaya Corsow, across from Karel's Beach Bar, tel. 599/7–8434. AE, MC, V. Inexpensive (downstairs)–Moderate (upstairs).*

China Garden Restaurant and Bar. Despite its name, this place has an everything-you-could-ever-want menu, from American sandwiches to shark's-fin soup, steaks, lobster, even omelets. But Cantonese dishes are still the specialty. Try the goat Chinese style, anything in black-bean sauce, or one of the sweet-and-sour dishes. Lots of locals turn up between 5 and 7 PM to have a drink and watch the latest in sports on the bar's cable TV. At press time, the sleazy decor was scheduled for a change. *47 Kaya Grandi, tel. 599/7–8480. Reservations advised in high season. AE, DC, MC, V. Closed Tues. Budget.*

Mona Lisa Bar & Restaurant. This restaurant offers authentic Dutch fare, along with a few Indonesian dishes, at unbeatable prices. Its most famous plate is the pork tenderloin *sate* drizzled with a special peanut-butter sauce. Somehow, Mona Lisa has become renowned for fresh vegetables, though God knows where they come from, since nearly everything in Bonaire has to be imported. This is a late-night hangout for local schmoozing and light snacks, which are served until about 2 AM. *15 Kaya Grandi, tel. 599/7–8718. MC, V. Closed Sun. Budget–Inexpensive.*

Je-Mar Health Shop. Bonaire's answer to the health craze, this tiny shop serves tofu burgers and salads alongside aisles of health food products. Decor is nonexistent. It's open weekdays from 7 AM–7 PM. *Kaya Grandi, tel. 599/7–5012. MC, V. Closed weekends. Budget.*

Lodging

Hotels on Bonaire cater primarily to avid divers who spend their days under water and come up for air only for evening festivities. Hence, hotel facilities tend to be modest, with small swimming pools and limited service. Groomed sandy beaches are less important to these hotels than efficient dive shops. In the last few years, several apartment complexes have been built, offering modern amenities at moderate prices. But even rooms in many affordable resorts here offer the same fully equipped kitchens found in apartment complexes—together with the facilities of a full-scale hotel. Most of the true budget properties on Bonaire are older than the more recently built complexes, but many have undergone renovations that include air-conditioning, modern bathrooms, microwave ovens in kitchens, and upgraded furnishings. Unlike budget accommodations on many other islands, Bonaire's guest houses are often within walking distance of a beach.

Most hotels, apartment resorts, guest houses, and villas are located along the west coast just north or south of Kralendijk. Large hotels offer several meal plans, with a full American breakfast (BP) averaging $9 a person, and a breakfast and dinner plan (MAP) costing about $35 per person per day. Only one hotel, the Divi Flamingo Beach Resort & Casino, offers an all-inclusive option, with all meals, drinks, and dives included in the value-oriented package. Always ask for a hotel's package rate, as it usually includes breakfast, airport transfers, some diving, taxes, service charges, and gratuities at a rate that is less than à la carte prices. High season runs from mid-December until mid-April, with prices reduced anywhere from 15%–30% the rest of the year.

Highly recommended lodgings are indicated by a star ★.

Category	Cost*
Moderate	$110–$150
Inexpensive	$80–$110
Budget	under $80

* All prices are for a standard double room for two in high season, excluding a $4.10 per person, per night government room tax and a 10% service charge. To estimate rates for hotels offering MAP, add about $35 per person per day to the above price ranges. For all-inclusives, add about $70 per person per day.

Hotels and Resorts

★ **Captain Don's Habitat.** With its recent expansion and massive renovation, the Habitat, once a sort of extended home of Captain Don Stewart, the island's wildest sharpshooting personality, can no longer pass itself off as a mere guest house for divers. Stewart's Curaçaon partners have poured money into this resort, adding a set of upscale rooms (Junior suites) and then a long row of private villas (the Hamlet section). Villas have three bedrooms and can be rented in their entirety (not affordable unless you are traveling with others) or by bedroom. The villas rank among the island's best: all with ocean-view verandas, full kitchens, and spacious, stylish arrangements. The rooms in the original 11 cottages are roomy but in need of renovation (which is scheduled to be completed by 1994). Only the rates for the cottages—with two bedrooms, they're ideal for two couples traveling together—and the villa deluxe studio apartments fall within our Moderate range. The atmosphere at the Habitat is laid-back and easygoing, with the emphasis on the staff's personal warmth rather than on spick-and-span efficiency. The beachfront property units are spaced widely apart, and the grounds have been landscaped with rocks and cacti. Be sure to meet Captain Don, who shows up twice a week just to say hello and tell his incredible tales, most of which are actually true. In August, the resort hosts two all-inclusive family weeks with a full schedule of activities and learning for children. A full dive center with seven boats, complete with a resident photo pro, rounds out the picture. *Kaya Gob. Debrot 103, Box 88, tel. 599/7-8290. U.S. representative: Habitat North American, tel. 800/327-6709, fax 599/7-8240. 11 cottages, 11 villas, 16 rooms. Facilities: 2 bars, restaurant, gift shop, pool, cruises, baby-sit-*

ting, laundry facilities, bicycles, dive center, photo labs. AE, DC, MC, V. EP, BP, MAP, FAP. Moderate.

★ **Sand Dollar Beach Club.** Studio apartments at this condominium resort—larger units do not fall within our Moderate price range—feature a European design with a tropical rattan decor. They're long and narrow, with either a queen-size sleep sofa or a foldout bed, a full kitchen, cable color TV, private balcony or patio, and a bathroom. Two couples traveling together will find excellent value in the spacious two bedroom/two bathroom units here. There's daily maid service (maids will do your laundry for $4 a load). Lots of Americans stay here, especially serious divers and their families. There's an on-premise PADI five-star dive center, a limited activities club for children, and two lighted tennis courts. The miniscule beach disappears at high tide. The resort's waterfront Green Parrot restaurant serves breakfast, lunch, and dinner, and there's a grocery store for those who like to cook. *Kaya Grandi, tel. 599/7–8738, fax 599/7–8760; in the U.S., tel. 800/766–6016 or 617/821–1012. 77 studio, 1-, 2-, and 3-bedroom units and 8 two-bedroom town houses. Facilities: restaurant, bar, dive center, photo lab, pool, 2 lighted tennis courts, outdoor showers, cable TV, strip shopping center, grocery/convenience store. AE, DC, MC, V. EP, BP, MAP, FAP. Moderate.*

Sorobon Beach Resort. This delightfully unpretentious, small resort is for naturalists who take its clothing-optional motto seriously. An intimate cluster of cottages on a private beach at Lac Bay, it attracts a mix of Europeans and Americans. Room rates are at the top end of our Moderate category. Chalets consist of two small one-bedroom units, each with simple furnishings, an older-style kitchen, and a shower bath. In keeping with the get-away-from-it-all concept, there's no air-conditioning, TV, or telephone. A daily shuttle will take you to town. Relax sitting around moonlight bonfires, playing ping-pong, or enjoying a shiatsu massage all on the beach. More diversion comes from a nature-oriented book and video library and a telescope to view the stunning night skies. The heady windsurfing in Lac Bay, a result of the unbeatable combo of shallow bay and strong trade winds, draws raves. But act blasé when the manager arrives wrapped in a towel. *Box 14, tel. 599/7–8080, fax 599/7–5363. 25 cottages. Facilities: kitchenettes, restaurant, bar, library, water-sports center. AE, MC, V. EP. Moderate.*

Divi Flamingo Beach Resort and Casino. The Divi Flamingo is the closest thing you'll find to a small village on Bonaire—a plantation-style resort that will serve your every need. Unfortunately, only the standard category accommodations fall into our Moderate price range, and these are in sore need of new furnishings and fresh paint. Despite showing signs of age, the resort still has an excellent dive facility and an upbeat activities program. Many guests choose the all-inclusive option, a good value for serious divers. The dive facility, Dive Bonaire, was founded by world-class expert Peter Hughes and features some of the best photo labs in the Caribbean. Several rooms are accessible to the handicapped, and the dive operation even has specially trained masters who teach and dive with the handicapped. The on-premise tennis pro offers free clinics Tuesday and Wednesday mornings, live bands perform several nights a week, and the island's only casino—billed as the world's only barefoot gaming center—is here as well. *J. A. Abraham Blvd., tel. 599/7–8285. U.S. representative: Divi Ho-*

tels, tel. 800/367–3484, fax 599/7–8238. 105 rooms, 40 time-share units. Facilities: casino, 2 restaurants, 2 pools, 2 dive shops, jewelry store, lighted tennis court, 3 bars, 2 car-rental desks, tour desk, Jacuzzi, boutique. AE, D, MC, V. EP, MAP, All-inclusive. Moderate.

Sunset Beach Hotel. Despite recent and sweeping renovations at this hotel (formerly the Bonaire Beach Hotel), tired-looking rooms and bathrooms still lack brightness and appeal. And no amount of renovation could change the location or the buildings, which are all set back from the shore, giving even the best rooms only garden views. Still, the 12 acres encompass one of the island's better hotel beaches (in contrast to the swimming pool, which is tiny), a miniature golf course, a water-sports concession that offers more than any other on the island, and a romantic thatch-roof restaurant overlooking the sea. Unfortunately, the food is not the island's best, and the superfriendly service is not always efficient. Divers come for the complete on-premise scuba center, Dive Inn, which has three dive boats. Nondivers can rent Sunfish, Windsurfers, and snorkeling gear, or go parasailing or boogie boarding. *Kaya Gob. Debrot 75, Box 333, tel. 599/7–8448. U.S./Canada rep: 800/333–1212 800/344–4439 or 800/223–9815, fax 599/7–8118. 142 rooms, 3 one-bedroom suites. Facilities: alfresco restaurant, bar/lounge, beach, dive center, water-sports center, water taxi to Klein Bonaire, miniature golf, shuffleboard, 2 lighted tennis courts, billiards, ping-pong, tour desk, gift shop, car rental. AE, MC, V. EP, MAP, FAP. Inexpensive.*

Buddy Dive Center. Europeans who tend to eschew luxury and require only basic amenities with matching rates enjoy this growing complex situated on the beach. In keeping with its no-frills style, the five units on the ground level have no air-conditioning and no TV; the five second-floor units have air-conditioning. These original 10 "apartments" are tiny but clean, with a kitchenette, tile floors, twin beds, a sleep sofa, and a shower-only bathroom. In early 1993, the first of two new buildings containing more upscale, spacious, and air-conditioned two- and three-bedroom apartments opened. A dive operation and pool is also on the premises. *Kaya Gob. Debrot, Box 231, tel 599/7–8065 or 800/359–0747, fax 599/7–2647. 10 apartments, 15 two- and three-bedroom condominium units. Facilities: pool with bar, dive shop. AE, MC, V. EP. Budget.*

Guests Houses The **Tourism Corporation of Bonaire** (Kaya Libertador Simon Bolivar 12, Kralendijk, Bonaire, Dutch Caribbean, tel. 599/7–8322 or 599/7–8649, fax 599/7–8408) will mail or fax a list of guest houses and bungalows offering rooms for rent.

★ **Bruce Bowker's Carib Inn.** Sixteen years ago, American diver Bruce Bowker started his small diving lodge out of a private home, continually adding on and refurbishing the air-conditioned inn. New rattan furnishings, completely renovated kitchens, and a family-style atmosphere have turned this inn into one of the island's best bets—and one that repeat guests book far in advance. Bowker knows everybody by name and loves to fill special requests. The two units with no kitchen have a refrigerator and electric kettle, but for more involved dining you'll have to leave the premises—there's no restaurant. (Richard's Waterfront Restaurant is right next door.) Those who prefer to cook can shop for supplies at the grocery store across the street. Nervous virgin divers will enjoy Bowker's small scuba classes (one or two people); PADI certification is available. *Box 68, tel. 599/7–8819. U.S. rep: ITR, tel. 800/223–9815 or 212/545–8649, fax 599/7–599/7–5295. 9 units. Facilities: pool, dive center, retail dive store, cable TV. AE, MC, V. EP. Budget.*

Leeward Inn. American owners Don and Ditta Balstra have restored this 80-year-old guest house and modernized its five rooms. Guests come for the friendly service and the inexpensive meals at the on-site Harthouse Cafe as well as for the budget-priced, basic accommodations. The pastel-painted rooms have light tile floors, twin beds, white Formica furnishings, and modern bathrooms (shower only, except for one handicap-accessible room). There are no TVs, no phones, and no air-conditioning (ceiling fans and tropical breezes keep things cool). The location, just three short blocks from the heart of Kralendijk, is a block from the sea and a 10-minute walk to the Divi Flamingo beach. *Kaya Grandi 60, Kralendijk, tel. 599/7–5516, 601/353–7547, or 800/748–8733, fax 599/7–5517. 4 rooms, 1 suite. Facilities: restaurant, dive shop. AE, MC, V. EP. Budget.*

Sunset Inn. This pleasant property has seven hotel rooms, a community kitchen, and a small public beach across the street. The Dive Inn dive shop is adjacent to the guest house and offers guests dive packages as well as PADI instruction. The rooms are smallish and basic, with showers, color TVs, refrigerators, and air-conditioning. *Kaya C.E.B. Hellmund 29, tel. 599/7–8448 or 800/344–4439, fax 599/7–8118. 7 units. AE, MC, V. EP. Budget.*

Villa and Apartment Rentals Island villa and apartment rentals run the gamut from apartments in resort hotels to efficiency units to stand-alone houses rented by the week. Generally resort hotel units (described in Hotels and Resorts, *above*) cost more, but they offer on-site facilities that may be worth the extra price. Two families traveling together will find a wide selection of properties to choose from. The **Tourism Corporation of Bonaire** (tel. 800/U-BONAIR) can help locate guest houses and smaller rental apartments.

Diversion. The Dutch owners decided Bonaire needed modern, amenity-laden apartments geared toward divers with a thin wallet but a yen for the upscale, so they built these seven one-bedroom apartments north of hotel row in 1991. For about $950 a week (minimum one-week stay), you get a medium-sized apartment overlooking the sea, daily maid service, unlimited scuba air tanks and weight belts, plus a minivan for driving to the island's gold mine of shore diving. Each apartment comes with a fully equipped kitchen, a porch, lockable "wet room" for scuba gear, telephone, cable TV, air-conditioned bedroom, and a sleep sofa in the living room. *Box 104, Kralendijk, tel. 599/7–8659 or 599/7–8427, fax 599/7–5327. 7 one-bedroom units. MC, V. Inexpensive.*

Sunset Oceanfront Apartments. One- and two-bedroom apartments that overlook the sea are available at this small complex with pool, located just a three-minute walk from downtown Kralendijk. All of the apartments feature color TVs, air-conditioned bedrooms, and small kitchenettes with refrigerator and microwave oven. *Kaya Lodewijk D. Gerarts 22, Kralendijk, tel. 599/7–8291 or 800/344–4439, fax 599/7–8865. 12 units. Facilities: pool. AE, MC, V. Moderate.*

Sunset Villas. Spread out around the island are these 17 properties, ranging from efficiency studio apartments to a four-bedroom villa. Several are on the water, but none have a beach or a pool. All of the villas sleep a minimum of four people, have air-conditioned bedrooms, and washing machines and dryers. In general, the furnishings in these properties are a bit old and run-down, although some units are nicer than others. Maid service is only once a week. *Sunset Resorts, Box 333, Kralendijk, tel. 599/7–8291 or 800/344–4439, fax 599/7–8118. 17 units. AE, MC, V. Budget–Moderate.*

Off-Season Bets Between mid-April and mid-December is low season on Bonaire, and the time when hotel rates go down by as much as 30%. Two people traveling together can stay in a spacious one-bedroom unit for less than $135 a night at the **Coral Regency** (Kaya Gob. Debrot 91, tel. 599/7–5580 or 800/327–8150) or in a one-bedroom unit at the **Sand Dollar Condominiums** (*see above*) for $155 a night.

The Arts and Nightlife

The Arts Slide shows of underwater scenes keep both divers and nondivers fascinated in the evenings. The best is Dee Scarr, a dive guide whose show "Touch the Sea" is presented Monday night at 8:45, from the beginning of November to the end of June, at **Captain Don's Habitat** (tel. 599/7–8290). Check with the Habitat for other shows throughout the week. **Sunset Beach Hotel** (tel. 599/7–8448) offers a free one-hour slide show every Wednesday evening at 7. **Divi Flamingo Beach Resort** (tel. 599/7–8285) offers a free underwater video, "Discover the Caribbean," on Sunday night at 7 PM.

The best singer on the island is guitarist **Cai-Cai Cecelia,** who performs with his duo Monday night at the **Divi Flamingo Beach Resort,** Wednesday night at **Sunset Beach Hotel,** and Thursday night at **Captain Don's Habitat.** He sings his own compositions, as well as Harry Belafonte classics. The **Kunuku Band** plays every Friday and Sunday happy hour at Captain Don's Habitat. The **M & M Duo** entertains three nights a week at the Chibi Chibi restaurant at the Divi Flamingo Beach Resort.

Nightlife Most divers are exhausted after they finish their third, fourth, or fifth dive of the day, which probably explains why there's only one disco in Bonaire. Nevertheless, **E Wowo** (Kralendijk, at the corner of Kaya Grandi and Kaya L. D. Gerharts, no phone) is usually packed in high season, so get there early. The name E Wowo means "eye" in Papiamento, illustrated with two flashing op-art eyes on the wall. Recorded music is loud, and the large circular bar seats a lot of action. The entrance fee varies according to the season.

For after-hours conversations, **The Rendez-Vous Restaurant** (Kaya L. D. Gerharts 3, tel. 599/7–8454) is open late, with light pastries and espresso, as are the **Mona Lisa Bar & Restaurant** (Kaya Grandi 15, tel. 599/7–8718) and **Raffles** (*see* Dining, *above*).

The popular bar **Karel's** (tel. 599/7–8434), on the waterfront across from the Zeezicht Restaurant, sits on stilts above the sea and is *the* place for mingling with islanders, dive pros, and tourists. Closed Monday.

Friday and Saturday nights are party time, when B»nairians gather along the main street of Kralendijk to dance to informal bands that set up on the sidewalk.

7 The British Virgin Islands

Tortola, Virgin Gorda, and Outlying Islands

*Updated by
Pamela Acheson*

Serene, seductive, and spectacularly beautiful even by Caribbean standards, the British Virgin Islands are happily free of the runaway development that has detracted from the charm of so many West Indian islands. The pleasures to be found here are of the understated sort—sailing around the multitude of tiny nearby islands; diving to the wreck of the RMS *Rhone*, sunk off Salt Island in 1867; exploring the twisting passages and sunlit grottoes of Virgin Gorda's famed Baths; and settling down on some breeze-swept terrace to admire the sunset. There are just over 50 islands in the archipelago. Tortola, about 10 square miles, is the largest of the British islands, and Virgin Gorda, with 8 square miles, ranks second. Scattered around them are the islands of Jost Van Dyke; Great Camanoe; Norman; Peter; Salt; Cooper; Dead Chest; the low-lying, coral Anegada; and others.

Some of the most luxurious and expensive resorts in the Caribbean are scattered throughout the B.V.I. In addition, yacht owners and those on expensive private charters make up a significant portion of the B.V.I.'s visitors, furthering the islands' reputation as a genteel, costly destination. Nevertheless, there are a number of reasonably priced hotels and restaurants here. Many—though not all—accommodations are on or near beaches, and some include cooking facilities, so renting a car or eating out aren't always necessities. Sailors will discover bare-boat charters at affordable rates. There are even a handful of campgrounds in the B.V.I., a relatively uncommon phenomenon in the Caribbean. Nightlife, too (what there is of it) can be a bargain. Many local bands and singers perform at informal open-air bars and restaurants; it's possible to hear great music for the price of a drink.

The lack of direct-air flights from the mainland United States helps the British islands retain the endearing qualities of yesteryear's Caribbean. One first has to get to Puerto Rico, 60 miles to the west, or to nearby St. Thomas in the United States Virgin Islands, and catch a small plane to the little airports on Beef Island/Tortola and Virgin Gorda. Many of the travelers who return year after year prefer arriving by water. Sailing has always been a popular activity in the B.V.I. The first arrivals here were a seafaring tribe, the Siboney Indians. Christopher Columbus was the first European to visit, during his second voyage to the New World, in 1493.In the ensuing years, the Spaniards passed through these waters seeking gold and preying on passing galleons crammed with Mexican and Peruvian gold, silver, and spices. Among the most notorious of these predatory men were Blackbeard Teach; Bluebeard; Captain Kidd; and Sir Francis Drake, who lent his name to the channel that sweeps through the two main clusters of the B.V.I.

In the 17th century, these colorful cutthroats were replaced by the Dutch, who were soon sent packing by the British. They established a plantation economy and brought in African slaves to work the cane fields while the plantation owners and their families reaped the benefits. When slavery was abolished in 1838, the plantation economy quickly faltered, and the majority of the white population returned to Europe. The islands dozed, a forgotten corner of the British empire, until the early 1960s. In 1966, a new constitution, granting greater autonomy to the islands, was approved.

What It Will Cost These sample prices, meant only as a general guide, are for high season. Price estimates are for high season. An inexpensive hotel will be about $100 a night; a budget hotel room can be had for about $60. A two-bedroom villa rents for around $250 a night—$125 per couple if shared. Dinner at a budget restaurant will cost about $9; a sandwich lunch is around $6. Expect to pay a hefty $3 for a beer at a restaurant, and a similar price for a glass of house wine or a rum punch. Four-wheel-drive vehicles rent for $40–$50 a day. Taxis are expensive here: A trip from Road Town to Cane Garden Bay on Tortola is about $15; on Virgin Gorda, it's $20 from Spanish Town to Leverick Bay. A single-tank dive averages $60; daily snorkel equipment rents for about $10.

Before You Go

Tourist Information Information about the B.V.I. is available through the **British Virgin Islands Tourist Board** (370 Lexington Ave., Suite 416, New York, NY 10017, tel. 212/696–0400 or 800/835–8530) or at the **British Virgin Islands Information Office** in San Francisco (1686 Union St., Suite 305, San Francisco, CA 94123, tel. 415/775–0344, 800/922–4873 in CA, or 800/232–7770). British travelers can write or visit the **BVI Information Office** (110 St. Martin's La., London WC2N 4DY, tel. 071/2404259).

Arriving and Departing
By Plane No nonstop service is available from the United States to the B.V.I.; connections are usually made through San Juan, Puerto Rico, or St. Thomas. U.S.V.I. Airlines serving both San Juan and St. Thomas include **American** (tel. 800/433–7300), **Continental** (tel. 800/231–0856), and **Delta** (tel. 800/323–2323). **Key**

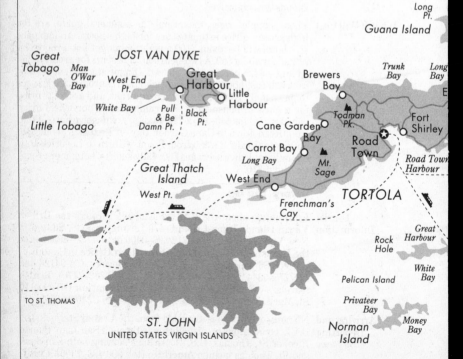

A T L A N T I C

Long
Pt.
Guana Island

Great
Tobago
Man
O'War
Bay

JOST VAN DYKE

West End
Pt.

Great
Harbour

Little
Harbour

Trunk
Bay

Long
Bay

White Bay
Pull
& Be
Damn Pt.

Black
Pt.

Brewers
Bay

Little Tobago

Cane Garden
Bay

Todman
Pk.

Fort
Shirley

E

Carrot Bay

Long Bay

Road
Town

Road Town
Harbour

Great Thatch
Island

West End

Mt.
Sage

TORTOLA

West Pt.

Frenchman's
Cay

Rock
Hole

Great
Harbour

TO ST. THOMAS

Pelican Island

White
Bay

Privateer
Bay

ST. JOHN
UNITED STATES VIRGIN ISLANDS

Norman
Island

Money
Bay

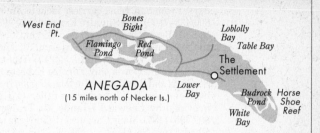
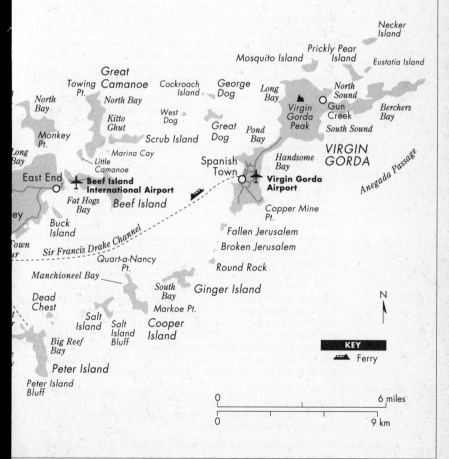

Airlines (tel. 800/786–2386) flies to St. Thomas from major cities through its Savannah, Georgia, hub on Thursdays and Sundays. From San Juan, carriers include **American Eagle** (tel. 800/433–7300), and **Sunaire Express** (809/495–2480), which fly to both Beef Island/Tortola and Virgin Gorda. Airlines flying to those same two destinations from St. Thomas are Sunaire Express and **Virgin Air** (tel. 809/495–1735); American Eagle flies to Virgin Gorda only. Sunaire Express also flies between St. Croix and Beef Island/Tortola. Regularly scheduled service between the B.V.I. and most other Caribbean islands is provided by **Leeward Islands Air Transport** (LIAT) (tel. 809/495–1187). Many Caribbean islands can also be reached via **Gorda Aero Service** (tel. 809/495–2271), a charter service.

From the Airport There is no bus service from the airports, and taxis (often in the form of minivans and open-air safari buses) are expensive. Fares are officially set, but can seem confusing. It's best to tell the taxi driver the number in your group and your destination and to make sure you understand the price before you get in the taxi (if the amount seems out of line, go to a different driver). Fare from the Beef Island/Tortola airport to Wickham's Cay I in Road Town (20 minutes) is a flat fee of $15 for one, two, or three people traveling together and $5 for each additional person traveling with the same party. The fare to West End (45 minutes) is a flat fee of $30 for one, two, or three people and $10 for each additional person. If there are no cabs, call the **B.V.I. Taxi Association** at Wickham's Cay I (tel. 809/494–2322). If you're planning to rent a car, **Airways Car Rental** (tel. 809/495–2161) is located across from the airport.

On Virgin Gorda, **Andy's Taxi** (tel. 809/495–5511) and **Mahogany Taxi Service** (tel. 809/495–5469) take people from the airport to the Spanish Town/Yacht Harbour area for $2 per person. Rates to Leverick Bay/North Sound are $20 a person, with reduced rates for children and large groups. Drivers meet incoming flights.

By Boat Various ferries connect St. Thomas, U.S.V.I., with Tortola and Virgin Gorda. **Native Son, Inc.** (tel. 809/495–4617), operates three ferries *(Native Son, Oriole, or Voyager Eagle),* and offers service between St. Thomas and Tortola (West End and Road Town) daily and between St. Thomas and Spanish Town, Virgin Gorda, on Wednesday and Sunday. **Smiths Ferry Services** (tel. 809/494–4430 or 809/494–2355) carries passengers between downtown St. Thomas and Road Town and West End on Monday through Saturday, offers daily service between Red Hook on St. Thomas and Tortola's West End, and travels between St. Thomas and Spanish Town on Sunday. **Inter-Island Boat Services'** *Sundance II* (tel. 809/776–6597) connects St. John and West End on Tortola daily. Fares are $17 one-way, $32 round-trip between St. Thomas and Tortola (any port); $16 one-way, $28 round-trip between St. John and Tortola; and $45 round-trip between St. Thomas and Virgin Gorda ($25 Virgin Gorda to St. Thomas, $20 St. Thomas to Virgin Gorda).

Passports and Visas Upon entering the B.V.I., U.S. and Canadian citizens are required to present some proof of citizenship, if not a passport then a birth certificate or voter-registration card with a driver's license or photo ID.

Lanºuage British English, with a West Indian inflection, is the language spoken.

strongly recommend renting a four-wheel drive vehicle. Driving is *à l'Anglais,* on the left side of the road. Speed limits are 30–40 mph outside town and 10–15 mph in residential areas. A valid B.V.I. driver's license is required and can be obtained for $10 at car rental agencies. You must be at least 25 and have a valid driver's license from another country to obtain one.

In Road Town, four-wheel-drive vehicles can be rented for $42 per day and at the special "one-day-free" weekly rate of $252 (passenger cars are $35) from Ms. Burke at **Budget** (Wickham's Cay I, tel. 809/494–2639). At West End, **Hertz** (tel. 809/495–4405) rents four-wheel-drive vehicles for $45 a day and $270 a week. Rentals are also available from **AVIS** (tel. 809/494–3322) and **National** (tel. 809/494–3197). On Virgin Gorda, try **Mahogany Rentals** (tel. 809/495–5469) or **Andy's Taxi and Jeep Rental** (tel. 809/495–5511).

Taxis Taxis are generally expensive in the B.V.I., with the exception of the $2 taxi-shuttles between Virgin Gorda's airport and the Spanish Town/Yacht Harbour area. On Tortola, expect to pay a flat rate of $15 for one, two, or three people ($5 each additional passenger) from Road Town to Cane Garden Bay, to Long Bay, and to West End. On Virgin Gorda, expect to pay $20 (for the first three people) from Spanish Town to Leverick Bay. On Tortola, there is a B.V.I. Taxi Association stand in Road Town near the ferry dock (tel. 809/494–3456) and Wickhams Cay I (tel. 809/494–2322) and one on Beef Island, at the airport (tel. 809/495–2466). You can also usually find a taxi at the Sopers Hole ferry dock, West End, where ferries from St. Thomas arrive. On Virgin Gorda, Mahogany or Andy's (*see above*) also provide taxi service.

Buses On Tortola, **Scato's Bus Service** (tel. 809/494–2365) has regular daily bus runs from Road Town (opposite the ferry dock) to Cane Garden Bay, Sebastians, West End, and back to Road Town. The fare is $3 one-way; if you tell the driver when you want to return, he'll make sure you get picked up. Call for schedules. There are no buses on Virgin Gorda.

Mopeds and **D.J.'s Scooters** (tel. 809/494–5071) rents mopeds for $9 per
Bicycles hour/single, $12 per hour/double, $26 per day/single, $37 per day/double. On Virgin Gorda, **Honda Scooter Rental** (tel. 809/495–5212) rents mopeds.

Telephones The area code for the B.V.I. is 809. To call anywhere in the B.V.I.
and Mail once you've arrived, dial only the last five digits. A local call from a public pay phone costs 25¢. Pay phones are frequently on the blink, but using them is often easier with a **Caribbean Phone Card,** available in $5, $10, and $20 denominations. The cards are sold at most major hotels and many stores and can be used all over the Caribbean. For credit-card or collect long-distance calls to the United States, look for special U.S.A. Direct phones that are linked to an AT&T operator, or dial 111 from a pay phone and charge the call to your MasterCard or Visa. U.S.A. Direct and pay phones can be found at most hotels and in towns.

There are post offices in Road Town on Tortola and in Spanish Town on Virgin Gorda. Postage for a first-class letter to the United States is 35¢ and for a postcard 20¢. (It might be noted that postal efficiency is not first-class in the B.V.I.) For a small fee, **Rush It** in Road Town (809/494–4421) or Spanish Town

Precautions Although there are generally no perils in drinking the water in these islands, it is a good idea to ask if the water is potable when you check in to your hotel. Insects, notably mosquitoes, are not usually a problem in these breeze-blessed isles, but it is always a good idea to bring some repellent along. Animals in the B.V.I. are not dangerous, but can be road hazards. Give goats, sheep, horses, and cows the right-of-way. Beware of the little varmints called no-see-ums. Apply some type of repellent liberally if you'll be near the water at twilight. No-see-um bites itch worse than mosquito bites and take longer to go away. Prevention is the best cure, but witch hazel (or a dab of gin or vodka) offers some relief if they get you.

Staying in the British Virgin Islands

Important Addresses On Tortola there is a **B.V.I. Tourist Board Office** at the center of Road Town near the ferry dock, just south of Wickham's Cay I (Box 134, Road Town, Tortola, tel. 809/494–3134). For all kinds of useful information about these islands, including rates and phone numbers, get a free copy of *The Welcome Tourist Guide*, available at hotels and other places.

Emergencies Dial 999 for a medical emergency. On Tortola there is **Peebles Hospital** in Road Town (tel. 809/494–3497). Virgin Gorda has two clinics, one in Spanish Town (tel. 809/495–5337) and one at North Sound (tel. 809/495–7310). Pharmacies in Road Town include **J.R. O'Neal Drug Store** (tel. 809/494–2292) and **Lagoon Plaza Drug Store** (tel. 809/494–2498). On Virgin Gorda, the Spanish Town pharmacy is **Medicure** (tel. 809/495–5182).

Currency British though they are, the B.V.I. use the U.S. dollar as the standard currency.

Taxes and Service Charges Hotels collect a 7% accommodations tax, which they will add to your bill along with a 10% service charge. Restaurants may put a similar service charge on the bill, or they may leave it up to you. For those leaving the B.V.I. by air, the departure tax is $5; by sea it is $4. There is no sales tax. Some merchants add a charge for credit-card purchases.

Getting Around
Boat Ferries run between Tortola and Virgin Gorda (both North Sound and Spanish Town), Jost Van Dyke, and Peter Island. All make two or three daily runs, unless otherwise noted. **Speedy's Fantasy** (tel. 809/495–5240) makes the run between Road Town, Tortola, and Spanish Town, Virgin Gorda daily. Fares are $10 one-way, $19 round-trip. Running daily between Virgin Gorda's North Sound (Bitter End Yacht Club) and Beef Island/Tortola are **North Sound Express** (tel. 809/494–2746) boats. Fares are $18 one-way, $36 round-trip. There are also daily boats between Tortola's CSY Dock just east of Road Town and Peter Island. Fare is $10 round-trip (free if you're having dinner on Peter Island; seven runs daily; tel. 809/494–2561 for schedule). **Jost Van Dyke Ferry Service** (no phone) makes the Jost Van Dyke–Tortola run daily via the *When* ferry. Fare is $7 one-way, $14 round-trip.

Cars Driving on Tortola and Virgin Gorda is not for the timid. Roller-coaster roads with breathtaking ascents and descents and tight turns that give new meaning to the term hairpin curves are the norm. It's a challenge well worth trying, however; the ever-changing views of land, sea, and neighboring islands are among the most spectacular in the Caribbean. Most people will

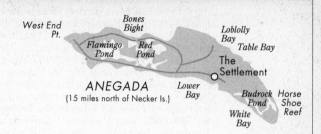

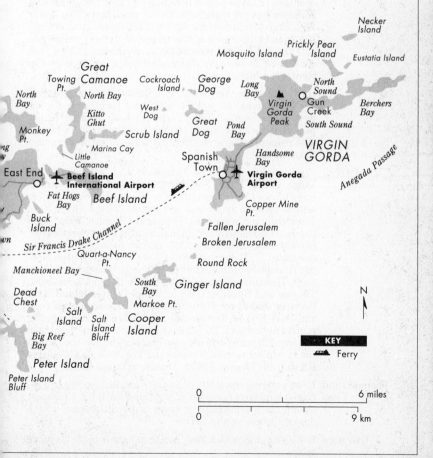

KEY

Ferry

| 0 | | | 6 miles |

| 0 | | | 9 km |

Airlines (tel. 800/786–2386) flies to St. Thomas from major cities through its Savannah, Georgia, hub on Thursdays and Sundays. From San Juan, carriers include **American Eagle** (tel. 800/433–7300), and **Sunaire Express** (809/495–2480), which fly to both Beef Island/Tortola and Virgin Gorda. Airlines flying to those same two destinations from St. Thomas are Sunaire Express and **Virgin Air** (tel. 809/495–1735); American Eagle flies to Virgin Gorda only. Sunaire Express also flies between St. Croix and Beef Island/Tortola. Regularly scheduled service between the B.V.I. and most other Caribbean islands is provided by **Leeward Islands Air Transport** (LIAT) (tel. 809/495–1187). Many Caribbean islands can also be reached via **Gorda Aero Service** (tel. 809/495–2271), a charter service.

From the Airport There is no bus service from the airports, and taxis (often in the form of minivans and open-air safari buses) are expensive. Fares are officially set, but can seem confusing. It's best to tell the taxi driver the number in your group and your destination and to make sure you understand the price before you get in the taxi (if the amount seems out of line, go to a different driver). Fare from the Beef Island/Tortola airport to Wickham's Cay I in Road Town (20 minutes) is a flat fee of $15 for one, two, or three people traveling together and $5 for each additional person traveling with the same party. The fare to West End (45 minutes) is a flat fee of $30 for one, two, or three people and $10 for each additional person. If there are no cabs, call the **B.V.I. Taxi Association** at Wickham's Cay I (tel. 809/494–2322). If you're planning to rent a car, **Airways Car Rental** (tel. 809/495–2161) is located across from the airport.

On Virgin Gorda, **Andy's Taxi** (tel. 809/495–5511) and **Mahogany Taxi Service** (tel. 809/495–5469) take people from the airport to the Spanish Town/Yacht Harbour area for $2 per person. Rates to Leverick Bay/North Sound are $20 a person, with reduced rates for children and large groups. Drivers meet incoming flights.

By Boat Various ferries connect St. Thomas, U.S.V.I., with Tortola and Virgin Gorda. **Native Son, Inc.** (tel. 809/495–4617), operates three ferries *(Native Son, Oriole,* or *Voyager Eagle),* and offers service between St. Thomas and Tortola (West End and Road Town) daily and between St. Thomas and Spanish Town, Virgin Gorda, on Wednesday and Sunday. **Smiths Ferry Services** (tel. 809/494–4430 or 809/494–2355) carries passengers between downtown St. Thomas and Road Town and West End on Monday through Saturday, offers daily service between Red Hook on St. Thomas and Tortola's West End, and travels between St. Thomas and Spanish Town on Sunday. **Inter-Island Boat Services'** *Sundance II* (tel. 809/776–6597) connects St. John and West End on Tortola daily. Fares are $17 one-way, $32 round-trip between St. Thomas and Tortola (any port); $16 one-way, $28 round-trip between St. John and Tortola; and $45 round-trip between St. Thomas and Virgin Gorda ($25 Virgin Gorda to St. Thomas, $20 St. Thomas to Virgin Gorda).

Passports and Visas Upon entering the B.V.I., U.S. and Canadian citizens are required to present some proof of citizenship, if not a passport then a birth certificate or voter-registration card with a driver's license or photo ID.

Lan⁰uage British English, with a West Indian inflection, is the language spoken.

(809/495–5821) offers most U.S. mail and UPS services via St. Thomas the next day.

Opening and Closing Times Stores are generally open Monday–Saturday 9–5. Bank hours are Monday–Thursday 9–2:30 and Friday 9–2:30 and 4:30–6.

Guided Tours For a 2½-hour tour around most of Tortola, get in touch with the **B.V.I. Taxi Association** (Wickham's Cay I, tel. 809/494–2875 or 809/494–2322; Airport, tel. 809/495–2378). Tours are $45 for a minimum of three people; $12 for each additional person. **Travel Plan Tours** (tel. 809/494–2872; cost: $25 per person) provides special tours for large groups (minimum 12). **Style's Taxi Service** (tel. 809/494–2260) also handles large groups but sometimes makes regular runs during high season to various beaches for $5 a person. Pickup is at the Chase Manhattan Bank in Road Town. Guided tours around the entire island of Virgin Gorda cost $30 for two people and can be arranged through **Andy's Taxi and Jeep Rental** (tel. 809/495–5511) or **Mahogany Rentals and Island Tours** (tel. 809/495–5469).

Exploring Tortola

Numbers in the margin correspond to points of interest on the Tortola map.

You can easily explore all of Tortola (or Virgin Gorda) in a single day with a rental car; this will even leave you time for a swim here and a snack there. If you'd rather do it in several concentrated hours or would prefer not to navigate the steep hills on your own, you can opt for a guided tour (*see* Guided Tours, *above*); the costs of car rentals or guided tours are roughly the same. The drives on Tortola are dramatic, with dizzying roller-coaster dips and climbs and glorious views. Distractions are the real danger here, from the glittering mosaic of azure sea, white skies, and emerald islets to the ambling cattle and grazing goats roadside.

Before setting out on your tour of Tortola, you may want to devote an hour or so to strolling down Main Street and along
❶ the waterfront in **Road Town,** the laid-back island capital. Locals don't use street names much because they know where everything is, so if you ask directions, ask how to get to such-and-such restaurant or store, rather than how to find the street. Start at the General Post Office facing **Sir Olva Georges Square,** across from the ferry dock and customs office. The hands of the clock atop this building permanently point to 10 minutes to 5, rather appropriate in this drowsy town where time does seem to be standing still.

The eastern side of Sir Olva Georges Square is open to the harbor, and a handful of elderly Tortolans can generally be found sitting under the square's shade trees and enjoying the breeze that sweeps in from the water here. The General Post Office and government offices occupy two other sides of the square, and small shops line the third side. From the front of the post office, follow Main Street to the right past a number of small shops housed in traditional pastel-painted West Indian buildings with high-pitched, corrugated tin roofs, bright shutters, and delicate fretwork trim.

On the left, about half a block from the post office, you'll encounter the **British Virgin Islands Folk Museum.** Founded in 1983, the museum has a large collection of artifacts from the

Tortola

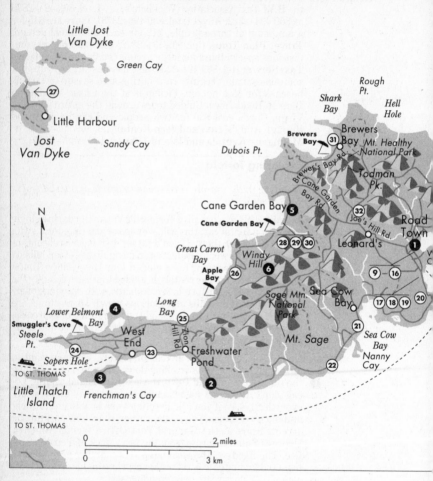

ATLANTIC OCEAN

Little Jost Van Dyke

Green Cay

Jost Van Dyke

Little Harbour

Sandy Cay

Rough Pt.

Shark Bay

Hell Hole

Brewers Bay

Brewers Bay

Mt. Healthy National Park

Dubois Pt.

Todman Pk.

Cane Garden Bay

Cane Garden Bay

Great Carrot Bay

Windy Hill

Leonard's

Road Town

Apple Bay

Sage Mtn. National Park

Sea Cow Bay

Long Bay

West End

Freshwater Pond

Mt. Sage

Sea Cow Bay

Nanny Cay

Lower Belmont Bay

Smuggler's Cove Steele Pt.

Sopers Hole

TO ST. THOMAS

Little Thatch Island

Frenchman's Cay

TO ST. THOMAS

N

0   2 miles
0   3 km

Exploring
Beef Island, **7**
Belmont Point, **4**
Callwood Distillery, **6**
Cane Garden Bay, **5**
Fort Recovery, **2**
Frenchman's Cay, **3**

Queen Elizabeth II Bridge, **8**
Road Town, **1**

Dining
The Apple, **26**
The Fishtrap, **15**
Hungry Sailor Garden Cafe, **9**
Jolly Roger, **24**
Marlene's, **14**
Midtown Restaurant, **10**

Pusser's Pub, **11**
Rhymers, **28**
Skyworld, **32**
The Struggling Man, **21**
Virgin Queen, **12**
The Whiz, **13**

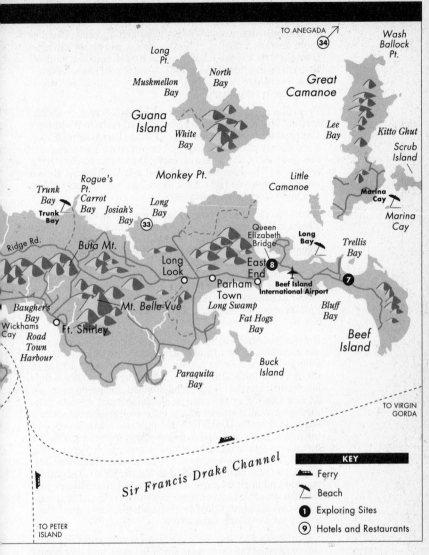

TO ANEGADA
34

Wash
Ballock
Pt.

Long
Pt.

North
Bay

Great
Camanoe

Muskmellon
Bay

Guana
Island

White
Bay

Lee
Bay

Kitto Ghut

Scrub
Island

Monkey Pt.

Little
Camanoe

Marina
Cay

Marina
Cay

Trunk
Bay

Rogue's
Pt.
Carrot
Bay

Josiah's
Bay

Long
Bay

33

Long
Bay

Trellis
Bay

Trunk
Bay

Ridge Rd.

Buta Mt.

Long
Look

Queen
Elizabeth
Bridge

Long
Bay

East
End

8

7

Parham
Town

Beef Island
International Airport

Baugher's
Bay

Mt. Belle-Vue

Long Swamp

Bluff
Bay

Beef
Island

Wickhams
Cay

Ft. Shirley

Fat Hogs
Bay

Road
Town
Harbour

Paraquita
Bay

Buck
Island

TO VIRGIN
GORDA

Sir Francis Drake Channel

KEY

Ferry

Beach

1 Exploring Sites

9 Hotels and Restaurants

TO PETER
ISLAND

Lodging

Anegada Beach
Campground, **34**

Brewer's Bay
Campground, **31**

B.V.I. Aquatic
Hotel, **23**

Cane Garden Bay
Beach Hotel, **30**

Fort Burt, **17**

Fort Recovery, **22**

Hotel Castle Maria, **18**

Jolly Roger Inn, **24**

Josiah's Bay
Cottages, **33**

Maria's by the Sea, **19**

Ole Works Inn, **29**

Sea View Hotel, **20**

Sebastian's on the
Beach, **25**

Tula's N&N
Campground, **27**

Village Cay Hotel &
Manna, **16**

Arawak Indians, some of the early settlers of the islands. Of particular interest are the triangular stones called *zemis,* which depict the Arawak gods Julihu and Yuccahu. The museum also has a display of bottles, bowls, and plates salvaged from the wreck of the RMS *Rhone,* a British mail ship sunk off Salt Island in a hurricane in 1867. *Main St., no phone. Admission free. Open Mon., Tues., Thurs., Fri. 10–4, Sat. 10–1, though hours may vary.*

From Main Street, turn right onto Challwell Street, cross Waterfront Drive, and proceed a few hundred yards to **Wickham's Cay** to admire the boats moored at **Village Cay Marina.** Enjoy a broad view of the wide harbor, home of countless sailing vessels and yachts, and a base of the well-known yacht-chartering enterprise The Moorings. You'll find a **B.V.I. Tourist Board** office to serve you right here, as well as banks, a post office, and more stores and boutiques.

When you've finished wandering about Wickham's Cay, take Fishlock Road up to the courthouse and make a right to get back on Main Street. At the police station, turn left onto Station Avenue and follow it to the **J.R. O'Neal Botanic Gardens.** These 2.8 acres of lush gardens include hothouses for ferns and orchids, special gardens of medicinal herbs and plants, and plants and trees indigenous to the seashore. A number of flower shows and special events are held here during the year. *Station Ave., tel. 809/494–4557. Admission free. Open Mon.– Sat. 8–4, Sun. noon–5.*

Retrace your steps to Sir Olva Georges Square to pick up your car. From Road Town, head southwest along Waterfront Drive. Follow the coastline for 5 miles or so of the easiest driving in the B.V.I.: no hills; little traffic; lots of curves to keep things interesting; and the lovely, island-studded channel on your left. At Sea Cows Bay the road bends inland just a bit to pass through a small residential area, but it soon rejoins the water's edge. Sir Francis Drake Channel provides a kaleidoscope of turquoise, jade green, and morning-glory blue on your left, and further entertainment is provided by pelicans diving for their supper. The next development you come to is **Nanny Cay.** Jutting out into the channel, this villagelike complex, with brightly painted buildings trimmed with lacy wood gingerbread, also contains a marina that can accommodate more than 200 yachts. A bar and restaurant, Peg Leg's Landing, offers a good place to stop for a soft drink and a view.

From Nanny Cay the route continues westward as St. John, the smallest of the three main U.S.V.I., comes into view across the channel. The road curves into **West End** past the ruins of
2 the 17th-century Dutch **Fort Recovery,** a historic fort 30 feet in diameter, on the grounds of Fort Recovery Villas. There are no guided tours, but the public is welcome to stop by. The road ends at **Sopers Hole.** The waterfront here is dominated by the boat terminal and customs office that service the St. Thomas/St. John/Tortola ferries. Turn around and head back, taking your very first right over a bridge, following signs to
3 **Frenchman's Cay,** and bear right on the other side of the bridge. There's a marina and a captivating complex of pastel-hued, West Indian–style buildings with shady second-floor balconies, colonnaded arcades, shuttered windows, and gingerbread trim; these showcase art galleries, boutiques, and restaurants.

Retrace your route out of West End, turn left, and head across the island on Zion Hill Road, a steep byway that rises and then drops precipitously to the other side of the island. Follow the road to the end and then turn left, drive up a steep hill, and be prepared for a dazzling view of **Long Bay,** a mile-long stretch

❹ of white sand secured on the west end by **Belmont Point,** a sugar-loaf promontory that has been described as "a giant green gumdrop." On this stretch of beach are the Long Bay Hotel, one of Tortola's more appealing resorts, and one of the island's two pitch-and-putt golf courses (Prospect Reef has the other). The large island visible in the distance is Jost Van Dyke. Follow North Coast Road northeast for about five minutes to **Capoon's Bay.**

Continue on to **Apple Bay** and the **Sugar Mill Hotel.** You'll want to inspect the 350-year-old mill that now serves as the hotel's main dining room, and owners Jeff and Jinx Morgan's superb collection of Haitian primitive art. With any luck you'll meet the Morgans, a delightful couple with a seemingly inexhaustible repertoire of island stories.

Back in the car, follow the North Coast Road over **Windy Hill,** a gripping climb that affords splendid vistas of the sea and sky.

❺ You'll descend to sea level at **Cane Garden Bay:** Its crystalline water and silky stretch of sand make this enticing beach one of Tortola's most popular getaways. Its existence is no secret, however, and it can get crowded, though never uncomfortably so.

❻ For a taste of old-time Tortola, pop into the **Callwood Distillery** (Cane Garden Bay, no phone). A tropical version of moonshine bubbles away here most days. If you purchase some of this potent brew, it will almost certainly be presented in an old gin or vodka bottle. Now, *that's* recycling.

Go up Cane Garden Bay Road, bearing right, and follow the mountainous Ridge Road eastward. The views from this twisting road are breathtaking; the dizzying turnoffs that lead to tranquil bays like **Trunk, Carrot** and **Josiah's** would make a Grand Prix racer blanch. To return to Road Town, take Joe's Hill Road, the first right after the sign to Skyworld. Follow this right and bear left (and down) when you come to the "Y." Whoever is driving may gasp at how steeply the road drops, but passengers will be "oohing" and "aahing" at the spectacular view of Road Town and the harbor.

If you want to keep exploring, continue along Ridge Road, which ultimately winds up at East End, the sleepy village that

❼ is the entryway to **Beef Island,** and the Beef Island Interna-
❽ tional Airport. The narrow **Queen Elizabeth II Bridge** connects Tortola and Beef Island, and you'll have to pay a toll to cross (50¢ for passenger cars, $1 for vans and trucks). It's worth it if only for the sight of the toll-taker extending a tin can attached to the end of a board through your car window to collect the fee. If you like interesting seashells, **Long Bay** on Beef Island has them for the picking.

From East End, proceed southwest on Blackburn Highway to Sir Francis Drake Highway, then west along the coast back to Road Town.

Virgin Gorda

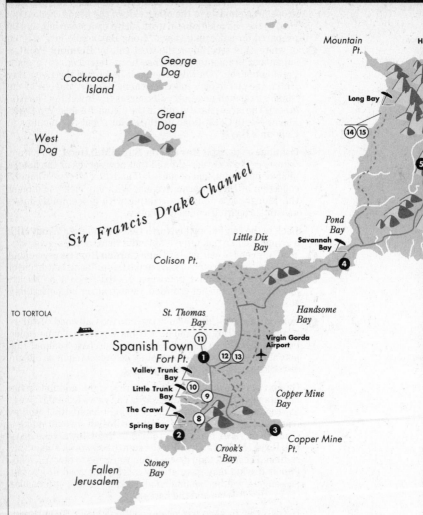

Mountain Pt.

Ha

George Dog

Cockroach Island

Great Dog

West Dog

Long Bay

14 15

5

Sir Francis Drake Channel

Pond Bay

Little Dix Bay

Savannah Bay

4

Colison Pt.

TO TORTOLA

St. Thomas Bay

Handsome Bay

Virgin Gorda Airport

Spanish Town

11

Fort Pt.

1

12 13

Valley Trunk Bay

10

Little Trunk Bay

9

Copper Mine Bay

The Crawl

8

Spring Bay

2

3

Copper Mine Pt.

Crook's Bay

Fallen Jerusalem

Stoney Bay

Exploring
The Baths, **2**
Black Rock, **4**
Copper Mine Point, **3**
Eustatia Sound, **7**
Saba Rock, **6**
Spanish Town, **1**
Virgin Gorda Peak National Park, **5**

Dining
The Bath and Turtle, **11**
The Crab Hole, **12**
Pusser's Leverick Bay, **16**
Teacher's Pet Ilma's, **9**

Lodging
Fischer's Cove Beach Hotel, **10**
Guavaberry Spring Bay Vacation Homes, **8**
Leverick Bay Resort, **17**

Mango Bay Resort, **14**
Paradise Beach Resort, **15**
The Wheelhouse, **13**

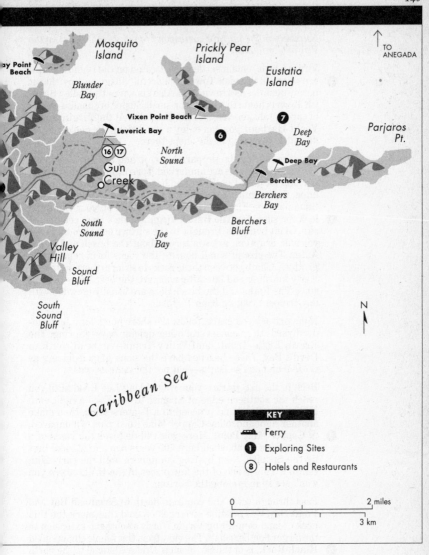

TO
ANEGADA

Mosquito
Island

Prickly Pear
Island

Eustatia
Island

ay Point
Beach

Blunder
Bay

Parjaros
Pt.

Vixen Point Beach

Leverick Bay

7

Deep
Bay

6

16 17

North
Sound

Deep Bay

Gun
Creek

Bercher's

Berchers
Bay

South
Sound

Joe
Bay

Berchers
Bluff

Valley
Hill

Berchers
Bluff

Sound
Bluff

South
Sound
Bluff

N

Caribbean Sea

KEY

Ferry

1 Exploring Sites

8 Hotels and Restaurants

0 —————————— 2 miles
0 —————————— 3 km

Exploring Virgin Gorda

Numbers in the margin correspond to points of interest on the Virgin Gorda map.

Virgin Gorda's main settlement, located on the island's southern wing, is **Spanish Town,** a peaceful village so tiny that it barely qualifies as a town at all. Also known as The Valley, Spanish Town is home to a marina, a small cluster of shops, a couple of car-rental agencies, and the ferry slip. At the **Virgin Gorda Yacht Harbour** you can enjoy a stroll along the dock front or do a little browsing in the shops there.

If you're driving, be prepared to stop and ask for directions, because many roads are unmarked. Turn right from the marina parking lot onto Lee Road and head through the more populated, flat countryside of the south for about 15 minutes. Continue past the Fischer's Cove Beach Hotel on your right and look for signs for **The Baths,** Virgin Gorda's most celebrated site. Giant boulders, brought to the surface eons ago by a vast volcanic eruption, are scattered about the beach and in the water. The size of small houses, the rocks form remarkable grottoes. Climb between these rocks to swim in the many pools. Early morning and late afternoon are the best times to visit, since The Baths and the beach here are usually crowded with day-trippers visiting from Tortola.

If it's privacy you crave, follow the shore north for a few hundred yards to reach several other quieter bays—Spring, The Crawl, Little Trunk, and Valley Trunk—or head south to Devil's Bay. These beaches have the same giant boulders as those found at The Baths—but not the same crowds.

Back in the car, retrace your route along Lee Road until you reach the southern edge of Spanish Town. Take a right onto Millionaire Road and proceed to a T-intersection, then make another right and follow Copper Mine Road, part of it unpaved, to **Copper Mine Point.** Here you will discover the ruins of a copper mine established here 400 years ago and worked first by the Spanish, then by English miners until the early 20th century. This is one of the few places in the B.V.I. where you won't see islands along the horizon.

Pass through town and continue north to **Savannah Bay** and **Pond Bay,** two pristine stretches of sand that mark the thin neck of land connecting Virgin Gorda's southern extension to the larger northern half. The view from this scenic elbow, called **Black Rock,** is of the Sir Francis Drake Channel to the north and the Caribbean Sea to the south. The road forks as it goes uphill. The unpaved left prong winds past the Mango Bay Club resort (and not much else) to Long Bay and not quite to Mountain Point. To continue exploring, take the road on the right, which winds uphill and looks down on beautiful South Sound.

You'll see a small sign on the left for the trail up to the 265-acre **Virgin Gorda Peak National Park** and the island's summit at 1,359 feet. It's about a 15-minute hike up to a small clearing, where you can climb a ladder to the platform of a wood observation tower. The view at the top is dazzling, if somewhat tree-obstructed. A bit farther on, the road forks again. The right fork leads to **Gun Creek,** where launches pick up passengers for the Bitter End, Biras Creek, and Drake's Anchorage, three of Virgin Gorda's upscale resorts.

The left fork will bring you to **Leverick Bay.** There is a resort here, with a cozy beach and marina, a restaurant, a cluster of shops, and some luxurious hillside villas to rent, all a little like a tucked-away tropical suburb. Low-gear your way up one of the narrow hillside roads (you're not on a driveway, it only seems that way) to one of those top-most Leverick dwellings, where you can park for a moment. Out to the left, across Blunder Bay, you'll see **Mosquito Island,** home of Drake's Anchorage Resort; the hunk of land straight ahead is **Prickly Pear,** which has been named a national park to protect it from development. At the neck of land to your right, across from Gun Creek, is **Biras Creek Hotel,** and around the bend to the north of that you'll see the Danish-roof buildings of the **Bitter End Yacht Club and Marina.** Between the Bitter End and Prickly Pear you should be able to make out **Saba Rock,** home of one of the Caribbean's best-known diving entrepreneurs, Bert Kilbride—a colorful character who knows where all the wrecks are and who is recognized and commissioned by the Queen of England as Honorary Keeper of the Wrecks.

That magical color change in the sea near Prickly Pear reveals **Eustatia Sound** and its extensive reef. Beyond that are Horseshoe Reef and the flat coral island of Anegada some 20 miles north, where most of those wrecks are and where bare-boaters are not permitted to sail because of the perilous reefs. But you can easily take a boat to Biras Creek, the Bitter End, or Drake's Anchorage. In fact, that's the only way you can get there.

Other British Virgin Islands

Jost Van Dyke, the sizable island north of Tortola's western tip, is a good choice for travelers in search of isolation and good hiking trails; it has several hostelries and a campground, but only two small settlements, few cars, and small generators for electricity. Three ferries daily (two on Sunday) go to Jost Van Dyke from Tortola; fare is $7 one-way. **Anegada,** about 20 miles north of Virgin Gorda's North Sound, is a flat mass of coral 11 miles long and 3 miles wide with a population of only about 250. Visitors are chiefly scuba divers, snorkelers, lovers of deserted beaches, and fishermen, some of whom come for the bonefishing.

Beaches

Beaches here have fewer facilities and fewer people than those of more populous islands. Try to get out on a boat at least one day during your stay in these islands, whether a dive-snorkeling boat or a day-trip sailing vessel. It's sometimes the best way to get to the most virgin Virgin beaches (some have no road access).

Tortola Tortola's north and west coasts have a number of postcard-perfect, palm-fringed white-sand beaches that curl luxuriantly around turquoise bays and coves. None are within walking distance of town, but hotels are located on several. Nearly all are accessible by car (preferably four-wheel drive), albeit down bumpy roads that corkscrew precipitously. Facilities tend toward the basic, but you can usually find a humble beach bar with rest rooms.

If you want to surf, **Apple Bay** (Capoon's Bay) is the spot. Sebastian's, the very casual hotel here, caters especially to those in search of the perfect wave. Good waves are never a sure thing, but January and February are usually high times here. **Josiah's Bay** is another favored place to hang 10. The water at **Brewers Bay** is good for either snorkeling (calm) or surfing (swells). There's a campground here, but in the summer you'll find almost nobody around. The beach and its old sugar mill and rum-distillery ruins are just north of Cane Garden Bay (up and over a steep hill), just past Luck Hill.

Beautiful **Cane Garden Bay** is Tortola's most popular beach and one of the B.V.I.'s best-known anchorages. The informal Cane Garden Bay Beach Hotel is here. You can rent sailboards and such, and for noshing or sipping you have a choice of going to Stanley's Welcome Bar; Rhymer's; The Wedding; or Quito's Gazebo, where local recording star Quito Rhymer sings island ballads four nights a week.

Long Bay on Beef Island offers scenery that draws superlatives and is visited only by a knowledgeable few. The view of Little Camanoe and Great Camanoe islands is appealing, and if you walk around the bend to the right, you can see little Marina Cay and Scrub Island. Take the Queen Elizabeth II Bridge to Beef Island and watch for a small dirt turnoff on the left before the airport. Drive across that dried-up marsh flat— there really is a beach (with interesting seashells) on the other side.

After bouncing your way to beautiful **Smuggler's Cove** (Lower Belmont Bay), you'll really feel as if you've found a hidden paradise (although don't expect to be alone on weekends). Have a beer or toasted cheese sandwich, the only items on the menu, at the extremely casual snack bar. There is a fine view of the island of Jost Van Dyke, and the snorkeling is good.

About the only thing you'll find moving at **Trunk Bay** is the surf. It's directly north of Road Town, midway between Cane Garden Bay and Beef Island, and you'll have to hike down a *ghut* (gully) from the high Ridge Road.

Virgin Gorda The best beaches are most easily reached by water, although they are accessible on foot, usually after a moderately strenuous hike of 10 to 15 minutes. But your persistence is amply rewarded.

Anybody going to Virgin Gorda must experience swimming or snorkeling among its unique boulder formations. But why go to **The Baths,** which is usually crowded, when you can catch some rays just north at **Spring Bay** beach, which is a gem, and, a little farther north, at **The Crawl.** Both are easily reached from The Baths on foot or by swimming.

Leverick Bay is a small, busy beach-cum-marina that fronts a resort restaurant and pool. Don't come here to be alone, but if you want a lively little place and a break from the island's noble quiet, take the road north and turn left before Gun Creek. The view of Prickly Pear Island is an added plus, and there's a dive facility right here to motor you out to beautiful Eustatia Reef just across North Sound.

It's worth going out to **Long Bay** (near Virgin Gorda's northern tip, past the Diamond Beach Club) for the snorkeling (Little Dix Bay resort has outings there). Going north from Spanish Town, go left at the fork near Pond Bay. Part of the route there is dirt road.

The North Shore has many nice beaches. From Biras Creek or Bitter End resorts you can walk to **Bercher's** and **Deep Bay** beaches. Two of the prettiest beaches in North Sound are accessible only by boat: Mosquito Island's **Hay Point Beach** and Prickly Pear's **Vixen Point Beach.**

Savannah Bay is a lovely long stretch of white sand, and though it may not always be deserted, it seems wonderfully private for a beach just north of Spanish Town (on the north side of where the island narrows, at Black Rock). From town it's about 30 minutes on foot.

Other Islands   Beaches on other islands, reachable only by boat, include Jost Van Dyke's **Great Harbour** and **White Bay; Marina Cay;** Peter Island's **Big Reef Bay, White Bay,** and **Dead Man's Bay;** Mosquito Island's **Limetree Beach, Long Beach,** and **Honeymoon Beach;** and Cooper Island's **Manchineel Bay.** Farther off, and reachable by plane as well as boat, is beach-ringed, reef-laced **Anegada.**

Sports and the Outdoors

Sailboarding   One of the best spots for sailboarding is at Trellis Bay on Beef Island. **Boardsailing B.V.I.** (Trellis Bay, Beef Island, tel. 809/495–2447) has rentals, private lessons, and group rates. Rentals are $20 the first half hour, $15 the second half hour, and $55 for the day. On Virgin Gorda, The **Nick Trotter Sailing School** (Bitter End Yacht Club, North Sound, tel. 809/495–2745) rents boards for two hours for $25, $10 each additional hour, and offers three-hour beginner courses for $50; a brush-up one-hour course is $25.

Sailing/Boating   The B.V.I. offer some of the finest sailing waters in the world, with hundreds of boats available for charter—with or without crew—as well as numerous opportunities for day sails. Bareboating is an affordable option for competent sailors if split among three or four couples. For sailors interested in renting a bare boat, contact **The Moorings** (1305 U.S. 19 S, Suite 402, Clearwater, FL 34624, tel. 800/535–7289). Based in Road Town, it is the largest operator in the islands and offers day sails as well as boat rentals.

A day sail or themed cruise is a must on the beautiful waters surrounding these islands. Although the cost per person may seem steep, it usually includes snorkel equipment rental, lunch or snacks, and sometimes drinks. The speedy *Island Hopper* (tel. 809/495–4870) leaves from Prospect Reef (but will pick up elsewhere for $5 extra per person) and takes a maximum of eight people virtually anywhere they want to go in the B.V.I. for beach or snorkeling trips. Cost is $35 per person half-day, $65 full-day. If you want the slower pace of sailboat, the 80-foot *White Squall* (Road Town, tel. 809/494–2564) offers a full day of snorkeling, beaching, barbecue lunch, sodas, and rum punch for $70 a person (lower off-season). The catamaran *Patouche II* (Wickham's Cay I, Road Town, tel. 809/496–0222) takes people on half-day snorkeling cruises to Norman Island for $43 per person, and offers half-day sunset sails with snorkeling and hors d'oeuvres for $53 a person. On Virgin Gorda, call **Harrigan's Rent-A-Boat** (Yacht Harbour, tel. 809/495–5542).

Scuba Diving and Snorkeling The famed wreck of the RMS *Rhone*, off Salt Island, is reason enough to dive during your B.V.I. stay. For snorkelers, perhaps the most popular spot is at the famed Baths on Virgin Gorda. Dive and snorkel sites also abound near the smaller islands of Norman, Peter, Cooper, Ginger, the Dogs, and Jost Van Dyke; the North Sound area of Virgin Gorda; Brewer's Bay and Frenchman's Cay on Tortola; and the wreck-strewn waters off Anegada. In addition to renting equipment, many of the dive operators here also offer instruction, hotel/dive packages, and snorkeling excursions. On Tortola, contact **Baskin-in-the-Sun** (Box 108, Road Harbour, tel. 809/494–2858 or 800/233–7938) or **Underwater Safaris Ltd.** (Box 139, Road Town, tel. 809/494–3235 or 800/537–7032). **Dive BVI** (VG Yacht Harbour, tel. 809/495–5513 or 800/848–7078) has locations at Leverick Bay and Spanish Town on Virgin Gorda and on Peter Island and offers special dive packages in conjunction with most of the Virgin Gorda hotels listed in this chapter. A single-tank dive from these operators costs about $60. Snorkel equipment rents for about $10.

Tennis Several resorts on Tortola have tennis courts for guests' use. Nonguests may use courts at **Prospect Reef** (Road Town, tel. 809/494–3311). On Virgin Gorda, nonguests can use the courts at **Biras Creek** (tel. 809/494–3555). Court fees average $5–$10 an hour.

Shopping

The British Virgins are not known as a shopping haven, and what there is is not cheap. Although you won't find many bargains, the shops listed below offer unusual and reasonably priced items.

Shopping Districts Most of the shops and boutiques on Tortola are clustered on and off Road Town's **Main Street** and at the **Wickhams Cay** shopping area adjacent to the Marina. There is also an ever-growing group of art, jewelry, clothing, and souvenir stores at **Sopers Hole** on Tortola's West End. On Virgin Gorda, there's a scattering of shops in the minimall adjacent to the bustling yacht harbor in Spanish Town.

Specialty Stores *Jewelry* **Felix Gold and Silver Ltd.** (Main St., Road Town, tel. 809/494–2406) handcrafts exceptionally fine jewelry in its on-site workshop. Choose from island or nautical themes or have something custom-made (in most cases, within 24 hours).

Samarkand (Main St., Road Town, tel. 809/494–6415) features handmade gold and silver pendants, earrings, bracelets, and pins.

Local Crafts **Caribbean Handprints** (Main St., Road Town, tel. 809/494–3717) creates silk-screened fabric and sells it by the yard or fashioned into dresses, shirts, pants, bathrobes, beach cover-ups, and beach bags.

Virgin Gorda Craft Shop (Virgin Gorda Yacht Harbour, no phone) features the work of island artisans and carries West Indian jewelry and crafts styled in straw, shells, and other local materials. It also stocks clothing and paintings by Caribbean artists.

Textiles **Zenaida** (Cutlass House, Wickham's Cay, Road Town, tel. 809/494–2113) displays the fabric finds of Argentinean Vivian Jenik Helm, who travels through South America, Africa, and India in search of batiks, hand-painted and hand-blocked fabrics, and interesting weaves that can be made into pareos or wall hangings. The shop also offers a selection of unusual bags, belts, sarongs, scarves, and ethnic jewelry.

Dining

Dining in the B.V.I. can be quite affordable if you are willing to stay out of fancy restaurants and sample local cuisine. On Tortola, there are a wide range of lunch and dinner choices, including hearty buffets. If you plan to cook, you'll find several excellent take-out places and grocery stores in Road Town. Stick with the local supermarkets rather than the more expensive yacht provisioning stores. **Bobby's Supermarket** (Wickham's Cay I) sells take-out and baked goods as well as grocery items. **Riteway** (Road Town and Pasea Estate) sells liquor and wine as well as groceries; the Pasea location usually has the island's best selection of vegetables. **Roadtown Wholesale Cash & Carry** (Pasea Estate) sells items in bulk at discount prices; consider if you are traveling with a large family or group. Even at the supermarkets, expect high prices. Liquor is cheap, but beer and soda are very expensive. (If you are traveling with children, pack several gallon packages of their favorite drink mix).

On more remote Virgin Gorda there are fewer restaurants to choose from, but it is still possible to eat out inexpensively. Groceries are more limited and more expensive than on Tortola. **The Commissary and Ship Store** (Yacht Harbour) and the smaller **Buck's Food Market** (Yacht Harbour) are your best bets.

Highly recommended restaurants are indicated by a star ★.

Category	Cost*
Moderate	$15–$25
Inexpensive	$10–$15
Budget	under $10

per person for three courses, excluding drinks and service; there is no sales tax in the B.V.I.

Tortola **The Apple.** This inviting restaurant is located in a small West Indian house not far from the cooling breezes of Little Apple Bay. Soft candlelight complements local seafood dishes such as fish steamed in lime butter, and conch or whelks in garlic sauce. *Little Apple Bay, tel. 809/495–4437. No credit cards. Moderate.*
The Fishtrap. Friday and Saturday nights, this charming open-air restaurant serves a barbecue with a terrific salad bar. Choose from grilled chicken, ribs, and several varieties of local fish. *Columbus Centre, Wickham's Cay I, Road Town, tel. 809/494–2636. AE, MC, V. Closed Sun. lunch. Moderate.*

★ **Virgin Queen.** This spot is popular with everyone from the sailing crowd to tourists to locals. The menu, a mix of West Indian and English pub, has daily specials that might include bangers and mash, shepherd's pie, barbecued chicken or fish, or stuffed chicken with peas and rice. Although some dishes are expensive, many lunch and dinner specials are under $10, and portions are hearty. The house specialty, the Queen's Pizza, is on the expensive side. *Fleming St., Road Town, tel. 809/494–2310. No reservations. No credit cards. Closed Sun. Moderate.*

Rhymer's. Located at Cane Garden Bay Beach Hotel, this casual beachfront restaurant features "eat-all-you-want" buffets that include barbecued ribs, conch, and other West Indian specialties on Tuesday, Saturday, and Sunday evenings for $15 a person. *Cane Garden Bay, tel. 809/495–4639. MC, V. Inexpensive–Moderate.*

★ **Skyworld.** This well-known restaurant with a spectacular view of the B.V.I. is expensive for dinner, but has quite reasonable lunch specials, many in the $5–$8 range. Sandwiches are served on delicious freshly baked bread. After lunch, visit the observation deck that sits atop the restaurant for the 360-degree view of numerous islands and cays. *Ridge Rd., tel. 809/494–3567. AE, MC, V. Budget–Inexpensive (for lunch).*

The Struggling Man. Barely more than a roadside shack, this pleasant place with raffish candy-cane decor offers striking views of Drake's Channel, and simple, tasty West Indian specialties. *Sea Cow Bay, tel. 809/494–4163. No reservations. No credit cards. Inexpensive.*

Hungry Sailor Garden Café. This patio restaurant is an offshoot of the adjoining and more expensive Captain's Table. Its blackboard menu includes close to 20 selections, most under $10. Good bets include shepherd's pie, flying fish, hamburgers, and Caesar salad. *Wickham's Cay I, tel. 809/494–3885. AE, MC, V. Budget–Inexpensive.*

Jolly Roger. A young boating crowd comes here day and night for pizza (also available for take-out), cheeseburgers, conch fritters, and nightly West Indian specials. The barbecues on Friday and Saturday nights (entrées $8.50–$13) feature live music. *West End, tel. 809/495–4559. MC, V. Budget–Inexpensive.*

Midtown Restaurant. Locals frequent this coffee shop for breakfast, lunch, and dinner. The menu features West Indian specialties including conch, whelk, salt fish, pork, and mutton. *Main St., Road Town, tel. 809/494–2764. No credit cards. Budget–Inexpensive.*

Pusser's Pub. This boisterous pub is open from late morning until late evening and serves English-style meat pies, pizza, deli sandwiches, and some Mexican items. Thursday night is "nickel beer night." *Waterfront Dr., Road Town, tel. 809/494–2467. AE, MC, V. Budget–Inexpensive.*

Marlene's. This take-out shop open all day sells cakes, pastries, West Indian baked or fried pâtés (meat baked in pastry dough), spicy *rotis* (curries wrapped in a West Indian version of a tortilla), and sandwiches. *Wickham's Cay I, Road Town, tel. 809/494–4634. No credit cards. Budget.*

The Whiz. This small, cafeteria-style restaurant has daily specials, sandwiches, and salads. Take-out is also available. *At the Round-A-Bout, Road Town, no phone. No credit cards. Closed Sun. Budget.*

Virgin Gorda **The Bath and Turtle.** This informal patio tavern with its
★ friendly staff is a popular spot to sit back and relax. Burgers,
well-stuffed sandwiches, pizzas, pasta dishes, and daily specials round out the casual menu. Live entertainment performs
on Wednesday and Sunday nights. *Virgin Gorda Yacht Harbour, tel. 809/495–5239. MC, V. Moderate.*

The Crab Hole. This homey hangout, serving Creole specialties
like callaloo soup, salt fish, and curried chicken roti, rocks with
live bands and a mostly local crowd on Saturdays. *The Valley,
tel. 809/495–5307. No credit cards. Inexpensive–Moderate.*

Pusser's Leverick Bay. It's a bit of a drive unless you are staying in Leverick Bay, but this restaurant and beach bar has
nightly specials that can be very reasonably priced, such as
Wednesday's Mexican Enchilada Night. Call ahead to see
what's on. *Leverick Bay, tel. 809/495–7369. AE, MC, V. Inexpensive–Moderate.*

Teacher's Pet Ilma's. This little hole-in-the-wall offers delightful local atmosphere and delicious native-style family dinners. *The Valley, tel. 809/495–5355. Reservations required. No
credit cards. No lunch. Inexpensive.*

Lodging

The number of rooms in the B.V.I. is small compared with other
destinations in the Caribbean. What is available is often in
great demand, and the prices are not low; the top-of-the-line
resorts here are among the most expensive in the Caribbean.
Nevertheless, these islands also have a number of affordable
properties, as well as some moderately priced rentals and even
a few campgrounds. Modest hotels we recommend are clean
and well-kept, but rooms may seem a little on the bare side.

Road Town hotels don't have beaches, but all have pools and
are within walking distance of grocery stores, restaurants,
nightlife, and shopping. Bus service is available to a number of
beaches around the island. Hotels outside Road Town are relatively isolated, but some are on or near a beach. If you stay
at one of these, you can do without a car for most of your trip,
but if you like to explore or want to visit deserted beaches
(some of the island's best are off the beaten track), you'll want
to rent a car for at least several days. On Virgin Gorda, you can
manage without a car if you're staying in the Spanish Town
area, but you may be walking up to a mile or more to shops,
restaurants, or beaches.

Highly recommended lodgings are indicated by a star ★.

Category	Cost*
Moderate	$130–$180
Inexpensive	$75–$130
Budget	under $75

**All prices are for a standard double room in high season,
excluding 7% hotel tax and 10% service charge. To estimate
rates for hotels offering MAP/FAP, add about $35 per
person per day to the above price ranges.*

Hotels **Sebastian's on the Beach.** The beach is the main attraction
Tortola here; the surfing on Little Apple Bay is considered among the

best in the B.V.I. Hang-10 types dote on Sebastian's casual atmosphere and the wide range of water sports available. The rooms are divided among three buildings, only one of which is on the beach—this is also the only building that has balconies in each room. Rooms here are moderately priced, while those facing the garden have lower rates. The appealing on-site restaurant overlooks the water. *Box 441, Road Town, tel. 809/495–4212, fax 809/495–4466. 26 rooms. Facilities: restaurant, bar, beach, water sports, commissary. AE. EP. Inexpensive–Moderate.*

Fort Burt. Set on a hill overlooking Road Harbour, the hotel is built within the walls of a Dutch fort dating from 1666. Guest rooms are rather threadbare, with a hodgepodge of furniture styles. It's at the edge of town, away from beaches, but there is a pool. *Box 187, Road Town, tel. 809/494–2587. 7 rooms. Facilities: bar, restaurant, pool. AE, MC, V. EP, MAP. Inexpensive.*

★ **Fort Recovery.** Built around the remnants of a Dutch fort, this appealing group of one- to four-bedroom bungalows stretches along a small beach facing Sir Francis Drake Channel. All units have excellent views and come with fully equipped kitchens and sliding glass doors that open onto patios facing the ocean. Bedrooms are air-conditioned; living rooms (not air-conditioned) are suitable as an additional bedroom for one child. Grounds are bright with tropical flowers. *Box 239, Road Town, tel. 809/495–4467, fax 809/495–4036. 10 units. Facilities: commissary. AE, MC, V. EP. Inexpensive.*

Hotel Castle Maria. This simple three-story hotel is within walking distance of downtown Road Town. Some rooms have kitchenettes, balconies, and air-conditioning. All have refrigerators and cable TV. The hotel is close to in-town diversions and has a freshwater pool, a bar, and a small tropical restaurant. *Box 206, Road Town, tel. 809/494–2553. 30 rooms. Facilities: restaurant, bar, pool. AE, MC, V. EP. Inexpensive.*

Maria's by the Sea. Perched like a sandpiper on the edge of Road Harbour, this simple hotel is an easy walk from in-town restaurants. The small rooms are decorated with white rattan furniture, floral-print bedspreads, and locally done murals. All rooms have kitchenettes and balconies, some of which offer harbor views. A freshwater pool is available for cooling dips. *Box 206, Road Town, tel. 809/494–2595. 14 rooms. Facilities: restaurant, bar, pool. AE, MC, V. EP. Inexpensive.*

Village Cay Hotel & Marina. Now under new management, this pleasant, compact hotel overlooks Road Town Harbour and several marinas. It is popular with yachters and those who want to be within easy walking distance of restaurants and shops. Rooms are nicely decorated in tropical prints; some have cathedral ceilings. There is a small pool. *Wickham's Cay I, Road Town, tel. 809/494–2771. 20 rooms. Facilities: restaurant, bar, pool, water sports. AE, MC, V. EP. Inexpensive.*

★ **Ole Works Inn.** Located on one of Tortola's most beautiful beaches, this exceptionally charming inn is owned by local recording star Quito Rhymer. A steeply pitched roof and lots of glass, wood, and island stone add a contemporary flair to what was once an old sugar mill. Attractive rooms have ceiling fans, air-conditioning, and refrigerators. *Cane Garden Bay, tel. 809/495–4837. 8 rooms, 1 honeymoon tower. Facilities: TV in lobby. MC, V. CP. Budget–Inexpensive.*

BVI Aquatic Hotel. The rates here are remarkably reasonable, but don't expect many extras at this unpretentious place. All rooms do come equipped with kitchenettes. You'll need a car if you're staying here; it's a bit out of the way, though the village of West End isn't too far to walk. There's a beach of sorts, but it's small and rocky. *Box 605, West End, tel. 809/495–4541. 14 rooms. Facilities: bar, restaurant. No credit cards. EP. Budget.*

Cane Garden Bay Beach Hotel. With one of the Caribbean's most beautiful beaches right on the doorstep, the setting here couldn't be lovelier. The rooms are nothing special, with brown-tile floors, blue-green walls, and multicolor bedspreads, though they are air-conditioned and have balconies, TVs, phones, and kitchenettes. But the warm waters of Cane Garden Bay beckon, and a wealth of water activities keep guests outdoors. The beach bar and terrace restaurant attract locals, day-trippers, and charter-boat types, so the atmosphere is always lively. *Box 570, Cane Garden Bay, tel. 809/495–4639. 25 rooms. Facilities: restaurant, bar, water sports. AE, MC, V. EP. Budget.*

Jolly Roger Inn. New management has spruced up this little inn at the harbor's edge of Sopers Hole. The seven rooms are small but clean and brightly painted in tropical pastels. There is no air-conditioning, but rooms are well ventilated. A restaurant (*see* Dining, *above*) fronts the building and has live music several nights a week. It's a good spot if you like to be in the midst of the action, but a bad one if you crave the water, because it has no beach or pool. *West End, tel. 809/495–4559. 6 rooms, 2 with bath, 4 with shared bath. Facilities: restaurant, bar, dinghy dock. AE, MC, V. EP. Budget.*

Sea View Hotel. Located at the edge of Road Town and within walking distance of stores and restaurants, this modest three-story establishment has rooms and studios with cable TV, but no air-conditioning. Ten rooms have kitchenettes. You'll have to drive to the beach, though there is a pool. *Box 59, Road Town, tel. 809/494–2483. 28 units. Facilities: pool. No credit cards. EP. Budget.*

Virgin Gorda **Guavaberry Spring Bay Vacation Homes.** You'll feel you're in a
★ tree house in these unusual hexagonal cottages perched on stilts and surrounded by chirping birds and swaying branches. The one- and two-bedroom units are situated on a hill, a short walk down to a tamarind-shaded beach and not far from the mammoth boulders and cool basins of the famed Baths. Although two-bedroom units fall into our Moderate range, they become a bargain when split between two couples. *Box 20, Virgin Gorda, tel. 809/495–5227, fax 809/495–7367. 10 one-bedroom units, 6 two-bedroom units. Facilities: commissary. No credit cards. EP. Inexpensive–Moderate.*

Leverick Bay Resort. This hotel overlooking a small, sandy beach offers 16 hillside rooms, decorated in pastels and with original artwork. All rooms have refrigerators, balconies, and lovely views of North Sound. Four two-bedroom condos (a bargain when shared by two couples) are also available. A Spanish Colonial–style main building houses a restaurant. *Box 63, tel. 809/495–7421, fax 809/495–7367. 20 units. Facilities: restaurant, bar, marina, pool, shopping arcade, water sports. AE, D, MC, V. EP. Inexpensive–Moderate.*

Fischer's Cove Beach Hotel. Set amid casually tended gardens, this informal beachside hotel features simply furnished two-unit cottages, some of which are oddly shaped to catch the breezes off the sea. Dining at the restaurant here offers a choice of Continental cuisine or such West Indian classics as crispy conch fritters, red snapper, and funghi, a polentalike side dish. *Box 60, The Valley, tel. 809/495–5252. 22 rooms. Facilities: restaurant, bar, water sports, disco. AE, MC, V. EP. Inexpensive.*

Mango Bay Resort. Sparkling white villas framed by morning glory and frangipani, handsome contemporary Italian decor, and a gorgeous ribbon of golden sand that all but vanishes at high tide make this an idyllic family retreat. Even for Virgin Gorda it's a study in isolation. *Box 1062, Virgin Gorda, tel. 809/495–5672. 8 villas. Facilities: water sports. No credit cards. EP. Inexpensive.*

Paradise Beach Resort. These one-, two-, and three-bedroom beachfront suites and villas were originally intended to be one with Mango Bay Resort and are consequently remarkably similar to that property. Units are handsomely decorated in Caribbean pastels. Jeeps are included in the daily rate. *Box 534, Virgin Gorda, tel. 809/495–5871. 9 units. Facilities: water sports. No credit cards. EP. Inexpensive.*

The Wheelhouse. This hotel, across from the Marina and half a mile from the nearest beach, is easy on the pocketbook for those seeking a no-frills vacation headquarters. The cinderblock building has rooms that are air-conditioned but small, and the restaurant and bar can get noisy. It is conveniently close to the Virgin Gorda marina and shopping center. *Box 66, tel. 809/495–5230. 12 rooms. Facilities: restaurant, bar. AE, MC, V. CP. Inexpensive.*

Campgrounds   **Anegada Beach Campground.** Tents and bare sites are available on a beautiful stretch of white sand on this remote coral island. Various tent sizes range from $20 to $36 a day. Bare sites are $10. *Anegada, tel. 809/495–8038. Facilities: snack bar, snorkel-equipment rental, commissary. No credit cards. Budget.*

Brewers Bay Campground. Both prepared ($20) and bare sites ($7) are located on Brewers Bay, one of Tortola's prime snorkeling spots. Check out the ruins of the distillery that gave the bay its name. *Box 185, Road Town, Tortola, tel. 809/494–3463. Facilities: bar, restaurant, commissary, water sports, baby-sitters available. No credit cards. Budget.*

Tula's N & N Campground. Located in Little Harbour on the tiny island of Jost Van Dyke, Tula's offers both tent ($10) and bare ($4 a person) sites. *Little Harbour, Jost Van Dyke, tel. 809/774–0774 or 809/775–3073. Facilities: snack bar, restaurant, commissary. No credit cards. Budget.*

Villa and Apartment Rentals   Villas are available in a wide range of prices in the B.V.I., and the less expensive ones, most of which are on Virgin Gorda, can be downright cheap if you split the cost among several families.

Tortola   **Josiah's Bay Cottages.** These out-of-the-way hexagonal cottages are furnished in tropical prints and have large picture windows and roomy balconies. It's a five-minute walk from here to the beach. *Box 306, tel. 809/494–6186. 9 units. Facilities: pool. AE, MC, V. Moderate.*

Rockview Holiday Homes. Although most of their properties are luxury, this company has several more modest villas on the hillside along the northwest side of the island. *Box 263, tel. 809/494–2550. 30 villas. AE, MC, V. Moderate.*

Virgin Gorda **Guavaberry Spring Bay.** The managers of these popular hexagonal cottages (*see above*) also handle one-, two-, and three-bedroom villas, some with private pools, in The Valley area of Virgin Gorda. Prices start in the Moderate range, but some units are very expensive. *Box 20, tel. 809/495–5227. No credit cards. Moderate.*

Virgin Gorda Villa Rentals. This company manages villas all over Virgin Gorda, from Leverick Bay to the southern tip of the island. Many villas have private swimming pools; all boast spectacular views. *Box 63, tel. 809/495–7421. AE, D, MC, V. Inexpensive–Moderate.*

Off-Season Bets Virtually every property in the B.V.I., including its most exclusive resorts, offers reduced rates off-season. Top-of-the-line properties including **Biras Creek Hotel** (tel. 809/494–3555); **Bitter End Yacht Club** (tel. 809/494–2746); **Drake's Anchorage Resort** (tel. 809/494–2254 or 800/624–6651); **Little Dix Bay Resort** (tel. 809/495–5555); and **Peter Island Hotel and Yacht Harbour** (tel. 809/494–2561 or 800/346–4451) offer a number of off-season packages. If you are willing to travel in the fall (when the weather can be quite beautiful though somewhat unpredictable), you can find truly exceptional price reductions— most of which are never publicized. It's best to call the hotel directly for these, about a month before you want to visit, and ask if any special rates or packages are available.

Nightlife

On Tortola, live bands play at **Pusser's Landing** (Sophers Hole, tel. 809/494–4554) Thursday through Sunday, the **Jolly Roger** (West End, tel. 809/495–4559) Friday and Saturday, **Sebastian's** (Apple Bay, tel. 809/495–4214) Saturday and Sunday, and **Bomba's Shack** (Apple Bay, tel. 809/495–4148) on Sunday, Wednesday, and every full moon. At **Quito's Gazebo** (Cane Garden Bay, tel. 809/495–4837), B.V.I. recording star Quito Rhymer sings island ballads. **Stanley's Welcome Bar** (Cane Garden Bay, tel. 809/495–4520) gets rowdy when crews stop by to party. On Virgin Gorda, **Andy's Chateau de Pirate** (Fischer's Cove Beach Hotel, The Valley, tel. 809/495–5252) has live music and dancing on the weekends. One of the busiest nocturnal spots in the B.V.I. is little Jost Van Dyke. Check out **Rudy's Mariner Rendezvous** (tel. 809/495–9282), **Foxy's Tamarind** (tel. 809/495–9258), and **Sydney's Peace and Love** (tel. 809/495–9271).

8 Cayman Islands

Grand Cayman, Cayman Brac, Little Cayman

Updated by
Joan Iaconetti

The venerable old *Saturday Evening Post* dubbed them "the islands that time forgot." But the past decade has changed all that: The Cayman Islands, a British Crown colony that includes Grand Cayman, Cayman Brac, and Little Cayman, are now one of the Caribbean's hottest destinations.

Your dollars certainly go farther on other Caribbean islands than they do here. In Grand Cayman, which positively reeks of suburban prosperity, the U.S. dollar is worth 80 Cayman cents, and the cost of living is 20% higher than in the United States. As the locals say about their paradise, "It's a great place to live, but I wouldn't want to be a tourist here." But not everyone on the island earns a banker's salary—despite the 544 offshore banks in George Town, Grand Cayman's capital—and an affordable vacation *is* possible here.

If you're willing to do some homework before your trip, cook most of your dinners, and forego expensive pastimes like sportfishing and jetskiing, Grand Cayman is well worth considering, especially for families and groups. Most of the available rooms are in condos; four or more people sharing an apartment or villa bring down lodging costs considerably. Plan an off-season summer visit, and prices dip another 20%–40%. Grand Cayman rewards the budget traveler with gorgeous beaches, pleasant accommodations, virtually zero crime, genuinely welcoming locals, and some of the best scuba diving in the hemisphere.

Island-hopping among the Caymans eats up time and money, and not all flights run daily; best to choose among the three and stay put. Gung-ho scuba divers who have no use for shopping or lolling on wide sandy beaches will prefer the summer-camp-for-adults atmosphere of Little Cayman (Jacques Cousteau called Bloody Bay Wall one of the world's best dives). Cayman Brac has more modern, comfortable hotels and better beaches. It offers dive excursions to nearby Little Cayman, as well as good spelunking in numerous caves. Both offer good value.

What It Will Cost These prices, meant only as a general guide, are for high season. Price estimates are for high season. An inexpensive hotel on Grand Cayman is about $90–$110 a night. A villa or apartment rental (usually two bedrooms or more) will cost $225 and up. An inexpensive restaurant dinner is $9–$12. A picnic lunch or pub hamburger will be around $4.75; fast food, $3–$4. A rum punch costs about $4 at most restaurants, as does (surprisingly) a beer. A glass of wine is a little less. Car rental averages $48. A cab from the airport to Seven Mile Beach will be $8–$12; from George Town to Seven Mile Beach, about $8. A single-tank dive costs $35–$40. Snorkel equipment rents for about $15 a day.

Before You Go

Tourist Information For the latest information on activities and lodging, write or call any of the following offices of the **Cayman Islands Department of Tourism** (6100 Waterford Bldg., 6100 Blue Lagoon Dr., Suite 150, Miami, FL 33126–2085, tel. 305/266–2300; 2 Memorial City Plaza, 820 Gessner, Suite 170, Houston, TX 77024, tel. 713/461–1317; 420 Lexington Ave., Suite 2733, New York, NY 10170, tel. 212/682–5582; 9525 West Bryn Mawr Ave., Suite 160, Rosemont, IL 60018, tel. 708/678–6446; 3440 Wilshire Blvd., Suite 1202, Los Angeles, CA 90010, tel. 213/738–1968; 234 Eglinton Ave. E., Suite 306, Toronto, Ont. M4P 1K5, tel. 416/485–1550; Trevor House, 100 Brompton Rd., Knightsbridge, London SW3 1EX, tel. 071/581–9960).

Don't fail to study the annually updated *Rates and Facts* booklet, available from any Tourist Office. You'll find a wealth of detailed information and prices on accommodations, sports, taxi and transportation rentals, plus maps and general information. (Restaurant listings are in a separate brochure.)

Arriving and Departing
By Plane **Cayman Airways** (tel. 800/422–9626) flies nonstop daily from Miami and four times a week from Tampa and Houston. It flies direct from Atlanta, with a stop in Tampa, four days a week. **Northwest Airlines** (tel. 800/447–4747) flies daily nonstop from Miami and, during high season, several times weekly from Memphis. **American Airlines** (tel. 800/433–7300) flies daily from Miami and Raleigh-Durham. **Cayman Airtours** (tel. 800/247–2966) offers package deals. Flights land at Owen Roberts Airport on Grand Cayman, Gerrard Smith Airport on Cayman Brac, and Edward Bodden Airfield on Little Cayman.

From the Airport A taxi from the airport on Grand Cayman to central Seven Mile Beach costs $8–$12; Seven Mile Beach to George Town is $8. Some hotels offer free pickup. Car rentals are also available.

Passports and Visas American and Canadian citizens do not have to carry passports, but they must show some proof of citizenship, such as a birth certificate or voter registration card, plus a return ticket. British and Commonwealth subjects do not need a visa, but must carry a passport.

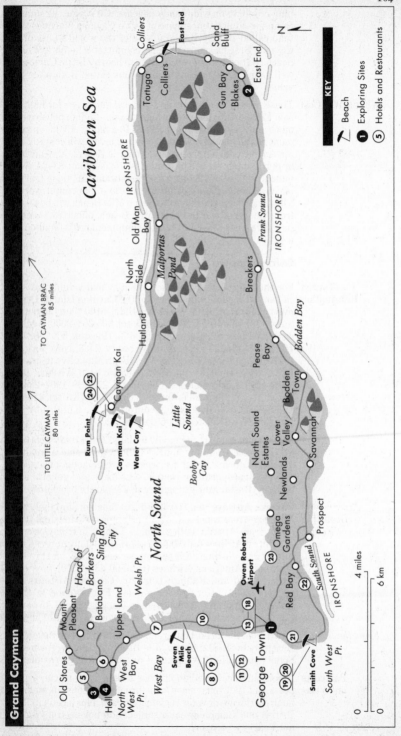

Grand Cayman

Caribbean Sea

TO LITTLE CAYMAN
80 miles

TO CAYMAN BRAC
85 miles

N

Old Stores

Hell ③ ④

North West Pt.

Mount Pleasant

⑤ ⑥

West Bay

Batabano

Upper Land

Head of Barkers

Sting Ray City

Welsh Pt.

North Sound

⑦

Seven Mile Beach

⑧ ⑨

⑪ ⑫

⑩

⑬ ⑱

Owen Roberts Airport

㉓

Omega Gardens

North Sound Estates

Lower Valley

Newlands

Little Sound

Booby Cay

Cayman Kai

Rum Point

㉔ ㉕

Cayman Kai

Water Cay

Hutland

Cayman Kai

North Side

Old Man Bay

IRONSHORE

Malportas Pond

Breakers

Frank Sound

IRONSHORE

Tortuga

Colliers

Colliers Pt.

East End

Sand Bluff

Gun Bay

Blakes

East End

②

Pease Bay

Bodden Bay

Bodden Town

Savannah

Prospect

South Sound

IRONSHORE

Red Bay

㉒

George Town

①

㉑

Smith Cove

⑲ ⑳

South West Pt.

South Cove

KEY

↗ Beach

❶ Exploring Sites

⑤ Hotels and Restaurants

0 — 4 miles

0 — 6 km

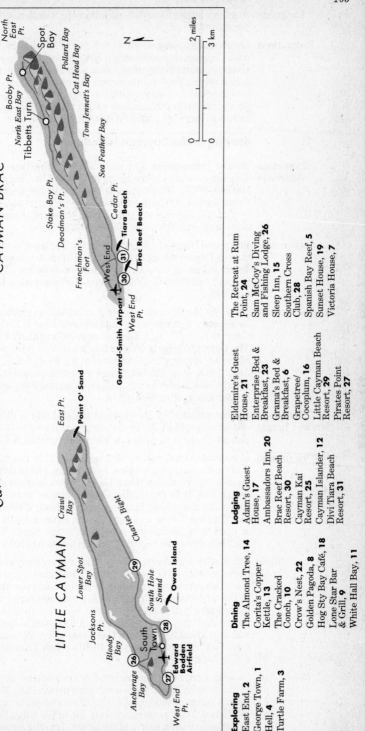

Caribbean Sea

CAYMAN BRAC

LITTLE CAYMAN

North East Pt.
Spot Bay
Booby Pt.
Pollard Bay
North East Bay
Cat Head Bay
Tibbetts Turn
Tom Jennett's Bay
Stake Bay Pt.
Deadman's Pt.
Sea Feather Bay
Frenchman's Fort
Cedar Pt.
West End
Tiara Beach
West End Pt.
Brac Reef Beach
Gerrard-Smith Airport

East Pt.
Point O' Sand
Crawl Bay
Charles Bight
Lower Spot Bay
Jacksons Pt.
South Hole Sound
Owen Island
Bloody Bay
South Town
Anchorage Bay
West End Pt.
Edward Bodden Airfield

N
0   2 miles
0   3 km

Exploring
East End, 2
George Town, 1
Hell, 4
Turtle Farm, 3

Dining
The Almond Tree, 14
Corita's Copper Kettle, 13
The Cracked Conch, 10
Crow's Nest, 22
Golden Pagoda, 8
Hog Sty Bay Café, 18
Lone Star Bar & Grill, 9
White Hall Bay, 11

Lodging
Adam's Guest House, 17
Ambassadors Inn, 20
Brac Reef Beach Resort, 30
Cayman Kai Resort, 25
Cayman Islander, 12
Divi Tiara Beach Resort, 31

Eldemire's Guest House, 21
Enterprise Bed & Breakfast, 23
Grama's Bed & Breakfast, 6
Grapetree/ Cocoplum, 16
Little Cayman Beach Resort, 29
Pirates Point Resort, 27

The Retreat at Rum Point, 24
Sam McCoy's Diving and Fishing Lodge, 26
Sleep Inn, 15
Southern Cross Club, 28
Spanish Bay Reef, 5
Sunset House, 19
Victoria House, 7

Language English is spoken everywhere; all local publications are in English as well.

Precautions Locals make a constant effort to conserve fresh water, so don't waste a precious commodity. Penalties for drug importation and possession of controlled substances include large fines and prison terms. Theft is uncommon, but be smart: Lock up your room and car and secure valuables as you would at home. Outdoors, marauding blackbirds called ching chings have been known to carry off jewelry if it is left out in the open.

Staying in the Cayman Islands

Important **Tourist Information:** The main office of the **Department of**
Addresses **Tourism** is located in the Harbour Center (N. Church St., tel. 809/949–0623). Information booths are in the George Town Craft Market, on Cardinal Avenue, open when cruise ships are in port (tel. 809/949–8342), and in the kiosk at the cruise ship dock in George Town (tel. 809/949–0623).

Emergencies **Police and Hospitals:** 911. **Pharmacies:** The most central pharmacy is **Cayman Drug,** (tel. 809/949–2597) in downtown George Town on Panton Street. **Airport Information:** For flight information, call 809/949–7733. **Divers' Recompression Chamber:** Call 555.

Currency Although the American dollar is accepted everywhere, you'll save money if you go to the bank and exchange U.S. dollars for Cayman Island (C.I.) dollars, which are worth about $1.25 each. The Cayman dollar is divided into a hundred cents with coins of 1¢, 5¢, 10¢, and 25¢, and notes of $1, $5, $10, $25, $50, and $100. There is no $20 bill. Prices are often quoted in Cayman dollars, so it's best to ask. All prices quoted here are in U.S. dollars unless otherwise noted.

Taxes and Hotels collect a 6% government tax and add a 10% service
Service Charges charge to your bill. Many restaurants add a 10%–15% service charge. There is no sales tax. The departure tax is $10.

Getting Around If your accommodations are along Seven Mile Beach, you can walk to the shopping centers, restaurants, and entertainment spots along West Bay Road. George Town is small enough to see on foot. If you're touring Grand Cayman by car, there's a well-maintained road that circles the island; it's hard to get lost. You won't need a car on Cayman Brac or Little Cayman (a good thing, since car rental doesn't exist here). Your hotel staff will drive you, though there's really nowhere to go.

Taxis Taxis offer islandwide service. Fares are determined by an elaborate rate structure set by the government, and although it may seem pricey for a short ride (fare from Seven Mile Beach to the airport ranges from $8 to $12), cabbies rarely try to rip off tourists. Ask to see the chart if you want to double-check the quoted fare. A cab from Seven Mile Beach to Georgetown will cost about $8. **Cayman Cab Team** offers 24-hour service (tel. 809/947–0859), as does **Holiday Inn Taxi Stand** (tel. 809/947–4491).

Rental Cars To rent a car, bring your current driver's license and the car-rental firm will issue you a temporary permit ($3). Most firms have a range of models available, from compacts to Jeeps to minibuses. Daily rates range from $35 to $55 a day. The major agencies have offices in a plaza across from the airport terminal, where you can pick up and drop off vehicles. Just remember, driving is on the left.

Car-rental companies are **Hertz** (tel. 809/949–2280), **Budget** (tel. 809/949–5605), **CICO-Avis** (tel. 809/949–2468), **Coconut** (tel. 809/949–4037), **Dollar** (tel. 809/949–2981), **Payless** (tel. 809/949–7074), **National** (tel. 809/949–4790), and **Marshall's Car Rental** (tel. 809/949–2127).

Bicycles, Scooters, and Motorcycles   Since Grand Cayman is flat as a pancake, why not zip around on a motor scooter or bike? (Don't forget the sun block.) Bicycles (about $12 a day), scooters ($20–$24 a day), and motorcycles ($30–$35 a day) can be rented from **Caribbean Motors Ltd.** (tel. 809/949–8878) and **Cayman Cycle Rentals** (several locations on Seven Mile Beach, tel. 809/947–4021).

Telephones and Mail   For international dialing to Cayman, the area code is 809. To call outside, dial 0 + 1 + area code and number. You can call anywhere, anytime through the Cable and Wireless system and local operators. To make local calls (25¢ at a pay phone), dial the seven-digit number.

Beautiful stamps and first-day covers are available at the main post office in downtown George Town weekdays from 8:30 to 4 and from the Philatelic office in West Shore Plaza, weekdays from 8:30 to 3:30. Sending a postcard to the United States, Canada, the Caribbean, or Central America costs C.I. 10¢. An airmail letter is C.I. 25¢ per half-ounce. To Europe and South America, the rates are C.I. 15¢ for a postcard and C.I. 50¢ per half ounce for airmail letters.

Opening and Closing Times   Banking hours are generally Monday–Thursday 9–2:30 and Friday 9–1 and 2:30–4:30. Shops are open weekdays 9–5, and on Saturday in George Town from 10 to 2; in outer shopping plazas, from 10 to 5. Shops are usually closed on Sunday except in hotels.

Guided Tours   **Evco Tours** (tel. 809/949–2118) offers six-hour, round-island tours from the Tortuga Club at the East End to the Turtle Farm and village of Hell in West Bay. All-day tours also can be arranged with **GreyLine** (tel. 809/949–2791), **Majestic Tours** (tel. 809/949–7773), **Reids** (tel. 809/949–6531), **Rudy's** (tel. 809/949–3208), and **Tropicana Tours** (tel. 809/949–0944). Half-day tours average $45 a person; full-day tours are around $65 a person, including lunch.

Exploring the Cayman Islands

Numbers in the margin correspond to points of interest on the Grand Cayman and Cayman Brac and Little Cayman maps.

George Town
❶   Begin exploring **George Town** at the **National Museum** on Harbour Drive, slightly south of the Cruise Ship Dock Gazebo. Small but fascinating, the museum has excellent displays and videos illustrating the history of Cayman plant, animal, human, and geological life. *Harbour Drive, tel. 809/949–8368. Admission: C.I. $5. Open Mon.–Sat. 9:30–4:30.*

Along the waterfront, heading along North Church Street toward town, notice part of the original wall of the old Fort George, which is being restored. Across the street is the Wholesome Bakery and Cafe, which adds the homey smell of baking bread to the sea breezes off George Town Harbour. Try one of its delicious meat patties. Turn left onto **Fort Street,** a main shopping street where you'll find the People's Boutique and a whole row of jewelry shops.

At the end of the block is the heart of downtown George Town. At the corner of Fort Street and **Edward Street,** notice the small clock tower dedicated to Britain's King George V and the huge fig tree, manicured into an umbrella shape. The Cayman Islands **Legislative Assembly Building** is next door to the 1919 **Peace Memorial Building.**

Turning right on Edward Street, you'll find the charming **Library,** built in 1939; it has English novels, current newspapers from the United States, and a small reference section. It's worth a visit just for the old-world atmosphere. Across the street is the new **Court House.** Down the next block, enter the "financial district," where banks from all over the world have offices.

Straight ahead is the **General Post Office,** also built in 1939, with its strands of decorative colored lights and some 2,000 private mailboxes on the outside. (Mail is not delivered on the island.) Behind the post office is **Elizabethan Square,** a new shopping and office complex on **Shedden Road** that houses various food, clothing, and souvenir establishments. The courtyard has a pleasant garden and fountain as well as outdoor tables at La Fontaine, a German restaurant.

Leave Elizabethan Square via Shedden Road and walk past Anderson Square and Caymania Freeport. Turn right back onto Edward Street, then left at the Royal Bank of Canada onto **Cardinal Avenue.** This is the main shopping area. On the right is the chic Kirk Freeport Plaza, known for its duty-free luxury items. Turn left on **Harbour Drive** and make your way back to Shedden Road, passing the English Shoppe, a souvenir outlet that looks more as if it belongs on Shaftesbury Avenue in London than in the West Indies, and the Cayside Galleries, with its maritime antiques and cameras.

Returning to town on Harbour Drive, makes for a leisurely stroll along a waterfront sidewalk. Cruise-ship passengers disembark at a new public park with a circular gazebo. Across the street is a pleasant church, the **Elmslie Memorial United.** Its vaulted ceiling with wood arches and sedate nave reflect the quietly religious nature of island residents.

The **Treasure Museum,** located on West Bay Road in front of the Hyatt Hotel, contains dioramas showing how Caymanians became seafarers, boat builders, and turtle breeders. An animated figure of Blackbeard the Pirate spins salty tales about the pirates and buccaneers who "worked" the Caribbean. Since the museum is owned by a professional treasure-salvaging firm, it's not surprising that there are a lot of artifacts from shipwrecks. There is even a gold bar that visitors can lift to appreciate its weight. *West Bay Rd., tel. 809/947–5033. Admission: C.I. $5. Open Mon.–Sat. 9–4:30 but hours can change; phone to check.*

The Outer Districts To see the rest of the island, rent a car or scooter, or take a guided tour (*see above*). A half-day guided tour (sufficient to see the major sites) is roughly comparable in cost to a single day of car rental. The flat road that circles the island is in good condition, with clear signs; you'd have to work to get lost here. Driving is on the left.

Venturing away from the Seven Mile Beach strip, travelers will encounter the more down-home character of the islands. Heading out on South Church Street, you can see some of the old houses, which feature elaborate Victorian gingerbread on modest frame homes. Heading east in a district called **Pantonville,** you'll come upon three pretty cottages with lacy woodwork. At **South Sound** are larger residences, some with fine detail and gracious verandas.

In the Savannah district, **Pedro's Castle,** built in 1780, lays claim to being the oldest structure on the island. Formerly a restaurant, it was purchased by the government in late 1991 for restoration as a historic landmark. At **Bodden Town,** you'll find an old cemetery on the shore side of the road. Graves with A-frame structures are said to contain the remains of pirates, but may actually be those of early settlers. A curio shop serves as the entrance to what's called the **Pirate's Caves;** you'll pass a minizoo en route to these partially underground caves. The natural formations are interesting, but the place is more hokey than spooky.

❷ The village of **East End** is the first recorded settlement on the island. Renowned local musician the "Violin Man," aka Radley Gourzong and His Happy Boys, lives here and occasionally performs his distinctive form of music (more akin to Louisiana's backwater zydeco than reggae). East End is also the site of a number of shipwrecks and **Morritt's Tortuga Club** (55 timeshare units), whose guests include avid divers and windsurfers.

At the other end of the island is the **West Bay** community, whose ❸ main attraction is the **Turtle Farm** established about 25 years ago, both as a conservation and a commercial enterprise. It releases about 5% of its stock back out to sea every year, harvests turtles for local restaurants, and exports the by-products. (Note: U.S. citizens are forbidden from importing turtle products.) Some 70,000 visitors a year now come to see turtles of all ages, from day-old hatchlings to huge 600-pounders that can live to be 100 years old. In the adjoining café, you can sample turtle soup or turtle sandwiches. *West Bay Rd., tel. 809/949–3893. Admission: $5 adults, $2.50 children 6–12. Open daily 9–5.*

The other area of West Bay that is of brief interest is the tiny ❹ village of **Hell,** which is little more than a patch of incredibly jagged rock formations called ironshore. The big attraction here is a small post office, which does a land-office business selling stamps and postmarking cards from Hell. You'll find plenty of T-shirt and souvenir shops. Almost unbelievably, a nearby nightclub, called the Club Inferno, is run by the McDoom family.

Cayman Brac

Brac, the Gaelic word for "bluff," aptly identifies this island's most distinctive feature, a rugged limestone cliff that runs down the center of the island's 12-mile length and soars to 140 feet at its eastern end. Lying 89 miles east of Grand Cayman, Cayman Brac is a spelunker's paradise: You can explore the island's half-dozen large caves, some of which are still used for hurricane shelter, via moped or taxi. Only 1,700 people live on this island, in communities such as Watering Place and Halfway Ground. Flora and fauna include unusual orchids, mangoes, papaya, and the Cayman Brac parrot. Parts of the island are unpopulated, so visitors can explore truly isolated areas both inland and along the shore. Two hotels catering to divers are located on sandy beaches on the southwest coast. Swimming is possible, but the bottom is rocky.

Little Cayman

Only 7 miles from Cayman Brac is Little Cayman Island, population 32. This is a true hideaway: few phones, fewer shops, no nightlife—just spectacular diving, great fishing, and laid-back camaraderie. In addition to privacy, the real attractions of Little Cayman are diving in spectacular Bloody Bay, off the north coast, and fishing, which includes angling for tarpon and bonefish. Visitor accommodations are mostly in small lodges.

And if Little Cayman ever gets too busy, there is one final retreat—**Owen Island,** just 200 yards offshore. Accessible by rowboat, it has a blue lagoon and a sandy beach. Take your own picnic if you plan to spend the day.

Beaches

Grand Cayman You may read or hear about the "dozens of beaches" of these islands, but that's more exaggeration than reality. Grand Cayman's west coast, the most developed area of the entire colony, is where you'll find its famous **Seven Mile Beach** (actually 5$^{1}/_{2}$ miles long) and its expanses of powdery white sand. The beach is litter-free and sans peddlers, so you can relax in an unspoiled, hassle-free (if somewhat crowded) atmosphere. This is also Grand Cayman's busiest vacation center, and most of the island's accommodations, restaurants, shopping centers, and water-sports shops are on this strip.

Smith Cove, off South Church Street in George Town, south of the Grand Old House, is a popular bathing spot with residents on weekends.

The best snorkeling locations are off **the ironshore** (coral ledge area) south of **George Town** on Grand Cayman's west coast and in the reef-protected shallows of the island's north and south coasts, where coral and fish life are much more varied and abundant.

Other good beaches include **East End,** at Colliers, by Morritt's Tortuga Club, which can be lovely when free of the seaweed tossed ashore by trade winds. Seldom discovered by visitors unless they're staying there are the beautiful beach areas of **Cayman Kai, Rum Point,** and, even more isolated and unspoiled, **Water Cay.** These are favored hideaways for residents and popular Sunday picnic spots.

Cayman Brac Both **Tiara Beach** and **Brac Reef Beach** resorts have fine small beaches, better for sunning than for snorkeling. Excellent snorkeling can be found immediately offshore of the now-defunct **Buccaneer's Inn** on the north coast.

Little Cayman The beaches of **Point o' Sand,** on the eastern tip, and **Owen Island,** off the south coast, are exquisite, isolated patches of powder that are great for sunbathing and worth a minisplurge to reach by car, bike, or boat.

Sports and the Outdoors

Diving and Snorkeling To say the Cayman Islands are a scuba diver's paradise is not overstating the case. Pristine water (often exceeding 100-foot visibility), breathtaking coral formations, and plentiful and exotic marine life await divers. Snorkeling here is equally wonderful, with countless shallow, offshore reefs. A must-see here is **Sting Ray City,** which has been called the "best 12-foot dive (or snorkel) in the world." Here dozens of sting rays, which have become tame from being fed first by fishermen and now divers, will play gracefully around you in what feels like an extraordinary interaction with alien life forms.

Divers are required to be certified and possess a C card or to take a short resort or full certification course. A certification course, including classroom, pool, and boat sessions as well as checkout dives, takes five or six days and costs $300–$350. A resort course usually lasts a day and costs about $75–$90. It introduces the novice to the sport and teaches the rudimentary skills needed to make a shallow, instructor-monitored dive.

All dive operations on Cayman are more than competent; among them are **Bob Soto's** (tel. 809/947–4631 or 800/262–7686), **Don Foster's** (tel. 809/949–5679), **Red Sail Sports** (tel. 809/949–8745 or 800/255–6425), **Quabbin Dives** (tel. 809/949–5597), and **Sunset Divers** (tel. 809/949–7111 or 800/854–4767). Request full information on all operators from the Department of Tourism (*see* Before You Go, *above*). Most operations can rent all diving gear, including equipment for underwater photography. A single-tank dive here averages $35–$40; a two-tank dive is about $55. Snorkel equipment rents for $10–$15 a day, so consider purchasing your own before you come.

On Cayman Brac, **Brac Aquatics** (tel. 809/858–7429 or 809/858–7323) and **Divi Tiara** (tel. 809/948–7553) offer scuba and snorkeling. On Little Cayman, each hotel has its own instructors.

Golf The **Grand Cayman–Britannia** golf course (tel. 809/949–1234), next to the Hyatt Regency on Seven Mile Beach, was designed by Jack Nicklaus. The course is really three in one—a nine-hole championship course, an 18-hole executive course, and a Cayman course, played with a Cayman ball that goes about half the distance of a regulation ball. Greens fees range from $25 to $50.

The first 9 holes of "The Links," located on the west coast of Grand Cayman, and the Cayman's first 18-hole championship course, were scheduled at press time to be ready by December 1993.

Sea Excursion The most impressive sights are underwater. Snorkeling, diving, glass-bottom-boat and submarine rides can be arranged at any of the major aquatic shops: **Atlantis Submarine** (tel. 809/949–7700), **Aqua Delights** (tel. 809/947–4786), **Bob Soto's Diving Ltd.** (tel. 809/947–4631), **Don Foster's Dive Grand Cayman** (tel. 809/949–5679), **Red Sail Sports** (tel. 809/949–8745), and the **Watersports Center** (tel. 809/947–0762). All-day snorkel excursions are about $40 a person.

Water Sports Water skis, Windsurfers, Hobie Cats, and jet skis are available at many of the aquatic shops along Seven Mile Beach (*see* Diving, *above*).

Shopping

Grand Cayman offers a vast selection of fine jewelry, including authentic sunken treasure and ancient coins made into jewelry. Though items can be pricey, many are unique; you may decide something is worth a splurge. Try **Venture Gallery** (tel. 809/949–8657) in the Westshore Shopping Center.

If you have a rental car, don't overlook an unlikely pastime: Garage sales. Yard sales and "leaving the island" sales are listed in the Friday *Caymanian Compass* publication, and early arrivals can get great bargains on scuba/snorkel equipment, books, and who knows what else.

Debbie van der Bol runs an arts and crafts shop called **Pure Art** (tel. 809/949–4433) on South Church Street and at the Hyatt Regency Hotel (tel. 809/347–5633). She features watercolors, woodcarvings, and lace-making by local artists, as well as her own sketches and cards. The **Heritage Crafts Shop** (tel. 809/949–7093), near the harbor in George Town, sells local crafts and gifts. The new **West Shore Shopping Center** on Seven Mile Beach near the Radisson offers good-quality island art, beachwear, and more. Original prints, paintings, and sculpture with a tropical theme are found at **Cayman Fine Art** (tel. 809/949–8007). The **Oasis Boutique** (tel. 809/947–4444) at the Holiday Inn has a superior selection of contemporary art pieces, jewelry, gifts, carvings, and clothing. T-shirt shops abound all over town.

Dining

Among Caribbean destinations, the Caymans are second only to the French islands for fine gourmet dining and prices to match. West Indian fare in local restaurants offers the best value and—often—taste. The following tips will cut costs.

You can skip lunch if you eat enough breakfast at the huge all-you-can-eat buffet at **Holiday Inn** (tel. 809/947–4444); cost is about $10. The **Wholesome Bakery** (tel. 809/949–7588), on the waterfront in George Town, offers full bacon-and-egg or waffle breakfasts for about $4. Enjoy fine dining and save almost 50% over dinner prices when you lunch at **Lantana's** (tel. 809/947–5595), the **Grand Old House** (tel. 809/949–9333), the **Wharf** (tel. 809/949–2231), and other fine restaurants. (Be sure to reserve.) Try **Champion House** (no phone; closed evening) on Eastern Avenue for large takeout portions of local dishes such as spicy beef stew, conch, breadfruit salad, cassava, and yams. A huge plateful ($6–$8) can be refrigerated for dinner.

Happy hours in West Bay Road hotels offer discounted drinks and free hors d'oeuvres daily between 5 and 7 or 8; graze enough, and you've replaced dinner. Try **Periwinkle** (tel. 809/947–5181), **Sunset House** (tel. 809/949–7111), **Ottmar's** (tel. 809/947–5879), the Radisson's **BWI** nightclub (tel. 809/949–0088), and **Indies Suites** (tel. 809/947–5025). Other weekly all-you-can-eat feeds of fajitas, seafood, or fish are listed Friday's *Cayman Compass*, available everywhere.

For the occasional quick, cheap meal, there are always the fast-food joints: On Seven Mile Beach you'll find Burger King, Pizza Hut, Subway, KFC, Domino's, TCBY Yogurt, and Wendy's.

The latter offers an all-you-can-eat salad bar, including pastas and Mexican food, for about $8.

While Grand Cayman's supermarkets are somewhat more expensive than those in the United States, they now feature salad bars and deli takeout salads for under $4 a pound—perfect for picnics or eating in. Try **Kirk's, Foster's Food Fair,** and **Hurley's,** all along Seven Mile Beach. Note that supermarket munchies such as potato chips and nachos cost about triple what they do stateside.

Many restaurants automatically add a 15% gratuity to your bill. If you're not sure, just ask; otherwise, you'll be tipping twice. Highly recommended restaurants are indicated by a star ★.

Category	Cost*
Moderate	$20–$30
Inexpensive	$10–$20
Budget	under $10

per person, excluding drinks and service

The Almond Tree. This eatery features architecture from the South Seas isle of Yap, with bones, skulls, and bric-a-brac from Africa, South America, and the Pacific. Sample good-value seafood entrées, including environmentally correct turtle steak, with "All-U-Can-Eat" entrées for C.I. $11 on Wednesday and Friday. Avoid the lobster and some seafood dishes to keep your bill within our Moderate price range. *North Church St., tel. 809/459–2893. Dinner reservations advised. AE, MC, V. Closed Tues. Moderate.*

The Cracked Conch. Specialties at this popular, often-crowded fish house include conch fritters, conch chowder, spicy Cayman-style snapper, and three types of turtle steak. The Key lime pie is divine. Take-out service is available. The bar has live entertainment and is a local hangout. *Selkirk's Plaza, West Bay Rd., tel. 809/947–5217. Reservations advised in winter. AE, MC, V. Moderate.*

★ **Crow's Nest.** With the ocean right in its backyard, this secluded small restaurant, located about a 15-minute drive south of George Town, is a great spot for snorkeling as well as lunching. The gourmet shrimp and conch dishes are excellent, as is the dessert of raisins and rum cake. One drawback: Insect repellent is required for patio dining in the evening. *South Sound, tel. 809/949–9366. Reservations required. MC, V. Closed Sun. Moderate.*

Golden Pagoda. The oldest Chinese restaurant in the Caymans features Mahlah chicken, butterfly shrimp, and chicken in black-bean sauce. Takeout is available. *West Bay Rd., tel. 809/949–5475. Dress: no shorts at dinner. AE, MC, V. Moderate.*

White Hall Bay. Formerly the Cook Rum, this casual and charming restaurant has now moved across the street to a rambling old house on the waterfront. The hearty West Indian menu includes turtle stew, salt beef and beans, and pepper pot stew. Follow up with dessert specials, such as yam cake and coconut cream pie. *N. Church St., tel. 809/949–8670. AE, D, MC, V. Moderate.*

Hog Sty Bay Cafe. People gather on the seaside patio of this English pub-style café on the harbor in George Town to socialize and watch the sun set. The simple menu of sandwiches, hamburgers, and Caribbean dishes is available at lunch and dinner; there's a happy hour on weekday evenings. *N. Church St., tel. 809/949–6163. AE, MC, V. Closed lunch Sat. Inexpensive–Moderate.*

Corita's Copper Kettle. Here is a tidy downtown diner featuring Jamaican breakfasts and such native specialties as conch and lobster burgers. The fare is tasty and plain. *Edward St., tel. 809/949–2696; Dolphin Center, tel. 809/949–7078. No reservations. No credit cards. Inexpensive.*

Lone Star Bar & Grill. This very casual sports bar with red-and-white checked tablecloths and booths offers indoor and outdoor seating. The menu is mostly Tex-Mex, with most dishes under $10. The bar here is open daily until 1 AM. *Seven Mile Beach, tel. 809/947–5175. AE, MC, V. Budget–Inexpensive.*

Lodging

While it takes work to make the Caymans an affordable destination, the wide range of accommodations on Grand Cayman gives you a head start. Divers will find money-saving packages offered through hotels and through **TourScan, Inc.** (tel. 800/962–2080 or 203/655–8091 in CT) and **Cayman Airtours** (tel. 800/247–2966).

Most of the hotels on Grand Cayman are on or very near Seven Mile Beach. Those that aren't either have their own beach—sometimes rocky coral, sometimes sandy—or are within a 10-minute walk. All hotels on Cayman Brac and Little Cayman are on the beach. More than half of the Caymans' rooms are in condominiums rather than hotels, with weekly rates ranging from $735 all the way to $7,000. Dozens rent in the $1,600-$2,300-a-week range; traveling with another couple brings the cost well into our Moderate price range and below. Some properties allow an extra person(s) to stay for $10–$20 a night over the regular rate, and many offer kitchens. Shopping the well-stocked supermarkets and cooking your own meals further cut costs.

Most of the larger hotels along Seven Mile Beach don't offer meal plans. The smaller properties that are more remote from the restaurants usually offer MAP or FAP. **Cayman Islands Hotel Reservations:** 800/327–8777.

Highly recommended lodgings are indicated by a star ★.

Category	Cost*
Moderate	$160–$200
Inexpensive	$110–$160
Budget	under $110

*All prices are for a standard double room for two, excluding 6% tax and a 10% service charge. To estimate rates for hotels offering MAP/FAP, add about $40 per person per day to the above price ranges.

Hotels
Grand Cayman

Cayman Kai Resort. Nestled next to a coconut grove, each sea lodge features a full kitchen, dining and living areas, and two screened-in porches overlooking the ocean. The hotel is on a beach on the north-central tip of the island—quite remote. You need a car to get anywhere, but many of the guests simply don't; they're content to stay put and dive. *Box 1112, North Side, Grand Cayman, tel. 809/947–9055 or 800/223–5427, fax 809/947–9055. 26 sea lodges, 1 villa. Facilities: restaurant, 2 bars, tennis court, diving, fishing and water-sports shop. AE, MC, V. EP. Moderate.*

★ **Sunset House.** Low-key and laid-back describe this resort with air-conditioned, motel-style rooms on the ironshore south of George Town, 4 miles from Seven Mile Beach. A well-run dive operation, congenial staff, popular bar, and excellent seafood restaurant make Sunset House a favorite with divers. It's easy to meet people most evenings in the relaxed atmosphere on the deck. Full dive services include free waterside lockers, three-tank dives to sites on the eastern end of the island, and Cathy Church's U/W Photo Center. It's a five-minute walk to a sandy beach, 10 minutes to George Town. Ask about the excellent dive packages. *Box 479, S. Church St., Grand Cayman, tel. 809/949–7111 or 800/854–4767, fax 809/949–7101. 57 rooms, 2 suites. Facilities: restaurant, bar, dive shop and u/w photo center, fresh and seawater pools, whirlpool, fishing and sailing charters. AE, D, MC, V. EP. Inexpensive–Moderate.*

Cayman Islander. New management has refurbished the pool and garden area and all rooms at this simple, locally run hotel. Improvements include new air-conditioning, brighter tropical decor, and phone and satellite TV in each room. The 9-acre flower garden includes a large pond with indigenous freshwater turtles. The five efficiency apartments have microwaves and refrigerators in the kitchenettes. There's a complete dive shop on-site, with dive packages available. The property offers great value in a great location, across the road from Seven Mile Beach. *Box 30081, Seven Mile Beach, Grand Cayman, tel. 809/949–0990 or 800/327–8777, fax 809/949–7896. 67 rooms, 5 efficiency apartments. Facilities: restaurant, bar/lounge, dive shop, pool, satellite TV. AE, MC, V. EP. Inexpensive.*

Sleep Inn. This two-story Choice Hotels affiliate is a stroll from Seven Mile Beach, close to the airport and just a mile from George Town's shops. Air-conditioned rooms are motel-modern, with the usual pastels and furnishings. The eight suites have a queen-size bed and sleeper sofa. All units feature satellite TV, phones, and super-sized showers. The Dive Inn dive shop is here, as are tours and car and motorcycle rentals. *Box 30111, Grand Cayman, tel. 809/949–9111, fax 809/949–6699. 116 rooms, 8 suites. Facilities: pool, whirlpool, poolside bar and grill, water-sports shop, boutique. AE, D, MC, V. EP. Inexpensive.*

★ **Spanish Bay Reef.** Grand Cayman's only all-inclusive resort is lovely, with by far the most secluded, authentically Caribbean feel of any property along the west shore. Pale pink, two-story stucco units are surrounded by flowering trees and bushes on their own small, sandy beach. An outdoor dining/bar area around the pool and overlooking the ocean includes tables under a semicircular white-latticed arcade. There's also a spacious, coral-stone indoor bar and dining area. Simple but comfortable guest units, with bright Caribbean print bedspreads and curtains, are connected by boardwalks; they feature air-conditioning, private balcony or patio, and satellite TV. The resort is located on the northwest tip of the island, several miles past Seven Mile Beach in West Bay. Spanish Bay Reef itself is a deep drop-off, which means superior beach diving and snorkeling; instruction in both is offered. Rates include round-trip transfers, all taxes and gratuities, unlimited shore diving, daily two-tank boat dive, use of bicycles (not in mint condition), and Jeeps (one per eight rooms). *Box 30867 SMB, Grand Cayman, tel. 809/949–3765, fax 809/949–1842. 46 units. Facilities: restaurant, disco, bar, pool, 2 Jacuzzis, dive shop, fishing charters. AE, D, DC, MC, V. All-inclusive. Budget–Inexpensive.*

Cayman Brac **Brac Reef Beach Resort.** Designed, built, and owned by Bracker Linton Tibbets, the resort lures divers and vacationers who come to savor the special ambience of this tiny island. Just-renovated accommodations, a pool, a beach, snorkeling, and the waterside two-story covered deck are additional reasons to stay here. *Box 56, Cayman Brac, tel. 809/948–7323, 800/327–3835, 800/233–8880 in FL. 40 rooms. Facilities: restaurant, 2 bars, pool, Jacuzzi, beach, dive shop, tennis, photo center. AE, MC, V. EP, MAP, FAP. Inexpensive–Moderate.*

Divi Tiara Beach Resort. This resort is dedicated to divers; it has an excellent diving facility complemented by the Divi chain's standards: tile floors, rattan furniture, louvered windows, balconies, and ocean views. *Box 238, Cayman Brac, tel. 809/948–7553; in the U.S., 800/FOR–DIVI. 70 rooms. Facilities: restaurant, bar, pool, Jacuzzi, tennis, dive operation, watersports center, fishing. AE, MC, V. EP. Inexpensive–Moderate.*

Little Cayman **Southern Cross Club.** Three family-style meals a day are included in the rates at this relaxing retreat that caters to fishermen and divers. Spacious, two-unit cottages have charming white wicker decor. You're on a pretty beach here, with good views. A motorboat makes trips to uninhabited Owen Island nearby. *Little Cayman, tel. 809/948–3255; in the U.S., 317/636–9501. 10 rooms. Facilities: diving, fishing, bird-watching in sanctuary. No credit cards. FAP. Moderate.*

Little Cayman Beach Resort. Considerably less rustic than other Little Cayman resorts, this new two-story property has 32 oceanfront rooms with modern furnishings in pastel tropical colors, tile floors, and satellite TVs. The formal dining room overlooking the pool and bar area seats 50 for family-style meals. Double hammocks are slung on the two-story pier. The resort offers diving and fishing packages. A second wing was scheduled to open by the end of 1993. *Little Cayman, tel. 809/948–4533 or 800/327–3835, fax 809/948–4507. 32 rooms. Facilities: dive shop, pool, Jacuzzi, bar/restaurant, dive packages. AE, MC, V. MAP, FAP. All-inclusive. Inexpensive–Moderate.*

Pirates Point Resort. Opened by Texan Gladys Howard, this comfortably informal beach resort has added four large rooms to its six octagonal units just a few minutes from the airstrip. The voluble Ms. Howard leads nature walks and is a cordon bleu chef. "Relaxing" rates include meals only; all-inclusive rates include mouth-watering meals, wine, dives, fishing, and picnics on uninhabited Owen Island. *Little Cayman, tel. 809/948–4210 or 800/654–7537, fax 809/948–4610. 10 rooms. Facilities: diving, fishing, restaurant. No credit cards. FAP, All-inclusive. Inexpensive–Moderate.*

Sam McCoy's Diving and Fishing Lodge. Be prepared for an ultracasual experience: This is really a large, ordinary family house with very simple bedrooms and baths. There's no bar or restaurant per se; guests just eat at a few tables outdoors or with Sam and his family. Fans like it for its very low rates and the owner's infectious good nature, and for the superb diving and snorkeling right offshore. In late 1991, Sam opened a new beach bar a few minutes away overlooking Bloody Bay. Totally secluded, it offers outdoor dancing and light snacks. Rates include all meals (not drinks), diving, and airport transfers. Guided bonefishing trips are $15 an hour. *Little Cayman, tel. 809/948–4526 or 800/626–0496, fax 809/949–6821. 6 rooms. Facilities: diving and fishing trips. No credit cards. FAP. Budget–Inexpensive.*

Guest Houses and B&Bs   Away from the beach and short on style and facilities, these nevertheless offer rock-bottom prices and a friendly atmosphere. Rooms are clean and simple, often with cooking facilities.

Ambassadors Inn. This peach-pink, motellike property is just across the road from the ironshore (rocky beach), a mile south of town on the southwest tip of the island. A large patio with open-air and indoor dining (breakfast and lunch) faces the swimming pool; the area is shaded by a gigantic sea-grape tree. The talking green parrot says "hello" as you return from your computer-assisted daily dive trip (maximum 12 divers). Simple rooms with private baths have pink and green flowered bedspreads, TVs, phones, and air-conditioning, and all but four have ceiling fans. Gung-ho divers return repeatedly for the great diving, the casual atmosphere, and the camaraderie. *Box 1789, Grand Cayman, tel. 809/949–7577 or 800/648–7748, fax 809/949–7050. 18 rooms. Facilities: restaurant, bar, pool, dive facilities. AE, MC, V. EP. Budget–Inexpensive.*

Grama's Bed & Breakfast. Graham and Madge Ebanks offer simple rooms with ceiling fans (air-conditioning is about $5 extra) in a remodeled two-story house. There are no cooking facilities in rooms, but there's an outdoor grill for guest use. Private screened patios overlook a freshwater pool, and the secluded, residential location offers a taste of real Caymanian life. A car is needed to get anywhere other than Seven Mile Beach, a few blocks away. It's 8 miles to town or the airport. *Box 198, West Bay, Grand Cayman, tel. 809/949–3798. 5 rooms. Facilities: pool, outdoor grill. No credit cards. BP. Budget–Inexpensive.*

Adam's Guest House. A mile south of George Town, this '50s-style ranch house offers spotless, bright rooms with air-conditioning and ceiling fans, microwave/toaster ovens, minifridges, and private entrances to each of its guest rooms and one 2-bedroom apartment. Owners Tom and Olga Adam are well-traveled, warm, and interesting. Their hospitality—along with their dog and exotic birds—make this a real home away from home. The beach is 4 miles away, but Smith Cove Bay, with its wonderful snorkeling, is a 10-minute stroll, and dive facilities are within a five-minute walk. *Box 312GT, George Town, Grand Cayman, tel. 809/949–2512. 5 units. No credit cards or personal checks; cash or travelers' checks only. EP. Budget.*

Eldemire's Guest House. Grand Cayman's first guest house is a mile from town and a half-mile from pretty Smith Cove beach. A rambling ranch house, it has large, simple, spotless guest rooms and one studio apartment; room decor tends toward pastel pink and blue. Each unit has private bath and ceiling fans, but no TV or phone. Guests have kitchen privileges and fridge space; there's an extra $10 charge per night for each extra person up to five. Eighty-two-year-old owner Erma E. clearly loves her work, which includes dispensing island lore and local recipes for coconut jelly and honey chicken wings. The house has a large screened porch, and a plant-filled yard has picnic table and barbecue pit. No dive packages, but full dive facilities are within a five-minute walk. It's a 15-minute drive to Seven Mile Beach. *Box 482, Grand Cayman, tel. 809/949–5387, fax 809/949–6987. 5 units. No credit cards. EP. Budget.*

Enterprise Bed & Breakfast. The two-story white frame house looks about as futuristic as a palm tree, but Captain Kirk would enjoy the posters of Star Trek actors and intergalactic "cities," snapshots of the owner in his Starship uniform, videos of every "Star Trek" show and film, and, in the large white rooms, magenta or electric-blue satin bedspreads. This is a "no-smoking inn" in a very quiet, rather treeless residential area that borders a small marsh and is 10 minutes by car from town and Seven Mile Beach; you'll need wheels. Rooms have either air-conditioning or ceiling fans, plus refrigerators and microwaves. Diving can be arranged through Aqua'Nauts Diving nearby. Bring your own Klingon. *Box 246, Savannah, Grand Cayman, tel. 809/947–6009. U.S. reservations: Box 8063, Calabasas, CA. 91372, tel. 800/484–9943, fax 818/348–0433. 8 rooms. No credit cards. BP. Budget.*

Villa and Condominium Rentals The Cayman Islands Department of Tourism provides a complete list of condominiums and rental apartments in the Moderate to Inexpensive range. Many of these are multibedroom units that become affordable when shared by two or more couples. Also try: **Reef House Ltd. Property Management** (Box 1540, Grand Cayman, tel. 809/949–7093); **Scales & Company Ltd.** (Box 1103, Grand Cayman, tel. 809/947–4325, fax 809/947–4320); and **Hospitality World Ltd.** (Box 30123, Grand Cayman, tel. 809/949–8098 or 800/232–1034, fax 809/949–7054). The following complexes, which bear a marked similarity to one another, are on Grand Cayman. All are well-maintained, directly on the beach, and near town, though you will need a car for grocery shopping.

Grapetree/Cocoplum. A half-mile from George Town on Seven Mile Beach, these sister condo units are adjacent to one another. Grapetree's two-bedroom, two-bath units are carpeted, with traditional wicker furnishings and beige and brown colors. Cocoplum's units are similar, with Caribbean pastel prints; its grounds have more plants and trees. Units in both are air-conditioned and have ceiling fans. The two share two pools and tennis courts. *Box 1802, West Bay Beach, Grand Cayman, tel. 809/949–5640, fax 809/949–0150. 51 units. Facilities: 2 freshwater pools, tennis courts. AE, MC, V. Moderate.*

The Retreat at Rum Point. It's got its own narrow beach with casuarina trees, far from the madding crowd on the north central tip of Grand Cayman, 27 miles from town and crowds. Up to six people can rent an air-conditioned, two-bedroom villa here (two or three people are comfortable in the one-bedroom units). Spacious rooms have full kitchens, ceiling fans, and blue-lavender upholstery on rattan furniture. Full dive facilities let you take advantage of the superb offshore diving; the famed North Wall is nearby. You'll be stranded without a car. *Box 46, North Side, Grand Cayman, tel. 809/947–9135, fax 809/947–9058. 23 units. Facilities: restaurant, bar, dive shop, freshwater pool, tennis courts, exercise room, sauna, racquetball court. MC, V. Moderate.*

Victoria House. Three miles north of town on the quieter northern end of Seven Mile Beach, this squarish white building houses bright, roomy one-, two-, and three-bedroom units with white tile floors and white walls, muted Caribbean prints, and rattan furniture. Amenities include TVs, telephones, full kitchens, air-conditioning, ceiling fans, ocean views, screened patios, and daily maid service. Guests have a range of activities to choose from, including tennis, shuffleboard, and occasional early-morning sightings of giant sea turtles on the beach. A car is recommended. *Box 636, West Bay Beach, Grand Cayman, tel. 809/947–4233, fax 809/947–5328. 25 units. Facilities: scuba, snorkeling, tennis, hammocks. AE, MC, V. Moderate.*

Off-Season Bets **TourScan, Inc.** (tel. 203/655–8091 or 800/962–2080) offers discount packages that include hotel and airfare for 53 properties in the Caymans, from simple to luxury resort, during both high and low seasons. Other plans and packages may be available through individual hotels. Study the *Rates and Facts* brochure from the Tourism Board and call or fax properties directly for complete information.

Nightlife

Each of the island hot spots attracts a different clientele. At the **Holiday Inn** (tel. 809/947–4444) a local dance band plays outdoors around the pool six nights a week. **Coconuts** (tel. 809/947–5757), the Caymans' original Comedy Club, features young American stand-up comedians. **Silver's Nightclub** (tel. 809/949–7777), at the Ramada Treasure Island Resort, is a spacious, tiered club that is usually filled to capacity. A lively house band plays Monday–Saturday nights. The **BWI High Energy Club** (tel. 809/949–0088), at the Radisson Resort Grand Cayman, offers recorded music and dancing six nights a week. Also at the Radisson, "The Comedy Zone" features stand-up comedians from the United States, Saturdays 8:30–10 PM ($16). **Island Rock Nightclub** (Falls Shopping Center, tel. 809/947–5366), a new disco and bar, features live bands some nights. For current entertainment, look at the freebie magazine *What's Hot*, which gives listings of music, movies, theater, and other entertainment possibilities.

9 Curaçao

Updated by
Laurie Senz

Thirty-five miles north of Venezuela and 42 miles east of Aruba is Curaçao, the largest of the islands in the Netherlands Antilles. Though the island claims 38 beaches, Curaçao does not have long stretches of sand or enchanting scenery. The island is dominated by an arid countryside, rocky coves, and a sprawling capital situated around a natural harbor. Until recently, the island's economy was based not on tourism but on oil refining and catering to offshore corporations seeking tax hedges. This has since changed, and although the atmosphere on Curaçao remains low-key, tourism has become a major economic force in the past five years.

Budget travelers are benefiting from this new attention to tourism. Many inexpensive resorts, hotels, and apartment units have sprung up in recent years. Visitors staying a week or longer can book one of the island's special "Break Away" packages. Dining and entertainment are equally affordable in Curaçao. Visitors who put taste ahead of ambience will enjoy the many Antillean eateries that serve hearty local dishes at easy-on-the-wallet prices. A number of good Chinese restaurants serve first-class Cantonese food, and there are always the fast-food standbys such as Burger King, McDonald's, KFC, and Pizza Hut. In the evening, many of the bigger resorts have two-for-the-price-of-one happy hours, with live music and free snacks; a night of bingo costs only a few dollars.

What It Will Cost These sample prices, meant only as a general guide, are for high season. Expect to pay about $100 for a modern room in an inexpensive hotel. A two-bedroom villa rental at a top place will run about $200 a night. A hearty meal for one at the covered market behind the post office is about $4; at a Chinese restaurant, $8; at a good seafood restaurant, $15. Cocktails average $3 here, while a beer is around $2. A taxi into town from most hotels will run $6, while a bus costs NAf .40. Car rentals begin at $33 a day during high season, but the average cost is more like $46 a day. Snorkel gear costs between $7 and $10 a day.

Before You Go

Tourist Information
Contact the **Curaçao Tourist Office** (400 Madison Ave., New York, NY 10017, tel. 212/751–8266 or 800/332–8266 and at 330 Biscayne Blvd., Suite 330, Miami, FL 33132, tel. 305/374–5811) for information.

Arriving and Departing
By Plane
ALM (tel. 800/327–7230) has four nonstop and 10 direct flights a week from Miami and four direct flights a week from Atlanta. For Atlanta departures, ALM has connecting services (throughfares) to most U.S. gateways with Delta. This arrangement makes ALM Curaçao's major carrier. ALM uses Curaçao as its hub to fly to Aruba, Bonaire, Caracas, Trinidad, Puerto Rico, and St. Maarten. ALM also offers a Visit Caribbean Pass, allowing easy interisland travel. **Air Aruba** (tel. 800/882–7822) has direct flights to Curaçao (flights make brief stops in Aruba) from both Miami and Newark airports. Air Aruba also has regularly scheduled service from Curaçao to Aruba and Bonaire. Every Saturday, **Key Air** (tel. 800/786–2386) offers connecting flights from Chicago; Baltimore/Washington, DC; Newark; Philadelphia; and Boston into its hub in Savannah, Georgia, for a nonstop flight into Curaçao.

From the Airport
Buses do run from the **International Airport Curaçao** into Willemstad, but unless you're staying in town, you will have to switch buses at either the Punda or Otrobanda Terminals to get to your hotel. The majority of hotels are located only a 15- to 20-minute drive from the airport, and a taxi will run $10 to $12 for up to four people. Be sure to agree on the fare, in U.S. dollars, before departure. Hotels located over a half-hour's ride from town usually provide free airport transfers for their guests; transfers are included in most packages.

Passports and Visas
U.S. and Canadian citizens traveling to Curaçao need only proof of citizenship and a valid photo ID. A voter's registration card or a notarized birth certificate (not a photocopy) will suffice—a driver's license will *not*. British citizens must produce a passport. All visitors must show an ongoing or return ticket.

Language
Dutch is the official language, but the vernacular is Papiamento—a mixture of Dutch, Portuguese, Spanish, and English. Developed during the 18th century by Africans, Papiamento evolved in Curaçao as the mode of communication between landowners and their slaves. These days, however, English, as well as Spanish and Dutch, are studied by schoolchildren. Anyone involved with tourism—shopkeepers, restaurateurs, and museum guides—speaks English.

Precautions
Mosquitoes on Curaçao do not seem as vicious and bloodthirsty as they do on Aruba and Bonaire, but that doesn't mean they don't exist. To be safe, keep perfume to a minimum, be prepared to use insect repellent before dining alfresco, and spray your hotel room at night—especially if you've opened a window.

Curaçao

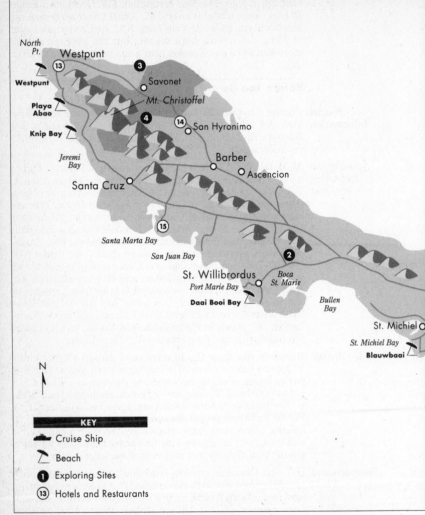

North Pt.

Westpunt

⓭ **Westpunt**

❸

○ Savonet

Mt. Christoffel

Playa Abao

❹ ⑭ San Hyronimo

Knip Bay

Jeremi Bay

Barber

○ Ascencion

Santa Cruz ○

⑮

Santa Marta Bay

San Juan Bay

❷

St. Willibrordus *Boca St. Marie*

Port Marie Bay

Daai Booi Bay

Bullen Bay

St. Michiel ○

St. Michiel Bay

Blauwbaai

N

KEY

🚢 Cruise Ship

⌐ Beach

❶ Exploring Sites

⑬ Hotels and Restaurants

Exploring
Amstel Brewery, **8**
Arawak Clay Products, **10**
Boca Tabla, **3**
Caracas Bay, **12**
Christoffel Park, **4**
Curaçao Seaquarium, **5**

Curaçao Underwater Marine Park, **6**
Hato Caves, **11**
Landhuis Brievengat, **9**
Landhuis Jan Kock, **2**
Senior Liqueur Factory, **7**
Willemstad, **1**

Dining
Belle Terrace, **20**
Bon Appetit, **24**
Cozzoli's Pizza, **21**
El Marinero, **23**
Garuda Indonesian Restaurant, **16**
Golden Star Restaurant, **28**

Grill King, **19**
Guacamaya Steakhouse, **25**
Jaanchi Christiaan's Restaurant, **13**
Rijsttafel Indonesia Restaurant, **27**

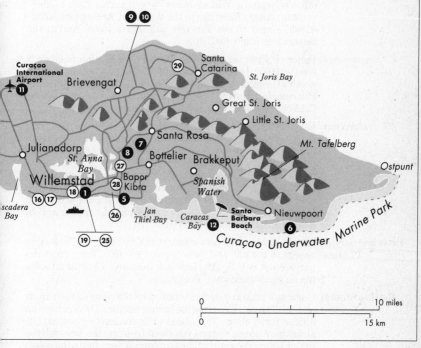

Caribbean Sea

Lodging
Avila Beach Hotel, **20**
Club Seru Coral, **29**
Coral Cliff Resort and Beach Club, **15**
Holiday Beach Hotel and Casino, **17**
Kadushi Cliffs, **14**
Lions Dive Hotel & Marina, **26**

Otrabanda Hotel & Casino, **18**
Van Der Valk Plaza Hotel and Casino, **22**

If you plan to go into the water, beware of long-spined sea urchins, which can cause pain and discomfort if you come in contact with them. Do not eat any of the little green applelike fruits of the manchineel tree: They're poisonous. In fact, steer clear of the trees altogether; raindrops or dewdrops dripping off the leaves can blister your skin. If contact does occur, rinse the affected area with water and, in extreme cases, get medical attention. Usually, the burning sensation won't last longer than two hours.

Staying in Curaçao

Important Addresses **Tourist Information:** The **Curaçao Tourism Development Foundation** has three offices on the island, where multilingual guides are ready to answer questions. You can also pick up maps, brochures, and a copy of *Curaçao Holiday*. The main office is located in Willemstad at Pietermaai No. 19 (tel. 599/9–616000); other offices are in the Waterfort Arches (tel. 599/9–613397), next to the Van Der Valk Plaza Hotel, and at the airport (tel. 599/9–686789).

Emergencies **Police** or **Fire:** tel. 114. The **Main Police Station** number is 599/9–611000. **Hospitals:** For medical emergencies, call **St. Elisabeth's Hospital** (tel. 599/9–624900) or an ambulance (tel. 112). **Pharmacies: Botica Popular** (Madurostraat 15, tel. 599/9–611269). Or ask at your hotel for the nearest one.

Currency U.S. dollars—in cash or traveler's checks—are accepted nearly everywhere, so there's no need to worry about exchanging money. However, you may need small change for pay phones, cigarettes, or soda machines. The currency in the Netherlands Antilles is the guilder, or florin as it is also called, indicated by an fl. or NAf. on price tags. The U.S. dollar is considered very stable; the official rate of exchange at press time was NAf 1.79 to U.S. $1. Note: Prices quoted here are in U.S. dollars unless indicated otherwise.

Taxes and Service Charges Hotels collect a 7% government tax and add a 12% service charge to the bill; restaurants add 10%–15%. The airport departure tax is U.S. $10 ($5.65 for Bonaire). There is no sales tax on goods purchased in Curaçao.

Getting Around *Taxis* Curaçao's taxis are easily identified by the signs on their roofs and the letters "TX" after the license number. Drivers have an official tariff chart. Taxis tend to be moderately priced, but since there are no meters, you should confirm the fare with the driver before departure. The fare from Willenstad to the hotels in Piscadera Bay is about $5; to the hotels by the Seaquarium, about $7. There is an additional 25% surcharge after 11 PM. Taxis are readily available at hotels; in other cases, call Central Dispatch at tel. 599/9–616711. Since crossing the Queen Juliana Bridge by cab can easily double your fare from town to your hotel, save money by beginning your ride from the same side of the canal as your hotel: Just stroll across the Queen Emma floating bridge and *then* get your cab.

Rental Cars You can rent a car from **Budget** (tel. 599/9–683420), **Avis** (tel. 599/9–681163), or **National Car Rental** (tel. 599/9–683489) at the airport or have it delivered free to your hotel. A typical rate is about $46 a day for a Toyota Starlet. The least expensive car-rental companies at press time were **Love Car Rental** (tel. 599/9–690444) and **Dollar** (tel. 599/9–690262). Their prices range from $33 for a Starlet to $50 for a four-door sedan. Off-season prices are about $25 a day. If you're planning to do country driving or rough it through Christoffel Park, a Jeep is best. All you'll need is a valid U.S. or Canadian driver's license.

Shuttle Vans All the major hotels outside of town offer free shuttle service into Willemstad. Shuttles coming from the Otrabanda side leave you at Rif Fort. From there it's a short walk north to the foot of the Queen Emma pontoon bridge. Shuttles coming from the Punda side leave you near the main entrance to Fort Amsterdam. Check the schedule with your hotel's front desk clerk, as the shuttles do not run every hour, and be sure to ask the driver for the return schedule from town back to your hotel.

Buses Yellow public buses, called convoys, are available from about 6 AM until 11:30 PM. At least six main routes can be used for sightseeing or beachcombing. Buses leave either from the Punda Bus Terminal at the downtown market place or the Otrabanda Bus Terminal located under the overpass. At press time, the fares ranged from NAf .40 to NAf .80 one-way. You'll need florins, so be sure to have enough coins. A number of private vans also function as buses. They list their destinations and show the word Bus on their license plates. Hail one from a bus stop, but be sure to check the route with the driver. The minimum fare for these private buses is NAf .50. The **Punda to Hato** route runs hourly from 6:15 AM and stops at the Senior Liqueur Factory, the zoo and botanical gardens, Landhuis Brievengat, and the Hato Caves. The **Punda to Dominquito** route departs hourly from 7:35 AM and stops at the Bolivar Museum, the Seaquarium, and the Jan Thiel Beach Club. The **Otrabanda to Wespunt** bus stops at Landhuis Ascension, Christoffel Park, and Westpunt beach. For prices and schedules, contact the **ABC Bus Company** (tel. 599/9–684733).

Telephones and Mail Phone service through the hotel operators in Curaçao is slow, but direct-dial service, both on-island and to the United States, is fast and clear. Hotel operators will put the call through for you, but if you make a collect call, do check immediately afterward that the hotel does not charge you as well. To call Curaçao direct, dial 011–599–9 plus the number in Curaçao. To place a local call on the island, dial the six-digit local number. A local call from a pay phone costs NAf .25. An airmail letter to anywhere in the world costs NAf 1.25, a postcard NAf .70.

Opening and Closing Times Most shops are open Monday–Saturday 8–noon and 2–6. Banks are open weekdays 8:00–3:30.

Guided Tours You don't really need a guide to show you downtown Willemstad—it's an easy taxi, bus, or free shuttle van ride from most major hotels and small enough for a self-conducted walking tour (follow the one outlined in the free tourist booklet *Curaçao Holiday*). To see the rest of the island, however, a guided tour can save you time and energy, though it is easy to cover the island yourself in a rented car. Most hotels have tour desks where arrangements can be made with reputable tour operators. For very personal, amiable service, try **Casper Tours** (tel. 599/9–653010 or 599/9–616789). For $25 per person, you'll be escorted around the island in an air-conditioned van, with stops at the Juliana Bridge, the salt pans, Knip Bay for a swim, the grotto at Boca Tabla, and lunch at Jaanchi Christiaan's, which is famous for its native cuisine. **Taber Tours** (tel. 599/9–376637) offers a 3½-hour city and country tour ($10) that includes visits to the Curaçao Liqueur Factory, the Curaçao Museum, and a shopping center. A full-day tour includes a visit to the Seaquarium and a snorkel trip; it costs $25 per person. Sightseeing by taxi costs $20 an hour for up to four people.

Boat Tours **Tabor Tours** (tel. 599/9–376637) offers a two-hour sunset cruise ($29.50 for adults, $20 for children under 12), with a feast of French bread, cheese, and wine. One-hour morning, afternoon, and evening cruises of Santa Anna Harbor are offered aboard the M/S *Hilda Veronica* (tel. 599/9–611257; cost: $7 adults, $4 children). A snorkeling, sailing, and lunch cruise to Klein Curaçao, an offshore island, is offered aboard the *Miss Anne* (tel. 599/9–671579; cost: $40), as are moonlight cruises for $15 per person and sunset cruises for $18, both including drinks.

Exploring Curaçao

Numbers in the margin correspond to points of interest on the Curaçao map.

Willemstad The capital city, **Willemstad,** is a favorite cruise stop for two
❶ reasons: The shopping is considered among the best in the Caribbean, and a quick tour of most of the downtown sights can be managed within a six-block radius. Santa Anna Bay slices the city down the middle: On one side is the Punda, and on the other is the Otrabanda (literally, the "other side"). Think of the Punda as the side for tourists, crammed with shops, restaurants, monuments, and markets. Otrabanda is less touristy, with lots of narrow winding streets full of private homes.

There are three ways to make the crossing from one side to the other: (1) drive or take a taxi over the Juliana Bridge; (2) traverse the Queen Emma Pontoon Bridge on foot; or (3) ride the free ferry, which runs when the bridge is open for passing ships.

Our walking tour of Willemstad starts at the **Queen Emma Bridge,** affectionately called the Lady by the natives. During the hurricane season in 1988, the 700-foot floating bridge practically floated right out to sea; it was later taken down for major reconstruction. If you're standing on the Otrabanda side, take a few moments to scan Curaçao's multicolored "face" on the other side of Santa Anna Bay. Spiffy rows of town houses combine the gabled roofs and red tiles of the island's Dutch heritage with the gay colors unique to Curaçao. The architecture makes a cheerful contrast to the stark cacti and the austere shrubbery dotting the countryside. Millions of dollars have been poured into restoring old colonial landmarks and upgrading and modernizing hotels. If you wait long enough, the bridge will swing open (at least 30 times a day) to let the seagoing ships pass through. The original bridge, built in 1888, was the brainchild of the American consul Leonard Burlington Smith, who made a mint off the tolls he charged for the bridge. Initially, the charge was 2¢ per person for those wearing shoes, free to those crossing barefoot. Today it's free to everyone.

Take a breather at the peak of the bridge and look north to the 1,625-foot-long **Queen Juliana Bridge,** completed in 1974 and standing 200 feet above water. That's the bridge you drive over to cross to the other side of the city, and although the route is time-consuming (and more expensive if you're going by taxi), the view from this bridge is worth it. At every hour of the day, the sun casts a different tint over the city, creating an ever-changing panorama; the nighttime view, rivaling Rio's, is breathtaking.

When you cross the Pontoon Bridge and arrive on the Punda side, turn left and walk down the waterfront, along **Handelskade.** You'll soon pass the ferry landing. Now take a close look at the buildings you've seen only from afar; the original red tiles of the roofs came from Europe and arrived on trade ships as ballast.

Walk down to the corner and turn right at the customs building onto Sha Caprileskade. This is the bustling **floating market,** where each morning dozens of Venezuelan schooners arrive laden with tropical fruits and vegetables. Fresh mangoes, papayas, and exotic vegetables vie for space with freshly caught fish and herbs and spices. It's probably too much to ask a tourist to arrive by 6:30 AM when the buying is best, but there's plenty of action to see throughout the afternoon. Any produce bought here, however, should be thoroughly washed before eating.

Keep walking down Sha Caprileskade. Head toward the Wilhelmina Drawbridge, which connects Punda with the once-flourishing district of **Scharloo,** where the early Jewish merchants first built stately homes. Scharloo is now a red-light district.

If you continue straight ahead, Sha Caprileskade becomes De Ruyterkade. Soon you'll come to the post office, which will be on your left. Behind it is the **Old Market** (Marche). Here you'll find local women preparing hearty Antillean lunches. For $4–$6 you can enjoy such Curaçao specialties as *funghi* (cornbread), *kesi yena* (Gouda cheese stuffed with meat), goat stew, fried fish, peas and rice, and fried plantains. After lunch, return to the intersection of De Ruyterkade and Columbusstraat and turn left.

Walk up Columbusstraat to the **Mikveh Israel-Emmanuel Synagogue,** founded in 1651 and the oldest temple still in use in the Western Hemisphere. One of the most important sights in Curaçao, it draws 20,000 visitors a year. Enter through the gates around the corner on Hanchi Snoa and ask the front office to direct you to the guide on duty. A unique feature is the brilliant white sand covering the synagogue floor, a remembrance of Moses leading his people through the desert; the Hebrew letters on the four pillars signify the names of the Four Daughters of Israel: Eve, Sarah, Rachel, and Esther. A fascinating museum (tel. 599/9–611633) in the back displays Jewish antiques (including a set of circumcision instruments) and artifacts from Jewish families collected from all over the world. The gift shop near the gate has excellent postcards and commemorative medallions. *Hanchi Di Snoa 29, tel. 599/9–611067. Open weekdays 9–11:45 and 2:30–5. English and Hebrew services conducted by an American rabbi are held Fri. at 6:30 PM and on Sat. at 10 AM. Jacket and tie required.*

Continue down Columbusstraat and cross Wilhelminaplein (Wilhelmina Park). Now you will be in front of the courthouse, with its stately balustrade, and the impressive Georgian facade of the Bank of Boston. The statue keeping watch over the park is of Queen Wilhelmina, a deceased popular monarch of the Netherlands, who gave up her throne to her daughter Juliana after her Golden Jubilee in 1948. Cut back across the park and turn left at Breedestraat. Take Breedestraat down to the Pontoon Bridge, then turn left at the waterfront. At the foot of the bridge are the mustard-colored walls of **Fort Amsterdam.** Take a few steps through the archway and enter another century. The entire structure dates from the 1700s, when it was actually the center of the city and the most important fort on the island. Now it houses the governor's residence, the Fort Church, the ministry, and several other government offices. Next door is the **Plaza Piar,** dedicated to Manuel Piar, a native Curaçaoan who fought for the independence of Venezuela under the liberator Simón Bolívar. On the other side of the plaza is the **Waterfort,** a bastion dating from 1634. The original cannons are still positioned in the battlements. The foundation, however, now forms the walls of the Van Der Valk Plaza Hotel. Following the sidewalk around the Plaza, you'll discover one of the most delightful shopping areas on the island, newly built under the **Waterfort arches** (*see* Shopping, *below*).

Western Side With so much to see and do, it's best to allow two full days to explore the island. If you only want to rent a car for one day, then use it for this itinerary, as the major sites on the Eastern Side itinerary are easy to get to by bus. Take a bathing suit and a few cold drinks and head to the Otrabanda side of town. Begin by stopping at the **Curaçao Museum** (tel. 599/9–623777 or 599/9–623873), located behind the Holiday Beach Hotel on Van Leeuwenhoekstraat. Built in 1853 and restored in 1942, it houses a collection of Indian artifacts as well as colonial and historical island memorabilia. Then turn back to the highway and head northwest until the road merges with Westpunt Highway (Weg Naar Wespunt). For a splendid view, and some unusual island ghost tales, follow this road to the intersection at Cunucu Abao, then veer left onto Weg Naar San Willibrordo
❷ until you come to **Landhuis Jan Kock** (tel. 599/9–648087), located across from the salt pans. Since the hours are irregular, be sure to call ahead to arrange a tour of this reputedly haunted mid-17th-century house, or stop by on Sunday mornings, when the proprietor serves delicious Dutch pancakes in the small restaurant behind her home.

Continuing north on this road, you'll come to the village of Soto. From here the road leads to the northwest tip of the island through landscape that Georgia O'Keeffe might have painted—towering cacti, flamboyant dried shrubbery, and aluminum-roof houses. Throughout this *cunucu,* or countryside, you'll see native fishermen hauling in their nets, women pounding cornmeal, and an occasional donkey blocking traffic. Landhouses, large estate houses from centuries past, dot the countryside, though most are closed to the public. Their facades, though, can often be glimpsed from the highway. Stop at Playa Abao, Knip Bay, or Westpunt for a swim. Rounding the northwest tip of the island, the road becomes Wespunt
❸ Highway again and heads south to **Boca Tabla,** where the sea has carved a magnificent grotto. Safely tucked in the back, you can watch and listen to the waves crashing ferociously against
❹ the rocks. A short distance farther is **Christoffel Park,** a fantastic 4,450-acre garden and wildlife preserve with the towering Mt. Christoffel at its center. Open to the public since 1978, the park consists of three former plantations with individual trails that take about one to 1½ hours each to traverse. You may drive your own car (heavy-treaded wheels) or rent a Jeep

with an accompanying guide ($15). Start out early (by 10 AM the park starts to feel like a sauna), and if you're going solo, first study the *Excursion Guide to Christoffel Park* (sold at the front desk), which outlines the various routes and identifies the flora and fauna found here. No matter what route you take, you'll be treated to interesting views of hilly fields full of prickly-pear cacti, divi-divi trees, bushy-haired palms, and exotic flowers that bloom unpredictably after April showers. There are also caves and ancient Indian drawings. For the strong of heart: Walk through the bat caves on the Savonet route (marked in blue); you'll hear bat wings rustling in the corners and see a few scary but nonpoisonous scorpion spiders scuttling over the walls. Make sure you're wearing the proper shoes; the ground is covered with guano (bird and bat droppings) that almost seems alive because of the millions of harmless mites. It's not all a shop of horrors, though—if you make it to the last chamber, you may see a magnificent white-faced barn owl that nests in the cave fissures.

As you drive through the park, keep a lookout for tiny deer, goats, and other small wildlife that might suddenly dart in front of your car. The snakes you could encounter—the whip snake and the minute silver snake—are not poisonous. White-tailed hawks may be seen on the green route, white orchids and crownlike passion flowers on the yellow route.

Climbing up the 1,239-foot Mt. Christoffel on foot is an exhilarating experience and a definite challenge to anyone who hasn't grown up scaling the Alps. The guidebook claims the round-trip will take you one hour, and Curaçaoan adolescent boys do make a sport of racing up and down, but it's really more like 2½ (sweaty) hours for a reasonably fit person who's not an expert hiker. And the last few feet are deadly. The view from the peak, however, *is* thrilling—a panorama of the island, including Santa Marta Bay and the tabletop mountain of St. Hironimus. On a clear day, you can even see the mountain ranges of Venezuela, Bonaire, and Aruba. *Savonet, tel. 599/9–640363. Admission: $5 adults, $3 children 6–15. Open Mon.–Sat. 8–5, Sun. 6–3.*

Eastern Side To explore the eastern side of the island, take the coastal road —Martin Luther King Boulevard—out from Willemstad past the zoo and botanical gardens (neither is exceptional) about 2 miles to Bapor Kibra. There you'll find the Seaquarium and the Underwater Park.

❺ The **Curaçao Seaquarium** is *the* place to see the island's underwater treasures without getting your feet wet. In fact, it's the world's only public aquarium where sea creatures are raised and cultivated totally by natural methods. You can spend several hours here, mesmerized by the 46 freshwater tanks full of more than 400 varieties of exotic fish and vegetation found in the waters around Curaçao, including sharks, lobsters, turtles, corals, and sponges. Look out for the over-five-foot-long mascot, Herbie the lugubrious jewfish. Four sea lions from Uruguay are the most recent pride of the aquarium. If you get hungry, stop at the excellent Italian restaurant or the steak house–cum–Mexican eatery. There are also glass-bottom boat tours and a viewing platform overlooking the wreck of the steamship SS *Oranje Nassau*, which sank in 1906 and now sits in 10 feet of water. A nearby 495-yard man-made beach of white sand is well suited to novice swimmers and children, and bathroom and shower facilities are available. A souvenir shop sells some of the best postcards and coral jewelry on the island. *Tel. 599/9–616666. Admission: $6 adults, $3 children. Open daily 9 AM–10 PM.*

6 **Curaçao Underwater Marine Park** (tel. 599/9–618131) consists of about 12½ miles of untouched coral reefs that have been granted the status of national park. Mooring buoys have been placed at the most interesting dive sites on the reef to provide safe anchoring and to prevent damage to the reef. The park stretches along the south shore from the Princess Beach Hotel in Willemstad to the eastern tip of the island.

7 Located on Salina Arriba, in the Landhouse Cholobo, the **Senior Liqueur Factory** (tel. 599/9–613526) distills and distributes the original Curaçao liqueur. Don't expect to find a massive factory—it's just a small showroom in the open-air foyer of a beautiful 17th-century landhouse. There are no guides, but you can read the story of the distillation process on posters, and you'll be graciously offered samples in various flavors. If you're interested in buying—the orange-flavored chocolate liqueur is fantastic over ice cream—you can choose from a complete selection, which is bottled in a variety of fascinating shapes, including Dutch ceramic houses.

8 In nearby Salina you can take a free tour of the **Amstel Brewery,** which offers insights into the world's only beer made from distilled seawater. Free tours (followed by all-you-can-drink beer tastings) are held Tuesday and Thursday mornings at 10 AM. *Closed June 15–Aug. 6.*

9 **Landhuis Brievengat** (tel. 599/9–378344) is a 10-minute drive northeast of Willemstad, near the Centro Deportivo sports stadium. On the last Sunday of the month (from 10 AM to 3 PM), this old estate holds an open house with crafts demonstrations and folkloric shows. You can see the original kitchen still intact, the 18-inch-thick walls, fine antiques, and the watchtowers, once used for lovers' trysts. The restaurant, which is open only on Wednesday, serves a fine *rijsttafel* (Indonesian smorgasbord). Every Friday night a party is held on the wide wraparound terrace, with two bands and plenty to drink.

10 Opposite the Industry Park at Brievengat, is **Arawak Clay Products,** which has a factory showroom of native-made crafts. You can purchase a variety of tiles, plates, pots, and tiny replicas of landhouses. Tour operators usually include a stop here. *Tel. 599/9–377658. Open Mon.–Sat. 7:30–5.*

11 Head northwest toward the airport to the island's newest attraction, **Hato Caves,** with hour-long guided tours that wind down into the various chambers to the water pools; voodoo chamber; wishing well; fruit bats' sleeping quarters; and Curaçao Falls, where a stream of silver joins with a stream of gold and is guarded by a limestone "dragon" perched nearby. Hidden lights illuminate the limestone formations and gravel walkways. One of the better Caribbean caves open to the public. *Tel. 599/9–680378. Admission: $4.25 adults, $2.75 children. Open Tues.–Sun. 10 AM–5 PM. Closed Mon.*

Wind southward past Spanish Water, where you'll pass several private yacht clubs that attract sports anglers from all over the world for international tournaments. And make a stop at **Santa Barbara Beach,** especially on Sundays, when the atmosphere

12 approaches party time (*see* Beaches, *below*). **Caracas Bay,** off Bapor Kibra, is a popular dive site, with a sunken ship so close to the surface that even snorkelers can balance their flippers on the helm.

Beaches

Curaçao has some 38 beaches, but unfortunately, many are extremely rocky and litter-strewn. Instead of long, powdery stretches of sand, you'll discover the joy of inlets: tiny bay openings to the sea marked by craggy cliffs, exotic trees, and scads of interesting pebbles. If your hotel, apartment, or guest house doesn't have a beach, you can hop a bus to one that does. Your front desk clerk can tell you which bus to take and when it runs, or call the **ABC Bus Company** (*see* Buses in Getting Around, *above*). All of the major hotels have a beach, although some are teeny and others are man-made. Nonguests are supposed to pay the hotels a beach fee, but often there is no one there to collect.

Hotels with the best beach properties include the new **Sonesta Beach Hotel** (impressively long), the **Princess Beach** (impressively sensuous), and the **Coral Cliff Resort** (impressively deserted).

One of the largest, more spectacular beaches on Curaçao is **Blauwbaai** (Blue Bay). There's plenty of white sand and lots of shady places, showers, and changing facilities, but since it's a private beach, you'll pay an entrance fee of about $2.50 per car. Take the road that leads past the Holiday Beach Hotel and the Curaçao Caribbean north toward Julianadorp. At the end of the stretch of straight road, a sign will instruct you to bear left for Blauwbaai and the fishing village of St. Michiel. The latter is a good place for diving.

Starting from the church of St. Willibrordus, signs will direct you to **Daai Booi Bay,** a sandy shore dotted with thatched shelters. The road to this public beach is a small paved highway flanked on either side by thick, lush trees and huge organ-pipe cacti. The beach is curved, with shrubbery rooted into the side of the rocky cliffs—a great place for swimming.

Knip Bay has two parts: Big (Groot) Knip and Little (Kleine) Knip. Only Little Knip is shaded with trees, but these are manchineels, so steer clear of them. Also beware of cutting your feet on beer bottle caps. Both have alluring white sand, but only Big Knip has changing facilities as well as several tiki huts for shade, and calm turquoise waters that are perfect for swimming and lounging. The protected cove, flanked by sheer cliffs, is usually a blast on Sundays, when there is live music. To get there, take the road to the Knip Landhouse, then turn right. Signs will direct you. In between the big and the little bay is a superb scenic route.

Playa Abao , northwest of Knip Bay, boasts crystal-clear turquoise water and a small beach. Sunday afternoons are crowded and festive. Amenities include a snack center and public toilets.

Westpunt, on the northwest tip of the island, is shady in the morning. It doesn't have much sand, but you can sit on a shaded rock ledge. On Sunday, watch the divers jump from the high cliff. The bay view is worth the trip. For lunch, stop at Jaanchi Christiaan's nearby (*see* Dining, *below*).

Santa Barbara, a popular family beach on the eastern tip, has changing facilities and a snack bar, but charges a small fee, usually around $3.35 per car.

Sports and the Outdoors

Golf　Visitors are welcome to play golf at the **Curaçao Golf and Squash Club** (tel. 599/9–373590) in Emmastad. The nine-hole course offers a challenge because of the stiff trade winds and the sand greens. Greens fees are $15. Golf clubs and pull carts are available for rent. *Open 8–12:30.*

Jogging　The **Rif Recreation Area,** locally known as the *corredor,* stretches from the water plant at Mundo Nobo to the Curaçao Caribbean Hotel along the sea. It consists of more than 1.2 miles of palm-lined beachfront, a wading pond, and a jogging track with an artificial surface, as well as a big playground. There is good security and street lighting along the entire length of the beachfront.

Tennis　Most hotels (including Sonesta Beach, Curaçao Caribbean, Las Palmas, Princess Beach, and Holiday Beach) offer well-paved courts, illuminated for day and night games, but these are only open to hotel guests. Your only option if you're not staying at one of these is the **Santa Catherina Sports and Country Club** (tel. 599/9–677028). Forty-five minutes of court time costs $7 during the day, $10 after 6 PM.

Water Sports　Curaçao has facilities for all kinds of water sports, thanks to the government-sponsored **Curaçao Underwater Marine Park** (tel. 599/9–618131), which includes almost a third of the island's southern diving waters. Scuba divers and snorkelers can enjoy more than $12^1/2$ miles of protected reefs and shores, with normal visibility from 60 to 80 feet (up to 150 feet on good days). With water temperatures ranging from 75° to 82°F, wet suits are generally unnecessary. No coral collecting, spearfishing, or littering is allowed. An exciting wreck to explore is the SS *Oranje Nassau,* which ran aground over 80 years ago and now hosts hundreds of exotic fish and unusually shaped coral.

Most hotels either offer their own program of water sports or will be happy to make arrangements for you. An introductory scuba resort course usually runs about $50–$65.

Underwater Curaçao (tel. 599/9–618131) offers complete vacation/dive packages in conjunction with the Lions Dive Hotel & Marina; as well as private and group lessons and dive excursions. A single dive costs $33. Its fully stocked dive shop, located between the Lions Dive Hotel and the Curaçao Seaquarium, offers equipment for sale or rent. Take a dive/snorkeling trip on the *Coral Sea,* a 40-foot twin diesel yacht-style dive boat. Landlubbers can see beneath the sea aboard the *Coral View,* a monohull flat-top glass-bottom boat that makes four excursions a day. The 30-minute ride costs $5.50 per person and requires a minimum of five people.

Seascape (tel. 599/9–625000, ext. 177), at the Curaçao Caribbean Hotel, specializes in snorkeling and scuba diving trips to reefs and underwater wrecks in every type of water vehicle— from pedal boats and water scooters to water skis and Windsurfers. A six-dive package costs $155 and includes unlimited beach diving plus one free night dive. Snorkeling gear costs about $5 an hour or $10 a day to rent. Die-hard fishermen with companions who prefer to suntan will enjoy the day trip to Little Curaçao, the "clothes optional" island between Curaçao and Bonaire, where the fish are reputed to be lively: Plan on $25 per person.

Peter Hughes Diving (tel. 599/9–614944, ext. 5047) at the Princess Beach Hotel rents equipment and conducts diving and snorkeling trips.

Coral Cliff Diving (tel. 599/9–642822) offers scuba certification courses ($320), a one-week windsurfing school ($170), a one-week basic sailing course ($255), and a full schedule of dive and snorkeling trips to Curaçao's southwest coast. It also rents pedal boats, Hobie Cats, and underwater cameras.

For windsurfing, check out the **Curaçao High Wind Center** (Princess Beach Hotel, tel. 599/9–614944). Lessons cost $20 an hour.

Shopping

Curaçao is not the shopper's haven that most guidebooks make it out to be. If you're looking for bargains on Swiss watches, cameras, crystal, or electronic equipment, do some comparison shopping back home and come armed with a list of prices. You can find some excellent buys on French perfumes and jewelry, especially gold, but again, know what things cost in your hometown before making any purchases. For many years, Curaçao catered to hordes of Venezuelan shoppers who adored American goods. In recent years, European merchandise has made inroads, but most of it is expensive designer clothing from Italy, Spain, and France.

Shopping Areas Most of the shops are concentrated in one place—**Punda**—in downtown Willemstad, within about a six-block area. The main shopping streets are **Heerenstraat, Breedestraat,** and **Madurostraat. Heerenstraat** and **Gomezplein** are pedestrian malls, closed to traffic, and their roadbeds have been raised to sidewalk level and covered with pink inlaid tiles.

The hippest shopping area lies under the **Waterfort arches,** along with a variety of restaurants and bars. Highly recommended here are **Bamali** (tel. 599/9–612258), which sells Indonesian batik clothing, leather bags, and charming handicrafts, and **The African Queen** (tel. 599/9–612682), an exotic bazaar of fine African jewelry, batik clothes, and Kenyan handbags handmade of coconut husk and sisal.

Good Buys **La Zahav N.V.** (Curaçao International Airport, tel. 599/9–689594) is one of the best places to buy gold jewelry—with or without diamonds, rubies, and emeralds—at true discount prices. The shop is located in the airport transit hall, just at the top of the staircase. **Boutique Liska** (Schottegatweg Oost 191-A, tel. 599/9–613111) is where local residents shop for smart women's fashion. **Toko Zuikertuintje** (Zuikertuintjeweg, tel. 599/9–370188), a supermarket built on the original 17th-century Zuikertuintje Landhuis, is where most of the local elite shop. Enjoy the free tea and coffee while you stock up on all sorts of European and Dutch delicacies. Shopping here for a picnic is a treat in itself.

Local Crafts Native crafts and curios are on hand at **Fundason Obra di Man** (Bargestraat 57, tel. 599/9–612413). Particularly impressive are the posters of Curaçao's architecture. **Arawak Clay Products** (Industry Park, Brievgat, tel. 599/9–377658) sells island-made ceramics such as tiles, plates, ashtrays, mugs, and tiny replicas of landhouses.

Dining

Restaurateurs in Curaçao believe in whetting appetites with a variety of cuisines and intriguing ambience: Dine under the boughs of magnificent old trees, in the romantic gloom of wine cellars in renovated landhouses, or on the ramparts of 18th-century forts. Curaçaoans partake of some of the best Indonesian food in the Caribbean, and they also find it hard to resist the French, Swiss, Dutch, and Swedish delights.

Even at budget prices, good food is abundant. In the Old Covered Market, located behind the post office in Willemstad, you can lunch on a large plate of grilled fish or chicken over rice, with plantains and vegetables, for $4–$6. Fast-food spots in the center of town are another option: Choose from Burger King, Pizza Hut, Kentucky Fried Chicken, or McDonald's. There are six Chinese restaurants serving Cantonese food, with lots of dishes under $10. Other good bets are the clean, no-frills local eateries serving Dutch/Curaçaon specialties; for $7–$9 you can get a dinner of pork chops, shrimp criollo (a spicy tomato-based sauce), goat stew, or fresh grilled kingfish served with funghi (cornbread pudding), plantains, vegetables, and rice. At Indonesian restaurants, a 16-course rijsttafel (smorgasbord of meats, chicken, fish, and vegetables) that will quell the hungriest appetite is served at your table for about $14 a person.

If you're cooking in, you'll find plenty of supermarkets and minigrocery stores on Curaçao. If you purchase your fruits or vegetables from either the floating market or the market behind the post office (*see* Exploring Willemstad, *above*), be sure to wash all produce well. You can also buy fresh fish at both markets. Meat is best purchased from a butcher or supermarket. The latter include: **Mangusa Supermarket** (Seru Mangusa 1), **Mini Market Jandoret** (Jandoret 62), **Bello Horizonte** (Aztekenweg 17), and **Broadway Supermarket** (Ontarioweg 1).

Even at budget restaurants, reservations are always helpful, and are especially advised during winter. Dress in restaurants is almost always casual, but if you feel like putting on your finery, there will be a place for you.

Highly recommended restaurants are indicated by a star ★.

Category	Cost*
Moderate	$15–$25
Inexpensive	$10–$15
Budget	under $10

per person, excluding drinks and service

Belle Terrace. Tucked into the quaint Avila Beach Hotel, this seaside restaurant sits beneath the boughs of an ancient tree. Each night it features a different specialty, from such Curaçao

dishes as *keshi yena* to *sopito* (fish and coconut soup) to salted
boiled breast of duck and filet mignon. In between stops at the
creative salad bar, watch the fish jumping out of the sea—they
fly up to 20 feet. *Avila Beach Hotel, Penstraat 130–134, tel.
599/9–614377. Reservations required. AE, DC, MC, V. Dinner
only. Moderate.*

★ **El Marinero.** This restaurant is a favorite of the island's governor. The setting is lighthearted nautical, with waiters
dressed in white sailor suits and the bow of a boat jutting out
of one wall. The owner, Luis Chavarria, dresses as the captain.
The service is both friendly and efficient, and the food is excellent. The chef whips up one superb seafood dish after another,
including such delicacies as shellfish soup, seviche, paella, and
conch. The sea bass Creole-style is delicious, as is the garlic
lobster. *Schottegatweg Noord 87-B, tel. 599/9–379833. Reservations advised. AE, DC, MC, V. Moderate.*

Guacamaya Steakhouse. The portions here are hearty, the chef
knows what *rare* means, and there's even a small selection of
seafood to satisfy the noncarnivore in the crowd. A large papier-mâché parrot sits on a brass perch, waiters stroll by in
Bermuda shorts and safari hats, and the drink of the house—a
guacamaya—is a tall, iced concoction the color of foliage. Try
the chateaubriand or the tenderloin medallions. There's also
steak tartare and a mixed skewer of chicken, pork, and beef
kebabs. *Schottegatweg-West 365, tel. 599/9–689208. Reservations
required. AE, DC, MC, V. Closed Mon. Moderate.*

Garuda Indonesian Restaurant. The special rijsttafel (Indonesian smorgasbord) features 19 trays of traditional vegetable,
chicken, meat, fish, and shrimp dishes, each with its own sauce.
The ocean breezes, bamboo and rattan decor, and Far Eastern
music add to the feeling of being a guest in a foreign land. Save
room for a dessert of *spekkok*, a multilayered pastry with nuts
that will melt in your mouth. *Curaçao Caribbean Hotel, tel.
599/9–626519. Open Tues.–Fri. lunch and dinner, Sat. and Sun.
dinner only. Reservations advised. AE, DC, MC, V. Inexpensive–Moderate.*

Rijsttafel Indonesia Restaurant. No steaks or chops here, just
one dish after another of exotic delicacies that make up the
traditional Indonesian banquet called rijsttafel. Choose from
16 to 25 traditional dishes that are set buffet-style around you.
Lesser appetites will enjoy the lighter meals, such as the fried
noodles, fresh jumbo shrimps in garlic, or combination meat-
and-fish platters. A "ladies only" ice cream comes with a red
rose; the coconut ice cream is packed in a coconut shell you can
take home. The walls are stocked with beautiful Indonesian
puppets ($25–$40) that make stunning gifts. *Mercurriusstraat
13–15, Salinja, tel. 599/9–612999. Open Mon.–Sat. for lunch and
dinner; Sun. for dinner only. Reservations required. AE, DC,
MC, V. Inexpensive–Moderate.*

Grill King. This casual, no-frills waterfront eatery is popular
with locals and tourists alike, especially on weekends, when a
keyboard player provides live entertainment. The sea crashing
against the rocks below makes an exciting backdrop to a meal
of succulent seafood or flame-broiled meats. Try the grilled
conch with a shrimp cocktail appetizer, the wahoo in criollo
sauce, or the Danish-style, baby-back ribs. Service is a bit slow
but always pleasant. *Waterfort Arches, tel. 599/9–616870. Reservations advised. AE, D, DC, MC, V. Closed Sun. lunch. Inexpensive.*

Bon Appetit. This popular breakfast spot is in the heart of the shopping district. The fare is reasonably priced, the portions are large, and the service is friendly and pleasant. Think of this as a Dutch diner, good for breakfast and lunch, less so for dinner. Try the Dutch pancakes with pineapple. *Hanchi di Snoa 4, tel. 599/9–616916. AE, DC, MC, V. Closed Sun. Budget–Inexpensive.*

Cozzoli's Pizza. Fast, cheap, hearty New York–style pizzas are offered here, along with calzones, sausage rolls, and lasagna. It is right in the middle of downtown Willemstad. *Breedestraat 2, tel. 599/9–617184. No credit cards. Budget.*

★ **Golden Star Restaurant.** This place looks and feels more like a friendly roadside diner than a full-fledged restaurant, but the native food is among the best in town. Owner Marie Burke turns out such Antillean specialties as *bestia chiki* (goat stew), shrimp Creole, and delicately seasoned grilled conch, all served with generous heaps of rice, fried plantains, and avocado. Steaks and chops are another option. *Socratestraat 2, tel. 599/9–654795. AE, DC, MC, V. Budget.*

Jaanchi Christiaan's Restaurant. Tour buses stop regularly at this open-air restaurant for lunch and for weird-sounding, mouth-watering native dishes. The main-course specialty is a hefty platter of freshly caught fish, potatoes, and vegetables. Curaçaoans joke that Jaanchi's iguana soup is "so strong it could resurrect the dead"—truth is, it tastes just like chicken soup, only better. But Jaanchi, Jr., says if you want iguana, you must order in advance "because we have to go out and catch them." He's not kidding. *Westpunt 15, tel. 599/9–640126. AE, DC, MC, V. Budget.*

Lodging

Curaçao has a number of excellent-value hotels priced at around $100 a night. For this price—maybe half of what you'd pay on more expensive islands—you get a pleasant room at a full-service hotel with restaurant, water-sports center, beach, and other facilities. It's possible to pay much less for a room in a small guest house or inn—around $50 a night—but know that you'll be taking a huge drop in quality. These properties generally have stark rooms, off-beach locations (though not always), and little or no facilities—you'll have to leave the property to get everything from snorkel gear to breakfast.

Hotels here tend to be in three main areas: On the beaches of Piscadera Bay (a few minutes west of the Otrabanda side of Willemstad); on the Bapor Kibra beachfront (an eight-minute drive from the Punda side of Willemstad); and in the Westpunt area at the northwest tip of the island. Beaches are within walking distance at all three locations. Almost every hotel in Curaçao participates in the tourist-board promoted "Break Away" package, which offers a number of extras for not much more money than room rates. If you're a diver, be sure to ask whatever hotel you call about scuba packages. Almost every hotel outside of Willemstad offers free shuttle service into town. There are no campgrounds on Curaçao and, so far, no all-inclusive resorts.

Highly recommended lodgings are indicated by a star ★.

Category	Cost*
Moderate	$120–$160
Inexpensive	$85–$120
Budget	under $85

All prices are for a standard double room for two and include tax and service charges. To estimate rates for hotels offering MAP/FAP, add about $20–$30 per person per day to the above price ranges.

Hotels
★

Avila Beach Hotel. The royal family of Holland and its ministers stay at this 200-year-old mansion for three good reasons: the privacy, the personalized service, and the austere elegance. Americans used to luxurious resorts will find the air-c»nditioned rooms rather plain and old-fashioned, but the double quarter-moon-shape beach is enchanting. The original guest rooms are charming but basic, with hardwood or tile floors and small baths (shower only). Most guests will prefer the newer La Belle Alliance section, on its own beach adjacent to the main property; where all units have either balconies or patios with sea views. The hotel has an outdoor dining area shaded by the leafy, intertwining boughs of an enormous tree. The Danish chefs, who specialize in a Viking pot, local dishes, and weekly smorgasbord, also smoke their own fish and bake their own bread. *Box 791, Penstraat 130134, Willemstad, tel. 599/9–614377 or 800/448–8355, fax 599/9–611493. 95 rooms. Facilities: restaurant, coffee shop, tennis court, bar, baby-sitting service, cable TV, shuttle bus to city center. AE, DC, MC, V. EP. Moderate.*

Holiday Beach Hotel and Casino. This ex–Holiday Inn is a four-story, 26-year-old structure built around a pool area. Over the past four years, rooms have been completely renovated and refurnished in a beige, emerald, and rose color scheme, with bleached wood and rattan furniture, TVs, and balconies. Half the rooms face the car park; most of the others face the pool area, and only a few have sea views. The hotel's best feature is its crescent beach, which is quite large for Curaçao and dotted with palm trees. You'll find lots of tour groups assembling in the spacious lobby and visiting the island's largest casino, off to the lobby's left. A beachside alfresco restaurant features a well-stocked, all-you-can-eat breakfast buffet. In the evening, international dishes and island specialties are served in addition to several weekly theme-buffet dinners. The lobby bar happy hour is one of the most popular on the island. While this hotel is an older property, the completed renovation, along with the friendly service, make it a good choice for those seeking value on a middle-of-the-road budget. *Box 2178, Otrabanda, Pater Euwensweg, Willemstad, tel. 599/9–625400, fax 599/9–624397. 197 rooms, 2 suites. Facilities: restaurant, bar, playground, 2 tennis courts, beauty shop, boutique, drugstore, gift shop, car-rental agent, baby-sitting service, casino. AE, DC, MC, V. EP. Moderate.*

Lions Dive Hotel & Marina. This recent addition to the Curaçao vacation scene is a hop, skip, and plunge away from the Seaquarium. The pink-and-green caravansary is set next to a quarter mile of private beach. The rooms are airy, modern, and light-filled, with tile floors, large bathrooms, and lots of windows. A pair of French doors leads out to a spacious balcony or terrace, and every room has a view of the sea. The Sunday-night happy hour is especially festive, with a local merengue band playing poolside. Pluses include a young, attractive staff who are eager to please and a scuba center that's top-notch. Dive packages are offered with Underwater Curaçao, and most, if not all, of the guests are dive enthusiasts. *Bapor Kibra, Curaçao, tel. 599/9–618100, fax 599/9–618200. 72 air-conditioned rooms. Facilities: restaurant, terrace bar, pool, scuba diving center with 2 dive boats, water-sports concession, video-rental shop. AE, DC, MC, V. CP. Inexpensive.*

Otrabanda Hotel & Casino. New in 1991, this city hotel is across the harbor from downtown Willemstad. The management appears more interested in keeping the locals gambling in the ground-floor casino than in attracting visitors to the small but clean and simple rooms. But with double rooms at $105 during high season, it offers good value. *Breedestradt (O), Otrabanda, tel. 599/9–627400, fax 599/9–627299. 45 rooms. Facilities: casino, coffee shop, restaurant, bar. AE, V. CP. Inexpensive.*

Van Der Valk Plaza Hotel and Casino. "Please don't touch the passing ships" is the slogan of the Van Der Valk Plaza, the only hotel in the world with marine-collision insurance. The ships do come close to the island's first high-rise hotel, built into the massive walls of a 17th-century fort at the entrance of Willemstad's harbor. Its proximity to town (within walking distance of the city center) makes it popular with business travelers, who aren't bothered by the lack of beachfront. (Guests have beach privileges at other hotels.) Rooms are sorely lacking in style, but long-range plans include renovation. All units do have color cable TV, air-conditioning, and a minifridge; some have balconies and sea views. A new, enlarged casino has recently been completed, and the lobby has been smartened. The ramparts rising from the sea offer a fantastic evening view of the twinkling lights of the city. *Box 229, Plaza Piar, Willemstad, tel. 599/9–612500, fax 599/9–616543. 254 rooms. Facilities: restaurant, coffee shop, casino, room service, 3 bars, dive shop, drugstore, gift shop, car-rental agent, tour desk, pool. Baby-sitter and house physician on call. AE, DC, MC, V. CP. Inexpensive.*

Coral Cliff Resort and Beach Club. Seclusion and rustic simplicity are everything here. A 45-minute ride from the center of Willemstad, the grounds boast a beach so enticing that it even attracts native islanders seeking a weekend retreat. (The beach is open to the public for a $5 admission charge.) The resort exudes a European atmosphere and is very popular with Dutch tourists. Americans used to luxurious or amenity-laden resorts will find the rooms stark and in sore need of modernizing. However, all are air-conditioned, have spectacular views of the sea, and are equipped with an old but functional kitchenette. The hotel recently installed a children's playground, a tennis court, and slot machines in the bar. All guests receive complimentary airport transfers. *Box 3782, Santa Marta Bay, tel. 599/9–641820 or 800/344–1212, fax 599/9–641781. 35 rooms. Facilities: pool, restaurant, bar, car-rental agent, marina, water-sports center, and PADI 4-star dive shop. AE, DC, MC, V. EP, BP, MAP, FAP. Budget.*

Villa and Apartment Rentals
As a rule, Curaçao's rental villas and cottages are not on the beach, although there are a few in the Westpunt area that overlook the sea and are a short walk from the water. For a complete list of rental units available, contact the **Curaçao Tourist Board** (Pietermaii 19, Willemstad, Curaçao, Netherland Antilles, tel. 599/9–616000, fax 599/9–612305). Most villas and cottages cater

to Europeans used to basic amenities and a no-frills atmosphere. Air-conditioning is not a standard feature, so be sure to request it. Two top-notch apartment complexes are listed below.

Kadushi Cliffs. Located in the lusher and more hilly western end of the island is this quiet time-share complex, with fabulous two-bedroom villas sitting atop a high bluff that overlooks the sea (and a bikini-sized beach far below). With a nightly rate of $200, the property is affordable only if you are one of two couples sharing a villa or are part of a large family. All of the units are identical, with two bedrooms, two full baths, and upscale appointments in an eye-pleasing beige, mauve, and aqua color scheme. Amenities include air-conditioning, ceiling fans, a fully equipped modern kitchen, tile floors, an enormous patio and sun deck, remote control color TVs, safe-deposit boxes, vaulted ceilings, and a queen-size sleep sofa in the living room. An al fresco restaurant serves international cuisine for lunch and dinner. Although the tiny beach below the property is accessible by a (steep) walk, you'll be happier here if you're renting a car, since town and larger beaches are far away. *Westpunt, tel. 599/9–640200 or 800/KADUSHI, fax 599/9–640282. 12 two-bedroom villas. Facilities: restaurant, pool, laundry facilities. AE, MC, V. Moderate.*

Club Seru Coral. This modern resort complex with bungalows and studio apartments opened in 1992 on Curaçao's east coast. The grounds feature both desert and tropical landscaping. Bungalows have two bedrooms, bath, fully equipped kitchen, and a combination dining/living room. The compact studio apartments are comparable to large hotel rooms with complete kitchenettes. All accommodations are air-conditioned and feature tile floors, twin beds, patios, color TVs, phones, radios, and safe-deposit boxes. There's a restaurant and pool here, and tennis-loving guests have full privileges at Santa Catherina Sports Club, located 2½ miles away. Guests enjoy free pickup from the airport, but since the resort is off the beach and a good 9 miles from town, a rental car is advised. *Koraal Partier 10, tel. and fax 599/9–678276. 41 units. Facilities: restaurant, bar, pool, children's pool, room service, car-rental desk, satellite TV, games room, baby-sitting, small grocery and liquor store, daily maid service. AE, D, DC, MC, V. Budget (studios)–Moderate (bungalows).*

Guest Houses and Inns Curaçao has a number of small budget hotels, guest houses, and inns charging less than $50 a day in high season. Many are off the beaten track and have few, if any, facilities, other than rooms with kitchenettes. Request a list from the tourist board (*see* Villa and Apartment Rentals, *above*), along with a detailed island map so that you can locate each place. If you're worried about what you might end up with, first book a hotel and then inspect your room at the guest house before deciding to stay there.

Off-Season Bets Prices at Curaçao's top hotels decrease by about 30% from mid-April to mid-December. Full-service resorts with excellent off-season rates in our Moderate category include the new **Sonesta Beach Hotel & Casino** (Box 6003, Piscadera Bay, tel. 599/9–368800 or 800/SONESTA, fax 599/9–627502); and the **Princess Beach Hotel and Casino** (M.L. King Blvd. 8, tel. 599/9–614944 or 800/327–3286, fax 599/9–614131).

Nightlife

The once-a-month open house at Landhuis Brievengat (*see* Exploring Curaçao, Eastern Side, *above*) is a great way to meet interesting locals—it usually offers a folkloric show, snacks, and local handicrafts. Every Friday night the landhouse holds a big party with two bands. The Sonesta Beach, Van Der Valk Plaza, Curaçao Caribbean, Holiday Beach, Las Palmas, and the Princess Beach hotels all have casinos that are open 1 PM–4 AM.

Blue Note Jazz Cafe (Schout bij N. Doormanweg 37, tel. 599/9–370685) has reopened under new management but still remains a singles bar–cum–Dutch pub that fills up fast. There is live jazz on Wednesday and Friday 8:30 PM–1 AM and Sunday noon–5 PM.

The Pub (Salina 144A, tel. 599/9–612190) is a crowded, energetic dancing and drinking club. The dress is casual to funky, so leave your heels at home. Open Friday 8–4, Saturday 9–4, Monday–Thursday and Sunday 9–3.

Infinity (tel. 599/9–613450), a tiny club underneath the Fort Nassau Restaurant, is a romantic disco, with semicircular alcoves, plush couches, curtains made of strings of lights, and a teeny dance floor. It doesn't get busy until the clock strikes the witching hour. Open Friday and Saturday 9–3, Monday–Thursday and Sunday 9–1.

Rum Runner (Otrobanda Waterfront, DeRouvilleweg 9, tel. 599/9–623038) is another casual hot spot, with an indoor/outdoor bar and eatery serving up tapas in an atmosphere reminiscent of a college fraternity hall. There's music nightly.

10 Dominica

*Updated by
Nigel Fisher*

The national motto emblazoned on the coat of arms of the Commonwealth of Dominica reads *"Après Bondi, c'est la ter."* It is a French-Creole phrase meaning "After God, it is the land." On this unspoiled isle, the land is indeed the main attraction . . . it turns and twists, towers to mountain crests, then tumbles to falls and valleys. It is a land that the Smithsonian Institution called a giant plant laboratory, unchanged for 10,000 years. Indeed, after a heavy rain you half expect to see things grow before your very eyes; the island is a virtual rainbow in entirely green hues.

The grandeur of Dominica (pronounced *dom-in-EE-ka*) is not man-made. This untamed, ruggedly beautiful land, located in the eastern Caribbean between Guadeloupe to the north and Martinique to the south, is a 305-square-mile nature retreat; 29 miles long and 15 miles wide, the island is dominated by some of the highest elevations in the Caribbean and is laced with 365 rivers, "one for every day of the year." Much of the interior is covered by a luxuriant rain forest, a wild place where you almost expect Tarzan to swing howling by on a vine. Straight out of Conan Doyle's *Lost World,* everything here is larger than life, from the towering tree ferns to the enormous insects. This exotic spot is home to such unusual critters as the Sisserou (or Imperial) parrot and the red-necked (or Jacquot) parrot, neither of which is found anywhere else in the world.

Dominica's rugged mountains and abundant forests and rivers have held the island back from rapid economic development. And the lack of good beaches has hindered the growth of tour-

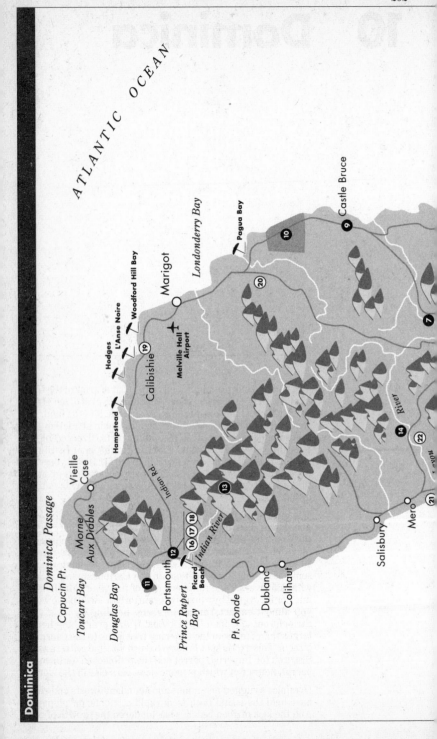

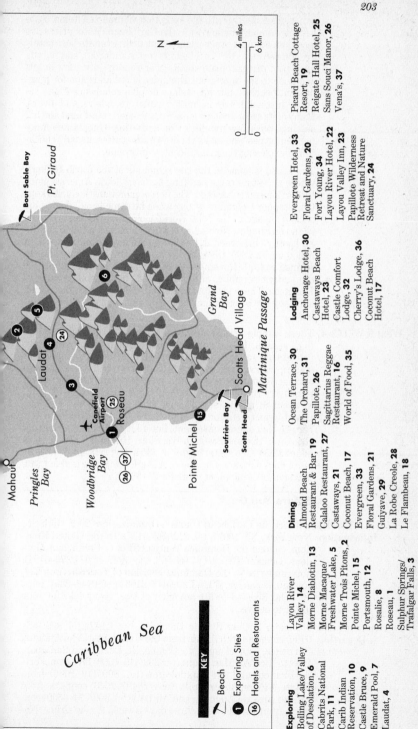

Caribbean Sea

KEY

Beach
Exploring Sites
(16) Hotels and Restaurants

Exploring
Boiling Lake/Valley of Desolation, **6**
Cabrits National Park, **11**
Carib Indian Reservation, **10**
Castle Bruce, **9**
Emerald Pool, **7**
Laudat, **4**
Layou River Valley, **14**
Morne Diablotin, **13**
Morne Macaque/Freshwater Lake, **5**
Morne Trois Pitons, **2**
Pointe Michel, **15**
Portsmouth, **12**
Rosalie, **8**
Roseau, **1**
Sulphur Springs/Trafalgar Falls, **3**

Dining
Almond Beach Restaurant & Bar, **19**
Calaloo Restaurant, **27**
Castaways, **21**
Coconut Beach, **17**
Evergreen, **33**
Floral Gardens, **21**
Guiyave, **29**
La Robe Creole, **28**
Le Flambeau, **18**
Ocean Terrace, **30**
The Orchard, **31**
Papillote, **26**
Sagittarius Reggae Restaurant, **16**
World of Food, **35**

Lodging
Anchorage Hotel, **30**
Castaways Beach Hotel, **23**
Castle Comfort Lodge, **32**
Cherry's Lodge, **36**
Coconut Beach Hotel, **17**
Evergreen Hotel, **33**
Floral Gardens, **20**
Fort Young, **34**
Layou River Hotel, **22**
Layou Valley Inn, **23**
Papillote Wilderness Retreat and Nature Sanctuary, **24**
Picard Beach Cottage Resort, **19**
Reigate Hall Hotel, **25**
Sans Souci Manor, **26**
Vena's, **37**

ism. Consequently, with the exception of imported items, costs here are among the lowest in the Caribbean. Hotel prices are less than on most other islands (but then, even its best hotels are almost basic by Caribbean resort standards), and for the most part prices remain steady year-round. Only a few hotels are close to the beach, but Dominica is not an island for magnificent beaches, nor for casinos or piña coladas or glitzy resorts. Instead, it's an island for explorers, hikers, and divers. Many of its accommodations are in secluded rain-forest and hill settings with few amenities or activities. Guests are independent types who make their own itineraries, usually chock-full of exploring the magnificent countryside.

The island is home to the last remnants of the Carib Indians, whose ancestors came paddling up from South America more than a thousand years ago. The fierce, cannibalistic Caribs kept Christopher Columbus at bay when he came to call during his second voyage to the New World. Columbus turned up at the island on Sunday, November 3, 1493. In between Carib arrows he hastily christened it Dominica (Sunday Island), and then sailed on. In 1805, the island became a British colony and remained so until November 3, 1978, when it became a fully independent republic, officially called the Commonwealth of Dominica. There are about 82,000 people living on the island, and they are some of the friendliest people in all of the Caribbean.

What It Will Cost These sample prices, meant only as a general guide, are for high season. For a standard double room at a moderately priced hotel, expect to pay about $110. Dinner at an inexpensive restaurant costs about $12. Beer prices at restaurants start at $1.50. Wine is prohibitive, but local rum is cheap; a rum punch at a restaurant costs about $2.50. Taxis are no bargain, at about $1 a mile, and because sites are scattered over the island, transportation costs mount. There is infrequent bus service that's less convenient, but a lot cheaper: A ride from Roseau in the southwest to Woodford Hill in the northeast is about $3.50. Car rental begins at $35 a day; rentals of three or more days will save you money. A single-tank dive is about $40, and snorkel equipment rents for $5–$6 a day.

Before You Go

Tourist Information Contact the **Caribbean Tourism Organization** (20 E. 46th St., New York, NY 10017, tel. 212/682–0435). In the United Kingdom, contact the **Dominica Tourist Office** (1 Collingham Gardens, London SW5 0HW, tel. 071/835–1937 or 071/370–5194). You can write to the **Dominica Division of Tourism** (Box 293, Roseau, Dominica, WI, tel. 809/448–2186 or 809/448–2351, telex 8642, fax 809/448–5840), but allow at least two weeks for your letter to arrive.

Arriving and Departing *By Plane* No major airlines fly into Dominica, but **LIAT** (tel. 809/462–0700) connects with flights from the United States on Antigua, Barbados, Guadeloupe, Martinique, St. Lucia, and San Juan, Puerto Rico. **Air Martinique** (tel. 809/449–1060) flies from Fort-de-France, and **Air Guadeloupe** (tel. 809/449–1060) from Pointe-à-Pitre. **Air Anguilla** (tel. 809/497–2643) connects from Puerto Rico via Anguilla, and **Air BVI** (tel. 809/774–6500) connects from Tortola, BVI, three days a week. A new airline, **Na-**

ture Island Express (tel. 809/449–2309), provides service to and from Barbados, St. Lucia, and St. Maarten daily.

From the Airport Canefield Airport can take only small aircraft, with lights available for night takeoffs. Dominica's older and larger **Melville Hall Airport,** on the northeast (Atlantic) coast, can manage larger commercial aircraft. If you have a choice, however, opt for Canefield, a 3-mile, $10 cab ride from the capital city of Roseau. Melville to Roseau, on the other hand, takes 90 minutes (albeit through glorious rain forest) and costs $50 for a private taxi. The usual system is a co-op cab, where all seats must be taken for about $17 a person.

By Boat **The Caribbean Express** (Fort-de-France, Martinique, tel. 596/60–12–38) has scheduled twice-weekly departures from Guadeloupe in the north to Martinique in the south, with stops at Les Saintes and Dominica. Fare is E.C. $104 (about U.S. $38) from Pointe-à-Pitre to Dominica and E.C. $122 (U.S. $45) from Fort-de-France.

Passports and Visas The only entry requirements for U.S. or Canadian citizens are proof of citizenship, such as a birth certificate or voter registration card bearing a photograph, and an ongoing or return airline ticket. British citizens are required to have passports, but visas are not necessary.

Language The official language is English, but most Dominicans also speak a French-Creole patois.

Precautions Be sure to bring insect repellent. If you are prone to car sickness, you will also want to bring along some pills. The roads twist and turn dramatically, and the (expert) local drivers barrel across them at a dizzying pace.

Staying in Dominica

Important Addresses **Tourist Information:** Contact the main office of the **Division of Tourism** (National Development Corp., Valley Rd., Roseau, tel. 809/448–2186 or 809/448–2351). The tourist desk at the **Old Market Plaza** (Roseau, tel. 809/448–2186) is open Monday 8–5, Tuesday–Friday 8–4, Saturday 9–1. The offices at **Canefield Airport** (tel. 809/449–1242) and **Melville Hall Airport** (tel. 809/445–7051) are open weekdays 6:15–11 AM and 2–5:30 PM.

Emergencies **Police, Fire, and Ambulance:** call 999. **Hospitals: Princess Margaret Hospital** (Federation Dr., Goodwill, tel. 809/448–2231 or 809/448–2233). **Pharmacies: Jolly's Pharmacy** (33 King George St., Roseau, tel. 809/448–3388).

Currency The official currency is the Eastern Caribbean dollar (E.C.), but U.S. dollars are accepted everywhere. At banks the rate is officially tied to the U.S. dollar, at a rate of E.C. $2.70 to U.S. $1. Local prices, especially in shops frequented by tourists, are often quoted in both currencies, so be sure to ask. Prices quoted here are in U.S. dollars unless noted otherwise.

Taxes and Service Charges Hotels collect a 5% government tax; restaurants a 3% tax. Most hotels and restaurants add a 10% service charge to your bill. Taxi drivers appreciate a 10% tip. There is a 3% sales tax. The departure tax is $8, or E.C. $20. A security service charge tax of $2 (E.C. $5) is also imposed.

Getting Around *Rental Cars* If it doesn't bother you to drive on the left over potholed mountainous roads with hairpin curves, rent a car and strike out on your own. Daily car-rental rates begin at $35 (weekly about $190), plus collision damage at $6 a day, and personal accident insurance at $2 a day, and you'll have to put down a deposit and purchase a visitor's driving permit for E.C. $20. You can rent a car from **Anselm's Car Rental** (3 Great Marlborough, Roseau, tel. 809/448–2730), **S.T.L. Rent-A-Car** (Goodwill Rd., Roseau, tel. 809/448–2340 or 809/448–4525), **Valley Rent-A-Car** (Goodwill Rd., Roseau, tel. 809/448–3233), or **Wide Range Car Rentals** (79 Bath Rd., Roseau, tel. 809/448–2198); **Budget Rent-A-Car** (Canefield Industrial Estate, Canefield, tel. 809/449–2080) offers daily rates, three-day specials, and weekly and monthly rates.

By Taxi   Taxis have fixed rates, though a little negotiation is always possible (except from the airport). A typical fare within Roseau is $5; a trip from Roseau to Portsmouth is $45. Taxis are hard to find after 6 PM, so you should make prior arrangements with a cabbie.

Telephones   To call Dominica from the United States, dial area code 809 and
and Mail   the local access code, 44. On the island, you need to dial only the five-digit number. A local call costs E.C. 25¢. Direct telephone, telegraph, telefax, teletype, and telex services are via **Cable & Wireless (West Indies) Ltd.** Card phones are becoming more common here. You can purchase the cards at the Cable & Wireless office and other locations. All pay phones are equipped for local and overseas dialing.

First-class (airmail) letters to the United States and Canada cost E.C. 60¢; postcards cost E.C. 35¢.

Opening and   Business hours are weekdays 8–1 and 2–4, Saturday 8–1.
Closing Times   Banks are open Monday–Thursday 8–1, Friday 8–1 and 3–5.

Guided Tours   A variety of hiking and photo safari tours are conducted by **Dominica Tours** (tel. 809/448–2638) in sturdy four-wheel-drive vehicles. Prices range from $25 to $75 per person, depending upon the length of the trip and whether picnics and rum punches are included. There are also boat tours that include snorkeling, swimming, and rum or fruit drinks. **Rainbow Rover Tours** (tel. 809/448–8650) are conducted in air-conditioned Land Rovers. Tours take in the island for a half or full day at a per-person cost of $30–$50, which includes food and drink. **Ken's Hinterland Adventure Tours** (tel. 809/448–4850) provides tours in vans with knowledgeable guides and can design expeditions to fit your needs. Prices vary according to the tour; an afternoon hike to the Valley of Desolation costs $20 and includes transportation to and from your hotel.

Any taxi driver will be happy to offer his services as a guide for $18 an hour, with tip extra. It's a good idea to get a recommendation from your hotel manager or the Dominica Tourist Board (*see* Tourist Information, *above*) before selecting a guide and driver. A tour to introduce you to the ruggedness of the island's terrain and its flora can be managed in four hours, but if you want to travel around the island, plan on seven.

Exploring Dominica

Numbers in the margin correspond to points of interest on the Dominica map.

The island's mountainous interior means getting anywhere takes longer than you think. Although you can get a quick overview of the island in one day of touring by car, you should supplement this with specialized hiking and sightseeing tours. The highways ringing the island's perimeter have been upgraded in recent years (in general, those in the north are better than those in the south).

Roseau
1
All the hotels and virtually all the island's population are on the leeward, or Caribbean, side of the island. Twenty thousand or so inhabitants reside in **Roseau,** a town on the flat delta of the Roseau River. Stop first in the Tourist Office in the **Old Market Plaza.** Then stroll through the center of town, where crafts shops and tiny cafés are tucked into old buildings made of wood, stone, and concrete. On Victoria Street is the **Fort Young Hotel,** originally built as a fort in the 18th century. Directly across the street is the **State House;** the **Public Library** and the **old Court House** are both nearby.

The National Park Office, fittingly located in the 40-acre Botanical Gardens in Roseau, can provide tour guides and a wealth of printed information. *Tel. 809/448–2401, ext. 417. Open Mon. 8–1 and 2–5, Tues.–Fri. 8–1 and 2–4.*

Head north to Woodbridge Bay Harbour and stroll along the harbor, where you can watch bananas, citrus, and spices being loaded onto ships.

Elsewhere on the Island
2
Morne Trois Pitons is a blue-green hill of three peaks, the highest of which is 4,403 feet. The mountain is usually veiled in swirling mists and clouds, and the 16,000-acre national park over which it looms is awash with cool mountain lakes, waterfalls, and rushing rivers. Ferns grow 30 feet tall, and wild orchids sprout from trees. Sunlight leaks through green canopies, and a gentle mist rises over the jungle floor.

3
The road from the capital to the Morne Trois Pitons National Park runs through the **Roseau River Valley.** About 5 miles out of Roseau, a side road branches, one direction leading to Wotten Waven, the other to **Sulphur Springs** (visible evidence of the island's volcanic origins) and the spectacular triple **Trafalgar Falls,** dropping 200 feet into a warm rock-strewn pool that's ideal for bathing.

4
5
The village of **Laudat** (about 7 miles from Roseau) is a good starting point for a venture into the park. Two miles northeast of Laudat, at the base of **Morne Macaque** (3,500 feet), you'll find **Freshwater Lake,** and farther on, **Boeri Lake,** with a fringe of greenery and purple hyacinths floating on the water.

6
From Freshwater Lake there are several sights to be seen, but the hiking trails are not for the faint of heart. **Boiling Lake** and the **Valley of Desolation** are reached by a rugged, all-day, 6-mile ramble, and you should go only with an experienced guide. There are *very* hot springs here that shift direction from time to time under an outer crust. Even experienced guides keep small groups of hikers (six to eight maximum) under their eye at all times (*see* Sports and the Outdoors, *below*).

Boiling Lake, the world's second-largest boiling lake, is like a caldron of gurgling gray-blue water. It is 70 yards wide, and the temperature of the water ranges from 180 to 197°F. Its depth is unknown. It is believed that the lake is not a volcanic crater but a flooded fumarole—a crack through which gases escape from the molten lava below. This is a serious expedition for serious hikers. You must be in excellent condition and bring your own drinking water.

The Valley of Desolation lies below Boiling Lake, and it lives up to its name. Harsh sulfuric fumes have destroyed virtually all the vegetation in what was once a lush forested area. Hikers in the Valley of Desolation are advised to stay on the trail to avoid breaking through the crust that covers the hot lava below.

❼ You'll have to backtrack to Roseau and head north toward Pont Casse to reach **Emerald Pool,** 3¹/₂ miles northeast of Pont Casse. It's a 10-minute walk along the road that leads to Castle Bruce. Lookout points along the trail provide sweeping views of the windward (Atlantic) coast and the forested interior. Emerald Pool is a swirling, fern-bedecked basin into which a 50-foot waterfall splashes.

A good map and steady nerves are necessary for driving along the rugged, ragged windward coast. A few miles east of Pont Casse there is a fork in the road where a right turn will take you to the southeast coast and a left, to the northeast coast.

❽ The south-coast road goes to **Rosalie,** where there is a river for swimming, a black-sand beach, an old aqueduct, and a water-wheel. There is also a waterfall that dashes down a cliff into the ocean. A hike leads to **Petite Soufrière.**

❾ The northerly road leads to the little fishing village of **Castle Bruce.** On the beach here you can watch dugout canoes being made from the trunks of *gommier* trees using traditional Carib methods (after the tree is cut it gets stretched). About 6 miles **❿** north of Castle Bruce lies the **Carib Indian Reservation,** which was established in 1903 and covers 3,700 acres. Don't expect a lot in the way of ancient culture and costume. The folks who gave the Caribbean its name live pretty much like other West Indians, as fishermen and farmers. However, they have maintained their traditional skills at wood carving, basket weaving, and canoe building. Their wares are displayed and sold in little thatch-top huts lining the road. The reservation's Roman Catholic church at Salibia has an altar that was once a canoe. Another point of interest on the reservation is **L'Escalier Tête Chien** ("trail of the snake staircase" in Creole patois)—a hardened lava flow that juts down to the ocean. Note: Do not attempt to walk to its end, where waves have pulled people from the rock to their death.

The Atlantic here is particularly fierce and roily, the shore marked with countless coves and inlets. The Carib still tell wondrous colorful legends of the island's origins. La Roche Pagua, they say, is home to a fragrant white flower; bathe in its petals and your loved one will obey your every command. By night, Londonderry Islets metamorphose into grand canoes to take the spirits of the dead out to sea.

Continuing north from the reservation, you'll go past lovely **Pagua Bay,** with its beach of dark sand. A bit farther along, near Melville Hall Airport, is **Marigot,** the largest (population: 5,000) settlement on the east coast. On the northeast coast, steep cliffs rise out of the Atlantic, which flings its frothy waters over dramatic reefs, and rivers crash through forests of mangroves and fields of coconut. The beaches at **Woodford Hill, Hampstead, L'Anse Noir,** and **Hodges** are excellent for snorkeling and scuba diving, though all this wind-tossed beauty can be dangerous to swimmers, since there are strong underwater currents as well as whipped-cream waves. From this vantage point you can see the French island of Marie Galante in the distance.

The road continues through banana plantations to Portsmouth, but a side road leads up to the village of **Vieille Case** and **Capucin Pointe** at the northernmost tip of the island. **Morne Aux Diables** soars 2,826 feet over this area and slopes down to **Toucari Bay** and **Douglas Bay** on the west coast, where there are spectacular dark-sand beaches.

⑪ Just 2 miles south of Douglas Bay, the 250-acre **Cabrits National Park** is surrounded on three sides by the Caribbean Sea. Local historian Lennox Honychurch has restored **Fort Shirley,** a military complex built between 1770 and 1815. Some of the buildings have been restored, and there is a small museum in the park. The park is connected to the mainland by a freshwater swamp, verdant with ferns, grasses, and trees, where you can see a variety of migrant birds. A new cruise-ship pier development with both berthing and passenger facilities is open at the port of Cabrits, below Fort Shirley. Present plans are to host only one ship at a time, which will make this a desirable stop on cruise itineraries.

⑫ **Portsmouth,** 2 miles south of Cabrits, is a peaceful little town with a population of about 5,000. **Prince Rupert Bay,** site of a naval battle in 1782 between the French and the English, is far and away the island's most beautiful harbor. There are more than 2 miles of sandy beaches fringed with coconut trees and most of the island's beachfront hotels. The **Indian River** flows to the sea from here, and a canoe ride takes you through an exotic rain forest thick with mangrove swamps. Board a rowboat (not power) for total tranquillity, to be able to hear fish jumping and exotic birds calling. The guides here are notoriously overeager: Choose carefully or ask your hotel to recommend someone.

Just south of Indian River is **Pointe Ronde,** the starting point ⑬ for an expedition to **Morne Diablotin,** at 4,747 feet the island's highest summit. This is not an expedition you should attempt alone; the uninhabited interior is an almost impenetrable primeval forest. You'll need a good guide (*see* Sports and the Outdoors, *below*), sturdy shoes, a warm sweater, and firm resolve.

The west-coast road dips down through the little villages of **Dublanc** (with a side road off to the Syndicate Estate), **Colihaut,** and **Salisbury** before reaching the mouth of the Layou ⑭ River. The **Layou River Valley** is rich with bananas, cacao, citrus fruits, and coconuts. The remains of Hillsborough Estate, once a rum-producing plantation, are here. The river is the island's longest and largest, with deep gorges, quiet pools and beaches, waterfalls and rapids—a great place for a full day's outing of swimming and shooting the rapids, or just sunning and picnicking. Plans are under way to build a large hotel and conference center in this area, the Shangri-la, which may disturb the peace in the area.

The road at the bend near Dublanc that leads to the Syndicate Estate also leads to the 200-acre site of the new **Project Sisserou.** This protected site has been set aside with the help of some 6,000 schoolchildren, each of whom donated 25¢ for the land where the endangered Sisserou parrot (found only in Dominica) flies free. At last estimate, there were only about 60 of these shy and beautiful birds, covered in rich green feathers with a mauve front.

Just south of Roseau the road forks, with a treacherous prong leading east to **Grand Bay,** where bay leaves are grown and distilled. If you continue due south from Roseau, you'll go ⑮ through **Pointe Michel,** settled decades ago by Martinicans who fled the catastrophic eruption of Mont Pelée. The stretch all the way from Roseau to Scotts Head at the southernmost tip of the island has excellent beaches for scuba diving and snorkeling.

Beaches

Don't come to Dominica in search of powdery white-sand beaches. The travel-poster beaches do exist on the northeast coast, but this is still an almost totally undeveloped area. The beaches that most visitors see are of dark sand, evidence of the island's volcanic origins. The best beaches are found at the mouths of rivers and in protected bays. Scuba diving, snorkeling, and windsurfing are all excellent here.

Layou River has the best river swimming on the island, and its banks are great for sunbathing.

Picard Beach, on the northwest coast, is the island's best beach. Great for windsurfing and snorkeling, it's a 2-mile stretch of brown sand fringed with coconut trees. The Picard Beach Cottage Resort and Coconut Beach hotels are along this beach.

Pagua Bay, a quiet, secluded beach of dark sand, is on the Atlantic coast.

Woodford Hill Bay, Hampstead, L'Anse Noir, and **Hodges,** all on the northeast coast, are excellent beaches for snorkeling and scuba diving. Strong underwater currents discourage swimmers.

In the southeast, near La Plaine, **Bout Sable Bay** is not much good for swimming, but the surroundings are stirringly elemental: towering red cliffs challenge the rollicking Atlantic.

The beaches south of Roseau to **Scotts Head** at the southernmost tip of the island are good for scuba diving and snorkeling because of the dramatic underwater walls and sudden drops.

The scuba diving is excellent at **Soufrière Bay,** a sandy beach south of Roseau. Volcanic vents puff steam into the sea; the experience has been described as "swimming in champagne."

Sports and the Outdoors

Hiking Trails range from the easygoing to the arduous. For the former, all you'll need are sturdy, rubber-soled shoes and an adventurous spirit.

For the hike to Boiling Lake or the climb up Morne Diablotin you will need hiking boots, a guide, and water. Guides will charge about $30–$35 per person and can be contacted through the Tourist Office or the Forestry Division (tel. 809/448–2401 or 809/448–2638).

Scuba Diving *Skin Diver* magazine recently ranked Dominica among the top five Caribbean dive destinations. There's no shore diving here, so you'll have to hook up with a dive shop to make boat arrangements. **Dive Dominica** (Castle Comfort, tel. 809/448–2188, fax 809/448–6088), with three boats, is one of the best dive shops in Dominica, run by owners Derek and Ginette Perryman, NAUI-approved instructors. They offer snorkeling and resort dives for beginners and, for the advanced set, dives on drop-offs, walls, and pinnacles—by day or night. Other dive operations include **Dominica Dive Resorts,** (Anchorage Hotel tel. 809/448–2638); **Winward Island Divers Ltd.** (Portsmouth Beach Hotel, tel. 809/445–5142). **Dive Castaways** (Castaways Hotel, tel. 809/449–6244); and **East Carib Dive Ltd.** (tel. 809/449–6602). The going rate at all of the above is about $40 for a single-tank dive, $65 for a two-tank dive, or $90 for a resort course with two open-water dives.

Snorkeling Major island operators rent equipment for about $5–$6 a day: **Anchorage Hotel** (tel. 809/448–2638), **Castaways Hotel** (tel. 809/449–6244), **Coconut Beach Hotel** (tel. 809/445–5393), **Portsmouth Beach Hotel** (tel. 809/445–5142), and **Picard Beach Cottage Resort** (tel. 809/445–5131).

Swimming River swimming is extremely popular on Dominica, and the best river to jump into is the Layou River (*see* Exploring Dominica, *above*). *Also see* Beaches, *above*, for our pick of the best beaches for swimming, snorkeling, or surfing.

Shopping

Gift Ideas The distinctive handicrafts of the Carib Indians include traditional baskets made of dyed larouma reeds and waterproofed with tightly woven balizier leaves. These crafts are sold on the reservation, as well as in Roseau's shops. Dominica is also noted for its spices, hot peppers, bay rum, and coconut-oil soap; its vetiver-grass mats are sold all over the world. All of these items represent good value.

Good gifts are stylized candles from **Starbrite Industries** (Canefield Industrial Site, tel. 809/449–1006) that come in the shape of the Dominican parrot, cupids, and trees, as well as more traditional shapes. Open weekdays 8–1 and 2–4. **The Old Mill Culture Centre and Historic Site** on Canefield Road presents exhibits on the historical, cultural, and political development of Dominica. In addition, the center exhibits and sells carvings from Dominican wood by master carver, Louis Desire, and his students. Open weekdays 9–1 and 2–4. There are gift shops at Papillote (wonderful wooden bowls) and Floral Gardens (domestic goods and crafts). (*See* Lodging, *below*.)

Stop in at **Caribana Handcrafts** (31 Cork St., Roseau, tel. 809/448–2761) or **Tropicrafts** (41 Queen Mary St., Roseau, tel. 809/448–2747), where you'll find soaps, spices, and stacks of handmade hats, baskets, and woven straw mats.

Dining

Except in Roseau, most restaurants on Dominica are attached to hotels. But even here, you'll have ample opportunity to sample the local cuisine; indeed, you'll be hard pressed to find anything else. Menus are remarkably similar throughout the island, although preparations differ. Produce and fish are mostly from local sources, and meals usually consist of meat, chicken, or fish in a Creole sauce, served with sweet green bananas, kushkush yams, breadfruit, and *dasheen* (a tuber similar to the potato and called taro elsewhere)—these and other staples are known as ground provisions. On virtually every menu you'll find "mountain chicken"—a euphemism for a large toad called *crapaud*. Two rare delicacies for the intrepid diner are *manicou* (a small opossum) and the tender, gamey *agouti* (a large, indigenous rodent); both are best smoked or stewed. Few restaurants are expensive here.

Highly recommended restaurants are indicated by a star ★.

Category	Cost*
Moderate	$15–$25
Inexpensive	$10–$15
Budget	under $10

per person, excluding drinks, service, and 3% sales tax

★ **La Robe Creole.** Roseau's best restaurant is a cozy place with wood rafters, ladder-back chairs, and colorful madras cloths. A specialty is callaloo and crab soup, made with dasheen and coconut. You can also have crêpes of lobster and conch, charcoal-grilled fish and meats, barbecued chicken, and salads. A good way to keep your check down is to order appetizers as your main course. The downstairs take-out annex, The Mouse Hole, is an inexpensive place to stock up for your picnic. *3 Victoria St., Roseau, tel. 809/448–2896. Reservations advised. AE. Closed Sun. Moderate.*

Evergreen. This large, airy dining room opens onto a terrace overlooking the sea. Dinner includes an interesting choice of soup and salad; entrées of chicken, fish, and beef are served with local fruits and vegetables such as kushkush and plantains. Homemade desserts include cake and ice cream. *Evergreen Hotel, Roseau, tel. 809/448–3288. Reservations advised. AE, V, MC. Moderate.*

Floral Gardens. You feel as if you're eating in a private home at this warm, welcoming restaurant. Large portions include local specialties such as crapaud and agouti. Service is slow. *Floral Gardens Hotel, Concord, tel. 809/445–7636. AE, MC, V. Moderate.*

Le Flambeau. This open-air beach restaurant at the Picard Beach Cottage Resort serves an American-style breakfast of pancakes and French toast. Lunch and dinner entrées are a little pricey and not memorable, but leave room for the homemade ice cream—peanut, coconut, or mixed berry. *Picard Beach Cottage Resort, Portsmouth, tel. 809/445–5131. AE, D, MC, V. Moderate.*

Ocean Terrace. Arrive early to witness a magnificent sunset from this terrace-restaurant overlooking the sea at the Anchorage Hotel. Grilled lamb chops with mint jelly, Creole-style fish court bouillon, and chilled lobster in a chive-vinaigrette marinade are among the à la carte specialties. There's a barbeque and live Caribbean entertainment on Thursday nights. *Anchorage Hotel, Roseau, tel. 809/448–2638. Reservations advised. AE, D, MC, V. Moderate.*

The Orchard. You can dine indoors in a spacious, unadorned dining room or in a pleasant covered courtyard surrounded by latticework. Chef Joan Cools-Lartique offers Creole-style coconut shrimp, lobster, black pudding, mountain chicken, and callaloo soup with crabmeat, among other delicacies, on a changing menu. Sandwiches are also on the menu. *31 King George V St., Roseau, tel. 809/448–3051. AE, D, MC, V. Moderate.*

Papillote. This open-air restaurant, with trellises of woven orchids and ferns, and popular with birds, butterflies, and tour groups, seems hacked from the undergrowth. Try the bracing callaloo soup, the knockout rum punches and, if they're on the menu, the succulent *souk* (tiny, delicate river shrimp). *Papillote Wilderness Retreat, tel. 809/448–2287. AE, D, MC, V. Moderate.*

Calaloo Restaurant. Up the stairs of a verandahed building smack on a busy Roseau street is this small, informal eatery decorated with local crafts. Changing lunch and dinner specials might include pepperpot soup, curried conch, or crab callaloo. Most everything here is homemade, including juices and ice cream. *63 King George V St., Roseau, tel. 809/448–3386. No credit cards. Inexpensive–Moderate.*

Almond Beach Restaurant & Bar. If you're visiting one of the island's northeast beaches, stop here for a lunch of callaloo soup, lobster, or octopus. Select from tantalizing fruit juices, including guava, passion fruit, tangerine, soursop, and papaya, or one of the bewitching rums, steeped for more than two months in various herbs and spices. Try the *pweve* (patois for pepper), the aniselike *nanie,* or *lapsenth,* a violet-scented pick-me-up and digestif. The delightful owners, Mr. and Mrs. Joseph, are experts in local culture and will arrange a traditional *bélé* dance performance for groups. *Calibishi, tel. 809/445–7783. No credit cards. Inexpensive.*

★ **Castaways.** The hotel's guests often lunch or dine here, but it's the Sunday brunch (which starts at 11 AM and goes to 6 PM) that's the real draw. The grill is fired up, and fresh fish, steak, chicken, and lobster are tossed on the fire. Side dishes of fresh fruits and vegetables, along with hot breads, round out the beach party. *Castaways Hotel, Mero, tel. 809/449–6244 or 809/449–6245. AE, MC, V. Inexpensive.*

Coconut Beach. This casual, low-key beachfront restaurant and bar is popular with visiting yacht owners (moorings are available) and students from the nearby medical school. Fresh tropical drinks, local seafood dishes, sandwiches, and *rotis* (Caribbean burritos) are served. *Coconut Beach Hotel, Portsmouth, tel. 809/445–5393. AE, D, MC, V. Inexpensive.*

Guiyave. Have a drink at the second-floor bar and then repair to the table-filled balcony for dining. Spareribs, lobster, rabbit, and mountain chicken are offered, along with homemade beef or chicken patties, spicy rotis, and a variety of light snacks and sandwiches. This restaurant is noted for its fresh tropical fruit juices (a local cherry, guava, passion fruit, and barbadine) and its homemade pies, tarts, and cakes. *15 Cork St., Roseau, tel. 809/448–2930. No credit cards. No dinner. Inexpensive.*

World of Food. Sit in the garden of the late Jean Rhys, the Dominican-born novelist who won Britain's Royal Literary Award. The spot has been turned into a garden bistro serving rotis, sandwiches, and other light meals. Locals come here in the evening, attracted by the girls who hang around the dance floor next door. *Field La., off Queen Mary St., Roseau, tel. 809/448–6125. No credit cards. Inexpensive.*

Sagittarius Reggae Restaurant. This funky place, plastered with astrological paraphernalia, serves johnnycakes that have Egg McMuffins beat by a country mile and sublime fresh fruit juices. Weekends it's transformed into a hopping club that blasts reggae and soca. *Portsmouth, no phone. No credit cards. Budget.*

Lodging

Most hotels here are locally owned, and standards are often not up to what many Caribbean travelers have come to expect. Rooms may be dark, bathrooms far from luxurious, and linens a bit threadbare at some properties. On the plus side, prices are low and owners are usually extremely warm and hospitable. It pays to compare rates and call for hotel brochures, as everything from barebones motels to charming hilltop properties tend to be comparably priced here.

The only beachfront hotels are in the Portsmouth area, the one exception being the Castaways on Mero Beach outside Roseau. Roseau's seaside facilities have a splendid view of the Caribbean but are beachless. There are also nature retreats hidden in the rain forest.

Most hotels offer an MAP plan; considering the paucity of good restaurants on Dominica and the difficulty getting around, this option makes sense. Dominica is one of the few Caribbean islands that knows no high or low seasons (although this may change as tourism increases). Nevertheless, you may be able to negotiate better rates than those posted when you call any of the hotels listed above for reservations during the summer.

Highly recommended lodgings are indicated by a star ★.

Category	Cost*
Moderate	$100–$150
Inexpensive	$60–$100
Budget	under $60

*All prices are for a standard double room for two, excluding 5% tax, 3% sales tax, and a 10%–15% service charge. To estimate rates for hotels offering MAP, add about $20 per person per day to the above price ranges.

Castaways Beach Hotel. This beachfront hotel in Mero, 11 miles north of Roseau, is popular with young and active people. Daytime activity centers on its mile-long, dappled gray beach; evenings, the focus is on the restaurant and terrace. Rooms have somewhat worn furnishings (plans are afoot to remedy this), double beds, and balconies that overlook the tropical garden; some units have air-conditioning. Cuisine at the popular restaurant is mainly French-Creole, island music plays most nights in the beach bar, and the all-day Sunday brunch/beach barbecue has a loyal following among island expats. Castaways offers good-value dive packages. *Box 5, Roseau, tel. 809/449– 6245 or 800/626–0581, fax 809/449–6246. 27 rooms. Facilities: beach, restaurant, 2 bars, tennis court, water-sports center, scuba, dive packages. AE, MC, V. EP, MAP. Moderate.*

★ **Fort Young Hotel.** Roseau's top downtown hotel, it reopened in the summer of 1989 following a total renovation. Now Dominican paintings and prints from the late 1700s meld with the massive stone walls of the 18th century, when this was Dominica's main fort. Set on a cliff in Roseau, the hotel features rooms with small balconies, air conditioning, ceiling fans, shower baths, cable TV, and modern furnishings. Oceanview rooms cost more but are worth it. Plans are to add 39 more rooms. *Box 519, Roseau, tel. 809/448–5000, fax 809/448–5006. 33 rooms. Facilities: pool, entertainment, bar, disco, restaurant. AE, MC, V. EP. Moderate.*

Picard Beach Cottage Resort. Eight small wood cottages dot the grounds of this former coconut plantation, on the island's northwest coast. Units have a simple, rustic appeal, with louvered windows, locally made furniture, and small porches. Rooms have kitchens, but the restaurant here serves large breakfasts as well as lunch and dinner. Beach and pool privileges are next door, at the Portsmouth Beach Hotel. *Box 34, Roseau, tel. 809/445–5131; in the U.S., 800/424–5500, fax 809/445–5599. 8 cottages. Facilities: beach, pool, dive center with scuba, snorkeling, and windsurfing, bar, restaurant. AE, MC, V. EP. Moderate.*

Reigate Hall Hotel. Perched high on a steep cliff and a $2 taxi ride from downtown Roseau, this is a lovely stone-and-wood facility. Units feature locally made furnishings, such as embroidered bedspreads, air-conditioning, and private balconies; the higher priced rooms 17 and 18 (still affordable) have sea views from their balconies. The restaurant is expensive for a full meal; count on $30 a person unless you forgo dessert and coffee. The nearest swimming beach is a $4 cab ride away, so you may find lazing around the pool more convenient. *Reigate, tel. 809/448–4031; in the U.S., 800/223–9815; in Canada, 800/468–0023, fax 809/448–4034. 14 rooms, 2 suites, 1 apartment. Facilities: restaurant, 2 bars, pool, sauna. AE, MC, V. EP, MAP. Inexpensive–Moderate.*

★ **Sans Souci Manor.** Three luxury apartments and one bungalow sit in a prosperous suburb high above Roseau. The huge two-bedroom apartments (where two couples can happily roam) have clay-tile floors, locally made wood and wicker furniture, fully equipped kitchens, large verandahs with sweeping views of Roseau and the hills, and museum-quality Caribbean and Latin American art. Urbane owner John Keller hosts a sophisticated crowd of Americans and Europeans, many of them repeat visitors. Dinners—for those who wisely opt for the MAP plan—are three-course affairs prepared by Mr. Keller, a gourmet cook, and served house-party style on his plant-filled terrace. Management will help make car rental and tour arrangements, or you can hire the property's own car and driver. Transfers from Canefield Airport are included in the rates, which are a jaw-dropping $105 a night (EP). *Box 373, St. Aroment, Roseau, tel. 809/448–2306, fax 809/448–6202. 3 apartments, 1 bungalow. Facilities: dining, honor bar, pool, airport transfers. AE, MC, V. Moderate.*

★ **Castle Comfort Lodge.** This small dive lodge run by the enthusiastic Derek and Ginette Perryman wins a loyal following for its first-rate dive shop and excellent-value dive packages. Rooms are nothing special, although the five oceanfront units are more modern and cheerful than many you will find on the island. The Perrymans can arrange various inland adventures and nature walks. *Box 63, Roseau, tel. 809/448–2188, fax 809/448–6088. 10 rooms. Facilities: restaurant, dive shop. AE, MC, V. EP. Inexpensive–Moderate.*

Evergreen Hotel. A recently completed expansion has added six bright, modern rooms with balconies and an airy bar and restaurant with terrace to this small hotel 2 miles from downtown Roseau. While the squeaky-clean new annex is somewhat lacking in authentic island charm (the older building, a stone and wood structure with a red roof, has more character), the former is where you want to stay. Air-conditioned rooms have bright print fabrics, rattan furnishings, large shower baths, and lovely sea views from private balconies. The original high-ceilinged dining room with veranda still serves breakfast and lunch; dinner is in the new restaurant. *Box 309, Roseau, tel. 809/448–3288, fax 809/448–6800. 16 rooms. Facilities: 2 restaurants, bar, pool. AE, MC, V. CP, MAP. Inexpensive–Moderate.*

Anchorage Hotel. Years of wear have taken their toll on this hotel although it still becomes an active scene during the season. Make sure you reserve one of the renovated rooms, with clay-tile floors and madras fabrics, in the two-story galleried section; don't bother with any of the other dark, lifeless units. Downtown Roseau is a 10-minute walk away, but the nearest beach requires a $4 cab ride. The hotel is headquarters for Dominica Tours (*see* Guided Tours, *above*). *Box 34, Roseau, tel. 809/448–2638, fax 809/448–5680. 32 rooms. Facilities: restaurant, bar, pool, squash court. AE, D, MC, V. EP. Inexpensive.*

Coconut Beach Hotel. Rooms and baths here are bare and depressing, and amenities are nonexistent (only those staying a week get utensils to use in their kitchenettes). But for those determined to stay on the island's best beach, lovely Picard *is* right outside your door. Another plus is an open-air bar and restaurant where a crowd of yachties (there are moorings here) and locals keep things lively. *Box 37, Roseau, tel. 809/445–5393, fax 809/445–5693. 22 rooms. Facilities: restaurant, bar, dive shop, yacht moorings. AE, D, MC, V. EP, MAP. Inexpensive.*

Layou River Hotel. This is a rambling estate property centered around the turbulent beauty of the Layou River. Swimmers take their dips here or in the large swimming pool, as the beach is a 10-minute drive down the Caribbean coast. Although the setting is lovely, the somewhat-musty rooms, with concrete floors and dull fabrics, seem in need of a facelift. At press time, a Chinese company was planning to build a 200-room hotel and convention center, the Shangri-la, across the road, and to incorporate the Layou River Hotel into the complex. *Box 8, Roseau, tel. 809/449–6281, fax 809/449–6793. 40 air-conditioned rooms. Facilities: restaurant, bar, pool. AE, D, MC, V. EP. Inexpensive.*

Layou Valley Inn. Tamara Holmes and her late husband built this tasteful house in the foothills of the National Preserve, under the peaks of Morne Trois Pitons. She's a Russian who once translated for NASA but now devotes her talents to the kitchen. The rooms are simple and clean, and the sunken lounge and glass-fronted dining area are comfortable, attractive areas where guests mingle. Unless you plan on going nowhere (there's a restaurant and nearby river bathing), you'll need a car—even buses pass only infrequently. *Box 196, Roseau, tel. 809/449–6203, fax 809/448–5212. 10 rooms. Facilities: restaurant, bar, swimming in mountain rivers, guided climbs* *to the Boiling Lake at extra cost. AE, MC, V. EP, MAP. Inexpensive.*

Papillote Wilderness Retreat and Nature Sanctuary. This inn is in the rain forest, only a short hike from the 200-foot Trafalgar Falls and near river bathing. The spectacular setting includes a botanical garden, created by owner Anne Jean-Baptiste, with a mind-boggling assortment of plants and flowers. Rooms are low-ceilinged and somewhat dark, with a rustic, log-cabin feel; some bathrooms are in need of renovation. Bird calls and rushing water are your background music at meals, served in an open-air restaurant. *Box 67, Roseau, tel. 809/448–2287, fax 809/448–2286. 10 rooms. Facilities: restaurant, bar, gift shop, nature tours. AE, DC, MC, V. EP, MAP. Inexpensive.*

Cherry's Lodge. In the center of Roseau, this somewhat scruffy wooden house offers simple, clean rooms with shower baths and furnished with nothing more than bed, table, and two chairs. A couple of rooms have balconies with views of street life. Least expensive rooms have shared baths and no balconies. It's a 15-minute drive to the beach. Choose this hotel only if Vena's (*see below*) is full. *20 Kennedy Ave., Roseau, tel. 809/448–2366. 4 rooms with bath, 4 with shared bath. No credit cards. EP. Budget.*

Floral Gardens. This 15-room motel looks like a Swiss Chalet—complete with latticed windows and flower boxes—plonked down on the edge of Dominica's rain forest reserve on the island's windward side. Although rooms seem carefully decorated with island crafts and homey fabrics, they are small and dark, with a slightly claustrophobic feel. New, larger units closer to the beautiful Layou River are scheduled for completion by 1994. The restaurant here (*see* Dining, *above*) is a favorite among residents and tour groups, and the hotel's location is near river bathing, hiking, and relaxing on northeast coast beaches. Congenial O.J. Seraphin, the former interim prime minister, is the owner here. *Concord, tel. and fax 809/445–7636. 15 rooms. Facilities: restaurant, gift shop. AE, MC, V. EP, MAP. Budget.*

Vena's. Adjoining the World of Food restaurant is this boarding-house-style hotel that's full of local color. Vena herself is a character. You'll need a sense of humor to stay here and join in the partying that goes on in the downstairs lounge on weekends. Rooms are tiny and very basic, but so is the $20-a-night price tag. *48 Cork St., Roseau, tel. 809/448–3286. 17 rooms, most with shared bath. Facilities: restaurant next door. No credit cards. EP. Budget.*

Cottage and Apartment Rentals The **Dominica Division of Tourism** (Box 293, Roseau, Dominica, WI, tel. 809/448–2186 or 809/448–2351) has a list of rental apartments, as well as hotels and guest houses, with rates. The selection ranges from small, concrete cottages ($400 a week) to more comfortable, attractive units at more than twice the price. Although rentals typically allow you to cut costs by preparing your own meals, this is not always the case on Dominica: Imported foods in grocery stores are expensive, and some rental units here don't even have kitchens. Considering that you will also need a car to get supplies and to get around, it may not make economic sense unless you are traveling with a large family or another couple.

Nightlife

Discos If you're not too exhausted from mountain climbing, swimming, and the like, you can join the locals on weekends at **The Warehouse** (tel. 809/449–1303), outside Roseau toward the airport, or the **Night Box** (Goodwill Road, no tel.), which attracts a rowdier clientele.

Nightclubs When the moon comes up, most visitors go down to the dining room in their resident hotel for the music or chat offered there, always liveliest on weekends.

The **Shipwreck,** in the Canefield Industrial area (tel. 809/449–1059), has live reggae and taped music on weekends, and a Sunday bash that starts at noon and continues into the night.

The best insider's spot is definitely **Wykie's La Tropical** (51 Old St., Roseau, tel. 809/448–8015). This classic Caribbean hole-in-the-wall is a gathering spot for the island's movers and shakers, especially during Friday's "Happy Hours" from 5 to 7, when they nibble on stewed chicken or black pudding, then stay on for a local calypso band or Jing-Ping—a group playing local music on the accordion, *quage* (a kind of washboard instrument), drums, and a *boom boom* (a percussive instrument). Another resident favorite is **Lenville** (tel. 809/446–6598), a very basic rum shop with barbecued chicken and dancing in the village of Coulivistrie.

11 Dominican Republic

*Updated by
Nigel Fisher*

Sprawling over two-thirds of the island of Hispaniola, the Dominican Republic is the spot where European settlement of the Western Hemisphere really began. Santo Domingo, its capital, is the oldest continuously inhabited city in this half of the globe, and history buffs who visit have difficulty tearing themselves away from the many sites that boast of antiquity in the city's 16th-century Colonial Zone. Sunseekers head for the beach resorts of Puerto Plata, Samaná, and La Romana; at Punta Cana, beachcombers tan on the Caribbean's longest stretch of white-sand beach. The highest peak in the West Indies is here: Pico Duarte (10,128 feet) lures hikers to the central mountain range, and ancient sunken galleons and coral reefs divert divers and snorkelers.

After Haiti, the Dominican Republic is the least expensive destination in the Caribbean. Low wages combined with an excess of hotel rooms keep lodging costs down. With more four- and five-star hotels under construction, prices aren't likely to climb in the near future. The island's resort hotels tend to be huge, self-contained properties designed to lure package-tour groups rather than independent travelers. A weekly rate at a hotel booked through your local travel agent is considerably less expensive than if you make your own reservations on a per-night basis. Most vacationers here are on one- to two-week packages that include tie-ins with low airfares. Although this means bargain prices, there are drawbacks: Travelers are not free to choose any hotel on the island and are often locked into hotel meal plans, which limit the opportunity to sample local

Dominican Republic

Cofresi Beach
Luperón Beach
36 — 45   46 47
Playa Dorada   Sosúa
35
Puerto Plata   31   Cabar Beach
Montecristi   32   33
Guayubin   Sosúa
Dajabón   La Unión International Airport
Moca
Santiago de los Caballeros   30   San Francisco de Macorís
29   Jarabacoa
HAITI   Bánica
San Juan
Lago Enriquillo   Neiba   Azua
Duvergé   Bani
Barahona
Pedernales   Bahía de Ocoa
HISPANIOLA
Oviedo
Isla Beato   Cabo Beato

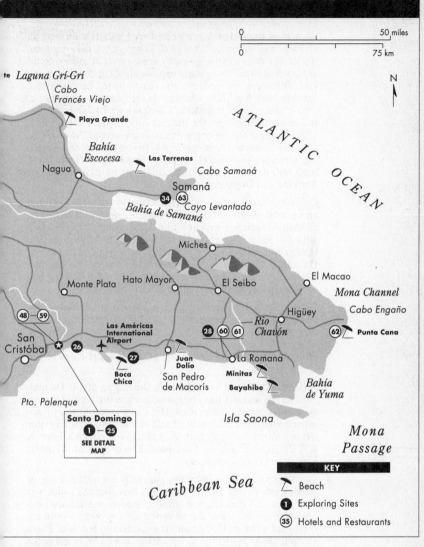

0   50 miles

0   75 km

N

te *Laguna Grí-Grí*

Cabo Francés Viejo

🏖 **Playa Grande**

A T L A N T I C

Bahía Escocesa **Las Terrenas**

Nagua

Samaná

O C E A N

Cabo Samaná

③④ ⑥③ 🏖

Cayo Levantado

Bahía de Samaná

Miches

Monte Plata   Hato Mayor   El Seibo   El Macao

Mona Channel

Cabo Engaño

④⑧—⑤⑨   **Las Américas International Airport**   ②⑧ ⑥⓪ ⑥①   Higüey   ⑥②🏖 **Punta Cana**

San Cristóbal   ②⑥   ✈   ②⑦   **Juan Dolio**   *Río Chavón*

Boca Chica   San Pedro de Macorís   La Romana

Minitas   **Bayahibe** 🏖   *Bahía de Yuma*

Pto. Palenque

Santo Domingo
① — ㉕
SEE DETAIL MAP

Isla Saona

Mona Passage

Caribbean Sea

KEY

🏖 Beach

① Exploring Sites

㉟ Hotels and Restaurants

Lodging

Bahía Beach, **63**

Caribbean Village Club and Resort, **40**

Club Méditerranée, **62**

Gran Hotel Lina and Casino, **52**

Heavens, **44**

Hostal Jimessón, **37**

Hostal Palacio Nicolás de Ovando, **48**

Hotel Cervantes, **50**

Hotel Cofresi, **35**

Hotel El Embajador and Casino, **49**

Hotel Hispaniola, **51**

Jack Tar Village, **45**

Playa Chiquita, **47**

Puerto Plata Beach Resort and Casino, **39**

Sand Castle, **46**

cuisine. This is increasingly the case as more resort hotels become all-inclusives.

Since most resort hotels are located on or a short walk from an idyllic beach, car rental is not vital. The most you may want one is a day or two to explore nearby areas; taxis or guided tours are other options. Few people explore all of the country in one visit. Distances are too large and the roads too harrowing for extended touring. Many who want to combine a beach vacation with exploration of the nation's heritage divide their visit between Santo Domingo, the nation's capital, and Puerto Plata, where many of the major resort hotels are located. An efficient, air-conditioned bus fleet operates between the two, and American Airlines sometimes offers flights that arrive in Santo Domingo and depart from Puerto Plata at no extra cost (*see* Arriving and Departing, *below*).

Columbus happened upon this island on December 5, 1492, and on Christmas Eve his ship, the *Santa María*, was wrecked on the Atlantic shore. He named it La Isla Española ("the Spanish island"). Santo Domingo, on the south coast where the Río Ozama spills into the Caribbean Sea, was founded in 1496 by Columbus's brother Bartholomew and Nicolás de Ovando, during the first half of the 16th century, it became the bustling hub of Spanish commerce and culture in the New World.

Hispaniola (a derivation of La Isla Española) has had an unusually chaotic history, replete with bloody revolutions, military coups, yellow-fever epidemics, invasions, and bankruptcy. The country has been relatively stable since the early 1970s, and administrations have been staunch supporters of the United States.

American influence looms large in Dominican life. If Dominicans do not actually have relatives living in the United States, they know someone who does; and many speak at least rudimentary English. Still, it is a Latin country, and the Hispanic flavor contrasts sharply with the culture of the British, French, and Dutch islands in the Caribbean. The Dominican Republic also reflects racial mixtures.

Dominican towns and cities are generally not quaint, neat, or particularly pretty. Poverty is everywhere, but the country is also alive and chaotic, sometimes frenzied, sometimes laid-back. Its tourist zones are as varied as they come—from extravagant Casa de Campo and the manicured hotels of Playa Dorada to the neglected streets of Jarabacoa in its gorgeous mountain setting and the world-weary beauty of the Samaná peninsula.

What It Will Cost These sample prices, meant only as a general guide, are for high season. The American dollar receives a very favorable rate of exchange in the Dominican Republic, so costs for locally produced items and services are among the least expensive in the Caribbean. A budget hotel in Puerto Plata is no more than $20 a night, while the same hotel in Santo Domingo will be about $30. Even the luxury hotels in Santo Domingo start their prices for a double room at around $120, and a moderately priced all-inclusive resort will run about $200 a couple. A simple meal of grilled fish or rice and chicken will be under $5 at a small restaurant, and a large bottle of beer adds only another $1.25. A rum punch costs around $2, while a glass of Bordeaux is something like $4.50 (which gives you a fair idea what ought to be your libation of choice).

Imported goods, on the other hand, are expensive. This is reflected in car rentals, which can be as much as $70 a day for a compact. But because wages are low, renting a car with a driver adds only another $30 for the day, including gasoline. To use another example, a two-hour taxi tour of Santo Domingo will cost around $20, but so will a 30-minute drive to the airport. With the exception of an efficient, air-conditioned bus service between Santo Domingo and Puerto Plata for $6, public transportation tends to be infrequent and unreliable. A single-tank dive is about $30; snorkel equipment rents for about $4 a day.

Before You Go

Tourist Information Contact the **Dominican Republic Department of Tourism** (Dominican Consulate, 1 Times Sq., 11th floor, New York, NY 10036, tel. 212/768–2480; 2355 Sanzedo Ave., Suite 305, Coral Gables, FL 33134, tel. 305/444–4592; 1464 Crescent St., Montreal, Quebec, Canada H3A 2B6, tel. 514/933–6126). The best source of information is the **Tourism Promotional Council** in Santo Domingo (tel. 800/752–1151). Be prepared to wait at least two weeks for requested materials.

Arriving and Departing
By Plane The Dominican Republic has two major international airports: Las Américas International Airport, about 20 miles outside Santo Domingo, and La Unión International Airport, about 25 miles east of Puerto Plata on the north coast. **American Airlines** (tel. 800/433–7300) has the most extensive service to the Dominican Republic. It and **Dominicana** (tel. 212/765–7310) fly nonstop from New York to Santo Domingo; American, **Continental** (tel. 800/231–0856), and Dominicana fly nonstop from New York to Puerto Plata; American and Dominicana fly nonstop from Miami to Santo Domingo; and American and Dominicana fly nonstop from Miami to Puerto Plata. Continental has connecting service from Puerto Plata to Santo Domingo; American offers connections to both Santo Domingo and Puerto Plata from San Juan, Puerto Rico; and American Eagle has two flights a day from San Juan to La Romana.

Several regional carriers serve neighboring islands. **ALM** (tel. 800/327–7230) connects Santo Domingo to St. Maarten and Curaçao. There is also limited domestic service available from La Herrera Airport in Santo Domingo to smaller airfields in La Romana, Samaná, and Santiago. A new airport is planned for Barahona.

Long-needed expansions and rehauls continue at both Las Américas and La Unión. A major fire in the old terminal at Las Américas has meant congestion in a new terminal that was built to ease such problems. La Unión's arrival hall is still pretty dismal, and you need to search left of the exit for the bank that will change money into Dominican pesos. Overworked customs and immigration officials are often less than courteous, and luggage theft is rife. Try to travel with carry-on luggage, and keep a sharp eye on it. Although seemingly hundreds of porters, taxi drivers, and hustlers are known to descend upon those leaving customs, order has started to emerge from chaos. Taxis now form lines and *usually* charge officially set rates. Porters are licensed, but if you can manage your own bags, we advise you to do so. If you have arranged for a hotel transfer, a representative should be waiting for you in the immigration hall.

From the Airport Taxis are available at the airport, and the 25-minute ride into Santo Domingo averages R.D. $250 (about U.S. $20). Taxi fares from the Puerto Plata airport average R.D. $200 (U.S. $16) to the town center and R.D. $230 (U.S. $19) to the Playa Dorado hotels. There is no bus service, but you can often team up with another traveler and share a taxi.

Passports and Visas U.S. and Canadian citizens must have either a valid passport or proof of citizenship, such as an original (not photocopied) birth certificate, and a tourist card. Legal residents of the United States must have an alien registration card (green card), a valid passport, and a tourist card. British citizens need only a valid passport; no entry visa is required. The requisite tourist card costs $10, and you should be sure to purchase it at the airline counter when you check in, and then fill it out on the plane. You can purchase the card on arrival at the airport, but you'll encounter long lines. Keep the bottom half of the card in a safe place because you'll need to present it to immigration authorities when you leave.

Language Before you travel to the Dominican Republic, you should know at least a smattering of Spanish. There is little effort to learn English here, unlike on other Caribbean islands. Guides at major tourist attractions and front-desk personnel in the major hotels speak a fascinating form of English, though they often have trouble understanding tourists. The people who serve you in the hotel coffee shop are usually speechless when English is spoken to them, as are people you meet in the streets of Santo Domingo. Traffic signs and restaurant menus, except at popular tourist establishments, are in Spanish. Using smiles and gestures will help, but a nodding acquaintance with the language or a phrase book is more useful.

Precautions Beware of the *buscones* at the airports. They offer to assist you, and do so by relieving you of your luggage and disappearing with it. Also avoid the black marketers, who will offer you a tempting rate of exchange for your U.S. dollars. If the police catch you changing money on the street, they'll haul you off to jail (the *calabozo*). Also, buy amber only from reputable shops. The attractively priced piece offered by the street vendor is more than likely plastic. Guard your wallet or pocketbook in Santo Domingo, especially around the Malecón (waterfront boulevard), which seems to teem with pickpockets.

Staying in the Dominican Republic

Important Addresses **Tourist Information:** The **Secretary of Tourism** is located in Santo Domingo, in a complex of government offices at the corner of Av. Mexico and 30 de Maizo (Oficinas Guberbamentales Building D, tel. 809/689–3655, fax 809/682–3806). Unless you are seeking special assistance, it is not worth making the trek here for the limited materials offered to tourists. There's also a tourist office in Puerto Plata (Playa Long Beach, tel. 809/586–3676). Both offices are officially open weekdays 9–2:30, but the Puerta Plata office often opens late and closes early.

Emergencies **Police:** In Santo Domingo, call 711; in Puerto Plata, call 586–2804; in Sosúa, call 571–2233. However, do not expect too much from the police, aside from a bit of a hassle and some paperwork that they will consider the end of the matter. In general, the police and bureaucrats take a hostile approach to visitors.

Hospitals: Santo Domingo emergency rooms that are open 24 hours are **Centro Médico Universidad Central del Este** (UCE) (Av. Máximo Gómez 68, tel. 809/682–1220), **Clínica Abreu** (Calle Beller 42, tel. 809/688–4411), and **Clínica Gómez Patino** (Av. Independencia 701, tel. 809/685–9131 or 685–9141). In Puerto Plata, you can go to **Clínica Dr. Brugal** (Calle José del Carmen Ariza 15, tel. 809/586–2519). In Sosúa, try the **Centro Médico Sosúa** (Av. Martinez, tel. 809/571–2305).

Pharmacies: The following pharmacies are open 24 hours a day: in Santo Domingo, **San Judas Tadeo** (Av. Independencia 57, tel. 809/689–2851 or 809/685–8165); in Puerto Plata, **Farmacia Deleyte** (Av. John F. Kennedy 89, tel. 809/571–2515); in Sosúa, **San Rafael** (Carretera Cabarete Km. 1, tel. 809/571–0777).

Currency The coin of the realm is the Dominican peso, which is divided into 100 centavos. It is written R.D. $ and fluctuates relative to the U.S. dollar. At press time, U.S. $1 was equivalent to R.D. $12.30. Always make certain you know in which currency any transaction is taking place (any confusion will probably not be to your advantage). There is a growing black market for hard currency, so be wary of offers to exchange U.S. dollars at a rate more favorable than the official one. Prices quoted here are in U.S. dollars unless noted otherwise.

Taxes and Service Charges Hotels and restaurants add a 21% government tax (which includes a 10% service charge) to your bill. Although hotels add the 10% service charge, it is customary to leave a dollar per day for the hotel maid. At restaurants and nightclubs you may want to leave an additional 5%–10% tip for a job well done. Taxi drivers expect a 10% tip. Skycaps and hotel porters expect at least five pesos per bag. U.S. visitors must buy a $10 tourist card before entering the Dominican Republic. All foreign visitors must pay a $10 departure tax. Both must be paid in U.S. dollars.

Getting Around Taxis, which are government regulated, line up outside hotels
Taxis and restaurants. The taxis are unmetered, and the minimum fare within Santo Domingo is about R.D. $50 (U.S. $4), but you can bargain for less if you order a taxi away from the major hotels. Hiring a taxi by the hour and with any number of stops is R.D. $125 (U.S. $10) per hour with a minimum of two hours. Be sure to establish the time that you start; drivers like to advance the time a little. Just be certain it is clearly understood in advance which currency is to be used in the agreed-upon fare. Taxis can also drive you to destinations outside the city. Rates are posted in hotels and at the airport. Sample fares from Santo Domingo are R.D. $930 (U.S. $75) to La Romana and R.D. $1,830 (U.S. $150) to Puerta Plata. Round-trips are considerably less than twice the one-way fare. **Taxi la Paloma** (tel. 809/562–3460), **Taxi Raffi** (tel. 809/689–5468), and **Centro Taxi** (tel. 809/687–6128) will transport you.

In a separate category are radio taxis, which are convenient if you'd like to schedule a pickup and academic if you don't speak Spanish. The fare is negotiated over the phone when you make the appointment. The most reliable company is **Apolo Taxi** (tel. 809/541–9595).

Avoid unmarked street taxis—there have been numerous incidents of assaults and robberies, particularly in Santo Domingo.

Buses *Públicos* are small blue-and-white or blue-and-red cars that run regular routes, stopping to let passengers on and off. The fare is two pesos. Competing with the públicos are the *conchos* or *colectivos* (privately owned busés), whose drivers tool around the major thoroughfares, leaning out of the window or jumping out to try to persuade passengers to climb aboard. It's a colorful, if cramped, way to get around town. The fare is about one peso. Privately owned air-conditioned buses make regular runs to Santiago, Puerto Plata, and other destinations. Avoid night travel because the country's roads are full of potholes. You should make reservations by calling **Metro Buses** (Av. Winston Churchill, tel. 809/566–6590, 809/566–6587, or 809/566–7126 in Santo Domingo; 809/586–6063 in Puerto Plata; 809/583–9111 in Santiago; and 809/584–2259 in Nagua) or **Caribe Tours** (Av. 27 de Febrero at Leopoldo Navarro, tel. 809/687–3171). One-way bus fare from Santo Domingo to Puerto Plata is R.D. $70 (U.S. $6).

Motorbike Taxis Known as *motoconchos,* these bikes are a popular and inexpensive way to get around such tourist areas as Puerto Plata, Sosúa, and Jarabacoa. Bikes can be flagged down both on the road and in town; rates vary from R.D. $3 anywhere in the town of Puerto Plata to R.D. $5 from Puerto Plata to Long Beach to R.D. $15–$20 from Puerto Plata to Playa Dorada.

Rental Cars You'll need a valid driver's license from your own country and a major credit card and/or cash deposit. Cars can be rented at the airports and at many hotels. Among the known names are **Avis** (tel. 809/532–2969), **Budget** (tel. 809/562–6812), **Hertz** (tel. 809/688–2277), and **National** (tel. 809/562–1444). Rates average U.S. $70 and up per day, depending upon the make and size of the car. Driving is on the right side of the road. Many Dominicans drive recklessly, often taking their half of the road out of the middle, but they will flash their headlights to warn against highway patrols.

If for some unavoidable reason you must drive on the narrow, unlighted mountain roads at night, exercise extreme caution. Many local cars are without headlights or taillights, bicyclists do not have lights, and cows stand by the side of the road. Traffic and directional signs are less than adequate, and unseen potholes can easily break a car's axle. The 80-kph (50-mph) speed limit is strictly enforced. Finally, keep in mind that gas stations are few and far between in some of the remote regions. Police are known to supplement their income by stopping drivers on various pretexts and eliciting a "gift." Locals give R.D. $20–R.D. $40.

Telephones and Mail To call the Dominican Republic from the United States, dial area code 809 and the local number. Connections are clear and easy to make. Trying to place calls from the Dominican Republic, however, is another matter. The system is archaic, although there is direct-dial service to the United States; dial 1, followed by area code and number.

Airmail postage to North America for a letter or postcard costs R.D. $2; to Europe, R.D. $4, and may take up to three weeks to reach the destination.

Opening and Closing Times Regular office hours are weekdays 8–noon and 2–5, Saturday 8–noon. Government offices are open weekdays 7:30–2:30. Banking hours are weekdays 8:30–4:30.

Guided Tours If you are staying in the Puerto Plata area and wish to visit Santo Domingo, it's easy enough to take the public bus, book your own hotel, and walk your way through Santo Domingo's old quarter yourself. For destinations outside Santo Domingo, however, you may find a guided tour helpful. The country is large, and tours—unlike those on smaller Caribbean islands—will go to specific areas rather than circumnavigating the island.

Prieto Tours (tel. 809/685–0102 or 809/688–5715) operates Gray Line of the Dominican Republic. It offers half-day bus tours of Santo Domingo, nightclub tours, beach tours, tours to Cibao Valley and the Amber Coast, and other itineraries. A half-day sightseeing tour of the capital is R.D. $200 (U.S. $16).

Turinter (tel. 809/685–4020) tours include dinner and a show or casino visit, a full-day tour of Samaná, as well as specialty tours (museum, shopping, fishing).

Apolo Tours (tel. 809/586–5329) offers a full-day tour of Playa Grande and tours to Santiago (including a casino tour) and Sosúa. It will also arrange transfers between your hotel and the airport and will customize trips along the north coast, including making hotel bookings. One tempting two-day trip goes from Puerto Plata along the Amber Coast to Samaná; the $90-a-person cost includes one night's lodging and dinner.

Exploring the Dominican Republic

Numbers in the margin correspond to points of interest on the Santo Domingo map.

The Dominican Republic is a large island, made larger by the narrow, often potholed and congested roads. Few tourists try to see it all on their first visit. More often, they will explore only an area that can be managed in a day's outing. All of the touring described below may be accomplished by public transportation, but the only regularly scheduled air-conditioned buses are those that run through the Cibao Valley between Santo Domingo and Puerto Plata.

The historic heart of Santo Domingo is easily explored on foot, though you may need a taxi for a few far-flung sights. For touring elsewhere, your options are to rent a car for a day or two, hire a car and driver (at not much additional cost), or take an organized tour (*see* Guided Tours, *above*). If you don't mind driving, a car will give you the most freedom. A guided tour gives you the least freedom, but is the cheapest option.

Santo Domingo We'll begin our tour where Spanish civilization in the New World began, in the 12-block area of **Santo Domingo** called the Colonial Zone. This historical area is now a bustling, noisy district with narrow cobbled streets, shops, restaurants, residents, and traffic jams. Ironically, all the noise and congestion make it somehow easier to imagine this old city as it was when it was yet a colony—when the likes of Columbus, Cortés, Ponce de León, and pirates sailed in and out, and colonists were settling themselves in the New World. Tourist brochures boast that "history comes alive here"—a surprisingly truthful statement.

Be aware that wearing shorts, miniskirts, and halters in churches is considered inappropriate. (Note: Hours and admission charges are erratic; check with the Tourist Office for up-to-date information.)

One of the first things you'll see as you approach the Colonial Zone is a statue only slightly smaller than the Colossus of Rhodes, staring out over the Caribbean Sea. It is **Montesina,** the Spanish priest who came to the Dominican Republic in the 16th century to appeal for human rights for Indians.

❶

❷ **Parque Independencia,** on the far western border of the Colonial Zone, is a big city park dominated by the marble and concrete **Altar de la Patria.** The impressive mausoleum was built in 1976 to honor the founding fathers of the country (Duarte, Sánchez, and Mella).

❸ To your left as you leave the square, the **Concepción Fortress,** within the old city walls, was the northwest defense post of the colony. *Calle Palo Hincado at Calle Isidro Duarte, no phone. Admission free. Open Tues.–Sun. 9–6.*

From Independence Square, walk eight blocks east on Calle El Conde and you'll come to **Parque Colón.** The huge statue of Columbus dates from 1897 and is the work of French sculptor Gilbert. On the west side of the square is the **old Town Hall** and on the east, the **Palacio de Borgella,** residence of the governor during the Haitian occupation of 1822–44 and presently the seat of the Permanent Dominican Commission for the **Fifth Centennial of the Discovery and Evangelization of the Americas.** Gallery spaces house architectural and archaeological exhibits pertaining to the Fifth Centennial.

❹

Towering over the south side of the square is the coral limestone facade of the **Catedral Santa María la Menor, Primada de América,** the first cathedral in America. Spanish workmen began building the cathedral in 1514 but left off construction to search for gold in Mexico. The church was finally finished in 1540. Its facade is composed of a mix of architectural styles, from late Gothic to Plateresque (the latter known for intricately carved stonework). Inside, the high altar is made of beaten silver, and in the Treasury there is a magnificent collection of gold and silver. Some of its 14 lateral chapels serve as mausoleums for noted Dominicans, including Archbishop Meriño, who was once president of the Dominican Republic. Of interest is the Chapel of Our Lady of Antigua, which was reconsecrated by John Paul II in 1984. In the nave are four baroque columns, carved to resemble royal palms, which for more than four centuries guarded the magnificent bronze and marble sarcophagus containing (say Dominican historians) the remains of Christopher Columbus. (Cuba and Spain also lay claim to the famed remains.) The sarcophagus has recently been moved to the Columbus Memorial Lighthouse—only the latest in the Great Navigator's posthumous journeys. When Columbus died in Spain in 1506, his last wish was to be buried in Santo Domingo, and, when the cathedral was finished, his remains were deposited there. After the French occupation of 1795, the Spaniards, determined to keep Columbus on Spanish soil, supposedly moved the remains to Cuba. Later, both Spain and Cuba got hold of exhumed corpses that they claimed were

❺

Santo Domingo

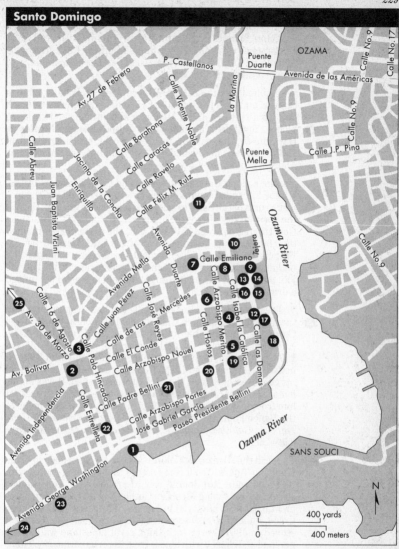

Alcázar de Colón, **9**

Calle Las Damas, **12**

Capilla de los Remedios, **14**

Casa de Bastidas, **17**

Casa de Tostado, **19**

Casa del Cordón, **8**

Catedral Santa María la Menor, **5**

Concepción Fortress, **3**

Hospital de San Nicolás de Bari, **6**

Hostal Palacio Nicolás de Ovando, **15**

Iglesia y Convento Domínico, **20**

Jardín Botánico Nacional Dr. Rafael M. Moscoso, **25**

La Atarazana, **10**

La Iglesia de Regina Angelorum, **21**

Malecón, **23**

Montesina, **1**

Museo de las Casas Reales, **13**

National Pantheon, **16**

Parque Colón, **4**

Parque Independencia, **2**

Plaza de la Cultura, **24**

Puerta de la Misericordia, **22**

San Francisco Monastery, **7**

Santa Bárbara Church, **11**

Torre del Homenaje, **18**

the remains of somebody named Columbus. Cuban and Spanish historians say it was Christopher; Dominican authorities say that it was Christopher's grandson Luís and that Christopher's remains rest in Santo Domingo. *Calle Arzobispo Meriño, tel. 809/689–1920. Admission free. Open Mon.–Sat. 9–4; Sun. masses begin at 6 AM.*

When you leave the cathedral, turn right, walk to Columbus Square, and turn left on Calle El Conde. Walk one more block and turn right on Calle Hostos and continue for two more blocks. You'll see the ruins of the **Hospital de San Nicolás de Bari,** the first hospital in the New World, which was built in 1503 by Nicolás de Ovando. *Calle Hostos, between Calle de Las Mercedes and Calle Luperón, no phone.*

Continue along Calle Hostos, crossing Calle Emiliano Tejera. Up the hill and about mid-block on your left you'll see the majestic ruins of the **San Francisco Monastery.** (If you look toward the horizon, you will see the impressive Columbus Lighthouse.) Constructed between 1512 and 1544, the monastery contained the church, chapel, and convent of the Franciscan order. Sir Francis Drake's demolition squad significantly damaged the building in 1586, and in 1673 an earthquake nearly finished the job, but when it's floodlit at night, the old monastery is indeed a dramatic sight.

Walk east for two blocks along Calle Emiliano Tejera. Opposite the Telecom building on Calle Isabel la Católica, the **Casa del Cordón** is recognizable by the sash of the Franciscan order carved in stone over the arched entrance. This house, built in 1503, is the Western Hemisphere's oldest surviving stone house. Columbus's son Diego Colón, viceroy of the colony, and his wife lived here until the Alcázar was finished. It was in this house, too, that Sir Francis Drake was paid a ransom to prevent him from totally destroying the city. The house is now home to the Banco Popular. *Corner of Calle Emiliano Tejera and Calle Isabel la Católica, no phone. Admission free. Open weekdays 8:30–4:30.*

To reach the **Alcázar de Colón,** walk one block east along Calle Emiliano Tejera. You'll come across the imposing castle, with its balustrade and double row of arches. The Renaissance structure has strong Moorish, Gothic, and Isabelline (an ornamental, late Gothic style) influences. The castle of Don Diego Colón, built in 1514, was painstakingly reconstructed and restored in 1957. Forty-inch-thick coral limestone walls were patched and shored with blocks from the original quarry. There are 22 rooms, furnished in a style to which the viceroy of the island would have been accustomed—right down to the dishes and the viceregal shaving mug. Many of the period paintings, statues, tapestries, and furnishings were donated by the University of Madrid. *Just off Calle Emiliano Tejera at the foot of Calle Las Damas, tel. 809/687–5361. Admission: R.D. $10. Open Mon. and Wed.–Fri. 9–5, Sat. 9–4, Sun. 9–1. Closed Tues.*

Across from the Alcázar, **La Atarazana** (the Royal Mooring Docks) was once the colonial commercial district, where naval supplies were stored. There are eight restored buildings, the oldest of which dates from 1507. It now houses crafts shops, restaurants, and art galleries.

To reach the **Santa Bárbara Church,** go back to Calle Isabel la Católica, turn right, and walk several blocks. This combination church and fortress, the only one of its kind in Santo Domingo, was completed in 1562. *Av. Mella, between Calle Isabel la Católica and Calle Arzobispo Meriño, no phone. Admission free. Open weekdays 8–noon. Sun. masses begin at 6 AM.*

⑫ Retrace your steps to Calle Isabel la Católica, go south to Calle de Las Mercedes, turn left, and walk one block right to **Calle Las Damas,** where you'll make a right turn to the New World's oldest street. The "Street of the Ladies" was named after the elegant ladies of the court who, in the Spanish tradition, promenaded in the evening.

On your left you'll see a sundial dating from 1753 and the **Casa de los Jesuitas,** which houses a fine research library for colonial history as well as the Institute for Hispanic Culture. *Admission free. Open weekdays 8–4:30.*

⑬ Across the street is the **Museo de las Casas Reales** (Museum of the Royal Houses). The collections in the museum are displayed in two early 16th-century palaces that have been altered many times over the years. Exhibits cover everything from antique coins to replicas of the *Niña,* the *Pinta,* and the *Santa María.* There are statue and cartography galleries, coats of armor and coats of arms, coaches and a royal courtroom, gilded furnishings, and Indian artifacts. The first room of the former Governor's Residence has a wall-size map marking the routes sailed by Columbus's ships on expeditions beginning in 1492. *Calle Las Damas, corner Calle Mercedes, tel. 809/682–4202. Admission: R.D. $10. Open Tues.–Sat. 9–4:45, Sun. 10–1.*

⑭ Across the street is the **Capilla de los Remedios** (Chapel of Our Lady of Remedies), which was originally built as a private chapel for the family of Francisco de Dávila. Early colonists also worshiped here before the completion of the cathedral. Its architectural details, particularly the lateral arches, are evocative of the Castilian-Romanesque style. *Calle Las Damas, at the foot of Calle Mercedes, no phone. Admission free. Open Mon.–Sat. 9–6; Sun. masses begin at 6 AM.*

⑮ Just south of the chapel on Calle Las Damas, the **Hostal Palacio Nicolás de Ovando** (*see* Lodging, *below*), now a highly praised hotel, was once the residence of Nicolás de Ovando, one of the principal organizers of the colonial city.

⑯ Across the street from the hotel looms the massive **National Pantheon.** The building, which dates from 1714, was once a Jesuit monastery and later a theater. Trujillo had it restored in 1955 with an eye toward being buried there. (He is buried instead at Père Lachaise in Paris.) An allegorical mural of his assassination is painted on the ceiling above the altar, where an eternal flame burns. The impressive chandelier was a gift from Spain's Francisco Franco. *Calle Las Damas, near the corner of Calle Mercedes, no phone. Admission free. Open Mon.–Sat. 10–5.*

⑰ Continue south on Calle Las Damas and cross Calle El Conde. Look on your left for the **Casa de Bastidas,** where there is a lovely inner courtyard with tropical plants and temporary exhibit galleries. *Calle Las Damas, just off Calle El Conde, no phone. Admission free. Open Tues.–Sun. 9–5.*

⑱ You won't have any trouble spotting the **Torre del Homenaje** (Tower of Homage) in the Fort Ozama. The fort sprawls two blocks south of the Casa de Bastidas, with a brooding crenellated tower that still guards the Ozama River. The fort and its tower were built in 1503 to protect the eastern border of the city. The sinister tower was the last home of many a condemned prisoner. *On Paseo Presidente Bellini, overlooking Río Ozama, no phone. Admission: R.D. $10. Open Tues.–Sun. 8–7.*

When you leave the fortress, turn left off Calle Las Damas onto Calle Padre Bellini. A two-block walk will bring you to **Casa de Tostado.** The house was built in the first decade of the 16th century and was the residence of writer Don Francisco Tostado. Its twin Gothic windows are the only ones that are still in existence in the New World. It now houses the **Museo de la Familia Dominicana** (Museum of the Dominican Family), which features exhibits on the well-heeled Dominican family in the 19th century. *Calle Padre Bellini, near Calle Arzobispo Meriño, tel. 809/689–5057. Admission: R.D. $10. Open Thurs.– Tues. 9–2.*

Walk two blocks west on Calle Padre Bellini to the corner of Avenida Duarte. The graceful building with the rose window is the **Iglesia y Convento Domínico** (Dominican Church and Convent), founded in 1510. In 1538, Pope Paul III visited here and was so impressed with the lectures on theology that he granted the church and convent the title of university, making it the oldest institution of higher learning in the New World. *Calle Padre Bellini and Av. Duarte, tel. 809/682–3780. Admission free. Open Tues.–Sun. 9–6.*

Continue west on Calle Padre Bellini for two blocks, and at the corner of Calle José Reyes you'll see another lovely church, **La Iglesia de Regina Angelorum** (Church of Regina Angelorum), which dates from 1537. The church was damaged during the Haitian regime, from 1822 to 1844, but you can still appreciate its Baroque dome, Gothic arches, and traceries. *Corner of Calle Padre Bellini and Calle José Reyes, tel. 809/682–2783. Admission free. Open Mon.–Sat. 9–6.*

Walk four blocks west on Calle Padre Bellini, turn left on Calle Palo Hincado, and keep going straight till you reach the **Puerta de la Misericordia** (Gate of Mercy), part of the old wall of Santo Domingo. It was here on the plaza, on February 27, 1844, that Ramón Mata Mella, one of the country's founding fathers, fired the shot that began the struggle for independence from Haiti.

Parque Independencia separates the old city from the new. Avenidas 30 de Marzo, Bolívar, and Independencia traverse the park and mingle with avenues named for George Washington, John F. Kennedy, and Abraham Lincoln. Modern Santo Domingo is a sprawling, noisy city with a population of close to 2 million.

Avenida George Washington, which features tall palms and Las Vegas–style tourist hotels, breezes along the Caribbean Sea. The Parque Litoral de Sur, better known as the **Malecón,** borders the avenue from the colonial city to the Hotel Santo Domingo, a distance of about 3 miles. The seaside park, with its cafés and places to relax, is a popular spot, but beware of pickpockets.

Avenida Máximo Gómez comes down from the north. Take a right turn on it, cross Avenida Bolívar, and you'll come to the landscaped lawns, modern sculptures, and sleek buildings of

㉔ the **Plaza de la Cultura.** Among the buildings are the **National Theater** (tel. 809/687–3191), which stages performances in Spanish; the **National Library,** in which the written word is Spanish; and museums and art galleries, whose notations are also in Spanish. The following museums on the plaza are open Tuesday–Saturday from 10 to 5, and admission to each is R.D. $10: The **Museum of Dominican Man** (tel. 809/687–3622) traces the migrations of Indians from South America through the Caribbean islands. The **Museum of Natural History** (tel. 809/689–0106) examines the flora and fauna of the island. In the **Gallery of Modern Art** (tel. 809/682–8260), the works of 20th-century Dominican and foreign artists are displayed.

㉕ North of town in the Arroyo Hondo district is the **Jardín Botánico Nacional Dr. Rafael M. Moscoso** (Dr. Rafael M. Moscoso National Botanical Gardens), the largest garden in the Caribbean. Its 445 acres include a Japanese Garden, a Great Ravine, a glen, a gorgeous display of orchids, and an enormous floral clock. You can tour the gardens by train, boat, or horse-drawn carriage. *Arroyo Hondo, no phone. Admission: R.D. $2. Open daily 10–6.*

In the 320-acre **Parque Zoológico Nacional** (National Zoological Park), not far from the Botanical Gardens, animals roam free in natural habitats. There is an African plain, a children's zoo, and what the zoo claims is the world's largest bird cage. *Av. Máximo Gómez at Av. de los Proceres, tel. 809/562–2080. Admission: R.D. $10. Open daily 10–6.*

The **Acuario Nacional** (National Aquarium)—whose construction was a controversial public expenditure during a time of crisis—is the largest aquarium in the Caribbean, with an impressive collection of tropical fish and dolphins. *In the Sans Souci district on the Avenida de las Américas. Admission: R.D. $10. Open daily 10–6.*

La Romana *Numbers in the margin correspond to points of interest on the Dominican Republic map.*

Head east on Las Américas Highway toward La Romana, about a two-hour drive along the southeast coast. All along the highway to Romana are small resort-hotel complexes where you can find refreshments or stay overnight. About 1½ miles ㉖ outside the capital, you'll come to the **Parque de los Tres Ojos** (Park of the Three Eyes). The "eyes" are cool blue pools peering out of deep limestone caves, and it's actually a four-eyed park. If you've a mind to, you can look into the eyes more closely by climbing down into the caves.

About 20 minutes east of the city is **Boca Chica Beach,** popular because of its proximity to the capital. Another 45 minutes or ㉗ so farther east is the city of **San Pedro de Macorís,** where the national sport and the national drink are both well represented. Some of the country's best *béisbol* games are played in **Tetelo Vargas Stadium,** which you can see off the highway to your left. The **Macorís Rum distillery** is on the eastern edge of the city.

The two big businesses around La Romana used to be cattle and sugarcane. That was before Gulf & Western created (and subsequently sold) the **Casa de Campo** resort, which is a very big business, indeed, and **Altos de Chavón,** a re-creation of a 16th-century village and art colony on the resort grounds.

Casa de Campo means "house in the country," and, yes, you could call it that. This particular "house" is a resort that sprawls over 7,000 acres, accommodates some 3,000 guests, and offers two public golf courses (one of them, a teeth-clencher called Teeth of the Dog, has seven holes that skirt the sea), 16 tennis courts, horseback riding, polo, archery, trap shooting, and every imaginable water sport. Oscar de la Renta designed much of the resort and has a boutique in Altos de Chavón. He also owns a villa at Casa de Campo.

㉘ **Altos de Chavón** sits on a bluff overlooking the Rio Chavón, about 3 miles east of the main facility of Casa de Campo. You can drive there easily enough, or you can take one of the free shuttle buses from the resort. In this re-creation of a medieval Spanish village there are cobblestone streets lined with lanterns, wrought-iron balconies, and courtyards swathed with bougainvillea. More than a museum piece, this village is a place where artists live, work, and play. There is an art school, affiliated with New York's Parsons School of Design; a disco; an archaeological museum; five restaurants; and a 5,000-seat outdoor amphitheater (used about four times a year) where Frank Sinatra and Julio Iglesias have entertained. The focal point of the village is **Iglesia St. Stanislaus,** which is named after the patron saint of Poland in tribute to the Polish Pope John Paul II, who visited the Dominican Republic in 1979 and left some of the ashes of St. Stanislaus behind.

The Cibao Valley to Puerto Plata This tour can be made by bus (fare: R.D. $70/U.S. $6), though you won't see as much: Although the bus does stop briefly in Santiago de los Caballeros, you have to get off and take a local bus from there if you want to see La Vega. Strictly as a means of transport from Santo Domingo to Puerto Plata, however, a bus is ideal.

The road north from Santo Domingo, known as Autopista Duarte, cuts through the lush banana plantations, rice and tobacco fields, and royal poinciana trees of the Cibao Valley. All along the road there are stands where, for a few centavos, you can buy ripe pineapples, mangoes, avocados, *chicharrones* (either fried pork rinds or chicken pieces), and fresh fruit drinks. To ㉙ the west is **Pico Duarte,** at 10,128 feet the highest peak in the West Indies.

In the heart of the Cibao is La Vega. Founded in 1495 by Columbus, it is the site of one of the oldest settlements in the New World. The inquisitive will find the tour of the ruins of the original settlement, **La Vega Vieja** (The Old La Vega), a rewarding ㉚ experience. About 3 miles north of La Vega is **Santo Cerro** (Holy Mount), site of a miraculous apparition of the Virgin and therefore of many local pilgrimages. The **Convent of La Merced** is located there, and the views of the Cibao Valley are breathtaking.

About 144 kilometers (90 miles) north of the capital, you'll come to the industrial city of **Santiago de los Caballeros,** where a massive monument honoring the Restoration of the Republic guards the entrance to the city. Many past presidents were born in Santiago, and it is currently a center for processing tobacco leaf. Cuban cigar-making skills are found here, and a tour of **La Aurora Tabacalera** (tel. 809/582–1131) gives the visitor an appreciation of this art.

The Amber Coast The Autopista Duarte ultimately leads (in three to four hours from Santo Domingo) to the Amber Coast, so called because of its large, rich, and unique deposits of amber. The coastal area around Puerto Plata is a region of splashy resorts. The north coast boasts more than 70 miles of beaches with condominiums and villas going up fast.

31 **Puerto Plata,** although now quiet and almost sleepy, was a dynamic city in its heyday. Visitors can get a feeling for this past in the magnificent Victorian **Glorieta** (Gazebo) in the central **Parque Independencia.** Next to the park, the recently refurbished **Catedral de San Felipe** recalls a simpler, colonial past. On Puerto Plata's own Malecón, the **Fortaleza de San Felipe** protected the city from many a pirate attack and was later used as a political prison. The fort is most dramatic at night.

Puerto Plata is also the home of the **Museum of Dominican Amber,** a lovely galleried mansion and one of several tenants in the Tourist Bazaar. The museum displays and sells the Dominican Republic's national stone. Semiprecious, translucent amber is actually fossilized pine resin that dates back about 50 million years, give or take a few millennia. The north coast of the Dominican Republic has the largest deposits of amber in the world (the only other deposits are found in Germany and the former Soviet Union), and jewelry crafted from the stone is the best-selling item on the island. *Calle Duarte 61, tel. 809/586–2848. Admission: R.D. $10. Open Mon.–Sat. 9–5.*

Southwest of Puerto Plata, you can take a cable car (when it is **32** working) to the top of **Mt. Isabel de Torres,** which soars 2,600 feet above sea level. On the mountain there is a botanical garden, a huge statue of Christ, and a spectacular view. The cable was first laid in 1754, although rest assured that it's been replaced since then. Lines can be long, and once on top of the mountain you may wonder if it was worth the time. Don't eat at the restaurant at the top—the food is awful. *The cable car operates Tues., Thurs., Fri., Sat., and Sun. 8–6. Round-trip is R.D. $20.*

On the eastern side of Puerta Plata, about 1.6 miles along the Malecón and past the Puerto Plata Beach Resort and Casino, is a small gathering of bars, discos, and restaurants in an area called Long Beach, where the oft-closed office of tourism is situated. If you're hungry, you can sample fresh fish at **Peter's Fisch Place,** Cantonese fare at the **Orient Express,** or pizza at **Los Pinos.** About 3 miles further east is the **Playa Dorada** complex, a resort area containing about a dozen hotels. Security guards act to limit access to locals here, but tourists not staying at the hotels are welcome to visit the casinos, discos, and restaurants within.

Back on the main road (Autopista), proceed another 6 miles **33** east to **Sosúa,** a small community settled during World War II by 600 Austrian and German Jews. After the war, many of them returned to Europe or went to the United States, and most of those who remained married Dominicans. Only a few Jewish families reside in the community today, and there is only one small, one-room synagogue. The flavor of the town is decidedly Spanish. There are numerous hotels, condominiums, and apartments in Sosúa. (The roads off the Autopista, incidentally, are horribly punctured with potholes.)

Sosúa has become one of the most frequently visited tourist destinations in the country, favored by French Canadians and Europeans. Hotels and condos are going up at breakneck speed. It actually consists of two communities, **El Batey** and **Los Charamicos,** which are separated by a cove and one of the island's prettiest beaches. The sand is soft and white, the water translucent and calm. The walkway above the beach is packed with tents filled with souvenirs, pizzas, and even clothing for sale—a jarring note in this otherwise idyllic setting.

Continue east on the Autopista past **Playa Grande.** The powdery white beach remains miraculously undisturbed and unspoiled by development.

34 The Autopista rolls along eastward and rides out onto a "thumb" of the island, where you'll find **Samaná.** Back in 1824, a sailing vessel called the *Turtle Dove,* carrying several hundred escaped American slaves from the Freeman Sisters' underground railway, was blown ashore in Samaná. The escapees settled and prospered, and today their descendants number several thousand. The churches here are Protestant; the worshipers live in villages called Bethesda, Northeast, and Philadelphia; and the language spoken is an odd 19th-century form of English.

About 3,000 humpback whales winter off the coast of Samaná from December to March. Plans are under way for organizing major whale-watching expeditions, such as those out of Massachusetts, that will boost the region's economy without scaring away the world's largest mammals.

In the meantime, sport fishing at Samaná is considered to be among the best in the world. A beautiful bay and beach round out Samaná's attractions. Tourism is finding its way here, and resort hotels are in the planning stages.

Beaches

The Dominican Republic has more than 1,000 miles of beaches, including the Caribbean's longest strip of white sand—Punta Cana. Many beaches are accessible to the public and may tempt you to stop for a swim. Be careful: Some have dangerously strong currents. Most of the nation's coastline is paralleled by a road, so access to these beaches is easy. You'll need a car to visit those away from your hotel, as public transportation is unreliable.

Boca Chica is the beach closest to Santo Domingo (2 miles east of Las Américas Airport, 21 miles from the capital), and it's crowded with city folk on weekends. Five years ago, this beach was virtually a four-lane highway of fine white sand. "Progress" has since cluttered it with plastic beach tables, chaise longues, pizza stands, and beach cottages for rent. But the sand is still fine, and you can walk far out into clear blue water, which is protected by natural coral reefs that help keep the big fish at bay.

About 20 minutes east of Boca Chica is another beach of fine white sand, **Juan Dolio.** The Villas del Mar Hotel and Punta Garza Beach Club are on this beach.

Moving counterclockwise around the island, you'll come to the La Romana area, with its miniature **Minitas** beach and lagoon, and the long white-sand, palm-lined crescent of **Bayahibe** beach, which is accessible only by boat. La Romana is the home of the 7,000-acre Casa de Campo resort, so you're not likely to find any private place in the sun here.

The gem of the Caribbean, **Punta Cana** is a 20-mile strand of pearl-white sand shaded by trees and coconut palms. Located on the easternmost coast, it is the home of Club Med, the new Melia Punta Cana, and the Bavaro Beach Resort.

Las Terrenas, on the north coast of the Samaná peninsula, looks like something from *Robinson Crusoe:* Tall palms list toward the sea, away from the mountains; the beach is narrow but sandy, and best of all, there is nothing man-made in sight—just vivid blues, greens, and yellows.

Playa Grande, on the north coast, is a long stretch of powdery sand that is slated for development. At present, it's undisturbed, but you'd better hurry if you want to enjoy it in solitude.

Farther west is the lovely beach at **Sosúa,** where calm waters gently lap at long stretches of soft white sand. Unfortunately the backdrop here is a string of tents, with hawkers pushing cheap souvenirs. You can get snacks and rent water-sports equipment from the vendors.

The ideal wind and surf conditions of **Cabarete Beach,** also on the north coast, have made it an integral part of the international windsurfing circuit.

On the north Amber Coast, **Puerto Plata** is situated in a developed and still-developing area that is about to outdo San Juan's famed Condado strip. The beaches are of soft ecru or white sand, with lots of reefs for snorkeling. The Atlantic waters are great for windsurfing, waterskiing, and fishing expeditions.

About an hour west of Puerto Plata lies **Luperón Beach,** a wide white-sand beach fit for snorkeling, windsurfing, and scuba diving. The Luperón Beach Resort is handy for rentals and refreshments.

Sports and the Outdoors

Although there is hardly a shortage of outdoor activities here, the resorts have virtually cornered the market on sports, including every conceivable water sport. Some hotels, particularly all-inclusives, offer their facilities only to guests. You can check with the Tourist Office for more details.

Bicycling Pedaling is easy on pancake-flat beaches, but there are also steep hills in the Dominican Republic. Bikes are available at **Villas Doradas** (Playa Dorada, Puerto Plata, tel. 809/586–3000), **Dorado Naco** (Dorado Beach, tel. 809/586–2019), **Jack Tar Village** (Puerto Plata, tel. 809/586–3800), and **Cofresi Beach Hotel** (Puerto Plata, tel. 809/586–2898). Be aware that cars, buses, and trucks can make biking hazardous on some roads; you'll be charged for any bike damage. Count on a $15 daily rental fee.

Boating Small-boat sailing is limited, though most resort hotels have a few tattered sailing dinghies for rent at about R.D. $100 (U.S. $8) an hour. Hobie Cats and paddleboats are available at **Heavens** (Playa Dorada, tel. 809/586–5250). Check also at **Casa de**

Campo (La Romana, tel. 809/682–2111) and **Club Med** (Punta Cana, tel. 809/567–5228).

Golf **Casa de Campo** has two 18-hole Pete Dye courses and a third for the private use of villa owners. These are among the best in the Caribbean; greens fees at the two nonprivate courses are $50 (including cart). Two new 18-hole courses are planned for the **Punta Cana Beach Resort** and the **Bávaro Beach.** The Playa Dorada hotels have their own 18-hole Robert Trent Jones–designed course; there is also a 9-hole course nearby at the **Costambar.** Guests in Santo Domingo hotels are usually allowed to use the 18-hole course at the **Santo Domingo Country Club** on weekdays—*after* members have teed off. There is a 9-hole course outside of town, at Lomas Lindas. A new Pete Dye course is under construction outside Santo Domingo.

Scuba Diving and Snorkeling Ancient sunken galleons, undersea gardens, and offshore reefs are the lures here, although the Dominican Republic offers less for the diver than many other Caribbean islands. For equipment and trips, contact **Mundo Submarino** (Santo Domingo, tel. 809/566–0344). A new Diving Instructors World Association (DIWA) scuba-certification school has opened at the **Demar Beach Club** in Boca Chica, outside the capital, offering three-day and one-week programs. A half-day of diving costs $30. Snorkel equipment is available at most resort hotels for about R.D. $50 (U.S. $4), but only around Punta Cana, off the beaches of Club Med, do you see much teeming marine life.

Tennis There must be a million nets laced around the island, and most of them can be found at the large resorts (*see* Lodging, *below*). If your hotel does not have courts, you can usually reserve court time at another nearby resort hotel (not at all-inclusive properties), for approximately $14 an hour.

Windsurfing Between June and October, **Cabarete Beach** offers what many consider to be optimal windsurfing conditions: wind speeds at 20–25 knots and 3- to 15-foot waves. The Professional Boardsurfers Association has included Cabarete Beach in its international windsurfing slalom competition. But the novice is also welcome to learn and train on modified boards stabilized by flotation devices. **CaribBIC Windsurfing Center,** on Caberete Beach (tel. 800/635–1155 or 800/243–9675), offers accommodations, equipment, training, and professional coaching. Most hotels have Windsurfers for rent at R.D. $120 (U.S. $10) an hour.

Shopping

The hot ticket in the Dominican Republic is amber jewelry. This island has the world's largest deposits of amber, and the prices here for the translucent, semiprecious stone are unmatched anywhere. The stones, which range in color from pale lemon to dark brown, are actually petrified resin from coniferous trees that disappeared from Earth about 50 million years ago. The most valuable stones are those in which tiny insects or small leaves are embedded. (Don't knock it till you've seen it.)

In the crafts department, hand-carved wood rocking chairs are big sellers, and they are sold unassembled and boxed for easy transport. Look also for the delicate ceramic lime figurines that symbolize the Dominican culture.

Bargaining is both a game and a social activity in the Dominican Republic, especially with street vendors and at the stalls in El Mercado Modelo. Vendors are disappointed and perplexed if you don't haggle. They also tend to be tenacious, so unless you really have an eye on buying, don't even stop to look—you may get stuck buying a souvenir just to get rid of an annoying vendor.

Shopping Districts **El Mercado Modelo** in Santo Domingo is a covered market in the Colonial Zone bordering Calle Mella. The restored buildings of **La Atarazana** (across from the Alcázar in the Colonial Zone) are filled with shops, art galleries, restaurants, and bars. The main shopping streets in the Colonial Zone are **Calle El Conde,** which has been transformed into an exclusively pedestrian thoroughfare, and **Calle Duarte.** (Some of the best shops on Calle Duarte are north of the Colonial Zone, between Calle Mella and Av. Las Américas). **Plaza Criolla** (corner of Av. 27 de Febrero and Av. Anacaona) is filled with shops that sell everything from scents to nonsense.

In Puerto Plata, the seven showrooms of the **Tourist Bazaar** (Calle Duarte 61) are in a wonderful old galleried mansion with a patio bar. Another cluster of shops is at the **Plaza Shopping Center** (Calle Duarte at Av. 30 de Marzo). A popular shopping street for jewelry and local souveniers is **Calle Beller.**

In **Altos de Chavón,** art galleries and shops are grouped around the main square.

Good Buys
Amber/Jewelry **Ambar Tres** (La Atarazana 3, Colonial Zone, Santo Domingo, tel. 809/688–0474) carries a wide selection of the Dominican product.

Dominican Art Galleries in Santo Domingo are **Arawak Gallery** (Av. Pasteur 104, tel. 809/685–1661) and **Galería de Arte Nader** (La Atarazana 9, Colonial Zone, tel. 809/688–0969). **Novo Atarazana** (Atarazana 21, tel. 809/689–0582) has a varied assortment of artifacts made by locals.

Wood Crafts Visit the stalls of **El Mercado Modelo** in the Colonial Zone and **El Conde Gift Shop** (Calle El Conde 153, tel. 809/682–5909), both in Santo Domingo.

In Puerto Plata, browse and shop at **Macaluso's** (Calle Duarte 32, tel. 809/586–3433) and at the **Collector's Corner Gallery and Gift Shop** (Plaza Shopping Center, no phone). In Santiago, try **Artesanía Lime** (Autopista Duarte, Km 21–2, Santiago, tel. 809/582–3754).

Dining

Dining out is a favorite form of entertainment for Dominicans, and they tend to dress up for the occasion. Most restaurants begin serving dinner around 6 PM, but the locals don't generally turn up until 9 or 10. There are French, Italian, and Chinese restaurants, as well as those serving traditional Dominican fare. Dining doesn't have to be expensive in the Dominican Republic, so long as you keep away from beef. Freshly caught fish is usually your best bet. A simple rice-and-beans lunch (*moro de habichuelas*) is cheap and filling. To save money, don't eat every meal in a full-service restaurant. Small stands and more casual restaurants offer tasty roast pork and goat dishes that cost less than $2. Small pieces of fried chicken (*chicharrones de pollo*) are great for nibbling while downing one of the first-rate local beers. And for snacking, you'll find luscious local fruit-mangoes, citrus fruits, passion fruit, and papaya—sold on the streets everywhere. Visits to food stores here are not so exciting. There is little variety, and even some staples you would expect to see on the shelves may be missing. Those who rent a house usually avoid the problem of provisions by employing a cook, who visits the market each morning.

Some favorite local dishes you should sample are paella, *sancocho* (a thick stew usually made with five different meats, though sometimes as many as seven), *arroz con pollo* (rice with chicken), *plátanos* (plantains) in all their tasty varieties, and *tortilla de jamón* (spicy ham omelet). Country snacks include *chicharrones* (fried pork rinds) and *galletas* (flat biscuit crackers). Many a meal is topped off with *majarete,* a tasty cornmeal custard. Presidente, Bohemia, and Quisqueya are the local beers, Bermúdez and Brugal the local rums. To end a meal, sip the dark brown, aged rum known as *añejo* over ice. Wine is on the expensive side because it has to be imported. Dominicans like their coffee strong (decaffeinated coffee is rare); if you're not of like mind, you may want to bring your own.

The dress code at D.R. restaurants is less easygoing than on many Caribbean islands. In Santo Domingo, smart casual is the rule at lunch, with something a little dressier at dinner, at least in more expensive restaurants. Casual rules at beach resorts, yet even here shorts are not appreciated at dinner. The reviews below indicate when something more than casual dress is appropriate.

Highly recommended restaurants are indicated by a star ★.

Category	Cost*
Moderate	$20–$30
Inexpensive	$10–$20
Budget	under $10

per person, excluding drinks, service, and sales tax (6%)

La Romana **Café del Sol.** At this outdoor café in a re-created medieval Spanish village, 3 miles east of Casa de Campo, you can lunch quite inexpensively on pizza, a light salad, or quiche while gazing at the distant mountain range. Dinner here is more elaborate and more expensive. *Altos de Chavón, tel. 809/523–3333, ext. 2346. No reservations. AE, DC, MC, V. Moderate.*

Villa Casita. This small and intimate restaurant serves creative Dominican cooking amid candles and muted lights. Start with octopus vinaigrette, spinach crêpes, or pasta with anchovies and clams before feasting on sea bass or local lobster. Piano music accompanies your dinner, and the polished wood bar is a relaxing place for cognac and coffee. *Francisco Richer 71, La Romana, tel. 809/556–2808. Dress: smart casual. AE, MC, V. Moderate.*

Puerto Plata **Cafemba.** The view of Fort San Felipe and the sunset over the mountain of Isabel de Torres set the scene for this refined dining room. Start with the carpaccio or the clams oreganata with Creole sauce. Follow this with grilled medallions of beef, chicken, or veal, each with its own sauce—red wine, pomodoro, and hollandaise—or the fillet of sea bass. Desserts are freshly made pastries chosen from a trolley. Service is slightly strained (waiters wear white gloves) but certainly attentive. *Bayside Hill Resort, Costambar, tel. 809/566–9206. Reservations advised. AE, DC, MC, V. Dinner only. Moderate.*

★ **Jimmy's.** The beef here is reasonably priced and some of the best in town. Within this old Victorian house you'll be served chateaubriand, filet mignon, and a variety of creatures from the sea. Be sure to top it all off with something flambéed. *Calle Beller 72, tel. 809/586–4325. Reservations advised. Jacket advised. AE, MC, V. Moderate.*

Peter's Fisch Place. One of several small restaurants in the section known as Long Beach, between Puerto Plata and Playa Dorada, Peter's stands out for its very fresh fish and its squeaky-clean European ambience, with stucco walls and checkered tablecloths. The cooking is simple; you can have your fish grilled in butter and herbs or in a Creole sauce. *Long Beach, no phone. No reservations. No credit cards. Inexpensive.*

Porto Fino. Fare here is a combination of Italian—lasagna is the most popular dish—and Dominican. Many rate the latter dishes, such as crab Creole, more tasty. Located on the same avenue as most of Puerto Plata's major restaurants, the café has minimal decor, with bright lighting and plain green walls. An outdoor terrace is much more pleasant. *Av. Hermanas Mirabel, tel. 809/586–2858. No reservations. AE, DC, MC, V. Inexpensive.*

Roma II. This is just an open-sided stand with a metal roof, but the pizzas, cooked in a wood-burning oven, are some of the best you'll ever eat. The pizza dough and pasta are made fresh daily. Other specialties include *spaghetti con pulpo* (spaghetti with octopus), *filete chito* (steak with garlic), and a host of other pastas and special sauces. *Corner Calle E. Prudhomme and Calle Beller, tel. 809/586–3904. No reservations. No credit cards. Budget.*

Santo Domingo
Continental

★ **Lina.** Lina was the personal chef of Trujillo, and she taught her secret recipes to the chefs of this stylish contemporary restaurant. The steak dishes here may strain the budget, but you cannot fail with the paella (so satisfying you won't need any appetizer or dessert) or the sea bass, cooked however you like. *Gran Hotel Lina, Av. Máximo Gómez at Av. 27 de Febrero, tel. 809/686–5000. Reservations required. Jacket required. AE, DC, MC, V. Moderate.*

Mesón de la Cava. The capital's most unusual restaurant is more than 50 feet below ground in a natural cave complete with stalagmites and stalactites. Guests clamber down a circular staircase (ducking rock protrusions) to dine on excellent seafood dishes. You'll need to keep to less expensive dishes and possibly forgo an appetizer or dessert to keep your meal within our Moderate range. Live music and dancing nightly until 1 AM. *Av. Mirador del Sur, tel. 809/533–2818. Reservations required. Jacket required. AE, DC, MC, V. Moderate.*

Fonda de la Atarazana. This patio restaurant in the Colonial Zone is especially romantic at night, when music and dancing are added. Try the kingfish, shrimp, or *chicharrones de pollo* (bits of fried Dominican chicken). *La Atarazana 5, tel. 809/689–2900. Dinner reservations advised. Dress: smart casual. AE, MC, V. Moderate.*

Lucky Seven. Baseball is the big deal here. Owner Evelio Oliva has two satellite dishes, and telecasts of six major-league games go on at once. Incidentally, there's also steak, chicken, and seafood to satisfy pre- or postgame appetites. *Casimiro de Moya and Av. Pasteur, tel. 809/682–7588. No reservations. No credit cards. Moderate.*

Dominican **El Castillo del Mar.** Another seafood restaurant on the Malecón, this one has an open-air setting by the sea. Start with fish soup, then feast on lobster thermidor or sea bass smothered in onions, tomatoes, peas, and basil. *Av. George Washington 2, tel. 809/688–4047. No reservations. MC, V. Inexpensive.*

★ **La Bahía.** This is an unpretentious spot where the catch of the day is tops. Conch appears in a variety of dishes. For starters, try the *sopa palúdica*, a thick soup made with fish, shrimp, and lobster, served with tangy garlic bread. Then move on to kingfish in coconut sauce or *espaguettis a la canona* (spaghetti heaped with seafood). *Av. George Washington 1, tel. 809/682–4022. No reservations. AE, MC, V. Budget.*

French **Café St. Michel.** The cream of pumpkin soup and steak tartare
★ should clue you in to why this popular restaurant has won many gastronomical awards. Desserts include a prize-winning chocolate torte and spectacular soufflés. *Av. Lope de Vega 24, tel. 809/562–4141. Reservations advised. Jacket advised. AE, MC, V. Moderate.*

Spanish **La Taverna.** In this bistrolike restaurant, every round of tapas (Spanish appetizers) seems tastier than the last. You'll find it hard to limit yourself as you choose from among shrimp dipped in Creole sauce, slices of zesty pizza, chicharrones, and *pastilitos* (meat pies). It's located next to its more expensive partner, El Caserio. *Av. George Washington 459, tel. 809/685–3392. No reservations. AE, DC, MC, V. Inexpensive.*

★ **Midimodo.** The slow, old-fashioned service here is fitting for the dining room of the oldest hotel in the New World. High ceilings, twirling fans, and colonnades breathe an ancient charm; modern pleasure comes from the Spanish food. This is a bargain if ever there was one. *Hostal Palacio Nicolás de Ovando, Calle Las Damas 44 (old quarter), tel. 809/687–3101. AE, MC, V. Budget.*

Lodging

The Dominican Republic has the largest hotel inventory in the Caribbean. Puerto Plata alone features 6,000 rooms and hosts 200,000 tourists a year. There are already so many adjoining resorts that when you go out for a stroll you have to flag landmarks to find your way back to the one where your luggage is. What the island's hotels lack in charm, they make up for in low rates. Even many of the larger resorts and all-inclusives here are affordable.

The D.R. may be the place to opt for an MAP or all-inclusive plan rather than trying to save money with an EP rate. Restaurants (and sporting facilities) within walking distance of hotels are scarce; even if you take an EP plan, you may find yourself eating at your hotel night after night anyway, but without the savings offered through an MAP or all-inclusive package.

More and more hotels here are becoming all-inclusives. If you plan to take advantage of sports facilities and eat and drink generously, you'll find many all-inclusives that are excellent value. And although you are dependent upon the hotel's kitchens, the difference between menus from one establishment to another is often marginal.

Small hotels at the bottom end of our Budget category tend to be pretty dingy rooms in urban centers, away from the better beaches. What you save may be offset by the cost of the car rental you'll need at these locations. Nor are rental properties much of an option in the Dominican Republic, except for the high-priced luxury villas at Casa de Campo.

Santo Domingo's hotels, while often providing rooms with views of the Caribbean, are at least 30 minutes away by car from any beach where you would want to swim. All of the other hotels listed, except for the lodging in Jarabacoa, are on the beach or close to the water. Those hotels on Playa Dorado that do not front the beach have shuttle buses that go there; in any case you are never more than a 10-minute walk away.

Highly recommended lodgings are indicated by a star ★.

Category	Cost*
Moderate	$80–$120
Inexpensive	$50–$80
Budget	under $50

All prices are for a standard double room for two, excluding 21% tax. To estimate rates for hotels offering MAP/FAP, add about $20–$25 per person per day to the above price ranges. For all-inclusives, add about $35–$40 per person per day.

The Amber Coast **Caribbean Village Club and Resort.** Formerly the Playa Dorada Princess, this resort has accommodations in 44 two-story pastel-colored villas. Rooms are air-conditioned, with remote-control cable TVs and minibars. The free-form pool has a swim-up terrace, and there's free shuttle service to the beach, or you can make the 10-minute hike. On the beach is the hotel's La Tortuga, a snack bar, and the water-sports facilities. Nightly entertainment and dancing take place in the patio lounge and lobby bar. *Playa Dorada, tel. 809/586–5350 or 800/852–4523, fax 809/320–5386. 310 rooms, 26 suites. Facilities: 2 restaurants, 3 bars/lounges, pool, 7 lighted tennis courts, health club, gym, spa, Jacuzzi, golf. AE, MC, V. CP, MAP. Expensive.*

Jack Tar Village. At this link in the all-inclusive chain of JTVs, everything, including drinks and golf greens fees, is included in the cost of your accommodations. The activities program is varied, enhanced by nightly entertainment and all manner of enjoyable pursuits. Accommodations are in Spanish-style villas set back from the beach in a large landscaped garden. There is free transportation to town, but the all-inclusive deal will probably keep you on the premises. *Box 368, Playa Dorada, tel. 809/586–3800 or 800/999–9182, fax 809/320–4161. 240 rooms. Facilities: 2 pools, 3 restaurants, 5 bars, casino, disco, golf, horseback riding, tennis, water-sports center. AE, MC, V. All-inclusive. Moderate.*

★ **Puerto Plata Beach Resort and Casino.** This is a 7-acre village with cobblestone pathways, colorful gardens, and rooms and suites in 23 two- and three-story buildings. Only the standard doubles are within our Moderate range during high season.

(During the summer, the one-bedroom suites also fall within this price category.) An activities center sets up water-sports clinics, rents bicycles, and so forth. The resort also caters to the little ones, with children's games and enclosures for them at the shallow end of the pool. Bogart's is the glitzy disco. Ylang-Ylang, named after the evening flower that blooms here, is a highly rated gourmet restaurant and catering service. This resort is just outside of town and a ways from Playa Dorada, which will be an added attraction to some. *Box 600, Av. Malecón, Puerto Plata, tel. 809/586–4243 or 800/223–9815, fax 809/586–4377. 170 rooms, 51 suites. Facilities: pool, 4 restaurants, bar, outdoor Jacuzzi, horseback riding, 3 lighted tennis courts, water-sports center. AE, MC, V. EP, MAP. Moderate.*

★ **Sand Castle.** The name says it all. This resort is a fantasy of curves, balconies, and balustrades set high above coral cliffs. Royal palms rise majestically from the beachside gardens. Rooms are simple and comfortable—extremely beige. Your stay here will be made more enjoyable if you have a room with a view, especially of the small curving beach down below. The hotel is by itself on a peninsula, with the village of Sosúa nearby. Organized activities keep you as busy as you want. *Puerto Chiquito, Sosúa, tel. 809/571–2420 or 800/445–5963, fax 809/571–2000. 240 rooms. Facilities: 4 restaurants, 5 bars, 2 pools, Jacuzzi, cable TV, shopping, disco, convention center, beach house, horseback riding, bicycling, snorkeling, deep-sea fishing, scuba diving, waterskiing, parasailing. AE, MC, V. EP, MAP. Moderate.*

Heavens. The accent at this compact, all-inclusive property is on fun and active playtime. From exercise to merengue lessons, Heavens caters to the young (not the young at heart), and children are welcome, too. Outside guests may use the facilities with a daily ($45) pass. The decor is composed of stylized palms in rattan, cloth, and metal, and the health-conscious Rainbow Restaurant is the only Dominican eatery to offer a separate smoking section. Locals frequent the high-tech Andromeda disco, but ask for a room away from it—things can get noisy. This is one of Playa Dorado's smaller resorts, with buildings jostling each other for space and a pool area densely packed with chaise longues. *Box 576, Playa Dorada, Puerta Plata, tel. 809/586–5250 or 800/835–7697, fax 809/320–4733. 150 rooms and suites. Facilities: pool, 2 restaurants, disco, bar, cable TV, horseback riding, water aerobics, windsurfing, sailing, snorkeling and scuba, merengue lessons. AE, MC, V. All-inclusive. Moderate.*

Hotel Cofresi. The rooms here are simply furnished with twin beds, but the setting is breathtaking. The all-inclusive resort is built on the reefs along the Atlantic, which spritzes its waters into the peaceful man-made lagoon and pools along the beach. There are jogging and exercise trails, paddleboats for the lagoon, scuba-diving clinics, and evening entertainment, including a disco. The cost covers drinks and all. *Box 327, Costambar, tel. 809/586–2898, fax 809/586–8064. 145 rooms, 5 suites. Facilities: 2 restaurants, 3 bars, disco, nightclub, 2 pools (1 saltwater), bicycling, horseback riding, paddleboats, tennis, water-sports center. AE, MC, V. All-inclusive. Moderate.*

★ **Playa Chiquita.** In this Sosúa resort you register in a broad breezeway that leads past the free-form pool right to the small private beach. The all-suite, air-conditioned complex has contemporary tropical decor, with terra-cotta floors, cable TVs, double or king-size beds, wet bar, kitchenettes, and patios or balconies. A sun deck overlooks the ocean. The pool has a swim-up bar for adult guests and a shallow section for children. Plans are to have doubled the number of rooms by the end of 1993, but construction may continue into 1994. In the meantime, a new casino has opened. *Sosúa, tel. 809/689–6191 or 800/922–4272, fax 809/571–2460. 90 rooms. Facilities: restaurant, coffee shop, pool, gift shop, horseback riding, casino, water sports. MC, V. EP, MAP. Inexpensive.*

Punta Goleta Beach Resort. This all-inclusive resort is set on 100 tropical acres across the road from the Cabarete beach, where wind-surfing is king. All the hotel's rooms are air-conditioned, and most have terraces or patios with gingerbread trim. There is a lot of activity, such as volleyball in the pool or on the beach, frog and crab racing, board games, merengue lessons, disco, and boating on the lagoon. Villas here are not affordable. *Box 318, Cabarete, tel. 809/571–0700, fax 809/571–0707. 126 rooms, 10 villas. Facilities: 2 restaurants, 4 bars, disco, jogging track, pool, lagoon, horseback riding, golf, tennis, water-sports center. AE, DC, MC, V. All-inclusive. Moderate.*

★ **Hostal Jimessón.** One of the few hotels in downtown Puerto Plata, the Jimessón is a gingerbread-trimmed, century-old clapboard house right out of New Orleans. There are rocking chairs on the front porch, and the parlor houses a veritable museum of antique grandfather clocks, Victrolas, and mahogany and wicker furniture. Other superb, homey touches include a live parrot, hanging plants, and the owners' genuine hospitality. Unfortunately, air-conditioned guest rooms, in a newer concrete addition in back, share none of the main house's charm; they have budget-conscious bathrooms and are furnished with only a bed and table. Though only a few city blocks from the seafront, the better beaches are a couple of miles away. The numerous and varied restaurants of Puerto Plata are within easy walking distance. *Calle John F. Kennedy 41, Puerto Plata, tel. 809/586–5131, fax 809/586–6313. 22 rooms. Facilities: bar, cable TV. AE, MC, V. EP. Budget.*

Hotel Montemar. Located on the Malecón, between Puerto Plata and Playa Dorada, this is a good choice for a cost-conscious holiday. All rooms have an ocean view. Superior rooms are air-conditioned, but small standard rooms are not. The beach across the road is not recommended for swimming, but there's transportation to the beaches at Playa Dorada. Daily activities are scheduled. *Box 382, Puerto Plata, tel. 809/586–2800 or 800/332–4872, fax 809/586–2009. 95 rooms. Facilities: restaurant, coffee shop, bar, 2 tennis courts, beach club, golf, horseback riding. AE, MC, V. EP, MAP, FAP. Inexpensive.*

Jarabacoa
★ **Hotel Hogar.** Tasty home-cooked meals and a very friendly staff add to the charm of this simple establishment right in the middle of town (only a block from the bus station). Look for the huge Montecarlo cigarette sign hanging out front. The rooms are spartan but serviceable and come with their own mosquito netting. *Calle Mella 34, Jarabacoa, tel. 809/574–2739. 9 rooms. Facilities: restaurant. No credit cards. CP. Budget.*

Punta Cana **Bávaro Beach Resort.** More than 20 miles of the Caribbean's best beach are to be found in front of this four-star luxury resort, where only rooms not facing the beach make it into our Moderate price category. Units are in five low-rise buildings by the beach or overlooking the gardens. Each room is air-conditioned and has a private balcony or terrace and refrigerator. Despite a social director and a wide variety of daily activities, this very large property feels impersonal. *Higüey, tel. 809/682–2162 or 800/336–6612, fax 809/682–2169. 1,001 rooms. Facilities: 3 restaurants, 3 bars, 2 pools, cable TV, archery, bicycles, horseback riding, tennis, disco, water sports. AE, MC, V. MAP. Moderate.*

Club Mediterranée. Everything but hard liquor is included in the price you pay for a stay in this 70-acre facility on the Punta Cana beach. Its air-conditioned, double-occupancy rooms are in three-story beach and coconut-grove lodgings, with twin beds and showers. There's a disco on the beach, plus the whole spectrum of Club Med activities, from archery to yoga. *Punta Cana, tel. 809/687–2767 or 800-CLUBMED; in NY, 212/750–1670, fax 809/565–2558. 332 rooms. Facilities: 2 restaurants, bar, disco, pool, 14 tennis courts (6 lighted), golf driving range and putting green, archery, boccie ball, volleyball, boat rides, soccer, ping-pong, aerobics classes, water-sports center. AE, MC, V. All-inclusive (drinks not included). Moderate.*

Samaná **Bahía Beach.** On a cliff above the beach in one of the best game-fishing areas of the Caribbean, the Bahía offers air-conditioned rooms with ocean view on the mainland, plus fan-cooled cottages on Cayo Levantado, a nearby island. This is a favorite with young Dominicans. *Samaná Bay, tel. 809/685–6060. 85 rooms in the main hotel, 29 on the island. Facilities: restaurant, bar, pool, 2 tennis courts, disco, water sports. AE, MC, V. All-inclusive. Inexpensive.*

Santo Domingo **Hotel Hispaniola.** This hotel is older and less costly than its sister hotel, the Hotel Santo Domingo, next door. It draws a younger, more active crowd, who gather at the modern disco and recently refurbished casino. There are two restaurants here, Las Cañas and La Pizetta, as well as the Hispaniola Bar, which has a small dance area. Air-conditioned guest rooms are rather worn, with stained carpets, but they are spacious and have phones and TVs. The staff is helpful and will take the time to advise you on your travel plans. A slight drawback is the hotel's location at the opposite end of the Malecón to the historic quarter, and a good 10-minute walk to most of the action. *Av. Independencia and Abraham Lincoln, tel. 809/221–7111 or 800/223–6620, fax 809/535–4050. 163 rooms, 2 suites. Facilities: 2 restaurants, bar, pool, disco, casino, 3 tennis courts. AE, DC, MC, V. EP. Moderate.*

Hotel El Embajador and Casino. The rooms in this air-conditioned hotel are spacious, with carpeting, twin or king-size beds, radios, cable TVs, and balconies with either a mountain or an ocean view (the latter are preferable and affordable). An executive concierge floor is good for business travelers. The pool is a popular weekend gathering place for resident foreigners. *Av. Sarasota 65, Santo Domingo, tel. 809/221–2131 or 800/457–0067, fax 809/532–4494. 304 rooms, 12 suites. Facilities: casino, pool, free transport to beach, 4 tennis courts, 2 restaurants, 2 bars, shopping arcade, facilities for the disabled. AE, DC, MC, V. EP. Moderate.*

Gran Hotel Lina and Casino. This balconied hotel, on Avenida Máximo Gómez near the Plaza de la Cultura, has a staid but secure ambience. The rooms are air-conditioned, spacious, and carpeted, with double beds, minifridges, huge marble baths, and cable TVs. The staff is friendly and helpful. *Box 1915, Santo Domingo, tel. 809/686–5000 or 800/942–2461, fax 809/686–5521.*

205 rooms, 15 suites. Facilities: casino, Spanish restaurant, piano bar, nightclub, coffee shop, health club, 2 tennis courts, pool facilities for the disabled. AE, DC, MC, V. EP. Inexpensive.

★ **Hostal Palacio Nicolás de Ovando.** The oldest hotel in the New World, and one of the few in the Colonial Zone, was home to the first governor in the early 1500s. The decor is Spanish, with carved mahogany doors, beamed ceilings, tapestries, arched colonnades, and three courtyards with splashing fountains. The air-conditioned rooms have views of the port, the pool, or the Colonial Zone. Dominican specialties are served in the restaurant (see Dining, above). This is Santo Domingo's only hotel with the charm of antiquity; with prices at the low end of this category, it's the city's most delightful bargain. Unfortunately, its location is against it: At nighttime, the area can be deserted and unpleasant for walking alone. Calle Las Damas 44, Apdo. 89-2, Santo Domingo, tel. 809/687–3101, fax 809/686–5170. 55 rooms. Facilities: restaurant, bar, TV, pool. AE, MC, V. EP. Inexpensive.

Hotel Cervantes. In the heart of the capital's residential district and five blocks from the Malecón, this modern four-story hotel is popular with traveling businessmen and tourists wanting inexpensive, clean, and functional accommodations. All rooms have air-conditioning, either a king-size bed or two queen-size beds, and a small sitting area with a table and chairs. Colors are pastel modern. The hotel's restaurant prides itself on its steaks and other meats, and the front office staff cheerfully provides advice on what to see and do in the capital. Calle Cervantes 202, Santo Domingo, tel. 809/686–8161, fax 809/686–5754. 180 rooms. Facilities: restaurant, pool, sauna, barber shop, free parking. AE, DC, MC, V. EP. Budget.

Off-Season Bets Although Santo Domingo hotel prices remain fairly constant year-round, beach resorts drop rates by up to 40% during the off-season. Some of the D.R.'s top hotels become affordable at this time, among them Playa Dorada's **Paradise Beach Resort and Club** (Box 337, Playa Dorada, tel. 809/586–3663 or 800/223–9815, fax 809/320–4858). This well-designed property, a cluster of low-rise buildings with white tile roofs and latticed balconies, offers its all-inclusive package for a price that just dips into our Moderate category; it's also one of only four Playa Dorada resorts that actually front the beach. The new, luxury **Hotel Gran Bahia** (Box 2024, Santo Domingo, tel. 809/538–3111 or 800/372–1323, fax 809/538–2764), at La Samaná, with spacious rooms, also slips into our Moderate price category. You may also wish to investigate discounts at the huge **Casa de Campo** complex (Box 140, La Romana, tel. 809/523–3333 or 800/223–6620, fax 809/523–8548), where certain summer packages make double rooms affordable.

The Arts and Nightlife

Get a copy of the magazine *Vacation Guide* and the newspaper *Touring*, both of which are available free at the Tourist Office and at hotels, to find out what's happening around the island. Also look in the *Santo Domingo News* and the *Puerto Plata News* for listings of events. The monthly *Dominican Fiesta!* also provides up-to-date information.

Casinos These are the raison d'être for many visitors to the island. There's no cover charge in D.R. casinos, and everyone from high-stakes rollers to those with a few quarters frequents them. Most of the casinos are concentrated in the larger hotels of Santo Domingo, but there are others here and there, and all offer blackjack, craps, and roulette. Casinos are open daily 3 PM–4 AM. You must be 18 to enter, and jackets are required. In Santo Domingo, the most popular casinos are in the **Dominican Concorde** (Calle Anacaona, tel. 809/562–8222), the **Jaragua** (Av. Independencia, tel. 809/686–2222), the **Embajador** (Av. Sarasota, tel. 809/533–2131), the **Gran Hotel Lina** (Av. Máximo Gómez, tel. 809/689–5185), the **Naco Hotel** (Av. Tiradentes 22, tel. 809/562–3100), and the **San Géronimo** (Av. Independencia 1067, tel. 809/533–8181).

Cafés **Café Atlantico** (Prolongación Mexico 152 at Abraham Lincoln, tel. 809/565–1840) is responsible for bringing happy hour and Tex-Mex cooking to the Dominican Republic. It has been attracting well-to-do Dominicans and an international crowd for more than six years. Usually young, very lively, and very friendly, the late-afternoon yuppie crowd comes for the music, the food, the exotic drinks, and the energetic atmosphere. You may even find owner-host Gustavo spinning your favorite record. The wine and cheese bar **Exquesito** (Av. Tiradentes 8, tel. 809/541–0233) has an odd decor that mixes traditional Dominican with deconstructivist provincial Italian. The fare includes French cheeses, Italian antipasti, and a local version of the deli. A recent annex to the Café St. Michel, the **Grand Café** (Av. Lope de Vega 26, tel. 809/562–4141) attracts a relaxed local crowd. You can escape the music by going upstairs to the Tree House. The menu is informal and generally light, but try the Creole oxtail *fradiabolo* served with crabmeat patties.

Music and Dance An active and frenzied young crowd dances to new wave; house; and, of course, merengue at **Alexander's** club (Av. Pasteur 23, tel. 809/685–9728). The neon palm tree outside **Bella Blue** (Av. George Washington 165, tel. 809/689–2911) beckons nightbirds to this Malecón dance club, where the crowd is definitely over 21, and no jeans are allowed. A favorite of locals for live music featuring local merengue bands, **Las Palmas** (Hotel Santo Domingo, Av. Independencia at Abraham Lincoln, tel. 809/535–1511) has a happy hour from 6 to 8 PM. The newest sensation is **Guacara Taina** (tel. 809/530–2666), a cultural center/disco set in a cave. It hosts folkloric dances by day and becomes the city's hottest night spot in the late evening. When all the partying is over and the *nuit blanche* is coming to an end, capitaleños will guide you to **La Aurora** (Av. Hermanos Deligne, no phone), a pediatric clinic turned lush after-hours supper club. Savor typical dishes, even sancocho, at four in the morning. Here you'll see not only party goers but also the musicians who entertained them. It's a spot of preference for Santo Domingo's hottest band, 4:40.

12 Grenada

Updated by
Carolyn Price

Grenada, 21 miles long and 12 miles wide, is bordered by dozens of beaches and secluded coves; crisscrossed by nature trails; and filled with spice plantations, tropical forests, and select hotels clinging to hillsides overlooking the sea.

Known as the Isle of Spice, Grenada is a major producer of nutmeg, mace, cinnamon, cocoa, and many other common household spices. The pungent aroma of spices fills the air at the outdoor markets, where they're sold from large burlap bags; in the restaurants, where chefs believe in using them liberally; and in the pubs, where cinnamon and nutmeg are sprinkled on the rum punches. If the Irish hadn't beaten them to the name, Grenadians might have called their land the Emerald Isle, for the lush pine forests and the thick brush on the hillsides give it a great, green beauty that few Caribbean islands duplicate.

Located in the Eastern Caribbean 90 miles north of Trinidad, Grenada is the most southerly of the Windward Islands. It is a nation composed of three inhabited islands and a few uninhabited islets: Grenada island is the largest, with 120 square miles and about 86,000 people; Carriacou, 16 miles north of Grenada, is 13 square miles and has a population of about 5,000; and Petit Martinique, 5 miles northeast of Carriacou, has 486 acres and a population of 700. Although Carriacou and Petit Martinique are popular for day trips and fishing and snorkeling excursions, most of the tourist action is on Grenada. Here, too, you will find the nation's capital, St. George's, and its largest harbor, St. George's Harbour.

Grenada (and Carriacou)

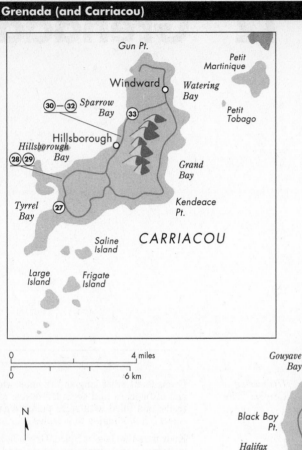

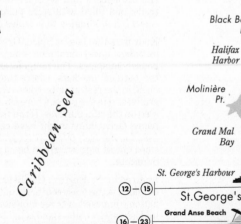

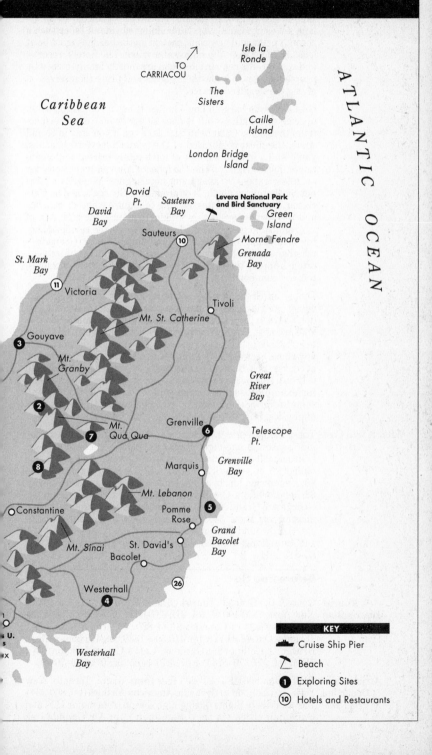

TO CARRIACOU

Isle la Ronde

The Sisters

Caille Island

London Bridge Island

Caribbean Sea

David Pt.

David Bay

Sauteurs Bay

Levera National Park and Bird Sanctuary

Green Island

Sauteurs ⑩

Morne Fendre

Grenada Bay

St. Mark Bay

⑪ Victoria

Tivoli

Mt. St. Catherine

❸ Gouyave

Mt. Granby

Great River Bay

❷

❼ Mt. Qua Qua

Grenville ❻

Telescope Pt.

❽

Marquis

Grenville Bay

Mt. Lebanon

○ Constantine

Pomme Rose

❺

Mt. Sinai

St. David's

Bacolet

Grand Bacolet Bay

Westerhall

㉖

❹

ATLANTIC OCEAN

KEY

⛴ Cruise Ship Pier

⌇ Beach

❶ Exploring Sites

⑩ Hotels and Restaurants

Westerhall Bay

U.

s

X

Although Grenada's tourism industry is undergoing an expansion, it is a controlled expansion, counterbalanced by the island's West Indian flavor. No building can stand taller than a coconut palm, and new construction on the beaches must be at least 165 feet from the high-water mark. The hotels, resorts, and restaurants remain small and are mostly family-owned by people who get to know their guests and pride themselves on giving personalized service.

Grenada is no bargain hop—in fact it has a reputation as an upscale destination—but it does sit lower on the price spectrum than some Caribbean islands. Even if you stay in Grand Anse, the most celebrated of the island's leeward beaches, you'll find a limited number of moderately priced, well-maintained hotels right on the Caribbean. Alternatively, consider even less expensive apartment hotels, guest houses, or inexpensive hotels up north, in or around St. George's, and on Carriacou. For all properties, be sure to inquire whether beaches and restaurants are within walking distance; the high cost of car rental and gas on Grenada can outweigh the savings of hotels in far-flung locations. Most accommodations on Grenada—whether expensive or budget—remain open during off-season, often dropping their rates by as much as 40%. Group packages, too, are common here.

Dining on Grenada need not be expensive either. Relatively cheap eateries are as common as pricey restaurants, and you don't have to pay a lot to take advantage of the island's remarkable produce. Public transportation, not available on all Caribbean islands, can convey you around the island's perimeter for anywhere between E.C. $1 and E.C. $6. There are drawbacks, of course: Schedules are unpredictable (you'd never be able to rely on a ride back to your hotel from St. George's after dinner, for example); seating arrangements are, well, cuddly; and some of the local drivers like to challenge accepted properties of physics. Still, the option exists for the open-minded.

What It Will Cost These sample prices, meant only as a general guide, are for high season. A one-night stay at a budget hotel is $40; a two-bedroom villa rental costs about $2,500 a week. An inexpensive dinner for one ranges from $15 to $20. A fast-food meal is $4–$6; a sandwich lunch, about $2.50–$3.50. Rum punch is about $2 here, while a Carib beer is $1.30. A taxi ride from St. George's to Grand Anse is $7. Rental cars with standard transmission cost about $45 a day. Jeeps and automatic-drive vehicles are around $5 more. A gallon of gas is about $2.25. A single-tank dive costs about $40; snorkel-equipment rental is $5–$10 a day.

Before You Go

Tourist Information Contact the **Grenada Tourist Office** (820 2nd Ave., Suite 900D, New York, NY 10017, tel. 212/687–9554 or 800/927–9554 fax 212/573–9731; in Canada: Suite 820, 439 University Ave., Toronto, Ont. M5G 1Y8, tel. 416/595–1339; fax 416/595–8278; in Britain: 1 Collingham Gardens, Earl's Court, London SW5 0HW, tel. 071/370–5164 or 071/370–5165; fax 071/370–7040).

Arriving and Departing **BWIA** (tel. 800/JET–BWIA) flies from Miami, Toronto, New York, and London to Grenada. **American Airlines** (tel. 800/334–7400) has daily flights during high season from major U.S. and Canadian cities via their San Juan hub; **Air Canada** (tel.

By Plane

800/776–3000) flies from Toronto to Barbados, where **LIAT** (Leeward Islands Air Transport, tel. 809/440–2796 or 809/440–2797) connects with flights to Grenada. LIAT has scheduled service between Barbados, Grenada, and Carriacou and also serves Trinidad and Venezuela.

From the Airport Taxis (usually in the form of modern Mitsubishi minivans) are available at Point Salines International Airport to take you to your hotel. Rates to St. George's and the hotels of Grand Anse and L'Anse aux Epines are about $10–$13. In Eastern Caribbean currency, this amounts to about E.C. $25–E.C. $35. A charge of E.C. $10 is tacked on to any ride taken after 6 PM. Some of the less centrally located hotels offer a free airport pickup, so inquire when you make your reservations. Unfortunately, there's no public transportation from the airport, so unless you've made arrangements in advance of your arrival, you're stuck with a cab ride.

Passports and Visas Passports are not required of U.S., Canadian, and British citizens, provided they have two proofs of citizenship (one with photo) and a return air ticket. A passport, even an expired one, is the best proof of citizenship; a driver's license with photo *and* an original birth certificate or voter registration card will also suffice.

Language English is the official language of Grenada.

Precautions Secure your valuables in the hotel safe. A problem with walking late at night in the Grand Anse/L'Anse aux Epines hotel districts is the lack of street lights (although 50 have recently been added). It's still dark enough to bump into things, maybe even into one of the cows that graze silently by the roadside.

Staying in Grenada

Important Addresses **Tourist Information:** The **Grenada Tourist Office** is located in St. George's (the Carenage, tel. 809/440–2279, fax 809/440–2123). It has maps, brochures, and information on accommodations, tours, and other services.

Emergencies **Police, Fire,** and **Ambulance:** In St. George's, Grand Anse, and L'Anse aux Epines, call 911. For other areas, check with your hotel. **Hospitals: St. George's Hospital** (tel. 809/440–2051, 809/440–2052, 809/440–2053). **Pharmacies: Gitten's** (Halifax St., St. George's, tel. 809/440–2165) is open Monday–Wednesday and Friday–Saturday 8–5, Thursday 8–noon and 1–5. **Gittens Drugmart** (Grand Anse, tel. 809/444–4954) is open weekdays and Saturday 9–8, Sunday and public holidays 9–noon. **Parris' Pharmacy Ltd.** (Victoria St., Grenville, tel. 809/442–7330), on the windward side of the island, is open Monday–Wednesday and Friday 9–4:30, Thursday 9–1, and Saturday 9–7.

Currency Grenada uses the Eastern Caribbean (E.C.) dollar. At press time, the exchange rate in banks was E.C. $2.67 to U.S. $1. Be sure to ask which currency is referred to when you make purchases and business transactions; prices are often quoted in E.C. dollars. Money can be exchanged at any bank or hotel. However, hotels are unable by law to give foreign currency in change or on departure. U.S. currency and traveler's checks are widely accepted. Most hotels and major restaurants accept credit cards. Prices quoted here are in U.S. dollars unless indicated otherwise.

Taxes and Service Charges Hotels add an 8% government tax; restaurants add a 10% tax. In addition, hotels and some restaurants add a 10% service charge to your bill. If not, a 10%–15% gratuity at mealtime should be added for a job well done.

The departure tax is E.C. $35 (about U.S. $13) for adults and E.C. $17.50 (about U.S. $6.50) for children ages 5 to 12. Children under 5 are exempt.

Getting Around

Buses Minivans ply the winding road between St. George's and Grand Anse Beach, where many of the hotels are located. Hail one anywhere along the way, pay E.C. $1, and hold on to your hat. They are available from about 6 to 8 daily except Sundays and public holidays. You can get anywhere on the island by minivan for E.C. $1–E.C. $6—a bargain by any standard—but be prepared for packed vehicles, unpredictable schedules, and some hair-raising maneuvers on mountainous roads and byways.

Taxis Taxis—also in the form of minivans, though without the crush of passengers—are plentiful, and rates are posted at the hotels and at the pier on the Carenage in St. George's. The trip from the airport to Grand Anse is E.C. $25, and from the airport to St. George's, E.C. $30. A charge of E.C. $10 is added to all fares for rides taken after 6 PM. Cabs are plentiful at all hotels, at the pier, and near the Tourist Office on the Carenage.

For trips outside St. George's, you'll be charged E.C. $4 (U.S. $1.50) a mile for the first 10 miles, and E.C. $3 (U.S. $1.12) a mile thereafter. From St. George's pier to L'Anse aux Epines, for example, count on a $12 fare; to Grand Anse, about $7; to the golf course, $6. Most tourists use taxis liberally, but the budget-minded should confine their use to getting back to their hotel after dark. For a guided tour of the island, you're better off pricewise using an established tour agency (*see* Guided Tours, *below*) than a taxi and driver.

Boats Twice a week, boats depart the Carenage in St. George's for Carriacou. Trips take about four hours; cost is $20 round-trip.

Rental Cars Driving here is not a leisurely venture. The main coastal road is windy and occasionally steep and narrow; potholes are part of the scenery. Driving is on the left side of the road. To rent a car, you will need a valid driver's license, with which you may obtain a local permit at a cost of E.C. $30. Rental cars cost about $45 a day or $250 a week with unlimited mileage. A Jeep and automatic drive run about $50 a day, and $275 a week. Gas costs about $2.25 per gallon. Your hotel can arrange a rental for you. Car-rental agencies in St. George's are numerous. **David's** (tel. 809/440–2399, 809/440–3038, or 809/444–4310) maintains four offices: Point Salines International Airport, the Ramada Renaissance Hotel, Archibold Avenue in St. George's, and South Wind Cottages in Grand Anse. **Avis** at Spice Isle Rental (tel. 809/440–3936 or 809/440–2624, after hours: 809/444–4563) is on Paddock and Lagoon roads in St. George's. Look for **McIntyre Bros. Ltd.** (tel. 809/440–2044 or 809/440–2901; after hours: 809/440–4053) on Lagoon Road in the capital.

Telephones and Mail Telephone service on the island has greatly improved in the last few years. Grenada can be dialed directly from the United States and Canada. The area code is 809. Long-distance calls from Grenada can now be dialed directly as well. The price of a local call from a pay phone is E.C. 25¢. Public booths at many locations accept U.S. quarters as well as E.C. 25¢ and E.C.$1 coins.

Airmail rates for letters to the United States and Canada are E.C. 75¢ for a half-ounce letter and E.C. 35¢ for a postcard.

Opening and Closing Times Store hours are generally weekdays 8–noon and 1–4, Saturday 8–noon; they are closed Sunday. Banks are open Monday-Thursday 8–noon, Friday 8–noon and 2:30–5.

Guided Tours **New Trends Tours** (Siesta Apartment Hotel, Grand Anse, tel. 809/444–1236, fax 809/444–4836) offers a wide selection of tours, as does **Arnold's Tours** (611 Archibald Ave., St. George's, tel. 809/440–0531 or 809/440–2213, fax 809/440–4118). Both agencies will customize their offerings for individual clients, but "Around the Island" is typically a seven-hour trip up the west coast to a spice plantation at Gouyave, then to the Mascoll plantation house, Morne Fendue, for lunch. The return route is through the east-coast town of Grenville and across scenic St. David's Parish. The tour costs about $35 per person.

A number of car-rental agencies and tour operators in St. George's offer standard tours such as the "Royal Drive," which includes the town of St. George's; scenic Westerhall Point, across the island on the Atlantic; a small fishing village; a sugar-processing factory; and Grand Anse Beach. The half-day excursion should run you about $25 or less. Agencies that offer such tours include **Otways Tours** (the Carenage, tel. 809/440–2558, 809/440–2423, fax 809/440–4179) and, in Grand Anse, **Carib Tours,** just south of the shopping center (tel. 809/444–4363 or 809/444–4364, fax 809/444–4560). A complete circle of the island takes about seven hours, but that's rushing it. To get a taste of the natural beauty of Grenada's interior, hook up with **Henry's Safari Tours** (tel. 809/444–5313, fax 809/444–4847), which offers tours ranging from three to seven hours. Henry will take you anywhere, and at whatever pace you're capable. You can pay up to $100 if you're on your own; hook up with three or more people, however, and the cost per person drops to $15–$35.

Exploring Grenada

Numbers in the margin correspond to points of interest on the Grenada (and Carriacou) map.

A half-day guided tour (usually around $25) makes a good introduction to Grenada and will familiarize you with the island's highlights. Take it from there. If you find yourself intrigued with a particular spot, you can probably return via public transportation, walk (depending upon distances), or combine the two. You may want to rent a car for an additional day to beach-hop or return to a favorite site, but keep in mind the steep daily rental rate and price of gas. Be prepared for challenging driving conditions even on the major coastal road that circles the island. (For more information, *see* Guided Tours and Getting Around, *above.*)

Our first itinerary is a walking tour of St. George's. It's easy and fun; you should have time to cover everything in a day and still enjoy a seafood lunch on the Carenage. The East and West Coast tours are driving tours that require more than a day to complete, but budget travelers can combine highlights from both tours and visit them via public transportation or in a single day of driving. The Grand Anse tour comprises beach, boutiques, restaurants, and nightlife in an easily traversed area. Round up your sightseeing by asking one of the American medical students here where *they* go to relax over a Carib beer.

St. George's   Grenada's capital city and major port is one of the most picturesque and truly West Indian towns in the Caribbean. Pastel warehouses cling to the curving shore along the horseshoe-shaped Carenage, the harborside thoroughfare; rainbow-colored houses rise above it and disappear into the green hills. A

❶   walking tour of **St. George's** can be made in about two hours, particularly with the help of the Department of Tourism's free brochure, *Historical Walking Tour of St. George's*, which directs you to 21 points of historical interest. Pick it up at the office on the Carenage (*see below*).

Start on the **Carenage,** a walkway along St. George's Harbour and the town's main thoroughfare. Ocean liners dock at the pier at the eastern end, and the **Delicious Landing** restaurant (tel. 809/440–3948), with outdoor tables, is at the western end. In between are the **public library,** a number of small **shops,** the **Grenada Tourist Office,** and two more good restaurants, **Rudolf's** and the **Nutmeg** (*see* Dining, *below*), the latter boasting a huge open window that provides a great view of the harbor.

You can reach the **Grenada National Museum** by walking along the west end of the Carenage and taking Young Street west to Monckton Street. The museum has a small, interesting collection of ancient and colonial artifacts and recent political memorabilia. *Young and Monckton Sts., tel. 809/440–3725. Admission: $1 adults, 25¢ children under 18. Open weekdays 9–4:30; Sat. 10–1:30.*

Walk west along Young Street, turn left on Cross Street, and you'll reach the **Esplanade,** the thoroughfare that runs along the ocean side of town. At the intersection of Cross Street and the Esplanade is the **Yellow Poui Art Gallery** (tel. 809/440–3878), which keeps irregular hours (tourist brochures put it this way: "Open by appointment or by chance"). The studio displays art from Grenada, Jamaica, Trinidad, and Guyana and canvases by British, German, and French artists now living here. On the nearby Esplanade you'll find a row of tiny shops that sell such treats as guava jelly and coconut fudge. *Shopping hours: weekdays 9:15–12:15 and 1:15–3:15, Sat. 9:15–12:15; closed Sun. Appointments may be scheduled after hours.*

Take the Esplanade north to Granby Street and turn right. Granby Street will take you to **Market Square,** which comes alive every Saturday morning from 8 to noon with vendors selling baskets and fresh produce, including tropical fruit you can eat on the spot. Don't miss it!

Walk back on Granby Street to Halifax Street and turn left. At the intersection of Halifax and Church streets is **St. Andrew's Presbyterian Church,** built in 1830. Follow Church Street east to Gore Street, to **St. George's Anglican Church,** built in 1828. It's lined with plaques representing Grenada in the 18th and 19th centuries. Continue up Church Street to the **York House,** built around 1800. Now home to the Senate and Supreme Court, it's open to the public for unstructured visits. Go back to Market Hill and turn left to reach **St. George's Methodist Church,** built in 1820, on Green Street near Tyrrel Street.

Take Tyrrel Street east to the corner of Park Lane to see the **Marryshow House.** Built in 1917, it combines Victorian and West Indian architecture. The Marryshow also houses the **Marryshow Folk Theatre,** Grenada's first cultural center. Plays, West Indian dance and music, and poetry readings are presented here on occasion. *Tyrrel St., near Bain Alley, tel. 809/440–2451. Admission free. Open weekdays 8:30–4:30, Sat. 9–1.*

Head back west on Tyrrel Street and turn left onto Church Street. **Fort George** is at the southern tip of Church Street. The fort, rising above the point that separates the harbor from the ocean, was built by the French in 1705. The inner courtyard now houses the police headquarters. *Church St., no phone. Outer courtyard open to the public. Admission free. Open daily during daylight hours.*

The fastest way from the Carenage to the Esplanade is through the **Sendall Tunnel,** slightly north of Fort George. Take it if you're too tired to walk up the steep hill.

The West Coast The coast road north from St. George's winds past soaring mountains and valleys covered with banana and breadfruit trees, palms, bamboo, and tropical flowers. You can drive to ❷ **Concord Falls,** about 8 miles north of St. George's, then hike 2 miles to the main falls; it's another hour from there to a second, spectacular waterfall. Use the small changing room at the main falls to don your bathing suit; during the dry months when the currents aren't too strong, you can take a dip under the cascades. About 15 minutes farther north is the town of **Gouyave,** center of the nutmeg industry.

❸ **Dougaldston Estate,** near the entrance to the town, has a spice factory where you can see cocoa, nutmeg, mace, cloves, cinnamon, and other spices in their natural state, laid out on giant trays to dry in the sun. Old women walk barefoot through the spices, shuffling them to ensure even drying. *Gouyave, no phone. Admission free. Open weekdays 9–4.*

The East Coast Start your tour at **Westerhall,** a residential area about 5 miles ❹ southeast of St. George's, known for its beautiful villas, gardens, and panoramic views. From here, take a dirt road north ❺ to **Grand Bacolet Bay,** a jagged peninsula on the Atlantic where the surf pounds against deserted beaches. Some miles north is ❻ **Grenville,** the island's second-largest city. From here you can watch schooners set sail for the outer islands. As in St. George's, Saturday is market day, and the town fills with local people doing their shopping for the week. Cooking enthusiasts may want to see the town's spice-processing factory, which is open to the public.

If you take the interior route back to St. George's, you'll get a full sense of the lush, mountainous nature of the island. There is only one paved road that cuts across the island. Leaving Grenville and heading for St. George's, you'll wind upward through the rain forest until you're surrounded by mist, then you'll descend onto the sunny hillsides. In the middle of the ❼ island is **Grand Etang National Park.** The lake, in the crater of an extinct volcano here, is a 13-acre glasslike expanse of cobalt-blue water. The area is a bird sanctuary and forest reserve, where you can fish and hike. *Main interior road, halfway between Grenville and St. George's, tel. 809/442–7425. Admission free. Open weekdays 8–4.*

8 At **Annandale Falls and Visitors' Centre,** a mountain stream cascades 50 feet into a pool surrounded by such exotic tropical flora as liana vines and elephant ears. This is a good swimming and picnic spot. *Main interior road, 15 min east of St. George's, tel. 809/440–2452. Suggested donation: $1. Open daily 9–5.*

Grand Anse and the South End Most of the island's hotels and its nightlife are in Grand Anse or the adjacent community of L'Anse aux Epines (launce-au-peen), which means Cove of Pines. Here you will find one of the two campuses of **St. George's University Medical School.** Chez Josephine, its unofficial beachfront cafeteria, serves drinks and light snacks. **9**

The second campus is in **True Blue,** a residential area near L'Anse aux Epines. To reach it, take Grand Anse Road south toward the airport and turn left just before you reach the airport. Although the road is unnamed, it is the only one off Grand Anse Road.

The **Grand Anse Shopping Centre** has a supermarket/liquor store, a clothing store, shoe store, a fast-food joint, and several small gift shops with good-quality souvenirs.

Grenada's Grenadines **Carriacou, Petit Martinique,** and a handful of uninhabited specks that comprise the nation of Grenada are north of Grenada island and part of the Grenadines, a chain of 32 tiny islands and cays.

Carriacou is a little island (13 square miles) with a lot of punch. A hideaway with "over a hundred rum shops and only one gasoline station," this place moves the fastest Manhattan metabolism down several notches and exudes the kind of ebullient spirit and goodwill you hope for (but don't always find) in a Caribbean retreat. Don't come here if you don't want peace, if you do want luxurious amenities, or if you would suffer coldly a parrot on your breakfast table.

Getting to Carriacou is not cheap (*see* Getting Around, *above*), so a day trip here is a somewhat pricey way to spend a few hours. However, budget travelers may want to consider staying on this little island for a few days. Room rates in Spartan accommodations are rock bottom, and finding budget dining is easy. Carriacou is a wonderful place to hang out if you really want to relax—as in perfecting the art of doing nothing. Moreover, the quality of the scuba diving and snorkeling here at times surpasses that of the larger island's.

Beaches

Grenada has some 80 miles of coastline, 65 bays, and 45 white-sand beaches, many with secluded little coves. All the beaches are public and within an easy cab ride of St. George's. Most are located on the Caribbean, south of St. George's in the Grand Anse and L'Anse aux Epines areas, where most of the hotels are clustered. Virtually every hotel, apartment complex, and residential area has its own beach or tiny cove.

The loveliest and most popular beach is **Grand Anse,** about a 10-minute taxi ride from St. George's. It's a gleaming, 2-mile curve of sand and clear, gentle surf. You'll find rougher waters and shorter stretches of sand at **L'Anse aux Epines,** but the windward side of the island has its advantages: Rainfall is slightly less, and the little cove beaches are less populated, thereby discouraging hawkers and Romeos in search of the perfect foreign companion.

Morne Rouge Beach is on the Caribbean side, about 1 mile south of Grand Anse Bay and 3 miles south of St. George's Harbour. The beach forms a half-mile-long crescent and has a gentle surf excellent for swimming. A small café serves light meals during the day. In the evening, there's the disco, Fantazia 2001 (*see* Nightlife, *below*).

Levera National Park and Bird Sanctuary is at the northern tip of the island, where the Caribbean meets the Atlantic. The southernmost Grenadines are visible in the distance. The surf is rougher here than on the Caribbean beaches, but it is great for body surfing or watching the waves roll in. In 1991, this area, with its thick mangroves for food and protection, became an official sanctuary for nesting seabirds and seldom-seen tropical parrots. Also of interest here are fine Arawak ruins and petroglyphs.

Sports and the Outdoors

Bicycling Level ground is about as common here as are reindeer, but that doesn't stop the aerobically primed. What's more, 15-speed mountain bikes are cheaper than four-wheel-drive vehicles and can get you to a lot of the same places. Try **Ride Grenada** (L'Anse aux Epines, tel. 809/444–1157).

Diving and A single-tank dive costs about $40 here. **Dive Grenada** on Grand
Snorkeling Anse Beach (at Ramada Renaissance, tel. 809/444–4371 or 809/444–4372, ext. 638, fax 809/444–4800) offers a variety of scuba courses, including certification. It also transports experienced divers to reefs and shipwrecks. Their single-tank dive ($40) includes tank, weights, boat trip, and dive leader; a night dive is $5 extra. Head for Carriacou for mind-bending marine beauty. The water-sports center at the **Silver Beach Resort** (Silver Beach, tel. 809/443–7337, fax 809/443–7165) offers training, equipment rental, and water-sports activities for all skill levels.

Snorkel-equipment rental on Grenada costs between $5 and $10 per day. **The Moorings** (*see* Sailing, *below*) rents gear for $40 a week. Beginners will be happy bobbing up and down the waters at Grand Anse, but the more experienced should inquire about outlying spits, islands, and shipwrecks where more colorful and abundant underwater life appears.

Golf The **Grenada Golf Club** in Grand Anse (tel. 809/444–4128) has an 18-hole golf course that charges $16 for greens fees; your hotel will make arrangements for you.

Hiking Grenada is a mountainous, volcanically-formed terrain, and inland regions are covered with riots of lush green, tropical growth. You'll need a guide for interior jaunts. Trails aren't always marked, and you may find yourself blazing through tangled jungle mass or sliding down muddy slopes on your derrière. **Henry's Safari Tours** (*see* Guided Tours, *above*) offers lower rates for three or more in a group. If you don't want to use a guide, stick to tame walks such as hiking from Concord Falls to the upper falls (*see* Exploring, *above*).

Sailing The **Moorings' Club Mariner** (tel. 800/535–7289 in the U.S., tel. 800/633–7348 in Canada), located at the Secret Harbour Hotel, offers a full-day sail for $40 a person, and a half-day sail to

Calivigny Island for $25 a person. A trip to Hog Island is $15 a person, lower for groups of five or more. Costs include snorkel-equipment rental, but guests are expected to bring or buy their own lunch and drinks. For qualified sailors, the Moorings offers a 23.5-foot Beneteau for $30 an hour; a 21-foot Impulse for $25 an hour, and a 15-foot Precision for $20. For $15 an hour, you can climb aboard a little dinghy with an outboard engine. The major hotels on Grand Anse Beach have water-sports centers where you can rent small sailboats, Windsurfers, jet skis, aqua bikes, and Sunfish.

Tennis Several hotels have tennis courts that are free to their guests, but most of these are at expensive properties that are out of our affordable price ranges. If there are no courts where you're staying, you can play at some private clubs on the island or pay a court rental at a resort. Count on an average hourly fee of $10.

Shopping

The best souvenirs in Grenada are little spice baskets filled with cinnamon, nutmeg, mace, bay leaf, vanilla, and ginger. You can find them in practically every shop, but your best bet is the Saturday morning market in downtown St. George's. Bananas are a steal here, and big, palm-tied bundles of cinnamon bark resembling cords of wood cost about $2. Note: Do not take photographs at the market without asking an individual's permission. Vendors who stroll the beach in Grand Anse also sell spice baskets as well as fabric dolls, T-shirts, hats, fans, visors woven from green palm, and black-coral jewelry. (Be aware that environmental groups discourage tourists from buying coral that is designated as endangered species, because the reefs are not always harvested carefully.) Shops are open weekdays 8–4. Many are closed noon–1. Saturday hours are 8–noon. Shops are generally closed Sunday, but some make exceptions when cruise ships are in port.

Good Buys Stick to island handicrafts. While even some of these can be
St. George's expensive, many are more reasonably priced. **Tikal** (Young St., tel. 809/440–2310) carries mainly premium-priced goods, but you can find mahogany walking sticks for $19 and brightly colored batik pareos for $38. Carved wood comes in a variety of forms—a slender letter opener whittled from local wood costs $5.40. **Spice Island Perfumes** on the Carenage (tel. 809/440–2006) has shelves of T-shirts, spice baskets ($3.25), and hand-painted cotton caftans.

Grand Anse Try **Imagine** (Grand Anse Shopping Complex, tel. 809/444–4028) for assorted island creations. The books, postcards, and notepaper here aren't bargains, but woven hats and baskets are more reasonable. Those who don't consider $15–$20 for a pair of pierced earrings to be an extravagance can find lovely West Indian jewelry here.

Dining

Restaurants here come in all price ranges; you'll find them serving entrées priced anywhere from $4 to $20. Unlike most Caribbean islands, which have a scarcity of fresh produce, Grenada has everything from cabbages and tomatoes to bananas, mangoes, papaya (called pawpaw), plantains, melons, callaloo (similar to spinach), breadfruits, oranges, tangerines, limes, *christophines* (similar to squash), avocados—the list is endless. In addition, fresh seafood of all kinds, including lobster and oyster, is also plentiful. Conch, known here as *lambi*, is very popular and appears on most menus in some form, usually as a stew. Be sure to try one of the exotic ice creams made from avocado or nutmeg. Almost all the Grenadian restaurants serve local dishes, which are varied enough to be continually interesting. Rum punches are served everywhere, but no two places make them exactly alike. The local beer, Carib, is also very popular.

If you're renting a self-contained unit and want to save money by cooking, ply your way through the crowds at the Saturday morning market in St. George's for fresh fruits and vegetables. Then look over the selection at **D'Green Grocers**, on the main road between Grand Anse Shopping Complex and the new Le Marquis mall, where everything except the apples is fresh and locally harvested. You can stock up on paper products here, too. Another option are the more expensive, large supermarkets, including **Foodland** (Lagoon Rd., St. George's) and **Food Fair** (at the Carenage and in Grand Anse). Stay away from the marine minimarkets unless you're desperate: They cater to jet-set yachtsmen with megabucks who've probably never heard of comparison shopping.

Highly recommended restaurants are indicated by a star ★.

Category	Cost*
Moderate	$20–$40
Inexpensive	$10–$20
Budget	under $10

*per person, excluding drinks, service, and sales tax (10%)

Grenada **Betty Mascoll's Great House.** Although it's a one-hour drive
★ from St. George's, this restaurant is definitely worth the trip. The owner, Mrs. Mascoll, serves only lunch—and what a lunch! The buffet usually includes her legendary pepper pot, a stew of pork, oxtail, and other meats, rumored to have been bubbling for years. The rum punches, fragrant with fresh nutmeg, are truly intoxicating. *St. Patrick's Parish, near Sauteurs, tel. 809/440–9330. Reservations required. No credit cards. Moderate.*

★ **Canboulay.** At this pink-washed building trimmed in bright green and cobalt blue, you'll find perhaps the finest food on the island, and certainly the most subtle and sophisticated use of local produce. Erik and Gina-Lee Johnson, a Trinidadian couple with backgrounds in architecture and business administration, designed this recent addition to the Grenadian culinary family. Menus change every few months, but recent winners include tomato fettucine topped with garlic and lemon-flavored fish sauce, fresh tuna with a tangy citrus pepper sauce, and seasoned shrimp, rolled in coconut and a light beer batter, then fried and served with sweet pineapple relish. Desserts here will revive flagging appetites, with such marvels as Alamanda Ice, a flower-shaped cookie filled with vanilla ice cream and passion fruit and served with a guava, carambola, and cherry *coulis*. The most expensive entrée here is E.C. $85 (U.S. $32), but that includes starter, salad or sorbet (we recommend the latter), main course served with vegetables and a choice of rice or tuber, dessert, coffee, Grenadian frivolities (candied sweets), and government tax. It's a gem. *Morne Rouge, St. George's, tel. 809/444–4401. Reservations advised. Dress: casual but elegant. AE, D, MC, V. Closed Sat. lunch and Sun. Moderate.*

The Boatyard. Smack in the middle of a marina, this restaurant is a lively place, filled with embassy personnel and expatriates. Lunches include burgers, fish-and-chips, and deep-fried shrimp. Dinner features club steaks, lobster, and different types of meat and seafood brochettes. In season (late Dec.-mid-Apr.) there's a steel band on Saturday night, jazz on Sunday, and disco music on Friday night. *L'Anse aux Epines, tel. 809/444–4662. MC, V. Moderate.*

The Nutmeg. Fresh seafood is the specialty of this second-floor restaurant that has a great view of the harbor. Try the grilled turtle steaks, lobsters, or shrimp. *The Carenage, St. George's, tel. 809/440–2539. Dress: informal. AE, D, MC, V. Moderate.*

Rudolf's. This informal, publike place offers fine West Indian fare. Skip the attempts at haute cuisine "Viennoise" or "Parisienne," and enjoy the crab back, lambi, and delectable nutmeg ice cream. This is *the* place for eavesdropping on local gossip. Even for Grenada the rum punches are lethal. *The Carenage, St. George's, tel. 809/440–2241. No credit cards. Closed Sun. Moderate.*

Cot Bam. Wedged between the Coyaba Hotel and the Medical School on Grand Anse beach, this bar/restaurant/night spot with a tin roof and bamboo railings is a place to kick back and enjoy. Order a chicken *roti* (curried meat, potatoes, and beans wrapped in a giant tortilla) served with coleslaw for E.C. $6 and a Carib beer, and you're set for the evening. It's within walking distance of all the Grand Anse hotels; the staff is a delight; and you can hop over in your shorts after a long day at the beach to dance or socialize with abandon. *Grand Anse, tel. 809/444–2050. Open Sun.–Thurs. 10 AM–midnight, Fri.–Sat. 10 AM–3 AM. AE. Inexpensive.*

★ **Mama's.** This restaurant is more like a diner, West Indian style and very charming. One of Mama's daughters will set generous helpings of local specialties before you—probably some roast turtle, lobster salad, christophine salad, cabbage salad, or fried plantain, as well as such exotica as armadillo, opossum, and sea urchin. Menus don't list prices, but the broad buffet offerings are available at a fixed E.C. $45 per person. Request the iguana in advance. You will not leave hungry. *Lagoon Rd., St. George's, tel. 809/440–1459. Reservations required. No credit cards. Inexpensive.*

Tabanka. German-owned and managed, this spanking white, open-air café overlooking the water is a new addition to the Grand Anse community. It specializes in fresh everything: juices, pastries, sorbets, and coffees. Dinners include a pepper steak concoction for about $20, Spanish omelet ($10), fresh fish, and lamb chops ($14). Lunchtime orders won't set you back more than $5 or $6. *Grand Anse, tel. 809/444–1300. No credit cards. Open 10 AM–11 PM. Inexpensive.*

Hooters. Opened in October 1992, Hooters fills Grand Anse's need for a West Indian fast-food spot. This small, white cement structure with a tin roof and orange trim is located in the Le Marquis Shopping Centre. Inside, waitresses wear baseball caps, and seating consists of stools at the counter or umbrella-canopied picnic tables (unfortunately situated next to a noisy roadway). Order a fish burger, conch salad, or potato roti, all of which run about $2. If you're having a french-fries attack, an order here sells for about $1. *Le Marquis Shopping Centre, Grand Anse, tel. 809/444–3170. No credit cards. Closed Sun. lunch and Mon. Budget.*

Sugar and Spice. This is a favorite of medical students and mothers with ice-cream–addicted offspring. It's a quick, easy-on-the-wallet stop in the Grand Anse shopping center, and the food is fair to middling. Pizza by the slice is about $1.30, and a ham-and-cheese sub goes for $1.70. *Grand Anse Shopping Complex, tel. 809/444–4597. No credit cards. Closed Sun. lunch and Mon. Budget.*

Carriacou **Barba's Oyster Shell.** This place is elemental, but it is the only one that offers Carriacou's rare and succulent mangrove oysters. *Tyrrel Bay, Carriacou, tel. 809/443–7454. No credit cards. Inexpensive.*

Scrapers. At Tyrrel Bay, Scrapers serves up lobster, conch, and an assortment of fresh catches, along with an artless spirit and decor seasoned with occasional calypsonian serenades (owner Steven Gay "Scraper" is a pro). Order a rum punch and exercise your right to do nothing. Lunch fare is a bargain—a big bowl of callalou soup and a cheeseburger cost about $5. *Tyrrel Bay, Carriacou, tel. 809/443–7403. AE, D, MC, V. Budget–Inexpensive.*

Lodging

Grenada has a healthy number of affordable accommodations. Even in Grand Anse there are a few moderately priced hotels right on the beach. Another option is to stay at an apartment hotel, which allows you to save on meals and taxes; granted, you may not be sitting on the sand at some of these places, but an easy five- or 10-minute amble will get you there. For even greater savings, look into guest houses or less elegant hotel accommodations in the north, in or around the capital, and in Carriacou; some of these will even pick you up at the airport free of charge. Many of these properties have access to lovely stretches of sand and provide all meals at their in-house restaurant, which means you won't have to rent a car for the duration of your stay. Do make inquiries when you call, as the high cost of car rental and gas prices here can outweigh the savings at more remote accommodations. Campgrounds are virtually nonexistent on Grenada, and most villa rentals creep into the extravagant range (with some exceptions; *see below*).

The off-season is the time to really save here; prices are discounted 20%–40%. The availability of meal plans (listed in the service information of each review, *below*) can vary with the season; assume those specified apply year-round unless otherwise noted.

Highly recommended lodgings are indicated by a star ★.

Category	Cost*
Moderate	$100–$150
Inexpensive	$50–$100
Budget	under $50

*All prices are for a standard double room for two, excluding 8% tax and a 10% service charge. To estimate rates for hotels offering MAP, add about $30–$40 per person per day to the above price ranges.

Hotels
Grenada
★

Blue Horizons Cottage Hotel. This comfortable hotel with handsome mahogany furnishings is a very good value; it is set among the palms around a large, sunny lawn and swimming pool on 6½ acres. Grand Anse Beach is a six-minute walk down the hill, where the sister hotel, the Spice Island Inn (a more expensive property), sprawls along 1,600 feet of beach. Water sports are free for guests at either hotel. Guests may eat at either property, and evening entertainment alternates between the two. *Box 41, Grand Anse, St. George's, tel. 809/444–4316, 809/444–4592 or 800/223–9815 in the U.S., fax 809/444–2815. 32 suites with terraces. Facilities: restaurant, 2 bars, lounge, pool. AE, MC, V. EP, CP, MAP. Moderate.*

The Flamboyant Hotel and Cottages. Once a week, you'll find a wildly diverse crowd of Italians, Germans, Americans, British, Grenadians, and Dutch gathered on the terrace of the Flamboyant's Beachside restaurant, engaged in the ferociously competitive sport of crab racing. This sums up the atmosphere at this fifth largest hotel in Grenada, a jovial place presided over by charming managing director Lawrence Lambert. The hotel is set on a hillside overlooking Grand Anse Beach (a short walk down a path will get you there), and a 10-minute drive from downtown St. George's. Rooms are fresh and airy, with white walls and dark-wood furnishings. *Box 214, St. George's, tel. 809/444–4247, fax 809/444–1234. 16 rooms, 20 suites (with kitchenettes), 2 cottages. Facilities: freshwater swimming pool, bar, restaurant, satellite TV, free use of snorkeling equipment. AE, D, MC, V. EP, BP, MAP. Inexpensive–Moderate.*

La Sagesse Nature Center. Set its own beach 10 miles from Point Salines Airport, the center has a guest house with basic but spacious rooms. There are an old sugar mill and rum distillery at the entrance. Mangroves, a salt-pond bird sanctuary, and hiking trails provide a peaceful, unspoiled setting. It's a good bet for nature lovers and those who don't fancy rousing nightlife. The restaurant here serves breakfast, lunch, and dinner, and most of the rooms have small kitchens. Mike Meranski, the American owner/manager, cheerfully runs guests into town for grocery supplies and shopping when he takes his daughter to school. *Box 44, St. David's, tel. 809/444–6458, fax 809/444–6458. 4 double rooms. Facilities: restaurant, bar, beach, satellite TV. MC, V. EP, MAP. Inexpensive.*

Bailey's Inn. This family-run property overlooking St. George's and the Carenage provides a laid-back, restful environment. From here, the capital's attractions are a leisurely walk away. Muriel Bailey's West Indian cuisine makes liberal use of local produce; a full American meal plan is available. All rooms have private baths and ceiling fans, and two apartments have kitchenettes. It's a 10–15-minute drive to Grand Anse Beach. *Springs, Box 82, St. George's, tel. 809/440–2912, fax*

809/440–4179. 12 rooms, 2 apartments. Facilities: dining room, bar, boutique. No credit cards. EP, CP, MAP. Budget.

Victoria Hotel. Overlooking the Caribbean, the Victoria is situated on the northwest coast of Grenada, not far from Sauteurs Bay and Levera National Park and Bird Sanctuary. This fresh and charming property is a cut above the typical budget hotel, with open-air, high-ceilinged corridors on the second story and a wood-paneled bar and restaurant on the first floor. The single and double rooms are small, and closet space is at a minimum, but tall, sloped ceilings elongate the cozier units and allow for ample entry of light. All rooms have fans, private shower and bath, and TV. The hotel offers free airport transfers (which would otherwise cost you $30–$40). Public transportation is easily accessible to Sauteurs to the north, and to St. George's or Grand Anse to the south (you'll need the latter, as the sandy, postage-stamp sized area outside the hotel barely qualifies as a beach). The restaurant serves breakfast, lunch, and dinner. This is the sort of spot for those who'll enjoy the natural spirit of the island by day, then gather to share their exploits at night over conch and Carib beer. *Queen St., Victoria, St. Mark's, tel. 809/444–9367 or 809/444–8104. 6 doubles, 4 singles. Facilities: restaurant, bar. AE, MC, V. EP. Budget.*

Carriacou **Cassada Bay Resort.** Cabins here, on the south side of Carriacou, shimmy down the side of a hilltop overlooking the sea, and offer an unadorned but peaceful hideaway. The hotel offers free transport to a private island for snorkeling and windsurfing (the property is not on the beach). You'll get hooked on the lemonade here, some of the finest this side of the equator. *Carriacou, tel. 809/443–7494, fax 809/443–7672. 20 doubles. Facilities: restaurant, bar, water-sports center. AE, DC, MC, V. EP, CP, MAP. Moderate.*

Silver Beach Resort. This 18-room hotel is tucked away on stretches of pristine beach. All rooms have private patios and ocean views. An owner-managed hotel, it has the biggest scuba facilities in the Grenadines and, incidentally, is the best place on the island for a hearty, early-morning breakfast in its open-air restaurant by the water. *Silver Beach, Carriacou, tel. 809/443–7337, fax 809/443–7165. 12 doubles (2 with kitchenettes), 6 cottages with kitchenettes. Facilities: snorkeling, windsurfing, spearfishing, day trip to offshore islets, boutique, gift shop, complete scuba certification course, in-house bus, complimentary transfers from Carriacou airport, car rental. AE, MC, V. EP, CP, MAP. Inexpensive–Moderate.*

Scrapers Bay View Holiday Cottages. Mighty Skyscraper opened his place on Tyrrel Bay in August 1992. Though clean and well maintained, this slightly funky property is not for those who need the antiseptic familiarity of chain hotels (bathroom facilities, for instance, are curtained). Seven units, four of which have kitchens, are housed in duplex cottages across the road from the bay and beach. You can get along without a car here, though you may feel confined after three or four days. Lively nightlife and cordial hosts await you; Mr. Skyscraper won't hesitate to tell you he makes the best rum punch in the Caribbean. *Tyrell Bay, Carriacou, tel. 809/443–7403. 7 rooms. Facilities: restaurant/bar, souvenir shop. AE, D, MC, V. EP. Budget.*

Hope's Inn. Six rooms here come dirt cheap, but you'll have to accustom yourself to common toilets and curtained showers in the hallway. The structure is bright white with maroon trim, aqua stairways, and an occasional splash of pink on exterior walls. Fans are provided, and a large kitchenette on the second floor can be used by guests. A restaurant and bar are slated to open by winter of 1993. You'll need a car to get to the beach. *L'Esterre, Carriacou, tel. 809/443–7457. 6 rooms. Facilities: kitchenette. No credit cards. EP. Budget.*

Villas and Apartment Rentals Villas aren't cheap in Grenada, although you'll find more affordable options in Carriacou. But there are exceptions. The furnished villa in Grand Anse (*see below*) even falls in our Budget range if shared by four adults (two children can be accommodated comfortably as well). Malcolm and Rosamond Cameron of **Down Island** (tel. and fax 809/443–8182) run a sterling rental management service on Carriacou that offers several highly desirable properties.

Grenada **Tapawingo.** This two-bedroom villa, on a hillside in Grand Anse near the Ramada Renaissance hotel, can be rented by the week or month. Although it doesn't boast the luxury amenities, such as pool and gardening service, of more expensive hideaways, this 2,500-square-foot residence does have maid service, and comes at a reasonable price. You'll need to call by July for a December booking. *Grand Anse, tel. 809/444–2848, fax 809/444–2822. Moderate.*

Wave Crest Holiday Apartments. Joyce Dabrieo, a former nurse, takes great pains to keep these 20 sunny rooms—all with balconies and air-conditioning—spotless and well-maintained. Apartments have kitchens. The buildings are surrounded by landscaped flower gardens. Wave Crest is an excellent value, and lies within a five-minute walk of Grand Anse beach. *Box 278, St. George's, tel. 809/444–4116, fax 809/444–4847. 4 rooms, 14 one-bedroom apartments, 2 two-bedroom apartments. AE, D, MC, V. Inexpensive.*

Carriacou **Villa Serenity.** This hacienda-style lodging with polished wood floors and outdoor railed terrace looks out over Hillsborough Bay. A main section housing a combination living/dining room plus a galley-style kitchen has a stone patio with sea and mountain view. A second structure is comprised of two bedrooms, both with private baths. A 15-minute walk brings you to a little sandy swimming cover; it's an even shorter walk to catch a bus to town, but if you want more mobility, a car is advisable. *Down Island Rental, tel. and fax 809/443–8182. Facilities: maid service 3 times a week. Moderate.*

Studio "Nice One." A wraparound veranda at this 600-square-foot accommodation has terrific views of the harbor and outlying islands. Airy and casual, Nice One comes equipped with a kitchen, futon sofa bed, and tiled shower room. Fans, mosquito nets, and some strategically hung hammocks on the patio will convert any drifter to a lifetime commitment to the island. A five-minute walk will get you to the beach; a 10-minute walk takes you to the bus that goes into town. *Down Island Rental, tel. and fax 809/443–8182. Facilities: single camp bed for third person, part-time maid service available (at extra cost). Inexpensive.*

Off-Season Bets Many of the premium-priced hotels in Grenada drop their room rates drastically during the summer. All of the following qualify for a Moderate listing during the off season: **Calabash** (Box 382, St. George's, tel. 809/444–4234); **Coyaba** (Box 336, Grand Anse, St. George's, tel. 809/444–4129); **Ramada Renaissance** (Box 441, Grand Anse, St. George's, tel. 809/444–4371); and **Secret**

Harbour (Box 11, St. George's, tel. 809/444–4439). The same goes for a handful of villas—call **Bain & Bertrand Realtors** (tel. 809/444–2848) regarding their three-bedroom **Spice of Life** located in L'Anse aux Epines, or **Down Island Rental** (tel. 809/443–8182) in Carriacou for word on their **Villa "Down Island,"** with plunge pool and maid service.

Nightlife

Fantazia 2001 (Gem Apartments premises, Morne Beach, tel. 809/444–4224) is a popular disco on Morne Rouge Beach where soca, reggae, and cadance are local steps, in addition to international tapes. There is a small cover charge on Friday and Saturday nights. **Le Sucrier** (Grand Anse, tel. 800/444–1068) has reopened in the Sugar Mill on Wednesday, Thursday, Friday, and Saturday from 9 PM to 3 AM, with live jazz on Thursday and "oldies" night on Wednesday. Friday night only is "the" night at the **Boatyard Restaurant and Bar** (L'Anse aux Epines beach in the Marina, tel. 809/444–4662), from 11 PM till sunup, with international discs spun by a smooth-talkin' local DJ. Check out **Cot Bam** (tel. 809/444–2050) on Grand Anse Beach for a night of dancing, dining, and socializing. The place is open until 3 AM on Friday and Saturday, and it definitely hits the spot for visitors who want something simple, lively, and friendly for little money. Don't forget the **Beachside Terrace** (St. George's, tel. 809/444–4247) at the Flamboyant Hotel in Grand Anse. Crab racing on Monday nights, a live steel band on Wednesdays, and a beach barbecue with calypso music on Friday evenings draw an international set who savor a casual, unpretentious environment.

On Carriacou, rum flows freely at the **Hillsborough Bar** (Carriacou, tel. 809/443–7932), a small, white, flat-topped structure on the main street of the island's seat of government—a town of about 600 citizens.

13 Guadeloupe

Updated by
Nigel Fisher

It's a steamy hot Saturday in mid-August. There may be a tropical depression brewing somewhere to the west. It's that time of year. But the mood in Pointe-à-Pitre, Guadeloupe's commercial center, is anything but depressed. Amid music and laughter, women adorned with gold jewelry and the traditional madras and foulard parade through the streets. Balanced on their heads are huge baskets decorated with miniature kitchen utensils and filled with mangoes, papayas, breadfruits, christophines, and other island edibles. The procession wends its way to the Cathédrale de St-Pierre et St-Paul, where a high mass is celebrated. A five-hour feast with music, song, and dance will follow.

The Fête des Cuisinières (Cooks' Festival) takes place annually in honor of St. Laurent, patron saint of cooks. The parading *cuisinières* are the island's women chefs, an honored group. This festival gives you a tempting glimpse of one of Guadeloupe's stellar attractions—its cuisine. The island's more than 200 restaurants serve some of the best food in all the Caribbean.

Guadeloupe looks like a giant butterfly resting on the sea between Antigua and Dominica. Its two wings—Basse-Terre and Grande-Terre—are the two largest islands in the 659-square-mile Guadeloupe archipelago, which includes the little islands of Marie-Galante, La Désirade, and Les Saintes, as well as French St. Martin and St. Barthélemy to the north. Mountainous 312-square-mile Basse-Terre (lowland) lies on the leeward side, where the winds are "lower." Smaller, flatter Grande-

Terre (218 square miles) gets the "bigger" winds on its windward side. The Rivière Salée, a 4-mile seawater channel flowing between the Caribbean and the Atlantic, forms the "spine" of the butterfly. A drawbridge over the channel connects the two islands.

If you're seeking resorts and white sandy beaches, your target is Grande-Terre. By contrast, Basse-Terre's Natural Park, laced with mountain trails and washed by waterfalls and rivers, is a 74,100-acre haven for hikers, nature lovers, and anyone yearning to peer into the steaming crater of an active volcano. If you want to get away from it all, head for the islands of Les Saintes, La Désirade, and Marie-Galante.

As a diverse archipelago, Guadeloupe offers vacations of every style and budget. Though splashy hotels with every amenity exist here, the island is more about variety than luxury. Self-contained resorts near the beach aren't cheap, but many offer good value for those who'll spend their vacation around the pool and beach. Guadeloupe also has smaller, less expensive inns (*Relais Créoles*) and small apartments and cottages (*gîtes*). Many of the latter have their own kitchens, so you can sample the French goods on the shelves of local supermarkets.

Restaurants tend to be expensive here, as does car rental—and on an island as large as Guadeloupe, you'll probably want your own wheels. Driving around the island is the best way to appreciate its variety. Indeed, variety's the name of the game here: Night owls and nature enthusiasts, hikers and bikers, scuba divers, sailors, mountain climbers, beachcombers, and hammock potatoes all can indulge themselves in Guadeloupe.

Sugar, not tourism, is Guadeloupe's primary source of income. French is the official language here. But even if your tongue twirls easily around a few French phrases, you will sometimes receive a bewildered response. The Guadeloupeans' Creole patois greatly affects their French pronunciation. However, don't despair—most hotels and many of the restaurants have some English-speaking staff.

What It Will Cost These sample prices, meant only as a general guide, are for high season. Guadeloupe has many small hotels in the $100-a-night range or a little below. Resort hotels on the beach start at about $150. A week's rental of a small apartment may be about $300–$400. Food is wonderful here, and prices show it: It's hard to come away from a good dinner for less than $20 a person without wine. You can save by getting takeout and picnic fare from local stores, where imported goods are plentiful and affordable (an average-quality bottle of Bordeaux is about $7). A beer is $2.50 and up at a restaurant; a *ti'* punch varies from less than $2 in a small café to about $3.50 at a hotel bar. You'll probably need a car to get around; public transportation is limited, and there's lots to see. Plan on about $60 a day. Cab fares are fixed; from the airport to Pointe-à-Pitre it's about $7; from Gosier to St-François, about $24. A single-tank dive averages $40; snorkel equipment rental is about $10 a day.

Before You Go

Tourist Information For information contact the **French West Indies Tourist Board** by calling France-on-Call at 900/990–0040 (50¢ per minute) or

Guadeloupe

Le Normandie, **49**
Le Rocher de
Malendure, **40**
Les Gommiers, **39**
Les Pieds dans
l'Eau, **71**
L'OursinBlanc, **70**
Pizzeria Napoli, **59**
Relais des Iles, **44**
Relais du Moulin, **68**

Lodging
Auberge de la
Distillerie, **48**
Auberge des
Anacardies, **46**
Auberge du Grand
Large, **61**
Bois Joli, **47**
Callinago-PLM
Azur, **56**
Canella Beach, **58**
Cap Sud Caraibes, **57**
Centre UCPA, **73**
Club Med
Caravelle, **64**
Gîte de M. Jean
Kancel, **74**
Golf Marine Club
Hotel, **69**
Grand Anse Hotel, **42**
La Maison de la
Marie-Galante, **50**
La Sucrerie du
Comté, **36**
La Toubana, **65**
Le Barrière de
Corail, **67**
Le Domaine de l'Anse
des Rochers, **72**
Les Flamboyants, **60**
Mini-Beach, **66**
Relais du Moulin, **68**
Village Creole, **45**

write to the **French Government Tourist Office** (610 5th Ave., New York, NY 10020; 9454 Wilshire Blvd., Beverly Hills, CA 90212; 645 N. Michigan Ave., Chicago, IL 60611; 2305 Cedar Spring Rd., Dallas TX 75201). In Canada contact the French Government Tourist Office (1981 McGill College Ave., Suite 490, Montreal, P.Q. H3A 2W9, tel. 514/288–4264 or 1 Dundas St. W, Suite 2405, Toronto, Ont. M5G 1Z3, tel. 416/593–4723 or 800/361–9099). In the United Kingdom, contact the tourist office (178 Piccadilly, London, United Kingdom W1V 0AL, tel. 071/499–6911).

Arriving and Departing

By Plane **American Airlines** (tel. 800/433–7300) is usually the most convenient, with year-round daily flights from more than 100 U.S. cities direct to San Juan and nonstop connections to Guadeloupe via American Eagle. **Minerve Airlines** (tel. 800/765–6065), a French charter carrier, has flights Friday–Sunday from New York during the December–March peak season. **Air Canada** (tel. 800/422–6232) flies direct from Montreal and Toronto. **Air France** (tel. 800/237–2747) flies nonstop from Paris and Fort-de-France, and has direct service from Miami, San Juan, and Port-au-Prince. **Air Guadeloupe** (tel. 599/5–44212) flies daily from St. Martin and St. Maarten, St. Barts, Marie-Galante, La Désirade, and Les Saintes. **LIAT** (tel. 212/269–6925) flies from St. Croix, Antigua, and St. Maarten in the north and is your best bet from Dominica, Martinique, St. Lucia, Grenada, Barbados, and Trinidad.

From the Airport You'll land at La Raizet International Airport, 2½ miles from Pointe-à-Pitre. Cabs are lined up outside the airport. The metered fare is about 35F to Pointe-à-Pitre, 60F to Gosier, and 170F to St-François. Or, for 5F, you can take a bus from the airport to downtown Pointe-à-Pitre. If you plan to rent a car for your entire vacation, you may want to collect it at the airport (*see* Getting Around, *below*).

Passports and Visas U.S. and Canadian citizens need only proof of citizenship. A passport is best (even one that expired up to five years ago). Other acceptable documents are a notarized birth certificate with a raised seal (not a photocopy) or a voter registration card accompanied by a government-authorized photo ID. A free temporary visa, good only for your stay in Guadeloupe, will be issued to you upon your arrival at the airport. British citizens need a valid passport but no visa. In addition, all visitors must hold an ongoing or return ticket.

Language The official language is French. Everyone also speaks a Creole patois, which you won't be able to understand even if you're fluent in French. In the major tourist hotels, most of the staff knows some English. However, communicating may be more difficult in the smaller hotels and restaurants in the countryside. Some taxi drivers speak a little English. Arm yourself with a phrase book, a dictionary, patience, and a sense of humor.

Precautions Put your valuables in the hotel safe. Don't leave them unattended in your room or on the beach. Keep an eye out for motorcyclists riding double. They sometimes play the notorious game of veering close to the sidewalk and snatching shoulder bags. It isn't a good idea to walk around Pointe-à-Pitre at night, because it's almost deserted after dark. If you rent a car, always lock it with luggage and valuables stashed out of sight. The rough Atlantic waters off the northeast coast of Grande-Terre are dangerous for swimming. Ask permission before taking a picture of an islander, and don't be surprised if the answer is a firm "No." Guadeloupeans are also deeply religious and traditional. Don't offend them by wearing short shorts or swimwear off the beach.

Staying in Guadeloupe

Important Addresses **Tourist Information:** The **Office Départemental du Tourisme** has offices in Pointe-à-Pitre (23 rue Delgrès, corner rue Schoelcher, tel. 590/82–09–30), in Basse-Terre (Maison du Port, tel. 590/81–24–83), and in St-François (Ave. de l'Europe, tel. 590/88–48–74). All offices are open weekdays 8–5, Saturday 8–noon. A tourist information booth is at the airport.

Emergencies **Police:** In Pointe-à-Pitre (tel. 590/17 or 590/82–00–17), in Basse-Terre (tel. 590/81–11–55). **Fire:** In Pointe-à-Pitre (tel. 590/18 or 590/82–00–28), in Basse-Terre (tel. 590/81–19–22). **SOS Ambulance:** tel. 590/82–89–33. **Hospitals:** There is a 24-hour emergency room at the main hospital, **Centre Hopitalier de Pointe-à-Pitre** (Abymes, tel. 590/82–98–80 or 590/82–88–88). There are 23 clinics and five hospitals located around the island. The Tourist Office or your hotel can assist you in locating an English-speaking doctor. **Pharmacies:** Pharmacies alternate in staying open around the clock. The Tourist Office or your hotel can help you locate the one that's on duty.

Currency Legal tender is the French franc, which comprises 100 centimes. At press time, U.S. $1 bought 5.3F and £1 bought 8.50F, but currencies fluctuate daily. Check the current rate of exchange. Some places accept U.S. dollars, but it's best to change your money into the local currency. Credit cards are accepted in most major hotels, restaurants, and shops, less so in smaller places and in the countryside. Prices are quoted here in U.S. dollars unless otherwise noted.

Taxes and Service Charges A *taxe de séjour* varies from hotel to hotel but never exceeds $1.50 per person, per day. Most hotel prices include a 10%–15% service charge; if not, it will be added to your bill. Restaurants are legally required to include 15% in the menu price. No additional gratuity is necessary. A VAT tax is included in hotel and restaurant tariffs. Tip skycaps and porters about 5F. Many cab drivers own their own cabs and don't expect a tip. You won't have any trouble ascertaining if a 10% tip is expected.

Getting Around *Taxis* Fares are regulated by the government and posted at the airport, at taxi stands, and at major hotels. During the day you'll pay about 35F from the airport to Pointe-à-Pitre, about 60F to Gosier, and about 170F to St-François. A 15–20-minute ride from Gosier to St-François costs about 120F. Between 9 PM and 7 AM, fares increase 40%. If your French is in working order, you can contact radio cabs at 590/82–15–09, 590/83–64–27, and 590/84–37–65.

Buses Modern public buses run from 5:30 AM to 7:30 PM and connect Guadeloupe's major towns to Pointe-à-Pitre. Fares range from 5F to 25F. They stop along the road at bus stops and shelters marked *arrêtbus*, but you can also flag one down along the route. Although buses are an inexpensive way to get around, they run infrequently, and are especially crowded before and after school.

Vespas or Bikes If you opt to tour the island by bike, you won't be alone. Biking is a major sport here, as well as an inexpensive way to get around. Bike rental averages 50F a day (75F for mountain bikes). On Grand-Terre, the terrain is flat and poses no strain. If you're in reasonably good shape you can use a bike to get from one town to another here. Mountainous Basse-Terre, on the other hand, is best for short bike excursions. For rentals contact **Veló-Vert** (Pointe-à-Pitre, tel. 590/83–15–74); **Cyclo-Tours** (Gosier, tel. 590/84–11–34); **Le Flamboyant** (St-François, tel. 590/84–45–51); and **Rent-a-Bike** (Meridien Hotel, St-François, tel. 590/84–51–00). Mountain bikes with 18 speeds are available from **VTT Evasion** (Ste-Rose, tel. 590/28–85–60). For information on escorted bike tours, *see* Guided Tours, *below.*

Vespas can be rented at **Vespa Sun** (Pointe-à-Pitre, tel. 590/82–17–80), **Location de Motos** (Meridien Hotel, St-François, tel. 590/88–51–00), and **Dingo Location Scooter** (Gosier, tel. 590/90–97–01). A day's rental is about 100F, with a $200 deposit or a major credit card.

Rental Cars Your valid driver's license will suffice for up to 20 days, after which you'll need an international driver's permit. Guadeloupe has 1,225 miles of excellent roads (marked as in Europe), and driving around Grande-Terre is relatively easy. On Basse-Terre it will take more effort to navigate the hairpin bends that twist through the mountains and around the eastern shore. Guadeloupeans are skillful drivers, but they do like to drive fast. Cars can be rented at **Avis** (tel. 590/82–33–47 or 800/331–1212), **Budget** (tel. 590/82–95–58 or 800/527–0700), **Hertz** (tel. 590/82–00–14 or 800/654–3131), and **National-Europcar** (tel. 590/82–50–51 or 800/468–0008). There are rental offices at the airport as well as at the major resort areas. Car rentals cost a bit more on Guadeloupe than on the other islands. Count on about $60 a day for a small rental car.

By Boat **Trans Antilles Express** (tel. 590/91–13–43) and **Transport Maritime Brudey Frères** (tel. 590/90–04–48) provide ferry service to and from Marie-Galante, Les Saintes, and La Désirade. The *Jetcat* and *Madras* ferries depart daily from the pier at Pointe-à-Pitre for Marie Galante starting at 8 AM (check the schedule). The trip takes one hour, and the fare is 160F round-trip. Recently introduced are one-day excursions from St-François operated by **Multi Marine Charter** (tel. 590/83–32–67). For Les Saintes, Trans Antilles Express connects daily from Pointe-à-Pitre at 8 AM and from Terre-de-Haut at 4 PM. The trip takes 60 minutes and costs 160F round-trip. The *Princess Caroline* leaves Trois Rivières for the 30-minute trip to Les Saintes Monday–Saturday at 8:30 AM, Sunday at 7:30 AM. The return ferry leaves at 3 PM. Allow 1½ hours to get from Pointe-à-Pitre to Trois Rivières. The *Socimade* runs between La Désirade and St-François, departing Monday, Wednesday, Friday–Sunday at 8:30 AM, Tuesday at 3 PM, Thursday at 4:30 PM. Return ferries depart Monday, Wednesday, Friday, Saturday at 6:15 AM and 4 PM, Tuesday and Thursday at 6:15 AM, Sunday at 4 PM. Fare is 130F. These schedules are subject to change and should be verified through your hotel or at the Tourist Office.

Telephones and Mail To call from the United States, dial 011 + 590 + the local six-digit number. (To call person-to-person, dial 01–590.) To call the United States from Guadeloupe, dial 19 + 1 + the area code and phone number. It is not possible to place collect or credit card calls to the United States from Guadeloupe. To make calls outside of your hotel, purchase a Telecarte at the post office or other outlets marked *Telecarte en Vente Ici.* Telecartes look like credit cards and are used in special booths marked "Telecom." Local and international calls made with the cards are cheaper than operator-assisted calls. Coin-operated phones are rare but can be found in restaurants and cafés. To dial locally in Guadeloupe, simply dial the six-digit phone number. A local call costs 1F.

Postcards to the United States cost 3.50F; letters up to 20 grams, 4.40F. Stamps can be purchased at the post office, *café-tabacs,* hotel newsstands, or souvenir shops. Postcards and letters to the United Kingdom cost 3.40F.

Opening and Closing Times Banks are open weekdays 8–noon and 2–4. Credit Agricole, Banque Populaire, and Société Générale de Banque aux Antilles have branches that are open Saturday. During the summer most banks are open 8–3. Banks close at noon the day before a legal holiday that falls during the week. As a rule, shops are open weekdays 8 or 8:30–noon and 2:30–6, but hours are flexible when cruise ships are in town.

Guided Tours There are set fares for taxi tours to various points on the island. The Tourist Office or your hotel can arrange for an English-speaking taxi driver and even organize a small group for you to share the cost of the tour. One popular itinerary is a six-hour trip from Gosier to Basse-Terre and the Soufrière volcano; cost is approximately $85 per car (not per person).

George-Marie Gabrielle (Pointe-à-Pitre, tel. 590/82–05–38) and **Petrelluzzi Travel** (Pointe-à-Pitre, tel. 590/82–82–30) both offer half- and full-day excursions around the island. A modern bus with an English-speaking guide will pick you up at your hotel. Costs average $60 for a half-day tour, $85 for a full day, including lunch.

Le Relais du Moulin (near Ste-Anne, tel. 590/88–23–96) arranges bicycle tours on Grand-Terre. For more challenging excursions into the mountainous terrain of Basse-Terre, try the **Velo Club V.C.G.F.** (801 Résidence du Port, Pointe-à-Pitre, tel. 590/91–60–31). For information about cycling vacations in Guadeloupe, contact **Country Cycling Tours** (140 W. 83rd St., New York, N.Y. 10024, tel. 212/874–5151).

Exploring Guadeloupe

Numbers in the margin correspond to points of interest on the Guadeloupe map.

Although a guided tour will take you to many of the sites described below, a rental car will be cheaper (unless there are several of you sharing the cost of a taxi tour). Roads are well marked. Pointe-à-Pitre can be managed on foot.

Pointe-à-Pitre
❶ **Pointe-à-Pitre** is a city of some 100,000 people in the extreme southwest of Grande-Terre. It lies almost on the "backbone" of the butterfly, near the bridge that crosses the Salée River. In this bustling, noisy city, with its narrow streets, honking horns, and traffic jams, there is a faster pulse than in many other Caribbean capitals, though at night the city streets are deserted.

Life has not been easy for Pointe-à-Pitre. The city has suffered severe damage over the years as a result of earthquakes, fires, and hurricanes. The most recent damage was done in 1979 by Hurricane Frederick, in 1980 by Hurricane David, and in 1989 by Hurricane Hugo. Standing on boulevard Frébault, you can see on one side the remaining French colonial structures and on the other the modern city. However, downtown is rejuvenating itself while maintaining its old charm. The recent completion of the Centre St-John Perse has transformed old warehouses into a new cruise-terminal complex comprising a hotel (the Hotel St-John), three restaurants, space for 80 shops, and the headquarters for Guadeloupe's Port Authority.

Stop at the Office of Tourism, in Place de la Victoire across from the quays where the cruise ships dock, to pick up maps and brochures. *Bonjour, Guadeloupe*, the free visitors' guide, is very useful. Outside the tourist office stalls take over the sidewalk, selling everything from clothes to kitchen utensils. Across the road alongside the harbor, a gaggle of colorfully dressed women sell fruits and vegetables.

When you leave the office, turn left, walk one block along rue Schoelcher, and turn right on rue Achille René-Boisneuf. Two more blocks will bring you to the **Musée St-John Perse.** The restored colonial house is dedicated to the Guadeloupean poet who won the 1960 Nobel Prize in Literature. (Nearby, at No. 54, rue René-Boisneuf, a plaque marks his birthplace.) The museum contains a complete collection of his poetry, as well as some of his personal effects. There are also works written about him and various mementos, documents, and photographs. *Corner rues Noizières and Achille René-Boisneuf, tel. 590/90–01–92. Admission: 10F. Open weekdays 8–12:30 and 2:30–5:30, Sat. 8–12:30.*

Rues Noizières, Frébault, and Schoelcher are Pointe-à-Pitre's main shopping streets. In sharp contrast to the duty-free shops is the bustling **Marketplace,** which you'll find by backtracking one block from the museum and turning right on rue Frébault. Located between rues St-John Perse, Frébault, Schoelcher, and Peynier, the market is a cacophonous and colorful place where housewives bargain for papayas, breadfruits, christophines, tomatoes, and a vivid assortment of other produce.

Take a left at the corner of rues Schoelcher and Peynier. The **Musée Schoelcher** honors the memory of Victor Schoelcher, the 19th-century Alsatian abolitionist who fought slavery in the French West Indies. The museum contains many of his personal effects, and the exhibits trace his life and work. *24 rue Peynier, tel. 590/82–08–04. Admission: 5F. Open weekdays 9–noon and 2:30–5:30.*

Walk back along rue Peynier past the market for three blocks. You'll come to **Place de la Victoire,** surrounded by wood buildings with balconies and shutters. Many sidewalk cafés have opened up on this revitalized square, making it a good place for lunch or light refreshments. The square was named in honor of Victor Hugues's 1794 victory over the British. The sandbox trees in the park are said to have been planted by Hugues the day after the victory. During the French Revolution, Hugues's guillotine in this square lopped off the heads of many a white aristocrat. Today the large palm-shaded park is a popular gathering place. The Tourist Office is at the harbor end of the square.

Rue Duplessis runs between the southern edge of the park and La Darse, the head of the harbor, where fishing boats dock and fast motorboats depart for the choppy ride to Marie-Galante and Les Saintes.

Rue Bebian is the western border of the square. Walk north along it (away from the harbor) and turn left on rue Alexandre Isaac. You'll see the imposing **Cathedral of St. Peter and St. Paul,** which dates from 1847. Mother Nature's rampages have wreaked havoc on the church, and it is now reinforced with iron ribs. Hurricane Hugo took out many of the upper windows and shutters, but the lovely stained-glass windows survived intact.

Grande-Terre This round-trip tour of **Grande-Terre** will cover about 85 miles. You may want to visit its sights and towns on several short trips—a bike is an option here—rather than one long tour. Head south out of Pointe-à-Pitre on Route N4 (named the "Riviera Road" in honor of the man-made beaches and resort hotels of Bas-du-Fort, essentially an extension of Pointe-à-Pitre). The road goes past the marina, which is always crowded with yachts and cabin cruisers. The numerous boutiques and restaurants surrounding the marina make it popular in the evening.

The road turns east and heads along the coast. In 2 miles you'll **❷** sight **Fort Fleur d'Epée,** an 18th-century fortress that hunkers on a hillside behind a deep moat. This was the scene of hard-fought battles between the French and the English. You can explore the well-preserved dungeons and battlements, and on a clear day take in a sweeping view of Iles des Saintes and Marie-Galante.

❸ The **Guadeloupe Aquarium** is just past the fort off the main highway. This aquarium, the Caribbean's largest and most modern, also ranks third in all of France. *Place Créole (just off Rte. N4), tel. 590/90–92–38. Admission: 15F adults, 10F children. Open weekdays 8:30–12:30 and 2:30–5:30, Sat. 8:30–5:30.*

❹ **Gosier,** a major tourist center 2 miles farther east, is a busy place indeed, with big hotels and tiny inns, cafés, discos, shops, and a long stretch of sand. The Creole Beach, the Auberge de la Vieille Tour, and the Canella Beach are among the hotels here.

Breeze along the coast through the little hamlet of St-Felix and **❺** on to **Ste-Anne,** about 8 miles east of Gosier. Only ruined sugar mills remain from the days in the early 18th century when this village was a major sugar-exporting center. Sand has replaced sugar as the town's most valuable asset. The soft white-sand beaches here are among the best in Guadeloupe. The Club Med Caravelle occupies a secluded spot on the Caravelle Beach to the west of town, and there are several small *Relais Créoles* (small inns) with their "feet in the sand." The hotel La Toubana sits on a bluff with its bungalows tumbling down to the beach, and the Relais du Moulin occupies one of the old sugar mills. On a more spiritual note, you'll pass Ste-Anne's lovely cemetery with stark-white aboveground tombs.

Don't fret about leaving the beaches of Ste-Anne behind you as you head eastward. The entire south coast of Grande-Terre is scalloped with white-sand beaches. Eight miles along, just **❻** before coming to the blue-roof houses of **St-François,** you'll come to the Raisins-Clairs beach, another beauty.

St-François was once a simple little village primarily involved with fishing and tomatoes. The fish and tomatoes are still here, but so are some of the island's ritziest hotels. This is the home of the Hamak and Le Méridien's new extension, La Cocoteraie, two very plush properties. Avenue de l'Europe runs between the well-groomed 18-hole Robert Trent Jones municipal golf course and the man-made marina. On the marina side, a string of shops, hotels, and restaurants caters to tourists.

❼ To reach **Pointe des Châteaux,** take the narrow road east from St-François and drive 8 miles out onto the rugged promontory that is the easternmost point on the island. The Atlantic and the Caribbean waters join here and crash against huge rocks, carving them into castlelike shapes. The jagged, majestic cliffs are reminiscent of the headlands of Brittany. The only human contribution to this dramatic scene is a white cross high on a hill above the tumultuous waters. From this point there are spectacular views of the south and east coasts of Guadeloupe and of the distant cliffs of La Désirade.

About 2 miles from the farthest point, a rugged dirt road crunches off to the north and leads to the nudist beach Pointe Tarare.

A mile closer to St-François is another beach, Anse de la Gourde, where at least half of a bikini is kept on. The half-mile stretch of coarse white sand and reef-protected waters makes it a choice beach; off the car park is **La Langouste** (tel. 590/88–52–19), a popular lunch spot on the weekends.

Take Route N5 north from St-François for a drive through fragrant silvery-green seas of sugarcane. About 4 miles beyond

❽ St-François you'll see **Zévalos,** a handsome colonial mansion that was once the manor house of the island's largest sugar plantation.

❾ Four miles northwest you'll come to **Le Moule,** a port city of about 17,000 people. This busy city was once the capital of Guadeloupe. It was bombarded by the British in 1794 and 1809 and by a hurricane in 1928. Canopies of flamboyants hang over narrow streets where colorful vegetable and fish markets do a brisk business. Small buildings are of weathered wood with shutters, balconies, and bright awnings. The town hall, with graceful balustrades, and a small 19th-century neoclassical church are on the main square. Le Moule also has a beautiful crescent-shape beach. A mile east, a reef protects an excellent windsurfing beach; rent boards from the **Tropical Club Hotel** (tel. 590/93–97–97).

❿ North of Le Moule archaeologists have uncovered the remains of Arawak and Carib settlements. The **Edgar-Clerc Archaeological Museum,** 3 miles out of Le Moule in the direction of Campêche, contains Amerindian artifacts from the personal collection of this well-known archaeologist and historian. There are several rooms with displays pertaining to the Carib and Arawak civilizations. *La Rosette, tel. 590/23–57–43. Admission free. Open Mon., Wed.–Fri., and Sun. 9:30–12:30 and 2:30–5:30, Sat. 9:30–5:30.*

From Le Moule you can turn west on Route D101 to return to Pointe-à-Pitre or continue northwest to see the rugged north coast.

To reach the coast, drive 8 miles northwest along Route D120 to Campêche, going through Gros-Cap.

At 1½ miles beyond Campêche, turn north on Route D122.

⓫ **Porte d'Enfer** (Gate of Hell) marks a dramatic point on the

coast where two jagged cliffs are stormed by the wild Atlantic
waters. One legend has it that a Madame Coco strolled out
across the waves carrying a parasol and vanished without a
trace.

⑫ Four miles from Porte d'Enfer is **La Pointe de la Grande Vigie,**
the northernmost tip of the island. Park your car and walk
along the paths that lead right out to the edge. There is a splendid view of the Porte d'Enfer from here, and on a clear day you
can see Antigua 35 miles away.

⑬ **Anse-Bertrand,** the northernmost village in Guadeloupe, lies 4
miles south of La Pointe de la Grande Vigie along a gravel road.
Drive carefully. En route to Anse-Bertrand you'll pass another
good beach, Anse Laborde. The area around Anse-Bertrand
was the last refuge of the Caribs.

⑭ Route N6 will take you 5 miles south to **Port-Louis,** a fishing
village of about 7,000. As you come in from the north, look for
the turnoff to Souffleur Beach, once one of the island's petti-
est, but now a little shabby. The sand is fringed by flamboyant
trees whose brilliant orange-red flowers bloom during the
summer and early fall. The beach is crowded on weekends, but
during the week it's blissfully quiet. The sunsets here are something to write home about.

From Port-Louis the road leads 5 miles south through mangrove swamps to Petit Canal, where it turns inland. Three
miles east of Petit Canal, turn right on the main road. Head 6
⑮ miles south to **Morne-à-l'Eau,** an agricultural city of about
16,000 people. Morne-à-l'Eau's unusual amphitheater-shape
cemetery is the scene of a moving (and photogenic) candlelight
service on All Saints' Day. Take Route N5 out of town along
gently undulating hills past fields of sugarcane and dairy
farms.

Just south of Morne-à-l'Eau are the villages of **Jabrun du Sud**
and **Jabrun du Nord,** which are inhabited by the descendants
of the blancs matignon, the whites who hid in the hills and valleys of the Grands Fonds after the abolition of slavery in 1848.

Continue on Route N5 to Pointe-à-Pitre.

Basse-Terre There is high adventure on the butterfly's west wing, which
swirls with mountain trails and lakes, waterfalls, and hot
springs. Basse-Terre is the home of the Old Lady, as the Soufrière volcano is called locally, as well as of the capital, also
called Basse-Terre.

Guadeloupe's de rigueur tour takes you through the 74,100-
acre **Parc Naturel,** a sizable chunk of Basse-Terre. (The park's
administrative headquarters is in Basse-Terre, tel. 590/80–24–
25.) Before going, pick up a *Guide to the Natural Park* from the
Tourist Office, which rates the hiking trails according to difficulty.

The Route de la Traversée (La Traversée) is a good paved road
that runs east–west, cutting a 16-mile-long swath through the
park to the west-coast village of Mahaut. La Traversée divides
Basse-Terre into two almost equal sections. The majority of
mountain trails falls into the southern half. It takes a very full
day just to drive around Basse-Terre, making brief stops in the
Parc Naturel and some of the major attractions in the southern
part of the island. Wear rubber-soled shoes, and take along

both swimsuit and sweater, and perhaps food for a picnic. A mountain-bike tour of at least three days is an excellent way to further explore the tropical rain-forest-clad mountains, hiking trails, and deserted beaches.

Begin your tour by heading west from Pointe-à-Pitre on Route N1, crossing the Rivière Salée on the Pont de la Gabare drawbridge. At the Destrelan traffic circle turn left and drive 6 miles south through sweet-scented fields of sugarcane to the Route de la Traversée (aka D23), where you'll turn west.

As soon as you cross the bridge, you'll begin to see the riches produced by Basse-Terre's fertile volcanic soil and heavy rainfall. La Traversée is lined with masses of thick tree-ferns, shrubs, flowers, tall trees, and green plantains that stand like soldiers in a row.

Five miles from where you turned off Route N1, you'll come to a junction. Turn left and go a little over a mile south to **Vernou.** Traipsing along a path that leads beyond the village through
⑯ the lush forest, you'll come to the pretty waterfall at **Saut de la Lézarde,** the first of many you'll see.

Back on La Traversée, 3 miles farther, you'll come to the next
⑰ one, **Cascade aux Ecrevisses.** Park your car and walk along the marked trail that leads to a splendid waterfall dashing down into the Corossol River (a fit place for a dip). Walk carefully— the rocks along the trail can be slippery.

⑱ Two miles farther along La Traversée you'll come to the **Parc Tropical de Bras-David,** where you can park and explore various nature trails. The **Maison de la Forêt** (admission free, open daily 9–5) has a variety of displays that describe (for those who can read French) the flora, fauna, and topography of the Natural Park. There are picnic tables where you can enjoy your lunch in tropical splendor.

Two and a half miles more will bring you to the two mountains
⑲ known as **Les Mamelles** (the breasts)—Mamelle de Petit-Bourg at 2,350 feet and Mamelle de Pigeon at 2,500 feet. There is a spectacular view from the pass that runs between the Mamelles to the south and a lesser mountain to the north. From this point, trails ranging from easy to arduous lace up into the surrounding mountains. There's a glorious view from the lookout point, 1,969 feet up the Mamelle de Pigeon. If you're a climber, you'll want to spend several hours exploring this area.

You don't have to be much of a hiker to climb the stone steps
⑳ leading from the road to the **Zoological Park and Botanical Gardens.** Titi the Raccoon is the mascot of the Natural Park. There are also cockatoos, iguanas, and turtles. A snack bar is open for lunch daily except Monday. *La Traversée, tel. 590/98-83–52. Admission: 20F adults, 10F children. Open daily 9–5.*

On the winding 4-mile descent from the mountains to **Mahaut,** you'll see patches of the blue Caribbean through the green trees. In the village of Mahaut, turn left on Route N2 for the drive south along the coast. In less than a mile you'll come to **Malendure.** The big attraction here is offshore on **Pigeon Island.** Club Nautilus and Chez Guy, both on the Malendure Beach, conduct diving trips, and the glass-bottom *Aquarium* and *Nautilus* make daily snorkeling trips to this spectacular site.

㉑ From Malendure, continue through neighboring **Bouillante,**
㉒ where hot springs burst up through the earth, and **Vieux-Habi-
tants,** one of the oldest settlements on the island. Pause to see
the restored church, which dates from 1650, before driving 8
miles south to the capital city.

㉓ **Basse-Terre,** the capital and administrative center, is an active
city of about 15,000 people. Founded in 1640, it has had even
more difficulties than Pointe-à-Pitre. The capital has endured
not only foreign attacks and hurricanes but sputtering threats
from La Soufrière as well. More than once it has been evacuated when the volcano began to hiss and fume. The last major
eruption was in the 16th century. But the volcano seemed active
enough to warrant the evacuation of more than 70,000 people
in 1975.

The centers of activity are the port and the market, both of
which you'll pass along boulevard Général de Gaulle. The 17th-
century **Fort St. Charles** at the extreme south end of town, and
the **Cathedral of Our Lady of Guadeloupe** to the north, across
the Rivière aux Herbes, are worth a short visit. Drive along
boulevard Felix Eboue to see the colonial buildings that house
government offices. Follow the boulevard to the **Jardin Pichon**
to see its beautiful gardens. Stop off at **Champ d'Arbaud,** an
Old World square surrounded by colonial buildings. Continue
along the boulevard to the **Botanical Gardens.** A steep, narrow
㉔ road leads 4 miles up to the suburb of **St-Claude,** on the slopes
of La Soufrière. In St-Claude there are picnic tables and good
views of the volcano. You can also get a closer look at the volcano
by driving up to the Savane à Mulets. From there leave your
car and hike the strenuous two-hour climb (with an experienced guide) to the summit at 4,813 feet, the highest point in
the Lesser Antilles. Water boils out of the eastern slope of the
volcano and spills into the Carbet Falls.

㉕ Drive 2 miles farther north from St-Claude to visit **Matouba,** a
village settled by East Indians whose descendants still practice
ancient rites, including animal sacrifice. If you've an idle 10
hours or so, take off from Matouba for a 19-mile hike on a
marked trail through the Monts Caraïbes to the east coast.

Descend and continue east on Route N1 for 4 miles to **Gour-**
㉖ **beyre.** Visit **Etang As de Pique.** Reaching this lake, located 2,454
feet above the town, is another challenge for hikers, but you
can also reach it in an hour by car via paved Palmetto Road.
The 5-acre lake, formed by a lava flow, is shaped like an *as de
pique* (ace of spades).

From Gourbeyre you have the option of continuing east along
Route N1 or backtracking to the outskirts of Basse-Terre and
taking the roller-coaster Route D6 along the coast. Either
route will take you through lush greenery to **Trois-Rivières.**

㉗ Not far from the ferry landing for Les Saintes, the **Parc Ar-
chéologique des Roches Gravées** contains a collection of pre-
Columbian rock engravings. Pick up an information sheet at
the park's entrance. Displays interpret the figures of folk and
fauna depicted on the petroglyphs. The park is set in a lovely
botanical garden that is off the beaten track for many tourists,
so it remains a haven of tranquillity. *Trois-Rivières, no phone.
Admission: 4F. Open daily 9–5.*

Continue through banana fields and the village of Bananier for 5 miles to reach the village of **St-Sauveur,** gateway to the magnificent **Chutes du Carbet** (Carbet Falls). Three of the chutes, which drop from 65 feet, 360 feet, and 410 feet, can be reached by following the narrow, steep, and spiraling Habituée Road for 5 miles up past the **Grand Etang** (Great Pond). At the end of the road you'll have to proceed on foot. Well-marked but slippery trails lead to viewing points of the chutes.

Continue along Route N1 for 3 miles toward **Capesterre-Belle-Eau.** You'll cross the Carbet River and come to **Dumanoir Alley,** lined with century-old royal palms.

Three miles farther along, through fields of pineapples, bananas, and sugarcane, you'll arrive at **Ste-Marie,** where Columbus landed in 1493. In the town there is a monument to the Great Discoverer.

Seventeen miles farther north, you'll return to Pointe-à-Pitre.

Iles des Saintes This eight-island archipelago, usually referred to as **Les Saintes,** dots the waters off the south coast of Guadeloupe. The islands are Terre-de-Haut, Terre-de-Bas, Ilet à Cabrit, Grand Ilet, La Redonde, La Coche, Le Pâté, and Les Augustins. Columbus discovered the islands on November 4, 1493, and christened them Los Santos in honor of All Saints' Day.

Arrival on Terre-de-Haut requires a choppy 35-minute ferry crossing from Trois-Rivières or a 60-minute ride from Pointe-à-Pitre. Ferries leave Trois-Rivières at about 8:30 AM (7:30 AM on Sunday) and return about 3 PM. From Pointe-à-Pitre the usual departure time is 8 AM, with return at 4 PM. Check with the Tourist Office for up-to-date ferry schedules. Round-trip fare is 160F.

Of the islands, only Terre-de-Haut and Terre-de-Bas are inhabited, with a combined population of 3,260. Les Saintois, as the islanders are called, are fair-haired, blue-eyed descendants of Breton and Norman sailors. Fishing is the main source of income for les Saintois, and the shores are lined with their fishing boats and *filets bleus* (blue nets dotted with burnt-orange buoys). The fishermen wear hats called *salakos,* which look like inverted saucers or coolie hats. They are patterned after a hat said to have been brought here by a seafarer from China or Indonesia.

With 5 square miles and a population of about 1,500, Terre-de-Haut is the largest island and the most developed for tourism. Its big city is Bourg, which boasts one street and a few bistros, cafés, and shops. Clutching the hillside are trim white houses with bright red or blue doors, balconies, and gingerbread frills.

Terre-de-Haut's ragged coastline is scalloped with lovely coves and beaches, including the nudist beach at Anse Crawen. The beautiful bay, complete with sugarloaf, has been called a mini Rio. This is a quiet, peaceful getaway, but it may not remain unspoiled. At present, tourism accounts for 20%–30% of the economy. Although government plans call for a total of only 250 hotel rooms, the tourist-related industries are making a major pitch for visitors.

There are three paved roads on the island, but don't even think about driving here. The roads are ghastly, and backing up is a minor art form choreographed on those frequent occasions when two vehicles meet on one of the steep, narrow roads. There are four minibuses that transport passengers from the airstrip and the wharf and double as tour buses. However, the island is so small you can get around by walking. It's a mere five-minute stroll from the airstrip and ferry dock to downtown Bourg.

32 **Fort Napoléon** is a relic from the period when the French fortified these islands against the Caribs and the English, but nobody has ever fired a shot at or from it. The nearby museum contains a collection of 250 modern paintings. You can also visit the well-preserved barracks, prison cells, and museum and admire the surrounding botanical gardens. From the fort you can see Fort Josephine across the channel on the Ilet à Cabrit. *Bourg, no phone. Admission: 10F. Open daily 9–noon.* For such a tiny place, Terre-de-Haut offers a variety of hotels and restaurants. For details, *see* Dining and Lodging, *below.* The recently opened **Centre Nautique des Saintes** (Plage de la Coline, tel. 590/99–54–25) rents equipment and leads dive excursions offshore.

Marie-Galante The ferry to this flat island departs from Pointe-à-Pitre at 8 AM, 2 PM, and 5 PM with returns at 6 AM, 9 AM, and 3:45 PM. (Schedules often change, especially on the weekends, so check at the tourist office or the harbor offices.) The round trip costs **33** 160F. You'll put in at **Grand Bourg,** its major city, with a population of about 8,000. A plane will land you 2 miles from Grand Bourg. If your French, or phrase book, is good enough, you can negotiate a price with the taxi drivers for touring the island.

Covering about 60 square miles, Marie-Galante is the largest of Guadeloupe's islands. It is dotted with ruined 19th-century sugar mills, and sugar is still one of its major products (the others are cotton and rum). The island is one of the last refuges of the Caribs when they were driven from the mainland by the French; today it's a favorite retreat of Guadeloupeans, who come on weekends to enjoy the beach at Petit-Anse.

Columbus sighted the island on November 3, 1493, the day before he landed at Ste-Marie on Basse-Terre. He named it for his flagship, the *Maria Galanda,* and sailed on. There are several places near the ferry landing where you can get an inexpensive meal of seafood and Creole sauce. If you want to stay over, you can choose from Le Salut, in St-Louis (15 rooms, tel. 590/97–02–67), Auberge de l'Arbre à Pain (7 rooms, tel. 590/97–73–69) or Auberge de Soledad (18 rooms, tel. 590/97–75–44) in Grand Bourg, or Hotel Hajo (6 rooms, tel. 590/97–32–76) in Capesterre. An entertainment complex in Grand Bourg, El Rancho, has a 400-seat movie theater, restaurant, terrace grill, snack bar, disco, and a few double rooms.

La Désirade According to legend, La Désirade is the "desired land" of Columbus's second voyage. He spotted the island on November **34** 3, 1493. The 8-square-mile island, 5 miles east of St-François, was for many years a leper colony. The main settlement is Grande-Anse, where there is a pretty church and a hotel called La Guitoune. Nothing fancy, but the restaurant serves excellent seafood. Most of the 1,600 inhabitants are fishermen.

There are good beaches here, notably Souffleur and Baie Mahault, and there's little to do but loll around on them. The island is virtually unspoiled by tourism and is likely to remain so, at least for the foreseeable future.

Three or four minibuses meet the flights and ferries, and you can negotiate with one of them to give you a tour. Ferries depart from St-François Monday, Wednesday, Friday–Sunday 8:30; Tuesday and Thursday 4:30. The return ferry departs (at varying hours) afternoons daily except Tuesday and Thursday. However, be sure to check schedules. Cost is 130F.

Beaches

Generally Guadeloupe's beaches, all free and open to the public, have no facilities. For a small fee, hotels allow nonguests to use changing facilities, towels, and beach chairs. You'll find long stretches of white sand on Grande-Terre. On the south coast of Basse-Terre the beaches are gray volcanic sand, and on the northwest coast the color is golden-tan. There are several nudist beaches (noted below), and topless bathing is prevalent at the resort hotels. Note that the Atlantic waters on the northeast coast of Grande-Terre are too rough for swimming. Except for Ilet du Gosier, all beaches are accessible from the road; even the smallest beach is sign-posted with a track leading to the sands.

Ilet du Gosier is a little speck off the shore of Gosier where you can bathe in the buff. Make arrangements for water-sports rentals and boat trips to the island (cost: 50F)through the Creole Beach Hotel in Gosier (tel. 590/84–26–26). Take along a picnic for an all-day outing. *Beach closed weekends.*

Some of the island's best beaches of soft white sand lie on the coast of Grande-Terre from Ste-Anne to Pointe des Châteaux.One of the longest and prettiest stretches is just outside the town of Ste-Anne at **Caravelle Beach,**though there are rather dilapidated shacks and cafés scattered about the area. Protected by reefs, the beach makes a fine place for snorkeling. At the hotel La Toubana (tel. 590/88–25–78) in the hills above, you can rent fins and masks, as well as canoes and Windsurfers. Club Med, with its staggering array of activities, occupies one end of this beach.

Just outside of St-François is **Raisin-Clairs,** home of Le Méridien (tel. 590/88–51–00), which rents Windsurfers, water skis, and sailboats.

Between St-François and Pointe des Châteaux, **Anse de la Gourde** is a beautiful stretch of sand that becomes very popular on weekends. A restaurant and snack bar are at the entrance to the beach.

Tarare is a secluded strip just before the tip of Pointe des Châteaux; many bathe naked there. There is a small bar/café located where you park the car, a four-minute walk from the beach.

Located just outside of Deshaies on the northwest coast of Basse-Terre, **La Grande Anse** is a secluded beach of soft beige sand sheltered by palms. There's a large parking area but no facilities other than the Karacoli restaurant, which sits with its "feet in the water," ready to serve you rum punch and Creole dishes.

From here south along the western shore of Basse-Terre, signs point the way to small beaches. By the time you reach Pigeon

Island, the sand starts turning gray; as you work your way farther south, it becomes black.

From **Malendure** beach, on the west coast of Basse-Terre, Pigeon Island lies just offshore. Jacques Cousteau called it one of the 10 best diving places in the world. The Nautilus Club (tel. 590/98–85–89) and Chez Guy (tel. 590/98–81–72) at Malendure are two of the island's top scuba operations. There are also glass-bottom boat trips for those who prefer keeping their heads above water.

Souffleur, on the west coast of Grande-Terre, north of Port-Louis, has brilliant, flamboyant trees that bloom in the summer. There are no facilities on the beach, but you can buy the makings of a picnic from nearby shops. Be sure to stick around long enough for a super sunset.

Place Crawen, Les Saintes' quiet, secluded beach for skinny-dipping, is a half-mile of white sand on Terre-de-Haut. Facilities are within a five-minute walk at Bois Joli hotel (tel. 590/99–50–38).

Petit-Anse, on Marie-Galante, is a long gold-sand beach crowded with locals on weekends. During the week it's quiet, and there are no facilities other than the little seafood restaurant, La Touloulou.

Sports and the Outdoors

Bicycling *See* Getting Around, *above.*

Boating All beachfront hotels rent Hobie Cats, Sunfish, pedal boats, motorboats, and water skis. Small boat rental runs about 50F an hour; water skiing is about 75F for 15 minutes.

Golf **Golf Municipal Saint-François** (St-François, tel. 590/88–41–87) has an 18-hole Robert Trent Jones course, an English-speaking pro, a clubhouse, a pro shop, and electric carts for rental. Expect to pay 250F for a day's greens fees.

Hiking Basse-Terre's Natural Park is laced with fascinating trails, many of which should be attempted only with an experienced guide. Trips for up to 12 people are arranged by **Organisation des Guides de Montagne de la Caraibe (O.G.M.C.)** (Maison Forestière, Matouba, tel. 590/80–05–79) or **Association des Amies de Parc Naturel** (BP 256 Basse-Terre 97100, tel. 590/81–45–43 in Basse-Terre or 590/82–88–16 in Pointe-à-Pitre); cost is about 100F per person for a four- to five-hour hike. The cost does not include lunch, and you are advised to wear sturdy shoes with strong ankle support.

Scuba Diving The main diving area is the Cousteau Underwater Park off Pigeon Island (west coast of Basse-Terre). Guides and instructors here are certified under the French CMAS rather than PADI or NAUI. To explore the wrecks and reefs, contact **Nautilus Club** (Bouillante, tel. 590/98–85–69) or **Chez Guy** (Bouillante, tel. 590/98–81–72). Both of these outfits arrange dives elsewhere around Guadeloupe. Chez Guy also arranges weekly packages that include accommodations in bungalows. On the Isle des Saintes, the new **Centre Nautique des Saintes** (Plage de la Coline, Terre de Haut, tel. 590/99–54–25) rents dive and snorkel equipment and will arrange dives. A single-tank dive averages 200F.

Sea Excursions and Snorkeling Most hotels rent snorkeling gear for around 50F a day and post information about excursions. The *Papyrus* (Marina Bas-du-Fort, tel. 590/90–92–98) is a glass-bottom catamaran that offers full-day outings replete with rum, dances, and games, as well as moonlight sails. An evening cruise with buffet and drinks is 225F per person.Glass-bottom boats also make 90-minute excursions to Pigeon Island (*see* Outfitters in Scuba Diving, *above*) for 65F a person. The sailing school **Evasion Marine** (locations in St-François and Bas-du-Fort, tel. 590/84–46–67) offers excursions on board the *Ginn Fizz*, the *Ketch*, or the *Sloop*. Prices vary depending on the cruise; a full-day trip to Marie-Galante, for example, is 225F.

Tennis Courts are located at the following hotels: **Pullman Auberge de la Vieille Tour** (tel. 590/84–23–23), **Club Med Caravelle** (tel. 590/88–21–00), **Golf Marine Club Hotel** (tel. 590/88–60–60), **Le Méridien** (tel. 590/88–51–00), **Relais du Moulin** (tel. 590/88–23–96), and **Toubana** (tel. 590/88–25–78). Games can also be arranged through the **St-François Tennis Club** (tel. 590/88–41–87). Courts rent for approximately 75F an hour.

Windsurfing Immensely popular here, windsurfing rentals and lessons are available at all beachfront hotels. Windsurfing buffs congregate at the UCPA hotel club (tel. 590/88–54–84) in St-François. You can also rent a *planche-à-voile* (Windsurfer) at **Holywind** (Residence Canella Beach, Pointe de la Verdure, Gosier, tel. 590/90–44–84) and at the **Tropical Club Hotel** (Le Moule, tel. 590/93–97–97). Le Moule benefits from constant Atlantic trade winds. Windsurfers rent for 45F an hour; three hours of instruction cost about 200F.

Shopping

You'll find shopping less of a temptation here than it is on Martinique, where the selection is larger and the language less of a barrier. But shopping in Pointe-à-Pitre is fun at the street stalls around the harbor quay, in front of the tourist office, and at the market. The more touristy—and more expensive—shops are down at the Jean-Perse cruise terminal, where an attractive new mall is home to two dozen shops. Get an early start–it's hot and sticky by midday.

Many stores offer a 20% discount on luxury items purchased with traveler's checks or, in some cases, major credit cards. You can find good buys on anything French—perfumes, crystal, china, cosmetics, fashions, scarves—but check stateside prices before leaving home to make sure you're really saving money here. As for local handcrafted items, you'll see a lot of junk, but you can also find island dolls dressed in madras, finely woven straw baskets and hats, salako hats made of split bamboo, madras table linens, and wood carvings. And, of course, the favorite Guadeloupean souvenir—rum.

Shopping Areas In Pointe-à-Pitre the main shopping streets are **rue Schoelcher, rue de Nozières,** and **rue Frébault.** The **Jean-Perse Cruise Terminal** in Pointe-à-Pitre has a complex of smart shops that tend to be more expensive than stores in the older part of town.Bas-du-Fort's two shopping districts are the **Mammouth Shopping Center** and the **Marina,** where there are 20 or so boutiques and several restaurants. In **St-François** there are also several shops surrounding the marina. Many of the resorts have fashion boutiques. There are also a number of duty-free shops at Raizet Airport.

Good Buys For dolls, straw hats, baskets, and madras table linens, try **Au**
Native Crafts **Caraibe** (4 rue Frébault, Pointe-à-Pitre, no phone). Anthuriums and other plants that pass muster at U.S. customs are packaged at **Casafleurs** (42 rue René-Boisneuf, tel. 590/82–31–23, and Raizet Airport, tel. 590/82–33–34) and **Floral Antilles** (80 rue Schoelcher, tel. 590/82–18–63, and Raizet Airport, tel. 590/82–97–65). **Mariposa** (13 Galerie du Port, St-François, tel. 590/88–69–38) offers a collection of local crafts, and **L'Imagerie Créole** (Bas-du-Fort, tel. 590/90–87–28) also carries native-art antiques. For imaginative, thought-provoking paintings and sculpture, visit the **Centre d'Art Haitien** (Rue Delgres, Pointe-à-Pitre, tel. 590/82–54–46 and at 65 Montauban, Gosier, tel. 590/84–04–84).

Rum and Tobacco **Delice Shop** (45 rue Achille René-Boisneuf, Pointe-à-Pitre, tel. 590/82–98–24) and **Ets Azincourt** (13 rue Henry IV, Pointe-à-Pitre, tel. 590/82–21–02) have good choices of island rum as well as tobacco.

Dining

The food here is superb. You'll find numerous reasonably priced restaurants serving creative, delicious food, but as a rule dining here is not cheap. Expect to pay about $25 for a good Creole dinner, less for lunch, more (sometimes double) at a formidable French restaurant serving haute cuisine. You may want to budget for at least one splurge meal here.

Many of Guadeloupe's restaurants feature seafood (shellfish is a great favorite), often flavored with rich herbs and spices à la Creole. Favorite appetizers are *accras* (codfish fritters), *boudin* (highly seasoned pork sausage), and *crabes farcis* (stuffed land crabs). Christophine is a vegetable pear (plantain is considered a vegetable banana—served as a side dish) prepared in a variety of ways. *Blaff* is a spicy fish stew. Lobster, turtle steak, and *lambi* (conch) are often among the main dishes, and homemade coconut ice cream is a typical dessert. The island boasts 200 restaurants, including those serving classic French, Italian, African, Indian, Vietnamese, and South American fare. The local libation of choice is the *'ti punch* (little "poonch," as it is pronounced)—a heady concoction of rum, lime juice, and sugarcane syrup.

Buying groceries is a pleasure on Guadeloupe, where import items from Europe are widely available and relatively affordable. You can save money on some meals by purchasing takeout for picnics or for eating back at your lodgings. The supermarket at the marina in Bas-du-Fort is popular, as is a smaller market off av. de l'Europe in St-François. For vegetables and tropical fruits, shop the market on the quay at Pointe-à-Pitre. You'll find minimarkets in the center of every town and village.

Unless you're fluent in French and Creole, you'll want to keep with you a small booklet, *Ti Gourmet Guadeloupe*, which lists restaurants, defines menu terms, and gives some indication of prices. The booklet is free from the Tourist Office and many hotels. Though the French are wont to bare all on the beach, dress is much more decorous in restaurants. Outside of informal beachside eateries, "smart casual" or "casual chic" is the rule of thumb. Unless stated otherwise in our reviews below, men need not wear jackets.

Highly recommended restaurants are indicated by a star ★.

Category	Cost*
Moderate	$25–$35
Inexpensive	$15–$25
Budget	under $15

per person, excluding drinks

Grande-Terre

★ **Le Balata.** Dinner will test the budget at this commanding restaurant, high on a bluff above the main Gosier Bas-du-Fort highway, but the romance may justify the splurge. Pierre and Marie Cecillon present classic Lyonnaise cuisine with Creole touches. Begin with shellfish in a cucumber sauce or homemade foie gras, then contemplate the catch of the day with parsley butter. A special businessman's lunch is available at 110F, including wine. Choose a table by the window (reserve early), and enjoy the magnificent view of Fort Fleur d'Epée. *Route de Labrousse, Gosier, tel. 590/90–88–25. AE, DC, V. Closed Sat. lunch, Sun., and Aug. Moderate.*

Jardin Gourmand. The Ecotel Hotel's dining room is a training ground for student cooks, waiters, and waitresses. The menu changes with the visiting French master chefs and apprentices, but usually includes red snapper and lobster prepared in various ways. Exotic Creole courses are sometimes offered: Try the octopus gratinéed with a pink sauce or shark in coconut milk. For dessert the delicious frozen nougat with banana is a good choice. Don't be tempted by the *menu de dégustation,* which is out of our price range. *Ecotel, Montauban, Gosier, tel. 590/84–15–66. Reservations advised. Jacket required. AE, DC, MC, V. No lunch. Moderate.*

Le Flibustier. This rustic hilltop farmhouse is a favorite with staffers from neighboring Club Med. A complete dinner of mixed salad, grilled lobster, coconut ice cream, 'ti punch, and half a pitcher of wine is $46, which is barely over our price limit when you consider that drinks are included. You may also order à la carte off the blackboard menu. It's a lively, fun place that warms up after 8 PM. *La Colline, Fonds Thézan (between Ste-Anne and St-Felix), tel. 590/88–23–36. No credit cards. Closed Mon., Sun. lunch. Moderate.*

★ **Relais du Moulin.** The restaurant of this inn overlooks a restored windmill. By day, sunlight floods through large windows; by night, candles flicker on crisp white cloths. Not all entrées are affordable here, but you can enjoy such dishes as the fish of the day baked in a Creole sauce or stuffed chicken breast. Crème caramel in coconut sauce is among the sumptuous desserts. *Châteaubrun (between Ste-Anne and St-François), tel. 590/88–13–78. Reservations advised. AE, DC, MC, V. Moderate.*

La Grande Pizzeria. Open late and very popular, this seaside spot serves pizza; pasta; salads; and some Milanese, Bolognese, and other Italian seafood specialties. Keep to the pizzas and you'll have a satisfying meal for under 90F, but prices will climb if you order the veal or other more elaborate dishes. *Bas-du-Fort, tel. 590/90–82–64. Inexpensive.*

★ **La Maison de la Marie-Galante.** By selecting wisely and limiting yourself to two or three courses, dinner will be under 125F, and lunch even less at this restaurant on the Place de la Victoire. You can choose to eat either on the patio or inside, wh"ch is pristinely decorated with a mural and white tablecloths over peach linens. The menu ranges from roast pork or onion quiche to more creative dishes, such as poached fish with a puree of aubergine. *16 bis pl. de la Victoire, Pointe-à-Pitre, tel. 590/90-10–41. No credit cards. Inexpensive–Moderate.*

La Mouette. Tables in a gazebo and in the front yard set the tone for barefoot and bathing-suit lunching here. Grilled lobster, curried goat, ragoûts, accras, and stuffed or roasted trunkfish are on the menu. Though there are some elaborate dishes–with prices to match—you are better off enjoying lighter fare while concentrating on locale. *Pointe des Châteaux, tel. 590/88–43–53. No credit cards. Closed Tues. and Sun. dinner. Inexpensive.*

★ **Chez Violetta-La Creole.** Head of Guadeloupe's association of cuisinières (women chefs), award-winning Violetta Chaville presents an à la carte menu of traditional Creole dishes. Tables have checkered cloths, and waitresses wear madras and foulard garb. Neat and smart, the restaurant is popular with American visitors. *Eastern outskirts of Gosier Village, tel. 590/84–10–34. No credit cards. Moderate–Inexpensive.*

Folie Plage. North of Anse-Bertrand, this lively spot is especially popular with families on weekends. In addition to the reliable Creole food of Prudence Marcelin, there is a children's wading pool, a boutique, and a disco on weekends. Superb court bouillon and imaginative curried dishes are among the specialties. *Anse Laborde, tel. 590/22–11–17. Reservations advised. No credit cards. Inexpensive.*

L'Amour en Fleurs. Close to Club Med (and very popular with its guests), this is an unpretentious little roadhouse, where the award-winning Madame Trésor Amanthe prepares spicy *blaffs* (fish stews) and a tasty blend of conch, octopus, rice and beans, and court bouillon. Don't miss the homemade coconut ice cream. *Ste-Anne, tel. 590/88–23–72. No credit cards. Inexpensive.*

Le Normandie. This hotel restaurant is quite a bargain for lunch (slightly more expensive in the evening). Take a table on the terrace and watch the activity in the square while relishing the plat du jour, often roast pork or brochettes of shrimp. For appetizer, sample the homemade pâtés or oven-baked bread with chopped oyster and garlic topping. You can also stay here in one of nine air-conditioned rooms, each with a private bath, for about 320F. *Hotel Normandie, 14 pl. de la Victoire, Pointe-à-Pitre, tel. 590/82–37–15. MC, V. Budget.*

L'Oursin Blanc. This little restaurant facing the sea is run by a mother-and-son team: He fishes and she cooks. It's a great place for the freshest of catches, and you may even be persuaded to go fishing yourself—what you bring back, *Maman* will grill for you. *St-François, tel. 590/88–77–97. No credit cards. Budget.*

Les Pieds dans l'Eau. At the left of the UCPA windsurfing center is this simple, bare-bones restaurant facing the water. The menu is varied, with Creole dishes, salads, and fish. If you want to splurge on lobster, the prices here are lower than anywhere else on the island. *Rue du Front-de-Mer, St-François, tel. 590/88–66–02. No credit cards. Budget.*

Pizzeria Napoli. As you enter Gosier, on the left-hand side of the main road you'll find this inexpensive, casual eatery with terrace dining. The large pizzas (toppings include a vegetarian) are good value, but you may also wish to try one of the fresh pâtes. *Montauban, Gosier, tel. 590/84–32–49. No credit cards. Budget.*

Basse-Terre **La Touna.** If you can't get a table at Le Rocher de Malendure, proceed down the shore to the casual La Touna. Waves wash the edge of this open-fronted restaurant, where the fresh fare includes home-smoked local fish caught by the owner. Sauces are your choice of Creole or French. *Pigeon, Bouillante, tel. 590/78–70–10. MC, V. Lunch only. Closed Thurs. Inexpensive-Moderate.*

★ **Le Rocher de Malendure.** The setting on a bluff above Malendure Bay overlooking Pigeon Island makes this restaurant worth a special trip for lunch. The tiered terrace is decked with flowers, and the best choices of the menu are the fresh fish, but there are also such meat selections as veal in raspberry vinaigrette and tournedos in three sauces. The owners, M. and Mme. Lesueur, also have five bungalows for rent at very reasonable prices. Even if you don't want a large lunch, stop here for a drink and perhaps a plate of accras. *Malendure Beach, Bouillante, tel. 590/98–70–84. Reservations advised on weekends. DC, MC, V. Lunch daily, dinner Fri., Sat. Moderate.*

★ **Chez Clara.** Clara Laseur (whose English is excellent) gave up a jazz-dancing career in Paris to run her family's seaside restaurant. She takes the orders for the Creole fare here, and the place is often so crowded with her friends and fans that you may have to wait at the hexagonal bar before being seated at a table on the upper deck, furnished with smart white wicker chairs and decorated with plants. Unfortunately, the restaurant's success has meant climbing prices for some of its more elaborate dishes. *Ste-Rose, tel. 590/28–72–99. Reservations advised. MC, V. Closed Wed., Sun. dinner, Oct. Moderate.*

Le Karacoli. The restaurant has its feet firmly planted in the sands of Grande-Anse, a great place for a swim. Lucienne Salcede's rustic seaside restaurant is well established and well regarded. Creole boudin is a hot item here, as are accras. Other offerings include coquilles Karacoli, court-bouillon, fried chicken, and turtle ragoût. For dessert, try the banana flambé. *Grande-Anse, north of Deshaies, tel. 590/28–41–17. MC, V. No dinner Sat.–Thurs.; closed Fri. Inexpensive.*

Chez Jacky. Jacqueline Cabrion serves Creole and African dishes in her cheerful seaside restaurant. Creole boudin is featured, as are lobster (grilled, vinaigrette, or fricassee), fried crayfish, and ragoût of lamb. There's also a wide selection of omelets, sandwiches, and salads. For dessert, try peach melba or banana flambé. *Anse Guyonneau, Pte. Noire, tel. 590/98–06–98. AE, MC, V. Closed Sun. dinner. Inexpensive.*

Les Gommiers. Lovely peacock chairs grace the bar of this stylish restaurant. The changing menu may list beef tongue in mango sauce, lobster in sauce piquante, fillet of beef Roquefort, escalopes of veal, and grilled entrecôte. Banana split and profiteroles are on the dessert list. Light lunches include salade Niçoise. *Rue Baudot, Pte. Noire, tel. 590/98–01–79. MC, V. Closed Mon., Wed. dinner. Inexpensive.*

Iles des Saintes, Terre-de-Haut

★ **Le Foyal.** This delightful seaside terrace restaurant serves a sophisticated mélange of Creole and Continental dishes. Begin with a warm crêpe filled with lobster, conch, octopus, and fish; crabe farci; or *rillettes* of smoked fish. House specialties include an assiette of smoked fish served cold and stuffed fish fillet served in a white-wine sauce. A special plate for children under 10 is also offered. *Anse Mirre, tel. 590/99–50–92. No credit cards. Inexpensive.*

★ **Relais des Iles.** Select your lobster from the *vivier* (tank) and enjoy the splendid view from this hilltop eatery while your meal is expertly prepared by Bernard Mathieu. Imaginative things are done with local vegetables. For dessert, try the melt-in-your-mouth chocolate mousse. Choose your spirits from an excellent wine list. *Rte. de Pompierre, tel. 590/99–53–04. Reservations advised in high season. No credit cards. Inexpensive–Moderate.*

Lodging

Resort hotels on the beach start at about $150 a night here; most of them are clustered around Gosier, Bas-du-Fort, and, more recently, Ste-Anne and St-François. Properties tend to be on the beach, with restaurants and shops within walking distance; a car is necessary only if you wish to explore the rest of the island. Many of the affordable large hotels belong to French chains and cater to tour groups. Expect friendly service but not necessarily individuality or charm. Guadeloupe also has many small hotels (*Relais Créoles*) in the $100-a-night range. These are usually owner-managed, often away from the beach, and without the amenities—tennis courts, pools, room service—of large hotels. Less expensive still are the *gîtes*, which are small apartments, cottages, and rooms in private houses. These can be rented through a central agency (*see* Home and Apartment Rental, *below*). Like Relais Créoles, gîtes tend to be off the beaten track and removed from beaches.

Highly recommended lodgings are indicated by a star ★.

Category	Cost*
Moderate	$150–$225
Inexpensive	$75–$150
Budget	under $75

*All prices are for a standard double room, excluding a taxe de séjour, which varies from hotel to hotel, and a 10%–15% service charge. To estimate rates for hotels offering MAP, add about $25–$35 per person per day to the above price ranges. To estimate rates for All-inclusives, add about $40 per person per day.

Hotels, Resorts, and Inns

Club Med Caravelle. Occupying 50 secluded acres at the western end of a magnificent white-sand beach, this version of the well-known villages has air-conditioned twin-bed rooms, some with balconies. Activities include a French-English language lab, yoga, volleyball, calisthenics, and water sports. This property has never been the smartest of Club Med's villages, but it draws a fun-loving younger crowd, most of whom are from France, and serves as the home port for Club Med's sailing cruises. *Ste-Anne 97180, tel. 590/88–21–00 or 800/258–2633, fax 590/88–06–06. 275 rooms. Facilities: restaurant, pub, boutiques, 6 lighted tennis courts (with pro), pool, water-sports center. AE. All-inclusive (drinks not included). Moderate.*

La Toubana. Red-roof bungalows are sprinkled on a hilltop overlooking the Caravelle Peninsula, arguably the best beach on the island. The bungalows are air-conditioned, and all rooms have private bath, phone, and an ocean view. Seven suites have kitchenettes and private gardens. The pool is rather small. There's evening entertainment at the French-Creole restaurant, including a piano bar. Pets are welcome. Despite the renovations made after Hurricane Hugo, La Toubana requires more work and maintenance. *Box 63, Ste-Anne 97180, tel. 590/88–25–78 or 800/223–9815, fax 590/88–38–90. 45 rooms, 12 suites. Facilities: restaurant, bar, pool, tennis court, watersports center. AE, DC, V. CP, MAP. Moderate.*

Canella Beach. One of the latest additions to the Gosier hotels is this 150-room resort built to resemble a Creole village. Guests have a choice of one-level and duplex unites. Each has its own terrace or balcony and a small kitchenette. Duplexes with separate sitting areas exceed our Moderate price range. Water sports are complimentary, and there is a beach bar for refreshments. Set back from the beach are the swimming pool and tennis courts. The enthusiastic manager, Jean-Pierre Reuff, enjoys speaking English. The Verandah restaurant offers Creole and French dishes and indoor and outdoor seating. *Pointe de la Verdure, 97190 Gosier, tel. 590/90–44–00 or 800/233–9815, fax 590/90–44–44; 212/545–8469 in NY. 150 rooms. Facilities: restaurant, pool, tennis courts, water sports, excursions arranged to nearby islands. AE, DC, MC, V. EP. Moderate.*

Cap Sud Caraibes. This is a tiny Relais Créole on a country road between Gosier and Ste-Anne, just a five-minute walk from a quiet beach. English is not the first language here, but every attempt is made to make you feel at home. Individually decorated rooms are air-conditioned, and each has a balcony and an enormous bath. There's a big kitchen that guests are welcome to share. The nearest grocery store is a five-minute walk away. *Gosier 97190, tel. 590/85–96–02, fax 590/85–80–39. 12 rooms. Facilities: airport transfers, bar, dry-cleaning and laundry facilities, snorkeling equipment. CP. Moderate.*

Golf Marine Club Hotel. Although this small hotel within a new area of shops and restaurants is moderately priced, its name overpromises: It is not a club—the municipal golf course is across the street—and it has neither marina nor beach. Guests must walk two blocks to the nearest public beach. The rooms, however, are clean, pristine, and softly decorated in light blues. Each room has a balcony, but those facing the street tend to be noisy—reserve one looking onto the gardens. A third of the rooms—called mezzanine suites—are out of our Moderate price range. The patio terrace facing the small pool serves breakfast, lunch, and dinner in a relaxed, informal setting. *Avenue de l'Europe, B.P. 204, St-François 97118, tel. 590/88–60–60, fax 590/88–74–67. 52 rooms, 24 suites. Facilities: restaurant, pool. AE, DC, MC, V. CP. Moderate.*

Le Domaine de l'Anse des Rochers. Although its standard rates exceed our Moderate range, package deals are common at this large new hotel on the coast a few miles from St-François. Rooms are spread among six buildings and 34 villas, and have red clay-tile floors, rich russet-patterned bedspreads, and functional bathrooms. The man-made beach at one end of this 27-acre complex (if you're at the other end, you may be tempted to use a car) is not a standout. The huge swimming pool, however, is dramatically set and seems to cascade into the sea. Unlike most other large resort hotels on Guadeloupe, Le Domaine is somewhat removed from the bustle (St-François is about 6 miles away); guests are more dependent on the hotel's facilities than they would be in St-François's or Gosier's hotels. *Anse des Rochers, St-François 97118, tel. 590/93–90–00, fax 590/93–91–00. 360 rooms. Facilities: 2 restaurants, beach snack bar, pool, disco, 2 lighted tennis courts, archery, conference rooms. AE, DC, MC, V. EP, CP, MAP. Moderate.*

★ **Relais du Moulin.** A restored windmill serves as the reception room for this Relais Créole tucked in Châteaubrun, near Ste-Anne. A spiral staircase leads up to a TV/reading room from which there is a splendid view. Accommodations are in air-conditioned bungalows; the rooms are immaculate and tiny, with twin beds, small terraces, and kitchenettes. The hotel is on a small hill, and there is usually a pleasant cooling breeze. The beach is a 10-minute hike away. Guests are advised to have their own rental cars. Horseback riding can be arranged, and bikes are available. The owner-manager speaks English. *Châteaubrun, Ste-Anne 97180, tel. 590/88–23–96 or 800/223–9815, fax 590/88–03–92. 40 rooms. Facilities: restaurant, bar, pool, tennis court, archery. AE, MC, V. CP. Moderate.*

Callinago-PLM Azur. Within the Gosier area on a peninsula 2 miles from town, this hilltop complex above the beach offers a choice between the Callinago Hotel and the Callinago Village. Travelers on a budget will want to choose the hotel, which offers air-conditioned rooms with full baths, phones, and private balconies with views of the sea or the gardens. The village, with studios and duplex apartments, exceeds our Moderate range, but may be a good choice for large families. With dancing in the bar and frequent entertainment by folkloric groups and steel bands, this property suits those with a party spirit. *Box 1, Gosier 97110, tel. 590/84–25–25 or 800/223–9862, fax 590/84–24–90. 154 units. Facilities: 2 restaurants, bar, car rental, dive shop, pool, water-sports center. AE, DC, MC, V. CP. Moderate.*

★ **Auberge de la Distillerie.** This is an excellent choice for those who want to stay on Basse-Terre, close to the Natural Park and its hiking trails. The small country inn has air-conditioned studios with phones (you'll have to share a bath) and a TV lounge. There's also a rustic wood chalet that sleeps two to four people. Boat trips are arranged on the Lezarde River, in which you can also swim. The nearest beaches have black sand and are a 20-minute drive away. *Vernou 97170, Petit-Bourg, tel. 590/94–25–91 or 800/223–9815, fax 590/94–11–91. 7 studios, 1 chalet. Facilities: restaurant, bar, piano bar. AE, V. EP, CP, MAP. Inexpensive.*

Auberge du Grand Large. This casual family-style inn on the grand Ste-Anne beach has bungalows on the beach or tucked in a garden. All are air-conditioned with private baths. The restaurant serves Creole specialties. Pets are welcome. *Ste-Anne 97180, tel. 590/88–20–06, fax 590/88–16–69. 10 rooms. Facilities: restaurant, bar. AE, MC. EP. Inexpensive.*

Grand Anse Hotel. Located near the ferry landing in Trois-Rivières on Basse-Terre, this Relais Créole offers air-conditioned bungalows with shower baths, phones, and little balconies. The view of the mountains is spectacular. It's less than a mile from a black-sand beach, and water sports can be arranged. A good choice for nature lovers. *Trois-Rivières 97114, tel. 590/92–92–21 fax 590/92–93–69. 16 bungalows. Facilities: restaurant, bar. V. CP. Inexpensive.*

La Maison de la Marie-Galante. Opened in 1990, this small hotel in the heart of Pointe-à-Pitre facing Place de la Victoire has small, neat rooms. Most have twin beds and few furnishings; the toilet is separate from the small private bathroom, which has a shower but no tub. The staff speaks English and is wonderfully helpful. The current prices make this small hotel a tremendous value if you wish to stay in town—you'll need to take a bus to get to the beach. *16 bis Place de la Victoire, Pointe-à-Pitre 97110, tel. 590/90–10–41, fax 590/90–22–75. 9 rooms. Facilities: restaurant. No credit cards. CP. Inexpensive.*

La Sucrerie du Comté. These pristine white bungalows on a former sugar plantation on the north coast of Basse-Terre offer clean, simple, air-conditioned accommodations at reasonable prices. Though the rooms are small, the pool in the center court, the al fresco restaurant, and the bar lounge are large, pleasant gathering spots. The atmosphere is friendly and informal. The enthusiastic young French owner, M. Girard Jean-Luc, will have you speaking French in no time as you try the homemade fruit punches lined up in great jars on the bar. Situated a mile inland from the sea, La Sucrerie is a 15-minute walk from numerous small beaches; you'll need a car to better appreciate your stay here. *Comté de Lohéac, Ste-Rose 97115, tel. 590/28–60–17, fax 590/28–65–63. 26 rooms. Facilities: restaurant, bar, pool, tennis court. MC, V. CP. Inexpensive.*

Mini-Beach. This small hotel, at the northern end of Ste-Anne's beach, has recently added a central living and dining area with wicker chairs, hanging plants, and an open-hearth kitchen. There are six simple rooms with private bath, in the houses, and three one-room bungalows. One bungalow is at the water's edge, another is on the beach near the main house, the third is in the gardens. All are very simply furnished, but more than adequate for a beachcombing life. Ste-Anne's restaurants are nearby. *BP 77, Ste-Anne 97180, tel. 590/88–21–13, fax 590/88–19–29. 9 rooms. Facilities: restaurant, pool table. MC, V. CP. Inexpensive.*

Les Flamboyants. This small hotel is located just outside Gosier, with spectacular views from the promontory over the sea and Ilet du Gosier. Choose between rooms in the main building, where *petit déjeuner* (breakfast) is included in the room rate, or pay 40F more for a room with kitchen in one of the bungalows (breakfast not included). You can walk to Gosier restaurants and stores and to the beach. *Chemin Ste-Anne, Gosier 97190, tel. 590/84–14–11, fax 590/84–53–56. 6 rooms, 8 bungalow rooms. Facilities: pool. MC, V. EP, CP. Inexpensive.*

La Barrière de Corail. Be prepared for Spartan rooms at budget prices. This series of bungalows, most with kitchenettes, offers good value. The beach is only a few yards away, and the shops of Ste-Anne are within easy walking distance. *Durivage, Ste-Anne 97180; for reservations, write: Mme. Giroux, MABC, rue Béban, Pointe-à-Pitre 97110, tel. 590/88–20–03. 14 bungalows. MC, V. EP. Budget.*

Centre UCPA. Most of the guests at this small, clean hotel come from France on package vacations, and all of them seem to be windsurfing fanatics: You'll feel most at home if you speak French and share their enthusiasm for the sport. The hotel is off a small beach, with reefs offshore and ideal sailing conditions. Creature comforts are few; fellow guests, young and energetic. *Rue du Front-de-Mer, St-François, tel. 590/88–64–80. 24 rooms. Facilities: restaurant, windsurfing. No credit cards. EP. Budget.*

Gîte de M. Jean Kancel. In a quiet residential area just outside St-François and less than 50 yards from the sea, this private house offers three neat units, each with a small mezzanine floor with couch for extra sleeping space. There is a fully equipped, shared kitchen for guests, and a garden full of avocado, banana, and orange trees. You can walk to Ste-François's beach, shops, and restaurants. *2 allée Boissard, St-François, tel. 590/82–00–64. 3 rooms. Facilities: shared kitchen. No credit cards. EP. Budget.*

Iles des Saintes **Village Creole.** Baths by Courrèges, dishwashers, freezers, satellite TV/videos, and international direct-dial phones are among the amenities in this apartment hotel on Terre-de-Haut in the Iles des Saintes. Units are duplexes, with bedrooms upstairs and kitchen/dining areas down. Ghyslain Laps, the English-speaking owner, will help you whip up meals in the kitchen. If you'd prefer not to cook, he can provide you with a cook and housekeeper for an extra charge. The beach is an easy walk away. *Pte. Coquelet 97137, Terre-de-Haut, tel. 590/99–53–83 (telex 919671), fax 590/99–55–55. 22 duplexes. Facilities: airport shuttle service, daily maid service, scooter and boat rentals, water-sports center. MC, V. EP. Inexpensive–Moderate.*

★ **Auberge des Anacardies.** Trimmed with trellises, topped by dormers, and formerly owned by the mayor, this inn offers air-conditioned, twin-bed rooms with phones and baths. Casement windows open to a splendid view of the gardens, the hills, and the bay. From here it's a five-minute walk to the sea, 10 minutes to the nearest swimming beach. Furnishings are an odd assortment of antiques. This hostelry has the island's only swimming pool, and the new owners, Jean-Paul Coles and Didier Spindler, have installed a sauna alongside. A new bungalow has also been built next to the main house. Steak au poivre and grilled lobster are among the restaurant's offerings. *La Savane 97137, Terre-de-Haut, tel. 590/99–50–99, fax 590/99–54–51. 11 rooms. Facilities: restaurant, bar, pool. AE, MC, V. CP. Inexpensive.*

★ **Bois Joli.** In high season, you'll need to reserve a room here three months in advance. Facing the "Sugarloaf" on the island's beautiful bay, the hotel consists of modern rooms in bungalows, 14 of which are air-conditioned. Private baths were recently added to every room. The more modern and fresher rooms are in the recently added, fully equipped bungalows. The hotel restaurant serves wonderful clams in Creole sauce on a terrace that overlooks the sea. Water sports can be arranged, and the Anse Crawen nudist beach is a five-minute walk away. Pets are allowed. *Terre-de-Haut 97137, tel. 590/99–52–53 or 800/223–9815, fax 590/99–55–05. 26 rooms. Facilities: restaurant, 2 bars, pool, airport transfers. MC, V. EP, MAP. Inexpensive.*

Home and Apartment Rental For information about villas, apartments, and private rooms in modest houses, contact **Gîtes de France** (Association Guadeloupéenne des Gîtes de France, Office du Tourisme de la Guadeloupe, B.P. 759, Pointe-à-Pitre 97110, tel. 590/91–64–33, fax 590/91–45–40). Rentals average $400 a week and usually require a minimum stay of one week. For additional information about apartment-style accommodations, contact the **ANTRE Association** (tel. 590/88–53–09).

Campgrounds Camping is not well developed on Guadeloupe. The island has two campgrounds with tent sites and shower and toilet facilities: **Camping La Traverse** (Anse de la Grande Plaine, Pointe-Noire 97116, tel. 590/98–21–23) and **Camping Les Sables D'Or** (Plage de Grand Anse, Deshaies 97126, tel. 590/28–44–60).

Off-Season Bets Hotel prices drop by approximately 40% after April 15 and remain bargains until December 15. Among hotels that become more affordable then are: **Pullman Auberge de la Vielle-Tour** (Gosier 97190, tel. 590/84–23–23, fax 590/84–33–43), with its own small beach, a swimming pool, and some of the best French cuisine on the island; and the action-packed **Le Méridien** (St-François 97118, tel. 590/88–51–00, fax 590/88–40–71), on the beach in St-François.

The Arts and Nightlife

Cole Porter notwithstanding, Guadeloupeans maintain that the beguine began here (the Martinicans make the same claim for their island). Many of the resort hotels feature dinner dancing, as well as entertainment by steel bands and folkloric groups.

Discos A mixed crowd of locals and tourists frequents the discos. Night owls should note that carousing is not cheap. Most discos charge an admission of at least $8, which includes one drink. Drinks cost about $5 each. Some of the enduring hot spots are **Le Foufou** (Hotel Frankel, Bas-du-Fort, tel. 590/84–35–59), the very Parisian **Elysée Matignon** (Rte. des Hôtels, Bas-du-Fort, tel. 590/90–89–05), **Ti Raccoon** (Creole Beach Hotel, Pointe de la Verdure, tel. 590/84–26–26), **Le Caraibe** (Salako, Gosier, tel. 590/84–22–22), **New Land** (Rte. Riviera, Gosier, tel. 590/84–37–91), the **Bet-a-Feu** (Le Méridien, St-François, tel. 590/88–51–00), and the local down-home **Neptune disco** (Quartier Cayenne, St-François, tel. 590/88–48–65) on weekends.

Bars and Nightclubs Generally, nightclubs don't charge a cover, but they can be expensive. **La Toubana** (Ste-Anne, tel. 590/88–25–78) offers a popular piano bar; **Le Jardin Brésilien** (Marina, Bas-du-Port, tel. 590/90–99–31) has light music in a relaxed setting on the waterfront.

14 Jamaica

Updated by
Jordan Simon

The third-largest island in the Caribbean (after Cuba and Puerto Rico), the English-speaking nation of Jamaica enjoys a considerable self-sufficiency based on tourism, agriculture, and mining. Its physical attractions include jungle mountaintops, clear waterfalls, and unforgettable beaches, yet the country's greatest resource may be the Jamaicans themselves. Although 95% of the population trace their bloodlines to Africa, their national origins lie in Great Britain, the Middle East, India, China, Germany, Portugal, South America, and many of the other islands in the Caribbean. Their cultural life is a wealthy one; the music, art, and cuisine of Jamaica are vibrant, with a spirit easy to sense but as hard to describe as the rhythms of reggae or the flourish of the streetwise patois.

In addition to such pleasure capitals of the north coast as Montego Bay and Ocho Rios, Jamaica has a real capital in Kingston. For all its congestion and for all the disparity between city life and the bikinis and parasails to the north, Kingston is the true heart and head of the island. This is the place where politics, literature, music, and art wrestle for acceptance in the largest English-speaking city south of Miami, its actual population of nearly 1 million bolstered by the emotional membership of virtually all Jamaicans.

In recent years, Jamaica has become synonymous with the all-inclusive resort phenomenon: Pay one price for a hassle-free vacation. Many of these are luxurious, high-priced properties, but the more affordable establishments are a smart choice for active travelers wanting to take advantage of the many sports

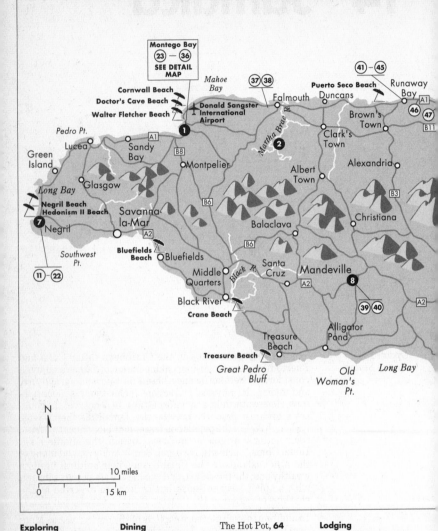

Montego Bay
(23) — (36)
SEE DETAIL
MAP

Mahoe Bay

(37)(38)

Puerto Seco Beach Duncans Runaway Bay

Cornwall Beach Falmouth

Doctor's Cave Beach (41) — (45)

Walter Fletcher Beach ↑ **Donald Sangster International Airport** **Brown's Town**

(46)(47)

A1

Pedro Pt. Clark's Town B11

Lucea A1 (2)

Green Island Sandy Bay Albert Town Alexandria

B8

Long Bay ○Montpelier B3

Glasgow B6

Negril Beach Savanna-la-Mar Balaclava Christiana

Hedonism II Beach

(7) A2

Negril B6

Southwest Pt. **Bluefields Beach** ○Bluefields Santa Cruz Mandeville

(11) — (22) Middle Quarters *Black R.* A2

Black River (8)

Crane Beach (39)(40)

Alligator Pond A2

Treasure Beach

Treasure Beach *Old Woman's Pt.* *Long Bay*

Great Pedro Bluff

N
↑

0 ___ 10 miles
0 ___ 15 km

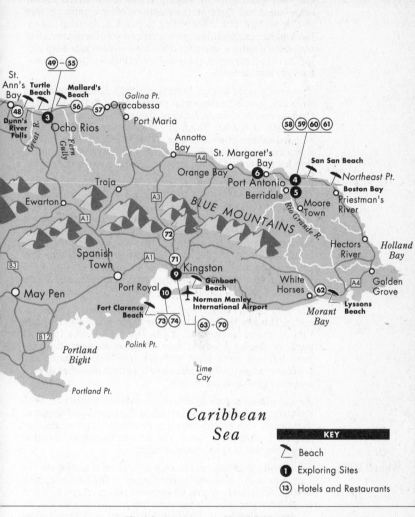

Caribbean
Sea

KEY

⌐ Beach

1 Exploring Sites

13 Hotels and Restaurants

FDR, Franklyn D.
Resort, **42**
Fisherman's Inn Dive
Resort, **37**
Goblin Hill, **60**
H.E.A.R.T. Country
Club, **43**
Hedonism II, **12**
Hibiscus Lodge, **49**
Hotel Four
Seasons, **65**

Hotel Oceana, **68**
Jamaica Grande, **48**
Jamaica, Jamaica, **44**
Jamaica Palace, **61**
Jamaica Pegasus, **69**
Jamel Continental, **47**
Mandeville Hotel, **40**
Morant Bay Villas, **62**
Morgan's Harbour
Hotel, Beach Club,
and Yacht Marina, **74**

Negril Cabins, **20**
Negril Gardens, **14**
Negril Inn, **13**
Parkway Inn, **53**
Pine Grove Mountain
Chalets, **72**
Rock Cliff Hotel, **21**
Sandals Ocho Rios, **54**
Seasplash, **18**
Shaw Park Beach
Hotel, **55**

Tamarind Tree
Hotel, **45**
Thrills, **22**
Trelawny Beach
Hotel, **38**
Wyndham
Kingston, **70**

and other activities offered at all-inclusives. Budget travelers to Jamaica who can do without sports galore and several drinks daily will save more by staying at one of the island's small inns—most are right on the beach or offer complimentary shuttle service. For those willing to rough it, Jamaica has extensive camping facilities, good vantage points for appreciating the island's natural splendor. Fine local restaurants help visitors avoid overpriced hotel restaurants; look for "jerk centers" in every sizable town.

The first people known to have reached Jamaica were the Arawaks, gentle Indians who paddled their canoes from the Orinoco region of South America about a thousand years after the death of Christ. Then, in 1494, Christopher Columbus stepped ashore at what is now called Discovery Bay. Having spent four centuries on the island, the Arawaks had little notion that his feet on their sand would mean their extinction within 50 years.

The Spaniards were never impressed with Jamaica; their searches found no precious metals, and they let the island fester in poverty for 161 years. When 5,000 British soldiers and sailors appeared in Kingston Harbor in 1655, the Spaniards did not put up a fight. The arrival of the English, and the three centuries of rule that followed, provided Jamaica with the surprisingly genteel underpinnings of its present life—and the rousing pirate tradition, fueled by rum, that enlivened a long period of Caribbean history.

The very British 18th century was a time of prosperity in Jamaica. This was the age of the sugar baron, who ruled his plantation great house and made the island the largest sugar-producing colony in the world. Because sugar fortunes were built on slave labor, however, production became less profitable when the Jamaican slave trade was abolished in 1807 and slavery was ended in 1838.

As was often the case in colonies, a national identity came to supplant allegiance to the British in the hearts and minds of Jamaicans. This new identity was given official recognition on August 6, 1962, when Jamaica became an independent nation with loose ties to the Commonwealth.

What It Will Cost These sample prices, meant only as a general guide, are for high season. An inexpensive hotel room on the beach is about $100; a moderately priced all-inclusive resort can be as much as $350 for a couple. Dinner at an inexpensive restaurant, including one cocktail, costs about $20. A jerk pork and chicken lunch is around $5. A rum punch or glass of wine is about $2.50; a Red Stripe beer, $2. Rental car prices here are on the high side—about $60 a day. A taxi ride from the airport to your hotel can cost anywhere from $10 to $30; within town, figure on $1–$5. It's about $10 for a Great House tour, around $3 for admission to a natural attraction. A single-tank dive averages $50; snorkel equipment rents for about $5.

Before You Go

Tourist Information Contact the **Jamaica Tourist Board** (866 2nd Ave., New York, NY 10017, tel. 212/688–7650 or 800/223–5225, fax 212/759–5012; 36 S. Wabash Ave., Suite 1210, Chicago, IL 60603, tel. 312/346–1546, fax 312/346–1667; 1320 S. Dixie Hwy., Coral Gables, FL

33146, tel. 305/665–0557, fax 305/666–7239; 8214 Westchester, Suite 500, Dallas, TX 75225, tel. 214/361–8778, fax 214/361–7049; 3440 Wilshire Blvd., Suite 1207, Los Angeles, CA 90010, tel. 213/384–1123, fax 213/384–1123; 1 Eglinton Ave. E, Suite 616, Toronto, Ont. M4P 3A1, tel. 416/482–7850, fax 416/482–1730; 111 Gloucester Place, London W1H3PH, tel. 071/224–0505, fax 071/224–0551).

Arriving and Departing By Plane Donald Sangster International Airport in Montego Bay (tel. 809/952–3009) is the most efficient point of entry for visitors destined for Montego Bay, Round Hill-Tryall, Ocho Rios, Runaway Bay, and Negril. Norman Manley Airport in Kingston (tel. 809/924–8024) is better for visitors to the capital or Port Antonio. **Trans Jamaica Airlines** (tel. 809/923–8680) provides shuttle services on the island.

Air Jamaica (tel. 800/523–5585) and **American Airlines** (tel. 212/619–6991 or 800/433–7300) fly nonstop from New York. Air Jamaica also flies nonstop from Miami and has service from Atlanta, Baltimore, Orlando, and Philadelphia. **BWIA** (tel. 800/JET–BWIA) flies from San Juan. **Continental** (tel. 800/231–0856) flies in daily from Newark, **Northwest Airlines** (tel. 212/563–7200 or 800/447–4747) flies in daily from Minneapolis and Tampa, and **Aeroflot** (tel. 809/929–2251) flies in from Havana. **Air Canada** (tel. 800/776–3000) offers service from Toronto and Montreal in conjunction with Air Jamaica, and both **British Airways** (tel. 800/247–9297) and Air Jamaica connect the island with London.

From the Airport All-inclusive resorts provide free transfers from the airport, as do many small hotels when you stay on a special package; always inquire when booking, as the hotel may throw it in if asked. There is no public transportation to and from the airports. Taxi rates are not fixed, but sample fares to popular destinations are posted in public areas. Always set the price in advance, figuring $10–$15 to Kingston or Montego Bay from their respective airports, two or three times that to Negril, Ocho Rios, or Port Antonio.

Passports and Visas Passports are not required of visitors from the United States or Canada, but every visitor must have proof of citizenship, such as a birth certificate or a voter registration card (a driver's license is *not* enough). British visitors need passports but not visas. Each visitor must possess a return or ongoing ticket. Declaration forms are distributed in flight in order to keep customs formalities to a minimum.

Language The official language of Jamaica is English. Islanders usually speak a patois among themselves, and they may use it when they don't want you to understand something.

Precautions Do not let the beauty of Jamaica cause you to relax the caution and good sense you would use in your own hometown. Never leave money or other valuables in your hotel room; use the safe-deposit boxes that most establishments make available. Carry your funds in traveler's checks, not cash, and keep a record of the check numbers in a secure place. Never leave a rental car unlocked, and never leave valuables even in a locked car. Finally, resist the call of the wild when it presents itself as a scruffy-looking native offering to show you the "real" Jamaica. Jamaica *on* the beaten path is wonderful enough; don't take chances by wandering far from it. And ignore efforts, however persistent, to sell you a ganja joint.

Staying in Jamaica

Important Addresses **Tourist Information:** The main office of the **Jamaica Tourist Board** is in Kingston (Tourism Centre Bldg., New Kingston Box 360, Kingston 5, tel. 809/929–9200). There are also JTB desks at both Montego Bay and Kingston airports and in all resort areas.

Emergencies **Police, Fire, and Ambulance:** Police and Air-Rescue is 119; fire department and ambulance is 110. **Hospitals: University Hospital** at Mona in Kingston (tel. 809/927–1620), **Cornwall Regional Hospital** (Mt. Salem, in Montego Bay, tel. 809/952–5100), **Port Antonio General Hospital** (Naylor's Hill in Port Antonio, tel. 809/993–2646), and **St. Ann's Bay Hospital** (near Ocho Rios, tel. 809/972–2272). **Pharmacies: Pegasus Hotel** in Kingston (tel. 809/926–3690), **McKenzie's Drug Store** (16 Strand St. in Montego Bay, tel. 809/952–2467), and **Great House Pharmacy** (Brown's Plaza in Ocho Rios, tel. 809/974–2352).

Currency The Jamaican government abolished the fixed rate of exchange for the Jamaican dollar, allowing it to be traded publicly and subject to market fluctuations. At press time the Jamaican dollar was worth about J$22 to U.S.$1. Currency can be exchanged at airport bank counters, exchange bureaus, or commercial banks. Prices quoted below are in U.S. dollars unless otherwise noted.

Taxes and Service Charges Hotels collect a 5% government tax on room occupancy. Most hotels and restaurants add a 10% service charge to your bill. Otherwise, figure on tipping 10%–15%. The departure tax is approximately $10.

Getting Around *Taxis* Some but not all of Jamaica's taxis are metered. If you accept a driver's offer of his services as a tour guide, be sure to agree on a price *before* the vehicle is put into gear. All licensed taxis display red Public Passenger Vehicle (PPV) plates, as well as regular license plates. Cabs can be summoned by telephone or flagged down on the street. Taxi rates are per car, not per passenger, and 25% is added to the metered rate between midnight and 5 AM. A ride from most hotels in resort areas to downtown will run $10–$15 round-trip. For long trips, you're better off renting a car. Licensed minivans are also available and bear the red PPV plates. Figure on anywhere from $1 to $5 in town.

Rental Cars Jamaica has dozens of car-rental companies throughout the island. Because rentals can be difficult to arrange once you've arrived, you *must* make reservations and send a deposit before your trip. (Cars are scarce, and without either a confirmation number or a receipt you may have to walk.) Best bets are: **Avis** (tel. 800/331–1212), **Dollar** (tel. 800/800–4000), **Hertz** (tel. 800/654–3131), and **National** (tel. 800/227–3876). In Jamaica, try the branch offices in your resort area: **United Car Rentals** (tel. 809/952–3077), or **Jamaica Car Rental** (tel. 809/924–8217). You must be at least 21 years old to rent a car, and you must have a valid driver's license (from any country). You may be required to post a security of several hundred dollars before taking possession of your car; ask about it when you make the reservation. Daily rates average $60.

Traffic keeps to the left in Jamaica. Be cautious until you are comfortable with it.

Trains The diesel train run by the **Jamaica Railway Corporation** (tel. 809/922–6620) between Kingston and Montego Bay reveals virtually every type of scenery Jamaica has to offer in a trip of nearly five hours. At press time operation was temporarily suspended.

Buses Buses are the mode of transportation Jamaicans use most, and consequently some buses are very crowded and slow. Yet the service is quite good between Kingston and Montego Bay and between other major destinations. Schedule or route information is available at bus stops or from the driver. Stops are usually small roadside shelters, with a dilapidated but clearly marked sign. Service between major points is regular but rarely sticks to a timetable. Although the ride is somewhat uncomfortable, the price is right, and the experience is an excellent way to meet Jamaicans. The fare from Kingston to Montego Bay runs approximately $5. There are also buses from Montego Bay to Ocho Rios or Negril, and from Kingston to Port Antonio.

Telephones and Mail The area code for all Jamaica is 809. Direct telephone, telegraph, telefax, and telex services are available. Local calls are J$5.

At press time, airmail postage from Jamaica to the United States or Canada was J$1.10 for letters, J$.90 for postcards. Local mail cost J$.50.

Opening and Closing Times Normal business hours for stores are weekdays 8–4, Saturday 8–1. Banking hours are generally Monday–Thursday 9–2, Friday 9–noon and 2:30–5.

Guided Tours The best Great Houses tours include Rose Hall, Greenwood, and Devon House. Plantations to tour are Prospect and Brimmer's Hall. Tours cost $7–$10. The increasingly popular waterside folklore feasts are offered on the Dunn's, Great, and White rivers. These cost $40–$60 per person and include a meal and usually drinks and transfers. The significant city tours are those in Kingston, Montego Bay, and Ocho Rios. Quality tour operators include **Estate Tours Services** (tel. 809/974–2058), **Greenlight Tours** (tel. 809/952–4490), **Jamaica Tours** (tel. 809/952–8074), **Martin's Tours** (tel. 809/922–5246), and **Tropical Tours** (tel. 809/952–1110). Costs average $20–$25. The highlight of the **Hilton High Day Tour** (tel. 809/952–3343), which has been dubbed "Up, Up, and Buffet," is a meet the people, experience Jamaican food, and learn some of Jamaica's history day, all on a private estate ($55, including transportation). **South Coast Safaris Ltd.** has guided boat excursions that go some 10 miles (round-trip) up the Black River and into the mangroves and marshlands, aboard the 25-passenger *Safari Queen* and 25-passenger *Safari Princess* (tel. 809/962–0220 or 809/965–2513). The cost is $30 per person.

Fifteen years ago Jamaica introduced the Meet the People concept that has become so popular in the Caribbean. One of the best free attractions anywhere, it allows visitors to get together with islanders who have compatible interests and expertise. The nearly 600 Jamaican families who participate in Meet the People on a voluntary basis offer their guests a spectrum of activities, ranging from time at a business or home to musical or theatrical performances. The program's theme is Forget Me Not, the name of a tiny blue flower that grows on

Jamaican hillsides. It's important to arrange your occasion in advance of your trip through the Jamaica Tourist Board.

Exploring Jamaica

Numbers in the margin correspond to points of interest on the Jamaica map.

The astonishing diversity of Jamaica's attractions makes renting a car the most desirable way to get to know the island. If you only intend to explore the area near your hotel, you will save money by hiring a taxi or taking a guided tour (*see above*).

Montego Bay The number and variety of its attractions make **Montego Bay,**
❶ on the island's northwest corner, the logical place to begin an exploration of Jamaica. Confronting the string of high-rise developments that crowd the water's edge, you may find it hard to believe that little of what is now Montego Bay (the locals call it MoBay) existed before the turn of the century.

Rose Hall Great House, perhaps the greatest in the West Indies in the 1700s, enjoys its popularity less for its architecture than for the legend surrounding its second mistress, Annie Palmer, who was credited with murdering three husbands and the plantation overseer who was her lover. The story is told in two novels sold everywhere in Jamaica: *The White Witch of Rose Hall* and *Jamaica White.* The great house is east of Montego Bay, just across the main highway from the Rose Hall resorts. *Tel. 809/953–2323. Admission: $10 adults, $6 children. Open daily 9:30–6.*

Greenwood Great House, 15 miles east of Montego Bay, just off the main highway, has no spooky legend to titillate visitors, but it's much better than Rose Hall at evoking the atmosphere of life on a sugar plantation. The Barrett family, from which the English poet Elizabeth Barrett Browning was descended, once owned all the land from Rose Hall to Falmouth, and the family built several great houses on it. The poet's father, Edward Moulton Barrett ("the Tyrant of Wimpole Street"), was born at Cinnamon Hill, currently the private estate of country singer Johnny Cash. Highlights of Greenwood include oil paintings of the Barretts, china made especially for the family by Wedgwood, a library filled with rare books printed as early as 1697, fine antique furniture, and a collection of exotic musical instruments. *Tel. 809/953–1077. Admission: $8. Open daily 9–6.*

One of the most popular excursions in Jamaica is rafting on the
❷ **Martha Brae River.** The gentle waterway takes its name from that of an Arawak Indian who killed herself because she refused to reveal the whereabouts of a local gold mine to the Spanish. According to legend, she finally agreed to take them there and, on reaching the river, used magic to change its course and drowned herself along with the greedy Spaniards. Her *duppy* (ghost) is said to guard the mine's entrance to this day. Bookings are made through hotel tour desks. The trip is $32 per raft (two per raft) for the 1½-hour river run, about 28 miles from most hotels in Montego Bay. There are gift shops, a bar/restaurant, and swimming pool at the top of the river where you purchase tickets. To make arrangements call 809/952–0889.

Ocho Rios Perhaps more than anywhere else in Jamaica, **Ocho Rios**—67
❸ miles east of Montego Bay—presents a striking contrast of

natural beauty and recreational development. The Jamaicans can fill the place by themselves, especially on a busy market day, when cars and buses from the countryside clog the heavily traveled coastal road that links Port Antonio with Montego Bay. Add a tour bus or three and the entire passenger list from a cruise ship, and you may find yourself mired in a considerable traffic jam.

Yet a visit to Ocho Rios is worthwhile, if only to enjoy its two chief attractions—Dunn's River Falls and Prospect Plantation. A few steps from the main road in Ocho Rios await some of the most charming inns and oceanfront restaurants in the Caribbean. Lying on the sand of what will seem to be your private cove or swaying in a hammock with a tropical drink in your hand, you'll soon forget the traffic that's only a stroll away.

The dispute continues as to the origin of the name Ocho Rios. Some claim it's Spanish for "eight rivers"; others maintain that the name is a corruption of *chorreras*, which describes a seemingly endless series of cascades that sparkle from the limestone rocks along this stretch of coast. For as long as anyone can remember, Jamaicans have favored Ocho Rios as their own escape from the heat and the crowds of Kingston.

Dunn's River Falls (tel. 809/974–2857) is an eye-catching sight: 600 feet of cold, clear mountain water splashing over a series of stone steps to the warm Caribbean. The best way to enjoy the falls is to climb the slippery steps. Don a swimsuit, take the hand of the person ahead of you, and trust that the chain of hands and bodies leads to an experienced guide. Those who lead the climbs are personable fellows who reel off bits of local lore while telling you where to stop. *Admission: $1.50 adults, 75¢ children.*

Prospect Plantation Tour (tel. 809/974–2058) is the best of several offerings that delve into the island's former agricultural lifestyle. It's not just for specialists; virtually everyone enjoys the beautiful views over the White River Gorge and the tour by jitney (a canopied open-air cart pulled by a tractor) through a plantation with exotic fruits and tropical trees planted over the years by such celebrities as Winston Churchill and Charlie Chaplin. Horseback riding over 1,000 acres is available. *Admission: about $10.*

Port Antonio
❹

Every visitor's presence in **Port Antonio** pays homage to the beginnings of Jamaican tourism. Early in the century the first tourists arrived here on the island's northeast tip, 133 miles east of Montego Bay, drawn by the exoticism of the island's banana trade and seeking a respite from the New York winters. In time it became the tropical darling of a fast-moving crowd and counted Clara Bow, Bette Davis, Ginger Rogers, Rudyard Kipling, J. P. Morgan, and William Randolph Hearst among its admirers. Its most passionate devotee was the actor Errol Flynn, whose spirit still seems to haunt the docks, devouring raw dolphin and swigging gin at 10 AM. Flynn's widow, Patrice Wymore Flynn, owns a boutique in the Palace Hotel and operates a working cattle farm.

Although the action has moved elsewhere, the area can still weave a spell. Robin Moore wrote *The French Connection* here, and Broadway's tall and talented Tommy Tune found inspiration for the musical *Nine* while being pampered at Trident.

With the help of recent renovations, a stroll through the town suggests a step into the past. A couple of miles north of Port Antonio's main street, **Queen Street** in the residential Titchfield area offers fine Georgian architecture. **DeMontevin Lodge** (21 Fort George St., on Titchfield Hill, tel. 809/993–2604), owned by the Mullings family (the late Gladys Mullings was Errol Flynn's cook), and the nearby **Musgrave Street** (the Craft Market is here) are in the traditional sea-captain style that one finds along coasts as far away as New England.

The town's best-known landmark is **Folly,** on the way to Trident, a Roman-style villa in ruins on the eastern edge of East Harbor. The creation of a Connecticut millionaire in 1905, the manse was made almost entirely of concrete. Unfortunately, the cement was mixed with seawater, and it began to crumble as it dried. According to local lore, the millionaire's bride took one look at her shattered dream, burst into tears, and fled forever. Little more than the marble floor remains today.

❺ Rafting on the **Rio Grande River** (yes, Jamaica has a Rio Grande, too) is a must. This is the granddaddy of the river-rafting attractions, an 8-mile-long, swift green waterway from Berrydale to Rafter's Rest. Here the river flows into the Caribbean at St. Margaret's Bay. The trip of about three hours is made on bamboo rafts pushed along by a raftsman who is likely to be a character. You can pack a picnic lunch and eat it on the raft or along the riverbank; wherever you lunch, a vendor of Red Stripe beer will appear at your elbow. A restaurant, bar, and souvenir shops are at Rafter's Rest (tel. 809/993–2778), a pleasant spot to relax, even if you don't want to pay the approximately $42 per two-person raft trip.

❻ Another interesting excursion takes you to **Somerset Falls,** a sun-dappled spot crawling with flowering vines; you can climb its 400 feet with some assistance from a concrete staircase. A brief raft ride takes you part of the way. **Athenry Gardens** (tel. 809/993–3740), a 16-acre tropical wonderland, and **Nonsuch Cave** are some 6 miles northeast of Port Antonio in the village of Nonsuch. The cave's underground beauty has been made accessible by concrete walkways, railed stairways, and careful lighting. *Admission to Somerset Falls: $2; to Athenry/Nonsuch: $5.*

A short drive east from Port Antonio deposits you at **Boston Bay,** which is popular with swimmers and has been enshrined by lovers of jerk pork. The spicy barbecue was originated by the Arawaks and perfected by runaway slaves called the Maroons. Eating almost nothing but wild hog preserved over smoking coals enabled the Maroons to survive years of fierce guerrilla warfare with the English.

Crystal Springs, about 18 miles west of Port Antonio, has more than 15,000 orchids, and hummingbirds dart among the blossoms, landing on visitors' outstretched hands. Hiking and camping are available here.

Negril Situated 52 miles southwest of Montego Bay on the winding **❼** coast road, **Negril** is no longer Jamaica's best-kept secret. In fact, it has begun to shed some of its bohemian, ramshackle atmosphere for the attractions and activities traditionally associated with Montego Bay. Applauding the sunset from Rick's Cafe may still be the highlight of a day in Negril, yet increasingly the hours before and after have come to be filled with conventional recreation.

One thing that has not changed around this west coast center (whose only true claim to fame is a 7-mile beach) is the casual approach to life. As you wander from lunch in the sun to shopping in the sun to sports in the sun, you'll find that swimsuits are common attire. Want to dress for a special meal? Slip a caftan over your bathing suit.

After sunset, activity centers on **West End Road,** Negril's main (and only) thoroughfare, which comes to life in the evening with bustling bistros and ear-splitting discos. West End Road may still be unpaved, yet it leads to the town's only building of historical significance, the **Lighthouse.** All anyone can tell you about it, however, is that it's been there for a while. Even historians find it hard to keep track of the days in Negril.

Negril today stretches along the coast north from the horseshoe-shaped **Bloody Bay** (named during the period when it was a whale-processing center), along the calm waters of **Long Bay** to the Lighthouse section and the landmark **Rick's Cafe** (tel. 809/957–4335). Sunset at Rick's is a tradition, one not unlike the event observed at Mallory Square in Key West. Here there are jugglers and fire-eaters, 50-foot cliffs, and divers who go spiraling downward into the deep green depths.

In the 18th century Negril was where the English ships assembled in convoys for the dangerous ocean crossing. Not only were there pirates in the neighborhood, but the infamous Calico Jack and his crew were captured right here, while they guzzled the local rum. All but two of them were hanged on the spot; Mary Read and Anne Bonney were pregnant at the time, and their executions were delayed.

Mandeville
8

More than a quarter of a century after Jamaica achieved its independence from Great Britain, **Mandeville** seems like a hilly tribute to all that is genteel and admirable in the British character. At 2,000 feet above sea level, 70 miles southeast of Montego Bay, Mandeville is considerably cooler than the coastal area 25 miles to the south. Its vegetation is more lush, thanks to the mists that drift through the mountains. The people of Mandeville live their lives around a village green, a Georgian courthouse, tidy cottages and gardens, even a parish church. The entire scene could be set down in Devonshire, were it not for the occasional poinciana blossom or citrus grove.

Mandeville is omitted from most tourist itineraries even though its residents are increasingly interested in showing visitors around. It is still much less expensive than any of the coastal resorts, and its diversions include horseback riding, cycling, croquet, hiking, tennis, golf, and people-meeting. The town itself is characterized by its orderliness. You may stay here several days, or a glimpse of the lifestyle may satisfy you and you'll scurry back to the steamy coast. **Manchester Club** features tennis, nine holes of golf, and well-manicured greens; **Mrs. Stephenson's Gardens** are lovely, with orchids and fruit trees; the natural **Bird Sanctuary** at Marshalls Pen (tel. 809/962–2260) shows off 25 species indigenous to Jamaica; and **Marshall's Penn Great House** offers an array of walking tours. The cool, crisp air will make you feel up to any stroll in Mandeville. Further information on Mandeville is available from the Mandeville office of the JTB (tel. 809/962–1072), or through the visitors information center at the Hotel Astra (tel. 809/962–3265 or 809/962–3377).

Kingston   The reaction of most visitors to the capital city, situated on the southeast coast of Jamaica, is anything but love at first sight. In fact, only a small percentage of visitors to Jamaica see it at all. **Kingston,** for the tourist, may seem as remote from the resorts of Montego Bay as the loneliest peak in the Blue Mountains. Yet the islanders themselves can't seem to let it go. Everybody talks about Kingston, about their homes or relatives there, about their childhood memories. More than the sunny havens of the north coast, Kingston is a distillation of the true Jamaica. Parts of it may be dirty, crowded, often raucous, yet it is the ethnic cauldron that produces the cultural mix that is the nation's greatest natural resource. (The Jamaican motto is "Out of many, one people.") Kingston is a cultural and commercial crossroads of international and local movers and shakers, art-show openings, theater (from Shakespeare to pantomime), and superb shopping. Here, too, the University of the West Indies explores Caribbean art and literature, as well as science. As one Jamaican put it, "You don't really know Jamaica until you know Kingston."

The best way to approach this city is from within, staying in one of the quiet residential sections and dining with the local inhabitants in restaurants that seem to have no names (people refer to them by their addresses, such as 73 or 64, and everyone knows where to meet). The first-time business or pleasure traveler may prefer to begin with New Kingston, a former racetrack property that now glistens with hotels, office towers, apartments, and boutiques. Newcomers may feel more comfortable settling in here and venturing forth from comfort they know will await their return.

Kingston's colonial past is very much alive away from the high rises of the new city. **Devon House** (tel. 809/929–6602), is reached through the iron gates at 26 Hope Road. Built in 1881 and bought and restored by the government in the 1960s, the mansion has period furnishings. Shoppers will appreciate Devon House, for the firm Things Jamaican has converted portions of the space into some of the best crafts shops on the island. On the grounds you'll find one of the few mahogany trees to survive Kingston's ambitious but not always careful development. Further information on Kingston is available at the Kingston JTB Office (tel. 809/929–9200).

Among nearby residences, **Kings House,** farther along Hope Road, is the home of Jamaica's governor-general, and **Vale Royal** on Montrose Road is home to the prime minister. The latter structure, originally built as a plantation house in the 1700s, is one of the few still standing in the capital that has a lookout tower for keeping an eye on ships in the harbor. *Tel. 809/927–6424. King's House is open weekdays 10–5.*

Once you have accepted the fact that Kingston doesn't look like a travel poster—too much life goes on here for that—you may see your trip here for precisely what it is: the single best introduction to the people of Jamaica. Near the waterfront, the **Institute of Jamaica** (tel. 809/922–0620) is a museum and library that traces the island's history from the Arawaks to current events. The charts and almanacs here make fascinating browsing; one example, the famed Shark Papers, is made up of damaging evidence tossed overboard by a guilty sea captain and later recovered from the belly of a shark.

From the Institute, push onward to the **University of the West Indies** (tel. 809/927–1660) in the city's Mona section. A cooperative venture begun after World War II by several West Indian governments, the campus is set in an eye-catching cradle of often misty mountains. In addition to a bar and a disco where you can meet the students (they pay dues, while tourists enter free), the place seems a monument to the conviction that education and commitment lead to a better life for the entire Caribbean.

Jamaica's rich cultural life is evoked at the **National Gallery** (12 Ocean Blvd., tel. 809/922–1561), which was once at Devon House and can now be found at Kingston Mall near the reborn waterfront section. The artists represented here may not be household words in other nations, yet the paintings of such intuitive masters as John Dunkley, David Miller, Sr., and David Miller, Jr., reveal a sensitivity to the life around them that transcends academic training. Among other highlights from the 1920s through the 1980s are works by Edna Manley and Mallica Reynolds, better known as Kapo. Reggae fans touring the National Gallery will want to look for Christopher Gonzalez's controversial statue of Bob Marley.

Reggae fans will also want to see **Tuff Gong International** (56 Hope Rd.). Painted in Rastafarian red, yellow, and green, this recording studio was built by Marley at the height of his career. The house has since become the **Bob Marley Museum** (tel. 809/927–9152), with impromptu tours given by just about anyone who may be around. Certainly there is much here to help the outsider understand Marley, reggae, and Jamaica itself. The Ethiopian flag is a reminder that Rastas consider the late Ethiopian emperor Haile Selassie to be the Messiah, a descendant of King Solomon and the Queen of Sheba. A striking mural by Everald Brown, *The Journey of Superstar Bob Marley*, depicts the hero's life from its beginnings in a womb shaped like a coconut to enshrinement in the hearts of the Jamaican people.

A distinct change of pace is offered by the **Royal Botanical Gardens at Hope** (tel. 809/927–1257), a cooling sanctuary donated to Jamaica by the Hope family following the abolition of slavery. Some 200 acres explode with tropical trees, plants, and flowers, each clearly labeled and lovingly discussed by qualified guides. Free concerts are given here on the first Sunday of each month.

10 Unless your visit must be very brief, you shouldn't leave Kingston without a glimpse of "the wickedest city in the world." **Port Royal** has hardly been that since an earthquake tumbled it into the sea in 1692, yet the spirits of Henry Morgan and other buccaneers add a great deal of energy to what remains. The proudest possession of **St. Peter's Church,** rebuilt in 1725 to replace Christ's Church, is a silver communion plate donated by Morgan himself.

You can no longer down rum in Port Royal's legendary 40 taverns, but you can take in a draft of the past at the **Archaeological and Historical Museum** (tel. 809/924–8706), located within the Police Training School building, and explore the impressive remains of Fort Charles, once the area's major garrison. On the grounds are a small **Maritime Museum** and a tipsy, angled structure known as **Giddy House.** Nearby is a graveyard in which rests a man who died twice. According to the tombstone, Lewis Goldy was swallowed up in the great earthquake of 1692, spewed into the sea, rescued, and lived another four decades in "Great Reputation." Port Royal attractions are open daily 9–5.

Admirers of Jamaica's wonderful coffee may wish to tour the **Blue Mountains.** The best way to do so is in your own rental car, driving into the mountains from Kingston along Highway A3. Before departing, you should obtain directions either to **Pine Grove** or to the Jablum coffee plant at **Mavis Bank,** then follow the hand-lettered signs after you leave A3. It's an exciting excursion and a virtual pilgrimage for many coffee lovers. Pine Grove, a working coffee farm that doubles as an inn, has a restaurant that serves the owner Marcia Thwaites's Jamaican cuisine. Mavis Bank is delightfully primitive—considering the retail price of the beans it processes. There is no official tour; ask someone to show you around.

Beaches

Jamaica has some 200 miles of beaches, some of them still uncrowded. The beaches listed below are public places, and they are among the best Jamaica has to offer. In addition, nearly every resort has its own private beach, complete with towels and water sports. Some of the larger resorts (all-inclusives such as Grand Lido or Hedonism II) sell day passes to nonguests. Costing $40–$50, these include meals and drinks, as well as use of facilities. Most hotels are on beaches or provide a free shuttle. The following beaches have public sections; access is only denied in those areas adjoining major hotels. Generally, the farther west you travel, the lighter and finer the sand.

Doctor's Cave Beach at Montego Bay shows a tendency toward population explosion, attracting Jamaicans and tourists alike; at times it may resemble Fort Lauderdale at spring break. The 5-mile stretch of sugary sand has been spotlighted in so many travel articles and brochures over the years that it's no secret to anyone. On the bright side, Doctor's Cave is well fitted for all its admirers with changing rooms, colorful if overly insistent vendors, and a large selection of snacks.

Two other popular beaches in the Montego Bay area are **Cornwall Beach,** farther up the coast, smaller and also lively, with lots of food and drink available, and **Walter Fletcher Beach,** on the bay near the center of town. Fletcher offers protection from the surf on a windy day and therefore unusually fine swimming; the calm waters make it a good bet for children, too.

Ocho Rios appears to be just about as busy as MoBay these days, and the busiest beach is usually **Mallard's. The Jamaica Grande** hotel, formerly The Mallards Beach and Americana hotels, is here, spilling out its large convention groups at all hours of the day. Next door is **Turtle Beach,** which islanders consider the place for swimming in Ocho Rios.

In Port Antonio, head for **SanSan Beach** or **Boston Bay.** Any of the shacks spewing scented smoke along the beach at Boston Bay will sell you the famous peppery delicacy jerk pork.

Puerto Seco Beach at Discovery Bay is a sunny, sandy beach.

Around Kingston, **Gunboat Beach** is the most popular choice. **Fort Clarence,** a black-sand beach in the Hellshire Hills area southwest of the city, has changing facilities and entertainment. Sometimes Kingstonians are willing to drive 32 miles east to the lovely golden **Lyssons Beach** in Morant Bay or, for a small negotiable fee, to hire a boat at the Morgan's Harbor Marina at Port Royal to ferry them to **Lime Cay.** This island, just beyond Kingston Harbor, is perfect for picnicking, sunning, and swimming.

Not too long ago, the 7 miles of white sand at **Negril Beach** offered a beachcomber's vision of Eden. Today much of it is fenced off. The nude beach areas are sectioned off, and some new resorts are building accommodations overlooking their nude beaches, thereby adding a new dimension to the traditional notion of "ocean view."

Those who seek beaches off the main tourist routes will want to explore Jamaica's unexploited south coast. Nearest to "civilization" is **Bluefields Beach** near Savanna-la-Mar, south of Negril along the coast. **Crane Beach** at Black River is another great discovery. And the best of the south shore has to be **Treasure Beach,** 20 miles farther along the coast beyond Crane.

Sports and the Outdoors

The Tourist Board licenses all operators of recreational activities, which should ensure you of fair business practices as long as you deal with companies that display the decals.

Golf   The best courses may be found at **Caymanas** (tel. 809/997–8026) and **Constant Spring** (tel. 809/924–1610) in Kingston; **Half Moon,** (tel. 809/953–2560), **Rose Hall,** (tel. 809/953–2650), **Try-all,** (tel. 809/952–5110), and **Ironshore** (tel. 809/953–2800) in Montego Bay; and **Runaway Bay** (tel. 809/973–2561) and **Upton** (tel. 809/974–2528) in Ocho Rios. A nine-hole course in the hills of Mandeville is called **Manchester Club** (tel. 809/962–2403), and **Prospect Estate** (tel. 809/974–2058) in Ocho Rios has an 18-hole mini-golf course.

Tennis   Many hotels have tennis facilities that are free to their guests, but some will allow you to play for a fee, usually about $7 a person per hour. The sport is a highlight at **Tyrall** (tel. 809/952–5110), **Round Hill Hotel and Villas** (tel. 809/952–5150), and **Half Moon Club** (tel. 809/953–2211) in Montego Bay; **Swept Away** (tel. 809/957–4061) in Negril; and **Sans Souci Hotel & Spa** (tel. 809/974–2353) and **Ciboney** (tel. 809/974–5503) in Ocho Rios.

Water Sports   The major areas for swimming, windsurfing, snorkeling, and scuba diving are Negril in the west and Port Antonio in the east. Equipment rental is not cheap, primarily because so many all-inclusives and major resorts offer facilities free to guests. All the large resorts rent equipment for a deposit and/or a fee. Figure on $5 for snorkeling gear, $20 for a half-hour of windsurfing, and $50 for a single-tank dive. **Blue Whale Divers** (tel. 809/957–4438); **Sun Divers,** Poinciana Beach Hotel, Negril (tel. 809/957–4069), and Ambiance Hotel, Runaway Bay, (tel. 809/973–2346); **Fantasea Divers** at the Beach Bar of the Sans Souci Hotel & Spa (Ocho Rios, tel. 809/975–4504); and **Seaworld Resorts Ltd.** (Montego Bay, tel. 809/953–2180, fax 809/952–5018) offer certification courses and dive trips. **Lady Godiva Ltd. at San San Beach** (tel. 809/993–3318), in Port Antonio, has scuba diving, snorkeling, windsurfing, a glass-bottom boat, and sailing; excursions start at $25 a person.

Shopping

Jamaican crafts take the form of resortwear, hand-loomed fabrics, silk-screening, wood carvings, paintings, and other fine arts.

Jamaican rum is a great take-home gift. So is Tia Maria, Jamaica's world-famous coffee liqueur. The same goes for the island's prized Blue Mountain and High Mountain coffees and its jams, jellies, and marmalades.

A must to avoid are the "crafts" stalls in MoBay and Ocho Rios that are literally filled with "higglers" desperate to sell touristy straw hats, T-shirts, and cheap jewelry. You may find yourself purchasing an unwanted straw something just to get out alive.

Cheap sandals are good buys in shopping centers throughout Jamaica. While workmanship and leathers don't rival the craftsmanship of those found in Italy or Spain, neither do the prices (about $20 a pair). In Kingston there's **Lee's** (New Kingston Shopping Center, tel. 809/929–8614). In Ocho Rios, the **Pretty Feet Shoe Shop** (Ocean Village Shopping Centre, tel. 809/974–5040) is a good bet. In Montego Bay, try **Overton Plaza** or **Westgate Plaza.**

Things Jamaican (Devon House, Hope Rd., Kingston, tel. 809/929–6602; Fort St., MoBay, tel. 809/952–5650) has two outlets and two airport stalls that display and sell some of the best native crafts made in Jamaica, at competitive prices. The Devon House branch offers items that range from carved wood bowls and trays to reproductions of silver and brass period pieces.

Reggae tapes by world-famous Jamaican artists such as Bob Marley, Ziggy Marley, Peter Tosh, and Third World, can be found easily in U.S. or European record stores, but a pilgrimage to **Randy's Record Mart** (17 N. Parade, Kingston, tel. 809/922–4859) should be high on the reggae lover's list. Also worth checking is the **Record Plaza** (Tropical Plaza, Kingston, tel. 809/926–7645), **Record City** (1 William St., Port Antonio, tel. 809/993–2836), and **Top Ranking Records** (Westgate Plaza, Montego Bay, tel. 809/952–1216). While Kingston is the undisputed place to make purchases, the determined will somehow (usually with the help of a local) find **Jimmy Cliff's Records** (Oneness Sq., MoBay, no phone), owned by reggae star Cliff.

Blue Mountain coffee can be found at **John R. Wong's Supermarket** (1 Tobago Ave., Kingston, tel. 809/926–4811) and the **Sovereign Supermarket** (Hope Rd., tel. 809/927–5955). If they're out of stock, you'll have to settle for High Mountain coffee, the natives' second preferred brand. If you're set on Blue Mountain, you may try **Magic Kitchen Ltd.** (Village Plaza, Kingston, tel. 809/926–8894). Jamaican-brewed rums and Tia Maria can be bought at either the Kingston or MoBay airports before your departure.

Silk batiks, by the yard or made into chic designs, are at **Caribatik** (tel. 809/954–3314), the studio of the late Muriel Chandler, 2 miles east of Falmouth. Drawing on patterns in nature, Chandler translated the birds, seascapes, flora, and fauna into works of art.

Sprigs and Things (Miranda Ridge Plaza, Gloucester Ave., MoBay, tel. 809/952–4735) is where artist Janie Soren sells T-shirts featuring her hand-painted designs of birds and animals. She also paints canvas bags and tennis dresses.

Annabella Proudlock sells her unique wood Annabella Boxes, the covers depicting reproductions of Jamaican paintings, at a restored great house, Harmony Hall (an eight-minute drive from Ocho Rios, east on A1; tel. 809/975–4222). Reproductions of paintings, lithographs, and signed prints of Jamaican scenes are also for sale, along with hand-carved wood combs—all magnificently displayed. Harmony Hall is also well known for its year-round art shows by local artists.

Dining

Sampling the island's cuisine introduces you to virtually everything the Caribbean represents. Every ethnic group that has made significant contributions on another island has made them on Jamaica, too, adding to a Jamaican stockpot that is as rich as its melting pot. So many Americans have discovered the Caribbean through restaurants owned by Jamaicans that the very names of the island's dishes have come to represent the region as a whole. Moreover, restaurants specializing in the savory local cuisine, such as the "jerk centers" found in every major town, are invariably less expensive than restaurants serving Continental cuisine. This is especially true in Negril, which caters to a young, carefree crowd. Its West End Road (bush country just 20 years ago) is lined with shacks where it is virtually impossible to order a bad meal—or a weak rum punch.

Outside of informal local eateries, restaurants can be expensive, particularly those with sensational views or located in major hotels. Kingston has the widest selection; its ethnic restaurants offer Italian, French, Rasta natural foods, Cantonese, German, Thai, Indian, Korean, and Continental fare. If you want to sample an all-inclusive, you can purchase a day pass (usually $50–$60 a person) that entitles you to full use of the facilities plus meals (sometimes drinks, too).

If you plan to cook where you are staying, the supermarkets with the greatest produce, lowest prices, and widest selection are Kingston's **Lane** and **Poppeen Center** supermarkets (both New Hope Rd.), Ocho Rios's **General Food Supermarket** (Ocean Village Shopping Centre, next to JTB Office), and Negril's **Hi-Lo Supermarket** (Sunshine Arcade). Several daily markets (weekends are best) in Kingston are located near the bus station downtown. Ocho Rios has a good one on weekends that's located near the clock tower on the main road.

Jamaican food represents a cuisine all its own. Here are a few typically Jamaican dishes:

Rice and Peas. A traditional dish, known also as coat of arms and similar to the *moros y cristianos* of Spanish-speaking islands: white rice cooked with red beans, coconut milk, scallions, and seasoning.

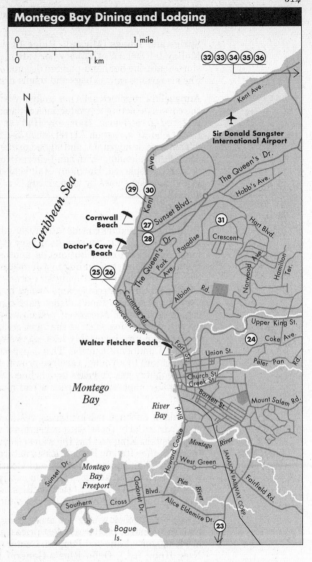

Montego Bay Dining and Lodging

Pepper pot. The island's most famous soup—a peppery combination of salt pork, salt beef, okra, and the island green known as callaloo—is green, but at its best it tastes as though it ought to be red.

Curry Goat. Young goat cooked with spices is more tender and has a gentler flavor than the lamb for which it was a substitute for immigrants from India.

Akee and Saltfish. Salted fish was once the best islanders could do between catches, so they invented this incredibly popular dish that joins saltfish (in Portuguese, *bacalao*) with *akee*, a vegetable (introduced to the island by Captain Bligh of *Bounty* fame) that reminds most people of scrambled eggs.

Jerk Pork. Created by the Arawaks, jerk pork is the ultimate island barbecue. The pork (the purist cooks the whole pig) is covered with a paste of hot peppers, berries, and other herbs and cooked slowly over a coal fire. Many think that the "best of the best" jerk comes from Boston Beach in Port Antonio.

Patties, which originated in Haiti, are spicy meat pies that elevate street food to new heights.

Dress at restaurants is casual (casual but neat at better establishments), unless stated otherwise. Highly recommended restaurants are indicated by a star ★.

Category	Cost*
Moderate	$20–$30
Inexpensive	$10–$20
Budget	under $10

*per person, excluding drinks and service charge (or tip)

Kingston **Hotel Four Seasons.** The Four Seasons has been pleasing local residents for more than 25 years with its cuisine from the German and Swiss schools, as well as local seafood. The setting tries to emulate Old World Europe without losing its casual island character. *18 Ruthven Rd., tel. 809/926–8805. Reservations advised. AE, DC, MC, V. Moderate.*

Ivor Guest House. Serving international and Jamaican cuisines, this elegant yet cozy restaurant has an incredible view of Kingston, from 2,000 feet above sea level. Go for dinner, when the restaurant seems dramatically suspended between the stars above and the glittering Kingston lights below. Owner Hellen Aitken is an animated and cordial hostess. There are also three delightfully quaint, antique-crammed guest rooms in this peaceful charmer. *Jack's Hill, tel. 809/977–0033. Reservations required. AE, MC, V. Moderate.*

★ **The Hot Pot.** Jamaicans love the Hot Pot for breakfast, lunch, and dinner. Fricassee chicken is the specialty, along with other local dishes, such as mackerel run-down (salted mackerel cooked down with coconut milk and spices) and akee and salted cod. The restaurant's fresh juices "in season" are the best—tamarind, sorrel, coconut water, soursop, and cucumber. *2 Altamont Terr., tel. 809/929–3906. V. Inexpensive.*

Gloria's Rendezvous. This brightly painted, ramshackle Port Royal eatery is wildly popular with Kingston locals escaping the sultry city heat on weekends. Delectable grilled fish and chicken are the draw. *5 Queen St., Port Royal, tel. 809/924–8578. No credit cards. Budget–Inexpensive.*

Minnie's Ethiopian Herbal Health Food. The late Bob Marley loved Minnie's cooking (she was his personal cook), and so does much of Kingston. Only fresh foods and Rasta-style cooking (no salt, no meat, etc.) are offered here. There are about 30 tables scattered over two floors of a simple wooden space, with local folk sipping fresh juices (soursop, carrot, beetroot, papaya, June plum, orange sorrel, neaseberry, Otaheite apple, mango, straight cane juice), or sampling red-pea stew, gungopea stew, steam fish, akee, callaloo, and vegetable run-down. On Friday nights (from about 8 to 11), there are reggae musicians or poetry readings. *176 Old Hope Rd., tel. 809/927–9207. AE, MC, V. Budget–Inexpensive.*

Peppers. This casual outdoor bar is the "in" spot in Kingston, particularly on weekends. Sample the jerk pork and chicken with the local Red Stripe beer. *31 Upper Waterloo Rd., tel. 809/925–2219. No credit cards. Budget–Inexpensive.*

Chelsea Jerk Centre. This new Kingston restaurant is little more than a cafeteria, with an outdoor terrace that could double as a basketball court. But it doesn't bother those who crowd the tables to munch on superlative jerk pork, chicken, and fish. *7 Chelsea Ave., tel. 809/926–6322. No credit cards. Budget.*

Montego Bay **Hemingway's Pub.** Opened in 1990, this eatery has been a great success with the local business community, which enjoys the pub lunches and dinners. The fish-and-chips here is a classic. It's an air-conditioned casual bar/restaurant with satellite TV and the added bonus of a terrace for watching the sun go down. *At Miranda Ridge Plaza, Gloucester Ave., tel 809/952–8606. No credit cards. Inexpensive–Moderate.*

★ **Le Chalet.** Don't let the French name fool you. This Denny's look-alike, set in a nondescript shopping mall, serves heaping helpings of some of the best Chinese and Jamaican food in MoBay, including succulent curried goat and *escoveitch* fish (seasoned with onions, tomato, garlic, and peppers). The staff will even pick you up from your hotel. *32 Gloucester Ave., tel. 809/952–5240. AE, MC, V. Budget–Inexpensive.*

Lone Star Café. This unassuming, cheerful little place, enlivened by flowers and fire-engine-red chairs, is set in a shopping center across from the Holiday Inn. Tacos, enchiladas, and other Mexican standards are given uniquely Jamaican spices and preparations; the result is oddly satisfying variations on familiar dishes. *Rose Hall Shopping Center, tel. 809/953–2584. AE, DC, MC, V. Budget–Inexpensive.*

★ **Pork Pit.** This open-air hangout three minutes from the airport must introduce more travelers to Jamaica's fiery jerk pork than any other place on the island. The Pork Pit is a local phenomenon down to the Red Stripe beer, yet it's accessible in both location and style. Plan to arrive around noon, when the jerk begins to be lifted from its bed of coals and pimento wood. *Adjacent to Fantasy Resort Hotel, tel. 809/952–1046. No reservations. No credit cards. Budget.*

Negril **Café au Lait.** The proprietors of Café au Lait are French and Jamaican, and so is the cuisine. Local seafood and produce are prepared with delicate touches and presented in a setting overlooking the sea. *Mirage Resort on Lighthouse Rd., tel. 809/957–4471. Reservations advised. MC, V. Moderate.*

Tan-ya's. This al fresco restaurant is on the edge of the beach of its hotel, Seasplash. It features Jamaican delicacies with an international flavor for breakfast, lunch, and dinner. Try the excellent deviled crab backs or the snapper Florentine stuffed with callaloo. *Seasplash Hotel, Norman Manley Blvd., Negril, tel. 809/957–4041. AE, DC, MC, V. Moderate.*

★ **Cosmo's Seafood Restaurant and Bar.** Owner Cosmo Brown has made this seaside open-air bistro one of the best places in town to spend a lunch, an afternoon, and maybe stay on for dinner. (He's also open for breakfast. In fact, he only closes from 5 to 6:30 PM for a scrub-down.) The fresh fish is the featured attraction, and the conch soup that's the house specialty is a meal in itself. There's also lobster (grilled or curried), fish-and-chips, and the catch of the morning. Customers often drop cover-ups to take a beach dip before coffee and dessert, then return later to lounge in chairs scattered under almond and sea-grape trees. (There's an entrance fee for the beach alone, but it's less than $1.) *Norman Manley Blvd., tel. 809/957-4330. MC, V. Inexpensive.*

Paradise Yard. Locals enjoy this alfresco restaurant on the Savana-La-Mar side of the roundabout in Negril. Sit back and relax in the casual atmosphere while eating Jamaican dishes or the house special, Rasta Pasta. Open for breakfast, lunch, and dinner. *Negril, tel. 809/957-4006. V. Budget-Inexpensive.*

Tigress Inn. This humble maize-and-white café is a magnet for local seafood lovers, who come for the copious portions of rice, coleslaw, and stewed or steamed catch of the day for $6.50. For $14 you can get an enormous lobster, prepared in one of five ways, and all the fixings. *West End Rd., tel. 809/957-4372. MC, V. Budget-Inexpensive.*

Ocho Rios **Almond Tree.** One of the most popular restaurants in Ocho
★ Rios, the Almond Tree offers Jamaican dishes enlivened by a European culinary tradition. The swinging rope chairs of the terrace bar and the tables perched above a lovely Caribbean cove are great fun. You'll find pumpkin and pepper pot soups, *suprêmes de volaille Jamaican* (chicken breasts layered with bananas and ham), and the house special, grouper Caprice, grilled with various island spices. All but the most expensive seafood dishes fall within our Moderate range. *83 Main St., Ocho Rios, tel. 809/974-2813. Reservations required. AE, DC, MC, V. Moderate.*

The Ruins. A 40-foot waterfall dominates the open-air Ruins restaurant, and in a sense it dominates the food as well. Surrender to local preference and order the Lotus Lily Lobster, a stir-fry of the freshest local shellfish, then settle back and enjoy the tree-shaded deck and the graceful footbridges that connect the dining patios. *DaCosta Dr., tel. 809/974-2442. Reservations advised. AE, DC, MC, V. Moderate.*

★ **Evita's.** The setting here is a sensational, nearly 100-year-old gingerbread house high on a hill overlooking Ocho Rios's Bay (but also convenient from MoBay). More than 18 kinds of pasta are served here, ranging from lasagna Rastafari (vegetarian) to *rotelle alla Eva* (crabmeat with white sauce and noodles). There are also excellent fish dishes—sautéed fillet of red snapper with orange butter, red snapper stuffed with crabmeat— and several meat dishes, among them grilled sirloin with mushroom sauce and barbecued ribs glazed with honey-and-ginger sauce. *Mantalent Inn, Ocho Rios, tel. 809/974-2333. Reservations required. AE, MC, V. Inexpensive-Moderate.*

Double V Jerk Centre. This partially alfresco hut with dirt floor is a great place to park yourself for a frosty Red Stripe beer and fiery, crispy jerk pork or chicken. Lively at lunch (when you can tour the minizoo and botanical garden), it rocks at night with an informal disco. *109 Main Rd., tel. 809/974-2084. No credit cards. Budget.*

Lodging

The island has a variety of destinations to choose from, each of which offers its own expression of the Jamaican experience. Jamaica was the birthplace of the Caribbean all-inclusive, the vacation concept that took the Club Med idea and gave it a lusty, excess-in-the-tropics spin. From Negril to Ocho Rios, resorts make their strongest statement by including everything, even drinks and cigarettes, in a single price. Unfortunately, that one price you pay often seems to factor in a carton of cigarettes and 10 piña coladas daily. For that reason, a number of Jamaica's all-inclusives have not been included here: Their rates are simply too high, even considering all the "freebies" that come with the price tag.

Those who don't opt for the all-inclusive route will still find their choices on Jamaica plentiful. If you plan to sample the varied cuisine at the island's many restaurants, you'll probably want to stay in a hotel offering EP rates. Other properties offer MAP or FAP packages that include extras such as airport transfers and sightseeing tours. Even if you don't want to be tied down to a meal plan, it pays to inquire, as the savings can be considerable. Backpacking types can explore the island's camping options (*see* Camping, *below*). Consider also geography when choosing where to stay:

Montego Bay has miles of hotels, villas, apartments, and duty-free shops set around Doctor's Cave Beach. Although lacking much cultural stimulus, the area is a comfortable island backdrop for the many conventions and conferences it hosts.

Ocho Rios, on the northwest coast halfway between Port Antonio and Montego Bay, long enjoyed the reputation of being Jamaica's most favored out-of-the-way resort, but the late-blooming Negril has since stolen much of that distinction. Ocho Rios's hotels and villas are all situated within short driving distance of shops and one of Jamaica's most scenic attractions, Dunn's River Falls.

Port Antonio, described by poet Ella Wheeler Wilcox as "the most exquisite port on earth," is a seaside town nestled at the foot of verdant hills toward the east end of the north coast.

Negril, some 50 miles west of Montego Bay, has become a byword for the newest crop of all-inclusive resorts. Negril itself is only a small village, so there isn't much of historical significance to seek out. Then again, that's not what brings the sybaritic singles and couples here. The crowd is young, hip, laid-back, and open to alternative lifestyles. You'll find some of the island's best accommodation bargains here.

Mandeville, 2,000 feet above the sea, is noted for its cool climate and proximity to secluded south coast beaches. The smallest of the resort areas, **Runaway Bay** has a handful of modern hotels and an 18-hole golf course.

Kingston is the most culturally active place on Jamaica. Some of the island's finest hotels are located here, and those high towers are filled with rooftop restaurants, English pubs, serious theater and pantomime, dance presentations, art museums and galleries, jazz clubs, upscale supper clubs, and disco dives. The beaches around the city are not terribly attractive and are sometimes polluted. Hotels here do not run shuttles to better beaches, so if you stay here count on a good 20- to 30-minute drive.

Highly recommended lodgings are indicated by a star ★.

Category	Cost EP*	Cost AI**
Moderate	$150–$225	$250–$350
Inexpensive	$75–$150	
Budget	under $75	

*EP prices are for a standard double room for two, excluding 6% tax and any service charge. To estimate rates for hotels offering MAP, add about $30–$40 per person per day to the above price ranges. For FAP, add about $60 per person per day (these rates may include extras).
**All-inclusive prices are per couple and include tax, service, all meals, drinks, facilities, lessons, airport transfers.*

Falmouth **Trelawny Beach Hotel.** The dependable Trelawny Beach resort offers seven stories of rooms overlooking 4 miles of beach. In recent years it has become semi-all-inclusive (lunch and liquor are excluded) with an emphasis on families. Children under 12 get free room and board during the off-season when they share accommodations with their parents. *Box 54, Falmouth, tel. 809/954-2450, fax 809/954-2173. 350 rooms. Facilities: 2 dining rooms, 4 lighted tennis courts, pool, complimentary use of water-sports equipment, shopping arcade, beauty salon, disco, nightly entertainment. AE, DC, MC, V. EP, MAP. Moderate.*

★ **Fisherman's Inn Dive Resort.** A charming red tile-and-stucco building fronts a phosphorescent lagoon at this welcoming, well-run hotel. At night the hotel restaurant offers a free boat ride to diners; dip your hand in the water, and the bioluminescent microorganisms glow. The bright breezy rooms all face the water and have air-conditioning, satellite TV, patio, and full bath. Excellent dive packages are available. *Falmouth P.O., tel. and fax 809/954-3427. 12 rooms. Facilities: restaurant, bar, pool, water sports (include PADI shop). AE, MC, V. EP, MAP. Inexpensive.*

Kingston **Jamaica Pegasus.** The Jamaica Pegasus is one of two fine business
★ hotels in the New Kingston area. The 17-story complex near downtown is virtually a convention center, with some good restaurants, handsome old-world decor, and at least a little pampering. The Polo Bar Lounge in the hotel lobby is a comfortable place to sit and have a drink. *Box 333, Kingston, tel. 809/926-3690, fax 809/929-4062. 350 rooms, 13 suites. Facilities: restaurants, cocktail lounge, shops, Olympic-size pool, jogging track, health club, 2 lighted tennis courts. AE, DC, MC, V. EP, MAP. Moderate.*

Wyndham Kingston. The main competition to Jamaica Pegasus on the Kingston business beat, the high-rise Wyndham Kingston also has 17 stories but adds seven cabana buildings, with additional apartment units planned for completion in 1994. A recent renovation upgraded existing facilities. The pleasant modern rooms have air-conditioning, satellite TV, direct-dial phones, and hair dryers. *Box 112, Kingston, tel. 809/926-5430, fax 809/929-7439. 300 rooms, 14 suites. Facilities: Olympic-size pool, gardens, conference space for 800, meeting rooms, 2 lighted tennis courts, health club, 2 restaurants, 3 bars, disco. AE, DC, MC, V. EP, MAP. Moderate.*

Morgan's Harbour Hotel, Beach Club, and Yacht Marina. A favorite of the sail-into-Jamaica set, this small property boasts 22 acres of beachfront at the very entrance to the old pirate's town. Rooms are decorated in either a provincial or an 18th-century nautical style that the pirate Captain Morgan would have appreciated. *Port Royal, Kingston, tel. 809/924–8487, fax 809/924–8562. 46 rooms, 5 suites. Facilities: full-service marina, pier bar, restaurant, disco, access to Lime Cay and other cays. AE, MC, V. EP. Inexpensive–Moderate.*

Hotel Oceana. This high rise is near the National Gallery, government offices, and the ferry to Port Royal. While it lacks the finesse of the Pegasus or Wyndham, the rooms are quieter and extremely comfortable, with floral decor, fine mountain or harbor views, and all amenities. *Box 986, Kingston, tel. 809/922–0920, fax 809/922–3928. 250 rooms. Facilities: 2 restaurants, 2 bars, beauty salon, cocktail lounge, shopping arcade, pool. AE, DC, MC, V. EP, MAP. Inexpensive.*

Hotel Four Seasons. This rambling, converted Edwardian mansion is a bit frayed around the edges, but that only contributes to its shabby, genteel charm. The comfortable, spacious rooms all include telephones, cable TVs, air-conditioning, and full baths; many feature period antiques. The clientele is an amiable blend of Europeans, honeymooners, and locals. It's a refreshing change of pace from other Kingston accommodations, which range from efficient business hotels to plain guest houses, with little in between. *18 Ruthven Rd., Kingston 10, tel. 809/926–8805, fax 809/929–5964. 39 rooms. Facilities: restaurant, bar, access to nearby pool. AE, MC, V. EP, MAP. Budget-Inexpensive.*

Pine Grove Mountain Chalets. Hibiscus, oleander, and frangipani drape the steep winding road that leads to this rustic, tranquil retreat nestled in the Blue Mountains overlooking Kingston. The landscaped grounds are dotted with sculpted topiary and laced with brick walkways, with strategically placed vantage points for drinking in the sublime views. The simply outfitted units all include TVs, shower baths, and full kitchens, and are decorated in pastel prints and earth tones. The restaurant serves delicious local cuisine at reasonable prices. The friendly owners often arrange hikes up Blue Mountain peak and trips to their coffee plantation. At press time, an additional 15 units were slated for completion by summer 1993. *Content Gap P.A., St. Andrew, tel. 809/922–8705. 27 studios. Facilities: restaurant. No credit cards. EP, MAP, FAP. Budget.*

Morant Bay Villas. If you really want to get away from it all, stay at one of these Spartan villas in the middle of nowhere between Kingston and Port Antonio. You'll experience true local flavor (95% of the clientele are Jamaican families) at unbeatable tariffs ($40 and under). Units all have private baths, fans, and TVs. Larger units have kitchenettes; smaller rooms have minifridges. The beach is rocky and poky, but glorious Lyssons is a 30-minute walk away. *Morant Bay, St. Thomas, tel. 809/982–2418. 25 units. Facilities: restaurant, bar. No credit cards. EP, MAP. Budget.*

Mandeville **Astra Hotel.** A hotel with guest-house charm, the Astra is situ-
★ ated 2,000 feet up in the hills, providing an ideal getaway for nature lovers and outdoors enthusiasts. *Ward Ave., Box 60, Mandeville, tel. 809/962–3265, fax 809/962–1461. 22 rooms. Facilities: restaurant and bar, swimming pool, golf course and tennis court nearby, horseback riding, bird-watching, fitness center, satellite TV. AE, V. EP. Inexpensive.*

Mandeville Hotel. The Victorian Mandeville Hotel, set in tropical gardens, has redecorated for the 1990s. There's now a flower-filled garden terrace for breakfast and lunch, and simple private rooms. *Box 78, Mandeville, tel. 809/962–2460, fax 809/962–0700. 60 rooms. Facilities: restaurant, cocktail lounge, golf privileges at nearby Manchester Club. AE, MC, V. EP. Inexpensive.*

Montego Bay   **Holiday Inn Rose Hall.** Here the great equalizer of hotel chains has done much to raise a run-down campground to the level of a full-service property, with activities day and night and many tour facilities. Although the rooms are cheerful enough, the hotel is big and noisy, with drab hallways and public areas. The quietest rooms are those farthest from the pool. *Box 480, Montego Bay, tel. 809/953–2485. 520 rooms. Facilities: pool, watersports center, 3 restaurants, 4 bars, exercise room, shops. AE, DC, MC, V. EP. Moderate.*

Seacastles. This new apartment resort, with colonnaded verandas alternating with imposing turrets, resembles a cross between Camelot and a West Indian plantation great house. The units are located in six "castles" spread over 14 acres and constructed around a central courtyard with splashing fountain. The studio apartments are smallish and rather plain, but quite adequate; suites have a little more character. The still-developing beach is pleasant and tree-shaded, and everything you could possibly need is on the premises. Seacastles is especially popular with families: Up to two children under 12 can both stay (in parents' room) and eat for free. *Box 1, Rose Hall, Montego Bay, tel. 809/953–3250, fax 809/953–3062. 198 studios and suites. Facilities: 3 restaurants, 3 bars, pool, 2 lighted tennis courts, water-sports center, car rental, laundry service. AE, DC, MC, V. EP, MAP, FAP. Moderate.*

Wyndham Rose Hall. The veteran Wyndham Rose Hall, a self-contained resort built on the 400-acre Rose Hall Plantation, mixes recreation with a top-flight conference setup. This typical bustling business hotel with modern amenities is popular with groups, but is somewhat lacking in charm. *Box 999, Montego Bay, tel. 809/953–2650, fax 809/953–2617. 489 rooms, 19 suites. Facilities: 3 pools, water sports, 6 tennis courts, golf course, 4 restaurants, coffee shop, nightclub, lounge, fitness center, laundry service, shopping arcade. AE, DC, MC, V. EP. Moderate.*

Reading Reef Club. Four miles southwest of Montego Bay airport, this owner-operated resort is ideal for families and honeymooners who appreciate its seclusion and its quiet, understated elegance. Another of Jamaica's fine small-hotel values, it offers simply but tastefully furnished rooms and an excellent pasta/seafood restaurant, the Safari. Golf and horseback riding can be arranged. There is a small, adequate beach at the property. *Box 225, Reading, Montego Bay, tel. 809/952–5909 or 800/223–6510, fax 809/952–7217. 26 rooms, 2 suites. Facilities: private beach, pool, dive shop, water sports, restaurant. AE, MC, V. EP, MAP. Inexpensive–Moderate.*

Cariblue Beach Resort. This rather dilapidated but ultrafriendly hotel is a favorite with divers. The unassuming but comfortable rooms feature phones, air-conditioning, private baths, and radios. All but a few have an unobstructed ocean view. Calling this a beach resort is a tad grandiose (the sandy stretch is rather paltry), but the nautically minded guests are usually out on the water. The prow-shaped patio of the fine seafood restaurant is a popular gathering place at happy hour. *Ironshore, Box 610, Montego Bay. 20 rooms. Facilities: restau-*

rant, bar, pool, water-sports and dive shop. AE, MC, V. EP, MAP. Inexpensive.

Fantasy Resort. After a brief stint as an all-inclusive resort, this property has gone back to standard hotel status. The resort sports high-rise design and a Mediterranean flair. All nine stories have terraces with ocean views. A small beach is across the street. This efficient and pleasant property is a good buy and usually booked solid with tour groups. *Opposite Cornwall Beach, Box 161, Montego Bay, tel. 809/952–4150, fax 809/952–3637. 119 rooms. Facilities: open-air bar, dining room, pool, disco, shopping arcade. AE, DC, MC, V. EP. Inexpensive.*

★ **Richmond Hill Inn.** The hilltop Richmond Hill Inn, a quaint, 200-year-old great house originally owned by the Dewars clan, attracts repeat visitors by providing spectacular views of the Caribbean and a great deal of peace, compared with MoBay's hustle. Decor here tends toward the dainty, with frilly lace curtains and doilies and lots of lavenders and mauves. The hotel offers a free shuttle to beaches, about 10–15 minutes away. *Union St., Box 362, Montego Bay, tel. 809/952–3859. 15 rooms, 5 suites. Facilities: pool, terrace dining room, coffee shop, bar, free beach shuttle. AE, MC, V. EP, MAP, FAP. Inexpensive.*

Sandals Inn. Now a part of the Sandals group, the cozy Sandals Inn operates as an all-inclusive for couples. Its charming rooms have balconies facing the sea, and it is convenient to shopping and tours in Montego Bay. Be forewarned that there's no escaping the festivities at this intimate resort. The PA system might blast you out of your room. While there is a small beach just across the street, many guests prefer to take the free shuttle to other Sandals properties, with their extensive beaches and facilities. *Box 412, Montego Bay, tel. 809/952–4140 or 800/SANDALS, fax 809/952–6913. 52 rooms. Facilities: beach privileges, pool, restaurants, pub, satellite TV, gift shop, lighted tennis court, fitness center. AE, DC, MC, V. All-inclusive. Moderate.*

★ **Toby Inn.** This quiet oasis amid the bustle of downtown MoBay is everything a small budget hotel should be—pleasant, comfortable, and conveniently located. The property is shaded by almond and grapefruit trees filled with chirping birds and is only half a block from the small public beach (major beaches are a five- to 10-minute walk away). The small but homey rooms are located either in individual cottages or balconied buildings surrounding the lively pool area. The Oriental/Jamaican restaurant is civilized, inexpensive, and very good. *1 Kent Ave., Box 467, Montego Bay, tel. 809/952–4370, fax 809/952–6591. 72 rooms. Facilities: restaurant, bar, 2 pools, tennis court, boutique, beauty salon. AE, MC, V. EP, MAP, FAP. Budget–Inexpensive.*

Verney House Hotel. This intimate little inn tucked in the hills above Montego Bay couldn't be less touristy, nor its owner more cordial. The clean, fresh rooms include full baths, phones, ceiling fans, TVs, and air-conditioning. The charming restaurant is alive with hanging plants and flowers. With the feel of a private home, this is definitely real Jamaica, including the warm reception. There's a free shuttle (a 10- to 15-minute drive) to the beach. *3 Leader Ave., Box 18, Montego Bay, tel. 809/952–2875. 28 rooms. Facilities: restaurant, bar, pool, free beach shuttle. AE, MC, V. EP, MAP. Budget.*

Negril
★ **Hedonism II.** Here is the resort that introduced the all-inclusive to Jamaica a little over 15 years ago. Still wildly successful,

Hedonism appeals most to vacationers who like a robust mix of physical activities, all listed daily on a chalkboard. A recent $2 million refurbishment spruced up the public areas. The rooms are modern and handsome, with lots of blond wood. The clientele is 60% single. *Box 25, Negril, tel. 809/957–4200 or 800/858–8009, fax 809/957–4289. 280 rooms. Facilities: watersports center, including scuba diving; fitness center and trapeze and trampoline clinics; open-air buffet dining room, disco and bar; horseback riding, 6 lighted tennis courts, shuffleboard, volleyball, squash. AE, MC, V. All-inclusive. Moderate.*

Negril Inn. One of Jamaica's prettiest palm-speckled sandy beaches is the center of almost everything the all-inclusive Negril Inn does for its guests. *Negril, tel. 809/957–4209 or 800/634–7456, fax 809/957–4365. 46 rooms. Facilities: restaurant, dancing, entertainment, satellite TV, lounge, 2 tennis courts, disco, water-sports center. AE, MC, V. All-inclusive. Moderate.*

Seasplash. The deluxe, tastefully decorated suites in these Mediterranean-style villas boast lovely garden or sea views. All units have full baths, air-conditioning, kitchenettes, phones, and satellite TVs. Tropical color schemes feature lilacs and mauves. The rates are a bargain, considering the lovely, fully equipped rooms and the tranquil grounds. *Norman Manley Blvd., Box 123, Negril, tel. 809/957–4041, fax 809/957–4049. 2 rooms, 14 suites. Facilities: restaurant, bar, pool, Jacuzzi, boutique, minigym. AE, MC, V. EP, MAP, FAP. Moderate.*

★ **Charela Inn.** Each of the air-conditioned, elegantly appointed rooms at this intimate inn offers a balcony or a covered patio. The owners' French-Jamaican roots find daily expression in the kitchen, and there's an excellent selection of wines. The beach here is part of the glorious 7-mile Negril crescent. *Box 33, Negril, Westmoreland, tel. 809/957–4277. 26 rooms, 4 suites. Facilities: restaurant. DC, MC, V. EP, MAP. Inexpensive–Moderate.*

Negril Cabins. These timber cottages are nestled amid lush vegetation and towering royal palms. Rooms are unadorned, but have a fresh, natural look. The gleaming beach is right across the road. A most convivial place, and highly popular with young Europeans. *Negril P.O., tel. 809/957–4350, fax 809/957–4381. 24 rooms. Facilities: restaurant, bar. AE, MC, V. EP. Inexpensive.*

Negril Gardens. A study in colonial pink and white, the new Negril Gardens bills itself as the "friendly alternative" to Negril's all-inclusive scene. It is attractive and offers a nice beach with water sports. *Negril, Westmoreland, tel. 809/957–4408, fax 809/957–4374. 54 rooms. Facilities: terrace restaurant, tennis, pool, water sports. AE, MC, V. EP. Inexpensive.*

Rock Cliff Hotel. These whitewashed villas perched near the cliffs are a terrific value. The only drawback is the lack of a beach, though the friendly owners and fellow guests often ferry those without wheels; otherwise the public beach is a 25-minute walk away, or you can clamber down the rocks to the small sunbathing area. The charming rooms all have invigorating sea views and breezes, mahogany furnishings, air-conditioning, and full baths. *West End Rd., Box 67, Negril, tel. 809/957–4331, fax 809/957–4108. 31 rooms, 2 suites. Facilities: restaurant, bar, pool, Jacuzzi, gift shop, water-sports center including 5-star PADI dive shop. AE, MC, V. EP, MAP. Inexpensive.*

Thrills. The beach is a 10-minute drive, a 20-minute bike ride, or a 30-minute walk away from this modest, hopping little inn, but the cliffs just 200 yards distant are a spectacular site for snorkeling. The spare but pleasant rooms are decorated in muted earth tones and feature louvered blinds, private shower baths, ceiling fans, and patios. *Box 99, Negril, tel. 809/957–4390, fax 809/957–4153. 28 rooms. Facilities: restaurant, bar, disco, pool, bike rental. AE, MC, V. EP, MAP. Budget.*

Ocho Rios **Boscobel Beach.** Boscobel Beach is a parent's dream for a Ja-
★ maican vacation, an all-inclusive that makes families feel wel-
come. The cheery day-care centers, divided by age group, should be a model for the rest of the Caribbean. Everybody is kept busy all week for a single package price, and everyone leaves happy. Regular (not junior) suites are not affordable un-less shared with another couple. There's a fine beach here. *Box 63, Ocho Rios, tel. 809/974–3291 or 800/858–8009, fax 809/975– 3270. 208 rooms, half of them junior suites. Facilities: satellite TV, gym, Jacuzzi, windsurfing, scuba diving, sailing, snor-keling, 3 restaurants, 5 bars, 2 pools, disco, day-care center, bou-tique, 4 lighted tennis courts, volleyball, golf at Jamaica, Jamaica/Runaway Bay. AE, DC, MC, V. All-inclusive. Moder-ate.*

Couples. No singles, no children. The emphasis at Couples is on romantic adventure for just the two of you, and the all-in-clusive concept eliminates the decision making that can intrude on social pleasure. Couples has the highest occupancy rate of any resort on the island—and perhaps the most suggestive logo as well. There may be a correlation. *Tower Isle, St. Mary, tel. 809/975–4271, fax 809/975–4439. 172 rooms, 12 suites. Facili-ties: pool, satellite TV, island for nude swimming, 3 lighted ten-nis courts, Nautilus gym, 2 air-conditioned squash courts, a water-sports center that includes scuba diving, horseback rid-ing, nightly entertainment, golf at Runaway Bay, 3 Jacuzzis, 3 restaurants, 3 bars, shopping arcade. AE, DC, MC, V. All-inclu-sive. Moderate.*

The Enchanted Garden. Set on 20 acres in the former Carinosa Gardens, this all-inclusive resort opened in the winter of 1991– 92. The stunning gardens showcase tropical plants, flowers, and a dramatic series of streams and waterfalls. The futuristic pink cinderblock buildings seem incongruous amid the natural splendor, but the rooms are comfortable, and you're never far from the soothing sound of rushing water. There is an aviary and a seaquarium where you can enjoy a delicatessen lunch or tea surrounded by tanks of fish and hanging orchids. *Box 284, Ocho Rios, tel. 809/974–1400 or 800/654–1337, fax 809/974–5623. 60 rooms, 40 suites. Facilities: spa, disco, gift shop, beauty par-lor, satellite TV, aviary, 4 restaurants, hillside gardens, 2 lighted tennis courts, golf and horseback riding nearby. Daily transpor-tation and picnic to private beach. AE, MC, V. All-inclusive. Moderate.*

Jamaica Grande. Ramada bought the Americana (Divi-Divi) and the Mallards Beach Resort and created Jamaica Grande, now the largest conference hotel in Jamaica. At press time, a major refurbishment program and the addition of a conference center were scheduled to be completed for summer 1993, at a cost of $20 million. This property's clientele is mostly families, couples, conference attendees, and incentive-travel winners. The resort's focal point is the fantasy pool with waterfall, sway-ing bridge, and swim-up bar. Accommodations in the south building are a bit roomier; those in the north boast slightly better views. The staff is quite friendly for such a large, rather charmless property. *Box 100, Ocho Rios, tel. 809/974–2201, fax 809/974–5378. 691 rooms, 21 suites. Facilities: 5 restaurants, water-sports center, fitness center, disco, 4 tennis courts, children's day-care center, 3 pools, gaming parlor, shopping arcade, beauty salon, lighted tennis court. AE, DC, MC, V. EP. Moderate.*

Sandals Ocho Rios. The Sandals concept follows its successful formula at this couples-only, all-inclusive nine-acre resort. The mix of white and sand colors contrasts nicely with the vegetation and the sea. The accommodations are airy and pleasant, with king-size beds, air-conditioning, satellite TV, direct-dial phones, hair dryers, and safe-deposit boxes. Geared to the super couple, this Sandals seems to offer even more daily activities than do the other all-inclusives. *Ocho Rios, tel. 809/974–5691 or 800/327–1991, fax 809/974–5700. 237 units. Facilities: 3 restaurants, 4 bars, gift shop, 3 pools, 2 lighted tennis courts, disco, fitness center, satellite TV, water-sports center. AE, DC, MC, V. All-inclusive. Moderate.*

Shaw Park Beach Hotel. This popular property offers a pleasant alternative to downtown high rises. Rooms are fairly nondescript, but comfortable. There's a smallish beach on the property, and the grounds are colorful and well tended. The Silks disco is a favorite for late-night carousing. *Cutlass Bay, Box 17, Ocho Rios, tel. 809/974–2552 or 800/243–9420, fax 809/974–5042. 118 rooms. Facilities: restaurant, water sports, disco, pool, massage. AE, DC, MC, V. EP. Moderate.*

Jamel Continental. This spotless, upscale tropical motel is set on its own beach in a relatively undeveloped area close to all the activities of Ocho Rios and Runaway Bay. The well-appointed units are spacious and breezy; all feature a balcony with sea view, full bath, phone, air-conditioning, and satellite TV. In addition to the usual floral prints and pastel hues, there are unexpected touches, such as mahogany writing desks and Oriental throw rugs. The moderately priced restaurant serves fine local dishes, and the staff is friendly and helpful. *2 Richmond Estate, Priory, St. Ann, tel. 809/972–1031. 17 rooms, 3 suites. Facilities: restaurant, bar, pool, gift shop. MC, V. EP, MAP, FAP. Inexpensive.*

★ **Hibiscus Lodge.** This gleaming white building with a blue canopy sits amid beautifully manicured lawns laced with trellises, overlooking its own tiny private beach. The impeccably neat, cozy rooms all have at least a partial sea view, terrace, air-conditioning, and full bath. This German-run property may be Jamaica's best bargain, attracting a discriminating (and jubilant) crowd. *Box 52, Ocho Rios, tel. 809/974–2676, fax 809/974–1874. 26 rooms. Facilities: pool, restaurant, piano bar, lighted tennis court. AE, DC, MC, V. EP, MAP, FAP. Budget–Inexpensive.*

Parkway Inn. In this downtown Ocho Rios property that's popular with Jamaican businesspeople, plain but dainty rooms feature air-conditioning, telephones, and private baths. The upstairs restaurant is a local favorite for moderately priced Chinese/Jamaican specialties such as curried goat, baked crab, and shrimp fried rice. The beach is a 10-minute walk away. *Main St., Ocho Rios, tel. 809/974–2667. 21 rooms. Facilities: restaurant, bar. MC, V. EP, MAP. Budget.*

Port Antonio **Goblin Hill.** This lush 13-acre estate sits atop a hill overlooking SanSan cove. Each attractively appointed villa at this peaceful, relaxing oasis comes with its own dramatic view, plus a housekeeper-cook. Rates are at the high end of our Moderate category. *Box 26, Port Antonio, tel. 809/993–3286, fax 809/925–6248.*

28 villas. Facilities: pool, 2 tennis courts. AE, MC, V. EP. Moderate.

Jamaica Palace. Built to resemble an Edwardian mansion, this imposing five-year-old property rises in an expanse of white pillared marble. Inside is more white, contrasting with black lacquer and gilded oversize furniture. Each room has a semicircular bed and original European *objets d'art* and Oriental rugs; some are more lavish than others. There is a 114-foot swimming pool shaped like Jamaica. The beach is a 10- to 15-minute walk away. *Box 227, Port Antonio, tel. 809/993–2021. 54 rooms, 5 suites, 20 junior suites. Facilities: restaurant, 2 bars, swimming pool, baby-sitters on request, boutique. AE, MC, V. EP, MAP. Inexpensive–Moderate.*

Bonnie View Plantation Hotel. Accommodations here are Spartan, mattresses are a tad lumpy, and the furnishings a bit frayed. But the hotel certainly lives up to its name: Locals and Europeans flock here for the sublime views and air of tranquillity. The nicest rooms (more expensive) are those with private verandas. But you can open your window for a burst of invigorating mountain air, or hang out in the restaurant and savor the unparalleled water panoramas. Beachcombers are forewarned: It's a good 25-minute drive to the ocean. *Box 82, Port Antonio, tel. 809/993–2752, fax 809/993–2862. 20 rooms. Facilities: pool, sun deck. AE, DC, MC, V. EP. Inexpensive.*

DeMontevin Lodge. This historic place offers the ambience of a more genteel time. The rooms are basic and spotless, with circular fans overhead. Outsiders are welcome for very tasty home cooking at lunch or dinner, with prior reservations. The better beaches are on the other side of town from here, a 10- to 15-minute drive away. *Fort George St. on Titchfield Hill, Port Antonio, tel. 809/993–2604. 15 rooms. Facilities: bar, restaurant. AE. EP. Inexpensive.*

Runaway Bay **FDR, Franklyn D. Resort.** Jamaica's first all-suite, all-inclusive resort for families, the FDR opened in 1990. The sugary pink buildings of this casual property are grouped in a horseshoe around the swimming pool and face the ocean. Units are light and roomy. Rates are at the high end of our Moderate category, unless you share one of the larger suites with another family. *Runaway Bay, tel. 809/973–3067 or 800/654–1FDR, fax 809/973–3071. 67 suites. Facilities: pool, water sports, beach, gym, restaurant, satellite TV, lighted tennis court, golf, disco, piano bar, miniclub for children with supervised activities. AE, MC, V. All-inclusive. Moderate.*

Jamaica, Jamaica. This all-inclusive was a pioneer in emphasizing the sheer Jamaicanness of the island over the generic sensuality. The cooking is particularly first-rate. Spartan lodgings resemble tropical dorm rooms, but are nevertheless comfortable, with all amenities including hair dryers and safe-deposit boxes. The American and European clientele who stay here don't seem to mind; Germans, Italians, and Japanese flock here for the superb golf school (plans are afoot to make the already excellent course more challenging) and colorful reef surrounding the beach. Guests must be over 16. *Box 58, Runaway Bay, tel. 809/973–2436, fax 809/973–2352. 238 rooms, 4 suites. Facilities: water-sports center, 2 lighted tennis courts, horseback riding, 2 restaurants, PADI 5-star dive center, 2 bars, gym, sundries shop, sightseeing tours, disco, nightly entertainment, 3 Jacuzzis, 18-hole golf course with golf school nearby. AE, DC, MC, V. All-inclusive. Moderate.*

Club Caribbean. This all-inclusive resort reopened its doors in winter 1990 after a $3 million renovation. A series of typically Caribbean cottages, half with kitchenettes, line the long but narrow gray-sand beach. Sixty cottages have bunk rooms instead of kitchenettes and are very reasonably priced. The rooms are simple but clean, with rattan furnishings and floral prints. The resort is very popular with European families (children under 12 stay free). *Box 65, Runaway Bay, tel. 809/973–3507, fax 809/973–3509. 128 rooms. Facilities: pool, shopping arcade, JAMAQUA PADI 5-star dive center, water-sports center, tennis courts, massage and exercise, day-care center with children's program, 2 restaurants. AE, MC, V. All-inclusive. Moderate.*

★ **H.E.A.R.T. Country Club.** It's a shame more visitors don't know about this place, perched above Runaway Bay and brimming with Jamaica's true character. While training young islanders interested in the tourism industry, it also provides a remarkably quiet and pleasant stay for guests. The employees make an effort to please, and the tranquil restaurant serves delicious local and Continental specialties. An excellent beach is a 20-minute hike (uphill coming back) or a 5- to 10-minute drive away. *Box 98, St. Ann, tel. 809/973–2671, fax 809/973–2693. 20 rooms. Facilities: satellite TV, golf, beach shuttle, restaurant. AE, MC, V. EP, MAP. Inexpensive.*

Tamarind Tree Hotel. Only a three-minute walk from the beach, this whitewashed building has pastel trim and fluttering blue awnings. The smallish but bright rooms all contain TVs, direct-dial phones, and full baths. The cottages include a kitchenette and are a superb buy for large families. *Box 235, Runaway Bay, tel. 809/973–2678. 16 rooms, 3 three-bedroom cottages. Facilities: restaurant, pool, disco. AE, MC, V. EP, MAP. Budget–Inexpensive.*

Villa and Apartment Rental Although Jamaica has some luxurious villas, many more are comfortable, reasonably priced properties. While a few are located on beaches, most are situated in the hills, making a car a virtual necessity. Recommended management companies for villas and apartment complexes include **Relax Villas** (Montego Bay, tel. 809/952–7218); **Sunshine Rental Villas** (Ocho Rios, tel. 809/974–5025); and **Jamswing Villas and Condos** (Runaway Bay, tel. 809/973–4847). For a complete listing, contact the **Jamaica Association of Villas and Apartments** (tel. 800/221–8830). Member companies must adhere to certain guidelines.

Camping There are extensive camping facilities throughout the island, most of them clean, safe, and well-run. The acknowledged leader in the field is **JATCHA** (Jamaica Alternative Tourism Camping and Hiking Association, Box 216, Kingston 7, tel. 809/927–2097). For $15 they'll send information on more than 100 recommended properties, as well as maps and a questionnaire to ascertain your particular needs. Their personalized service will do everything from make reservations to suggesting a tailor-made itinerary.

Off-Season Bets While exclusive properties such as Half Moon and Trident remain out of our price range even during the off-season, several all-inclusives become affordable. In Montego Bay, these include: **Sandals Montego Bay** (Box 100, Montego Bay, tel. 809/952–5510 or 800/SANDALS, fax 809/952–0816) and **Sandals Royal Caribbean** (Box 167, Montego Bay, tel. 809/953–2231 or 800/SANDALS, fax 809/953–2788). In Negril, try **Swept**

Away (Long Bay, Negril, tel. 809/957–4061 or 800/545–7937, fax 809/957–4060).

The Arts and Nightlife

Jamaica—especially Kingston—supports a lively community of musicians. For starters there is reggae, popularized by the late Bob Marley and the Wailers and performed today by son Ziggy Marley, Jimmy Tosh (the late Peter Tosh's son), Gregory Isaccs, the Third World, Jimmy Cliff, and many others. If your experience of Caribbean music has been limited to steel drums and Harry Belafonte, then the political, racial, and religious messages of reggae may set you on your ear; listen closely and you just might hear the heartbeat of the people.

Nightlife and Bars For the most part, the liveliest late-night happenings throughout Jamaica are in the major resort hotels. Some of the best music will be found in Negril at **De Buss** (tel. 809/957–4405) and at the hot, hot spot **Kaiser's Cafe** (tel. 809/957–4070), as well as at the **Disco** at Hedonism II (tel. 809/957–4200), and **Horselips** (no tel.). The most popular spots in Kingston today are **Mingles** at the Courtleigh (tel. 809/929–5321), **Illusions** in the New Lane Plaza (tel. 809/929–2125), and **Jonkanoo** in the Wyndham New Kingston (tel. 809/926–5430).

In Port Antonio, if you have but one night to disco, do it at **The Roof Club,** 11 West Street. On weekends, from elevenish on, this is where it's all happening. The principal clubs in Ocho Rios are **Acropolis** on Main Street (tel. 809/974–2633), **Silks** in the Shaw Park Beach Hotel (tel. 809/974–2552), and the **Little Pub on Main Street** (tel. 809/974–2324), which produces Caribbean revues. The hottest places in Montego Bay are the **Cave** disco at the Seawinds Beach Resort (tel. 809/952–4070), **Sir Winston's Reggae Club** on Gloucester Street (tel. 809/952–2084), and the **Witches Hideaway** at **Holiday Inn** (tel. 809/953–2485).

15 Martinique

Updated by
Nigel Fisher

Not for naught did the Arawaks name Martinique Madinina, which means "Island of Flowers." This is one of the most beautiful islands in the Caribbean, lush with exotic wild orchids, frangipani, anthurium, jade vines, flamingo flowers, and hundreds of vivid varieties of hibiscus. Trees bend under the weight of such tropical treats as mangoes, papayas, bright red West Indian cherries, lemons, limes, and bananas. Acres of banana plantations, pineapple fields, and waving green seas of sugarcane show the bounty of the island's fertile soil.

The towering mountains and verdant rain forest in the north lure hikers, while underwater sights and sunken treasures attract snorkelers and scuba divers. Martinique appeals as well to those whose idea of exercise is turning over every 10 or 15 minutes to get an even tan or whose adventuresome spirit is satisfied by finding booty in a duty-free shop. Francophiles in particular will find the island enchanting.

This 425-square-mile island is 4,261 miles from Paris, but its spirit (and language) is French with more than a mere soupçon of West Indian spice. Tangible, edible evidence of that fact is the island's cuisine—a tempting blend of classic French and Creole dishes.

Martinique became an overseas department of France in 1946 and a *région* in 1974, a status not unlike that of an American state vis-à-vis the federal government. The island has benefited from the economic growth in Europe; the standard of living and salaries here are some of the highest in the West Indies. Unfortunately for the budget traveler, this is reflected in the

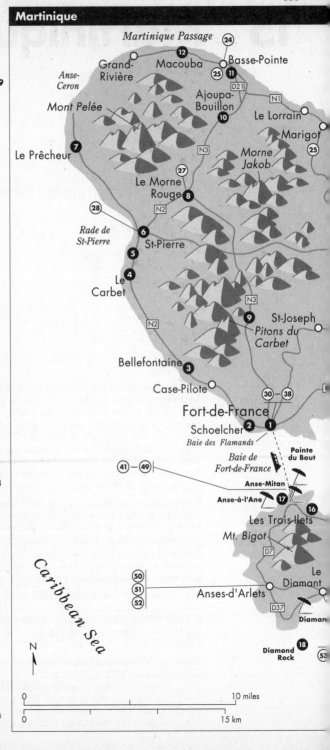

Martinique

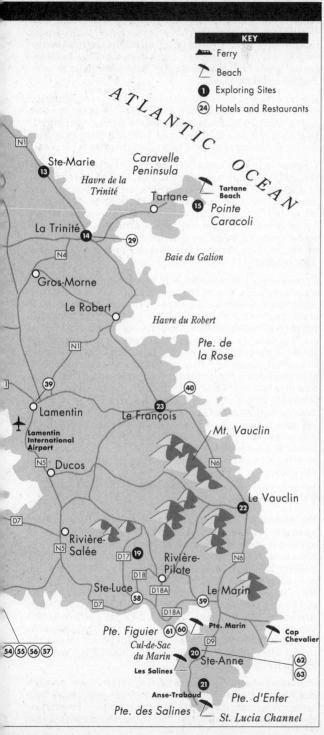

KEY

🛳 Ferry

🏖 Beach

1 Exploring Sites

24 Hotels and Restaurants

ATLANTIC OCEAN

Ste-Marie **13**

Caravelle Peninsula

Havre de la Trinité

Tartane **15**

Tartane Beach

Pointe Caracoli

La Trinité **14** **29**

Baie du Galion

Gros-Morne

Le Robert

Havre du Robert

Pte. de la Rose

39

Lamentin

40

23 Le François

Lamentin International Airport

Mt. Vauclin

Ducos

Le Vauclin

22

Rivière-Salée

19

Rivière-Pilote

Ste-Luce

58

Le Marin

59

Pte. Figuier **61** **60**

Pte. Marin

Cap Chevalier

Cul-de-Sac du Marin

54 **55** **56** **57**

20 Ste-Anne

62

Les Salines

63

21

Anse-Trabaud

Pte. d'Enfer

Pte. des Salines

St. Lucia Channel

prices. Dining in particular is expensive here, although you can comfort yourself with the knowledge that you're getting what you paid for: The quality of cuisine here is higher than on many Caribbean islands. Visitors on a budget find they can economize by picnicking. Grocery stores have tempting foods imported from France, and wine is more affordable than on English-speaking islands.

Rental cars and taxis are also costly. If you are planning a beach-combing vacation, take a small hotel close to the water so you won't require transportation throughout your stay. If your main activity will be exploring, look for lodging away from the beach; the lower cost will help offset the price of car rental.

Despite these high costs, Martinique's hotel prices compare favorably with other Caribbean islands. You can find a number of moderately priced hotels located on or near beaches, and many of these offer package deals that make them yet more affordable (always inquire when you call). Downright budget hotels are harder to find, but small apartments, cottages, and rooms in private homes are available through the island's Gîtes de France office. Most of these smaller properties are away from beaches.

What It Will Cost These sample prices, meant only as a general guide, are for high season. Martinique has many small hotels in the $100-a-night range. Resort hotels on the beach start at about $150. A small apartment rents for about $45 a day. Expect to pay $20 per person for dinner—more than on some islands, but the food tends to be better. Wine is reasonably priced; a recent vintage Médoc is about $7 at the grocery store, and a bottle of house wine at a restaurant can be as low as $12. Local beer is $2.50–$3 at a restaurant; a rum punch ranges from less than $2 at a local rum shop to at least $3.50 at a restaurant. Public transportation is limited, so one of your biggest costs here will be a car. An average daily rental is $60. Taxis are also expensive. Cost from the airport to Fort-de-France is about $15, and about $28 to Pointe du Bout. A *vedette*, or ferry, from Fort-de-France to Pointe du Bout costs 12F (about U.S. $2.50). A single-tank dive here is around $55, while snorkel equipment rents for about $10 a day.

Before You Go

Tourist Information For information contact the **French West Indies Tourist Board** by calling France-on-Call at 900/990–0040 (50¢ per minute) or write to the **French Government Tourist Office** (610 5th Ave., New York, NY 10020, tel. 212/757–1125; 9454 Wilshire Blvd., Beverly Hills, CA 90212, tel. 213/272–2661; 645 N. Michigan Ave., Chicago, IL 60611, tel. 312/337–6301; 2305 Cedar Spring Rd., Dallas TX 75201, tel. 214/720–4010). In Canada, contact the French Government Tourist Office (1981 McGill College Ave., Suite 490, Montreal, P.Q. H3A 2W9, tel. 514/288–4264; 1 Dundas St. W, Suite 2405, Toronto, Ont. M5G 1Z3, tel. 416/593–4723 or 800/361–9099). In the United Kingdom, contact the tourist office (178 Piccadilly, London, United Kingdom W1V 0AL, tel. 071/499–6911).

Arriving and Departing *By Plane* The most frequent flights from the United States are on **American Airlines** (tel. 800/433–7300), which has year-round daily service from more than 100 U.S. cities to San Juan. From there, the airline's American Eagle flies to Martinique with a stop first at Guadeloupe. **Minerve Airlines** (tel. 212/980–4546 or 800/765–6065), a French charter company, now flies Friday, Saturday, and Sunday nonstop from New York's JFK during the winter season (December through April). **Air France** (tel. 800/237–2747) flies direct from Miami and San Juan; **Air Canada** (tel. 800/422–6232) has service from Montreal and Toronto; **LIAT** (tel. 809/462–0700), with its extensive coverage of the Antilles, flies from Antigua, St. Maarten, Guadeloupe, Dominica, St. Lucia, Barbados, Grenada, and Trinidad and Tobago. **Air Martinique** (tel. 596/51–09–90) has service to and from St. Martin, Dominica, and Guadeloupe.

From the Airport You'll arrive at Lamentin International Airport, which is about a 15-minute taxi ride from Fort-de-France and about 40 minutes from the Trois-Ilets peninsula, where most of the hotels are located.

Cab fare to Fort-de-France is 70F, and 150F to Trois-Islets. A 40% surcharge is in effect between 8 PM and 6 AM. This means that if you arrive at Lamentin at night, depending on where your hotel is, it may be cheaper to rent a car from the airport than to take a one-way taxi. A bus departs hourly 6–6 to downtown Fort-de-France (cost: 10F).

Passports and Visas U.S. and Canadian citizens must have a passport (an expired passport may be used, as long as the expiration date is no more than five years ago) or proof of citizenship, such as an original (not photocopied) birth certificate or a voter registration card accompanied by a government-authorized photo identification. British citizens are required to have a passport. In addition, all visitors must have a return or ongoing ticket.

Language Many Martinicans speak Creole, which is a mixture of Spanish and French. Try *sa ou fe* for hello. In major tourist areas you'll find someone who speaks English, but the courtesy of using a few French words, even if it is *Parlez-vous anglais*, is appreciated. The people of Martinique are extremely courteous and will help you through your French. Even if you do speak fluent French, you may have a problem understanding the accent of the country people. Most menus are written in French, so a dictionary is helpful.

Precautions Exercise the same safety precautions you would in any other big city: Leave valuables in the hotel safe-deposit vault and lock your car, with luggage and valuables stashed out of sight. Don't leave jewelry or money unattended on the beach. Beware of the *ma«cenillie* (manchineel) trees. These pretty trees with little green fruits that look like apples are poisonous. Sap and even raindrops falling from the trees onto your skin can cause painful, scarring blisters. The trees have red warning signs posted by the Forestry Commission.

If you plan to ramble through the rain forest, be careful where you step. Poisonous serpents, cousins of the rattlesnake, slither through this lush tropical Eden. Except for the area around Cap Chevalier, the Atlantic waters are rough and should be avoided by all but expert swimmers.

Staying in Martinique

Important Addresses **Tourist Information:** The **Martinique Tourist Office** (Blvd. Alfassa, tel. 596/63–79–60) is open Monday–Thursday 7:30–12:30 PM and 2:30–5:30, Friday 7:30–12:30 and 2:30–5, Saturday 8–

noon. The office's free maps and booklet, *Martinique Info*, are useful. The Tourist Information Booth at Lamentin Airport is open daily until the last flight has landed.

Emergencies **Police:** Call 17. **Fire:** Call 18. **Ambulance:** Call 70–36–48 or 71–59–48. **Hospitals:** There is a 24-hour emergency room at **Hôpital La Meynard** (Châteauboeuf, just outside Fort-de-France, tel. 596/50–15–15). **Pharmacies:** Pharmacies in Fort-de-France include **Pharmacie de la Paix** (corner rue Victor Schoelcher and rue Perrinon, tel. 596/71–94–83) and **Pharmacie Cypria** (Blvd. de Gaulle, tel. 596/63–22–25). **Consulate:** The **United States Consulate** (14 rue Blénac, Fort-de-France, tel. 596/63–13–03).

Currency The coin of the realm is the French franc, which consists of 100 centimes. At press time, the rate was 5.30F to U.S. $1, but check the current exchange rate before you leave home. U.S. dollars are accepted in some of the tourist hotels, but for convenience, it's better to convert your money into francs. Banks give a more favorable rate than do hotels. A currency exchange service, **Change Caraibes,** is located at the Arrivals Building at Lamentin Airport (tel. 596/51–57–91; open weekdays 8–7:30, Sat. 8:30–2) and at the Galerie des Flibustiers in Fort-de-France (tel. 596/60–28–40; open weekdays 8–5:30, Sat. 8:30–1). Note: Prices quoted here are in U.S. dollars unless indicated otherwise.

Major credit cards are accepted in hotels and restaurants in Fort-de-France and the Pointe du Bout areas; few establishments in the countryside accept them. There is a 20% discount on luxury items paid for with traveler's checks or with certain credit cards.

Taxes and A resort tax varies from hotel to hotel; the maximum is $1.50
Service Charges per person per day. Rates quoted by hotels usually include a 10% service charge; some hotels add the 10% to your bill. All restaurants include a 15% service charge in their menu prices.

Getting Around Taxi stands are located at Lamentin Airport, in downtown
Taxis Fort-de-France, and at major hotels. They are expensive. Rates are regulated by the government, but local taxi drivers are an independent lot, and prices often turn out to be higher than the minimum "official" rate. The official rate is established at the beginning of each year and is listed in the tourist brochures, which you can get on your arrival at the tourist office at the airport. When taxi drivers overcharge, passengers have little recourse. You can either cause a fuss by contacting the police or show the driver the "officially quoted rate" in the brochure and hope that he accepts it. The cost from the airport to Fort-de-France is about 70F; from the airport to Pointe du Bout, about 150F. A 40% surcharge is in effect between 8 PM and 6 AM.

Buses Public buses and eight-passenger minivans (license plates bear the letters TC) are an inexpensive means of getting from point to point around the island. Buses are always crowded and are not recommended for the timid traveler, especially during rush hours. However, it's the cheapest way of travel next to hitchhiking, which is quite popular in Martinique. The routes radiate from Fort-de-France to major towns including St-Pierre, Basse-Pointe, La Trinité, Le Marin, and Lamentin. In Fort-de-France, the main terminal for the minivans is at Pointe Simon on the waterfront. There are frequent departures from early morning until 8 PM; fares range from $1 to $5.

Ferries Weather permitting, vedettes operate daily between Fort-de-France and the Marina Méridien in Pointe du Bout and between Fort-de-France and Anse-Mitan and Anse-à-l'Ane. The Quai d'Esnambuc is the arrival and departure point in Fort-de-France. At press time, the one-way fare was 12F; round-trip, 20F. The trip takes 20 minutes. Ferry schedules are listed in the visitors' guide, *Martinique Info,* available at the Tourist Office.

The **Caribbean Express** (tel. 590/60–12–38) offers daily, scheduled interisland service aboard a 128-foot, 227-passenger motorized catamaran, linking Martinique with Guadeloupe, and Dominica. Fares run approximately 25% below economy airfares.

Bicycles or Motorbikes Bikes and motorbikes can be rented from **Vespa** (tel. 596/71–60–03), **Funny** (tel. 596/63–33–05), or **T. S. Autos** (tel. 596/63–42–82), all in Fort-de-France. Cost is about $10 a day for bikes; about $35 for a small motorbike. Bikes are a cheap option for short trips to the beach. For longer trips, however, you need very strong legs to manage mountainous interior roads.

Rental Cars Having a car will make your stay in Martinique much more pleasurable. Although most of the larger hotels are on a beach, you may want to visit other beaches, especially Les Salines, the island's best (*see* Beaches, *below*). Moreover, budget hotels are generally not within walking distance of the water, making a car essential. Martinique has about 175 miles of well-paved and well-marked roads (albeit with international signs). Streets in Fort-de-France are narrow and clogged with traffic; country roads are mountainous with hairpin curves. The Martinicans drive with aggressive abandon, but are surprisingly courteous and will let you into the flow of traffic. When driving up-country, take along the free map supplied by the Tourist Office and you should have no trouble finding your way. If you want a more detailed map, the *Carte Routière et Touristique* is available at bookstores. There are plenty of gas stations in the major towns, but a full tank of gas will get you all the way around the island with gallons to spare.

A valid driver's license is needed to rent a car for up to 20 days. After that, you'll need an international driver's permit. Major credit cards are accepted by most car-rental agents. Rates are about $60 per day (unlimited mileage). Lower daily rates with per-mile charges, which usually turn out to be higher overall rates, are sometimes available. Question agents closely. Among the many agencies are **Avis** (tel. 596/70–11–60 or 800/331–1212), **Budget** (tel. 596/63–69–00 or 800/527–0700), **Hertz** (tel. 596/60–64–64 or 800/654–3131), and **Europcar/National Car Rental** (tel. 596/51–20–33 or 800/328–4567). Most hotels have a car-rental desk. For Jeep rentals, try **Suncar** (tel. 596/76–25–36), with an office in the Diamant Novotel. If you book a rental car from the United States at least 48 hours in advance, you can qualify for a hefty discount.

Telephones and Mail To call Martinique from the United States, dial 011 plus 596 plus the local six-digit number. To place an interisland call, dial the local six-digit number. To call the United States from Martinique, dial 19–1, area code, and the local number. For Great Britain, dial 19–44, area code (without the first zero), and the number.

It is not possible to make collect or credit calls from Martinique to the United States. There are few coin telephone booths on the island, and those are usually in hotels and restaurants. Most public telephones now use Telecartes, which are sold in denominations of 50F, 80F, and 100F and may be purchased from post offices, café-tabacs, and hotels. These are inserted into the telephone box; units are deducted from your card according to time and distance of each call you make. Long-distance calls made with Telecartes are less costly than are operator-assisted calls.

Airmail letters to the United States cost 4.40F for up to 20 grams; postcards, 3.80F. For Great Britain, the cost is 3.80F and 3.00F, respectively. Stamps may be purchased from post offices, café-tabacs, or hotel newsstands.

Opening and Closing Times Stores that cater to tourists are generally open weekdays 8:30–6; Saturday 8:30–1. Banking hours are weekdays 7:30–noon and 2:30–4.

Guided Tours For a personalized tour of the island, ask the Tourist Office to arrange for a tour with an English-speaking taxi driver. There are set rates for tours to various points on the island; prices are per car, so sharing the ride with two or three other sightseers keeps the cost down. The island is so large that you can't begin to see everything in a day. Before opting for a personalized tour, decide what you want to see. The northern part of the island, especially around St-Pierre, is a good choice.

Madinina Tours (tel. 596/61–49–49) offers half- and full-day jaunts, with lunch included in the all-day outings. Boat tours are also available. Madinina has tour desks in most of the major hotels.

Parc Naturel Régional de la Martinique (Regional Nature Reserve, tel. 596/73–19–30) organizes guided hiking tours year-round. Descriptive folders are available at the Tourist Office. Rates and tours vary, but a morning hike costs about $10 per person.

Exploring Martinique

Numbers in the margin correspond to points of interest on the Martinique map.

The starting point of the tour is the capital city of Fort-de-France, where almost a third of the island's 320,000 people live. From here, we'll tour St-Pierre, Mont Pelée, and other points north; go along the Atlantic coast; and finish with a look at the sights in the south.

Fort-de-France **Fort-de-France** lies on the beautiful Baie des Flamands on the island's Caribbean (west) coast. With its narrow streets and pastel buildings with ornate wrought-iron balconies, the capital city is reminiscent of the French Quarter in New Orleans. However, where New Orleans is flat, Fort-de-France is hilly. Public and commercial buildings and residences cling to its hillsides behind downtown.

Stop first at the **Tourist Office,** which shares a building with Air France on the boulevard Alfassa, right on the bay near the ferry landing. English-speaking staffers provide excellent, free material, including detailed maps; a visitors' guide called *Martinique Info,* which lists events; and *Une Histoire d'Amour*

Entre Ciel et Mer, an 18-page booklet in English, with a series of seven self-guided tours that are well worth your while.

Thus armed, walk across the street to **La Savane.** The 12½-acre landscaped park is filled with gardens, tropical trees, fountains, and benches. It's a popular gathering place and the scene of promenades, parades, and impromptu soccer matches. A statue of Pierre Belain d'Esnambuc, leader of the island's first settlers, is upstaged by Vital Dubray's flattering white Carrara marble statue of the Empress Josephine, Napoleon's first wife. Sculpted in a high-waisted Empire gown, Josephine gazes toward Trois-Ilets across the bay, where in 1763 she was born Marie-Joseph Tascher de la Pagerie. Near the harbor is a **marketplace** where high-quality local crafts are sold. On the edge of the Savane, you can catch the **ferry** for the beaches at Anse-Mitan and Anse-à-l'Ane and for the 20-minute run across the bay to the resort hotels of Pointe du Bout. The ferry is more convenient than a car for travel between Pointe du Bout and Fort-de-France.

Rue de la Liberté runs along the west side of La Savane. Look for the main post office (rue de la Liberté, between rue Blénac and rue Antoine Siger). Just across rue Blénac from the post office is the **Musée Departementale de Martinique,** which contains exhibits pertaining to the pre-Columbian Arawak and Carib periods. On display are pottery, beads, and part of a skeleton that turned up during excavations in 1972. One exhibit examines the history of slavery; costumes, documents, furniture, and handicrafts from the island's colonial period are on display. *9 rue de la Liberté, tel. 596/71–57–05. Admission: 5F. Open weekdays 9–1 and 2–5, Sat. 9–noon.*

Leave the museum and walk west (away from La Savane) on rue Blénac along the side of the post office to rue Victor Schoelcher. There you'll see the Romanesque **St-Louis Cathedral,** the steeple of which rises high above the surrounding buildings. The cathedral has lovely stained-glass windows. A number of Martinique's former governors are interred beneath the choir loft.

Rue Schoelcher runs through the center of the capital's primary shopping district, which consists of a six-block area bounded by rue de la République, rue de la Liberté, rue de Victor Severe, and rue Victor Hugo. Stores feature Paris fashions (at Paris prices) and French perfume, china, crystal, and liqueurs, as well as local handicrafts.

Three blocks north of the cathedral, make a right turn on rue Perrinon and go one block. At the corner of rue de la Liberté is the **Bibliothèque Schoelcher,** the wildly elaborate public library that's a Byzantine-Egyptian-Romanesque pastiche. It's named after Victor Schoelcher, who led the fight to free the slaves in the French West Indies in the 19th century. The eye-popping structure was built for the 1889 Paris Exposition, after which it was dismantled, shipped to Martinique, and reassembled piece by ornate piece on its present location.

Follow rue Victor Severe five blocks west, just beyond the Hôtel de Ville, and you'll come to Place Jose-Marti. The **Parc Floral et Culturel** will acquaint you with the variety of exotic flora on this island. There's also an aquarium showing fish that can be found in these waters. *Place Jose-Marti, Sermac, tel. 596/71–66–25. Admission free. Open Mon.–Sat. 9–noon and 3–6.*

The North From here out, you'll need to rent a car or take a guided tour of the island's highlights. A car is best for touring, as it permits meandering down small roads and stopping to take in views. If there are four or more splitting the cost, a full-day car rental should be cheaper than a half-day guided tour. You can try touring by bus, but you'll end up having to spend several nights on the road. Ten-speed bikes are possible for stretches of the tours, but not for their entirety. The tour of the north is divided into two sections: a short day's trip and a long day's (even overnight) excursion. Martinique's "must do" is the drive north along the coast from Fort-de-France to St-Pierre. The 40-mile round-trip to St-Pierre can be made in an afternoon, although there is enough to see to fill an entire day. The drive to the north coast will appeal primarily to nature lovers, hikers, and mountain climbers. If you are interested in climbing Mont Pelée or hiking, plan to spend at least a night on the road (*see* Sports and the Outdoors, *below,* for guided hikes). Bear in mind that a 20-mile mountain drive takes longer than driving 20 miles on the prairie.

Head west out of Fort-de-France on Route N2. You'll pass ❷ through the suburb of **Schoelcher,** home of the University of the French West Indies and Guyana. Just north of Schoelcher is Fond-Lahaye, where the road begins to climb sharply. About 4½ miles farther along, you'll come to the fishing village of **Case-Pilote,** named after a Carib chief to whom the French took kindly and called Pilote.

Continuing along the coastal road, you'll see red-roof houses ❸ clinging to the green mountainside on the way to **Bellefontaine,** 4 miles north. This is another fishing village, with pastel houses on the hillsides and colorful *gommier* canoes (fishing boats made from gum trees) bobbing in the water. One of the houses here is built in the shape of a boat.

❹ Continue north along the coast until you get to **Le Carbet.** Columbus is believed to have landed here on June 15, 1502. In 1635, Pierre Belain d'Esnambuc arrived here with the first French settlers.

Le Carbet is home to the **Zoo de Carbet,** also called the Amazona Zoo, which features animals from the Caribbean, Amazon, and Africa, including rare birds, snakes, wildcats, and caimans. *Le Coin, Le Carbet, tel. 596/78–00–64. Admission: 15F adults, 10F children. Open daily 9–6.*

Just north of Carbet is **Anse-Turin,** where Paul Gauguin lived for a short time in 1887 with his friend and fellow artist Charles ❺ Laval. The **Musée Gauguin** traces the history of the artist's Martinique connection through documents, letters, and reproductions of some of the paintings he did while on the island. There is also a display of Martinican costumes and headdresses. *Anse-Turin, tel. 596/77–22–66. Admission: 10F. Open daily 10–5.*

❻ **St-Pierre,** the island's oldest city, now has a population of about 6,000. At the turn of this century, St-Pierre was a flourishing city of 30,000 and was called the Paris of the West Indies. In spring 1902, nearby Mont Pelée began to rumble and spit out ash and steam. By the first week in May, all wildlife had wisely vacated the area. City officials, however, ignored the warnings, needing voters in town for an upcoming election. At 8 AM on May 8, 1902, the volcano erupted, belching forth a cloud of burning ash with temperatures over 3,600°F. In the space of three minutes, Mt. Pelée transformed the Paris of the West Indies into Martinique's Pompeii. The entire town was destroyed, and its inhabitants were instantly calcified. There was only one survivor, a prisoner named Siparis, who was saved by the thick walls of his underground cell. (He was later pardoned and for some years afterward was a sideshow attraction at the Barnum & Bailey Circus.) You can wander through the site to see the ruins of the island's first church, built in 1640; the theater; the toppled statues; and Siparis's cell. *For a guided tour of the area, contact Syndicat d'Initiative, La Guinguette Restaurant, tel. 596/77–15–02. Tours: 15F adults, 10F children. Open weekdays 9–noon.*

The **Musée Vulcanologique** was established in 1932 by American volcanologist Franck Perret. His collection includes photographs of the old town, documents, and a number of relics excavated from the ruins, including molten glass, melted iron, and contorted clocks stopped at 8 AM, the time of the disaster. *St-Pierre, tel. 596/78–15–16. Admission: 10F adults, 1F children. Open daily 9–noon and 3–5.*

Walk along St-Pierre's main street parallel to the sea, and drop in at La Vogue St-Pierre Hotel and restaurant (tel. 596/78–14–36). The barroom close to the street is a local hangout, but the dining room facing the sea offers reasonably priced Creole food. In St-Pierre, Route N2 turns inland toward Morne Rouge, but before going there, you may want to follow the **7** coastal road 8 miles north to **Le Prêcheur.** En route, you'll pass what is called the Tomb of the Carib Indians. The site is actually a formation of limestone hills from which the last of the Caribs are said to have flung themselves to avoid capture by the French. The village of Le Prêcheur was the childhood home of Françoise d'Aubigné, who was later to become the Marquise de Maintenon and the second wife of Louis XIV.

Return to St-Pierre and drive 4 miles east on Route N2 to reach **8** **Le Morne Rouge.** Lying on the southern slopes of Mont Pelée, the town of Morne Rouge, too, was destroyed by the volcano. It is now a popular resort spot, with spectacular mountain scenery. This is the starting point for a climb up the 4,600-foot mountain, but you must have a guide (*see* Sports and the Outdoors, *below*).

At this point, you have the option of returning to Fort-de-France or continuing on for a tour of the north and Atlantic coasts.

If you choose to return to the capital, take the Route de la Trace (Rte. N3) south from Le Morne Rouge. The winding, two-lane paved road is one of the island's great drives, snaking through dense tropical rain forests.

9 La Trace leads to **Balata,** where you can see the **Balata Church,** a replica of Sacré-Coeur Basilica in Paris, and the **Jardin de Balata** (Balata Gardens). Jean-Philippe Thoze, a professional landscaper and devoted horticulturalist, spent 20 years creating this collection of thousands of varieties of tropical flowers and plants. There are shaded benches where you can relax and take in the panoramic views of the mountains. *Rte. de Balata, tel. 596/72–58–82. Admission: 30F adults, 10F children. Open daily 9–5.*

From Balata, Route N3 continues 8 miles south to the capital city.

If you've opted to continue exploring the north and Atlantic coasts, take Route N3 north from Morne Rouge. You'll pass through Petite Savane and wind northeast to the flower-filled village of **Ajoupa-Bouillon,** a 17th-century settlement in the midst of pineapple fields.

A mile and a half east of Ajoupa-Bouillon, Route N3 dead-ends at Route N1, which runs north–south. Turn left and drive 3 miles through sugarcane, pineapple, and banana fields to **Basse-Pointe,** which lies at sea level on the Atlantic coast. Just before reaching Basse-Pointe you'll pass a Hindu temple, one of the relics of the East Indians who settled in this area in the 19th century. The view of the eastern slope of Mont Pelée is lovely from here.

On the approach to Basse-Pointe, you'll see a small road (D21) off to the left. This road leads to the estimable **Leyritz Plantation,** which has been a hotel for several years. Guests have the questionable pleasure of staying in the converted slave cabins. Visit the plantation's **Musée de Poupées Végétales,** which contains a collection of exotic "doll sculptures," in which a local plant is shaped into figurines depicting famous women of French history. They are the work of local artisan Will Fenton. *Musée de Poupées Végétales, Leyritz Plantation, tel. 596/78–53–92. Admission: 15F. Open daily 7–5.*

Three miles along, you'll come to **Macouba** on the coast. From here, the island's most spectacular drive leads 6 miles to **Grand-Rivière,** on the northernmost point. Perched on high cliffs, this village affords magnificent views of the sea; the mountains; and, on clear days, the neighboring island of Dominica. From Grand-Rivière, you can trek 11 miles on a well-marked path that leads through lush tropical vegetation to the beach at Anse-Ceron on the northwest coast. The beach is lovely and the diving is excellent, but the currents are very strong and swimming is not advised.

From Grand-Rivière, backtrack 13 miles to the junction of Routes N1 and N3.

From the junction, continue 10 miles on Route 1 along the Atlantic coast, driving through the villages of Le Lorrain and Marigot to **Ste-Marie,** a town of about 20,000 Martinicans and the commercial capital of the island's north. There is a lovely mid-19th-century church in the town and, on a more earthy note, a rum distillery.

The **Musée du Rhum,** operated by the St. James Rum Distillery, is housed in a graceful galleried Creole house. Guided tours of the museum take in displays of the tools of the trade and include a visit to the distillery. And, yes, you may sample the product. *Ste-Marie, tel. 596/69–30–02. Admission free. Open weekdays 9–5, weekends 9–1.*

La Trinité, a subprefecture in the north, is 6 miles to the south in a sheltered bay. From La Trinité, the **Caravelle Peninsula** thrusts 8 miles into the Atlantic Ocean. Much of the peninsula is under the auspices of the Regional Nature Reserve and offers places for trekking, swimming, and sailing. This is the home of the **Morne Pavilion,** an open-air sports and leisure center operated by the nature reserve (*see* Sports and the Outdoors, *below*). To reach it, turn right before Tartane on the Spoutourne Morne Pavilion road. The beach at Tartane is popular for its cooling Atlantic breezes.

⑮ At the eastern tip of the peninsula, you can root through the ruins of the **Dubuc Castle.** This was the home of the Dubuc de Rivery family, which owned the peninsula in the 18th century. According to legend, young Aimée Dubuc de Rivery was captured by Barbary pirates, sold to the Ottoman Empire, became a favorite of the sultan, and gave birth to Mahmud II.

Return to La Trinité and take Route N4, which winds about 15 miles through lush tropical scenery to Lamentin. There you can pick up Route N1 to Fort-de-France or Route N5 to D7 and the southern resort areas.

The South The loop through the south is a round-trip of about 100 miles. This excursion will include the birthplace of the Empress Josephine, Pointe du Bout and its resort hotels, a few small museums, and many large beaches. Since you will likely stay in the southern part of the island, you may wish to explore these areas on the days you try out different beaches. You can go from Fort-de-France to Ste-Anne in an hour or less on the highway. Buses ply the road frequently, and you'll see a number of people hitchhiking.

From Fort-de-France, take Route N1 to Route N5, which leads south through Lamentin, where the airport is located. A 20-mile drive will bring you to Rivière-Salée, where you'll make a ⑯ right turn on Route D7 and drive 4¹/₂ miles to the village of **Les Trois-Ilets.**

Named after the three rocky islands nearby, it is a lovely little village with a population of about 3,000. It's known for its pottery, straw, and wood works and as the birthplace of Napoleon's Empress Josephine. On the village square, you can visit the simple church where she was baptized Marie-Joseph Tascher de la Pagerie. To reach the museum and the old sugar plantation where she was born, drive a mile west on Route D7 and turn left on Route D38.

A stone building that held the kitchen of the estate is now home to the **Musée de la Pagerie.** (The main house blew down in the hurricane of 1766, when Josephine was three.) It contains an assortment of memorabilia pertaining to Josephine's life and loves (she was married at 16 in an arranged marriage to Alexandre de Beauharnais). There are family portraits; documents, including a marriage certificate; a love letter written to her in 1796 by Napoleon; and various antique furnishings, including the bed she slept in as a child. *Trois-Ilets, tel. 596/68–34–55. Admission: 15F adults, 3F children. Open Tues.–Sun. 9–5.*

The **Maison de la Canne** will teach you everything you ever wanted to know about sugarcane. Exhibits take you through three centuries of sugarcane production, with displays of tools, scale models, engravings, and photographs. *Trois-Ilets, tel. 596/68–32–04. Admission: 15F. Open Tues.–Sun. 9–5:30.*

⑰ You can reach **Pointe du Bout** and the beach at **Anse-Mitan** by turning right on Route D38 west of Trois-Ilets and just past the **Golf de l'Impératrice Joséphine** (a golf course). This area is filled with resort hotels, among them the Bakoua and the Méridien. The Pointe du Bout marina is a colorful spot where a whole slew of boats are tied up. The ferry to Fort-de-France leaves from this marina. More than anywhere else on Martinique, Pointe du Bout caters to the vacationer. A cluster of boutiques, ice-cream parlors, and car-rental agencies forms the hub from which restaurants and hotels of varying caliber radiate.

When you return to Route D7, turn right and head west. Less than five miles down the road you will reach **Anse-à-l'Ane,** where there is a pretty white-sand beach complete with picnic tables. There are also numerous small restaurants and inexpensive guest-house hotels for the budget traveler. South from Anse-à-l'Ane, Route D7 turns into a 10-mile roller coaster en route to **Anse-d'Arlets,** a quiet backwater fishing village. You'll see fishermen's nets strung up on the beach to dry and pleasure boats on the water. In recent years, activity here has centered on the restaurants and small shops lining the shore. A popular gathering spot for Sunday brunch is **Ti Sable** (tel. 596/68–62–44), a restaurant on the beach at the northern edge of the village. **Bidjoul** (*see* Dining, *below*), in the center of the village, makes a good vantage point from which to view the sunset.

From the center of town, take Route D37 along the coast down to Morne Larcher and on to **Le Diamant.** The road—narrow, twisting, and hilly—offers some of the best shoreline views in Martinique. Be sure to pull to the side at a scenic spot from which you can stare out at **Diamond Rock,** a mile or two offshore.

18

In 1804, during the squabbles over possession of the island between the French and the English, the latter commandeered the rock, armed it with cannons, christened it HMS *Diamond Rock,* and proceeded to use it as a warship. For almost a year and a half, the British held the rock, bombarding any French ships that came along. The French got wind of the fact that the British were getting cabin fever on their isolated ship-island and arranged a supply of barrels of rum for those on the rock. The French easily overpowered the inebriated sailors, ending one of the most curious engagements in naval history.

Le Diamant is a small, friendly village with a little fruit-and-vegetable market on its town square. Next to the town square is **Longchamp** (tel. 596/76–25–47), an ice-cream/pizza restaurant, but the adventurous will want to cross the street and enter a dark bar called **Maully's** (no phone). You'll be the only tourist here, but on your second *'ti punch* (little punch), the locals will warm to you.

Back on the road (D7), it's about 5 miles to the junction of the island's main highway to the south (N5). If you go to the north, you'll be back in Fort-de-France within a half hour. Instead, go south along the coast.

Some 10 miles down the coastline lies **Ste-Luce,** another fishing village with a pretty white beach. From Ste-Luce, you can take Route D17 north 1 mile to the **Forêt de Montravail,** where arrows point the way to Carib rock drawings.

19

From Ste-Luce you can proceed directly to Ste-Anne, curving around the beautiful cul-de-sac inlet through **Le Marin.** Continue until you reach the pretty village of **Ste-Anne,** where a Roman Catholic church sits on the square facing a lovely white beach; there are several restaurants here, and a market to buy

20

picnic fixings. Not far away, at the southernmost tip, is the island's best beach, **Les Salines.** It's 1½ miles of soft white sand, calm waters, and relative seclusion (except on weekends).

In sharp contrast to the north, this section of the island is dry. The soil does not hold moisture for long. A rutted track—suitable for vehicles, but not for queasy stomachs—leads all the way to **Pointe des Salines** and slightly beyond. The gnarled, stubby trees have given the area the name **Petrified Forest,** in part because the sight is unexpected in a place known as the Island of Flowers.

Though there is a restaurant, **Aux Delices de la Mer** (tel. 596/76–73–75), near the point facing the channel that separates Martinique from St. Lucia, many people bring their own refreshments and picnic in the shade of the palms.

Backtrack 9 miles to Le Marin. The adventuresome should take a detour a mile before reaching town. Take the small road on your right that leads to **Cap Chevalier.** After less than 2 miles, the road forks. The road to the left dead-ends at a small community and does not justify the 4 miles of driving. The fork to the right, however, runs for about 4 miles to a tiny cove with five or six one-man fishing boats and racks where the fishermen dry their nets. The scene is definitely worth a photograph.

If you retrace your steps for half a mile, you will come to a turnoff on the right. Less than a mile down this road there is a long, empty beach that rarely has more than four or five couples taking sun and a cool dip in the Atlantic waters.

㉒ To get out of Cap Chevalier, you must go back toward Le Marin. On the outskirts of Le Marin, Route N6 branches off to the right and goes north 7 miles to **Le Vauclin,** where it skirts the highest point in the south, **Mt. Vauclin** (1,654 feet). Le Vauclin is an important fishing port on the Atlantic coast, and the return of the fishermen shortly before noon each day is a big event.

㉓ Continue north 9 miles on Route N6 to **Le François,** a sizable city of some 16,000 Martinicans. This is a great place for snorkeling. Offshore are a number of shallow basins with white-sand bottoms between the reefs.

There is a lovely bay 6 miles farther along at **Le Robert.** You'll also come to the junction of Route N1, which will take you west to Fort-de-France, 12½ miles away.

Beaches

All Martinique's beaches are open to the public, but hotels charge a fee for nonguests to use changing rooms and facilities. There are no official nudist beaches, but topless bathing is prevalent at the large resort hotels. Unless you're an expert swimmer, steer clear of the Atlantic waters, except in the area of Cap Chevalier and the Caravelle Peninsula. The soft, white-sand beaches begin south of Fort-de-France and continue; to the north the beaches are made up of hard-packed gray volcanic sand. The soft white beaches of **Pointe du Bout** are man-made, superb, and lined with luxury resorts.

Anse-Mitan was created by Mother Nature, who placed it just to the south of Pointe du Bout and sprinkled it with white sand. The waters around this beach offer superb snorkeling opportunities. Small family-owned bistros are half hidden in palm trees nearby.

On the beach at **Anse-à-l'Ane,** you can spread your lunch on a picnic table, browse through the nearby shell museum, and cool off in the bar of the Calalou Hotel.

Diamant, the island's longest beach (2½ miles), has a splendid view of Diamond Rock, but the waters are sometimes rough and the currents are strong.

Anse-Trabaud is on the Atlantic side, across the southern tip of the island from Ste-Anne. There is nothing here but white sand and the sea.

Les Salines is a 1½-mile cove of soft white sand lined with coconut palms. A short drive south of Ste-Anne, Les Salines is awash with families and children during holidays and on weekends, but quiet and uncrowded during the week even at the height of the winter season. This beach, especially the far end, is peaceful and beautiful. Take along a picnic, including plenty of liquids; there is only one restaurant, Aux Delices de la Mer (tel. 596/76–73–71), close to Pointe des Salines.

Near Les Salines, **Pointe Marin** stretches north from Ste-Anne. A good windsurfing and waterskiing spot, it also has restaurants, campsites, sanitary facilities, and a 10F admission charge. Club Med occupies the northern edge, and Ste-Anne, with several good restaurants, is near at hand.

The Atlantic surf rolls onto **Cap Chevalier,** a windswept beach with hard-packed sand. Swimming here is only for the strong, but the emptiness of the shore appeals to those seeking respite from crowds. Small trees act as shade, but there are no refreshment stands, so bring your own.

Sports and the Outdoors

Bicycling The Parc Naturel Régional de la Martinique (tel. 596/64–42–59) has designed biking itineraries off the beaten track. Bikes can be rented from **Funny** (tel. 596/63–33–05), **Discount** (tel. 596/66–33–05), and **T S Location Sarl** (tel. 596/63–42–82), all located in Fort-de-France. In Ste-Luce, try **Marquis Moto** (no phone). VTT (Vélo Tout Terrain), or mountain, bikes, specially designed with 18 speeds to handle all terrains, may be rented from **VTTilt** (Anse-Mitan, tel. 596/66–01–01). Average daily cost for a 10-speed bike is 50F; mountain bikes are a few francs more.

Golf At **Golf de l'Impératrice Joséphine** (tel. 596/68–32–81) there is an 18-hole Robert Trent Jones course with an English-speaking pro, fully equipped pro shop, bar, and restaurant. It's located at Trois-Ilets, a mile from the Pointe du Bout resort area and 18 miles from Fort-de-France. Greens fees are 300F for 18 holes.

Hiking Inexpensive guided excursions are organized year-round by the **Parc Naturel Régional de la Martinique** (Regional Nature Reserve, Caserne Bouille, Fort-de-France, tel. 596/73–19–30). The tourist board can also arrange for a guide. The most interesting—and demanding—hikes are in the volcanic, mountainous area around Le Morne Rouge. Terrain is steep and thickly forested. You'll need a guide, especially when low clouds descend and the visibility drops to near zero. Costs vary, but count on 50F for a morning hike. While you do need a guide to hike inland, you can walk around the island's northern tip between Le Prêcheur and Grand-Rivière—a three- to four-hour hike—on your own.

Sailing Hobie Cats, Sunfish, and Sailfish can be rented by the hour from hotel beach shacks. Sunfish rentals average 50F an hour; Windsurfers, about 40F an hour.

Scuba Diving Among the island's dive operators are **Bathy's Club** (Méridien, tel. 596/66–00–00), **Cressma** (Fort-de-France, tel. 596/61–34–36 or 596/58–04–48), **CSCP** (Le Port, Case-Pilote, tel. 596/78–73–75), **Oxygène Bleu** (Longpre, Lamentin, tel. 596/50–25–78), **Planète Bleue** (La Marina, Trois-Ilets, tel. 596/66–08–79), **Sub Diamant Rock** (Novotel, tel. 596/76–42–42), and **Tropicasub** (La Guinguette, St-Pierre, tel. 596/77–15–02). Single-tank dives start at 175F. Snorkel equipment rents for about $10 a day; rental is available at the dive shops listed.

Sea Excursions The *Aquarium* (Fort-de-France, tel. 596/61–49–49) is a glass-bottom boat that does excursions. Costs vary, but an afternoon excursion with snorkeling and a picnic is about 100F. For information on other sailing, swimming, snorkeling, and beach picnic trips, contact **Affaires Maritimes** (tel. 596/71–90–05).

Tennis In addition to its links, the **Golf de l'Impératrice Joséphine** (Trois-Ilets, tel. 596/68–32–82) has three lighted tennis courts. There are also courts at the **Bakoua Beach Hotel** (tel. 596/66–02–02); **Buccaneer's Creek/Club Med** (tel. 596/76–74–52); **Diamant-Novotel** (tel. 596/76–42–42); **La Batelière Hotel** (tel. 596/61–49–49); **Leyritz Plantation** (tel. 596/78–53–92); the **Méridien Hotel** (tel. 596/66–00–00); **Brise Marine** (tel. 596/62–46–94); **Diamant Bleu** (tel. 596/76–42–15); **Hotel PLM Azur Carayou** (tel. 596/66–04–04); **La Caravelle** (tel. 596/58–37–32); **Le Calalou** (tel. 596/68–31–67); **La Margelle** (tel. 596/76–40–19); **Relais Caraibes** (tel. 596/74–44–65); and **Rivage Hotel** (tel. 596/66–00–53). For additional information about tennis on the island, contact **La Ligue Régionale de Tennis** (Petit Manoir, Lamentin, tel. 596/51–08–00). An hour's court time averages 50F for nonguests.

Shopping

Although it's possible to save money on French fragrances and designer scarves, fine china and crystal, leather goods, and liquors and liqueurs in Fort-de-France, these items won't be cheap (even with the 20% discount on luxury items paid for by traveler's checks and major credit cards). Bargain shoppers are better off sticking with local items. Look for Creole gold jewelry, such as loop earrings, heavy bead necklaces, and slave bracelets; white and dark rum; and handcrafted straw goods, pottery, and tapestries. In addition, U.S. Customs allows you to bring some of the local flora into the country.

Local Handicrafts A wide variety of dolls, straw goods, tapestries, pottery, and other items are available at the **Caribbean Art Center** (Centre de Métiers Arts, opposite the Tourist Office, blvd. Alfassa, Fort-de-France, tel. 596/70–32–16). The **Galerie d'Art** (89 rue Victor Hugo, tel. 596/63–10–62) has some unusual and excellent Haitian art—paintings, sculptures, ceramics, and intricate jewelry cases—at reasonable prices.

Rum Rum can be purchased at the various distilleries, including **Du-quesnes** (Fort-de-France, tel. 596/71–91–68), **St. James** (Ste-Marie, tel. 596/69–30–02), and **Trois Rivières** (Ste-Luce, tel. 596/62–51–78).

Dining

As in France, eating well is part of living well. Here you'll find the same interest in food, the same lingering over meals—and the same willingness to pay high prices for memorable cuisine. Notice that our price chart, below, lists a moderately priced meal as $30–$50. Generally, you'll spend more on dining here than on many Caribbean islands. It's tough to find budget alternatives to the typical restaurant meal. There are no fast-food outlets on Martinique, although you can find places in Fort-de-France and Pointe du Bout for light snacks such as crêpes Suzettes. Many smaller restaurants will prepare a plate of appetizers in lieu of a full meal. As a rule of thumb, at restaurants where reservations are not necessary, it is acceptable to order just one main course or substitute appetizers. At any restaurant where you are advised to make reservations, you are expected to dine well; i.e., three courses plus wine.

It used to be argued that Martinique had the best food in all the Caribbean, but many believe this top-ranking position has been lost to some of the other islands of the French West Indies—Guadeloupe, St. Barts, even St. Martin. Nevertheless, Martinique remains an island of restaurants serving classic French cuisine and Creole dishes, its wine cellars filled with fine French wines. Some of the best restaurants are tucked away in the countryside, and therein lies the problem. The farther you venture from tourist hotels, the less likely you are to find English-speaking folk. But that shouldn't stop you from savoring the countryside cuisine. The local Creole specialties are *colombo* (curry), *accras* (cod or vegetable fritters), *crabe farcis* (stuffed land crab), *écrevisses* (freshwater crawfish), *boudin* (Creole blood sausage), *lambi* (conch), *langouste* (clawless Caribbean lobster), *soudons* (sweet clams), and *oursins* (sea urchin). The local favorite libation is *'ti punch*, a "little punch," concocted of four parts white rum, one part sugarcane syrup (some people like a little more syrup), and a squeeze of lime.One of the delights of Martinique is grocery shopping for picnic fare or take-out meals to eat at your lodgings. You'll find minimarkets in the center of every town and village, but for a truly mouth-watering experience, visit the **Euromarche** in Lamentin, just off the main Fort-de-France–Rivière highway (N5). This is one of the most complete *hypermarchés* (supermarket) in the Western Hemisphere. Whether you are stocking the larder for a week or planning a simple picnic, you'll be tempted by the breads, pâtés, cheeses, and wines. Choose carefully, and you'll have the makings of a delicious gourmet meal for two that costs less than $15.

Outside of Fort-de-Franc restaurants, dress is casual (anything more is indicated in individual reviews below). Shorts, however, are not appreciated at any restaurant other than al fresco cafés on the beach.

Highly recommended restaurants are indicated by a star ★.

Category	Cost*
Moderate	$30–$50
Inexpensive	$20–$30
Budget	under $20

*per person, excluding drinks and service

Anse-d'Arlets **Tamarin Plage Restaurant.** The lobster tank in the middle of the room gives you a clue to the specialty here, but there are other recommendable offerings as well. Fish soup or Creole boudin are good starters, then consider court-bouillon, chicken fricassee, or curried mutton. The beachfront bar is a popular local hangout. *Anse-d'Arlets, tel. 596/68–67–88. No credit cards. Moderate.*

Bidjoul. The small side street off the main road is Anse-d'Arlets's main drag, with numerous modest restaurants on either side. The latest addition is the small Bidjoul, with tables on the sand under a canopy and across the road a tiny indoor dining room. The salads are huge and the grilled fish as fresh as could be. So is the fish at neighboring restaurants, but customers like the enthusiastic owner here; it's the popular gathering spot to watch the sun set into the Caribbean. *Anse-d'Arlets, tel. 596/68–65–28. No reservations. No credit cards. Budget.*

Anse-Mitan/ **La Matador.** Fresh flowers adorn each table in this simply fur-
Pte. du Bout nished terrace restaurant. Creole boudin, quiche, or sea urchins are good for openers. Main dishes include turtle steak, Creole bouillabaisse, lobster thermidor, and fillet of beef with port wine and mushrooms. This pretty restaurant with checkered tablecloths would be more enjoyable if it had a view of the sea instead of the road and the Bambou Hotel. *Anse-Mitan, tel. 596/68–05–36. Reservations advised in high season. AE, DC, MC, V. Closed Wed. Moderate.*

L'Amphore. Dining is either on the front terrace, where there's a nice view of the bay, or in a gas-lit garden. Lobster, selected from a tank, is the menu's highlight, but there are Creole specialties and classic French dishes as well. During dinner, a guitarist strums and sings in several languages. *Anse-Mitan, tel. 596/66–03–09. No credit cards. Closed Mon., and Tues. lunch. Moderate.*

★ **La Villa Creole.** The steak béarnaise, curried dishes, conch, court-bouillon, and other dishes are all superb. But the real draw here is owner Guy Dawson, a popular singer and guitarist who entertains during dinner, either solo or en duo with Roland Manere or Guy Vadeleux. The setting is romantic, with oil lamps flickering in the lush back garden of this very popular place. *Anse-Mitan, tel. 596/66–05–53. Reservations essential. AE, DC, V. Dinner only. Closed Sun. Moderate.*

Bambou Restaurant. This casual place, right on the beach, serves omelets and salads, as well as lamb cutlets, curried chicken, steak au poivre, codfish pie, and sole meunière. For dessert there's coconut flan or banana or pineapple flambé. *Bambou Hotel, Anse-Mitan, tel. 596/66–01–39. AE, DC, MC, V. Inexpensive.*

Le Poisson d'Or. At this alfresco spot—the first restaurant on the right-hand side as you enter Pointe du Bout—choose from among such Creole dishes as fried conch, poached local fish, and scallops sautéed in white wine. You can order just a main course, but the menu of the day is usually a good bet for a more substantial dinner. Choose a table in the front part of the terrace to benefit from any passing breezes. *Pointe du Bout, tel. 596/66–01–80. No reservations. No credit cards. Closed Mon. Budget.*

Basse-Pointe **Restaurant Mally.** Unpretentious and popular, Mally Edjam's home has a few tables inside and only four on the side porch under an awning. The lady is a legend on the island and will serve you the likes of papaya soufflé; spicy Creole concoctions, such as curried pork and stuffed land crabs; and fresh local vegetables. Her exotic confitures of guava, pineapple, and cornichon top off the feast, along with a yogurt or light coconut cake. *Rte. de la Côte Atlantique, tel. 596/75–51–18. Reservations required. No credit cards. Budget.*

Fort-de-France **Diamant Creole.** Claudine Victoire's popular seven-table restaurant is on the second floor of a little red-and-white house. The old-fashioned Creole dishes served include tiny local clams in white wine or with chives and shallots, fish or conch brochette, Creole paella, and soups and local vegetables not offered on most island menus. *7 blvd. de Verdun, tel. 596/73–18–25. Reservations advised. AE, MC, V. Closed Sun. Moderate.*

La Biguine. Downstairs is a cozy, casual café with red-and-white checkered cloths, and upstairs, a more formal candlelit dining room. Local fish poached in Creole sauce, shark cooked in tomato sauce, and duck fillet with pineapple or orange sauce are among the à la carte offerings, with homemade tarts for dessert. It's a convenient place for lunch, and there is a special fixed-price businessmen's menu. *11 Rte. de la Folie, tel. 596/71–47–75. Reservations required for dinner. Jacket required for dinner. AE. No lunch Sat.; closed Sun. Moderate.*

★ **Le Coq Hardi.** Crowds flock here for the best steaks and grilled meats in town. You can pick out your own steak and feel confident that it will be cooked to perfection. Steak tartare is the house specialty, or choose tournedos Rossini (with artichoke hearts, foie gras, truffles, and Madeira sauce), entrecôte Bordelaise, prime rib, or T-bone steaks. For dessert, there's a selection of sorbets, profiteroles, and pear belle Hélène. *Km 0.6, rue Martin Luther King, tel. 596/71–59–64. Reservations advised. AE, DC, MC, V. Closed Wed. and Sat. lunch. Moderate.*

Chez Gaston. Its cozy upstairs dining room, very popular with local residents, features a Creole menu that includes such items as ox-foot soup, conch kebabs, and simmered sea urchins. The brochettes are especially recommended. The kitchen stays open late, and there's a small dance floor. The downstairs section serves snacks all day. A French phrase book will be very helpful. *10 rue Felix Eboue, tel. 596/71–45–48. No credit cards. Inexpensive.*

Le Crew. The meals here are served family-style in rustic dining rooms, where the bill of fare features a few Creole dishes and lots of typical French bistro dishes: fish soup and stuffed mussels, snails, country pâté, frogs' legs, tripe, grilled chicken, and steak. The portions are ample, and there's a daily 60F three-course tourist menu that simplifies ordering. *42 rue Ernst Deproge, tel. 596/73–04–14. No credit cards. Closed Sat. evening and Sun. Inexpensive.*

★ **Le Second Soufflé.** The chef uses fresh vegetables and fruits—nutrition is a top priority here—to make soufflés ranging from *aubergine* (eggplant) to *filet de ti-nain* (small green bananas) with chocolate sauce. With prices around 40F and a wonderful location near the cathedral, this little restaurant is a delightful find. *27 rue Blénac, tel. 596/63–44–11. No reservations. No credit cards. Closed Sat. lunch. Budget.*

Le Diamant **Le Diam's.** For an inexpensive meal that may consist of crisp and tasty pizzas or a grilled fish of the day, this casual, open-sided restaurant facing the village square is hard to beat. Checkered tablecloths and wicker furniture are the only decor; the overhead fan helps to keep a breeze moving through the dining room. *Place de l'Eglise, tel. 596/76–23–28. No reservations. MC, V. Closed Tues. and Wed. lunch. Budget..*

Le François **Club Nautique.** While this little place is not going to turn up in
★ *Architectural Digest,* the food that comes fresh daily out of the sea is exquisitely prepared. Have a couple of rum punches, then dig into turtle steak or charcoal-broiled lobster. The restaurant is right on the beach, and boat trips leave here for snorkeling in the nearby coral reefs. *Le François, tel. 596/54–31–00. AE, DC, MC, V. Lunch only. Inexpensive.*

Le Morne Rouge **Auberge de la Montagne Pelée.** This restaurant is open for dinner by reservation only, but the real treat is lunch on a clear day, when you can see Mont Pelée's summit from the terrace. Creole and French dishes are featured, including a Caribbean-style pot-au-feu, with whitefish, scallops, salmon, crayfish, and tiny vegetables. *Rte. de l'Aileron, tel. 596/52–32–09. Reservations essential. MC, V. Moderate.*

Morne-des-Esses **Le Colibri.** In the northwestern reaches of the island, this is
★ the domain of Clotilde Palladino, who presides over the kitchen while her children serve. Choice seating is at one of the seven tables on the back terrace. For starters, try *buisson d'écrevisses,* six giant freshwater crayfish accompanied by a tangy tomato sauce flavored with thyme, scallions, and tiny bits of crayfish. Stuffed pigeon, lobster omelets, suckling pig, and coconut chicken are among the main dishes. Keep an eye on prices here, as some menu items will push your bill out of our Moderate range. *Morne-des-Esses, tel. 596/69–91–95. Reservations essential. AE, DC, MC, V. Closed Mon. Moderate.*

Ste-Anne **Athanor.** Formerly the L'Arbre à Pain, this new restaurant offers an ambitious menu that includes everything from pizza to Creole dishes and meats with French sauces. Recommended are the grilled lobster and the grilled fish in a shallot-and-rum sauce. Seating is in a plant-filled room or in a small garden at the back. *Rue de Bord de Mer, Ste-Anne, tel. 596/76–97–60. No credit cards. Moderate.*

La Dunette. Located in the center of Ste-Anne with the sea washing its foundations, this restaurant in a small hotel has a terrace shaded by bright blue awnings. The wrought-iron chairs and tables are surrounded by hanging plants. Your choices for lunch or dinner include fish soup, grilled fish or lobster, poached sea urchins, pork en brochette with pineapple, and several curried dishes. *Ste-Anne, tel. 596/76–73–90. Reservations advised in high season. MC, V. Closed Wed. Inexpensive.*

Poï et Virginie. Facing the jetty in the center of Ste-Anne is this popular restaurant with bamboo walls, ceiling fans, and colorful, fresh-cut flowers. The menu is extensive—from meats to fish—but the specialty is the lobster and crab salad. Lunchtime is busy, especially on weekends; get here soon after noon if you want a table facing the bay, with views of St. Lucia in the distance. *Rue de Bord de Mer, Ste-Anne, tel. 596/76–76–86. No reservations. AE, DC, MC, V. Closed Mon. Inexpensive.*

Le Chatrou. On the beach near the entrance to Club Med, you'll find this wood chalet, with the best grilled fish on the beach. The prix-fixe menu is a bargain at 70F; à la carte offerings include *fricassée de chatroux* (cuttlefish). Fresh vegetables accompanying the meal and cheerful, friendly service are added pluses. *A La Plage, Pointe Marin, Ste-Anne, tel. 596/76–77–16. No reservations. No credit cards. Budget.*

Ste-Luce **La Petite Auberge.** This country inn is hidden behind a profusion of tropical flowers, just across the main road from the beach. Fresh seafood is turned into such dishes as *filet de poisson aux champignons* (fish cooked with mushrooms), *crabe farci*, and fresh langouste in a Creole sauce. Or sample *canard à l'ananas* (duck with pineapple), *poulet Créole* (chicken Creole), or entrecôte Creole. They're all winners. *Plage du Gros Raisins, Ste-Luce, tel. 596/62–47–26. No credit cards. Moderate.*

St-Pierre **La Factorérie.** Alongside the ruins of the Eglise du Fort is this open-air restaurant connected to the agricultural training school, where students raise crops. The food is pleasant and the view is outstanding. Dishes include grilled langouste, grilled chicken in a piquant sauce, fricassée de lambi, and the fresh catch of the day. This restaurant is convenient for lunch when visiting St-Pierre, but it's probably not worth a special trip. *Quartier Fort, St-Pierre, tel. 596/78–12–53. No credit cards. Closed Sat. and Sun. evenings. Inexpensive.*

Lodging

Martinique has a number of moderately priced large resort hotels, designed to accommodate large groups, primarily from Europe. This may explain the impersonality and lack of charm at many of these hotels, as well as prices that are quite reasonable for the Caribbean. Most of these hotels are on or near a beach, and many of them offer attractive packages that are cheaper than their standard room rates; ask about them when you call.

Other affordable options include smaller hotels and inns (*Relais Créoles*) and the modest apartments and cottages known as *gîtes*. The latter are simple accommodations, usually available by the week, that range from separate cottages to rooms in a private home to bed-and-breakfast–style properties. The Martinique office of **Gîtes de France** (9 blvd. du Général-de-Gaulle, BP 1122, Fort-de-France 97248, tel. 596/73–67–92, fax 596/63–55–92) has a list of more than 100 properties and serves as a reservation center.

Most of the major hotels are clustered in Pointe du Bout and Anse-Mitan on the Trois-Ilets peninsula, across the bay from Fort-de-France, or in the Le Diamant and Ste-Anne resort areas. You'll find other lodgings—particularly budget properties—scattered around the island.

Many larger hotels offer MAP plan in their weekly rates; if you don't have a car, a meal plan makes economic sense. Even those offering only EP often include buffet breakfast in their package rates. At Relais Creoles, breakfast usually consists of cold cuts, an array of breads, juice, and hot beverages.

Highly recommended lodgings are indicated by a star ★.

Category	Cost*
Moderate	$120–$180
Inexpensive	$70–$120
Budget	under $70

All prices are for a standard double room for two in high season, excluding $1.50 per person per night tax and a 10% service charge. To estimate rates for hotels offering MAP, add about $35 per person per day to the above price ranges.

Hotels, Inns, and Gîtes

Anse-Mitan/ Pte. du Bout

Bambou. The young and hardy will enjoy this complex of rustic A-frame "chalets" with shingled roofs. The rooms are paneled in pink; they are tiny and Spartan, albeit with such conveniences as air-conditioning, phones, and shower baths. During high season, entertainment is featured five nights a week. You're on the water here, but a five-minute walk brings you to a better beach by Le Bakoua hotel. *Anse-Mitan 97229, tel. 596/66–01–39 or 800/224–4542, fax 596/66–05–05. 118 rooms. Facilities: restaurant and bar, pool, water-sports center. AE, DC, MC, V. CP, MAP. Moderate.*

PLM Azur-Carayou. The reception area of this tropical-style hotel has rattan furniture and, overhead, quaint wood rafters. The rooms, built around the large swimming pool in the garden, are air-conditioned and equipped with TVs, direct-dial phones, and well-stocked minibars. Only those without sea views are affordable here, so ask about prices when you call. There are lots of sporting options for daytime activity, and a popular disco, Le Vésou, for evening. The hotel has its own small but pleasant beach. It's well run, and the staff is helpful and friendly. *Pointe du Bout 97229, tel. 596/66–04–04 or 800/221–4542, fax 596/66–00–57. 200 double rooms. Facilities: 3 restaurants, 2 bars, 2 tennis courts, pool, archery, scuba diving, fishing, waterskiing, sailing. AE, DC, MC, V. EP, MAP. Moderate.*

★ **PLM Azur La Pagerie.** La Pagerie, with its garden courtyard and lattice balconies, looks as if it were plucked from southern Louisiana and planted near the marina in Pointe du Bout; on an island not known for attractive hotels, this is an exception. Fully air-conditioned, the hotel has small rooms and studios, some with kitchenettes, all with private baths. Although the hotel has no beach or water-sports activities, it is within a short stroll of resort hotels, restaurants, and the beach. The al fresco restaurant by the pool serves lunch and dinner. The local expat and sailing crowd likes to stop by for a round or two of evening cocktails. *Pointe du Bout 97229, tel. 596/66–05–30, fax 596/66–00–99. U.S. reservations, 800/221–4542; in NY, 212/757–6500. 98 rooms. Facilities: restaurant, bar, pool. AE, MC, V. EP. Inexpensive–Moderate.*

Auberge de l'Anse-Mitan. This beachfront hotel, established in 1930, is the island's oldest family-run inn. The rooms are Spartan, but all are air-conditioned and have shower baths. Views are either of the bay or the tropical garden at the back, and some rooms have balconies. Informal meals are served on the terrace for guests. Located at the end of the road along the beachfront, things are peaceful and quiet here—even more so if you don't speak French. *Anse-Mitan 97229, tel. 596/66–01–12, fax 596/66–01–05; in Canada, 800/468–0023; in NY, 212/840–6636. 26 rooms. Facilities: restaurant, bar. AE, DC. CP. Inexpensive.*

Rivage Hotel. Maryelle and Jean Claude Riveti's garden studios have kitchenettes, air-conditioning, TVs, phones, and private baths. The hotel is right across the road from the beach. Breakfast and light meals are served in the friendly, informal snack bar. You get good value for your money, and you should have no difficulty communicating: English, Spanish, and French are spoken. *Anse-Mitan 97229, tel. 596/66–00–53, fax 596/66–06–56. 17 rooms. Facilities: snack bar, pool, poolside barbecue pit. MC, V. EP. Budget.*

Anses d'Arlets **Hotel Tamarind Plage.** Across the road from the sea and 100 yards from the center of the village, this modest hotel offers basic comforts and a congenial atmosphere. Rooms have air-conditioning, TVs, and shower-baths. Try for one of the upper-story units with a balcony and a view of the sea. There's always a buzz of activity around the hotel, especially in the evenings, when the bar attracts a cheerful crowd that spills onto the veranda. *Anse d'Arlet, tel. 596/68–67–88. 26 rooms. Facilities: restaurant, bar. MC, V. EP. Inexpensive.*

Gîte de Mme. Rachel Melinard. This two-story cottage with a small veranda has superb views of the sea; it's a 10-minute walk to the nearest swimming beach. The cottage accommodates four people and has a well-equipped kitchen. Buy your fresh fish in the morning off the boats that pull onto the shore, a five-minute walk away. Rental is by the week, but you can request a three-day stay. *Anse d'Arlets. Reservations: Gîte #109, Gîtes de France, 9 blvd. du Général-de-Gaulle, BP 1122, Fort-de-France 97248, tel. 596/73–67–92, fax 596/63–55–92. No credit cards. EP. Budget.*

Basse-Point **Leyritz Plantation.** Sleeping on a former sugar plantation in
★ either the old-fashioned furnished rooms at the manor house or in one of the restored former slave cabins is a novelty that may appeal to you. The place is authentic—and isolated on 16 acres of lush vegetation in the northern part of the island. Except for the occasional tour bus carrying cruise-ship passengers passing through, it is very quiet here—a sharp contrast to the frenzied level of activity at the hotels in Pointe du Bout. The new owners are improving the property and have installed a health spa with a nutrition and fitness program, a swimming pool, a meeting room, and an enlarged boutique. Not all rooms are affordable here, so check prices when you call. The restaurant, too, can be pricey, although careful ordering can keep the bill within your budget. There's free transportation to the beach, which is about 30 minutes away. *Basse-Pointe 97218, tel. 596/78–53–92, fax 596/78–92–44. 53 rooms. Facilities: restaurant, bar, spa, health-and-fitness center, horseback riding, tennis courts, pool. DC, MC. CP. Moderate.*

Fort-de-France **Impératrice.** Overlooking La Savane park in the center of the city, the Impératrice's air-conditioned rooms are in a 1950s five-story building (with an elevator). The rooms in the front are either the best or the worst, depending upon your sensibilities: They are noisy, but they overlook the city's center of activity. All rooms have a TV and a private bath; 20 have balconies. Children under 8 stay free in the room with their parents, children 8–15 stay at 50% of the room rate. The hotel also has a popular sidewalk café. Public transportation to the beach is nearby, as is the ferry that will shuttle you to Pointe du Bout. *Fort-de-France 97200, tel. 596/63–06–82 or 800/223–9815, fax 596/72–66–30; in Canada, 800/468–0023; in NY, 212/251–1800. 24 rooms. Facilities: restaurant, café, bar. AE, DC, MC, V. CP. Moderate.*

Lafayette. For those who want to be right in the heart of town, this place is a real find. The choicest rooms are those with French windows. All rooms have air-conditioning, phones, and TVs. You'll need to take a bus or taxi to the beach, where guests have free use of the Bakoua Hotel's facilities. Although this hotel's main claim to fame is its superb dining room, you'll find most of the restaurant's prices will strain your budget. *5 rue de la Liberté, Fort-de-France, tel. 596/73–80–50 or 800/223–9815, fax 596/60–97–75. 24 rooms. Facilities: restaurant, bar, complimentary use of Bakoua Hotel beach facilities. AE, DC, V. EP. Inexpensive.*

Hotel Malmaison. The best bargain in Fort-de-France is this small hotel with white-and-green exterior. It's owned by a Frenchman who's lived on Martinique for 40 years. All rooms have air-conditioning, TVs, minibars, and private baths. Some units have colonial-style beds with sculptured frames, and a few of the higher priced ones have a small living room. For the best value, choose a corner room that has more light and views of the Savane. Beaches are a taxi or ferry ride away. *7 rue de la Liberté, Fort-de-France 97200, tel. 596/63–90–85. 20 rooms. MC, V. EP. Budget.*

Lamentin **Martinique Cottages.** These garden bungalows in the countryside have kitchenettes, cable TVs, and phones. The restaurant here, La Plantation, is a gathering spot for gourmets. The beaches are about a 15-minute drive away. The cottages are difficult to find, and you should take advantage of the property's airport transfers. *Lamentin 97232, tel. 596/50–16–08, fax 596/50–26–83. 16 rooms. Facilities: restaurant, bar, pool, Jacuzzi. AE, MC, V. EP. Inexpensive.*

La Trinité **Saint Aubin.** This restored colonial house is in the countryside above the Atlantic coast. The rooms are modern, with air-conditioning, TVs, phones, and private baths. This is a peaceful retreat, and only 3 miles from La Trinité, 2 miles from the Spoutourne sports center and the beaches on the Caravelle Peninsula. The inn's restaurant is reserved for hotel guests and is closed during June and October. The new owner is trying to improve the property, but it still requires some refurbishing if it is to be more than a guest house. *Box 52, La Trinité, 97220, tel. 596/69–34–77, 800/223–9815, 800/468–0023 in Canada, 212/840–6636 in NY; fax 596/69–41–14. 15 double rooms. Facilities: restaurant, bar, pool. AE, DC, MC, V. CP. Moderate.*

Le Diamant **Diamant-Novotel.** This self-contained resort occupies half an island in an ideal windsurfing location. Air-conditioned, spacious guest rooms have small balconies facing either the sea or the pool. Furnishings are cane and wickerwork painted pastel peach and green, and the floors are tile. The four beaches on the 5-acre property are small. The dining room is large and unromantic, set up to accommodate groups, but there is a pleasant terrace bar where a local band plays on most nights. A smaller, more formal restaurant is open during peak season. Scuba packages are offered. The staff speaks English. Note: The daily rate here exceeds our price category, but weekly packages bring costs into the Moderate range. *Le Diamant 97223, tel. 596/76–42–42 or 800/221–4542, fax 596/76–22–87. 180 rooms. Facilities: 2 restaurants, 3 bars, 2 tennis courts, pool, dive shop, car-rental desk, water-sports center. AE, DC, MC, V. CP, MAP. Moderate.*

★ **Diamant Les Bains.** Although manager Hubert Andrieu and his family go all out to make their guests comfortable, you won't feel quite at home unless you speak at least a little French. A few of the rooms are in the main house, where the restaurant is located, but most are in bungalows, some just steps away from the sea. Those closest to the water are at the top end of our Moderate price range. All rooms are air-conditioned, with private baths, TVs, and phones; eight have kitchenettes. Ask about weekly package rates. *Le Diamant 97223, tel. 596/76–40–14 or 800/223–9815, 800/468–0023 in Canada, 212/251–1800 in NY; fax 596/76–27–00. 24 rooms. Facilities: restaurant, bar, car rental, pool, water-sports center. DC, MC. CP, MAP. Closed Sept. Moderate.*

Diamant Marine. The hotel tends to cater to French families on tour packages, and this high turnover and large-group clientele contribute to the impersonality of the staff and the wear and tear on facilities. The resort consists of self-contained mini-apartments (sleeping room with kitchenette and balcony) in a stucco building. Motellike rooms are painted in pastel colors. The main part of the hotel is some 100 feet above the beach, and rows of dwelling units are tiered on the hillside down to the shore. The pool is just above the beach. Although this arrangement is visually attractive, the climb up the steps from the pool and beach to the main house and restaurant is strenuous. *Point de la Chery, near Diamant, tel. 596/76–46–00 or 800/221–4542, fax 596/76–25–99. 149 rooms. Facilities: restaurant, 2 bars, 2 pools (1 for children), water sports, deep-sea fishing, 2 tennis courts. AE, V. CP, MAP. Moderate.*

★ **Relais Caraibes.** Of all the hotels on Martinique, this one comes closest to having the individuality and authenticity of a country inn. It's a colony of bungalows on manicured grounds, with Diamond Rock dominating the seascape. Each of the 12 bungalows has a bedroom, a small salon with a sofa bed, a kitchenette, and a bathroom. During high season, the price for large one-bedroom units tops out at $190, but standard units are at the top end of our Moderate range. There are also three rooms in the main house. The decorations are objects the owner has brought from trips to her native Paris. The pool is perched at the edge of the cliff that drops to the sea—a very dramatic setting. The hotel is a mile off the main road, and guests will need cars to get around. (The beach, however, is a short walk away.) The restaurant here tends to be expensive at dinner; you may want to travel 2 miles into Diamant for a lighter meal. *Point de la Chery, Diamant 97223, tel. 596/76–44–65 or 800/223–9815, fax 596/76–21–20. 15 rooms. Facilities: restaurant, bar, pool, private beach, boat, scuba instruction. AE, MC, V. CP. Moderate.*

Le Marin **The Last Resort.** John and Véronique Deschamps' bed-and-breakfast on rue Osman Duquesnay is in the former gendarmerie annex. Language will be no problem here, since the Deschampses once lived in Sausalito. You'll have to be flexible enough to share a bathroom with the other guests on your floor. Rooms are not air-conditioned, but sea breezes keep nights cool. A small communal kitchen is available, and an excellent family-style dinner is served nightly. You can walk to the beach from here. *Le Marin 97290, tel. 596/74–83–88, fax 596/74–76–41. 7 rooms with shared bath. Facilities: restaurant. No credit cards. CP, MAP. Budget.*

Le Morne Rouge **Auberge de la Montagne Pelée.** There are three rooms and six studios with kitchenettes in this hillside inn that faces the famed volcano. Accommodations are simple. The restaurant serves Creole food; its view from the terrace is spectacular. Keep in mind that this hotel is in the mountains, an hour's drive to Atlantic beaches. The inn was closed for renovations at press time, but should reopen for the 1993–94 season. *Le Morne Rouge 97260, tel. 596/52–32–09, fax 596/73–20–75. 12 rooms. Facilities: restaurant. No credit cards. EP. Inexpensive.*

Ste-Anne **Club Med/Buccaneer's Creek.** Occupying 48 landscaped acres, Martinique's Club Med is an all-inclusive village with plazas, cafés, restaurants, boutique, and a small marina. Air-conditioned pastel cottages contain twin beds and private shower baths. The only money you need spend here is for bar drinks, scuba diving, personal expenses, and excursions into Fort-de-France or the countryside. There's a white-sand beach, a plethora of water sports, and plenty of nightlife. *Pointe Marin 97180, tel. 596/76–72–72, 800/CLUBMED, or 212/750–1670 in NY; fax 596/72–76–02. 300 rooms. Facilities: 2 restaurants and bars, 6 tennis courts (4 lighted), fitness and water-sports center, nightclub, disco. AE, V. All-inclusive (drinks not included). Moderate.*

★ **La Dunette.** Refurbished in 1992, this small hotel in Ste-Anne is one of the best buys in this price category. Rooms are not spacious, but they are comfortable, with TVs, air-conditioning, and full baths; make sure yours faces the sea and St. Lucia beyond. The beach in front of the hotel is adequate for a morning dip, but head for Pte. Marin, about a mile away, for more serious sunbathing. An outside patio 50 feet from the water's edge serves as the restaurant (*see* Dining, *above*); there's a small bar for morning coffee and evening aperitifs. A minimarket across the street from the hotel and a vegetable market a block away make assembling a picnic a simple matter. The friendly staff speaks some English. *Ste-Anne 97227, tel. 596/76–73–90, fax 596/76–76–05. 18 rooms. Facilities: restaurant, bar. MC, V. EP. Inexpensive.*

Campgrounds It is acceptable to pitch a tent in designated locations on Martinique. One popular site is at Anse-Mitan (tel. 596/68–31–30); the 62F cost for two people includes access to coin-operated showers. Ste-Anne is another popular site, with a municipal campground (tel. 596/76–72–79) just outside the Club Med. The Tourist Office (tel. 596/63–79–60) can advise on other locations.

Villas and Apartment Rentals Besides the apartment-style accommodations listed with Gîtes de France (*see above*), units here range from studios to four-bedroom apartments. Weekly rates start at around $220 and climb from there. Contact **Villa Rental Service** (Centrale de Réservation, 20 rue Ernest Deproge, B.P. 823, Fort-de-France 97208, tel. 596/71–56–11, fax 596/63–11–64).

Off-Season Bets Between April 15 and December 15, you can take advantage of hotel rates that are as much as 40% lower than peak-season prices. Among hotels with rates that decrease dramatically are **Le Bakoua** (Box 589, Fort-de-France, tel. 596/66–02–02 or 800/221–4542, fax 596/66–00–71), often considered Martinique's leading resort hotel; and **Habitation Lagrange** (Marigot 97225, tel. 596/53–60–60, fax 596/53–50–58), a former sugar plantation with a restored 18th-century manor house. Only **Relais Caraibes's** (*see above*) small rooms squeak into our Moderate price category during high season, but even the suites at this charming cliffside inn overlooking Diamond Rock are affordable during the off-season.

The Arts and Nightlife

Be sure to catch a performance of **Les Grands Ballets de Martinique** (tel. 596/63–43–88). The troupe of young, exuberant dancers, singers, and musicians is one of the best folkloric groups in the Caribbean. They perform on alternate nights at the Bakoua, Méridien, La Batelière, and Carayou-PLM Azur.

Discos Your hotel or the Tourist Office can put you in touch with the current "in" places. It's also wise to check on opening and closing times and admission charges. For the most part, the discos draw a mixed crowd of locals and tourists, the young and the not so young. Some of the currently popular places are **L'Oeil** (Petit Cocotte, Ducos, tel. 596/56–11–11), **La Cabane de Pêcheur** (Diamant-Novotel, tel. 596/76–42–42), **Le Must** (20 blvd. Allegre, Fort-de-France, tel. 596/60–36–06), **Le New Hippo** (24 blvd. Allegre, Fort-de-France, tel. 596/71–74–60), **Le Sweety** (rue Capitaine Pierre Rose, Fort-de-France, no phone), **Le Vesou** (Carayou-PLM Azur, tel. 596/66–04–04), **VonVon** (Méridien, tel. 596/66–00–00), and **Zipp's Dupe Club** (Dumaine, Le François, tel. 596/54–47–06).

Zouk and Jazz Currently the most popular music is zouk, which mixes the Caribbean rhythm and an Occidental tempo with Creole words. Jacob Devarieux (Kassav) is the leading exponent of this style and is occasionally on the island. More likely, though, you will hear zouk music played by one of his followers at the hotels and clubs. The **Neptune** (Diamant, tel. 596/76–34–23) is a current hot place for zouk. In season, you'll find one or two jazz combos playing at clubs and hotels, but only at **Coco Lobo** (next to the Tourist Office in Fort-de-France, tel. 596/63–63–77) are there regular jazz sessions.

16 Montserrat

*Updated by
Simon Worrall*

Measuring only 11 miles by 8 miles, Montserrat is a small, friendly island that has escaped much of the large-scale development common in other parts of the Caribbean. Mass tourism is rare, package deals almost unheard of. When you see the airstrip, you'll understand why; 747s can't land here. And that's part of the attraction.

Montserrat is startlingly lush and green, thanks to its fertile, volcanic soil, which is responsible for the black-sand beaches found on most of the island (although there are some beautiful stretches of "beige" sand on the northwest coast). Three mountain ranges dominate the landscape: Silver Hills to the north; Centre Hills; and the southern range, home to Galway's Soufrière, a 3,000-foot inactive volcano.

Monserrat neither caters to nor discourages the budget traveler. It lacks the exclusive feel and outrageously expensive resorts of some Caribbean islands, but it's not known for particularly cheap hotels or restaurants either. Nevertheless, most accommodations are moderately priced, including some of the rental villas for which the island is known. A healthy handful of small hotels and guest houses offer cheaper alternatives. Activities tend to be inexpensive and sporty; bicycling and hiking are popular. It's the kind of place that attracts independent travelers who want a low-key, away-from-it-all vacation. If you want to pump iron, drink piña coladas, and boogie until dawn, you'll probably be bored. If you like seclusion, nature, peace, and quiet, you'll love it.

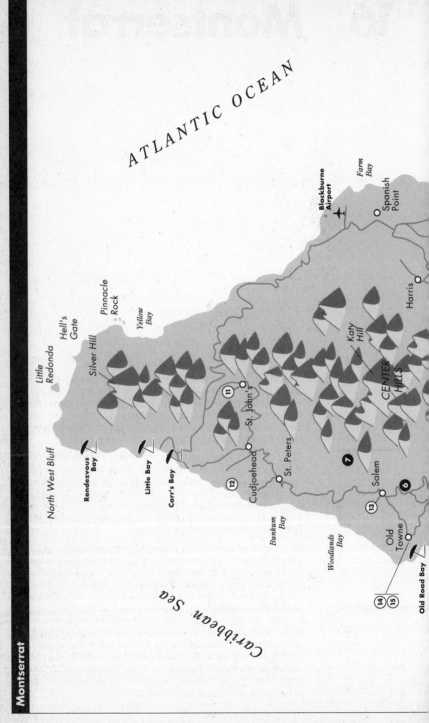

ATLANTIC OCEAN

Caribbean Sea

Little
Redonda

Hell's
Gate

Pinnacle
Rock

Silver Hill

Yellow
Bay

North West Bluff

Rendezvous
Bay

Little Bay

Carr's Bay

Bunkum
Bay

Woodlands
Bay

St. John's

Cudjoehead

St. Peters

Katy
Hill

CENTER
HILLS

Harris

Blackburne
Airport

Farm
Bay

Spanish
Point

Salem

Old
Towne

Old Road Bay

⑪

⑫

⑬

⑭
⑮

❼

❻

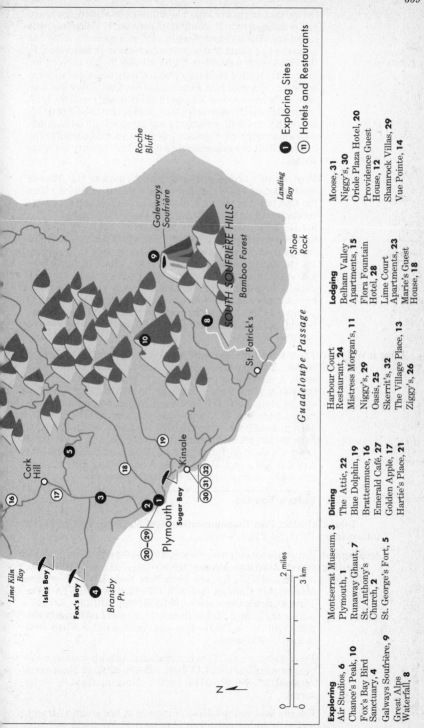

● Exploring Sites

⑪ Hotels and Restaurants

Guadeloupe Passage

Roche Bluff

Landing Bay

Shoe Rock

SOUTH SOUFRIÈRE HILLS

Galleways Soufrière

Bamboo Forest

St. Patrick's

Cork Hill

Kinsale

Plymouth

Sugar Bay

Lime Kiln Bay

Isles Bay

Fox's Bay

Bransby Pt.

N

0   2 miles

0   3 km

Exploring
Air Studios, **6**
Chance's Peak, **10**
Fox's Bay Bird
Sanctuary, **4**
Galways Soufrière, **9**
Great Alps
Waterfall, **8**

Montserrat Museum, **3**
Plymouth, **1**
Runaway Ghaut, **7**
St. Anthony's
Church, **2**
St. George's Fort, **5**

Dining
The Attic, **22**
Blue Dolphin, **19**
Brattenmuce, **16**
Emerald Café, **27**
Golden Apple, **17**
Hartie's Place, **21**

Harbour Court
Restaurant, **24**
Mistress Morgan's, **11**
Niggy's, **29**
Oasis, **25**
Skerrit's, **32**
The Village Place, **13**
Ziggy's, **26**

Lodging
Belham Valley
Apartments, **15**
Flora Fountain
Hotel, **28**
Lime Court
Apartments, **23**
Marie's Guest
House, **18**

Moose, **31**
Niggy's, **30**
Oriole Plaza Hotel, **20**
Providence Guest
House, **12**
Shamrock Villas, **29**
Vue Pointe, **14**

On the map the island looks like a flint-ax head, with the sharp end pointing north. It was first discovered by Columbus, who sailed past the leeward coast in 1493 and named it after the monastery of Santa Maria de Montserrate near Barcelona. In the 17th Century, dissident Irish Catholics fleeing persecution in St. Kitts settled on Montserrat and gave the island its nickname, the Emerald Isle. Place names like Carr's Bay and Kinsale, and surnames like Maloney and Frith, still recall the Irish connection, and though today the island is a British Crown Colony with a resident governor, your passport will be stamped with a shamrock. St. Patrick's Day is also enthusiastically celebrated, albeit to commemorate a major 18th-century slave uprising.

Most visitors arrive at Blackburne Airport on the Atlantic (east) coast and then transfer to the west coast. This is where the best beaches and most of the island's villas and hotels are concentrated, in a 5-by-2 mile area around the capital of Plymouth. As you drive around Montserrat's northern tip from the airport en route to your hotel, you will notice the landscape change from the rocky, windswept Atlantic coast to the luxuriant vegetation of the island's west side, where hibiscus, bougainvillea, giant philodendron, frangipani, avocado, mango, papaya, breadfruit, christophines, coconut palms, and flamboyant trees run riot. Notice, too, the spectacular view unfold across the Caribbean to the mysterious island of Rodondo and, beyond it, to St. Kitts, a sequence of indigo blue peaks on the horizon.

What It Will Cost These sample prices, meant only as a general guide are for high season. A two-bedroom villa sleeping four costs about $900 a week. A moderately priced hotel will be around $125 a night, but you can find budget hotels for about $30 a night. A B&B will be around $60–$80 for two. A budget restaurant dinner ranges from $6 to $8. A rum punch costs anywhere from $2 to $4. A glass of house wine will be $1.50–$2; a beer, $1–$2. A taxi from the airport to Plymouth runs about $11, from town to the beach it's about $5. Cars rent for $35–$40 a day; mountain bike rental is $20 a day, $110 a week. A single-tank dive will cost about $40; snorkel equipment rents for about $5.

Before You Go

Tourist Information Contact **Pace Communications** (485 5th Ave., New York, NY 10017, tel. 212/818–0100).

Arriving and Departing *By Plane* Antigua is not only the gateway, it's the best way to reach Montserrat. **American Airlines** (tel. 800/334–7200) and **BWIA** (tel. 800/JET–BWIA) fly here from New York; **BWIA** flies from Miami; **Air Canada** (tel. 800/422–6232) and BWIA from Toronto; **British Airways** (tel. 081/897–4000 in Britain, 800/247–9297 in the United States) from London; and **Lufthansa** transports visitors via Puerto Rico and Antigua (tel. 800/645–3880 in the United States).

From Antigua's V.C. Bird International Airport, you can make your connections with **LIAT** (tel. 809/491–2200) or **Montserrat Airways** (tel. 809/491–2713) for the 15-minute flight to Montserrat.

You will land on the 3,400-foot runway at Blackburne Airport, on the Atlantic coast, about 11 miles from Plymouth.

From the Airport Taxis meet every flight, and the government-regulated fare from the airport to Plymouth is E.C. $29 (U.S. $11).

Passports and Visas U.S. and Canadian citizens need only proof of citizenship, such as a passport, a notarized birth certificate, or a voter registration card. A driver's license is *not* sufficient. British citizens must have a passport; visas are not required. All visitors must hold an ongoing or return ticket.

Language It's English with more of a lilt than a brogue. You'll also hear a patois that's spoken on most of the islands.

Precautions Ask for permission before taking pictures. Some residents may be reluctant photographic subjects, and they will appreciate your courtesy. Most Montserratians frown at the sight of skimpily dressed tourists; do not risk offending them by strolling around in swimsuits.

Staying in Montserrat

Important Addresses **Tourist Information:** The **Montserrat Department of Tourism** (Church Rd., Plymouth, tel. 809/491–2230) is open weekdays 8–noon and 1–4.

Emergencies **Police:** tel. 809/491–2555. **Hospitals:** There is a 24-hour emergency room at **Glendon Hospital** (Plymouth, tel. 809/491–2552). **Pharmacies: Lee's Pharmacy** (Evergreen Dr., Plymouth, tel. 809/491–3274) and **Daniel's Pharmacy** (George St., Plymouth, tel. 809/491–2908).

Currency The official currency is the Eastern Caribbean dollar (E.C.$), often called beewee. At press time, the exchange rate was E.C. $2.70 to U.S. $1. U.S. dollars are readily accepted, but you'll often receive change in beewees. Note: Prices quoted here are in U.S. dollars unless noted otherwise.

Taxes and Service Charges Hotels collect a 7% government tax and add a 10% service charge. If they do not, leave a 10% or 15% tip. Taxi drivers should be given a 10% tip. The departure tax is E.C. $25. Most restaurants add a 10%–15% service charge.

Getting Around Taxis, private vehicles, or the M11 (a play on the local registration numbers, meaning your own two legs) are the main means of transport on the island. As the island is small (only 39 square miles) and most of the accommodations concentrated in a small area on the west coast, biking is also popular. Whatever you choose, you are unlikely to be more than a 10-minute walk from a beach. Even the villas perched on the hillside in the Woodlands district are within walking distance of the sea, although you'll need a car to get to the supermarkets in Plymouth. If you're staying in a hotel, it's not essential to rent a car for your entire stay. Many visitors rent for a day to see the sights, and spend the rest of their time swimming and hiking.

Taxis These are available at the airport, the main hotels, and at the Taxi Stand in Plymouth (tel. 809/491–2261). As distances from your accommodation to Plymouth are likely to be less than 5 miles, fares are not expensive. The journey from the Vue Point Hotel to Plymouth, for instance, costs E.C. $13; from Woodlands to Plymouth, E.C. $18. The Department of Tourism publishes a list of taxi fares to most destinations.

Car Rentals The island has more than 150 miles of good roads. If you like to drive, you'll enjoy the switchback hill roads and hairpin curves. Just remember that driving is on the left, and watch out for potholes and the occasional goat. You'll need a valid driver's license, plus a Montserrat license, which is available at the airport or the police station. The fee is E.C. $30. Rental cars cost about $35–$40 per day. The smaller companies, whose prices are generally 10%–25% cheaper, will negotiate, particularly off-season. The local Avis outlet is **Pauline Car Rentals** (Plymouth, tel. 809/491–2345 or 800/331–1084). Other agencies are **Budget** (Blackburne Airport, tel. 809/491–6065), **Fenco** (Plymouth, tel. 809/491–4901), **Jefferson's Car Rental** (Dagenham, tel. 809/491–2126), and **Reliable** (Marine Dr., Plymouth, tel. 809/491–6990).

Public Transportation There is no public bus service as such; instead, an informal network of privately run minibuses ply the main routes between Plymouth and the villages. They generally start moving early, about 6:30 AM, bringing local people in to work or shop, and then leave town again at 3–4 PM, at the end of the islanders' working day. Outside these times, most service is haphazard, so if you use a minibus to get to Plymouth, you'll probably have to spend all day in town. The main route travels from St. John's, in the north, down the west coast to Plymouth. The main pickup point in Plymouth is the courtyard in front of the Osborne Wholesale Department on Parliament Street; another is at Papa's grocery store on Church Street. (Outside of Plymouth, there are no fixed pickup points; just flag down the vehicle.) Fare for the full route is a mere E.C. $3. The Department of Tourism publishes a list of routes and approximate fares.

Mountain Bikes Montserrat is good mountain-bike country: small, with relatively traffic-free roads and lots of challenging hills to try out all those gears. Potholes will present a constant challenge, as will the heat and steep gradients. Even so, biking is a great way to get around this island, where the majority of facilities, shops, and accommodations are concentrated in a small area on the west coast. At **Island Bikes** (Harney St., Plymouth, tel. 809/491–4686), Butch Miller and Susan Goldin, the bustling, can-do Americans who run the outfit, are self-confessed biking junkies and know the island like the backs of their own saddles. Rentals are $20 a day, $110 a week. The couple also conducts guided tours, which include refreshments and a sag wagon for the faint of heart, and can arrange bed-and-bike package tours.

Telephones and Mail To call Montserrat from the United States, dial area code 809 and access code 491 plus the local four-digit number. International direct-dial is available on the island; both local and long-distance calls come through clearly. To call locally on the island, you need to dial only the local four-digit number. A local call costs E.C. 25¢.

Airmail letters and postcards to the United States and Canada cost E.C. $1.15 each. Montserrat is one of several Caribbean islands whose stamps are of interest to collectors. You can buy them at the main post office in Plymouth (open Mon. and Tues., Thurs. and Fri. 8:15–3:30, Wed. and Sat. 8:15–11:30 AM).

Opening and Closing Times Most shops are open Monday–Saturday 8–5. Banking hours are Monday–Thursday 8–1, Friday 3–5.

Guided Tours These are priced by car, not by person, so if you're part of a group or even a couple, your cost will be only marginally more expensive than renting a car. **Runaway Tours** (tel. 809/491–2776 or 809/491–2800) offers a five-hour tour of the island that in-

American Express offers Travelers Cheques built for two.

American Express® Cheques *for Two*. The first Travelers Cheques that allow either of you to use them because both of you have signed them. And only one of you needs to be present to purchase them.

Cheques *for Two* are accepted anywhere regular American Express Travelers Cheques are, which is just about everywhere. So stop by your bank, AAA* or any American Express Travel Service Office and ask for Cheques *for Two*.

cludes Galway's Soufrière, St. George's Fort, and the Fox's Bay Bird Sanctuary. The hefty $110 cost is reduced to $75 a person for a party of two, or $58 for a party of three (children under 12, $33). The price includes refreshments and a meal, usually at the Emerald Café. Sturdy walking shoes are recommended. Other companies include **Carib World Tours** (tel. 809/491–2713) and **Best Foot Forward** (tel. 809/491–5872).

A number of taxi drivers will also act as tour guides. The best is Charles Frith, known to everyone simply as **Mango** (tel. 809/491–2134), an enormously likable Montserratian with a good grasp of the island's geography, boundless patience, and a soft-spoken, slow charm that is typically Monserratian. Also recommended are **John Ryner** (tel. 809/491–2190) and the aptly named **Be-Beep Taylor** (tel. 809/491–3787). Prices (fixed by the Department of Tourism) are E.C. $30 (U.S. $11) per hour or E.C. $130 (U.S. $48) for a five-hour day tour. Refreshments are extra.

Exploring Montserrat

Numbers in the margin correspond to points of interest on the Montserrat map.

Plymouth
❶

About a third of the island's population of 12,500 live in **Plymouth,** the capital city that faces the Caribbean on the southwest coast. The town is neat and clean, its narrow streets lined with trim Georgian structures built mostly of stones that came from Dorset as ballast on old sailing vessels. Most of the town's sights are set right along the water. On the south side, a bridge over the Fort Ghaut ("gut," or ravine) leads to Wapping, where most of the restaurants are located.

We'll begin at **Government House** on the south side of town just above Sugar Bay. The frilly Victorian house, decorated with a shamrock, dates from the 18th century. The beautifully landscaped grounds are open from 10 to noon.

Follow Peebles Street north and cross the bridge. Just over the bridge at the junction of Harney, Strand, and Parliament streets you'll see the **Market,** where islanders bring their produce every Saturday—a very colorful scene.

From the market, walk along Strand Street for one block to the tall white **War Memorial**, a tribute to the soldiers of both World Wars. Next to the monument is the **Post Office and Treasury,** a galleried West Indian–style building by the water, where you can buy stamps that make handsome souvenirs.

Walk away from the water on George Street, which runs alongside the War Memorial. The town's main thoroughfare, Parliament Street, cuts diagonally north–south through the town. A left turn onto Parliament Street, at the corner of George Street, will take you to the Methodist Church and the Court House. If you continue straight on George Street, you'll come to the Roman Catholic Church. North of the church is the **American University of the Caribbean,** a medical school with many American students.

Elsewhere on the Island

The main sites on Montserrat can be seen in a day. Although a guided tour is somewhat more expensive than renting a car (*see* Guided Tours, *above*), it does allow you to see the island through an insider's eyes. A car, on the other hand, gives you more freedom, particularly for lunch and swim stops, and is cheaper.

Tour 1 Take Highway 2, the main road north out of Plymouth. On the outskirts of town there's a stone marker that commemorates ❷ the first colony in 1632. Just north of town is **St. Anthony's Church,** consecrated some time between 1623 and 1666. It was rebuilt in 1730 following one of the many clashes between the French and the English in the area. Two silver chalices displayed in the church were donated by freed slaves after emancipation in 1834. An ancient tamarind tree stands near the church.

Richmond Hill rises northeast of town. Here you will find the ❸ **Montserrat Museum** in a restored sugar mill. The museum contains maps, historical records, artifacts, and all sorts of memorabilia pertaining to the island's growth and development. *Richmond Hill, tel. 809/491–5443. Admission free (donations accepted). Open Sun. and Wed. 2:30–5 (but telephone to be sure).*

Take the first left turn past the museum to Grove Road; it will ❹ take you to the **Fox's Bay Bird Sanctuary,** a 15-acre bog. Marked trails lead into the interior, which is aflutter with egrets, herons, coots, and cuckoo birds.

The **Bransby Point Fortification** is also in this area and contains a collection of restored cannons.

Backtrack on Grove Road to Highway 2, drive north and turn ❺ right on Highway 4 to **St. George's Fort.** It's overgrown and of little historical interest, but the view from the hilltop is well worth the trip.

Highway 2 continues north past the **Belham Valley Golf Course** to **Vue Pointe Hotel,** on the coast at Lime Kiln Bay. A few miles ❻ inland, at Centre Hills, you will find the old **Air Studios,** a recording studio founded in 1979 by former Beatles producer George Martin. Sting, Boy George, and Paul McCartney have all cut records here, but following Hurricane Hugo, Martin closed up shop.

About 1½ miles farther north, a scenic drive takes you along ❼ **Runaway Ghaut.** Two centuries ago, this peaceful green valley was the scene of bloody battles between the French and the English. Local legend has it that "those who drink its water clear they spellbound are, and the Montserrat they must obey." **Carr's Bay, Little Bay,** and **Rendezvous Bay,** the island's three most popular beaches, are along the northwest coast.

Tour 2 This tour of Soufrière, the rain forest, and the southern mountains will be considerably more arduous than the first. It involves hiking from the end of access roads to the sites themselves. You can do this tour in half a day if you race through it, but if you do any significant hiking or biking, you could easily spend a day. A guide may help, as there are few markers on the paths, and the access roads are not always easy to find. But anyone with a bit of hiking experience and a modicum of common sense will have no problem. To hire a knowledgeable guide, contact the Department of Tourism or ask at your hotel. The guide's fee will be about $6 per person for the rain-forest hike to the Great Alps Waterfall. Wear rubber-soled shoes.

A 15-minute drive south of Plymouth on Old Fort Road will bring you to the village of **St. Patrick's.** From there, a scenic drive takes you to the starting point of the moderately strenu-

8 ous 30- to 45-minute hike through thick rain forests to **Great Alps Waterfall.** The falls cascade 70 feet down the side of a rock and splash into a shallow pool, where you can see a rainbow in the mist.

9 A rugged road leads eastward to **Galways Soufrière,** a highlight of any trip to Montserrat. Millions of years ago, Galways was the submarine volcano that created the island; it's still techni-cally active, though it releases no lava. From where you park your car, a small path leads through bushes to an outcrop of rock above the crater. Exercise caution here, as the viewing area is small. From above, the soufrière doesn't look like much, but once you have made your way down a second stony path onto the valley floor, you feel as though you have walked into a scene from *Journey to the Center of the Earth*. Steaming, milky-colored streams flow over pink- and rust-colored rocks. Steam gushes from vents in the rock. Brilliant, lemon-yellow crystals hang like clusters of cheap jewelry. Look up, and you will see rust-red cliffs and, beyond them, the lush green vegetation of surrounding hills. Note: If you go on your own, exercise cau-tion. The ground is extremely hot and unstable, and people have been known to slip and lose all the skin on their legs.

10 The island's highest point, **Chance's Peak,** pokes up 3,000 feet through the rain forests. The climb to the top is arduous, but if you do make it to the top, what little breath you may have left will be taken away by the view (*see* Hiking, *below*). Also in this area is the old **Galways Estate,** a plantation built in the late 17th century by prosperous Irishmen John and Henry Blake, who came to Montserrat from Galway. All that now remains of the fine estate is the ruins of the house and factory and some rusted machinery.

Beaches

The sand on the beaches on Montserrat's south coast is of vol-canic origin; usually referred to as black, it's actually light to dark gray. On the northwest coast, the sand is beige or white. Black sand absorbs more heat than white, and sandals are re-commended. The best of Montserrat's beaches are, like every-thing else, on the west coast. (The water on the rocky east coast is rough, and the areas are inaccessible.) Most are in lovely little coves surrounded by steep, lush hillsides, where hotels generally perch. In the small, developed area where you will probably be staying, you will rarely be farther than a 10-minute walk from the water.

There are excellent beaches close to the main villa and hotel developments at **Old Road Bay, Isles Bay,** and **Fox's Bay.** Fur-ther north, the most popular destinations for swimming and sunning are **Rendezvous Bay, Little Bay,** and **Carr's Bay,** where the sand is beige-gray. Unless you arrive by boat, it's a 30-minute drive from Plymouth over potholed dirt tracks to reach Carr's Bay and Little Bay. From Little Bay, you must hike to Rendezvous Bay. The most pleasant way to reach the northern beaches is by boat (*see* Sports and the Outdoors, *below*).

Sugar Bay, to the south of Plymouth, is a beach of fine gray volcanic sand. The Yacht Club overlooks this beach. The beaches in a«d around Plymouth itself are adequate, but not the island's best.

Sports and the Outdoors

Most of the sports facilities on Montserrat, apart from hiking and biking, are run from the larger hotels and tend to be expensive for nonguests.

Boating Boats are available through **Captain Martin,** who has a 46-foot trimaran and takes guests for a full-day sail to neighboring islands from 10 AM to 5 PM for about $40 (tel. 809/491–5738), or through **Vue Pointe Hotel** (tel. 809/491–5210). The latter offers sailing and snorkeling excursions to Rendezvous Bay, Little Bay, and Carr's Bay. Cost is $20 a person and includes a sandwich lunch and snorkel equipment.

Golf The **Montserrat Golf Course** (no phone), in the picturesque Belham Valley, is "slope rated" by the USGA (in other words, it's damnably hilly) and must be one of the few golf courses in the world whose hazards include gopher holes and iguanas, which collect golf balls. The number of holes (11) is also somewhat eccentric, though by playing a number of them twice, you can get your 18. Four fairways run along the ocean. The rest are uphill and down dale. The greens fee is E.C. $60.

Hiking Small, green, and hilly, Montserrat is an excellent place to hike, assuming you can take the heat. If you want to do an Indiana Jones, then head for the South Soufrière Hills at the southern tip of the island. It is the wildest and most unspoiled part of Montserrat and includes, among its highlights, the **Bamboo Forest,** a large tract of semi–rain forest inhabited by frogs, numerous plants, and more than 100 species of birds. Among the latter is the national emblem, *iaterus oberi* (Montserrat oriole), also known locally as the Tannia Bird. Don't expect to see one, though, as its habitat was severely damaged by Hurricane Hugo and it is only now beginning to reestablish itself. As no roads lead into the area and there are no marked paths, you need a guide. **Joseph Peters** (tel. 809/491–6850) will take you on a two–three-hour tour and describe flora and fauna; his rates are negotiable. Also try **James Daley,** at the Department of Agriculture (tel. 809/491–2546).

A climb up **Chance's Peak** is well worth the effort. Wooden steps have been laid into the mountainside, and several viewing platforms await at the top. If you're a mountain goat, you can get up and down in two hours. But we recommend bringing a picnic lunch and making a half-day trip of it. Either way you can expect some muscle aches the next day.

A hike to **Galways Soufrière** rewards the intrepid with otherworldly sights from the volcano's crater (*see* Exploring, *above*).

Mountain Biking *See* Getting Around, *above*.

Snorkeling, Scuba Diving, and Water Sports **Dive Montserrat** (tel. 809/491–8812) operates from the Vue Pointe Hotel, offering one- or two-tank dives, night dives, and instruction from a PADI-certified teacher. The **Sea Wolf Diving School** (tel. 809/491–7807) in Plymouth offers PADI and specialty courses. Costs at both are about $40 for a one-tank dive and $60 for a two-tank dive. **Danny Water Sports** (tel. 809/491–5645), also operating out of the Vue Pointe, offers fishing ($30 an hour), Sunfish sailing ($10 an hour), waterskiing ($10 an hour), and windsurfing ($10 an hour). Both Sea Wolf and Danny Water Sports rent snorkeling equipment ($5–$10 per day).

Tennis There are lighted tennis courts at the **Vue Pointe Hotel** (tel. 809/491–5210), the **Montserrat Golf Club** (tel. 809/491–5220), and the **Montserrat Springs Hotel** (tel. 809/491–2481).

Shopping

Montserrat is one of the few Caribbean islands where a local craft industry has remained (just about) intact. A few good bargains are still to be had, mainly in pottery, straw goods, and shell and coral jewelry. The island's most famous product used to be sea-island cotton, prized for its high quality and softness. Unfortunately, ever since Hurricane Hugo, the already limited amount grown has dwindled further. A few boutiques still offer sea-island cotton, but it's not cheap. Montserratian stamps are prized by collectors; they can be purchased at the Post Office or at the Philatelic Bureau, just across the bridge in Wapping. Two lip-smacking local food products are Cassell's hot sauce, available at most supermarkets, and Perk's Punch, an effervescent rum-based concoction manufactured by J.W.R. Perkins, Inc. (tel. 809/491–2596).

Good Buys **Montserrat Shirts** (Parliament St., tel. 809/491–2892) has a
Clothes good selection of T-shirts and sandals. **Etcetera** (John St., tel. 809/491–3299) has colorful, lightweight cotton dresses and a small, but fine, selection of local crafts. (If you're lucky, you may see someone making a hat of coconut palm fronds). **The Lime Tree** (Parliament St., tel. 809/491–3656) carries cotton clothing for men and boys, with some snappy styling. **The Montserrat Sea Island Cotton Co.** (corner of George and Strand Sts., Plymouth, tel. 809/491–7009) has long been famous for its cotton creations. Should you really need to purchase a T-shirt, stop in at **Sea Isle Style** (Parliament St., Plymouth, tel. 809/491–2892).

Crafts **The Tapestries of Montserrat** (Parliament St., tel. 809/491–2520) is a gallery of hand-tufted creations—from wall hangings and pillow covers to tote bags and rugs—all with fanciful yarn creations of flowers, carnival figures, animals, and birds. You can tour the gallery and create your own design for a small fee. **Carol's Corner** (Vue Pointe Hotel, tel. 809/491–5210) copper bookmarks and books ranging from cookbooks to art books. Drop by **Dutcher's Studio** (Old Towne, tel. 809/491–5823) to see hand-cut, hand-painted objects made from old bottles. Don't miss the morning iguana feeding. **Island House,** on John Street, stocks Haitian art, Caribbean prints, and clay pottery. **Jus' Looking** (George St., Plymouth, tel. 809/491–4076) features the island's best selection of indigenous crafts, including hand-painted pillows from Antigua, lacquered boxes from Tortola, Caribelle Batik's line of richly colored fabrics and—watch out—even an Arawak love potion. There is also a selection of local poetry and history books.

Dining

For its size, Montserrat offers a variety of affordable dining options, from gourmet-quality restaurants to local cafés and bistros. Many of these may look like the proverbial hole-in-the-wall, but if you're lucky you'll be served delicious Caribbean home cooking. The island has a lively assortment of **rum shops**—the Caribbean version of local bars—packed with islanders on Friday nights; you can join in and get a drink and a simple meal. One of the best is the **Cork Hill Rum Shop** in Salem. On Fridays you'll find music, the best spare ribs on the island, and chicken and fried fish cooked by local women in their homes and brought to the bar for sale. At the **Treasure Cove,** in the village of Kinsale, a traditional string band featuring guitars, pipes, and tambourines often plays.

For those renting villas, Plymouth has several large, well-stocked supermarkets. The biggest is **Rams Emdee** (Church Rd.). It's run by the same Indian family that manages the Flora Fountain Hotel down the street, which accounts for the store's good selection of Indian foods and spices. Another large, modern store is **Angelo's** (Church Rd.). Most villages, including Kinsale, St. Patrick's, and Salem, have little general stores selling basics like matches, canned goods, fruits and vegetables, and—a basic here—Guinness. **Pete's 24 Hour Bakery** (George St.), which makes delicious rye, whole wheat, and French breads is worth the half-mile trip out of Plymouth. **Economy Bakery** (Church St.; closed Sat.) is also good.

At Plymouth's Strand Street **market** on Fridays and Saturdays, the best produce is gone by midday (it opens at 4:30 AM). You'll forget about the grubby buildings when you see the busloads of ample island women in colorful cotton print dresses; the piles of sugarcane and green bananas, and the singsong haggling and banter at the stalls.

Montserrat's national dish is goatwater stew, made with goat meat and vegetables, similar to Irish stew. Goat meat is reminiscent of mutton. Mountain chicken (*crapaud,* actually enormous frogs) is also a great favorite. Yam, breadfruit, christophine (a green vegetable), lime, mango, papaya, and a variety of seafood are served in most restaurants. Home-brewed ginger beer, one of the finest traditional drinks of the West Indies, is available at many cafés.

Dress is casual unless otherwise stated. Highly recommended restaurants are indicated by a star ★.

Category	Cost*
Moderate	$20–$30
Inexpensive	$10–$20
Budget	under $10

*Per person, excluding drinks and service. If the service charge is not added to the bill, leave a 10%–15% tip.

Emerald Café. Dining is relaxed at 10 tables inside and on the terrace, where there are white tables shaded by blue umbrellas. Burgers, sandwiches, salads and grilled dishes are served at lunchtime. Dinner features tournedos sautéed in spicy butter, broiled or sautéed Caribbean lobster, T-bone steak, mountain chicken diable, and kingfish, broiled or sautéed. The homemade pastries, such as Island Coconut Pie, are superb. There's also an ample list of liqueurs and wines, a full bar, and entertainment on weekends. *Wapping, Plymouth, tel. 809/491–*

3821. *Dinner reservations advised in season. No credit cards. Closed Sun. Moderate.*

Oasis. A 200-year-old stone building houses this restaurant, where you can dine outdoors on the patio. Entrées include mountain chicken, jumbo shrimp Provençale, and red snapper with lime butter. Owners Eric and Mandy Finnamore are well known for their fish-and-chips. *Wapping, Plymouth, tel. 809/491–2328. Reservations advised in season. No credit cards. Closed Wed. Moderate.*

The Attic. The story of the Attic is the story of Montserrat itself since Hurricane Hugo. The (formerly) third-story Attic had a sister restaurant on the second story called The Pantry. Compliments of Hugo, the Attic ended up in the Pantry, where owners John and Jeanne Fagon decided it would stay! For breakfast, lunch, and dinner, 12 busy tables supply town folk with specialties of ocean perch, pork chops with "pantry" sauce, breaded shrimp, and lobster tail. *Marine Dr., Plymouth, tel. 809/491–2008. No credit cards. Inexpensive.*

★ **Blue Dolphin.** It's short on ambience, the chairs are Naugahyde, and the menu's scrawled on a blackboard without prices or descriptions, but the seductive aromas wafting from the kitchen announce that the Blue Dolphin serves some of the best food on the island, including luscious pumpkin fritters, mouthwatering lobster, and meltingly tender mountain chicken. The restaurant is on the northeastern edge of Plymouth. *Amersham, tel. 809/491–3263. No credit cards. Inexpensive.*

★ **Brattenmuce.** You can't miss the canary-yellow facade and bright croton bushes of this property that sits above the road from Plymouth to Belham Valley, about 10 minutes by car out of town. It's run by Matt Hawthorne and Bruce Munro, two Canadians who have been in Montserrat since 1985. They serve good old-fashioned favorites: meat loaf and creamed potatoes, curried pork chops, and chicken cordon bleu. On Games Night each Wednesday, E.C. $25 gets you a three-course meal and free use of the Scrabble boards and Trivial Pursuit. Fridays, there's a fish dinner (E.C. $25–$35) and Saturdays, a steak barbecue (E.C. $40). The lunch menu includes omelets, burgers, and sandwiches. For those who want to stay over, Rogie's, above the restaurant, has simple rooms to let. *Belham Valley, tel. 809/419–7564. No credit cards. Reservations advised in high season. Closed Mon. in season. Open Wed., Fri., and Sat. dinner and Sun. lunch only in off-season. Inexpensive.*

Golden Apple. In this large, galleried stone building, you'll be served huge plates of good local cooking: the special goatwater stew (weekends only) cooked outside over an open fire; pilau (chicken-and-rice curry); conch, stewed or curried; and mountain chicken. Guests eat off cheerful red-and-white checked tablecloths, and families will appreciate the relaxed atmosphere. A grocery store is adjacent. Fun and funky. *Cork Hill, tel. 809/491–2187. No credit cards. Inexpensive.*

★ **Niggy's.** In his previous life, the owner was a British character actor in Hollywood before trading in the spotlight for a place behind the bar in this simple, attractive restaurant. It was an immediate hit when it opened in the fall of 1992 (the British governor eats here regularly). It doesn't look like much from the outside—a simple clapboard cottage with yellow bella flowers trailing over the gate—but the food, served at picnic-style benches under a trellis of flowering plants, is excellent and good value. Dishes include steak fillet, scampi, conch, and clam and scallops. The owner will regale you with tales of Hollywood at the bar—an ingeniously converted fishing boat—and the whole place feels like a set for a Caribbean remake of *Casablanca*. There are two simple, clean guest rooms in the back. The property is a 10-minute drive from the center of Plymouth. *Kinsale, tel. 809/491–7489. No credit cards. Dinner only. Inexpensive.*

Ziggy's. On top of a barrel at the entrance to their restaurant, John and Marcia Punter, Montserratians who returned home after 28 years in the United Kingdom, display all the fruits and vegetables that grow on the island, among them ginger, nutmeg, yams, plantain, christophine, and coconuts. This is one of the first clues that what used to be a simple waterfront café and bar has become one of the best bistros on the island. The furnishings are sparse, but the waterside setting is very pleasant, and the menu—everything from curried mutton and rice to lasagna—one of the most varied on the island. Unfortunately, there was uncertainty about the restaurant's lease at press time. *Wapping, Plymouth, tel. 809/491–2237. Reservations advised. No credit cards. Closed Wed. Inexpensive.*

Harbour Court Restaurant. This simple street café is the best place on the island for granny-watching. At lunchtime, Plymouth's pensioner set comes here for fried chicken or a hamburger. The dining area—only a brown-and-white fence divides it from the street—is simple but clean, with ceiling fans and a corrugated roof. The owner, Mr. Watts, is a charming man. His specialty is homemade fruit drinks, including soursop and sorrel. The homemade ginger beer will bring tears to your eyes. On Friday nights there is a steel band. *Plymouth, tel. 809/491–2826. No credit cards. Budget.*

Hartie's Place. The very pleasant Hartie and her husband lived in New York's Bronx for 20 years before returning here to open this mom-and-pop hamburger restaurant in a wing of their house, about a half mile outside Plymouth on a hill overlooking the sea. The space is small, but clean and well kept; it's become the favorite of students from the American University of the Caribbean, the medical school just up the street. As well as hamburgers, Hartie makes simple Italian dishes such as fettucine and meat sauce and lasagna; there's also a big breakfast menu and free delivery around town. *Plymouth, tel. 809/491–7576. No credit cards. Budget.*

Mistress Morgan's. Saturday is goatwater-stew day at Mistress Morgan's, and from 11:30 onward you can join the carloads of locals who make the trek up to the north of the island to eat their fill (for E.C. $20) at one of four picnic tables in a simple, unadorned room with sea-foam walls. Down-home food such as souse, baked chicken, and the aforementioned goatwater is served just the way it should be, with the flesh falling off the bone and brimming with dumplings and innards. *Airport Rd., St. John's, tel. 809/491–5419. No credit cards. Budget.*

Skerrit's. Leroyd Skerrit has been serving local delicacies such as goatwater stew, red snapper, and pig's tail and chicken soup for nearly a decade at this tiny restaurant off the beaten track in a safe but run-down neighborhood in the village of Kinsale. The restaurant consists of a couple of alcove-sized rooms with Formica-topped tables seating no more than 12. But Mr. Skerrit is a good cook, the produce is fresh, the juices—passion fruit, ginger beer, lime—thirst-quenching; for E.C. $12 you can eat your fill. *Aymers Ghaut, Kinsale, tel. 809/491–3728. No credit cards. Budget.*

The Village Place. In its heyday this funky bar and disco on a hillside was *the* hangout for rock glitterati including Eric Clapton, Sting, and Elton John, who were on the island to record at Montserrat's legendary Air Studios. Mick Jagger is even known to have eaten owner Andy Lawrence's secret recipe of chicken spiced with paprika and thyme. These days, though, Andy's allure is just a little faded: The local bands are rarely that good; the drinking is heavy-duty; and on Saturdays, it is crowded and loud. A must for rock nostalgics; otherwise a detour wouldn't hurt much. *Salem, tel. 809/491–5202. No credit cards. No lunch. Closed Tues. Budget.*

Lodging

Accommodations on Montserrat are generally small: The two largest hotels, the Vue Pointe and Montserrat Springs, have only 86 rooms between them. The rest are small guest houses. What the island does have are villas—nearly twice as many as hotel rooms. Villas are not only affordable here; given their comforts and conveniences, they're preferable to the hotels (*see* Villa and Apartment Rentals, *below*). Montserrat's lodging prices tend to fall abruptly from the $150–$200 range to the $40 range, with not much in between. The two mid-price hotels, the Flora Fountain and the Oriole Plaza, are in the center of Plymouth and cater mainly to businesspeople.

Almost all hotels and villa developments are on the milder west coast, where the beaches are. Accommodations in and around Plymouth are within walking distance of a beach (not necessarily the best one). Wherever you stay, you're unlikely to be further than 10 minutes by car from a beach and shops.

Highly recommended lodgings are indicated by a star ★.

Category	Cost*
Moderate	$75–$150
Inexpensive	$40–$75
Budget	under $40

*All prices are for a standard double room for two, excluding 7% tax and a 10% service charge. To estimate rates for hotels offering MAP, add about $35–$40 per person per day to the above price ranges.

Hotels   **Vue Pointe.** The moment you arrive here you feel as though
★ both the staff and the owners, Cedric and Carol Osborne, really care about your well-being. The gracious Monday night cocktail parties that the Osbornes host at their house are a perfect example. Guests are taken up in minibuses and treated to drinks, delicious homemade hors d'oeuvres, and good conversation. Accommodations are in 12 rooms or 28 octagonal cottages that spill down to the gray-sand beach on Old Road Bay. Each cottage has a large bedroom, great view, cable TV, phone, and spacious bathroom. In the main building, a large lounge and bar overlooks the pool. The Wednesday night barbecue, with steel bands and other entertainment, is a well-attended island event for locals and guests alike. A 150-seat conference

center serves as a theater and disco, and for water-sports enthusiasts, there is scuba diving, snorkeling, and fishing. *Box 65, Plymouth, tel. 809/491–5210, fax 809/491–4813. 12 rooms, 28 cottages. Facilities: restaurant, bar, gift shop, pool, 2 lighted tennis courts, water-sports center. AE, MC, V. EP, MAP. Moderate.*

Flora Fountain Hotel. It caters primarily to businesspeople (only 35% of the clientele are tourists) or to those who appreciate an old, rambling hotel in the heart of town. The two-story building has been created around an enormous fountain that's sometimes lighted at night, with small tables scattered in the inner courtyard. There are 18 serviceable rooms, all with tile bath and air-conditioning. All rooms have phones but not all have TVs, so ask if it's important to you. The restaurant has a chef from Bombay who serves simple sandwiches and fine Indian dishes, particularly on Friday night, which is Indian buffet night. *Box 373, Church Rd., Plymouth, tel. 809/491–6092, fax 809/491–2568. 18 rooms. Facilities: restaurant and bar. AE, D, MC, V. EP, CP, MAP, FAP. Inexpensive.*

Oriole Plaza Hotel. Located in the center of town and a five-minute walk from the town's only beach, Wapping Beach, this simple but well-maintained hotel caters mostly to businesspeople. Rooms off a long corridor upstairs include suites, with two double beds and a balcony, and doubles. All rooms have ceiling fans (no air-conditioning), cable TV, and phones. Three rooms at the back of the building are simpler—and cheaper—but have the advantage of opening onto a sunny wooden landing from which you can see Chance's Peak. BB's, the restaurant in the downstairs foyer, serves marlin, lobster, or mountain chicken at reasonable prices. Children under 12 stay free in their parents'room; a third adult can stay in a double for $15 extra. *Box 250, Plymouth, tel. 809/419–6982, fax 809/491–6690. 12 rooms, 2 suites. Facilities: restaurant and bar. AE, MC, V. EP. Inexpensive.*

Guest Houses and B&Bs
★

Providence Guest House. On an island where it is almost impossible to find good bed-and-breakfast accommodations, this guest house perched on a bluff high above the ocean, with spectacular views of St. Kitts and Redonda, stands out like an oasis in the desert. Formerly a plantation house, the beautiful stone-and-wood building with a spider-box balustrade, wraparound veranda, and gleaming swimming pool edged with tiles from Trinidad, has been lovingly restored by its present owners, a young English professor of psychology and his Haitian-born wife. It now ranks as one of the finest examples of traditional Caribbean architecture on the island. In its day, it was home to such luminaries as Paul McCartney and Stevie Wonder. The two guest rooms are on the ground floor and open directly onto the pool area; one has a bath as well as a shower and is considerably larger. Both have the original timbered ceilings and massive stone walls (which keep them cool), and are decorated with red quarry tiles and attractive pastel fabrics. If there is any drawback to this idyll, it is the location. The nearest restaurant is 3 miles away in Belham Valley, and the nearest beach is a hike down the hillside. But the owners have provided a kitchenette by the pool where guests can cook their own meals and will prepare evening meals on request. A large, varied breakfast, with eggs, oatmeal, and fruits from the garden (in season) is included in the room rate. *Providence Estate House, Montserrat, tel. 809/491–6476. 2 rooms. Facilities: swimming pool, kitchenette, cable TV. No credit cards. BP. Moderate.*

Marie's Guest House. This well-kept modern bungalow, set on a half-acre of garden, is half a mile from Plymouth, on the main road north. Marie, a soft-spoken islander with a reserved manner, keeps the place neat and tidy. Rooms have mosquito nets, tasteful fabrics, good solid furniture, and tiled bathrooms. One drawback is the distance from the beach—about 10 minutes by car. At the front of the house there's a communal living-dining room area where guests can make their own simple meals. *The Groves, Plymouth, tel. 809/419–2745. 4 rooms. No credit cards. EP. Budget.*

Moose. This budget hotel, on a rocky beach that's a 10-minute walk to south Plymouth, is named for its owner, a former weight lifter. For a modest fee he will let you pump iron in his homemade gym at the back of the building (it's the only one on the island). Rooms, up a flight of wooden steps at the front of the building, are basic, with standing fans and simple, wood-framed beds. But Moose's wife, Ida, cooks excellent conch fritters and lobster at low prices in the simple restaurant downstairs. As there are also two lively bars in the courtyard at the back, the rooms are probably not the quietest on the island. *Kinsale, tel. 809/491–3146. 8 rooms. Facilities: restaurant and bar. No credit cards. EP. Budget.*

★ **Niggy's.** This pretty clapboard cottage with yellow bella flowers trailing over the gate is south of Plymouth (about five minutes by car), and half a mile from a passable beach. It is mostly a restaurant and bar (*see* Dining, *above*). But the owner, a one-time British character actor who gave up a life in Hollywood for the bucolic pleasures of Montserrat, also rents two simple, clean rooms with ceiling fans and showers. Backpackers are frequent guests. *Kinsale, tel. 809/491–7489. No credit cards. CP. Budget.*

Villa and Apartment Rental

Montserrat is primarily a villa destination, and many of the properties can be had for less than $700 a week. For $500 a week in high season, for instance, you can rent a house with a tropical garden, pool, daily maid service, stunning ocean views, and enough space for two families. Off-season rates are as much as 50% lower (and usually negotiable), and summer travelers can pick up some true bargains. The best villa developments are on the west coast of the island, within 20 minutes by car of Plymouth. The majority are in the districts of Old Towne, Olveston, and Woodlands. The latter, with its steep hillsides covered in luxuriant vegetation and magnificent ocean views, is especially noteworthy. Because most villas are in the hills outside Plymouth, you'll need to rent a car, unless you don't mind a 20-minute hike every time you go shopping or to the beach.

D.R.V. Edwards (Box 58, Marine Dr., Plymouth, tel. 809/491–2431, fax 809/491–4660) has 22 villas in Old Towne, Woodlands, and Isles Bay. A split-level villa sleeping six and set on an acre of landscaped gardens with pool costs about $1,200 a week ($700 off-season). The company also rents two-bedroom condominiums for $450 a week.

Neville Bradshaw Agencies (Box 270, Plymouth, tel. 809/491–5270, fax 809/491–5069) has a wide range of villas, mostly in Old Towne and Isles Bay, ranging from $750 a week for a one-bedroom villa to $2,500 for a marble-tiled house with pool that sleeps eight. In addition, Montserrat has a few apartment and condominium complexes for short-term vacation rental:

★ **Belham Valley Apartments.** Mainly an upscale restaurant, this property on a hillside overlooking Belham Valley River includes three self-catering units on its hibiscus-filled grounds. The cottage, studio apartment, and two-bedroom apartment all have stereo, phone, cable TV, and ceiling fan (no air-conditioning). It's a five-minute walk to the beach and a 15-minute drive to Plymouth. Sadly, meals at the excellent restaurant are not included in the room rate. *Box 409, Plymouth, tel. 809/491–5553. 3 units. Facilities: restaurant, daily maid service. AE, MC. Moderate.*

Shamrock Villas. These one- and two-bedroom apartments and town-house condominiums with kitchens are in a hillside development a few minutes drive from Plymouth. There is no air-conditioning or maid service. The nearest beach, shared with the Monserrat Springs Hotel and a three-minute walk away, is not the most attractive, but the price—$450 a week in high season—compensates. *Box 180, Plymouth, tel. 809/491–2974. 50 units. Facilities: pool. AE, MC, V. Inexpensive.*

Lime Court Apartments. This slightly run-down, white colonial-style apartment building is in the center of town, opposite the Parliament building. All units have kitchenettes, including a stove and microwave oven, and private shower baths. The downstairs apartments tend to be dark, airless, and—with the sound of the generator and the puttering of the fridges—not that peaceful. But the large, well-equipped penthouse sleeping four, up a flight of steps at the top of the building, has a fine view from the balcony over the red corrugated rooftops of the town to the sea beyond. *Box 250, Parliament St., Plymouth, tel. 809/491–3656. 8 apartments. Facilities: maid service, cable TV. AE, MC, V. Budget–Inexpensive.*

Off-Season Bets Montserrat's two finest resort hotels, the **Vue Pointe** (*see above*) and the **Montserrat Springs** (Box 259, Plymouth, tel. 809/491–2482) offer reductions of 40% in the off-season. Reasonable villa rates go down further, and some luxury villas become affordable (*see* Villa and Apartment Rental, *above*).

Nightlife

The hotels offer regularly scheduled barbecues and steel bands, and the small restaurants feature live entertainment in the form of calypso, reggae, rock, rhythm and blues, and soul.

The Plantation Club (Wapping, upstairs over the Oasis, tel. 809/491–2892) is a lively late-night place with taped rhythm and blues, soul, and *soca* (Caribbean music). **La Cave** (Evergreen Dr., Plymouth, no phone), featuring West Indian–style disco with Caribbean and international music, is popular among the young locals. **Nepcoden** (Weekes, no phone), with its ultraviolet lights, peace signs, and black walls, is a throwback to the '60s. In this cellar restaurant you can eat *rotis*, a large pancake filled with curried vegetables, or chicken for $6.

17 Puerto Rico

*Updated by
Karl Luntta*

No city in the Caribbean is steeped in Spanish tradition as is Puerto Rico's Old San Juan. Built as a fortress in the 16th Century the old city is now full of restored buildings, museums, art galleries, bookstores, and 200-year-old houses with balustraded balconies of filigreed wrought iron overlooking narrow cobblestone streets. This Spanish tradition also spills over into the island's countryside, from its festivals celebrated in honor of various patron saints in the little towns to the *paradores,* those homey, inexpensive inns whose concept originated in Spain.

Out in the countryside, amid its quiet colonial towns, lie Puerto Rico's natural attractions. The extraordinary 28,000-acre Caribbean National Forest, more familiarly known as the El Yunque rain forest, is home to more than 240 species of trees. There are forest reserves with trails to satisfy the most dedicated hiker, vast caves to tempt spelunkers, coffee plantations, old sugar mills, and hundreds of beaches.

With its countless small inns and guest houses, inexpensive eateries serving local dishes, and opportunities for camping and hiking, Puerto Rico is one of the Caribbean's best bets for budget travelers. Beyond the glitzy hotels in San Juan and sprawling resorts out on the island, Puerto Rico's lodgings include affordable, often charming paradors, as well as bed-and-breakfasts and campgrounds. Most hotels stay open year-round, and from mid-April to mid-December, many reduce their rates by as much as 20%–40%. Even those that don't

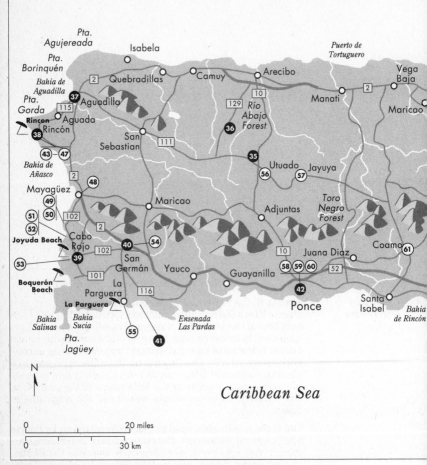

Pta.
Agujereada
Pta.
Borinquén
Isabela
*Puerto de
Tortuguero*
Vega
Baja
*Bahia de
Aguadilla*
Quebradillas
Camuy
Arecibo
2
Manati
2
Pta.
Gorda
37
Aguadilla
115
129
36
*Río
Abajo
Forest*
10
Maricao
Rincon
Aguada
38
Rincón
San
Sebastian
111
35
43 – **47**
*Bahia de
Añasco*
2
48
56
Utuado
Jayuya
57
Mayagüez
Maricao
Adjuntas
*Toro
Negro
Forest*
49
51 **50**
102
2
54
Coamo
61
52
Joyuda Beach
Cabo
Rojo
40
10
Juana Diaz
53
39
102
San
Germán
Yauco
Guayanilla
58 **59** **60**
52
Santa
Isabel
*Bahia
de Rincón*
**Boquerón
Beach**
101
La
Parguera
116
42
Ponce
La Parguera
*Bahia
Salinas*
*Bahia
Sucia*
*Ensenada
Las Pardas*
55
Pta.
Jagüey
41

N

Caribbean Sea

0 _____ 20 miles
0 _____ 30 km

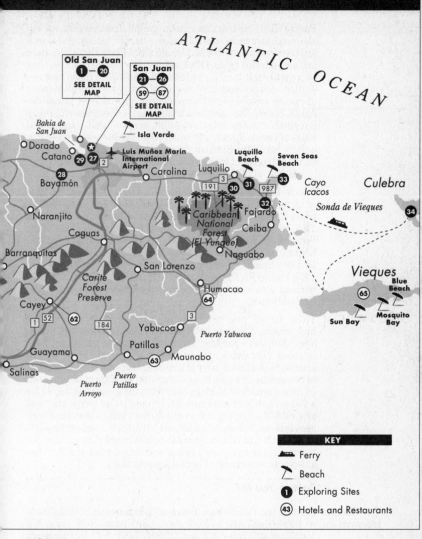

KEY

🚢 Ferry

⌒ Beach

❶ Exploring Sites

㊸ Hotels and Restaurants

Lodging

Beside the Pointe, **44**

Hotel Caribe Playa, **63**

Hotel Joyuda
Beach, **52**

Hotel Meliá, **60**

Hotel Villa
Cofresi, **45**

The Lazy Parrot, **47**

Palmas del Mar, **64**

Parador Baños de
Coamo, **61**

Parador Boquemar, **53**

Parador Casa
Grande, **56**

Parador Hacienda
Gripiñas, **57**

Parador Oasis, **54**

Parador Perichi's, **51**

Parador Villa
Antonio, **46**

Parador Villa
Parguera, **55**

Sea Gate, **65**

advertise lower rates are often willing to negotiate when you call.

Puerto Rico's restaurants run the gamut, from elegant, expensive establishments to small cafés, roadside kiosks, and standard fast-food places like McDonald's and Pizza Hut. Cafés here are a wonderful value. Often set up near public beaches, they serve authentic local fare such as *empanadillas* (fried pastries stuffed with crabmeat, lobster, or other meats) and all manner of *comida criolla,* a local blend of Spanish and West Indian delights. Puerto Rico also boasts hundreds of beaches with every imaginable water sport available, acres of golf courses and miles of tennis courts, and small colonial towns where you can quietly savor the Spanish flavor. Every town honors its individual patron saint with an annual festival, which is usually held in the central plaza and can last from one to 10 days.

Puerto Rico, 110 miles long and 35 miles wide (about the size of Connecticut), was populated by several tribes of Indians when Columbus landed on the island on his second voyage in 1493. In 1508, Juan Ponce de León, the frustrated seeker of the Fountain of Youth, established a settlement on the island and became its first governor, and in 1521, founded Old San Juan. In 1899, Spain ceded the island to the United States, and in 1917, Puerto Ricans became U.S. citizens. In 1952, Puerto Rico became a semiautonomous commonwealth territory of the United States.

What It Will Cost These sample prices, meant only as a general guide, are for high season. A budget hotel will cost about $40; a guest house, about $50; and a parador, about $60. A budget restaurant meal is about $10; snacks for two from a roadside kiosk will be around $7. A glass of beer at a restaurant is about $1.25; a glass of house wine or a piña colada is around $2. Expect to pay about $6 for a six-pack of Medalla beer from the grocery store; $7 for a 750 ml bottle of local rum (26 brands!). Car rental starts at around $30 a day. A taxi from the airport to the Condado Beach area is about $12; from the airport to Old San Juan, around $16. A two-tank dive ranges from $35 to $50. Snorkeling excursions, which include equipment rental and lunch, start at $35. Snorkel-equipment rental at beaches starts at $5.

Before You Go

Tourist Information Contact the **Puerto Rico Tourism Company** (tel. 800/223–6530 or 800/866–STAR; 575 5th Ave., 23rd floor, New York, NY 10017, tel. 212/599–6262, fax 212/818–1866; 3575 W. Cahuenga Blvd., Suite 560, Los Angeles, CA 90068, tel. 213/874–5991, fax 213/874–7257; 200 S.E. 1st St., Suite 700, Miami, FL 33131, tel. 305/381–8915, fax 305/381–8917).

In addition, sales representatives are located in Atlanta, Boston, Dallas, Detroit, Denver, Houston, Orlando, Philadelphia, St. Louis, San Francisco, Toronto, and Washington, DC. Their addresses can be obtained by calling the toll-free numbers above.

Overseas offices include 67–69 Whitfield St., London W1P 5RL, United Kingdom, tel. 071/636–6558, fax 071/255–2131.

Arriving and Departing The Luis Muñoz Marín International Airport (tel. 809/462–3147), east of downtown San Juan, is the Caribbean hub for
By Plane **American Airlines** (tel. 800/433–7300). American has daily non-

stop flights from New York, Newark, Miami, Boston, Philadelphia, Chicago, Nashville, Los Angeles, Dallas, Baltimore, Hartford, Raleigh-Durham, Washington, DC, and Tampa; it also provides nonstop service from Miami to Ponce and Aguadilla, and connecting flights through San Juan to Ponce. **Delta** (tel. 800/221–1212) has nonstop service from Atlanta and Orlando, as well as connecting service from major cities. **Northwest** (tel. 800/447–4747) has recently added nonstop flights from Detroit to San Juan. **TWA** (tel. 800/892–4141) flies nonstop from New York and Miami. **United** (tel. 800/241–6522) flies nonstop from Washington, DC, and Chicago. **USAir** (tel. 800/428–4322) offers nonstop flights from Philadelphia and Charlotte. **Northwest Airlines** (tel. 800/447–4747) flies nonstop from Detroit. **Kiwi International Airlines** (tel. 800/538–5494) has nonstop service from Orlando daily except Tuesdays and Wednesdays. Puerto Rico–based **Carnival Airlines** (tel. 800/437–2110) offers nonstop flights from Newark to San Juan, Ponce, and Aguadilla.

Foreign carriers include **Air France** (tel. 800/237–2747), **British Airways** (tel. 800/247–9297), **BWIA** (tel. 800/538–2942), **Iberia** (tel. 800/772–4642), **LACSA** (tel. 800/225–2272), **LIAT** (tel. 809/791–3838), and **Lufthansa** (tel. 800/645–3880).

Connections between Caribbean islands can be made through **Air Jamaica** (tel. 809/791–3870 or 800/523–5585), **Dominicana Airline** (tel. 809/724–7100), and **Sunaire Express** (tel. 809/791–4755 or 800/595–9501).

From the Airport **Airport Limousine Service** (tel. 809/791–4745) provides minibus service to hotels in the Isla Verde, Condado, and Old San Juan areas at basic fares of $2.50, $3.50, and $4.50, respectively; the fares, which are set by the Public Service Commission, can vary, depending on the time of day and number of passengers. Limousines of **Dorado Transport Service** (tel. 809/796–1214) serve hotels and villas in the Dorado area for $6 per person. Taxi fare from the airport to Isla Verde is about $6–$10; to the Condado area, $12–$15; and to Old San Juan, $15–$18. Be sure the taxi driver starts the meter.

Larger hotels around the island will arrange transportation for you from San Juan to the hotel, but transfers are rarely free. To the Palmas del Mar in Humacao, for instance, the charge is $16 one-way. Your other option if you're staying out on the island is to rent a car, particularly if you intend to explore the island (*see* Getting Around, *below*).

Passports and Visas Puerto Rico is a commonwealth of the United States, and U.S. citizens do not need passports to visit the island. British citizens must have passports. Canadian citizens need proof of citizenship (preferably a passport).

Language Puerto Rico's official languages are Spanish and English. Outside San Juan, it's wise to carry along a Spanish phrase book.

Precautions San Juan, like any other big city and major tourist destination, has its share of crime, so guard your wallet or purse on the city streets. Puerto Rico's beaches are open to the public, and muggings occur at night even on the beaches of the posh Condado and Isla Verde tourist hotels. Don't leave anything unattended on the beach. Leave your valuables in the hotel safe, and stick to the fenced-in beach areas of your hotel. Always lock your car

and stash valuables and luggage out of sight. Avoid deserted
beaches day or night.

Staying in Puerto Rico

Important   Call the government-sponsored **Puerto Rico Tourism Com-**
Addresses   **pany** (tel. 809/721–2400), and pick up a free copy of *¿Qué Pasa?*,
the official visitors guide, at its information offices, located at
Luis Muñoz Marín International Airport, Isla Verde (tel.
809/791–1014 or 809/791–2551); **301 Calle San Justo,** Old San
Juan (tel. 809/723–3135 or 809/723–0017); and **La Casita,** near
Pier 1 in Old San Juan (tel. 809/722–1709). Out on the island,
information offices are located in **Ponce** (Casa Armstrong-Poventud, Plaza, Las Delicias, tel. 809/840–5695 or 809/844–8240);
Aguadilla (Rafael Hernandez Airport, tel. 809/890–3315); and
in each town's city hall on the main plaza, open weekdays from
8 AM to noon and 1 to 4:30 PM.

Emergencies   **Police, fire, and medical emergencies:** Call 911. **Hospitals:** Hospitals in the Condado/Santurce area with 24-hour emergency
rooms are **Ashford Community Hospital** (1451 Av. Ashford, tel.
809/721–2160) and **San Juan Health Centre** (200 Av. De Diego,
tel. 809/725–0202). **Pharmacies:** In San Juan, **Walgreens** (1130
Av. Ashford, tel. 809/725–1510) operates a 24-hour pharmacy.
Walgreens operates more than 20 pharmacies throughout the
island. In Old San Juan, try **Puerto Rico Drug Company** (157
Calle San Francisco, tel. 809/725–2202).

Currency   The U.S. dollar is the official currency.

Taxes and   The government tax on room charges is 7% (9% in hotels with
Service Charges   casinos). Some hotels add a service charge (10%–15%) to your
bill. Restaurants may or may not. If it hasn't been added, a
15%–20% tip is appropriate. There is no departure tax.

Getting Around   Puerto Rico's 3,500 square miles is a lot of land to explore.
Taxis   While it is possible to get from town to town via público (*see
below*), we don't recommend traveling that way unless your
Spanish is good and you know exactly where you're going. The
public cars stop in each town's main square, leaving you on your
own to reach the beaches, restaurants, paradors, and sightseeing attractions. You'll do much better if you rent a car. The cost
is a little lower than a guided tour from San Juan, and having
a car allows you to stop, look, swim, and eat at your own pace.
Also, the longer you rent, the lower the cost—sometimes down
to $21 a day. This is just as well, since a complete tour of Puerto
Rico and its outlying islands will take a week or more. If you're
staying in the Old San Juan area and don't plan to tour the
island, however, you're better off without a car. Parking is mis-
erable and driving worse. Hotels here are within walking distance of restaurants and are a short cab ride from the beach.

Metered cabs authorized by the Public Service Commission
(tel. 809/751–5050) start at $1 and charge 10¢ for every addi-
tional 1/10 mile, 50¢ for every suitcase, and $1 for home or busi-
ness calls. Waiting time is 10¢ for each 45 seconds. Be sure the
driver begins the meter.

In and around the San Juan airport and hotel and tourist areas,
a typical taxi fare will rarely exceed $20. A cab from Old San
Juan to Condado Beach is about $6. From Isla Verde to Old San
Juan, expect to pay $14–$17; from Miramar to Condado,
around $3–$5. It's possible to charter a taxi for $12–$15 an hour

(a drive across Puerto Rico from east to west takes just over two hours); this may prove an economical option for groups wanting to view area sights. In general, however, taking a taxi from San Juan to other island destinations is a pricey proposition; with rates for rental cars averaging $30 a day, you're better off with your own wheels. You can usually find taxis at each town's main plaza, or have your hotel order one.

Buses The **Metropolitan Bus Authority** (tel. 809/767–7979) operates *guaguas* (buses) that thread through San Juan. The fare is 25¢ around San Juan, 50¢ from San Juan to Catano, 75¢ from San Juan to Hato Rey, and 75¢ from Hato Rey to Catano. Buses run in exclusive lanes, *against the traffic* on major thoroughfares, stopping at upright yellow posts marked *Parada* or *Parada de Guaguas*. The main terminals are Intermodal Terminal, Calles Marina and Harding, in Old San Juan, and Capetillo Terminal in Rio Piedras, next to the Central Business District.

Other cities around the island also operate bus services; 25¢ is a standard fare. Traveling by bus is potentially a fun way to do the local scene, and the price is certainly right. However, buses are often crowded, and schedules are less than rigid. Unless your Spanish is good enough to help you figure out why you have ended up nowhere near where you wanted to be, you should consider other means of transportation.

Públicos *Públicos* (public cars) with yellow license plates ending with *P* or *PD* scoot to towns throughout the island, stopping in each town's main plaza. The 17-passenger cars operate primarily during the day, with routes and fares fixed by the Public Service Commission. In San Juan, the main terminals are at the airport and at Plaza Colón on the waterfront in Old San Juan.

Públicos are best for traveling from town center to town center during off-peak times. During rush hours on weekdays (about 8–9 AM and 4–5 PM), públicos are often full; the same is true for weekend travel to popular beaches and recreation areas. Sample fares: San Juan to Fajardo, $3; San Juan to Ponce, $7; San Juan to Rincón, $7; San Juan to Mayaguez, $8; Aguadilla to Mayaguez, $1.75; and Ponce to Cabo Rojo, $5.

Trolleys If your feet fail you in Old San Juan, climb aboard the free open-air trolleys that rumble and dip like roller coasters through the narrow streets. Departures are from La Puntilla and from the marina, but you can board anywhere along the route.

Ferries The ferry between Old San Juan and Catano costs a mere 50¢ one-way. The ferry runs every half hour from 6:15 AM to 10 PM. The 400-passenger ferries of the **Fajardo Port Authority** (tel. 809/863–0705), which carry cargo as well as passengers, make the 80-minute trip twice daily between Fajardo and the island of Vieques (one-way $2 adults, $1 children under 12, free for children under 3), and the one-hour run between Fajardo and the island of Culebra daily (one-way $2.25 adults, $1 children).

Rental Cars U.S. driver's licenses are valid in Puerto Rico for three months. All major U.S. car-rental agencies are represented on the island, including **Avis** (tel. 809/721–4499 or 800/331–1212), **Hertz** (tel. 809/791–0840 or 800/654–3131), and **Budget** (tel. 809/791–3685 or 800/527–0700). Local rental companies, sometimes less expensive, include **Caribbean Rental** (tel. 809/724–3980) and **L & M Car Rental** (tel. 809/725–8416), fax 809/725–8307). Prices start at about $30 (plus insurance), with unlimited mileage. Discounts are offered for long-term rentals, and some discounts are offered for AAA or 72-hour advance bookings. Most car rentals have shuttle service to or from the airport and the pickup point.

If you plan to drive across the island, arm yourself with a good map and be prepared for unmarked mountain roads. Outside the mountains, roads are generally well marked; however, a good road map is helpful when traveling to more remote areas. Some car rental agencies distribute free maps when you pick up your car. Good maps are also found at **The Book Store** (255 Calle San José, Old San Juan, tel. 809/724–1815). Many service stations in the central mountains do not take credit cards. Speed limits are posted in miles, distances in kilometers, and gas prices in liters.

Telephones and Mail The area code for Puerto Rico is 809. Since Puerto Rico uses U.S. postage stamps and has the same mail rates (19¢ for a postcard, 29¢ for a first-class letter), you can save time by bringing stamps from home.

Opening and Closing Times Shops are open from 9 to 6 (from 9 to 9 during Christmas holidays). Banks are open weekdays from 8:30 to 2:30 and Saturday from 9:45 to noon.

Guided Tours Old San Juan can be seen either on a self-guided walking tour or on the free trolley. To explore the rest of the city and the island, consider renting a car. (We do, however, recommend a guided tour of the vast El Yunque rain forest.) If you'd rather not do your own driving, there are several tour companies you can call. Most San Juan hotels have a tour desk that can make arrangements for you. The standard half-day tours (at $10–$15) are of Old and New San Juan, Old San Juan and the Bacardi Rum Plant, Luquillo Beach and El Yunque rain forest. All-day tours ($15–$30) include a trip to Ponce, a day at El Comandante Racetrack, or a combined tour of the city and El Yunque rain forest.

Leading tour operators include **Borinquén Tours, Inc.** (tel. 809/725–4990), **Gray Line of Puerto Rico** (tel. 809/727–8080), **Normandie Tours, Inc.** (tel. 809/725–6990 or 809/722–6308), **Rich Sunshine Tours** (tel. 809/729–2929), **Rico Suntours** (tel. 809/722–2080 or 809/722–6090), **United Tour Guides** (tel. 809/725–7605 or 809/723–5578), and **Loose Penny Tours** (tel. 809/261–3030 or 800/468–4786).

Boat Tours In San Juan and most coastal towns, you'll find excursion boats that tour the coast and outlying islands. Though price tags for daylong excursions seem steep, the trips are actually a good value, as they usually include a meal, drinks, snorkeling, and sometimes exploring or other activities. You might want to consider one for a splurge. In San Juan, **Castillo Watersports** (tel. 809/791–6195 or 809/726–5752) offers a day sail from $60 a person that includes transfers, lunch, drinks, and snorkeling instructions. **Caribbean School of Aquatics** (tel. 809/723–4740 or 809/728–6606) offers a less-expensive day-sail package from $39 a person, or a sail on the small *Fun Cat* for less. In Fajardo, **Captain Jayne Sailing Charters** (tel. 809/791–5174) will take you on a six-passenger, 26-foot sailboat to a small, deserted island about 3 miles offshore for snorkeling and exploring. The $60-per-person cost includes transfers from San Juan, lunch, drinks, and snorkeling gear. Also out of Fajardo, the 35-passenger *Spread Eagle* (tel. 809/852–1879) departs at 10 AM for an hour-long sail to outlying islands. The $45 fare includes lunch; round-trip transfers from San Juan are an additional $10. Additional boat tour operators can be found by contacting local marinas. In San Juan, try **Club Nautico Marina** (tel. 809/722–0177) or **San Juan Bay Marina** (tel. 809/721–8062). In Fajardo, a major center of nautical activity, try **Isleta Marina** (tel. 809/863–0370), **Puerto Chico Marina** (tel. 809/863–0834), **Puerto del Rey** (tel. 809/250–1250) or **Villa Marina** (tel. 809/728–2450). In Humacao, contact **Marina de Palmas** (tel. 809/852–6000).

Exploring Puerto Rico

Numbers in the margin correspond to points of interest on the Old San Juan Exploring map.

Old San Juan Old San Juan, the original city founded in 1521, contains authentic and carefully preserved examples of 16th- and 17th-century Spanish colonial architecture, some of the best in the New World. More than 400 buildings have been beautifully restored in a continuing effort to preserve the city. Graceful wrought-iron balconies, decorated with lush green hanging plants, extend over narrow streets paved with blue-gray stones (*adequines*, originally used as ballast for Spanish ships). The old city is partially enclosed by the old walls, dating from 1633, that once completely surrounded it. Designated a U.S. National Historic Zone in 1950, Old San Juan is chockablock with shops, open-air cafés, private homes, tree-shaded squares, monuments, plaques, pigeons, and people. The traffic is awful. Get an overview of the inner city on a morning's stroll (bearing in mind that this "stroll" includes some steep climbs). However, if you plan to immerse yourself in history or to shop, you'll need two or three days.

El Morro and Fort San Cristóbal are described in our walking tour: You may want to set aside extra time to see them, especially if you're an aficionado of military history. UNESCO has designated each fortress a World Heritage Site; each is also a National Historic Site. Both are administered by the National Park Service; you can take one of its tours or wander around on your own.

Sitting on a rocky promontory on the northwestern tip of the old city is **Fuerte San Felipe del Morro** ("El Morro"), a fortress built by the Spaniards between 1540 and 1783. Rising 140 feet above the sea, the massive six-level fortress covers enough territory to accommodate a nine-hole golf course. It is a labyrinth of dungeons, ramps and barracks, turrets, towers, and tunnels. Built to protect the port, El Morro has a commanding view of the harbor. Its small, air-conditioned museum traces the history of the fortress. *Calle Norzagaray, tel. 809/729–6960. Admission free. Open daily 9:15–6.*

Pass San José Plaza, a short two blocks from the entrance to El Morro, and head a block east to the **San Juan Museum of Art and History,** a must-see. A bustling marketplace in 1855, this handsome building is now a modern cultural center that houses exhibits of Puerto Rican art. Multi-image audiovisual shows present the history of the island; concerts and other cultural events take place in the huge courtyard. The museum was closed for repairs at press time, but exhibitions are temporarily

Old San Juan Exploring

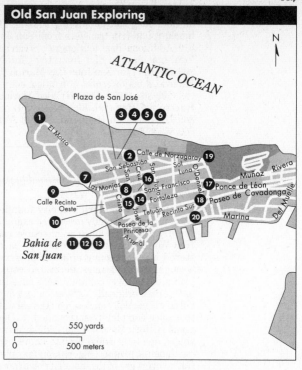

held at the **Miensal Building** (tel. 809/722–1824), 200 Calle San Francisco, weekdays 8–noon and 1–4. *Calle Norzagaray, at the corner of Calle MacArthur, tel. 809/724–1875.*

3 Turn back west toward San José Plaza to **La Casa de los Contrafuertes,** on Calle San Sebastián. This building is also known as the Buttress House because wide exterior buttresses support the wall next to the plaza. The house is one of the oldest remaining private residences in Old San Juan. Inside is the Pharmacy Museum, a re-creation of an 18th-century apothecary shop. *101 Calle San Sebastián, Plaza de San José, tel. 809/724–5949. Admission free. Open Wed.–Sun. 9–4:30.*

4 The **Pablo Casals Museum,** a bit farther down the block, contains memorabilia of the famed cellist, who made his home in Puerto Rico for the last 16 years of his life. The museum holds manuscripts, photographs, and his favorite cellos, in addition to recordings and videotapes of Casals Festival concerts (the latter shown on request). *101 Calle San Sebastián, Plaza de San José, tel. 809/723–9185. Admission free. Open Tues.–Sat. 9:30–5:30, Sun. 1–5; closed Mon.*

5 In the center of the plaza, next to the museum, is the **San José Church.** With its series of vaulted ceilings, it is a splendid example of 16th-century Spanish Gothic architecture. The church, which is one of the oldest Christian houses of worship in the Western Hemisphere, was built in 1532 under the supervision of the Dominican friars. The body of Ponce de León, the Spanish explorer who came to the New World seeking the Fountain of Youth, was buried here for almost three centuries before being removed in 1913 and placed in the cathedral (*see below*). *Calle San Sebastián, tel. 809/725–7501. Admission free. Open Mon.–Sat. 8:30–4, Sun. mass at 12:15 PM.*

⑥ Next door is the **Dominican Convent.** Built by Dominican friars in 1523, the convent often served as a shelter during Carib Indian attacks and, more recently, was headquarters for the Antilles command of the U.S. Army. Now home to the Institute of Puerto Rican Culture, the beautifully restored building contains an ornate 18th-century altar, religious manuscripts, artifacts, and art. Classical concerts are occasionally held here. *98 Calle Norzagaray, tel. 809/724–0700. Admission free. Chapel museum open Wed.–Sun. 9–noon and 1–4:30.*

⑦ From San José Plaza, walk west on Calle Beneficencia to **Casa Blanca.** The original structure on this site, not far from the ramparts of El Morro, was a frame house built in 1521 as a home for Ponce de León. But Ponce de León died in Cuba, never having lived in it, and it was virtually destroyed by a hurricane in 1523, after which Ponce de León's son-in-law had the present masonry home built. His descendants occupied it for 250 years. From the end of the Spanish-American War in 1898 to 1966, it was the home of the U.S. Army commander in Puerto Rico. A museum devoted to archaeology is here. *1 Calle San Sebastián, tel. 809/724–4102. Admission free. Open Wed.–Sun. 9–noon and 1–4.*

⑧ Head east on Calle Sol and down Calle Cristo to **San Juan Cathedral.** This great Catholic shrine of Puerto Rico had humble beginnings in the early 1520s as a thatch-topped wood structure. Hurricane winds tore off the thatch and destroyed the church. It was reconstructed in 1540, when the graceful circular staircase and vaulted ceilings were added, but most of the church dates from the 19th century. The remains of Ponce de León are in a marble tomb near the transept. *153 Calle Cristo, tel. 809/722–0861. Open daily 8:30–4. Masses: Sat. 7 PM, Sun. 9 AM and 11 AM, weekdays 12:15 PM.*

Across the street from the cathedral you'll see the Gran Hotel El Convento, which was a Carmelite convent more than 300 years ago. Go west alongside the hotel on Caleta de las Monjas **⑨** toward the city wall to the **Plazuela de la Rogativa.** In the little plaza, statues commemorate the legend that the British, while laying siege to the city in 1797, mistook the flaming torches of a *rogativa* (religious procession) for Spanish reinforcements and beat a hasty retreat. The monument was donated to the city in 1971 on its 450th anniversary.

⑩ One block south on Calle Recinto Oeste you'll come to **La Fortaleza,** which sits on a hill overlooking the harbor. La Fortaleza, the Western Hemisphere's oldest executive mansion in continual use, home of 170 governors and official residence of the present governor of Puerto Rico, was built as a fortress. The original primitive structure, built in 1540, has seen numerous changes over a period of three centuries, resulting in the present collection of marble and mahogany, medieval towers, and stained-glass galleries. Guided tours are conducted every hour on the hour in English, on the half-hour in Spanish. Tours that include a visit to the mansion's second floor, a must-see, are held at 10 and 10:50 in English, 9:30 and 10:30 in Spanish. *Tel. 809/721–7000. Admission free. Open weekdays (except holidays) 9–4.*

⓫ At the southern end of Calle Cristo is **Cristo Chapel.** According to legend, in 1753 a young horseman, carried away during festivities in honor of the patron saint, raced down the street and plunged over the steep precipice. A witness to the tragedy promised to build a chapel if the young man's life could be saved. Historical records maintain the man died, though legend contends that he lived. Inside is a small silver altar, dedicated to the Christ of Miracles. *Open Tues. 10–4 and on most Catholic holidays.*

⓬ Across the street from the chapel, the 18th-century **Casa del Libro** has exhibits devoted to books and bookbinding. The museum's 5,000 books include rare volumes dating back 2,000 years; more than 200 of these books were printed before the 16th century. *255 Calle Cristo, tel. 809/723–0354. Admission free. Open Tues. 11–4:30 and 7:30–10 PM, Wed.–Sat. (except holidays) 11–4:30.*

⓭ The **Fine Arts Museum** (253 Calle Cristo, tel. 809/723–2320), in a lovely colonial building next door, occasionally presents special exhibits. The museum usually holds the Institute of Puerto Rican Culture's collection of paintings and sculptures, but was closed for restoration at press time.

⓮ Follow the wall east one block and head north on Calle San José two short blocks to **Plaza de Armas,** the original main square of Old San Juan. The plaza, bordered by Calles San Francisco, Fortaleza, San José, and Cruz, has a lovely fountain with 19th-century statues representing the four seasons.

⓯ West of the square stands **La Intendencia,** a handsome three-story neoclassical building. From 1851 to 1898, it was home to the Spanish Treasury. Recently restored, it is now the headquarters of Puerto Rico's State Department. *Calle San José, at the corner of Calle San Francisco, tel. 809/722–2121, ext. 230. Admission free. Tours at 2 and 3 in Spanish, 4 in English. Open weekdays 8–noon and 1–4:30.*

⓰ On the north side of the plaza is **City Hall,** called the *Alcaldía.* Built between 1604 and 1789, the alcaldía was fashioned after Madrid's city hall, with arcades, towers, balconies, and a lovely inner courtyard. A tourist information center and an art gallery are on the first floor. *Tel. 809/724–7171, ext. 2391. Open weekdays 8–noon and 1–4.*

⓱ Four blocks east on the pedestrian mall of Calle Fortaleza, you'll find **Plaza de Colón,** a bustling square with a statue of Christopher Columbus atop a high pedestal. Originally called St. James Square, it was renamed in honor of Columbus on the 400th anniversary of the discovery of Puerto Rico. On the north side of the plaza is a terminal for buses to and from San Juan.

⓲ Walk two blocks north from Plaza de Colón to Calle Sol and turn right. Another block will take you to **San Cristóbal,** the 18th-century fortress that guarded the city from land attacks. Even larger than El Morro, San Cristóbal was known as the Gibraltar of the West Indies. *Tel. 809/724–1974. Admission free. Open daily 9:15–6.*

⓳ South of Plaza de Colón is the magnificent **Tapia Theater** (Calle Fortaleza at Plaza de Colón, tel. 809/722–0407), named after the famed Puerto Rican playwright Alejandro Tapia y Rivera. Built in 1832, remodeled in 1949 and again in 1987, the municipal theater is the site of ballets, plays, and operettas. Stop by the box office to see what's showing and find out if you can get tickets.

㉒ Stroll from Plaza de Colón down to the **Port,** where the **Paseo de la Princesa** is spruced up with flowers, trees, and street lamps. Across from Pier 3, where the cruise ships dock, local artisans display their wares at the Plazoleta del Puerto.

San Juan *Numbers in the margin correspond to points of interest on the San Juan Exploring, Dining, and Lodging map.*

You'll need to resort to taxis, buses, públicos, or a rental car to reach the points of interest in "new" San Juan.

Avenida Muñoz Rivera, Avenida Ponce de León, and Avenida Fernández Juncos are the main thoroughfares that cross Puerta de Tierra, just east of Old San Juan, to the business and tourist districts of Santurce, Condado, and Isla Verde.

㉑ In Puerta de Tierra is Puerto Rico's **Capitol,** a white marble building that dates from the 1920s. The grand rotunda, with mosaics and friezes, was completed a few years ago. The seat of the island's bicameral legislature, the Capitol contains Puerto Rico's constitution and is flanked by the modern buildings of the Senate and the House of Representatives. There are spectacular views from the observation plaza on the sea side of the Capitol. Pick up an informative booklet about the building from the House Secretariat on the second floor. *Av. Ponce de León, tel. 809/721–7305 or 809/721–7310. Admission free. Open weekdays 8:30–5.*

㉒ At the eastern tip of Puerta de Tierra, behind the splashy Caribe Hilton, the tiny **Fort San Jeronimo** is perched over the Atlantic like an afterthought. Added to San Juan's fortifications in the late 18th century, the structure barely survived the British attack of 1797. Restored in 1983 by the Institute of Puerto Rican Culture, it is now a military museum with displays of weapons, uniforms, and maps. *Tel. 809/724–5949. Admission free. Open Wed.–Sun. 9:30–noon and 1:30–4:30.*

Dos Hermanos Bridge connects Puerta de Tierra with Miramar, Condado, and Isla Grande. Isla Grande Airport, from which you can take short hops to the islands of Vieques and Culebra, is on the bay side of the bridge.

On the other side of the bridge, the Condado Lagoon is bordered by Avenida Ashford, which threads past the high-rise Condado hotels and El Centro Convention Center, and Av. Baldorioty de Castro Expreso, which barrels all the way east to the airport and beyond. Due south of the lagoon is Miramar, a primarily residential area with fashionable, turn-of-the-century homes and a cluster of hotels and restaurants.

㉓ **Santurce,** which lies between Miramar on the west and the Laguna San José on the east, is a busy mixture of shops, markets, and offices. The classically designed **Sacred Heart University** is the home of the **Museum of Contemporary Puerto Rican Art.** *Tel. 809/268–0049. Open weekdays 9–4.*

㉔ Internationally acclaimed performers appear at the **Centro de Bellas Artes (Fine Arts Center).** This completely modern facility, the largest of its kind in the Caribbean, has a full schedule

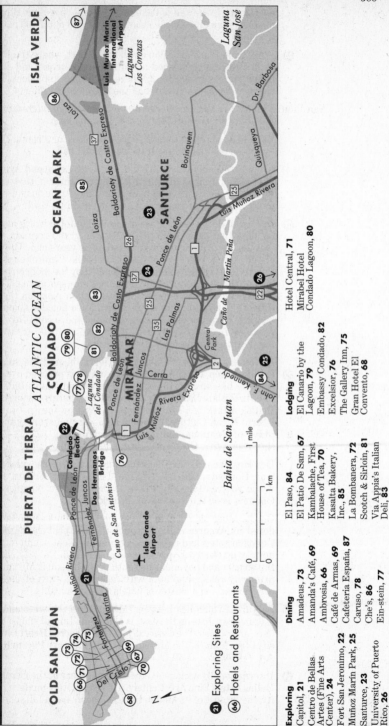

San Juan Exploring, Dining, and Lodging

388

Exploring
Capitol, **21**
Centro de Bellas Artes (Fine Arts Center), **24**
Fort San Jeronimo, **22**
Muñoz Marín Park, **25**
Santurce, **23**
University of Puerto Rico, **26**

Dining
Amadeus, **73**
Amanda's Café, **69**
Ambrosia, **66**
Café de Armas, **69**
Cafetería España, **87**
Caruso, **78**
Che's, **86**
Ein-stein, **77**

El Paso, **84**
El Patio De Sam, **67**
Kambalache, First House of Tea, **70**
Kasalta Bakery, Inc., **85**
La Bombanera, **72**
Scotch & Sirloin, **81**
Via Appia's Italian Deli, **83**

Lodging
El Canario by the Lagoon, **79**
Embassy Condado, **82**
Excelsior, **76**
The Gallery Inn, **75**
Gran Hotel El Convento, **68**

Hotel Central, **71**
Mirabel Hotel Condado Lagoon, **80**

21 Exploring Sites
66 Hotels and Restaurants

of concerts, plays, and operas. *Corner of Av. De Diego and Av. Ponce de León, tel. 809/724-4751.*

South of Santurce is the "Golden Mile"—Hato Rey, the city's bustling new financial hub. Isla Verde, with its glittering beachfront hotels, casinos, discos, and public beach, is to the east, near the airport.

Northeast of Isla Verde, Boca de Cangrejos sits between the Atlantic and Torrecilla Lagoon—a great spot for fishing and snorkeling. Southeast of Miramar, Avenida Muñoz Rivera skirts along the northern side of the mangrove-bordered **San Juan Central Park,** a convenient place for jogging and tennis. The park was built for the 1979 Pan-American Games. *Cerra St. exit on Rte. 2, tel. 809/722-1646. Admission free. Open Mon. 2-10, Tues.-Sat. 8-10, Sun. 10-6.*

Las Américas Expressway, heading south, goes by Plaza Las Américas, the largest shopping mall in the Caribbean, and ㉕ takes you to **Muñoz Marín Park,** an idyllic tree-shaded spot dotted with gardens, lakes, playgrounds, and picnic areas. Cable cars connect the park with the parking area. *Next to Las Américas Expwy., west on Av. Piñero, tel. 809/763-0568 or 809/763-0787. Admission free; parking $1 per vehicle. Open Tues.-Sun. 9-5:30; closed Mon.*

Río Piedras, a southern suburb of San Juan, is home to the ㉖ **University of Puerto Rico,** located between Avenida Ponce de León and Avenida Barbosa. The campus is one of two sites for performances of the Puerto Rico Symphony Orchestra. Theatrical productions and other concerts are also scheduled here throughout the year. The University Museum has permanent archaeological and historical exhibits and occasionally mounts special art displays. *Next to the university's main entrance on Av. Ponce de León, tel. 809/764-0000, ext. 2452 or 2456. Open weekdays 9-9, Sat. 8-3:30; closed Sun. and holidays.*

The university's main attraction is the **Botanical Garden,** a lush garden with more than 200 species of tropical and subtropical vegetati»n. Footpaths through the thick forests lead to a graceful lotus lagoon, a bamboo promenade, an orchid garden, and a palm garden. *Intersection of Rtes. 1 and 847 at the entrance to Barrio Venezuela, tel. 809/763-4408. Admission free. Open Tues.-Sun. 9-5; when Mon. is a holiday, it is open Mon. and closed Tues.*

San Juan Environs *Numbers in the margin correspond to points of interest on the Puerto Rico map.*

From San Juan, follow Route 2 west toward Bayamón and ㉗ you'll spot the **Caparra Ruins,** where, in 1508, Ponce de León established the island's first settlement. The ruins are that of an ancient fort. Its small **Museum of the Conquest and Colonization of Puerto Rico** contains historical documents, exhibits, and excavated artifacts. (You can see the museum's contents in less time than it takes to say the name.) *Km 6.6 on Rte. 2, tel. 809/781-4795. Admission free. Open weekdays 9-5, weekends and holidays 10-6.*

㉘ Continue on Route 2 to **Bayamón.** In the Central Park, across from Bayamón's city hall, there are some historical buildings and a 1934 sugarcane train that runs through the park (open daily 8 AM-10 PM). On the plaza, in the city's historic district, stands the 18th-century Catholic church of Santa Cruz and the old neoclassical city hall, which now houses the **Francisco Oller Art and History Museum** (open weekdays 8–noon and 1–4).

㉙ The **Bacardi Rum Plant,** along the bay, conducts 45-minute tours of the bottling plant, museum, and distillery, which has the capacity to produce 100,000 gallons of rum a day. (Yes, you'll be offered a sample.) *Km 2.6 on Rte. 888, tel. 809/788–1500. Admission free. Tours Mon.–Sat., except holidays, 9:30–3:30; closed Sun.*

Out on the Island **East and South** Our first excursion out on the island will take us east, down the coast to the south, and back up to San Juan. The first leg of the **㉚** trip—to Luquillo Beach and the nearby **Caribbean National Forest,** commonly known as **El Yunque,** can easily be done in a day. (There'll be heavy traffic and a crowded beach on weekends, when it seems as if the whole world heads for Luquillo.) The full itinerary will take two to three days, depending upon how long you loll on the beach and linger over the mountain scenery.

To take full advantage of the 28,000-acre El Yunque rain forest, go with a tour (*see* Guided Tours, *above*). Dozens of trails lead through the thick jungle (it sheltered the Carib Indians for 200 years), and the tour guides take you to the best observation points. Some of the trails are slippery, and there are occasional washouts.

Take Route 3 east from San Juan and turn right (south) on Route 191, about 25 miles from the city. The **Sierra Palm Visitor Center** is on Route 191, Km 11.6 (open daily 9:30–5). Nature talks and programs at the center are in Spanish and English and by appointment only.

El Yunque, named after the good Indian spirit Yuquiyu, is in the Luquillo Mountain Range. The rain forest is verdant with feathery ferns, thick ropelike vines, white tuberoses and ginger, miniature orchids, and some 240 different species of trees. More than 100 billion gallons of precipitation fall annually. Rain-battered, wind-ravaged dwarf vegetation clings to the top peaks. (El Toro, the highest, is 3,532 feet.) El Yunque is also a bird sanctuary and is the base of the rare Puerto Rican parrot. Millions of tiny, inch-long *coquis* (tree frogs) can be heard singing (or squawking, depending on your sensibilities). *For further information, call the Catalina Field Office, tel. 809/887–2875 or 809/766–5335; or write Caribbean National Forest, Box B, Palmer, PR 00721.*

㉛ To reach **Luquillo Beach,** take Route 191 back to Route 3 and continue east 5 miles to Km 35.4. One of the island's best and most popular strands, Luquillo was once a flourishing coconut plantation. Coral reefs protect its calm, pristine lagoon, making it an ideal place for a swim. The entrance fee is $1 per car, and there are lockers, showers, and changing rooms (*see* Beaches, *below*).

㉜ Back on Route 3, it's 5 miles to **Fajardo,** a major fishing and sailing center with thousands of boats tied and stacked in tiers at three large marinas. Boats can be rented or chartered here, and the *Spread Eagle* catamaran can take you out for a full day of snorkeling, swimming, and sunning (*see* Boat Tours, *above*). Fajardo is also the embarkation point for ferries to the islands of Culebra (fare $2.25) and Vieques ($2).

North of Fajardo on Route 987, just past the Seven Seas Recreational Area, is the entrance to **Las Cabezas de San Juan Nature Reserve.** Opened in 1991, the reserve contains mangrove swamps, coral reefs, beaches, a dry forest, all of Puerto Rico's natural habitats rolled into a microcosmic 316 acres. Nineteenth-century El Faro, one of the island's oldest lighthouses, is restored and still functioning; its first floor contains a small nature center that has an aquarium and other exhibits. The reserve is open, by reservation, to tours only, except from Friday to Sunday. *Rte. 987, tel. 809/722–5882, 809/722–5882 weekends. Admission: $4 adults, $1 children under 12. Tours given by reservation only Fri.–Sun. at 9:30, 10:30, and 1:30. Open to groups by reservation only at other times.*

A trip to the islands of Culebra or Vieques first involves a trip to Fajardo to catch a ferry. If you're driving, you can park in a local lot (about $3 a day) or take your car on the ferry. Cost for the latter depends upon the size of the car; the cheapest will be $26.50 round-trip to Culebra, $26 round-trip to Vieques. Reservations and payment must be made four days to a week in advance. You can also rent a car on either island. Plan on a full day, with overnight stay, to fully see each island.

Culebra has lovely white-sand beaches, coral reefs, and a wild-life refuge. In the sleepy town of **Dewey,** on Culebra's southwestern side, check at the Visitor Information Center at city hall (tel. 809/742–3291) about boat rentals. For car rentals, try **Prestige Car Rental** (tel. 809/742–3242). On **Vieques,** Sun Bay public beach has picnic facilities; Blue Beach is superb for snorkeling; and Mosquito Bay is luminous even on moonless nights. You can stay overnight at the government-sponsored Parador Villa Esperanza (tel. 809/741–8675) on Vieques, which has, among other amenities, its own marina and fleet of sailboats. For car rentals, contact **Vias Car Rental** (tel. 809/741–8173). Back on the main island, resume your ramble on Route 3, heading south past the U.S. Naval Base, and ride through the sugarcane fields to **Humacao.** South of Humacao (take Route 906) is the 2,700-acre Palmas del Mar, the island's largest resort community, with homes, condos, villas, and hotels.

Stay on Route 3 through **Yabuco,** tucked up in the hills, and **Maunabo** and **Patillas,** where you can pick up routes that will take you through the Cayey Mountains. Route 184 north skirts Lake Patillas and cuts smack through the **Carite Forest Reserve.** Stay on Route 184 until it meets Route 1, where you'll shoot northward back to San Juan.

Western Island If you're short of time, drive the 64 miles from San Juan to Ponce. On the Las Américas Expressway, Route 52, which cuts through the splendid mountains of Cordillera Central, the trip takes 90 minutes and costs $2 in tolls.

If time is not a major problem, plan a one- or two-day tour to explore the western regions of the island. This route covers Aguadilla, Rincón, San Germán, and Ponce. There's much to see along the way—caves and coves, karst fields and coffee plantations, mountains, beaches, and even a zoo.

Start out going west on Route 2. In Arecibo, pick up Route 10 and go south. Make a right on Route 111, and you'll find the **Caguana Indian Ceremonial Park,** used 800 years ago by the Taino tribes for recreation and worship. Mountains surround a 13-acre site planted with royal palms and guava. According to Spanish historians, the Tainos played a game similar to soccer, and in this park there are 10 courts bordered by cobbled walkways. There are also stone monoliths, some with colorful petroglyphs, and a small museum. *Rte. 111, Km 12.3, tel. 809/894–7325. Admission free. Open daily 8:30–4:30.*

Drive west on Route 111 and then north on Route 129 to Km
36 18.9, where you'll find the **Río Camuy Cave Park,** a 268-acre reserve that contains one of the world's largest cave networks. Guided tours take you on a tram down through dense tropical vegetation to the entrance of the cave, where you continue on foot over underground trails, ramps, and bridges. The caves, sinkholes, and subterranean streams are all spectacular (the world's second-largest underground river runs through here). Be sure to call ahead; the tours allow only a limited number of people. *Rte. 129, Km 18.9, tel. 809/898–3100 or 809/756–5555. Admission: $6 adults, $4 children. Parking $1. Open Wed.–Sun. and holidays 8–4. Last tour starts at 3:50.*

37 Backtrack to Route 111, which twists westward to **Aguadilla** on the northwest coast. In this area, somewhere between Aguadilla and Añasco, south of Rincón, Columbus dropped anchor on his second voyage in 1493. Both Aguadilla and **Aguada,** a few miles to the south, claim to be the spot where his foot first hit ground, and both towns have plaques to commemorate the occasion.

38 Route 115 from Aguadilla to **Rincón** is one of the island's most scenic drives, through rolling hills dotted with pastel-colored houses. Rincón, perched on a hill, overlooks its beach, which was the site of the World Surfing Championship in 1968. Skilled surfers flock to Rincón in winter, when the water is rough and challenging.

Pick up Route 2 for the 6-mile drive through **Mayagüez,** Puerto Rico's third-largest city, with a population approaching 100,000. Due south of Mayagüez, via the coastal Route 102, is
39 **Cabo Rojo,** once a pirates' hangout and now a favorite resort area of Puerto Ricans. The area has long stretches of white-sand beaches on the clear, calm Caribbean Sea, as well as many seafood restaurants. There are also several paradors in the region. **Boquerón,** at the end of Route 101, has one of the best beaches on the island, as well as two-room cabins for rent. Parking is $1 per car.

40 From Cabo Rojo continue east on Route 102 to **San Germán,** a quiet Old World town that's home to the oldest intact church under the U.S. flag. Built in 1606, Porta Coeli (Gates of Heaven) overlooks one of the town's two plazas, where the townspeople continue the Spanish tradition of promenading at night. The church is now a museum of religious art, housing 18th- and 19th-century paintings and statues. *Tel. 809/892–5845. Admission free. Open Wed.–Sun. 8:30–noon and 1–4:30.*

The fishing village of **La Parguera,** an area of simple seafood restaurants, mangrove cays, and small islands, lies south of San Germán at the end of Route 304. This is an excellent scuba-div-
41 ing area, but the main attraction is **Phosphorescent Bay.** Boats tour the bay, where microscopic dinoflagellates (marine plankton) light up like Christmas trees when disturbed by any kind of movement.

From San Germán, Route 2 traverses splendid peaks and valleys; pastel houses cling to the sides of steep green hills. East of Yauco, the road dips and sweeps right along the Caribbean **❷** and into **Ponce.**

Puerto Rico's second-largest city, with a population of 300,000, underwent a massive restoration for the 1992–93 quincentennial celebrating Columbus's discovery of the New World and for the 300th anniversary of the city's first settlement. For the event, the town installed 19th-century-style sidewalks bordered in pink marble and gas lamps. The red-and-black **Parque de Bombas,** a former firehouse dating from 1882, opened as a museum in 1990.

Ponce's charm stems from its mix of neoclassical, Creole, and art deco styles. Stop in and pick up information about this seaside city at the columned **Casa Armstrong-Poventud,** the home of the Institute of Puerto Rican Culture and Tourism Information Offices. Stroll around the **Plaza Las Delicias,** with its perfectly pruned India-laurel fig trees, graceful fountains, gardens, and park benches. View **Our Lady of Guadalupe Cathedral,** and walk down Calles Isabel and Christina, lined with turn-of-the-century wooden houses with wrought-iron balconies. Continue as far as Calles Mayor and Christina to the white stucco **La Perla Theater,** fronted by Corinthian columns. Be sure to allow time to visit the **Ponce Museum of Art,** worth seeing for the architecture alone. The modern two-story building was designed by Edward Durell Stone, who designed New York's Museum of Modern Art, has glass cupolas and a pair of curved staircases. The collection includes late Renaissance and Baroque works from Italy, France, and Spain, as well as contemporary art by Puerto Ricans. *Av. Las Américas, tel. 809/840–0511 or 809/848–0505. Admission: $3 adults, $2 children under 12. Open Mon. and Wed.–Fri. 9–4, Sat. 10–4, Sun. 10–5.*

Beaches

All Puerto Rico's beaches are open to the public by law (except for the man-made beach at the Caribe Hilton in San Juan). Many Puerto Rico beaches are within walking distance of hotels, if not right on the beach; other large hotels offer transport to beaches. Thirteen government-run *balnearios* (public beaches), have lockers, showers, picnic tables, and sometimes playgrounds and overnight facilities. Admission is free and parking $1 for a car. Most balnearios are open Tuesday–Sunday 9–6 in winter, 8–5 in summer. Listed below are some major balnearios.

Boquerón Beach is broad, with hard-packed sand and a fringe of coconut palms. It has picnic tables, cabin and bike rentals, a basketball court, minimarket, scuba diving, and snorkeling. *On the southwest coast, south of Mayagüez, Rte. 101, Boquerón.*

A white sandy beach bordered by resort hotels, **Isla Verde** is lively and popular with city folk. It offers picnic tables and good snorkeling, with equipment rentals nearby. *Near metropolitan San Juan, Rte. 187, Km 3.9, Isla Verde.*

Coral reefs protect the crystal-clear lagoon of crescent-shaped, palm-fringed **Luquillo Beach** from the Atlantic waters, making it ideal for swimming. As one of the largest and most well known, it gets crowded on weekends. There are picnic tables and tent sites. *30 mi east of San Juan, Rte. 3, Km 35.4.*

An elongated beach of hard-packed sand, **Seven Seas** is always popular with bathers. It has picnic tables and tent and trailer sites; snorkeling, scuba diving, and boat rentals are nearby. *Rte. 987, Fajardo.*

Sun Bay, a white-sand beach on Vieques, has picnic tables and tent sites, and offers such water sports as snorkeling and scuba diving. Boat rentals are nearby. *Rte. 997, Vieques.*

The famous **Condado Beach,** along Ashford Avenue in San Juan, is accessible from all hotels on the strip and from public walkways located along the road. To reach the long beaches of **Rincón, Cabo Rojo,** or **Parguera,** simply park your car along the road and walk.

Surfing   The best surfing beaches are along the Atlantic coastline from Borinquén Point south to Rincón. The surf is best from October through April; in summer, try Aviones and La Concha beaches in San Juan and Casa de Pesca in Arecibo. All have surf shops nearby.

Sports and the Outdoors

Bicycling   The broad beach at Boquerón makes for easy wheeling. You can rent bikes at **Boquerón Balnearios** (Rte. 101, Boquerón, Dept. of Recreation and Sports, tel. 809/722–1551). In the Dorado area on the north coast, bikes can be rented at the **Hyatt Regency Cerromar Beach Hotel** (tel. 809/796–1234) or the **Hyatt Dorado Beach Hotel** (tel. 809/796–1234). The average rate is $4 an hour.

Boating   Virtually all the resort hotels on San Juan's Condado and Isla Verde strips rent paddleboats, Sunfish, Windsurfers, and the like. Average cost is $35 an hour. Contact **Condado Plaza Hotel Watersports Center** (tel. 809/721–1000, ext. 1361), **Caribbean School of Aquatics** (La Concha Hotel, Av. Ashford, Condado, tel. 809/723–4740), or **Castillo Watersports** (ESJ Towers, Isla Verde, tel. 809/791–6195). Sailing and boat rentals are also available at **Playita Boat Rental** (1010 Av. Ashford, Condado, tel. 809/722–1607). For information on excursion boats, *see* Boat Tours in Guided Tours, *above.*

Golf   There are two 18-hole courses shared by the **Hyatt Dorado Beach Hotel** and the **Hyatt Regency Cerromar Beach Hotel** (Dorado, tel. 809/796–1234, ext. 3238 or 3013). You'll also find 18-hole courses at **Palmas del Mar Resort** (Humacao, tel. 809/852–6000, ext. 54), **Club Ríomar** (Río Grande, tel. 809/887–3964 or 809/887–3064), **Punta Borinquén** (Aguadilla, tel. 809/890–2987), **Berwind Country Club** (Río Grande, tel. 809/876–3056), and **Bahia Beach Plantation** (Río Grande, tel. 809/256–5600). Greens fees for nonguests at hotels range from $35 to $50 for 18 holes, and up to $35 for a nine-hole course. Golf carts cost $15–$30 per course; club rental, $15; and shoe rental, $5. Prices are generally lower at clubs, where greens fees and cart can total as little as $28.

Hiking   Dozens of trails lace **El Yunque** (information is available at the Sierra Palm Visitor Center, Rte. 191, Km 11.6). You can also hit the trails in **Río Abajo Forest** (south of Arecibo) and **Toro Negro Forest** (east of Adjuntas). Each reserve has a ranger station.

The trails are generally well marked, but maps and guides are available at the reserve ranger stations. Some trails, such as the rugged El Toro passage at El Yunque, are tougher than others; rangers can advise you of levels of difficulty. Trails are generally harder to hike during and after rainfall. You'll need hiking shoes, sun block, insect repellent, a hat, first-aid kit, canteen— and camera and film.

Snorkeling and Scuba Diving
Snorkeling and scuba-diving instruction and equipment rentals are available at **Caribbean School of Aquatics** and **Calypso Watersports** (La Concha Hotel, Av. Ashford, Condado, tel. 809/723–3903), **Coral Head Divers** (Marina de Palmas, Palmas del Mar Resort, Humacao, tel. 809/850–7208 or 800/221–4874), **La Cueva Submarina Training Center** (Plaza Cooperativa, Isabela, tel. 809/872–3903 or evenings 809/872–1094), **Marine Sports & Dive Shop** (Ponce, tel. 809/844–6175 or 809/752–8484), and **Parguera Divers Training Center** (Road 304, MM3-2, Lajas, tel. 809/899–4171). Escorted half-day dives range from $35 to $50 and generally include two tanks of air. Packages, which include lunch and other extras, start at $60. Night dives are available at close to double the price. Snorkeling excursions, which include equipment rental and lunch, start at $35. Snorkel equipment rents at beaches for about $5.

Caution: Puerto Rico's coral-reef waters and mangrove areas can be dangerous to novices. Unless you're an expert or have an experienced guide, avoid unsupervised areas and stick to the water-sports centers of major hotels.

Tennis
There are 17 lighted courts at **San Juan Central Park** (Calle Cerra exit on Rte. 2, tel. 809/722–1646); six lighted courts at the **Caribe Hilton Hotel** (Puerta de Tierra, tel. 809/721–0303, ext. 1730); eight courts, four lighted, at **Carib Inn** (Isla Verde, tel. 809/791–3535, ext. 6); and two lighted courts at the **Condado Plaza Hotel** (Condado, tel. 809/721–1000, ext. 1775). Out on the island, there are 14 courts, two lighted, at **Hyatt Regency Cerromar Beach Hotel** (Dorado, tel. 809/796–1234, ext. ...); seven courts, two lighted, at the **Hyatt Dorado Beach** (Dorado, tel. 809/796–1234, ext. 3220); 20 courts, four lighted, at **Palmas del Mar Resort** (Humacao, tel. 809/852–6000, ext. ...); and three lighted courts at the **Mayagüez Hilton Hotel** (Mayagüez, tel. 809/831–7575, ext. 2150). In the pricey hotels, court fees for nonguests can be as high as $25 an hour, with $6 lighting fees for night play. At San Juan Central Park, cost is $2 per person for an hour of court time.

Windsurfing
Windsurfing rentals are available at **Caribbean School of Aquatics, Castillo Watersports, Playita Boat Rental** (*see* Boating, *above,* for all information) and at **Lisa Penfield Windsurfing Center** (El San Juan Hotel, tel. 809/726–7274). Average rental is $15–$25 an hour, $10–$17 for two or more hours.

Shopping

San Juan is not a free port, and you won't find bargains on electronics and perfumes. You can find reasonable prices on china, crystal, and jewelry in and around major towns, but for true bargains, stick to local crafts and those from other Caribbean islands.

Shopping for local Caribbean crafts can be great fun. You'll run across a lot of tacky things you can live without, but you can also find some treasures, and in many cases you'll be able to watch the artisans at work. For details, contact the Tourism Artisan Center, tel. 809/721–2400, ext. 248.

The work of some Puerto Rican artists has brought them international acclaim: The paintings of Francisco Oller hang in the Louvre, and the portraits of Francisco Rodon are in the permanent collections of New York's Museum of Modern Art and Metropolitan Museum. Look for their works, and those of other native artists, in San Juan's stylish galleries.

Popular souvenirs and gifts include *santos* (small, hand-carved figures of saints or religious scenes), hand-rolled cigars, handmade lace, carnival masks, and fancy men's shirts called *guayaberas.* Also, some folks swear that Puerto Rican rum is the best in the world.

Shopping Districts **Old San Juan** is full of shops, especially on Cristo, Fortaleza, and San Francisco streets. The **Las Américas Plaza** south of San Juan is one of the largest shopping malls in the Caribbean, with 200 shops, restaurants, and movie theaters. Other malls out on the island include **Plaza del Carmen** in Caguas and the **Mayagüez Mall.**

Good Buys You can get discounts on Hathaway shirts and Christian Dior
Clothing clothing at **Hathaway Factory Outlet** (203 Calle Cristo, tel. 809/723–8946) and reductions on men's, women's, and children's raincoats at the **London Fog Factory Outlet** (156 Calle Cristo, tel. 809/722–4334).

Local Crafts For one-of-a-kind buys, head for **Puerto Rican Arts & Crafts** (204 Calle Fortaleza, Old San Juan, tel. 809/725–5596), **Plazoleta del Puerto** (Calle Marina, Old San Juan, tel. 809/722–3053), **Don Roberto** (205 Calle Cristo, tel. 809/724–0194), and **J. Rivera** (107 Calle Cristo, Old San Juan, tel. 809/724–1004). The **Haitian Gallery** (corner of Fortaleza and O'Donnell, Old San Juan, tel. 809/724–1053) carries Puerto Rican crafts and a selection of folksy, often inexpensive paintings from around the Caribbean.

Galería Palomas (207 Calle Cristo, Old San Juan, tel. 809/724–8904) is popular. **Galería Botello** (208 Calle Cristo, Old San Juan, tel. 809/723–9987, and Plaza Las Américas, tel. 809/724–7430) features a display of antique *santos* (religious sculptures).

Other galleries worth visiting are **Galería San Juan** (204–206 Calle Norzagaray, Old San Juan, tel. 809/722–1808 or 809/723–6515) and **Corinne Timsit International Galleries** (104 Calle San Jose, Old San Juan, tel. 809/724–1039 or 809/724–0994).

Dining

Over the past 10 years, phone-book listings of restaurants in Puerto Rico have quadrupled. Included among these are countless unique and inexpensive eateries. You can dine in kiosks set up near beaches, or tiny roadside cafés with Formica tabletops and some of the best food on the island. What you eat will likely be *comida criolla,* a mix of Spanish, African, and Indian cooking that uses an abundance of tomatoes, garlic, peppers, and cilantro with rice, local vegetables and fruits, and fried seafood. The prices in small cafés are an attraction in themselves: $5 will get you a full plate of empanadillas (flaky turnovers filled with crab, lobster, or conch) and *asopao* (chicken or shellfish gumbo with rice).

Puerto Rico has not escaped the global fast-food industry: Even small interior towns you'll find a McDonald's, Burger King or the like. Puerto Rico's own family-style **El Meson** features American-size burgers as well as *Cubano* sandwiches (made with roast pork, ham, Swiss cheese, pickles, and mustard), breakfast sandwiches, and Puerto Rican coffee. The inexpensive **Taco Maker** chain offers tacos, burritos, enchiladas, and the usual Tex-Mex fare.

Supermarkets and small grocers are located throughout the island, with many prices comparable to stateside's. Sugar, fish, local vegetables, rum, and local coffees are the best deals. In Old San Juan, try the **Capitol Supermarket** or **SJ Supermarket** on Calle San Francisco, across from the Plaza de Armas. **Mother Earth** (Plaza Las Américas, Hato Rey) is a health-food shop that's worth a stop if you're shopping in the mall. **Salud!** (1350 Av. Ashford, Condado) also has an excellent selection of health food. Well-stocked chain supermarkets, such as **Pueblo,** are located in every major center on the island.

A unique aspect of Puerto Rican cooking is its generous use of local vegetables. Plantains are cooked a hundred different ways—*tostones* (fried green), *amarillos* (baked ripe), and as chips. Rice and beans with tostones or amarillos are basic accompaniments to every dish. Locals cook white rice with *achiote* (annatto seeds) or saffron, brown rice with *gandules* (pigeon peas), and black rice with *frijoles* (black beans). *Garbanzos* (chick-peas) and white beans are served in many daily specials. A wide assortment of yams is served baked, fried, stuffed, boiled, smashed, and whole. *Sofrito*—a garlic, onion, sweet pepper, coriander, oregano, and tomato purée—is used as a base for practically everything.

Beef, chicken, pork, and seafood are all rubbed with *adobo,* a garlic-oregano marinade, before cooking. *Arroz con pollo* (chicken with rice), *sancocho* (beef and tuber soup), asopao, *empanada* (breaded cutlet), and *encebollado* (steak smothered in onions) are all typical plates.

Fritters, also popular, are served in food kiosks along the highways, notably at Luquillo Beach, as well as at cocktail parties. You may find empanadillas, *surrullitos* (cheese-stuffed corn sticks), *alcapurias* (stuffed green banana croquettes), and *bacalaitos* (codfish fritters).

Local *pan de agua* is an excellent French loaf bread, best hot out of the oven. It is also good toasted and should be tried in a Cubano sandwich.

Local desserts include flans, puddings, and fruit pastes served with native white cheese. Home-grown mangoes and papayas are sweet, and *pan de azucar* (sugar bread) pineapples make the best juice on the market. Fresh *parcha* (passion fruit) and the fresh juice of *guarapo* (sugarcane) and *guanabana* (similar to papaya) are sold cold from trucks along the highway. Puerto Rican coffee is excellent served espresso-black or generously cut *con leche* (with hot milk).

Local legend has it that the birthplace of the piña colada is the Gran Hotel El Convento, but you'd be hard-pressed to find a shoddy version of this famous local drink served anywhere. Rum can also be mixed with cola (known as a *cuba libre*), soda, tonic, juices, water, served on the rocks, or even straight up. Puerto Rican rums range from light white mixers to dark, aged sipping liqueurs. Look for Bacardi, Don Q, Ron Rico, Palo Viejo, and Barillito.

Unless stated otherwise, dress is casual at the restaurants listed below, and reservations are not necessary. Highly recommended restaurants are indicated by a star ★.

Category	Cost*
Moderate	$15–$25
Inexpensive	$10–$15
Budget	under $10

per person, excluding drinks and service

Old San Juan
★
Amadeus. In an atmosphere of gentrified Old San Juan, this restaurant offers a nouvelle Caribbean menu. The roster of appetizers includes tostones with sour cream and caviar, marlin seviche, and crabmeat tacos. Entrées range from grilled dolphin with coriander butter to chicken lasagna and tuna- or egg-salad sandwiches. *106 Calle San Sebastián, tel. 809/722–8635 or 809/721–6720. Reservations required. AE, MC, V. Closed Mon. Moderate.*

Amanda's Cafe. This airy cafe, on the north side of the city, offers seating inside or out, with a view toward the Atlantic and the old city wall. The cuisine is Mexican, French, and Caribbean. The nachos and margaritas are the best in town. *424 Calle Norzagaray, tel. 809/722–1682. AE, MC, V. Moderate.*

El Patio de Sam. With its warm, faux-brick interior, indoor patio, and wide selection of beers, this is a popular late-night gathering place. Specialties are steaks and seafood. Try the malagueña casserole (eggs baked in a criolla sauce). *102 Calle San Sebastián, tel. 809/723–1149. AE, DC, MC, V. Inexpensive-Moderate.*

Ambrosia. At the bottom of Calle Cristo, this restaurant serves fresh, frozen fruit drinks at the bar, while the menu features pastas, veal, and chicken. The daily lunch specials usually include quiche and lasagna served with large mixed salads—a good value. *205 Calle Cristo, tel. 809/722–5206. AE, MC, V. Inexpensive.*

Café de Armas. Soak up local atmosphere and dig into down-home comida criolla at this bare-bones restaurant conveniently located on the Plaza de Armas. Breakfast, lunch, and early dinners are served, and the menu changes daily. Try the *filete de chillo en salsa criolla* (snapper in Creole sauce) or *salchichas guisadas* (sausage, tomato, and potato stew). *On the Plaza de Armas, tel. 809/722–2601. No credit cards. Open Mon.–Sat. 6:30 AM–5 PM, Sun. 11–5. Budget.*

Kambalache, First House of Tea. Coffee and exotic teas from around the world are the draw at this small café. Here you can sample, among others, vanilla rum, dragon well, cinnamon bark, or Taiwan broken-leaf tea. Fresh pastries and sandwiches are served, and a liquor license is in the works. Seating is inside or out, on the busy street in front of Cristo Chapel. *252 Calle Cristo, tel. 809/724–5654. AE, MC, V. Closed Tues. Budget.*

La Bombonera. Established in 1903, this café and restaurant is known for its strong Puerto Rican coffee and *Mallorca*—a Spanish pastry made of light dough, toasted, buttered, and sprinkled with powdered sugar. Full breakfasts are served as well. It's a favorite Sunday-morning gathering place for locals and tourists alike. *259 Calle San Francisco, tel. 809/722–0658. AE, MC, V. Open daily 7:30 AM–8 PM. Budget.*

San Juan   **Che's.** The most established and casual of three Argentinian restaurants within a few blocks of one another, Che's features juicy *churrasco* (barbecue) steaks, lemon chicken, and grilled sweetbreads. The hamburgers are huge, and the french fries are fresh. The list of Chilean and Argentinean wines is also decent. *35 Calle Caoba, Punta Las Marias, tel. 809/726–7202. Reservations advised on weekends. AE, DC, MC, V. Moderate.*

★ **Scotch & Sirloin.** Tucked back among the tropical overgrowth overlooking the lagoon, the Scotch & Sirloin has been San Juan's most consistently fine steakhouse. Aquariums light up the otherwise dark bar, and the fresh salad bar serves moist banana bread. Steaks are aged in-house and cooked precisely to order. Sit outside on the patio by the lagoon. *La Rada Hotel, 1020 Av. Ashford, Condado, tel. 809/722–3640. Reservations advised. AE, DC, MC, V. Dinner only. Moderate.*

Ein-Stein. If you tire of tropical cuisine, come to this Teutonic outpost near the main shopping centers of Av. Ashford. Decor is dark-wood Germanic, and traditional dishes are prepared tableside on *de heisse stein,* or hot stone. Standards are rich Wiener schnitzel, sauerbraten, and a wide range of sausages. Imported German wines and beer round out the experience. *53-A Calle Aguadilla, Condado, tel. 809/723–1757. AE, DC, MC, V. Inexpensive–Moderate.*

Caruso. This bistrolike restaurant across from the Hotel La Concha and Condado Beach, features solid Italian fare in an unassuming atmosphere. Any of the pastas from the extensive list are a good buy; fish dishes are the most expensive menu items. Pizza and takeout are also offered. *1104 Av. Ashford, Condado, tel. 809/723–6876. AE, MC, V. Inexpensive.*

El Paso. This family-run restaurant serves genuine Creole food seasoned for locals. Specialties include asopao, pork chops, and breaded empanadas. There's always tripe on Saturday and arroz con pollo on Sunday. *405 Av. De Diego, Puerto Nuevo, tel. 809/781–3399. AE, DC, MC, V. Inexpensive.*

Via Appia's Italian Deli. The only true sidewalk café in San Juan, this eatery serves pizzas, sandwiches, cold beer, and pitchers of sangria. It is a good place to people-watch. *1350 Av. Ashford, Condado, tel. 809/725–8711. AE, MC, V. Inexpensive.*

Cafeteria España. This is a busy Spanish cafeteria serving strong coffee, assorted croquettes, toasted sandwiches, soups, and a large selection of pastries. Spanish candies, canned goods, and other gourmet items for sale are packed into floor-to-ceiling shelves that add a cozy note. *Centro Commercial Villamar, Baldorioty de Castro Marginal, Isla Verde, tel. 809/727–4517 and 809/727–3860. No credit cards. Budget.*

★ **Kasalta Bakery, Inc.** Walk up to the counter and order an assortment of sandwiches, cold drinks, strong café con leche, and pastries. Try the Cubano sandwich. *1966 Calle McLeary, Ocean Park, tel. 809/727–7340. No credit cards. Budget.*

Out on the Island   **La Rotisserie.** An institution in Mayagüez, this fine dining room offers the best value for the money in town with its lavish breakfast and lunch buffets. The restaurant is known for grilled steaks and fresh seafood. A different food festival is featured nightly: Italian, buffet, seafood, Latin night. *Hilton International Mayagüez, Hwy. 2, Km 152.5, Mayagüez, tel. 809/831–7575. Reservations advised. AE, D, DC, MC, V. Moderate.*

The Black Eagle. On the restaurant's veranda, you dine literally on the water's edge, with lapping waves as background music. House specialties include breaded conch fritters, fresh fish of the day, lobster, and prime meats that are imported by the owner. *Hwy. 413, Km 1, Barrio Ensenada, Rincón, tel. 809/823–3510. AE, DC, MC, V. Moderate.*

La Casona de Serafin. This informal oceanside bistro, with bleached walls and mahogany furniture, specializes in steaks, seafood, and Puerto Rican Creole dishes. Try sampling tostones, asopao, and surrullitos. *Hwy. 102, Km 9, Playa Joyuda, Cabo Rojo, tel. 809/851–0066. AE, MC, V. Moderate.*

Restaurant El Ancla. This courteous, relaxed spot by the water serves seafood and Puerto Rican specialties. Entrées come with tostones, *papas fritas,* and garlic bread. The menu ranges from lobster and shrimp to chicken, beef, and asopao. The piña coladas, with or without rum, and the flan are especially good. *Av. Hostos Final 9, Playa-Ponce, tel. 809/840–2450. AE, DC, MC, V. Moderate.*

Sand and the Sea. Looking down onto Guayama and out across the sea, this mountain cottage is a retreat into Caribbean living. The menu leans toward steaks and barbecues; there's a good carrot vichyssoise and excellent baked beans. Bring a sweater—it cools down to 50°F at night. *Hwy. 715, Km 5.2, Cayey, tel. 809/745–6317. AE, DC, MC, V. Moderate.*

El Bohio. Join the locals for fresh seafood at this informal restaurant overlooking the sea, about a 10- to 15-minute drive south of Mayagüez. Selections range from red snapper to lobster and shrimp. *Hwy. 102, Playa Joyuda, Cabo Rojo, tel. 809/851–2755. AE, DC, MC, V. Inexpensive–Moderate.*

Parador Perichi's. An extensive wine selection, with many bottles under $20, and fresh seafood distinguish this informal restaurant attached to a small inn on Joyuda Beach. Service here is excellent. Try the house specialty, a lavish lobster parmesan. *Hwy. 102, Km 14.3, Playa Joyuda, Cabo Rojo, tel. 809/851–3131. AE, D, DC, MC, V. Inexpensive.*

Fox Delicias Mall. This mall food court in Ponce, bustling with hungry shoppers and carousing teenagers, is like a scene from home, but with a Puerto Rican twist. Food stalls include Le Kafe, serving pastries, flans, and strong Puerto Rican coffee, and the local food specialists Criollisimo, with empanadillas, asopao, and barbecued dishes. *On the Plaza Las Delicias, Ponce. No credit cards. Budget.*

Lodging

Accommodations on Puerto Rico come in all shapes and sizes. There are high-rise beachfront hotels in San Juan that cater to the epicurean, and self-contained luxury resorts that cover hundreds of acres out on the island. But these pricey properties are only half the story on Puerto Rico. Affordable lodging abounds, most noticeably in the government-sponsored *paradores,* country inns modeled after Spain's successful parador system. They are required to meet certain standards, such as proximity to a sightseeing attraction or beach and a kitchen serving native cuisine. Parador prices range from $50 to $80 for a double room. Reservations for all paradors can be made by calling 800/443–0266, or 809/721–2884 in Puerto Rico.

Guest houses—traditionally either private homes that rent rooms or small inns—can range from charming dwellings with colorful decor and welcoming owners to stark rooms with little or no amenities and indifferent hosts. Villa rentals, while available on Puerto Rico, generally prove more expensive than a small guest house or parador, unless you are traveling with a large group and split the cost. However, you can find one- or two-bedroom villas for as little as $450–$750 per week in the off-season (*see* Villa and Apartment Rentals, *below*).

Keep in mind that the terms "guest house" and "villa" are subject to differing interpretations. Either could really be a small inn; sometimes you'll get a self-contained apartment unit, sometimes a studio with kitchen facilities, and sometimes just a standard hotel room. In all cases, call ahead to discern exactly what is being offered.

Most of the hotels below are within walking distance of a beach. An exception is in Old San Juan, where hotels are generally a short taxi ride from Condado Beach. In the few cases when a hotel or inn in a resort town is not on or near the water, transportation to the beach is usually provided (check when you call). However, if you're staying outside the San Juan area, it's best to have a car anyway, for easy access to sights and restaurants around the island.

Most hotels operate on the EP plan (meals not included in room rates). In some larger hotels, FAP (breakfast, lunch, dinner) and MAP (breakfast and dinner) plans are available. Weigh costs carefully, as meal plans may or may not save you money. Very few Puerto Rican hotels are all-inclusive. If you book the hotel yourself, be sure to ask about any packages the hotel may be offering. Many smaller hotels are willing to negotiate, particularly in the off-season. Also inquire whether rates include sports facilities and airport transfers.

Highly recommended lodgings are indicated by a star ★.

Category	Cost*
Moderate	$75–$125
Inexpensive	$40–$75
Budget	under $40

All prices are for a standard double room for two, excluding 7% tax (9% for hotels with casinos) and a 10% service charge. To estimate rates for hotels offering MAP/FAP, add about $20–$25 per person per day to the above price ranges.

Hotels and Resorts
Old San Juan
★

Gran Hotel El Convento. Standard rates at Puerto Rico's most famous hotel are generally out of our price range during high season, but its many specials and discounts make it worth your while to call. The light brown stucco building, with its dark wood paneling and arcades, was a Carmelite convent in the 17th century. All the rooms are air-conditioned, with twin beds and wall-to-wall carpeting. Fourteen rooms have balconies (ask for one with a bay view). The hotel's central location on Calle Cristo across from the San Juan Cathedral puts restaurants and city sights within walking distance. There are 25% discounts for seniors, and children under 18 stay free when sharing their parents' room. *100 Calle Cristo, 00902, tel. 809/723–9020 or 800/468–2779, fax 809/721–2877. 99 rooms. Facilities: pool, 2 restaurants and bar, free transport to beach. AE, D, DC, MC, V. EP. Moderate.*

The Gallery Inn. Owners Jan D'Esopo and Manuco Gandia restored one of the oldest private residences in the area and turned it into a rambling, classically Spanish guest house with winding, uneven stairs, private balconies, individually decorated rooms, and gardens hidden throughout. Overlooking the Atlantic along the north wall of Old San Juan, with views of El Morro and San Cristóbal forts, this small inn and art gallery has a compelling and singular panorama that is one of the best in the old city. Rooms are individually decorated with Spanish and French colonial antiques, and all open up to the inn's gardens. The gallery is also a working studio, and you may run into models posing in any of the suites in the house. The inn even offers a package that combines a five-night stay with the creation of your portrait bust. *204–206 Calle Norzagaray, 00901, tel. 809/722–1808 or 809/725–3829, fax 809/724–7360. 5 rooms, 3 suites. Facilities: self-service bar, roof bar, restaurant for guests only. AE, MC, V. EP. Moderate.*

Hotel Central. One of the older hotels in Old San Juan, this no-frills inn is also one of the city's better bargains. The dark-paneled main lobby, reminiscent of grandmother's sitting room, is furnished with an eclectic array of musty furniture that has seen many, and better, days. Rooms are small and sparsely furnished, with ceiling fans but no air-conditioning, telephones, or TVs. But they are clean and possess a travel-worn integrity, and each has its own small bath, with plenty of hot water. Located a stone's throw from the Plaza de Armas, the hotel is central to sights, shopping, and some of Puerto Rico's finest restaurants. *202 Calle San Jose, 00901, tel. 809/722–2751 or 809/721–9667. 62 rooms. Facilities: restaurant. No credit cards. EP. Budget.*

San Juan **Excelsior.** Recently spruced up with English carpets in the corridors and new sculptures in the lobby, this hotel is a five-minute walk to Condado Beach and one block from the Condado Lagoon. Each room has a private bath with phone and hair dryer. Although the decor is standard, this hotel is a very good value for its price range. Complimentary coffee, newspaper, and shoeshine are offered each morning. *801 Av. Ponce de León, Miramar 00907, tel. 809/721–7400 or 800/223–9815, fax 809/723–0068. 140 rooms, 60 with kitchenette. Facilities: pool, cocktail lounge, 2 restaurants, fitness rooms, free parking and free transportation to the beach. AE, MC, V. EP. Moderate.*

Mirabel Hotel Condado Lagoon. Located south of Av. Ashford in the Condado shopping area, this high-rise hotel is within easy walking distance of both Condado Beach and the Condado Lagoon. Characterless rooms are comfortable but have a homely 1970s look. Each has a double bed, air-conditioning, a small refrigerator, telephone, and TV. *6 Calle Clemenceau, Condado, 00907, tel. 809/721–0170, fax 809/724–4356. 46 rooms, 2 suites. Facilities: freshwater pool, coffee shop. AE, DC, MC, V. EP. Moderate.*

El Canario by the Lagoon. This bright, cheery inn has a convenient location, a block from Condado Beach and close to shopping and restaurants. The standard rooms are sparse but functional, each with a private bath, double bed, balcony, air-conditioning, telephone, and TV. Superior rooms have updated decor and views of Condado Lagoon. The complimentary breakfast the hotel advertises is Continental. *4 Calle Clemenceau, Condado, 00907, tel. 809/722–5058 or 800/533–2649, fax 809/723–8590. 40 rooms. Facilities: breakfast restaurant, small refrigerators available on request. AE, DC, MC, V. CP. Inexpensive–Moderate.*

Out on the Island **Parador Baños de Coamo.** This recently renovated mountain inn with lush grounds is on Route 546, Km 1, northeast of Ponce, located at the hot sulfur springs that are said to be the fountain of youth of Ponce de León's dreams. All rooms are air-conditioned and have private baths. *Box 540, Coamo, 00640, tel. 809/825–2186 or 800/443–0266. 48 rooms. Facilities: adult pool, children's pool, tennis, restaurant, lounge. AE, D, DC, MC, V. EP. Moderate.*

Parador Boquemar. Located on Route 101 near the beach in a small, unpretentious fishing village, this parador has air-conditioned rooms, all with minifridges, telephones, TVs, and private baths. Some rooms have balconies. *Box 133, Cabo Rojo, 00622, tel. 809/851–2158 or 800/443–0266. 64 rooms. Facilities: adult pool, children's pool, restaurant. AE, DC, MC, V. EP. Moderate.*

Hotel Joyuda Beach. This low-slung hotel is a new addition to Joyuda Beach. Rooms aren't large, but feature air-conditioning, double beds, satellite TV, telephones, and private baths. The beach is long, with good snorkeling at its reef. Also close is Isla de Rationes, a popular snorkeling and picnicking spot. A pool is planned. Children under 12 sleep free in their parents' room. *Carr. 102, Km 11.7, Playa Joyuda, Cabo Rojo, 00623, tel. 809/851–5650, fax 809/255–3750. 41 rooms, 2 cabana-villas with kitchenettes. Facilities: restaurant, beach bar. AE, MC, V. EP. Inexpensive–Moderate.*

Hotel Villa Cofresi. This apartment hotel on Rincón Beach is on the outskirts of Rincón, with its shops and restaurants. It offers studios, one-bedroom, and two-bedroom apartments (the latter can sleep up to a crowded eight). Accommodations are not elegant and lack phones, but do include kitchenettes, private baths, air-conditioning, and TVs. It's a good place for those who like to roll out of bed and onto the beach. *Box 1193, Rincón, 00677, tel. 809/823–7045 or 809/823–2450. 60 units. Facilities: restaurant, lounge, patio bar, pool. AE, DC, MC, V. EP. Inexpensive–Moderate.*

★ **Parador Villa Antonio.** This family-owned parador on Rincón beach is a sprawling, modern apartment-and-cottage complex with lushly landscaped grounds. Most appealing here are the cottages, especially those on the beach. Most are two-bedroom; a few have two bedrooms upstairs and two down and are rented as two units. Each unit is equipped with air-conditioning, kitchen, living room, TV, private bath, and balcony, but there are no phones in rooms. Even the most expensive units, the beachfront cottages, are Moderate here, and become Inexpensive when shared by two couples. A playground and games room keep children occupied. There's no restaurant, but nearby Rincón has many. *Box 68, Rincón, 00677, tel. 809/823–2645, 809/823–2285, or 800/443–0266, fax 809/823–3380. 55 apart-*

ments. *Facilities: 2 lighted tennis courts, pool, barbecue areas. AE, DC, MC, V. EP. Inexpensive–Moderate.*

Hotel Meliá. This family-owned and operated hotel has been a landmark in Ponce since 1908. Its slightly shabby exterior gives way to the old-world charm of its lobby, with its inlaid ceilings and dark wood. Rooms are clean and air-conditioned, with telephones, TVs, large closets, and private baths. Deluxe rooms have balconies; those overlooking the plaza are best. There's a Continental breakfast served on the rooftop terrace—cold toast, juice, and tepid coffee—but you're better off eating elsewhere. Rates stay the same year-round. *Box 1431, Ponce, 00733, tel. 809/842–0260 or 800/443–0266, fax 809/841–3602. 75 rooms. Facilities: restaurant, bar, lounge, rooftop terrace. AE, DC, MC, V. EP. Inexpensive.*

Parador Casa Grande. This restored hacienda sits on 107 acres of a former coffee plantation, where cottages snuggle along wood walkways among lush green hills. Each unit has four spacious balconied rooms; No. 9 is way in the back—quiet, with a lovely mountain view. Rooms have no air-conditioning, but the cool mountain air would make it redundant. There are trails for hikers, hammocks for loafers, and occasional music for romantics. *Box 616, Utuado, 00761, tel. 809/894–3939 or 800/443–0266. 20 rooms. Facilities: pool, restaurant, lounge. AE, MC, V. EP. Inexpensive.*

★ **Parador Hacienda Gripiñas.** Don't stay here if you're looking for a beach vacation: The sea is more than 30 miles away. Instead, this white hacienda is for those looking for a romantic mountain hideaway. It has polished wood, beam ceilings, a spacious lounge with rocking chairs, and splendid gardens. The large airy rooms with private baths are decorated with native crafts. A very romantic hideaway. *Rte. 527, Km 2.5, Box 387, Jayuya, 00664, tel. 809/828–1717, 809/721–2884, or 800/443–0266. 19 rooms. Facilities: restaurant, lounge, pool, hiking and horseback-riding trails. AE, MC, V. EP. Inexpensive.*

Parador Oasis. The Oasis, not far from San Germán's two plazas, was a family mansion 200 years ago. You'll get a better taste for its history in the older front rooms; rooms in the new section in the rear are small and somewhat motelish. All rooms offer air-conditioning, phones, TVs, and private baths. It's 12 miles to the nearest beach. *72 Calle Luna, Box 144, San Germán, 00753, tel. 809/892–1175 or 800/443–0266. 50 rooms. Facilities: restaurant, pool, Jacuzzi, lounge, gym, sauna. AE, DC, MC, V. EP. Inexpensive.*

Parador Perichi's. On Route 102 along famous Joyuda Beach and minutes from Mayagüez, this hotel has first-rate access to the beach and to knockout sunsets. Decor is modern, simple, and bright. All rooms have air-conditioning, TVs, phones, and balconies. Most have views of the ocean, but ask for one that faces the beach. The award-winning restaurant draws crowds (*see* Dining, *above*). Look for live bands and dancing on weekends in the open-air bar area. *Carr. 102, Km 14.3, Playa Joyuda, Cabo Rojo, 00623, tel. 809/851–3131 or 800/443–0266. 25 rooms. Facilities: game room, pool, restaurant, and lounge. AE, D, DC, MC, V. EP. Inexpensive.*

Parador Villa Parguera. This parador is a stylish hotel on Phosphorescent Bay, with large, colorfully decorated, air-conditioned rooms, all with TVs and private baths. A spacious dining room, overlooking the swimming pool and the bay beyond, serves excellent native and international dishes. Children under 10 stay free in their parents' room. Ask about honeymoon packages. *Rte. 304, Box 273, Lajas 00667, tel. 809/899–3975 or 800/443–0266. 62 rooms. Facilities: saltwater pool, restaurant, lounge, some facilities for disabled. AE, D, DC, MC. EP. Inexpensive.*

Beside the Pointe. Directly on the thundering beach of Rincón, this small activity-oriented property attracts surfers from around the world, especially from November to April. The hotel consists of studio, one-bedroom, and two-bedroom apartments (the latter sleeping up to five) in two buildings. Room decor is nonexistent, but all units have fans, private baths, and kitchen facilities with large refrigerators. A small beach bar/restaurant is decorated with photos of guests. *Box 4430, Rincón, 00677, tel. 809/823–8550 or 809/823–5683. 3 efficiency studios, 9 apartments. Facilities: bar, restaurant, laundry. MC, V. EP. Budget–Inexpensive.*

★ **Hotel Caribe Playa.** The '60s-style buildings of this small charmer sit 90 feet from the water on 45 lush acres that include a coconut plantation—picturesque indeed. Simple rooms, located in three two-story buildings, face the sea and catch the virtually nonstop breezes, which cool the rooms and keep insects at bay. All rooms sleep four and are clean and comfortable, with kitchenettes, fans, and private baths. Top-floor rooms have balconies. Children under 10 stay free in their parents' room. Restaurants and food stores are nearby, but the owners will cook for guests by arrangement. The hotel is just south of Humacao on Rte. 3. *HC 764, Buzon 8490, Pantillas, 00723, tel. 809/839–6339 or 800/221–4483. 28 efficiencies, 4 rooms. Facilities: library with TV and public phone, beachside barbecues, small restaurant for guests. AE, D, MC, V. EP. Budget–Inexpensive.*

Guest Houses and B&Bs

Embassy Condado. A block from Condado Beach in San Juan, this small, modern two-story guest house is in the right place for the right price. The 15 rooms can be combined to make singles, doubles, or suites; all have private baths, air-conditioning and ceiling fans, TVs, and kitchenettes or access to one. Several rooms have fold-out beds to accommodate an extra person. There's a rooftop sun deck and an outdoor café that looks over Condado Beach and the ocean. Across the road, Panche Restaurant, owned and operated by the guest house, serves French cuisine. *1126 Seaview, Condado, San Juan, 00907, tel. 809/725–8284 or 809/725–2400. 15 rooms. Facilities: café, rooftop sun deck. AE, MC, V. EP. Inexpensive.*

Sea Gate. Occupying 2 acres of a hilltop on the island of Vieques, this whitewashed hotel is a family-run operation. Proprietors John, Ruthye, and Penny Miller will meet you at the airport or ferry, drive you to the beaches, arrange scuba-diving and snorkeling trips, and give you a complete rundown on their adopted home. Accommodations include three-room efficiencies with full kitchens and terraces. All have fans, but no air-conditioning (the hilltop breezes are just fine), and no phones; TVs are available on request. *Box 747, Vieques, 00765, tel. 809/741–4661. 16 efficiencies (sleep 3), one 2-bedroom cottage (sleeps 4). No credit cards. EP. Budget–Inexpensive.*

★ **The Lazy Parrot.** Clearly one of the best deals in Rincón, this small, bright guest house is in the hills above Rincón's famous surfing beaches (it's best to have a car to get around). It's owned and operated by Steve and Francia Lantz, transplanted Americans who came to surf and somehow couldn't leave.

Rooms are small but comfortable, and each has two bunk beds, fan, private bath, and a writing desk. The outdoor patio is where the inn's locally famous "Texas-size" breakfasts are served: lobster omelets, pancakes, hash browns, pineapple bread, and more. A recently completed dining room serves breakfast, lunch, and dinner Tuesday–Sunday in high season and Thursday–Sunday in low season. Rates do not include meals. *Carr. 413, Km 4.1, Box 430, Rincón, 00743, tel. 809/823–5654. 6 rooms. Facilities: dining room, patio, gift shop. AE, MC, V. EP. Budget.*

Villa and Apartment Rentals Villa and condominium or apartment rentals in Puerto Rico are not as common as on some Caribbean islands, and very few of them are meant to be budget accommodations. Rather, most are deluxe homes in luxury areas, complete with maids, cooks, and gardeners, and can cost anywhere from $1,000 a night and up. If you're part of a large group or you'd like to investigate off-season rates, contact **Condo World** (26645 W. Twelve Mile Rd., Southfield, MI 48034, tel. 800/521–2980).

Camping The Puerto Rico Tourism Company currently recognizes 35 camping areas in locations ranging from Natural Resources parks such as El Yunque National Forest to Luquillo Beach and many of the *balnearios* (public beaches) around the island. Camping facilities can include *casetas* (small cottages), huts, lean-tos, and even small trailer homes. Cost ranges from $5–$12. Tent sites are also available, with an average cost of 50¢ per person. The facilities can be rustic, some with cold showers, some with no water or toilets at all. Contact the **Recreation Department** (tel. 809/722–1771 or 809/722–1551) or the **Department of Natural Resources** (tel. 809/723–1717).

Off-Season Bets Roughly mid-April through mid-December, many of Puerto Rico's more expensive properties drop their prices to qualify in our Moderate range. In addition, these and other hotels may offer limited special deals or packages, so inquire when you call. In San Juan, try **Hotel La Concha** (Box 4195, Condado, 00905, tel. 809/721–6090 or 800/468–2822) or the **Excelsior** (801 Av. Ponce de Leon, Miramar, 00907, tel. 809/721–7400 or 800/223–9815). The **Hyatt Dorado Beach** (Rte. 693, Dorado 00646, tel. 809/796–1234 or 800/233–1234, fax 809/796–2022) and **Hyatt Cerromar Beach** (Dorado 00646, tel. 809/796–1234 or 800/233–1234, fax 809/796–4647) frequently offer packages, although some of these are pricey even off-season.

The Arts and Nightlife

¿Qué Pasa?, the official visitors guide, has current listings of events in San Juan and out on the island. Also, pick up a copy of the *San Juan Star, Quick City Guide,* or *Sunspot,* and check with the local tourist offices and the concierge at your hotel to find out what's doing.

Music, Dance, and Theater **LeLoLai** is a year-round festival that celebrates Puerto Rico's Indian, Spanish, and African heritage. Performances take place each week, moving from hotel to hotel, showcasing the island's music, folklore, and culture. Because it is sponsored by the Puerto Rico Tourism Company and major San Juan hotels, passes to the festivities are included in some packages offered by participating hotels. Others can purchase tickets for $8 (adults) and $6 (children) for the series. *Contact the Condado*

Convention Center, tel. 809/723–3135. Reservations can be made by telephoning 809/722–1513.

Casinos By law, all casinos are in hotels; most are in San Juan. It goes without saying that frequenting casinos is not a good way to stretch your vacation money. That said, Puerto Rico's casinos have no cover charge or drinking, so it *is* possible to visit and get away with no more than spending some loose change at the slot machine. Alcoholic drinks are not permitted at the gaming tables, although free soft drinks, coffee, and sandwiches are often available. Dress for the larger casinos tends to be on the formal side, and the atmosphere is refined. The law permits casinos to operate noon–4 AM, but individual casinos set their own hours, which change with the season.

Casinos are located in the following San Juan hotels: **Condado Plaza Hotel, Caribe Hilton, Carib-Inn, Clarion Hotel, Ramada, Dutch Inn, Sands,** and **El San Juan.** Elsewhere on the island, there are casinos at the **Hyatt Regency Cerromar** and **Hyatt Dorado Beach hotels,** at **Palmas del Mar,** and at the **Hilton International Mayagüez.**

Discos In Old San Juan, young people flock to **Neon's** (203 Calle Tanca, tel. 809/725–7581) and **Lazers** (251 Calle Cruz, tel. 809/721–4479).

Nightclubs El San Juan's **Tropicoro** presents international revues, occasional top-name entertainers, and a flamenco show four times a week. In Old San Juan, the Hotel El Convento's **Ponce de León Salon** (tel. 809/723–9020) puts on flamenco shows. Young professionals gather at **Peggy Sue** (1 Av. Roberto, tel. 809/722–4750), where the design is 1950s and the music includes oldies and current dance hits.

18 Saba

Updated by
Jordan Simon

This 5-square-mile fairy-tale isle is not for everybody. If you're looking for exciting nightlife or lots of shopping, forget Saba, or take the one-day trip from St. Maarten. There are only a handful of shops, even fewer inns and eateries, and only 1,200 friendly but shy inhabitants. Beach lovers should also take note that Saba is a beachless volcanic island, ringed with steep cliffs that plummet sharply to the sea.

So, why Saba? Saba is a perfect hideaway, a challenge for adventurous hikers (Mt. Scenery rises above it all to a height of 2,855 feet); a longtime haven for divers; and, for Sabans, heaven on water. It's no wonder that they call their island the Unspoiled Caribbean Queen. Saba is also one of the Caribbean's most affordable islands. Only two hotels raise their rates during high season, and the island's plushest rental property, boasting four bedrooms, a huge pool, and a dazzling ocean view, rents for under $250 a night in winter.

Saba may be the prettiest island in the Caribbean. It's certainly the most immaculate, with a once-upon-a-time storybook enchantment. The island's uncomplicated lifestyle has persevered: Saban ladies still hand-embroider the very special, delicate Saba lace and brew the potent rum-based liquor Saba Spice, sweetened with secret herbs and spices. In tiny, toylike villages, narrow paths are bordered by flower-draped walls and neat picket fences. Tidy houses with red roofs and gingerbread trim are planted in the mountainside among the bromeliads, palms, hibiscuses, orchids, and Norwegian pines.

Saba is part of the Netherlands Antilles Windward Islands, 28 miles—a 15-minute flight—from St. Maarten. The island is a volcano, extinct for 5,000 years (no one even knows where the crater was). Sabans are a hardy lot. To get from Fort Bay to The Bottom—the town that's actually at the top of the island— the early Sabans carved 900 steps out of the mountainside. Everything that arrived on the island, from a pin to a piano, had to be hauled up. Those rugged steps remained the only way to get about the island until The Road was built by Josephus Lambert Hassell (a carpenter who took correspondence courses in engineering) in the 1940s. An extraordinary feat of engineering, the handmade road took 20 years to build, and if you like roller coasters, you'll love it. The 6½-mile, white-knuckle route begins at sea level in Fort Bay, zigs up to 1,968 feet, and zags down to 131 feet above sea level at the airport. This makes a car or scooter the most desirable mode of transportation, although walking is possible (if tiring) and hitchhiking practiced regularly.

What It Will Cost These sample prices, meant only as a general guide, are for high season. A one-bedroom cottage in town rents for about $60 a night; an inexpensive one-bedroom apartment is about $50. Dinner at an inexpensive restaurant will be about $15; lunch at a budget restaurant, about $7. A rum punch costs around $2.50; a glass of beer will be $1.50–$2. Rental cars average $35 a day. A taxi from Windwardside hotels to local dive shops is about $10; from hotels in the Bottom to dive shops, $6. Expect to pay about $45 for a single-tank dive; snorkel equipment rents for about $5 a day.

Before You Go

Tourist Information Contact the very helpful **Saba Tourist Information Office** (c/o **Medhurst & Assoc. Inc.,** 271 Main St., Northport, NY 11768, tel. 516/261–7474, 212/936–0050, or 800/344–4606) or, in Canada, **New Concepts in Travel** (410 Queens Quai W, Suite 303, Toronto, Ont. M5V 2Z3, Canada, tel. 416/362–7707).

Arriving and Departing
By Plane Unless you parachute in, you'll arrive from St. Maarten via **Windward Islands Airways** (tel. 599/5–42255 or 599/5–44237) at Juancho E. Yrausquin Airport.

From the Airport Your only option is to take a cab; to Windwardside, it's about $5.

By Boat *Style,* an open-air vessel with an open bar, departs St. Maarten's Great Bay Marina, Phillipsburg, for the one-hour trip to Fort Bay three times weekly at 9 AM and returns at 3 PM (fare-$45; tel. 599/5–22167 in St. Maarten).

Passports and Visas U.S. citizens need proof of citizenship. A passport is preferred, but a birth certificate or voter registration card will do (a driver's license will *not* do). British citizens must have a British passport. All visitors must have an ongoing or return ticket.

Language Saba's official language is Dutch, but everyone on the island speaks English.

Precautions Everyone knows everyone else on the island, and crime is virtually nonexistent. Take along insect repellent, sunscreen, and sturdy, no-nonsense shoes that get a good grip on the ground.

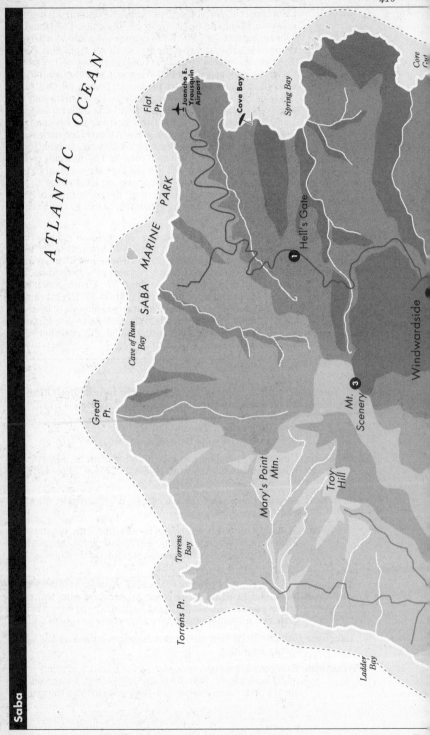

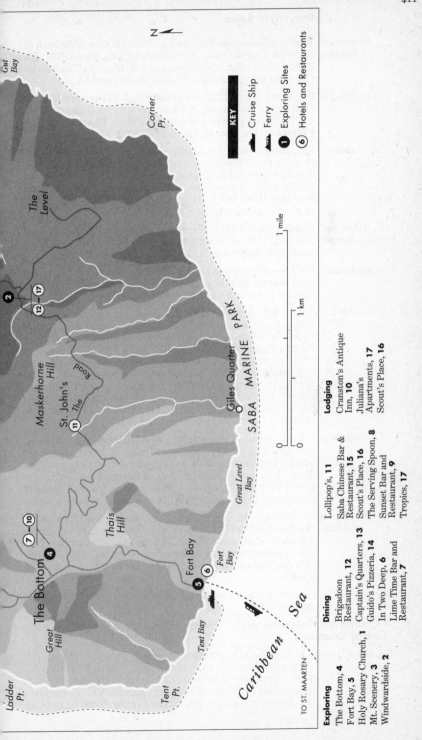

N

KEY

Cruise Ship
Ferry
1 Exploring Sites
6 Hotels and Restaurants

Exploring
The Bottom, **4**
Fort Bay, **5**
Holy Rosary Church, **1**
Mt. Scenery, **3**
Windwardside, **2**

Dining
Brigadoon Restaurant, **12**
Captain's Quarters, **13**
Guido's Pizzeria, **14**
In Two Deep, **6**
Lime Time Bar and Restaurant, **7**

Lollipop's, **11**
Saba Chinese Bar & Restaurant, **15**
Scout's Place, **16**
The Serving Spoon, **8**
Sunset Bar and Restaurant, **9**
Tropics, **17**

Lodging
Cranston's Antique Inn, **10**
Juliana's Apartments, **17**
Scout's Place, **16**

TO ST. MAARTEN

Caribbean Sea

Staying in Saba

Important Addresses

Tourist Information: The amiable Glenn Holm is at the helm of the **Saba Tourist Office** (Windwardside, tel. 599/4–62231, fax 599/4–62350) weekdays 8–noon and 1–5. If needed, the tourist office will help secure accommodations in guest houses.

Emergencies

Police: call 599/4–63237; **Hospitals:** The **A. M. Edwards Medical Center** (The Bottom, tel. 599/4–63288) is a 10-bed hospital with a full-time physician and various clinics; **Pharmacies:** The **Pharmacy** (The Bottom, tel. 599/4–63289).

Currency

U.S. dollars are accepted everywhere, but Saba's official currency is the Netherlands Antilles florin (also called guilder). The exchange rate fluctuates but is around NAf 1.80 to U.S. $1. Prices quoted here are in U.S. dollars unless noted otherwise. **Barclays Bank** in Windwardside is the island's only major bank; it's open weekdays 8:30–2.

Taxes and Service Charges

Hotels collect a 5% government tax. Most hotels and restaurants add a 10%–15% service charge to your bill. The departure tax is $2 from Saba to St. Maarten or St. Eustatius.

Getting Around

Saba is easily explored by car or on foot (if you're hardy and in good shape), making guided tours unnecessary. Many people manage to survive without transportation.

Rental Cars

Saba's one and only road—The Road—is a serpentine affair with many a hairpin (read hair-raising) curve. To drive it, contact **Doc's Car Rentals** (Windwardside, tel. 599/4–62271); **Scout's Place** (Windwardside, tel. 599/4–62205); or **Juliana's** (Windwardside, tel. 599/4–62269). A car rents for about $35 per day, with a full tank of gas and unlimited mileage. (If you run out of gas, call the island's only gas station, down at Fort Bay, tel. 599/4–63272. It closes at noon.) Scooters can be rented at **Steve's** (tel. 599/4–62507), next to Sandra's Salon & Boutique, for $30–$35 per day, less by the week.

Hitchhiking

Carless Sabans get around the old-fashioned ways—walking and hitchhiking (very popular and safe). If you choose to get around by thumbing rides, you'll need to know the rules of The Road. To go from The Bottom, sit on the wall opposite the Anglican Church; to go from Fort Bay, sit on the wall opposite Saba Deep dive center, where the road begins to twist upward.

Telephones and Mail

To call Saba from the United States, dial 011/599/4 followed by the five-digit number, which always begins with a "6." On the island, it is only necessary to dial the five-digit number. Telephone communications are excellent on the island, and direct-dial long distance is in effect. There are no pay phones on the island.

To airmail a letter to the United States costs NAf 1.30; a postcard, NAf 60¢.

Opening and Closing Times

Businesses and government offices on Saba are open weekdays 8–5.

Guided Tours

All 10 of the taxi drivers who meet the planes at Yrausquin Airport also conduct tours of the island. The cost for a full-day tour is $8 per person with a minimum of four people. If you're just in from St. Maarten for a day trip, have your driver make lunch reservations for you at **The Serving Spoon** or the **Cap-**

tain's Quarters (*see* Dining, *below*). Guides are available for hiking; contact the tourist office.

Exploring Saba

Numbers in the margin correspond to points of interest on the Saba map.

Touring the island's sights by car will take only half a day. Guided tours here make for a pleasant introduction to Saba, but the island is so small that you shouldn't have any problem driving on your own. Begin your tour with a trip from Flat Point, at the airport, up to Hell's Gate. Because there is only one road, we'll continue along its hairpin curves up to Windwardside, and then on to The Bottom and down to Fort Bay.

There are 20 sharp curves on The Road between the airport and Hell's Gate. On one of these curves, poised on Hell's Gate's hill, is the stone **Holy Rosary Church,** which looks medieval but was built in 1962. In the **Community Center** behind the church, village ladies sell blouses, handkerchiefs, tablecloths, and tea towels embellished with the very special and unique Saba lace. These same ladies also turn out innocent-sounding Saba Spice—each according to her own family recipe—a rum-based liqueur that will knock your socks off.

The Road spirals past banana plantations, oleander bushes, and stunning views of the ocean below. In **Windwardside,** the island's second-largest village, teetering at 1,968 feet, you'll see rambling lanes and narrow alleyways winding through the hills and a cluster of tiny, neat houses and shops.

On your right as you enter the village is the **Church of St. Paul's Conversion,** a colonial building with a red-and-white steeple. Your next stop should be the **Saba Tourist Office** (just down the road), for brochures and books. Then browse through the **Square Nickel,** the **Breadfruit Gallery,** the **Weaver's Cottage, Saba Tropical Arts,** and the **Island Craft Shop.**

The **Saba Museum,** surrounded by lemongrass and clover, lies just behind the Captain's Quarters. There are small signs marking the way to the 150-year-old house, which has been set up to look much as it did when it was a sea captain's home. Its furnishings include a handsome mahogany four-poster bed with pineapple design; an antique organ; and, in the kitchen, a rock oven and a hearth. Among the old documents on display is a letter a Saban wrote after the hurricane of 1772, in which he sadly says, "We have lost our little all." The first Sunday of each month, the museum holds croquet matches on its grounds; all-white attire is requested at this formal but fun social event. *Windwardside, no phone. Admission: $1 donation requested. Open weekdays 10–12:30 and 1–3.*

Near the museum are the stone and concrete steps—1,064 of them—that rise to **Mt. Scenery.** The steps lead past giant elephant ears, ferns, begonias, mangoes, palms, and orchids, up to a mahogany grove at the summit: six identifiable ecosystems in all. Signs name the trees, plants, and shrubs. On a cloudless day the view is spectacular. Begin this half-day excursion in the early morning; bring a picnic lunch (your hotel will pack one), nonslip shoes, a jacket, and water.

4 You'll be zigzagging downhill, past the small settlement of St. John's, from Windwardside to **The Bottom,** which sits in its bowl-shape valley 820 feet above the sea. The Bottom is the seat of government and the home of the lieutenant-governor. The large house next to Wilhelmina Park has fancy fretwork, a high-pitched roof, and wraparound double galleries.

On the other side of town is the **Wesleyan Holiness Church,** a small stone building, dating from 1919, with bright white fretwork. Stroll by the church, beyond a place called The Gap, and you'll come to a **lookout point** where you can see the rough-hewn steps leading down to Ladder Bay. Ladder Bay, with 524 steps, and Fort Bay, with its 200 steps, were the two landing sites from which Saba's first settlers had to haul themselves and their possessions. Sabans sometimes walk down to Ladder Bay to picnic. If you follow suit, remember the 524 steps back *up* to The Road. (Hitchhiking from down there will get you nowhere!)

5 The last stop on The Road is **Fort Bay,** which is the jumping-off place for two of the island's dive operations (*see* Scuba Diving and Snorkeling, *below*) and the St. Maarten ferry docks. There's also a gas station, a 277-foot deep-water pier that accommodates the tenders from ships that call here, and the information center for the **Saba Marine Park** (*see* Scuba Diving and Snorkeling, *below*). On the quay is a decompression chamber, one of the few in the Caribbean, and **Saba Deep's** dive shop, above which is its new snack bar, **In Two Deep.**

Beaches

Well's Bay, a small beach near Mary's Point that used to exist roughly half the year, hasn't reappeared since Hurricane Hugo. **Cove Bay,** a 20-foot strip of rocks and pebbles laced with gray sand, is now the only place for sunning (and moonlight dips after a Saturday night out).

Sports and the Outdoors

Boating **Saba Deep** (tel. 599/4–63347 or 599/4–62201) occasionally conducts one-hour round-island cruises that include cocktails, hors d'oeuvres, and a sunset you won't soon forget for $25 a person.

Hiking You can't avoid some hiking, even if you just go to mail a postcard. The big deal, of course, is Mt. Scenery, with 1,064 slippery steps leading up to the top (*see* Exploring Saba, *above*). For information about Saba's 18 recommended botanical hiking trails, check with Glenn Holm at the Tourist Office (*see* Important Addresses, *above*). Botanical tours are available upon request. A guided hike through the undeveloped back side of Mt. Scenery, a strenuous, all-day trip, will cost about $50. Except for this backside of Mt. Scenery, trails throughout the island are clearly marked. Other popular hikes include The Ladder (very steep, with splendid views of the coastal bluffs), the Maskerhorne Hill Trail (moderate difficulty, offering magnificent panoramic views and abundant plant life) and the easy, rambling Sandy Cruz Track. The Old Sulphur Mine Walk from Lower Hell's Gate leads to bat caves—with typical sulfuric stench—that can be explored by the truly intrepid. Exercise caution!

Scuba Diving and Snorkeling The island's first settlers probably found the **Saba Bank** (a fertile fishing ground 3 miles southwest of Saba) a crucial point in their decision to set up house here. In more recent times, divers have enjoyed Saba's coral gardens and undersea mountains. **Saba Marine Park** was established in 1987 to preserve and manage Saba's marine life. The park circles the entire island, dipping down to 200 feet, and is zoned for diving, swimming, fishing, boating, and anchorage. One of the unique features of Saba's diving is the submerged pinnacles (islands that never made it!) at about the 70-foot depth mark. Here all forms of sea creatures rendezvous. The park offers talks and slide shows for divers and snorkelers and provides brochures and literature. *Harbor Office, Fort Bay, tel. 599/4–63295. Open weekdays 8–5. Call first to see if anyone's around.*

Saba Deep (tel. 599/4–63347) and Sea Saba (tel. 599/4–62246) will take you to explore Saba's 25 dive spots. Both offer rental equipment and certified instructors, as well as hotel-dive packages. For inquiries from the United States, direct dial 599/4–63347. Sea Saba's Joan Bourque, whose accomplished photographs are displayed at island galleries, also offers underwater photography lessons. **Wilson's Diving** (tel. 599/4–63410) in Fort Bay specializes in shorter dive trips for visitors over from St. Maarten for the day.

A single-tank excursion costs $45 per person. You can save about $50 weekly if you book a dive package, which includes daily round-trip transportation from your lodgings.

Shopping

Gift Ideas The island's most popular purchases are Saba lace and Saba Spice. Every weekday Saban ladies display and sell their creations at the Community Center in Hell's Gate. Many also sell their wares from their houses; just follow the signs. Collars, tea towels, napkins, purses, and other small items are relatively inexpensive, ranging from $8–$20, but larger items, such as tablecloths, can be pricey. You should also know that the fabric requires some care—it is not drip-dry. Saba Spice may *sound* as delicate as Saba lace, and the aroma is as sweet as can be. However, the base for the liqueur is 151-proof rum, and all the rest is window dressing.

Shops Saba's famed souvenirs can be found in almost every shop. For good buys in local watercolors and fabrics in Windwardside, stop in at **Saba Tropical Arts, The Square Nickel, Island Craft Shop, Piggy's Boutique, Lynn's Gallery,** and the **Breadfruit Gallery** downstairs from the Tourist Office. Ruth Buchanan's especially lovely clothing designs are available at local galleries and at her own **Weaver's Cottage.** In The Bottom, the **Saba Artisan Foundation** (tel. 599/4–63260) turns out hand-screened fabrics that you can buy by the yard or already made into resort clothing for men, women, and children. Look also for the superlative *Saban Cottages: A Book of Watercolors,* sold at the Tourist Office and several stores.

Dining

In most of Saba's restaurants you pretty much have to take potluck. If you don't like what's cooking in one place, you can check out the other restaurants. However, it won't take you long to run out of options, and nowhere will you find gourmet-style cooking.

The markets carry a limited selection of canned goods, produce, and toiletries. Best are **Saba Drug and Superette** (Windwardside) and **My Store** (The Bottom). There are daily fresh produce markets at The Bottom and the Agricultural Garden in Booby Hill. You'll also find posted flyers advertising everything from freshly baked bread to frozen fish fillets. The **Corner Deli and Gourmet Shop** (Windwardside) is *the* place to pick up tasty picnic provisions, with a sophisticated selection of fresh salads, breads, roast chicken, and charcuterie.

Unless stated otherwise, restaurants listed below do not require reservations; dress is always casual. Highly recommended restaurants are indicated by a star ★.

Category	Cost*
Moderate	$20–$25
Inexpensive	$10–$20
Budget	under $10

per person, excluding drinks and service

★ **Captain's Quarters.** Dining is comfortable on a cool porch surrounded by flowers and mango trees. New chef Manuela's cuisine artfully blends Dutch, Indonesian, French, and Creole influences. Examples include *Kapucijners,* a classic Dutch meat and bean stew served with cole slaw, pickles, cucumbers, bacon, and onions; and *nasi goreng* (Indonesian fried rice). The fish (whatever's fresh that day) is prepared with a variety of sauces, including lime butter. Her $18 three-course Saba menu and $20 chef's menu are wonderful bargains. *Windwardside, tel. 599/4–62201. Reservations advised. AE, MC, V. Closed Sept. Moderate.*

Brigadoon Restaurant. From the first floor of a colonial building, one can enjoy the street scene passing before this new, open-front restaurant. Fresh fish grilled and with a light Creole sauce is the specialty, but there are also chicken and steak dishes, lobster, and flavorful creations such as shrimp encrusted with salt and pepper. Sandwiches provide a light snack. *Windwardside, tel. 599/4–62380. AE, D, MC, V. Closed lunch. Moderate.*

Lollipop's. Lollipop is the affectionate nickname for owner Carmen, celebrated for her "sweet" disposition. The outdoor terrace, with stonework and a charming aqua-and-white trellis, is a tranquil place to sample her fine land crab, goat, and fresh grilled fish. *St. John's, tel. 599/4–63330. No credit cards. Inexpensive–Moderate.*

Scout's Place. Here Diana Medero cooks up her version of chicken cordon bleu, braised steak with mushrooms, and curried goat. You can also opt simply to order a sandwich—the crab is best. Wednesday breakfast serves as the unofficial town meeting for expatriate locals, offering the visitor a slice of Saba life. *Windwardside, tel. 599/4–62295. Reservations advised. Dinner starts at 7:30. MC, V. Inexpensive–Moderate.*

Saba Chinese Bar & Restaurant. This restaurant is a plain house with plastic tablecloths where you can get, among other things, sweet-and-sour pork or chicken, cashew chicken, and some curried dishes. *Windwardside, tel. 599/4–62268. Reservations advised. No credit cards. Closed Mon. Inexpensive.*

★ **The Serving Spoon.** Queenie Simmons's sky-blue house adjoins the eight-table restaurant, where plates come heaped with huge portions. Stop by and ask her what she's preparing for the day. It might be meatballs with rice, baked onion chicken, or curried goat with butter. Eighteen dollars (you can haggle) buys all you can eat and then some. *The Bottom, tel. 599/4–63225. Reservations required. No credit cards. No lunch. Inexpensive.*

Lime Time Bar and Restaurant. It's a little ramshackle, but a classic Caribbean hangout, with pool table, peeling paint, mouth-watering Creole food (goat stew, curried fish), and live music weekends. *The Bottom, tel. 599/4–63351. No credit cards. Budget–Inexpensive.*

Sunset Bar & Restaurant. Artificial flowers and colorful place mats brighten this humble, homey place. Authentic Creole food includes heavenly johnnycakes, bread-tart pudding, and lip-smacking ribs. *The Bottom, tel. 599/4–63332. No credit cards. Budget–Inexpensive.*

Guido's Pizzeria. You'll find pizza with several toppings at this pleasant, cool spot, as well as burgers and fish-and-chips. *Windwardside, tel. 599/4–62230. No credit cards. Budget.*

In Two Deep. This delightful lunch spot, with its stained glass window and mahogany bar, is run by the owners of Saba Deep. Here you can sample excellent soups, sandwiches (especially the reuben), and smoothies (try the lemon pucker). The bar is plastered with humorous sayings, and customers seem equally high-spirited. *Fort Bay, tel. 599/4–63347. No credit cards. No dinner. Budget.*

Tropics. This new poolside café across the street from Juliana's offers great views of the Caribbean. This is a place for snacks—sandwiches and burgers—rather than full meals. *Windwardside, tel. 599/4–62469. No credit cards. Budget.*

Lodging

Like everything else on Saba, the guest houses are tiny and tucked into tropical gardens. The selection is limited, and because most restaurants are located in the guest houses, you should take advantage of meal plans, available for about $30 a person above standard room rates. Accommodations are reasonably priced. All are located in Windwardside or The Bottom. You'll find that most of your fellow guests are young, laid-back Europeans "doing the Caribbean."

Highly recommended lodgings are indicated by a star ★.

Category	Cost*
Moderate	$75–$100
Inexpensive	$50–$75
Budget	under $50

All prices are for a standard double room for two, excluding 5% tax and a 10%–15% service charge. To estimate rates for hotels offering MAP, add about $30 per person per day to the above rates.

Hotels **Juliana's Apartments.** Mrs. Juliana Johnson offers eight comfortable, tidy studios and a 2¹/₂-room apartment with private bath, balcony, kitchenette, living/dining room, bedroom, and a large porch facing the sea. The decor is best described as motel modern, with rustic touches and earth tones. Across the street is a pool and a café, Tropics, for breakfast and light meals. *Windwardside, tel. 599/4–62269; in the United States, 800/223–9815; in Canada, 800/468–0023. 8 rooms, 1 1-bedroom apartment. Facilities: pool, restaurant. AE, MC, V. EP. Moderate.*

★ **Scout's Place.** Billed as "Bed 'n Board, Cheap 'n Cheerful," Scout's Place is near the post office and within walking distance of Sea Saba Dive Center. Ten new rooms, all with four-poster beds, reproductions of antiques, private balconies, and private baths with hot water, have been added to the original four plain rooms, which have *no* hot water. *Windwardside, tel. 599/4–62205. 14 rooms, 12 with private bath. Facilities: restaurant, pool, bar, gift shop. D, MC, V. EP, MAP. Moderate.*

Cranston's Antique Inn. The six cozy rooms (only one with private bath) are popular with the surfing set. Most rooms have four-poster beds and elegant hardwood floors. The pool bar has live music some weekends. *The Bottom, tel. 599/4–63203. 6 rooms, 1 with private bath. Facilities: pool, bar, restaurant. No credit cards. EP. Inexpensive.*

Apartment Rentals More than 20 apartments and wood cottages, all with hot water and modern conveniences, are available for weekly and monthly rentals. For listings, check with the Saba Tourist Office (*see* Important Addresses, *above*) or with Medhurst Associates (*see* Tourist Information, *above*). Most of these are pleasant and well-maintained. The most expensive properties, located in the hills outside the towns, boast spectacular ocean views and luxurious settings; these cost $100–$175 a night for two people. Three- and four-bedroom cottages with pools are around $250–$275 a night for three or four couples. Units in Windwardside and The Bottom range from $40–$90 a night.

Off-Season Bets The charming **Captain's Quarters** (Windwardside, tel. 599/4–62201 or 800/468–0023) is Saba's most elegant hostelry, brimming with lace and Victorian furnishings. During low season, rates drop to $100 a night for a double.

The Arts and Nightlife

Guido's Pizzeria (Windwardside, tel. 599/4–62330) is transformed into the Mountain High Club and Disco, on Saturday night, and you can dance till 2 AM on Sunday. Do the nightclub scene at **The Lime Tree Bar & Restaurant** (The Bottom, tel. 599/4–63256) and the **Birds of Paradise, aka The Cozy Corner Club** (The Bottom, tel. 599/4–62240), or just hang out at **Scout's Place** or the **Captain's Quarters.** Consult the bulletin board in each village for a listing of the week's events.

19 St. Barthélemy

Updated by
Jordan Simon

Scale is a big part of St. Barthélemy's charm: a lilliputian harbor; red-roof bungalows dotting the hillsides; minimokes—really glorified golf carts—buzzing up narrow roads or through the neat-as-a-pin streets of Gustavia; and exquisite coves and beaches, most undeveloped, all with pristine stretches of white sand. Just 8 square miles, St. Barts is for people who like things small and perfectly done. It's for Francophiles, too. The French cuisine here is tops in the Caribbean, and gourmet lunches and dinners are rallying points of island life. A French *savoir vivre* pervades, and the island is definitely for the style-conscious—casual but always chic. This is no place for the beach-bum set.

Nor is St. Barts, generally, a destination for the budget-minded. Development has largely been in luxury lodgings and gourmet restaurants, and, with the decline in the dollar, island-wide prices have increased sharply in recent years. There is no public transportation on St. Barts, so getting anywhere other than on foot isn't cheap either. If you're on a budget, but are determined to come to St. Barts, there are ways to save. What you have to remember, however, is that *affordable* here is a relative term. It could mean spending $150 a night for a no-frills hotel, or sharing a modest villa ($1,000–$2,000 a week) with another couple and using minimokes to get to the beach. You can definitely save money by cooking at home, restricting yourself to the occasional splurge meal (well worth it on St. Barts).

Longtime visitors speak wistfully of the old, quiet St. Barts. While development *has* quickened the pace, the island has not been overrun with prefab condos or glitzy resorts. The largest

St. Barthélemy

Ile Chevreau

Pte. à Colombier

Colombier

La Petite Anse

Flamands

36 — 39

Anse à Galets

40

Anse de Petit Jean

41

Colombier

35

Anse de Cayes

4 St. Jean

28 — 34

Corossol

2

42

Baie de St. Jean

Corossol Beach

Public Beach

St. Jean Airport

Les Islettes La Baleine

TO ST. MARTIN

Les Saintes

Gustavia

1

8 — 15

Petit Anse de Galet

Lurin

16

17

Morn

Caribbean Sea

Anse du Gouverneu

Grande Pt.

KEY

Ferry

Beach

1 Exploring Sites

8 Hotels and Restaurants

TO ILE FRÉGATE

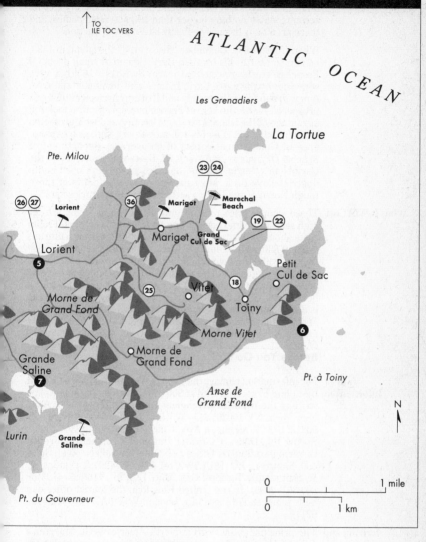

ATLANTIC OCEAN

Les Grenadiers

La Tortue

Pte. Milou

Lorient

Marigot

Marechal
Beach

Lorient

Marigot

Grand
Cul de Sac

Petit
Cul de Sac

Morne de
Grand Fond

Vitet

Toiny

Grande
Saline

Morne Vitet

Morne de
Grand Fond

Pt. à Toiny

Anse de
Grand Fond

Lurin

Grande
Saline

N

Pt. du Gouverneur

0   1 mile

0   1 km

Lodging

Auberge de la
Petite Anse, **40**

Baie des Anges, **37**

Baie des Flamands, **38**

Castelets, **17**

Grand Cul de Sac
Beach Hotel/St.
Barths Beach
Hotel, **22**

Hostellerie des Trois
Forces, **25**

La Normandie, **26**

Le P'tit Morne, **41**

Les Mouettes, **27**

Marigot Bay Club, **23**

Presqu'ile, **14**

Sea Horse Club, **24**

Sunset Hotel, **15**

Tropical Hotel, **31**

Village St. Jean, **34**

White Sand Beach
Cottages, **39**

hotel has only 76 rooms, and the remaining 650 rooms are scattered in cottages and villas around the island. The tiny airport accommodates nothing bigger than 19-passenger planes, and there aren't any casinos or flashy late-night attractions.

When Christopher Columbus "discovered" the island in 1493, he named it after his brother, Bartholomeo. A small group of French colonists arrived from nearby St. Kitts in 1656 but were wiped out by the fierce Carib Indians who dominated the area. A new group from Normandy and Brittany arrived in 1694 and prospered—with the help of French buccaneers, who took full advantage of the island's strategic location and well-protected harbor. Today the island is still a free port, and, as a dependency of Guadeloupe, is part of an overseas department of France. Dry, sunny, and stony, St. Barts was never one of the Caribbean's "sugar islands" and thus never developed an industrial slave base. Most natives are descendants of those tough Norman and Breton settlers of three centuries ago.

What It Will Cost These sample prices, meant only as a general guide, are for high season. An inexpensive one-bedroom villa or a hotel room costs about $175 a night. Dinner at an inexpensive restaurant is about $30; a snack lunch, $8–$10. Groceries to cook a dinner for two will run about $25; a bottle of wine, such as a vin du pays or beaujolais, will be around $10. A rum punch or cocktail at a restaurant is around $4; a glass of wine, about $3; and a beer, $2.50. Taxi fare between Gustavia and major beach areas is about $10, up to $15 from the airport to the farthest hotel. Jeep or minimoke rental is $40–$45 a day. A single-tank dive averages $55; snorkel equipment rents for about $12 a day.

Before You Go

Tourist Information For information contact the **French West Indies Tourist Board** by calling France-on-Call at 900/990–0040 (50¢ per minute) or write to the **French Government Tourist Office** (610 5th Ave., New York, NY 10020; 9454 Wilshire Blvd., Beverly Hills, CA 90212; 645 N. Michigan Ave., Chicago, IL 60611; 2305 Cedar Spring Rd., Dallas TX 75201). In Canada, contact the French Government Tourist Office (1981 McGill College Ave., Suite 490, Montreal, P.Q. H3A 2W9, tel. 514/288–4264; 1 Dundas St. W, Suite 2405, Toronto, Ont. M5G 1Z3, tel. 416/593–4723 or 800/361–9099). In the United Kingdom, the tourist office can be reached at 178 Piccadilly, London W1V 0AL (tel. 071/499–6911).

Arriving and Departing
By Plane The principal gateway from North America is St. Maarten's Juliana Airport, where several times a day you can catch a 10-minute flight to St. Barts on either **Windward Islands Airways** (tel. 590/27–61–01) or **Air St. Barthélemy** (tel. 590/27–71–90). **Air Guadeloupe** (tel. 590/27–61–90) and Air St. Barthélemy offer daily service from Espérance Airport in St. Martin, the French side of the same island. Air Guadeloupe also has direct flights to St. Barts from Guadeloupe, Antigua, and San Juan, while **Virgin Air** (tel. 590/27–71–76) operates daily flights between St. Barts and both St. Thomas and San Juan. Reconfirmation on all return interisland flights, even during off-peak seasons, is strongly recommended. Windward, Air St. Barthélemy, and Virgin Air also offer charter service.

From the Airport Airport taxi service costs $5 to $15 (to the farthest hotel). Since the cabs are unmetered, you may be charged more if you make stops on the way. Cabs meet all flights, and a taxi dispatcher (tel. 590/37–66–31) operates from 8:30 AM until the last flight of the day arrives. Several major car rental companies have airport desks. Few affordable hotels offer complimentary transfers, but by all means inquire when booking.

By Boat Catamarans leave Philipsburg in St. Maarten at 9 AM daily, arriving in Gustavia's harbor around 11 AM. These are one-day, round-trip excursions (about $50, including open bar), with departures from St. Barts at 3:30 PM. If there's room, one-way passengers ($25) are often taken as well. Contact **Bobby's Marina** in Philipsburg (tel. 599/5–23170) for reservations. *St. Barth Express,* a 12-seat open powerboat, and *La Dame du Coeur* leave Gustavia at 7:30 AM and 3:30 PM on a varying daily schedule. The crossing to Marigot, St. Martin, takes one hour. The boat departs from Marigot at 9 AM and 3:45 PM on the same varying schedule and goes directly to St. Barts. One-way fare is $30. The **Yacht Charter Agency** (tel. 590/27–62–38) in Gustavia handles reservations. The *Princess* motorboat makes the same run every Wednesday; book through **La Marine Service** (tel. 590/27–70–34) in Gustavia.

Passports and Visas U.S. and Canadian citizens need either a passport (one that expired no more than five years ago will suffice) or other proof of citizenship, such as a notarized birth certificate with a raised seal or a voter registration card, both accompanied by photo identification. A visa is required for stays of more than three months. British citizens need a valid passport.

Language French is the official language, though a Norman dialect is spoken by some longtime islanders. Most hotel and restaurant employees speak English.

Precautions Roads are narrow and sometimes very steep, so check the brakes and gears of your rental car *before* you leave the lot. Some hillside restaurants and hotels require a bit of uphill walking, so, inquire ahead.

Staying in St. Barthélemy

Important Addresses **Tourist Information:** The **Office du Tourisme** (tel. 590/27–87–27) is open weekdays 8:30–12:30 and 2–6. The office is closed on weekends and Wednesday afternoons.

Emergencies **Hospitals: Gustavia Clinic** (tel. 590/27–60–35 or 590/27–60–00) is on the corner of rue Jean Bart and rue Sadi Carnot. For the doctor on call, dial 590/27–76–03. **Pharmacies:** There is a pharmacy in Gustavia on rue de la République (tel. 590/27–61–82), and one in St. Jean (tel. 590/27–66–61).

Currency The French franc is legal tender. At press time, the exchange rate was 5.3F to U.S.$1. U.S. dollars are accepted everywhere; credit cards are accepted at most shops, hotels, and restaurants. Note: Prices quoted here are in U.S. dollars unless indicated otherwise.

Taxes and Service Charges A 16F departure tax is charged regardless of where you're heading. Some hotels add a 10%–15% service charge to bills; others include it in their tariffs. All restaurants are required to include a 15% service charge in their published prices. It is especially important to remember this when your credit-card receipt is presented to be signed with the tip space blank, or you could end up paying a 30% service charge. Most taxi drivers own their vehicles and do not expect a tip.

Getting Around A car is not a necessity if you're staying on the water, although
Taxis you'll find a vehicle gives you freedom for beach-hopping. If you're staying in the hills, you'll have to have a car. The small hotels do not offer shuttle service (unless you befriend the staff). Hitchhiking is safe but fairly uncommon, and there's no public transportation.

You may arrange cab service by calling 590/27–66–32, 590/27–60–59, or 590/27–63–12. Note: Fares are 50% higher from 8 PM to 6 AM and on Sundays and holidays. Fares average $10 between Gustavia and major beach areas.

Rental Cars The island's steep, curvy roads require careful driving. Check the rental car's brakes before you drive away. Jeeps, sturdier than the chic but rickety minimokes, are preferable. **Avis** (tel. 590/27–71–43), **Budget** (tel. 590/27–67–43), and **Europcar** (tel. 590/27–73–33) are represented at the airport, among others. Check with several of the rental counters for the best price. **Mathew Aubin** (tel. 590/27–73–03) often has special discounts. All accept credit cards. You must have a valid driver's license, and in high season there may be a three-day minimum. Suzuki Jeeps, open-sided Gurgels (VW Jeep), and minimokes—all with stick shift only—rent in season for $40–$45 a day, with unlimited mileage and limited collision insurance. Car-rental reservations are advised, especially during February and around Christmas. Some hotels have their own car fleets; reserve one when you book. Many hotels offer 24-hour emergency road service, which most rental companies do not.

Motorbikes These rent for about $25 per day and require a $100 deposit. Call **Rent Some Fun** (tel. 590/27–70–59). Two people can ride one motorbike, but rental companies discourage this.

Telephones To phone St. Barts from the United States, dial 011–590 and
and Mail the local number. To call the United States from St. Barts, dial 19–1, the area code, and the local number. For St. Martin, dial 3 and the number. For local information, dial 12. Public telephones do not accept coins; they accept Telecartes, a type of prepaid credit card that you can purchase from the post offices at Lorient and Gustavia, as well as at the gas station next to the airport. Making an international call with a Telecarte is less expensive than making the call from your hotel. You can purchase Telecartes in amounts from 31F to 93F.

Mail is slow. It can take up to three weeks for correspondence between the United States and the island. Post offices are in Gustavia and Lorient. It costs 3.10F to mail a postcard to the United States, 3.90F to mail a letter.

Opening and Businesses and offices close from noon to 2 during the week
Closing Times and all day Sunday. Shops in Gustavia are open weekdays 8:30–noon and 2–5, and until noon on Saturday. Shops across from the airport and in St. Jean also open on Saturday afternoons and until 7 PM on weekdays. The banks are open weekdays 8–noon and 2–3:30.

Guided Tours Tours are by minibus or taxi. An hour-long tour costs about $40 for up to three people and $50 for up to eight people. A five-hour island tour costs about $100 per vehicle. Itineraries are negotiable; other officially recommended tours (of 45 and 90 minutes) are available. Tours can be arranged at hotel desks, through the Tourist Office, or by calling any of the island's taxi operators, including **Hugo Cagan** (tel. 590/27–61–28) and **Florian La Place** (Taxi Drivers Group, tel. 590/27–63–58). If you don't speak French, be sure to request a driver whose English is good.

Exploring St. Barthélemy

Numbers in the margin correspond to points of interest on the St. Barthélemy map.

You're best off renting a car if you want to explore the island at your own pace. Those staying on or near a major beach, who won't need a car to get to the water, may opt for a guided half-day tour as an introduction to the island's charms.

Gustavia and the West ❶ With just a few streets on three sides of its tiny harbor, **Gustavia** is easily explored in a two-hour stroll, including time to browse through shops or visit a café. This will leave you the rest of the afternoon for a trip to the west coast to enjoy a picnic and a swim.

Park your car harborside on the rue de la République, where flashy catamarans, yachts, and sailboats are moored, then head to the **Tourist Office** right on the pier. Here you should pick up an island map and a free copy of *St. Barth Magazine,* a monthly publication on island happenings. Then settle in at either **Bar de l'Oubli** or **Gustavia's Le Select** (*see* Nightlife, *below*), two cafés at the corner of rue de la France and rue de la République, for coffee and croissants and a quick leaf through the listings of the week's events.

As you stroll through the little streets, you will notice that plaques sometimes spell out names in both French and Swedish, a reminder of the days when the island was a Swedish colony. You'll see ultrachic boutiques along **rue du Roi Oscar II** and **rue du Général de Gaulle**.

Enjoy the colorful spectacle of the local **market,** where ladies from Guadeloupe and Dominica preside over their tropical fruit and vegetable arrangements. And if you feel like a swim, drive around the end of the harbor to **Petit Anse de Galet.** This quiet little *plage* is also called Shell Beach after the tiny shells heaped ankle-deep in some places.

On the other side of the harbor, at the point, the new **Municipal Museum** details the island's history. *No phone. Admission: 10F. Open weekdays 8–noon and 1:30–5:50, Sat. 8:30–noon, closed Sun.*

Head south back the way you came and turn off at the sign for Lurin. The views up the winding road overlooking the harbor are spectacular. After about five minutes, look for a sign to Plage du Gouverneur. A small rocky route off to the right will take you bumping and grinding down a steep incline to **Anse du Gouverneur,** one of St. Barts's most beautiful beaches, where pirate's treasure is said to be buried. If the weather is clear, you will be able to see the islands of Saba, St. Eustatius, and St. Kitts.

Corossol and Flamands ❷ Starting at the intersection on the hilltop overlooking the airport (known as Tourmente), take the road to Public Beach and on to **Corossol,** a two-street fishing village with a little beach. Corossol is where the island's French provincial origins are most evident. Residents speak an old Norman dialect, and some of the barefoot older women still wear traditional garb—ankle-length dresses and starched white sunbonnets called *quichenottes* (*kiss-me-not* hats). The women don't like to be photographed, but they're not shy about selling you some of their handmade straw work—handbags, baskets, broad-brim hats, and delicate strings of birds—made from lantania palms. The palms were introduced to the island 100 years ago by fore-sighted Father Morvan, who planted a grove in Corossol and Flamands, thus providing the country folk with a living that is still pursued today. Here, too, is the **Inter Oceans Museum** (tel. 590/27–62–97), with a small but excellent collection of marine shells from around the world. *Tel. 590/27–62–97. Admission: 20F. Open daily 10–5.*

❸ From Corossol, head down the main road about a mile to **Anse des Flamands,** a wide beach with several small hotels, and many rental villas. From here, take a brisk hike to the top of what is believed to be the now-extinct volcano that gave birth to St. Barts. From the peak you can take in the gorgeous view of the islands.

A drive to the end of Flamands Road brings you to a rocky footpath that leads to the island's most remote beach, **Anse de Colombier.** It's a 30-minute hike down the footpath to reach the beach.

St. Jean, Grand Cul de Sac, Saline **❹** Brimming with bungalows, bistros, sunbathers, and windsurfing sails, the half-mile crescent of sand at **St. Jean** is the island's most famous beach. Lunch at a beachside bistro, such as **Chez Francine** (*see* Dining, *below*), perhaps interrupted by a swim in the surf, is de rigueur, followed by a stroll through nearby boutiques.

❺ Leaving St. Jean, take the main road to **Lorient.** On your left are the royal palms and rolling waves of Lorient Beach. Lorient, site of the first French settlement, is one of the island's two parishes, and a newly restored church, historic headstones, a school, post office, and gas station mark the spot.

Turn right before the gleaming white Lorient cemetery. In a short while you'll reach a dusty cutoff to your right. The pretty little Creole house on your left is home to Ligne de Cosmetiques M (*see* Shopping, *below*). Behind it is one of St. Barthélemy's treasured secrets, **Le Manoir,** a 1610 Norman manor that was painstakingly disassembled, shipped, and re-constructed in 1984 by the charming Jeanne Audy Rowland in tribute to the island's Viking forebears. The tranquil surround-ing courtyard and garden contain a waterfall and a lily-strewn pool. Mme. Rowland graciously allows visitors; you don't need an appointment, but you do need to speak some French, as Ma-dame speaks little English.

Retrace your route back to Lorient and continue along the coast. Turn left at the Mont Jean sign. Your route rolls around the island's pretty windward coves, past **Pointe Milou,** an ele-gant residential colony, and on to **Marigot,** where you can pick up a bottle of fine wine at **La Cave.** The bargain prices may surprise you (*see* Shopping, *below*).

The winding road passes through the mangroves, ponds, and beach of **Grand Cul de Sac,** where there are plenty of excellent beachside restaurants and water-sports concessions. Over the

❻ hills beyond Grand Cul de Sac is the much photographed **Toiny coast.** Drystone fences crisscross the steep slopes of Morne Vitet along a rocky shoreline that resembles the rugged coast of Normandy. The road turns inland and up the slopes of Morne de Grand Fond. At the first fork (less than a mile), the road to the right leads back to Lorient. A left-hand turn at the next intersection will bring you within a few minutes to a dead end **❼** at **Grande Saline.** Ten years ago the big salt ponds of Grande Saline were shut down after a half-century of operation. The place looks desolate, but climb the short hillock behind the ponds for a surprise—the long arc of **Anse de Grande Saline.**

Beaches

There are nearly 20 *plages* (beaches), each with a distinctive personality and all of them public. Topless sunbathing is common, but nudism is forbidden. St. Jean, Flamands, and Grand Cul de Sac are the liveliest, with the greatest concentration of hotels and activities. Here are the main attractions:

St. Jean is like a mini Côte d'Azur—beachside bistros, bungalow hotels, bronze beauties, and lots of day-trippers. The reef-protected strip is divided by Eden Rock promontory, and there's good snorkeling west of the rock. **Lorient** is popular with St. Barts's families and surfers, who like its rolling waves. **Marigot** is a quiet fishing beach with good snorkeling along the rocky far end. Shallow, reef-protected **Grand Cul de Sac** is especially nice for small children and Windsurfers; it has excellent lunch spots and lots of pelicans. Around the point, next to the Guanahani Hotel, is tiny **Marechal Beach,** which offers some of the best snorkeling on the island. Secluded **Grande Saline,** with its sandy ocean bottom, is just about everyone's favorite beach and is great for swimmers. Despite the law, young and old alike go nude on this beach. It can get windy here, so go on a calm day. **Anse du Gouverneur** is even more secluded and equally beautiful, with good snorkeling and views of St. Kitts, Saba, and St. Eustatius. A five-minute walk from Gustavia is **Petit Anse de Galet,** named after the tiny shells on its shore. Both **Public Beach** and **Corossol Beach** are best for boat- and sunset-watching. The beach at **Colombier** is the least accessible but the most private; you'll have to take either a rocky footpath from La Petite Anse or brave the 30-minute climb down a cacti-bordered trail from the top. **Flamands** is the most beautiful of the hotel beaches—a roomy strip of silken sand. Back toward the airport, the surf at **Anse de Cayes** is rough for swimming, but great for surfing.

Sports and the Outdoors

Boating St. Barts is a popular yachting and sailing center, thanks to its location midway between Antigua and St. Thomas. You can take an hour's cruise on the glass-bottom boat *L'Aquascope* by contacting **Marine Service** (Quai de Yacht Club, Gustavia, tel. 590/27–70–34); cost is $35 a person, $16 children under 12.

Diving and Snorkeling **Marine Service** (tel. 590/27–70–34), operates a PADI diving center, with scuba-diving trips for about $50 per person, gear included. Or try **Club La Bulle** (tel. 590/27–68–93) or PADI-certified **Dive with Dan** (tel. 590/27–64–78). Snorkeling off the beaches here is not wonderful; you might want to consider splurging on a snorkel excursion. These cost around $50 a person (gear, drinks, and snacks usually included). Contact the **Yacht Charter Agency** (tel. 590/27–62–38). A single-tank dive on St. Barts averages $55; snorkel equipment rents for about $12 a day.

Tennis There are two tennis courts at the **Guanahani** (tel. 590/27–66–60), **Le Flamboyant Tennis Club** (tel. 590/27–69–82), and the **Sports Center of Colombier** (tel. 590/27–61–07). The **Manapany** (tel. 590/27–66–55), the **Taiwana** (tel. 590/27–65–01), the **Isle de France** (tel. 590/27–61–81), which also has the island's only squash court, **Les Ilets de la Plage** (tel. 590/27–62–38), and the **St. Barths Beach Hotel** (tel. 590/27–62–73) each have one court. Court fees average $25–$30 an hour for nonguests.

Windsurfing Windsurfing fever is high here. Boards can be rented for about $20 an hour at water-sports centers along St. Jean and Grand Cul de Sac beaches. Lessons are offered for about $40 an hour at **Grand Bay Watersports** (Guanahani, tel. 590/27–66–60), **St. Barth Wind School** (St. Jean, tel. 590/27–70–96), and **Wind Wave Power** (St. Barths Beach Hotel, tel. 590/27–62–73). A new windsurfing school has opened at the **El Sereno Beach Hotel** (tel. 590/27–64–80) on Grand Cul de Sac Bay.

Shopping

Befitting St. Barts's chic reputation, you'll find superb duty-free items here, but few really good buys. Often you can get better prices back home for such items as perfume and designer clothes. The best bargains are crafts such as straw work and pottery.

Shopping Areas Shops are clustered in **Gustavia, St. Jean's Commercial Center,** and the **Villa Creole,** a cottage complex also in St. Jean. More shops are located across from the airport at **La Savane Commercial Center.**

Good Buys Stop in Corossol to pick up some of the intricate straw work
Island Crafts (wide-brim beach hats, mobiles, handbags) that the ladies of Corossol create by hand. They practice the even finer art of haggling: Expect to pay at least $25 per item. For a very special kind of basket, visit **René Brin,** the last practitioner of a dying art form. His beautiful and sturdy fishermen's baskets each take three weeks to make and will last 30 years. For directions to his house/workshop in Lurin, contact Elise Magras at the Tourist Information Center (tel. 590/27–87–27). In Gustavia, look for hand-turned pottery at **St. Barth's Pottery** (tel. 590/27–62–74) and exotic coral and shark's tooth and shell jewelry at the **Shell Shop** (no phone). Superb local skin care products are available at **Ligne de Cosmetiques M** (tel. 590/27–82–63).

Wine and The island's wine shops stock an excellent selection of French
Gourmet Shops wines for under $20, including many Bordeaux petit châteaux and good, solid Burgundy and Loire labels. Values are comparable to discount shops stateside. Wine lovers will especially enjoy **La Cave** (Marigot, tel. 590/27–63–21), where an excellent collection of French vintages is stored in temperature-controlled cellars. Also check out **La Cave du Port Franc** (tel. 590/27–71–75), on the far side of the harbor, for vintage wines and objets d'art. Both offer surprising values. Look for the local Belon's P Punch, which packs a wallop.

For exotic groceries or picnic fixings, stop by St. Barts's fabulous gourmet delis in Gustavia: **La Rotisserie** (tel. 590/27–63–

13) on rue du Roi Oscar II (branches in Villa Creole and Pointe Milou) and **Taste Unlimited** (tel. 590/27–70–42) on rue du Général de Gaulle. In Grand Fond, stop by **La Cuisine à Michel** (no phone), a simple shack doling out delectable $10 take-out meals.

Dining

Dining out is a ritual on St. Barts. The quality of fare is generally high, and so are the prices, which are among the steepest in the Caribbean. The stiff tariffs reflect both the island's culinary reputation and the difficulty of obtaining fresh ingredients. Several top restaurants offer prix-fixe lunch menus that, while less elaborate than dinner, amply display their chefs' culinary expertise. One is the elegant **Carl Gustav** (tel. 590/27-82–83), perched high above Gustavia harbor; the $27 lunch menu costs less than half what you'd pay at dinner. Generally, the island's Italian, Creole, and French/Creole restaurants tend to be less expensive than the French establishments.

If you're renting a villa, you'll save by eating at home. **Le Mono Shop** (Marigot) and **JoJo Alimentation** (Lorient) are small but well-stocked supermarkets with a good selection of produce. **Chez JoJo**, next door to the latter, is a popular burger stand with great fries. For impromptu picnics, you can't do better than **Cuisine à Michel** or the higher-priced **La Rotisserie** (*see* Shopping, *above*). The latter also has a few tables to enjoy fine pizzas and salads for $10–$15.

Accras (salt cod fritters) with Creole sauce (minced hot peppers in oil), spiced christophine (a kind of squash), *boudin Créole* (a very spicy blood sausage), and a lusty *soupe de poissons* (fish soup) are some of the delicious and ubiquitous Creole dishes.

Dress code is for the most part casual, although long pants for men and a skirt or dress for women are usually *de rigueur* in the tonier spots. Some restaurants close in September and October, so call ahead. Highly recommended restaurants are indicated by a star ★.

Category	Cost*
Moderate	$30–$45
Inexpensive	$20–$30
Budget	under $20

per person, excluding drinks, service, and sales tax (4%)

Chez Pompi. This delightful cottage, located on the road to Toiny, might have sprung from a Cézanne canvas. Pompi (a.k.a. Louis Ledée) is an artist of some repute whose naive artworks clutter the walls of his tiny studio. You can browse and chat with M. Pompi while enjoying his fine Creole and country French cuisine. Daily specials might include stewed chicken or boeuf bourguignonne. *Petit Cul de Sac, tel. 590/27–75–67. No credit cards. Closed Sun. Moderate.*

★ **Eddy's Ghetto.** The combination of imaginatively prepared, modestly priced fare—crab salad, ragoût of beef, crème caramel—served in a disarmingly fun-loving atmosphere made this restaurant into an instant success when it opened a few years ago. The crowd is lively, the wine list impressive. *Gustavia, just off rue du Général de Gaulle. No phone. Reservations requested. No credit cards. Moderate.*

La Frégate. Solange Greaux is the charming hostess, Thierry and Jean-Pierre the inventive chefs at this casual restaurant decorated with nautical paraphernalia. You may order something from the grill (selecting one of 11 sauces) or opt for the fine regular menu. There are also two reasonable set-priced Creole menus. *Anse des Flamands, tel. 590/27–64–85. Reservations advised. MC, V. Moderate.*

★ **La Toque Lyonnaise.** In pleasant outdoor dining at Grand Cul de Sac, chef Michel Fredric creates a three-course *menu de dégustation* for 240F. This price includes service, which means it just makes it into our Moderate price category (à la carte is more). In fact, personable owner Marc Llepez is committed to keeping prices down and plans to open an adjoining, more casual eatery. If you're going to splurge, this is the place to do it. The chef has quickly learned to adapt classical recipes to the sultry surroundings. Courses vary, but a popular menu starts with a roquefort terrine with pears poached in Sauternes, followed by a salmon steak in "passion" sabayon, then a superb cinnamon apple tart. *El Sereno Beach Hotel, Grand Cul de Sac, tel. 590/27–64–80. Reservations advised. AE, DC, MC, V. Dinner only. Moderate.*

★ **Le Patio.** Gourmet pizzas, salads, pastas, brochettes, and hamburgers are offered for lunch. In the evening there's all that, plus fancier Italian fare—all reasonably priced, especially the homemade pasta. You'll like the breezy outdoor and indoor dining rooms, the views of the bay, and the friendly family service. *St. Jean, tel. 590/27–61–39. MC, V. Closed Wed. Moderate.*

Le Pelican. Energetic Gilbert has one of the most deservedly popular seashore restaurants for lunch. At picnic tables under awnings, start with baby shrimp in avocado and follow it with the local grilled fish or chicken brochettes. For those who like it hot and spicy, be sure to ask for Gilbert's chili sauce. At dinner inside, the menu is more elaborate and expensive (still affordable with careful ordering), with a pianist and chanteuse accompanying your meal. Locals cluster around the piano bar for late-night desserts long after other restaurants have locked their doors. *St. Jean Bay, tel. 590/27–64–64. AE, MC, V. Moderate.*

Marigot Bay Club. Generous portions and consistent quality help make this 16-table beachside place a favored lunch and dinner spot. Lightly spiced Creole dishes and simple fish and seafood entrées are featured, and the friendly owners are always on hand to explain the menu. *Marigot, tel. 590/27–75–45. Reservations required. AE, V. Closed Sun. and lunch Mon. Moderate.*

Maya's. Set right on Public Beach, with sweeping ocean views, this is one of the hippest eateries on the island. The fare is simple but freshly prepared, with only four or five choices per course, such as lobster brochettes or curried chicken. There's no prix-fixe menu, but only the lobster or shrimp are out of our price range. The scrumptious cakes and pies are baked on the premises. The schizophrenic service can move from haughty to harried to helpful all in one evening. *Public Beach, tel. 590/27–73–61. Reservations advised. AE, D, MC, V. Moderate.*

New Born. This unadorned but pleasant restaurant offers the closest thing to authentic Creole cooking on St. Barts. The fresh seafood is caught right off the beach, steps away. Mouthwatering accras, turtle steak, salt cod salad, and coconut flan may make up one memorable dinner. *Anse des Cayes, tel. 590/27–67–07. Reservations advised. MC, V. Moderate.*

Gloriette. This beachside bistro serves delicious local dishes such as crunchy accras and grilled red snapper with Creole sauce. Light salads and Creole dishes are served at lunch, and the house wine is always good. *Grand Cul de Sac, tel. 590/27–75–66. No credit cards. Closed Sun. evening. Inexpensive–Moderate.*

La Marine. Mussels from France arrive on Thursday and in-the-know islanders are there to eat them at dockside picnic tables. The menu always includes fresh fish, hamburgers, and omelets. *Rue Jeanne d'Arc, Gustavia, tel. 590/27–70–13. No credit cards. Inexpensive–Moderate.*

★ **Le Rivage.** This popular and very casual Creole establishment on the beach at Grand Cul de Sac serves delicious lobster salad, accras, and fresh grilled fish. The relaxed atmosphere and surprisingly low prices make for a very enjoyable time. *Grand Cul de Sac. tel. 590/27–60–70. AE, MC, V. Closed Thurs. Inexpensive–Moderate.*

★ **L'Escale.** This pretty, cheery, and very popular restaurant is located on the waterfront on the far side of Gustavia's harbor. Chef Eric Dugast cooks up the best pizza on the island, while Pierre Lebrech prepares first-rate filet mignon, seafood, and pastas. Friendly service and low prices are a plus. *Gustavia, tel. 590/27–81–06. MC, V. Closed Tues. Dinner only. Inexpensive–Moderate.*

Chez Francine. Swimsuit-clad patrons lunch on the terrace or at wood tables set in the sand. Fewer day-trippers from St. Martin find their way here than they do to the Pelican, so it is quieter and has better prices. The lunch-only menu features grilled chicken, beef, and lobster, all served with crispy french fries for $15. *St. Jean Bay, tel. 590/27–60–49. MC, V. No dinner. Inexpensive.*

Topolino. Popular with families, Topolino's offerings range from hearty Italian dishes to pizza. Trap your own lobster in the pond. *St. Jean, tel. 590/27–70–92. MC, V. Inexpensive.*

Brasserie La Créole. Good breakfast omelets, croissants, and fresh fruit juices are served at open-air tables at this restaurant in the St. Jean shopping complex. For lunch and dinner there are salads, grilled dishes, and sandwiches. *St. Jean, tel. 590/27–68–09. AE. Budget–Inexpensive.*

Bar de l'Oubli. This strategically located bistro/bar is a favorite watering hole of French expatriates and a great spot for people-watching. Come for delicious breakfast omelets, salads, and *croques monsiers. Gustavia, corner of rues de la France and de la République, no phone. No credit cards. Budget.*

La Luna. This tiny restaurant with terrace is rapidly becoming an early evening hot spot. Locals love the "ambience très sympathique" and the Mexican/Creole fare, including sensational salads. Try the conch or Cannonball (crab, conch, and cheese). *Gustavia, no phone. No credit cards. Budget.*

Le Select/Cheeseburger in Paradise. Located catty-corner from Bar de l'Oubli, this atmospheric spot is popular with a crowd of Americans and nautical types. The bar is decorated with assorted memorabilia, including postcards from exotic ports of call and yellowing magazine covers. Cheeseburger in Paradise, named for the song by honorary St. Barthian Jimmy Buffet, occupies the adjoining garden and serves typical fast-food fare. *Gustavia, corner of rues de la France and de la République, tel. 590/27–86–87. No credit cards. Budget.*

Santa Fe. This hilltop hangout with terrific views is a popular spot for sundowners, sunsets, and the island's best hamburgers. Sunday afternoons find it jammed with Americans and Brits cheering their favorite teams on the closed-circuit TV. *Morne Lurin, tel. 590/27–61–04. No credit cards. Closed Mon. Budget.*

Lodging

Expect to be shocked at accommodation prices here. You pay for the privilege of staying on the island rather than for the hotel. Even at $500 a night, bedrooms tend to be small, but that does not diminish the lure of St. Barts for those who can afford it. Away from the beaches are a number of small hotels and a multitude of rental bungalows that offer less expensive accommodations, though staying at these means you'll need a car to get to the beach. To try for cheaper lodging on or within walking distance of a beach, head for St. Jean. It (and to a lesser extent Flamands and Grand Cul de Sac) offers the greatest variety of accommodations, as well as restaurants, shops, and activities. Unlike some islands, St. Barts has few charming guest houses. It does have villas, however; more modest ones offer a tremendous savings, especially if you're willing to forgo a pool, TV, or ocean view. Most of the top hotels close for a month or two during the off-season, but that shouldn't concern budget travelers: Even the 50% discount these offer when they *are* open during off-season won't bring their rates below astronomical. Most hotels here offer CP or EP, with MAP sometimes available.

Highly recommended lodgings are indicated by a star ★.

Category	Cost*
Moderate	$175–$225
Inexpensive	$125–$175
Budget	under $125

*All prices are for a standard double room for two, excluding a 10%–15% service charge; there is no government room tax. To estimate rates for hotels offering MAP, add about $50–$60 per person per day to the above price ranges.

Hotels **Baie des Anges.** Units in these low-slung coral and white cottages fronting Flamands Beach are simply but pleasantly appointed, with rattan furniture, air-conditioning, kitchenettes, and shower baths. The pricier moderate rooms open onto the beach; the inexpensive–moderate rooms have partial water views and are only steps from the beach themselves. *Anse de Flamands, tel. 590/27–63–63, fax 590/27–83–44. 9 rooms. Facilities: beach, snack bar. AE, MC, V. EP. Inexpensive–Moderate.*

Baie des Flamands. Upper-level rooms have balconies, and lower-level ones have terrace kitchenette units in this recently refurbished motel-style hotel. One of the first hotels on the island, it is still run by a St. Barts family, with a gentle, laid-back island ambience, and is popular with families and tour groups. It has a good restaurant and an outstanding beach location. *Box 68, Anse des Flamands 97133, tel. 590/27–64–85, fax 590/27–83–98. 24 rooms with baths. Facilities: restaurant, bar, saltwater pool, TV/library room, rental cars. AE, MC, V. CP. Moderate.*

Castelets. After a brief stint as the Italian Sapore di Mare, this small retreat has reverted to its original name and French roots. Antiques-furnished rooms are in terraced chalets, with the exception of two in the main house, that are connected by steep paths. The rooms are of varying sizes and prices, but all are affordable with the exception of the two largest villas. The pool is small, but the views from this property, situated atop Morne Lurin, are breathtaking. Since the hotel is inland and off by itself, you will need a car. *Box 60, Morne Lurin 97133, tel. 590/27–61–73 or 800/322–VILLAS, fax 590/27–85–27. 10 rooms, 1 2-bedroom suite. Facilities: restaurant, small pool. AE, MC, V. CP. Moderate.*

Grand Cul De Sac Beach Hotel and **St. Barths Beach Hotel.** These side-by-side properties stretch out on a narrow peninsula between lagoon and sea. Both are comfortable, unpretentious, and popular with families and tour groups, who take advantage of the full range of sports available on the hotels' beach. Upper-level rooms are best at the two-story St. Barths Beach Hotel; the best rooms at Grand Cul de Sac Beach Hotel, a group of small air-conditioned bungalow units with kitchenettes, are right on the beach. The windows are screenless, and if they are left open, mosquitoes can be a problem. There's limited parking for cars not rented through the owner's agency. *Box 81, Grand Cul de Sac 97133, tel. 590/27–62–73, fax 590/27–75–57. 35 rooms; 16 bungalows. Facilities: 2 restaurants, bar, saltwater pool, tennis court, windsurfing school and watersports center, TV/library room, car rental, boutique. AE, MC, V. EP. Moderate.*

Marigot Bay Club. Jean Michel Ledee's pleasant apartments across from his popular seaside restaurant feature comfortable furniture, louvered doors and windows, air-conditioning, twin beds, kitchen/living areas, and large terraces with good views. It's a five- to 10-minute walk to the nearest beach. *Marigot 97133, tel. 590/27–75–45, fax 590/27–70–70. 6 apartments. Facilities: restaurant. AE, V. EP. Moderate.*

Sea Horse Club. Next door to the Marigot Bay Club, this property has suites and a beautifully landscaped garden. All rooms have living room, kitchen, terrace, and shower bath. The beach is within walking distance. *Marigot 97133, tel. 590/27–75–36, fax 590/27–60–52. 11 suites. AE, MC, V. EP. Moderate.*

Tropical Hotel. Up the hill from St. Jean's Beach (a five-minute walk), this cozy gingerbread complex encircles a lush garden and small pool. Air-conditioned rooms have either fresh pastels or sparkling white furnishings with red-tile floors. The ambience is friendly. *Box 147, St. Jean 97133, tel. 590/27–64–87, fax 590/27–81–74. 20 rooms. Facilities: restaurant, reception bungalow with bar and wide-screen video lounge, pool. AE, MC, V. CP. Moderate.*

★ **Village St. Jean.** This stone-and-redwood resort, up a short, steep hill from St. Jean's Beach, is now run by the second generation of the Charneau family. It has acquired a strong following over the years. The accent is on service, privacy, and wholesomeness. There are a variety of accommodations with air-conditioning and fine views of the sea. (The largest units are too expensive.) A patio restaurant serves pizza-type fare by the small new pool. This is a good value. *Box 23, St. Jean 97133, tel. 590/27–61–39, fax 590/27–77–96. 24 rooms. Facilities: restaurant, bar, pool, small grocery, boutique, games room, library. MC, V. EP. Moderate.*

White Sand Beach Cottages. The road in front of the place is a little ramshackle, but these tiny cottages are pleasant, air-conditioned, and well equipped. The cottage on the beach is the best. *Anse des Flamands 97133, tel. 590/27–63–66, fax 590/27–70–69. 4 cottages with kitchenettes. Facilities: sun deck, MC, V. EP. Inexpensive–Moderate.*

★ **Hostellerie des Trois Forces.** This rustic mountaintop inn is an idiosyncratic delight, with rooms charmingly decorated according to astrological color schemes. All feature a minibar, a terrace with ocean view, and air-conditioning or a ceiling fan. Most have four-poster beds. The aroma of a wood-burning fireplace and the tinkle of wind chimes float through the pleasant restaurant. Hubert de la Motte (he's a Gemini, by the way) is the personable owner, who may even arrange a reading for you by one of his psychic friends. You'll want a car: It's a 15-minute drive to the beach. *Morne Vitet, tel. 590/27–61–25, fax 590/27–81–38. 12 rooms. Facilities: restaurant, bar, pool. AE, MC, V. CP. Inexpensive.*

Auberge de la Petite Anse. Minimal decor but comfortable rooms with terraces and air-conditioning are offered in eight bungalows just above the beach, which you reach by a short walk down a rocky path. A grocery, bar, and restaurant are within walking distance. *Box 117, Anse des Flamands, tel. 590/27–64–60. 16 rooms with kitchenettes. AE, V. Budget–Inexpensive.*

La Normandie. This small inn offers reasonably priced rooms, a restaurant, and dancing in the evening on a glass floor set over the pool. Ask for one of the two air-conditioned rooms. You can walk to the beach from here (about 10 minutes). *Lorient 97133, tel. 590/27–61–66, fax 590/27–68–64. 8 rooms. Facilities: pool, restaurant. V. EP. Budget–Inexpensive.*

★ **Le P'tit Morne.** There is good value in these mountainside studios, each with a private balcony, air-conditioning, and panoramic views of the coastline below. A snack bar serving breakfast and light lunches recently opened, but each room has a small kitchenette that is adequate for creating light meals or making picnic lunches. It's relatively isolated here, with the beach a 10-minute drive away. *Box 14, Colombier 97133, tel. 590/27–62–64, fax 590/27–84–63. 14 rooms. Facilities: pool, snack bar, reading room. AE, MC, V. CP. Budget–Inexpensive.*

★ **Les Mouettes.** Good family accommodations are provided in bungalows overlooking the island's best surfing beach. Six separate, spacious bungalows have double beds as well as twin beds or a foldout sofa. Each room has a shower, patio, and kitchenette. *Lorient 97133, tel. 590/27–60–74. 6 rooms. Facilities: car rental. No credit cards. EP. Budget–Inexpensive.*

Presqu'ile. Set on the far side of the Gustavia marina in a slightly dilapidated building, the Presqu'ile has small, basic, and unadorned rooms, but they are clean, with air-conditioning, shower baths, and refrigerators. The brightest rooms are those with a marina view. The beach is a 15- to 20-minute walk away. *Gustavia, tel. 590/27–64–60, fax 590/27–72–30. 14 rooms. Facilities: restaurant. No credit cards. CP. Budget.*

Sunset Hotel. This basic hotel is located on the main drag of Gustavia overlooking the marina. Spartan rooms are clean and have air-conditioning, shower baths, and refrigerators. The smaller rooms have no view, but are quieter. It's a 15–20-minute walk to Shell Beach. *Gustavia, tel. 590/26–77–21, fax 590/27–83–40. 8 rooms. MC, V. CP. Budget.*

Villas, Condos, Apartments For the price of an inexpensive hotel room, you can get your own little cottage, and for the price of a room at an expensive hotel, you'll get a villa with several bedrooms and your own swimming pool. Moreover, the island's restaurants are so expensive that having a kitchen of your own makes sense. What you sacrifice in room service and the amenities of a hotel, you'll gain in privacy, more room, and money saved. Don't forget to factor in the almost always necessary cost of car rental. Villas, apartments, and condos can be rented through **SIBARTH** (tel. 590/27–62–38), which handles about 200 properties. **WIMCO** (tel. 800/932–3222) is the agency's representative in the United States. Rents average $1,000–$2,000 per week for one-bedroom villas, $3,500 for three-bedroom villas, and more for houses with pools. **Villas St. Barts** (tel. 590/27–74–29) has about 100 properties. Manager Joe Ledée speaks English and meets his clients at the airport.

Off-Season Bets As noted above, very few of the expensive properties qualify as Moderate during the off-season, even at 50% reductions. Among the charming hotels whose prices drop sufficiently in low season are the casually chic **El Serena Beach Hotel and Villas** at Grand Cul de Sac Beach (Box 19, Grand Cul de Sac 97133, tel. 590/27–64–80); **Filao Beach** (Box 167, St. Jean 97133, tel. 590/27–64–84), a member of the prestigious Relais et Châteaux group; and the colonial-style **François Plantation** (Colombier 97133, tel. 590/27–78–82), located in the hills above Flamands. Note that many of the top hotels here close in September and October.

Nightlife

St. Barts is a mostly-in-bed-by-midnight island. However, some of the hotels and restaurants provide late-night fun. Cocktail hour finds the barefoot boating set gathered in the garden of **Gustavia's Le Select** (tel. 590/27–86–87); the more sophisticated up at **L'Hibiscus's** (tel. 590/27–64–82) jazz bar; the French at **Bar de l'Oubli** (no phone). Then it's a long, leisurely meal, followed by an after-dinner drink on a breezy terrace—possibly your own. The young and the hip (and all those who go by one name—Liza, Cher, Madonna, and so on) gather after 10 at Gustavia's aptly named **Le Petit Club** (no phone). Locals also flock to **Le Pelican** (tel. 590/27–64–64) and the retro hip **American Bar-Video** (tel. 590/27–86–07) next door to L'Escale. **La Licorne** (no phone), a disco, can be lively on weekends, as can **Club Hurricane** (no phone) in St. Jean.

20 St. Eustatius

*Updated by
Jordan Simon*

The flight approach to the tiny Dutch island of St. Eustatius, commonly known as Statia (pronounced *STAY-sha*) in the Netherlands Antilles, is almost worth the visit itself. The plane circles The Quill, a 1,968-foot-high extinct volcano that encloses a stunning primeval rain forest within its crater. Here you'll find giant elephant ears, ferns, flowers, wild orchids, fruit trees, wildlife, and birds hiding in the trees. The entire island is alive with untended greenery—bougainvillea, oleander, and hibiscus.

Sleepy Statia is one of the few "undiscovered" Caribbean destinations left, which translates into superb bargains. There's no official high season; all but the three priciest properties offer the same year-round rates. You won't find high-rise developments, traffic lights, cruise ships, or package deals (they'd be redundant on a tropical isle whose rates are already a steal). You *will* find splendid hiking and diving, friendly people, and deserted black-sand beaches. Most visitors are content with a day visit from nearby St. Maarten. But should you stay over, you'll discover an unusual island that attracts a funky mix of European expatriates and young Dutch on holiday.

Statia is in the Dutch Windward Triangle, 178 miles east of Puerto Rico and 35 miles south of St. Maarten. Oranjestad, the capital and only "city" (note quotes), is on the western side facing the Caribbean. The island is anchored at the north and the south by extinct volcanoes, like the Quill, that are separated by a central plain. The island is a wonderful playground for hikers and divers. Myriad ancient ships rest on the ocean floor alongside 18th-century warehouses that were slowly buried in the sea by storms.

This 12-square-mile island, past which Columbus sailed in 1493, had prospered almost from the day the Dutch Zeelanders colonized it in 1636. In the 1700s, a double row of warehouses crammed with goods stretched for a mile along the bay, and there were sometimes as many as 200 ships tied up at the duty-free port. The island was called the Emporium of the Western World and Golden Rock. Holland, England, and France fought one another for possession of the island, which changed hands 22 times. In 1816, it became a Dutch possession and has remained so to this day.

During the American Revolution, when the British blockaded the North American coast, food, arms, and other supplies for the revolutionaries were diverted through the West Indies, notably through neutral Statia. On November 16, 1776, the brig-of-war *Andrew Doria*, commanded by Captain Isaiah Robinson of the Continental Navy, sailed into Statia's port flying the Stars and Stripes and fired a 13-gun salute to the Royal Netherlands standard. Governor Johannes de Graaff ordered the cannons of Fort Oranje to return the salute, and that first official acknowledgment of the new American flag by a foreign power earned Statia the nickname "America's Childhood Friend."

What It Will Cost These sample prices, meant only as a general guide, are for high season. An inexpensive efficiency apartment with bath and kitchenette will cost about $50 a day. For a moderately priced dinner, expect to pay about $20; picnic fixings for two are about $10. A glass of wine or a rum punch at a restaurant costs about $2.50; two beers and live music at a local spot will be about $5. Car rental is $40–$45 daily. A taxi from Oranjestad to the Quill is about $10. A single-tank dive ranges from $40 to $50 a person; snorkel equipment rents for about $5.

Before You Go

Tourist Information Contact the **Saba and St. Eustatius Tourist Information Office** (c/o Medhurst & Associates, Inc., 271 Main St., Northport, NY 11768, tel. 516/261–7474 or 800/344–4606), which will advise and reserve guest-house accommodations.

Arriving and Departing
By Plane **Windward Islands Airways** (tel. 599/5–44230 or 599/5–44237) makes the 20-minute flight from St. Maarten four times a day, the 10-minute flight from Saba daily, and the 15-minute flight from St. Kitts daily. **LIAT** (tel. 809/462–0700) has twice-weekly flights from St. Kitts.

From the Airport Planes put down at the **Franklin Delano Roosevelt Airport,** where taxis meet all flights and charge about $4 for the drive into town. There's an Avis outlet at the airport, should you decide to rent a car (*see* Getting Around, *below*).

Passports and Visas All visitors must have proof of citizenship. A passport is preferred, but a birth certificate or voter registration card will do. (A driver's license will *not* do.) British citizens need a valid passport. All visitors need a return or ongoing ticket.

Language Statia's official language is Dutch (it's used on government documents), but everyone speaks English. Dutch is taught as

438

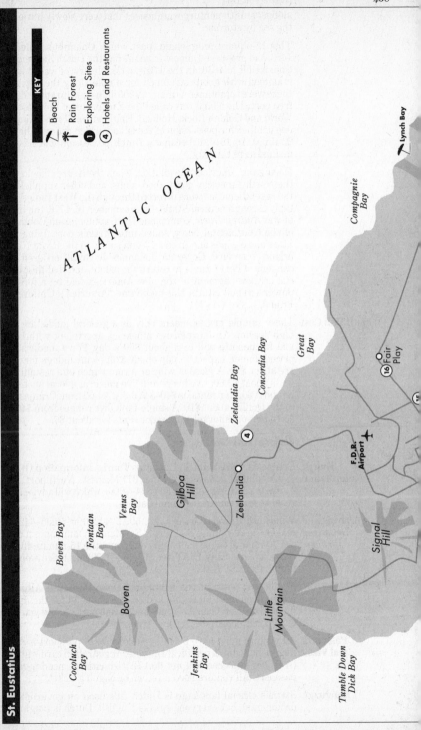

St. Eustatius

ATLANTIC OCEAN

KEY

⌐ Beach
✳ Rain Forest
❶ Exploring Sites
④ Hotels and Restaurants

Boven Bay

Cocoluch Bay

Fontaan Bay

Venus Bay

Boven

Jenkins Bay

Gilboa Hill

Little Mountain

Tumble Down Dick Bay

Signal Hill

Zeelandia

④ Zeelandia Bay

Concordia Bay

Great Bay

F.D.R. Airport ✈

❶⑥ Fair Play

Compagnie Bay

⌐ Lynch Bay

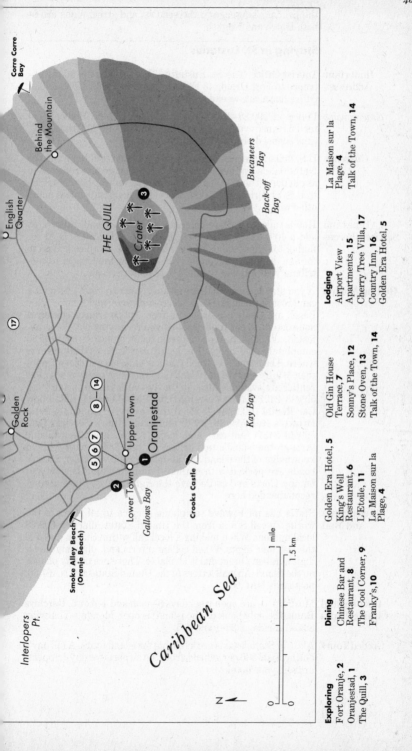

Exploring
Fort Oranje, **2**
Oranjestad, **1**
The Quill, **3**

Dining
Chinese Bar and
Restaurant, **8**
The Cool Corner, **9**
Franky's, **10**
Golden Era Hotel, **5**
King's Well
Restaurant, **6**
L'Etoile, **11**
La Maison sur la
Plage, **4**
Old Gin House
Terrace, **7**
Sonny's Place, **12**
Stone Oven, **13**
Talk of the Town, **14**

Lodging
Airport View
Apartments, **15**
Cherry Tree Villa, **17**
Country Inn, **16**
Golden Era Hotel, **5**
La Maison sur la
Plage, **4**
Talk of the Town, **14**

Interlopers
Pt.

Caribbean Sea

Smoke Alley Beach
(Oranje Beach)

Golden Rock

English Quarter

Behind
the Mountain

Corre Corre
Bay

THE QUILL

Crater

Bucaneers
Bay

Back-off
Bay

Gallows Bay

Lower Town

Upper Town

Oranjestad

Crooks Castle

Kay Bay

0   1 mile
0   1.5 km

N

the primary language in the schools, and street signs are in both Dutch and English.

Staying in St. Eustatius

Important Addresses
Tourist Office: The **St. Eustatius Tourist Office** is at the entrance to Fort Oranje (3 Fort Oranjestraat, tel. 599/38–2433). Office hours are weekdays 8–noon and 1–5.

Emergencies
Police: tel. 599/38–2333. **Hospitals: Queen Beatrix Medical Center** (25 Prinsesweg, tel. 599/38–2211 and 599/38–2371) has a full-time licensed physician on duty.

Currency
U.S. dollars are accepted everywhere, but legal tender is the Netherlands Antilles florin (NAf). Florins are also referred to as guilders. The exchange rate fluctuates but is about NAf 1.80 to U.S. $1. Prices quoted here are in U.S. dollars unless noted otherwise.

Taxes and Service Charges
Hotels collect a 7% government tax. All hotels and restaurants add a 10%–15% service charge. The departure tax is $3 for flights to other islands of the Netherlands Antilles and $5 to foreign destinations. You may be asked at the airport to contribute your leftover guilders to the latest cause.

Getting Around
If you stay in or around Oranjestad, you can get by without a car. Most of the historical sites, restaurants, and Smoke Alley Beach are easily accessible on foot. Public transportation is nonexistent. A car is advisable if you're staying outside Oranjestad, although most people seem to hitchhike (it's considered completely safe here). The hardy can walk virtually everywhere. The island is so small that any taxi ride will cost no more than $10. To explore the island (and there isn't very much), car rentals are available through the **Avis** outlet at the airport (tel. 599/38–2421 and 800/331–1084) for $40–$45 per day. **Rainbow Car Rental** (tel. 599/38–2586) has several Hyundai for rent. **Brown's** (tel. 599/38–2266) and **Lady Ama's Services** (tel. 599/38–2451) rent cars and Jeeps; rentals are also available through the island's taxi drivers. A taxi driver with a broad knowledge of the island and its folklore is Mr. Daniel. Statia's roads are pocked with potholes, and the going is slow and bumpy. Goats and cattle have the right-of-way. Bikes are not recommended here.

Telephones and Mail
Statia has microwave telephone service to all parts of the world. To call Statia from the United States, dial 011–599/38 local number. When making a local call within Statia, just dial the last four digits. When calling interisland, dial only the 4-digit number. Direct dial is available. There are no pay phones on the island. Airmail letters to the United States are NAf 1.30; postcards NAf .60.

Opening and Closing Times
Most offices are open weekdays 8–noon and 1–4 or 5. **Barclays Bank** (the only bank on the island) is open Monday–Thursday 8:30–1, Friday 8:30–1 and 4–5.

Guided Tours
All 10 of Statia's taxis are available for island tours. A full day's outing costs $35 per vehicle, from the airport (for day-trippers) or from your hotel.

Exploring St. Eustatius

Numbers in the margin correspond to points of interest on the St. Eustatius map.

The major—some say only—attractions of Statia are Oranjestad and The Quill. A guided island tour (*see above*) can be accomplished in less than two hours.

Oranjestad Statia's capital and only town, **Oranjestad** sits on the western
❶ coast facing the Caribbean. It's a split-level town: Upper Town and Lower Town. History buffs will enjoy poking around the ancient Dutch Colonial buildings, which are being restored by the Historical Foundation. Both Upper Town and Lower Town are easily explored on foot.

The first stop is the **Tourist Office,** which is right at the entrance to Fort Oranje. You can pick up maps, brochures, and a listing of 12 marked hiking trails. You can also arrange for guides and guided tours.

When you leave the Tourist Office, you will be at the entrance
❷ to **Fort Oranje.** With its three bastions, the fort has clutched these cliffs since 1636. In 1976, Statia participated in the U.S. bicentennial celebration by restoring the old fort, and now gleaming black cannons point out over the ramparts. In the parade grounds a plaque, presented in 1939 by Franklin D. Roosevelt, reads, "Here the sovereignty of the United States of America was first formally acknowledged to a national vessel by a foreign official." A few government offices are within the fort, and restoration continues.

From the fort, cross over to Wilhelminaweg (Wilhelmina Way) in the center of Upper Town. The **St. Eustatius Historical Foundation Museum** is in the Doncker/de Graaff house, a lovely building with slim columns and a high gallery. British Admiral Rodney, who captured Oranjestad and confiscated islanders' possessions in the 18th century, is believed to have lived here. The house, acquired by the foundation in 1983 and completely restored, is Statia's most important intact 18th-century dwelling. Exhibits trace the island's history from the 6th century to the present. The most recent addition is a pre-Columbian annex across the street. Ruins and artifacts of a newly discovered tribe called the Saladoid have been excavated. *12 Van Tonningenweg, tel. 599/38–2288. Admission: $1 adults, 50¢ children. Open weekdays 9–5, weekends 9–noon.*

Return to Fort Oranjestraat (Fort Orange St.) and turn left. Continue to **4 Fort Oranjestraat,** at the corner of Kerkweg (Church Way). The big yellow house, with a stone foundation, shingled walls, and gingerbread trim, is typical of the houses built in the West Indies around the turn of the century. Just behind it is **Three Widows Corner,** a tropical courtyard where you'll see two more examples of Statian architecture in a town house and another gingerbread house.

Now head west down Kerkweg to the edge of the cliff, where you'll find the **Dutch Reformed Church,** built in 1775. Ancient tales can be read on the gravestones in the 18th-century cemetery adjacent to the church.

Continue on Kerkweg and take the next two left turns onto Synagogepad (Synagogue Path) to **Honen Dalim** ("She Who Is

Charitable to the Poor"), one of the Caribbean's oldest syna-
gogues. Dating from 1738, it is now in ruins, but is slated for
restoration.

❸ **The Quill,** the volcanic cone rising in the southern sector, is 3
miles south of Oranjestad on the main road. Most people drive
to the slopes and then park their cars alongside the road; the
main tracks begin from Welfare Road. A variety of trails are
mostly fairly easy, and all afford sensational views of Oranjestad and surrounding Caribbean islands. The truly challenging treks are the Panoramic route surrounding the crater and
those descending into the rain forest itself, a dense wonderland
of exotic vegetation including wild banana and lime trees.

Follow Prinsesweg back to the main square and zigzag down
the cobblestone Fort Road to Lower Town. Most of the 18th-
century warehouses and shops here are in disrepair, but the
restoration of the 18th-century cotton mill on the land side of
Bay Road, now the **Old Gin House Hotel,** is impressive. The
palms, flowering shrubs, and park benches along the water's
edge are the work of the Historical Foundation members.

Beaches

Statia is not an island for beach lovers. Beaches are rather poky
and occasionally rocky. The nicest are on the Atlantic side, but
here the water is generally too rough for swimming. Sand is
mainly black (actually varying shades of gray). It is possible to
hike around the coast at low tide, though a car is recommended
to reach the more remote Atlantic stretches.

Smoke Alley Beach (also called **Oranje Beach**) is the nicest and
most accessible. The beige-and-black-sand beach is on the Caribbean, off Lower Town, and is relatively deserted until late
afternoon, when the locals arrive.

A 30-minute hike down an easy marked trail behind the Mountain Road will bring you to **Corre Corre Bay** and its gold-sand
cove. Two bends north, **Lynch Bay** is somewhat protected from
the wild swells that pound the Atlantic side of the island. Here,
especially around Concordia Bay, the surf is rough and there
is sometimes a dangerous undertow.

Beachcombers enjoy searching for Statia's famed blue glass
beads. Manufactured in the 17th century by the Dutch West
Indies Company, the blue glass beads were traded for rum,
slaves, cotton, and tobacco. They were also awarded to faithful
slaves or included as a part of marriage settlements between
the groom and the bride's father. Try looking after a heavy rain,
but don't be too disappointed if you come up empty-handed.

Sports and the Outdoors

Hiking The big thrill here is The Quill, the 1,968-foot extinct volcano
with its crater full of rain forest. You'll need a guide for descending into the crater (about $20); the Tourist Office has re-
commendations. The office can also supply a map and a list of
marked trails throughout the island. If you're hiking The Quill,
wear layers: It can be cool at the summit and steamy in the
interior. Local boys climb The Quill by torchlight for delectable
sand crabs. You can join them, then ask your hotel to prepare

your catch for dinner. The tourist board can make arrangements.

Scuba Diving If you've never gone to an undersea supermarket, here's your chance. The "supermarket" is actually two parallel shipwrecks less than 50 yards apart and is but one of many wrecks and 18th-century submerged seaports here. **Dive Statia** (tel. 599/38–2435), is a fully equipped dive shop offering certification courses; most of the hotels offer their dive packages with Dive Statia. For single-tank dives (including transportation from your hotel), figure $40–$50, less for a weekly package.

Snorkeling Crooks Castle has several stands of pillar coral, giant yellow sea fans, and sea whips. Jenkins Bay and Venus Bay are other favorites with snorkelers. For equipment rental, contact **Dive Statia** (*see* Scuba Diving, *above*). Daily rates are $5–$10.

Tennis At the **Community Center** there's a lone tennis court that's even lighted at night. It has changing rooms, but you'll have to bring your own rackets and balls. The cost is $2.

Shopping

Shopping on Statia is duty-free and somewhat limited. Barbara Lane shows her own sophisticated ceramic pieces, together with paintings and woven sculptures by local artists, at **The Park Place Gallery** (tel. 599/38–2452) across from the Cool Corner in the center of town. Mazinga Gift Shop on Fort Oranje Straat in Upper Town (tel. 599/38–2245) is a small department store selling jewelry, cosmetics, liquor, beachwear, sports gear, stationery, books, and magazines.

Dining

Just about everything here is affordable, especially local eateries. You'll likely run into the same crowd wherever you go. The variety of cuisines here is unexpected, given the size of the island. Besides the traditional West Indian fare, you can find French and Chinese food. Surprisingly, the island's Dutch heritage is not reflected in the cuisine.

If you'd rather cook in, there are five supermarkets concentrated around the capital. Best are **Windward Island Agencies** (Heiligerweg, tel. 599/38–2372) and **Duggin's Shopping Center** (DeWindtweg, tel. 599/38–2241). Go on Monday or Tuesday for the best selection. Bread fanatics should put their morning order in at **William Schmidt's house** (Van Peereweg, Upper Town, no phone). He bakes fresh loaves every morning.

Highly recommended restaurants are indicated by a star ★.

Category	Cost*
Moderate	$20–$25
Inexpensive	$10–$20
Budget	under $10

per person, excluding drinks and service

Golden Era Hotel. The restaurant and bar of this establishment are somewhat stark, but the Creole food is good and the setting is right on the water. Sunday-night buffets, a steal at $14.50, are popular, served outside by the pool and ocean, with a local band providing entertainment. *Golden Era Hotel, Lower Town, Oranjestad, tel. 599/38–2345. AE, D, MC, V. Moderate.*

King's Well Restaurant. "Good food, cold drinks and easy prices" reads the hand-painted sign at this breezy terrace eatery overlooking the sea. It's run by a fun-loving Dutch couple, who serve fine grilled chicken and fish along with authentic *rostbraten* and schnitzels. *Bay Rd., Lower Town, Oranjestad, tel. 599/38–2538. No credit cards. Moderate.*

La Maison sur la Plage. The view here is of the Atlantic, the cloths are crisp and white, and the fare is French. For dinner, openers include fish soup and quiche Lorraine. Among the entrées are duck breast with green-peppercorn sauce and *entrecôte forestière* (sirloin with mushrooms, cream, and red wine). Try the crêpes à l'orange for dessert. *Zeelandia, tel. 599/38–2256. Reservations required. AE, MC, V. Moderate.*

★ **Old Gin House Terrace.** Dining is delightful on the oceanside terrace of this hotel. The menu may include peanut soup, fillet of orange roughy, lobster Antillean (lobster chunks stewed with onions, red wine, Pernod, and a dash of hot pepper), plain burgers and dillyburgers (with sour cream and dill sauce), lobster salad, and sandwiches. Lunch is more casual and offers lighter fare. *Old Gin House, Lower Town, Oranjestad, tel. 599/38–2319. Reservations advised. AE, D, MC, V. Moderate.*

Talk of the Town. Breakfast, lunch, and dinner are served at this pleasant restaurant midway between the airport and town. Caribbean, Oriental, and American dishes are offered. *L. E. Sadlerweg, near Upper Town, tel. 599/38–2236. MC, V. Moderate.*

Chinese Bar and Restaurant. Owner Kim Cheng serves up tasty Oriental and Caribbean dishes—*Bami goreng* (Indonesian chow mein), pork chops Creole—in hearty portions at his unpretentious establishment. Dining indoors can be slightly claustrophobic, but just ask your waitress if you may tote your Formica-top table out onto the terrace. She'll probably be happy to lend a hand and then serve you under the stars. *Prinsesweg, Upper Town, Oranjestad, tel. 599/38–2389. No credit cards. Inexpensive.*

★ **Franky's.** Come here for good local barbecue: ribs, chicken, lobster, and fish served later than at most other places on Statia. Try the bullfoot soup and the goatwater stew. The less adventurous can get pizza on the weekend, when there is live music. *Ruyterweg, Upper Town, Oranjestad, tel. 599/38–2575. No credit cards. Inexpensive.*

L'Etoile. West Indian dishes, such as spicy stuffed land crab and goat meat, are prepared by Caren Henriquez in a simple snack bar/restaurant. You can also get hot dogs, hamburgers, and spareribs. *Heiligerweg, Upper Town, Oranjestad, tel. 599/38–2299. No credit cards. Inexpensive.*

Stone Oven. Such West Indian specialties as goatwater stew are featured here. You can eat either indoors in the little house or outside on the palm-fringed patio. *16A Feaschweb, Upper Town, Oranjestad, tel. 599/38–2247. Reservations required. No credit cards. Budget–Inexpensive.*

The Cool Corner. Grab a beer and a snack of sandwiches or fish fritters and join in the local gossip. It's located near the Tourist Office. *Fort Oranjestraat, tel. 599/38–2523. No credit cards. Closed Sun. Budget.*

Sonny's Place. The enticing aromas of conch fritters and roti emanate from this open-air gazebo that often swings with live music on weekends. Try the scrumptious fresh fruit juices for a quick pick-me-up. *Fort Oranjestraat, no phone. No credit cards. Budget.*

Lodging

There are only three full-service hotels and a few apartment rentals on the island. Units in these already-scarce accommodations have become even harder to find recently, thanks to an influx of Dominicans and Jamaicans seeking work. You may also compete for a room with young Dutch on driving-license packages designed to save time and money over lessons back home. As a rule, cheerful is the best you can expect; while the better properties are clean and efficiently run, many resemble hippie communes. Hotels here generally do not offer meal plans.

Highly recommended lodgings are indicated by a star ★.

Category	Cost*
Moderate	$75–$100
Inexpensive	$50–$75
Budget	under $50

All prices are for a standard double room for two, excluding 7% tax and a 10%–15% service charge.

Hotels **Golden Era Hotel.** This is a harborfront hotel whose rooms are neat, small, air-conditioned, and motel-modern. All have little terraces, but only half have a full or partial view of the sea. The other rooms look out over concrete or down onto the roof of the restaurant. Not particularly attractive, the hotel nevertheless is central, by the water, and enjoys a cheerful clientele. *Box 109, Oranjestad, tel. 599/38–2345 or 800/223–6510. 19 rooms, 1 suite. Facilities: pool, restaurant, bar. AE, D, MC, V. EP. Moderate.*

La Maison sur la Plage. French-born Michelle Greca's *maison* (house) is actually eight Spartan cottages, where you have a choice of twin, double, or king-size beds. Each cottage has a bath and a private veranda where a Continental breakfast is served. Repairs from recent hurricanes have so far been makeshift rather than improvements. There's a stone-and-wood bar and a *très* French dining room bordered by a trellis and greenery. The *plage* is a 2-mile crescent of gray sand slapped by the wild waters of the Atlantic. The undertow here can be dangerous, so do your swimming in the pool. *Box 157, Zeelandia, tel. 599/38–2256 or 800/845–9504. 8 cottages with 10 rooms. Facilities: pool, restaurant, bar, lounge. AE, MC, V. EP. Moderate.*

★ **Talk of the Town.** These bright and simply furnished rooms are for those who don't need a view. There is a deck with lounge chairs for guests' use, and a restaurant downstairs. The hotel is on the road between the airport and town. This is an excellent value, and one of the liveliest places on the island. *L. E. Saddlerweg, tel. 599/38–2236. 17 rooms with shower. Facilities: restaurant, bar. MC, V. EP. Inexpensive.*

Country Inn. Cows graze in the pasture outside Iris and Wendell Pompier's comfortable guest house, whose simply furnished rooms all feature cable TV, air-conditioning, and shower baths. The owners do their utmost to make you feel at home, even offering impromptu additions to the Continental breakfasts and lifts into town. The clientele is an appealing mix of students and nature lovers. *Concordia, tel. 599/38–2484. 6 rooms. Facilities: breakfast room. No credit cards. CP. Budget–Inexpensive.*

Apartment Rentals Statia has only a handful of apartments, though a spate of small developments and guest houses have sprung up recently to meet demand. Most of these average $50 or less per night. The apartments are very basic by most American standards; if you're considering one not recommended below, it's a good idea to inspect it before committing. Check with the Tourist Office for listings. The only luxury accommodation is **Cherry Tree Villa,** which sprawls over 17 lush acres. The moderately priced two-bedroom villa sleeps four, and its luxe touches include a Cuisinart, dishwasher, microwave oven, outdoor Jacuzzi facing the sea, and the use of a car. A Hobie Cat and a 32-foot skippered yacht are available for an extra charge. *Cherry Hill, tel. 314/569–2501 or 599/38–2478. No credit cards. Moderate.*

★ The **Airport View Apartments** are one of the island's best values. Located near the airport, these are inexpensive studios with carpeted floors, small refrigerators, TVs, air-conditioning, coffee makers, private baths, and either two double or twin beds. There's an outdoor patio with a barbecue pit and a meeting room that can accommodate 12. *Oranjestad, tel. 599/38–2299. 9 units. Facilities: bar, restaurant, pool. No credit cards. Budget.*

Nightlife

Statia's five local bands stay busy, dividing their time among gigs at the occasional Saturday-night dances at the **Community Center** (*see* Sports and the Outdoors, *above*); alfresco soirees at the **Chinese Bar and Restaurant** (*see* Dining, *above*) and **Sonny's Place** in Oranjestad; and Saturday nights at the **Cool Corner** (*see* Exploring St. Eustatius, *above*). Sunday nights find everyone at the **Golden Era Hotel** (*see* Lodging, *above*). **Talk of the Town** (*see* Lodging, *above*) is the place to be for live music Friday nights; weekend nights at **Franky's** (*see* Dining, *above*) are also popular. The **Lago Heights Club and Disco** (no phone), known to all as Gerald's, at the shopping center in Chapelpiece, has dancing and a late-night barbecue.

21 St. Kitts and Nevis

Updated by
Harriet Edleson

Tour groups are not attracted to islands that have no nonstop flights from the United States, virtually no glittering nightlife or shopping, and no high-rise hotels. Visitors here tend to be self-sufficient, sophisticated types who know how to amuse themselves and appreciate the warmth and character of country inns.

As you might expect, this atmosphere of understated luxury comes at a price: Both St. Kitts and Nevis are expensive. Their resorts and plantation-house hotels tend to attract the upscale traveler. Moreover, the islands are small and offer fewer cheap lodging and dining alternatives than larger, more diverse destinations. Nevertheless, St. Kitts does have a few mid-priced hotels and some condominiums with kitchen facilities, as well as one all-inclusive resort that represents good value. Nevis has two affordable plantation-house hotels and—for those on a tighter budget—a few simple cottage complexes and guest houses.

Tiny though it is, St. Kitts, the first English settlement in the Leeward Islands, crams some stunning scenery into its 65 square miles. The island is fertile and lush with tropical flora and has some fascinating natural and historical attractions: a rain forest replete with waterfalls, thick vines, and secret trails; a central mountain range dominated by the 3,792-foot Mt. Liamuiga, whose crater has been long dormant; and Brimstone Hill, the Caribbean's most impressive fortress, which was known in the 17th century as the Gibraltar of the West Indies. The island is home to 35,000 people and hosts some

60,000 visitors annually. The shape of St. Kitts has been variously compared to a whale, a cricket bat, and a guitar. It's roughly oval, 19 miles long and 6 miles wide, with a narrow peninsula trailing off toward Nevis, 2 miles across the strait.

Nevis (pronounced NEE-*vis*) rises out of the water in an almost perfect cone, the tip of its 3,232-foot central mountain smothered in clouds. It's lusher and less developed than its sister island. Nevis is known for its natural beauty—long beaches with white and black sand, lush greenery—for a half-dozen mineral spa baths, and for the restored sugar plantations that now house some of the Caribbean's most elegant hostelries. The islands offer plenty of activity for the energetic-mountain climbing, swimming, tennis, horseback riding, snorkeling. But the going is easy here, with hammocks for snoozing, lobster bakes on palm-lined beaches, and quiet dinners on romantic verandas.

Nevis is linked with St. Kitts politically. The two islands, together with Anguilla, achieved self-government as an Associated State of Great Britain in 1967. In 1983, St. Kitts and Nevis became a fully independent nation. Nevis papers sometimes run fiery articles advocating independence from St. Kitts, and the two islands may separate someday. However, it's not likely that a shot will be fired, let alone one that will be heard around the world.

What It Will Cost These sample prices, meant only as a general guide, are for high season. On St. Kitts, a moderately priced hotel will be about $150 a night; a budget one-bedroom condominium costs about $85 a night. On Nevis, a room at one of the more affordable plantation-house hotels costs $175 a night. A room at a budget guest house is about $45 a night. Dinner at an inexpensive restaurant on either island is about $15; a sandwich lunch is $1.50–$3. On Nevis, a fixed-price dinner at some of the island's plantation dining rooms is $25–$35 (others are more). A rum punch is $3–$4 on either island; a beer is about $2.50. Figure on $35–$40 a day for car or Jeep rental. On St. Kitts, cab fare from the airport to Basseterre is only about $6, but fare to more distant hotels can approach $20. On Nevis, cab fare from the airport to the Mt. Nevis hotel is $15; from Charlestown to Oualie Beach, it's about $9. A single-tank dive on both islands costs around $45; snorkel equipment rents for about $10.

Before You Go

Tourist Information Contact the **St. Kitts & Nevis Tourist Board** (414 E. 75th St., New York, NY 10021, tel. 212/535–1234, fax 212/734–6511) or the **St. Kitts & Nevis Tourist Office** (11 Yorkville Ave., Suite 508, Toronto, Ont., Canada M4W 1L3, tel. 416/921–7717; 10 Kensington Ct., London W85 DL, tel. 071/376–0881, fax 071/937–3611; 3166 S. River Rd., Suite 33, Des Plaines, IL 60018, tel. 708/699–7583).

Arriving and Departing
By Plane **American** (tel. 800/433–7300) and **Delta** (tel. 800/221–1212) fly from the United States to Antigua, St. Croix, St. Thomas, St. Maarten, and San Juan, Puerto Rico, where connections can be made on regional carriers such as **American Eagle,** part of the **American Airlines** system (tel. 800/433–7300); **LIAT** (tel. 809/465–2511, or tel. 212/251–1717 in NY); **Windward Island Airways** (tel. 809/465–0810); and **Air BVI** (tel. 800/468–2485).

British Airways (tel. 800/247–9297) flies from London to Antigua, **Air Canada** (tel. 800/422–6232) flies from Toronto to Antigua, and American flies from Montreal to San Juan. **Air St. Kitts-Nevis** (tel. 809/465–8571) and **Carib Aviation** (tel. 809/465–3055, St. Kitts; 809/469–9295, Nevis; fax 809/469–9185) are reliable air-charter operations providing service from St. Kitts to other islands. Carib Aviation also flies from Antigua to Nevis.

From the Airport Taxis meet every flight at the airports on both islands. The taxis are unmetered, but fixed rates are posted at the airport and at the jetty. On St. Kitts the fare from the airport to the closest hotel in Basseterre is E.C. $16 (U.S. $6); to the farthest point, E.C. $52 (U.S. $20). On Nevis, a taxi from Newcastle Airport to Golden Rock is about $15; to Pinney's Beach Hotel, it's about $11. Be sure to clarify whether the rate quoted is in E.C. or U.S. dollars.

By Boat The 150-passenger, government-operated ferry MV *Caribe Queen* makes the 45-minute crossing from Nevis to St. Kitts daily except Thursday (which is maintenance day) and Sunday. The schedule is a bit erratic, so confirm departure times with the tourist office. Round-trip fare is U.S. $8. A new, air-conditioned, 110-passenger ferry, MV *Spirit of Mount Nevis*, makes the run twice daily except Wednesday. The fare is U.S. $12 round-trip. Call **Nevis Cruise Lines** (tel. 809/469–9373) for information and reservations.

Passports and Visas U.S. and Canadian citizens need only produce proof of citizenship (voter registration card or birth certificate; a driver's license will not suffice). British citizens must have a passport; visas are not required. All visitors must have a return or ongoing ticket.

Language English with a West Indian lilt is spoken here.

Precautions Visitors, especially women, are warned not to go jogging on long, lonely roads.

St. Kitts

Staying in St. Kitts

Important Addresses **Tourist Information:** St. Kitts/Nevis Department of Tourism (Pelican Mall, Bay Rd., Box 132, Basseterre, tel. 809/465–2620 and 809/465–4040, fax 809/465–8794) and the **St. Kitts-Nevis Hotel Association** (Box 438, Basseterre, tel. and fax 809/465–5304).

Emergencies **Police:** Call 911. **Hospitals:** There is a 24-hour emergency room at the **Joseph N. France General Hospital** (Basseterre, tel. 809/465–2551). **Pharmacies:** In Baøseterre, **Skerritt's Drug Store** (Fort St., tel. 809/465–2008) and **City Drug** (Fort St., Basseterre, tel. 809/465–2156). In Frigate Bay, **City Drug** (Sun 'n' Sand, Frigate Bay, tel. 809/465–1803).

Currency Legal tender is the Eastern Caribbean (E.C.) dollar. At press time, the rate of exchange was E.C. $2.70 to U.S. $1. U.S. dollars are accepted practically everywhere, but you'll almost always get change in E.C.s. Prices quoted here are in U.S. dollars unless noted otherwise. Most large hotels, restaurants, and

St. Kitts

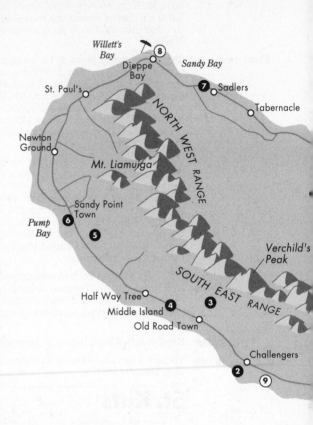

KEY

🚢 Ferry

🏖 Beach

① Exploring Sites

⑧ Hotels and Restaurants

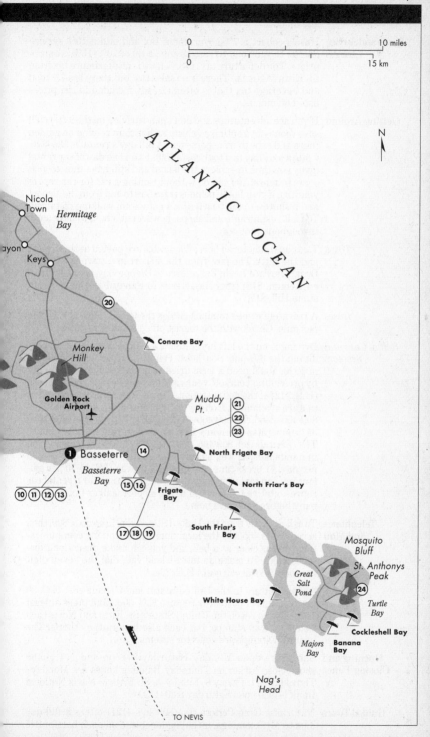

shops accept major credit cards, but small inns and shops usually do not.

Taxes and Service Charges Hotels collect a 7% government tax and add a 10% service charge to your bill. In restaurants, a tip of 10%–15% is appropriate. The departure tax is $8. (There is no departure tax from St. Kitts to Nevis.) There is no sales tax, but there is a 7% food and beverage tax that is often already included in the prices listed on menus.

Getting Around If you are adventurous and don't mind driving on the left, you'll save money by renting a vehicle rather than relying on guided tours and cabs to transport you. (A full day's rental is $35–$40, while a half-day taxi tour costs $50). Even one day of car rental gives you time to explore the island and still have time to visit some beaches. You can do without renting a car for the rest of your trip if your hotel includes transfers to and from the airport and a shuttle to the beach (if it's not within walking distance). To visit restaurants and shops, however, it's best to have a car throughout your stay.

Taxis Taxis are unmetered here; fixed rates are posted at the airport and the jetty. The fare from the airport into town is $5; from Ocean Terrace Inn in Basseterre to Dieppe Bay, near the Golden Lemon, $18; from Basseterre to Sandy Point near Brimstone Hill, $17.

Buses A privately owned minibus circles the island. Fare is E.C. 25¢ per mile. Check with the tourist office about schedules.

Rental Cars and Scooters Driving is on the left here. Roads are in reasonably good condition; the 6½-mile Southeast Peninsula Road was completed in 1990. You'll need a local driver's license, which you can get by presenting yourself, your valid driver's license, and E.C. $30 (U.S. $12) at the police station, Cayon Street, Basseterre. Rentals are available at **Holiday** (tel. 809/465–6507) and **Caines** (tel. 809/465–2366, fax 809/465–6172). Delise Walwyn (tel. 809/465–8449) operates **Economy Car,** which also rents scooter bikes. **TDC Rentals** (tel. 809/465–2991, fax 809/469–1329) can put you in minimokes, as well as cars. Car rentals run about U.S. $35 per day. At press time, the price of gas was U.S. $1.70 per gallon. You can make arrangements ahead of time for a rental car representative to meet you at the airport; call or fax the company before you leave home.

Telephones and Mail To call St. Kitts from the United States, dial area code 809, then access code 465 and the local number. Telephone communications are as clear as a bell, and you can make direct long-distance calls. To make an intra-island call, dial the seven-digit number. A local call costs E.C. 25¢.

Airmail letters to the United States and Canada cost E.C. 80 per half ounce; postcards require E.C. 50¢. Mail takes at least 7–10 days to reach the United States. St. Kitts and Nevis each issues its own stamps, but each also honors the other's. The beautiful stamps are collector's items.

Opening and Closing Times Shops are open Monday–Saturday 8–noon and 1–4. Some shops close earlier on Thursday. Banking hours are Monday–Thursday 8–1, Friday 8–1 and 3–5. St. Kitts & Nevis National Bank is also open Saturday 8:30–11 AM.

Guided Tours Naturalist **Greg Periera** (tel. 809/465–4121) offers a full-day hike to Mt. Liamuiga, including lunch and an open bar, for $45 a person. He also offers a half-day rain-forest hike, including lunch and open bar, for $35; and a plantation tour with West Indian lunch for $45. **Tropical Tours** (tel. 809/465–4167) offers rain-forest ($35 a person) and island ($12 a person) tours. **Denise Walyn** (tel. 809/465–2631) offers cab or minivan tours of Caribelle Batik and Brimstone Hill ($45 for up to four people) and a rain-forest tour for $30 a person (minimum four people). **Kriss Tours** (tel. 809/465–4042) offers rain-forest tours with lunch and a drink for $35 a person, and volcano tours, also with lunch and drink, for $40.

Taxi tours of the island take about four hours and cost about U.S. $50. Both **Little** and **Big Mac** (tel. 809/465–2016) are reliable, helpful drivers, as are **Jimmy Herbert** (tel. 809/465–4694) and **Pat Riley** (tel. 809/465–2444).

Exploring St. Kitts

Numbers in the margin correspond to points of interest on the St. Kitts map.

Basseterre
❶
The capital city of **Basseterre,** set in the southern part of the island, is an easily walkable town, graced with tall palms and small, beautifully maintained houses and buildings of stone and pastel-colored wood. You can see the town's main sights in a half hour or so.

Your first stop is at the **St. Kitts Tourist Board** (Tourism Complex, Bay Rd.) to pick up maps. Turn left when you leave there and walk past the handsome Treasury Building. It faces the octagonal **Circus,** which contains a fanciful memorial to Thomas Berkeley, a former president of the Legislative Assembly. Duty-free shops fill the streets and courtyards leading off from around the Circus. The **St. Kitts Philatelic Bureau** (open weekdays 8–4) is nearby on the second floor of the Social Security Building (Bay Rd.).

The colorful **Bay Road produce market** is open on weekends only. On the waterfront, next to the Treasury Building, is the air-conditioned **Shoreline Plaza,** with its tax-free shops, and nearby is the landing for the ferries to Nevis.

From the Circus, Bank Street leads to **Independence Square,** with lovely gardens on the site of a former slave market. The square is surrounded on three sides by Georgian buildings.

Walk up West Square Street, away from the bay, to Cayon Street, turn left, and walk one block to **St. George's Anglican Church.** This handsome stone building with crenellated tower was built by the French in 1670 and called Nôtre Dame. The British burned it down in 1706 and rebuilt it four years later, naming it after the patron saint of England. Since then, it has suffered fire, earthquake, and hurricanes and was once again rebuilt in 1859.

Elsewhere on the Island
Main Road traces the perimeter of the island, circling the central mountain ranges. Head west on it out of Basseterre to explore the rest of St. Kitts. For the first few miles, you'll be driving through gently rolling hills, past old sugar plantations and ancient stone fences covered with vines, and through tiny villages with tiny houses of stone and weathered wood. Allow three to four hours for an island tour.

You won't have any trouble identifying the villages as you come across them; small white welcome signs, placed by members of the 4-H Club, are posted outside each village. Just outside Challengers is **Bloody Point,** where in 1629, French and British soldiers joined forces to repel a mass attack by the Caribs. The scenery on the drive into **Old Road Town** is spectacular.

From Old Road Town, take the road through the rain forest to visit **Romney Manor,** where batik fabrics are printed at **Caribelle Batik** (*see* Shopping, *below*). The house is set in 6 acres of gardens, with exotic flowers, an old bell tower, and a 350-year-old saman tree (sometimes called a rain tree). Inside, you can watch artisans hand-printing fabrics using the 2,500-year-old Indonesian process known as batik.

The village after Old Road Town is **Middle Island,** where Thomas Warner, the "gentleman of London" who brought the first settlers here, died in 1648 and is buried beneath a green gazebo in the churchyard of **St. Thomas Church.**

The road continues through the village of Half-Way Tree to **Brimstone Hill,** the most important historic site on St. Kitts. From the parking area it's a long walk to the 38-acre fortress, but the exercise is well worth it if military history and/or spectacular views interest you. After routing the French in 1690, the English erected a battery on top of Brimstone Hill, and by 1736, there were 49 guns in the fortress. In 1782, the French lay siege to the fortress, which was defended by 350 militia and 600 regular troops of the Royal Scots and East Yorkshires. A plaque in the old stone wall marks the place where the fort was breached. When the English finally surrendered, the French allowed them to march from the fort in full formation out of respect for their bravery. (The English afforded the French the same honor when the latter surrendered the fort a mere year later.) A hurricane seriously damaged the fortress in 1834, and in 1852 it was evacuated and dismantled.

The citadel has been partially reconstructed and its guns remounted. You can see what remains of the officers' quarters, the redoubts, barracks, the ordnance store, and the cemetery. Its museums display, among other things, weaponry, uniforms, photographs, and old newspapers. In 1985, Queen Elizabeth visited Brimstone Hill and officially opened it as part of a national park. There's a splendid view from here that includes Montserrat and Nevis to the southeast, Saba and Statia to the northwest, and St. Barts and St. Maarten to the north. *Main Rd., Brimstone Hill. Admission: $5 adults, $2.50 children. Open daily 9:30–5:30.*

Continuing on through seas of sugarcane, past breadfruit trees and old stone walls, you'll come to **Sandy Point Town.** The houses here are West Indian–style raised cottages. The **Roman Catholic Church** has lovely stained-glass windows.

Farther along, just outside the village of **Newton Ground,** are the remains of an old sugar mill and some ancient coconut palms. Outside the village of **St. Paul's** is a road that leads to **Rawlins Plantation,** a restored sugar plantation that's popular for dining and lodging. The fishing town of **Dieppe Bay** is at the northernmost point of the island. Its tiny black-sand beach is backed by **The Golden Lemon,** one of the Caribbean's most famous inns. **Black Rocks** on the Atlantic coast just outside the town of Sadlers, in Sandy Bay, are lava deposits, spat into the sea ages ago when the island's volcano erupted. They have since been molded into fanciful shapes by centuries of pounding surf. The drive back to Basseterre around the other side of the island is a pleasant one, through small, neat villages with centuries-old stone churches and pastel-colored cottages.

Beaches

All beaches on the island are free and open to the public, even those occupied by hotels. The powdery white-sand beaches are all at the southern end of the island and on the peninsula. The best way to see the beaches is to rent a vehicle for a day, bring your swimsuit and a picnic lunch, and make the rounds.

The South East Peninsula Road leads from the foot of Timothy Hill to Major's Bay on the southern tip of the island, providing access to some of the island's best beaches. Among them are the twin beaches of **Banana Bay** and **Cockleshell Bay,** which together cover more than 2 miles.

Other good peninsula beaches are **Friar's Bay** (on both the Atlantic and the Caribbean sides) and **White House Bay.** North of these beaches is talcum-powder-fine **Frigate Bay,** on the Caribbean. On the Atlantic, **North Frigate Bay** is 4 miles wide.

Beaches elsewhere on the island are of gray-black volcanic sand. **Conaree Bay** on the Atlantic side is a narrow strip where the water is good for bodysurfing (no facilities). Snorkeling and windsurfing are good at **Dieppe Bay,** on the north coast, where the Golden Lemon Hotel is located.

Sports and the Outdoors

Boating Sunfish can be rented at **Tropical Surf** in Turtle Bay (tel. 809/496–9086) and **R.G. Watersports** in Frigate Bay (tel. 809/465–8050) for $15 an hour.

Golf The **Royal St. Kitts Golf Club** (tel. 809/465–8339) is an 18-hole championship course in the Frigate Bay area. It costs $30 to play here, with cart rental an additional $30. There is a 9-hole course at **Golden Rock** (tel. 809/465–8103).

Hiking Trails in the central mountains vary from easy to don't-try-it-by-yourself. **Greg Pereira** (tel. 809/465–4121) and **Kriss Tours** (tel. 809/465–4042) lead guided hikes (*see* Guided Tours, *above*).

Scuba Diving and Snorkeling Kenneth Samuel of **Kenneth's Dive Centre** (tel. 809/465–7043 or 809/465–2670) is a PADI-certified dive master who takes small groups of divers with C cards to nearby reefs. Auston MacLeod, a PADI-certified dive master/instructor and owner of **Pro-Divers** (tel. 809/465–3223 or 809/465–2754), offers resort and certification courses. He also has Nikonos camera equipment for rent. A single-tank dive costs $35–$40; a double is about $60. Snorkel equipment rents for about $10.

There are more than a dozen excellent dive sites on St. Kitts, all with a variety of sea life and color. **Coconut Tree Reef,** one of the largest in the area, includes sea fans, sponges, and anemones. **Black Coral Reef** features the rare black coral tree. **Brassball Wreck** is a shallow-water wreck, good for snorkeling and photography. **Redonda Bank** is an extensive area of reef that's just beginning to be explored. The shallow **Tug Boat** is a good spot for snorkelers.

Sea Excursions **Leeward Island Charters** (tel. 809/465–7474) offers day and overnight charters on two catamarans—the 47-foot *Caona* or the 70-foot *Spirit of St. Kitts.* Day sails are from 9:30 to 4:30 and include barbecue, open bar, and snorkeling equipment. **Tropical Tours** (tel. 809/465–4167) offers moonlight cruises on the 52-foot catamaran *Cileca III* and glass-bottom-boat tours. *Tropical Dreamer* (tel. 809/465–8224) is another catamaran available for day and sunset cruises. For the ultimate underwater trip, call **Blue Frontier Ltd.** (tel. 809/465–4945); owner Lindsey Beck will take even nondivers for a half-hour ride off Frigate Bay in his two-man submarine. **Kantours** (tel. 809/465–2098) will take you on a Banana Bay Beach Safari for a day of snorkeling and swimming and an evening barbecue. Excursions average $45 a person, including lunch, drinks, and snorkel equipment. **Pro-Divers** (*see above*) offers half-day snorkeling trips for $25 a person.

Tennis There are two lighted courts at **Jack Tar Village/Royal St. Kitts** (tel. 809/465–2651) and a functional grass court at **Rawlins Plantation** (tel. 809/465–6221). Hotel courts are free during the day; night play on lighted courts costs about $5.

Waterskiing and **Tropical Surf** (tel. 809/469–9086) at Turtle Bay rents Wind-
Windsurfing surfers, surfboards, and boogie boards. **R.G. Watersports** (tel. 809/465–8050) has windsurfing and waterskiing equipment. Windsurfing costs $10 an hour; waterskiing is $15 for 15 minutes.

Shopping

Worth a splurge are the batik fabrics, scarves, caftans, and wall hangings of Caribelle Batik; cost of batik wall hangings ranges from $25 to $70. Locally produced jams, jellies, and herb teas make good gifts, as do handcrafts of local shell, straw, and coconut. CSR (Cane Spirit Rothschild) is a "new cane-spirit drink" that's distilled from fresh sugarcane right on St. Kitts.

Shopping Districts Most shopping plazas are near The Circus in downtown Basseterre. Some shops have outlets in other areas, particularly in Dieppe Bay. The **Pelican Mall**, opened in 1991, has 26 stores, a restaurant, tourism offices, and a bandstand. This shopping arcade is designed to look like a traditional Caribbean street. **TDC Mall** is just off The Circus in downtown Basseterre. At press time, the Ballaho Building, right on The Circus, was being renovated; it will house Spencer Cameron Fabrics, Island Hopper, the Ballaho Restaurant, and more. **Shoreline Plaza** is next to the Treasury Building, right on the waterfront in Basseterre. **Palms Arcade** is on Fort Street, also near The Circus.

Good Buys **Lemonaid** (Dieppe Bay, tel. 809/465–7359) has select Caribbean handicrafts, antiques, and clothing by John Warden. **Caribelle Batik** (Romney Manor, tel. 809/465–6253), **The Kittitian Kitchen** (Palms Arcade, Basseterre, and at the Golden Lemon, Dieppe Bay, no phone), and **Palm Crafts** (also in Palms Arcade, tel. 809/465–2599) all sell those special somethings (island crafts, jams and jellies, batik). **Spencer Cameron Fabrics** (Ballaho Bldg., The Circus) has silk, cotton, and muslin fabrics hand-painted with clever, colorful designs that include monkeys and tropical flowers. **Spencer Cameron Art Gallery** (South Square St., tel. 809/465–4047) has historical reproductions of Caribbean island charts and prints, in addition to owner Rosey

Cameron's popular Carnevale clown prints and other work by Caribbean artists. **Splash** (tel. 809/465–9279) in the Pelican Mall, carries colorful ceramics, including eye-catching work by local artist Paula Fiorel.

Dining

Dining in St. Kitts can be affordable if you avoid plantation dining rooms. There are a number of good restaurants with reasonably priced menu items. Most restaurants offer a variety of West Indian specialties, such as curried mutton, Arawak chicken (seasoned rice and almonds served on breadfruit leaf), pepper pot, and honey-glazed garlic spare ribs.

There's little in the way of fast food here, but quick, cheap lunches can be had at the temporary snack stands set up on beaches around the island. If you're cooking in, **Ram's Supermarket** and **Scotch House** in Basseterre have provisions; in the Frigate Bay area, try **City Drug Store.** You can buy picnic fare at **Ocean Terrace Inn** (*see below*).

Highly recommended restaurants are indicated by a star ★.

Category	Cost*
Moderate	$25–$35
Inexpensive	$15–$25
Budget	under $15

*per person, excluding drinks, service (10%), and tax (7%)

★ **The Golden Lemon.** Though it's out of our price range for dinner, come here for the excellent Sunday brunch ($15) and reasonably priced lunches ($10 lobster sandwich). Owner Arthur Leaman creates the recipes himself for the West Indian, Continental, and American cuisines served in his hotel, and he never repeats them more than once in a two-week period. The patio, lush with bougainvillea and ferns, is a popular spot for the Sunday brunch, which can include banana pancakes, rum beef stew, and spaghetti with white clam sauce. *Dieppe Bay, tel. 809/465–7260. Reservations required. Dress: casually elegant. AE. Moderate.*

The Lighthouse Gourmet Restaurant. Overlooking the harbor of Basseterre and close to town, this restaurant offers panoramic views and both West Indian and Continental cuisines. *Deepwater Port Rd., tel. 809/465–8914. AE, MC, V. Closed Sun. and Mon. Moderate.*

★ **Ocean Terrace Inn.** Popular with locals and visitors, who dine by candlelight inside or on a balcony overlooking the bay. Lobster is the specialty here—grilled, broiled, and thermidor. The chef's special, which includes appetizer, soup, entrée, vegetables, dessert, and coffee, costs $35—a price that barely makes it into our Moderate category, but is an excellent value. The lunch menu includes sandwiches for $5–$9. At the Friday-night buffet, steak barbecue alternates with West Indian specialties. The 7:30 dinner is followed by entertainment and dancing. *Fortlands, Basseterre, tel. 809/465–2754. Reservations required. AE, MC, V. Moderate.*

★ **Ballahoo.** Curried conch, beef Stroganoff, salads, and sand-wiches are served in a delightful upstairs gallery overlooking Pelican Gardens and The Circus in the heart of town. *Fort St., Basseterre, tel. 809/465–4197. AE, MC, V. Closed Sun. Inexpen-sive.*

Coconut Cafe. This restaurant offers casual beachfront din-ing—breakfast, lunch, and dinner—at the Colony's Timothy Beach Resort on Frigate Bay. Enjoy fresh grilled seafood while watching the sunset. *Frigate Bay, tel. 809/465–3020. AE, D, MC, V. Inexpensive.*

★ **Fisherman's Wharf.** At the Ocean Terrace Inn, this informal waterfront eatery serves the island's best conch chowder, grilled lobster, and fish. It's a lively spot on weekend nights. *Fortlands, Basseterre, tel. 809/465–2754. No credit cards. Inex-pensive.*

OTI Turtle Beach Bar and Grill. Located at the end of the new South East Peninsula Road, this informal restaurant is on a beautiful stretch of beach facing Nevis and is a great place for lunch or dinner. Better yet, spend the day. Try the conch salad with garlic, tandoori chicken, fresh fish, or lobster on the grill. *Turtle Bay, tel. 809/469–9086. Reservations required for dinner. AE, MC, V. Inexpensive.*

PJ's Pizza. You'll find excellent pizza right next to the Island Paradise Condominiums. Other Italian dishes are also served, as are sandwiches. *Frigate Bay, tel. 809/465–8373. No credit cards. Closed Sun. and Mon. Budget–Inexpensive.*

The Atlantic Club. This oceanside eatery on the island's east coast makes a good lunch stop for everything from West Indian food to seafood, club sandwiches, hamburgers—and divine piña coladas. Genford Gumbs, a Nevisian who worked at the Golden Lemon for 15 years, opened this simple restaurant and outdoor bar next to his Morgan Heights Condominiums in 1992. The portions are hearty, and the prices can't be beat. *Morgan Heights Condominiums, Main Rd. near Basseterre, tel. 809/465–8633. AE, D, MC, V. Closed Sun. Budget.*

Blue Horizon. On the cliffs of Bird Rock, this restaurant and bar afford a panoramic view of Basseterre and Nevis. The menu is French, but uses local ingredients. The rustic atmos-phere features indoor and outdoor dining; parents welcome the supervised playground for children. *Basseterre, tel. 809/465–5863. Reservations advised. AE, MC, V. Budget.*

Chef's Place. This is a great place to have an inexpensive West Indian meal and meet the local businesspeople. The best seats are on the outdoor white veranda; try the local version of jerk chicken, moist rather than dry, or the goat stew. *Upper Church St., Basseterre, tel. 809/465–6176. No credit cards. Closed Sun. Budget.*

Lodging

St. Kitts does not have an abundance of hotels, and what it has are mostly expensive. You'll have to bypass the unique resorts and restored plantations the island is known for and concen-trate on more modest properties, located for the most part in Basseterre and in the Frigate Bay area. Apartment rentals are another possibility (*see below*).

Highly recommended lodgings are indicated by a star ★.

Category	Cost*
Moderate	$115–$175
Inexpensive	$90–$115
Budget	under $90

*All prices are for a standard double room for two, excluding 7% tax and a 10% service charge. To estimate rates for hotels offering MAP, add about $35 per person per day to the above price ranges. For all-inclusives, add about $75 per person per day.

Hotels
★ **Colony's Timothy Beach Resort.** This is the only hotel in the Frigate Bay area that sits directly on the calm, Caribbean beach. The rooms and suites are decorated in modern style with island accents; bathrooms are attractive. Not all rooms are affordable here, so ask when you call; less expensive units have mountain views. Guests can participate in a variety of water and land activities, including nearby golf. The management is attentive and friendly, and the hotel's Coconut Cafe (see Dining, above) is a local favorite. Ideal for couples and families willing to trade atmosphere for a beach location, modern comfort, and good prices. Box 81, Frigate Bay, tel. 809/465–8597 or 800/621–1270, fax 809/465–7723; Colony Reservations Worldwide, 800/777–1700. 60 rooms. Facilities: pool, restaurant, water activities, nearby golf, shopping. AE, MC, V. EP. Moderate.

Jack Tar Village Beach Resorts and Casino. An almost completed $2-million renovation has breathed new life into this Jack Tar Village. What was once worn and overworked is now the kind of lively, all-inclusive, resort this chain is known for. Grounds have been relandscaped, and guest rooms updated with cheerful bedspreads, drapes, and bathrooms. About 10% of the rooms booked at least 60 days in advance go for $129 per person during high season; once these are filled, rates for the remaining rooms cost $160 a person. (The two suites here are not affordable.) One price covers all activities—of which there are many—including greens fees for the 18-hole golf course (mandatory cart rental is extra). You can walk to the nearby Atlantic beach, or take the free shuttle to a beach on the Caribbean side. Nightly live entertainment, a disco, and the island's only casino keep the action going late into the night. Box 406, Frigate Bay, tel. 809/465–8651 or 800/999–9182, fax 809/465–8651. 240 rooms, 2 suites. Facilities: 2 restaurants, 3 bars, casino, 2 pools, 2 lighted tennis courts, facilities for the disabled, water-sports center, access to golf course, supervised children's activities. AE, MC, V. All-inclusive. Moderate.

Sun 'n Sand Beach Village. These studio and two-bedroom, self-catering cottages are immaculately clean and right by a beach and pool on the Atlantic side of the island. Furnishings are simple and tropical, with tile floors, terraces, twin or queen-size beds, and private shower baths. Studios are air-conditioned; apartments have window air conditioners in bedrooms and ceiling fans in living rooms. Bedroom apartments have convertible sofas in living rooms and fully equipped kitchens with microwave ovens and full-size refrigerators. Box 341, Frigate Bay, tel. 809/465–8037, 800/621–1270, or 800/223–6510, fax 809/465–6745. 32 studios, 18 2-bedroom cottages. Facilities: restaurant, pool, children's pool, 2 lighted tennis courts, grocery store, nearby drugstore, gift shop. AE, D, MC, V. CP, MAP. Moderate.

Frigate Bay Beach Hotel. The third fairway of the island's golf course adjoins the property, and the nearby beach is reached by complimentary shuttle buses. The whitewashed, air-conditioned buildings contain standard rooms as well as condominium units with fully equipped kitchens. There are hillside and poolside units; the latter are more expensive. Standard rooms are large but simply furnished, with tile floors and sliding glass doors leading to a terrace or balcony. There's a pool with swim-up bar and a friendly staff. *Box 137, Basseterre, tel. 809/465–8936, 809/465–8935, or 800/223–9815, fax 809/465–7050. 64 rooms. Facilities: pool, restaurant, bar. AE, D, MC, V. EP, MAP. Inexpensive–Moderate.*

★ **Ocean Terrace Inn.** Affectionately called OTI, this centrally located family-run hotel in Basseterre has friendly service and an assortment of affordable rooms. All units are air-conditioned, with cable TVs and radios. There are rooms with kitchenettes and condominium units with private terraces overlooking one of the inn's two pools. Fisherman's Wharf restaurant (*see* Dining, *above*) is famed island-wide for its seafood, and the hotel's Pelican Cove Marina has its own fleet of boats. There is a shuttle daily to the hotel's beach at Turtle Bay, where you'll find a restaurant/bar and all water sports. *Box 65, Basseterre, tel. 809/465–2754, 800/223–5695, or 800/524–0512, fax 809/465–1057. 52 rooms. Facilities: 2 pools, outdoor Jacuzzi, 2 restaurants, 2 bars, fleet of boats, water-sports center. AE, MC, V. EP, MAP. Inexpensive–Moderate.*

Bird Rock Beach Resort. Perched on a bluff overlooking the Caribbean, this new hotel has two-story units containing air-conditioned rooms and suites with direct-dial telephones, cable TV, and balconies. The tile-floored rooms are simply furnished with rattan furniture and floral fabrics. The hotel has its own beach and pool with a swim-up bar. There is an informal dining room next to the pool and shuttle service to the Lighthouse Gourmet Restaurant. It's just five minutes from the airport, town, golf, and Frigate Bay beaches. *Box 227, Basseterre, tel. 809/465–8914 or 800/621–1270, fax 809/465–1675. 24 rooms. Facilities: 2 restaurants, bar, pool, tennis court, shuttle service to golf. AE, MC, V. EP, MAP. Inexpensive.*

Fairview Inn. The main building of this hotel is an 18th-century great house, with graceful white verandas and Oriental rugs on hardwood floors. The rooms are in cottages sprinkled around the backyard, which happens to be a mountain of considerable size. Rooms have functional furnishings and simple private baths with showers or bathtubs. Some have air-conditioning, some fans, some neither. The Fairview is well known for its superb West Indian cuisine, served in the great house (dress: casual elegant). At press time the hotel was undergoing a change in management. *Box 212, Basseterre, tel. 809/465–2472 or 800/223–9815, fax 809/465–1056. 30 rooms. Facilities: restaurant, 2 bars, pool. AE, D, MC, V. EP. Inexpensive.*

Fort Thomas Hotel. Popular with tour groups, it's set on 8 acres on a hillside in the outskirts of Basseterre, on the site of an old fort. The rooms are spacious, and all have private baths, air-conditioning, radios, and phones; TVs can be rented. There's a free shuttle bus to the beach. *Box 407, Basseterre, tel. 809/465–2695, fax 809/465–7518. 64 rooms. Facilities: pool, games room, restaurant, bar. AE, D, MC, V. EP. Budget.*

Condo and Apartment Rentals The **St. Kitts Tourist Board** (Box 132, Basseterre, St. Kitts, tel. 809/465–2620) has information on condominium and apartment rentals.

Morgan Heights Condominiums. Situated along the Atlantic coast, 10 minutes by car from Basseterre, this small condominium complex was built in 1992 by Glenford Gumbs, who also owns the Atlantic Club restaurant next door (*see* Dining, *above*). Air-conditioned two-bedroom units (which can be divided and rented as one-bedroom units) are clean and comfortable, with contemporary furnishings. They feature kitchens, ceramic tile floors, wicker furniture, and covered patios overlooking the water. Room amenities include cable color TVs and telephones. The beach is a 10-minute drive away. Plans are to add 10 more units by the end of 1994. *Box 536, Basseterre, tel. 809/465–8633 or 809/465–9210, fax 809/465–9272. 5 2-bedroom units that can be rented as 1-bedroom units. Facilities: restaurant, freshwater pool. AE, D, MC, V. EP. Budget–Inexpensive.*

Gateway Inn. Located at the entrance to Frigate Bay, this inn has 10 air-conditioned apartments with telephones, cable TV, kitchens, and laundry facilities. It's a 10-minute walk to the beach or the public golf course. *Box 64, Frigate Bay, tel. 809/465–7155/7158/7159, fax 809/465–9322. 10 rooms. EP. Budget.*

Guest Houses There are at least 20 guest houses available to visitors. The quality varies, so it's a good idea to inspect your room and be prepared with an alternate hotel should you not like what you see. Although many guest houses provide charming accommodations, warm service, and even fine cooking, the clear advantage is the cost, which can be as low as $30 a night. Most of the best properties are located in Basseterre, including **Llewellyn's Haven** (Infirmary Rd., Basseterre, tel. 809/465–2941); **On the Square** (14 Independence Sq., Box 81, Basseterre, tel. 809/465–2485/2071); **Park View Guest House** (Box 64, Basseterre, tel. 809/465–2100); **Rose's Guest House** (New Pond Site, Basseterre, tel. 809/465–4651/2434); and **Windsor Guest House** (Box 122, Basseterre, tel. 809/465–2894).

Off-Season Bets Although the expensive properties on St. Kitts are generally out of our price range even in the off-season, more moderately priced establishments listed above become even cheaper, with rates averaging 20% lower. At **Jack Tar Village** (*see above*), for instance, all-inclusive rates per person per night start at $89. Many St. Kitts hotels also offer packages with various amenities; these offer considerable savings over standard room rates and separate amenity payments. For instance, **Ocean Terrace Inn** (*see above*) offers a variety of seven-night packages, including windsurfing ($458 per person), diving ($649 per person), and honeymoon/romantic break ($495 per person) packages.

Nightlife

Most of the Kittitian nightlife revolves around the hotels, which host folkloric shows, calypso music, and steel bands.

Discos On Saturday night head for the **Turtle Beach Bar and Grill** (Turtle Bay, tel. 809/496–9086), where there is a beach dance-disco. Play volleyball into the evening, then dance the night away under the stars. At **J's Place** (across from Brimstone Hill, tel. 809/465–6264), you and the locals can dance far into the night on Friday and Saturday. **Reflections Night Club** (tel. 809/465–7616), upstairs at Flex Fitness Center, is the newest

Kittitian night spot. It's open Tuesday through Sunday from 9 until well past midnight. Cover charge is E.C. $10 Thursday, Friday, and Saturday nights.

Nevis

Staying in Nevis

Important **Tourist Information:** The **Tourism Office** (tel. 809/469–5521) is
Addresses on Main Street in Charlestown. The office is open Monday and Tuesday 8–4:30 and Wednesday–Friday 8–4.

Emergencies **Police:** Call 911. **Hospitals:** There is a 24-hour emergency room at **Alexandra Hospital** (Charlestown, tel. 809/469–5473). **Pharmacies: Evelyn's Drugstore** (Charlestown, tel. 809/469–5278) is open weekdays 8–5, Saturday 8–7:30, and Sunday 7 AM–8 PM; and the **Claxton Medical Centre** (Charlestown, tel. 809/469–5357) is open Monday–Wednesday and Friday 8–6, Thursday 8–4, Saturday 7:30–7, and Sunday 6–8 PM.

Currency Legal tender is the Eastern Caribbean (E.C.) dollar (E.C. $2.70 to U.S. $1). The U.S. dollar is accepted everywhere, but you'll almost always get change in E.C.s. Prices quoted here are in U.S. dollars unless noted otherwise. Credit cards are accepted at many hotels and restaurants on the island, though some of the inns will take only personal checks.

Taxes and Hotels collect a 7% government tax. Most hotels add a 10%
Service Charges service charge to your bill. For a job well done, a 10%–15% gratuity should be left in addition. In restaurants, leave a 10%–15% tip. There is a 7% food and beverage tax that is usually included in the prices listed on menus. Taxi drivers should get a 10% tip. The departure tax is $8. There is no sales tax.

Getting Around Because Nevis is small and many hotels are located on the
Rental Cars beach or have their own shuttles, you can do without a car. If you're staying in a more remote area, however, it may be a necessity. If you do rent, be aware of the following conditions: The island's roads are pocked with crater-size potholes; driving is on the left; goats and cattle crop up out of nowhere to amble along the road; and if you deviate from Main Street, you're likely to have trouble finding your way around. **Skeete's Car Rental** (Newcastle Village, at the airport, tel. 809/469–9458) has Toyota Corollas, Suzuki Jeeps, and Mitsubishi Lancers; **TDC Rentals, Ltd.** (Charlestown, tel. 809/469–5690) and **Striker's Car Rental** (Hermitage, tel. 809/469–2654) have minimokes and compacts; **Nisbett Rentals Ltd.** (tel. 809/469–1913 or 809/469–6211) rents cars, minimokes, and Jeeps. None of them charges for mileage, and all of them accept major credit cards. Arrive in Nevis with a valid driver's license, and your car-rental agency will help you obtain a local license at the police station. The cost is E.C. $30 (U.S. $12). Rental costs about $35 a day for a Jeep and about $25 for a minimoke.

Taxis Taxi service is available at the airport. Some of the island's fleet includes **Kurtley Maynard** (tel. 809/469–1973), **Ralph Hutton** (tel. 809/469–1767), and **Luther Morton** (tel. 809/469–1858). Sample taxi rates: from the airport to Mt. Nevis Hotel, about $15; from the airport to Charlestown, $12; from Charlestown to Oualie Beach near Hurricane Hill, about $9; from the ferry to Golden Rock, $10. Be sure to clarify whether the rate quoted is in E.C. or U.S. dollars.

Telephones and Mail To call Nevis from the United States, dial area code 809, followed by 469 and the local number. Communications are excellent, both on the island and with the United States, and direct-dial long distance is in effect. A local call costs E.C. 25¢.

Airmail letters to the United States and Canada require E.C. 80¢ per half ounce; postcards, E.C. 50¢. It takes 7–10 days for mail to reach home. Nevis and St. Kitts have separate stamp-issuing policies, but each honors the other's stamps.

Opening and Closing Times Shops are open Monday–Saturday 8–noon and 1–4 (until 5 on Saturday). Banking hours vary but are generally Monday–Thursday 8–3; Friday 8–5. **St. Kitts-Nevis-Anguilla National Bank** and the **Bank of Nevis** are open Saturday 8:30–11 AM.

Guided Tours Nevis's 36 square miles can be seen in a few hours. Guided tours generally include the birthplace of Alexander Hamilton, Charlestown, the Nelson Museum, Bath Springs, and one or more plantations. **Taxi drivers** make knowledgeable guides; cost is about $50 for a 3½-hour tour.

Exploring Nevis

Numbers in the margin correspond to points of interest on the Nevis map.

Charlestown About 1,200 of the island's 9,300 inhabitants live in **Charles-**
❶ **town,** the capital of Nevis. It faces the Caribbean, about 12½ miles south of Basseterre in St. Kitts. If you arrive by ferry, as most people do, you'll walk smack onto Main Street from the pier. You can tour the capital city in a half-hour or so.

Turn right on Main Street and look for the **Nevis Tourist Office** (on your right as you enter the main square). Pick up a copy of the Nevis Historical Society's self-guided tour of the island and stroll back onto Main Street.

While it is true that Charlestown has seen better days—it was founded in 1660—it's easy to imagine how it must have looked in its heyday. The buildings may be weathered and a bit the worse for wear now, but there is still evidence of past glory in their fanciful galleries, elaborate gingerbread, wood shutters, and colorful hanging plants.

The stonework building with the clock tower at the corner of Main and Prince William streets houses the **courthouse** and **library.** A fire in 1873 severely damaged the building and destroyed valuable records. The current building dates from the turn of the century. You're welcome to poke around the second-floor library (open Mon.–Sat. 9–6), a cooling retreat. If you intend to rent a car, go to the **police station** across from the courthouse for your local driver's license.

The little park opposite the courthouse is **Memorial Square,** dedicated to the fallen of World Wars I and II.

When you return to Main Street from Prince William Street, turn right and go past the pier. Main Street curves and becomes Craddock Road, but keep going straight and you'll be on Low Street. The **Alexander Hamilton Birthplace,** which contains the **Museum of Nevis History,** is on the waterfront, covered in bougainvillea and hibiscus. This Georgian-style house

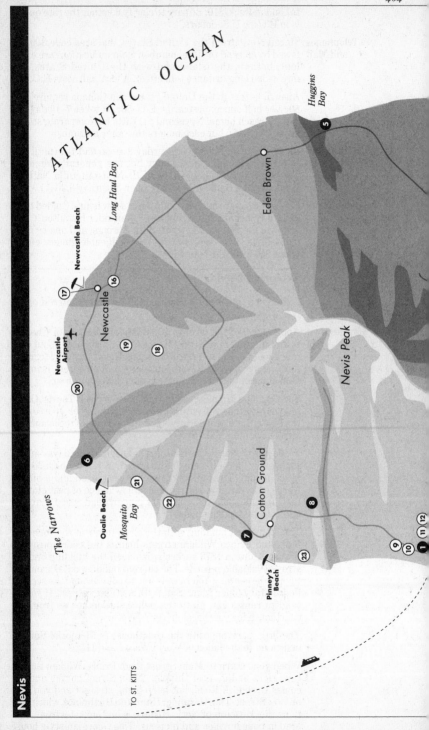

Nevis

TO ST. KITTS

ATLANTIC OCEAN

The Narrows

Mosquito Bay

Long Haul Bay

Huggins Bay

Oualie Beach

Pinney's Beach

Newcastle Beach

Newcastle Airport

Newcastle

Eden Brown

Cotton Ground

Nevis Peak

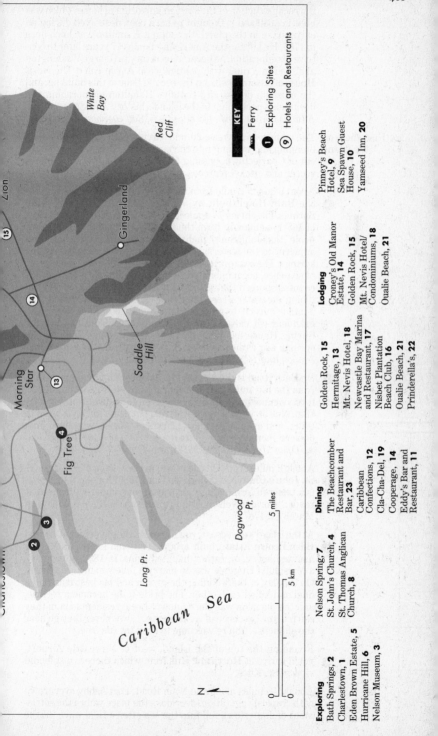

N

Caribbean Sea

Long Pt.

Dogwood Pt.

Morning Star

Fig Tree

Saddle Hill

Gingerland

White Bay

Red Cliff

0 ——— 5 km

0 ——— 5 miles

KEY

🚢 Ferry

1 Exploring Sites

9 Hotels and Restaurants

Exploring

Bath Springs, **2**
Charlestown, **1**
Eden Brown Estate, **5**
Hurricane Hill, **6**
Nelson Museum, **3**

Nelson Spring, **7**
St. John's Church, **4**
St. Thomas Anglican
Church, **8**

Dining

The Beachcomber
Restaurant and
Bar, **23**
Caribbean
Confections, **12**
Cla-Cha-Del, **19**
Cooperage, **14**
Eddy's Bar and
Restaurant, **11**

Golden Rock, **15**
Hermitage, **13**
Mt. Nevis Hotel, **18**
Newcastle Bay Marina
and Restaurant, **17**
Nisbet Plantation
Beach Club, **16**
Oualie Beach, **21**
Prinderella's, **22**

Lodging

Croney's Old Manor
Estate, **14**
Golden Rock, **15**
Mt. Nevis Hotel/
Condominiums, **18**
Oualie Beach, **21**

Pinney's Beach
Hotel, **9**
Sea Spawn Guest
House, **10**
Yamseed Inn, **20**

is a reconstruction of the statesman's original home, which was built in 1680 and is thought to have been destroyed during an earthquake in the mid-19th century. Hamilton was born here in 1755. He left for the American colonies 17 years later to contrive his education; he became secretary to George Washington and died in a duel with political rival Aaron Burr. The **Nevis House of Assembly** sits on the second floor of this building, and the museum downstairs contains Hamilton memorabilia and documents pertaining to the island's history. *Low St., no phone. Admission free. Open weekdays 8–4, Sat. 10–noon. Closed Sun.*

Elsewhere on the Island The main road makes a 20-mile circuit, with various offshoots bumping and winding into the mountains. Take the road south out of Charlestown, passing **Grove Park** along the way, where soccer and cricket matches are played.

2 About a quarter-mile from the park you'll come to the ruins of the **Bath Hotel** (built by John Huggins in 1778) and **Bath Springs.** The springs—some icy cold, others with temperatures of 108°F—emanate from the hillside and spill into the "great poole" that John Smith mentioned in 1607. Huggins's hotel was adjacent to the waters, with the Spring House built over the springs. The swanky hotel, which charged the outrageous price of sixpence, accommodated 50 guests. Eighteenth-century accounts reported that a stay of a few days, bathing in and imbibing the waters, resulted in miraculous cures. It would take a minor miracle to restore the decayed hotel to anything like grandeur—it closed down in the late 19th century—but the Spring House has been partially restored, and some of the springs are as hot as ever. *Bathing costs $2. Open weekdays 8–noon and 1–3:30, Sat. 8–noon. Closed Sun.*

3 On Bath Road is the **Nelson Museum,** containing memorabilia from the life and times of Admiral Lord Nelson, including letters, documents, paintings, and even furniture from his flagship. Nelson was based in Antigua, but came to Nevis often to court, and eventually marry, Frances Nisbet, who lived on a 64-acre plantation here. *Bath Rd., tel. 809/469–0408. Admission: $2. Open Mon.–Wed. 8–4:30, Thurs.–Fri. 8–4, Sat. 8–noon.*

4 About 2 miles from Charlestown, in the village of Fig Tree, is **St. John's Church,** which dates from 1680. Among its records is a tattered, prominently displayed marriage certificate that reads: "Horatio Nelson, Esquire, to Frances Nisbet, Widow, on March 11, 1787."

5 At the island's east coast, you'll come to the government-owned **Eden Brown Estate,** built around 1740 and known as Nevis's haunted house, or, rather, haunted ruins. In 1822, apparently, a Miss Julia Huggins was to marry a fellow named Maynard. On the day of the wedding the groom and his best man had a duel and killed each other. The bride-to-be became a recluse, and the mansion was closed down. Local residents claim they can feel the presence of . . . someone . . . whenever they go near the old house. You're welcome to drop by. It's free.

6 Rounding the top of the island, west of Newcastle Airport, you'll arrive at **Hurricane Hill,** from which there is a splendid view of St. Kitts.

About 1½ miles along the Main Road, **Fort Ashby,** overgrown with tropical vegetation, overlooks the place where the settlement of Jamestown fell into the sea after a tidal wave hit the coast in 1680. Needless to say, this is a favored target of scuba divers.

7 At nearby **Nelson Spring,** the waters have considerably decreased since the 1780s, when young Captain Horatio Nelson periodically filled his ships with fresh water here.

Before driving back into Charlestown, a little over a mile down **8** the road, stop to see the island's oldest church, **St. Thomas Anglican Church.** The church was built in 1643 and has been altered many times over the years. The gravestones in the old churchyard have stories to tell, and the church itself contains memorials to the early settlers of Nevis.

Beaches

All the beaches on the island are free to the public. There are no changing facilities, so you'll have to wear a swimsuit under your clothes. If you're doing a cab tour, you may arrange with your driver to drop you off at the beach and pick you up later. Most hotels are either located on the beach or provide transportation.

Pinney's Beach is the island's showpiece. It's almost 4 miles of soft, white sand backed by a cyclorama of palm trees, and it's on the calm Caribbean Sea. The palm-shaded lagoon is a scene right out of *South Pacific.* Several of the mountain inns have private cabanas and pavilions on the beach.

Oualie Beach, at Mosquito Bay, just north of Pinney's, is a black-sand beach where Oualie Beach Club (tel. 809/469–9518) can mix you a drink and fix you up with water-sports equipment.

Newcastle Beach is the beach location of Nisbet Plantation. Popular among snorkelers, it's a broad strand of soft, white sand shaded by coconut palms on the northernmost tip of the island, on the channel between St. Kitts and Nevis.

Sports and the Outdoors

Boating Hobie Cats and Sunfish can be rented from **Oualie Beach Club** (tel. 809/469–9518).

Hiking The center of the island is Nevis peak, which soars up to 3,232 feet, flanked by Hurricane Hill on the north and Saddle Hill on the south. To scale Mt. Nevis is a daylong affair that requires a guide. Your hotel can arrange it and pack a picnic lunch. Expect to pay about $45 a person for an all-day hike. The **Nevis Academy** (tel. 809/469–2091, fax 809/469–2113), headed by David Rollinson, offers ecorambles (slower tours) and hikes; the cost is $20 per person.

Tennis There are 10 tennis courts at the **Four Seasons Resort Nevis** (tel. 809/469–1111; fee $15 an hour), and two at **Pinney's Beach Hotel** (tel. 809/469–5207; fee $2 an hour). **Hermitage** (tel. 809/469–3477) and **Golden Rock** (tel. 809/469–3346) offer courts to nonguests at no charge.

Water Sports The village of **Jamestown** was washed into the sea around Fort Ashby; the area is a popular spot for snorkeling and diving. Reef-protected **Pinney's Beach** offers especially good snorkeling.

Snorkeling and waterskiing trips can be arranged through **Scuba Safaris** (tel. 809/469–9518), **Oualie Beach** (tel. 809/469–9518) and **Newcastle Bay Marina** (tel. 809/469–9395). Windsurfers can also be rented at both places. Scuba Safaris offers resort and NAUI-certification courses and a five-day dive package with two dives per day for $300 a person. The average cost of a single-tank dive on Nevis is $45, $80 for a two-tank dive. Snorkel equipment rents for about $10 a day.

Winston Crooke (tel. 809/469–9615) rents windsurfing equipment and provides instruction. A two-hour beginners class is $50 per person. Equipment rental is $12 an hour.

Shopping

Rare is the traveler who heads for Nevis on a shopping spree. However, there are some surprises, notably the island's stamps and batik and hand-embroidered clothing.

For dolls and baskets handcrafted in Nevis, visit **The Sandbox Tree** (tel. 809/469–5662) in Evelyn's Villa, Charlestown. Among other items available here are hand-painted chests. This is an appealing shop even if you are only browsing. The **Nevis Handicraft Co-op Society** (tel. 809/469–5509), next door to the Tourism Office, offers work by local artisans, including clothing, woven goods, and homemade jellies. Heading out of town, just past Alexander Hamilton's birthplace, you'll see the **Nevis Crafts Studio Cooperative.** Here Alvin Grante, a multitalented Nevisian artisan, displays his works and those of Ashley Phillips: hand-blocked prints and watercolors of the local landscape and architecture, hand-painted T-shirts, and baskets.

Stamp collectors should head for the **Philatelic Bureau,** just off Main Street opposite the Tourist Office. St. Kitts and Nevis are famous for their decorative, sometimes valuable, stamps. An early Kittitian stamp recently brought in $7,000.

Other local items of note are the batik caftans, scarves, and fabrics found in the Nevis branch of **Caribelle Batik** (in the Arcade of downtown Charlestown, tel. 809/469–1491).

Dining

Nevis is known for its memorable plantation dinners, ranging from candlelit meals in elegant dining rooms to family-style dinners and West Indian buffets. Although not all of these are affordable, there are three plantations on the island that serve fixed-price dinners costing $25–$35, including wine, per person. Another option is to visit at lunch, when some serve less expensive à la carte items. Besides these dining rooms, the island has a number of casual eateries serving inexpensive lunches and dinners. If you're renting a place with a kitchen, you can get fresh produce from the public market in Charlestown. **Super Foods** sells liquor as well as groceries.

Highly recommended restaurants are indicated by a star ★.

Category	Cost*
Moderate	$25–$35
Inexpensive	$15–$25
Budget	under $15

per person, excluding drinks and service

★ **Cooperage.** An old stone dining room provides an elegantly rustic setting for fixed-price or à la carte meals. The lunch menu includes Jamaican jerk chicken or pork; conch; sandwiches of lobster, tuna, and chicken salad; and steak burgers. The pricier dinner menu features grilled seafood, beef, lamb, veal, chicken, and pork. The $20 lobster is the most expensive item at dinner. *Croney's Old Manor Estate, tel. 809/469–3445. Reservations required. AE, D, MC, V. Moderate.*

Golden Rock. Come here for an alfresco lunch under an umbrella table. Salads include lobster and shrimp, chef, chicken, and tuna; sandwiches include lobster, shrimp, ham, tuna, and chicken, as well as hamburgers and cheeseburgers. Dinner is in an opulent dining room with handsome tablecloths and soft candlelight. West Indian and Continental dishes are served. *Golden Rock, tel. 809/469–3346. Reservations required. AE, MC, V. Closed Sun. Moderate.*

Hermitage. The atmosphere here is subdued, with white cloths, candlelight, and a backdrop of white latticework on the porch. Begin your meal with carrot-and-tarragon soup, then follow with West Indian red snapper in ginger sauce, and finish with a rum soufflé. The Hermitage is known for having the best rum punch on the island—no small accomplishment. *Hermitage Plantation, tel. 809/469–3477. Reservations required. AE, MC, V. Personal checks accepted. Moderate.*

Mt. Nevis Hotel. The airy 60-seat dining room, where tables are set with fine china and silver, opens onto the terrace and pool, beyond which spreads a splendid daytime view of St. Kitts in the distance. Starters include fish chowder and lobster bisque. Entrées may be red snapper, lobster, or sirloin steak embellished with mushrooms and onions. *Mt. Nevis Hotel/Condominiums, Newcastle, tel. 809/469–9373. Reservations advised. AE, D, MC, V. Moderate.*

Nisbet Plantation Beach Club. The beach- and poolside restaurant here, also known as Coconuts, is a pretty, breezy spot for a casual lunch. Menu items include sandwiches, seafood salads, and burgers. (The antiques-filled dining room in the Great House is out of our price range.) *Nisbet Plantation, tel. 809/469–9325. AE, MC, V. Lunch only. Inexpensive.*

Eddy's Bar and Restaurant. Located in the center of Charlestown, this is a popular in-town gathering spot for locals. Island specialties and stir-fry dishes are fine; especially good is the conch chowder. Stop by between 5 and 8 on Wednesdays for happy hour, when drinks are half-price and snacks are free. *Main St., Charlestown, tel. 809/469–5958. Reservations advised. AE, MC, V. Closed Sun. Inexpensive.*

Caribbean Confections. Drop by this friendly Charlestown establishment for local color and quick foods such as sandwiches, homemade pastries, peanut-butter cookies, and popcorn. The full menu includes mutton stew with peas, rice, and salad. On Saturdays, free hors d'oeuvres at 6 PM are followed by a courtyard buffet dinner and entertainment for $19 a person. The restaurant also serves breakfast. *Main St. (across from Tourist Office), Charlestown, tel. 809/469–5685. Reservations advised for Sat. buffet. MC, V. Budget–Inexpensive.*

Cla-Cha-Del. Locals know it as a place for authentic West Indian fare in an informal atmosphere. Seafood is also good here. On Saturdays, try the goatwater or bullhead stew. *Shaw's Rd., Newcastle, tel. 809/469–9640. Reservations required for dinner. No lunch Sun. Budget–Inexpensive.*

Prinderella's. Although its perfect beachside setting made it a prime target for Hurricane Hugo, owners Ian and Charlie Mintrim have rebuilt and reopened their popular restaurant. Lunch features flying fish and chips, grilled lobster, and salmon. On Tamarind Bay, with views across the channel to St. Kitts, it's a great spot for a sunset drink. *Jones Bridge, tel. 809/469–9291. AE, MC, V. No dinner Sun.–Mon. Budget–Inexpensive.*

Oualie Beach. This low-key, casual bar and restaurant on Oualie Bay is the perfect stop during a round-the-island tour or after a long day on the beach. Try the delicious homemade soups, including ground-nut or breadfruit vichyssoise. Then move on to Creole conch stew or lobster crêpes. *Oualie Beach, tel. 809/469–9735. MC, V. Budget–Inexpensive.*

The Beachcomber Restaurant & Bar. The prices at this casual spot on Pinney's Beach can't be beat anywhere on the island. You can select from grilled items, including steak, wahoo, snapper, and lobster, or opt for more informal fare, such as cheeseburgers, tuna or chef's salads, and conch chowder. The special is linguini with calamari and lobster. Service is friendly. *Pinney's Beach, tel. 809/469–1192. MC, V. Budget.*

Newcastle Bay Marina and Restaurant. The pizza here is excellent, but even non–pizza lovers will enjoy sitting back on the deck and looking out to sea. Try the conch chowder, a sandwich, or a salad. This complex, part of the Mt. Nevis hotel, will soon include a fitness facility and live entertainment on certain evenings. *Newcastle Bay Marina, tel. 809/469–9373. AE, D, MC, V. Closed Wed. and mid-Apr.–mid-Dec. Budget.*

Lodging

Restored sugar plantations are Nevis's trademark lodging. Two of the island's five plantations have rates that fall into the top end of our Moderate category in high season. You'll do better in low season (*see* Off-Season Bets, *below*), when more of the plantations become affordable. Most of these operate on the Modified American Plan (MAP; breakfast and dinner included in room rate). Besides these fairly pricey accommodations, choices are somewhat limited, with a handful of budget hotels and guest houses.

Highly recommended lodgings are indicated by a star ★.

Category	Cost*
Moderate	$115–$175
Inexpensive	$90–$115
Budget	under $90

All prices are for a standard double room for two, excluding 7% tax and a 10% service charge. To estimate rates for hotels offering MAP, add about $35–$40 per person per day to the above price ranges.

Croney's Old Manor Estate. Vast tropical gardens surround this restored sugar plantation. Many guest rooms have high ceilings, king-size four-poster beds, and colonial reproductions, but some units are a bit gloomy and dark. The outbuildings, such as the smokehouse and jail, have been imaginatively restored, and the old cistern is now the pool. This is the home of The Cooperage, one of the island's best restaurants (*see* Dining, *above*). There's transportation to and from the beach. The hotel is not recommended for children under 12. *Box 70, Charlestown, tel. 809/469–3445, 800/223–9815, or 800/892–7093, fax 809/469–3388. 14 rooms. Facilities: pool, 2 restaurants, 2 bars. AE, MC, V. EP, MAP. Moderate.*

★ **Golden Rock.** Co-owner Pam Barry is a direct descendant of the original owner of this 200-year-old estate. She has decorated the five cottages in a style befitting a plantation. Rooms have handsome four-poster beds of mahogany or bamboo, native grass rugs, rocking chairs, and island-made fabrics of floral prints; all have patios. The restored sugar mill is a two-level suite for honeymooners or families, and the old cistern is now a spring-fed swimming pool. The estate covers 150 mountainous acres and is surrounded by 25 acres of lavish tropical gardens. Enjoy the Atlantic view and cooling breeze from the bar. A shuttle transports guests to Pinney's and Windward beaches. *Box 493, Gingerland, tel. 809/469–3346, fax 809/469–2113. 16 rooms. Facilities: restaurant, bar, pool, tennis court. AE, MC, V. Personal checks accepted. EP, MAP. Moderate.*

Mt. Nevis Hotel/Condominiums. Standard rooms and suites at this hotel are done up with handsome white wicker furnishings, glass-top tables, and colorful island prints. All units have a balcony, direct-dial phone, cable TV, and VCR. Suites with kitchens are only affordable in the off-season. The main building houses the casual restaurant and terrace-bar, overlooking the pool and St. Kitts beyond. Shuttle service is provided to the water-sports center and outdoor restaurant at Newcastle Beach. The hotel has its own ferry, used for moonlight cruises when it's not carrying passengers to and from St. Kitts. *Box 494, Newcastle, tel. 809/469–9373 (collect), fax 809/469–9375. 32 rooms. Facilities: pool, restaurant, bar, water sports, beach club. AE, D, MC, V. EP, MAP. Moderate.*

Oualie Beach. Six (more are being built) white West Indian cottages line the shore facing the channel to St. Kitts—a great view. The rooms are bright, roomy, and simply furnished. There is a full dive shop here offering NAUI-certified instruction, and dive packages are available. Sunfish and Windsurfers may be rented. Breakfast, lunch, and dinner are served at an informal restaurant and bar. *Oualie Beach, tel. 809/469–9735, fax 809/469–9176. 6 rooms. Facilities: restaurant, bar, water-sports center. MC, V. EP, MAP. Inexpensive.*

Pinney's Beach Hotel. These bungalows and rooms are smack on Pinney's Beach, but be prepared for basic, no-frills accommodations. All rooms are air-conditioned; some of the cottages are set around a garden. You'll be more comfortable in one that opens directly onto the beach. *Pinney's Beach, tel. 809/469–5207 or 312/699–7570 in the U.S. 48 rooms. Facilities: 2 restaurants, 2 bars, 2 tennis courts, pool. AE, MC, V. EP. Inexpensive.*

Sea Spawn Guest House. If you're willing to forsake all extras, this place is among the least expensive on the island. Rooms are bare but clean. Guests pay $7 to use a communal kitchen. Breakfast, lunch, and dinner are served in the restaurant. It's a two-minute walk to Pinney's Beach and a 10-minute walk to Charlestown. Service is not especially friendly. *Old Hospital Rd., Charlestown, tel. 809/469–5239, fax 809/469–5706. Facilities: dining room, lounge, beach cabana, common kitchen. MC, V. EP. Budget.*

Yamseed Inn. This pale yellow bed-and-breakfast has its own beach on the northernmost part of Nevis, overlooking St. Kitts. Friendly innkeeper Sybil Siegfried presides; her breakfasts include eggs, fresh fruits, and breads. Guests will need a car to get to restaurants and shops. *On the beach, Newcastle, tel. 809/469–9361. 4 rooms. 3-night minimum. No credit cards. BP. Budget.*

Villa and Cottage Rentals Nevis has several villa and cottage complexes that offer an affordable alternative to hotels and guest houses. Among them are **Pinney's Village Complex** (Box 508, Charlestown, tel. 809/469–1811; $31–$65 a night); **Hurricane Cove Bungalows** (Mosquito Bay, tel. 809/469–9462; $75–$115 a night); and **Castle Bay Villas** (Newcastle, tel. 809/469–9088/9490; $125–$150 a night).

Off-Season Bets Although the plantations tend to be expensive, an off-season visit brings more of these charming properties within reach, including the **Hermitage** (St. Johns, Figtree Paris, tel. 809/469–3477) and **Nisbet Plantation Beach Club** (Newcastle, St. James Parish, tel. 809/469–9325).

Nightlife

The hotels usually bring in local calypso singers and steel or string bands one night a week. On Friday night the Shell All-Stars steel band entertains in the gardens at **Croney's Old Manor** (tel. 809/469–3445). The **Golden Rock** (tel. 809/469–3346) brings in the Honeybees String Band to jazz up the Saturday-night buffet. Have dinner and a dance on Wednesday nights at **Pinney's Beach Hotel** (tel. 809/469–5207).

For hi-fi calypso, reggae, and other island music on weekends, young locals head for **Mariner's Pub & Bar** (tel. 809/469–1993) near Fort Ashby and **Dick's Bar** (no phone) in Brickiln.

22 St. Lucia

*Updated by
Nigel Fisher*

Oval, lush St. Lucia, 27 miles long and 14 miles wide, sits at the southern end of the Windward Islands. It has two topographical features, apart from its beaches, that earn it a special place in the Caribbean tableau of islands: the twin peaks of the Pitons (Petit and Gros), which rise to more than 2,400 feet, and the bubbling sulfur springs in the town of Soufrière, part of a low-lying volcano that erupted thousands of years ago and now attracts visitors with its curative waters.

This is a ruggedly beautiful island, with towering mountains, lush green valleys, and acres of banana plantations. Yachtsmen put in at Marigot Bay, one of the Caribbean's most beautiful secluded bays. The diving is good, and so is the liming—the St. Lucian term for "hanging out." The honeymoon set has found out that St. Lucian law requires residence for only four days for couples to acquire a marriage license.

In recent years, St. Lucia has become home to an increasing number of all-inclusive resorts, many of them upscale properties with luxury amenities and high price tags. Inexpensive lodging alternatives are not plentiful, nor is cheap dining. Car rental costs more than on many other islands, and public transportation is limited.

Still, an affordable vacation on St. Lucia is far from impossible. Moderately priced all-inclusives do exist here (*see* Lodging, *below*), as well as a few budget properties. And off-season travel—always a smart idea in the Caribbean—is even more appealing on St. Lucia, where two of the most charming hotels on the islands drop their rates enough to make them an excel-

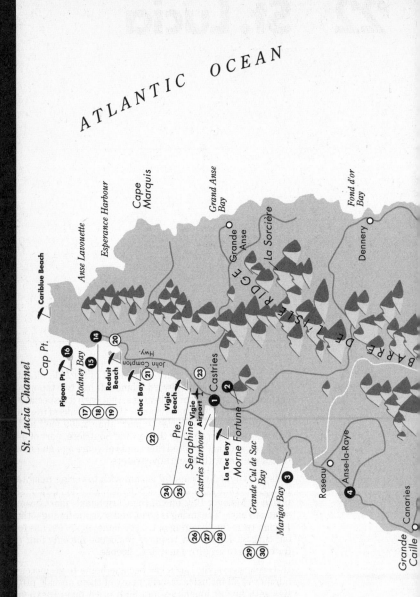

ATLANTIC OCEAN

St. Lucia Channel

Cap Pt.

Cariblue Beach

Pigeon Pt. 16

14

20

Rodney Bay

15

17 18 19

Reduit Beach

Choc Bay

21

John Compton Hwy.

22

Vigie Beach

Pte.

Seraphine Vigie

Castries Harbour Airport

1 Castries

23

2

24 25

La Toc Bay

Morne Fortune

26 27 28

Grande Cul de Sac Bay

29 30

Marigot Bay

3

Anse Lavonette

Esperance Harbour

Cape Marquis

Grand Anse Bay

Grande Anse

La Sorcière

BARRE DE L'ISLE RIDGE

Fond d'or Bay

Dennery

Roseau

Anse-la-Raye

4

Grande Caille

Canaries

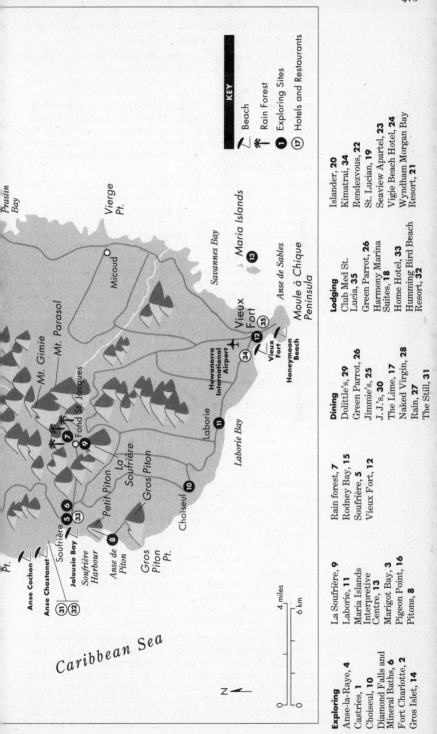

lent value (*see* Off-Season Bets, *below*). Route taxis (usually minivans) ply fixed routes here and offer intrepid travelers the chance to get around cheaply.

The history of this 238-square-mile island resembles that of many in the Caribbean. After a 150-year struggle between the French and the English for control of St. Lucia, during which the island changed hands 14 times, the British took permanent possession in 1814. On February 22, 1979, St. Lucia became an independent state within the British Commonwealth of Nations, with a resident governor-general appointed by the queen. Still, there are many relics of French occupation, notably the island patois, the Creole cuisine, and the names of the places and the people.

What It Will Cost These sample prices, meant only as a general guide, are for high season. While you can find budget accommodation in motellike lodgings, expect to pay $125 a night or more at an inexpensive, full-service hotel. A moderately priced all-inclusive resort will cost about $300 or more per couple per night. Transportation, be it taxi or rental car, is also high: A car costs about $60 a day. Public transportation is limited, but a minivan, or route taxi, from Castries to Rodney Bay is about $2; from Castries to Vieux Fort, it's about $5.50. Fish is reasonably priced here, but imported goods, such as coffee, are expensive. Expect to pay about $20 a person for a modest dinner; at least $5 for lunch at an inexpensive café. Wine is prohibitively expensive; stick to local rum punches or beer, which starts at about $1.75 in restaurants. A single-tank scuba dive is about $45; snorkel equipment rents for about $5 a day.

Before You Go

Tourist Information Contact the **St. Lucia Tourist Board** (820 2nd Ave., 9th floor, New York, NY 10017, tel. 212/867–2950 or 800/456–3984, fax 212/370–7867; in Canada: 151 Bloor St. W, Suite 425, Toronto, Ont., Canada M5S 1S4, tel. 416/867–2950, fax 416/961–4317; in the United Kingdom: 10 Kensington Court, London W8 5DL, tel. 071/937–1969, fax 071/937–3611).

Arriving and Departing There are two airports on the island. Wide-body planes land at Hewanorra International Airport on the southern tip of the island. Vigie Airport, near Castries, handles interisland and charter flights. **BWIA** (tel. 800/327–7401) has direct service from Miami. **American** (tel. 800/433–7300) has daily service from New York, Dallas, and other major U.S. cities, with a stopover in San Juan and continuing service via **American Eagle** . **Air Canada** (tel. 800/422–6232) flies from Toronto to Barbados and Antigua, connecting with flights to St. Lucia. **LIAT**'s(tel. 809/462–0701) small island hoppers fly into Vigie Airport, linking St. Lucia with Barbados, Trinidad, Antigua, Martinique, Dominica, Guadeloupe, and other islands.

From the Airport Taxis are unmetered, and although the government has issued a list of suggested fares, these are not regulated. You should negotiate with the driver *before* you get in the car, and be sure that you both understand whether the price you've agreed upon is in E.C. or U.S. dollars. The drive from Hewanorra to Castries takes about 75 minutes and should cost about U.S. $45—almost as much as a full day's car rental. A taxi to Castries from Vigie Airport, on the other hand, is only about $5. If you plan to rent a car for your entire stay, consider picking it up at the airport.

Passports and Visas U.S., Canadian, and British citizens must produce a valid passport. A driver's license alone will *not* do. In addition, all visitors must have a return or ongoing ticket.

Language The official language is English, but you'll also hear some French and patois.

Precautions Bring along industrial-strength insect repellent to ward off the mosquitoes and sand flies. Centipede bites, though rare and not lethal, can be painful and cause swelling. If you're bitten, you should see a doctor. If you happen to step on a sea urchin, its long black spines may lodge under the skin; don't try to pull them out, because you could cause infection. Apply ammonia or an ammonia-based liquid as quickly as possible, and the spine will retreat, allowing you to ease it out. Don't touch or even sit under a manchineel tree, whose poisonous fruit and leaves cause skin blisters. The waters on the Atlantic (east) coast can be rough, with dangerous undertows—avoid swimming there. Vendors and self-employed guides in places like Sulphur Springs (where your entrance fee includes a guided tour) can be tenacious. If you do hire a guide, be sure the fee is clearly fixed up front. As a courtesy rather than a precaution, you should always ask before taking an islander's picture and be prepared to part with a few coins in return.

Staying in St. Lucia

Important Addresses **Tourist Information: St. Lucia Tourist Board** is based at the Pointe Seraphine duty-free complex on Castries Harbor (tel. 809/452–4094 or 809/452–5968). The office is open weekdays 8–4:30. There is also a tourist information desk at each of the two airports (Vigie, tel. 809/452–2596, and Hewanorra, tel. 809/454–6644).

Emergencies **Police:** Call 999. **Hospitals:** Hospitals with 24-hour emergency rooms are **Victoria Hospital** (Hospital Rd., Castries, tel. 809/452–2421) and **St. Jude's Hospital** (Vieux Fort, tel. 809/454–6041). **Pharmacies:** The largest pharmacy is **Williams Pharmacy** (Williams Bldg., Bridge St., Castries, tel. 809/452–2797).

Currency The official currency is the Eastern Caribbean dollar (E.C.$). Figure about E.C. $2.70 to the U.S. $1. U.S. dollars are readily accepted, but you'll usually get change in E.C. dollars. Major credit cards are widely accepted, as are traveler's checks. Prices quoted here are in U.S. dollars unless indicated otherwise.

Taxes and Service Charges Hotels collect an 8% government tax; a 10% service charge is added to your bill. Most restaurants also add 10% service to the bill. Tip taxi drivers 10%. There is no sales tax. The departure tax is $11, or E.C. $27.

Getting Around Discovering St. Lucia using public transportation is difficult. You will probably want to budget for either renting a car for at least two days or taking a guided tour (*see below*).

Buses There's no organized service, but minivans, or route taxis, cruise the island and, like taxis, will stop when hailed. You can also catch a minivan in Castries by hanging around outside Clarke Cinema (corner Micoud and Bridge Sts.). This is the cheapest way to get around the island. The fare varies according to distance. A ride from Castries to Rodney Bay is E.C. $5; to Vieux Fort, E.C. $15. Be sure you are being charged the minivan and not the private taxi rate.

Taxis Taxis are always available at the airport, the harbor, and in front of the major hotels. Most hotels post the names and phone numbers of drivers and a table of fares set by the taxi commission. Learn the fare before you agree to a journey. The cost from Hewanorra Airport to Castries, for example, is $45.

Rental Cars Driving is on the left. Roads are congested around Castries and in the north; to the south, traffic is light. Expect occasional kidney-punching potholes. To rent a car, you have to be 25 years or older and hold a valid driver's license. You must buy a temporary St. Lucian license at the airports or police headquarters (Bridge St., Castries) for $16. Rental agencies include **Avis** (tel. 809/452–2700 or 800/331–2112), **Budget** (tel. 809/452–0233 or 800/527–0700), **Dollar** (tel. 809/452–0994), and **National** (tel. 809/452–8028 or 800/328–4567). Rates are high—from $60 a day.

Telephones and Mail To call St. Lucia from the United States, dial area code 809, access code 45, and the local five-digit number. You can make direct-dial long-distance calls from the island, and the connections are excellent. To place interisland calls, dial the local five-digit number. A local call costs E.C. 25¢.

Postage for airmail letters to the United States and Canada is E.C. 95¢ and E.C. $1.10 to Great Britain up to one ounce; postcard postage is E.C. 65¢ and E.C. 70¢, respectively.

Opening and Closing Times Shops are open weekdays 8–12:30 and 1:30–4, Saturday 8–noon. Banks are open Monday–Thursday 8–2, Friday 8–1 and 3–5.

Guided Tours **Taxi drivers** take special guide courses and offer the most personalized way to see the island. Four can share a car and cut rates; otherwise, costs are steep. A six-hour tour around the island costs $120 (tip additional) and takes approximately six hours. Hourly taxi rates are about $20. The **Carib Touring Company** (tel. 809/452–6791) and **Sunlink International** (tel. 809/452–8232) offer a variety of half- and full-day tours. A full-day tour of southern St. Lucia, including the Pitons and Mt. Soufrière, costs $25 per person. **Barnard's Travel** (Bridge St., Castries, tel. 809/452–2214) and **St. Lucia Representative Services Ltd.** (tel. 809/452–3762) also offer half- and full-day island tours.

Exploring St. Lucia

Numbers in the margin correspond to points of interest on the St. Lucia map.

Castries
❶ **Castries,** on the northwest coast, is a busy city with a population of about 60,000. It lies in a sheltered bay surrounded by green hills. Ships carrying bananas, coconut, cocoa, mace, nutmeg, and citrus fruits for export leave from **Castries Harbour,** one of the busiest ports in the Caribbean. Cruise ships dock here, too, though most now use the new cruise terminal at **Pointe Seraphine,** a Spanish-style complex that includes duty-free shops. The Tourist Board is here, so you may want to drop by to collect free maps and brochures. It is also the starting point for many island tours.

The John Compton Highway connects the duty-free complex to downtown Castries. To reach the downtown center from Pointe Seraphine's transportation terminal, you can stroll for 20 minutes or take a cab.

Castries, with Morne Fortune (the Hill of Good Luck) rising behind it, has had more than its share of bad luck over the years, including two hurricanes and four fires. As a result, it lacks the colorful colonial buildings found in other island capitals. Most of the buildings are modern, and the town has only a few sights of historical note.

Head first to **Columbus Square,** a green oasis ringed by Brazil, Laborie, Micoud, and Bourbon streets. At the corner of Laborie and Micoud streets there is a 400-year-old saman tree. A favorite local story is of the English botanist who came to St. Lucia many years ago to catalogue the flora. Awestruck by this huge old tree, she asked a passerby what it was. "Massav," he replied, and she gratefully jotted that down in her notebook, unaware that "massav" is patois for "I don't know."

Directly across the street is the Roman Catholic **Cathedral of the Immaculate Conception,** which was built in 1897.

Some of the 19th-century buildings that managed to survive fire, winds, and rains can be seen on Brazil Street, the southern border of the square.

Head north on Laborie Street and walk past the government buildings on your right. On the left, William Peter Boulevard is one of Castries's shopping areas. "The Boulevard" connects Laborie Street with Bridge Street, another shopping street.

Continue north for one more block on Laborie Street and you'll come to Jeremie Street. Turn right, and you'll see the **market** on the corner of Jeremie and Peynier streets. On Saturday mornings, the market is thronged with a colorful crowd of shoppers and farmers selling produce.

Elsewhere on the Island

Morne Fortune

You'll need a full day to explore the island south of Castries. A rental car gives you greater flexibility and is cheaper than a guided tour, if shared among three or four people. Leaving Castries, head due east on Bridge Street to ascend **Morne Fortune.** The drive will take you past the **Government House,** the official residence of the governor-general of St. Lucia. If you want to take a picture of the house, ask the guard on duty before focusing your camera. You cannot take pictures when the governor-general is in residence.

You'll want to stop before the hill's summit to embrace the views. To the north is the Vigie Peninsula, once heavily fortified and now home to the island's greatest concentration of resort playgrounds. The island rising on the horizon is Martinique. To the south you'll see the twin peaks of the Pitons.

2 **Fort Charlotte** on the Morne was begun in 1764 by the French as the Citadelle du Morne Fortune. It was completed 20 years later, but during those years many battles were fought here, and the fortress changed hands a number of times. The Inniskilling Monument is a tribute to one of the most famous battles, fought in 1796, when the 27th Foot Royal Inniskilling Fusiliers wrested the Hill of Good Fortune from the French. Admission to Fort Charlotte is free, and you can wander at will to see the Four Apostles Battery; the Combermere Barracks, which are now part of an educational complex; and the redoubts, guard room, stables, and cells. Stop in the Military Cemetery. It was first used in 1782, and the faint inscriptions on the tombstones tell the tales of the French and English soldiers who died here. Six former governors of the island are buried here as well.

South of Castries The road from Castries to Soufrière travels through beautiful country. Keep in mind, though, that the many hairpin curves make this road a difficult drive. You'll also be handling a right-hand drive vehicle on the left side of a curving road. From Anse-la-Raye to Soufrière, you may run into construction delays as crews work to widen the road; at press time, this work was scheduled for completion by the end of 1993.

❸ In the area of Roseau, make a detour and drive to **Marigot Bay.** In 1778, British Admiral Samuel Barrington took his ships into this secluded bay within a bay and covered them with palm fronds to hide them from the French. The resort community today is a great favorite of yachtspeople. You can swim, snorkel, or lime with the yachting crowd at one of the bars. A 24-hour water taxi connects the various points on the bay.

If you continue south, you'll be in the vicinity of one of the island's two rum distilleries. Major production of sugar ceased here in about 1960, and distilleries now make rum with imported molasses. You're also in banana country, with acres of banana trees covering the hills and valleys. More than 127 different varieties are grown on the island.

In the mountainous region ahead you'll see **Mt. Parasol,** and if you look hard enough through the mists, you may be able to make out **Mt. Gimie,** St. Lucia's highest peak, rising to 3,117
❹ feet. The next village you'll come to is **Anse-la-Raye.** The beach here is a colorful sight, with fishing nets hanging on poles to dry and brightly painted fishing boats bobbing in the water. The fishermen of Anse-la-Raye still make canoes the old-fashioned way, by burning out the center of a log.

Soufrière As you approach the town of **Soufrière,** you'll be in the island's
❺ breadbasket, where most of the mangoes, breadfruit, tomatoes, limes, and oranges are grown. The town, which dates from the mid-18th century, was named after the nearby volcano and has a population of about 9,000 people. The Soufrière Harbour is the deepest harbor on the island, accommodating cruise ships that nose right up to the wharf. The nearby jetty contains an excellent small-crafts center. The **Soufrière Tourist Information Centre** (Bay St., tel. 809/454–7419) can provide information about the attractions in the area, which, in addition to the Pitons, include La Soufrière, billed as the world's only drive-in volcano, and its sulfur springs; the Diamond Mineral Baths; and the rain forest. You can also ask at the Tourist Center about Soufrière Estate, on the east side of town, replete with botanical gardens and minizoo.

❻ Adjoining Soufrière Estate are the **Diamond Falls and Mineral Baths,** which are fed by an underground flow of water from the sulfur springs. Louis XVI provided funds for the construction of these baths for his troops to "fortify them against the St. Lucian climate." During the Brigand's War, just after the French Revolution, the baths were destroyed. They were restored in 1966, and you can see the waterfalls and gardens before slipping into your swimsuit for a dip in the steaming curative waters. *Soufrière. Admission: E.C. $5. Open daily 10– 5.*

7 The island's dense tropical **rain forest** is to the east of Soufrière on the road to Fond St. Jacques. The trek through the lush landscape takes three hours, and you'll need a guide. Mt. Gimie (St. Lucia's highest peak), Piton Canaries, Mt. Houlom, and Piton Tromasse are all part of this immense forest reserve. The views of the mountains and valleys are spectacular.

8 For the best land view of the **Pitons,** take the road south out of Soufrière. The road is awful and leads up a steep hill, but if you persevere, you'll be rewarded by the sight of the twin peaks. The perfectly shaped pyramidal cones, covered with tropical greenery, were formed of lava from a volcanic eruption 30 million to 40 million years ago. The tallest is Petit Piton (2,619 feet) and its twin, Gros Piton (2,461 feet). Gros Piton is actually shorter but fatter than its twin.

To the south of Soufrière, your nose will note the left turn that **9** takes you to **La Soufrière,** the drive-in volcano, and its **sulfur springs.** There are more than 20 pools of black, belching, smelly sulfurous waters and yellow-green sulfur baking and steaming. Although the sign proclaims this to be the world's only drive-in volcano, it is not strictly a volcano at all, but a fault in the substratum rock. Take the guided tour offered by the Tourist Board. *La Soufrière. Admission: E.C. $3 (including guided tour). Open daily 9–5.*

Follow the road farther south and you'll come next to the **10** coastal town of **Choiseul,** home to wood-carving and pottery shops. At the turn of the road past the Anglican Church, built in 1846, a bridge crosses the river Dorée, so named because the riverbed is blanketed with fool's gold. In La Fargue, just to the south, the **Choiseul Arts & Craft Centre** (tel. 809/452–3226) sells superb traditional Carib handicrafts, including pottery, wickerwork, and braided khus-khus grass mats and baskets.

11 The next stop is **Laborie,** a little fishing village where you can buy cheese, bread, and fish.

12 Now drive along the southern coast of the island to **Vieux Fort,** St. Lucia's second-largest city and home of Hewanorra International Airport. Drive out on the **Moule à Chique Peninsula,** the southernmost tip of the island. If you look to the north, you can see all of St. Lucia and, if the day is especially clear, you can spot the island of St. Vincent 21 miles to the south. Looking straight down, you can see where the waters of the Caribbean blend with the bluer Atlantic.

13 At the **Maria Islands Interpretive Centre** you can find out all there is to know about the Maria Islands Nature Reserve. The reserve consists of two tiny islands in the Atlantic off the southeast coast of St. Lucia. The 25-acre Maria Major and its little sister, 4-acre Maria Minor, are inhabited by rare species of lizards and snakes that share their home with fregate birds, terns, doves, and other wildlife. *Moule à Chique, no phone. Admission: Wed.–Sat. E.C. $3, Sun. E.C. 50¢. Open Wed.–Sun. 9:30–5.*

A good road leads from Vieux Fort through the towns on the Atlantic coast. The road will take you past **Honeymoon Beach,** a wide, grassy, flat Anse l'Islet peninsula jutting into the ocean.

Drive through Micoud and, a few miles farther north, Dennery, both of which are residential towns overlooking the Atlantic. At Dennery the road turns west and climbs across the Barre de l'Isle Ridge through a tiny rain forest with dense vegetation. There are trails along the way that lead to lookout points where you can get a view of the National Forest Preserve. This bumpy road will take you all the way back to Castries.

The North End The east coast north of Castries is home to most of St. Lucia's
and Gros Islet resort hotels and some of the island's best beaches. There is little need to make this a specific tour, especially if you are staying at one of these hotels. During the day, route taxis continuously travel between Castries and Pigeon Point.

14 If you're driving, take the John Compton Highway north out of town for about five minutes to the Vigie Airport. **Gros Islet** to the north is normally a quiet little fishing village not unlike Anse-la-Raye to the south; but on Friday nights, it is transformed by a lively street festival—or jump-up—to which the whole island is invited.

15 **Rodney Bay,** named after Admiral Rodney, is an 80-acre manmade lagoon that's home to a host of hotels and restaurants.

Pigeon Point **Pigeon Point,** jutting out on the northwest coast, was Pigeon
16 Island until a causeway was built to connect it to the mainland. Tales are told of the pirate Jambe de Bois (Wooden Leg), who used to hide out here. This 40-acre area, a strategic point during the struggles for control of the island, is now a national park, with long sandy beaches, calm waters for swimming, and areas for picnicking.

The **Pigeon Point Museum** includes the ruins of barracks, batteries, and garrisons dating from the French and English battles. *Pigeon Point, no phone. Admission: E.C. $3. Open Mon.–Sat. 9–4.*

Beaches

All of St. Lucia's beaches are public, and many are flanked by hotels where you can rent water-sports equipment and have a rum punch. Unlike many islands, St. Lucia does not have any major hotel strip, where property after property lines a single beach. Rather, hotels tend to have their own stretches of sand; visitors usually keep to the beach where they are staying. There are also secluded beaches, accessible only by water, to which hotels can arrange boat trips. It is not advisable to swim along the windward (east) coast, where the Atlantic waters are rough and sometimes dangerous.

Pigeon Point off the northern shore has secluded white-sand beaches, fine for picnicking and swimming. You can walk to the beaches from the main road.

Reduit Beach is a long stretch of beige sand between Choc Bay and Pigeon Point and is home to the St. Lucian Hotel, which offers numerous water sports. You can walk or drive here from the main road.

Vigie Beach and **Choc Bay,** north of Castries Harbour, have fine beige sand and calm waters; both are within walking distance of the main road.

La Toc Bay is near Castries Harbour and is accessible by car or taxi. The sand here is beige.

Anse Cochon, on the Caribbean coast, is a black-sand beach accessible only by boat. The waters are superb for swimming and snorkeling.

Anse Chastanet is a gray-sand beach just north of Soufrière, with a backdrop of green hills and the island's best reefs for snorkeling and diving. Anse Chastanet Hotel, located here, has a dive shop and bar on the beach. You'll need a vehicle to travel from Soufrière down the rutted road that leads to the hotel and beach.

Jalousie Bay, south of Soufrière, is a bay several miles deep between the Pitons. Accessible only by boat, it offers great snorkeling and diving.

Vieux Fort, at the southernmost tip, has a long secluded stretch of gray volcanic sand and waters protected by reefs. **Honeymoon Beach** is another sandy escape just west of Vieux Fort. You'll need a car to reach either one.

Sports and the Outdoors

Most hotels offer Sunfish, water skis, fins, masks, and other water-sports equipment free to guests and for a fee to nonguests.

Golf   At **Sandals St. Lucia** (tel. 809/452–3081), the former Cunard La Toc, there is a 9-hole course. There is also a 9-plus-9 course at **Cap Estate Golf Club** (tel. 809/452–8523). Greens fees at both are about E.C. $15, and clubs are available for rental.

Hiking   The island is laced with trails, but you should not attempt the challenging peaks on your own. Your hotel or the Tourist Board can provide you with a guide. It's not unusual to pay $60 a day for a guided hike, and even more to scale the Pitons. These are serious, demanding excursions, usually with a maximum of four hikers per guide. You'll need strong legs and proper footwear. Discuss the level of fitness required with the guide before deciding to go. **The St. Lucia National Trust** (tel. 809/452–5005), established to preserve the island's natural and cultural heritage, can advise on less difficult nature walks and trails. This organization tours several sites, including Pigeon Island, the Maria Islands, and Fregate Island.

Jogging   You can jog on the beach by yourself or team up with the **Roadbusters** (tel. Jimmie at 809/452–5142 or evenings at 809/452–4790) at no cost.

Scuba Diving   Scuba St. Lucia (tel. 809/454–7000) is a PADI five-star training facility that offers daily beach and boat dives, resort courses, underwater photography, and day trips. **Marigot Bay Resort** (tel. 809/453–4357) offers a full scuba program that includes certification. Dive trips are also arranged through **Buddies Scuba** (tel. 809/452–5288) and through most of the hotels. The cost of a single-tank dive starts at $45. Snorkel equipment rents for about $5 a day. **Anse Chastenet** (tel. 809/454–7000 or 800/545–2459), a hotel located close to some of the island's best dive sites, offers seven-day dive packages that include two dives daily.

Sea and Snorkeling Excursions The 140-foot square-rigger *Brig Unicorn* (tel. 809/452–6811) sails to Soufrière, with steel bands, a swim stop, rum punch, and soda. Its sister schooner, the *Buccaneer,* also does outings. **Captain Mike's** (tel. 809/452–0216) provides swimming and snorkeling cruises; the *Sailing Bus* (tel. 809/452–8725) offers a full-day sail from Rodney Bay to Marigot; and **Jacob's Watersports** (tel. 809/452–8281) features speedboat and snorkeling cruises. Sea and snorkeling excursions can also be arranged through **Maho** (tel. 809/452–3762) and **The Surf Queen** (tel. 809/452–3762) or through your hotel. These excursions range from $15 for snorkeling to $70 for a lunch cruise.

Squash There is one squash court at **Cap Estate Golf Course** (tel. 809/452–8523), and two at **Club St. Lucia** (tel. 809/452–0551) and **The St. Lucian Yacht Club** (Rodney Bay, tel. 809/452–8350).

Tennis All the major hotels have their own tennis courts, but many of them prohibit nonguests from playing. Those that do allow nonguests charge about $10 for 45 minutes of court time. Failing that, **Club St. Lucia** (tel. 809/452–0551), with its seven lighted courts, offers temporary memberships to nonguests.

Waterskiing Contact **Jacob's Watersports** (tel. 809/452–8281). Rentals are also available at most of the hotels for about $20 for 15 minutes.

Windsurfing The **St. Lucian Hotel** is the local agent for Mistral Windsurfers (tel. 809/452–8351). Also contact **Marigot Bay Resort** (tel. 809/453–4357) and **Jacob's Watersports** (tel. 809/452–8281). Most hotels rent Windsurfers to nonguests for about $10 an hour ($35 for instruction).

Shopping

Shopping on St. Lucia is low-key, and you won't find many bargains. The island's best-known products are the unique hand-silk-screened and hand-printed designs of Bagshaw Studios. Bagshaw products are designed, printed, and sold only on St. Lucia. In addition, there are native-made wood carvings, pottery, and straw hats and baskets. Local products offer your best hope for bargains. Some of the straw baskets at the Castries market, for example, can be had for a few dollars; those filled with spices make unusual gifts.

Remember that duty-free products such as designer clothing and perfume are not cheap, even without taxes. Check prices in your hometown before your trip: They may be lower than they are in the Caribbean.

Shopping Areas St. Lucia entered the duty-free market with the opening of **Pointe Seraphine,** a Spanish-style complex by the harbor, with shops selling designer perfumes, china and crystal, jewelry, watches, leather goods, liquor, and cigarettes. Native crafts are also sold in the shopping center. Castries has a number of shops, mostly on **Bridge Street** and **William Peter Boulevard,** selling locally made souvenirs. The barnlike interior of the **Castries Market** is chockablock with stalls selling crafts and local products, such as hand-sewn dolls and pressed cocoa powder. There is also a shopping arcade at the **St. Lucian hotel.**

Good Buys
Fabrics and Clothing Bagshaw's silk-screened fabrics and clothing can be found at Pointe Seraphine. **Windjammer Clothing Company** (tel. 809/452–1040) has its main store at Vigie Cove and an outlet at Pointe Seraphine. **Caribelle Batik** (Old Victoria Rd., The

Morne, Castries, tel. 809/452–3785) creates batik clothing and wall hangings. Visitors are welcome to watch the craftspeople at work. **The Batik Studio** at Humming Bird Beach Resort (Soufrière, tel. 809/454–7232) offers superb sarongs, scarves, and wall panels.

Native Crafts Trays, masks, and figures are carved from mahogany, red cedar, and eucalyptus trees in the studio adjacent to **Eudovic's** (Morne Fortune, 15 min. south of Castries, tel. 809/452–2747). Hammocks, straw mats, baskets and hats, and carvings, as well as books and maps of St. Lucia, are at **Noah's Arkade** (Bridge St., Castries, and Pte. Seraphine, tel. 809/452–2523).

Dining

With so many visitors staying at all-inclusives, the selection of independent restaurants here is limited. You'll find the widest choice of moderately priced, publike places in and around Rodney Bay. The best area for sampling the local fare (mostly grilled meats) is Gros Islet, especially during its Friday-night street party (*see* Nightlife, *below*).

If you're planning to cook, you'll find the basics in most grocery stores here. Stores in Rodney Bay supply charter boats and offer better quality imported goods, such as coffees and canned foods. Buy your breads and pastries at **Bread Baskets** (tel. 809/452–0647) in Rodney Bay or the **Central Bakery Amurbroise** (Marianne St., no phone) in Castries. For vegetables and fruits, don't miss the Castries market on the corner of Jeremie and Peynier streets (*see* Exploring St. Lucia, *above*).

Mangoes, plantains, breadfruits, limes, pumpkins, cucumbers, pawpaws (pronounced poh-poh here, known as papaya elsewhere), yams, christophines (a green vegetable), and coconuts are among the fruits and vegetables that appear on menus throughout the island. Every menu lists the catch of the day (especially flying fish), along with the ever-popular lobster. Chicken, pork, and barbecues are also big-time here. Most of the meats are imported—beef from Argentina and Iowa, lamb from New Zealand. The French influence is strong in St. Lucian restaurants, and most chefs cook pre–nouvelle cuisine with a Creole flair. This is not an island for the calorie- and cholesterol-conscious.

Highly recommended restaurants are indicated by a star ★.

Category	Cost*
Moderate	$20–$30
Inexpensive	$10–$20
Budget	under $10

per person, excluding drinks and service

Green Parrot. The best reason for dining here is the view over Castries and the harbor. The Continental menu includes poached fish fillet with mushroom cream and white-wine sauce glaze; *tournedos cordon rouge* (steak fillet topped with foie gras and Madeira sauce); and *escalope de volaille Viennoise* (grilled chicken breast served with mushrooms). To keep your bill within bounds, avoid pricey items such as lobster. There is lively entertainment on Wednesday and Saturday nights, with limbo and belly dancers. *Red Tape La., Morne Fortune, tel. 809/452–3399. Reservations essential. Jacket advised. AE, MC, V. Moderate.*

Dolittle's. Take the water taxi across from the Hurricane Hotel to this waterside eatery, named after the Rex Harrison movie shot here. Callaloo soup is among the openers. Main dishes include marinated red snapper; ask about the daily specials. If you're not hungry, come here for a drink and watch the boats drowsing in gorgeous blue-green Marigot harbor. *Marigot de Roseau on Marigot Bay, tel. 809/453–4246. Reservations advised. AE, MC, V. No dinner. Moderate.*

★ **Jimmie's.** The bar here is a popular meeting place, and the restaurant is a romantic spot for dinner. Specialties include Madras fish, seafood risotto, and a lip-smacking salt fish and green fig (the national dish—and an acquired taste). There's also a wide choice of seafood, meat, chicken, and vegetable dishes. *Vigie Cove, Castries, tel. 809/452–5142. No reservations. AE, MC, V. Moderate.*

★ **The Lime.** The Lime is a favorite Rodney Bay spot for liming, or hanging out. A casual place with lime-colored gingham curtains, straw hats decorating the ceiling, and hanging plants, it offers a businessman's three-course lunch. Starters may include homemade pâté or stuffed crab back. Entrée choices may be medallions of pork fillet with the chef's special orange-and-ginger sauce, stewed lamb, or fish fillet poached in white wine and mushroom sauce. Expatriates and locals gather here in the evenings. Judicious ordering will keep your meal in the Inexpensive range. *Rodney Bay, tel. 809/452–0761. Reservations advised for dinner. MC, V. Closed Tues. Inexpensive–Moderate.*

Naked Virgin. Tucked away in the quiet Castries suburb of Marchand (just opposite a local post office—keep asking), this pleasant hangout offers terrific Creole cuisine. The owner, Mr. Paul John, has worked in many of the island's major hotels and his concoction, the Naked Virgin, could be the best punch you've ever tasted. *Marchand Rd., Castries, tel. 809/452–5594. Reservations advised. AE, MC, V. Inexpensive.*

Rain. This restaurant is in a Victorian building, and the balcony overlooking Columbus Square is a favored spot. It's usually crowded, and the tables are a tad too close together, but you can still soak up the atmosphere, especially after a few Downpours—their knockout tropical punches and frozen concoctions. Lunchtime offerings include Creole soup, *crabe farci*, rain burgers, quiches, and salads; Creole chicken is a specialty. At night, the Champagne Buffet of 1885 is a lavish but moderately priced seven-course feast. The frequent specials here allow you to dine inexpensively. *Columbus Sq., Castries, tel. 809/452–3022. Reservations advised. AE, MC, V. Inexpensive-Moderate.*

The Still. Converted from an old rum distillery, this restaurant is on the grounds of a working plantation, which supplies most of the meats and produce served. The emphasis is on local foods—christophines, breadfruits, yams, and callaloo as well as seafood, pork chops, and beef dishes. A popular Creole buffet is served at lunch. *Soufrière, tel. 809/454–7224. Reservations advised. MC, V. No dinner. Inexpensive.*

★ **J.J.'s.** Not only are the prices right here, but the food is some of the best on the island. Superbly grilled fish with fresh vegetables is tops. Tables are on a terrace above the road, and the welcome is friendly and casual. On Friday nights the music blares, and the locals come for liming and dancing in the street. *Marigot Bay Rd. (3 mi before the bay), Marigot, tel. 809/453–4076. No reservations. No credit cards. Budget.*

Lodging

St. Lucia's Caribbean coast is splashed with hotels, most of them along the strip from Castries to Cap Estate. The island is known for its upscale, all-inclusive resorts, but it is also home to more moderately priced all-inclusives. Even at lesser-priced properties, however, only the least expensive rooms are what we would consider affordable during high season (*see* price chart, *below*). The island has few options in the strictly budget range. You won't find the inexpensive hotels, guest houses, or apartment and cottage rentals that are plentiful on some Caribbean islands. Given this, you may be better off budgeting most of your money for lodging in order to opt for an all-inclusive, especially as transportation can be expensive if you stay away from the beach in a small hotel. You should reserve four months in advance for a room during high season.

Highly recommended lodgings are indicated by a star ★.

Category	Cost*
Moderate	$125–$200
Inexpensive	$60–$125
Budget	under $60

*All prices are for a standard double room for two, excluding 8% tax and a 10% service charge. To estimate rates for hotels offering MAP/FAP, add about $35–$40 per person per day to the above price ranges. To estimate rates for all-inclusives, add about $75 per person per day.

Hotels **Club Med St. Lucia.** This four-story hotel is on a 95-acre beachfront property on the southeast coast, where the Atlantic waters are rough. Recent refurbishment helped freshen the property. Air-conditioned rooms feature ocean views. All the usual Club Med activities are here, including nightly entertainment. Hewanorra International Airport is five minutes away. *Vieux Fort, tel. 809/455–6001 or 800/CLUBMED, fax 809/452–0958. 256 rooms. Facilities: restaurant, bar, boutique, fitness center, 8 tennis courts, pool, horseback riding, water-sports center. AE, DC, MC, V. All-inclusive (drinks not included). Moderate.*

Harmony Marina Suites. On Rodney Bay Marina and a 10-minute hike from the beach, this two-story apartment hotel has one-bedroom apartments, four of which have fully equipped electric kitchens. All have wall-to-wall carpeting, twin beds, showers, TVs with VCRs, balconies or patios, and token-operated air conditioners. Poolside rooms, away from the marina, are quieter. Windsurfing is free; other water sports are available. The Mortar and Pestle restaurant features "haute cuisine des Caraibes." *Box 155, Castries, tel. 809/452–8756 or 800/223–6510, fax 809/452–8677. 21 units. Facilities: restaurant, minimarket, pool, water-sports center, VCR and books libraries. MC, V. EP. Moderate.*

Rendezvous. Formerly Couples, this all-inclusive resort on Malabar Beach is still for couples only. Things tend to be quite active, with volleyball in the pool and on the beach, aerobics, and water exercises. The activities desk can arrange anything, including a wedding. Accommodations are in rooms, suites, and oceanfront cottages; only the standard rooms make it into our price range during high season. There is nightly live music for dancing, and a piano bar that closes when the last couple leaves. This is at the high end of our Moderate range for all-inclusives, so consider it only if you plan to take advantage of its many offerings. *Box 190, Malabar Beach, tel. 809/452-4211 or 800/544-2883, fax 809/452-7419. 100 rooms. Facilities: 2 restaurants, 3 bars, 2 pools, 2 lighted tennis courts, sauna, Jacuzzi, exercise room, bicycles, horseback riding, water-sports center, dive shop, catamaran. AE, MC, V. All-inclusive. Moderate.*

St. Lucian. The lobby is broad and white, with potted plants and upholstered sofas, from which a corridor leads to the gardens, pool area, and beach. This was once two hotels, and the rooms are spread out over considerable acreage, some on Reduit Beach, some in gardens. All have individually controlled air conditioners, two double beds, clock radios, direct-dial phones, and patios or terraces. Discounted package tours from Britain have taken their toll on this resort, and the furnishings have that well-worn look, but there is lots of action. This is the home of Splash, one of the island's hottest discos, and the local agent for Mistral Windsurfers. Water sports, including windsurfing lessons, are free to hotel guests. *Box 512, Castries, tel. 809/452-8351, fax 809/452-8331. 222 rooms. Facilities: 2 restaurants, 3 bars, disco, pool, laundry/dry cleaning, 2 lighted tennis courts, dive shop, boutiques, ice-cream parlor, beauty salon, minimarket, water-sports center. AE, DC, MC, V. EP, MAP. Moderate.*

Wyndham Morgan Bay Resort. The expanding Wyndham Hotel group took over this property from the Hotel Pullman and opened this modestly priced all-inclusive in 1992. Most of the rooms, with floral linens and peach wicker furniture, offer partial and angled sea views from each of the eight three-story buildings, lined up on a small rise above the pool and restaurant area. All have air-conditioning, cable TV, phone, and hair dryer. Standard double rooms are at the top end of our price range, but the resort does offer packages that are worth inquiring about when you call. Drinks are generous, and guests seem to spend most of their time at the bar/pool area. The beach—small, with cloudy water—is a disappointment. *Box 2216, Gros Islet, tel. 809/450-2511, fax 809/450-1050. 240 rooms. Facilities: 2 restaurants, 2 bars, beach grill, boutique, 4 tennis courts, pool, games room, Jacuzzi, exercise room, sauna, satellite TV, water-sports center. AE, D, MC, V. All-inclusive. Moderate.*

Green Parrot. This stone-and-stucco hotel is high in the Morne above Castries. Originally a single block of rooms, the hotel has expanded to three rows of buildings staggered up the hillside. The air-conditioned rooms have basic motel-style furnishings, but they are large and have patios or balconies that command magnificent views of Castries and its harbor. A free shuttle bus takes guests to Castries and Vigie Beach, a 15-minute drive away. There is a formal restaurant for guests and visitors, and a more casual one for guests only. *Box 648, Castries, tel. 809/452-3399, fax 809/453-2272. 60 rooms. Facilities: 2 restaurants, bar, games room, pool, nightclub. AE, MC, V. EP, MAP. Inexpensive.*

Humming Bird Beach Resort. This charming spot has oodles of ambience and an ideal location at the edge of Soufrière, fronting a small, grayish-sand beach. Four-poster beds and African sculpture adorn the best rooms—priced at the high end of this category—while less expensive units are plainly furnished. The bar is a popular watering hole for yachtsmen in from their boats, and the alfresco restaurant offers a range of fare from light snacks to full dinners. Joyce Alexander, the owner, is a marvelous, dynamic hostess who, when not making improvements to her small hotel, designs batiks for the adjoining boutique. *Box 280, Soufrière, tel. 809/454–7232. 10 units. Facilities: restaurant, bar, pool. MC, V. EP, MAP. Inexpensive.*

Islander. This upscale motel just 300 yards from Reduit Beach (there is a shuttle bus) offers air-conditioned, carpeted rooms with king-size beds, refrigerators, balconies, cable TV, and phones. Twenty of the rooms have kitchenettes, as do six apartments. Supermarkets, restaurants, and the nightlife of Rodney Bay are a few steps away. *Box 907, Castries, tel. 809/452–8757 or 800/223–9815, fax 809/452–0958. 56 rooms, 6 apartments. Facilities: restaurant, bar, pool, movie room, shuttle bus to beach. AE, D, MC, V. EP. Inexpensive.*

Vigie Beach Hotel. A glassed-in bar sits on the mile-long Vigie Beach, and a path leads through gardens up to the hotel. Air-conditioned rooms are spacious, with modern decor, double beds, balconies with garden or beach view, TVs, and phones. You'll be sunning to the sound of small planes, since the hotel is located adjacent to Vigie Airport. The staff seems genuinely unconcerned. *Box 395, Castries, tel. 809/452–5211, fax 809/452–5434. 47 rooms. Facilities: restaurant, 2 bars, pool, Jacuzzi. AE, D, DC, MC, V. EP. Inexpensive.*

Home Hotel. Expect bare-bones rooms with shared baths and a cheerful welcome in this family home in the center of town, in the shadow of the church steeple. Rooms are clean and basic, each with a double bed, table, and two chairs. There's a kitchen where you can make breakfast and snacks; small grocery stores and cafés are about a block away. It's only a short walk to the harbor, the bay, and the gray-sand beach. *Soufrière, tel. 809/454–7318. 7 rooms with shared baths. No credit cards. EP. Budget.*

Kimatrai. This is a clean family-owned and -operated hotel on the southeast coast, just above Vieux Fort and five minutes from the Hewanorra International Airport. The beach is a quarter of a mile away, but you'll be swimming in sometimes-rough Atlantic waters. Accommodations include double rooms, self-contained apartments, and chalets. Apartments and chalets have kitchens and an extra room that can serve as a living room or additional sleeping space. All units are air-conditioned with private showers. A car will make your stay here more convenient, especially as grocery stores are a 20-minute hike away. *Box 238, Vieux Fort, tel. 809/454–6328. 25 units. Facilities: restaurant, bar. No credit cards. EP. Budget.*

Seaview Apartel. It's located across from the Vigie Airport and next to the main road, so expect noise here. If you can put up with that, you'll get spacious accommodations with bedroom, bathroom, and living room; seven units have a fully equipped kitchen. There are no facilities or staff on hand, but you'll be paying a third of what you pay for a standard double room in a moderately priced hotel. A grocery store is a block away and a restaurant is nearby. Beaches are a 15-minute walk away, or you can catch a route taxi. *Box 527, Castries, tel. 809/450–1627, fax 809/453–1611. 10 apartments. No credit cards. EP. Budget.*

Apartment Rentals St. Lucia has limited short-term home and apartment rentals. The **Top of the Morne Apartments** (tel. 809/452–3603, fax 809/453–1433), above Castries, has modern studio units with kitchens and patios overlooking a pool for about $150 a night. **Le Cure Villas** (tel. 800/387–2726) has apartments starting at $190 a night. Comparable units are offered by **Island Hideaways** (tel. 800/832–2302). **Villa Apartments** (tel. 809/452–2691), a local agent, has properties with slightly lower rates. Also contact the **Tourist Board** (tel. 809/452–4094 or 809/452–5968) for additional listings.

Off-Season Bets Prices fall by a good 40% from mid-April to mid-December. Among hotels that become affordable during the off-season is **Anse Chastenet** (Box 7000, Soufrière, tel. 809/454–7000 or 800/545–2459, fax 809/454–7097). This secluded property near Soufrière is known for its dramatic architecture, its mountain-side setting (with views of the Pitons), and its dive packages. Equally charming is **Ladera** (Box 225, Soufrière, tel. 809/459–7323 or 800/841–4145), an idyllic hillside retreat amid lush foliage. Romantic rooms with hardwood and wicker furnishings and charming print fabrics have only three walls and stunning views of the Pitons. **Windjammer Landing Villas** (Box 1504, Labrelotte Bay, Castries, tel. 809/452–1913 or 800/743–9609, fax 809/452–0907), north of Castries, is a luxury resort complex of one-bedroom villas with fully equipped kitchens. A shuttle bus transports guests between villas and the main reception area, where the pool and alfresco dining are steps from the beach.

Nightlife

Most of the action is in the hotels, which feature entertainment of the island variety—limbo dancers, fire-eaters, calypso singers, and steel band jump-ups. Many offer entertainment packages, including dinner, to nonguests.

Splash (St. Lucian Hotel, tel. 809/452–8351) is a sophisticated place with a good dance floor and splashy lighting effects. Open Monday–Saturday from 9 PM. At the **Halcyon Wharf Disco** (Halcyon Beach Club, tel. 809/452–5331) you can dance on the jetty under the stars every night.

On weekends, locals usually hang out at **The Lime** (Rodney Bay, tel. 809/452–0761) or at **Capone's** (Rodney Bay, tel. 809/452–0284), an art deco place right out of the Roaring '20s, with a player piano and rum drinks. The **Green Parrot** (The Morne, tel. 809/452–3399) is in a class all by itself. Chef Harry Edwards hosts the floor show, which features limbo dancers. Harry has been known to shimmy under the pole himself. There are also belly dancers. Great fun; semiformal attire.

On Friday nights, sleepy Gros Islet becomes like Bourbon Street during Mardi Gras, as the entire village is transformed into a street fair. Vendors and stalls sell beer and fried chicken. At the far end of the street, mammoth stereos loudly beat out sounds as locals and strangers let their hair down. **Monroe's** (Grande Rivière, Gros Islet, tel. 809/452–8131) is probably the best spot for meeting locals. **The Banana Split** (St. Georges St., Gros Islet, tel. 809/452–8125) offers entertainment and special theme nights, with a perpetual "spring break" atmosphere. It can get rowdy, so it's best to travel in a group and keep your wits about you. Another Friday night street scene and a popular alternate venue for liming can be found just before you enter Marigot Bay. The music is supplied by **J. J.'s Restaurant** (tel. 809/453–4076), and the popular fare is curried goat. More and more locals are choosing to come here instead of the more touristy Gros Islet happening.

23 St. Martin St. Maarten

Updated by
Jordan Simon

There are frequent nonstop flights from the United States to St. Maarten/St. Martin, so you don't have to spend half your vacation getting here—a critical advantage if you have only a few days to enjoy the sun. The 37-square-mile island is home to two sovereign nations, St. Maarten (Dutch) and St. Martin (French), so you can experience two cultures for the price of one (although the Dutch side has lost much of its European flavor).

This island, particularly the Dutch side, is ideal for people who like to stay busy. It's hard to be bored when you're surrounded by sparkling beaches, fine restaurants, duty-free shopping, and activities from water sports to golf, discos to casinos. The island depends on tourism and strives to appeal to the whole spectrum of travelers (anyone can fit in here). This makes bustling St. Martin/St. Maarten—despite its reputation—more affordable than more moderately priced spots that lack its range of options. The fierce competition between properties translates into package deals, especially in the off-season or for large tour groups—you can save a lot by hooking up with a wholesale travel agent's specials. The island also offers apartments, small inns, and guest houses (those on the French side have more charm but are pricier). Best of all, with few exceptions, even the cheapest accommodations are either on or within walking distance of beaches. If you frequent local Creole restaurants rather than swank French boîtes, you'll be pleasantly surprised by the quality of the kitchens and the fairly low prices.

On the negative side, St. Maarten/St. Martin has been thoroughly discovered and developed; you are likely to find yourself sharing beachfronts with tour groups or conventioneers. Yes, there is gambling, but the table limits are so low that hardcore gamblers will have a better time gamboling on the beach. It can be fun to shop, and there's an occasional bargain, but many goods, particularly electronics, are cheaper in the United States.

What It Will Cost These sample prices, meant only as a general guide, are for high season. An inexpensive hotel room on either the Dutch or French side averages $125 a night; a budget guest house is about $50. An inexpensive restaurant dinner will be about $25; lunch at a *lolo*, or Creole snack bar, is about $8. A beer or glass of wine costs around $2.50; a rum punch is about $3. A taxi ride from Marigot to the nearest beach is about $5. A round-trip ride between Marigot and Philipsburg is about $20; a bus ride between the two costs 80¢–$2. Car rental is about $35 for a subcompact. Cost for a single-tank dive ranges from $45 to $50; snorkel equipment rents for about $10.

Before You Go

Tourist Information For information about the Dutch side, contact the **St. Maarten Tourist Office** (275 7th Ave., New York, NY 10001, tel. 212/989–0000) or the **St. Maarten Information Office** (243 Ellerslie Ave., Willowdale, Toronto, Ont., Canada M2N 1Y5, tel. 416/223–3501). Information about French St. Martin can be obtained through the **French West Indies Tourist Board** by calling France-on-Call at 900/990–0040 (50¢ per minute), or you can write to the **French Government Tourist Office** (610 5th Ave., New York, NY 10020; 9454 Wilshire Blvd., Beverly Hills, CA 90212; 645 N. Michigan Ave., Chicago, IL 60611; 2305 Cedar Spring Rd., Dallas TX 75201; 1981 McGill College Ave., Suite 490, Montreal. P.Q. H3A 2W9, tel. 514/288–4264; 1 Dundas St. W, Suite 2405, Toronto, Ont. M5G 1Z3, tel. 416/593–4723 or 800/361–9099; 178 Piccadilly, London W1Z OAL, tel. 071/493–6594).

Arriving and Departing
By Plane There are two airports on the island. L'Espérance on the French side is small and handles only island-hoppers. Bigger planes fly into Juliana International Airport on the Dutch side. The most convenient carrier from the United States is **American Airlines** (tel. 800/433–7300), with daily nonstop flights from New York and Miami, as well as connections from more than 100 U.S. cities via its San Juan hub. **Continental Airlines** (tel. 800/231–0856) has daily flights from Newark. **LIAT** (tel. 809/462–0701) flies from Antigua; **ALM** (tel. 800/327–7230) from Aruba, Bonaire, Curaçao, the Dominican Republic, and from Atlanta and Miami via Curaçao. ALM also offers a Visit Caribbean Air Pass, which offers savings for traveling to several Caribbean islands. **Air Martinique** (tel. 596/51–08–09) connects the island with Martinique twice a week. **Windward Islands Airways** (Winair, tel. 599/54–42–30), which is based on St. Maarten, has daily scheduled service to Saba, St. Eustatius, St. Barts, Anguilla, St. Thomas, and St. Kitts/Nevis. **Air Guadeloupe** (tel. 590/90–37–37) has several flights daily to St. Barts and Guadeloupe from both sides of the island. **Air St. Barthélemy** (tel. 590/27–71–90) has frequent service between Juliana and St. Barts. Tour and charter services are available

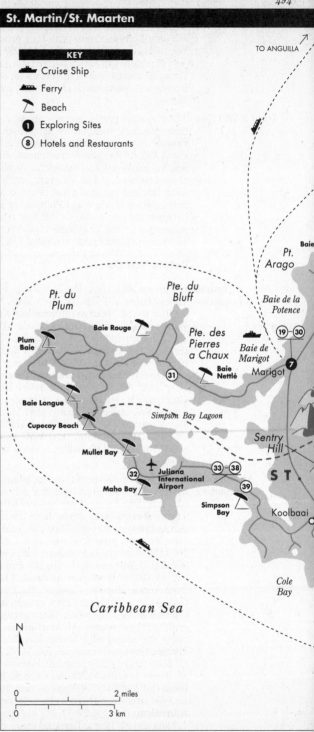

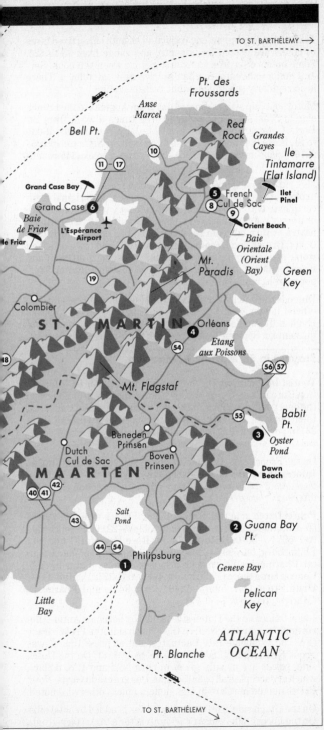

TO ST. BARTHÉLEMY →

Pt. des
Froussards

Anse
Marcel

Bell Pt.

Red
Rock

Grandes
Cayes

Ile →
Tintamarre
(Flat Island)

Grand Case Bay

⑪ ⑰

⑩

Ilet
Pinel

⑤ French
⑧ Cul de Sac

Grand Case ⑥

L'Espérance
Airport

Baie
de Friar

le Friar

⑨ Orient Beach

Baie
Orientale
(Orient
Bay)

Green
Key

Mt.
Paradis

⑲

Colombier

S T.   M A R T I N

Orléans

④

Etang
aux Poissons

⑱

⑤⑥ ⑤⑦

Mt. Flagstaf

⑤④

Babit
Pt.

⑤⑤

③ Oyster
Pond

Beneden
Prinsen

Boven
Prinsen

Dutch
Cul de Sac

Dawn
Beach

M A A R T E N

⑩ ⑪ ㊷

Salt
Pond

② Guana Bay
Pt.

㊸

㊹ ⑤④

① Philipsburg

Geneve Bay

Little
Bay

Pelican
Key

ATLANTIC
OCEAN

Pt. Blanche

TO ST. BARTHÉLEMY →

from Winair and **St. Martin Helicopters** (Dutch side, tel. 599/5–4287).

From the Airport   Taxi rates are government-regulated on both sides; fixed fares to hotels are posted prominently and range from $5 to $25. Some hotels offer free transfers; inquire when you book. Several major car rental companies have desks at Juliana. There is no regularly scheduled public transportation.

By Boat   Motorboats zip several times a day from Anguilla to the French side at Marigot ($9 one-way), three times a week from St. Barts. Catamaran service is available daily from the Dutch side to St. Barts ($40 one-way). The 50-passenger *Style* (tel. 599/5–22167) slaps across from Saba three times a week ($45 round-trip).

Passports and Visas   U.S. citizens need proof of citizenship. A passport (valid or not expired more than five years) is preferred. An original birth certificate with raised seal (or a photocopy with notary seal), or a voter registration card is also acceptable. All visitors must have a confirmed room reservation and an ongoing or return ticket. British and Canadian citizens need valid passports. You won't need your passport traveling between the Dutch and French sides of the island; there is no customs. Border flags, not patrols, mark the crossings.

Language   Dutch is the official language of St. Maarten and French is the official language of St. Martin, but almost everyone speaks English. If you hear a language you can't quite place, it's Papiamento, a Spanish-based Creole of the Netherlands Antilles.

Staying in St. Martin/St. Maarten

Important Addresses   **Tourist Information:** On the Dutch side, the **Tourist Information Bureau** is on Cyrus Wathey (pronounced *watty*) Square in the heart of Philipsburg, at the pier where the cruise ships send their tenders. The executive office is on Walter Nisbeth Road 23 (Imperial Building) on the third floor. *Tel. 599/5–22337. Open weekdays 8–noon and 1–5, except holidays.*

On the French side, there is the smart and very helpful **Tourist Information Office** on the Marigot pier. *Tel. 590/87–57–21. Open weekdays 8–12:30 and 2–5, Sat. 8–noon. Closed holidays and the afternoon preceding a holiday.*

Emergencies   **Police:** Dutch side (tel. 599/5–22222), French side (tel. 590/85–50–16); **Ambulance:** Dutch side (tel. 599/5–22111), French side (tel. 590/87–50–06); **Hospitals: St. Rose Hospital** (Front St., Philipsburg, tel. 599/5–22300) is a fully equipped 55-bed hospital. **Pharmacies:** Pharmacies are open Monday–Saturday 7–5. **Central Drug Store** (Philipsburg, tel. 599/5–22321), **Mullet Bay Drug Store** (tel. 599/5–42801, ext. 342), and **Pharmacie** (Marigot, tel. 590/87–50–79).

Currency   Legal tender on the Dutch side is the Netherlands Antilles florin (guilder), written NAf; on the French side, the French franc (F). The exchange rate fluctuates, but at press time it was about NAf 1.79 to U.S. $1 and 5.3F to U.S. $1. On the Dutch side, prices are usually given in both NAf and U.S. dollars, which are accepted all over the island, as are credit cards. Note: Prices quoted here are in U.S. dollars unless otherwise noted.

Taxes and Service Charges   On the Dutch side, a 5% government tax is added to hotel bills. On the French side, a *taxe de séjour* (visitor's tax) is tacked onto hotel bills (the amount differs from hotel to hotel, but the maximum is $3 per day, per person). Departure tax from Juliana Airport is $5 to destinations within the Netherlands Antilles and $10 to all other destinations. It will cost you 15F to depart by plane from l'Espérance Airport or by ferry to Anguilla from Marigot's pier.

In lieu of tipping, service charges (15% on the Dutch side; 10%–15% on the French) are added to hotel bills all over the island, and, by law, are included in all menu prices on the French side. On the Dutch side, most restaurants add 10%–15% to the bill. Taxi drivers expect a 10% tip.

Getting Around Chances are, you won't have to rent a car for the duration of your stay here. One day of driving (or a guided tour, roughly the same cost) is sufficient to see the major sites. After that, you can take taxis to Marigot, Philipsburg, and the casinos (if your hotel doesn't have a shuttle service). Most hotels here are on or within walking distance of the beach.

Taxis Taxi rates are government regulated, and authorized taxis display stickers of the St. Maarten Taxi Association. There is a taxi service, headed by Raymond Helligar, at the Marigot port near the Tourist Information Bureau. Fixed fares apply from Juliana Airport and the Marigot ferry to the various hotels and around the island. Fares are 25% higher between 10 PM and midnight, 50% higher between midnight and 6 AM. Sample rates are: Marigot to Philipsburg, $10–$12, Marigot to the nearest beach, $5.

Buses One of the island's best bargains at 80¢ to $2, depending on destination, buses operate frequently between 7 AM and 7 PM and run from Philipsburg through Cole Bay to Marigot.

Rental Cars You can book a car at Juliana Airport, where all major rental companies have booths, but to give taxi drivers work, you must collect the car at the rental offices located off the airport complex. (The Hertz office is closest to the airport, just a quarter-mile away.) There are also rentals at every hotel area. Rental cars are inexpensive—approximately $35 a day for a subcompact car plus collision damage waiver. All foreign driver's licenses are honored, and major credit cards are accepted. **Avis** (tel. 800/331–1212), **Budget** (tel. 800/527–0700), **Dollar** (tel. 800/421–6868), **Hertz** (tel. 800/654–3131), and **National** (tel. 800/328–4567) have offices on the island. Scooters rent for $20–$25 a day at **Rent 2 Wheels** (Nettlé Bay, tel. 590/87–20–59).

Telephones and Mail To call the Dutch side from the United States, dial 011–599 + local number; for the French side, 011–590 + local number. To phone from the Dutch side to the French, dial 06 + local number; from the French side to the Dutch, 3 + local number. Keep in mind that a call from one side to another is an overseas call, not a local call. Telephone communications, especially on the Dutch side, leave something to be desired. At the Landsradio in Philipsburg, there are facilities for overseas calls and an AT&T USADIRECT telephone, where you are directly in touch with an AT&T operator who will accept collect or credit-cards calls. On the French side, it is not possible to make collect calls to the United States, and there are no coin phones. If you need to use public phones, go to the special desk at Marigot's post office and buy a Telecarte (it looks like a credit card), which gives you 40 units for around 31F or 120 units for 93F. There is a small kiosk next to the tourist office in Marigot where you can make credit card phone calls. The operator will assign you a PIN (personal identification number), valid for as long as you specify. Calls are $4 per minute to the United States.

Letters from the Dutch side to the United States and Canada cost NAf 1.30; postcards, NAf 60¢. From the French side, letters up to 20 grams, 4.10F; postcards, 3.50F.

Opening and Closing Times Shops on the Dutch side are open Monday–Saturday 8–noon and 2–6; on the French side, Monday–Saturday 9–noon or 12:30 and 2–6. Some of the larger shops on both sides of the island open Sunday and holidays when the cruise ships are in port. Some of the small Dutch and French shops set their own capricious hours.

Banks on the Dutch side are open Monday–Thursday 8–1 and Friday 4–5. French banks open weekdays 8:30–1:30 and 2–3 and close afternoons preceding holidays.

Guided Tours A 2½-hour taxi tour of the island costs $35 for one or two people, $10 for each additional person. Your hotel or the Tourist Office can arrange it for you. Best bet is the 20-passenger vans of **St. Maarten Sightseeing Tours** (Philipsburg, tel. 599/5–22753), which offer, among other options, a 2½-hour complete island tour for $12 per person. On the French side, **Société Touristique de St. Martin** (tel. 590/87–56–20) also runs excellent island-wide tours. These range from two to five hours and cost $30–$50.

Exploring St. Martin/St. Maarten

Numbers in the margin correspond to points of interest on the St. Martin/St. Maarten map.

You can explore the island in your own rental car or take a guided tour (*see above*). The two are roughly equivalent in cost, and one day is more than sufficient to see the major sites.

St. Maarten
❶ The Dutch capital of **Philipsburg,** which stretches about a mile along an isthmus between Great Bay and the Salt Pond, has three more-or-less parallel streets: Front Street, Back Street, and Pond Fill. Front Street has been recently recobbled, cars discouraged from using it, and the pedestrian area widened. Shops, restaurants, and casinos vie for the hordes coming off the cruise boats. Head for **Wathey Square** and stroll out on the pier. **Great Bay** is rolled out before you, and the beach stretches alongside it for about a mile. The square bustles with vendors, souvenir shops, and tourists.

Directly across the street from Wathey Square, you'll see a striking white building with a cupola. It was built in 1793 and has since served as the commander's home, a fire station, and a jail. It now serves as the town hall, court house, and post office.

The square is in the middle of the isthmus on which Philipsburg sits. To your right and left the streets are lined with hotels, duty-free shops, fine restaurants, and cafés, most of them in pastel-colored West Indian cottages gussied up with gingerbread trim. Narrow alleyways lead to arcades and flower-filled courtyards where there are yet more boutiques and eateries.

A half-block away across the street, **Simart'n Museum,** in a restored 19th-century West Indian house, hosts rotating cultural exhibits and the permanent historical display entitled "Forts of St. Maarten/St. Martin." If you'd like to clamber through the ruins themselves, take the dirt path at the Great Bay Hotel parking lot to Fort Willem for a spectacular view of Philipsburg and the surrounding islands. *119 Front St., Philipsburg, tel. 599/5–32125. Admission: $1. Open Mon.–Sat. 10–6, Sun. 9:30–noon.*

Little lanes called *steegjes* connect Front Street with Back Street, which has fewer shops and is considerably less congested.

Our drive begins at the western end of Front Street. The road (it will become Sucker Garden Road) leads north along Salt Pond and begins to climb and curve just outside of town. Take ❷ the first right to **Guana Bay Point,** from which there is a splendid view of the island's east coast, tiny deserted islands, and small St. Barts, which is anything but deserted. Sucker Garden Road continues north through spectacular scenery. Continue along a paved roller-coaster road down to **Dawn Beach,** one of the island's best snorkeling beaches.

❸ **Oyster Pond** is the legendary point where two early settlers, a Frenchman and a Dutchman, allegedly began to pace in opposite directions around the island to divide it between their respective countries. (The official boundary marker is on the other side of the island.)

St. Martin From Oyster Pond, follow the road along the bay and around ❹ Etang aux Poissons (Fish Lake), all the way to **Orléans.** This settlement, which is also known as the French Quarter, is the oldest on the island. Noted local artist and activist Roland Richardson makes his home here. He holds open studio on Thursdays from 10 to 6 to sell his art. He's a proud islander ready to share his wealth of knowledge about the island's cultural history.

A rough dirt road leads northeast to **Orient Beach,** the island's best-known nudist beach. There's even a pricey rustic resort catering to "naturists." Offshore, little **Ilet Pinel** is an uninhabited island that's fine for picnicking, sunning, and swimming.

❺ Farther north you'll come to **French Cul de Sac,** where you'll see the French colonial mansion of St. Martin's mayor nestled in the hills. Little red-roof houses look like open umbrellas tumbling down the green hillside. The scenery here is glorious, and the area is great for hiking. There is a lot of construction, however, as the surroundings are slowly being developed. From the beach here, three shuttle boats make the five-minute trip ($5) to Ilet Pinel.

The road swirls south through green hills and pastures, past flower-entwined stone fences. Past L'Espérance Airport is the ❻ town of **Grand Case.** Though it has only one mile-long main street, it's known as the "Restaurant Capital of the Caribbean": More than 20 restaurants serve French, Italian, Indonesian, and Vietnamese fare, as well as fresh seafood. The budget-minded will appreciate the lolos—barbecue stands along the waterfront. **Grand Case Beach Hotel** is at the end of this road and has two beaches to choose from for a short dip. Better yet, travel down the road about 5 miles toward Marigot

and on the right is a turnoff to **Friar's Beach,** a small, picturesque cove that attracts a casual crowd of locals. A small snack
bar, **Kali's,** owned by a welcoming gentleman wearing dreadlocks, serves refreshments. From here, you can turn inland and
follow a bumpy tree-canopied road to **Pic du Paradis,** at 1,278
feet the highest point on the island; it affords breathtaking vistas of the Caribbean.

➐ Just before entering the French capital of **Marigot,** you will
notice a new shopping complex on the left. At the back of it is
Match (tel. 590/87–92–36), now the largest supermarket on the
French side, carrying a broad selection of tempting picnic makings—from country pâté to foie gras—and a vast selection of
wines. If you are a shopper, a gourmet, or just a Francophile,
you'll want to tarry awhile in Marigot. Marina Port La Royale
is the shopping complex at the port, but Rue de la République
and Rue de la Liberté, which border the bay, are also filled with
duty-free shops, boutiques, and bistros. The harbor area has
stalls selling everything from fruits and vegetables to
handmade crafts. Across from these stalls on pier road leading
to the ferries for Anguilla is the helpful **French Tourist Office,**
where you may collect an assortment of free maps and brochures.

You are likely to find more creative and fashionable buys in
Marigot than in Philipsburg; if you are not a shopper, rest in
one of the open-air cafés. **Le Bar de la Mer** (tel. 590/87–81–79)
on the harbor is a popular gathering spot in the early evening,
though the bar and restaurant are open all day.

The road due south of Marigot to Philipsburg passes the official
boundary, where a simple border marker, erected by the Dutch
and French citizenry to commemorate 300 years of peaceful
coexistence, bears the dates "1648 to 1948." Straddling the border is a mammoth condominium hotel complex, the Port de
Plaisance, where Sheraton has constructed the extravagant
Mont Fortune casino adjacent to the hotel.

At the airport, the road from Marigot to the north and Simpson
Bay to the west join together and lead to Philipsburg, passing
the cutoff to Divi Little Bay Beach Resort.

The other road from Marigot leads west and hugs the coastline
to cross a small bridge to Sandy Ground and then along Baie
Nettlé, with its many new, reasonably priced hotels. Soon
thereafter, on the right, you'll come to the Mediterranean-style
village resort of **La Belle Creole,** commanding Pointe du Bluff.
Then you'll begin to see some of the island's best beaches—
Baie Rouge, Plum Baie, and **Baie Longue**—clinging to its westernmost point. They are all accessible down bumpy but short
dirt roads and make lovely swimming and picnicking spots.

At the end of Baie Longue and running eastward along the
south coast is **La Samanna,** the fashionable jet-set resort. Just
after this hotel you'll reenter Dutch territory at **Cupecoy
Beach.** You'll have to endure the huge, garish vacation condo-
hotel complexes of Mullet Bay and Maho Bay before you reach
Juliana Airport and Philipsburg.

Beaches

The island's 10 miles of beaches are all open to the public.
Beaches occupied by resort properties charge a small fee

(about $3) for changing facilities, and water-sports equipment can be rented in most of the hotels. You cannot, however, enter a beach via a hotel unless you are a paying guest. Some of the 37 beaches are secluded, some are located in the thick of things. Topless bathing is virtually de rigueur on the French side, where the beaches are generally better than on the Dutch side. If you take a cab to a remote beach, be sure to arrange a specific time for your driver to return, and don't leave valuables unattended on the beach. Virtually all hotels are located on or near a beach; the more moderate properties are clustered around **Nettlé Bay** (outside Marigot) and **Grand Case Beach** on the French side, **Great Bay** (Philipsburg) on the Dutch side. Following are other popular stretches.

Hands down, **Baie Longue** is the best beach on the island. It's a beautiful, mile-long curve of white sand on the westernmost tip of the island. This is a good place for snorkeling and swimming, but beware of a strong undertow when the waters are rough. You can sunbathe in the buff, though only a few do. Pack a lunch. There are no facilities.

Beyond Baie Longue is **Plum Baie,** where the beach arcs between two headlands and the occasional sunbather discloses all.

Baie Rouge is one of the most secluded beaches on the island. This little patch of sand is located at the base of high cliffs and is backed by private homes rather than by hotels. Some rate it the prettiest beach of the island, although it can have rough waves. A small snack/soda stand is located at the entrance.

Orient Beach is the island's best-known "clothes optional" beach—it's on the agenda for voyeurs from visiting cruise ships. You can enter from the parking area or through the **Club Orient** (tel. 590/87–33–85), which has chalet self-catering bungalows for rent, shops, and rental water-sports equipment.

The long white-sand beach at **Dawn Beach–Oyster Pond** is partly protected by reefs (good for snorkeling), but the waters are not always calm. When the waves come rolling in, this is the best spot on the island for bodysurfing.

Ilet Pinel is a little speck off the northeast coast, with about 500 yards of beach where you can have picnics and privacy. There are no facilities. Putt-putts are available to take you from Orient Beach.

Simpson Bay is a long half-moon of white sand near Simpson Bay Village, one of the last undiscovered hamlets on the island. In this small fishing village you'll find refreshments, the **Ocean Explorers** (*see* Sports and the Outdoors, *below*) for water-sports rentals, and neat little ultra-Caribbean town homes.

Ecru-color sand, palm and sea-grape trees, calm waters, and the roar of jets lowering to nearby Juliana Airport distinguish the beach at **Maho Bay.** Concession stand, beach chairs, and facilities are available.

At **Mullet Bay,** the powdery white-sand beach is crowded with guests of the Mullet Bay Resort.

Cupecoy Beach is a small shifting arc of white sand fringed with eroded limestone cliffs, just south of Baie Longue on the western side of the island, near the Dutch-French border. On the first part of the beach, swimwear is worn, but farther up, sun worshipers start shedding their attire. There are no facilities, but a truck is often parked at the entrance, with a vendor who sells cold sodas and beers.

Sports and the Outdoors

All the resort hotels have activities desks that can arrange virtually any type of water sport.

Boating Motorboats, speedboats, Dolphins, pedal boats, sailboats, and canoes can be rented at **Lagoon Cruises & Watersports** (tel. 599/5–52801, ext. 1873), **Caribbean Watersports** (tel. 599/5–42801), and **Orient Watersports** (tel. 590/87–33–85). Rates average $15–$20 an hour.

Sun Yacht-Charters (tel. 800/772–3500), based in Oyster Pond, has a fleet of 30 Centurion sailboats for hire. The cost of a week's bare-boat charter for a 36-foot Centurion with six berths runs $2,590 in peak winter season. Also in Oyster Pond, **The Moorings** (tel. 800/535–7289 or 590/87–32–55) has a fleet of Beneteau yachts, 38–50 feet in length. **Dynasty** (Marigot's Port La Royale Marina, tel. 590/87–85–21) offers an excellent fleet of Dynamique yachts. Both have bare-boat rentals that are comparable to charters'.

Fitness **Le Privilège** (tel. 590/87–37–37), a sports complex at Anse Marcel above Meridien L'Habitation, features a full range of exercise equipment. **Fitness Caraibes** (tel. 590/87–97–04), a toning center run by Marc Bozzetto, is at Nettlé Bay. On the Dutch side, **L'Aqualigne** at the Pelican Resort (tel. 599/5–54330) is a health spa with gym, sauna, and beauty and weight-loss treatments. Day passes average $5.

Golf Travelers on a budget might do well to leave the golf clubs behind. **Mullet Bay Resort** (tel. 599/5–42081) has an 18-hole championship course, but greens fees for nonguests are a whopping $95 per day in high season ($65 in low).

Jet- and Waterskiing Rent equipment through **Caribbean Watersports** (tel. 599/5–42801 or 599/5–44363) and **Maho Watersports** (tel. 599/5–44387) on the Dutch side; on the French side, try **Orient Watersports** (tel. 590/87–33–85). Rental is about $40 for a half-hour.

Parasailing A great high can be arranged through **Lagoon Cruises & Watersports** (tel. 599/5–52898). Cost is $30–$40 for 15 minutes.

Running The **Road Runners Club** (Pelican Resort Activities Desk, tel. 599/5–42503) meets weekly for its 5K or 10K run.

Scuba Diving On the Dutch side is Proselyte Reef, named for the British frigate HMS *Proselyte*, which sank south of Great Bay in 1802. As popular as wreck dives are reef, night, cave, and drift dives. Off the northeast coast of the French side, dive sites include Ilet Pinel, for good shallow diving; Green Key, a prolific barrier reef; and Flat Island (also known as Ile Tintamarre) for sheltered coves and subsea geologic faults. NAUI- and PADI-certified dive centers offer instruction, rentals, and trips at **Tradewinds Dive Center/Maho Watersports** (tel. 599/5–54387), **St. Maarten Divers** (tel. 599/5–22446), and **Ocean Explorers Dive Shop** (599/5–45252). On the French side, PADI-certified **Lou Scuba** (tel. 590/87–28–58) has opened at the Laguna Beach Hotel at Nettlé Bay. **Blue Ocean** (tel. 590/87–89–73) is PADI-

and CMAS-certified. Single-tank dives average $45–$50, with package deals available.

Sea Excursions Day sails and cruises average a hefty $50 a person, but they do include snorkel gear, drinks, and snacks. You may want to consider one for a splurge. Half-day sails cost around $30 and cocktail cruises, $35. You can take a day-long picnic sail to nearby islands or secluded coves aboard the 45-foot ketch *Gabrielle* (tel. 599/5–23170) or the 41-foot ketch *Pretty Penny* (tel. 599/5–2167). The catamaran *Bluebeard II* (tel. 599/5–42801 or 599/5–42898), moored in Marigot, sails around Anguilla's south and northwest coasts to Prickly Pear, where there are excellent coral reefs for snorkeling and powdery white sands for sunning. The luxurious 75-foot motor catamaran *White Octopus* (tel. 599/5–23170) does full-moon and cocktail cruises, complete with calypso music. During the day the *White Octopus* makes the run to St. Barts, departing at 9 AM from Bobby's Marina and returning at 5 PM. In St. Martin, sailing, snorkeling, and picnic excursions to nearby islands can be arranged through **Orient Watersports** (Club Orient, tel. 590/87–33–85), **L'Habitation** (tel. 590/87–33–33), **La Belle Creole** (tel. 590/87–58–66), and **La Samanna** (tel. 590/87–51–22).

Snorkeling Coral reefs teem with marine life, and clear water allows visibility of up to 200 feet. Some of the best snorkeling on the Dutch side can be had around the rocks below Fort Amsterdam off Little Bay Beach, the west end of Maho Bay, Pelican Key and the rocks near the Caravanserai Hotel, and the reefs off Dawn Beach and Oyster Pond. On the French side, the area around Orient Bay, Green Key, Ilet Pinel, and Flat Island (or Tintamarre) is especially lovely for snorkeling, and has been officially classified a regional underwater nature reserve. Arrange rentals and trips through **Watersports Unlimited** (tel. 599/5–23434), **Red Ensign Watersports** (tel. 599/5–22929), **Ocean Explorers** (tel. 599/5–45252), and **Orient Watersports** (tel. 590/87–89–73). Half- and full-day trips, usually including picnic lunch, run anywhere from $40 to $70 per person. Snorkel equipment rents for about $10 a day.

Tennis There are four lighted courts at **Dawn Beach Hotel** (tel. 599/5–22944); four lighted courts at **Pelican Resort** (tel. 599/5–42503); three asphalt courts at **Little Bay and Belair Beach Resorts** (tel. 599/5–22333 or 599/5–23362); four courts at **Maho Reef & Beach** (tel. 599/5–42115); six lighted courts at **Le Privilège** (Anse Marcel, tel. 590/87–59–28), which also has squash and racquetball courts; 14 lighted courts at **Port de Plaisance** (tel. 599/5–45222); four lighted Omni courts at **La Belle Creole** (tel. 590/87–58–66); three lighted courts at **Nettlé Bay Beach Club** (tel. 590/87–97–04); two lighted courts at **Mont Vernon Hotel** (tel. 590/87–62–00) and at **Simson Beach Marine Hotel** (tel. 590/87–54–54); 16 all-weather courts at **Mullet Bay Resort** (tel. 599/5–42081); two unlighted courts at **Oyster Bay Hotel** (tel. 590/87–54–72) and **Oyster Pond Hotel** (tel. 599/5–22206); and one lighted court each at **Grand Case Beach Club** (tel. 590/87–51–87) and the **Coralita Beach Hotel** (tel. 590/87–31–81). Court fees for nonguests cost $15–$25 an hour.

Windsurfing Rental and instruction are available at **Little Bay Beach Hotel** (tel. 599/5–22333, ext. 186), **Maho Watersports** (tel. 599/5–44387), **Orient Watersports** (590/87–33–85), and **Red Ensign Watersports** (tel. 599/5–22929). Equipment and lessons cost $20–$30 an hour.

Shopping

About 180 cruise ships call at St. Maarten each year, and they do so for about 500 reasons. That's roughly the number of duty-free shops on the island.

You'll find the best buys on goods manufactured outside the United States. Prices can be 25%–50% below those in the United States and Canada on European luxury items. But check stateside prices before you leave home—they may be cheaper. In general, you will find more fashion on the French side in Marigot.

St. Maarten's best-known "craft" is its guavaberry liqueur, made from rum and the wild local berries (not to be confused with guavas) that grow only on this island's central mountains. Other than that, you're unlikely to find any great local buys.

Prices are quoted in florins, francs, and dollars; shops take credit cards and traveler's checks. Most shopkeepers, especially on the Dutch side, speak English. Although most merchants are reputable, there are occasional reports of inferior or fake merchandise passed off as the real thing. Generally, if you can bargain excessively, it's probably not worth it.

Shopping Areas In St. Maarten: **Front Street,** Philipsburg, is one long strip lined with sleek boutiques and cozy shops gift-wrapped in gingerbread. **Old Street,** near the end of Front Street, has 22 stores, boutiques, and open-air cafés. (If more than one cruise ship is in port, avoid Front Street. It's so crowded you won't be able to move.) There are almost 100 boutiques in **Mullet** and **Maho** shopping plazas, as well as at the **Simpson Bay Yacht Club** complex.

In St. Martin: Wrought-iron balconies, colorful awnings, and gingerbread trim decorate Marigot's smart shops, tiny boutiques, and bistros in the **Marina Port La Royale; Galerie Peri-gourdine;** and on the main streets, **Rue de la Liberté** and **Rue de la République.**

Island Specialties Caribelle batik, hammocks, handmade jewelry, the local guavaberry liqueur, and herbs and spices are stashed at **The Shipwreck Shop** (Philipsburg, tel. 599/5–22962).

Dining

It may seem that this island has no monuments. Au contraire, there are many of them, all dedicated to gastronomy. You'll scarcely find a touch of Dutch; the major influences are French and Italian. This season's "in" eatery may be next season's remembrance of things past, as things do have a way of changing rapidly. The generally steep prices reflect both the island's high culinary reputation and the difficulty of obtaining fresh ingredients. Not surprisingly, the hotel restaurants on the French side are usually more sophisticated, but at prices that would make almost anyone but a Rockefeller go Dutch.

Although most of the haute restaurants are appropriate only for splurges, some offer prix-fixe menus that represent tremendous savings over à la carte prices. Creole restaurants are generally less expensive than their classic and nouvelle French counterparts. The greatest concentration of moderately priced, open-air eateries can be found in Philipsburg and in

Marigot's Marina Port La Royale. In addition, look for Creole snack bars serving tasty budget island specialties along Philipsburg's steegjes, and French fast-food cafés and sidewalk croissanteries offering omelets or *steak frites* in Marigot.

If you're cooking at your lodgings, the selection, quality, and prices are so good at Marigot's **Match** that it's worth coming over if you're staying on the Dutch side. Otherwise, try **Stop and Shop** (Juliana Airport), either **Food Center** (Bush Road or Cole Bay), or **Ram's Cash and Carry** (Cay Hill).

Reservations are not required unless noted in our text. Dress is casual unless stated otherwise. Highly recommended restaurants are indicated by a star ★.

Category	Cost*
Moderate	$30–$40
Inexpensive	$20–$30
Budget	under $20

per person, excluding drinks and service

Dutch Side **Captain Oliver.** A glorious cockatoo presides over the entrance to this engaging bistro, perched over the marina at Oyster Pond. Although the staff and cuisine are French, the restaurant is just over the Dutch border. Seafood is king here, in such dishes as lobster flambéed in cognac or tuna in a rollicking pink pepper sauce. You can catch your own lobster in the pool. *Oyster Pond, tel. 590/87–30–00. Reservations advised. AE, MC, V. Moderate.*

L'Escargot. A lovely 19th-century house wrapped in verandas is home to one of St. Maarten's oldest French restaurants. Starters include baked brie en croûte in kiwi sauce. There is also, of course, a variety of snail dishes. For an entrée, try red snapper grilled on a bed of red beets. There's a fun cabaret Sunday nights; no cover charge with dinner. *76 Front St., Philipsburg, tel. 599/5–22483. AE, MC, V. Moderate.*

Island Bar and Restaurant. This unassuming Caribbean coffee shop serves delectable and authentic Creole cooking. Try the conch or bullfoot soup, a sultry spicy bouillon, followed by juicy ribs or goat meat. Wash it down with a potent Peanut Punch. *Bush Rd., Cul de Sac, tel. 599/5–25162. No credit cards. Inexpensive–Moderate.*

Wajang Doll. Indonesian dishes are served in the garden of this West Indian–style house. The specialty is *rijsttafel*—the Indonesian rice table that offers 14 or 19 dishes in a complete dinner. *137 Front St., Philipsburg, tel. 599/5–22687. AE, MC, V. Inexpensive–Moderate.*

Chesterfield's. Burgers and salads are served at lunch, but menus are more elaborate for dinner on this indoor/outdoor terrace overlooking the marina. Menu offerings include French onion soup, roast duckling with fresh pineapple and banana sauce, and chicken cordon bleu. The Mermaid Bar is a popular spot with yachtsmen. *Great Bay Marina, Philipsburg, tel. 599/5–23484. AE, MC, V. Inexpensive.*

Harbour Lights. This modest family-run spot is in a historic building built in 1870. The interior is warm, with peach and coral walls and native-print tablecloths. Choose among excellent rotis and *pilau* (a fragrant, spiced rice dish) and even bet-

ter stewed or curried chicken, meats, and seafood. Try one of
the knockout cocktails, all made with the local guavaberry liqueur. *30 Back St., Philipsburg, tel. 599/5–23504. AE, MC, V. Inexpensive.*

Shiv Sagar. Authentic East Indian cuisine, emphasizing
Kashmiri and Mughlai specialties, is served in this small mirrored room fragrant with cumin and coriander. Marvelous tan-
dooris and curries are offered, but try one of the less-familiar
preparations like Amritsari fish. There's also a large selection
of vegetarian dishes. *3 Front St., Philipsburg, tel. 599/5–22299.
AE, D, MC, V. Inexpensive.*

★ **Turtle Pier Bar & Restaurant.** Chattering monkeys and
squawking parrots greet you at the entrance to this classic Caribbean hangout, teetering over the lagoon and festooned with
creeping vines. The genial owner Sid Wathey, whose family is
one of the island's oldest, leaves most of the business details to
his American wife, Lorraine. They've fashioned one of the
funkiest, most endearing places in the Caribbean, with cheap
beer on draft, huge American breakfasts, all-you-can-eat ribs
dinners for $9.95, and eclectic live music several nights a week.
A lively crowd gathers at the bar during the daily happy hour,
4–8. *Airport Rd., tel. 599/5–52230. No credit cards. Inexpensive.*

Don Carlos. This plant-filled room adorned with sombreros is
a popular local hangout, with surprisingly good Mexican fare
and killer margaritas. You can also order excellent local specialties and juicy burgers. *Airport Rd., Simpson Bay, tel. 599/5–
53112. No credit cards. Budget–Inexpensive.*

Cheri's Café. This has been an island hot spot for years, with
terrific live entertainment nightly that draws curious crowds
from the neighboring Casino Royale. (It's also the closest thing
to a classic singles bar on St. Maarten.) Food is mainly good old
American grub: huge burgers and sandwiches and fine grilled
items. *Cinnamon Grove Shopping Center, Maho Beach, tel.
599/5–53361. No credit cards. Budget–Inexpensive.*

French Side **Case Anny.** Creole cooking is the specialty of Anne-Marie Boissard's seaside terrace restaurant. She turns out Creole boudin,
crabe farci, and *lambi* (conch) Provençal. *Rue d'Anguille,
Marigot, tel. 599/87–53–38. AE, MC, V. Moderate.*

★ **Cha Cha Cha Caribbean Café.** Everyone eventually seems to
end up at this island hot spot, a chichi dive with Japanese gardens and gaudy colors, run by Pascal and Christina Chevillot.
But food is not a sideline here; you'll find mouth-watering haute
Creole cuisine, reasonably priced. Try the giant prawns in passion-fruit butter or the grilled snapper with avocado, washed
down with a Grand Case Sunset, made with rum, fruit juices,
and grenadine. *Grand Case, tel. 590/87–53–63. MC, V. Dinner
only. Moderate.*

Don Camillo da Enzo. Country-style decor and excellent service distinguish this small eatery. Both northern and southern
Italian specialties are featured. Some favorites are the carpaccio, green gnocchi in Gorgonzola cream sauce, and veal medallions in marsala sauce. *Port La Royale, Marigot, tel.
590/87–52–88. AE, MC, V. Moderate.*

La Résidence. An intimate setting with soft lighting and a tin-
kling fountain, this restaurant offers such specialties as fresh
snapper baked in foil with olive oil and spices, and bouillabaisse. You'll keep your bill within reason by ordering the prix-
fixe *menu gastronomique* or one of the chicken or local fish

dishes. The soufflés are sensational. *Marigot, tel. 590/87–70–37. AE, MC, V. Moderate.*

Maison sur le Port. Watching the sunset from the palm-fringed terrace is not the least of pleasures in this old West Indian house. Delicious food includes sautéed boneless duck breast (*filet*) in mango sauce and red snapper steamed with leeks and champagne. Avoid expensive seafood items to keep dinner in our Moderate price range. Lunch, with Chef Jean-Paul Fahrner's imaginative salads, is a better value. *On the port, Marigot, tel. 590/87–56–38. AE. Moderate.*

★ **Bistrot Nu.** This friendly and enormously popular late-night spot serves traditional brasserie-style food, from *coq au vin* to fish soup, snails, pizza, and seafood, until 2 AM. For simple, unadorned fare at a reasonable price, this may be the best spot on the island. *Rue de Hollande, Marigot, tel. 590/87–77–39. MC, V. Inexpensive–Moderate.*

L'Alabama. This extravagant eatery looks like it was hacked out of the jungle: it's crawling with plants and decorated in lavish florals. The food artfully blends classic French cuisine and island influences in such dishes as minced beef sautéed in orange, red wine, and curry; and red snapper in a delicate lime-and-ginger butter sauce. *Grand Case, no tel. MC, V. Inexpensive–Moderate.*

Le Charolais. Steak, steak, and more steak (the chef is a licensed butcher in France) are the specialties at this pleasant, upscale diner with French farmhouse decor and exposed brick walls. You can also get a tasty leg of lamb Provençal or seafood casserole. The prix-fixe menus at $15–$20 are a wonderful bargain. *Rue Felix Eboue, Marigot, tel. 590/87–93–19. MC, V. Inexpensive–Moderate.*

Le Marocain. This exotic oasis in the middle of Marigot resembles a pasha's posh digs, with lush potted plants, intricate mosaics, hand-painted tiles, and wood carvings. The food is as colorful and enticing as the ambience and decor, with wonderfully perfumed *tajines* (casseroles of chicken or meat) and *pastillas* (fragrant pastries filled with spices, raisins, and meat or chicken) among the standouts. *Rue de Hollande, Marigot, tel. 590/87–83–11. No credit cards. No lunch. Closed Mon. Inexpensive–Moderate.*

Le Plaisance. Probably the most popular of several relaxing, open-air restaurants and pizzerias fronting the Marina Port La Royale, thanks to its piano bar and live nightly entertainment. Pizzas, pasta, and salads are featured, as well as a more ambitious French-Creole menu in the evenings. *Port La Royale, Marigot, tel. 590/87–85–00. AE, MC, V. Inexpensive.*

Mark's Place. This barnlike restaurant is an institution on Sundays. You may start with pumpkin soup or stuffed crab, then follow with linguine bolognese or curried goat. Daily specials are posted on a blackboard. The homemade pies and pastries are scrumptious. *French Cul de Sac, tel. 590/87–34–50. AE, MC, V. Closed Mon. Inexpensive.*

David's Pub. Presided over by a British expat, it's quintessentially English right down to the dart board. You can get draft Guinness and such house specialties as fish-and-chips soused in malt vinegar, beef Wellington, and steak-and-ale pie. The raucous trivia nights on Tuesdays and Fridays draw a lively and erudite crowd. *Rue de la Liberté Marigot, tel. 590/87–51–58. AE, MC, V. Budget–Inexpensive.*

★ **Yvette's.** An endearing dining room of valentine red, with classical music softly playing, is presided over by the kindly Yvette,
with her down-home manner and delicious food. Plates are
piled high with smashing Creole specialties: *accras* (fritters),
stewed chicken with rice and beans, and conch and dumplings.
This is the kind of place that is so good you're surprised to see
other tourists—but word gets around. *Orléans, tel. 590/87–32–
03. AE (5% surcharge). Budget–Inexpensive.*

★ **Lolos.** These barbecue stands are a St. Martin institution, dishing out heaping helpings of scrumptious grilled lobster, chicken
or fish, rice and peas, and johnnycakes. You'll find lolos lining
Marigot harbor in the marketplace and between the tourist
office and Anguilla ferry. But the best are in Grand Case. **Cynthia's** sauce recipe is the most coveted, but **Jimbo** lolo is the
hippest. It stays open until midnight for French punks and
American wanna-bes. *Marigot and Grand Case, no tel. No
credit cards. Budget.*

Surf Club South. This beach shack, seemingly held together by
business cards and silly photos, is straight from southern California via Jersey City. It rocks every happy hour, when beers
and hot dogs are both a buck. Otherwise, there are filling deli
heros, chili, and pastas (all garlic and attitude) for $5–$6. *Grand
Case, no tel. No credit cards. Budget.*

Lodging

Big, splashy resorts with casinos are a prominent feature here,
especially on the Dutch side of the island. Although standard
rates at many of these are not affordable for the budget traveler, most offer group package rates through travel wholesal-
ers. Bargains are rife on Dutch side, which is paying the price
of overbuilding with cut-rate tariffs and other incentives.

In general, the French resorts are more intimate and romantic,
but Dutch properties compensate with clean, functional, comfortable rooms with lots of amenities. Most of the larger Dutch
resorts feature time-share annexes; the units are often available for those vacationers who prefer the condo lifestyle at
comparable rates.

Both St. Martin and St. Maarten also have less expensive small
inns and guest houses. Often locally owned, these have few of
a large hotel's amenities, but they are a cheap and sometimes
charming introduction to the local scene. Budget guest houses
on the French side usually have more character and ambience
than their spartan Dutch counterparts. In addition to inns and
guest houses, you'll find many signs here advertising rooms to
let in private homes, especially around Grand Case on the
French side. These are the cheapest alternative of all ($20–$30
a night), but you are advised to inspect rooms carefully before
committing.

Keep in mind that truly budget accommodations tend to be a
hike from beaches. Those we've recommended are on established bus routes and no more than a half-hour's walk from the
nearest major beach. Exceptions are those in Philipsburg and
Grand Case, which boast their own beaches as well as restaurants and nightlife.

As with most Caribbean islands, you'll save substantially if you
travel off-season, although many hotels close for refurbish-

ment during some of these months (usually August/September).

Highly recommended lodgings are indicated by a star ★ .

Category	Cost*
Moderate	$150–$200
Inexpensive	$80–$150
Budget	under $80

All prices are for a standard double room for two, excluding 5% tax (Dutch side), a taxe de séjour (set by individual hotels on the French side), and a 10%–15% service charge. To estimate rates for hotels offering MAP, add $35–$50 per person per day to the above price ranges. For all-inclusives, add about $75 per person per day.

Hotels
Dutch Side

Holland House. This is a centrally situated hotel, with the shops of Front Street at its doorstep and a mile-long backyard called Great Bay Beach, which, unfortunately, is slightly polluted from the cruise ships and freighters anchored in the bay. (Rooms 104 through 107 open directly onto the beach.) Each room has contemporary tropical furnishings, balcony, kitchenette, satellite cable TV, and air-conditioning. Its delightful open-air restaurant overlooking the water serves reasonably priced dinners. *Box 393, Philipsburg, tel. 599/5–22572 or 800/223–9815; in NY, 212/840–6636, fax 599/5–24673. 52 rooms, 2 suites. Facilities: beach, restaurant, lounge, gift shop. AE, DC, MC, V. EP. Moderate.*

★ **Horny Toad Guesthouse.** This is one of the most charming properties on the island, thanks to the caring touch of owners Bette and Earle Vaughan who keep things as immaculate as if it were their own home (which it is most of the year). The eight apartments on the beach, all with kitchenettes and sizable baths, are individually and thoughtfully decorated. (The many repeat guests usually request the same room.) The blue-and-white sun terrace echoes the delft-colored buildings themselves. Mornings bring chirping birds and fresh flowers. *Simpson Bay, tel. 599/5–54323, fax 599/5–53316. 2 studios, 6 1-bedroom apartments. Facilities: library, barbecue. No credit cards. EP. Moderate.*

La Vista. Quaint Antillean buildings connect by brick walkways lined with hibiscus and bougainvillea at this intimate property with personal service. The hotel has its own rocky beach, but guests have the use of facilities at the adjacent Pelican Resort on Simpson Bay beach. All the accommodations are air-conditioned suites with cable TVs, direct-dial phones, balconies, and lovely white iron queen-size beds. *Box 40, Pelican Key, tel. 599/5–43005 or 800/365–8484, fax 599/5–43010. 24 suites. Facilities: horseback riding, pool, restaurant, tennis. AE, MC, V. EP. Moderate.*

Mary's Boon. This informal inn has enormous rooms with kitchenettes, seaside patios, and ceiling fans. Meals are served family-style, and there is an honor bar. The inn is on Simpson Bay's big beach. The many repeat guests don't seem fazed by the roar of the jets landing at the nearby airport. *Box 2078, Philipsburg, tel. 599/5–44235 or 212/986–4373 in the U.S. 12 studios. Facilities: restaurant, bar. No credit cards. EP. Moderate.*

Seaview Hotel & Casino. This is another good buy on Front Street and Great Bay Beach. The air-conditioned, twin-bed rooms are modest, cheerful, and clean. All rooms have baths (some with showers only), satellite TV, and phones. The four rooms above the sea have the best views. *Box 65, Philipsburg, tel. 599/5–22323 or 800/223–9815, 212/545–8469 in NY, 800/468–0023 in Canada; fax 599/5–24356. 45 rooms. Facilities: breakfast room, casino. AE, MC, V. EP. Inexpensive.*

Sea Breeze Hotel. This spotless motel is located in a quiet residential area, a 15-minute walk from the beach. The plain but tidy rooms include air-conditioning, phones, cable TVs, and minifridges. *Cay Hill, tel. 599/5–26054, fax 599/26057. 20 rooms. Facilities: pool, restaurant, bar, sundry shop. AE, MC, V. EP. Budget–Inexpensive.*

Caribbean Hotel. You expect Sadie Thompson to vamp through those beaded glass curtains any minute. Frankly, this hotel is recommended more for its funky atmosphere, than for its facilities, which are passable and clean. It's on a second floor above Front Street, across the street from the beach. The rooms have tile floors, air-conditioning, TVs, and private baths. Those in the back are quieter. *Box 236, Philipsburg, tel. 599/5–22028. 50 rooms. Facilities: restaurant, bar. AE, MC, V. EP. Budget.*

Royal Inn Motel. The staff is indifferent at best here, but rates are rock-bottom and the beach is a 10-minute walk away. Rooms are clean, if lacking in charm, and feature kitchenettes, cable TV, air-conditioning, and phones. *A.T. Illidge Rd., Over the Pond, tel. 599/5–24284. 17 rooms. Facilities: bar, restaurant, disco. No credit cards. EP. Budget.*

French Side **Alizéa.** The Alizéa is located on Mont Vernon hill and offers splendid views over Orient Bay. It's a 10-minute walk to the beach on Orient Bay, but you will need a car to go elsewhere on the island. An open-air feeling pervades the hotel from its terrace restaurant, where the food is superb, to the 26 guest apartments with kitchenettes, decorated with contemporary wood furnishings and pastel fabrics. Rooms vary in style and design, but all are tasteful and each has a large private patio balcony that makes breakfast a special treat. *Mont Vernon 25, 97150, tel. 590/87–33–42, fax 590/87–41–15. 8 1-bedroom bungalows, 18 studios. Facilities: pool, restaurant. AE, MC, V. CP. Moderate.*

★ **Captain Oliver.** At Oyster Pond facing a beautiful horseshoe-shape bay, this small hotel, is for those who want to be away from the hustle of St. Maarten. The exceptionally clean, fresh air-conditioned units have bay or garden views, patio decks, satellite TVs, minibars, direct-dial phones, and kitchenettes. The property straddles the border: Stay in France, dine in the Netherlands. Sail-and-stay packages can be arranged by the friendly, helpful staff. Standard rooms are high-end Moderate; suites here are out of our price range. *Oyster Pond, 97150, tel. 590/87–40–26 or 800/223–9862, fax 590/87–40–84. 50 rooms. Facilities: restaurant, snack bar. AE, DC, MC, V. CP. Moderate.*

Pavillon Beach Hotel. Every room of this small, fairly new hotel faces the sea and comes with a private balcony. The spacious rooms with tile floors and warm colored fabrics have clean bathrooms that come with a hair dryer and fixed-head shower (no tubs). On the balcony is a small but fully equipped kitchenette. The rooms on the ground level allow you to walk right onto the beach, but do require that you close yourself in at night with sliding shutters; you may prefer the upper-story rooms. The managers, Paul and Marie-Florence, are wonderfully warm-hearted and helpful. Prices are high-end Moderate. *Plage de Grand Case, RN 7, Grand Case 97150, tel. 590/87–96–46 or 800/223–9815 in the U.S., fax 590/87–71–04. 17 rooms. Facilities: kitchenettes, in-room safes. MC, V. EP. Moderate.*

★ **Marine Hotel Simson Beach.** This may be the best buy on the hotel "strip" known as Nettlé Bay. Rooms and duplex suites are cheerfully decorated, most with water views, and all have kitchenettes, safes, cable TV, and direct-dial phones. The youthful, fun-loving clientele including budget-conscious Europeans, enjoy the many extras, such as a huge breakfast buffet and nightly local entertainment. *Box 172, Nettlé Bay, tel. 590/87–54–54, fax 590/87–92–11. 120 studios, 45 1-bedroom duplexes. Facilities: pool, water-sports center, restaurant, bar, car and bike rental, minimart, laundromat, dive shop. AE, MC, V. BP. Inexpensive–Moderate.*

Coralita Beach Hotel. The entrance is a bit unprepossessing, like something out of a Graham Greene novel about well-bred Europeans down on their luck. But the ultraneat, fresh rooms haven't gone to seed. They are large and breezy, most with air-conditioning and kitchenette. Sunday brunch is one of the island's liveliest. As the name suggests, the hotel is right on the beach, though you'll need a car for restaurant hopping. A little worn, but quite congenial and an excellent bargain. *BP 175, Oyster Pond 97150, tel. 590/87–31–81, fax 590/87–51–77. 24 studios. Facilities: pool, bar, restaurant, tennis court, game room. AE, MC, V. EP. Inexpensive.*

Jardins de Chevrise. Perched on a hill overlooking Orient Bay and just a few minutes' (steep) walk from the beach, these peaceful, simply appointed but appealing efficiencies contain balconies, kitchenettes, and air-conditioning. *52 Mont Vernon 97150, tel. 590/87–37–79, fax 590/87–38–03. 30 studios and 1-bedroom bungalows. Facilities: pool, grill. AE, MC, V. EP. Inexpensive.*

★ **La Residence.** Its Marigot location makes this hotel popular with business travelers. Accommodations have shower baths, phones, safes, cable TVs, minibars, and air-conditioning. You've a choice among double rooms, studios, mezzanine loft beds, and apartments with or without kitchenettes. You'll have to take a cab to get to the beach. *Rue du Général de Gaulle, Marigot 97150, tel. 590/87–70–37, fax 590/87–90–44. 20 rooms. Facilities: restaurant, lounge, sundry shop. AE, MC, V. CP. Inexpensive.*

La Royale Louisiana. Located in downtown Marigot in the boutique shopping area, this upstairs hotel is pleasant and pretty. White and pale green galleries overlook the flower-filled courtyard. There's a selection of twin, double, and triple air-conditioned duplexes, all with private baths (tubs and showers), TVs, VCRs, and phones. It's a 20-minute walk to the nearest beach. *Rue du Général de Gaulle, Marigot 97150, tel. 590/87–86–51, fax 590/87–86–51. 68 rooms. Facilities: restaurant, snack bar, beauty salon. AE, DC, MC, V. CP. Inexpensive.*

Marina Royale Hotel. This busy little hotel on the Marina Port La Royale is very popular with young French families and businesspeople on holiday. The bright, simple rooms all feature kitchenettes, cable TVs, air-conditioning, and direct-dial phones. The beach is about a 20-minute stroll away. *Port La Royale, Marigot, tel. 590/87–52–46, fax 590/87–92–88. 62 rooms.*

Facilities: pool, restaurant, bar, shopping arcade. AE, MC, V. CP. Inexpensive.

Rosely's. This whitewashed motel is set in the hills just behind Marigot, a good 25-minute walk from the nearest beach. The rooms are cheerful, with kitchenettes and air-conditioning, and the ambience friendly, thanks to helpful management and the primarily island and French student clientele. *Concordia, Marigot, tel. 590/87–70–17, fax 590/87–70–20. Facilities: snack bar, pool. AE, MC, V. CP. Budget–Inexpensive.*

Guest Houses
Dutch Side

Beach House. This unexpectedly tranquil oasis amid the bustle of downtown Philipsburg gives you the best of both worlds: The beach and the shops and restaurants of Philipsburg are right at your doorstep. Gleaming white halls with gorgeous carved mahogany doors lead to tidy, well-appointed rooms with cable TVs, kitchenettes, safe-deposit boxes, ocean-view balconies, and air-conditioning. *161 Front St., Philipsburg, tel. 599/5–22456, fax 599/5–30308. 8 one-bedroom apartments. AE, MC, V. EP. Inexpensive.*

Residence La Chatelaine. This gleaming pink-and-white apartment hotel sits right on the beach and is within walking distance of restaurants. The ultra-feminine Maryanne Chatelaine floats through the property, and her delicate, slightly frilly touch is evident in the light, pastel rooms with lacy mosquito netting imported from Amsterdam. Individually decorated units each feature a full kitchen, small bath, and ceiling fan. Some also include cable TV, dishwasher, and lovely old mahogany four-poster beds. *Box 2056, Simpson Bay, tel. 599/5–54269, fax 599/5–53195. 13 studios, 4 apartments. Facilities: pool, boutique. AE, MC, V. EP. Inexpensive.*

Calypso Guest House. The homey rooms in this sparkling white building open onto an airy skylit hall with terra-cotta floor. The units themselves are a bit dim but comfortable, with air-conditioning, kitchenettes, and TVs. It's a five-minute walk to the beach, and the Philipsburg bus stops right at the door. *Box 65, Simpson Bay, tel. 599/5–44233. 1 studio, 7 apartments. Facilities: bar, restaurant. AE, MC, V. EP. Budget–Inexpensive.*

Ernest's Guest House. These clean, spacious units in a nondescript, motel-style facility are surprisingly nice for the price—$40—and feature cable TVs, phones, and air-conditioning. The only drawback is the location: a 20-minute walk from Great Bay beach, although the bus stops nearby. You can walk to local restaurants, though. *Bush Rd., Cay Hill, tel. 599/5–22003. 13 rooms. Facilities: pool. No credit cards. EP. Budget.*

French Side
★

Passangrahan Royal Guest House. It's entirely appropriate that the bar here is named Sidney Greenstreet. This is the island's oldest inn, and it looks like a set for an old Bogie–Greenstreet film. The building was once Queen Wilhelmina's residence (there's a picture of her in the lobby) and the government guest house. You'll find better facilities than are usual in a guest house, including its location right on Great Bay Beach. Wicker peacock chairs, slowly revolving ceiling fans, balconies shaded by tropical greenery, king-size mahogany four-poster beds, and a broad tile veranda are some of the hallmarks of this guest house. Afternoon tea is served. There are no TVs or phones. *Box 151, Philipsburg 97150, tel. 599/5–23588, fax 599/5–22885. 30 rooms and suites. Facilities: rental bikes, bar, restaurant. AE, MC, V. EP. Inexpensive–Moderate.*

Chez Martine. The rooms in this Antillean-style house overlooking Grand Case Bay are pleasingly furnished with wicker and pastel prints. All are air-conditioned and have minibars, but lack ocean views. The personable owners, Elaine and Jean Pierre Bertheau, tell fascinating tales of their days in Morocco. It's right on Grand Case Beach, with lots of restaurants nearby. Regrettably, the property's own very fine restaurant is quite expensive. *BP 637, Grand Case 97150, tel. 590/87–51–59, fax 590/87–87–30. 6 rooms. Facilities: restaurant, laundry service. AE, MC, V. EP. Inexpensive.*

★ **Hevea.** This is a small white guest house with smart awnings in the heart of Grand Case. The rooms are dollhouse small, but will appeal to romantics. There are beam ceilings, washstands, and carved wood beds with lovely white coverlets and mosquito nets. The air-conditioned rooms, studios, and apartment are on the terrace level; fan-cooled studios and apartments are on the garden level. Hotel guests can take advantage of the superb three-course *menu touristique* for $25 in the romantic burgundy dining room. *Grand Case 97150, tel. 590/87–56–85 or 800/423–4433, fax 590/87–83–88. 8 units. Facilities: restaurant. MC, V. EP. Inexpensive.*

Gracie Mansion Guest House. This is an immaculate little guest house, its whitewashed walls, teal roofs, and coral balconies contrasting brilliantly with the azure sky and water. On Oyster Pond and a short stroll from a poky beach, it's a peaceful retreat. Units are furnished in tasteful but idiosyncratic fashion, with satellite TVs, kitchenettes, balconies, fans, and small shower baths. You'll want a car. *Baie Lucas 97150, tel. 599/5–70787. 2 studios, 3 apartments. Facilities: snack bar, car rental. AE, MC, V. EP. Budget.*

Le Cigalon. Look behind drying wash and luxuriant, barely contained gardens to find this somewhat ramshackle, rambling old house. You pass through a flower-draped arbor into a welcoming little restaurant (which serves superb local food, with a *plat du jour* for $7). Seven rooms have private shower baths, two share a bath. All are air-conditioned; the nicest have hand-painted murals. A funky place, indeed, but as inexpensive as they come—$20–$25—and well worth the 20-minute beach trek. *Rue Fichot, Marigot 97150, tel. 590/87–08–19. 9 rooms, 2 with shared bath. Facilities: restaurant, bar. No credit cards. EP. Budget.*

Home and Apartment Rentals

Both sides of the island offer a variety of homes, villas, condominiums, and apartments. Information in the United States can be obtained through **Caribbean Home Rentals** (Box 710, Palm Beach, FL 33480, tel. 407/833–4454), **Jane Condon Corp.** (211 E. 43rd St., New York, NY 10017, tel. 212/986–4373), or **St. Maarten Villas** (707 Broad Hollow Rd., Farmingdale, NY 11735, tel. 516/249–4940). On the island, contact **Carimo** (tel. 590/87–57–58), **Ausar** (tel. 590/87–51–07), or **St. Maarten Rentals** (tel. 599/5–44330). Both tourist boards publish lists of recommended villas and guest houses that meet minimum standards in various price categories. The least expensive apartment complexes are located in Grand Case; all are fairly basic, clean, and priced in the budget–inexpensive range.

Off-Season Bets

While the most glamorous properties remain outside our price range, several top resorts lower their rates by up to 50% during the off-season. It also pays to inquire about special packages that can make an otherwise pricey property affordable. Most of the megaresorts on the Dutch side, as well as their sister time-share developments, are good off-season bets. You'll be where all the activity is, with a tremendous range of facilities at your disposal. Foremost among these are **Mullet Bay Resort and Casino** (Mullet Bay, tel. 599/5–52807 or 800/642–6401); **Pelican Resort and Casino** (Simson Bay, tel. 599/5–54330 or 800/451–5510); and **Maho Beach Hotel & Casino** (Maho Bay, tel. 599/5–42115 or 800/835–6246). The refined **Oyster Pond Hotel** (Oyster Pond, tel. 599/5–22206 or 800/372–1323) is a quieter property with great charm. On the French side, good bets are the bustling **Mont Vernon** (Oriental Bay, tel. 590/87–62–00 or 800/543–4300) and the pretty and popular **Anse Margot** (Nettlé Bay, tel. 590/87–92–01 or 800/333–1970). All are located on lovely stretches of beach.

Nightlife

To find out what's doing on the island, pick up any of the following publications: *St. Maarten Nights, What to Do in St. Maarten, St. Maarten Events,* or *St. Maarten Holiday*—all distributed free in the tourist office and hotels. *Discover St. Martin/St. Maarten,* also free, is a glossy magazine that includes articles about the island's history and the latest on shops, discos, restaurants—even archaeological digs.

There's rarely a cover charge at casinos and discos here. Dress is casual at both.

Casinos Table limits in St. Maarten casinos are quite low; it's hard to lose a lot of money unless you're a hard-core gambler on a bad streak. All 10 of the casinos have craps, blackjack, roulette, and slot machines. You must be 18 years old to gamble. The casinos are located at the **Great Bay Beach Hotel, Divi Little Bay Beach Hotel, Pelican Resort, Mullet Bay Hotel, Seaview Hotel** and the **Coliseum** in Philipsburg, **St. Maarten Beach Club, Port de Plaisance,** and **Casino Royale** at Maho Beach.

Discos **Last Stop** (A. T. Illidge Road, no tel.) and **The Tropics** (by Madame Estate in the Royal Inn Motel, no tel.) are hot, somewhat rowdy discos frequented by locals. There have been reports of drug activity at the latter. **Studio 7** (tel. 599/5–42115) attracts a young crowd in its ultramodern digs atop Casino Royale across from Maho Beach Resort. Casino Royale also produces the splashy "Paris Revue Show." **Le Club** (Mullet Bay, tel. 599/5–42801) draws a mixed crowd of locals and tourists. French nationals and locals flock to **L'Atmosphère** (no phone) on the second floor of L'Auberge de Mer in Marigot for the best in salsa and soca. **Night Fever** (Colombier, outside Marigot, no phone) attracts a young crowd of locals who gyrate to the latest Eurodisco beat.

24 St. Vincent and the Grenadines

By Joan Iaconetti

St. Vincent and the Grenadines form a necklace of lush, mountainous islands that beckon the traveler, sailor, and day-tripper more intrigued by blooming flowers than by Bloomingdale's. The fertile volcanic soil has helped to create the oldest botanical gardens in the Western Hemisphere, and rich, aromatic valleys of bananas, coconuts, and arrowroot cover these relatively undeveloped islands.

St. Vincent, with a population of about 99,000, is only 16 miles long and 9 miles wide, but it delights those who have discovered the stunning natural beauty both below and above its crystal seas. Visitors are usually seasoned travelers willing to exchange modern creature comforts for the Robinson Crusoe–like escape this unspoiled island offers. The Grenadines, an even more remote destination, appeal to adventurous singles and couples who prefer active sports to glitz and gambling. In contrast to St. Vincent's beaches of black volcanic sand, the Grenadines offer powdery white bays and coves on both the calm leeward and surfy windward shores.

St. Vincent and the Grenadines are home to both the most expensive and the most affordable accommodations in the Caribbean, with little in between. Several of the Grenadines, for instance, are patronized almost exclusively by jet-setters and the highest society, who breeze in and out of the private villas and single-resort islands here. If you steer clear of these tony enclaves, however, you'll find more than enough bargains. Although St. Vincent and the Grenadines are relatively costly to fly to, you can nonetheless live on a comparative shoestring once you arrive—if you don't mind taking brightly painted minivans instead of taxis, cooking some of your own meals, and sharing your Spartan room or apartment with gecko lizards and other harmless island critters. Beaches are almost always within walking distance (on St. Vincent, you will need wheels to get from Kingstown to Villa Beach), and numerous hotels offer attractive dive packages. Experienced sailors can charter bareboats at reasonable cost, and groups of four or six will find even a crewed yacht within their budget on St. Vincent. Thanks to the friendly, unpretentious atmosphere, visitors with even minimal charm and manual dexterity often find themselves invited to day-sail by the many yacht owners or bareboaters who frequent the Grenadines.

Remember, though, that unspoiled involves tradeoffs: no casinos, no shopping, no nightlife, and often no hot water in the clean but bordering-on-primitive budget hotels. Getting anything accomplished (even buying groceries) always takes more time and effort than you think . . . but sooner or later, everything seems to work out.

What It Will Cost These sample prices, meant only as a general guide, are for high season. Expect to pay from $50 to $80 a night for a budget hotel or a B&B for two. A two-bedroom apartment rents for $500–$600 a week. Plan on about $6 for a budget restaurant meal, about $5 for a sandwich lunch. Supermarket prices are higher than in the United States, as most food must be shipped in. A beer costs about $1.75 here. A glass of house wine or rum punch can be anywhere from $1.50 to $3. Car rental is about $35–$50 a day for a stick-shift model. Taxi fares cost about $3–$4 around Kingstown, about $8 from Kingstown to Villa Beach. A single-tank dive here is about $50; snorkel equipment rents for around $8 a day.

Before You Go

Tourist Information The **St. Vincent and the Grenadines Tourist Office** (801 2nd Ave., 21st floor, New York, NY 10017, tel. 212/687–4981 or 800/729–1726, fax 212/949–5946; or 6505 Cove Creek Pl., Dallas, TX 75240, tel. 214/239–6451, fax 214/239–1002; in Canada: 100 University Ave., Suite 504, Toronto, Ont. M5J 1V6, tel. 416/971–9666, fax 416/971–9667; in the United Kingdom: 10 Kensington Court, London W8 5DL, tel. 071/937–6570, fax 071/937–3611). Write for a visitors guide, filled with useful, up-to-date information.

Arriving and Departing Most U.S. visitors fly via **American** (tel. 800/433–7300) into Barbados or St. Lucia, then take a small plane to St. Vincent's **By Plane** E.T. Joshua Airport or to Bequia, Mustique, Canouan, Union, or Palm. (Other destinations require a boat ride on either a scheduled ferry, a chartered boat, or your hotel's launch.) Other airlines that connect with interisland flights are **BWIA** (tel. 800/JET–BWIA), **British Airways** (tel. 800/247–9297), **Air Canada** (tel. 800/776–3000), and **Air France** (tel. 800/237–2747).

LIAT (Leeward Islands Air Transport, tel. 809/462–0700; in NY, 212/251–1717; in the U.S., 800/253–5011), **Air Martinique** (tel. 809/458–4528), and **SVGAIR** (tel. 809/456–9246; in the U.S., 800/677–3195; in FL, 813/799–1858) fly interisland. Delays are common, but usually not outrageous. A surer way to go is with **Mustique Airways** (tel. 809/458–4380 or 809/458–4818. In the United States, contact Anchor Travel at tel.

800/526–4789 or in New Jersey, 201/891–1111). Its six- or eight-seat charter flights meet and wait for your major carrier's arrival even if it's delayed (bring earplugs if you're supersensitive to noise).

From the Airport Taxis and/or buses are readily available at the airport on every island. A taxi from the E.T. Joshua airport to Kingstown, St. Vincent, will cost $5–$7 (E.C. $15–$20); bus fare is less than 75¢. If you have a lot of luggage, it might be best to take a taxi—buses (actually minivans) are very short on space.

Passports and Visas U.S. and Canadian citizens must have a passport; all visitors must hold return or ongoing tickets. Visas are not required.

Language English is spoken everywhere in the Grenadines, often with a Vincentian patois or dialect.

Precautions Insects are a minor problem on the beach during the day, but when hiking and sitting outdoors in the evening, you'll be glad you brought industrial-strength mosquito repellent. Beware of the manchineel tree, whose little green apples look tempting but are toxic. Even touching the sap of the leaves will cause an uncomfortable rash. Most trees on hotel grounds are marked with signs; on more remote islands, the bark may be painted red. Hikers should watch for Brazil wood trees/bushes, which look and act similar to poison ivy. When taking photos of market vendors, private citizens, or homes, be sure to ask permission first and expect to give a gratuity for the favor. There's relatively little crime here, but don't tempt fate by leaving your valuables lying around or your room or car unlocked.

Staying in St. Vincent and the Grenadines

Important Addresses **Tourist Information:** The **St. Vincent Board of Tourism** (tel. 809/457–1502) is located on the second floor of a marked building on Egmont Street.

Emergencies **Police:** (tel. 809/457–1211). **Hospitals:** (tel. 809/456–1185). **Pharmacies: Deane's** (tel. 809/457–1522), **Reliance** (tel. 809/456–1734), both in Kingstown; on Bequia **Bequia Pharmacy** (tel. 809/458–3296).

Currency Although U.S. and Canadian dollars are taken at all but the smallest shops, Eastern Caribbean currency (E.C.$) is accepted and preferred everywhere. At press time, the exchange rate was U.S. $1 to E.C. $2.67; banks give a slightly better rate of exchange.

Price quotes on the islands are normally given in E.C. dollars; however, when you negotiate taxi fares and such, be sure you know which type of dollar you're agreeing on. Note: Prices quoted here are in U.S. dollars unless indicated otherwise.

Taxes and Service Charges The departure tax from St. Vincent and the Grenadines is $6 (E.C. $15). Restaurants and hotels charge a 5% government tax, and if a 10% service charge is included in your bill, no additional tip is necessary. Hotels charge a 5% tax and an additional 10% for service.

Getting Around The islands' roads make San Francisco's look almost flat, and they're not always well-maintained. For those not used to driving on the left, the whole experience can be unnerving. You may prefer to spend money on taxis or minibuses.

Taxis Fares run $3–$4 around Kingstown, $8 from Kingstown to Villa Beach. You can hire a taxi and driver for sightseeing (*see* Guided Tours, *below*) at $15 an hour.

Minivans Public buses come in the form of brightly painted minivans with names like "Struggling Man" and "Who to Blame." They are crowded, noisy, full of local color, and cheap—usually E.C. $1–$2. They cover all of St. Vincent. Route directions are on a sign in the windshield; just wave from the road and the driver will stop for you; the terminal in Kingstown is at Market Square on Bay Street.

On Bequia, most taxis are pickup trucks with benches in the back and canvas covers for when it rains. Transportation isn't really necessary—or indeed, obtainable—on the other islands. If you need to go somewhere, your hotel's vehicle will give you a lift.

Rental Cars Rental cars cost $45–$50 per day; driving is on the left. Many roads are not well marked or maintained. We recommend a taxi or minibus tour before going out on your own in order to familiarize yourself with directions and road conditions.

To rent a car you'll need a temporary Vincentian license (unless you already have an International Driver's License), which costs E.C. $20. Among the rental firms are **Johnson's U-Drive** (tel. 809/458–4864) at the airport and **Kim's Auto Rentals** (tel. 809/456–1884), which has a larger selection of slightly more expensive rental cars that must be rented by the week.

Telephones and Mail The area code for St. Vincent and the Grenadines is 809. If you use Sprint or MCI in the United States, you may need to access an AT&T line to dial direct to St. Vincent and the Grenadines. From St. Vincent, you can direct-dial to other countries; ask the hotel operator for the proper country code and the probable charge, surcharge, and government tax on the call. Local information is 118; international is 115.

When you dial a local number from your hotel in the Grenadines, you can drop the 45-prefix. Few hotels have phones in the rooms. Pay phones are E.C. 25¢.

Mail between St. Vincent and the United States takes two to three weeks. Airmail postcards cost 45¢; airmail letters cost 65¢ an ounce.

Opening and Closing Times Stores and shops in Kingstown are open weekdays 8–4. Many close for lunch from noon to 1 or so. Saturday hours are 8–noon. Banks are open weekdays 8–noon, Fridays from 2 or 3 to 5. The post office is open weekdays 8:30–3, Saturdays 8:30–11:30.

Guided Tours Tours can be informally arranged through taxi drivers who double as informal but knowledgeable guides. Your hotel or the Tourism Board will recommend a driver. When choosing a driver/guide, look for the Taxi Driver's Association decal on the windshield and talk with the driver long enough to be sure you can understand his patois over the noise of the engine. Settle the fare first ($30–$40 is normal for a two- or three-hour tour). To prearrange a taxi tour, contact the Taxi Driver's Association (tel. 809/457–1807).

St. Vincent

Exploring St. Vincent

Numbers in the margin correspond to points of interest on the St. Vincent map.

Kingstown's shopping/business district, cathedrals, and sights can easily be seen in a half-day tour. Outlying areas, botanical gardens, and the Falls of Baleine will each require a full day of touring. City maps are in the "Discover SVG" booklet, available everywhere.

Kingstown The capital and port of St. Vincent, **Kingstown** is at the south-
❶ eastern end of the island. Begin your tour on Bay Street, near Egmont Street. Kingstown's boutiques feature such local crafts as cotton batik hangings and clothing, floor mats, baskets, and black coral jewelry.

The **fish/vegetable market** on Bay Street is a hectic, lively place, especially on Saturdays before 11 AM. Note: Keep a tight grip on your valuables in the market. Unusual gifts for stamp collectors are at the **post office** on Granby Street east of Egmont. St. Vincent is known worldwide for its particularly beautiful and colorful issues, which commemorate flowers, undersea creatures, and architecture.

Follow Back Street (also called Granby Street) west past the Methodist Church to **St. George's Cathedral,** a yellow Anglican church built in the early 19th century. The dignified Georgian architecture includes simple wood pews, an ornate hanging candelabra, and stained-glass windows. The gravestones tell the history of the island.

Across the street is **St. Mary's Roman Catholic Cathedral,** built in 1823 and renovated in the 1930s. The renovations resulted in a strangely appealing blend of Moorish, Georgian, and Romanesque styles in black brick.

A few minutes away by bus is St. Vincent's famous **Botanical Gardens.** Founded in 1765, it is the oldest botanical garden in the Western Hemisphere. Captain Bligh brought the first breadfruit tree to this island; a direct descendant of it is in the gardens. St. Vincent parrots and green monkeys are housed in cages, and unusual trees and bushes cover the well-kept grounds. Local guides offer their services for $2–$4 an hour. *Information: c/o Minister of Agriculture, Kingstown, tel. 809/457–1003. Open weekdays 7–4, Sat. 7–11 AM, Sun. 7–6.*

The tiny **National Museum** houses ancient Indian clay pottery found by Dr. Earle Kirby, St. Vincent's resident archaeologist. Dr. Kirby's historical knowledge is as entertaining as it is extensive. Contact him for a guided tour, since the labels in the museum offer little information. *Tel. 809/456–1787. Suggested donation: $1. Open Wed. 9–noon, Sat. 3–6.*

❷ Flag another taxi for the 10-minute ride to **Fort Charlotte,** built in 1806 to keep Napoleon at bay. The fort sits 636 feet above sea level, with cannons and battlements perched on a dramatic promontory overlooking the city and the Grenadines to the south, Lowman's Beach and the calm east coast to the north.

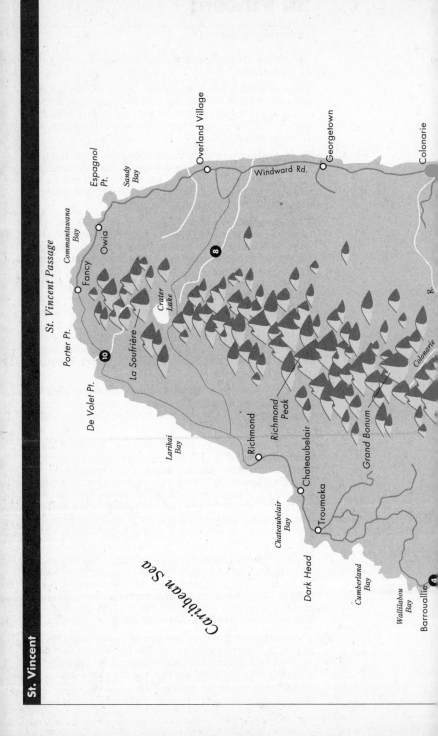

521

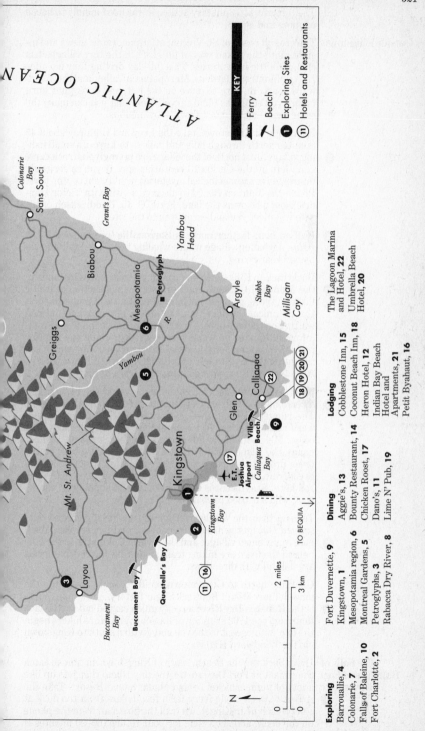

ATLANTIC OCEAN

Colonarie Bay
Sans Souci
Grant's Bay
Yambou Head
Biabou
Mesopotamia
Petroglyph
Greiggs
Yambou R.
Argyle
Stubbs Bay
Milligan Cay
Mt. St. Andrew
Glen
Colliaqua
Villa
Calliaqua Beach
Layou
Kingstown
Kingstown Bay
E.T. Joshua Airport
Calliaqua Bay
Buccament Bay
Questelle's Bay
Buccament Bay

TO BEQUIA

KEY

Ferry
Beach
1 Exploring Sites
11 Hotels and Restaurants

N

0   2 miles
0   3 km

Exploring
Barrouallie, 4
Colonarie, 7
Falls of Baleine, 10
Fort Charlotte, 2
Fort Duvernette, 9
Kingstown, 1
Mesopotamia region, 6
Montreal Gardens, 5
Petroglyphs, 3
Rabacca Dry River, 8

Dining
Aggie's, 13
Bounty Restaurant, 14
Chicken Roost, 17
Dano's, 11
Lime N' Pub, 19

Lodging
Cobblestone Inn, 15
Coconut Beach Inn, 18
Heron Hotel, 12
Indian Bay Beach Hotel and Apartments, 21
Petit Byahaut, 16
The Lagoon Marina and Hotel, 22
Umbrella Beach Hotel, 20

The fort saw little military action; it was used mainly to house paupers and lepers.

Outside Kingstown The coastal roads of St. Vincent offer panoramic views and insights into the island way of life. Life in the tiny villages has changed little in centuries. This full-day driving tour includes Layou, Montreal Gardens, Mesopotamia Valley, and the Windward coast. Be sure to drive on the left, and honk your horn before you enter the blind curves. Note that you can make the same tour—albeit more slowly—by minibus.

❸ Beginning in Kingstown, take the Leeward Highway about 45 minutes north through hills and valleys to **Layou,** a small fishing village. Just north of the village are **petroglyphs** (rock carvings) left by the Caribs 13 centuries ago. If you're seriously interested in archaeological mysteries, you'll want to stop here. Phone the Tourism Board to arrange a visit with Victor Hendrickson, who owns the land. For E.C. $5, Hendrickson or his wife will meet you and escort you to the site.

❹ Half an hour farther north is **Barrouallie** (pronounced *BARrelly*), a whaling village where whaling boats are built and repaired year-round.

❺ Backtrack to Kingstown and continue toward Mesopotamia to the **Montreal Gardens,** another extensive collection of exotic flowers, trees, and spice plants. It's not as well maintained as the Botanical Gardens, but the aroma of cocoa and nutmeg wafting on the cool breeze is enticing. Spend an hour with well-informed guides or wander on your own along the narrow paths. Vincentian newlyweds often spend their honeymoons in the garden's tiny cottage, appropriately named Romance. *Tel. 809/458–5452. Suggested donation: $1. Open daily.*

❻ Now drive southeast (roads and signs aren't the best, so ask directions at Montreal Gardens) to the **Mesopotamia region.** The rugged, ocean-lashed scenery along St. Vincent's windward coast is the perfect counterpoint to the lush, calm west coast. Mesopotamia is full of dense forests, streams, and bananas, the island's major export. The blue plastic bags on the trees protect the fruit from damage in high winds. Coconut, breadfruit, sweet corn, peanuts, and arrowroot grow in the rich soil here. St. Vincent is the world's largest supplier of arrowroot, which is used to coat computer paper.

❼ Turn north on the Windward Highway up the jagged coast road toward Georgetown, St. Vincent's second-largest city. You'll pass many small villages and the town of **Colonarie.** In the hills behind the town are hiking trails. Signs are limited, but locals are helpful with directions.

❽ Continue north to **Georgetown,** amid coconut groves and the long-defunct Mount Bentinck Sugar factory. A few miles north is the **Rabacca Dry River,** a rocky gulch carved out by the lava flow from the 1902 eruption of La Soufrière. Here hikers begin the two-hour ascent to the volcano. Return south to Kingstown via the Windward Highway.

The Falls of Drive back to Villa Beach, south of Kingstown, in time to catch
Baleine and Fort the sunset at **Fort Duvernette,** the tiny island that juts up like
Duvernette a loaf of pumpernickel behind Young Island Resort. Take the
❾ *African Queen*–style ferry for a few dollars from the dock at Villa Beach near Kingstown (call the boatman from the phone on the dock) and set a time for your return (60–90 minutes is

plenty for exploring). When you arrive at the island, climb the 100 or more steps carved into the mountain. Views from the 195-foot summit are terrific, but avoid the overgrown house near the top, where you'll encounter (harmless) bats. Rusting cannons from the early 1800s are still here, aimed not at sea-going invaders but at the marauding Caribs.

❿ Nearly impossible to get to by car, the **Falls of Baleine** are an absolute must to see on an escorted all-day boat trip. A motor-boat ride by **Dive St. Vincent** (*see* Sports and the Outdoors, *below*) costs $40 a person and includes drinks and a snorkel stop. When you arrive, be prepared to climb from the boat into shallow water to get to the beach. Local guides help visitors make the 15-minute sneakers-and-swimsuit trek over the boul-ders in the stream leading to the falls; a walkway allows the less adventurous to enjoy them as well. Swim in the freshwater pool, climb under the 63-foot falls (they're chilly), and relax in this bit of utterly untouched Eden.

Beaches

Most of the hotels and white-sand beaches are near Kingstown; black-sand beaches ring the rest of the island. A taxi or minivan ride is necessary to get to most beaches, unless you're staying on Villa Beach. The placid west coast, site of **Villa Beach** (white sand), **Questelle's Bay** (black sand), and **Buccament Bay** (black sand), is good for swimming; the beaches at Villa and the CSY Yacht Club are small but safe, with dive shops nearby. The ex-posed Atlantic coast is dramatic, but the water is rough and unpredictable. No beach has lifeguards, so even experienced swimmers are taking a risk. The windward side of the island has no beachfront facilities.

Sports and the Outdoors

Hiking Dorsetshire Hill, about 3 miles from Kingstown, rewards you with a sweeping view of city and harbor; picturesque Queen's Drive is nearby. Mt. St. Andrew, on the outskirts of the city, is a pleasant climb through a rain forest on a well-marked trail.

But the queen of climbs is La Soufrière, St. Vincent's active volcano (which last erupted, appropriately enough, on Friday the 13th in 1979). Approachable from both windward and lee-ward coasts, this is *not* a casual excursion for inexperienced walkers; you'll need stamina and sturdy shoes for this climb of just over 4,000 feet. Be sure to check the weather before you leave; hikers have been sorely disappointed to reach the top only to find the view completely obscured by enveloping clouds.

Climbs are all-day affairs; a LandRover and guide can be ar-ranged through your hotel or a knowledgeable taxi driver. The four-wheel-drive vehicle takes you past Rabacca Dry River through the Bamboo Forest. From there it's a two-hour hike to the summit, and you can arrange in advance to come down the other side of the mountain to the Chateaubelair area. Ex-pect to pay about $25 a person.

Sailing and The Grenadines are the perfect place to charter a sailboat or
Charter Yachting catamaran (bareboat or complete with captain, crew, and cook) to weave you around the islands for a day or a week. Boats of all sizes and degrees of luxury are available. **Barefoot Yacht Charters** (tel. 800/677–3195) and **Nicholson Yacht Charters** (tel.

809/460–1530, 809/460–1059 or 800/662–6066) offer bareboats and crewed yachts of varying sizes. Prices vary, but expect to pay around $1,900 a week ($1,300 off-season) for a 32′ bareboat that sleeps four to six. A 36′ bareboat sleeping six to eight is $2,850 a week ($2,350 off-season). The **Lagoon Marina** (tel. 809/458–4308) in St. Vincent offers 44′ captained sailboats for $400 a day ($300 off-season).

Much more common on St. Vincent than formal charter companies are individuals who live on their boats and charter when they can, on an informal basis. Every hotel and yacht service office can refer you to competent captains. Realize that for lower rates (about $140 a day per person for a crewed charter) and short notice, you may forgo formal contracts and insurance. If you go this route, be very clear about what you want and expect, and what the boat and captain offer in terms of itinerary, food, and activities. Agree on costs, and get it in writing, even if it's penciled on the back of an envelope.

Hotels can refer you to the many privately owned boats that will take you on a day-sail to nearby islands for about $50 a person (lunch and drinks often included).

Water Sports The constant trade winds are perfect for windsurfing, and 80-foot visibility on numerous reefs means superior diving. Many divers find St. Vincent and Bequia far less crowded and nearly as rich in marine life as Bonaire and the Caymans; snorkeling in the Tobago Cays is among the world's best.

Dive St. Vincent (tel. 809/457–4714), on Villa Beach, just across from Young Island, is where NAUI instructor Bill Tewes and his staff offer beginner and certification courses, trips to the Falls of Baleine ($40, including drinks and snorkeling), and attractive dive/hotel packages. A single-tank dive is about $50.

Depending on the weather, Young Island has some of the area's most colorful snorkeling. Nonguests of this private island can phone the resort for permission to take the ferry and rent equipment from the resort's water-sports center.

Shopping

St. Vincent isn't a duty-free port, but appealing local crafts (batik, baskets) and resortwear can be found at **Noah's Arkade** (tel. 809/457–1513) on Bay Street. The best batiks are at **Batik Carib** (tel. 809/456–1666) and **Sprotties** (tel. 809/458–4749), also on Bay Street. The **St. Vincent Craftsmen Center** (tel. 809/457–1288), in the northwest end of Kingstown on James Street above Granby Street, sells grass floor mats and other woven items.

Dining

No one visits these islands for the food. Virtually every eatery (usually humble local cafés) serves the same West Indian dishes, plus hamburgers and fried chicken baskets with french fries. More sophisticated seafood cuisine in prettier surroundings is available in a few hotels, but these are generally not affordable. There's a lone Kentucky Fried Chicken in Kingstown (locals love it).

Popular for both lunch and dinner are *rotis* (Caribbean "burritos" filled with curried chicken or meat and potatoes), fried chicken, fish-and-chips, "salt fish and bakes" (salty, spiced and flaked fish in a fried biscuit), and conch. Callaloo soup is a spinachlike concoction; a large bowl with homemade bread can make a whole lunch. Sandwiches are available everywhere, as are American-style ham-and-egg breakfasts. For groceries, try **Greave's** (say it like Graves) on Upper Bay Street near the dock or **Bonadie's** on Lower Middle Street.

Highly recommended restaurants are indicated by a star ★.

Category	Cost*
Moderate	$10–$20
Inexpensive	$6–$10
Budget	under $6

per person, excluding drinks and sales tax (5% on credit-card purchases only)

Aggie's. Come here for West Indian seafood specialties of conch, shrimp, fish, lobster (when available), whelks, and local souse (chopped, marinated raw conch). A variety of soups rounds out the menu at this informal, pleasant restaurant. *Grenville St., Kingstown, tel. 809/456–2110. No credit cards. No lunch Sun. Inexpensive–Moderate.*

Chicken Roost. This eatery is handy if you're waiting at the airport. The rotis, sandwiches (including shark), pizzas, and ice cream can't be beat. Open daily till midnight. *Opposite airport, tel. 809/456–4939. No credit cards. Inexpensive.*

Lime N' Pub. Locals and sailors enjoy drinks, burgers, and West Indian cooking at this relaxed spot on Villa Beach. *Opposite Young Island, tel. 809/458–4227. Inexpensive.*

Bounty Restaurant. West Indian dishes, such as rotis and fried meat patties, homemade soursop ice cream, and fast food are offered in this popular local restaurant in town. *Halifax St., Kingstown, tel. 809/456–1776. No credit cards. Open weekdays 8 AM–5 PM, Sat. 8 AM–1:30 PM; closed Sun. Budget–Inexpensive.*

Dano's. Stop in while you're strolling around Kingstown for good, cheap Caribbean rotis and lots of local color. *Middle St., Kingstown, tel. 809/457–2020. No credit cards. Closes 6 PM. Closed Sun. Budget.*

Lodging

Affordable lodging in St. Vincent—of which there is plenty—is often bare-bones simple to the point of primitive: a bed, a nightstand, a place to hang your clothes, maybe a dresser. Bring your own shampoo and soap. Hot water is a rarity (although how cold can the water get in 84-degree weather?). Most visitors report 24 hours of mild shock and frustration until they settle into Caribbean time, and realize that the simple life really does offer its own rewards. Gorgeous hibiscus and bougainvillea grow outside your window, the sea is usually steps away, and most managers of small hotels treat guests as valued friends.

Villa Beach, where most budget hotels are located, is the only white-sand beach on St. Vincent. It's a 10-minute minivan ride to Kingstown for groceries or restaurants; the Lime N' Pub (*see* Dining, *above*) is right on Villa. In most cases it's probably cheaper to forgo meal plans and eat at these inexpensive local eateries.

Highly recommended lodgings are indicated by a star ★.

Category	Cost*
Moderate	$80–$130
Inexpensive	$60–$80
Budget	under $60

All prices are for a standard double room for two, excluding 5% tax and a 10% service charge. To estimate rates for hotels offering MAP/FAP, add about $35 per person per day to the above price ranges.

The Lagoon Marina and Hotel. The spacious, modern rooms—some with air-conditioning, others with just ceiling fans—have cathedral ceilings and private patios. The long shallow-water beach that curves around Blue Lagoon offers a view of anchored sailboats; this is the place for trading stories with yacht owners. A beach bar has music and dancing on weekends. The secluded swimming pool is up a circuitous stone walk, set among flowering bushes. The hotel has three 44-foot sailboats sleeping up to six each (four are more comfortable) available for charter at $400 a day ($300 in off-season). *Box 133, St. Vincent, tel. 809/458–4308; U.S. agent: Charms Caribbean Vacations, tel. 800/742–4276. 19 rooms. Facilities: pool, bar, restaurant. AE, V. EP. Moderate.*

Petit Byahaut. The truly adventurous will enjoy staying in private room-size screened tents that sit on platforms (cabins are being built) in this secluded valley 2 miles north of Kingstown. Accessible only by boat, Petit Byahaut is a haven for divers, snorkelers, hikers, and anyone tired of civilization. *Petit Byahaut Bay, St. Vincent, tel. and fax 809/457–7008. 5 tents. Facilities: restaurant, bar, gardens, solar-heated showers, water sports. No credit cards. FAP. Moderate.*

Cobblestone Inn. This pre-1814 stone building in Kingstown used to be a sugar warehouse; wicker furniture now fills its large, airy rooms. Room No. 5 overlooks the street and is sunny but a bit noisy. The nearest beach is 3 miles away. The plant-filled courtyard leads to a rooftop bar that's popular for breakfast and lunch. *Box 867, St. Vincent, tel. 809/456–1937. 19 rooms. Facilities: bar, restaurant. AE, V. CP. Inexpensive–Moderate.*

Coconut Beach Inn. New management has transformed this inn on the beach into a charming, lively place for families and singles. Simple, sunny rooms with private baths have no air-conditioning, but there's a cool breeze going all the time. If Cleo is still cooking, be sure to have dinner here. *Indian Bay, Box 355, St. Vincent, tel. 809/458–4231. 8 rooms. Facilities: bar, restaurant, water-sports center nearby. AE, V. CP. Inexpensive–Moderate.*

Indian Bay Beach Hotel and Apartments. Just outside Kingstown, this property has its own tiny beach and is close to Villa Beach and water-sports facilities. Choose a standard room or a one- or two-bedroom apartment. All are air-conditioned, with simple wood furnishings and bright patterned curtains. A large terrace affords views of Young Island. Enjoy seafood and West Indian cuisine at the A La Mer restaurant here. *Box 538,*

St. Vincent, tel. 809/458–4001, fax 809/457–4777. 10 rooms, 4 apartments. Facilities: restaurant. AE, MC, V. EP. Inexpensive.

Umbrella Beach Hotel. The hotel's small and simple rooms with kitchenettes are set in a garden on Villa Beach. The three best rooms face the water. Next door is the French, St. Vincent's best restaurant, where lunch is affordable. The hotel serves a full, hot breakfast, which you can enjoy on your own tiny porch or in the garden. Here you'll find superior value and location for the price. *Box 530, St. Vincent, tel. 809/458–4651, fax 809/457–4930. 9 rooms. Facilities: bar, restaurant. MC, V. EP. Inexpensive.*

Heron Hotel. Right out of a Somerset Maugham novel, this Kingstown inn is on the second floor of a converted Georgian plantation's warehouse. Pleasantly eccentric travelers, young and old, stay here to be near the dock for the early boat. Air-conditioned rooms are faded but atmospheric, and No. 15 is large and has a sitting area. It's a 40¢ minivan or $8 taxi ride to Villa Beach. *Box 226, St. Vincent, tel. 809/457–1631. 12 rooms. Facilities: courtyard, dining room. AE, MC, V. CP. Budget.*

Apartment Rentals Apartments for short-term rental are bare-bones simple; architecture and design are, well, undistinguished. Each has at least a small porch, but none have ocean views, air-conditioning, or meal plans. None take credit cards either. Services and amenities are limited to linens and a few functional kitchen implements (you might want to bring your favorite omelet pan). Whichever one you stay in, you'll need a car to get to the beach and main tourist areas. Kingstown is usually a 10- to 15-minute ride away. Apartments include: **Belleville Apartments** (Box 746, St. Vincent, tel. 809/458–4776); **Breezeville Apartments** (Box 222, St. Vincent, tel. 809/458–4004); **Paradise Inn** (Villa Beach, St. Vincent, tel. 809/457–4795); **Ricks Apartments** (Cane Hall, St. Vincent, tel. tel. 809/458–5544, fax 809/456–2593); and **Tranquility Beach Apartments** (Box 71, St. Vincent, tel. and fax 809/458–4021).

Off-Season Bets In terms of cost, there isn't much of an off-season here; lower shoulder and summer rates at the luxury resorts are still too high for budget travelers. However, some budget hotels trim their already affordable rates even further; it pays to make inquiries.

Nightlife

Don't look for fire-eaters and limbo demonstrations on St. Vincent. Nightlife here consists mostly of hotel barbecue buffets and jump-ups, so called because the lively steel-band music makes listeners jump up and dance.

The Attic (on Grenville St., above the Kentucky Fried Chicken, tel. 809/457–2558), a jazz club with modern decor, features international artists and steel bands. There is a small cover charge; call ahead for hours and performers.

Vidal Browne, manager of **Young Island** (tel. 809/458–4826), hosts sunset cocktail parties with hors d'oeuvres once a week on Fort Duvernette, the tiny island behind the resort. On that night, 100 steps up the hill are lit by flaming torches, and a string band plays. Reservations are necessary for nonguests.

Basil's Too (tel. 809/458–4205) offers lunch, dinner, and dancing amid painted murals, all set on Villa Beach overlooking Young Island.

The Grenadines

The Grenadines are wonderful islands to visit for fine diving and snorkeling opportunities, good beaches, and unlimited chances to laze on the beach with a picnic, waiting for the sun to set so you can go to dinner. For travelers seeking privacy and peace or active water sports and informal socializing, these are the islands of choice. But for those on a budget, the choice is limited. Some of the Grenadines, such as Palm Island and Petit St. Vincent, contain nothing but one very expensive resort. Mustique, that tony society hideaway where the average beach cottage costs $3 million, is no place for the shoestring traveler trying to stretch a dollar. In fact, only two of the several islands that have tourist accommodations are what we consider truly affordable, and we devote our space to these. In addition, day sails to the tiny, uninhabited Tobago Cays for world-class snorkeling, as well as to Canouan and Union islands, are another fairly inexpensive option.

Arriving and Departing

By Plane   **Mustique Airways** (tel. 809/458–4380 or 809/458–4818) now flies into Bequia's new airport daily from Barbados. Flights from St. Vincent cost E.C. $45 one way. There are three flights daily. A shared taxi from Mitchell Airstrip to Friendship Bay is $6; to Port Elizabeth, $10.

By Ferry   The SS *Admiral I* and the SS *Admiral II* motor ferries leave Kingstown for Bequia weekdays at 9 AM, 10:30 AM, 4:30 PM, and, depending on availability, 7 PM. Saturday departures are at 12:30 PM and 7 PM; Sunday, 9 AM and 5:15 PM. Schedules are subject to change, so be sure to check times upon your arrival. All scheduled ferries leave from the main dock in Kingstown. The trip takes 70–90 minutes and costs $4. The SS *Snapper* mail boat travels south on Mondays and Thursdays at about 10 AM, stopping at Bequia, Canouan, Mayreau, and Union, and returns north on Tuesdays and Fridays. The cost is under $10. Weekday service between St. Vincent and Bequia is also available on the island schooner *Maxann O*, which leaves St. Vincent weekdays at about 12:30 PM and returns from Bequia 6:30 AM. Fare is $4.

The *St. Vincent and the Grenadines Visitor's Guide*, available in hotels and at the airport, has complete interisland schedules.

Bequia

Nine miles south of St. Vincent is Bequia, the second-largest Grenadine. Admiralty Bay is one of the finest anchorages in the Caribbean. With superb views, snorkeling, hiking, and swimming, the island has much to offer the international mix of backpackers and luxury yacht owners who frequent its shores.

Important   **Tourist Information:** The **Bequia Tourism Board** (tel. 809/458–
Addresses   3286) is located on the main dock.

Emergencies **Police** (tel. 809/456–1955). **Medical Emergencies** (tel. 999). **Hospital** (tel. 809/458–3294).

Getting Around Bicycle and scooter rentals can be found at the **Almond Tree Boutique** (no phone) on the main waterfront street in Port Elizabeth. Cost ranges from $20 to $35 a day. Drive on the left and use caution: Road improvements have made for overly speedy traffic.

Guided Tours To see the views, villages, and boat-building around the island, hire a taxi (Gideon and Curtis are recommended) and negotiate the fare in advance; expect to pay about $25–$30 for a two-hour tour. Water taxis, available from any dock, will take you by Moonhole, a private community of stone homes with glassless windows, some decorated with bleached whale bones. The fare is about $11.

For those who prefer sailboats to motorboats, Arne Hansen and his catamaran *Toien* can be booked through the **Frangipani Hotel** (tel. 809/458–3255). Day sails to Mustique run $35–$40 per person, including drinks. *Friendship Rose*, a large, hand-built schooner, will ferry you to the Tobago Cays for an all-day excursion that includes lunch; snorkeling; and beer, wine, or soft drinks. Cost is $60 a person; book through the **Local Color Boutique** (tel. 809/458–3202).

In addition, you'll see several signs on boats in the bay advertising day sails and charter. Ask your hotel for recommendations, then discuss price and itineraries thoroughly with your chosen captain before deciding (*see* Sailing and Charter Yachting in St. Vincent, *above*).

Beaches A half-hour walk from the Plantation House Hotel will lead you over rocky bluffs to **Princess Margaret Beach,** which is quiet and wide, with a natural stone arch at one end. Though it has no facilities, this is a popular spot for swimming, snorkeling, or simply relaxing under palms and sea-grape trees. Snorkeling and swimming are also excellent at **Lower Bay,** a wide, palm-fringed beach that can be reached by taxi or by hiking beyond Princess Margaret Beach; wear sneakers, not flip-flops. Facilities for windsurfing and snorkeling are here, and the **De Reef** restaurant features waiters who will eventually find you on the sand when your lunch is ready. **Friendship Bay** can be reached by land taxi and is well equipped with windsurfing and snorkeling rentals and an outdoor bar. **Industry Bay** boasts towering palm groves, a nearly secluded beach, and a memorable view of several uninhabited islands. The tiny three-room Crescent Bay Lodge is here; its huge bar offers drinks and late lunches (tel. 809/458–3400).

Sports and the Outdoors **Water Sports** Of Bequia's two dozen dive sites, the best are **Devil's Table,** a shallow dive rich in fish and coral; a sailboat wreck nearby at 90 feet; the 90-foot drop at **The Wall,** off West Cay; the **Bullet,** off Bequia's north point for rays, barracuda, and the occasional nurse shark; the **Boulders** for soft corals, tunnel-forming rocks, and thousands of fish; and **Moonhole,** shallow enough in places for snorkelers to enjoy.

Dive Bequia (tel. 809/458–3504, fax 809/458–3886) and **Sunsports** (tel. 809/458–3577, fax 809/458–3907) offer one- and two-tank dives, night dives, and certified instruction, plus snorkel excursions and equipment rental. Single-tank dives are about $50; snorkel gear rents for about $15 a day.

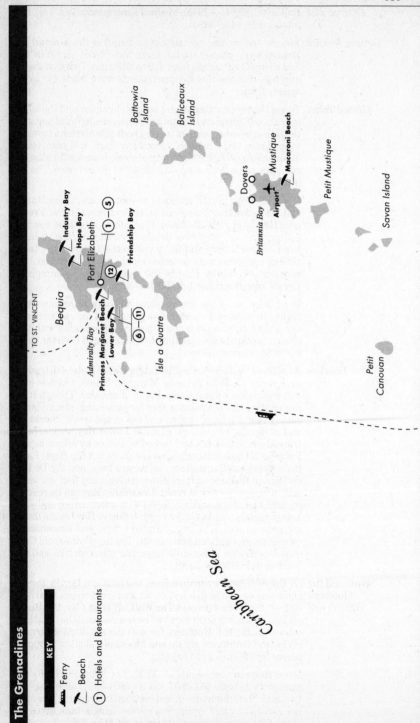

The Grenadines

KEY

⚓ Ferry

⚱ Beach

① Hotels and Restaurants

TO ST. VINCENT

Bequia

Admiralty Bay
Princess Margaret Beach
Lower Bay ⑥ — ⑪
Port Elizabeth ⑫
Industry Bay
Hope Bay
Friendship Bay ① — ⑤

Isle a Quatre

Battowia Island

Baliceaux Island

Dovers

Mustique
Airport
Britannia Bay
Macaroni Beach
Petit Mustique

Savan Island

Petit Canouan

Caribbean Sea

530

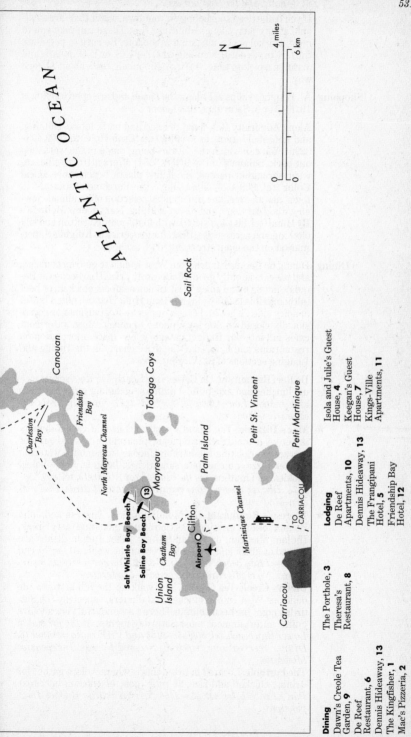

ATLANTIC OCEAN

N

4 miles
6 km

Canouan

Friendship
Bay

Charleston
Bay

Sail Rock

Tobago Cays

North Mayreau Channel

Mayreau

Salt Whistle Bay Beach

Saline Bay Beach

Palm Island

Chatham
Bay

Union
Island

Clifton

Airport

Petit St. Vincent

Martinique Channel

Petit Martinique

TO
CARRIACOU

Carriacou

Dining
Dawn's Creole Tea
Garden, **9**
De Reef
Restaurant, **6**
Dennis Hideaway, **13**
The Kingfisher, **1**
Mac's Pizzeria, **2**

The Porthole, **3**
Theresa's
Restaurant, **8**

Lodging
De Reef
Apartments, **10**
Dennis Hideaway, **13**
The Frangipani
Hotel, **5**
Friendship Bay
Hotel, **12**

Isola and Julie's Guest
House, **4**
Keegan's Guest
House, **7**
Kings-Ville
Apartments, **11**

If you'd like to go snorkeling on your own, water taxis are available at any jetty along Admiralty Bay. These can take you to most snorkel spots, including Moonhole. Be sure to negotiate the fare in advance, including whether U.S. or E.C. dollars, and arrange a pickup time. A trip to Moonhole costs about $4 each way.

Shopping All Bequia's shops are along the beach and are open weekdays 10:30–5 or 6, Saturdays 10:30–noon.

Along Admiralty Bay, hand-printed and batik fabric, clothing, and household items are sold at the **Crab Hole** (tel. 809/458–3290). You can watch the fabrics being made in the workshop out back. **Solana's** (tel. 809/458–3554) offers attractive beachwear, saronglike pareos, and handy plastic beach shoes. **Local Color** (tel. 809/458–3202), above the Porthole restaurant in town, has an excellent and unusual selection of handmade jewelry, wood carvings, and resort clothing. Next door is **Melinda's By Hand** (tel. 809/458–3409), with hand-painted cotton and silk clothing and accessories. Shop for groceries at **Knight's Supermarket** on the main street in Port Elizabeth.

Dining Dining on Bequia ranges from West Indian to gourmet cuisine, and it's consistently good. Moderately priced barbecues at Bequia's hotels mean spicy West Indian seafood, chicken, or beef (although it is usually tougher than Hulk Hogan), plus a buffet of spicy side dishes and sweet desserts. Restaurants are occasionally closed on Sundays; phone to check. Most waterfront cafés fall into our Budget category. For price information on restaurants and hotels, *see* the price charts in the Dining and Lodging sections of St. Vincent, *above.*

De Reef Restaurant. On Lower Bay Beach, De Reef serves casual lunches and exceptional dinners, including gingered lamb and seafood. *Lower Bay, tel. 809/458–3447. No credit cards. Inexpensive–Moderate.*

★ **Mac's Pizzeria.** The island's best lunches and casual dinners are enjoyed amid fuchsia bougainvillea on the covered outdoor terrace overlooking the harbor. Choose from mouth-watering lobster pizza, quiche, pita sandwiches, lasagna, home-baked cookies, and muffins. *On the beach, Port Elizabeth, tel. 809/458–3474. Dinner reservations required. No credit cards. Inexpensive–Moderate.*

★ **Theresa's Restaurant.** On Monday nights, Theresa and John Bennett offer a rotating selection of enormous and tasty Greek, Indian, Mexican, or Italian buffets. West Indian dishes are served at lunch and dinner the rest of the week. *At the far end of Lower Bay beach, tel. 809/458–3802. Dinner reservations required. No credit cards. Inexpensive–Moderate.*

Dawn's Creole Tea Garden. The walk up the hill is worth the delicious West Indian lunches and dinners, especially the Saturday night barbecue buffet. There's a wonderful view and live guitar entertainment most Saturday nights. *At the far end of Lower Bay beach, tel. 809/458–3154 and VHF radio channel 16. Dinner reservations required. No credit cards. Inexpensive–Moderate.*

The Porthole. Located in town, this is where sailors gather for drinks, chicken and rice, or *rotis* (goat or chicken burritos). *Port Elizabeth, tel. 809/458–3458. No credit cards. Budget–Inexpensive.*

The Kingfisher. It serves genuine West Indian fast food for those with no cholesterol worries. Try a salt fish and bake (fried, spicy flaked fish on a fried biscuit) at this tiny, lunch-only spot on the main street. *Port Elizabeth, no phone. No credit cards. Lunch only. Budget.*

Lodging **Friendship Bay Hotel.** This sprawling white house on a hill, with large terraces and sweeping views, overlooks another group of pretty, coral stone accommodations close to the beach (the latter, alas, out of our price range). The property offers a beautiful curve of white-sand beach and tropical plant-filled grounds. A lively barbecue/jump-up happens Saturday nights around the Mau Mau Beach Bar, whose seats around the bar are swings, cleverly built to keep you upright even after potent rum punches. Recent management changes may mean uneven service when you visit. *Box 9, Bequia, St. Vincent, tel. 809/458–3222, fax 809/458–3840. 27 rooms. Facilities: water-sports center, restaurant, 2 bars, boutique. AE, MC, V. CP, MAP. Moderate.*

★ **The Frangipani Hotel.** This local guest house has long been known as a gossip center for international yachties and tourists. Surrounded by flowering bushes, eight moderately priced garden units are built of stone, with private verandas and baths. Five simple, budget-priced rooms with no hot water are in the main house; only one has a private bath. The hotel is right on Admiralty Bay, with a tiny beach of its own. Main tourist beaches are a $3 taxi-ride away. There's a pleasant indoor-outdoor dining area and bar in the garden facing the bay (some dinner selections are expensive). String bands appear on Mondays, with folk singers on Friday nights during tourist season. The Thursday-night steel-band jump-up is a must. *Box 1, Bequia, St. Vincent, tel. 809/458–3255. 14 rooms, 4 with shared bath. Facilities: tennis, bar, restaurant, water-sports center, yacht services. MC, V. EP. Budget–Moderate.*

Isola and Julie's Guest House. Right on the water in Port Elizabeth, these two separate buildings share a small restaurant and bar. Furnishings (which are few) run to early Salvation Army, but the food is great and the rooms are airy and light, with private baths; some have hot water. *Box 12, Isola and Julie's Guest House, Bequia, St. Vincent, tel. 809/458–3304, 809/458–3323, or 809/458–3220. 25 rooms. Facilities: bar, restaurant. No credit cards. EP, MAP. Budget–Inexpensive.*

Kings-Ville Apartments. A few minutes' stroll from lovely, lively Lower Bay Beach, these two-bedroom apartments with kitchens and hot water are short on furniture and style, but they're more than adequate for a budget vacation. There's no air-conditioning, but you will find linens and kitchen utensils. From here it's a half-hour walk to town. *Lower Bay, Box 41, Bequia, St. Vincent, tel. 809/458–3404. 2 apartments. No credit cards. Budget–Inexpensive.*

Keegan's Guest House. This is the place for budget-minded beach lovers who want quiet, friendly surroundings. Located on Lower Bay, this *very* simple place offers family-style West Indian breakfasts and dinners that are included in its rock-bottom rates. Rooms 3, 4, and 5 have a shared bath and are cheaper, although there is no hot water to be found (you really do get used to it). *Bequia, St. Vincent, tel. 809/458–3254 or 809/458–3530. 11 rooms. Facilities: dining room. No credit cards. EP, MAP. Budget.*

De Reef Apartments. Just 100 yards from gorgeous Lower Bay Beach, these simple, un-air-conditioned apartments with kitchens are sparsely furnished. Expect a bed, a table, and a few plastic outdoor chairs. *Lower Bay, Box 47, Bequia, St. Vincent, tel. 809/458–3484 or 809/458–3447. 3 apartments. No credit cards. Budget.*

Off-Season Bets For divers, **Dive Bequia** (c/o Plantation House, Box 16, Bequia, St. Vincent, tel. 809/458–3504, fax 809/458–3886), located on the grounds of the posh Plantation House, offers a summer package of seven nights in a private cabana, unlimited boat diving, welcome rum punch, and a day-long excursion for diving and a picnic to an uninhabited island. Would-be divers can complete a full NAUI dive-certification course at the same time. Cost is $700 per person double occupancy; if you won't be diving, deduct $100.

Mayreau

The tiny island of Mayreau has 182 residents, no phones, and one of the area's most beautiful beaches. Farm animals outnumber citizens here. The Caribbean is often mirror-calm, yet just yards away on the southern end of this narrow island is the rolling Atlantic surf. Except for water sports and hiking, there's nothing to do, and visitors like it that way. This is the perfect place for a meditative or vegetative vacation.

Guided Tours You can swim and snorkel in the Cays or nearby islands on day trips with charter yachts arranged by **Undine Potter** at the Salt Whistle Bay Resort (from the U.S., tel. 800/263–2780; in the Grenadines, marine radio VHF channel 68 or 16). Note that the Salt Whistle Bay's snorkel equipment has seen better days. Buy or rent your own before you arrive. Trips cost $20–$30 a person, depending on length and type of boat.

Beaches Dennis Hideaway (*see* Dining and Lodging, *below*) overlooks Union Island and long, golden **Saline Bay Beach,** which offers excellent swimming; cruise ships occasionally anchor for picnics here. Hike a half-hour over Mayreau's mountain (wear shoes; bare feet or flip-flops are a big mistake) to spectacular views of the Tobago Cays atop the hill at the small church. Continue on and you'll come to one of the Caribbean's most beautiful beaches, **Salt Whistle Bay,** an exquisite half-moon of powdery white sand, shaded by perfectly spaced palms and flowering bushes, with the rolling Atlantic a stroll away. Have a drink or lunch (a minisplurge) at the Salt Whistle Bay Club.

Sports and the Outdoors Scuba diving can be arranged through **Grenadines Dive** (tel. 809/458–8138 or 809/458–8122), based on nearby Union Island.

Dining and Lodging **Dennis Hideaway.** It would still be *the* place to go even if it weren't practically the only place on the island. Dennis (who plays the guitar two nights a week) is a charmer, the food is great, the drinks are strong, and the view is heaven. Spacious, clean rooms are simple, without hot water or amenities, but do have private baths. A separate building houses the restaurant, where West Indian fixed-price dinners are served. *Saline Bay, tel. 809/458–8594. 3 rooms. Facilities: restaurant. Reservations advised. No credit cards. Restaurant: Moderate–Expensive. Lodging: EP. Inexpensive–Moderate.*

25 Trinidad and Tobago

Updated by
Nigel Fisher

Trinidad and Tobago, the southernmost islands in the West Indies chain, could not be more dissimilar. Trinidad's cosmopolitan capital, Port-of-Spain, bustles with shopping centers, modern hotels, sophisticated restaurants, and an active nightlife. It is also home to a riotous Carnival, the birthplace of steelband music, and a busy port. The 1.3 million Trinidadians know prosperity from oil (Trinidad is one of the biggest producers in the Western Hemisphere), a steel plant, natural gas, and a multiplicity of small businesses. More than half of them—Indians, Africans, Europeans, Asians, and Americans, each with their own language and customs—live in Port-of-Spain. And because it is one of the most active commercial cities in the West Indies, most visitors are business travelers.

Trinidad's capital may be noisy and its way of life somewhat frenetic, but its countryside is rich in flora and fauna, home to more than 400 species of birds and 700 varieties of orchids. Because Trinidad has not been developed as a resort island, prices are lower than on other Caribbean islands, though this also means fewer tourist facilities. The island's best beaches are along the north coast, an hour's drive west of Port-of-Spain, where most hotels are located. These accommodations tend to be inexpensive guest houses or small inns, with friendly, informal atmosphere and home-cooked meals. Dining here can be cheap for those who take advantage of *roti* stands and humble eateries serving generous portions of Indian and West Indian food. A rental car makes mobility easier, but those with patience can save considerably by using public transportation.

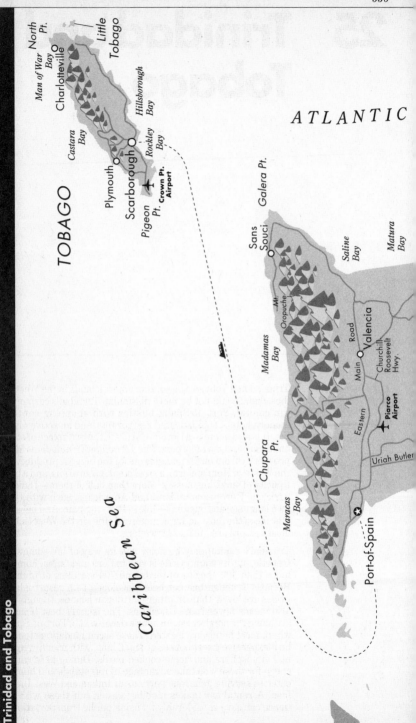

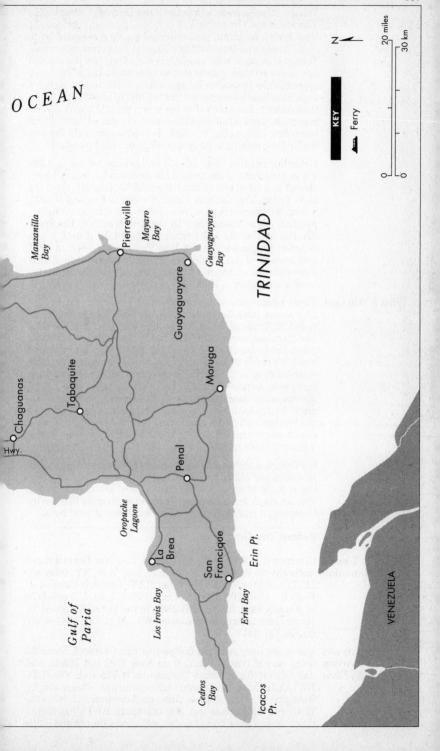

Tobago, 22 miles away, offers the lazier life most tourists seek. The Robinson Crusoe island is more laid-back; the pace is slower, with beautiful, near-deserted beaches, secluded bays, small hotels, and little fishing villages. Goats outnumber cars. Tobago is popular with snorkelers and divers; its Buccoo and Speyside reefs are underwater wonderlands. You'll find fewer opportunities to save on Tobago, where hotels tend to be more expensive beach resorts, and where dining is often limited to these same pricey hotels. But because most of Tobago's accommodations are a stroll from the water, a rental car isn't critical here. And unlike hilly Trinidad, Tobago is relatively flat and traffic-free, making getting around by bicycle a pleasure.

Columbus reached these islands on his third voyage in 1498. Three prominent peaks around the southern bay where he anchored prompted him to name the land La Trinidad, after the Holy Trinity. Trinidad was formally ceded to England in 1802, ending 300 years of Spanish rule. Tobago's history is more complicated. It was "discovered" by the British in 1508. The Spanish, Dutch, French, and British all fought for it until it was ceded to England under the Treaty of Paris in 1814. In 1962, both islands—T & T, as they're commonly called—gained their independence within the British Commonwealth, finally becoming a republic in 1976.

What It Will Cost These sample prices, meant only as a general guide, are for high season (mid-December–mid-April) for Tobago, and year-round for Trinidad, which has no high season outside Carnival (*see* Carnival, *below*). On Trinidad, a room in a comfortable guest house may be had for $55 a night; in an international hotel, it's about $125. Meals run from $30 for dinner at a fine establishment to $1 for a roti from a stand, while a buffet Indian curry meal costs less than $10. Locally made beer is about $1.25 in a rum shop (local bar), about $2.50 in a classier place. If you are willing to use local transportation, getting around Trinidad can be cheap: $3 for an hour's trip. A rental car is about $40 a day. A single-tank dive costs about $40; daily snorkel-equipment rental, about $5.

On Tobago, a night's lodging is around $90 for a modest accommodation and $120 for a beach hotel with resort facilities. Dining is more often at a hotel than a local restaurant, so the simpler snack foods found on Trinidad are harder to come by. Generally, it makes sense to take a meal plan at your hotel.

Before You Go

Tourist Information Contact the **Trinidad and Tobago Tourism Development Authority** (25 W. 43rd St., Suite 1508, New York, NY 10036, tel. 212/719–0540 or 800/232–0082, fax 212/719–0988; in Canada: 40 Holly St., Suite 102, Toronto, Ont. M4S 3C3, tel. 416/486–4470 or 800/268–8986, fax 416/440–1899; in the United Kingdom: 8a Hammersmith Broadway, London W6 7AL, tel. 081/741–4466, fax 081/741–1013).

Arriving and Departing
By Plane There are daily nonstop flights to Piarco Airport, about 30 miles east of Port-of-Spain, from New York and Miami, and daily direct flights from Toronto on **BWIA** (tel. 800/JET-BWIA), Trinidad and Tobago's national airline. You can also fly from one or more of these cities on **American** (tel. 800/433–7300) and **Air Canada** (tel. 800/422–6232). BWIA has flights three times a week from London and serves Boston and Balti-

more once a week. There are flights from Amsterdam and Paramaribo via **KLM Royal Dutch Airlines** (tel. 800/777–5553). **ALM** (tel. 800/327–7230) flies from Atlanta and Miami via Curaçao. There are numerous interisland flights in the Caribbean by BWIA and **LIAT** (tel. 809/462–0701). All flights to Trinidad alight at Piarco Airport. Most round-trip fares include a free round-trip ticket to Tobago from Piarco, about a $50 value, so be sure to check with your agent. BWIA and LIAT flights from Trinidad to Crown Point Airport in Tobago take about 15 minutes and depart several times a day. For those wishing to circumvent Trinidad entirely, LIAT has direct service from Barbados to Tobago.

Package tours aren't generally touted as heavily as they are for other Caribbean islands, but there are bargains to be had, especially around Carnival. Contact **Pan Caribe Tours** (Box 3223, Austin, TX 78764, tel. 512/267–9209 or 800/525–6896).

From the Airport A taxi ride from the airport to downtown Port-of-Spain costs TT $80 (about U.S. $19), more after midnight. A bus does run every hour into South Quay Bus Terminal for TT $5, but you will probably need a taxi from there to your hotel, and that may run another TT $40 (about U.S. $9.50).

By Boat The Port Authority runs a ferry service between Trinidad and Tobago; the ferry leaves once a day, except Saturday. The trip takes about six hours (flying is preferable); round-trip fare is TT $60, about U.S. $14; cabin fare is $22 (one-way double occupancy), with an extra charge for vehicles. Tickets are sold at offices in Port-of-Spain (tel. 809/625–4906) and at Scarborough, in Tobago (tel. 809/639–2181).

Passports Citizens of the United States, the United Kingdom, and Can-
and Visas ada who expect to stay for less than two months may enter the country with a valid passport. A visa is required for a stay of more than two months.

Language The official language is English, although no end of idiomatic expressions are used by the loquacious Trinis. You will also hear smatterings of French, Spanish, Chinese, and Hindi.

Precautions Insect repellent is a must during the rainy season (June–December) and is worth having around anytime. If you're prone to car sickness, bring your preferred remedy. Trinidad is only 11 degrees north of the equator, and the sun here can be intense. Even if you tan well, it's a good idea to use a strong sun block, at least for the first few days.

Staying in Trinidad and Tobago

Important **Tourist Information: Trinidad & Tobago Tourism Development**
Addresses **Authority** (134–138 Frederick St., Port-of-Spain, tel. 809/623–1932, fax 809/623–3848; Piarco Airport, tel. 809/664–5196). For Tobago, write to the **Tobago Division of Tourism** (N.I.B. Mall, Scarborough, tel. 809/639–2125) or drop in at its information booth at Crown Point Airport (tel. 809/639–0509) when you arrive.

Emergencies **Police:** Call 999. **Fire and Ambulance:** Call 990. **Hospitals: Port-of-Spain General Hospital** is on Charlotte Street (tel. 809/625–7869). **Tobago County Hospital** is on Fort Street in Scarborough (tel. 809/639–2551). **Pharmacies: Oxford Pharmacy** (tel. 809/627–4657) is at Charlotte and Oxford streets near the Port-of-Spain General Hospital. **Ross Drugs** (tel. 809/639–2658) is in Scarborough.

Currency The Trinidadian dollar (TT$) has been devalued twice in recent years. The current exchange rate is about U.S. $1 to TT $4.25. The major hotels in Port-of-Spain have exchange facilities whose rates are comparable to official bank rates. Most businesses on the island will accept U.S. currency if you're in a pinch. Note: Prices quoted here are in U.S. dollars unless indicated otherwise.

Taxes and Service Charges Restaurants and hotels add a 15% Value Added Tax (VAT). Many hotels and restaurants add a 10% service charge to your bill. If the service charge is not added, you should tip 10%–15% of the bill for a job well done. The airport departure tax is TT $50, or about U.S. $12.

Getting Around
Route Taxis In Port-of-Spain, where the streets are often jammed with traffic and drivers who routinely play chicken with one another, taxis are your best bet. Once away from the congestion of downtown, however, a car is by far the easiest way to travel. Since your hotel is likely to be in the suburbs, going carless means waiting for route taxis or private cabs. Though it's possible to *get* to the north coast by route taxi, you'll need a car to explore from one point to another. In Tobago you will be better off renting a car or Jeep than relying on taxi service, which is less frequent and much more expensive.

Route—or shared—taxis ply fixed routes to and from Port-of-Spain. They collect and drop off passengers anywhere along a set route and serve as a better alternative to buses. Route taxis come in two sizes: minibuses (often referred to as maxi-taxis) and regular sedans. The maxi-taxis are marked with stripes and are easy to recognize, but the only way to identify the sedans as taxis is by the *H* at the start of the license plate. However, although this will tell you whether the vehicle is a taxi, it does *not* distinguish whether it is a route taxi or a private taxi (*see below*). Therefore it is essential to make sure what you are getting in is a route taxi, or you'll end up paying private taxi fare. Fares are nominally fixed, but unless you have knowledge of the proper fare, you'll likely pay a dollar or two above what a local would pay. From Port-of-Spain, the departure point is at the corner of Prince and George streets. Fare to Maracas Bay is TT $7 and to Blanchisseuse Bay, TT $15.

Private Taxis When you choose a private taxi instead of a route taxi, you are hiring all the seats, and your driver goes straight to the destination you specify. Private taxis are useful for longer trips or trips to more remote destinations not covered by route taxis. There are set rates, though they are not always observed, particularly at Carnival. To be sure, pick up a rate sheet from the Tourism Office. An average ride within Port-of-Spain costs TT $20 (U.S. $5).

Buses Buses cover the island and are inexpensive, but they are very old and very crowded. Travelers generally opt for a route taxi (*see above*) instead. The South Quay Bus Terminal is the main departure point for buses.

Rental Cars/ Scooters **Auto Rentals** (tel. 809/675–2258) has eight locations, or try **Bacchus Taxi Service** (37 Tragerete Rd., Port-of-Spain, tel. 809/622–5588). All agencies require a large deposit, and you must make reservations well in advance of your arrival. Figure on paying $30–$45 per day.

On Tobago, try **Sweet Jeeps** (Sandy Point, tel. 809/639–8533) or **Tobago Travel** (Box 163, Tobago, tel. 809/639–8778). You can also rent **motor scooters** from **Banana Rentals** (c/o Kariwak Village, Crown Point, tel. 809/639–8441). Rentals average $25–$35 a day.

As befits one of the world's largest exporters of asphalt, Trinidad's roads are fairly well paved. In the outback, however, they are often narrow, twisting, and prone to washouts in the rainy season. Inquire about conditions before you take off, particularly if you're heading toward the north coast. Never drive into downtown Port-of-Spain during afternoon rush hour. Driving is on the left.

Telephones and Mail The area code throughout the two islands is 809. For telegraph, telefax, teletype, and telex, contact **Textel** (1 Edward St., Port-of-Spain, tel. 809/625–4431). Cables can be sent from the Tourism Office and major hotels. To place an intra-island call, dial the local seven-digit number. To reach the United States by phone, dial 1, the appropriate area code, and the local number. A local call costs TT 25¢.

Postage for first-class letters to the United States is TT $2.25; postcards, TT $2.

Opening and Closing Times Most shops open weekdays 8–6:30, Saturday 8–noon. Banking hours are Monday–Thursday 9–2, Friday 9–1 and 3–5.

Guided Tours **Trinidad and Tobago Sightseeing Tours** (Galleria Shopping Centre, Western Main Rd., St. James, Port-of-Spain, tel. 809/628–1051) has a variety of sightseeing packages, from a tour of the city to an all-day drive to the other side of the island. Another reputable agency is **Hub Travel Limited** (Hilton Hotel lobby, tel. 809/625–3155; Piarco Airport, tel. 809/664–4359). A three-hour tour of the city is TT $60 (U.S. $14), while a full-day tour along the north coast to the ASA Wright Nature Centre is TT $150 (U.S. $35). Almost any **taxi driver** in Port-of-Spain will be willing to take you around the town and to the beaches on the north coast, and you can haggle for a cheaper rate. Count on paying TT $80 (U.S. $19) an hour for up to four people if you hire a taxi for four or more hours. For a complete list of tour operators and sea cruises, contact the Tourism Office. For nature guides *see* Sports and the Outdoors, *below*.

Carnival

Trinidad always seems to be either anticipating, celebrating, or recovering from a festival, the biggest of which is **Carnival**. Carnival occurs each year between February and early March (in 1994, it's February 14 and 15). Trinidad's version of the pre-Lenten bacchanal is reputedly the oldest in the Western Hemisphere; there are festivities all over the country, but the most lavish is in Port-of-Spain. Carnival officially lasts only two days, from *J'ouvert* (sunrise) on Monday to midnight the following day. If you're planning to go, it's a good idea to arrive in Trinidad a week or two early to enjoy the events leading up to Carnival. Not as overwhelming as its rival in Rio or as debauched as Mardi Gras in New Orleans, Trinidad's fest has the warmth and character of a massive family reunion.

Carnival is about extravagant costumes: Individuals prance around in imaginative outfits. Colorfully attired troupes—called *mas*—that sometimes number in the thousands march to the beat set by steel bands. You can visit the various mas "camps" around the city where these elaborate costumes are put together—the addresses are listed in the newspapers—and perhaps join one that strikes your fancy. Fees run anywhere from $35 to $100; you get to keep the costume. Children can also parade in a Kiddie Carnival that takes place on Saturday morning a few days before the real thing.

Throwing a party is not the only purpose of Carnival; it's also a showcase for calypso performers. Calypso is music that mixes dance rhythms with social commentary, sung by characters with such evocative names as Shadow, the Mighty Sparrow, and Black Stalin. As Carnival approaches, many of these singers perform nightly in calypso tents, which are scattered around the city. You can also visit the pan yards of Port-of-Spain, where steel orchestras such as the Renegades, Desperadoes, Catelli All-Stars, Invaders, and Phase II rehearse their arrangements of calypso.

For several nights before Carnival, costume makers display their talents, and the steel bands and calypso singers perform in spirited competitions in the grandstands of the racetrack in Queen's Park, where the Calypso Monarch is crowned. At sunrise, or J'ouvert, the city starts filling up with metal-frame carts carrying steel bands, flatbed trucks hauling sound systems, and thousands of revelers who squeeze into the narrow streets. Finally, at the stroke of midnight on "Mas Tuesday," Port-of-Spain's exhausted merrymakers go to bed. The next day everybody settles back to business.

Understandably, prices escalate during Carnival. Lodging rates are about 45% higher, and hotels usually require a minimum three-night stay. Reservations should be made long in advance.

Exploring Trinidad

Numbers in the margin correspond to points of interest on the Trinidad map.

Port-of-Spain Start this walking tour early in the day, as the city becomes hot by midafternoon. It is not really surprising that a sightseeing tour of **Port-of-Spain** begins at the port. Though it is no longer as frenetic as it was during the oil boom of the 1970s, **King's Wharf** entertains a steady parade of cruise and cargo ships, a reminder that the city started from this strategic harbor. Across Wrightson Road is **Independence Square,** not a square at all, but a wide, dusty thoroughfare crammed with pedestrians, car traffic, taxi stands, and peddlers of everything from shoes to coconuts. Flanked by government buildings and the familiar twin towers of the Financial Complex (familiar because its facade also adorns one side of all TT dollar bills), the square is representative of this city's chaotic charm.

Near the east end of Wrightson Road stands the Roman Catholic **Cathedral of the Immaculate Conception,** built in 1832 under the aegis of an Anglican governor, Sir Ralph Woodford. Its treasures consist of a Florentine-marble altar, iron framework from England, and stained glass from Ireland.

Up Picton Road are **Fort Chacon** and **Fort Picton,** erected to ward off invaders by the Spanish and British regimes, respectively. The latter is a martello tower with a fine view of the gulf.

At the corner of Prince and Frederick streets, look across **Woodford Square** toward the magnificent **Red House,** a Renaissance-style building that takes up an entire city block. Trinidad's House of Parliament takes its name from a paint job done in anticipation of Queen Victoria's Diamond Jubilee in 1897. Woodford Square has served as the site of political meetings, speeches, public protests, and occasional violence. The original Red House, in fact, was burned to the ground in a 1903 riot. The present structure was built four years later. The chambers are open to the public.

The view of the south side of the square is framed by the Gothic spires of **Trinity,** the city's other cathedral, and by the impressive **public library** building. *Tel. 809/623–6142. Open weekdays 7–3.*

Continue north along Pembroke Street and note the odd mix of modern and colonial architecture, gingerbread and graceful estate houses, and stucco storefronts. Pembroke crosses Keate Street at **Memorial Park.** A short walk north leads to the greater green expanse of **Queen's Park,** more popularly called the **Savannah.**

Proceeding west along the Savannah, you'll come upon some architectural delights: the elegant lantern-roof **George Brown House;** what remains of the **Old Queen's Park Hotel;** and a series of astonishing buildings constructed in a variety of 19th-century styles, known as the **Magnificent Seven.** Notable among these buildings are **Killarney,** patterned after Balmoral Castle in Scotland, with an Italian-marble gallery surrounding the ground floor; **Whitehall,** constructed in the style of a Venetian palace by a cacao-plantation magnate and currently the office of the prime minister; **Roomor,** a flamboyantly Baroque colonial-period house with a preponderance of towers, pinnacles, and wrought-iron trim that suggests an elaborate French pastry; and the **Queen's Royal College,** in German Renaissance style, with a prominent tower clock that chimes on the hour.

The **racetrack** at the southern end of the Savannah is the setting for music and costume competitions during Carnival and, when not jammed with calypso performers, costumes, or horses, tends toward quietude.

The northern end of the Savannah is devoted to plants. A rock garden, known as the **Hollow,** and a fish pond add to the rusticity. The **Botanic Gardens,** across the street, date from 1820. In the midst of the meticulous lattice of walkways is the Emperor Valley Zoo. The official residences of the president and prime minister are on these grounds. *Admission: TT $1. Open daily 9:30–6.*

Out on the Island The intensely urban atmosphere of Port-of-Spain belies the tropical beauty of the countryside surrounding it. To find that, you'll need a car, and six to eight hours. This tour keeps mainly to the northern section of the island. The central and southern portions of Trinidad are mostly endless sugar plantations and a coastline dotted with oil rigs. San Fernando is Trinidad's major industrial center.

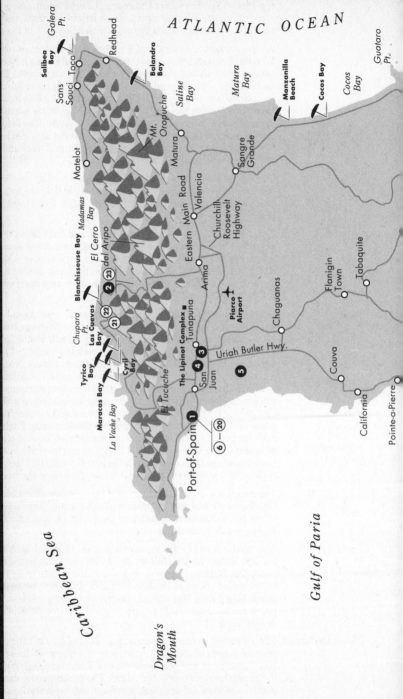

Trinidad

Caribbean Sea

ATLANTIC OCEAN

Galera Pt.

Guataro Pt.

Salibea Bay

Redhead

Balandra Bay

Sans Souci Toco

Saline Bay

Matura Bay

Manzanilla Beach

Cocos Bay

Cocos Bay

Mt. Oropuche

Matelot

Matura

Madamas Bay

Sangre Grande

Blanchisseuse Bay

El Cerro del Aripo

Eastern Main Road

Valencia

② ㉓

Chupara Pt.

Las Cuevas Bay

Churchill Roosevelt Highway

㉒

㉑

Arima

Flanigin Town

Tabaquite

Tyrico Bay

Cyril Bay

The Lipinot Complex

Tunapuna

Piarco Airport

Chaguanas

Maracas Bay

El Tucuche

④ ③

⑤

Uriah Butler Hwy.

La Vache Bay

San Juan

Couva

①

⑥ — ⑳

Port-of-Spain

Dragon's Mouth

Gulf of Paria

California

Pointe-a-Pierre

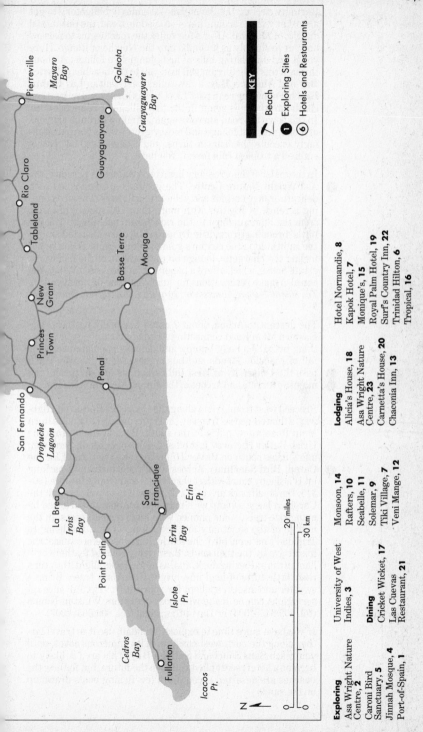

KEY

／ Beach

1 Exploring Sites

⑥ Hotels and Restaurants

Exploring
Asa Wright Nature
Centre, **2**
Caroni Bird
Sanctuary, **5**
Jinnah Mosque, **4**
Port-of-Spain, **1**

University of West
Indies, **3**

Dining
Cricket Wicket, **17**
Las Cuevas
Restaurant, **21**

Monsoon, **14**
Rafters, **10**
Seabelle, **11**
Solemar, **9**
Tiki Village, **7**
Veni Mange, **12**

Lodging
Alicia's House, **18**
Asa Wright Nature
Centre, **23**
Carnetta's House, **20**
Chaconia Inn, **13**

Hotel Normandie, **8**
Kapok Hotel, **7**
Monique's, **15**
Royal Palm Hotel, **19**
Surf's Country Inn, **22**
Trinidad Hilton, **6**
Tropical, **16**

Begin by circling the Savannah—seemingly obligatory to get almost anywhere around here—to Saddle Road, the residential district of **Maraval.** After a few miles the road begins to narrow and curve sharply as it climbs into the Northern Range. Here you'll find undulating hills of lush, junglelike foliage. An hour through this hilly terrain will lead you to the beaches at **Tyrico Bay** and **Maracas Bay;** a few miles past that is **Las Cuevas Beach.** Follow the road past Las Cuevas for several miles, then climb into the hills again to the tiny village of **Blanchisseuse.** In this town the road narrows again, winding through canyons of moist, verdant foliage and mossy grottoes. As you painstakingly execute the hairpin turns, you'll begin to think you've entered a tropical rain forest. You have.

In the midst of this greenery lies a bird-watcher's paradise, the ❷ **Asa Wright Nature Centre.** The grounds are festooned with delicate orange orchids and yellow tube flowers. The surrounding acreage is atwitter with more than 100 species of birds, from the hummingbird to the rare nocturnal oilbird. The oilbirds' breeding grounds in Dunston Cave are included among the sights along the center's guided hiking trails. If you're not feeling too energetic, lounge on the veranda of the handsome estate house, which offers a panorama of the Arima Valley. You can also make reservations for lunch (call one day in advance). *Tel. 809/667–4655. Admission: $6 adults, $3 children. Open daily 9–5.*

The descent to **Arima,** about 7 miles, is equally pastoral. The Eastern Main Road connecting Arima to Port-of-Spain is anything but: It's a busy, bumpy, and densely populated corridor full of roadside stands and businesses. Along the way you'll ❸ pass the **University of West Indies** campus in Curepe and the ❹ majestic turrets and arches of the **Jinnah Mosque** in St. Joseph.

Proceed west from Arima along the Churchill-Roosevelt Highway, a limited-access freeway that runs parallel to the Eastern Main Road a few miles to the south. Both avenues cross the Uriah Butler Highway just outside Port-of-Spain in San Juan; a few miles south on Butler Highway, take the turnoff for the ❺ **Caroni Bird Sanctuary.** Across from the sanctuary's parking lot is a sleepy canal with several boats and guides for hire ($6–$15; the small ones are best). These will take you through the Caroni, a large swamp with mazelike waterways bordered by mangrove trees, some plumed with huge termite nests. In the middle of the sanctuary are several islets that are home to Trinidad's national bird, the scarlet ibis. Just before sunset the ibis arrive by the thousands, their richly colored feathers brilliant in the gathering dusk, and, as more flocks alight, they turn their little tufts of land into bright Christmas trees. Bring a sweater and insect repellent for your return trip. Advance reservations can be made with boat operators Winston Nanan (tel. 809/645–1305) or David Ramsahai (tel. 809/663–2207).

If you have more time to explore Trinidad, use it to travel farther along the northwest coast, with its numerous coves, until you reach **Sans Souci** and **Salibea Bay**. This area is likely to become a hotel resort playground in the future, but for now the beaches are deserted except for a few fishing boats drawn up on the sands.

Exploring Tobago

Numbers in the margin correspond to points of interest on the Tobago map.

A driving tour of Tobago, from Scarborough to Charlotteville and back, takes about four hours.

❶ **Scarborough,** is a sleepy, charming place nestled around **Rockley Bay,** settled two centuries ago.

❷ The road east from Scarborough soon narrows as it twists through **Mt. St. George,** a village that clings to a cliff high above the ocean. Fort King George is a lovely, tranquil spot commanding sweeping views of the bay, with a restored 18th-century English fort and barracks, a fine arts center, and lush landscaped gardens.

❸ The sea dips in and out of view as you pass through a series of small settlements and the town of Roxborough. About an hour's drive will bring you to **King's Bay,** an attractive crescent-shape beach. Just before you reach the bay there is a bridge with an unmarked turnoff that leads to a gravel parking lot; beyond that, a landscaped path leads to a waterfall with a rocky pool where you can refresh yourself. You may meet enterprising locals who'll offer to guide you to the top of the falls, a climb that you may find not worth the effort.

❹ After King's Bay the road rises dramatically; just before it dips again there's a marked lookout with a vista of **Speyside,** a small fishing village, and several offshore islands.

❺ Past Speyside the road cuts across a ridge of mountains that separates the Atlantic side of Tobago from the Caribbean. On the far side is **Charlotteville,** a remote fishing community, albeit the largest village on the island. Fishermen here announce the day's catch (usually flying fish, red fish, or bonito) by sounding their conch shells. The paved road ends a few miles outside Charlotteville, in Camberton. Returning to Speyside, take a

❻ right at the sign for **Flagstaff Hill.** Follow a well-traveled dirt road for about 1¹/2 miles to a radio tower. It's one of the highest points in Tobago, surrounded by ocean on three sides and with a view of the hills, Charlotteville, and Bird of Paradise Island in the bay.

Beaches

Trinidad Contrary to popular notion, Trinidad has far more beaches than Tobago; the catch is that Tobago's beaches are close to hotels, and Trinidad's are not. There are, however, some worthy sites within an hour's drive of Port-of-Spain, spread out along the north-coast road.

Maracas Bay is a long stretch of sand with a cove and a fishing village at one end. It's a local favorite, so it can get crowded on weekends. Parking sites are ample, and there's a snack bar and rest facilities. **Cyril Bay,** a pebble-and-sand cove reachable only by foot, is laced with small waterfalls and is an idyllic picnic spot. **Tyrico Bay** is a small beach lively with surfers who flock here to enjoy the excellent surfing. The strong undertow may be too much for some swimmers. A few miles farther along the north-coast road is **Las Cuevas Bay,** a narrow, picturesque strip of sand named for the series of partially submerged and ex-

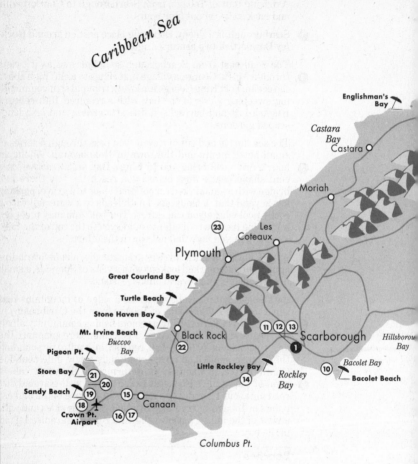

Caribbean Sea

Englishman's Bay

Castara Bay

Castara

Moriah

Les Coteaux

Plymouth

Great Courland Bay

Turtle Beach

Stone Haven Bay

Mt. Irvine Beach

Black Rock

Scarborough

Hillsborough Bay

Buccoo Bay

Pigeon Pt.

Store Beach

Little Rockley Bay

Rockley Bay

Bacolet Bay

Bacolet Beach

Sandy Beach

Canaan

Crown Pt. Airport

Columbus Pt.

Exploring
Charlotteville, **5**
Flagstaff Hill, **6**
King's Bay, **3**
Mt. St. George, **2**
Scarborough, **1**
Speyside, **4**

Dining
Blue Crab, **11**
Cocrico Inn, **23**
Dillon's, **15**
Jemma's Village Kitchen, **8**
The Old Donkey Cart House, **12**
Papillon, **22**

Rouselles, **13**
Store Bay Centre, **20**
Teaside, **14**
The Village, **16**

Lodging
Blue Waters Inn, **7**
Cocrico Inn, **23**
The Golden Thistle Hotel, **17**
Harris Cottage, **10**
Kariwak Village, **16**

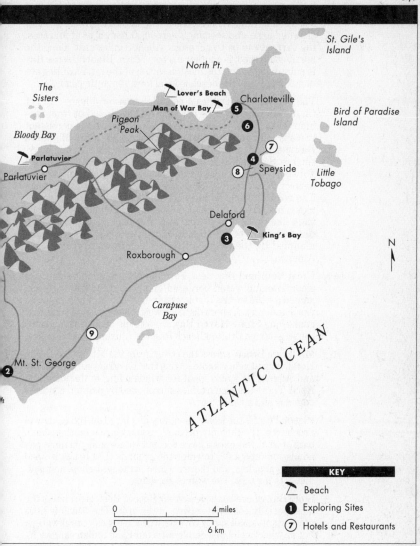

The Sisters

North Pt.

Lover's Beach

Charlotteville

St. Gile's Island

Bird of Paradise Island

Man of War Bay

5

6

7

4

8

Speyside

Little Tobago

Pigeon Peak

Bloody Bay

Parlatuvier

Parlatuvier

Delaford

King's Bay

3

Roxborough

Carapuse Bay

N

9

Mt. St. George

2

ATLANTIC OCEAN

KEY

Beach

1 Exploring Sites

7 Hotels and Restaurants

0   4 miles

0   6 km

Richmond Great House, **9**
Sandy Point Beach Club, **18**
Store Bay Holiday Resort, **19**
Tropikist, **21**

plorable caves that ring the beach. A food stand offers tasty snacks, and vendors hawk fresh fruit across the road. It's less crowded here, and seemingly serene, although, as at Maracas, the current can be treacherous. About 8 miles east, along the north-coast road, is another narrow beach. **Blanchisseuse Bay** is palm-fringed and the most deserted of the lot. Facilities are nonexistent, but the beach is ideal for a romantic picnic.

The drive to the northeast coast takes several hours. To get there you must take the detour road to Arima, but "goin' behind God's back," as the Trinis say, does reward the persistent traveler with gorgeous vistas and secluded beaches. **Balandra Bay,** sheltered by a rocky outcropping, is popular among body-surfers. **Salibea Bay,** just past Galera Point, which juts toward Tobago, is a gentle beach with shallows and plenty of shade—perfect for swimming. Snack vendors abound in the vicinity. The road to **Manzanilla Beach** and **Cocos Bay** to the south, nicknamed the Cocal, is lined with stately palms whose fronds vault like the arches at Chartres. Manzanilla has picnic facilities and a view of the Atlantic, though its water is occasionally muddied by the Orinoco River, which flows in from South America.

Tobago **Great Courland Bay,** near Fort Bennett, is a long stretch of clear, tranquil water, bordered on one end by **Turtle Beach,** named for the turtles that lay their eggs here at night between April and May. A short distance west, there's a side road that runs along **Stone Haven Bay,** a gorgeous beach that's across the street from Grafton Beach Resorts, a luxury hotel complex.

Mt. Irvine Beach, across the street from the Mt. Irvine Beach Hotel, is an unremarkable setting that has great surfing in July and August. It's also ideal for windsurfing in January and April. There are picnic tables surrounded by painted concrete pagodas and a snack bar.

Pigeon Point is the locale inevitably displayed on Tobago travel brochures. It's the only privately owned beach on the island, part of what was once a large coconut estate, and you must pay admission (about $2) to enter the grounds. The beach is lined with royal palms, and there's a food stand, gift shop, and paddleboats for rent. The waters are calm.

Store Bay, where boats depart for Buccoo Reef, is probably the most socially convivial setting in the area. The beach is little more than a small sandy cove between two rocky breakwaters, but six shacks sell delectable *rotis* (an East Indian sandwich), *pilau* (rice and peas), and messy but marvelous crab and dumplings. Miss Jean's is generally considered the best. Farther west along Crown Point, **Sandy Beach** is abutted by several hotels. You won't lack for amenities around here.

Just west of Scarborough, take Milford Road off the main highway to the shores of **Little Rockley Bay.** The quiet beach is craggy and not much good for swimming, but offers a pleasing view of Tobago's capital across the water.

After driving through Scarborough, continue south on Bacolet Street 4 miles to **Bacolet Beach,** a dark-sand beach that was the setting for the films *Swiss Family Robinson* and *Heaven Knows, Mr. Allison.*

The road from Scarborough to Speyside has plenty of swimming sites. **King's Bay Beach,** surrounded by steep green hills, is the most appealing—the bay hooks around so severely that you feel as if you're swimming in a lake.

Man of War Bay in Charlotteville is flanked by one of the prettiest fishing villages in the Caribbean. You can lounge on the sand and purchase the day's catch for your dinner. Farther west across the bay is **Lover's Beach,** so called because of its pink sand and because it can be reached only by boat. You can hire one of the locals to take you across.

Parlatuvier, on the north side of the island, is best approached via the road from Roxborough. The beach here is a classic Caribbean crescent, a scene peopled by villagers and local fishermen. The next beach over, **Englishman's Bay,** is equally seductive and completely deserted.

Sports and the Outdoors

Bird-watching Bird-watchers can fill up their books with notes on the variety of species to be found in Trinidad at the **Asa Wright Nature Centre,** the **Caroni Bird Sanctuary** (*see* Exploring Trinidad, *above*), and the **Pointe-à-Pierre Wild Fowl Trust,** which is located within the confines of a petrochemical complex (42 Sandown Rd., Pt. Cumana, tel. 809/637–5145). In Tobago, naturalist **David Rooks** offers walks inland and trips to offshore bird colonies (tel. 809/639–4276); a morning's walk with a small group of no more than eight is TT $55 (U.S. $13).

Golf There are nine golf courses in the country, the best of which are the **Mt. Irvine Golf Club** (tel. 809/639–8871) in Tobago and **Moka Golf Course** in Maraval (tel. 809/629–2314), just outside Port-of-Spain. Greens fees average TT $60 (U.S. $14).

Scuba Diving Tobago draws scuba-diving aficionados from around the world. You can get supplies and instruction at **Dive Tobago** (tel. 809/639–3695), **Sean Robinson** (tel. 809/639–1279), **Tobago Marine Sports Ltd.** (tel. 809/639–0291), **Tobago Scuba** (tel. 809/660–4327), and **Tobago Dive Experience** (Grafton Beach, tel. 809/639–0191; in Trinidad, tel. 809/639–1263). On Trinidad contact **Scuba Shop Ltd.** (Mirabella, tel. 809/658–2183). Cost of a single-tank dive averages $40.

Snorkeling The best spots for snorkeling are on Tobago, of which **Buccoo Reef** is easily the most popular—perhaps too popular. Over the years the reef has been damaged by the ceaseless boat traffic and by the thoughtless visitors who take pieces of coral for souvenirs. Even so, it's still a trip worth experiencing, particularly if you have children. For $8 (tickets are available in almost any hotel), you board a Plexiglas-bottom boat at either Store Bay or Buccoo Beach; the 15-minute trip to the reef, 2 miles offshore, is made only at low tide. Operators provide rubber shoes, masks, and snorkels but not fins, which are helpful in the moderate current.

There is also good snorkeling by the beach near the **Arnos Vale Hotel** and at **Blue Waters,** and the government is slowly developing reefs around Speyside that rival if not surpass Buccoo. Most beachside hotels on Tobago rent snorkeling equipment; the cost is around $5 a day.

Tennis The following hotels and clubs have tennis courts: **Arnos Vale** (tel. 809/639–2881), **Mt. Irvine** (tel. 809/639–8817); **Blue Waters Inn** (tel. 809/660–4341); **Tranquility Lawn Tennis Club** (Victoria Ave., Port-of-Spain, tel. 809/625–4182); **Trinidad Country Club** (tel. 809/622–3470); **The Trinidad Hilton** (tel. 809/624–3211); and **Turtle Beach** (tel. 809/639–2851). Court fees are about TT $45 (U.S. $10) an hour.

Shopping

Thanks in large part to Carnival costumery, there's no shortage of fabric shops on the islands. The best bargains for Oriental and East Indian silks and cottons can be found in downtown Port-of-Spain, on **Frederick Street** and around **Independence Square.** Other good buys are such duty-free items as Angostura Bitters and Old Oak or Vat 19 rum, all widely available.

Local Crafts The Tourism Office can provide an extensive list of local artisans who specialize in everything from straw and cane work to miniature steel pans. **The Village** (Nook Ave. by the Hotel Normandie) has several shops that specialize in indigenous fashions. Around the corner is **Art Creators** (7 St. Ann's Rd., tel. 809/624–4369), a top-notch gallery. On Tobago, **The Hangover Cafe and Art Gallery** (Pigeon Point Gate, tel. 809/639–7940) sells watercolors, handicrafts, and T-shirts. **The Cotton House** (Bacolet and Windward Rds., tel. 809/639–3695) is a good bet for jewelry and imaginative batik work.

Records For the best selection of calypso and soca music, check out **Rhyner's Record Shop** (54 Prince St., 809/623–5673; Cruise Ship Complex, tel. 809/627–8717) or **Metronome** (83 Western Main Rd., tel. 809/622–4157), both in Port-of-Spain.

Dining

Dining can be very inexpensive. Small stands and cafés throughout Port-of-Spain sell such snacks as rotis (a kind of East Indian burrito, usually filled with curried chicken and potatoes) for less than an American dollar. Fewer budget options exist on Tobago, where dining is primarily in hotel restaurants, but even here prices are reasonable. If your lodgings include kitchen facilities, you'll find plenty of minimarkets on Trinidad well-stocked with local and imported foods; stores are few and far between on Tobago.

Trinidad Port-of-Spain doesn't lack for variety when it comes to eateries, with imaginative hybrids of European, Oriental, East Indian, and Caribbean fare. In addition to the establishments below, there are plenty of East Indian and Chinese restaurants and pizzerias (don't expect New York–style pizza).

Trinidadians are particularly fond of *callaloo,* a soup or stew of dasheen leaves (similar to spinach) and okra, flavored with anything from pork to coconut, pureed and served at every restaurant on the island. It's hard to believe anything this green and swampy-looking can taste so delicious. Other items in a Trinidadian menu worth sampling are *coocoo,* a dumpling of cornmeal and coconut (similar to polenta); roti (*see above*); *pilau,* a rice-and-peas dish inspired by Chinese cuisine; tamarind ball, a dessert made from the sweet-sour tamarind; and peanut shake, a peanut butter–flavored milk shake.

No Trinidadian dining experience can be complete, of course, without a rum punch with fresh fruit and the legendary Angostura Bitters, made by the same company that produces the excellent Old Oak rum. Carib beer and Stag are recommended for washing down the spicier concoctions. Dark-beer aficionados can try Royal Extra Stout (R.E.), which is even sweeter than Guinness.

Tobago With few exceptions, the restaurants in Tobago are located in hotels and guest houses; several of the large resort complexes also feature some form of nightly entertainment. The food isn't as eclectic as on Trinidad, generally favoring local styles, but in terms of quality and service Tobagonian "home cooking" more than holds its own.

Highly recommended restaurants are indicated by a star ★.

Category	Cost*
Moderate	$20–$30
Inexpensive	$10–$20
Budget	under $10

per person, excluding drinks, service, and sales tax (15%)

Trinidad **Solemar.** Joe Brown, formerly chef at the Trinidad Hilton, has won a strong following for dinner with his sophisticated menu, which combines a strong French influence with local seafood (try the stuffed grouper baked in banana leaves) and imported meats. You'll have to avoid high-end à la carte dishes here. The setting resembles a greenhouse; potted plants flow over the sides of shelves, and trellises support orchids. *6 Nook Ave., St. Ann's, Port-of-Spain, tel. 809/624–1459. AE, DC, MC, V. Closed Sun. Moderate.*

Rafters. Behind a stone facade with green rafters is a former rum shop, now a pub and restaurant, that's an urban institution. The pub is the center of activity, especially Friday night. In late afternoons the place begins to swell with Port-of-Spainers generally loosening up as they order from the tasty selection of burgers and barbecue. *6A Warner St., Port-of-Spain, tel. 809/628–9258. AE, DC, MC, V. Closed weekend lunch. Moderate.*

Seabelle. This restaurant is hard to find—there's no sign or street number, and the entrance looks like the door to a private home—which is part of its charm. The ambience is beatnik—with 1950s jazz on the stereo, and a darkened bar where time almost stands still. The accent is on seafood. There are only seven tables, so call for reservations—and directions. *27 Mucurapo Rd., St. James, Port-of-Spain, tel. 809/622–3594. Reservations essential. No credit cards. Moderate.*

Tiki Village. Cosmopolitan Port-of-Spainers are as passionate about their Oriental food as New Yorkers and San Franciscans are. Everyone touts their favorite, but this eatery, a serious version of Trader Vic's, is the most reliable. What it lacks in kitsch, it compensates for in fine Oriental food. Polynesian-inspired dishes include sweet-and-sour vegetables, snapper with honey-and-lime sauce, and a wonderful assortment of appetizers. *Kapok Hotel, 16–18 Cotton Hill, Port-of-Spain, tel. 809/622–6441. AE, D, DC, MC, V. Moderate.*

★ **Veni Mange.** The best lunches in town are served inside this small stucco house. Credit Allyson Hennessy, a Cordon Bleu–trained cook who has become a celebrity of sorts because of a TV talk show she hosts, and her sister-partner Rosemary Hezekiah. The cuisine here is Creole. Formerly open only for lunch, this popular restaurant now serves dinner too; the Wednesday evening buffet is a good way to sample the regional cuisine. *13 Lucknow St., St. James, Port-of-Spain, no phone. No credit cards. Inexpensive.*

Cricket Wicket. This casual eatery and local night spot serves reasonably good hamburgers and fried chicken. After 8 PM, the interest shifts from food to beer, rum, and the beat of music. *149 Trageret Rd., Port-of-Spain, tel. 809/622–1808. No credit cards. Budget.*

Monsoon. Dark green Formica tables, lavender walls, and a few sprigs of flowers comprise the simple decor of this Indian restaurant. The specialties are curries: goat, shrimp, chicken, and beef, made with spices imported from India and served with chutney, potatoes, and chick-peas. Wednesday evenings bring a special buffet. *Corner of Tragerete Rd. and Picton St., Newtown, Port-of-Spain, tel. 809/628–7684. AE, DC, MC, V. Closed Sun. Budget.*

Las Cuevas Restaurant. This local fishermen's hangout doubles as a beachside snack bar. The menu is limited; your best bet is a wholesome and tasty bake 'n shark (shark burger). If you want a full meal, go for the fish of the day. It was probably caught this morning. *Las Cuevas, no telephone. No credit cards. Open 11–7. Budget.*

Tobago
★ **Blue Crab.** This lunch spot is perched on a wide porch above a busy corner of downtown Scarborough. Best bets are the fish chowder or flying fish with callaloo and vegetables, prepared with élan by cook Ken Sardinha. His wife, Alison, is one of Tobago's most gracious hostesses. Dinner is officially served only on Wednesday and Friday nights, but the proprietors will open the restaurant for a supper upon the request of even one couple. *Corner of Main and Fort Sts., Scarborough, tel. 809/639–2737. AE, MC, V. No dinner except Wed. and Fri. Moderate.*

Cocrico Inn. A café with a bar against one wall, the Cocrico offers delectable home cooking. The three rotating chefs frequently use fresh fruits and vegetables grown in the neighborhood. They zealously guard their recipes, including a marvelous coocoo and lightly breaded, subtly spiced grouper. There is nothing fancy here, just delicious food. *Corner of North and Commissioner Sts., Plymouth, tel. 809/639–2661. AE, V. Moderate.*

Dillon's. This cozy recent arrival, with checked tablecloths and local artwork adorning the walls, offers friendly service, imaginatively prepared seafood, and delicate garlic bread. *Airport Rd. near Crown Point, tel. 809/639–8765. AE, MC, V. Closed Mon. Moderate.*

The Old Donkey Cart House. The name is something of a curiosity, since this attractive restaurant is set in and around a green-and-white colonial house, about a 2-mile drive south of Scarborough. There's outdoor dining in a garden with twinkling lights. The cuisine is standard Caribbean, nothing special, but German side dishes and an extensive selection of Rhine and Moselle wines set it apart. *Bacolet St., Scarborough, tel. 809/639–3551. AE, V. Closed Wed. Moderate.*

Papillon. Named after one of the proprietor's favorite books, this seafood restaurant is a homey room with an adjoining patio. Well-prepared, standard Caribbean fare has a few adventurous touches. *Buccoo Bay Rd., Mt. Irvine, tel. 809/639–0275. AE, DC, MC, V. No lunch Sun. Moderate.*

★ **Rouselles.** A charming setting, attentive service, and a rotating menu make this one a winner. Featured are pork chops in ginger, calypso chicken, grouper in a tangy Creole sauce, and beet or christophine pie. The $15 tasting menu is an amazing bargain. *Old Windward Rd., Bacolet, tel. 809/639–4738. Lunch only by reservation. AE, MC, V. Inexpensive–Moderate.*

★ **The Village.** Steel-band music plays gently in the background at this romantic candlelit spot under a thatched roof, where waitresses are clad in colorful island prints. The prix-fixe, four-course menu changes daily and may include christophine soup, green fig salad, or shrimp with two sauces (sweet and sour, and Creole). Co-owner Cynthia Clovis creates sophisticated variations on Caribbean cuisine; everything she prepares is fresh and bursting with flavor. *Kariwak Village, Crown Point, tel. 809/639–8442. AE, DC, MC, V. Moderate.*

Teaside. This peaceful teahouse is an oasis of civility, the ideal place to watch the sun disappear behind Trinidad on the horizon. The pastel structure looks Japanese, but the service is *terribly* British. Pizzas, tasty cakes, and more than 25 selections of tea are offered. *Lambeau Rd., tel. 809/639–4306. No credit cards. No dinner. Inexpensive.*

Jemma's Village Kitchen. Just outside of Speyside on the main road, this local house perches on stilts by the ocean's shore. Jemma produces tasty Tobagonian cooking spiced with Indian herbs—the chicken is a popular choice—and while the decor is as basic as could be, the ocean views are inspiring. *Speyside, tel. 809/660–4066. No credit cards. Budget.*

Store Bay Centre. In a small park across the road from the beach are a collection of small take-out restaurants serving local fare such as fish burgers, rotis, and fried chicken. Make your selection and carry it to one of the tables set under a thatched roof. If you're with a group, each person can select from one of several restaurants and together enjoy a large, varied meal for little money. *Store Bay, no telephone. No credit cards. Open 11 AM–7 PM. Budget.*

Lodging

Lodging prices in Trinidad and Tobago are among the lowest in the Caribbean, and Trinidad's are slightly lower than Tobago's. Even Trinidad's top city hotel, the Trinidad Hilton, falls just within our Moderate category for a standard double room. On Trinidad, most lodging is located within the vicinity of Port-of-Spain, far from any beach. The larger of these Port-of-Spain hotels cater mainly to the business traveler or convention groups. As a consequence, a number of small inns and guest houses have sprung up to meet the needs of tourists. These offer a congenial, family-type atmosphere where guests intermingle. Unlike Trinidad's properties, almost every one of Tobago's hotels are on or within walking distance of the ocean.

On both islands, private homes have begun opening their doors to paying guests. These can be reserved through the tourist offices on either island, or contact the **Trinidad and Tobago Bed and Breakfast Association** (Box 3231, Diego Martin, or Park

Lane Court, Ameythst Dr., El Dorado, Tunupana, tel. 809/663–5265; on Tobago, Mr. Lloyd Anthony, Tony's House, Carnbee, Tobago, tel. 809/639–8836), which only admits members after an inspection for safety and cleanliness. We recommend that you only consider those listed with this organization or the tourist office. Most private homes are away from the beach.

During Carnival week and Christmas, you should book reservations far in advance; expect to pay about 40%–50% more for lodging at these times. From mid-December to mid-April, Tobago's hotel rates average 30% higher than the rest of the year.

Most establishments offer a choice of EP, CP, or MAP meal plans. Since most of the Trinidad accommodations listed below are a few blocks from any breakfast shop, you may want to elect for a CP plan, but an MAP plan on Trinidad will limit your dinner options. On Tobago, however, MAP is a sensible choice if you don't have a car; it's an especially good idea on the east side of the island, where there is a dearth of restaurants. Lodgings with cooking facilities are the exception rather than the rule.

Highly recommended lodgings are indicated by a star ★.

Category	Cost*
Moderate	$100–$150
Inexpensive	$50–$100
Budget	under $50

All prices are for a standard double room for two, excluding 15% tax and a 10% service charge. To estimate rates for hotels offering MAP/FAP, add about $25–$35 per person per day to the above price ranges.

Trinidad **Asa Wright Nature Centre.** Set in a lush rain forest about 90 minutes east of Port-of-Spain and an hour's drive from the nearest beach, this handsome lodge, constructed in 1908 by a tycoon for his young bride, attracts international legions of bird-watchers and nature photographers. There are impressive views of the verdant Arima Valley and the Northern Range from the verandah, where tea is served each afternoon. The rooms are uncomplicated and comfortably furnished. Three meals a day and an evening rum punch are included in the rates. Reserve at least six months in advance. (For more information about the center, *see* Exploring, *above.*) *Bag 10, Port-of-Spain; write Caligo Ventures, Box 21, Armonk, NY 10504, tel. 914/273–6333 or 800/426–7781. 23 rooms. Facilities: restaurant. No credit cards. FAP. Moderate.*

★ **Trinidad Hilton.** Perched above Port-of-Spain, the Hilton radiates the feeling of comfort and competence. This is Port-of-Spain's most stylish hotel, with prices to match; everything but the standard rooms here exceed our Moderate price range. Each room either has a balcony, which opens to a fine view of Savannah Park and the city and sea beyond, or overlooks the equally inviting Olympic-size pool, shaded by trees. La Boucan, the hotel's formal restaurant, tends to be expensive; the Pool Terrace, with live entertainment on Monday nights, is less. The hotel frequently bustles with conventioneers, which may be its only drawback. Ask for a special corporate rate when you book.

Lady Young Rd., Box 442, Port-of-Spain, tel. 809/624–3211, fax 624–4485. 442 rooms. Facilities: 2 restaurants, bar, satellite TV, pool, health club, tennis courts, drugstore, gift shops, car rental, taxi service. AE, DC, MC, V. EP. Moderate.

Hotel Normandie. Built in the 1930s by French Creoles on the ruins of an old coconut plantation, the Normandie has touches of Spanish, English colonial, and even postmodern architecture, giving the place an agreeably artsy patina that offsets the drab lighting and slightly tatty decor. The standard rooms have a motel ambiance, and even those facing the small courtyard pool are dark and uninspiring. The exception are the loft rooms ($20 more). The shopping gallery here has a small café for light meals, but the hotel's main restaurant, La Fantasie, makes for expensive dining. You can catch one of the buses that run along the nearby main road for the 10-minute ride to downtown. *10 Nook Ave., St. Ann's Village, Port-of-Spain, tel. and fax 809/624– 1181. 48 rooms, 13 loft rooms. Facilities: restaurant and bar, pool, gallery, café, shops, car rental, taxi service. AE, DC, MC, V. EP. Inexpensive–Moderate.*

★ **Kapok Hotel.** Although now part of the Golden Tulip hotel chain, this hotel has been run by the Chan family for years and all but gleams with cheerful efficiency. It's a great location, just off the north end of the park, near the zoo and Presidential Palace, and away from the worst traffic. The Café Savanna here, which serves local seafood and grills, may stretch your budget, but do sample the Chinese and Polynesian specialties at Tiki Village (*see* Dining, *above*). Rooms are furnished with wicker; more expensive ones (still within our affordable range) command a pleasing view on the park side. *16–18 Cotton Hill, Port-of-Spain, tel. 809/622–6441 or 800/333–1212, fax 809/622– 9677. 71 rooms. Facilities: pool, 2 restaurants, taxi service. AE, DC, MC, V. EP. Inexpensive–Moderate.*

Alicia's House. The Govia family named their house after their daughter and have a knack of treating guests as long-lost cousins. Only a 10-minute walk or a TT $2 ride in a route taxi from the Savannah, this private home has expanded to a 15-room inn, but still retains a family atmosphere. Accommodations range from rooms with four beds to closet-sized units with one or two twin beds. Furnishings are basic, but each has air-conditioning and a private shower or bath. The pool is large enough for a quick dip while relaxing on the patio. A lounge area has a TV and piano for guests to play. The food is home-style; an odor of curry prevails. *7 Coblentz Gardens, St. Ann's, Port-of-Spain, tel. 809/623–2802, fax 809/622–8560. 15 rooms. Facilities: breakfast room, pool, lounge, Jacuzzi. MC, V. EP, CP, MAP. Inexpensive.*

Carnetta's House. When Winston Borell retired as director of tourism for Trinidad and Tobago, he and his wife, Carnetta, opened their surburban two-story house to guests. The choice room, Le Flamboyant, opens onto the garden's patio. All rooms have private shower baths, telephones, radios, and TV. There is air-conditioning, but cool breezes usually do the trick. Winston's garden is a fascinating introduction to tropical plants. Carnetta uses the garden's herbs in her cooking—some of the best you'll find in Port-of-Spain. The couple is a font of information on what to see and do in Trinidad, and will make arrangements for you. *28 Scotland Terr., Andalusia, Maraval, Port-of-Spain, tel. 809/628–2732, fax 809/628–7717. 5 rooms. Fa-*

cilities: lounge, dining room, laundry facilities, car-rental, airport transfers. AE, DC, MC, V. EP, BP, MAP. Inexpensive.

Chaconia Inn. This upscale motel has cheerful decor, a good restaurant, and great entertainment on weekends (soca queen Denyse). All rooms have TVs and phones. The property has undergone financial difficulties that seemed to have been resolved at press time, but call ahead. The inn is in Maraval, an upper-middle-class suburb that's a 10-minute ride from downtown by bus or taxi. *106 Saddle Rd., Maraval, Port-of-Spain, tel. 809/628–8603, fax 809/628–3214. 35 rooms and apartments. Facilities: pool, restaurant, nightclub. AE, DC, MC, V. EP. Inexpensive.*

★ **Monique's.** This homey guest house is a nest of congeniality only minutes by car from downtown. Of the 11 rooms, one is specifically designed for the disabled. All rooms have private baths. Meals are available on request, and owner Mike Charbonne will occasionally organize a picnic to the couple's 100-acre plantation near Blanchisseuse. *114 Saddle Rd., Maraval, Port-of-Spain, tel. 809/628–3334, fax 809/622–3232. 11 rooms. Facilities: dining room, common-room area with TV. AE. EP, CP, MAP. Inexpensive.*

Royal Palm Hotel. Completed at the end of 1992, this hotel within a shopping plaza offers especially good value for those who make use of the fully equipped kitchens in every room. The superior rooms at $10 more give you a larger sitting area that is separate from the bedroom, but even the standard rooms are quite spacious. All rooms have air-conditioning, TVs, and direct-dial phones. A coffee shop is planned for late 1993, but more substantial restaurant fare may be had at the two restaurants (one serving Oriental and Creole fare, and the other Middle Eastern) in the surrounding shopping plaza. Buses and taxis can whisk you from the hotel to downtown in about 10 minutes. *7 Saddle Rd., Maraval, Port-of-Spain, tel. and fax 809/628–6042. 70 rooms, 5 suites. Facilities: pool. AE, MC, V. EP. Inexpensive.*

Surf's Country Inn. Six new guest rooms have been added in buildings adjoining this popular fish restaurant. On a hillside overlooking the sea, these new accommodations will offer the traveler the chance to stay comfortably on the north coast after a day of swimming and surfing, instead of returning to Port-of-Spain. *Blanchisseuse, tel. 809/669–2475. 6 rooms. Facilities: restaurant, bar. No credit cards. EP, BP. Budget.*

Tropical. This small budget hotel in the residential suburb of Mareval, a 10-minute drive from downtown Port-of-Spain, offers bare-bones accommodations that are made cheerful by wild tropical colors in the rooms. All have individually controlled air-conditioning. Service is friendly and helpful. *6 Rookery Nook, Maraval, Port-of-Spain, tel. 809/622–5815, fax 809/622–4249. 16 rooms. Facilities: pool, restaurant. AE. EP. Budget.*

Tobago **Blue Waters Inn.** It's easy to miss the sign for this gem of a
★ hotel, nestled on the shore of Batteaux Bay; the entrance appears to drop over a cliff. It's part of the charm of this rustic retreat, where birds fly through a dining room ornamented with driftwood, and the sincere hospitality of owner Mrs. McClean greets you. A variety of beamed rooms and cabins includes new (and higher priced) units with kitchenettes. Only a few rooms have air-conditioning. The beach here is free of currents; nature walks are popular along the 48 acres of grounds. *Batteaux Bay, Speyside, Tobago, tel. 809/660–4341, fax*

809/639–4180. 29 rooms. Facilities: 2 tennis courts, TV lounge, dive instruction, gift shop, restaurant, bar. AE, DC, MC, V. EP, MAP. Moderate.

Richmond Great House. This is a restored late-18th-century plantation house with high-beamed ceilings on a 1,500-acre citrus estate. The common rooms have a great view, but what holds your gaze are the African sculptures and furniture collected by the professor who owns the place. Guests can choose one of the two rooms in the main house or one of four guest cottages. The beach is a 10-minute drive away, so you'll probably need a car here. Visitors may drop in for lunch, but be sure to telephone ahead that morning. *Belle Garden, Tobago, tel. 809/660–4467. 6 rooms. Facilities: dining room, pool, TV lounge. MC, V. MAP. Moderate.*

Cocrico Inn. Named after the national bird of Tobago, this inn built around a courtyard and small pool is set on a quiet side street in the village of Plymouth, a 10-minute walk from the beach. Although the impression is a little like a roadside motel, with large rooms, rather drab furnishings, and stained carpets, the hosts are genuinely welcoming, the restaurant serves a combination of good local and American fare, and guests can walk to the village, the marina, and beaches. *North and Commissioner Sts., Box 287, Plymouth, Tobago, tel. 809/639–2961, fax 809/639–6565. 16 rooms. Facilities: restaurant, bar, pool, gift shop. AE, MC, V. EP, MAP. Inexpensive.*

★ **Kariwak Village.** The resort's motif is inspired by the Carib and Arawak Indians, but modern creature comforts are much in evidence. There's a suitably tropical bar, highly praised Caribbean cooking, and open-air dining. The owners, Cynthia and Allan Clovis, create a warm and congenial atmosphere, with an emphasis on personal attention. Nine cabanas, which resemble equatorial igloos, have been divided into 18 cozy apartments, all of which look onto the pool. The beach is a five-minute walk away. The gift shop features a thoughtful selection of local crafts and books; local Tobago artists often show work here. This hotel is very popular with couples wanting a peaceful retreat, but with the action of Crown Point nearby. *Crown Point, tel. 809/639–8442, fax 809/639–8441, write Box 27, Scarborough, Tobago. 18 rooms. Facilities: shuttle service to beach, pool, restaurant, bar, scooter rentals, live entertainment weekends, TV lounge. AE, DC, MC, V. EP, MAP. Inexpensive..*

Sandy Point Beach Club. Spacious, modern villas have all the amenities, including satellite TV, but facilities look a little tired these days. The six apartments have one bedroom and a lounge that can double as sleeping quarters for another couple. The laid-back attitude and friendliness of the staff is infectious, and activities from volleyball on the beach to festive dinners encourage guests to join in the party spirit. The beach is so close that the sea actually washes the base of the bar. The village of Crown Point is within walking distance. *Crown Point, Tobago, tel. 809/639–8533 or 800/223–6510, fax 809/639–8495. 36 rooms, 6 apartments. Facilities: 2 pools, restaurant, 2 bars, car rentals, dive shop, boutique, laundry. DC, MC, V. EP. Inexpensive.*

Tropikist. This amiable, gleaming-white little beach hotel spread out across Store Bay attracts a fun, youngish crowd who appreciate its bargain prices, sparkling cleanliness, and beachfront location. The lively atmosphere is generated by the gaiety of the guests rather than the hotel's austere architecture and plain decor. *Store Bay, tel. 809/639–8512, fax 809/638–*

1110. 30 rooms. Facilities: beach, pool, restaurant, bar, disco, volleyball. AE, DC, MC, V. EP. Inexpensive.

The Golden Thistle Hotel. The look here is that of a respectable 1950s motel. All rooms include kitchenettes. You can make the 15-minute walk to the beach and local eateries, but a rental bike may give you more flexibility. *Store Bay Rd., Crown Point, Tobago, tel. and fax 809/639–8521. 36 rooms. Facilities: pool, bar, TV room, restaurant. DC, V. EP. Budget.*

Harris Cottage. Unlike most of the guest houses on Tobago— old clapboard homes converted on an ad hoc basis to accept boarders—the Harris Cottage is a new stone-and-stucco structure built on a half-acre of land. This is a family home, the kind of place where kids run in and out. The comfortable, air-conditioned rooms with private baths are in an addition abutting the house. Breakfast is served on a small terrace, and meals are by request throughout the day. It's about 10 minutes by bicycle from Scarborough, and a 10-minute walk from the beach. *Bacolet, near Scarborough, tel. 809/639–8810. 8 rooms. Facilities: dining room, TV lounge. No credit cards. BP. Budget.*

Store Bay Holiday Resort. Close to the airport and less than a mile from the beach, this impersonal, motellike property has air-conditioned rooms that look upon a pool. Furnishings are plain and the carpets somewhat worn, but rooms have fully equipped kitchens. *Store Bay Rd., Crown Point, tel. 809/622– 2141, fax 809/639–8810. 15 rooms. Facilities: snack bar, pool, reading room with TV. MC, V. EP. Budget.*

Off-Season Bets Other than Carnival time, Trinidad does not have a high season, and consequently no off-season when hotel rates dip. On Tobago, prices drop by about 30% from mid-April to mid-December. Among affordable hotels at this time is **Grafton Beach Resorts** (Black Rock, Tobago, tel. 809/639–0191, fax 809/639– 0030), the best-run resort on the island. It's located along the beach and has a large swimming pool, tennis and squash courts, and good restaurants.

The Arts and Nightlife

Trinidad Trinidadian culture doesn't end with music, but it definitely begins with it. While both calypso and steel bands are best displayed during Carnival, the steel bands play at clubs, dances, and fetes throughout the year. There's no lack of nightlife in Port-of-Spain. Popular now is "sweet parang," a mixture of Spanish patois and calypso sung to tunes played on a string instrument like a mandolin.

Mas Camp Pub (corner of Ariapata and French Sts., Woodbrook, tel. 809/627–8449) is Port-of-Spain's most comfortable and dependable night spot. There are tables, a bar, an ample stage in one room, and an open-air patio with more tables and a bar with a TV. There's a kitchen if you're hungry, and **Hush,** which makes delicious fruit-flavored ice cream, is right next door. **Cricket Wicket** (149 Tragarete Rd., tel. 809/622–1808), a popular watering hole with a cupola-shape bar in the center, is a fine place to hear top bands, dance, or just sit and enjoy the nocturnal scenery (*see* Dining, *above*). The main area for liming in Trinidad is on **Western Main Road.** From 6 PM, locals gather here to see and be seen until the early hours of the morning. Currently the favorite hangout is **Swanky's** (69 Western Main Rd., tel. 809/622–0569), which you'll easily recognize by the large number of people gathered on the sidewalk outside drinking beer.

In the late afternoons the locals come to **Rafters** (6A Warner St., tel. 809/628–9258) to wind down and wind up. Later in the evening, it's mainly tourists and resembles a college frat party.

Tobago Nightlife on Tobago is generally confined to hotel-sponsored entertainment, which runs the gamut from steel-band performances to limbo dancers. Turtle Beach produces the most extravagant—and touristy—spectacles Wednesday and Sunday. In addition, **Kariwak Village** (tel. 809/639–8442) features a mélange of calypso and jazz. La Tropicale at the **Della Mira Guest House** (tel. 809/639–3531) in Scarborough features dancing on weekends and occasional live performances, usually during Carnival season. The **Foundation for the Arts** occasionally sponsors authentic calypso concerts, usually at Signal Hill High School. For information contact the Tourist Office at 809/639–2125.

Locals head for the discos—John Grant near Store Bay and the rambunctious Christie's in Scarborough—the Tobagan equivalent of a singles bar. The Starting Gate, an unlikely but ingratiating cross between an English pub and a community social hall, rocks with a DJ on weekends. The Drifter is another popular hangout.

Sunday nights at Buccoo, there is an informal hop, affectionately dubbed Sunday School, which takes place in the village at Henderson's disco. It's great fun. "Blockos" (spontaneous block parties) spring up all over the island; look for the hand-painted signs. Also of interest on Sundays are Harvest parties, when a particular village hosts a street party complete with food, soft drinks (guests buy their own beer), and music. Tobagonians from other villages come to see friends and make new ones. These occur throughout the year and are a great way to meet the locals.

26 Turks and Caicos Islands

*Updated by
Laurie Senz*

The Turks and Caicos Islands are relatively unknown except to collectors of beautiful beaches and scuba divers, who religiously return to these waters year after year. First settled by the English more than 200 years ago, the British Crown Colony of Turks and Caicos is renowned in two respects: Its booming banking and insurance institutions lure investors from the United States and elsewhere; and its offshore reef formation entices divers to a world of colorful marine life surrounding its 40 islands, only eight of which are inhabited.

The Turks and Caicos are two groups of islands in an archipelago lying 575 miles southeast of Miami and about 90 miles north of Haiti. Some 15,000 people live on the eight large islands and more than 40 small cays that have a total landmass of 193 square miles. The Turks Islands include Grand Turk, which is the capital and seat of government, and Salt Cay, with a population of about 200. According to local legend, these islands were named by early settlers who thought the scarlet blossoms on the local cactus resembled the Turkish fez.

Some 22 miles west of Grand Turk, across the 7,000-foot-deep Christopher Columbus Passage, is the Caicos group, which includes South, East, West, Middle, and North Caicos and Providenciales. South Caicos, Middle Caicos, North Caicos, and Providenciales (nicknamed Provo) are the only inhabited islands in this group; Pine Cay, Parrot Cay and Salt Cay are the only inhabited cays. "Caicos" is derived from *cayos,* the Spanish word for cay, and is believed to mean "string of islands."

These islands are one of the few places in the Caribbean where visitors can still experience a small-town ambience along with their sun, sea, and sand, but alas small town does not mean low prices. There are no fast-food restaurants or budget motel franchises on Turks and Caicos, and the hefty importation tax is reflected in everything from orange juice to room rates. Island-hopping among the Turks and Caicos is relatively expensive: A $30 round-trip on the ferry, plus taxi hire once you get there. Generally, these islands are best traveled by tourists who can pay at least moderate prices. Nevertheless, the recent introduction of major airlines and hotels has given rise to affordable niches. (Provo, for instance, now claims a bed-and-breakfast that charges $65 for up to two people.) Cost-conscious travelers willing to ferret out the smattering of affordable restaurants and rooms will find the islands accessible.

With an eye toward tourism dollars to create jobs and increase the standard of living, the government has devised a long-term development plan to improve the Turks' and Caicos' visibility in the Caribbean tourism market.

What It Will Cost These sample prices, meant only as a general guide, are for high season. A moderately priced small inn or hotel within walking distance of the beach is $125–$150 a night. Dinner at a moderately priced restaurant costs about $25; it's $10 or less at a budget spot. A rum punch is about $4 at a restaurant; a glass of wine averages $3.25, and a beer, about $2.50. Car rental is about $40 a day. A bus into town from most hotels on Providenciales runs $2–$4 one-way. A new public bus system on Grand Turk charges 50¢ one-way to any scheduled stop. Single-tank dives cost $30–$35; snorkel equipment rents for $7–$10 a day.

Before You Go

Tourist Information The **Turks and Caicos Islands Tourist Board** has a toll-free number on the islands (tel. 800/241–0824). **The Caribbean Tourist Organization** (20 E. 46th St., New York, NY 10017, tel. 212/682–0435) is another reliable source of information. In the United Kingdom, contact **Morris-Kevan International Ltd.** (International House, 47 Chase Side, Enfiled Middlesex EN2 6NB, tel. 081/367–5175). For hotel information, contact **The Turks & Caicos Resort Association** (tel. 800/2TC–ISLES).

Arriving and Departing
By Plane **Cayman Airways** (tel. 800/422–9626) flies from Miami to Provo daily except Wednesday and from Miami to Grand Turk on Tuesday. **American Airlines** (tel. 800/433–7300) flies daily between Miami and Provo. **Turks & Caicos Islands Airways** (tel. 809/94–64352 or 809/94–62709) serves Nassau from Provo three days a week.

From the Airport Taxis are available at the airports; expect to share a ride. Rates are fixed. A trip from Provo's airport to hotels is about $15. On Grand Turk, a cab from the airport to town is about $4; to hotels outside town, $5–$10. **Executive Tours** (tel. 809/94–64524, fax 809/94–15391) offers shuttle service on Provo between town and 11 key hotels and destinations for between $2 and $4. On Grand Turk, some hotels will arrange a pickup at the time you make reservations.

Turks and Caicos Islands

Mary Cays

Parrot Cay

Fort George Cay
Pine Cay

Big Water Cay
Little Water Cay

Providenciales

Caicos Passage

Sandy Point, **9**

North Caicos

Spanish Point

Highas Cay

Juniper Hole

Middle

South Bluff

Jubber Point

Northwest Point

West Caicos

C A I C O S   I S L A

Southwest Point

Vine Point

Ocean Hole

C A I C O S   B A N K

N

0 ____ 14 miles

0 ____ 21 km

White Cay

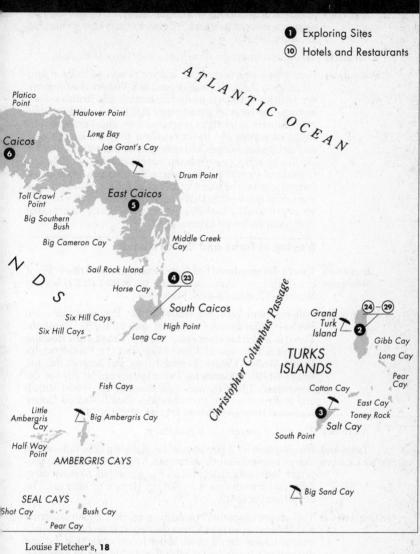

● Exploring Sites
⑩ Hotels and Restaurants

ATLANTIC OCEAN

Platico Point
Haulover Point
Long Bay
Joe Grant's Cay
Caicos ⑥
Drum Point
Toll Crawl Point
East Caicos ⑤
Big Southern Bush
Big Cameron Cay
Middle Creek Cay
N D S
Sail Rock Island
Horse Cay
④ ㉓
South Caicos
Six Hill Cays
High Point
Six Hill Cays
Long Cay
Fish Cays
Little Ambergris Cay
Big Ambergris Cay
Half Way Point
AMBERGRIS CAYS
SEAL CAYS
Shot Cay
Bush Cay
Pear Cay

Christopher Columbus Passage

Grand Turk Island
㉔—㉙
②
Gibb Cay
Long Cay
Pear Cay
TURKS ISLANDS
Cotton Cay
East Cay
Toney Rock
③ *Salt Cay*
South Point
Big Sand Cay

Louise Fletcher's, **18**
Prospect of Whitby Hotel, **22**
Salt Raker Inn, **26**
Treasure Beach Villas, **20**
Turks Head Inn, **29**
Turtle Cove Inn, **21**

Passports and Visas U.S. citizens need some proof of citizenship such as a birth certificate plus a photo ID or a current passport. British subjects require a current passport. All visitors must have an ongoing or return ticket.

Language The official language of the Turks and Caicos is English.

Precautions Petty crime does occur here, and you're advised to leave your valuables in the hotel's safe-deposit box. Visitors must remember to drive in the left lane while touring this British colony. Many of the recently paved roads lack lines and signs, while others are rocky enough to require a four-wheel-drive vehicle. Bring sunscreen and insect repellent to guard against day- and nighttime scourges, and watch out for manchineel, a native shrub with milky, poisonous sap that can cause painful blisters. Outside of Providenciales, where desalinators have transformed much of the island into a riot of flowers, water remains a precious commodity. Drink only from the decanter of fresh water provided by the hotel, but tap water is safe for brushing your teeth and other hygiene uses.

Staying in Turks and Caicos Islands

Important Addresses **Tourist Information:** The **Government Tourist Office** (Front St., Cockburn Town, Grand Turk, tel. 809/94–62321) is open Monday–Thursday 8–4:30, Friday 8–5.

Emergencies **Police:** Grand Turk, tel. 809/94–62299; Providenciales, tel. 809/94–64259; South Caicos, tel. 809/94–63299. **Hospitals:** There is a 24-hour emergency room at **Grand Turk Hospital** (Hospital Rd., tel. 809/94–62333) and the **Providenciales Health-Medical Center** (Leeward Hwy. and Airport Rd., tel. 809/94–64910). **Pharmacies:** Prescriptions can be filled at the **Government Clinic** (Grand Turk Hospital, tel. 809/94–62040) and in Provo, at the **Providenciales Health-Medical Center** (Leeward Hwy. and Airport Rd., tel. 809/94–64910).

Currency The unit of currency is U.S. dollars.

Taxes and Service Charges Hotels collect a 7% government tax and add a 10%–15% service charge to your bill. In a restaurant, a tip of 10%–15% is appropriate; some establishments add it to your bill, so check carefully. Taxi drivers expect a small tip. There is no sales tax. The departure tax is $15.

Getting Around Those more interested in swimming and diving than exploring will find that a cab to and from the airport is probably the only transportation they'll need. Major hotels are within walking distance of a beach, and others offer shuttle service. However, budget restaurants and other attractions on Provo are located about a $10 taxi trip from most hotels, making a scooter or rental car advisable for those not taking a meal plan at their hotel.

Taxis Taxis are unmetered, and rates, posted in the taxis, are regulated by the government. A trip between Provo's airport and most major hotels runs $15. On Grand Turk, a trip from the airport to town is about $4; from the airport to hotels outside town, $5–$10.

Ferries **Caicos Express** (tel. 809/94–67111 or 809/94–67258) offers two scheduled interisland ferries between Provo, Pine Cay, Middle Caicos, Parrot Cay, and North Caicos daily except Sunday.

Tickets cost $15 each way. Caicos Express also offers various guided tours to the out islands (*see* Guided Tours, *below*).

Rental Cars On Provo, **Budget** (tel. 809/94–64079) and **Highway** (tel. 809/94–52623) offer the lowest rates. On Grand Turk, try **Dutchie's Car Rental** (tel. 809/94–62244). Rates average $40–$50 per day.

Scooters Scooters are available at **The Honda Shop** (tel. 809/94–65585) and **Scooter Rental** (tel. 809/94–64684) for $25 per 24-hour day.

Buses A bus into town from most hotels on Providenciales runs $2–$4 one-way. A new public bus system on Grand Turk charges 50¢ one-way to any scheduled stop.

Telephones and Mail You can call the islands direct from the United States by dialing 809 and the number. To call the U.S. from Turks and Caicos, dial direct from most hotels, from some pay phones, and from **Cable and Wireless,** which has offices in Provo (tel. 809/94–64499) and Grand Turk (tel. 809/94–62200) that are open Monday–Thursday 8–4:30, Friday 8–4. You must dial 0, followed by the country code (1 for the United States and Canada; 44 for the United Kingdom), area code, and local number. To make local calls from public phones, you must purchase debit cards. Available in increments of $5, $10, and $20, these are inserted into phones like credit cards.

Postal rates for letters to the United States, Bahamas, and the Caribbean are 50¢ per half-ounce; postcards, 35¢. Letters to the United Kingdom and Europe, 65¢ per half-ounce; postcards, 45¢. Letters to Canada, Puerto Rico, and South America, 65¢; postcards, 45¢.

Opening and Closing Times Most offices are open weekdays from 8 or 8:30 till 4 or 4:30. Banks are open Monday–Thursday 8:30–2:30, Friday 8:30–12:30 and 2:30–4:30.

Guided Tours The cheapest and easiest way to see Provo is by bus. **Executive Tours** (tel. 809/94–64524) and **Turtle Tours** (tel. 809/94–65585) offer bus tours for $10 a person that take in all major sites and include a stop for drinks. Make reservations at least one day in advance. Although a bus tour is cheaper per person than a taxi tour, Providenciales is so small that a taxi tour costing $25 an hour for up to four people can take in the major sights in about an hour. (However, a full tour of the Conch Farm can run about 45 minutes to an hour, so be sure to get your driver to drop you off at the Conch Farm at the end of your taxi tour, then hop a cab back to your hotel.) Contact **Nell's Taxi** (tel. 809/94–65585 or 809/94–64393). There are no bus tours on Grand Turk, but a one-hour taxi tour is sufficient to see the island. Cost is $30 ($25 for each additional hour) for up to four people. Another good way to see the island is by bicycle (*see* Sports and the Outdoors, *below*).

If you'd like to tour any of the other islands, you'll find it's cheaper to go with an organized tour than to try to do it on your own. You can take a ferry on your own to Pine Cay, Parrot Cay, or North Caicos, but once you reach the islands, you would still need to hire a cab to get to the main attractions and beaches. **Caicos Express** (tel. 809/94–67111) offers various tours to and around these islands. Round-trip ferry passage to Middle Caicos, a two-hour cavern tour, land transportation, and swimming at Mudjian Harbour costs $76 per person—less than round-trip airfare alone would be, and a lot less hassle than going by yourself. A tour of North Caicos for $85 a person begins with a ferry tour of the Caicos Cays, followed by either a guided tour of North Caicos or a rental car to explore on your own, lunch at the island's leading hotel, and a guided tour of the Caribbean king crab farm. For $60 a person, Caicos Express's *Express Island Hopper* departs Turtle Cove Yacht Club for a six-hour boat run down the beaches of Provo, Pine, and Big Water Cays, a stop to feed the wild iguanas at Little Water Cay, a viewing of the submerged cannons off Ft. George's Cay National Park, shelling and swimming at Dellis Cay, and lunch with rum punch or soda.

Exploring Turks and Caicos Islands

Numbers in the margin correspond to points of interest on the Turks and Caicos Islands map.

Providenciales In the mid-18th century, so the story goes, a French ship was wrecked near here and the survivors were washed ashore on an island they gratefully christened La Providentielle. Under ❶ the Spanish, the name was changed to **Providenciales.**

Provo's 44 square miles are by far the most developed in the Turks and Caicos. With its rolling ridges and 12-mile beach, the island is a prime target for developers. More than 17 years ago a group of U.S. investors, including the DuPonts, Ludingtons, and Roosevelts, opened up this island for visitors and those seeking homesites in the Caribbean. In 1990 the island's first luxury resort, the **Ramada Turquoise Reef Resort & Casino,** opened, and with it, the island's first gourmet Italian restaurant. Provo is also the home of Club Mediterranée's showpiece, Club Med Turkoise, built in 1984. About 8,000 people live on Provo, a considerable number of whom are expatriate U.S. and Canadian businesspeople and retirees.

If you're exploring the island on your own, begin at **Sapadilla Bay**'s scenic view of inlets leading from the sea. From there, take in a guided tour and lecture at the world's only **conch farm.** Then drive by the ruins of the **Richmond Plantation** before heading to **Blue Hill,** a typical island community. Wrap up the day by driving to one of a few elevated spots on the island to enjoy a colorful sunset over **Chalk Sound.**

Downtown Provo, near Providenciales International Airport, is a cluster of stone and stucco buildings that house car-rental agencies, law offices, boutiques, banks, and other businesses.

Provo is home to the **Island Sea Center** (tel. 809/94–65330), on the northeast coast, where tourists can learn about the sea and its inhabitants. Here you'll find the **Caicos Conch Farm** (tel. 809/94–65849), a major mariculture operation where the mollusks are farmed commercially. You can tour the farm's facilities and geodesic dome, watch a video show, and take photos at the "hands-on" tank. Established by the PRIDE Foundation (Protection of Reefs and Islands from Degradation and Exploitation) and now funded by Into the Blue, the **JoJo Dolphin Project** is also here. It's named after a 7-foot male bottlenose dolphin who cruises these waters and enjoys playing with local divers. You can watch a video on JoJo and learn how to interact with him safely if you see him on one of your dives.

Grand Turk Horses and cattle wander around as if they owned the place, and the occasional donkey cart clatters by, carrying a load of water or freight. Fewer than 4,000 people live on this 7½ - square-mile island, although it's well known to divers for its Grand Turk's Wall, with a sheer drop to 7,000 feet.

② Front Street, the main drag, lazes along the western side of the island and eases through **Cockburn Town,** the colony's capital and seat of government. Buildings in the capital reflect the 19th-century Bermudian style of architecture, and the narrow streets are lined with low stone walls and old street lamps, now powered by electricity.

The **Turks & Caicos National Museum** opened last year in the restored Guinep House. One of the oldest native stone buildings in the islands, the museum now houses the Molasses Reef wreck of 1513, the earliest shipwreck discovered in the Americas, and natural history exhibits that include artifacts left by African, North American, Bermudian, French, Hispanic, and Taino settlers. *Tel. 809/94–62160. Admission: $5. Open weekdays 10–4, Sat. 10–1.*

Salt Cay A privately hired boat can ferry you from Grand Turk to this tiny 2½-square-mile dot that's home to about 200 people. The island was once a leading producer of salt, and visitors can still **③** see the old windmills, salt sheds, and salt ponds. **Balfour Town** boasts a few restaurants where you can stop for lunch and a drink, and a few stores stocking picnic provisions.

South Caicos **Cockburn Harbour,** the best natural harbor in the Caicos chain, **④** is home to the South Caicos Regatta, held each year in May. This 8½-square-mile island was once an important salt producer; today it's the heart of the fishing industry. Spiny lobster and queen conch may be found in the shallow Caicos bank to the west and are harvested for export by local processing plants. Bonefishing here is some of the best in the West Indies.

At the northern end of the island there are fine, white-sand beaches; the south coast is great for scuba diving along the drop-off; and the windward (east) side is excellent for snorkeling, where large stands of elkhorn and staghorn coral shelter a variety of small tropical fish.

East Caicos Uninhabited and accessible only by boat, **East Caicos** has on its **⑤** north coast a magnificent 17-mile beach. It was once a cattle range and the site of a major sisal-growing industry.

Middle Caicos The largest (48 square miles) and least-developed of the inhabited Turks and Caicos Islands, Middle Caicos is home to lime- **⑥** stone **Conch Bar Caves,** with their eerie underground salt lakes and milk-white stalactites and stalagmites. Archaeologists have discovered Arawak and Lucayo Indian artifacts in the caves and the surrounding area. Since telephones are a rare commodity here, the boats that dock here and the planes that land on the little airstrip provide the island's 270 residents with their main connection to the outside world.

North Caicos The **Prospect of Whitby Hotel** is on the north end of this 41- **⑦** square-mile island. To the south of Whitby is **Flamingo Pond,** a nesting place for the beautiful pink birds. If you take a taxi tour of the island, you'll see the ruins of the old plantations and, **⑧ ⑨** in the little settlements of **Kew** and **Sandy Point,** a profusion of tropical trees bearing limes, papayas, and custard apples. The beaches here are superb for shelling and lolling, and the waters offshore offer excellent snorkeling, scuba diving, and fishing.

Beaches

There are more than 230 miles of beaches in the Turks and Caicos Islands, ranging from secluded coves to miles-long stretches. Most beaches are soft coralline sand. Tiny uninhabited cays offer complete isolation for nude sunbathing and skinny-dipping. Many are accessible only by boat. All hotels in Provo and Grand Turk are within walking distance of a beach.

Big Ambergris Cay, an uninhabited cay about 14 miles beyond the Fish Cays, has a magnificent beach at **Long Bay.**

East Caicos, an uninhabited island accessible only by boat, boasts a magnificent 17-mile beach along its north coast.

Governor's Beach, a long white strip on the west coast of **Grand Turk,** is one of the nicest beaches on this island.

The north and east coasts of **North Caicos** are bordered by great beaches for swimming, scuba diving, snorkeling, and fishing. **Pine Cay,** a private upscale retreat, has a 2½-mile strip of beach—the most beautiful in the archipelago.

A fine white-sand beach stretches 12 miles along the northeast coast of **Providenciales.** Other splendid beaches are at **Sapadilla Bay** and rounding the tip of the northwest point of the island.

There are superb beaches on the north coast of **Salt Cay,** as well as at **Big Sand Cay** 7 miles to the south.

Only in **South Caicos** are the beaches small and unremarkable, but the vibrant reef makes it a popular destination for divers.

Sports and the Outdoors

Bicycling Much of Provo is steep, and the many unpaved roads kick up clouds of dust with each passing motorist. Still, there is very little on the island that can't be seen by bike, and it's an inexpensive way to explore. Bikes can be rented at **Island Princess Hotel** at The Bight (tel. 809/94–64260) for $8 per day. In Grand Turk, **Salt Raker Inn** (Duke St., tel. 809/94–62260) rents bikes to guests for $10 per day, $40 per week; **Hotel Kittina** (tel. 809/94–62232) also rents bikes to nonguests for $10 a day.

Boating **Dive Provo** (Ramada Turquoise Reef Resort, Provo, tel. 809/94–65040) rents single-seater kayaks for $10 an hour and two-seaters for $15 an hour. They also rent laser sailboats for $20 an hour and provide beginner instruction for the sailboats for $40 (up to two hours).

Golf This arid archipelago introduced a 6,529-yard golf course on Providenciales in 1992. **Provo Golf Club** (tel. 809/94–695991) is an 18-hole par-72 championship course, designed by Karl Litten. The turf is sprinkled in green islands over 12 acres of natural limestone outcroppings, creating a desert-style design of narrow "target areas" and sandy waste areas—a formidable challenge to anyone playing from the championship tees. Greens fees are $65 plus $15 for a mandatory electric cart.

Scuba Diving Diving is the top attraction here. (All divers must carry and present a valid certificate card.) These islands are surrounded by a reef system of more than 200 square miles—much of it unexplored. Grand Turk's famed wall drops more than 7,000 feet and is one side of a 22-mile-wide channel called the Christopher Columbus Passage. From January through March, an estimated 6,000 eastern Atlantic humpback whales swim through this passage en route to their winter breeding grounds. There are undersea cathedrals, coral gardens, and countless tunnels. Among the operations that provide instruction, equipment rentals, underwater video equipment, and trips are **Omega Divers** (Hotel Kittina, Grand Turk, tel. 809/94–62232 or 800/255–1966), **Blue Water Divers** (Salt Raker Inn, Grand Turk, tel. 809/94–62432), **Off the Wall Divers** (Grand Turk, tel. 809/94–62159 or 809/94–62517), **Barracuda Divers** (South Caicos, tel. 809/94–63360), **Dive Provo** (Ramada Turquoise Reef Resort, Provo, tel. 809/94–65040), **Flamingo Divers** (Provo, tel. 809/94–64193), **Provo Turtle Divers** (Provo, tel. 809/94–64232 or 800/328–5285), and **Porpoise Divers** (Salt Cay, tel. 809/94–66927). Single-tank dives cost $30–$35, two-tank dives average $60, and night dives run about $40. Scuba gear rental costs about $15 when you book a boat dive.

Note: A modern decompression chamber is located on Provo (tel. 809/94–64242) on the grounds of the Erebus Inn compound. Divers in need on Grand Turk are airlifted to Provo—a 30-minute flight.

Sea Excursions The *Island Diver* (tel. 809/94–64393), a 70-foot motor cruiser, does barbecue and snorkel cruises to uninhabited islands. A half-day snorkel and sail cruise on the 37-foot catamaran *Beluga* (tel. 809/94–65040) is $39 a person; sunset cruises are $25 a person, $40 a couple. Cruises aboard the 56-foot trimaran *Tao* (tel. 809/94–64393) cost $59 a person for a day-long trip that includes snorkeling, lunch, and drinks. **Dive Provo** (tel. 809/94–65040) offers two-hour glass-bottom boat rides for $20 a person. The Provo Turtle Divers' 20-foot glass-bottom *Grouper Snooper* (Provo, tel. 809/94–64232) offers sightseeing and snorkeling excursions.

Snorkeling **Dive Provo** (Provo, tel. 809/94–65040), **Blue Water Divers** (tel. 809/94–62432), **Omega Divers** (Grand Turk, tel. 809/94–62232), **Provo Turtle Divers** (Provo, tel. 809/94–64232), **Turtle Cove Inn** (Provo, tel. 809/94–64203), and **Flamingo Divers** (Provo, tel. 809/94–64193) offer snorkeling, boat trips, and equipment rentals. Boat trips cost $25–$35 and include all snorkel gear. Gear rental alone costs $7–$10.

Tennis There are two lighted courts at **Turtle Cove Inn** (Provo, tel. 809/94–64203), eight courts (four lighted) at **Club Med Turkoise** (Provo, tel. 809/94–64491), one court at the **Meridian Club** (Pine Cay, tel. 800/225–4255), two courts at the **Erebus Inn** (Grand Turk, tel. 809/94–64240), and two courts at the **Ramada Turquoise Reef Resort** (Provo, tel. 809/94–65555). Guests at all of the resorts play free. Nonguests can play at the Erebus Inn for $10 an hour (day), $20 an hour (evening). Club Med Turkoise has a half-day tennis package for nonguests for $50.

Waterskiing Water-skiers will find the calm turquoise water ideal for long-distance runs. **Dive Provo** (Ramada Turquoise Reef Resort, Provo, tel. 809/94–65040) will take you at $35 for a 15-minute run.

Windsurfing Rental and instruction are available at **Prospect of Whitby Hotel** (North Caicos, tel. 800/346–67119) and **Dive Provo**

(Ramada Turquoise Reef Resort, Provo, tel. 809/94–65040). The latter offers the Mistral School program for $20 an hour and rents boards for the same price.

Shopping

These are not shop-'til-you-drop islands. The only craft items native to the Turks and Caicos are the beautiful baskets woven from the indigenous top plant; these are sold at the airport.

Greensleeves (MarketPlace, Provo, tel. 809/94–64147) is the place to go for paintings by local artists, island-made rag rugs, baskets, jewelry, and sisal mats and bags.

Local Color (MarketPlace, and at Le Deck Hotel, Provo, tel. 809/94–65547) sells art and sculpture made by local artists, as well as native basketry, hand-painted tropical clothing, tie-dyed pareos, and silk-screened T-shirts.

Dining

Like everything else on these islands, dining out is a laid-back affair, which is not to say that it is cheap. Because of the high cost of importing all edibles, the cost of a meal is usually higher than that of a comparable meal in the United States. The most reasonably priced dishes are usually the local conch and the catch of the day. Reservations are not required, and dress is casual.

As recently as seven years ago, grocery shopping was limited to what the twin-engine plane delivered from Miami once a week. Today, however, Provo's grocery stores, **Island Pride Supermarket** (Butterfield Sq.) and **BWI Trading** downtown offer delicacies such as fresh arugula. Prices reflect the ubiquitous import tax, but as high as they seem, they remain the budget alternative to eating out. Gourmet items and whole-bean coffee ground to order are available at **Top O'The Cove** on Leeward Hwy. On Grand Turk, get groceries at **Sarah's Shopping Centre** (Frith St.).

Highly recommended restaurants are indicated by a star ★.

Category	Cost*
Moderate	$15–$25
Inexpensive	$10–$15
Budget	under $10

per person, excluding drinks, service, and sales tax (7%)

Grand Turk **Salt Raker Inn.** In this rustic, informal patio restaurant you may start with tomato and mozzarella salad or melon and ginger. Popular entrées include lobster in cream and sherry sauce, barbecued steak, and seafood curry. For dessert, try apple pie. The Sunday dinner and sing-along is a fun way to end the week. *Salt Raker Inn, tel. 809/94–62260. AE, D, MC, V. Inexpensive-Moderate.*

Sandpiper. Candles flicker on the Sandpiper's terrace beside a flower-filled courtyard. The restaurant's blackboard specialties may include pork chops with applesauce, lobster, filet mignon, or seafood platter. *Hotel Kittina, tel. 809/94–62232. AE, D, MC, V. Inexpensive.*

The Poop Deck. Known for its savory island fare, this restaurant serves conch in a variety of guises. The 25 seats fill up fast with locals and expats who come for the spicy island-fried chicken. Dinners cost $7–$10, and come with rice or potato and a salad. *Front St., no phone. No credit cards. Budget.*

Regal Beagle This popular local eatery is the place to get native specialties, such as cracked conch, minced lobster, and fish-and-chips. The atmosphere is casual, the portions large, and the prices easy on your wallet. *Hospital Rd., tel. 809/94–62274. No credit cards. Budget.*

Providenciales **Dora's.** Open seven days from 7 AM until the last person leaves
★ the bar, this immaculate restaurant specializes in island fare— turtle, shredded lobster, and tasty conch chowder. With its comfortable booths, pretty print-and-lace tablecloths, hanging plants, and Haitian art, Dora's is a favorite haunt of locals and expatriates alike. Soups ($4) come with homemade bread, and entrées such as lobster, conch Creole, cracked conch, and grilled pork come with a choice of vegetable. The popular $20 all-you-can-eat buffet on Mondays and Thursdays includes the full seafood menu plus transportation to and from your hotel. It's a little out of the way, but worth the trip. *Leeward Hwy., tel. 809/94–64558. AE, D, MC, V. Budget–Moderate.*

★ **Sharney's Restaurant and Bar.** Although most of the prices at this restaurant in the Erebus Inn are in our Moderate range, you can enjoy a budget lunch or dinner here by ordering from the abbreviated bar menu. Served from 10 AM to 10 PM, the menu offers gourmet ravioli with fillings that change daily ($6), hamburgers ($7), finger foods, and regional favorites such as conch chowder and conch fritters. In their lunch and dinner menus, new local owners are concentrating on English favorites prepared to order, and their lunch of fish-and-chips ($10) doesn't disappoint: Moist chunks of native grouper lightly battered and served with crisply thin, skin-on potatoes. The view from the restaurant is incomparable, and a band provides music on Friday nights. *Erebus Inn, Turtle Cove Rd., tel. 809/94–64204. AE, D, MC, V. Budget–Moderate.*

★ **Hey, José.** This patio restaurant with atrium is popular for such Tex-Mex treats as tacos, tostadas, nachos, burritos, fajitas, and margaritas. You can build your own pizza. *Leeward Hwy., tel. 809/94–64812. AE, MC, V. Closed Sun. Budget–Inexpensive.*

Hong Kong Restaurant. A no-frills place with plain wood tables and chairs, the Hong Kong offers lobster with ginger and green onions, chicken with black-bean sauce, sliced duck with salted mustard greens, and sweet-and-sour chicken. Dine in, delivery, and takeout are all options. *Leeward Hwy., tel. 809/94–65678. AE, MC, V. Budget–Inexpensive.*

Jimmy's Dinner House & Bar. This favorite local spot features red-checked tablecloths flanked by polished oak chairs with green upholstery. The menu includes pizza, pasta, ribs, and steaks. Early Bird specials, served 5:30–7:30 PM for $9.95, include panfried grouper, charbroiled sirloin steak, and a hot beef sandwich served with salad. *At Turtle Cove, tel. 809/94–15575. AE, MC, V. No lunch. Budget.*

★ **Top O' the Cove Gourmet Delicatessen.** Open every day from 7 AM to 3:30 PM, this tiny café and delicatessen is the island's best surprise, offering a rare cup of real cappuccino or espresso, 50 varieties of cheese pâtés, whole-bean coffees, boutique wines, and a breakfast and lunch menu with the lowest prices on Provo. Continental breakfasts to eat in or take out top out at $2.95 for a meat or ham-and-egg croissant, while assorted muffins and doughnuts sell for less than $1. The costliest lunch—a club sub—is $5.95; the most expensive salad, an antipasto platter, is $4.95. *Leeward Hwy., tel. 809/94–64694. No credit cards. No dinner. Budget.*

Yum Yum's. One of the newer eateries in town, this restaurant features native dishes, deli sandwiches, ice cream, yogurt, and fresh pastries served in a modern, air-conditioned setting. *Town Centre Mall, Butterfield Sq., tel. 809/94–64480. No credit cards. Budget.*

Lodging

In general, Provo hotels and inns are a bit more expensive than those on Grand Turk, Middle Caicos, or South Caicos. North Caicos and Salt Cay both tend to have either inexpensive guest houses or expensive hideaway resorts, with few or no moderately priced inns. Although we do list a couple of properties on the out islands, most affordable lodging is located on Provo or Grand Turk. Rustic places on the more remote islands are rustic indeed, and in most cases we do not recommend them.

Affordable accommodations here range from renovated properties with charm, air-conditioning, and modern amenities to basic digs with simple furnishings and few extras. Most budget inns and guest houses are not on the beach, although those on Provo and Grand Turk are usually within walking distance or are a short bus ride away. These cheaper properties generally do not have a restaurant or meal plans. On Provo, where inexpensive restaurants are usually off the beaten track, you will need to rent a car to get to your meals, or consider staying at a more expensive hotel and taking a meal plan. If you're staying in town on Grand Turk, you'll be within walking distance of several inexpensive restaurants.

If you're a diver, you can save money by taking advantage of one of the many packages offered by properties here. These provide considerable savings, so inquire when you call.

Highly recommended lodgings are indicated by a star ★.

Category	Cost*
Moderate	$110–$140
Inexpensive	$95–$110
Budget	under $95

*All prices are for a standard double room for two, excluding 7% tax and a 10% service charge. To estimate rates for hotels offering MAP, add $30–$45 per person per day to the above price ranges.

Grand Turk
★ **Hotel Kittina.** This family-owned hostelry is the largest hotel on Grand Turk. The sleek, balconied, air-conditioned suites with kitchens, which sit on a gleaming white-sand beach, barely squeak into our Moderate price range, but you'll find more affordable units in the older main house across the street, which oozes island atmosphere. These main-house rooms are simple;

strong winds blow through the rooms and keep things so cool you don't need the ceiling fans. Be sure to catch the hotel's occasional Friday-night poolside barbecue. *Duke St., Box 42, Grand Turk, tel. 809/94–62232 or 800/548–8462, fax 809/94–62877. 23 rooms, 20 suites. Facilities: restaurant, 2 bars, pool, boutique, Omega Dive Shop, T&C Travel Agency, scooter rentals, windsurfing, baby-sitting, room service, boat rentals, ice-cream parlor. AE, MC, V. EP, MAP. Inexpensive–Moderate.*

★ **Coral Reef Resort.** These modern, air-conditioned efficiency, one-, and two-bedroom units sit on a ridge on the eastern coast, where you can stroll out of your room and onto the beach. It's a combination apartment-hotel, with each unit boasting contemporary furnishings and a complete electric kitchen. *Box 10, Grand Turk, tel. 809/94–62055 or 800/243–4954, fax 809/94–62911. 21 rooms. Facilities: restaurant, bar, tennis, pool, boutique, mini-fitness center, water sports arranged with dive operations. AE, MC, V. EP, MAP. Inexpensive.*

Salt Raker Inn. Across the street from the beach, this galleried house was the home of a Bermudian shipwright 180 years ago. The rooms are not elegant, but are individually decorated and have a homey atmosphere. Accommodations include a garden house with screened porches. *Duke St., Box 1, Grand Turk, tel. 809/94–62260, fax 809/94–62432. In U.K., 44 Birchington Rd., London NW6 4LJ, tel. 071/328–6474. 9 rooms, 1 suite. Facilities: restaurant, bar, dive packages with Blue Water Diving. AE, D, MC, V. EP. Inexpensive.*

Turks Head Inn. Grand Turk's only bed-and-breakfast is located in one of the island's oldest buildings, a white and peach colonial inn dating from the mid-1800s. No two rooms are alike, and each is furnished with antiques. Two of the six have enclosed balconies that lengthen the rooms in order to accommodate rollaway beds for up to two children. Guests have a view of the garden and easy access to the beach, located across the road. The simple, air-conditioned rooms feature private shower baths and TVs; there are no telephones. Breakfast is included in the room rate (which is the same year-round), and you can negotiate additional meal plans with the owner, Xavier Tonneau. *Duke St., Box 58, Grand Turk, tel. 809/94–62466, fax 809/94–62825. 6 units. Facilities: restaurant, bar, dive packages. AE, MC, V. CP. Budget.*

Providenciales **Le Deck Hotel & Beach Club.** Just three years old, this 27-room ★ pink hostelry was built in classic Bermudian style around a tropical courtyard that opens onto a tiki hut- and palm tree-dotted beach on Grace Bay. Popular with divers, it offers clean rooms with tile floors, color TV, and air-conditioning. The atmosphere is informal and lively, with a mostly thirtysomething-and-over crowd. *Grace Bay, Box 144, Provo, tel. 809/94–65547 or 800/528–1905, fax 809/94–65770. 27 rooms, including 2 honeymoon suites. Facilities: restaurant, bar, pool, boutique, water sports. AE, D, MC, V. CP, MAP. Moderate.*

★ **Erebus Inn Resort.** Popular with divers, this hotel has a prime location within walking distance of major dive operations, five affordable restaurants, and a shopping center. Guests can walk or take the hotel's shuttle to the beach and Smith's Reef. Deluxe poolside rooms, which fall into the lower end of our Moderate range, are air-conditioned, with 13-channel cable TVs and phones. Four units in the older chalet are less expensive and have twin beds and shower baths; they do not have TVs, and air-conditioning costs an additional $20. *Turtle Cove, Box*

238, *Provo, tel. 809/94–64240, fax 809/94–64704. 30 rooms. Facilities: restaurant, bar, 2 pools (1 saltwater), fitness center, aqua aerobics, 2 lighted tennis courts. AE, MC, V. EP, MAP. Inexpensive–Moderate.*

Turtle Cove Inn. Occupying 1¹/₂ acres, this quiet two-story inn is geared toward tennis players, divers, and boaters. It offers free boat shuttles to a nearby beach and snorkeling reef and is an easy walk to several nearby beaches. Tile-floored rooms overlook a flagstone terrace and pool and include a TV, phone, and air-conditioning; eight also have minifridges. A handful of good restaurants are within walking distance. The hotel will arrange sailing, fishing, snorkeling, scuba, parasailing, and dune buggy excursions, as well as island picnics. *Box 131, Provo, tel. 809/94–64203 or 800/633–7411, fax 809/94–64040. Facilities: 2 restaurants, 2 bars, lounge, game room, 2 lighted tennis courts, pool, marina, 3 dive shops nearby. AE, D, MC, V. EP. Inexpensive–Moderate.*

Louise Fletcher's. The ambience at Provo's only bed-and-breakfast is more utilitarian British than quaint New England. With "natural" air-conditioning and a nearby pay phone, this tidy house with beach-towel curtains is not for those bent on luxury, but you will get clean lodging at a cheap price. The property is a long block from the beach; bicycles are available for rental. The two apartments each have a private bath, kitchen, and separate entrances. The guest room has a shared bath and access to the owner's kitchen. Continental breakfast and the company of the charming Canadian proprietress's dog and cat are included for the $65-a-day price for up to two, or $440 a week ($15 for an extra person). *Box 273, Provo, tel. 809/94–65878. 2 apartments, 1 room. Facilities: bicycle rental. No credit cards; personal checks accepted. CP. Budget.*

South Caicos **Club Carib Harbor Hotel.** Within walking distance of the township, this small resort overlooking Cockburn Harbour and the fishing district has simple, functional rooms with air-conditioning and color TV in the six waterfront suites. The other 12 units are single rooms, without air-conditioning. The hotel is on the beach, with a restaurant on the premises and another nearby. Be prepared for very basic accommodations. *Box 1, South Caicos, tel. 809/94–63360. 12 rooms, 6 suites. Facilities: restaurant, bar. AE, D, MC, V. EP, MAP. Inexpensive.*

North Caicos **Prospect of Whitby Hotel.** This secluded retreat is a quiet get-★ away located on a 7-mile-long beach. If you want them, diversions can include windsurfing, snorkeling, and bonefishing. The spacious rooms are tasteful island-basic with air-conditioning. Suites are out of our price range unless shared (they can sleep up to five). Most guests eat at the hotel, where the food is excellent; there is another hotel with restaurant within walking distance. *Kew Post Office, North Caicos, tel. 809/94–67119, fax 809/94–67114. 28 rooms, 4 suites. Facilities: restaurant, bar, pool, bicycles, tennis, windsurfing, tour desk. AE, MC, V. EP, MAP. Moderate.*

Villa and Most of the rentals on Turks and Caicos are on Provo, although **Apartment Rental** you can find a few cottage rentals on the out islands. At press time, there were no recommended rentals on Grand Turk.

Casaurina Cottages. Overlooking the south side of Providenciales are these pleasant, newly modernized one- and two-bedroom apartments. Each comes with a kitchen, a sleep sofa in the living room, weekly maid service, cable TV, a phone, and a ceiling fan. There is no air-conditioning, which can make them uncomfortable in the summer. Chairs and lounges are provided for use on the adjacent beach or large sun deck. All rooms come with twin beds, and each cottage accommodates four people. *Provo, tel. 809/94–64687, fax 809/94–64895. 3 units. No credit cards. Moderate.*

Treasure Beach Villas. These one- and two-bedroom self-catering apartments have fully equipped kitchens, fans, and Provo's 12 miles of white sandy beach for beachcombing and snorkeling. It's best to have a car or scooter here, or you can take the bus to the nearby grocery store and restaurants. *The Bight, tel. 809/94–64325, fax 809/94–64108. Box 8409, Hialeah, FL 33012. 8 single, 10 double rooms. Facilities: pool, tennis court. AE, D, MC, V. EP. Inexpensive–Moderate.*

Off-Season Bets Late April to the end of November is off-season here, when hotel rates drop 15%–20%. **Ramada Turquoise Reef Resort & Casino** (Box 205, Provo, tel. 809/94–65555 or 800/228–9898) and the **Club Med Turkoise** (Provo, tel. 809/94–65500 or 800/CLUB-MED) are two upscale resorts that have rooms available in our Moderate range. If apartment rental appeals to you, the pricey **Ocean Club** (Box 240, Provo, tel. 809/94–65880 or 800/223–6510) has efficiency suites and ocean-view studios.

Nightlife

On Provo, a full band plays native, reggae, and contemporary music on Tuesday and Thursday nights at the **Erebus Inn** (tel. 809/94–64240). **Le Deck** (tel. 809/94–65547) offers one-armed bandits every night. The island's liveliest lounge can be found at the **Ramada Turquoise Reef Resort** (tel. 809/94–65555) disco, where a musician plays to the mostly tourist crowd. The Ramada is also the location of **Port Royale** (tel. 809/94–65508), the island's only gambling casino. **Disco Elite** (Airport Rd., no phone) sports strobe lights and an elevated dance floor.

27 The U.S. Virgin Islands

St. Thomas, St. Croix, St. John

Updated by Heidi Waldrop and Denise Nolty

It is the combination of the familiar and the exotic found in the United States Virgin Islands that defines this "American Paradise" and explains much of its appeal. The effort to be all things to all people—while remaining true to the best of itself—has created a sometimes paradoxical blend of island serenity and American practicality in this U.S. territory 1,000 miles from the southern tip of the U.S. mainland.

The postcard images you'd expect from a tropical paradise are here: Stretches of beach arc into the distance, and white sails skim across water so blue and clear it stuns the senses; red-roof houses add their spot of color to the green hillsides' mosaic, along with the orange of the flamboyant tree, the red of the hibiscus, the magenta of the bougainvillea, and the blue stone ruins of old sugar mills. The other part of the equation are all those things that make it so easy and appealing to visit this cluster of islands. The official language is English, the money is the dollar, and there's cable TV, Pizza Hut, and McDonald's.

Your destination here will be St. Thomas (13 miles long); its neighbor St. John (9 miles long); or, 40 miles to the south, St. Croix (23 miles long). A pro/con thumbnail sketch of these three might have it that St. Thomas is bustling (hustling) and the place for shopping and discos (commercial glitz and overdevelopment); St. Croix is more Danish, picturesque, and rural (more provincial and duller, particularly after dark); and St. John is matchless in the beauty of its National Park Service-protected land and beaches (a one-village island mostly for the rich or for campers). Surely not everything will suit your fancy, but chances are that between the three islands you'll find your own idea of paradise.

With all this diversity, the budget traveler has plenty of options. Amid the glittering, $300-a-night resorts on St. Thomas, you'll find small hotels, bed-and-breakfasts, and condominium rentals. Those staying at campgrounds on St. John, where a bare site on the beach can be had for as little as $14 a night, share the same magnificent parkland and beaches as are enjoyed by guests at luxury resorts. On St. Croix, small inns and less-expensive properties are the rule rather than the exception.

The U.S.V.I. offer other ways to save. Plenty of nonstop flights to St. Thomas, with direct service to St. Croix, mean you won't have the additional cost of an island-hopper flight. (St. John is just a $7 ferry ride from St. Thomas.) On St. Thomas you can find cheap eats (if you don't mind fast food) and a fairly good bus system that can get you around much of the island.

What It Will Cost These sample prices, meant only as a general guide, are for high season. Expect to pay around $90 a night for an inexpensive hotel. Bed-and-breakfast places can be as low as $55 for two (with shared bath); for a private bath, prices climb to $75–$135 for two. A two-bedroom villa sleeping four rents for $1,500–$3,000 a week. You can pay as little as $14 a night for a tent site on St. John, but it's about $80 for one of the lovely tent-cottages at Maho Bay Camp. On St. Thomas, a budget lunch costs about $6; a dinner, about $10. At the West Indian and Latin restaurants on St. Croix and St. John, a filling dinner can be had for $5–$7. Rum punches cost around $3.50; a glass of house wine ranges from $3 to $4.50; a glass of beer, $2.50–$3. While car rental on St. Thomas is steep—daily rates range from $45 to $55—it's more reasonable on the other two islands, with economy cars renting for about $25–$30 a day. A taxi ride from Charlotte Amalie to the beach is about $4 a person for two people sharing a cab. A single-tank dive costs about $55 (including all equipment rental) on St. Thomas, a little less on St. Croix and St. John. Snorkel equipment rents for about $10 a day.

Before You Go

Tourist Information Information about the United States Virgin Islands is available through the following **U.S.V.I. Government Tourist Offices** (225 Peachtree St., Suite 760, Atlanta, GA 30303, tel. 404/688–0906, fax 404/525–1102; 122 S. Michigan Ave., Suite 1270, Chicago, IL 60603, tel. 312/461–0180, fax 312/461–0765; 3460 Wilshire Blvd., Suite 412, Los Angeles, CA 90010, tel. 213/739–0138, fax 213/739–2005; 2655 Le Jeune Rd., Suite 907, Coral Gables, FL 33134, tel. 305/442–7200, fax 305/445–9044; 1270 6th Ave., New York, NY 10020, tel. 212/582–4520, fax 212/581–3405; 900 17th Ave. NW, Suite 500, Washington, DC 20006, tel. 202/293–3707, fax 202/785–2542; 1300 Ashford St., Condado, Santurce, Puerto Rico 00907, tel. 809/724–3816, fax 809/724–7223; and 2 Cinnamon Row, Plantation Wharf, York Place, London, England SW11 3TW, tel. 071/978–5262, telex 27231, fax 071/924–3171).

You can also call the Division of Tourism's toll-free number (tel. 800/USVI–INFO).

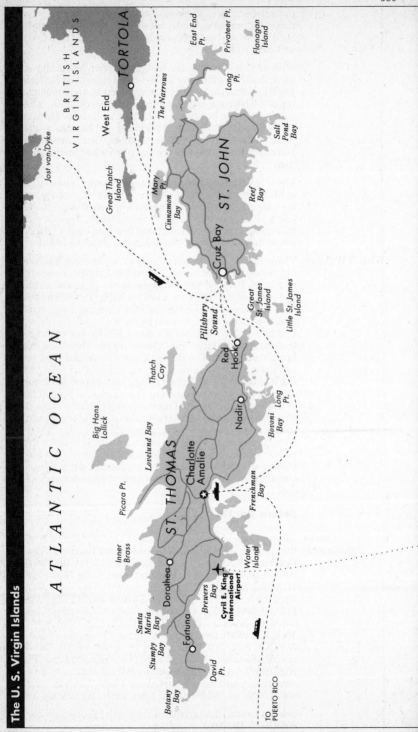

The U. S. Virgin Islands

ATLANTIC OCEAN

TORTOLA

West End

BRITISH
VIRGIN ISLANDS

Jost van Dyke

Great Thatch
Island

The Narrows

Mary
Pt.

Cinnamon
Bay

Cruz Bay

ST. JOHN

East End
Pt.

Privateer Pt.

Flanagan
Island

Long
Pt.

Salt
Pond
Bay

Reef
Bay

Pillsbury
Sound

Great
St. James
Island

Little St. James
Island

Thatch
Cay

Red
Hook

Big Hans
Lollick

Loveland Bay

Nadir

Long
Pt.

Bovoni
Bay

Frenchman
Bay

Picara Pt.

ST. THOMAS

Charlotte
Amalie

Inner
Brass

Dorothea

Water
Island

Santa
Maria
Bay

Brewers
Bay

Cyril E. King
International
Airport

Stumpy
Bay

Fortuna

Botany
Bay

David
Pt.

TO
PUERTO RICO

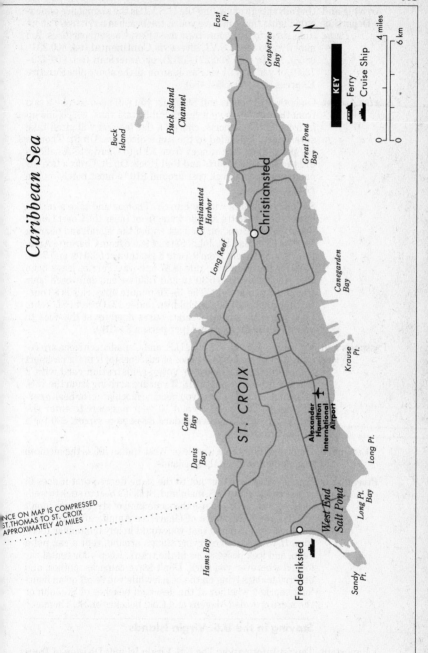

Caribbean Sea

East Pt.

Grapetree Bay

Buck Island Channel

Buck Island

Great Pond Bay

Christiansted Harbor

Christiansted

Long Reef

Canegarden Bay

Krause Pt.

ST. CROIX

Alexander Hamilton International Airport

Cane Bay

Davis Bay

Long Pt.

Long Pt. Bay

Hams Bay

West End Salt Pond

Frederiksted

Sandy Pt.

NCE ON MAP IS COMPRESSED
ST.THOMAS TO ST. CROIX
APPROXIMATELY 40 MILES

KEY

Ferry

Cruise Ship

N

4 miles

6 km

Arriving and Departing
By Plane
One advantage of visiting the U.S.V.I. is the abundance of non-stop flights that can have you at the beach in a relatively short time, three to four hours from most East Coast departures. You may fly into the U.S.V.I. direct via **Continental** (tel. 800/231–0856), **Delta** (tel. 800/221–1212), or **American** (tel. 800/433–7300), or you may fly via San Juan on all the above plus **Sunaire Express** (tel. 809/495–2480).

From the Airport
On both St. Thomas and St. Croix you will need to take a taxi from the airport to your hotel. Public taxi vans, which line up in front of the airports, charge a flat fee and will often take several people headed in the same direction. On St. Thomas the per-person rate ranges from $3 into Charlotte Amalie to $10 to East End resorts and Red Hook. On St. Croix a taxi for one or two people will cost around $10 to most hotels on the island.

St. John travelers will fly into St. Thomas and take a taxi to either the Charlotte Amalie waterfront (near the Coast Guard dock) or Red Hook, on the east end of the island, and board a ferry to Cruz Bay, St. John. Ferries leave from Charlotte Amalie every two hours from 9 AM to 3 PM, then at 5:30 PM and 7 PM. Fare for the 45-minute ride is $7 one-way. Ferries leave from Red Hook weekdays 6:30 AM and 7:30 AM, and daily each hour from 8 AM to midnight. The 15–20-minute ferry ride is $3 one-way for adults, $1.50 for children under 12. Once in St. John, take one of the open-air safari buses lined up at the dock to your hotel or campground (per person $3–$10).

Passports and Visas
Upon entering the U.S.V.I., U.S. and Canadian citizens are required to present some proof of citizenship, if not a passport then a birth certificate or voter-registration card with a driver's license or photo ID. If you are arriving from the U.S. mainland or Puerto Rico, you need no inoculation or health certificate. Britons need a valid 10-year passport to enter the U.S.V.I. (cost: £15 for a standard 32-page passport, £30 for a 94-page passport).

Language
English, often with a Creole or West Indian lilt, is the medium of communication in these islands.

Precautions
Crime exists here, but not to the same degree that it does in larger cities on the U.S. mainland. Still, it's best to stick to well-lit streets at night and use the same kind of street sense (don't wander the back alleys of Charlotte Amalie after five rum punches, for example) that you would in any unfamiliar territory. If you plan on carrying things around, rent a car, not a Jeep, and lock possessions in the trunk. Keep your rental car locked wherever you park. Don't leave cameras, purses, and other valuables lying on the beach while you're off on an hour-long snorkel, whether at the deserted beaches of St. John or the more crowded Magens and Coki beaches on St. Thomas.

Staying in the U.S. Virgin Islands

Important Addresses
Tourist Information: The **U.S. Virgin Islands Division of Tourism** has an office in St. Thomas (Box 6400, Charlotte Amalie, U.S. Virgin Islands 00804, tel. 809/774–8784, fax 809/774–4390), St. Croix (Box 4538, Christiansted, U.S. Virgin Islands 00822, tel. 809/773–0495, and on the pier, Strand St., Frederiksted, U.S. Virgin Islands 00840, tel. 809/772–0357), and St. John (Box 200, Cruz Bay, U.S. Virgin Islands 00830, tel. 809/776–6450).

There are two **Visitor Centers** in Charlotte Amalie: one across from Emancipation Square and one at Havensight Mall. In St. Croix, go to the Old Scale House at the waterfront in Christiansted, across from Fort Christiansvaern. The **National Park Service** also has visitor centers at the ferry areas on St. Thomas (Red Hook) and St. John (Cruz Bay).

Emergencies **Police:** Dial 915. **Hospitals:** The emergency room of **St. Thomas Hospital** (tel. 809/776–8311) in Sugar Estate, Charlotte Amalie, is open 24 hours a day. In Christiansted there is the **St. Croix Hospital and Community Health Center** (6 Diamond Bay, north of Sunny Isle Shopping Center, on Route 79, tel. 809/778–6311 or 809/778–5895), and in Frederiksted, the **Frederiksted Health Center** (tel. 809/772–1992 or 809/772–0750). On St. John contact the **Morris F. DeCastro Clinic** (Cruz Bay, tel. 809/776–6400) or call an **emergency medical technician** (tel. 809/776–6222).

Air Ambulance: Bohlke International Airways (tel. 809/778–9177) operates out of the airport in St. Croix. **Air Medical Services** (tel. 800/443–0013) and **Air Ambulance Network** (tel. 800/327–1966) also service the area from Florida.

Coast Guard: For emergencies on St. Thomas or St. John, call the **Marine Safety Detachment** (tel. 809/776–3497) from 7 to 3:30 weekdays; on St. Croix, call 809/773–7614. If there is no answer, call the **Rescue Coordination Center** (tel. 809/722–2943) in San Juan, open 24 hours a day.

Pharmacies: Sunrise Pharmacy has two branches on St. Thomas, one in Red Hook (tel. 809/775–6600) and another in the Wheatley Center (tel. 809/774–5333). **Drug Farm Pharmacy's** main store (tel. 809/776–7098) is located across from the General Post Office; another branch (tel. 809/776–1880) is located next to St. Thomas Hospital. On St. Croix, try **People's Drug Store, Inc.** (tel. 809/778–7355) in Christiansted or **D & D Apothecary Hall** (tel. 809/772–1890) in Frederiksted. On St. John, contact the **St. John Drug Center** (tel. 809/776–6353) in Cruz Bay.

Currency The U.S. dollar is the medium of exchange.

Taxes and Service Charges A 7½% tax is added to hotel rates. Some hotels and restaurants add a 10% or 15% service charge to your bill, generally only if you are part of a group of 15 or more. There is no sales tax in the U.S.V.I. Departure tax for the U.S.V.I. is included in the cost of your airplane ticket.

Getting Around Although sprawling St. Thomas is not a walker's island, you can get by here without a car. Most hotels and condominium complexes are on or near a beach. Those that aren't often provide a shuttle bus (free or for a few dollars) to a beach. Most of the less-expensive B&Bs and inns are in the old historic district downtown or scattered throughout the hills above Charlotte Amalie; both locations are a short taxi or bus ride from some of the island's best beaches. You may find a car necessary for trips to restaurants and shops, though. Even if you opt not to rent a car for your entire vacation, you may want to rent one for a day in order to explore the less-frequented areas of the island.

St. Croix is a big island, and visitors usually find their freedom severely curtailed without a car. The public taxi runs only between Christiansted and Frederiksted along Centerline Road, not to any of the hotels along the coast. On St. John, you can get by without renting a car if you stay in Cruz Bay or one of the more popular hotels where taxis are likely to stop. If you are renting a private house or condo, you'll probably need a car to come down out of the hills.

Car   Any U.S. driver's license is good for 90 days here; the minimum age for drivers is 18, although many agencies won't rent to anyone under the age of 25. Driving is on the left side of the road (although your steering wheel will be on the left side of the car). Many of the roads are narrow and the islands are dotted with hills, so there is ample reason to drive carefully. Jeeps are particularly recommended on St. John, where dirt roads prevail.

On St. Thomas, you can rent a car from **ABC Rentals** (tel. 809/776–1222 or 800/524–2080), **Anchorage E-Z Car** (tel. 809/775–6255), **Avis** (tel. 809/774–1468), **Budget** (tel. 809/776–7575), **Cowpet Car Rental** (tel. 809/775–7376 or 800/524–2072), **Dependable** (tel. 809/774–2253 or 800/522–3076), **Discount** (tel. 809/776–4858), **Hertz** (tel. 809/774–1879), **Sea Breeze** (tel. 809/774–7200), **Sun Island** (tel. 809/774–3333), or **Thrifty** (tel. 809/776–8600). Average cost is $52 a day (unlimited mileage), but you can get a standard shift car without air-conditioning for $43.

On St. Croix, call **Atlas** (tel. 809/773–2886), **Avis** (tel. 809/778–9355), **Budget** (tel. 809/778–9636), **Caribbean Jeep & Car** (tel. 809/773–4399), **Hertz** (tel. 809/778–1402), **Olympic** (tel. 809/773–9588 or 722–1617), and **Thrifty** (tel. 809/773–7200).

On St. John, call **Avis** (tel. 809/776–6374), **Budget** (tel. 809/776–7575), **Cool Breeze** (tel. 809/776–6588), **Delbert Hill Taxi and Jeep** (tel. 809/776–6637), **Hertz** (tel. 809/776–6695), **O'Connor Jeep** (tel. 809/776–6343), **St. John Car Rental** (tel. 809/776–6103), or **Spencer's Jeep** (tel. 809/776–7784). Economy rental cars on St. Croix and St. John average $25–$30 a day.

Taxis   Taxis of all shapes and sizes are available at various ferry, shopping, resort, and airport areas on St. Thomas and St. Croix and respond quickly to a call. U.S.V.I. taxis do not have meters, but rather a list of standard per-person fares to popular destinations. Rates are less if more than one person is traveling to the same destination. Sample fares to popular tourist destinations on St. Thomas: town to Havensight Mall, $2.50; town to Magens Bay, $6.50 for one, $4 per person for more than one; town to Red Hook, $9 for one, $5.50 per person for more than one. In Charlotte Amalie, taxi stands are located across from **Emancipation Gardens** (in front of Little Switzerland behind the post office) and along the waterfront. Away from Charlotte Amalie, you'll find taxis available at all major hotels and at such public beaches as Magens Bay and Coki Point. Calling taxis will work, too, but allow plenty of time.

Taxis on St. Croix, generally station wagons or minivans, are a phone call away from most hotels and are available in downtown Christiansted, at the Alexander Hamilton Airport, and at the Frederiksted pier during cruise-ship arrivals. Rates, set by law, are prominently displayed at the airport. The public taxi van, running along Centerline Road between Frederiksted and Christiansted, costs $1.50 one way. Private taxis (the same vans, but they don't stop to pick up other passengers along the way) typically cost $10 for a trip from the airport to Christiansted or to most North Shore hotels.

On St. John, buses and taxis are the same thing: open-air safari buses. You'll find them congregated at the Cruz Bay Dock, ready to take you to any of the beaches or other island destinations, but you can also pick them up anywhere on the road by signaling. Taxis from Cruz Bay to the popular North Shore beaches cost around $5 per person. It's a bit more expensive to reach the attractions on the other side of the island: A ride to Annaberg Plantation or Coral Bay can run $10 per person.

Buses Service is minimal, but the deluxe mainland-size buses on St. Thomas are a reasonable and comfortable way to get from east and west to town and back (there is no service north, however). Fares are $1 between outlying areas and town and 75¢ in town. St. Croix and St. John have no public bus system, and residents rely on the kindness of taxi vans and safari buses for mass transportation.

Ferries Ferries ply two routes between St. Thomas and St. John—either between the Charlotte Amalie waterfront and Cruz Bay or between Red Hook and Cruz Bay. The schedules for daily service between Red Hook, St. Thomas, and Cruz Bay, St. John: Ferries leave Red Hook weekdays 6:30 and 7:30 AM, and all week long hourly 8 AM–midnight. They leave Cruz Bay for Red Hook hourly 6 AM–10 PM and at 11:15 PM. The 15–20 minute ferry ride is $3 one way for adults, $1.50 for children under 12. Ferries leave from Charlotte Amalie every two hours from 9 AM to 3 PM, then at 5:30 PM and 7 PM. They leave Cruz Bay for Charlotte Amalie every two hours from 7:15 AM to 1:15 PM, and also at 3:45 PM and 5:15 PM. Fare for the 45-minute ride is $7 one-way.

Telephones and Mail The area code for all the U.S.V.I. is 809, and there is direct dialing to the mainland. Local calls from a public phone cost 25¢ for each five minutes. On St. John, the place to go for any telephone or message needs is **Connections** (tel. 809/776–6922). On St. Thomas, it's **Islander Services** (tel. 809/774–8128) behind the Greenhouse Restaurant in Charlotte Amalie or **East End Secretarial Services** (tel. 809/775–5262, fax 809/775–3590), upstairs at the Red Hook Plaza. On St. Croix, visit the **Business Bureau** (42–43 Strand St., Christiansted, tel. 809/773–7601) or **St. Croix Communications Centre** (61 King St., Frederiksted, tel. 809/772–5800).

By 1994 the telephone exchange throughout St. John will be switched to **693.** At press time the change had not been integrated. When you dial the current listing, a recording will redirect you if necessary.

The main **U.S. Post Office** on St. Thomas is near the hospital, with branches in Charlotte Amalie and Frenchtown; there's a post office at Christiansted and Fredriksted on St. Croix and at Cruz Bay on St. John. Postal rates are the same as elsewhere in the United States: 29¢ for a letter, 19¢ for a postcard to anywhere in the United States, 45¢ for a half-ounce letter mailed to a foreign country.

Opening and Closing Times On **St. Thomas,** Charlotte Amalie's Main Street–area shops are open weekdays and Saturday 9–5. Havensight Mall shops (next to the cruise-ships dock) hours are the same, though shops sometimes stay open until 9 on Friday, depending on how many cruise ships are staying late at the dock. You may also find some shops open on Sunday if a lot of cruise ships are in port. **St. Croix** store hours are usually weekdays 9 to 5, but you will find some shops in Christiansted open in the evening. On **St. John,** store hours are similar to those on the other two islands, and Wharfside Village shops in Cruz Bay are often open into the evening.

Guided Tours On St. Thomas, the **V.I. Taxi Association City-Island Tour** (tel. 809/774–4550) gives a two-hour tour aimed at cruise-ship passengers that includes stops at Drake's Seat and Mountain Top. You can join an air-conditioned taxi-van tour for about $12 a person or pay $35 for two people and have your own taxi. **Tropic Tours** (tel. 809/774–1855) offers half-day shopping and sightseeing tours of St. Thomas by bus on Mondays, Wednesdays, Fridays, and Saturdays for $18 per person and full-day snorkeling tours to St. John daily for $40 per person (including lunch). It picks up at all the major hotels. For a chance to wait hidden on a beach on St. Croix while the magnificent hawksbill turtles come ashore to lay their eggs in the spring, write or call the **Virgin Islands Conservation Society** (Box 3839, St. Croix 00822, tel. 809/773–1989); there is no charge to participate.

Van tours of St. Croix are offered by **St. Croix Safari Tours** (tel. 809/773–6700) and **Smitty's** (tel. 809/773–9188). The tours, which depart from Christiansted and last about three hours, cost from $20 per person. You might also try to strike a bargain with one of the taxi-van drivers you'll see congregating on King Street in Christiansted, outside the tourist office, though their prices are likely to be comparable to those of the safari tour. If you get enough people together, however, you could save money.

On St. John, taxi drivers are your best bet for an informal driving tour of the island. You'll find a multitude of these personable men gathered at the clock in Cruz Bay. A couple can take a two-hour tour for $30; three or more people bring the price down to $12 a person. The park service conducts guided tours onshore and off shore. Prices range from a $3 hike to Reef Bay to a $40 Round-the-Island snorkel tour. Contact the **St. John National Park Visitor Center** (Cruz Bay, tel. 809/776–6201).

Exploring St. Thomas

Numbers in the margin correspond to points of interest on the St. Thomas map.

Charlotte Amalie This tour of historic (and sometimes hilly) **Charlotte Amalie**
❶ and environs is on foot, so wear comfortable shoes, start early, and stop often to refresh. A note about the street names: In deference to the island's heritage, the streets downtown are labeled by their Danish names. Locals will use both the Danish name and the English name (such as Dronnigen's Gade and Main Street).

Begin at the waterfront. Waterfront and Main streets are connected by cobblestone-paved alleys kept cool by overhanging green plants and the thick stone walls of the warehouses on either side. The alleys (particularly Royal Dane Mall and Palm Passage, Main Street between the post office and Market Square, and Bakery Square on Back Street) are where you'll find the unique and glamorous—and duty-free—shops for which Charlotte Amalie is famous (*see* Shopping, *below*).

At the end of Kronprindsens Alley north of the waterfront is the pale-pink Roman Catholic **Cathedral of St. Peter and St.**

Paul, consecrated as a parish church in 1848. The ceiling and walls of the church are covered in the soft tones of murals painted in 1899 by two Belgian artists, Father Leo Servais and Brother Ildephonsus. The San Juan–marble altar and side walls were added in the 1960s. *Tel. 809/774–0201. Open Mon.– Sat. 8–5.*

At **Market Square,** east of the church on Main Street, try to block out the signs advertising cameras and electronics and imagine this place as it was in the early 1800s, when plantation owners stood on the delicately draped wrought-iron balconies and chose from the slaves for sale below. Today in the square, a cadre of old-timers sell papaya, taina roots, and herbs, and sidewalk vendors offer a variety of African fabrics and artifacts, tie-dyed cotton clothes at good prices, and fresh-squeezed fruit juices. Go east on Back Street, then turn left on Store Tvaer Gade; walk a short block, and take a left on Bjerge Gade.

As you walk up Bjerge Gade, you'll end up facing a weather-beaten but imposing two-story red house known as the **Crystal Palace,** so-named because it was the first building on the island to have glass windows. The Crystal Palace anchors the corner of Bjerge and Crystal Gade. Here the street becomes stairs, which you can climb to Denmark Hill and the old Greek Revival **Danish Consulate building** (1830)—look for the red-and-white flag.

Descend to Crystal Gade and go east. At Number 15, you'll come to the **St. Thomas Synagogue.** Its Hebrew name translates as the Congregation of Blessing, Peace, and Loving Deeds. Since the synagogue first opened its doors in 1833, it has held a weekly Sabbath service, making it the oldest synagogue building in continuous use under the American flag and the second oldest (after the one on Curaçao) in the Western Hemisphere. *15 Crystal Gade, tel. 809/774–4312. Open weekdays 9–4.*

One block east, down the hill, you'll come to the corner of Nye Gade. On the right corner is the St. Thomas **Dutch Reformed Church,** founded in 1744, burned in 1804, and rebuilt to its austere loveliness in 1844. The unembellished cream-color hall exudes peace—albeit monochromatically. The only touches of another color are the forest green shutters and carpet. *Tel. 809/776–8255. Open weekdays 9–5.*

Continue on Crystal Gade one block east and turn left (north) on Garden Street. The **All Saints Anglican Church** was built in 1848 from stone quarried on the island. Its thick, arched window frames are lined with the yellow brick that came to the islands as ballast aboard merchant ships. The church was built in celebration of the end of slavery in the Virgin Islands in 1848. *Tel. 809/774–0214. Open Mon.–Sat. 6 AM–3 PM.*

Return down Garden Street and go east on Kongen's Gade. Keep walking up the hill to the east and you'll find yourself at the foot of the **99 Steps,** a staircase "street" built by the Danes in the 1700s. (If you count the stairs as you go up, you'll discover, like thousands before you, that there are more than 99.)

Up the steps you'll find the neighborhood of **Queen's Street.** The homes are privately owned except for one guest house— **Blackbeard's Castle.** Its tower was built in 1679 and is believed

Outer
Brass

Picara
Pt.

Inner
Brass

Tropaco
Pt.

Vluck
Pt.

Hull Bay

Magens
Bay

Stumpy
Pt.

Santa
Maria
Bay

26

Magens Bay

Crown Mt.

6

Target
Pt.

Bordeaux
Bay

Stumpy
Bay

10

Dorthea

Signal
Hill

7

West Cay

Botany
Bay

9

8

Fortuna
Hill

Fortuna

Perseverance
Bay

**Brewers
Beach**

Contant

28

Barents
Bay

Fortuna
Bay

Brewers
Bay

Frenchtown

David
Pt.

**Cyril E. King
International
Airport**

Altona

29 **30**

Red Pt.

27

Crown
Bay

Hassel
Island

**Lindbergh
Beach**

Water
Island

Limestone
Bay

Caribbean Sea

TO PUERTO RICO

TO
ST. CROIX

Exploring
Charlotte Amalie, **1**
Coral World, **4**
Drake's Seat, **6**
Fairchild Park, **8**
Four Corners, **9**
Havensight Mall, **2**

Mountain Top, **7**
Red Hook, **3**
Tillet's Gardens, **5**
U.S. Department of
Agriculture Inspection
Station, **10**

Dining
Alexander's Cafe, **29**
Bryan's Bar and
Restaurant, **26**
The Chart House, **30**
Eunice's Terrace, **25**

For the Birds, **19**
Gladys' Café, **11**
I'll Take
Manhattan, **17, 21**
That Pizza Shoppe, **18**
Wok and Roll, **22**
Zorba's Cafe, **12**

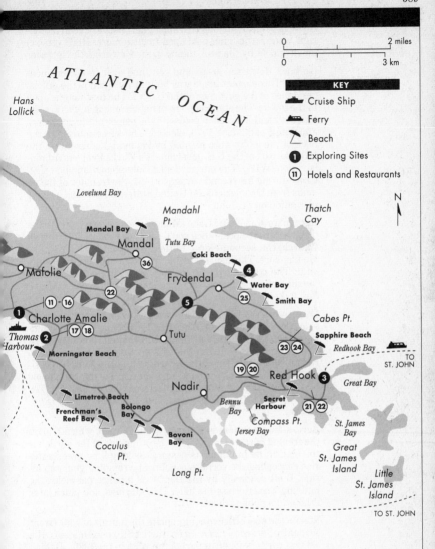

ATLANTIC OCEAN

Hans Lollick

Lovelund Bay

Mandahl Pt.

Thatch Cay

Mandal Bay

Mandal

Tutu Bay

Coki Beach

Mafolie

36

Frydendal

Water Bay

4

22

5

25

Smith Bay

11 **16**

Charlotte Amalie

Cabes Pt.

Sapphire Beach

Thomas Harbour

1

2

17 **18**

Tutu

23 **24**

Redhook Bay

TO ST. JOHN

Morningstar Beach

19 **20**

Red Hook

3

Great Bay

Limetree Beach

Nadir

Bennu Bay

Secret Harbour

St. James Bay

Frenchman's Reef Bay

Bolongo Bay

Compass Pt.

21 **22**

Coculus Pt.

Bovoni Bay

Jersey Bay

Great St. James Island

Little St. James Island

Long Pt.

TO ST. JOHN

KEY

⛴ Cruise Ship

⛴ Ferry

〉 Beach

1 Exploring Sites

11 Hotels and Restaurants

0 — 2 miles
0 — 3 km

N

to have been used by the notorious pirate Edward Teach. The castle is now the site of a charming guest house, a good restaurant, and a swimming pool open to customers. Here you can lunch and sit by the pool, taking in the view from the terrace.

Go back down the steps and continue east to **Government House.** This elegant home was built in 1867 and is the official residence of the governor of the U.S.V.I. The first floor is open to the public. The staircases are of native mahogany, as are the plaques hand-lettered in gold with the names of the governors appointed and, since 1970, elected. The three murals at the back of the lobby were painted by Pepino Mangravatti in the 1930s as part of the U.S. government's Works Projects Administration (WPA). The murals depict Columbus's landing on St. Croix during his second voyage in 1493, the transfer of the islands from Denmark to the United States in 1917, and a sugar plantation on St. John.

Return west on Norre Gade (Main Street) toward town. In the block before the post office you'll pass the **Frederick Lutheran Church,** the second-oldest Lutheran church in the Western Hemisphere. The inside is highlighted by a massive mahogany altar. The pews, each with its own door, were once rented to families of the congregation. *Tel. 809/776–1315. Open Mon.–Sat. 9–4.*

Directly across from the Lutheran Church, through a small side street, you'll see **Fort Christian,** St. Thomas's oldest standing structure, built 1672–87, and a U.S. national landmark. The clock tower was added in the 19th century. This remarkable redoubt has, over time, been used as a jail, governor's residence, town hall, courthouse, and church. Its dungeons now house a museum featuring artifacts of U.S.V.I. history. *Tel. 809/776–4566. Open weekdays 8:30–4:30, Sat. 9:30–4, Sun. noon–4.*

Across from the fort is **Emancipation Garden,** which honors the freeing of slaves in 1848. On the other side of the garden is the **legislature building,** its pastoral-looking lime-green exterior concealing the vociferous political wrangling going on inside. Built originally by the Danish as a police barracks, the building was later used to billet U.S. Marines, and much later it housed a public school.

Stop in the **post office** to contemplate the murals of waterfront scenes by *Saturday Evening Post* artist Stephen Dohanos. His art was commissioned as part of the WPA in the 1930s. Behind the post office, on the waterfront side of Little Switzerland, are the hospitality lounge and **V.I. Visitor's Information Center.**

As you head back toward Market Square along Main Street, you'll pass the Tropicana Perfume Shop, between Store Tvaer Gade and Trompeter Gade. The building the shop is in is also known as the **Pissarro Building,** the birthplace of French Impressionist painter Camille Pissarro.

The South Shore and East End Exploring St. Thomas by car gives you the most freedom to see the sights at your own pace. You can tour the island outside Charlotte Amalie in a day and even take an hour or so to linger on one of the island's beaches. If you prefer a cheaper alternative, guided tours of St. Thomas highlights are offered (*see* Guided Tours, *above*). Leaving Charlotte Amalie, take Veterans Drive (Route 30) east along the waterfront. Once you bear to the right at **Nelson Mandela Circle** (Yacht Haven is on your right), you'll make quicker progress. You may want to stop at **②** **Havensight Mall,** across from the dock. This shopping center is a less crowded (and less charming) version of the duty-free shopping district along Main Street in town.

Route 30 is narrow, winds up and down, and changes names several times along the way; it is Frenchman's Bay Road just outside town (sharp left turn), then becomes Bovoni Road around Bolongo Bay. As you travel it, you will be treated to some southerly vistas of the Caribbean Sea (and, on clear days, St. Croix, 40 miles away). The road becomes Route 32 and then is called Red Hook Road as it passes by **Benner Bay.** Staying **③** on Route 32 brings you into **Red Hook,** where you can catch the ferry to St. John (parking available for $5 a day). Red Hook has grown from a sleepy little town connected to the rest of the island only by dirt roads (or by boat) to an increasingly self-sustaining village. There's shopping and a deli at American Yacht Harbor, and you can stop in at The Big Chill for a frozen yogurt or croissant sandwich. Or walk along the docks and visit with sailors and fishermen, and stop for a beer at Piccola Marina Cafe or the Warehouse bar.

Above Red Hook the main road swings toward the north shore and becomes Route 38, or Smith Bay Road, taking you past Sapphire Beach, a resort and restaurant with water-sports rentals and a popular snorkeling and windsurfing spot. As you come to Smith Bay, you'll pass the lush green landscaping of Stouffer Grand Beach Resort, and then you'll see a turn-off to **④** the right for Coki Point Beach and **Coral World,** with its three-level underwater observatory, the world's largest reef tank, and an aquarium with more than 20 TV-size tanks providing capsulized views of sea life. A new semisubmarine (a craft that is half-submarine, half-boat, allowing passengers to come up on deck) offers 20-minute undersea tours for $12 per person. Coral World's staff will answer your questions about the turtles, iguanas, parrots, and flamingos that inhabit the park, and there's a restaurant, souvenir shop, and the world's only underwater mailbox, from which you can send postcards home. *Tel. 809/775–1555. Admission: $14 adults, $9 children. Open daily 9–6.*

⑤ Continue west on Route 38 and you'll come to **Tillet's Gardens,** where local artisans craft stained glass, pottery, and ceramics. Tillet's paintings and fabrics are also on display.

North Shore, Center Islands, and West The north shore is home to many inviting attractions, not to mention much lusher vegetation than is found on the rest of the island. The most direct route from Charlotte Amalie is Mafolie Road (Route 35), which can be picked up east of Government Hill.

⑥ In the heights above Charlotte Amalie is **Drake's Seat,** the mountain lookout from which Sir Francis Drake was supposed to have kept watch over his fleet and looked for enemy ships of the Spanish fleet. Magens Bay and Mahogany Run are to the north, with the British Virgin Islands and Drake's Passage to the east. Off to the left, or west, are Fairchild Park, Mountain Top, Hull Bay, and such smaller islands as the Inner and Outer Brass islands. The panoramic vista is especially breathtaking (and romantic) at dusk, and if you arrive late in the day you'll miss the hordes of day-trippers on taxi tours who stop a

Drake's Seat to take a picture and buy a T-shirt from one of the vendors there. The vendors are gone by the afternoon.

⑦ West from Drake's Seat is **Mountain Top,** not only a mecca for souvenir shopping, but also the location of the establishment that claims to have invented the banana daiquiri. There is a restaurant here, and, at more than 1,500 feet above sea level, some spectacular views as well.

⑧ Below Mountain Top is **Fairchild Park,** a gift to the people of the U.S.V.I. from the philanthropist Arthur Fairchild.

If you head west from Mountain Top on Crown Mountain Road
⑨ (Route 33) you'll come to **Four Corners.** Take the extreme right turn and drive along the northwestern ridge of the mountain through **Estate Pearl, Sorgenfri,** and **Caret Bay.** There's not much here except peace and quiet, junglelike foliage, and breathtaking vistas. You may want to stop at one of the inviting plant stores run by the talkative French. Near Bryan's Plants
⑩ you'll pass the **U.S. Department of Agriculture Inspection Station.** If you buy a plant, be sure to stop here to get the plant's roots sprayed for diseases and to get a certificate to present to U.S. customs when you leave the territory. Continue west to Brewer's Bay, then follow Route 30 east back to Frenchtown and Charlotte Amalie.

Exploring St. Croix

Numbers in the margin correspond to points of interest on the St. Croix map.

You can see some of St. Croix's sites by public transportation— the taxi-van route goes from Christiansted, the heart of the island past the St. George Botanical Gardens, Whim Greathouse, and on to Frederiksted—and you can get off and on the taxi anywhere along the line. But you should plan on renting a car for at least one day to tour the coastal roads and explore the lush rain forest on the West End. If you don't dally too long at some sandy stretch of beach, one day should be plenty to see the main points of interest.

❶ This tour starts in the historic, Danish-style town of **Christiansted,** St. Croix's commercial center. Many of the structures, which are built from the harbor up into the gentle hillsides, date from the 18th century. An easy-to-follow walking tour begins at the **visitor's bureau,** set at the harbor. The building was constructed in 1856, and once served as a scale house, where goods passing through the port were weighed and inspected. Directly across the parking lot, at the edge of D. Hamilton Jackson Park (the park is named for a famed labor leader, journalist, and judge), is the **Old Customs House.** Completed in 1829, this building now houses the island's national park offices. To the east stands yellow **Fort Christiansvaern.** Built by the Danish from 1738 to 1749 to protect the harbor against attacks on commercial shipping, the fort was repeatedly damaged by hurricane-force winds and was partially rebuilt in 1772. It is now part of the National Historic Site and is the best-preserved of the remaining Danish-built forts in the Virgin Islands. Five rooms, including military barracks and a dungeon, have been restored to demonstrate how the fort looked in the 1840s, when it was at its height as a military establishment. There is also an exhibit that documents the Danish military's 150-year presence in Christiansted. *Box 160, Christiansted 00822, tel. 809/773–1460. Admission: $2 (includes admission to Steeple Building); free to children under 16 and senior citizens. Open weekdays 8–5, weekends and holidays 9–5. Closed Christmas.*

Cross Hospital Street from the customs house to reach the **post office building.** Built in 1749, it once housed the Danish West India & Guinea Company warehouse. To the south of the post office, across Company Street, stands the maroon-and-white **Steeple Building.** Built by the Danes in 1754, the building once housed the first Danish Lutheran church on St. Croix. It is now a national-park museum and contains exhibits documenting the island's habitation by Native Americans through an extensive array of archaeological artifacts. There are also displays on the architectural development of Christiansted and the African-American experience in the town during Danish colonial rule. *Box 160, Christiansted 00822, tel. 809/773–1460. Admission: $1 (includes admission to fort). Open Wed. and weekends 9–4.*

One of the town's most elegant buildings is **Government House,** on King Street. Built as a home for a Danish merchant in 1747, the building today houses U.S.V.I. government offices and the U.S. district court. Slip into the peaceful inner courtyard to admire the still pools and gardens. A sweeping staircase leads visitors to a second-story ballroom, still the site of official government functions.

To leave Christiansted and begin a driving tour, take Hospital Street from the tourist office and turn right onto Company Street. Follow Company Street for several blocks and turn right with the flow of traffic past the police station. Make a quick left onto King Street, and follow it out of town. At the second traffic light, make a right onto Route 75, Northside Road. A few miles up the road, you can make a side trip by turning right, just past the St. Croix Avis building, onto Route ❷ 751, which leads you past the St. Croix by the Sea hotel to **Judith's Fancy,** where you can see the ruins of an old great house and the tower left from a 17th-century château that was once home to the governor of the Knights of Malta. The "Judith" comes from the first name of a woman buried on the property. From the guardhouse at the entrance to the neighborhood, follow Hamilton Drive to its end for a view of Salt River Bay, where Christopher Columbus anchored in 1493.

After driving back to Route 75, continue west for 2 miles and turn right at Tradewinds Road onto Route 80, which quickly ❸ returns to the grassy coastline and **Cane Bay.** This is one of St. Croix's best beaches for scuba diving, and near the small stone jetty you may see a few wet-suited, tank-backed figures making their way out to the drop-off (a bit farther out there is a steeper drop-off to 12,000 feet). Rising behind you is Mt. Eagle, St. Croix's highest peak, at 1,165 feet. Leaving Cane Bay and passing North Star beach, follow the beautiful coastal road as it dips briefly into the forest, then turn left. There is no street sign, but you'll know the turn: The pavement is marked with the words "The Beast" and a set of giant paw prints—the hill you are about to climb is the infamous Beast of the America's Paradise Triathalon, an annual St. Croix event in which participants must bike up this intimidating slope.

St. Croix

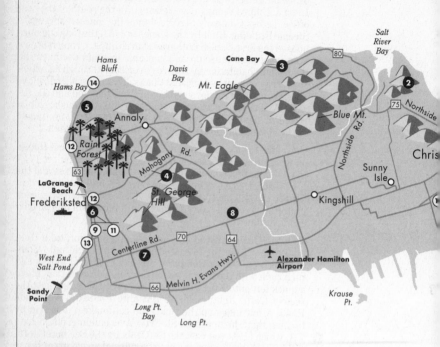

TO
ST. THOMAS

Salt
River
Bay

*Hams
Bluff*

*Davis
Bay*

Cane Bay ③

80

②

Hams Bay ⑭

Mt. Eagle

75 *Northside*

⑤

Annaly ○

Blue Mt.

Northside Rd.

Chris

⑫ *Rain
Forest*

Mahogany Rd.

63

④

*Sunny
Isle*

*LaGrange
Beach*

⑫

*St. George
Hill*

⑧

○ Kingshill

①

Frederiksted

⑥

⑨ ⑪

⑬

Centerline Rd. 70

64

⑦

✈ **Alexander Hamilton
Airport**

*West End
Salt Pond*

66 *Melvin H. Evans Hwy.*

**Sandy
Point**

*Long Pt.
Bay*

*Krause
Pt.*

Long Pt.

KEY

⚓ Cruise Ship

↗ Beach

🌴 Rain Forest

① Exploring Sites

⑨ Hotels and Restaurants

Caribbean Sea

Exploring
Cane Bay, **3**
Christiansted, **1**
Estate Mount
Washington
Plantation, **5**

Estate Whim
Plantation Museum, **7**
Frederiksted, **6**
Judith's Fancy, **2**
Mahogany Road, **4**
St. George Village
Botanical Gardens, **8**

Dining
Blue Moon, **9**
Camille's, **16**
La Guitarra, **18**
LaGrange Beach
Club, **12**
Le St. Tropez, **11**
Stixx on the
Waterfront, **17**

Lodging
Cottages by the
Sea, **13**
The Frederiksted, **10**
Hilty House, **15**
Paradise Sunset
Beach, **14**
The Pink Fancy, **19**

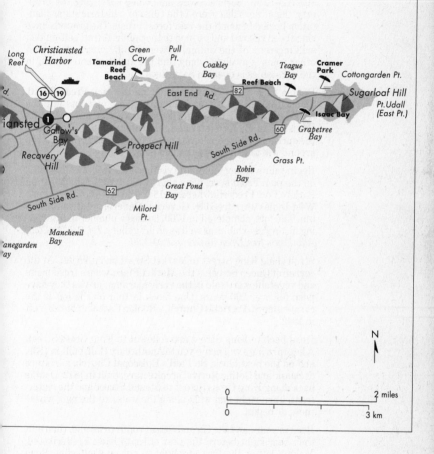

Buck Island

Buck Island Beach

Long
Reef

*Christiansted
Harbor*

*Green
Cay*

*Pull
Pt.*

**Tamarind
Reef
Beach**

*Coakley
Bay*

Reef Beach

*Teague
Bay*

**Cramer
Park**

Cottongarden Pt.

'd.

(16) (19)

East End Rd.

82

Sugarloaf Hill

Pt. Udall
(East Pt.)

iansted

(1)

*Gallow's
Bay*

60

Isaac Bay

*Grapetree
Bay*

Prospect Hill

South Side Rd.

*Recovery
Hill*

Grass Pt.

*Robin
Bay*

62

*Great Pond
Bay*

South Side Rd.

*Milord
Pt.*

*Manchenil
Bay*

'anegarden
'ay

N

0   2 miles

0   3 km

Follow this road, Route 69, as it twists and climbs up the hill and south across the island. The golf course you pass on the right is a Robert Trent Jones course, part of the Carambola resort complex. You will eventually bear right to join Route 76,

❹ **Mahogany Road.** Follow Mahogany Road through the heart of the rain forest until you reach the end of the road at Ham's Bluff Road (Route 63), running along the west coast of the island. Turn right and, after a few miles, look to the right side of

❺ the road for the **Estate Mount Washington Plantation** (tel. 809/772–1026). Several years ago, while surveying the property, the owners discovered the ruins of a historic sugar plantation buried beneath the rain forest brush. The grounds have since been cleared and opened to the public. A free, self-guided walking tour of the animal-powered mill, rum factory, and other ruins is available daily, and the antique shop located in the old stables is open on Saturdays.

❻ Double back along Ham's Bluff Road to reach **Frederiksted,** founded in 1751. A single, long cruise-ship pier juts into the sparkling sea from this historic coastal town, noted less for its Danish than for its Victorian architecture (dating from after the uprising of former slaves and the great fire of 1878). A stroll around will take no more than an hour.

Begin your walking tour at the **visitor center** (tel. 809/772–0357) on the pier. From here, it's a short walk across Emancipation Park to **Fort Frederik** where, in 1848, the slaves of the Danish West Indies were freed by Governor General Peter van Scholten. The fort, completed in 1760, houses a number of interesting historical exhibits as well as an art gallery. *Tel. 809/772–2021. Admission free. Open weekdays 8:30–4:30.*

Stroll along King Street to Market Street and turn left. At the corner of Queen Street is the **Market Place,** where fresh fruits and vegetables are sold in the early morning, just as they have been for over 200 years. One block farther on the left is the coral-stone **St. Patrick's Church,** a Roman Catholic church built in 1842.

Head back to King Street and follow it to King Cross Street. A left turn here will bring you to **Apothecary Hall,** built in 1839, and on the next block, **St. Paul's Episcopal Church,** a mixture of classic and Gothic Revival architecture, built in 1812. Double back along King Cross Street to Strand Street and the waterfront. Turn right and walk along the water to the pier, where the tour began.

Back in your car, take Strand Street south to its end, turn left, then bear right before the post office to leave Frederiksted. Make a left at the first stoplight to get on Centerline Road (Queen Mary Highway). A few miles along this road, on the

❼ right, is the **Estate Whim Plantation Museum.** The lovingly restored estate, with a windmill, cook house, and other buildings, will give you a true sense of what life was like on St. Croix's sugar plantations in the 1800s. The oval-shaped, high-ceilinged great house has antique furniture, decor, utensils, and the largest apothecary exhibit in the West Indies. Notice the fresh and airy atmosphere: The waterless moat around the great house was used not for defense but for gathering cooling air. It is built of stone, coral, and lime. You will also find a museum gift shop. *Box 2855, Frederiksted 00841, tel. 809/772–0598. Admission: $5 adults, $1 children. Open Tues.–Sat. 10–4.*

Continue along Centerline Road to the St. George Estate. Turn
⑧ left here to reach the **St. George Village Botanical Gardens,** 17
acres of lush and fragrant flora amid the ruins of a 19th-century
sugarcane plantation village. *Box 3011, Kingshill 00851–3011, tel.
809/772–3874. Admission: $3 adults, $1 children. Open Tues.–Sat.
10–3.*

Continue east along Centerline Road all the way back to Christiansted.

Exploring St. John

*Numbers in the margin correspond to points of interest on the
St. John map.*

Tiny St. John can easily be seen in one day by car—after all,
there's only one steep, winding road running all the way around
the island.

❶ **Cruz Bay** town dock is the starting point for just about everything on St. John. Take a leisurely stroll through the streets of
this colorful, compact town: There are plenty of shops to
browse in, and plenty of watering holes where you can stop to
take a breather.

Follow the waterfront out of town (about 100 yards) to another
dock at the edge of a parking lot. At the far side of the lagoon
here you'll find the **National Park Service Visitors Center** (tel.
809/776–6201), where you can pick up a handy guide to St.
John's hiking trails and see various large maps of the island.

Begin your driving tour traveling north out of Cruz Bay. You'll
pass **Mongoose Junction,** recently expanded to include Mongoose Junction II, one of the prettiest shopping areas to be
found. At the half-mile mark you'll come to the well-groomed
gardens and beaches of **Caneel Bay,** purchased from the Danish
West India Company and developed in the 1950s by Laurance
Rockefeller, who then turned over much of the island to the
U.S. government as parkland. Caneel Bay Beach (home of two
friendly stingrays) is reached by parking in the Caneel parking
lot and walking through the grounds (ask for directions).

Continue east on North Shore Road, with all the sense of anticipation that you can muster; you are about to see, one after
another, four of the most beautiful beaches in all of the Caribbean. The road is narrow and hilly (it was actually just expanded, believe it or not) with switchbacks and steep curves
that make driving a challenge. **Hawksnest,** the first beach you
will come to, is where Alan Alda shot scenes for his film *The
Four Seasons.* Just past Hawksnest Hill, swing left to Peace
❷ Hill, sometimes called Sugarloaf Hill, to the ***Christ of the Caribbean*** statue and an old sugar-mill tower. Park in the small
unmarked parking lot and walk about 100 yards up a rocky
path. The area is grassy, and views do not get much better than
this. *Christ of the Caribbean* was erected in 1953 by Colonel
Julius Wadsworth and donated, along with 9 acres of land, to
the national park in 1975.

Your next stop, and that of quite a few tourist-filled safari
buses, is **Trunk Bay,** a beautiful beach with an underwater trail
that's good for beginner snorkelers.

Continuing on the beach hunt, you'll come to wide **Cinnamon
Bay.** The snorkeling around the point to the right is good—look

St. John

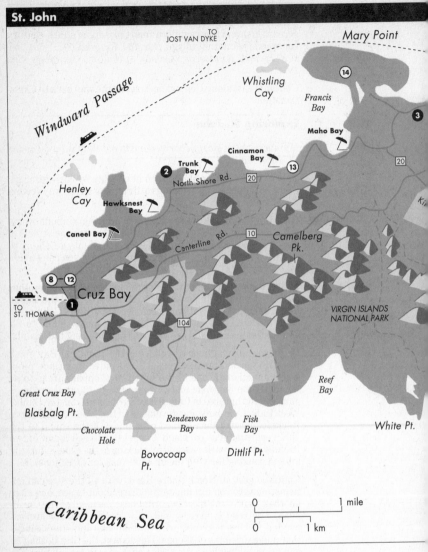

TO JOST VAN DYKE

TO ST. THOMAS

Windward Passage

Mary Point

Whistling Cay

Francis Bay

(14)

(3)

Maho Bay

Henley Cay

Trunk Bay

(2)

Cinnamon Bay

(13)

North Shore Rd.

20

20

Hawksnest Bay

Ki

Caneel Bay

Centerline Rd.

10

Camelberg Pk.

(8) — (12)

Cruz Bay

(1)

104

VIRGIN ISLANDS NATIONAL PARK

Great Cruz Bay

Blasbalg Pt.

Chocolate Hole

Bovocoap Pt.

Rendezvous Bay

Dittlif Pt.

Fish Bay

Reef Bay

White Pt.

Caribbean Sea

0			1 mile
0		1 km	

Exploring
Annaberg Plantation, **3**
Bordeaux Mountain, **7**
Christ of the Caribbean statue, **2**
Coral Bay, **4**
Cruz Bay, **1**
East End, **5**
Salt Pond, **6**

Dining
The Fish Trap, **8**
Inn at Tamarind Court, **10**
Lime Inn, **9**
Luscious Licks, **12**
Shipwreck Landing, **15**

Lodging
Cinnamon Bay Campground, **13**
The Inn at Tamarind Court, **10**
Maho Bay Camp, **14**
Raintree Inn, **11**

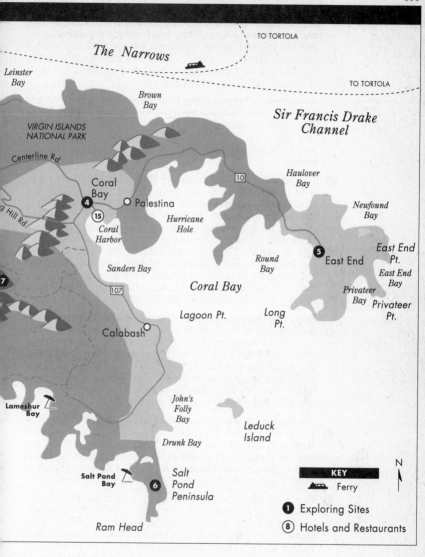

for the big angelfish and the swarms of purple triggerfish that live here. The national-park campground is at Cinnamon Bay and includes a snack bar, bathhouse, boutique, restaurant, general store, water-sports equipment rental, and a self-guided museum. Across the road from the beach parking lot is the beginning of the Cinnamon Bay hiking trail; look for the ruins of a sugar mill to mark the trailhead.

As you leave Cinnamon, the road flattens out, and you'll find yourself on a shaded lane running under flowering trees. **Maho Bay** comes almost to the road here, and you may want to stop and take a dip. The Maho Bay Campground is here, too—a wonderful mélange of open-air cottages nestled in the hillside above.

❸ The partially restored **Annaberg Plantation** at Leinster Bay, built in the 1780s and once an important sugar mill, is just ahead on North Shore Road. As you stroll around, look up at the steep hillsides and imagine cutting sugarcane against that grade in the hot sun. Slaves, Danes, and Dutchmen toiled here to harvest the sugarcane that produced sugar, molasses, and rum for export. There are no official visiting hours, no charge for entry, and no official tours, although some well-informed taxi drivers will show you around. For more information on talks and cultural demonstrations, contact the National Park Service Visitors Center (tel. 809/776–6201).

❹ From Annaberg keep to the left and go south, then head uphill and bear left at the junction to Route 10, to **Coral Bay,** named for its shape rather than for its underwater life. The word *coral* comes from *krawl*, Danish for *corral*. The community at the dry, eastern end of the island is the ultimate in laid-back style. The small wood-and-stucco West Indian homes here house everyone from families born here to newer residents who offer palm readings and massage.

❺ The road forms a loop around Coral Bay. Head northeast along Route 10 to Hurricane Hole at the remote and pristine **East End,** only a 15- to 20-minute ride from Coral Bay, where Arawak Indians are believed to have first settled on the island 2,000 years ago. At **Haulover Bay,** only a couple of hundred yards separate the Atlantic Ocean from the Caribbean.

❻ Route 107 takes you south to the peninsula of **Salt Pond,** which is only about 1 foot above sea level. If you're weary of driving, you can hike the trail south to the spectacular cliffs of **Ram Head.** In any case, you or your rented car can't proceed much farther on 107 without venturing onto a truly rocky road that heads west. Be sure at least to get a view of **Lameshur Bay,** one of the best snorkeling places on St. John and an area used for underwater training by the U.S. Navy.

❼ Once you've run out of road on Route 107, retrace your route to Coral Bay and go west (left) on Route 10 again, which takes you over the heights of the island toward Cruz Bay. On your left is the turnoff for **Bordeaux Mountain,** at 1,277 feet St. John's highest peak. This is also an area of rain forest. Stop for a moment hereabouts and you'll find bay trees. Crackle a leaf from one, and you'll get a whiff of the spicy aroma that you may recognize from the bay rum for which St. John is famous. To appreciate the Bordeaux Mountain region fully, save some time during your stay to hike the **Reef Bay Trail.** Join a hike led by a National Park Service ranger, who can identify the trees and plants on the hike down, fill you in on the history of the Reef Bay Plantation, and tell you about the carvings you'll find in the rocks at the bottom of the trail. You can continue straight back into Cruz Bay on Route 10.

Beaches

All beaches on these islands are open to the public, but often you will have to walk through a resort to reach them. Once there, you'll find that resort guests will often have access to lounge chairs and beach bars that are off limits to you; for this reason, you may feel more comfortable at one of the beaches not associated with a resort. Whichever one you choose, remember to remove your valuables from the car.

St. Thomas The majority of St. Thomas's beaches are on the eastern half of the island. The closest to Charlotte Amalie is **Morningstar Beach,** in the shadow of the huge Frenchman's Reef Hotel. Snorkeling is good here when the current doesn't affect visibility. Take a taxi or the hotel's Red Reefer ferry, which plies the waters of the harbor from downtown every half hour (fare: $3 one-way). World-famous **Magens Bay** is just a taxi ride over the hill behind Charlotte Amalie. Nestled between two peninsulas, this lively, popular beach has a spectacular half-mile arc of white sand and calm, protected waters. **Coki Beach,** next to Coral World, is a popular snorkeling spot for cruise-ship passengers. If you are visiting Coral World, you can use the lockers and changing rooms for free. **Sapphire Beach,** at Sapphire Beach Resort and Marina, has excellent snorkeling and a lovely view of St. John and the British Virgin Islands. Water-sports gear is available for rent here. Among the coves of the southeast tip of the island is **Secret Harbour** beach, a quiet spot with good snorkeling, near the low-key condo resort set among palm trees.

St. Croix **Buck Island** and its reef, which is under environmental protection, can be reached only by boat; it is a must outing on any visit to St. Croix. Its beach is beautiful, but its finest treasures are those you can see when you plop off the boat and adjust your face mask, snorkel, and flippers. The waters are not always gentle at **Cane Bay,** a breezy northshore beach, but the scuba diving and snorkeling are wondrous, and there are never many people around. Just swim straight out to see elkhorn and brain corals. Less than 200 yards out is the drop-off or so-called Cane Bay Wall. **Tamarind Reef Beach** is a small but attractive beach east of Christiansted. Both Green Cay and Buck Island seem smack in front of you and make the view arresting. Snorkeling is good. There are several popular West End beaches along the coast north of Frederiksted. Tiny **LaGrange Beach** is connected to a casual restaurant/bar of the same name, and the beach at the **West End Beach Club** features a bar, water sports, and volleyball. South of Frederiksted, try the beach at the **King Frederik Hotel,** where palm trees can provide plenty of shade for those who need it, and there is a fine beachside restaurant (*see* Dining, *below*) for a casual lunch on weekends. It's a bit of a hike, but if you don't have a car you can take the taxi-van to Frederiksted and walk to these three beaches—if you're friendly with the driver, he may drop you off for free.

St. John **Caneel Bay** is actually seven white-sand beaches on the north shore, six of which can be reached only by water if you are not a hotel guest. The main beach (ask for directions) provides easy access to the public. **Hawksnest Beach** is becoming more popular every day; it's narrow and lined with sea-grape trees. There are rest rooms, cooking grills, and a covered shed for picnicking. It's popular for group outings, but most of the time it's quiet. **Trunk Bay** is probably St. John's most photographed beach, and the most popular spot for beginning snorkelers, because of its underwater trail. It's the St. John stop for cruise-ship passengers who choose a snorkeling tour for the day. To avoid the crowd, check cruise-ship listings in *St. Thomas This Week* to find out what days the highest number are in port. There are changing rooms, a snack bar, picnic tables, and snorkeling equipment for rent. **Cinnamon Bay,** a long, sandy beach facing beautiful cays, serves the adjoining national-park campground. Facilities (showers, toilets, commissary, restaurant, beach shop) are open to all. There's good snorkeling off the point to the right, and rental equipment is available. These north shore beaches are all accessible by public taxi from Cruz Bay, for about $5 one way. **Salt Pond Bay,** on the southeastern coast of St. John, is a scenic area with a beach designed for the adventurous. It's a short hike down a hill from the parking lot, and the only facility is an outhouse. The beach is a little rockier here, but there are interesting tide pools and the snorkeling is good. Take special care to leave nothing valuable in the car; reports of thefts are numerous here.

Sports and the Outdoors

Golf On St. Thomas, scenic **Mahogany Run** (tel. 809/775–5000), with a par-70, 18-hole course and a view of the B.V.I., lies to the north of Charlotte Amalie and has the especially tricky "Devil's Triangle" trio of holes. On St. Croix, **The Buccaneer's** (tel. 809/773–2100) 18-hole course is just east of Christiansted. Yet more spectacular is **Carambola** (tel. 809/778–5638), in the valleyed northwestern part of the island, designed by Robert Trent Jones. **The Reef Club** (tel. 809/773–8844), at the northeastern part of the island, has nine holes. Greens fees average $60 per person, which may or may not include cart rental.

Hiking The very developed St. Thomas has little hiking to recommend. Similarly, options on St. Croix are limited to the dirt roads that wind up through the rain forest (try joining the scenic road either in the hills above Carambola or from Creque Dam Road on the West End). St. John, on the other hand, is hikers' heaven. The staff at the park ranger station in Cruz Bay will be happy to help direct you to a trail suitable to your abilities. Some of the more popular are the 1-mile Lind Point trail that runs from behind the visitor center to Salomon Beach, the Cinnamon Bay nature trail, and the 3-mile Reef Bay trail, which leads downhill to the south shore.

Scuba Diving/ There are numerous dive operators on the three islands, and
Snorkeling some of the hotels offer dive packages. Many of the operators listed below also offer snorkeling trips; call individual operators for details. The typical cost of a two-tank dive is $80; a single-tank dive, $55; and a night dive, $65.

St. Thomas **Aqua Action Watersports** (Box 15, Red Hook 00802, tel. 809/775–6285) is a full service, PADI five-star shop with all levels of instruction. They also rent sea kayaks and Windsurfers.

Joe Vogel Diving Co. (Box 7322, 00801, tel. 809/775–7610 for the shop), the oldest certified diving operation in the U.S.V.I., leaves from the West Indies Inn for day or night, reef or wreck dives. It has both PADI and NAUI instructors and will dive even if only one person shows up.

St. Thomas Diving Club (Box 7337, St. Thomas, U.S.V.I. 00801, tel. 809/776–2381), a divers' resort at Bolongo Bay, has a PADI five-star facility with sales, rentals, and introductory and certification courses. **Underwater Safaris** (Box 8469, St. Thomas, U.S.V.I. 00801, tel. 809/774–1350) is conveniently located in Long Bay at the Ramada Yacht Haven Marina—which is also home to the U.S.V.I. charter boat fleet. It is a PADI five-star dive operation that specializes in Buck Island dives to the wreck of the WWI cargo ship *Cartenser Sr.*

St. Croix **Dive Experience, Inc.** (Box 4254, Strand St., Christiansted 00822–4254, tel. 809/773–3307 or 800/542–2066) is a PADI five-star training facility providing the range from certification to introductory dives.

Dive St. Croix (59 King's Wharf, Box 3045, Christiansted 00820, tel. 809/773–3434 or 800/523–3483, fax 809/773–9411), takes divers to walls and wrecks—more than 50 sites—and offers introductory, certification, and PADI, NAUI, and SSI C-card completion courses. It has custom packages with five hotels and is the only dive operation on the island allowed to run dives to Buck Island.

V.I. Divers, Ltd. (Pan Am Pavilion, Christiansted 00820, tel. 809/773–6045 or 800/544–5911) is a PADI five-star training facility with a 35-foot dive boat and hotel packages.

St. John **Cruz Bay Watersports Co., Inc.** (Box 252, 00830, tel. 809/776–6234 or 800/835–7730; fax 809/776–8303) is a PADI five-star diving center with two locations in Cruz Bay. Owner/operators Patty and Marcus Johnson offer regular reef, wreck, and night dives aboard three custom dive vessels.

Low Key Water Sports (Box 431, 00831, tel. 809/776–7048), located at the Wharfside Village, offers PADI certification and resort courses, one- and two-tank dives, wreck dives, and specialty courses.

St. John Watersports (Box 70, 00830, tel. 809/776–6256) is a five-star PADI center located in the Mongoose Junction shopping mall.

Sea Excursions and Day Sails On St. Thomas, **Coconut Charters** (Suite 202, Red Hook Plaza, 00802, tel. 809/775–5959) has a sunset sail for $35 a person. **Tropic Tours** (tel. 809/774–1855) offers a full-day snorkeling trip to St. John for $40 a person; cost includes snorkel gear and lunch. Call at least a day ahead for reservations.

On St. Croix, try **Mile-Mark Charters** (Box 3045, 59 King's Wharf, Christiansted 00822, tel. 809/773–2628 or 800/524–2012, fax 809/773–9411) or **Big Beard's Adventure Tours** (Box 4534, Pan Am Pavilion, Christiansted 00822, tel. 809/773–4482) for trips to the underwater snorkeling trail at Buck Island. Cost is $35–$40, including snorkel gear, but you'll need to bring your own lunch. Captain Heinz's trimaran, the *Teroro II* (Box 2881, Christiansted, tel. 809/773–3161) departs for full- ($40 a person) or half-day ($30 a person) Buck Island trips from Green Cay Marina.

On St. John, **Connections** (Box 37, 00831, tel. 809/776–6922) represents a dozen of the finest local boats; many of its employees have worked on the boats they book.

Tennis Most hotels rent time to nonguests for $9–20 an hour. For re-
St. Thomas servations call **Bluebeard's Castle Hotel** (tel. 809/774–1600, ext.
195 or 196), **Bolongo Bay** (tel. 809/775–1800, ext. 486), **Mahogany Run Tennis Club** (tel. 809/775–5000), or **Sugar Bay Plantation Resort** (tel. 809/777–7100, ext. 2007). There are two public
courts at **Sub Base** (next to the Water and Power Authority),
open on a first-come, first-served basis.

St. Croix There are courts open to nonguests ($7–$10 an hour) at **The
Buccaneer** (tel. 809/773–2100), **Chenay Bay Beach Resort** (tel.
809/773–2918), **St. Croix by the Sea** (tel. 809/778–8600), **The Reef**
(tel. 809/773–9250), and **Club St. Croix** (tel. 809/773–4800) hotels. Public courts can be found at Conegata Park (two) and
Fort Frederik (two), though they may not be in the best condition. Court fees cost $7–$10 an hour at St. Croix hotels.

St. John The **Hyatt Regency** (tel. 809/776–7171) has six lighted courts
open to nonguests for $10 an hour, and a pro shop.

Shopping

St. Thomas Most people would agree that St. Thomas lives up to its self-
described billing as a shopper's paradise, but duty-free doesn't
necessarily mean bargain shopping. You can, however, find certain items costing 20%–30% less than they do stateside. Among
the best buys are liquor, linens, imported china, crystal (most
stores ship), perfume, and cosmetics. Island crafts, at reasonable prices, offer good value.

Most stores take major credit cards, and there is no sales tax
in the U.S.V.I.

Shopping Districts The prime shopping area in **Charlotte Amalie** is between Post
Office and Market squares and consists of three parallel
streets running east to west (Waterfront, Main Street, and
Back Street) and the alleyways connecting them. A new addition is **Vendors Plaza.** Located on the waterfront at Emancipation Gardens, this is a centralized location for all the vendors
who used to clog the sidewalks with their merchandise. Best
bets here are T-shirts and locally made jewelry.

Havensight Mall, next to the cruise-ship dock, though not as
charming as Charlotte Amalie, has parking and many of the
same stores. West of town, the pink stucco **Nisky Center** is more
of a hometown shopping center than a tourist area, but there's
an excellent bookstore (next to a bakery and yogurt shop), as
well as a bank, gift shops, and clothing stores.

Books and **Dockside Bookshop** (Havensight Mall, Bldg. IV, tel. 809/774–
Magazines 4937). Books written in and about the Caribbean and the Virgin
Islands range from literature to chartering guides to books on
seashells and tropical flowers.

China and Crystal **A.H. Riise Gift Shops** (Main St. and Riise's Alley and Havensight Mall; tel. 809/776–2303). A.H. Riise carries Waterford,
Wedgwood, Royal Crown, and Royal Doulton at good prices.
Outside the Charlotte Amalie branch are local artwork and
hand-painted postcards.

The English Shop (Waterfront, tel. 809/776–5399, and Havensight Mall, tel. 809/776–3776). This store offers china and crystal from major European and Japanese manufacturers.

Little Switzerland (two locations—5 and 38—on Main St., one behind the post office, and one at Havensight Mall; tel. 809/776–2010). All of this establishment's shops carry crystal from Lalique, Baccarat, Waterford, Riedel, and Orrefors, and china from Villeroy & Boch and Wedgwood, among others.

Clothing **Java Wraps** (24 Palm Passage, tel. 809/774–3700). Indonesian batik creations are the specialty here. Also choose from beach cover-ups, swimwear, and leisurewear for women, men, and children.

Local Color (Garden St., tel. 809/774–3727). St. Thomas artist Kerry Topper exhibits her island designs on cool cotton clothing. Also on display are wearable art by other local artists, unique jewelry, wall hangings, wood sculptures, and big-brim straw hats dipped in fuchsia, turquoise, and other tropical colors.

Arts and Crafts **The Caribbean Marketplace** (Havensight Mall, Bldg. III, tel. 809/776–5400). Caribbean handicrafts include Caribelle batiks from St. Lucia; bikinis from the Cayman Islands; and Sunny Caribee spices, soaps, teas, and coffees from Tortola.

The Gallery (Veteran's Dr., tel. 809/776–4641). The Gallery carries Haitian art, along with works by a number of Virgin Islands artists.

Jim Tillet's Gardens (Estate Tutu, tel. 809/775–1405) is an oasis where you can watch craftspeople and artisans produce silk-screened fabrics, pottery, candles, watercolors, and more.

The Straw Factory (Garden St., tel. 809/774–4849) is packed with straw items fashioned by local craftspeople. Hats and baskets are abundant.

Linens **Shanghai Silk and Handicrafts** (Royal Dane Mall, tel. 809/776–8118) and **Shanghai Linen** (Waterfront, tel. 809/776–2828). Both do a brisk trade in linens and silks.

Mr. Tablecloth (Main St., tel. 809/774–4343). The friendly staff will help you choose from a floor-to-ceiling array of linens.

Liquor and Wine **A.H. Riise Liquors** (Main St. and Riise's Alley and Havensight Mall; tel. 809/774–6900). This Riise venture offers a large selection of liquors, cordials, wines, and tobacco. They also stock imported cigars, fruits in brandy, and barware from England.

Al Cohen's Discount Liquor (across from Havensight Mall, Long Bay Rd., tel. 809/774–3690). This warehouse-style store has a large wine department.

Music **Parrot Fish Records and Tapes** (Back St., tel. 809/776–4514). Standard stateside tapes and compact discs are stocked here, plus a good selection of Caribbean artists, including local groups. For a catalogue of calypso, soca, steel band, and reggae music, write to Parrot Fish (Box 9206, St. Thomas 00801).

Perfumes **Tropicana Perfume Shoppes** (2 Main St., tel. 809/774–0010, and 14 Main St., tel. 809/774–1834). Tropicana has the largest selection of fragrances for men and women in all of the Virgin Islands; both shops give small free samples to customers.

St. Croix Although it doesn't offer as many shopping opportunities as St. Thomas, St. Croix has an array of smaller stores with unique merchandise. In Christiansted, the best shopping areas are the

Pan Am Pavilion and Caravelle Arcade, off Strand Street and along King and Company streets.

China and Crystal **The Royal English Shop** (5 Strand St., Frederiksted, tel. 809/772–2040). Saint-Louis and Beyer crystal and Wedgwood china are carried here at prices significantly lower than those on the mainland.

Little Switzerland (Hamilton House, 56 King St., Christiansted, tel. 809/773–1976). The St. Croix branch of this Virgin Islands institution features a variety of Rosenthal flatware, Lladro figurines, Waterford and Baccarat crystal, Lalique figurines, and Wedgwood and Royal Doulton china.

Clothing **Polo/Ralph Lauren Factory Store** (52 C Company St., Christiansted, tel. 809/773–4388). The factory outlet for this popular, upscale clothing line presents men's and women's clothes at huge discounts.

Crafts and Gifts **American West India Company** (1 Strand St., Christiansted, tel. 809/773–7325). In the market for some Jamaican allspice or perhaps a piece of Haitian metalwork? Goods from around the Caribbean, including St. Croix, are available here.

Designworks (3 Queen Cross St., Christiansted, tel. 809/773–5355). This store features "everything for the home," from Danish candles and hand-woven palm baskets to heavy Mexican glassware and Marimekko fabrics imported from Finland, at reasonable prices.

Folk Art Traders (1B Queen Cross St. at Strand St., Christiansted, tel. 809/773–1900). The owners travel to Haiti, Jamaica, Guayana, and elsewhere in the Caribbean to find their wares, including baskets, masks, pottery, and ceramics. From inexpensive trinkets to costly artwork.

Liquor **Tradewind's Liquor Store** (King St., Frederiksted, tel. 809/772–0718). Duty-free liquor is available at this popular combination bar/deli/liquor store.

Woolworth's (Sunny Isle Shopping Center, Centerline Rd., tel. 809/778–5466). This department store carries a huge line of discount, duty-free liquor.

Perfumes **St. Croix Shoppes** (53AB Company St., Christiansted tel. 809/773–2727). One of these side-by-side shops specializes solely in Estée Lauder and Clinique products, while the other carries a full line of fragrances, all at lower-than-stateside prices.

St. Croix Perfume Center (1114 King St., Christiansted, tel. 809/773–7604). An extensive array of fragrances, including all major brands, is available here.

St. John You won't find many bargains on pricey St. John, but you'll enjoy strolling through the lovely shopping centers here anyway. Two levels of cool stone-wall shops, set off by colorfully planted terraces and courtyards, make **Mongoose Junction** one of the prettiest shopping malls in the Caribbean. **Wharfside Village,** on the other side of Cruz Bay, is a painted-clapboard village with shops and restaurants.

Dining

Almost every cuisine you can imagine is available in the U.S.V.I. In upscale hotels, prices are comparable to those in expensive international cities, but local eateries serving delicious, filling, and inexpensive West Indian cuisine provide plenty of alternatives. St. Thomas has a variety of delis and Chinese restaurants, and all islands have their fair share of fast-food joints.

St. Thomas, the most cosmopolitan of the islands, has the largest variety of restaurants. While eating dinner in full-service restaurants can be on the expensive side, lower-priced lunch menus let you enjoy pricey ambience with an affordable bottom line. Two that serve up a spectacular view with good food are **Blackbeard's Castle** (tel. 809/776–1234), which overlooks Charlotte Amalie Harbor and offers a moderately priced Sunday brunch, and the **Seagrape** restaurant (tel. 809/775–6100), a few steps from the surf at Sapphire Beach Resort and Marina. Fast-food eateries on St. Thomas include Burger King, Arby's, McDonald's, Pizza Hut, and Kentucky Fried Chicken.

If you are renting a house or a condo and doing your own cooking, check out the **Pueblo** supermarket chain, with locations at Sub Base; Long Bay, across from Havensight Mall; and at the Four Winds and Lockhart Gardens Shopping Centers. **Gourmet Gallery,** at Yacht Haven Marina, has an excellent and fair-priced wine selection, as well as condiments, cheeses, and specialty ingredients for everything from tacos to curries to chow mein. For fresh fruits and vegetables, go to the **Fruit Bowl,** at Wheatley Center.

On St. Croix and St. John, dozens of West Indian and Latin restaurants will serve you a filling dinner of fish or goat with a salad, vegetable, and potato, rice, or plantain for $5–$7. These include **La Guitarra** (tel. 809/773–8448), **Vel's** (tel. 809/772–2160), **Motown** (tel. 809/772–9882), and **Stars of the West** (tel. 809/772–9039), on St. Croix; and **Fred's** (tel. 809/776–6363) on St. John. Cheap lunches are available at the many little coffee shops and roadside lunch trucks on St. Croix and St. John. Pâté (here, a hot meat- or fish-filled pastry) or johnny cakes (deep-fried pastries), washed down with locally bottled Brow soda, make an authentic and very inexpensive meal.

For a fast-food fix on St. Croix, visit the Pizza Hut or Burger King in Christiansted, and the Wendy's or Kentucky Fried Chicken in Frederiksted. St. John has a Wendy's in Cruz Bay. Christiansted and Frederiksted on St. Croix do not have supermarkets; you'll have to make do with a few corner stores. There are supermarkets at the **Villa LaReine** and **Sunny Isle** shopping centers. On St. John, the **Pine Peace Mini- Mart,** in Cruz Bay, has the best prices and selection on the island. Also in Cruz Bay is **Smiling Al's Natural Food Store,** which stocks unusual items.

Highly recommended restaurants are indicated by a star ★.

Category*	Cost*
Moderate	$15–$25
Inexpensive	$10–$15
Budget	under $10

*per person, excluding drinks and service.

St. Thomas **Alexander's Cafe.** This charming restaurant is a favorite with
★ the people in the restaurant business on St. Thomas—always
a sign of quality. Local media types, wine aficionados (the al-
ways-changing wine list offers the best value on the island), and
people just out to relax pack this place seven nights a week.
Alexander is Austrian, and the schnitzels are delicious and reasonably priced; the baked-brie-and-fruit plate and pasta specials are fresh and tasty. Save room for strudel. *24A Honduras,
Frenchtown, tel. 809/776–4211. Reservations advised. AE,
MC, V. Closed Sun. Moderate.*

The Chart House. Located in an old great house on the tip of
the Frenchtown peninsula, this restaurant features kebab and
teriyaki dishes, lobster, Hawaiian chicken, and a large salad
bar. *Villa Olga, Frenchtown, tel. 809/774–4262. Reservations accepted for 10 or more. AE, D, DC, MC, V. Moderate.*

Eunice's Terrace. Repeat visitors to Eunice's will find that this
excellent West Indian cook has gone up in the world—literally.
She's built a two-story restaurant behind the former one-
room-with-porch affair that made her famous. The new restaurant is roomy and has a spacious bar, but much the same menu
of native dishes, including conch fritters, fried fish, local sweet
potato, funghi, and green banana. *Rte. 38, near Stouffer's Grand
Beach Resort and Coral World, Smith Bay, tel. 809/775–3975. AE,
MC, V. Moderate.*

For the Birds. Located right on the beach near Compass Point,
this laid-back, friendly restaurant serves up sizzling fajitas,
barbecued baby-back ribs, seafood, or steak. By 10 PM it turns
into a jovial joint with dancing, pool, and live entertainment.
*Scott Beach, near Compass Point, East End, tel. 809/775–6431. Re-
servations required for 6 or more. AE, MC, V. Dinner only. Moderate.*

Zorba's Cafe. Tired of shopping? Summon up one last ounce of
energy and head up Government Hill to Zorba's. Sit and have
a cold beer or bracing iced tea in the 19th-century stone-paved
courtyard surrounded by banana trees. Greek salads and appetizers, moussaka, and an excellent vegetarian plate top the
menu. *Government Hill, Charlotte Amalie, tel. 809/776–0444. AE,
MC, V. Closed Sun. Moderate.*

Bryan's Bar and Restaurant. Located high on the cool north
side of the island, overlooking Hull Bay, this surfer's bar offers
some of the best food on the island. Dining is by lantern light
at wood booths inside or at picnic tables outside. The chefs surf
by day and cook by night, serving up gargantuan portions of
grilled fish, steaks, and burgers. A local hangout complete with
pool table, it's casual and reasonably priced. *Hull Bay, tel. 809/774–
3522. No credit cards. No lunch. Inexpensive–Moderate.*

Gladys's Café. Even if the food and prices didn't make this a recommended café, it would be worth going to for Gladys's smile. An Antiguan by birth, Gladys developed a following in the downtown
business community as a waitress at Palm Passage before opening
her own restaurant in a courtyard off Main Street. Try the Carib-

bean lobster roll. *Main St., Charlotte Amalie, tel. 809/774–6604. AE. No dinner. Inexpensive.*

I'll Take Manhattan. If you're planning a beach picnic or lunch on the run, visit this New York–style deli featuring high quality meats, a good selection of cheeses and sausages, a variety of sandwiches and salads, and freshly baked bread and desserts. Free delivery service. *Two locations: Raphune Hill and Red Hook Plaza, tel. 809/775–6328. No credit cards. Raphune Hill branch closed Sun. Budget.*

That Pizza Shoppe. This family-run café is a great place to pick up pizza after a day at the beach. Unusual selections here include the Santa Fe, with red onion, minced garlic, feta cheese, and Canadian bacon; and a barbecued chicken pizza. If you want, you can get your pie unbaked but ready for the oven in its own pizza pan. Pick up ice cream, frozen yogurt, freshly baked cookies, or pie for dessert. They also deliver. *Raphune Hill, tel. 809/776–2626. No credit cards. Closed Sun. Budget.*

Wok & Roll. Tucked in a corner just below the Warehouse Bar in Red Hook, this unpretentious nook has brought tasty take-out Chinese to the East End. You'll find all the standards, from fried rice and chow mein to sweet and sour pork, at good prices. *Red Hook, across from the ferry dock, tel. 809/775–6246. No credit cards. Inexpensive.*

St. Croix **Blue Moon.** This terrific little bistro in Frederiksted, popular for its live jazz on Friday nights, has an eclectic, often changing menu that draws heavily on Cajun and French influences. Try the hearty seafood chowder as an appetizer or a light meal. Leave room for the bittersweet chocolate torte. *17 Strand St., Frederiksted, tel. 809/772–2222. AE. Closed July–Sept. Closed Mon. and lunch. Moderate.*

Le St. Tropez. A dark-wood bar and soft lighting add to the Mediterranean atmosphere at this pleasant bistro, tucked into a courtyard off Frederiksted's main thoroughfare. Diners seated either inside or on the adjoining patio enjoy light French fare, including quiches, salads, brochettes, and crêpes. Daily specials often highlight fresh local seafood. *67 King St., Frederiksted, tel. 809/772–3000. AE, MC, V. Closed Sun. Moderate.*

LaGrange Beach Club. Take a seat just steps from the lapping surf and soak in the unbeatable views while you order a casual, well-prepared meal. A quick beachside lunch might include potato skins, chili, or burgers. At dinner, check the daily specials (seafood is emphasized). The restaurant is a 10-minute walk along Rte. 63 north from Frederiksted. *Rte. 63, Frederiksted, tel. 809/772–0100. MC, V. Inexpensive.*

Stixx on the Waterfront. Enjoy casual dining on a deck overlooking the harbor in Christiansted. The restaurant serves up hearty weekend brunches, good pizza, burgers, and daily specials. Try their rum Hurricanes, served in a variety of strengths. *Pan Am Pavilion, Christiansted, tel. 809/773–5157. AE. Inexpensive.*

★ **Camille's.** This tiny, lively spot is perfect for lunch or a light supper. Sandwiches and burgers are the big draw here, though the daily seafood special, often wahoo or mahimahi, is also popular. *Queen Cross St., Christiansted, tel. 809/773–2985. No credit cards. Closed Sun. Budget.*

La Guitarra. To sample some authentic West Indian/Latin cooking, head for this small restaurant for stew beef, conch stew, or fried pork chops, all served with rice, beans, and salad.

39–40 Queen Cross St., Market Square, Christiansted, tel. 809/773–8448. No credit cards. Closed Sun. Budget.

St. John **The Fish Trap.** Resting on a series of open-air wooden balconies
★ among banana trees and coconut palms, this favorite of locals serves up six kinds of fresh fish nightly, along with tasty appetizers such as conch fritters and fish trap chowder. The menu also includes steak, pasta, and chicken. *Downtown, Cruz Bay, tel. 809/776–9817. AE, D, MC, V. No lunch. Closed Mon. Moderate.*

★ **Lime Inn.** This busy, roofed, open-air restaurant has an ornamental garden and beach-furniture chairs. There are several shrimp and steak dishes and such specials as sautéed chicken with artichoke hearts in lemon sauce. On Wednesday night there's an all-you-can-eat shrimp feast. *Downtown, Cruz Bay, tel. 809/776–6425. Reservations advised. AE, MC, V. Moderate.*

Shipwreck Landing. Start with a house drink, perhaps a fresh-squeezed concoction of lime, coconut, and rum, then move on to hearty taco salads, fried shrimp, teriyaki chicken, and conch fritters. The birds keep up a lively chatter in the bougainvillea that surround the open-air restaurant, and there's live music on Sunday nights in season. *Coral Bay, tel. 809/776–8640. MC, V. Inexpensive.*

Inn at Tamarind Court. The courtyard restaurant at this inn located at the east end of Cruz Bay is a local favorite. Terrific West Indian lunches—conch, grouper, or mutton served with plantains, potato salad, and sweet potatoes—are just $5. *Centerline Rd. north, bear right at Texaco, tel. 809/776–6378. No reservations. No credit cards. Budget.*

Luscious Licks. This funky hole-in-the-wall serves mostly healthy foods such as all-natural fruit smoothies, veggie pita sandwiches, and homemade muffins. For those who've gotta have them, specialty coffees and Ben & Jerry's ice cream are sold here. *Cruz Bay, tel. 809/776–6070. No credit cards. Budget.*

Lodging

Although it's common to associate the U.S.V.I. with pricey resorts chock-full of activities and amenities, the islands are also home to inexpensive hotels, small inns, campgrounds, and affordable rental properties. On St. Thomas, most moderately priced hotels and condominium complexes are on or near a beach. Guest houses and smaller hotels are not typically on the water, but many offer pools and shuttle service to nearby beaches. If you're staying in Charlotte Amalie and your hotel does not offer shuttle service to the beach, you can take a bus to nearby beaches or take the Red Reefer ferry across the water to Morningstar Beach.

In keeping with its small-town atmosphere, St. Croix offers a number of modest small hotels and guest houses. You'll need a car at these, as public transportation is almost nil. There are no beaches in Christiansted, but those staying in town can take a quick ferry to Cay Beach across the harbor (it's cheaper than a taxi to beaches outside town).

St. John has a handful of inexpensive inns in downtown Cruz Bay, a short safari-bus ride ($8–$13 a couple one-way) from nearby beaches. Many budget visitors, however, head straight for one of the two campgrounds here, where accommodations range from bare sites to breezy open-air tent-cabins. Both campgrounds have eating facilities and are on beautiful beaches, with National Park hiking all around. (Maho Bay guests must walk down a hill to get to the beach.) If you're traveling with a group or another couple, you may find you can afford one of the upscale villas on St. John, though hillside locations make a car mandatory.

Highly recommended lodgings are indicated by a star★

Category	Cost*
Moderate	$110–$200
Inexpensive	$75–$110
Budget	under $75

*All prices are for a standard double room, excluding 7.5% accommodations tax. To estimate rates for hotels offering MAP/FAP, add about $30–$40 per person per day to the above price ranges.

St. Thomas
Hotels and Resorts

Island Beachcomber. Although a fence and careful landscaping shield the nearby airport from view, they cannot keep out the sound of departing planes (usually between 2 and 5 PM daily). The hotel *is* right on Lindbergh Beach, however, and has a casual, laid-back ambience that attracts an unpretentious clientele. The beach is on a shallow bay, with a gentle surf that makes it ideal for children. Eleven rooms are right on the water; the others open onto a courtyard with the ocean visible through the trees. All rooms have refrigerators, air-conditioning, and ceiling fans. A reasonably priced restaurant rests under the palms a few feet from the surf. *Box 2579, 00803, tel. 809/774–5250 or 800/982–9898. 48 rooms. Facilities: restaurant, water sports. AE, D, DC, MC, V. EP. Moderate.*

Ramada Yacht Haven Hotel & Marina. This pink landmark anchoring the outer edge of Charlotte Amalie is part of sprawling Yacht Haven Marina. It's a lively spot, with a variety of shops, restaurants, bars, and a supermarket. Many of the clean, simple rooms—some with balcony—overlook the ever-changing vista of marina, cruise dock, and harbor. The Morningstar beach is a short cab ride away. *4 Long Bay Rd., Charlotte Amalie, 00802, tel. 809/774–9700 or 800/228–9898. 151 rooms. Facilities: 3 restaurants, 2 bars, 2 freshwater pools. AE, DC, MC, V. EP. Moderate.*

Windward Passage Hotel. This hotel surrounds a courtyard on the main thoroughfare in Charlotte Amalie, across from the harbor. The historic and shopping district, restaurants, and ferries are a few blocks away. Rooms are basic and clean, facing either the courtyard or a cityscape; those on the waterfront side have a sweeping view of the harbor and cruise ships. All rooms are air-conditioned with private balconies. Rates include a full buffet breakfast and a shuttle to the beach. *Box 640, Charlotte Amalie, 00801, tel. 809/774–5200 or 800/524–7389. 151 rooms. Facilities: restaurant, bar with nightly entertainment, cable TV, freshwater pool. AE, DC, MC, V. BP. Moderate.*

Bunker Hill Hotel. The rooms at this modestly furnished family-run hotel climb a series of levels around a pool and terrace, above the rooftops of the Charlotte Amalie historic district and shopping area. All rooms are air-conditioned; some have small balconies, some kitchenettes. The two suites have kitchens and broad porches. It's a $4 cab ride to Magens Bay or Lindbergh beach from here, or you can walk to the harborfront and take the water shuttle to Frenchman's Reef and Morningstar Beach. The quaint back streets around the hotel are often deserted at night; be sure to take a taxi after dark. *9 Commandant Gade, Charlotte Amalie, 00802, tel. 809/774–8056. 15 rooms. Facilities: restaurant, freshwater pool. MC, V. BP. Inexpensive.*

Guest Houses and B&Bs

Sea Horse Cottages. This simple, quiet retreat rests on a hillside overlooking Nazareth Bay, on the East End and a world away from the bustle of Charlotte Amalie. Island-style rooms with shuttered windows and screened-in porches all have private bath. Steps going down a hillside from the pool lead to a sunning platform built into the rocks and a cove for snorkeling and swimming. While you may want to rent a car in this somewhat isolated spot, you can get by without one if your agenda is purely one of relaxation. All rooms have kitchen facilities, and Red Hook grocery stores and restaurants are a $5 taxi ride away. *Box 2312, 00801, tel. 809/775–9231. 15 cottages. Facilities: freshwater pool. No credit cards. EP. Inexpensive.*

Heritage Manor. This European-style guest house is in the heart of Charlotte Amalie's historic and shopping district. The four units in the vintage 1830 main structure have gleaming tiles, brass beds, and 12-foot ceilings with expansive windows. Four more cluster around a tiny gem of a pool and a courtyard. Two units, a studio and a one-bedroom suite, have kitchens; all are air-conditioned. It's a short taxi, van, or bus ride to a number of nearby beaches. Guests should be cautious about wandering around after dark, as the hotel is in the back streets of town. *1A Snegle Gade, Box 90, Charlotte Amalie, 00804, tel. 809/774–3003 or 800/828–0757. 4 rooms with bath, 4 with shared bath. Facilities: breakfast room in central courtyard, freshwater pool. AE, MC, V. CP. Budget–Inexpensive.*

Island View Guest House. This lovely, clean guest house near Frenchtown rests amid tropical foliage on the south face of 1,500-foot Crown Mountain, the highest point on St. Thomas. Guests get a sweeping view of Charlotte Amalie harbor from the pool and shaded terrace, where breakfast is served. All rooms have ceiling fans and at least a partial view; half are air-conditioned, and three have kitchenettes. The nearest beach is Lindbergh, about a 10-minute drive away. *Box 1903, 00801, tel. 809/774–4270 or 800/524–2023. 12 rooms with bath, 2 with shared bath. Facilities: freshwater pool. AE, MC, V. CP. Budget–Inexpensive.*

Condominium and Villa Rentals

These are plentiful on St. Thomas. Almost all condominium complexes on the island are located on or near a beach on the East End, a short taxi ride from a supermarket but across the island from the bustle and shopping in Charlotte Amalie. Most villas on St. Thomas are nestled into the hillside and have a pool, but are far from beaches. Although rental units tend to be pricey, they are affordable—even economical for those who cook—for a family or two or more couples traveling together. Rental prices drop significantly during off season (*see below*). You can arrange rentals on St. Thomas and St. John through several agents, including **Leisure Enterprises** (Box 11192, 00801, tel. 809/775–3566 or 800/843–3566); **McLaughlin-Anderson Vacations** (100 Blackbeard's Hill, 00802, tel. 809/776–0635 or 800/537–6246); and **Ocean Property Management** (Box 8529,

00801, tel. 809/775–2600 or 800/874–7897). The following condominium and apartment complexes are good rental bets:

Crystal Cove. One of the older condo complexes on the island, Crystal Cove was built as part of a Harvard University–sponsored architectural competition. The unassuming buildings blend into the Sapphire Beach setting so well that egrets and ducks are right at home in the pond in the center of the property. There are studio, one-, and two-bedroom units, each with a porch or balcony. Good snorkeling is nearby. *Reservations: Property Management Caribbean, Rte. 6, 00802, tel. 809/775–6220 or 800/524–2038. Facilities: saltwater pool, 2 lighted tennis courts. AE, DC, MC, V. Moderate.*

Sapphire Village. Be prepared for a swinging-singles atmosphere, since many of the units are rented out long-term to refugees from northern winters, working here for the season. The best units overlook the marina and St. John; the beach is in sight and just a short walk down the hill. *Reservations: Property Management Caribbean, Rte. 6, 00802, tel. 809/775–6220 or 800/524–2038. 35 units. Facilities: pub, 2 pools, restaurant. AE, DC, MC, V. Moderate.*

Off-Season Bets Besides the up-to-50% drop in prices, you'll find even bigger savings with one of the many hotel packages available during the off-season. The "Summer Lovers Special" offered by **McLaughlin-Anderson** (100 Blackbeard's Hill, 00802, tel. 809/776–0635 or 800/537–6246) offers two people a private villa with pool for $1,500 a week—it's twice that in high season. At **Bolongo Inclusive Beach Resort** (50 Estate Bolongo, 00802, tel. 809/779–2844 or 800/524–4746), the off-season "Club Everything" includes a beachfront room; full breakfast; airport transfers; shuttle to town; use of tennis courts, snorkel gear, canoes, Sunfish sailboats, windsurfing equipment, and paddleboats; and vouchers for an all-day sail, a cocktail cruise, and a half-day snorkel tour on one of the resort's yachts—all for a daily rate of $190 for two. At **Sugar Bay Plantation** (Estate Smith Bay, 00802, tel. 809/777–7100 or 800/HOLIDAY, fax 809/777–7200), Holiday Inn's new Crowne Plaza Resort, an off-season rate of $165 for a double includes a daily full breakfast buffet with champagne; use of tennis, health club, and snorkel equipment; and a nightly cocktail party. Other luxury hotels that enter the affordable range in off-season include **Bluebeard's Castle** (Box 7480, Charlotte Amalie, 00801, tel. 809/774–1600 or 800/524–6599) and **Marriott's Frenchman's Reef and Morningstar Beach Resorts** (Box 7100, 00801, tel. 809/775–6550 or 800/MARRIOTT), both of which rest on hills high above Charlotte Amalie and the harbor. For a more intimate atmosphere, try **Blackbeard's Castle** (Box 6041, Charlotte Amalie, 00801, tel. 809/776–1234), an upscale inn and premier sunset-watching spot built on a hill just above town.

St. Croix **Cottages by the Sea.** Reminiscent of some lakeside bungalow
Hotels, Inns, and complex from the 1950s, these cottages on a beach just outside
B&Bs Frederiksted are a good deal, as long as you don't mind dark paneling and somewhat shabby decor. The small cinder-block units all have porches, and there is a community barbecue area at the edge of the sand (one of the nicest beaches around). The atmosphere is friendly and familiar—most of their business is from repeat guests. You can save plenty by stocking up on food supplies and barbecuing here often; the restaurant next door is also very good. *Box 1697, Frederiksted, 00840, tel. 809/772–*

0495. 20 units. Facilities: barbecue, restaurant/bar next door. AE, D, MC, V. EP. Inexpensive.

The Frederiksted. This modern four-story inn is your best bet for lodging in Frederiksted. Yellow-stripe awnings and tropical greenery create a sunny, welcoming atmosphere. The bright, pleasant guest rooms are outfitted with tiny balconies, refrigerators, and sinks, and are decorated with light-color rattan furniture and print bedspreads. Bathrooms are on the small side (most have shower baths) but are bright and clean. Though you can walk to the beach at LaGrange, north of town, you're better off driving. *20 Strand St., Frederiksted, 00840, tel. 809/773–9150 or 800/524–2025, fax 809/778–4009. 40 rooms. Facilities: restaurant, bar, outdoor pool, sun deck, live entertainment. AE, DC, MC, V. EP. Inexpensive.*

★ **The Pink Fancy.** This homey, restful place is located a few blocks west of the center of town away from tourist areas. The oldest of the four buildings here is a 1780 Danish town house, and old stone walls and foundations enhance the setting. The inn's efficiency units are some of the loveliest guest rooms in town. Clean and well tended, all rooms feature hardwood floors, tropical-print fabrics, wicker furniture, and air-conditioning. *27 Prince St., Christiansted, 00820, tel. 809/773–8460 or 800/524–2045, fax 809/773–6448. 13 rooms. Facilities: bar, pool. MC, V. CP. Inexpensive.*

Paradise Sunset Beach. You'll need a car to get to beaches and restaurants from this remote pink hotel, tucked away on a cliff on the island's northwest corner. The rooms are on the small side, and the furnishings are nothing special, but you will have air-conditioning and TV, as well as a pool and bar out on the common deck. Wander behind the hotel to visit the ruins of an old sugar mill. *Box 1788, Frederiksted, 00840, tel. 809/772–2499. 15 rooms. Facilities: pool, bar. AE, MC, V. EP. Budget–Inexpensive.*

Hilty House. This small bed-and-breakfast on a hilltop is a tranquil alternative to the island's many beach resorts. Follow a rutted dirt road up the hill to a shaded courtyard, and pass through picturesque iron gates to reach the inn's gardens. The house is a rambling, one-story affair that was once a rum distillery. The immense, high-ceilinged living room has a Mediterranean flavor; hand-painted Italian tile lines the walls, and the giant fireplace accommodates a spit. Of the five guest rooms, the master suite is the largest, with a four-poster bed and sunken shower over which is suspended a chandelier. On the other side of the house is a large pool with hand-painted tile. You must have a car to get anywhere—including beaches—from here. *Box 26077, Gallows Bay, 00824, tel. 809/773–2594. 5 rooms, 1 with bath across the hall. Facilities: pool. No credit cards. CP. Budget.*

Off-Season Bets Many hotels here knock $20–$50 off their prices during the off-season. At the lovely **Caravelle** (44A Queen Cross St., Christiansted, tel. 809/773–0687), prices drop to around $100. Off-season rooms at the **King Christian** (Box 3619, Christiansted, tel. 809/773–2285) go for $95. At **Club St. Croix** (3280 Estate Golden Rock, Christiansted, tel. 809/773–4800), studios go for about $140, and four can share a one-bedroom suite for $160. **Hibiscus Beach Hotel's** (4131 La Grande Princesse, tel. 809/773–4042 or 800/442–0121) $175 Superior rooms are just $100 in low season. **The Waves at Cane Bay** (Box 1749, Kingshill, tel. 809/778–1805) offers $70 rooms with kitchenettes during the summer.

St. John
Hotels

Raintree Inn. If you want to be in the center of town and bunk at an affordable, island-style place, go no farther. The dark-wood rooms, some with air-conditioning, have a simple, tropical-cabin decor. Three efficiencies here have kitchens and—if you don't mind climbing an indoor ladder—a comfortable sleeping loft. The Fish Trap restaurant is next door. Take a safari-bus to north coast beaches. *Box 566, Cruz Bay, 00831, tel. and fax 809/776–7449 or 800/666–7449. 11 rooms. AE, DC, MC, V. EP. Budget–Inexpensive.*

The Inn at Tamarind Court. Decor reflects prices, with mismatched and somewhat shabby furnishings, but you will save money. Choose among traditional hotel rooms (some with shared bath), suites, or a one-bedroom apartment. The front-courtyard bar is a friendly hangout that attracts singles, as well as home to one of Cruz Bay's best West Indian restaurants. *Box 350, Cruz Bay, 00831, tel. 809/776–6378. 20 rooms, some with shared bath. Facilities: restaurant and bar. AE, D, MC, V. CP. Budget.*

Villa and Apartment Rentals

Generally, renting a private apartment or villa on St. John is not cheap. What you save by doing your own cooking you'll quickly spend on car rental, which you'll need at the hillside properties far from beaches. If you are traveling with a group, however, renting is an affordable option. Try **Caribbean Villas and Resorts Management Company** (Box 458, Cruz Bay 00831, tel. 809/776–6152 or 800/338–0987, fax 809/779–4044), the island's largest rental agent. Although their luxurious, multibedroom homes are expensive, they can accommodate a large number of people. At **Jaden Cottages** (tel. 809/776–6423), you'll find two inexpensive cottages just five minutes outside Cruz Bay. The apartments at **Serendip** (Box 273, Cruz Bay 00831, tel. 809/776–6646) are a bit shabby, but a good budget option.

Campgrounds
★

Maho Bay Camp. Eight miles from Cruz Bay, this private campground is a lush hillside community of three-room tent cottages (canvas and screens) linked by boardwalks, stairs, and ramps that also lead down to the beach. The 16-by-16-foot shelters have beds, dining table and chairs, electric lamps (and outlets), propane stoves, ice coolers, kitchenware, and cutlery. It's nicer than most campgrounds you'll come across, and prices reflect this: You'll pay $80 a night to rough it in style. The camp has the chummy feel of a retreat and is very popular, so book well in advance. *Cruz Bay, 00830, tel. 212/472–9453 or 800/392–9004. 113 tent cottages. Facilities: restaurant, commissary, barbecue areas, bathhouses (showers, sinks, and toilets), water sports. No credit cards. Inexpensive.*

Cinnamon Bay Campground. Tents, cottages with four one-room units in each cottage, and bare sites are available at this National Park Service location surrounded by jungle and set at the edge of big, beautiful Cinnamon Bay Beach. The tents are 10 feet by 14 feet, with flooring, and come with living, eating, and sleeping furnishings and necessities; the 15-by-15-foot cottages have twin beds. Bare sites, which come with a picnic table and a charcoal grill, must be reserved no earlier than eight months prior to arrival. The bare sites are cheap—at press time they were $14 a site—but tents and cottages range from $62 to $79 for two people per night. *Cruz Bay, 00830–0720, tel. 809/776–6330 or 800/223–7637. 44 tents, 40 cottages, 26 bare sites. Facilities: commissary, bathhouses (showers and toilets), cafeteria, water sports. AE, MC, V. Budget–Inexpensive.*

Off-Season Bets Many individual real estate companies here run special deals on house rentals during the off-season. For instance, a house renting for $1,300 a week during high season may go for $850 in the summer. The price for a bay-view condo at **Lavender Hill Estates** (Box 8306, Cruz Bay, tel. 809/776–6969) drops from $210 to $125 per night; a two-bedroom penthouse sleeping four is just $150 a night. Similar price breaks are available at **Gallows Point** (Box 58, Cruz Bay, tel. 809/776–6434 or 800/323–7229), where summer rates are typically 50% off. Inexpensive hotels become even more inexpensive: Rooms at the **Raintree Inn** *(see above)* and the **Inn at Tamarind Court** *(see above)* are around $60. The price of a tent at **Cinnamon Bay** *(see above)* drops from $62 to $40; at **Maho Bay** *(see above)*, an $80 tent-cottage is $55.

Nightlife

St. Thomas At **Barnacle Bill's** (tel. 809/774–7444), Bill Grogan has turned
Night Spots this Crown Bay landmark with the bright-red lobster on its roof into a musicians' home away from home.

Castaways (tel. 809/776–8410) is the watering hole and dance floor for the crews, owners, and those chartering the fleet of boats anchored at Yacht Haven.

Club 2 (tel. 809/776–4655) is a disco-style club located at the top of Crown Mountain Road, behind the Nisky area, with a spectacular view of glittering harbor lights from the terrace.

The Old Mill (tel. 809/776–3004) located in—you guessed it—an old mill, is a lively spot with a small dance floor and a good sound system.

At **Walter's Living Room** (tel. 809/776–3880) on Back Street, you may find a late-night jam going on. Back Street can be a little dicey late at night, so keep your wits about you.

Piano Bars **Blackbeard's Castle** (tel. 809/776–1234), atop Blackbeard's Hill, and **Raffles** (tel. 809/775–6004), on the East End, offer piano bars, each with its own flavor. The player at Raffles has been entertaining with his show "Gray, Gray, Gray" for many years and shouldn't be missed.

St. Croix Christiansted has a lively and eminently casual club scene near the waterfront. At **Hondo's Backyard** (53 King St., tel. 809/778–8103) you'll hear live guitar and vocals in an open-air courtyard with a bar and Cinzano umbrella–covered tables. The upstairs **Moonraker Lounge** (43A Queen Cross St., tel. 809/773–1535) presents a constant calendar of live music. To party under the stars, head to the **Wreck Bar** (tel. 809/773–6092), on Christiansted's Hospital Street, for crab races as well as rock-and-roll.

Although less hopping than Christiansted, Frederiksted restaurants and clubs have a variety of weekend entertainment. **Blue Moon** (17 Strand St., tel. 809/772–2222), a waterfront restaurant, is the place to be for live jazz on Friday 9 PM–1 AM. The **Lost Dog Pub** (King St., tel. 809/772–3526) is a favorite spot for a casual drink, a game of darts, and occasional live rock-and-roll on Sunday nights. For another outdoor lime, head up to Mahogany Road to the **Mt. Pellier Hut Domino Club** (50 Mt. Pellier, tel. 809/772–9914). Piro, the one-man band, plays on Sunday.

St. John Some friendly hubbub can be found at the rough-and-ready
Backyard (tel. 809/776–8553), the place for sports watching as
well as grooving to Bonnie Raitt et al. There's calypso and reggae on Wednesday and Friday at **Fred's** (tel. 809/776–6363).

Index

WHEREVER YOU TRAVEL, *H*ELP IS NEVER FAR AWAY.

From planning your trip to providing travel assistance along the way, American Express® Travel Service Offices* are always there to help.

ANTIGUA
Antours, St. John's
BWIA Sunjet House
Long & Thames Streets
809-462-4788

ARUBA
S.E.L. Maduro & Sons
Oranjestad
Rockefellerstraat 1
297-823-888

BARBADOS
Barbados International Travel
Bridgetown
McGregor Street
809-431-2423

CAYMAN ISLANDS
Cayman Travel Services
Shedden Road
Elizabethan Square
809-949-8755

CURAÇAO
S.E.L. Maduro & Sons
Willemstad
Breedes Straat
599-961-6212

DOMINICAN REPUBLIC
American Express, Santo Domingo
Avda. J.F. Kennedy #3
809-563-3233

GUADELOUPE
Petrelluzzi Travel, Pointe-à-Pitre
2 Rue Henry IV
590-830-399

JAMAICA
Stuart's Travel, Montego Bay
32 Market Street
809-952-4350

MARTINIQUE
Roger Albert Voyages, Fort-de-France
7 Rue Victor Hugo
596-715-555

PUERTO RICO
Travel Network, San Juan
1035 Ashford Ave.
809-725-0950

TRINIDAD & TOBAGO
The Travel Centre, Port-of-Spain
Uptown Mall, Level 2, Edward Street
809-625-4266

American Express Travel Service Offices* are also found in the following locations:

DOMINICA	**HAITI**	**ST. LUCIA**	**TURKS & CAICOS**
GRENADA	**MONTSERRAT**	**ST. MAARTEN**	**VIRGIN ISLANDS**
	ST. KITTS	**ST. VINCENT**	

INTRODUCING

Fodor's WORLDVIEW
TRAVEL UPDATE

At last, your own personalized list of what's going on in the cities you're visiting.

Keyed to the days when you're there, customized for your interests, and sent to you before you leave home.

Exclusive for purchasers of Fodor's Guides...

Fodor's WORLDVIEW
TRAVEL UPDATE

Introducing a revolutionary way to get customized, time-sensitive travel information just before your trip.

Now you can obtain detailed information about what's going on in each city you'll be visiting <u>before</u> you leave home—up-to-the-minute, objective information about the events and activities that interest you most.

Your Itinerary:
Customized reports available for 160 destinations

This is a special offer for purchasers of Fodor's guides – a customized Travel Update to fit your specific interests and your itinerary.

Travel Updates contain the kind of time-sensitive insider information you can get only from local contacts – or from city magazines and newspapers once you arrive. But now you can have the same information before you leave for your trip.

The choice is yours: current art exhibits, theater, music festivals and special concerts, sporting events, antiques and flower shows, shopping, fitness, and more.

The information comes from hundreds of correspondents and thousands of sources worldwide. Updated continuously, it's like having your own personal concierge or friend in the city.

You specify the cities and when you'll be there. We'll do the rest — personalizing the information for you the way no guidebook can.

It's the perfect extension to your Fodor's guide and the best way to make the most of your valuable travel time.

Reg
The
in th
domain
tion as J
worthwhile
the perform
Tickets are us
venue. Alter
mances are canc
given. For more in
Open-Air Theatre, In
NW1 4NP Open Air
Tel: 935-5756. Ends: 9-1
International Air Tattoo
Held biennially, the w
military air displ
demostr
tions

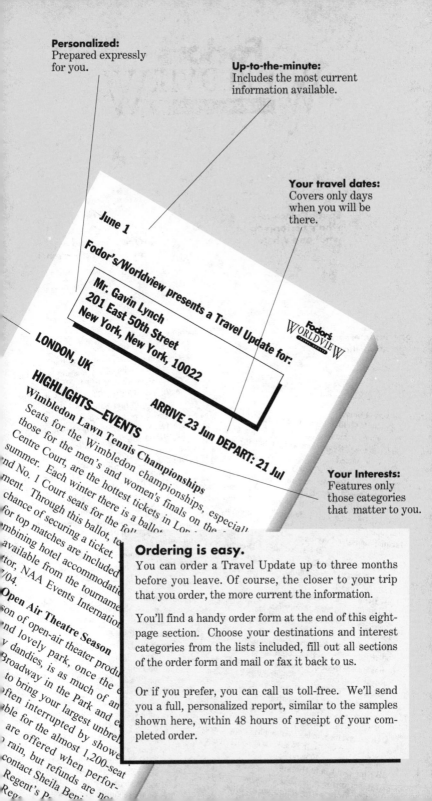

Personalized:
Prepared expressly
for you.

Up-to-the-minute:
Includes the most current
information available.

Your travel dates:
Covers only days
when you will be
there.

June 1

Fodor's/Worldview presents a Travel Update for:

Mr. Gavin Lynch
201 East 50th Street
New York, New York, 10022

WORLDVIEW

LONDON, UK

ARRIVE 23 Jun DEPART: 21 Jul

Your Interests:
Features only
those categories
that matter to you.

HIGHLIGHTS—EVENTS

Wimbledon Lawn Tennis Championships
Seats for the Wimbledon championships, especiall
those for the men's and women's finals on the
Centre Court, are the hottest tickets in Lo
summer. Each winter there is a ballo
nd No. 1 Court seats for the fol
ment. Through this ballot, te
chance of securing a ticket.
for top matches are included
mbining hotel accommodati
available from the tourna
tor, NAA Events Internation
7/04.

Open Air Theatre Season
son of open-air theater produ
nd lovely park, once the
y dandies, is as much of an
Broadway in the Park and e
to bring your largest unbrel
often interrupted by showe
ble for the almost 1,200-seat
are offered when perfor-
o rain, but refunds are no
contact Sheila Ben:
Regent's P
Reg

Ordering is easy.

You can order a Travel Update up to three months
before you leave. Of course, the closer to your trip
that you order, the more current the information.

You'll find a handy order form at the end of this eight-
page section. Choose your destinations and interest
categories from the lists included, fill out all sections
of the order form and mail or fax it back to us.

Or if you prefer, you can call us toll-free. We'll send
you a full, personalized report, similar to the samples
shown here, within 48 hours of receipt of your completed order.

**Special concerts—
who's performing
what and where**

**One-of-a-kind,
one-time-only events**

**Special interest,
in-depth listings**

Children — Events
Angel Canal Festival
The festivities include a children's funfair, entertainers, a boat rally and displays on the water. Regent's Canal. Islington. N1. Tube: Angel. Tel: 267 9100. 11:30am-5:30pm. 7/04.

Blackheath Summer Kite Festival
Stunt kite displays with parachuting teddy bears and trade stands. Free admission. SE3. BR: Blackheath. 10am. 6/27.

Megabugs
Children will delight in this infestation of giant robotic insects, including a praying mantic 60 times life size. Mon-Sat 10am-6pm; Sun 11am-6pm. Admission 4.50 pounds. Natural History Museum, Cromwell Road. SW7. Tube: South Kensington. Tel: 938 9123. Ends 10/01.

Childminders
This establishment employs only women, providing nurses and qualified nannies to

Music — Jazz & Blues
Tito Puente's Golden Men of Latin Jazz
The father of mambo and Cuban rumba king comes to town. Royal Festival Hall. South Bank. SE1. Tube: Waterloo. Tel: 928 8800. 8pm. 7/15.

Georgie Fame and The New York Band
Riding a popular tide with his latest album, the smoky-voiced Fame and his keyboard are on a tour yet again. The Grand. Clapham Junction. SW11. BR: Clapham Junction. Tel: 738 9000. 7:30pm. 7/07.

Jacques Loussier Play Bach Trio
The French jazz classicist and colleagues. Kenwood Lakeside. Hampstead Lane. Kenwood. NW3. Tube: Golders Green, then bus 210. Tel: 413 1443. 7pm. 7/10.

Tony Bennett and Ronnie Scott
Royal Festival Hall. South Bank. SE1. Tube: Waterloo. Tel: 928 8800. 8pm. 7/11.

Santana
Royal Festival Hall. South Bank. SE1. Tube: Waterloo. Tel: 928 8800. 8pm. 7/12.

Count Basie Orchestra and Nancy Wilson Trio
Royal Festival Hall. South Bank. SE1. Tube: Waterloo. Tel: 928 8800. 8pm. 7/14.

King Pleasure and the Biscuit Boys
Royal Festival Hall. South Bank. SE1. Tube: Waterloo. Tel: 928 8800. 6:30 and 9pm. 7/16.

Al Green and the London Community Gospel Choir
Royal Festival Hall. South Bank. SE1. Tube: Waterloo. Tel: 928 8800. 8pm. 7/13.

BB King and Linda Hopkins
Mother of the blues and successor to Bessie Smith, Hopkins meets up with "Blues Boy"

Music — Classical
Marylebone Sinfonia
Kenneth Gowen conducts music by Puccini and Rossini. Queen Elizabeth Hall. South Bank. SE1. Tube: Waterloo. Tel: 928 8800. 7:45pm. 7/16.

London Philharmonic
Franz Welser-Moest and George Benjamin conduct selections by Alexander Goehr, Messiaen, and some of Benjamin's own compositions. Queen Elizabeth Hall. South Bank. SE1. Tube: Waterloo. Tel: 928 8800. 8pm.

London Pro Arte Orchestra and Forest Choir
Murray Stewart conducts selections by Rossini, Haydn and Jonathan Willcocks. Queen Elizabeth Hall. South Bank. SE1. Tube: Waterloo. Tel: 928 8800. 7:45pm. 7/1

Kensington Symphony Orchestra

Here's what you get . . .

Detailed information about what's going on — precisely when you'll be there.

Show openings during your visit

Reviews by local critics

Exhibitions & Shows—Antique & Flower
Westminster Antiques Fair
Over 50 stands with pre-1830 furniture and other Victorian and earlier items. Thu-Fri 11am-8pm; Sat-Sun 11am-6pm. Admission 4 pounds, children free. Old Royal Horticultural Hall. Vincent Square. SW1. Tel: 0444/48 25 14. 6-24 thru 6/27.

Royal Horticultural Society Flower Show
The show includes displays of carnations, summer fruit and vegetables. Tue 11am-7pm; Wed 10am-5pm. Admission Tue 4 pounds, Wed 2 pounds. Royal Horticultural Halls. Greycoat Street and Vincent Square. SW1. Tube: Victoria. 7/20 thru 7/21.

Hampton Court Palace International Flower Show
Major international garden and flower show taking place in conjunction with the British

Theater — Musical
Sunset Boulevard
In June, the four Andrew Lloyd Webber musicals which dominated London's stages in the 1980s (Cats, Starlight Express, Phantom of the Opera and Aspects of Love) are joined by the composer's latest work, a show rumored to have his best music to date. The 1950 Billy Wilder film about a helpless young writer who is drawn into the world of a possessive, aging silent screen star offers rich opportunities for Webber's evolving style. Soaring, aching melodies, lush technical effects and psychological thrills are all expected. Patti Lupone stars. Mon-Sat at 8pm; matinee Thu-Sat at 3pm. In-person sales only at the box office; credit card bookings, Tel: 344 0055. Admission 15-32.50 pounds. Adelphi Theatre. The Strand. WC2. Tube: Charing Cross. Tel: 836 7611. Starts: 6/21

Leonardo A Portrait of Love
A new musical about the great Renaissance artist and inventor comes in for a London premier tested by a brief run at Oxford's Old Fire Stati autumn. The work explores the relations Vinci and the woman

Spectator Sports — Other Sports
Greyhound Racing: Wembley Stadium
This dog track offers good views of greyhound racing held on Mon, Wed and Fri. No credit cards. Stadium Way. Wembley. HA9. Tube: Wembley Park. Tel: 902 8833.

Benson & Hedges Cricket Cup Final
Lord's Cricket Ground. St. John's Wood Road. NW8. Tube: St. John's Wood. Tel: 289 1611. 11am. 7/10.

Business-Fax & Overnight Mail
Post Office, Trafalgar Square Branch
Offers a network of fax services, the Intelpost system, throughout the country and abroad. Mon-Sat 8am-8pm, Sun 9am-5pm. William IV Street. WC2.

Alberquerque • Atlanta • Atlantic City • N
Baltimore • Boston • Chicago • Cincinnati
Cleveland • Dallas/Ft.Worth • Denver • D
• Houston • Kansas City • Las Vegas • Los
Angeles • Memphis • Miami • Milwaukee
New Orleans • New York City • Orlando •
Springs • Philadelphia • Phoenix • Pittsburg
Portland • Salt Lake • San Antonio • San Di
San Franc • Wash • Louis • Tamp
Oslo • Wash • Island •
Hawaii • Kauai • Maui • Abacos • Bimini
Ber • County • Harbour • Islar
Antigua & B Huilla
Gorda • Barbados • Dominica • Gree
cia • St. Vincent • Trinidad &Tobago
ymans • Puerto Plata • Santo Domin
Aruba • Bonaire • Curacao • St. Ma
ec City • Montreal • Ottawa • Toro
ancouver • Guadeloupe • Martiniqu
elemy • St. Martin • Kingston • Ixt
o Bay • Negril • Ocho Rios • Ponce
n • Grand Turk • Providenciales • S
St. John • St. Thomas • Acapulco •
& Isla Mujeres • Cozumel • Guadal
a • Los Cabos • Manzanillo • Mazatl
City • Monterrey • Oaxaca • Puerto
do • Puerto Vallarta • Veracruz • I

Fodor's
WORLDVIEW
TRAVEL UPDATE

Interest Categories

For <u>your</u> personalized Travel Update, choose the categories you're most interested in from this list. Every Travel Update automatically provides you with *Event Highlights* – the best of what's happening during the dates of your trip.

1.	**Business Services**	Fax & Overnight Mail, Computer Rentals, Photocopying, Secretarial, Messenger, Translation Services

Dining

2.	**All Day Dining**	Breakfast & Brunch, Cafes & Tea Rooms, Late-Night Dining
3.	**Local Cuisine**	In Every Price Range—from Budget Restaurants to the Special Splurge
4.	**European Cuisine**	Continental, French, Italian
5.	**Asian Cuisine**	Chinese, Far Eastern, Japanese, Indian
6.	**Americas Cuisine**	American, Mexican & Latin
7.	**Nightlife**	Bars, Dance Clubs, Comedy Clubs, Pubs & Beer Halls
8.	**Entertainment**	Theater—Drama, Musicals, Dance, Ticket Agencies
9.	**Music**	Classical, Traditional & Ethnic, Jazz & Blues, Pop, Rock
10.	**Children's Activities**	Events, Attractions
11.	**Tours**	Local Tours, Day Trips, Overnight Excursions, Cruises
12.	**Exhibitions, Festivals & Shows**	Antiques & Flower, History & Cultural, Art Exhibitions, Fairs & Craft Shows, Music & Art Festivals
13.	**Shopping**	Districts & Malls, Markets, Regional Specialities
14.	**Fitness**	Bicycling, Health Clubs, Hiking, Jogging
15.	**Recreational Sports**	Boating/Sailing, Fishing, Ice Skating, Skiing, Snorkeling/Scuba, Swimming
16.	**Spectator Sports**	Auto Racing, Baseball, Basketball, Football, Horse Racing, Ice Hockey, Soccer

Please note that interest category content will vary by season, destination, and length of stay.

Destinations

The Fodor's/Worldview Travel Update covers more than 160 destinations worldwide. Choose the destinations that match your itinerary from this list. (Choose bulleted destinations only.)

United States (Mainland)
- Albuquerque
- Atlanta
- Atlantic City
- Baltimore
- Boston
- Chicago
- Cincinnati
- Cleveland
- Dallas/Ft. Worth
- Denver
- Detroit
- Houston
- Kansas City
- Las Vegas
- Los Angeles
- Memphis
- Miami
- Milwaukee
- Minneapolis/ St. Paul
- New Orleans
- New York City
- Orlando
- Palm Springs
- Philadelphia
- Phoenix
- Pittsburgh
- Portland
- St. Louis
- Salt Lake City
- San Antonio
- San Diego
- San Francisco
- Seattle
- Tampa
- Washington, DC

Alaska
- Anchorage/Fairbanks/Juneau

Hawaii
- Honolulu
- Island of Hawaii
- Kauai
- Maui

Canada
- Quebec City
- Montreal
- Ottawa
- Toronto
- Vancouver

Bahamas
- Abacos
- Eleuthera/ Harbour Island
- Exumas
- Freeport
- Nassau & Paradise Island

Bermuda
- Bermuda Countryside
- Hamilton

British Leeward Islands
- Anguilla
- Antigua & Barbuda
- Montserrat
- St. Kitts & Nevis

British Virgin Islands
- Tortola & Virgin Gorda

British Windward Islands
- Barbados
- Dominica
- Grenada
- St. Lucia
- St. Vincent
- Trinidad & Tobago

Cayman Islands
- The Caymans

Dominican Republic
- Puerto Plata
- Santo Domingo

Dutch Leeward Islands
- Aruba
- Bonaire
- Curacao

Dutch Windward Islands
- St. Maarten

French West Indies
- Guadeloupe
- Martinique
- St. Barthelemy
- St. Martin

Jamaica
- Kingston
- Montego Bay
- Negril
- Ocho Rios

Puerto Rico
- Ponce
- San Juan

Turks & Caicos
- Grand Turk
- Providenciales

U.S. Virgin Islands
- St. Croix
- St. John
- St. Thomas

Mexico
- Acapulco
- Cancun & Isla Mujeres
- Cozumel
- Guadalajara
- Ixtapa & Zihuatanejo
- Los Cabos
- Manzanillo
- Mazatlan
- Mexico City
- Monterrey
- Oaxaca
- Puerto Escondido
- Puerto Vallarta
- Veracruz

Europe
- Amsterdam
- Athens
- Barcelona
- Berlin
- Brussels
- Budapest
- Copenhagen
- Dublin
- Edinburgh
- Florence
- Frankfurt
- French Riviera
- Geneva
- Glasgow
- Interlaken
- Istanbul
- Lausanne
- Lisbon
- London
- Madrid
- Milan
- Moscow
- Munich
- Oslo
- Paris
- Prague
- Provence
- Rome
- Salzburg
- St. Petersburg
- Stockholm
- Venice
- Vienna
- Zurich

Pacific Rim Australia & New Zealand
- Auckland
- Melbourne
- Sydney

China
- Beijing
- Guangzhou
- Shanghai

Japan
- Kyoto
- Nagoya
- Osaka
- Tokyo
- Yokohama

Other
- Bangkok
- Hong Kong & Macau
- Manila
- Seoul
- Singapore
- Taipei

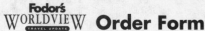

Order Form

THIS TRAVEL UPDATE IS FOR (Please print):

Name

Address

City	State		ZIP	
Country	Tel # (	)	-	

Title of this Fodor's guide:

Store and location where guide was purchased:

INDICATE YOUR DESTINATIONS/DATES: Write in below the destinations you want to order. Then fill in your arrival and departure dates for each destination.

			Month	Day		Month	Day
(Sample) LONDON	From:	6	/	21	To:	6 / 30	
1	From:	/		To:	/		
2	From:	/		To:	/		
3	From:	/		To:	/		

You can order up to three destinations per Travel Update. Only destinations listed on the previous page are applicable. Maximum amount of time covered by a Travel Update cannot exceed 30 days.

CHOOSE YOUR INTERESTS: Select up to eight categories from the list of interest categories shown on the previous page and circle the numbers below:

1   2   3   4   5   6   7   8   9   10   11   12   13   14   15   16

CHOOSE HOW YOU WANT YOUR TRAVEL UPDATE DELIVERED (Check one):

❏ Please mail my Travel Update to the address above **OR**

❏ Fax it to me at **Fax #** (   )   -

DELIVERY CHARGE (Check one)

	Within U.S. & Canada	Outside U.S. & Canada
First Class Mail	❏ $2.50	❏ $5.00
Fax	❏ $5.00	❏ $10.00
Priority Delivery	❏ $15.00	❏ $27.00

All orders will be sent within 48 hours of receipt of a completed order form.

ADD UP YOUR ORDER HERE. *SPECIAL OFFER FOR FODOR'S PURCHASERS ONLY!*

	Suggested Retail Price	Your Price	This Order
First destination ordered	$13.95	$ 7.95	$ 7.95
Second destination (if applicable)	$ 9.95	$ 4.95	+
Third destination (if applicable)	$ 9.95	$ 4.95	+
Plus delivery charge from above			+
		TOTAL:	$

METHOD OF PAYMENT (Check one):   ❏ AmEx   ❏ MC   ❏ Visa   ❏ Discover
                                                          ❏ Personal Check   ❏ Money Order

Make check or money order payable to: Fodor's Worldview Travel Update

Credit Card #   **Expiration Date:**

Authorized Signature

SEND THIS COMPLETED FORM TO:
Fodor's Worldview Travel Update, 114 Sansome Street, Suite 700, San Francisco, CA 94104

OR CALL OR FAX US 24-HOURS A DAY
Telephone **1-800-799-9609** • Fax **1-800-799-9619** (From within the U.S. & Canada)
(Outside the U.S. & Canada: Telephone 415-616-9988 • Fax 415-616-9989)

(Please have this guide in front of you when you call so we can verify purchase.)

Offer valid until 12/31/94.